𝔖𝔭𝔞𝔫𝔦𝔰𝔥
𝔈𝔵𝔭𝔩𝔬𝔯𝔞𝔱𝔦𝔬𝔫𝔰 𝔞𝔫𝔡 𝔖𝔢𝔱𝔱𝔩𝔢𝔪𝔢𝔫𝔱𝔰
𝔍𝔫 𝔄𝔪𝔢𝔯𝔦𝔠𝔞

FROM THE

𝔉𝔦𝔣𝔱𝔢𝔢𝔫𝔱𝔥 𝔱𝔬 𝔱𝔥𝔢 𝔖𝔢𝔳𝔢𝔫𝔱𝔢𝔢𝔫𝔱𝔥
𝔠𝔢𝔫𝔱𝔲𝔯𝔶

NARRATIVE AND CRITICAL

HISTORY OF AMERICA

EDITED

By JUSTIN WINSOR

LIBRARIAN OF HARVARD UNIVERSITY
CORRESPONDING SECRETARY MASSACHUSETTS HISTORICAL SOCIETY

VOL. II

BOSTON AND NEW YORK
HOUGHTON, MIFFLIN AND COMPANY
𝔗𝔥𝔢 𝔕𝔦𝔳𝔢𝔯𝔰𝔦𝔡𝔢 𝔓𝔯𝔢𝔰𝔰, 𝔠𝔞𝔪𝔟𝔯𝔦𝔡𝔤𝔢

NARRATIVE AND CRITICAL

HISTORY OF AMERICA

CONTENTS AND ILLUSTRATIONS.

[The Spanish arms on the title are copied from the titlepage of Herrera.]

CHAPTER VI.

CHAPTER VII.

CHAPTER III.

CHAPTER IV.

CHAPTER V.

CHAPTER VIII.

CHAPTER IX.

INTRODUCTION.

BY THE EDITOR.

———•———

DOCUMENTARY SOURCES OF EARLY SPANISH-AMERICAN HISTORY.

THE earliest of the historians to use, to any extent, documentary proofs, was Herrera, in his *Historia general*, first published in 1601.[1] As the official historiographer of the Indies, he had the best of opportunities for access to the great wealth of documents which the Spanish archivists had preserved; but he never distinctly quotes them, or says where they are to be found.[2] It is through him that we are aware of some important manuscripts not now known to exist.[3]

The formation of the collections at Simancas, near Valladolid, dates back to an order of Charles the Fifth, Feb. 19, 1543. New accommodations were added from time to time, as documents were removed thither from the bureaus of the Crown Secretaries, and from those of the Councils of Seville and of the Indies. It was reorganized by Philip II., in 1567, on a larger basis, as a depository for historical research, when masses of manuscripts from other parts of Spain were transported thither;[4] but the comparatively small extent of the Simancas Collection does not indicate that the order was very extensively observed; though it must be remembered that Napoleon made havoc among these papers, and that in 1814 it was but a remnant which was rearranged.[5]

---

[1] See further on Herrera *post*, p. 67.

[2] J. C. Brevoort, on "Spanish-American documents, printed or inedited," in *Magazine of American History*, March, 1879; Prescott, *Mexico*, ii. 91.

[3] "Of all the narratives and reports furnished to Herrera for his History, and of which he made such scanty and unintelligent use, very few have been preserved."— Markham, *Rites and Laws of the Yncas*, p. vii.

[4] An overcrowding of archives in the keeping of the Council of the Indies was sometimes relieved by sending part of them to Simancas. Bancroft, *Central America*, i. 281. Harrisse, *Christophe Colomb*, i. 33, says all, or nearly all, the papers relating to Columbus have been removed to Seville.

[5] Some of the documents at Simancas and in other repositories, beginning with 1485, have been edited in the Rolls Series (published for the English Government) by G. A. Bergenroth and by Gayangos (London, 1862–1879), in the *Calendar of Letters, Despatches, and State Papers relating to Negotiations between England and Spain*, contained in five volumes. Vol. i. comes through 1509; and the first paper in it is a complaint of Ferdinand and Isabella against Columbus for his participancy in the piratical service of the French in 1485. Various documents from the archives of Simancas are given in Ala-

Dr. Robertson was the earliest of the English writers to make even scant use of the original manuscript sources of information; and such documents as he got from Spain were obtained through the solicitation and address of Lord Grantham, the English ambassador. Everything, however, was grudgingly given, after being first directly refused. It is well known that the Spanish Government considered even what he did obtain and make use of as unfit to be brought to the attention of their own public, and the authorities interposed to prevent the translation of Robertson's history into Spanish.

In his preface Dr. Robertson speaks of the peculiar solicitude with which the Spanish archives were concealed from strangers in his time; and he tells how, to Spanish subjects even, those of Simancas were opened only upon a royal order. Papers notwithstanding such order, he says, could be copied only by payment of fees too exorbitant to favor research.[1] By order of Fernando VI., in the last century, a collection of selected copies of the most important documents in the various depositories of archives was made; and this was placed in the Biblioteca Nacional at Madrid.

In 1778 Charles III. ordered that the documents of the Indies in the Spanish offices and depositories should be brought together in one place. The movement did not receive form till 1785, when a commission was appointed; and not till 1788, did Simancas, and the other collections drawn upon, give up their treasures to be transported to Seville, where they were placed in the building provided for them.[2]

Muñoz, who was born in 1745, was commissioned in 1779 by the King with authority[3] to search archives, public and family, and to write and publish a *Historia*

man's *La República Mejicana*, three volumes, 1844–1849. We get glimpses in the *Historia* of Las Casas of a large number of the letters of Columbus, to which he must have had access, but which are now lost. Harrisse thinks it was at Simancas, that Las Casas must have found them; for when engaged on that work he was living within two leagues of that repository. It seems probable, also, that Las Casas must have had use of the Biblioteca Colombina, when it was deposited in the convent of San Pablo (1544–1552), from whose Dominican monks Harrisse thinks it possible that Las Casas obtained possession of the Toscanelli map. He regrets, however, that for the personal history of Columbus and his family, Las Casas furnishes no information which cannot be found more nearly at first hand elsewhere. See Harrisse, *Christophe Colomb*, i. 122, 125–127, 129, 133.

[1] Robertson prefixes to his *History* a list of the Spanish books and manuscripts which he had used.

"The English reader," writes Irving in 1828, when he had published his own *Life of Columbus*, "hitherto has derived his information almost exclusively from the notice of Columbus in Dr. Robertson's *History*; this, though admir-

ably executed, is but a general outline." — *Life of Irving*, ii. 313.

[2] Harrisse, *Christophe Colomb*, i. 35. He also refers to the notarial records preserved at Seville, as having been but partially explored for eluci dations of the earliest exploration. He found among them the will of Diego, the younger brother of Columbus (p. 38). Alfred Demersay printed in the *Bulletin de la Société de Géographie*, June, 1864, a paper, "Une mission geographique dans les archives d'Espagne et de Portugal," in which he describes, particularly as regards their possessions of documents relating to America, the condition at that time of the archives of the Torre do Tombo at Lisbon (of which, after 1842 and till his death, Santarem was archivist); those of the Kingdom of Aragon at Barcelona, and of the Indies at Seville; and the collections of Muñoz, embracing ninety-five vols. in folio, and thirty-two in quarto, and of Mata-Lanares, included in eighty folios, in the Academy of History at Madrid. He refers for fuller details to Tiran's *Archives d'Aragon et de Simancas* (1844), and to João Pedro Ribeiro's *Memorias Authenticas para a Historia do real Archivo*, Lisbon, 1819.

[3] This authority to search was given later, in 1781 and 1788.

del nuevo mundo. Of this work only a single volume,[1] bringing the story down to 1500, was completed, and it was issued in 1793. Muñoz gave in its preface a critical review of the sources of his subject. In the prosecution of his labor he formed a collection of documents, which after his death was scattered; but parts of it were, in 1827, in the possession of Don Antonio de Uguina,[2] and later of Ternaux. The Spanish Government exerted itself to reassemble the fragments of this collection, which is now, in great part, in the Academy of History at Madrid,[3] where it has been increased by other manuscripts from the archives at Seville. Other portions are lodged, however, in ministerial offices, and the most interesting are noted by Harrisse in his *Christophe*

AUTOGRAPH OF MUÑOZ.

Colomb.[4] A paper by Mr. J. Carson Brevoort on Muñoz and his manuscripts is in the *American Bibliopolist* (vol. viii. p. 21), February, 1876.[5] An English translation of Muñoz's single volume appeared in 1797, with notes, mostly translated from the German version by Sprengel, published in 1795. Rich had a manuscript copy made of all that Muñoz wrote of his second volume (never printed), and this copy is noted in the *Brinley Catalogue*, no. 47.[6]

"In the days of Muñoz," says Harrisse in his *Notes on Columbus*, p. 1, "the great repositories for original documents concerning Columbus and the early history of Spanish America were the Escurial, Simancas, the Convent of Monserrate, the colleges of St. Bartholomew and Cuenca at Salamanca, and St. Gregory at Valladolid, the Cathedral of Valencia, the Church of Sacro-Monte in Granada, the convents of St. Francis at Tolosa, St. Dominick at Malaga, St. Acacio, St. Joseph, and St. Isidro del Campo at Seville. There may be many valuable records still concealed in those churches and convents."

The originals of the letters-patent, and other evidences of privileges granted by the Spanish monarchs to Columbus, were preserved by him, and now constitute a part of the collection of the Duke of Veraguas, in Madrid. In 1502 Columbus caused several attested copies of them and of a few other documents to be made, raising the number of papers from thirty-six to forty-four. His care in causing these copies to be distributed among different custodians evinces the high importance which he held them to have, as testimonials to his fame and his prominence in the world's history.

---

[1] This volume is worth about five dollars.

[2] It was he who allowed Irving to use them.

[3] J. C. Brevoort, in the *Magazine of American History*, March, 1879. Cf. Prescott's *Ferdinand and Isabella* (1873), ii. 508, and his *Mexico*, preface.

[4] Vol. i. p. 56, referring to Fuster's "Copia de los manuscritos que recogió D. Juan Bautista Muñoz," in *Biblioteca Valenciana*, ii. 202–238.

[5] Harrisse, in his *Notes on Columbus*, p. 5, describes a collection of manuscripts which were sold by Obadiah Rich, in 1848 or 1849, to James Lenox, of New York, which had been formed by Uguina, the friend of Muñoz. There is in the Academy of History at Madrid a collection of documents said to have been formed by Don Vargas Ponçe.

[6] Harrisse (*Christophe Columb*, i. 65) refers to an unpublished fragment in the Lenox Library. The *Ticknor Catalogue* (p. 244) shows a discourse on Muñoz read before the Academy of History in 1833, as well as a criticism by Iturri on his single volume. Harrisse (*Christophe Colomb*, i. 65) gives the titles of other controversial publications on the subject of Muñoz's history. Muñoz died in 1799. It is usually said that the Spanish Government prevented the continuation of his work.

One wishes he could have had a like solicitude for the exactness of his own statements. Before setting out on his fourth voyage, he intrusted one of these copies to Francesco di Rivarolo, for delivery to Nicoló Odérigo, the ambassador of Genoa, in Madrid. From Cadiz shortly afterwards he sent a second copy to the same Odérigo. In 1670 both of these copies were given, by a descendant of Odérigo, to the Republic of Genoa. They subsequently disappeared from the archives of the State, and Harrisse [1] has recently found one of them in the archives of the Ministry of Foreign Affairs at Paris. The other was bought in 1816 by the Sardinian Government, at a sale of the effects of Count Michael-Angelo Cambiasi. After a copy had been made and deposited in the archives at Turin, this second copy was deposited in a marble custodia, surmounted by a bust of Columbus, and placed in the palace of the Doges in Genoa.[2] These documents, with two of the letters addressed (March 21, 1502, and Dec. 27, 1504) [3] to Odérigo, were published in Genoa in 1823 in the *Codice diplomatico Colombo-Americano*, edited with a biographical introduction by Giovanni Battista Spotorno.[4] A third letter (April 2, 1502), addressed to the governors of the Bank of St. George, was not printed by Spotorno, but was given in English in 1851 in the *Memorials of Columbus* by Robert Dodge, published by the Maryland Historical Society.[5]

The State Archives of Genoa were transferred from the Ducal Palace, in 1817, to the Palazzetto, where they now are ; and Harrisse's account [6] of them tells us what they do not contain respecting Columbus, rather than what they do. We also learn from him something of the "Archives du Notariat Génois," and of the collections formed by the Senator Federico Federici (d. 1647), by Gian Battista Richeri (*circa* 1724), and by others ; but they seem to have afforded Harrisse little more than stray notices of early members of the Colombo family.

Washington Irving refers to the "self-sustained zeal of one of the last veterans of Spanish literature, who is almost alone, yet indefatigable, in his labors in a country where at present literary exertion meets with but little excitement or reward." Such is his introduction of Martin Fernandez de Navarrete,[7] who was born in 1765,

---

[1] *Christophe Colomb*, i. 20.

[2] See *post*, p. 77. A third copy, made by Columbus' direction was sent to his factor in Hispaniola, Alonzo Sanchez de Carvajal. This is not known ; and Harrisse does not show that the archives of Santo Domingo offer much of interest of so early a date. A fourth copy was deposited in the monastery of the Cuevas at Seville, and is probably the one which his son, Diego, was directed to send to Gaspar Gorricio. Cf. Harrisse, *Christophe Colomb*, i. 16-23, 41, 46.

[3] This letter is given in fac-simile in the Navarrete Collection, French translation, vol. iii.

[4] This book was reprinted at Genoa in 1857, with additions, edited by Giuseppe Banchero, and translated into English, and published in 1823 in London, as *Memorials of a Collection of Authentic Documents*, etc. A Spanish edition was issued at Havana in 1867 (Leclerc, nos.

134, 135). Wagner, in his *Colombo und seine Entdeckungen* (Leipsic, 1825), makes use of Spotorno, and translates the letters. These and other letters are also given in Torre's *Scritti di Colombo ;* in the *Lettere autografe di Colombo*, Milan, 1863; and in Navarrete's *Coleccion*, vol. ii. following the text of those in the Veraguas collections. Cf. *North American Review*, xviii. 417 ; xxi. 398.

[5] Dodge also translated the other letters. Photographic fac-similes of these letters are in the Harvard College Library and in the Library of the Massachusetts Historical Society. See the *Proceedings* of the latter Society, February, 1870.

[6] *Christophe Colomb*, p. 11.

[7] Prescott, in the preface to his *Mexico*, speaks of him as "zealously devoted to letters ; while his reputation as a scholar was enhanced by the higher qualities which he possessed as

and as a young man gave some active and meritorious service in the Spanish navy. In 1789 he was forced by ill-health to abandon the sea. He then accepted a commission from Charles IV. to examine all the depositories of documents in the kingdom, and arrange the material to be found in illustration of the history of the Spanish navy.[1] This work he continued, with interruptions, till 1825, when he began at Madrid the publication of his *Coleccion de los viages y descubrimientos que hicieron por mar los Españoles desde fines del siglo XV.*,[2] which reached an extent of five volumes, and was completed in 1837. It put in convenient printed form more than five hundred documents of great value, between the dates of 1393 and 1540. A sixth and seventh volume were left unfinished at his death, which occurred in 1844, at the age of seventy-eight.[3] His son afterward gathered some of his minor writings, including biographies of early navigators,[4] and printed (1848) them as a *Coleccion de opúsculos;* and in 1851 another of his works, *Biblioteca maritima Española*, was printed at Madrid in two volumes.[5]

The first two volumes of his collection (of which volumes there was a second edition in 1858) bore the distinctive title, *Relaciones, cartas y otros documentos, concernientes á los cuatro viages que hizo el Almirante D. Cristóbal Colon para el descubrimiento de las Indias occidentales,* and *Documentos diplomáticos.* Three years later (1828) a French version of these two volumes appeared at Paris, which Navarrete himself revised, and which is further enriched with notes by Humboldt, Jomard, Walckenaer, and others.[6] This French edition is entitled : *Relation des quatres voyages entrepris par Ch. Colomb pour la découverte du Nouveau Monde de 1492 à 1504, traduite par Chalumeau de Verneuil et de la Roquette.* It is in three volumes, and is worth about twenty francs. An Italian version, *Narrazione dei quattro viaggi*, etc., was made by F. Giuntini, and appeared in two volumes at Prato in 1840–1841.[7]

Navarrete's literary labors did not prevent much conspicuous service on his part, both at sea and on land ; and in 1823, not long before he published his great Collection, he became the head of the Spanish hydrographic bureau.[8] After his death the Spanish Academy printed (1846) his historical treatise on the Art of Navigation and kindred subjects (*Disertacion sobre la historia de la náutica*[9]), which was an enlargement of an earlier essay published in 1802.

---

a man, — by his benevolence, his simplicity of manners, and unsullied moral worth."

[1] His projected work on the Spanish navy was never printed, though a fragment of it appeared in the *Memorias* of the Academy of History (*Ticknor Catalogue*, p. 247).

[2] Leclerc says it is "difficile à trouver," and prices it at 80 francs. The English price is from £2 to £3. A letter by Navarrete, descriptive of his *Coleccion*, is to be found in Zach's *Correspondance*, xi. 446. Cf. also Duflot de Mofras, *Mendoza et Navarrete*, Paris, 1845, quoted by Harrisse, *Christophe Colomb*, i. 67.

[3] There is a memoir of him, with a catalogue of his works, in the *Coleccion de documentos inéditos*, vol. vi.; and of those published and unpublished in his *Biblioteca maritima Española*, ii.

458–470. These sixth and seventh volumes have never been published. The sixth was to cover the voyages of Grijalva and Lopes de Villalobos. Harrisse (*Christophe Colomb*, i. 68) learned that the *Cartas de Indias* (Madrid, 1877) contains some parts of what was to appear in vol. vii.

[4] Columbus, Vespucius, Ojeda, Magellan, etc.

[5] It is an alphabetical (by Christian names, — a not uncommon Spanish fashion) record of writers on maritime subjects, with sketches of their lives and works.

[6] Cf. an article in the *North American Review*, xxiv. 265, by Caleb Cushing.

[7] These form vols. i. and ii. of Marmocchi's Collection (Leclerc, no. 133).

[8] Bancroft, *Central America*, i. 199.

[9] *Ticknor Catalogue*, p. 247.

While Navarrete's great work was in progress at Madrid, Mr. Alexander H. Everett, the American Minister at that Court, urged upon Washington Irving, then at Bordeaux, the translation into English of the new material which Navarrete was preparing, together with his Commentary. Upon this incentive Irving went to Madrid and inspected the work, which was soon published. His sense of the popular demand easily convinced him that a continuous narrative, based upon Navarrete's material, — but leaving himself free to use all other helps, — would afford him better opportunities to display his own graceful literary skill, and more readily to engage the favor of the general reader. Irving's judgment was well founded; and Navarrete never quite forgave him for making a name more popularly associated with that of the great discoverer than his own.[1] Navarrete afforded Irving at this time much personal help and encouragement. Obadiah Rich, the American Consul at Valencia, under whose roof Irving lived, furnished him, however, his chief resource in a curious and extensive library. To the Royal Library, and to that of the Jesuit College of San Isidro, Irving also occasionally resorted. The Duke of Veraguas took pleasure in laying before him his own family archives.[2] The result was the *Life and Voyages of Christopher Columbus;* and in the Preface, dated at Madrid in 1827,[3] Irving made full acknowledgment of the services which had been rendered to him. This work was followed, not long after, by the *Voyages and Discoveries of the Companions of Columbus;* and ever since, in English and other languages, the two books have kept constant company.[4]

Irving proved an amiable hero-worshipper, and Columbus was pictured with few questionable traits. The writer's literary canons did not call for the scrutiny which destroys a world's exemplar. "One of the most salutary purposes of history," he says, "is to furnish examples of what human genius and laudable enterprise may accomplish," — and such brilliant examples must be rescued from the "pernicious erudition" of the investigator. Irving's method at least had the effect to conciliate the upholders of the saintly character of the discoverer; and the modern school of the De Lorgues, who have been urging the canonization of Columbus, find Irving's ideas of him higher and juster than those of Navarrete.

Henri Ternaux-Compans printed his *Voyages, relations, et mémoires originaux pour servir à l'histoire de la découverte de l'Amérique,* between 1837 and 1841.[5]

---

[1] *Magazine of American History,* iii. 176. Cf., however, Navarrete's generous estimate of Irving's labors in the Introduction to the third volume of his *Coleccion.*

[2] The story of this undertaking is told in Pierre Irving's *Life of Washington Irving,* vol. ii. chaps. xiv., xv., xvi. The book was kindly reviewed by Mr. A. H. Everett in the *North American Review,* January, 1829 (vol. xxviii). Cf. other citations and references in Allibone's *Dictionary,* 942, and Poole's *Index,* p. 280. A portion, at least, of the manuscript of the book is in existence (*Massachusetts Historical Society's Proceedings,* xx. 201). Longfellow testified to Irving's devotion to his subject (*Proc.,* iv. 394). See *post,* p. 68.

[3] Irving also early made an abridged edition, to forestall the action of others.

[4] Their bibliography is fully given in Sabin, vol. ix. p. 150.

[5] It was completed in twenty volumes, and is now worth from 250 to 300 francs. See Leclerc, no. 562, for contents; Field's *Indian Bibliography,* no. 1,540; Alexander Young in *North American Review,* xlv. 222. Ternaux died in 1864. Santarem speaks of "the sumptuous stores of his splendid American library." Cf. H. H. Bancroft, *Central America,* ii. 759.

This collection included rare books and about seventy-five original documents, which it is suspected may have been obtained during the French occupation of Spain. Ternaux published his *Archives des voyages*, in two volumes, at Paris in 1840;[1] a minor part of it pertains to American affairs. Another volume, published at the same time, is often found with it, — *Recueil de documents et mémoires originaux sur l'histoire des possessions Espagnoles dans l'Amérique*, whose contents, it is said, were derived from the Muñoz Collection.

The Academy of History at Madrid began in 1842 a series of documentary illustrations which, though devoted to the history of Spain in general (*Coleccion de documentos inéditos para la historia de España*), contains much matter of the first importance in respect to the history of her colonies.[2] Navarrete was one of the original editors, but lived only to see five volumes published. Salvá, Baranda, and others have continued the publication since, which now amounts to eighty volumes, of which vols. 62, 63, and 64 are the famous history of Las Casas, then for the first time put in print.

In 1864 a new series was begun at Madrid, — *Coleccion de documentos inéditos relativos al descubrimiento, conquista y colonizacion de las posesiones Españolas en América y Oceania, sacados, en su mayor parte, del Real Archivo de Indias*. Nearly forty volumes have thus far been published, under the editing of Joaquin F. Pacheco, Francisco de Cárdenas, and Luis Torres de Mendoza at the start, but with changes later in the editorial staff.[3]

Mr. E. G. Squier edited at New York in 1860 a work called *Collection of Rare and Original Documents and Relations concerning the Discovery and Conquest of America, chiefly from the Spanish Archives, in the original, with Translations, Notes, Maps, and Sketches*. There was a small edition only, — one hundred copies on small paper, and ten on large paper.[4] This was but one of a large collection of manuscripts relative to Central America and Mexico which Mr. Squier had collected, partly during his term as *chargé d'affaires* in 1849. Out of these he intended a series of publications, which never went beyond this first number. The collection "consists," says Bancroft,[5] "of extracts and copies of letters and reports of *audiencias*, governors, bishops, and various governmental officials, taken from the Spanish archives at Madrid and from the library of the Spanish Royal Academy of History, mostly under the direction of the indefatigable collector, Mr. Buckingham Smith."

Early Spanish manuscripts on America in the British Museum are noted in its *Index to Manuscripts*, 1854–1875, p. 31; and Gayangos' *Catalogue of Spanish Manuscripts in the British Museum*, vol. ii., has a section on America.[6]

---

[1] Now worth from $12 to $15.

[2] Cf. contents in *Ticknor Catalogue*, p. 87.

[3] Cf. *Magazine of American History*, i. 256; ii. 256; (by Mr. Brevoort), iii. 175 (March, 1879); Sabin, *Dictionary*, vol. xiv. no. 58,072. Leclerc, *Bibliotheca Americana, Supplément*, no. 3,016, for 22 vols. (300 francs). Harrisse, referring to this collection, says: "It is really painful to see the little method, discrimination, and knowledge displayed by the editors." The docu-

ments on Columbus largely repeat those given by Navarrete.

[4] Sabin, *Dictionary*, vol. xiv. no. 58,270.

[5] H. H. Bancroft, *Central America*, i. 484; ii. 736.

[6] Collections like that of Icazbalceta on Mexico may be barely mentioned in this place, since their characteristics can better be defined in more special relations. Prescott had eight thousand manuscript pages of copies of docu-

Regarding the chances of further developments in depositories of manuscripts, Harrisse, in his *Notes on Columbus*,[1] says : " For the present the historian will find enough to gather from the Archivo General de Indias in the Lonja at Seville, which contains as many as forty-seven thousand huge packages, brought, within the last fifty years, from all parts of Spain. But the richest mine as yet unexplored we suppose to be the archives of the monastic orders in Italy ; as all the expeditions to the New World were accompanied by Franciscan, Dominican, Benedictine, and other monks, who maintained an active correspondence with the heads of their respective congregations. The private archives of the Dukes of Veraguas, Medina-Sidonia, and Del Infantado, at Madrid, are very rich. There is scarce anything relating to that early period left in Simancas ; but the original documents in the Torre do Tombo at Lisbon are all intact." [2]

Among the latest contributions to the documentary history of the Spanish colonization is a large folio, *Cartas de Indias, publícalas por primera vez el ministerio de fomento*, issued in Madrid in 1877 under the auspices of the Spanish Government. It contains one hundred and eight letters, covering the period 1496 to 1586, the earliest date being a supposed one for a letter of Columbus which is without date.[3]

---

ments relating to Mexico and Peru. Cf. Preface to his *Mexico*. In 1792 Father Manuel de la Vega collected in Mexico thirty-two folio volumes of papers, in obedience to an order of the Spanish Government to gather all documents to be found in New Spain "fitted to illustrate the antiquities, geography, civil, ecclesiastical, and natural history of America," and transmit copies of them to Madrid (Prescott, *Mexico*, iii. 409).

[1] This book was privately printed (ninety-five copies) for Mr. S. L. M. Barlow, of New York. It has thrice, at least, occurred in sales (Menzies, no. 894, — $57.50 ; J. J. Cooke, vol. iii. no. 580 ; Brinley, no. 17). It is an extremely valuable key to the documentary and printed references on Columbus' career. To a very small number (nine) of a separate issue of the portion relating to the letters of Columbus, a new Preface was added in 1865. Cf. Ernest Desjardin's *Rapport sur les deux ouvrages de bibliographie Américaine de M. Henri Harrisse* (Paris, 1867, p. 8), extracted from the *Bullétin de la Société de Géographie*. The article on Columbus in Sabin's *Dictionary* (iv. 274, etc.) is based on Harrisse, with revisions. Cf. references in H. H. Bancroft, *Central America*, i. 238; Saint-Martin, *Histoire de la géographie* (1873), p. 319; F. G. Cancellieri's *Dessertazioni epistolari bibliografiche sopra Colombo*, etc. (Rome, 1809).

[2] The Archives of Venice, at the beginning of this century, contained memorials of Columbus which can no longer be found (Marin, *Storia civile e politica del commercio de' Veneziani*, Venezia, 1800 ; Harrisse, *Bibl. Amer. Vet. Ad-*

ditions, p. xxi). This is perhaps owing to the Austrian depredation upon the Venetian archives in the Frari and Marciana in 1803–1805, and in 1866. Not a little, however, of use has been preserved in the *Calendar of State Papers in the Archives of Venice* published by the British Government, in the Rolls Series, since 1864. They primarily illustrate English history, but afford some light upon American affairs. Only six volumes (the last volume in three parts) have been printed. Mr. Rawdon Brown, who edited them, long a resident of Italy, dying at Venice, Aug. 25, 1883, at eighty, has sent, during his labors in this field, one hundred and twenty-six volumes of manuscript copies to the English Public Record Office.

[3] Of these, twenty-nine are also given in fac-simile ; there are besides about two hundred and fifty fac-similes of autographs. The volume is priced at 150 marks and 300 francs. Cf. Leclerc, no. 2,688. H. H. Bancroft (*Mexico*, ii. 606) says of the volume : " There are about two hundred and twenty-four pages of geographical notes, vocabulary, biographical data, a glossary, and cuts, maps, and indexes. The letters and fac-similes, from the first to the last, are valuable in a historic sense, and the vocabulary is useful ; but the biographical and historical data are not always reliable, numerous errors having been detected in comparing with official records and with memoranda of witnesses of the events related." Mr. Bancroft's own library is said to contain twelve hundred volumes of manuscript amassed for his own work ; but a large portion of them, it is supposed, do not concern the Spanish history of the Pacific coast.

The late Mr. George Dexter,[1] who has printed[2] a translation of this letter (together with one of another letter, Feb. 6, 1502, and one of Vespucius, Dec. 9, 1508), gives his reasons for thinking the date should be between March 15 and Sept. 25, 1493.[3]

At Madrid and Paris was published, in 1883, a single octavo volume, — *Costa-Rica, Nicaragua y Panamá en el siglo XVI., su historia y sus límites segun los documentos del Archivo de Indias de Sevilla, del de Simancas, etc., recogidos y publicados con notas y aclaraciones históricas y geográficas, por D. Manuel M. de Peralta.*

The more special and restricted documentary sources are examined in the successive chapters of the present volume.

[1] Mr. Dexter, a graduate of Harvard in 1858, after most serviceable labors as Recording Secretary of the Massachusetts Historical Society, resigned that position on account of ill health, and died at Santa Barbara, California, Dec. 18, 1883. The *Proceedings* of the Society for January, 1884, contain tributes to his memory. Various communications in earlier volumes of the same *Proceedings* show the painstaking of his research, and the accuracy of his literary method. The first chapter in Vol. IV. of the present *History* was his last effort in historical study, and he did not live to correct the proofs. His death has narrowed the circle of those helpful friends who have been ever ready to assist the Editor in his present labors.

[2] *Mass. Hist. Soc. Proc.*, xvi. 318 ; also issued separately. The letters of Columbus are also translated in the *Magazine of American History*, January, 1883, p. 53.

[3] An Italian version of the letters of Columbus and Vespucius, with fac-similes of the letters (*Tre lettere di Colombo ed Vespucci*), edited by Augusto Zeri, was printed (six hundred copies) at Rome in 1881. Cf. *Murphy Catalogue*, no. 642.

NARRATIVE AND CRITICAL

HISTORY OF AMERICA.

———•———

CHAPTER I.

COLUMBUS AND HIS DISCOVERIES.

BY JUSTIN WINSOR,
The Editor.

BEYOND his birth, of poor and respectable parents, we know nothing positively about the earliest years of Columbus. His father was probably a wool-comber. The boy had the ordinary schooling of his time, and a touch of university life during a few months passed at Pavia; then at fourteen he chose to become a sailor. A seaman's career in those days implied adventures more or less of a piratical kind. There are intimations, however, that in the intervals of this exciting life he followed the more humanizing occupation of selling books in Genoa, and perhaps got some employment in the making of charts, for he had a deft hand at design. We know his brother Bartholomew was earning his living in this way when Columbus joined him in Lisbon in 1470. Previous to this there seems to be some degree of certainty in connecting him with voyages made by a celebrated admiral of his time bearing the same family name, Colombo; he is also said to have joined the naval expedition of John of Anjou against Naples in 1459.[1] Again, he may have been the companion of another notorious corsair, a nephew of the one already mentioned, as is sometimes maintained; but this sea-rover's proper name seems to have been more likely Caseneuve, though he was sometimes called Coulon or Colon.[2]

---

[1] Irving's *Life of Columbus*, app. no. vii.

[2] Ferdinand Columbus tried to make his readers believe that his father was of some kinship with this corsair. The story of Columbus escaping on an oar from a naval fight off Cape St. Vincent, and entering Portugal by floating to the shore, does not agree with known facts in his life of the alleged date. (Harrisse, *Les Colombo,* p. 36.) Allegri Allegretti, in his *Ephemerides Senenses ab anno* 1450 *usque ad* 1496 (in Muratori, xxiii. 827), gives a few particulars regarding the early life of Columbus. (Harrisse, *Notes on Columbus,* p. 41.) Some of the latest researches upon his piratical life are given by Rawdon Brown in the *Calendar of State Papers,* 1864, covering 1202–1509, vol. i.

Columbus spent the years 1470–1484 in Portugal. It was a time when the air was filled with tales of discovery. The captains of Prince Henry of Portugal had been gradually pushing their ships down the African coast, and in some of these voyages Columbus was a participant. To one of his navigators Prince Henry had given the governorship of the Island of Porto Santo, of the Madeira group. To the daughter of this man, Perestrello,[1] Columbus was married; and with his widow Columbus lived, and derived what advantage he could from the papers and charts of the old navigator. There was a tie between his own and his wife's family in the fact that Perestrello was an Italian, and seems to have been of good family, but to have left little or no inheritance for his daughter beyond some property in Porto Santo, which Columbus went to enjoy. On this island Columbus' son Diego was born in 1474.

It was in this same year (1474) that he had some correspondence with the Italian *savant*, Toscanelli, regarding the discovery of land westward. A belief in such discovery was a natural corollary of the object which Prince Henry had had in view, — by circumnavigating Africa to find a way to the countries of which Marco Polo had given golden accounts. It was to substitute for the tedious indirection of the African route a direct western passage, — a belief in the practicability of which was drawn from a confidence in the sphericity of the earth. Meanwhile, gathering what hope he could by reading the ancients, by conferring with wise men, and by questioning mariners returned from voyages which had borne them more or less westerly on the great ocean, Columbus suffered the thought to germinate as it would in his mind for several years. Even on the voyages which he made hither and thither for gain, — once far north, to Iceland even, or perhaps only to the Faröe Islands, as is inferred, — and in active participation in various warlike and marauding expeditions, like the attack on the Venetian galleys near Cape St. Vincent in 1485,[2] he constantly came in contact with those who could give him hints affecting his theory. Through all these years, however, we know not certainly what were the vicissitudes which fell to his lot.[3]

It seems possible, if not probable, that Columbus went to Genoa and Venice, and in the first instance presented his scheme of western exploration to the authorities of those cities.[4] He may, on the other hand, have tried earlier to get the approval of the King of Portugal. In this case the visit to Italy may have occurred in the year following his departure from Portugal, which is nearly a blank in the record of his life. De Lorgues

---

[1] This name is sometimes given *Palestrello*.

[2] Rawdon Brown's *Calendar of State Papers in the Archives of Venice*, vol. i. (1864).

[3] Prescott (*Ferdinand and Isabella*, ed. 1873, vol. ii. p. 123) says: "The discrepancies among the earliest authorities are such as to render hopeless any attempt to settle with precision the chronology of Columbus's movements previous to his first voyage."

[4] It cannot but be remarked how Italy, in Columbus, Cabot, and Vespucius, not to name others, led in opening the way to a new stage in the world's progress, which by making the Atlantic the highway of a commerce that had mainly nurtured Italy on the Mediterranean, conduced to start her republics on that decline which the Turk, sweeping through that inland sea, confirmed and accelerated.

believes in the anterior Italian visit, when both Genoa and Venice rejected his plans; and then makes him live with his father at Savone, gaining a living by constructing charts, and by selling maps and books in Genoa.

It would appear that in 1484 Columbus had urged his views upon the Portuguese King, but with no further success than to induce the sovereign to despatch, on other pretences, a vessel to undertake the passage westerly in secrecy. Its return without accomplishing any discovery opened the eyes of Columbus to the deceit which that monarch would have put upon him, and he departed from the Portuguese dominions in not a little disgust.[1]

The death of his wife had severed another tie with Portugal; and taking with him his boy Diego, Columbus left, to go we scarcely know whither, so obscure is the record of his life for the next year. Muñoz claims for this period that he went to Italy. Sharon Turner has conjectured that he went to England; but there seems no ground to believe that he had any relations with the English Court except by deputy, for his brother Bartholomew was despatched to lay his schemes before Henry VII.[2] Whatever may have been the result of this application, no answer seems to have reached Columbus until he was committed to the service of Spain.

It was in 1485 or 1486 — for authorities differ[3] — that a proposal was laid by Columbus before Ferdinand and Isabella; but the steps were slow by which he made even this progress. We know how, in the popular story, he presented himself at the Franciscan Convent of Santa María de la Rábida, asking for bread for himself and his boy. This convent stood on a steep promontory about half a league from Palos, and was then in charge of the Father Superior Juan Perez de Marchena.[4] The appearance of the stranger first, and his talk next, interested the Prior; and it was under his advice and support after a while — when Martin Alonzo Pinzon, of the neighboring town of Palos, had espoused the new theory — that Columbus was passed on to Cordova, with such claims to recognition as the Prior of Rabida could bestow upon him.

It was perhaps while success did not seem likely here, in the midst of the preparations for a campaign against the Moorish kings, that his brother Bartholomew made his trip to England.[5] It was also in November, 1486, it

---

[1] Notwithstanding this disappointment of Columbus, it is claimed that Alfonso V., in 1474, had consulted Toscanelli as to such a western passage "to the land where the spices grow."

[2] There is great uncertainty about this English venture. Benzoni says Columbus's ideas were ridiculed; Bacon (*Life of Henry VII.*) says the acceptance of them was delayed by accident; Purchas says they were accepted too late. F. Cradock, in the Dedication of his *Wealth Discovered*, London, 1661, regrets the loss of honor which Henry VII. incurred in not listening to the project. (Sabin, v. 55.) There is much confusion of statement in the early writers. Cf. Las Casas, lib. i. cap. 29; Barcia, *Hist. del*

Almirante, cap. 10; Herrera, dec. i. lib. 2; Oviedo, lib. i. cap. 4; Gomara, cap. 15; Harrisse, *Bibl. Amer. Vet.*, p. 4.

[3] As, for instance, Oviedo and Bossi.

[4] The same whom Isabella advised Columbus to take "as an astrologer" on one of his later voyages. Cf. P. Augustin d'Osimo's *Christophe Colomb et le Père Juan Perez de Marchena; ou, de la co-opération des franciscains à la découverte de l'Amérique*, 1861, and P. Marcellino da Civezza's *Histoire générale des missions franciscaines*, 1863.

[5] Cf. Schanz on "Die Stellung der beiden ersten Tudors zu den Entdeckungen," in his *Englische Handelspolitik.*

would seem, that Columbus formed his connection with Beatrix Enriquez, while he was waiting in Cordova for the attention of the monarch to be disengaged from this Moorish campaign.

Among those at this time attached to the Court of Ferdinand and Isabella was Alexander Geraldinus, then about thirty years old. He was a traveller, a man of letters, and a mathematician; and it was afterward the boast of his kinsman, who edited his *Itinerarium ad regiones sub æquinoctiali plaga constitutas*[1] (Rome, 1631), that Geraldinus, in one way and another, aided Columbus in pressing his views upon their Majesties. It was through Geraldinus' influence, or through that of others who had become impressed with his views, that Columbus finally got the ear of Pedro Gonzales de Mendoza, Archbishop of Toledo. The way was now surer. The King heeded the Archbishop's advice, and a council of learned men was convened, by royal orders, at Salamanca, to judge Columbus and his theories. Here he was met by all that prejudice, content, and ignorance (as now understood, but wisdom then) could bring to bear, in the shape of Scriptural contradictions of his views, and the pseudo-scientific distrust of what were thought mere visionary aims. He met all to his own satisfaction, but not quite so successfully to the comprehension of his judges. He told them that he should find Asia that way; and that if he did not, there must be other lands westerly quite as desirable to dis-

COLUMBUS' ARMOR.[2]

cover. No conclusion had been reached when, in the spring of 1487, the Court departed from Cordova, and Columbus found himself left behind without encouragement, save in the support of a few whom he had convinced, — notably Diego de Deza, a friar destined to some ecclesiastical distinction as Archbishop of Seville.

[1] Stevens, *Historical Collection*, vol. i. no. 1,418; Leclerc, no. 235 (120 francs); Carter-Brown, vol. ii. no. 376; Sabin, vol. vii. no. 27,116; Murphy, no. 1,046. This book, which in 1832 Rich priced at £1 10*s*., has recently been quoted by Quaritch at £5 5*s*. Harrisse calls the book mendacious (*Notes on Columbus*, p. 37). The book was written in 1522; its author was born in 1465, and died in 1525 as bishop of Santo Domingo.

[2] This follows a cut in Ruge's *Geschichte des Zeitalters der Entdeckungen*, p. 245. The armor is in the Collection in the Royal Palace at Madrid.

During the next five years Columbus experienced every vexation attendant upon delay, varied by participancy in the wars which the Court urged against the Moors, and in which he sought to propitiate the royal powers by doing them good service in the field. At last, in 1491, wearied with excuses of pre-occupation and the ridicule of the King's advisers, Columbus turned his back on the Court and left Seville,[1] to try his fortune with some of the Grandees. He still urged in vain, and sought again the Convent of Rabida. Here he made a renewed impression upon Marchena; so that finally, through the Prior's interposition with Isabella, Columbus was summoned to Court. He arrived in time to witness the surrender of Granada, and to find the monarchs more at liberty to listen to his words. There seemed now a likelihood of reaching an end of his tribulations; when his demand of recognition as viceroy, and his claim to share one tenth of all income from the territories to be discovered, frightened as well as disgusted those appointed to negotiate with him, and all came once more to an end. Columbus mounted his mule and started for France. Two finance ministers of the Crown, Santangel for Arragon and Quintanilla for Castile, had been sufficiently impressed by the new theory to look with regret on what they thought might be a lost opportunity. Isabella was won; and a messenger was despatched to overtake Columbus.

The fugitive returned; and on April 17, 1492, at Santa Fé, an agreement was signed by Ferdinand and Isabella which gave Columbus the office of high-admiral and viceroy in parts to be discovered, and an income of one eighth of the profits, in consideration of his assuming one eighth of the costs. Castile bore the rest of the expense; but Arragon advanced the money,[2] and the Pinzons subscribed the eighth part for Columbus.

The happy man now solemnly vowed to use what profits should accrue in accomplishing the rescue of the Holy Sepulchre from the Moslems. Palos, owing some duty to the Crown, was ordered to furnish two armed caravels, and Columbus was empowered to fit out a third. On the 30th of April the letters-patent confirming his dignities were issued. His son Diego was made a page of the royal household. On May 12 he left the Court and hastened towards Palos. Here, upon showing his orders for the vessels, he found the town rebellious, with all the passion of a people who felt that some of their number were being simply doomed to destruction beyond that Sea of Darkness whose bounds they knew not. Affairs were in this unsatisfactory condition when the brothers Pinzon threw themselves and their own vessels into the cause; while a

[1] There are two views of Seville in Braun and Hogenberg's *Civitates orbis terrarum*, published at Antwerp in 1572, and again at Brussels (in French) in 1574. In one of the engravings a garden near the Puerta de Goles is marked "Guerta de Colon;" and in the other the words "Casa de Colon" are attached to the top of one of the houses. Muller, *Books on America*, 1877, no. 712. The book is in the Harvard College Library.

[2] Santangel supplied about seventeen thousand florins from Ferdinand's treasury. Bergenroth, in his Introduction to the Spanish State Papers, removes not a little of the mellow splendor which admirers have poured about Isabella's character.

PARTING OF COLUMBUS WITH FERDINAND AND ISABELLA.[1]

third vessel, the "Pinta," was impressed, — much to the alarm of its owners and crew.

And so, out of the harbor of Palos,[2] on the 3d of August, 1492, Columbus

---

[1] Fac-simile of the engraving in Herrera. It originally appeared in De Bry, part iv.

[2] Palos is no longer a port, such has been the work of time and tide. In 1548 the port is described in Medina's *Libro de grandezas y cosas*

de España. (Harrisse, *Bibl. Amer. Vet.*, no. 281.) Irving described it in 1828. Its present unmaritime character is set forth by E. E. Hale in *Amer. Antiq. Soc. Proc.*, ii. 159; *Seven Spanish Cities*, p. 17 ; and *Overland Monthly*, Jan., 1883, p. 42.

EARLY VESSELS.[1]

[1] This representation of the vessels of the early Spanish navigators is a fac-simile of a cut in Medina's *Arte de navegar*, Valladolid, 1545, which was re-engraved in the Venice edition of 1555. Cf. *Carter-Brown Catalogue*, vol. i. nos. 137, 204; Ruge, *Geschichte des Zeitalters der Entdeckungen*, pp. 240, 241; Jurien de la Gravière's *Les marins du XVe et du XVIe siècle*, vol. i. pp. 38, 151. In the variety of changes in methods of measurement it is not easy to find the equivalent in tonnage of the present day for the ships of Columbus's time. Those constituting his little fleet seem to have been light and swift vessels of the class called caravels. One had a deck amidships, with high forecastle and poop; and two were without this deck, though high, and covered at the ends. Captain G. V. Fox has given what he supposes were the dimensions of the larger one, — a heavier craft and duller sailer than the others. He calculates for a hundred tons, — makes her sixty-three feet over all, fifty-one feet keel, twenty feet beam, and ten and a half feet draft of water. She carried the kind of gun termed lombards, and a crew of fifty men. *U. S. Coast Survey Report*, 1880, app. 18; Becher's *Landfall of Columbus*; A. Jal's *Archéologie navale* (Paris, 1840); Irving's *Columbus*, app. xv.; H. H. Bancroft, *Central America*, i. 187; *Das Ausland*, 1867, p. 1. There are other views of the ships of Columbus' time in the cuts in some of the early editions of his Letters on the discovery. See notes following this chapter.

sailed with his three little vessels. The "Santa Maria," which carried his flag, was the only one of the three which had a deck, while the other two, the "Niña" and the "Pinta," were open caravels. The two Pinzons commanded these smaller ships, — Martin Alonzo the "Pinta," and Vicente the "Niña."

The voyage was uneventful, except that the expectancy of all quickened the eye, which sometimes saw over-much, and poised the mind, which was alert with hope and fear. It has been pointed out how a westerly course from Palos would have discouraged Columbus with head and variable winds. Running down to the Canaries (for Toscanelli put those islands in the lati-

BUILDING A SHIP.[1]

tude of Cipango), a westerly course thence would bring him within the continuous easterly trade-winds, whose favoring influence would inspirit his men, — as, indeed, was the case. Columbus, however, was very glad on the 22d of September to experience a west wind, just to convince his crew it was possible to have, now and then, the direction of it favorable to their return. He had proceeded, as he thought, some two hundred miles farther than the longitude in which he had conjectured Cipango to be, when the urging of Martin Alonzo Pinzon, and the flight of birds indicating land to be nearer in the southwest, induced him to change his course in that direction.[2]

[1] This follows a fac-simile, given in Ruge, *Geschichte des Zeitalters der Entdeckungen* p. 240, of a cut in Bernhardus de Breydenbach's *Peregrinationes*, Mainz, 1486.

[2] Cf. Irving, app. no. xvi., on the route of Columbus. Brevoort in his *Verrazano*, p. 101, describes the usual route of the early navigators from Spain to the West Indies. Columbus kept two records of his progress. One was an unworthily deceitful one (reminding us of an earlier deceit, when he tampered with the compass to mislead his crew), by which he hoped to check the apprehensions of his men arising from his increasing longitude; and the other a dead reckoning of some kind, in which he thought he was approximately accurate. The story of his capit-

About midnight between the 11th and 12th of October, Columbus on the lookout thought he saw a light moving in the darkness. He called a companion, and the two in counsel agreed that it was so.[1] At about two o'clock, the moon then shining, a mariner on the "Pinta" discerned unmistakably a low sandy shore. In the morning a landing was made, and, with prayer[2] and ceremony,

ulating to his crew, and agreeing to turn back in three days in case land was not reached, is only told by Oviedo on the testimony of a pilot hostile to Columbus.

[1] It may have been on some island or in some canoe; or just as likely a mere delusion. The fact that Columbus at a later day set up a claim for the reward for the first discovery on the strength of this mysterious light, to the exclusion of the poor sailor who first actually saw land from the "Pinta," has subjected his memory, not unnaturally, to some discredit at least with those who reckon magnanimity among the virtues. Cf. *Navarrete*, iii. 612.

[2] The prayer used was adopted later in similar cases, under Balboa, Cortes, Pizarro, etc. It is given in C. Clemente's *Tablas chronologicas*, Valencia, 1689. Cf. Harrisse, *Notes on Columbus*, p. 140; Sabin, vol. iv. no. 13,632; Carter-Brown, vol. ii. no. 1,376; Murphy, no. 599; and H. H. Bancroft's *Central America*, i. 371.

[3] This follows a map given in *Das Ausland*, 1867, p. 4, in a paper on Columbus' Journal, "Das Schiffsbuch des

COURSE OF COLUMBUS ON FIRST VOYAGE.[3]

possession was taken of the new-found island in the name of the Spanish sovereigns.

On the third day (October 14) Columbus lifted anchor, and for ten days sailed among the minor islands of the archipelago; but struck the Cuban coast on the 28th.[1]

Here the "Pinta," without orders from the Admiral, went off to seek some gold-field, of which Martin Alonzo Pinzon, its commander, fancied he had got some intimation from the natives. Pinzon returned bootless; but Columbus was painfully conscious of the mutinous spirit of his lieutenant.[2] The little fleet next found Hayti (Hispaniæ insula,[3] as he called it), and on its northern side the Admiral's ship was wrecked.

SHIP OF COLUMBUS'S TIME.[4]

Out of her timbers Columbus built a fort on the shore, called it "La Navidad," and put into it a garrison under Diego de Arana.[5]

Entdeckers von Amerika." The routes of Columbus' four voyages are marked on the map accompanying the *Studi biografici e bibliografici* published by the Società Geografica Italiana in 1882. Cf. also the map in Charton's *Voyageurs*, iii. 155, reproduced on a later page.

[1] Humboldt in his *Cosmos* (English translation, ii. 422) has pointed out how in this first voyage the descriptions by Columbus of tropical scenes convince one of the vividness of his impressions and of the quickness of his observation.

[2] Pinzons' heirs at a later day manifested hostility to Columbus, and endeavored to magnify their father's importance in the voyage. Cf. Irving, App. x. In the subsequent lawsuit for the confirmation of Columbus's right, the Pinzons brought witnesses to prove that it was their

urgency which prevented Columbus from giving up the voyage and turning back.

[3] This Latin name seems to have been rendered by the Spaniards La Española, and from this by corruption the English got Hispaniola.

[4] This follows a fac-simile, given in Ruge, *Geschichte des Zeitalters der Entdeckungen*, p. 241, of a cut in Bernhardus de Breydenbach's *Peregrinationes*, Mainz, 1486.

[5] There is a wide difference as reported by the early writers as to the number of men which Columbus had with him on this voyage. Ferdinand Columbus says ninety; Peter Martyr, one hundred and twenty; others say one hundred and eighty. The men he left at Hayti are reckoned variously at thirty-nine, forty-three, forty-eight, fifty-five, etc. Major, *Select Letters*, p. 12, reckons them as from thirty-seven to forty. The

With the rest of his company and in his two smaller vessels, on the 4th of January, 1493, Columbus started on his return to Spain. He ran northerly to the latitude of his destination, and then steered due east. He experienced severe weather, but reached the Azores safely; and then, passing on, entered the Tagus and had an interview with the Portuguese King. Leaving Lisbon on the 13th, he reached Palos on the 15th of March, after an absence of over seven months.

He was received by the people of the little seaport with acclamations and wonder; and, despatching a messenger to the Spanish Court at Barcelona, he proceeded to Seville to await the commands of the monarchs.

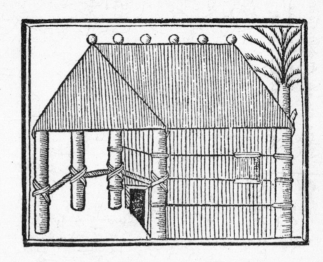

NATIVE HOUSE IN HISPANIOLA.[1]

He was soon bidden to hasten to them; and with the triumph of more than a conqueror, and preceded by the bedizened Indians whom he had brought with him, he entered the city and stood in the presence of the sovereigns. He was commanded to sit before them, and to tell the story of his discovery. This he did with conscious pride; and not forgetting the past,

CURING THE SICK.[2]

lists show among them an Irishman, "Guillermo Ires, natural de Galney, en Irlanda," and an Englishman, "Tallarte de Lajes, Ingles." These are interpreted to mean William Herries — probably "a namesake of ours," says Harrisse — and Arthur Lake. Bernaldez says he carried back with him to Spain ten of the natives.

[1] Fac-simile of a cut in Oviedo, edition of 1547, fol. lix. There is another engraving in Charton's *Voyageurs*, iii. 124. Cf. also Ramusio, *Nav. et Viaggi*, iii.

[2] This is Benzoni's sketch of the way in which the natives cure and tend their sick at Hispaniola. Edition of 1572, p. 56.

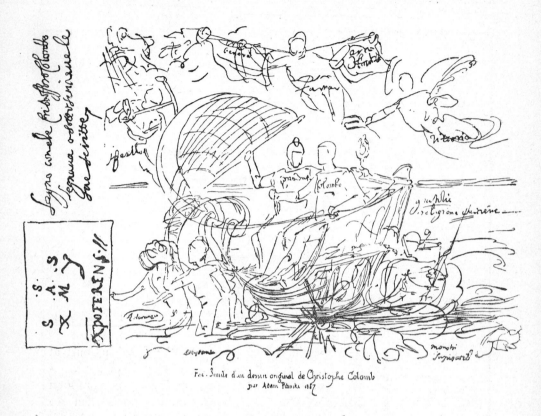

Fac-Simile d'un dessin original de Christophe Colomb
par Adam Pilinski 1867

THE TRIUMPH OF COLUMBUS.[1]

he publicly renewed his previous vow to wrest the Holy Sepulchre from the Infidel.

The expectation which had sustained Columbus in his voyage, and which he thought his discoveries had confirmed, was that he had reached

[1] This is a reduction of a fac-simile by Pilinski, given in Margry's *Les Navigations Françaises*, p. 360, — an earlier reproduction having been given by M. Jal in *La France maritime*. It is also figured in Charton's *Voyageurs*, iii. 139. The original sketch, by Columbus himself, was sent by him from Seville in 1502, and is preserved in the city hall at Genoa. M. Jal gives a description of it in his *De Paris à Naples*, 1836, i. 257. The figure sitting beside Columbus is Providence; Envy and Ignorance are hinted at as monsters following in his wake; while Constancy, Tolerance, the Christian Religion, Victory, and Hope attend him. Above all is the floating figure of Fame blowing two trumpets, one marked "Genoa," the other "Fama Columbi." Harrisse (*Notes on Columbus*, p. 165) says that good judges assign this picture to Columbus's own hand, though none of the drawings ascribed to him are authentic beyond doubt; while it is very true that he had the reputation of being a good draughtsman. Feuillet de Conches (*Revue contemporaine*, xxiv. 509) disbelieves in its authenticity. The usual signature of Columbus is in the lower left-hand corner of the above sketch, the initial letters in which have never been satisfactorily interpreted; but perhaps as reasonable a guess as any would make them stand for "SERVUS SUPPLEX ALTISSIMI SALVATORIS — CHRISTUS, MARIA, YOSEPH — *Christo ferens*." Others read, "SERVIDOR SUS ALTEZAS SACRAS, CHRISTO, MARIA, YSABEL [*or* YOSEPH]." The "Christo ferens" is sometimes replaced by "*El Almirante*." The essay on the autograph in the *Cartas de Indias* is translated in the *Magazine of American History*, Jan., 1883, p. 55. Cf. Irving, app. xxxv. Ruge, *Geschichte des Zeitalters der Entdeckungen*, p. 317; *Massachusetts Historical Society Proceedings*, xvi. 322, etc.

COLUMBUS AT HISPANIOLA.[1]

the western parts of India or Asia; and the new islands were accordingly everywhere spoken of as the West Indies, or the New World.

The ruling Pope, Alexander VI., was a native Valencian; and to him an appeal was now made for a Bull, confirming to Spain and Portugal respec-

[1] Fac-simile of engraving in Herrera, who follows DeBry.

tive fields for discovery.   This was issued May 4, 1493, fixing a line, on the thither side of which Spain was to be master; and on the hither side, Portugal.   This was traced at a meridian one hundred leagues west of the Azores and Cape de Verde Islands, which were assumed to be in the same longi-

HANDWRITING OF COLUMBUS.[1]

tude practically.   The thought of future complications from the running of this line to the antipodes does not seem to have alarmed either Pope or sovereigns; but troubles on the Atlantic side were soon to arise, to be promptly compounded by a convention at Tordesillas, which agreed (June 4, ratified June 7, 1494) to move the meridian line to a point three

[1] Last page of an autograph letter preserved   a photograph in Harrisse's *Notes on Columbus*, in the Colombina Library at Seville, following   p. 218.

hundred and seventy leagues west of the Cape de Verde Islands,—still without dream of the destined disputes respecting divisions on the other side of the globe.[1]

Thus everything favored Columbus in the preparations for a second voyage, which was to conduct a colony to the newly discovered lands.

ARMS OF COLUMBUS.[2]

Twelve hundred souls were embarked on seventeen vessels, and among them persons of consideration and name in subsequent history,—Diego,

[1] The line of 1494 gave Portugal, Brazil, the Moluccas, the Philippines, and half of New Guinea. Jurien de la Gravière, *Les marins du XVe et du XVIe siècle*, i. 86.

[2] As given in Oviedo's *Coronica*, 1547, fol. x., from the Harvard College copy. There is no wholly satisfactory statement regarding the origin of these arms, or the Admiral's right to bear

them. It is the quartering of the royal lion and castle, for Arragon and Castile, with gold islands in azure waves. Five anchors and the motto,

"A [*or* POR] CASTILLA Y A [*or* POR] LEON
    NUEVO MUNDO DIO [*or* HALLO] COLON,"

were later given or assumed. The crest varies in the Oviedo (i. cap. vii.) of 1535.

the Admiral's brother, Bernal Diaz del Castillo, Ojeda, and La Cosa, with the Pope's own vicar, a Benedictine named Buil, or Boil. Columbus and the destined colonists sailed from Cadiz on the 25th of September. The

ships sighted an island on the 3d of November, and continuing their course among the Caribbee Islands, they finally reached La Navidad, and found it a waste. It was necessary, however, to make a beginning somewhere; and a little to the east of the ruined fort they landed their supplies and began the laying out of a city, which they called Isabella.[1] Expeditions were sent inland to find gold. The explorers reported success. Twelve of the

FRUIT-TREES OF HISPANIOLA.[2]

ships were sent home with Indians who had been seized; and these ships were further laden with products of the soil which had been gathered. Columbus himself went with four hundred men to begin work at the interior mines; but the natives, upon whom he had counted for labor, had begun to fear enslavement for this purpose, and kept aloof. So mining did not flourish. Disease, too, was working evil. Columbus himself had been prostrated; but he was able to conduct three caravels westward, when he discovered Jamaica. On this expedition he made up his mind that Cuba

INDIAN CLUB.[3]

was a part of the Asiatic main, and somewhat unadvisedly forced his men to sign a paper declaring their own belief to the same purport.[4]

Returning to his colony, the Admiral found that all was not going well. He had not himself inspired confidence as a governor, and his fame as an explorer was fast being eclipsed by his misfortunes as a ruler. Some of his colonists, accompanied by the papal vicar, had seized ships and set sail

---

[1] Bancroft, *Central America*, i. 496, describes the procedures finally established in laying out towns.

[2] This is Benzoni's sketch, edition of 1572, p. 60.

[3] As given in Oviedo, edition of 1547, fol. lxi.

[4] Navarrete, ii. 143. It is the frequent recurrence of such audacious and arrogant acts on the part of Columbus which explains his sad failure as an administrator, and seriously impairs the veneration in which the world would rejoice to hold him.

for home. The natives, emboldened by the cruelties practised upon them, were laying siege to his fortified posts. As an offset, however, his brother Bartholomew had arrived from Spain with three store-ships; and later came Antonio de Torres with four other ships, which in due time were

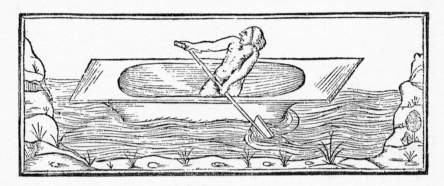

INDIAN CANOE.[1]

sent back to carry some samples of gold and a cargo of natives to be sold as slaves. The vessels had brought tidings of the charges preferred at Court against the Admiral, and his brother Diego was sent back with the ships to answer these charges in the Admiral's behalf. Unfortunately Diego was not a man of strong character, and his advocacy was not of the best.

In March (1495) Columbus conducted an expedition into the interior to subdue and hold tributary the native population. It was cruelly done, as the world looks upon such transactions to-day.

Meanwhile in Spain reiteration of charges

INDIAN CANOE.[2]

was beginning to shake the confidence of his sovereigns; and Juan Aguado, a friend of Columbus, was sent to investigate. He reached

---

[1] As depicted in Oviedo, edition of 1547, fol. lxi. There is another engraving in Charton's *Voyageurs*, iii. 106, called "Pirogue Indienne."

[2] Benzoni gives this drawing of the canoes of the coast of the Gulf of Paria and thereabout. Edition of 1572, p. 5.

COLUMBUS AT ISLA MARGARITA.[1]

Isabella in October, — Diego, the Admiral's brother, accompanying him.
Aguado did not find affairs reassuring; and when he returned to Spain
with his report in March (1496), Columbus thought it best to go too, and to
make his excuses or explanations in person. They reached Cadiz in June,
just as Niño was sailing with three caravels to the new colony.

[1] Fac-simile of engraving in Herrera.

Ferdinand and Isabella received him kindly, gave him new honors, and promised him other outfits. Enthusiasm, however, had died out, and delays took place. The reports of the returning ships did not correspond with the pictures of Marco Polo, and the new-found world was thought to

AMERICANS.[1]

be a very poor India after all. Most people were of this mind; though Columbus was not disheartened, and the public treasury was readily opened for a third voyage.

Coronel sailed early in 1498 with two ships, and Columbus followed with six, embarking at San Lucas on the 30th of May. He now discovered

[1] This is the earliest representation which we have of the natives of the New World, showing such as were found by the Portuguese on the north coast of South America. It has been supposed that it was issued in Augsburg somewhere between 1497 and 1504, for it is not dated. The only copy ever known to bibliographers is not now to be traced. Stevens, *Recoll. of James Lenox*, p. 174. It measures $13\frac{1}{2} \times 8\frac{1}{2}$ inches, with a German title and inscription, to be translated as follows : —

"This figure represents to us the people and island which have been discovered by the Christian King of Portugal, or his subjects. The people are thus naked, handsome, brown, well-shaped in body; their heads, necks, arms, pri-vate parts, feet of men and women, are a little covered with feathers. The men also have many precious stones on their faces and breasts. No one else has anything, but all things are in common. And the men have as wives those who please them, be they mothers, sisters, or friends; therein make they no distinction. They also fight with each other; they also eat each other, even those who are slain, and hang the flesh of them in the smoke. They become a hundred and fifty years of age, and have no government."

The present engraving follows the fac-simile given in Stevens's *American Bibliographer*, pp. 7, 8. Cf. Sabin, vol. i. no. 1,031; vol. v. no. 20,257; Harrisse, *Bibl. Amer. Vet.*, no. 20.

Trinidad (July 31), which he named either from its three peaks, or from the Holy Trinity; struck the northern coast of South America,[1] and skirted what was later known as the Pearl coast, going as far as the Island of Margarita. He wondered at the roaring fresh waters which the Orinoco pours into the Gulf of Pearls, as he called it, and he half believed that its exuberant tide came from the terrestrial paradise.[2] He touched the southern coast of Hayti on the 30th of August. Here already his colonists had established a fortified post, and founded the town of Santo Domingo. His brother Bartholomew had ruled energetically during the Admiral's absence, but he had not prevented a revolt, which was headed by Roldan. Columbus on his arrival found the insurgents still defiant, but was able after a while to reconcile them, and he even succeeded in attaching Roldan warmly to his interests.

Columbus' absence from Spain, however, left his good name without sponsors; and to satisfy detractors, a new commissioner was sent over with enlarged powers, even with authority to supersede Columbus in general command, if necessary. This emissary was Francisco de Bobadilla, who arrived at Santo Domingo with two caravels on the 23d of August, 1500, finding Diego in command, his brother the Admiral being absent. An issue was at once made. Diego refused to accede to the commissioner's orders till Columbus returned to judge the case himself; so Bobadilla assumed charge of the Crown property violently, took possession of the Admiral's house, and when Columbus returned, he with his brother was arrested and put in irons. In this condition the prisoners were placed on shipboard, and sailed for Spain. The captain of the ship offered to remove the manacles; but Columbus would not permit it, being determined to land in Spain bound as he was; and so he did. The effect of his degradation was to his advantage; sovereigns and people were shocked at the sight; and Ferdinand and Isabella hastened to make amends by receiving him with renewed favor. It was soon apparent that everything reasonable would be granted him by the monarchs, and that he could have all he might wish, short of receiving a new lease of power in the islands, which the sovereigns were determined to see pacified at least before Columbus should again assume government of them. The Admiral had not forgotten his vow to wrest the Holy Sepulchre from the Infidel; but the monarchs did not accede to his wish to undertake it. Disappointed in this, he proposed a new voyage; and getting the royal countenance for this scheme, he was supplied with four vessels of from fifty to seventy tons each, — the " Capitana," the " Santiago de Palos," the " Gallego," and the " Vizcaino." He

[1] The question of the priority of Columbus' discovery of the mainland over Vespucius is discussed in the following chapter. M. Herrera is said to have brought forward, at the Congrès des Américanistes held at Copenhagen in 1883, new evidence of Columbus's landing on the mainland. Father Manoel de la Vega, in his *Historia* *del descobrimiento de la America septentrional*, first published in Mexico in 1826 by Bustamante, alleges that Columbus in this southern course was intending to test the theory of King John of Portugal, that land blocked a westerly passage in that direction.

[2] Irving, app. xxxiii.

sailed from Cadiz May 9, 1502, accompanied by his brother Bartholomew and his son Fernando. The vessels reached San Domingo June 29.

Bobadilla, whose rule of a year and a half had been an unhappy one, had given place to Nicholás de Ovando; and the fleet which brought the new governor, — with Maldonado, Las Casas, and others, — now lay in the harbor waiting to receive Bobadilla for the return voyage. Columbus had been instructed to avoid Hispaniola; but now that one of his vessels leaked, and he needed to make repairs, he sent a boat ashore, asking permission to enter the harbor. He was refused, though a storm was impending. He sheltered his vessels as best he could, and rode out the gale. The fleet which had on board Bobadilla and Roldan, with their ill-gotten gains, was wrecked, and these enemies of Columbus were drowned. The Admiral found a small harbor where he could make his repairs; and then, July 14, sailed westward to find, as he supposed, the richer portions of India in exchange for the barbarous outlying districts which others had appropriated to themselves. He went on through calm and storm, giving names to islands, — which later explorers re-named, and spread thereby confusion on the early maps. He began to find more intelligence in the natives of these islands than those of Cuba had betrayed, and got intimations of lands still farther west, where copper and gold were in abundance. An old Indian made them a rough map of the main shore. Columbus took him on board, and proceeding onward a landing was made on the coast of Honduras August 14. Three days later the explorers landed again fifteen leagues farther east, and took possession of the country for Spain. Still east they went; and, in gratitude for safety after a long storm, they named a cape which they rounded Gracias á Dios, — a name still preserved at the point where the coast of Honduras begins to trend southward. Columbus was now lying ill on his bed, placed on deck, and was half the time in revery. Still the vessels coasted south. They lost a boat's crew in getting water at one place; and tarrying near the mouth of the Rio San Juan, they thought they got from the signs of the natives intelligence of a rich and populous country over the mountains inland, where the men wore clothes and bore weapons of steel, and the women were decked with corals and pearls. These stories were reassuring; but the exorcising incantations of the natives were quite otherwise for the superstitious among the Spaniards.

They were now on the shores of Costa Rica, where the coast trends southeast; and both the rich foliage and the gold plate on the necks of the savages enchanted the explorers. They went on towards the source of this wealth, as they fancied. The natives began to show some signs of repulsion; but a few hawk's-bells beguiled them, and gold plates were received in exchange for the trinkets. The vessels were now within the southernmost loop of the shore, and a bit of stone wall seemed to the Spaniards a token of civilization. The natives called a town hereabouts Veragua, — whence, years after, the descendants of Columbus borrowed the ducal title of his line. In this region Columbus dallied, not suspecting how thin the strip of country was which separated him from the great ocean whose farther waves washed his desired India. Then, still pursuing the coast, which now turned to the northeast, he reached Porto Bello, as we call it, where he found houses and orchards. Tracking the Gulf side of the Panama isthmus, he encountered storms that forced him into harbors, which continued to disclose the richness of the country.[1]

It became now apparent that they had reached the farthest spot of Bastidas' exploring, who had, in 1501, sailed westward along the northern coast of South America. Amid something like mutinous cries from the sailors, Columbus was fain to turn back to the neighborhood of Veragua, where the gold was; but on arriving there, the seas, lately so fair, were tumultuous, and the Spaniards were obliged to repeat the gospel of Saint John to keep a water-spout, which they saw, from coming their way, — so Fernando says in his Life of the Admiral. They finally made a harbor at the mouth of the River Belen, and began to traffic with the natives, who proved very cautious and evasive when inquiries were made respecting gold-mines. Bartholomew explored the neighboring Veragua River in armed boats, and met the chief of the region, with retainers, in a fleet of canoes. Gold and trinkets were exchanged, as usual, both here and later on the Admiral's deck. Again Bartholomew led another expedition, and getting the direction — a purposely false one, as it proved — from the chief in his own village, he went to a mountain, near the abode of an enemy of the chief, and found gold, — scant, however, in quantity compared with that of the crafty chief's own fields. The inducements were sufficient, however, as Columbus thought, to found a colony; but before he got ready to leave it, he suspected the neighboring chief was planning offensive operations. An expedition was accordingly sent to seize the chief, and he was captured in his own village; and so suddenly that his own people could not protect him. The craft of the savage, however, stood him in good stead; and while one of the Spaniards was conveying him down the river in a boat, he jumped overboard and disappeared, only to reappear, a few days later, in leading an attack on the Spanish camp. In this the Indians were repulsed; but it was the beginning of a kind of lurking warfare that disheartened the Spaniards. Meanwhile Columbus, with the ship, was outside the harbor's bar buffeting the gales. The rest of the prisoners who had been taken with the chief were confined in his forecastle. By concerted action some of them got out and jumped overboard, while those not so fortunate killed themselves. As soon as the storm was over, Columbus withdrew the colonists and sailed away. He abandoned one worm-eaten caravel at Porto Bello, and, reaching Jamaica, beached two others.

A year of disappointment, grief, and want followed. Columbus clung to his wrecked vessels. His crew alternately mutinied at his side, and roved

[1] H. H. Bancroft, *Central America*, vol. i. chap. iv., traces with some care the coast-findings of this voyage and the varying cartographical records.

about the island. Ovando, at Hispaniola, heard of his straits, but only tardily and scantily relieved him. The discontented were finally humbled; and some ships, despatched by the Admiral's agent in Santo Domingo, at last reached him, and brought him and his companions to that place, where Ovando received him with ostentatious kindness, lodging him in his house till Columbus departed for Spain, Sept. 12, 1504.

On the 7th of November the Admiral reached the harbor of San Lucas. Weakness and disease later kept him in bed in Seville, and to his letters of appeal the King paid little attention. He finally recovered sufficiently to go to the Court at Segovia, in May, 1505; but Ferdinand — Isabella had died Nov. 26, 1504 — gave him scant courtesy. With a fatalistic iteration, which had been his error in life, Columbus insisted still on the rights which a better skill in governing might have saved for him; and Ferdinand, with a dread of continued maladministration, as constantly evaded the issue. While still hope was deferred, the infirmities of age and a life of hardships brought Columbus to his end; and on Ascension Day, the 20th of May, 1506, he died, with his son Diego and a few devoted friends by his bedside.

The character of Columbus is not difficult to discern. If his mental and moral equipoise had been as true, and his judgment as clear, as his spirit was lofty and impressive, he could have controlled the actions of men as readily as he subjected their imaginations to his will, and more than one brilliant

HOUSE IN WHICH COLUMBUS DIED.[1]

opportunity for a record befitting a ruler of men would not have been lost. The world always admires constancy and zeal; but when it is fed, not by well-rounded performance, but by self-satisfaction and self-interest, and tarnished by deceit, we lament where we would approve. Columbus' imagination was eager, and unfortunately ungovernable. It led him to a great discovery, which he was not seeking for; and he was far enough right to make his error more emphatic. He is certainly not alone among the great men of the world's regard who have some of the attributes of the small and mean.

[1] This follows an engraving in Ruge, *Geschichte des Zeitalters der Entdeckungen*, p. 313, taken from a photograph. The house is in Valladolid.

CRITICAL ESSAY ON THE SOURCES OF INFORMATION.

IT would appear, from documents printed by Navarrete that in 1470 Columbus was brooding on the idea of land to the west. It is not at all probable that he would himself have been able to trace from germ to flower the conception which finally possessed his mind.[1] The age was ripened for it; and the finding of Brazil in 1500 by Cabral showed how by an accident the theory might have become a practical result at any time after the sailors of Europe had dared to take long ocean voyages. Columbus grew to imagine that he had been independent of the influences of his time; and in a manuscript in his own hand, preserved in the Colombina Library at Seville, he shows the weak, almost irresponsible, side of his mind, and flouts at the grounds of reasonable progress which many others besides himself had been making to a belief in the feasibility of a western passage. In this unfortunate writing he declares that under inspiration he simply accomplished the prophecy of Isaiah.[2] This assertion has not prevented saner and later writers[3] from surveying the evidences of the growth of the belief in the mind, not of Columbus only, but of others whom he may have impressed, and by whom he may have been influenced. The new intuition was but the result of intellectual reciprocity. It needed a daring exponent, and found one.

The geographical ideas which bear on this question depend, of course, upon the sphericity of the earth.[4] This was entertained by the leading cosmographical thinkers of that age, — who were far however from being in accord in respect to the size of the globe. Going back to antiquity, Aristotle and Strabo had both taught in their respective times the spherical theory; but they too were widely divergent upon the question of size, — Aristotle's ball being but mean in comparison with that of Strabo, who was not far wrong when he contended that the world then known was something more than one third of the actual circumference of the whole, or one hundred and twenty-nine degrees, as he put it; while Marinus, the Tyrian, of the opposing school, and the most eminent geographer before Ptolemy, held that the extent of the then known world spanned as much as two hundred and twenty-five degrees, or about one hundred degrees too much.[5] Columbus' calculations were all on the side of this insufficient size.[6] He wrote to Queen Isabella in 1503 that "the earth is smaller than people suppose." He thought but one seventh of it was water. In sailing a direct western course his expectation was to reach Cipango after having gone

[1] Helps says: "The greatest geographical discoveries have been made by men conversant with the book-knowledge of their own time." The age of Columbus was perhaps the most illustrious of ages. "Where in the history of nations," says Humboldt, "can one find an epoch so fraught with such important results as the discovery of America, the passage to the East Indies round the Cape of Good Hope, and Magellan's first circumnavigation, simultaneously occurring with the highest perfection of art, the attainment of intellectual and religious freedom, and with the sudden enlargement of the knowledge of the earth and the heavens?" *Cosmos*, Eng. tr., ii. 673.

[2] This manuscript is the *Libro de las profecias*, of which parts are printed in Navarrete. Cf. Harrisse, *Notes on Columbus*, p. 156, who calls it a "curious medley of quotations and puerile inferences;" and refers for an analysis of it to Gallardo's *Ensayo*, ii. 500. Harrisse thinks the hand is that of Ferdinand Columbus when a boy, and that it may have been written under the Admiral's direction.

[3] Irving, book i. chap. v.; Humboldt, *Examen critique* and *Cosmos ;* Major, *Prince Henry of Portugal*, chap. xix. and *Discoveries of Prince Henry*, chap. xiv.; Stevens, *Notes ;* Helps, *Spanish Conquest ;* and among the early writers, Las Casas, not to name others.

[4] Columbus, it is well known, advocated later a pear-shape, instead of a sphere. Cf. the "Tercer viage" in Navarrete.

[5] Robertson's *America*, note xii. Humboldt cites the ancients; *Examen critique*, i. 38, 61, 98, etc.

[6] Ferdinand Columbus says that the Arab astronomer, Al Fergani, influenced Columbus to the same end; and these views he felt were confirmed by the reports of Marco Polo and Mandeville. Cf. Yule's *Marco Polo*, vol. i. p. cxxxi.

about three thousand miles. This would actually have brought him within a hundred miles or so of Cape Henlopen, or the neighboring coast; while if no land had intervened he would have gone nine thousand eight hundred miles to reach Japan, the modern Cipango.[1] Thus Columbus' earth was something like two thirds of the actual magnitude.[2] It can readily be understood how the lesser distance was helpful in inducing a crew to accompany Columbus, and in strengthening his own determination.

Whatever the size of the earth, there was far less palpable reason to determine it than to settle the question of its sphericity. The phenomena which convince the ordinary mind to-day, weighed with Columbus as they had weighed in earlier ages. These were the hulling down of ships at sea, and the curved shadow of the earth on the moon in an eclipse. The law of gravity was not yet proclaimed, indeed; but it had been observed that the men on two ships, however far apart, stood perpendicular to their decks at rest.

Columbus was also certainly aware of some of the views and allusions to be found in the ancient writers, indicating a belief in lands lying beyond the Pillars of Hercules.[3] He enumerates some of them in the letter which he wrote about his third voyage, and which is printed in Navarrete. The Colombina Library contains two interesting memorials of his

---

[1] By a great circle course the distance would have been reduced to something short of five thousand eight hundred miles. (Fox in *U. S. Coast Survey Report*, 1880, app. xviii.) Marco Polo had not distinctly said how far off the coast of China the Island of Cipango lay.

[2] Cf. D'Avezac in *Bulletin de la Société de Géographie de Paris*, August – October, 1857, p. 97. Behaim in his globe placed China 120° west of Cape St. Vincent; and Columbus is supposed to have shared Behaim's views and both were mainly in accord with Toscanelli. Humboldt, *Examen Critique*, ii. 357.

[3] Not long from the time of his first voyage the *Orbis breviarium* of Lilius, which later passed through other editions and translations, summarized the references of the ancients (Stevens, *Bibl. Geog.* no. 1,670). But Harrisse, *Notes on Columbus*, p. 180, holds that the earliest instance of the new found islands being declared the parts known to the ancients, and referred to by Virgil in the 6th book of the Æneid, —

"Jacet extra sidera tellus," etc.,

is in the *Geographia* of Henricus Glareanus, published at Basle in 1527. Cf. also Gravier, *Les Normands sur la route des Indes*, Rouen, 1880, p. 24; Harrisse, *Bibl. Am. Vet.* 262. Mr. Murphy, in placing the 1472 edition of Strabo's *De Situ orbis* in his American collection, pointed to the belief of this ancient geographer in the existence of the American continent as a habitable part of the globe, as shown when he says: "Nisi Atlantici maris obstaret magnitudo, posse nos navigare per eundem parallelum ex Hispania in Indiam, etc." Cf. further, Charles Sumner's *Prophetic Voices concerning America*; also in his *Works*; Bancroft's *Native Races*, v. 68, 122; Baldwin's *Prehistoric Nations*, 399; Fontaine's *How the World was peopled*, p. 139; Las Casas, *Historia general*; Sherer, *Researches touching the New World*, 1777; *Recherches sur*

la géographie des anciens, Paris, 1797–1813; *Memoirs* of the Lisbon Academy, v. 101; Paul Gaffarel, *L'Amérique avant Colomb*, and his "Les Grecs et les Romains, ont ils connu l'Amérique?" in the *Revue de Géographie* (1881), ix. 241, etc.; Ferdinand Columbus' life of his father, and Humboldt's examination of his views in his *Examen critique*; Brasseur de Bourbourg's Introduction to his *Popul-Vuh*.

Glareanus, above referred to, was one of the most popular of the condensed cosmographical works of the time; and it gave but the briefest reference to the New World, "de regionibus extra Ptolemæum." Its author was under thirty when he published his first edition in 1527 at Basle. There is a copy in the Carter-Brown Library (*Catalogue*, i. 90). Cf. also *Bibl. Amer. Vet.*, 142; Huth, ii. 602; Weigel, 1877, p. 82, priced at 18 marks. It was reprinted at Basle, the next year, 1528 (Trömel, 3), and again in 1529. (*Bibl. Amer. Vet.*, 143, 147.) Another edition was printed at Freiburg (Brisgau) in 1530, of which there are copies in Harvard College and Carter-Brown (*Catalogue*, no. 95) libraries. (Cf. *Bibl. Amer. Vet.*, 147; Muller, 1877, no. 1,232.) There were other Freiburg imprints in 1533, 1536, 1539, 1543, and 1551. (*Bibl. Amer. Vet.*, 183, 212, 248; *Additions*, 121; Carter-Brown, i. 160; White Kennett, p. 12; Trömel, no. 12; Murphy, 1049.) There were Venice imprints in 1534, 1537, 1538, 1539, and 1544. (*Bibl. Amer. Vet.*, 225, 228, 259; *Additions*, 120; Lancetti, *Buchersaal*, i. 79.) An edition of Venice, without date, is assigned to 1549. (*Catalogue of the Sumner Collection in Harvard College Library*.) Editions were issued at Paris in 1542, with a folded map, "Typus cosmographicus universalis," in 1550 (Court, 144), and in 1572, the last repeating the map. (*Bibl. Amer. Vet.*, 139.) The text of all these editions is in Latin. Sabin, vol. vii. no. 27,536, etc., enumerates most of the editions.

connection with this belief.   One is a treatise in his own hand, giving his correspondence with Father Gorricio, who gathered the ancient views and prophecies ; [1] and the other is a copy of Gaietanus' edition of Seneca's tragedies, published indeed after Columbus' death, in which the passage of the *Medea*, known to have been much in Columbus' mind, is scored with the marginal comment of Ferdinand, his son, " Hæc prophetia expleta ē per patrē meus cristoforū colō almirātē anno 1492." [2]   Columbus, further, could not have been unaware of

Per me doctrina totum diuina Mathesis
Corpus habet: cuius glorior esse parens.

PTOLEMY.[3]

the opposing theories of Ptolemy and Pomponius Mela as to the course in which the further extension of the known world should be pursued.   Ptolemy held to the east and west theory, and Mela to the northern and southern view.

The Angelo Latin translation of Ptolemy's Greek *Geographia* had served to disseminate the Alexandrian geographer's views through almost the whole of the fifteenth century,

---

[1] Such as Plato's in his *Critias* and *Timæus,* and Aristotle's in his *De Mundo,* cap. iii., etc.

[2] Harrisse, *Bibliotheca Americana Vetustissima ; Additions,* no. 36.

[3] Fac-simile of a cut in *Icones sive imagines vivæ literis cl. virorum . . . cum elogiis variis per Nicolaum Reusnerum.   Basiliæ, CIƆ IƆ XIC,* Sig. A. 4.

for that version had been first made in 1409. In 1475 it had been printed, and it had helped strengthen the arguments of those who favored a belief in the position of India as lying over against Spain. Several other editions were yet to be printed in the new typo-

CL. PTOLOMAEVS ALEXAN-
drinus Mathematicus.

Per me Doctrinæ totum diuina Mathesis Corpus habet: cuius glorior esse parens.

PTOLEMY.[1]

graphical centres of Europe, all exerting more or less influence in support of the new views advocated by Columbus.[2] Five of these editions of Ptolemy appeared during the interval

[1] Fac-simile of cut in *Icones sive imagines virorum literis illustrium . . . ex secunda recognitione Nicolai Reusneri. Argentorati, CIƆIƆ XC,* p. 1. The first edition appeared in 1587. Brunet, vol. iv., col. 1255, calls the editions of 1590 and Frankfort, 1620, inferior.

[2] Bernaldez tells us that Columbus was a reader of Ptolemy and of John de Mandeville. Cf. on the spreading of Ptolemy's views at this time Lelewel, *Géographie du moyen âge,* ii. p. 122; Thomassy, *Les papes géographes,* pp. 15, 34. There are copies of the 1475 edition of Ptolemy in the Library of Congress and the Carter-Brown Library (cf. also *Murphy Catalogue,* no. 2,044); of the 1478 edition, the only copy in this country, so far as known, is the one in the Carter-Brown Library, added to that collection since its catalogue was printed. The Perkins copy in 1873 brought £80 (cf. *Livres payés en vente publique* 1,000 *francs,* etc., p. 137). It was the first edition

from 1475 to 1492.   Of Pomponius Mela, advocating the views of which the Portuguese were at this time proving the truth, the earliest printed edition had appeared in 1471. Mela's treatise, *De situ orbis*, had been produced in the first century, while Ptolemy had made his views known in the second; and the age of Vasco da Gama, Columbus, and Magellan were to prove the complemental relations of their respective theories.

It has been said that Macrobius, a Roman of the fifth century, in a commentary on the *Dream of Scipio*, had maintained a division of the globe into four continents, of which two were then unknown.   In the twelfth century this idea had been revived by Guillaume de Conches (who died about 1150) in his *Philosophia Minor*, lib. iv. cap. 3.   It was again later further promulgated in the writings of Bede and Honoré d'Autun, and in the *Micro-cosmos* of Geoffroy de Saint-Victor, — a manuscript of the thirteenth century still pre-served.[1]   It is not known that this theory was familiar to Columbus.   The chief directors of his thoughts among anterior writers appear to have been, directly or indirectly, Alber-tus Magnus, Roger Bacon, and Vincenzius of Beauvais;[2] and first among them, for importance, we must place the *Opus Majus* of Roger Bacon, completed in 1267.   It was from Bacon that Petrus de Aliaco, or Pierre d'Ailly (b. 1340; d. 1416 or 1425), in his *Ymago mundi*, borrowed the passage which, in this French imitator's language, so impressed Columbus.[3]

with maps.   Lelewel (vol. ii. p. 124) had traced the influence of the Agathodæmon (Ptolemean) maps on the cartography of the Middle Ages. The maps representing the growth of geograph-ical ideas anterior to Columbus will be exam-ined in another place.   The Ulm edition of Ptolemy, 1482, showed in its map of the world a part of what is now called America in repre-senting Greenland; but it gave it a distinct rela-tion to Europe, by making Greenland a peninsula of the Scandinavian north.   There seems reason to believe that this map was made in 1471, and it passes for the earliest engraved map to show that northern region, — "Engrone-land," as it is called.   If we reject the Zeno map with its alleged date of 1400 or thereabout (published long after Columbus, in 1558), the oldest known delinea-tions of Greenland (which there is no evidence that Columbus ever saw, and from which if he had seen them, he could have inferred nothing to advantage) are a Genoese manuscript map in the Pitti palace, which Santarem (*Histoire de la Car-tographie*, vol. iii. p. xix) dates 1417, but which seems instead to be properly credited to 1447, the peninsula here being "Grinlandia " (cf. Lele-wel, *Epilogue*, p. 167; *Magazine of American History*, April, 1883, p. 290); and the map of Claudius Clavus, assigned to 1427, which be-longs to a manuscript of Ptolemy, preserved in the library at Nancy.   This, with the Zeno map and that in the Ptolemy of 1482, is given in *Trois cartes précolombiennes représentant Groen-land, fac-simile présentés au Congrès des Améri-canistes à Copenhague ; par A. E. Nordenskiöld*, Stockholm, 1883.   In the Laon globe (1486–1487) "Grolandia " is put down as an island off the Norway coast.   There is a copy of this 1482 edition of Ptolemy in the Carter-Brown Library, and another is noted in the *Murphy Catalogue*, no. 2,046.   Its maps were repeated in the 1486

edition, also published at Ulm; and of this there was a copy in the Murphy Collection (no. 2,047, — bought by President White, of Cor-nell); and another belongs to the late G. W. Riggs, of Washington.   In 1490 the Roman edition of 1478 was reproduced with the same maps ; and of this there is a copy in the Carter-Brown Li-brary; and another is shown in the *Murphy Cata-logue* (no. 2,048).   A splendidly illuminated copy of this edition sold in the Sunderland sale (part v. no. 13,770) has since been held by Quaritch at £600.   See further on these early editions of Ptolemy in Winsor's *Bibliography of Ptolemy's Geography*, published by Harvard University.

[1] Gravier, *Les Normands sur la route des Indes*, Rouen, 1880, p. 37.

[2] Humboldt, *Cosmos* (Eng. ed.), ii. 619. The *Speculum naturale* of Vincenzius (1250) is an encyclopædic treatise, closely allied with other treatises of that time, like the *De rerum natura* of Cantipratensis (1230), and the later work of Meygenberg (1349).

[3] Humboldt, *Examen Critique*, i. 61, 65, 70; ii. 349.   Columbus quoted this passage in Octo-ber, 1498, in his letter from Santo Domingo to the Spanish monarch.   Margry, *Navigations Françaises*, Paris, 1867, p. 71, "Les deux Indes du XVᵉ siècle et l'influence Française sur Co-lomb," has sought to reflect credit on his country by tracing the influence of the *Imago mundi* in the discovery of the New World; but the bor-rowing from Bacon destroys his case. (Major, *Select Letters of Columbus*, p. xlvii ; Harrisse, *Notes on Columbus*, p. 84.)   If Margry's claim is correct, that there was an edition of the *Imago mundi* printed at Nuremberg in 1472, it would carry it back of the beginning of Colum-bus's advocacy of his views; but bibliographers find no edition earlier than 1480 or 1483, and most place this *editio princeps* ten years later,

An important element in the problem was the statements of Marco Polo regarding a large island, which he called Cipango, and which he represented as lying in the ocean off the eastern coast of Asia. This carried the eastern verge of the Asiatic world farther than the ancients had known ; and, on the spherical theory, brought land nearer westward from

ALBERTVS MAGNVS EPI
ſcopus Ratiſponenſis.

Magnus eram Sophiæ doctor, Præſulq; ſacrorum:
Abdita naturæ vis mihi nota liquet.
M. CCCIXCII.

ALBERTUS MAGNUS.[1]

as Humboldt does. It is generally agreed that the book was written in 1410. A copy of this first edition, of whatever date, is preserved in the Colombina Library in Seville ; and it was the copy used by Columbus and Las Casas. Its margins are annotated, and the notes, which are by most thought to be in the hand of Columbus, have been published by Varnhagen in the *Bulletin de la Société de Géographie de Paris*, January, 1858, p. 71, and by Peschel in his *Geschichte des Zeitalters der Entdeckungen*, p. 112, — who, however, ascribes the notes to Bartholomew Columbus. A fac-simile of part of them is given on p. 31. Cf. Major, *Prince Henry*, p. 349; Carter-Brown, vol. i. no. 3; *Murphy Catalogue*, no. 27, bought by Cornell Univ. and Dinaux, *Cardinal P. d'Ailly*, Cambray, 1824.

[1] Fac-simile of cut in Reusner's *Icones*, Strasburg, 1590, p. 4. There is another cut in Paulus Jovius's *Elogia virorum litteris illustrium*, Basle, 1575, p. 7 (copy in Harvard College Library).

Europe than could earlier have been supposed.   It is a question, however, if Columbus had any knowledge of the Latin or Italian manuscripts of Marco Polo, — the only form in which anybody could have studied his narrative before the printing of it at Nuremberg in 1477, in German, a language which Columbus is not likely to have known.   Humboldt

has pointed out that neither Columbus nor his son Ferdinand mentions Marco Polo ; still we know that he had read his book.   Columbus further knew, it would seem, what Æneas Sylvius had written on Asia. Toscanelli had also imparted to him what he knew.   A second German edition of Marco Polo appeared at Augsburg in 1481.   In 1485, with the *Itinerarius* of Mandeville,[1] published at Zwolle, the account — " De regionibus orientalibus " — of Marco Polo first appeared in Latin, translated from the original French, in which it had been dictated.   It was probably in this form that Columbus first saw it.[2]   There was a separate Latin edition in 1490.[3]

The most definite confirmation and encouragement which Columbus received in his views would seem to have come from Toscanelli, in 1474. This eminent Italian astronomer, who was now about seventy-eight years old, and was to die, in 1482, before Columbus and Da Gama had con-

MARCO POLO.[4]

summated their discoveries, had reached a conclusion in his own mind that only about fifty-two degrees of longitude separated Europe westerly from Asia, making the earth much smaller even than Columbus' inadequate views had fashioned it ; for Columbus had

[1] Mandeville had made his Asiatic journey and long sojourn (thirty-four years) thirty or forty years later than Marco Polo, and on his return had written his narrative in English, French, and Latin.   It was first printed in French at Lyons, in 1480.

[2] A copy of this edition is in the Colombina Library, with marginal marks ascribed to Columbus, but of no significance except as aids to the memory.   Cf. *Harper's Monthly*, xlvi. p. 1.

[3] There were other editions between his first voyage and his death, — an Italian one in 1496, and a Portuguese in 1502.   For later editions, cf. Harrisse, *Bibl. Am. Vet.*, no. 89 ; Navarrete, *Bibl. maritima*, ii. 668 ; Brunet, iii. 1,406 ; Saint-Martin, *Histoire de la Géographie*, p. 278.   The recent editions of distinctive merit are those, in English, of Colonel Yule ; the various texts issued in the *Recueil de voyages et de mémoires publiés par la Société de Géographie de Paris ;* and *Le livre de Marco Polo, rédigé en Français*

sous sa dictée en 1298, *par Rusticien de Pise, publ. pour la* 1e *fois d'après* 3 *MSS. inéd., av. variantes, comment. géogr. et histor., etc.,* par G. Pauthier. 2 vols.   Paris : Didot, 1865.   Cf. Foscarini, *Della lett. Ven.* 239 ; Zurla, *Di Marco Polo ;* Maltebrun, *Histoire de la Géographie ;* Tiraboschi, *Storia della lett. Ital,* vol. iv.; Vivien de Saint-Martin, *Histoire de la Géographie,* p. 272 ; and the bibliography of the MSS. and printed editions of the *Milione* given in Pietro Amat di S. Filippo's *Studi biog. e bibliog.,* published by the Società Geografica Italiana in 1882 (2d ed.).   A facsimile of a manuscript of the fourteenth century of the *Livre de Marco Polo* was prepared under the care of Nordenskiöld, and printed at Stockholm in 1882.   The original is in the Royal Library at Stockholm.

[4] This follows an engraving in Ruge's *Geschichte des Zeitalters der Entdeckungen,* p. 53.   The original is at Rome.   There is a copy of an old print in Jules Verne's *Découverte de la Terre.*

satisfied himself that one hundred and twenty degrees of the entire three hundred and sixty was only as yet unknown.[1] With such views of the inferiority of the earth, Toscanelli had addressed a letter to Martinez, a prebendary of Lisbon, accompanied by a map professedly based on information derived from the book of Marco Polo.[2] When Toscanelli received a letter of inquiry from Columbus, he replied by sending a copy of this letter and the map. As the testimony to a western passage from a man of Toscanelli's eminence, it was of marked importance in the conversion of others to similar views.[3]

It has always been a question how far the practical evidence of chance phenomena, and the absolute knowledge, derived from

[1] The actual distance from Spain westerly to China is two hundred and thirty-one degrees.

[2] Cf. Zurla, *Fra Mauro*, p. 152; Lelewel, ii. 107.

[3] The Italian text of Toscanelli's letter has been long known in Ferdinand Columbus' Life of his father; but Harrisse calls it "très-inexact et interpolée;" and, in his *Bibl. Am. Vet. Additions* (1872), p. xvi, Harrisse gives the Latin text, which he had already printed, in 1871, in his *Don Fernando Colon*, published at Seville, from a copy made of it which had been discovered by the librarian of the Colombina, transcribed by Columbus himself in a copy of Æneas Sylvius' (Pius II.'s) *Historia rerum ubique gestarum*, Venice, 1477, preserved in that library. Harrisse also gives a photographic fac-simile of this memorial of Columbus. Cf. D'Avezac, in the *Bulletin de la Société de Géographie de Paris*, October, 1873, p. 46; and Harrisse, *Les Cortereal*, p. 41. The form of the letter, as given in Navarrete, is translated into English in Kettell's *Journal of Columbus*, p. 268, and in Becher's *Landfall of Columbus*, p. 183. Cf. Lelewel, *Géographie du moyen âge*, ii. 130; *Bulletin de la Société de Géographie*, 1872, p. 49; Ruge, *Geschichte des Zeit-alters der Entdeckungen*, p. 225. H. Grothe, in his *Leonardo da Vinci*, Berlin, 1874, says that Da Vinci in 1473 had written to Columbus respecting a western passage to the Indies.

[4] On a copy of Pierre d'Ailly's *Imago mundi*, preserved in the Colombina Library at Seville, following a photograph in Harrisse's *Notes on Columbus*, p. 84.

ANNOTATIONS BY COLUMBUS.[4]

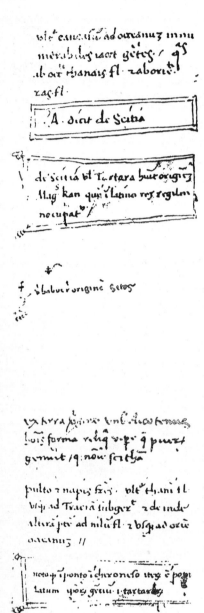

phagos:qui ultra bos habitauere Thoon
ſum paruas gentes quę australia caucaſı
que ponti Septentrionale latus:ultra Cau
anum innumirabiles iacent gentes:quas a
claudit ab orieti ut Ptholomęo placet R
ni Plinio & multis aliis lógiſſimus Caſp
qui hanc terram incolunt ſcytharum noı̄
uis Ptholomęus Sarmathas appellat:qu
eſt:& alios aſiaticos uocat a Thanai uſq
os Europes:qui germaniam inter Thana
ro ultra & intra Iinaum montem collocat
tum eſt.Scriptores alii Scytharum nomı
unt:quos a germanico limite uſque ad ıp
pelagus occupare arbitrantur:& ſicut hab
Ethyopibus tradiderunt : pari modo Se
quos cum Sarmathis confuderunt . Dic
tem apud Araxim flumen originem hab
ab initio nationem fuiſſe & modicę ter
ignobilitatem a uicinis contemptam:n
quendam bellicoſum: & militari uirtut
pliaſſe montanos: quod uſqʒ ad Cauça
uſqʒ ad occeanum & Meotidem flume
lam quoque adducit natam apud Scyt
bellicotenus hominis forma reliqua in
erit nomine ſcytham:qui omnı am arte
nomen ex ſe populis uocabulum indic
ros duo fratres extiterint ſumma uirtut
appellatus:q magnis rebus geſtis regn
populos Plutones:alteros napas uocit
nies regiones ultra Thanaim uſque ad
ſiſque deinde in alteram partem armıs
nerit:redactis in poteſtatem omnibus
tibus & uſqʒ ad orientis occeanum:&
protederit:multoſqʒ reges habuit mem

ANNOTATIONS BY COLUMBUS.[1]

[1] On a copy of the *Historia rerum ubique gestarum* of Æneas Sylvius, preserved in the Colombina Library at Seville, following a photograph in Harrisse's *Notes on Columbus*, appendix.

other explorers, bearing upon the views advocated by Columbus, may have instigated or confirmed him in his belief. There is just enough plausibility in some of the stories which are cited to make them fall easily into the pleas of detraction to which Columbus has been subjected.

A story was repeated by Oviedo in 1535 as an idle rumor, adopted by Gomara in 1552 without comment, and given considerable currency in 1609 by Garcilasso de la Vega, of a Spanish pilot, — Sanches, as the name is sometimes given, — who had sailed from Madeira, and had been driven west and had seen land (Hispaniola, it is inferred), and who being shipwrecked had been harbored by Columbus in his house. Under this roof the pilot is said to have died in 1484, leaving his host the possessor of his secret. La Vega claimed to have received the tale from his father, who had been at the Court of Spain in the time of Ferdinand and Isabella. Oviedo repeated it, but incredulously ; [1] and it was later told by Gomara, Acosta, Eden, and others. Robertson,[2] Irving,[3] and most later writers find enough in the indecision and variety of its shapes to discard it altogether. Peter Martyr, Bernaldez, and Herrera make no mention of it. It is singular, however, that Ferdinand de Galardi, in dedicating his *Traité politique des abassadeurs*, published at Cologne in 1666, to a descendant of Columbus, the Duke of Veraguas, mentions the story as an indisputable fact ; [4] and it has not escaped the notice of querulous writers even of our day.[5]

Others have thought that Columbus, in his voyage to Thule or Iceland,[6] in February, 1477, could have derived knowledge of the Sagas of the westerly voyages of Eric the Red and his countrymen.[7] It seems to be true that commercial relations were maintained between Iceland and Greenland for some years later than 1477; but if Columbus knew of them, he probably shared the belief of the geographers of his time that Greenland was a peninsula of Scandinavia.[8]

The extremely probable and almost necessary pre-Columbian knowledge of the northeastern parts of America follows from the venturesome spirit of the mariners to those seas for fish and traffic, and from the easy transitions from coast to coast by which they would have been lured to meet the more southerly climes. The chances from such natural causes are quite as strong an argument in favor of the early Northmen venturings as the somewhat questionable representations of the Sagas.[9] There is the same ground for representing, and similar lack of evidence in believing, the alleged voyage of João Vas Costa Cortereal to the Newfoundland banks in 1463–1464. Barrow finds authority for it in Cordeyro, who gives, however, no date in his *Historia Insulana das Ilhas a Portugal*, Lisbon, 1717; but Biddle, in his *Cabot*, fails to be satisfied with Barrow's uncertain references, as enforced in his *Chronological History of Voyages into the Arctic Regions*, London, 1818.[10]

[1] Navarrete, iii. 28.

[2] Note xvii.

[3] Appendix xi.

[4] Stevens, *Bibl. Geog.*, no. 1147, and Sabin, *Dictionary*, vii. no. 26,342, give different dates.

[5] Goodrich's *Life of the so-called Christopher Columbus*. Cf. Luciano Cordeiro, "Les Portugais dans la découverte de l'Amérique," in Congrès des Américanistes, 1875, i. 274.

[6] Humboldt sees no reason to doubt that Iceland was meant. (*Examen critique*, i. 105; v. 213; *Cosmos*, ii. 611.) It may be remarked, however, that "Thyle" and "Islanda" are both laid down in the Ptolemy map of 1486, which only signifies probably that the old and new geography were not yet brought into accord. Cf. *Journal of the American Geographical Society*, xii. 170, 177, where it is stated that records prove the mild

winter for Iceland in 1477, which Columbus represents at Thule.

[7] A like intimation is sustained by De Costa in *Columbus and the Geographers of the North*, Hartford, 1872; and it is distinctly claimed in Anderson's *America not discovered by Columbus*, 3d edition, 1883, p. 85. It is also surmised that Columbus may have known the Zeni map.

[8] Humboldt discusses the question whether Columbus received any incentive from a knowledge of the Scandinavian or Zeni explorations, in his *Examen critique*, ii. 104; and it also forms the subject of appendices to Irving's *Columbus*.

[9] This problem is more particularly examined in Vol. I. Cf. also Vol. IV. p. 3.

[10] Harrisse, *Les Cortereals*, p. 25, who points out that Behaim's globe shows nothing of such a voyage, — which it might well have done if the

Another of these alleged northern voyagers was a Polish navigator, John Szkolny, — a name which we get in various Latinized or other forms, as Scolve, Skolnus, Scolvus, Sciolvus, Kolno, etc., — who is said to have been on the Labrador coast in 1476, while in the service of Denmark.   It is so stated by Wytfliet,[1] Pontanus,[2] and Horn.[3] De Costa cites what is known as the Rouen globe, preserved in Paris, and supposed to belong to about 1540, as showing a legend of Skolnus reaching the northwest coast of Greenland in 1476.[4] Hakluyt quotes Gemma Frisius and Girava. Gomara, in 1553, and Herrera, in 1601, barely refer to it.[5]

There is also a claim for a Dieppe navigator, Cousin, who, bound for Africa, is said to have been driven west, and reached South America in 1488–1489.   The story is told by Desmarquets in his *Mémoires chronologiques pour servir à l'histoire de Dieppe,* i. 92, published at Paris, 1785.   Major, giving the story an examination, fully discredits it.[6]

There remains the claim for Martin Behaim, the Nuremberg cosmographer and navigator, which rests upon a passage in the Latin text of the so-called *Nuremberg Chronicle*[7] which states that Cam and Behaim, having passed south of the equator, turned west

voyage had been made; for Behaim had lived at the Azores, while Cortereal was also living on a neighboring island.   Major, *Select Letters of Columbus,* p. xxviii, shows that Faria y Sousa, in *Asia Portuguesa,* while giving a list of all expeditions of discovery from Lisbon, 1412-1460, makes no mention of this Cortereal.   W. D. Cooley, in his *Maritime and Island Discovery,* London, 1830, follows Barrow; but Paul Barron Watson, in his " Bibliography of pre-Columbian Discoveries " appended to the 3d edition (Chicago, 1883) of Anderson's *America not discovered by Columbus,* p. 158, indicates how Humboldt (*Examen critique,* i. 279), G. Folsom (*North American Review,* July, 1838), Gaffarel (*Études,* p. 328), Kohl (*Discovery of Maine,* p. 165), and others dismiss the claim.   If there was any truth in it, it would seem that Portugal deliberately cut herself off from the advantages of it in accepting the line of demarcation in 1493.

[1] Edition of 1597, folio 188.

[2] Follows Wytfliet in his *Rerum Danicarum historia,* 1631, p. 763.

[3] *Ulyssea,* Lugduni, 1671, p. 335.

[4] *Journal of the American Geographical Society,* xii. 170.   Asher, in his *Henry Hudson,* p. xcviii, argues for Greenland.

[5] Gomara, *Historia general de las Indias,* Medina, 1553, and Anvers, 1554, cap. xxxvii, folio 31 ; and Herrera, *Historia general,* Madrid, 1601, dec. 1, lib. 6, cap. 16.   Later writers have reiterated it. Cf. Humboldt, *Examen critique,* ii. 152, who is doubtful ; Lelewel, iv. 106, who says he reached Labrador ; Kunstmann, *Entdeckung Amerikas,* p. 45.   Watson, in his *Bibliography of the pre-Columbian Discoveries,* cites also the favorable judgment of Belleforest, *L'histoire universelle,* Paris, 1577 ; Morisotus' *Orbis maritimi,* 1643; Zurla's *Marco Polo,* 1818 ; C. Pingel in *Grönlands Historisk Mindesmaeker,* 1845 ; Gaffarel, *Étude,* 1869 ; and De Costa, *Columbus and the Geographers of the North,* 1872, p. 17.

[6] *America not discovered by Columbus,* p. 164. Estancelin, in his *Recherches sur les voyages et découvertes des navigateurs Normands en Afrique, dans les Indes orientales, et en Amérique ; suivies d'observations sur la marine, le commerce, et les établissemens coloniaux des Français,* Paris, 1832, claims that Pinzon, represented as a companion of Cousin, was one of the family later associated with Columbus in his voyage in 1492.   Léon Guérin, in *Navigateurs Français,* 1846, mentions the voyage, but expresses no opinion. Parkman, *Pioneers of France,* p. 169, does not wholly discredit the story.   Paul Gaffarel, *Étude sur les rapports de l'Amérique et de l'ancien continent avant Colomb,* Paris, 1869, and *Découverte du Brésil par Jean Cousin,* Paris, 1874, advocates the claim.   Again, in his *Histoire du Brésil Français,* Paris, 1878, Gaffarel considers the voyage geographically and historically possible. (Cf. also a paper by him in the *Revue politique et littéraire,* 2 mai, 1874.)   It is claimed that the white and bearded men whom, as Las Casas says, the natives of Hispaniola had seen before the coming of the Spaniards, were the companions of Cousin. Cf. Vitet's *Histoire de Dieppe,* Paris, 1833, vol. ii. ; David Asseline's *Antiquitez et chroniques de Dieppe, avec introduction par Hardy, Guérillon, et Sauvage,* Paris, 1874, two vols. ; and the supplemental work of Michel Claude Guibert, *Mémoires pour servir à l'histoire de Dieppe,* Paris, 1878, two vols. Cf. Sabin, vol. xii. no. 47,541 ; Dufossé, *Americana,* nos. 4,735, 9,027.

[7] The ordinary designation of Hartmann Schedel's *Registrum huius operis libri cronicarum cū figuris et ymagībus ab inicio mūdi,* Nuremberg, 1493, p. 290.   The book is not very rare, though much sought for its 2,250 woodcuts ; and superior copies of it bring from $75 to $100, though good copies are often priced at from $30 to $60. Cf. *Bibliotheca Spenceriana ;* Leclerc, no. 533 ; Carter-Brown, vol. i. nos. 12, 18 ; Huth, iv. 1305 ; Sunderland, no. 2,796 ; Harrisse, *Bibl. Amer. Vet.,* no. 13 ; Muller,

and (by implication) found land. The passage is not in the German edition of the same year, and on reference to the manuscript of the book (still preserved in Nuremberg) the passage is found to be an interpolation written in a different hand.[1] It seems likely to have been a perversion or misinterpretation of the voyage of Diego Cam down the African coast in 1489, in which he was accompanied by Behaim. That Behaim himself did not put the claim forward, at least in 1492, seems to be clear from the globe, which he made in that year, and which shows no indication of the alleged voyage. The allegation has had, however, some advocates; but the weight of authority is decidedly averse, and the claim can hardly be said to have significant support to-day.[2]

It is unquestionable that the success of the Portuguese in discovering the Atlantic islands and in pushing down the African coast, sustained Columbus in his hope of western discovery, if it had not instigated it.[3] The chance wafting of huge canes, unusual trunks of trees, and even sculptured wood and bodies of strange men, upon the shores of the outlying islands of the Azores and Madeira, were magnified as evidences in his mind.[4] When at a later day he found a tinned iron vessel in the hands of the natives of Guade-

Books on America, 1872, no. 1,402; Cooke, no. 2,961; Murphy, no. 2,219, with a note by that collector.

[1] Cf. Von Murr, Memorabilia bibliothecarum Norimbergensium, vol. i. pp. 254-256: "nec locus ille de America loquitur, sed de Africa."

[2] Watson's Bibliography of pre-Columbian Discoveries of America, p. 161, enumerates the contestants; and Harrisse, Bibl. Amer. Vet., nos. 13, 14, epitomizes the authorities. The earliest reference, after Schedel, seems to be one in Guillaume Postel's Cosmographicæ disciplinæ compendium, Basle, 1561, in which a strait below South America is named Behaim's Strait; but J. Chr. Wagenseil, in his Sacra parentalia, 1682, earliest urged the claim, which he repeated in his Historia universalis, while it was reinforced in Stüven's or Stuvenius' De vero novi orbis inventore, Frankfort, 1714. (Copy in Harvard College Library; cf. Carter-Brown, vol. iii. no. 195.) The first important counter-argument appeared in E. Tozen's Der wahre und erste Entdecker der Neuen Welt, Christoph Colon, gegen die ungegründeten Ausprüche, welche Americus Vespucei und Martin Behaim auf diese Ehre machen, vertheidiget, Göttingen, 1761. (Sabin, xii. 489.) Robertson rejected the claim; and so, in 1778, did C. G. von Murr, in his Diplomatische Geschichte des Ritters Behaim, published at Nuremberg (2d ed., Gotha, 1801; Jansen's French translation, Paris, 1801, and Strasburg, 1802; also appended to Amoretti's Pigafetta; English in Pinkerton's Voyages, 1812). A letter from Otto to Benjamin Franklin, in the American Philosophical Society's Transactions, 1786, ii. 263, urged the theory. Dr. Belknap, in 1792, in the Appendix to his Discourse on Columbus, dismissed it. Cladera, in his Investigaciones históricas sobre los principales descubrimientos de los Españoles, Madrid, 1794, was decidedly averse, replying to Otto, and adding a translation of Von Murr's essay. (Leclerc, nos. 118, 2,505.) Amoretti, in his Preface to Pigafetta's

Voyage, Paris, 1801, argues that Columbus' discoveries convinced Behaim of his own by comparison. Irving says the claim is founded on a misinterpretation of the Schedel passage. Humboldt, in his Examen critique, i. 256, enters into a long adverse argument. Major, in his Select Letters of Columbus, and in his Prince Henry, is likewise decided in opposition. Ghillany, in his Geschichte des Seefahrers Ritter Martin Behaim, is favorable. Gaffarel, Étude sur les rapports de l'Amérique et de l'ancien continent avant Colomb, Paris, 1869, is sceptical.

It seems to be a fact that Behaim made a map showing the straits passed by Magellan, which Pigafetta refers to; and it is also clear that Schöner, in globes made earlier, also indicated a similar strait; and Schöner might well have derived his views from Behaim. What we know of Behaim's last years, from 1494 to 1506, is not sufficient to fill the measure of these years; and advocates are not wanting who assign to them supposed voyages, on one of which he might have acquired a personal knowledge of the straits which he delineated. Such advocates are met, and will continue to be answered, with the likelier supposition, as is claimed, of the Straits in question being a happy guess, both on Behaim's and Schöner's part, derived from the analogy of Africa, — a southern extremity which Behaim had indeed delineated on his globe some years before its actual discovery, though not earlier than the existence of a prevalent belief in such a Strait. Cf. Wieser, Magalhâes-Strasse.

[3] Las Casas is said to have had a manuscript by Columbus respecting the information derived by him from Portuguese and Spanish pilots concerning western lands.

[4] These were accounted for by the westerly gales, the influence of the Gulf Stream not being suspected. Humboldt, Cosmos, English translation, ii. 662; Examen critique, ii. 249.

loupe, he felt that there had been European vessels driven along the equatorial current to the western world, which had never returned to report on their voyages.

Of the adventurous voyages of which record was known there were enough to inspire him ; and of all the mysteries of the Sea of Darkness,[1] which stretched away illimitably to the west, there were stories more than enough. Sight of strange islands had been often reported ; and the maps still existing had shown a belief in those of San Brandan [2] and Antillia,[3] and of the Seven Cities founded in the ocean waste by as many Spanish bishops, who had been driven to sea by the Moors.[4]

The Fortunate Islands [5] (Canaries) of the ancients — discovered, it is claimed, by the Carthaginians [6] — had been practically lost to Europe for thirteen hundred years, when, in the beginning of the fifteenth century (1402), Juan de Béthencourt led his colony to settle them.[7] They had not indeed been altogether forgotten, for Marino Sanuto in 1306 had delineated them on a map given by Camden, though this cartographer omitted them on later charts. Traders and pirates had also visited them since 1341, but such acquaintance had hardly caused them to be generally known.[8]   The Canaries, however, as well as the

[1] See Major's Preface to his *Prince Henry*. Cf. H. H. Bancroft, *Central America*, i. 373, for the successive names applied to the Atlantic.

[2] Cf. *Les voyages merveilleux de Saint-Brandan à la recherche du paradis terrestre. Légende en vers du XIe siècle, publiée avec introduction par Francisque-Michel*, Paris, 1878 ; and references in Poole's *Index*, p. 159.

[3] Humboldt points this island out on a map of 1425.

[4] Cf. Humboldt, *Examen critique*, ii. 156–245 ; Kunstmann, *Entdeckung Amerikas*, pp. 6, 35 ; D'Avezac on the "Isles fantastiques," in *Nouvelles annales des voyages*, April, 1845, p. 55. Many of these islands clung long to the maps. Becher (*Landfall of Columbus*) speaks of the Isle of St. Matthew and Isle Grande in the South Atlantic being kept in charts till the beginning of this century. E. E. Hale tells amusingly of the Island of Bresil, lying off the coast of Ireland and in the steamer's track from New York to England, being kept on the Admiralty charts as late as 1873. *American Antiquarian Society Proceedings*, Oct. 1873. Cf. Gaffarel, *Congrès des Américanistes*, 1877, i. 423, and Formaleoni's *Essai sur la marine ancienne des vénitiens ; dans lequel on a mis au jour plusieurs cartes tirées de la bibliothèque de St. Marc, antérieures à la découverte de Christophe Colomb, & qui indiquent clairement l'existence des isles Antilles. Traduit de l'italien par le chevalier d'Hénin*, Venise, 1788.

[5] There are seven inhabitable and six desert islands in the group.

[6] Cf. *Die Entdeckung der Carthager und Griechen auf dem Atlantischen Ocean*, by Joachim Lelewel, Berlin, 1831, with two maps (Sabin, x. 201) one of which shows conjecturally the Atlantic Ocean of the ancients (see next page).

[7] Two priests, Bontier and Le Verrier, who accompanied him, wrote the account which we have. Cf. Peter Martyr, dec. i. c. 1 ; Galvano, p. 60 ; Muñoz, p. 30 ; Kunstmann, p. 6.

[8] Charton (*Voyageurs*, iii. 75) gives a partial bibliography of the literature of the discovery and conquest. The best English book is Major's *Conquest of the Canaries*, published by the Hakluyt Society, London, 1872, which is a translation, with notes, of the Béthencourt narrative ; and the same author has epitomized the story in chapter ix. of his *Discoveries of Prince Henry*. There is an earlier English book, George Glas's *Discovery and Conquest of the Canary Islands*, London, 1764, 1767, which is said to be based on an unpublished manuscript of 1632, the work of a Spanish monk, J. de Abreu de Galineo, in the island of Palma. The Béthencourt account was first published in Paris, 1630, with different imprints, as *Histoire de la première descouverte et conqueste des Canaries*. Dufossé prices it at from 250 to 300 francs. The original manuscript was used in preparing the edition, *Le Canarien*, issued at Rouen in 1874 by G. Gravier (Leclerc, no. 267). This edition gives both a modern map and a part of that of Mecia de Viladestes (1413) ; enumerates the sources of the story ; and (p. lxvi) gives D'Avezac's account of the preservation of the Béthencourt manuscript. The Spanish translation by Pedro Ramirez, issued at Santa Cruz de Tenerife in 1847, was rendered from the Paris, 1630, edition.

. Cf. Nuñez de la Peña's *Conquista y antiguedades de las Islas de la Gran Canaria*, Madrid, 1676, and reprint, Santa Cruz de Tenerife, 1847 ; Cristóval Perez de el Christo, *Las siete Islas de Canaria*, Xeres, 1679 (rare, Leclerc, no. 644, — 100 francs) ; Viera y Clavijo, *Historia general de las Islas de Canaria*, Madrid, four volumes, 1772–1783 (Leclerc, no. 647, calls it the principal work on the Canaries) ; Bory de Saint Vincent, *Essais sur les Isles Fortunées*, Paris, an xi. (1803) ; *Les Iles Fortunées*, Paris, 1869. D'Avezac, in 1846, published a *Note sur la première expédition de Béthencourt aux Canaries*, and his "Isles d'Afrique" in the *Univers pittoresque* may be referred to.

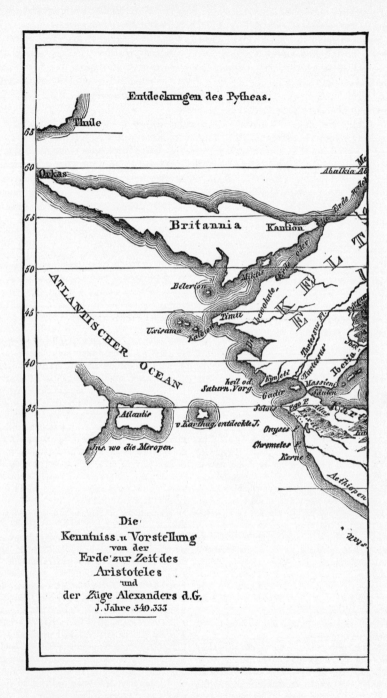

Entdeckungen des Pytheas.

Thule

Orkas

Britannia   Kantion

ATLANTISCHER OCEAN

Belerion

Urisama

Atlantis

Ins. wo die Meropen

Iberia

Aethiopen

Die
Kenntniss u Vorstellung
von der
Erde zur Zeit des
Aristoteles
und
der Züge Alexanders d.G.
J. Jahre 340.333

THE ATLANTIC OF THE ANCIENTS AS MAPPED BY LELEWEL.[1]

[1] This is part of a map of the ancient world given in Lelewel's *Die Entdeckung der Car-* *thager und Griechen auf dem Atlantischen Ocean,* Berlin, 1831.

Azores, appear in the well-known portolano of 1351,[1] which is preserved in the Biblioteca Mediceo-Laurenziana in Florence.   A chart of the Brothers Pizigani, dated in 1367, gives islands which are also identified with the Canaries, Azores, and Madeira ;[2] and the Canaries also appear on the well-known Catalan mappemonde of 1375.[3]   These Atlantic islands are again shown in a portolano of a period not much later than 1400, which is among the Egerton manuscripts in the British Museum, and is ascribed to Juan da Napoli ;[4] and in 1436 they are conspicuous on the detailed sea-chart of Andrea Bianco.   This portolano has also two islands on the extreme western verge of the sheet, — "Antillia" and "De la man Satanaxio," which some have claimed as indicating a knowledge of the two Americas.[5]   It was a map brought in 1428 from Venice by Dom Pedro, — which, like the 1351 map, showed the Azores, — that induced Prince Henry in 1431 to despatch the expedition which rediscovered those islands; and they appear on the Catalan map, which Santarem (pl. 54) describes as "Carte de Gabriell de Valsequa, faite à Mallorcha en 1439."   It was in 1466 that the group was colonized, as Behaim's globe shows.[6]

   The Madeira group was first discovered by an Englishman, — Machin, or Macham, — in the reign of Edward III. (1327–1378).   The narrative, put into shape for Prince Henry of Portugal by Francisco Alcaforado, one of his esquires, was known to Irving in a French translation published in 1671, which Irving epitomizes.[7]   The story, somewhat changed, is given by Galvano, and was copied by Hakluyt ;[8] but, on account of some strangeness and incongruities, it has not been always accepted, though Major says the main recital is confirmed by a document quoted from a German collection of voyages, 1507, by Dr. Schmeller, in the Memoirs of the Academy of Science at Munich, 1847, and which, secured for Major by Kunstmann, is examined by him in his *Prince Henry*.[9]   The group was rediscovered by the Portuguese in 1418–1420.[10]   Prince Henry had given the command of Porto Santo to Perestrello ; and this captain, in 1419, observing from his island a cloud in the horizon, found, as he sailed to it, the island now called Madeira.   It will be remembered that it was the daughter of Perestrello whom Columbus at a later day married.[11]

[1] It is given by Lelewel, *Géographie du Moyen Age ;* and has been issued in fac-simile by Ongania at Venice, in 1881.   It is also given in Major, *Prince Henry,* 1868 edition, p. 107, and in Marco Polo, edition by Boni, Florence, 1827. Cf. Winsor's *Kohl Collection of Early Maps,* issued by Harvard University.

[2] This chart is given by Jomard, pl. x., and Santarem, pl. 40. Ongania published in 1881 a Pizigani chart belonging to the Ambrosian Library in Milan, dated 1373.

[3] This map is given in *Manuscrits de la Bibliothèque du Roi,* vol. xiv. part 2; in Santarem, pl. 31, 40; Lelewel, pl. xxix. ; Saint-Martin's *Atlas,* pl. vii.; Ruge's *Geschichte des Zeitalters der Entdeckungen,* 1881, and full size in fac-simile in *Choix de documents géographiques conservés à la Bibliothèque Nationale,* Paris, 1883.

[4] Winsor's *Kohl Collection of early maps,* part i., no. 17.

[5] Cf. Santarem, *Histoire de la Cartographie,* iii. 366, and the references in Winsor's *Kohl Collection,* part i. no. 19; and *Bibliography of Ptolemy,* sub anno 1478. A sea-chart of Bartolomeus de Pareto, A. D. 1455, shows "Antillia" and an island farther west called "Roillo." Antillia is supposed also to have been delineated on Toscanelli's map in 1474. In 1476 Andreas Benincasa's portolano, given in Lelewel, pl. xxxiv. and Saint-Martin, pl. vii. shows an island "An-

tilio ;" and again in the portolano belonging to the Egerton manuscripts in the British Museum, and supposed to represent the knowledge of 1489, just previous to Columbus's voyage, and thought by Kohl to be based on a Benincasa chart of 1463, the conventional "Antillia" is called "Y de Sete Zitade." It is ascribed to Christofalo Soligo. Behaim's globe in 1492 also gives "Insula Antilia genannt Septe Citade." Cf. Harrisse, *Les Cortereal,* p. 116. The name "Antilhas" seems first to have been transferred from this problematical mid-ocean island to the archipelago of the West Indies by the Portuguese, for Columbus gave no general name to the group.

[6] Cf. Kunstmann, *Entdeckung Amerikas,* pp. I, etc.; Drummond, *Annales da Ilha Terceira ;* Ernesto do Canto, *Archivo dos Açores ;* Major's *Discoveries of Prince Henry,* chap. x.; *Quarterly Review,* xi. 191 ; Cordeyro's *Historia insulana,* Lisbon, 1717.

[7] Appendix xxv.

[8] Vol. ii. part 2, p. 1 ; also Purchas, ii. 1672.

[9] Edition of 1868, pp. xvii and 69; Kunstmann, *Entdeckung Amerikas,* p. 4.

[10] Cf. Gaspar Fructuoso's *Historia das Ilhas do Porto-Santo, Madeira, Desertas e Selvagens,* Funchal, 1873.

[11] Cf. *Studi biog. e bibliog.* i. 137, which places Perestrello's death about 1470.

It was not till 1460 [1] that the Cape De Verde Islands were found, lying as they do well outside of the route of Prince Henry's vessels, which were now following down the African coast, and had been pursuing explorations in this direction since 1415.

There have been claims advanced by Margry in his *Les navigations Françaises et la révolution maritime du XIVᵉ au XVIᵉ siècle, d'après les documents inédits tirés de France, d'Angleterre, d'Espagne, et d'Italie*, pp. 13–70, Paris, 1867, and embraced in his first section on "Les marins de Normandie aux côtes de Guinée avant les Portugais," in which he cites an old document, said to be in London, setting forth the voyage of a vessel from Dieppe to the coast of Africa in 1364. Estancelin had already, in 1832, in his *Navigateurs Normands en Afrique*, declared there were French establishments on the coast of Guinea in the fourteenth century, — a view D'Avezac says he would gladly accept if he could. Major, however, failed to find, by any direction which Margry could give him, the alleged London document, and has thrown — to say the least — discredit on the story of that document as presented by Margry.[2]

PRINCE HENRY.[3]

The African explorations of the Portuguese are less visionary, and, as D'Avezac says, the Portuguese were the first to persevere and open the African route to India.[4]

The peninsular character of Africa — upon which success in this exploration depended — was contrary to the views of Aristotle, Hipparchus, and Ptolemy, which held to an

---

[1] It has sometimes been put as early as 1440; but 1460 is the date Major has determined after a full exposition of the voyages of this time. *Prince Henry* (1868 edition), p. 277. D'Avezac *Isles de l'Afrique*, Paris, 1848.

[2] Prince Henry, edition of 1868, pp. xxiv and 127. Guibert, in his *Ville de Dieppe*, i. 306 (1878), refers, for the alleged French expedition to Guinea in 1364, to Villault de Belfond, *Relation des costes d'Afrique appelées Guinée*, Paris, 1669, p. 409; Vitet, *Anciennes villes de France*, ii. 1, Paris, 1833; D'Avezac *Découvertes dans l'océan atlantique antérieurement aux grands explorations du XVᵉ siècle*, p. 73, Paris, 1845; Jules Hardy, *Les Dieppois en Guinée en* 1364, 1864; Gabriel Gravier, *Le Canarien*, 1874.

[3] This follows a portrait in a contemporary manuscript chronicle, now in the National Library at Paris, which Major, who gives a colored fac-simile of it, calls the only authentic likeness,

probably taken in 1449–1450, and representing him in mourning for the death of his brother Dom Pedro, who died in 1449. There is another engraving of it in Jules Verne's *La Découverte de la Terre*, p. 112. Major calls the portrait in Gustave de Veer's Life of Prince Henry, published at Dantzig, in 1864, a fancy one. The annexed autograph of the Prince is the equivalent of IFFANTE DOM ANRIQUE. Prince Henry, who was born March 4, 1394, died

Nov 15, 1463. He was the third son of John I. of Portugal; his mother was a daughter of John of Gaunt, of England.

[4] Cf. Jurien de la Gravière's *Les marins du XVᵉ et du XVIᵉ siècle*, vol. i. chap. 2.

enclosed Indian Ocean, formed by the meeting of Africa and Asia at the south.[1] The stories respecting the circumnavigation of Africa by the ancients are lacking in substantial proof ; and it seems probable that Cape Non or Cape Bojador was the limit of their southern expeditions.[2] Still, this peninsular character was a deduction from imagined necessity rather than a conviction from fact. It found place on the earliest maps of the revival of geographical study in the Middle Ages. It is so represented in the map of Marino Sanuto in 1306, and in the Lorentian portolano of 1351. Major[3] doubts if the Catalan map of 1375 shows anything more than conjectural knowledge for the coasts beyond Bojador.

Of Prince Henry — the moving spirit in the African enterprise of the fifteenth century — we have the most satisfactory account in the *Life of Prince Henry of Portugal, surnamed the Navigator, and its Results . . . from Authentic Contemporary Documents*, by Richard Henry Major, London, 1868,[4] — a work which, after the elimination of the controversial arguments, and after otherwise fitting it for the general reader, was reissued in 1877 as *The Discoveries of Prince Henry the Navigator*. These works are the guide for the brief sketch of these African discoveries now to be made, and which can be readily followed on the accompanying sketch-map.[5]

Prince Henry had been with his father at the capture of Ceuta, opposite Gibraltar, in 1415, when the Portuguese got their first foothold in Africa. In 1418 he established a school of nautical observation at Sagres,[6] the southwestern promontory of his father's kingdom, and placed the geographer, Jayme,[8] of Majorca, in charge of it. The Prince at once sent out his first expedition down the Barbary coast ; but his vessel, being driven out of its course, discovered the Island of Porto Santo. Expedition after expedition reached, in successive years, the vicinity of Cape Bojador ; but an inexpressible dread of the uncertainty beyond deferred the passage of it till 1434. Cape Blanco was reached in 1445 ; Cape Verde shortly after ; and the River Gambia in 1447. Cadamosto and his Venetians pushed

SKETCH-MAP OF THE PORTUGUESE DISCOVERIES IN AFRICA.[7]

---

[1] Humboldt, *Examen critique*, i. 144, 161, 329; ii. 370; *Cosmos*, ii. 561; Jules Codine's *Mémoire géographique sur la mer des Indes*, Paris, 1868.

[2] Irving, app. xiv.

[3] *Prince Henry*, p. 116 (1868). Cf. *Studi biog. e bibliog. della Soc. Geog. Ital.*, ii. 57.

[4] The author tells, in his preface, the condition of knowledge regarding his subject which he found when he undertook his work, and recounts the service the Royal Academy of Sciences at Lisbon has done since 1779 in discovering and laying before the world important documents.

[5] Gustav de Veer's *Prinz Heinrich der Seefahrer, und seine Zeit*, Dantzig, 1864, is a more popular work, and gives lists of authorities. Cf. H. Monin in the *Revue de géographie*, December, 1878.

[6] There is some question if the school of Sagres had ever an existence; at least it is doubted in the *Archivo dos Açores*, iv. 18, as quoted by Harrisse, *Les Cortereal*, p. 40.

[7] Cf. Heinrich Wuttke's "Zur Geschichte der Erdkunde in der letzten hälfte des Mittelalters: Die Karten der Seefahrenden Völker süd Europas bis zum ersten Druck der Erdbeschreibung des Ptolemäus," in the *Jahrbuch des Vereins für Erdkunde in Dresden*, 1870; J. Codine's "Découverte de la côte d'Afrique par les Portugais pendant les années, 1484–1488," in the *Bulletin de la Société de Géographie de Paris*, 1876; Vivien de Saint-Martin's *Histoire de la géographie et des découvertes géographiques, depuis les temps les plus reculés jusqu'à nos jours*, p. 298, Paris, 1873 ; Ruge's *Geschichte des Zeitalters der Entdeckungen*, p. 81 ; Clarke's *Progress of Maritime Discovery*, p. 140; and G. T. Raynal's *Histoire philosophique et politique des établissemens et du commerce des Européens dans les deux Indes*, Geneva, 1780; Paris, 1820. Paulitschke's *Afrika-literatur in der Zeit von 1500 bis 1750*, Vienna, 1882, notes the earliest accounts.

[8] Cf. Harrisse, *Bibl. Amer. Vet.*, 261 ; adds 154.

still farther, and saw the Southern Cross for the first time.[1] Between 1460 and 1464 they went beyond Cape Mesurado. Prince Henry dying in 1463, King Alfonso, in 1469, farmed out the African commerce, and required five hundred miles to be added yearly to the limit of discovery southward. Not long after, Diego Cam reached the Congo coast, Behaim accompanying him. In 1487, after seventy years of gradual progress down six

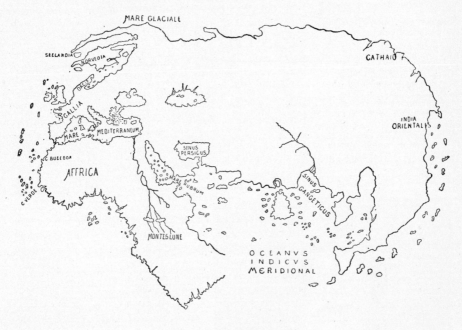

PORTUGUESE MAP, 1490.[2]

thousand miles of coast, southward from Cape Non, the Portuguese under Diego reached the Stormy Cape, — later to be called the Cape of Good Hope. He but just rounded it in May, and in December he was in Portugal with the news. Bartholomew, the brother of Columbus, had made the voyage with him.[3] The rounding of the Cape was hardly a surprise; for the belief in it was firmly established long before. In 1457–1459, in the map of Fra Mauro, which had been constructed at Venice for Alonzo V., and in which Bianco assisted, the terminal cape had been fitly drawn.[4]

[1] Major (p. xvi) has more or less distrust of Cadamosto's story as given in the *Paese nova-mente.* Cf. the bibliography in *Studi biog. e bib-liog. della Soc. Geog. Ital.,* i. 149 (1882); and Carter-Brown, i. 101, 195, 202, 211; also *Bibl. Amer. Vet. Add.,* no. 83.

[2] This map follows a copy in the Kohl Collection (no. 23), after the original, attached to a manuscript theological treatise in the British Museum. An inscription at the break in the African coast says that to this point the Portuguese had pushed their discoveries in 1489; and as it shows no indication of the voyages of Columbus and Da Gama, Kohl places it about 1490. It may be considered as representing the views current before these events, Asia following the Ptolemean

drafts. The language of the map being partly Italian and partly Portuguese, Kohl conjectures that it was made by an Italian living in Lisbon; and he points out the close correspondence of the names on the western coast of Africa to the latest Portuguese discoveries, and that its contour is better than anything preceding.

[3] "Through all which I was present," said Bartholomew, in a note found by Las Casas.

[4] The original is now preserved at Venice, in the Biblioteca Marciana. A large photographic fac-simile of it was issued at Venice, in 1877, by Münster (Ongania); and engraved reproductions can be found in Santarem, Lelewel, and Saint-Martin, besides others in Vincent's *Commerce and Navigations of the Ancients,* 1797 and

Such had been the progress of the Portuguese marine, in exemplification of the southerly quest called for by the theory of Pomponius Mela, when Columbus made his westerly voyage in 1492 and reached, as he supposed, the same coast which the Portuguese were seeking to touch by the opposite direction.[1] In this erroneous geographical belief Columbus remained as long as he lived,

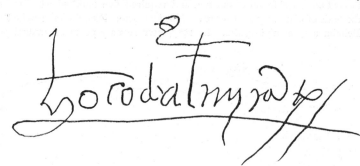

HO COMDE ALMIRANTE (*Da Gama's Autograph*).

— a view in which Vespucius and the earlier navigators equally shared;[2] though some, like Peter Martyr,[3] accepted the belief cautiously.   We shall show in another place how slowly the error was eradicated from the cartography of even the latter part of the sixteenth century.

During the interval when Columbus was in Spain, between his second and third voyages, Vasco da Gama sailed from Lisbon, July 8, 1497, to complete the project which had so long animated the endeavors of the rival kingdom. He doubled the Cape of Good Hope in Nov. 1497, and anchored at Calicut, May 20, 1498, — a few days before Columbus left San Lucas on his third voyage.   In the following August, Da Gama started on his return; and after a year's voyage he reached Lisbon in August, 1498. The Portuguese had now accomplished their end.   The *éclat* with which it would have been received had not

VASCO DA GAMA.[4]

1807; and in Ruge's *Geschichte des Zeitalters der Entdeckungen*, 1881. A copy on vellum, made in 1804, is in the British Museum.

[1] Cf. G. Gravier's *Recherches sur les navigations Européennes faites au moyen-âge*, Paris, 1878.

[2] Navarrete, i. 304, ii. 280; Bandini's *Amerigo Vespucci*, pp. 66, 83; Humboldt, *Examen critique*, i. 26, iv. 188, 233, 250, 261, v. 182–185; and his preface to Ghillany's *Behaim ;* Harrisse, *Ferdi-*

nand Colomb, pp. 121-127; Major's *Prince Henry*, p. 420; Stevens's *Notes*, p. 372. When the natives of Cuba pointed to the interior of their island and said "Cubanacan," Columbus interpreted it to mean "Kublai Khan;" and the Cuban name of Mangon became to his ear the Mangi of Sir John Mandeville.

[3] Dec. i. c. 8.

[4] This follows the engravings in Ruge's *Geschichte des Zeitalters der Entdeckungen*, p. 111, and in Stanley's *Da Gama*, published by the Hakluyt Society. The original belongs to the Count de Lavradio. Another portrait, with a view of Calicut, is given in Lafitau's *Découvertes des Portugais*, Paris, 1734, iii. 66.

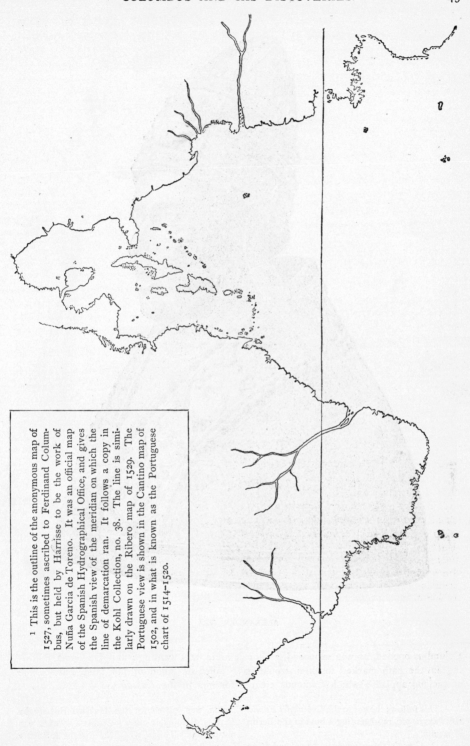

¹ This is the outline of the anonymous map of 1527, sometimes ascribed to Ferdinand Columbus, but held by Harrisse to be the work of Nuña Garcia de Toreno. It was an official map of the Spanish Hydrographical Office, and gives the Spanish view of the meridian on which the line of demarcation ran. It follows a copy in the Kohl Collection, no. 38. The line is similarly drawn on the Ribero map of 1529. The Portuguese view is shown in the Cantino map of 1502, and in what is known as the Portuguese chart of 1514-1520.

THE LINE OF DEMARCATION (*Spanish claim*, 1527).[1]

ALEXANDER VI.[1]

Columbus opened, as was supposed, a shorter route, was wanting; and Da Gama, follow-ing in the path marked for him, would have failed of much of his fame but for the auspicious applause which Camoens created for him in the *Lusiad*.[2]

[1] This follows the cut in the *Gazette des Beaux-Arts*, xxvii. 500, representing a bust in the Berlin Museum.

[2] Da Gama's three voyages, translated from the narrative of Gaspar Correa, with other docu-ments, was edited for the Hakluyt Society by H. E. J. Stanley, in 1869. Correa's account was not printed till 1858, when the Lisbon Academy issued it. Cf. Navarrete, vol. i. p. xli; Ramusio, i. 130; Galvano, p. 93; Major, *Prince Henry*, p. 391;

Da Gama at Calicut and Columbus at Cuba gave the line of demarcation of Alexander VI. a significance that was not felt to be impending, five years earlier, on the 3d and 4th of May, 1493, when the Papal Bull was issued.[1] This had fixed the field of Spanish and Portuguese exploration respectively west and east of a line one hundred leagues [2] west of the Azores, following a meridian at a point where Columbus had supposed the magnetic needle [3] pointed to the north star.[4] The Portuguese thought that political grounds were of more consideration than physical, and were not satisfied with the magnet governing the limitation of their search. They desired a little more sea-room on the Atlantic side, and were not displeased to think that a meridian considerably farther west might give them a share of the new Indies south and north of the Spanish discoveries; so they entered their protest against the partition of the Bull, and the two Powers held a convention at Tordesillas, which resulted, in June, 1494, in the line being moved two hundred and seventy leagues westerly.[5] No one but vaguely suspected the complication yet to arise about this same meridian, now selected, when the voyage of Magellan should bring Spaniard and Portuguese face to face at the Antipodes. This aspect of the controversy will claim attention elsewhere.[6] From this date the absolute position of the line as theoretically determined, was a constant source of dispute, and the occasion of repeated negotiations.[7]

Justin Winsor

Cladera, _Investigaciones históricas_; Saint-Martin, _Histoire de la géographie_, p. 337 ; Clarke, _Progress of Maritime Discovery_, p. 399; Ruge's _Geschichte des Zeitalters der Entdeckungen_ pp. 109, 135, 188, 189; Lucas Rem's _Tagebuch_, 1494-1542, Augsburg, 1861; Charton's _Voyageurs_, iii. 209 (with references), etc.

"Portugal," says Professor Seeley, "had almost reason to complain of the glorious intrusion of Columbus. She took the right way, and found the Indies; while he took the wrong way, and missed them . . . If it be answered in Columbus's behalf, that it is better to be wrong and find America, than to be right and find India, Portugal might answer that she did both," — referring to Cabral's discovery of Brazil (_Expansion of England_, p. 83).

[1] The Bull is printed in Navarrete, ii. 23, 28, 130; and in the app. of Oscar Peschel's _Die Theilung der Erde unter Papst Alexander VI. und Julius II._, Leipsic, 1871. Harrisse, _Bibl. Amer. Vet., Additions_, gives the letter of May 17, 1493, which Alexander VI. sent with the Bulls to his nuncio at the court of Spain, found in the archives of the Frari at Venice. Cf. also Humboldt, _Examen critique_, iii. 52 ; Solorzano's _Política Indiana; Sabin's Dictionary_, vol. i. no. 745; and the illustrative documents in Andres García de Céspedes' _Reg. de nav._, Madrid, 1606.

[2] There is more or less confusion in the estimates made of the league of this time. D'Avezac, _Bulletin de la Société de Géographie de Paris_, September and October, 1858, pp. 130–164, calls it 5,924 metres. Cf. also Fox, in the _U. S._

Coast Survey Report, 1880, p. 59; and H. H. Bancroft, _Central America_, i. 190.

[3] Cf. Humboldt, _Examen critique_, iii. 17, 44, 56, etc.

[4] Humboldt, _Examen critique_, iii. 54 ; _Cosmos_, v. 55. Columbus found this point of no-variation, Sept. 13, 1492. In the latter part of the sixteenth century, for a similar reason, St. Michael's in the Azores was taken for the first meridian, but the no-variation then observable at that point has given place now to a declination of twenty-five degrees.

[5] See the documents in Navarrete, ii. 116, and Peschel's _Theilung der Erde unter Papst Alexander VI. und Julius II._

[6] Cf., however, Juan y Ulloa's _Dissertacion sobre el meridiano de demarcacion_, Madrid, 1749; in French, 1776. Carter-Brown, vol. iii. no. 910; and "Die Demarcations-linie" in Ruge's _Das Zeitalter der Entdeckungen_, p. 267.

[7] In 1495 Jaume Ferrer, who was called for advice, sent a manuscript map to the Spanish Monarchs to be used in the negotiations for determining this question. (Navarrete; also Amat, _Diccionario de los escritores Catalanes._) Jaume's different treatises are collected by his son in his _Sentencias cathólicas_, 1545. (Leclerc, no. 2,765, 1,000 francs ; Harrisse, _Bibl. Am. Vet._, no. 261 ; _Additions_, no. 154.) This contains Jaume's letter of Jan. 27, 1495, and the Monarchs' reply of Feb. 28, 1495; and a letter written at the request of Isabella from Burgos, Aug. 5, 1495, addressed to "Christofol Colō en la gran Isla de Cibau."

NOTES.

A. FIRST VOYAGE. — As regards the first voyage of Columbus there has come down to us a number of accounts, resolvable into two distinct narratives, as originally proceeding from the hand of Columbus himself, — his Journal, which is in part descriptive and in part log, according to the modern understanding of this last term ; and his Letters announcing the success and results of his search. The fortunes and bibliographical history of both these sources need to be told :

JOURNAL. — Columbus himself refers to this in his letter to Pope Alexander VI. (1503) as being kept in the style of Cæsar's *Commentaries ;* and Irving speaks of it as being penned "from day to day with guileless simplicity." In its original form it has not been found ; but we know that Las Casas used it in his *Historia*, and that Ferdinand Columbus must have had it before him while writing what passes for his Life of his father. An abridgment of the Journal in the hand of Las Casas, was discovered by Navarrete, who printed it in the first volume of his *Coleccion* in 1825; it is given in a French version in the Paris edition of the same (vol. ii.), and in Italian in Torre's *Scritti di Colombo*, 1864. Las Casas says of his abstract, that he follows the very words of the Admiral for a while after recording the landfall ; and these parts are translated by Mr. Thomas, of the State Department at Washington, in G. A. Fox's paper on "The Landfall" in the *Report of the Coast Survey* for 1880. The whole of the Las Casas text, however, was translated into English, at the instigation of George Ticknor, by Samuel Kettell, and published in Boston as *A Personal Narrative of the First Voyage* in 1827 ;[1] and it has been given in part, in English, in Becher's *Landfall of Columbus*. The original is thought to have served Herrera in his *Historia General*.[2]

LETTERS. — We know that on the 12th of February, 1493, about a week before reaching the Azores on his return voyage, and while his ship was laboring in a gale, Columbus prepared an account of his discovery, and incasing the parchment in wax, put it in a barrel, which he threw overboard. That is the last heard of it.

He prepared another account, perhaps duplicate, and protecting it in a similar way, placed it on his poop, to be washed off in case his vessel foundered. We know nothing further of this account, unless it be the same, substantially, with the letters which he wrote just before making a harbor at the Azores. One of these letters, at least, is dated off the Canaries ; and it is possible that it was written earlier on the voyage, and post-dated, in expectation of his making the Canaries ; and when he found himself by stress of weather at the Azores, he neglected to change the place. The original of neither of these letters is known.

One of them was dated Feb. 15, 1493, with a postscript dated March 4 (or 14, copies vary, and the original is of course not to be reached; 4 would seem to be correct), and is written in Spanish, and addressed to the "Escribano de Racion," Luis de Santangel, who, as Treasurer of Aragon, had advanced money for the voyage. Columbus calls this a second letter ; by which he may mean that the one cast overboard was the first, or that another, addressed to Sanchez (later to be mentioned), preceded it. There was at Simancas, in 1818, an early manuscript copy of this letter, which Navarrete printed in his *Coleccion*, and Kettell translated into English in his book (p. 253) already referred to.[3]

In 1852 the Baron Pietro Custodi left his collection of books to the Biblioteca Ambrosiana at Milan; and among them was found a printed edition of this Santangel letter, never before known, and still remaining unique. It is of small quarto, four leaves, in semi-gothic type, bearing the date of 1493,[4] and was, as Harrisse and Lenox think, printed in Spain, — Major suggests Barcelona, but Gayangos thinks Lisbon. It was first reprinted at Milan in 1863, with a fac-simile, and edited by Cesare Correnti, in a volume, containing other letters of Columbus, entitled, *Lettere autografe edite ed inedite di Cristoforo Colombo*.[5] From this reprint Harrisse copied it, and gave an English translation in his *Notes on Columbus*, p. 89, drawing attention to the error of Correnti in making it appear on his titlepage that the letter was addressed to "Saxis,"[6] and testifying that, by collation, he

1 Cf. *North American Review*, nos. 53 and 55.
2 Cf. portions in German in *Das Ausland*, 1867, p. 1.
3 It is in Italian in Torre's *Scritti di Colombo*.
4 Brunet, *Supplément*, col. 277.
5 It appeared in the series *Biblioteca rara* of G. Daelli.
6 Cf. *Historical Magazine*, September, 1864.

had found but slight variation from the Navarrete text. Mr. R. H. Major also prints the Ambrosian text in his *Select Letters of Columbus*, with an English version appended, and judges the Cosco version could not have been made from it. Other English translations may be found in Becher's *Landfall of Columbus*, p. 291, and in French's *Historical Collections of Louisiana and Florida*, 2d series, ii. 145.

In 1866 a fac-simile edition (150 copies) of the Ambrosian copy was issued at Milan, edited by Gerolamo d' Adda, under the title of *Lettera in lingua Spagnuola diretta da Cristoforo Colombo a Luis de Santangel*.[1] Mr. James Lenox, of New York, had already described it, with a fac-simile of the beginning and end, in the *Historical Magazine* (vol. viii. p. 289, September, 1864, April, 1865) ; and this paper was issued separately (100 copies) as a supplement to the Lenox edition of Scyllacius. Harrisse[2] indicates that there was once a version of this Santangel letter in the Catalan tongue, preserved in the Colombina Library at Seville.

A few years ago Bergenroth found at Simancas a letter of Columbus, dated at the Canaries, Feb. 15, 1493, with a postscript at Lisbon, March 14, addressed to a friend, giving still another early text, but adding nothing material to our previous knowledge. A full abstract is given in the *Calendar of State Papers relating to England and Spain*, p. 43.

A third Spanish text of a manuscript of the sixteenth century, said to have been found in the Colegio Mayor de Cuenca, was made known by Varnhagen, the Minister of Brazil to Portugal, who printed it at Valencia in 1858 as *Primera epistola del Almirante Don Christóbal Colon*, including an account " de una nueva copia de original manuscrito." The editor assumed the name of Volafan, and printed one hundred copies, of which sixty were destroyed in Brazil.[3]

This letter is addressed to Gabriel Sanchez, and dated "sobre la isla de Sa. Maria, 18 de Febrero ;" and is without the postscript of the letters of Feb. 15. It is almost a verbatim repetition of the Simancas text. A reprint of the Cosco text makes a part of the volume; and it is the opinion of Varnhagen and Harrisse that the Volafan text is the original from which Cosco translated, as mentioned later.

Perhaps still another Spanish text is preserved and incorporated, as Muñoz believed, by the Cura de los Palacios, Andrés Bernaldez, in his *Historia de los reyes católicos* (chap. cxviii). This book covers the period 1488–1513; has thirteen chapters on Columbus, who had been the guest of Bernaldez after his return from his second voyage, in 1496, and by whom Columbus is called "mercador de libros de estampa." The manuscript of Bernaldez's book long remained unprinted in the Royal Library at Madrid. Irving used a manuscript copy which belonged to Obadiah Rich.[4] Prescott's copy of the manuscript is in Harvard College Library.[5] Humboldt[6] used it in manuscript. It was at last printed at Granada in 1856, in two volumes, under the editing of Miguel Lafuente y Alcántara.[7] It remains, of course, possible that Bernaldez may have incorporated a printed Spanish text, instead of the original or any early manuscript, though Columbus is known to have placed papers in his hands.

The text longest known to modern students is the poor Latin rendering of Cosco, already referred to. While but one edition of the original Spanish text appeared presumably in Spain (and none of Vespucius and Magellan), this Latin text, or translations of it, appeared in various editions and forms in Italy, France, and Germany, which Harrisse remarks[8] as indicating the greater popular impression which

---

[1] Harrisse, *Bibl. Amer. Vet. Additions*, p. vi., calls this reproduction extremely correct.

[2] *Bibl. Amer. Vet.*, p. xii.

[3] *Ticknor Catalogue*, p. 387 ; Stevens, *Hist. Coll.*, vol. i. no. 1,380 ; Sabin, iv. 277 ; Leclerc, no. 132. It was noticed by Don Pascual de Gayangos in *La America*, April 13, 1867. Cf. another of Varnhagen's publications, *Carta de Cristóbal Colon enviada de Lisboa á Barcelona en Marzo de 1493*, published at Vienna in 1869. It has a collation of texts and annotations (Leclerc, no. 131). A portion of the edition was issued with the additional imprint, " Paris, Tross, 1870." Of the 120 copies of this book, 60 were put in the trade. Major, referring to these several Spanish texts, says : " I have carefully collated the three documents, and the result is a certain conclusion that neither one nor the other is a correct transcript of the original letter," — all having errors which could not have been in the original. Major also translates the views on this point of Varnhagen, and enforces his own opinion that the Spanish and Latin texts are derived from different though similar documents. Varnhagen held the two texts were different forms of one letter. Harrisse dissents from this opinion in *Bibl. Amer. Vet. Additions*, p. vi.

[4] Cf. Irving's *Columbus*, app. xxix.

[5] Prescott's *Ferdinand and Isabella*, revised edition, ii. 108 ; Sabin, vol. ii. no. 4,918 ; Harrisse, *Notes on Columbus*, no. 7, who reprints the parts in question, with a translation.

[6] *Cosmos*, English translation, ii. 641.

[7] *Ticknor Catalogue*, p. 32.

[8] He points out how the standard *Chronicles* and *Annals* (Ferrebouc, 1521 ; Regnault, 1532 ; Galliot du Pré, 1549 ; Fabian, 1516, 1533, 1542, etc.), down to the middle of the sixteenth century, utterly ignored the acts of Columbus, Cortes, and Magellan (*Bibl. Amer. Vet.* p. ii).

the discovery of America made beyond Spain than within the kingdom; and the monthly delivery of letters from Germany to Portugal and the Atlantic islands, at this time, placed these parts of Europe in prompter connection than we are apt to imagine.[1] News of the discovery was, it would seem, borne to Italy by the two Genoese ambassadors, Marchesi and Grimaldi, who are known to have left Spain a few days after the return of Columbus.[2] The Spanish text of this letter, addressed by Columbus to Gabriel or Raphael Sanchez, or Sanxis, as the name of the Crown treasurer is variously given, would seem to have fallen into the hands of one Aliander de Cosco, who turned it into Latin, completing his work on the 29th of April. Harrisse points out the error of Navarrete and Varnhagen in placing this completion on the 25th, and supposes the version was made in Spain. Tidings of the discovery must have reached Rome before this version could have got there; for the first Papal Bull concerning the event is dated May 3. Whatever the case, the first publication, in print, of the news was made in Rome in this Cosco version, and four editions of it were printed in that city in 1493. There is much disagreement among bibliographers as to the order of issue of the early editions. Their peculiarities, and the preference of several bibliographers as to such order, is indicated in the following enumeration, the student being referred for full titles to the authorities which are cited:—

I. *Epistola Christofori Colom* [1493]. Small quarto, four leaves (one blank), gothic, 33 lines to a page. Addressed to Sanchis. Cosco is called Leander. Ferdinand and Isabella both named in the title. The printer is thought to be Plannck, from similarity of type to work known to be his.

Major calls this the *editio princeps*, and gives elaborate reasons for his opinion (*Select Letters of Columbus*, p. cxvi). J. R. Bartlett, in the *Carter-Brown Catalogue*, vol. i. no. 5, also puts it first; so does Ternaux. Varnhagen calls it the second edition. It is put the third in order by Brunet (vol. ii. col. 164) and Lenox (*Scyllacius*, p. xliv), and fourth by Harrisse (*Notes on Columbus*, p. 121; *Bibl. Amer. Vet.*, no. 4).

There are copies in the Lenox, Carter-Brown, and Huth (*Catalogue*, i. 336) libraries; in the Grenville (*Bibl. Gren.*, p. 158) and King's Collections in the British Museum; in the Royal Library at Munich; in the Collection of the Duc d'Aumale at Twickenham; and in the Commercial Library at Hamburg.[3] The copy cited by Harrisse was sold in the Court Collection (no. 72) at Paris in 1884.

II. *Epistola Christofori Colom, impressit Rome, Eucharius Argenteus* [Silber], *anno dñi MCCCCXCIII.* Small quarto, three printed leaves, gothic type, 40 lines to the page. Addressed to Sanches. Cosco is called Leander. Ferdinand and Isabella both named.

Major, who makes this the second edition, says that its deviations from No. I. are all on the side of ignorance. Varnhagen calls it the *editio princeps*. Bartlett (*Carter-Brown Catalogue*, no. 6) puts it second. Lenox (*Scyllacius*, p. xlv) calls it the fourth edition. It is no. 3 of Harrisse (*Bibl. Amer. Vet.*, no. 3; *Notes on Columbus*, p. 121). Graesse errs in saying the words "Indie supra Gangem" are omitted in the title.

There are copies in the Lenox, Carter-Brown, Huth (*Catalogue*, i. 336), and Grenville (*Bibl. Gren.*, p. 158) Libraries. It has been recently priced at 5,000 francs. Cf. *Murphy Catalogue*, 629.

III. *Epistola Christofori Colom.* Small quarto, four leaves, 34 lines, gothic type. Addressed to Sanxis. Cosco is called Aliander. Ferdinand only named.

This is Major's third edition. It is the *editio princeps* of Harrisse, who presumes it to be printed by Stephanus Plannck at Rome (*Notes on Columbus*, p. 117; *Bibl. Amer. Vet.*, vol. i.); and he enters upon a close examination to establish its priority. It is Lenox's second edition (*Scyllacius*, p. xliii). Bartlett places it third.

There are copies in the Barlow (formerly the Aspinwall copy) Library in New York; in the General Collection and Grenville Library of the British Museum; and in the Royal Library at Munich. In 1875 Mr. S. L. M. Barlow printed (50 copies) a fac-simile of his copy, with a Preface, in which he joins in considering this the first edition with Harrisse, who (*Notes on Columbus*, p. 101) gives a careful reprint of it.

IV. *De insulis inventis*, etc. Small octavo, ten leaves, 26 and 27 lines, gothic type. The leaf before the title has the Spanish arms on the recto. There are eight woodcuts, one of which is a repetition. Addressed to Sanxis. Cosco is called Aliender. Ferdinand only named. The words "Indie supra Gangem" are omitted in the title.

This is Major's fourth edition. Lenox makes it the *editio princeps* (as does Brunet), and gives fac-similes of the woodcuts in his *Scyllacius*, p. xxxvi. Bossi supposed the cuts to have been a part of the original manuscript, and designed by Columbus.[4] Harrisse calls it the second in order, and thinks Johannes Besicken may have been the printer (*Bibl. Amer. Vet.*, 2), though it is usually ascribed to Plannck, of Rome. It bears the arms of Granada; but there was no press at that time in that city, so far as known, though Brunet seems to imply it was printed there.

The only perfect copy known is one formerly the Libri copy, now in the Lenox Library, which has ten leaves. The Grenville copy (*Bibl. Gren.*, p. 158), and the one which Bossi saw in the Brera at Milan, now lost, had only nine leaves.

Hain (*Repertorium*, no. 5,491) describes a copy which seems to lack the first and tenth leaves; and it was proba-

---

[1] Murr, *Histoire diplomatique de Behaim*, p. 123.

[2] They are mentioned in Senarega's "De rebus Genuensibus," printed in Muratori's *Rerum Italicarum scriptores*, xxiv. 534. Cf. Harrisse, *Notes on Columbus*, p. 41.

[3] Harrisse says that when Tross, of Paris, advertised a copy at a high price in 1865, there were seven bidders for it at once. Quaritch advertised a copy in June, 1871. It was priced in London in 1872 at £140.

[4] This view is controverted in *The Bookworm*, 1868, p. 9. Cf. 1867, p. 103. The ships are said to be galleys, while Columbus sailed in caravels.

¶Epistola Christofori Colom : cui etas nostra multu debet: de
Insulis Indie supra Gangem nuper inuentis. Ad quas perqui/
rendas octauo antea mense auspicijs z ere inuictissimi Fernant
di Hispaniarum Regis missus fuerat:ad Magnificum dnm Ra
phaelem Sanxis:eiusdem serenissimi Regis Thesaurariu missa:
quam nobilis ac litteratus vir Aliander de Cosco ab Hispano
ideomate in latinum connertir : tertio kal's Maij. M.cccc.xciij.
Pontificatus Alecandri Sexti Anno primo.

Uoniam suscepte prouintie rem perfectam me consecutum
fuisse gratum tibi fore scio: has constitui exarare: que te
vniuscuiusq rei in hoc nostro itinere geste inuentecq ad/
moneant: Tricesimotertio die postq Gadibus discessi in mare
Indicu perueni:vbi plurimas insulas innumeris habitatas ho
minibus repperi:quarum omnium pro foelicissimo Rege nostro
preconio celebrato z vexillis extensis contradicente nemine pos/
sessionem accepi:primecq earum diui Saluatoris nomen impo/
sui:cuius fretus aurilio tam ad hanc:q ad ceteras alias perue/
nimus. Eam vo Indi Guanabanin vocant. Aliarum etia vnam
quanq nouo nomine nuncupaui. Quippe alia insulam Sancte
Marie Conceptionis. aliam Fernandinam. aliam Hysabellam.
aliam Iohanam. z sic de reliquis appellari iussi. Quamprimum
In eam insulam quã dudum Iohanã vocari dici appulimus:iu
xta eius littus occidentem versus aliquantulum processi:tamecq
eam magnã nullo reperto fine inueni:vt non insulam: sed cont/
nentem Chatai prouinciam esse crediderim:nulla tñ videns op/
pida municipiaue in maritimis sita confinib? preter aliquos vi/
cos z predia rustica:cum quorz incolis loqui nequibam. quare si
mul ac nos videbant surripiebant fugam. Progrediebar vltra:
existimans aliquã me vrbem villasue inuenturum. Denicq vides
q longe admodum progressis nihil noui emergebat:z hmõi via
nos ad Septentrionem deferebat:q ipse fugere exoptabã:terris
etenim regnabat bruma: ad Austrumcq erat in voto contendere:

COLUMBUS' LETTER NO. III.

bly this copy (Royal Library, Munich) which was followed
by Pilinski in his Paris fac-simile (20 copies in 1858), which
does not reproduce these leaves, though it is stated by
some that the defective British Museum copy was his
guide. Bartlett seems in error in calling this fac-simile a
copy of the Libri-Lenox copy.[1]

V. *Epistola de insulis de novo repertis*, etc. Small
quarto, four leaves, gothic, 39 lines; woodcut on
verso of first leaf. Printed by Guy Marchand in
Paris, about 1494. Addressed to Sanxis. Cosco is
called Aliander. Ferdinand only named.

This is Lenox's (*Scyllacius*, p. xlv.), Major's, and
Harrisse's fifth (*Notes on Columbus*, p. 122 ; *Bibl. Amer.
Vet.*, p. 5) edition.

The Ternaux copy, now in the Carter-Brown Library,
was for some time supposed to be the only copy known;
but Harrisse says the text reprinted by Rosny in Paris, in
1865, as from a copy in the National Library at Paris, corresponds to this. This reprint (125 copies) is entitled,
*Lettre de Christophe Colomb sur la découverte du nou-
veau monde. Publiée d'après la rarissime version Lat-
ine conservée à la Bibliothèque Impériale. Traduite en
Français, commentée* [etc.] *par Lucien de Rosny.* Paris:

[1] But compare his *Cooke Catalogue*, no. 575 ; also, *Pinart-Bourbourg Catalogue*, p. 249.

REVERSE OF TITLE OF NOS. V. AND VI.

J. Gay, 1865. 44 pages octavo. This edition was published under the auspices of the " Comité d'Archéologie Américaine." [1]

VI. *Epistola de insulis noviter repertis*, etc. Small quarto, four leaves, gothic, 39 lines; woodcut on verso of first leaf. Guiot Marchant, of Paris, printer. Addressed to Sanxis. Cosco is called Aliander. Ferdinand only named.

This is Major's sixth edition; Harrisse (*Notes on Columbus*, p. 122; *Bibl. Amer. Vet.*, no. 6) and Lenox (*Scyllacius*, p. xlvii) also place it sixth. There are fac-similes of the engraved title in Harrisse, Lenox, and Stevens's *American Bibliographer*, p. 66.

There are copies in the Carter-Brown, Bodleian (Douce), and University of Göttingen libraries; one is also shown in the *Murphy Catalogue*, no. 630.

John Harris, Sen., made a fac-simile edition of five copies, one of which is in the British Museum.

VII. *Epistola Cristophori Colom*, etc. Small quarto, four leaves, gothic, 38 lines. Addressed to Sanxis. Th. Martens is thought to be the printer.

This edition has only recently been made known. Cf. Brunet, *Supplément*, col. 276. The only copy known is in the Bibliothèque Royale at Brussels.

The text of all these editions scarcely varies, except in the use of contracted letters. Lenox's collation was reprinted, without the cuts, in the *Historical Magazine*, February, 1861. Other bibliographical accounts will be found in Graesse, *Trésor*; *Bibliotheca Grenvilliana*, i. 158; Sabin, *Dictionary*, iv. 274; and by J. H. Hessels in the *Bibliophile Belge*, vol. vi. The cuts are also in part reproduced in some editions of Irving's *Life of Columbus*, and in the *Vita*, by Bossi.[2]

In 1494 this Cosco-Sanchez text was appended to a drama on the capture of Granada, which was printed at Basle, beginning *In laudem Serenissimi Ferdinandi*, and ascribed to Carolus Veradus. The " De insulis nuper inventis " is found at the thirtieth leaf (*Bibl.*

[1] M. de Rosny was born in 1810, and died in 1871. M. Geslin published a paper on his works in the *Actes de la Société d'Ethnologie*, vii. 115. A paper by Rosny on the " Lettre de Christoph Colombe," with his version, is found in the *Revue Orientale et Américaine*, Paris, 1876, p. 81.

[2] The earliest English version of this letter followed some one edition of the Cosco-Sanchez text, and appeared in the *Edinburgh Review* in 1816, and was reprinted in the *Analectic Magazine*, ix. 513. A translation was also appended by Kettell to his edition of the *Personal Narrative*. There is another in the *Historical Magazine*, April, 1865, ix. 114.

Amer. Vet., no. 15; Lenox's *Scyllacius*, p. xlviii; Major, no. 7; *Carter-Brown Catalogue*, no. 13). There are copies in the Carter-Brown, Harvard College, and Lenox libraries.[1]

By October, in the year of the first appearance (1493) of the Cosco-Sanchez text, it had been turned into *ottava rima* by Guiliano Dati, a popular poet, to be sung about the streets, as is supposed; and two editions of this verse are now known. The earliest is in quarto, black letter, two columns, and was printed in Florence, and called *Questa e la Hystoria . . . extracte duna Epistola Christofano Colombo.* It was in four leaves, of coarse type and paper; but the second and third leaves are lacking in the unique copy, now in the British Museum, which was procured in 1858 from the Costabile sale in Paris.[2]

The other edition, dated one day later (Oct. 26, 1493), printed also at Florence, and called *La Lettera dell'isole*, etc., is in Roman type, quarto, four leaves, two columns, with a woodcut title representing Ferdinand on the European, and Columbus on the New World shore of the ocean.[3] The copy in the British Museum was bought for 1,700 francs at the Libri sale in Paris; and the only other copy known is in the Trivulgio Library at Milan.

In 1497 a German translation, or adaptation, from Cosco's Latin was printed by Bartlomesz Küsker at Strasburg, with the title *Eyn schön hübsch lesen von etlichen inszlen die do in kurtzen zyten funden synd durch dē künig von hispania, vnd sagt vō groszen wunderlichen dingen die in dē selbē inszlen synd.* It is a black-letter quarto of seven leaves, with one blank, the woodcut of the

title being repeated on the verso of the seventh leaf.[4] There are copies in the Lenox (Libri copy) and Carter-Brown libraries; in the Grenville and Huth collections; and in the library at Munich.

COLUMBUS' LETTER NO. VI.

The text of the Cosco-Sanchez letter, usually quoted by the early writers, is contained in the *Bellum Christianorum Principum* of Robertus Monarchus, printed at Basle in 1533.[5]

---

[1] It was priced by Rich in 1844 at £6 6s.; and by Robert Clarke, of Cincinnati, in 1876, at $200. There was a copy in the J. J. Cooke sale (1883), vol. iii. no. 574, and another in the Murphy sale, no. 2,602.

[2] Sabin, vol. v. no. 18,656; Major, p. xc, where the poem is reprinted, as also in Harrisse's *Notes on Columbus*, p. 186; *Bibl. Amer. Vet.*, no. 8, p. 461. This first edition has sixty-seven octaves; the second, sixty-eight. Stevens's *Hist. Coll.*, vol. i. no. 129, shows a fac-simile of the imperfect first edition.

[3] *Notes on Columbus*, p. 185; *Bibl. Amer. Vet.*, no. 9; *Additions*, no. 3; Lenox's *Scyllacius*, p. lii. The last stanza is not in the other edition, and there are other revisions. A fac-simile of the cut on the title of this Oct. 26, 1493, edition is annexed. Other fac-similes are given by Lenox, and Ruge in his *Geschichte des Zeitalters der Entdeckungen*, p. 247. This edition was reprinted at Bologna, 1873, edited by Gustavo Uzielli, as no. 136 of *Scelta di curiosità letterarie inedite*, and a reprint of Cosco's Latin text was included.

[4] Lenox's *Scyllacius*, p. lv, with fac-similes of the cuts; *Bibl. Amer. Vet.*, no. 19: *Notes on Columbus*, p. 123; *Huth*, i. 337. The elder Harris made a tracing of this edition, and Stevens had six copies printed from stone; and of these, copies are noted in the C. Fiske-Harris *Catalogue*, no. 553; Murphy, no. 632; Brinley, no. 14; Stevens's (1870) *Catalogue*, no. 459; and *Hist. Coll.*, vol. i. nos. 130, 131. The text was reprinted in the *Rheinisches Archiv*, xv. 17. It was also included in *Ein schöne newe Zeytung*, printed at Augsburg about 1522, of which there are copies in the Lenox and Carter-Brown libraries. *Scyllacius*, p. lvi; Brunet, *Supplément*, col. 277; Harrisse, *Bibl. Amer. Vet.*, no. 115. The latest enumeration of these various editions is in the *Studi biog. e bibliog. della Soc. Geog. Ital.*, 2d edition, Rome, 1882, p. 191, which describes some of the rare copies.

[5] Harrisse, *Bibl. Amer. Vet.*, no. 175; *Carter-Brown*, no. 105; Lenox, *Scyllacius*, p. lviii; Stevens, *Hist. Coll.*, vol. i. no. 163, and *Bibl. Geog.*, no. 2,383; Muller (1872), no. 387; J. J. Cooke, no. 2,183; O'Callaghan, no. 1,836. The letter is on pages 116–121 of the *Bellum*, etc. The next earliest reprint is in Andreas Schott's *Hispaniæ illustratæ*, Frankfort, 1603–1608, vol. ii. (Sabin, vol. viii. no. 32,005; Muller, 1877, no. 2,914; Stevens, 1870, no. 1,845). Of the later reproductions in other languages than English, mention may be made of those in Amati's *Ricerche Storico-Critico-Scientifiche*, 1828–1830; Bossi's *Vita di Colombo*, 1818; Urano's edition of Bossi, Paris, 1824 and 1825; the Spanish rendering of a collated Latin text made by the royal librarian Gon-

THE LANDING OF COLUMBUS.

B. LANDFALL. — It is a matter of controversy what was Guanahani, the first land seen by Columbus. The main, or rather the only, source for the decision of this question is the Journal of Columbus; and it is to be regretted that Las Casas did not leave unabridged the parts preceding the landfall, as he did those immediately following, down to October 29. Not a word outside of this Journal is helpful. The testimony of the early maps is rather misleading than reassuring, so conjectural was their geography. It will be remembered that land

zalez for Navarrete, and the French version in the Paris edition of Navarrete; G. B. Torre's *Scritti di Colombo*, Lyons, 1864 ; *Cartas y testamento di Colon*, Madrid, 1880. There is in Muratori's *Rerum Italicarum scriptores* (iii. 301) an account " De navigatione Columbi," written in 1499 by Antonio Gallo, of Genoa; but it adds nothing to our knowledge, being written entirely from Columbus's own letters.

The earliest compiled account from the same sources which appeared in print was issued, while Columbus was absent on his last voyage, in the *Nouissime Hystoriarum omnium repercussiones, que supplementum Supplementi Cronicarum nuncupantur . . . usque in annum* 1502, of Jacopo Filippo Foresti (called Bergomenses, Bergomas, or some other form), which was dated at Venice, 1502 (colophon, 1503), and contained a chapter " De insulis in India," on leaf 441, which had not been included in the earlier editions of 1483, 1484, 1485, 1486, and 1493, but is included in all later editions (Venice, 1506 ; Nuremberg, 1506 ; Venice, 1513, 1524 ; Paris, 1535), except the Spanish translation (Harrisse, *Bibl. Amer. Vet.*, nos. 42, 138, 204, and *Additions*, nos. 11, 75 ; Sabin, vol. vi. nos. 25,083, 25,084 ; Stevens, 1870, no. 175, $11 ; Carter-Brown, vol. i. nos. 19, 27 ; Murphy, no. 226 ; Quaritch, no. 11,757, £4). There are copies in the Library of Congress, the Carter-Brown and Lenox libraries, and in the National Library in Paris.

CUT IN THE GERMAN TRANSLATION OF THE FIRST LETTER OF COLUMBUS (TITLE).

was first seen two hours after midnight; and computations made for Fox show that the moon was near the third quarter, partly behind the observer, and would clearly illuminate the white sand of the shore, two leagues distant. From Columbus's course there were in his way, as constituting the Bahama group, — taking the enumeration of to-day, and remembering that the sea may have made some changes, — 36 islands, 687 cays, and 2,414 rocks. By the log, as included in the Journal, and reducing his distance sailed by dead reckoning — which then depended on observation by the eye alone, and there were also currents to misguide Columbus, running from nine to thirty miles a day, according to the force of the wind — to a course west, 2° 49′ south, Fox has shown that the discoverer had come 3,458 nautical miles. Applying this to the several islands claimed as the landfall, and knowing modern computed distances, we get the following table : —

ISLANDS.	Course.	Miles.	An Excess of
To Grand Turk .	W. 8° 1′ S.	2834	624
Mariguana .	W. 6° 37′ S.	3032	426
Watling . .	W. 4° 38′ S.	3105	353
Cat	W. 4° 20′ S.	3141	317
Samana . .	W. 5° 37′ S.	3071	387

Columbus speaks of the island as being "small," and again as "pretty large" (*bien grande*). He calls it very level, with abundance of water, and a very large lagune in the middle; and it was in the last month of the rainy season, when the low parts of the islands are usually flooded.

Some of the features of the several islands already named will now be mentioned, together with a statement of the authorities in favor of each as the landfall.

SAN SALVADOR, OR CAT. — This island is forty-three miles long by about three broad, with an area of about one hundred and sixty square miles, rising to a height of four hundred feet, the loftiest land in the group, and with no interior water. It is usual in the maps of the seventeenth and eighteenth centuries to identify this island with the Guanahani of Columbus. It is so considered by Catesby in his *Natural History of Carolina* (1731); by Knox in his *Collection of Voyages* (1767); by De la Roquette in the French version of Navarrete, vol. ii. (1828); and by Baron de Montlezun in the *Nouvelles annales des voyages*, vols. x. and xii. (1828–1829). Alexander Slidell Mackenzie, of the United States Navy, worked out the problem for Irving; and this island is fixed upon in the latter's *Life of Columbus*, app. xvi., editions of 1828 and 1848. Becher claims that the modern charts used by Irving were imperfect; and he calls "not worthy to be called a chart" the

Er Houptman der schiffung des mórs Cristoferus colon von Hispania schribt dem künig von Hispania võ
den inßlen des lands Indie uff dem fluß gangen genant. der do flüsset am mitten durch das lande india
in das indisch mór. Die er nelichen erfunden hat, vñ
die zu finden geschickt ist mit hilff vñ groser schiffung. Und
ouch etlich vorsagung võ den inßlen. Des großmechtigisten
künigs Fernãdo genant von Hispania. ¶ Nach dem vnnd ich
gefaren bin von dem gestadt des landsvon Hispania, das man
nennet Colũnas Hercules. oder von end der welt, bin ich gefaren in dry vnd dryssig tagen in das indisch mór. Do hab ich gefunden vil inßlen mit onzalber volcks wõhafftig. Die hab ich
all ingenõmen mit uff geworffnem baner vnsers mechtigisten
künigs. Und nyeman hat sich gewidert noch darwider gestelt
in keinerley weg. ¶ Die erst die ich gefundē hab, habe ich geheissen diui saluatoris. Das ist zu tuetsch des götlichen behal-
ters vñ selig machers. zu einer gedechtnyß syner wunderlichez
hohen maiestat die mir dar zu geholffen hat. vñ die von India
heissent sie gwanahũ ¶ Die ander hab ich geheissen vnß fro-
wen enpfengnyß. ¶ Uñ die dryt hab ich geheissen fernandinã
nach des künigs namen. Die vierde hab ich geheissen die Hub-
sche insel. ¶ Die fünffte iohänam. vnd hab also einer peglich
en yren namen gegeben. Und als bald ich kam in die inßel io-
hannam also genant do für ich an dem gestade hinuff gegen occident wertz, da fand ich die insel lang vnnd kein ende dar an.
Das ich gedacht es wer ein gantz land. vñ wer die prouintz zu
Cathei genant. Do sahe ich ouch keine stett noch schlösser am
gestade des móres. on etliche buren hüserfürst vnnd gestedel
vnd des selben glichen. Und mit den selben ynwonern mocht,

a ij

GERMAN TRANSLATION OF THE FIRST LETTER OF COLUMBUS (TEXT).

La Cosa map, which so much influenced Humboldt in following Irving, in his *Examen critique*
(1837), iii. 181, 186-222.

WATLING'S. — This is thirteen miles long by
about six broad, containing sixty square miles,
with a height of one hundred and forty feet, and
having about one third its area of interior water.
It was first suggested by Muñoz in 1793. Captain Becher, of the Royal Navy, elaborated the
arguments in favor of this island in the *Journal
of the Royal Geographical Society*, xxvi. 189, and
Proceedings, i. 94, and in his *Landfall of Columbus on his First Voyage to America*, London, 1856.
Peschel took the same ground in his *Geschichte*
des Zeitalters der Entdeckungen (1858). R. H.
Major's later opinion is in support of the same
views, as shown by him in the *Journal of the
Royal Geographical Society* (1871), xvi. 193, and
Proceedings, xv. 210. Cf. *New Quarterly Review*,
October, 1856.

Lieut. J. B. Murdock, U. S. N., in a paper on
"The Cruise of Columbus in the Bahamas,
1492," published in the *Proceedings* (April, 1884,
p. 449) of the United States Naval Institute,
vol. x, furnishes a new translation of the passages in Columbus' Journal bearing on the subject, and made by Professor Montaldo of the
Naval Academy, and repeats the map of the

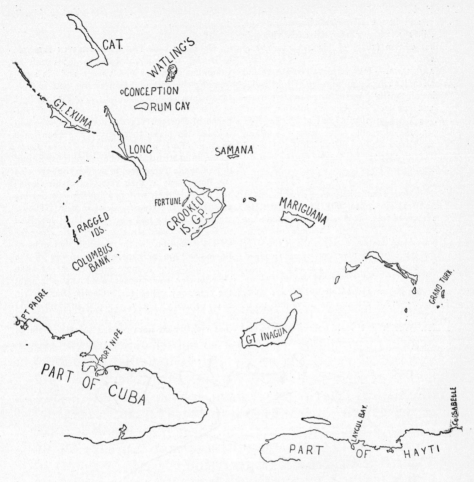

THE BAHAMA GROUP.[1]

modern survey of the Bahamas as given by Fox. Lieutenant Murdock follows and criticises the various theories afresh, and traces Columbus' track backward from Cuba, till he makes the landfall to have been at Watling's Island. He points out also various indications of the Journal which cannot be made to agree with any supposable landfall.

GRAND TURK. — Its size is five and one half by one and a quarter miles, with an area of seven square miles; its highest part seventy feet; and one third of its surface is interior water. Navarrete first advanced arguments in its favor in 1825, and Kettell adopted his views in the Boston edition of the *Personal Narrative of Columbus.* George Gibbs argued for it in the

---

[1] This map is sketched from the chart, made from the most recent surveys, in the United States Coast-Survey Office, and given in Fox's monograph, with the several routes marked down on it. Other cartographical illustrations of the subject will be found in Moreno's maps, made for Navarrete's *Coleccion* in 1825 (also in the French version); in Becher's paper in the *Journal of the Royal Geographical Society,* xxvi. 189, and in his *Landfall of Columbus;* in Varnhagen's *Das wahre Guanahani;* in Major's paper in the *Journal of the Royal Geographical Society,* 1871, and in his second edition of the *Select Letters,* where he gives a modern map, with Herrera's map (1601) and a section of La Cosa's; in G. B. Torre's *Scritti di Colombo,* p. 214; and in the section, "Wo liegt Guanahani?" of Ruge's *Geschichte des Zeitalters der Entdeckungen,* p. 248, giving all the routes, except that offered by Fox. See further on the subject R. Pietschmann's "Beiträge zur Guanahani-Frage," in the *Zeitschrift für wissenschaftliche Geographie* (1880), i. 7, 65, with map; and A. Breusing's "Zur Geschichte der Kartographie," in Ibid., ii. 193.

New York Historical Society's Proceedings (1846), p. 137, and in the *Historical Magazine* (June, 1858), ii. 161. Major adopted such views in the first edition (1847) of his *Select Letters of Columbus.*

MARIGUANA. — It measures twenty-three and one half miles long by an average of four wide; contains ninety-six square miles; rises one hundred and one feet, and has no interior water. F. A. de Varnhagen published at St. Jago de Chile, in 1864, a treatise advocating this island as *La verdadera Guanahani*, which was reissued at Vienna, in 1869, as *Das wahre Guanahani des Columbus.*[1]

SAMANA, OR ATTWOOD'S CAY. — This is nine miles long by one and a half wide, covering eight and a half square miles, with the highest ridge of one hundred feet. It is now uninhabited; but arrow-heads and other signs of aboriginal occupation are found there. The Samana of the early maps was the group now known as Crooked Island. The present Samana has been recently selected for the landfall by Gustavus V. Fox, in the *United States Coast Survey Report*, 1880, app. xviii., — "An attempt to solve the problem of the first landing-place of Columbus in the New World." He epitomized this paper

in the *Magazine of American History* (April, 1883), p. 240.

C. EFFECT OF THE DISCOVERY IN EUROPE. — During the interval between the return of Columbus from his first voyage and his again treading the soil of Spain on his return from the second, 1494, we naturally look for the effect of this astounding revelation upon the intelligence of Europe. To the Portuguese, who had rejected his pleas, there may have been some chagrin. Faria y Sousa, in his *Europa Portuguesa*, intimates that Columbus' purpose in putting in at the Tagus was to deepen the regret of the Portuguese at their rejection of his views; and other of their writers affirm his overbearing manner and conscious pride of success. The interview which he had with John II. is described in the *Lyuro das obras de Garcia de Resende.*[2] Of his reception by the Spanish monarchs at Barcelona,[3] we perhaps, in the stories of the historians, discern more embellishments than Oviedo, who was present, would have thought the ceremony called for. George Sumner (in 1844) naturally thought so signal an event would find some record in the "Anals consulars" of that city, which were formed to make note of

SIGN-MANUALS OF FERDINAND AND ISABELLA.

[1] *Sull' importanza d'un manoscritto inedito della Biblioteca Imperiale di Vienna per verificare quale fu la prima isola scoperta dal Colombo,* . . . *Con una carta geographica,* Vienna, 1869, sixteen pages. Varnhagen's paper first appeared in the *Anales de la Universedad de Chile,* vol. xxvi. (January, 1864).

[2] Evora, 1545, and often reprinted. Harrisse, *Notes on Columbus,* p. 45 : *Bibl. Amer. Vet.,* no. 265.

[3] A fac-simile of Irving's manuscript of his account of this reception is given in the *Mass. Hist. Soc. Proc.* XX. 201.

the commonest daily events; but he could find in them no indication of the advent of the discoverer of new lands.[1] It is of far more importance for us that provision was soon made for future records in the establishment of what became finally the " Casa de la Contratacion de las Indias," at this time put in charge of Juan de Fonseca, who controlled its affairs throughout the reign of Ferdinand.[2] We have seen how apparently an eager public curiosity prompted more frequent impressions of Columbus' letter in other lands than in Spain itself; but there was a bustling reporter at the Spanish Court fond of letter-writing, having correspondents in distant parts, and to him we owe it, probably, that the news spread to some notable people. This was Peter Martyr d' Anghiera. He dated at Barcelona, on the ides of May, a letter mentioning the event, which he sent to Joseph Borromeo; and he repeated the story in later epistles, written in September, to Ascanio Sforza, Tendilla, and Talavera.[3] There is every reason to suppose that Martyr derived his information directly from Columbus himself. He was now probably about thirty-seven years old, and he had some years before acquired such a reputation for learning and eloquence that he had been invited from Italy (he was a native of the Duchy of Milan) to the Spanish Court. His letters, as they have come down to us, begin about five years before this,[4] and it is said that just at this time (1493) he began the composition of his Decades. Las Casas has borne testimony to the value of the Decades for a knowledge of Columbus, calling them the most worthy of credit of all the early writings, since Martyr got, as he says, his accounts directly from the Admiral, with whom he often talked. Similar testimony is given to their credibleness by Carbajal, Gomez, Vergara,

and other contemporaries.[5] Beginning with Muñoz, there has been a tendency of late years to discredit Martyr, arising from the confusion and even negligence sometimes discernible in what he says. Navarrete was inclined to this derogatory estimate. Hallam[6] goes so far as to think him open to grave suspicion of negligent and palpable imposture, antedating his letters to appear prophetic. On the other hand, Prescott[7] contends for his veracity, and trusts his intimate familiarity with the scenes he describes. Helps interprets the disorder of his writings as a merit, because it is a reflection of his unconnected thoughts and feelings on the very day on which he recorded any transaction.[8]

What is thought to be the earliest mention in print of the new discoveries occurs in a book published at Seville in 1493, — Los tratados del Doctor Alonso Ortiz. The reference is brief, and is on the reverse of the 43d folio.[9] Not far from the same time the Bishop of Carthagena, Bernardin de Carvajal, then the Spanish ambassador to the Pope, delivered an oration in Rome, June 19, 1493, in which he made reference to the late discovery of unknown lands towards the Indies.[10] These references are all scant; and, so far as we know from the records preserved to us, the great event of the age made as yet no impression on the public mind demanding any considerable recognition.

D. SECOND VOYAGE (*Sept. 25, 1493, to June* 11, 1496). — First among the authorities is the narrative of Dr. Chanca, the physician of the Expedition. The oldest record of it is a manuscript of the middle of the sixteenth century, in the Real Academia de la Historia at Madrid.

---

[1] Prescott, *Ferdinand and Isabella* (1873), ii. 170; Major's *Select Letters*, p. lxvi; Harrisse, *Bibl. Amer. Vet., Additions*, p. ix.

[2] Irving's *Columbus*, app. xxxii.

[3] Humboldt (*Examen critique*, ii. 279-294) notes the letters referring to Columbus; and Harrisse, (*Notes on Columbus*, p. 129) reprints these letters, with translations. In the 1670 edition the Columbus references are on pp. 72-77, 81, 84, 85, 88-90, 92, 93, 96, 101, 102, 116.

[4] There are eight hundred and sixteen in all (1488 to 1525), and about thirty of them relate to the New World. He died in 1526.

[5] Prescott, *Ferdinand and Isabella* (1873), ii. 76.

[6] *Literature of Europe*, vol. i. cap. 4, § 88.

[7] *Ferdinand and Isabella* (1873), ii. 507, and p. 77. Referring to Hallam's conclusion, he says: " I suspect this acute and candid critic would have been slow to adopt it had he perused the correspondence in connection with the history of the times, or weighed the unqualified testimony borne by contemporaries to Martyr's minute accuracy."

[8] Harrisse, *Bibl. Amer. Vet.*, p. 282; Irving, *Columbus*, app. xxvii.; Brevoort's *Verrazano*, p. 87; H. H. Bancroft's *Central America*, i. 312. A bibliography of Martyr's works is given on another page.

[9] *Ticknor Catalogue*, p. 255; Harrisse, *Notes on Columbus*, p. 135; *Bibl. Amer. Vet.*, no. 10; Sabin, vol. xiv. no. 57,714.

[10] It is not certain when this discourse was printed, for the publication is without date. Harrisse, *Notes on Columbus*, p. 136; *Bibl. Amer. Vet.*, no. 11; Sabin, vol. iii. no. 11,175; *Carter-Brown Catalogue*, vol. i. no. 4. There are copies of this little tract of eight leaves in the Force Collection (Library of Congress), and in the Lenox and Carter-Brown libraries. Others are in the Vatican, Grenville Collection, etc. Cf. Court, no. 255.

From this Navarrete printed it for the first time,[1] under the title of " Segundo Viage de Cristobal Colon," in his *Coleccion*, i. 198.

Not so directly cognizant of events, but getting his information at second hand from Guglielmo Coma, — a noble personage in Spain, — was Nicolas Scyllacius, of Pavia, who translated Coma's letters into Latin, and published his narrative, *De insulis meridiani atque indici maris nuper inventis*, dedicating it to Ludovico Sforza, at Pavia (Brunet thinks Pisa), in 1594 or 1595. Of this little quarto there are three copies known. One is in the Lenox Library ; and from this copy Mr. Lenox, in 1859, reprinted it sumptuously (one hundred and two copies[2]), with a translation by the Rev. John Mulligan. In Mr. Lenox's Introduction it is said that his copy had originally belonged to M. Olivieri, of Parma, and then to the Marquis Rocca Saporiti, before it came into Mr. Lenox's hands, and that the only other copy known was an inferior one in the library of the Marquis Trivulzio at Milan. This last copy is probably one of the two copies which Harrisse reports as being in the palace library at Madrid and in the Thottiana (Royal Library) at Copenhagen, respectively.[3] Scyllacius adds a few details, current at that time, which were not in Coma's letters, and seems to have interpreted the account of his correspondent as implying that Columbus had reached the Indies by the Portuguese route round the Cape of Good Hope. Ronchini has conjectured that this blunder may have caused the cancelling of a large part of the edition, which renders the little book so scarce ; but Lenox neatly replies that " almost all the contemporaneous accounts are equally rare."

Another second-hand account — derived, however, most probably from the Admiral himself — is that given by Peter Martyr in his first Decade, published in 1511, and more at length in 1516.[4]

Accompanying Columbus on this voyage was Bernardus Buell, or Boil, a monk of St. Benoit, in Austria, who was sent by Pope Alexander VI. as vicar-general of the new lands, to take charge of the measures for educating and converting the Indians.[5] It will be remembered he afterward became a caballer against the Admiral. What he did there, and a little of what Columbus did, one Franciscus Honorius Philoponus sought to tell in a very curious book, *Nova typis transacta navigatio novi orbis Indiæ occidentalis*,[6] which was not printed till 1621. It is dedicated to Casparus Plautius, and it is suspected that he is really the author of the book, while he assumed another name, more easily to laud himself. Harrisse describes the book as having "few details of an early date, mixed with much second-hand information of a perfectly worthless character."

So far as we know, the only contemporary references in a printed book to the new discoveries during the progress of the second voyage, or in the interval previous to the undertaking of the third voyage, in the spring of 1498, are these : The *Das Narrenschiff* (Ship of Fools) of Sebastian Brant, a satire on the follies of society, published at Basle in 1494,[7] and reprinted in Latin in 1497, 1498, and in French in 1497, 1498, and 1499,[8] has a brief mention of the land previously unknown, until Ferdinand discovered innumerable people in the great Spanish ocean. Zacharias Lilio, in his *De origine et laudibus scientiarum*, Florence, 1496,[9] has two allusions. In 1497 Fedia Inghirami, keeper of the Vatican Archives, delivered a funeral oration on Prince John, son of Ferdinand and Isabella, and made a reference to the New World. The little book was probably printed in Rome. There is also a reference in the *Cosmographia* of Antonius Nebrissensis, printed in 1498.[10]

E. THIRD VOYAGE (*May* 30, 1498, *to Nov.* 20, 1500). — Our knowledge of this voyage is derived at first hand from two letters of Columbus himself, both of which are printed by Na-

---

[1] It is given in Italian in Torre's *Scritti di Colombo*, p. 372 ; and in English in Major's *Select Letters of Columbus*, repeated in the appendix of Lenox's reprint of Scyllacius. The " Memorial . . . sobre el suceso de su segundo viage á las Indias," in Navarrete, is also printed, with a translation, by Major, p. 72.

[2] They were all presentation-copies ; but one in Leclerc, no. 2,960, is priced 400 francs. The Menzies copy brought $35.

[3] Harrisse, *Bibl. Amer. Vet.*, no. 16 ; *Notes on Columbus*, p. 125. Cf. *Intorno ad un rarissimo opusculo di Niccolò Scillacio*, Modena, 1856, by Amadeo Ronchini, of Parma.

[4] Cf. a later note for the bibliography of Martyr.

[5] Harrisse, *Notes on Columbus*, p. 36, refers, for curious details about Buell, to Pasqual's *Descubrimiento de la situacion de la América*, Madrid, 1789, and the letter of the Pope to Boil in Rossi's *Del discacciamento di Colombo dalla Spagnuola*, Rome, 1851, p. 76.

[6] There are two copies in Harvard College Library. Cf. Rich (1832), no. 159, £2 2s. ; Carter-Brown, ii. no. 252 ; Quaritch, £6 16s. 6d. ; O'Callaghan, no. 1,841 ; Murphy, no. 1,971 ; Court, nos. 271, 272.

[7] Harrisse, *Bibl. Amer. Vet.*, no. 2.

[8] Carter-Brown, vol. i. nos. 16, 17, 276, 356 ; *Bibl. Amer. Vet.*, nos. 5, 6.

[9] Folios 11 and 40. Cf. *Bibl. Amer. Vet.*, no. 17 ; Sabin, vol. x. no. 41,067. Harrisse, *Notes on Columbus* p. 55, says Rich errs in stating that an earlier work of Lilio (1493) has a reference to the discovery.

[10] *Bibl. Amer. Vet.*, no. 7.

SEBASTIANVS BRANDVS
Iurisconsultus.

Iurisconsultus poteram, & simul esse Poëta:
Barbaries secli ni vetet ipsa mei.

SEBASTIAN BRANT.[1]

varrete, and by Major, with a translation. The first is addressed to the sovereigns, and follows a copy in Las Casas's hand, in the Archives of the Duque del Infantado. The other is addressed to the nurse of Prince John, and follows a copy in the Muñoz Collection in the Real Academia at Madrid, collated with a copy in the Columbus Collection at Genoa, printed by Spotorno.[2]

F. FOURTH VOYAGE (*May* 9, 1502, *to Nov.* 7, 1504). — While at Jamaica Columbus wrote

---

[1] Fac-simile of cut in Reusner's *Icones*, Strasburg, 1590.

[2] Harrisse, *Notes on Columbus*, no. 126. The *Coronica de Aragon*, of Fabricius de Vagad, which was published in 1499, makes reference to the new discoveries (*Bibl. Amer. Vet., Additions*, no. 9), as does the *Coronica van Coellen*, published at Cologne, 1499, where, on the verso of folio 339, it speaks of "new lands found, in which men roam like beasts" (Murphy, no. 254; Baer, *Incunabeln*, 1884, no. 172, at 160 marks; London Catalogue (1884), £12 10s.). In 1498, at Venice, was published Marc. Ant. Sabellicus' *In rapsodiam historiarum* (copy in British Museum), which has a brief account of Columbus' family and his early life. This was enlarged in the second part, published at Venice in 1504 (*Bibl. Amer. Vet.*, no. 21). An anchor lost by Columbus on this voyage, at Trinidad, is said to have been recovered in 1880 (*Bulletin de la Société Géographique d'Anvers*, v. 515).

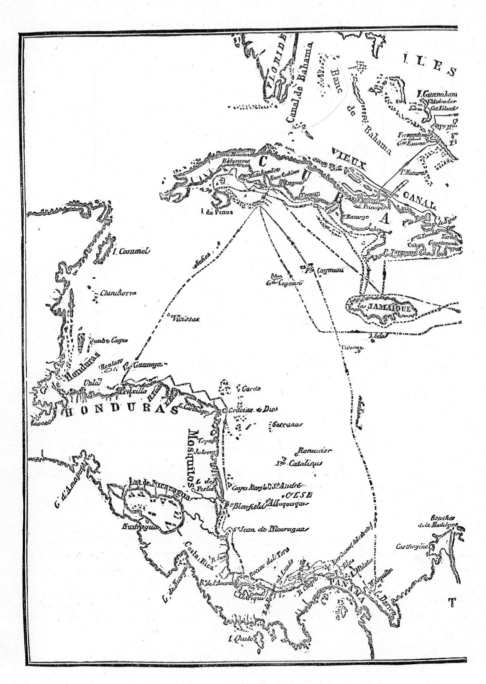

MAP OF COLUMBUS' FOUR VOYAGES (WESTERN PART).[1]

[1] A reproduction of the map in Charton's *Voyageurs*, iii. 179.

Carte générale des quatre Voyages de Colomb.

1er Voyage de Colomb ————————
2me   do   ----------------
3me   do   ················
4me   do   — · — · — · —

MAP OF COLUMBUS' FOUR VOYAGES.[1]   (EASTERN PART.)

[1] A reproduction of the map in Charton's *Voyageurs*, iii. 178.

to Ferdinand and Isabella a wild, despondent letter,[1] suggestive of alienation of mind. It brings the story of the voyage down only to July 7, 1503, leaving four months unrecorded. Pinelo says it was printed in the Spanish, as he wrote it; but no such print is known.[2] Navarrete found in the King's private library, at Madrid, a manuscript transcript of it, written, apparently, about the middle of the sixteenth century; and this he printed in his *Coleccion*.[3] It was translated into Italian by Costanzo Bayuera, of Brescia, and published at Venice, in 1505, as *Copia de la lettera per Colombo mandata*.[4] Cavaliere Morelli, the librarian of St. Mark's, reprinted it, with comments, at Bassano, in 1810, as *Lettera rarissima di Cristoforo Colombo*.[5] Navarrete prints two other accounts of this voyage, — one by Diego Porras;[6] the other by Diego Mendez, given in his last will, preserved in the Archives of the Duke of Veraguas.[7]

While Columbus was absent on this voyage, as already mentioned, Bergomas had recorded the Admiral's first discoveries.[8]

G. Lives and Notices of Columbus. — Ferdinand Columbus — if we accept as his the Italian publication of 1571 — tells us that the fatiguing career of his father, and his infirmities, prevented the Admiral from writing his own life. For ten years after his death there were various references to the new discoveries, but not a single attempt to commemorate, by even a brief sketch, the life of the discoverer. Such were the mentions in the *Commentariorum urbanorum libri* of Maffei,[9] published in 1506, and again in 1511; in Walter Ludd's *Speculi orbis*, etc.;[10] in F. Petrarca's *Chronica*;[11] and in the *Oratio*[12] of Marco Dandolo (Naples), — all in 1507. In the same year the narrative in the *Paesi novamente retrovati* (1507) established an account which was repeated in later editions, and was followed in the *Novus orbis* of 1532. The next year (1508) we find a reference in the *Oratio*[13] of Fernando Tellez at Rome; in the *Supplementi de le chroniche vulgare, novamente dal frate Jacobo Phillipo al anno* 1503 *vulgarizz., per Francesco C. Fiorentino* (Venice);[14] in Johannes Stamler's *Dyalogus*;[15] in the Ptolemy published at Rome with Ruysch's map; and in the *Collectanea*[16] of Baptista Fulgosus, published at Milan.

In 1509 there is reference to the discoveries in the *Opera nova* of the General of the Carmelites, Battista Mantuanus.[17] Somewhere, from 1510 to 1519, the *New Interlude*[18] presented Vespucius to the English public, rather than Columbus, as the discoverer of America, as had already been done by Waldseemüller at St. Dié. In 1511 Peter Martyr, in his first Decade, and Sylvanus, in his annotations of Ptolemy, drew attention to the New World; as did also Johannes Sobrarius in his *Panegyricum carmen de gestis heroicis divi Ferdinandi*

---

[1] *Que escribió D. Cristóbal Colon á los . . . . Rey y Reina de España.* Cf. Harrisse, *Notes on Columbus*, p. 127. It is given, with an English translation, in Major's *Select Letters;* also in the *Relazione delle scoperte fatte da C. Colombo, da A. Vespucci, e da altri dal 1492 al 1506, tratta dai manoscritti della Biblioteca di Ferrara e pubblicata per la prima volta ed annotata dal Prof. G. Ferraro*, at Bologna, in 1875, as no. 144 of the *Scelta di curiosità letterarie inedite o rare dal secolo* xiii *al* xvii. A French translation is given in Charton's *Voyageurs*, iii. 174.

[2] It is usually said that Ferdinand Columbus asserts it was printed; but Harrisse says he can find no such statement in Ferdinand's book.

[3] Vol. i. pp. 277–313.

[4] It is a little quarto of six leaves and an additional blank leaf (Lenox, *Scyllacius*, p. lxi; Harrisse, *Bibl. Amer. Vet.*, no. 36). There is a copy in the Marciana, which Harrisse compared with the Morelli reprint, and says he found the latter extremely faithful (*Bibl. Amer. Vet.*, no. 17).

[5] Leclerc, no. 129.

[6] In Italian in Torre's *Scritti di Colombo*, p. 396.

[7] This is also in Italian in Torre, p. 401, and in English in Major's *Select Letters*.

[8] Stevens (*Notes*, etc., p. 31) is said by Harrisse (*Bibl. Amer. Vet., Additions*, p. 35) to be in error in saying that Valentim Fernandez's early collection of Voyages, in Portuguese, and called *Marco Paulo*, etc., has any reference to Columbus.

[9] *Bibl. Amer. Vet.*, nos. 43, 67, and p. 463; *Additions*, nos. 22, 40; Thomassy, *Les papes géographes*.

[10] *Bibl. Amer. Vet.*, no. 49. See the chapter on Vespucius.

[11] Ibid., *Additions*, no. 27.

[12] Ibid., no. 28.

[13] Ibid., no. 30.

[14] Sabin, vol. vi. no. 24,395.

[15] *Bibl. Amer. Vet.*, nos. 51, 52; Murphy, no. 2,353; Stevens, *Bibl. Geog.*, no. 2,609. There are copies in the Library of Congress, Harvard College Library, etc.

[16] Sabin, vol. vii. no. 26,140; Carter-Brown, vol. i. no. 39; *Bibl. Amer. Vet.*, no. 34; Graesse, ii. 645; Brunet, ii. 1421. There were later editions in 1518, 1565, 1567, 1578, 1604, 1726, etc.

[17] *Bibl. Amer. Vet.*, no. 35.

[18] See Vol. III. pp. 16, 199; *Bibl. Amer. Vet.*, pp. 464, 518; and *Additions*, no. 38.

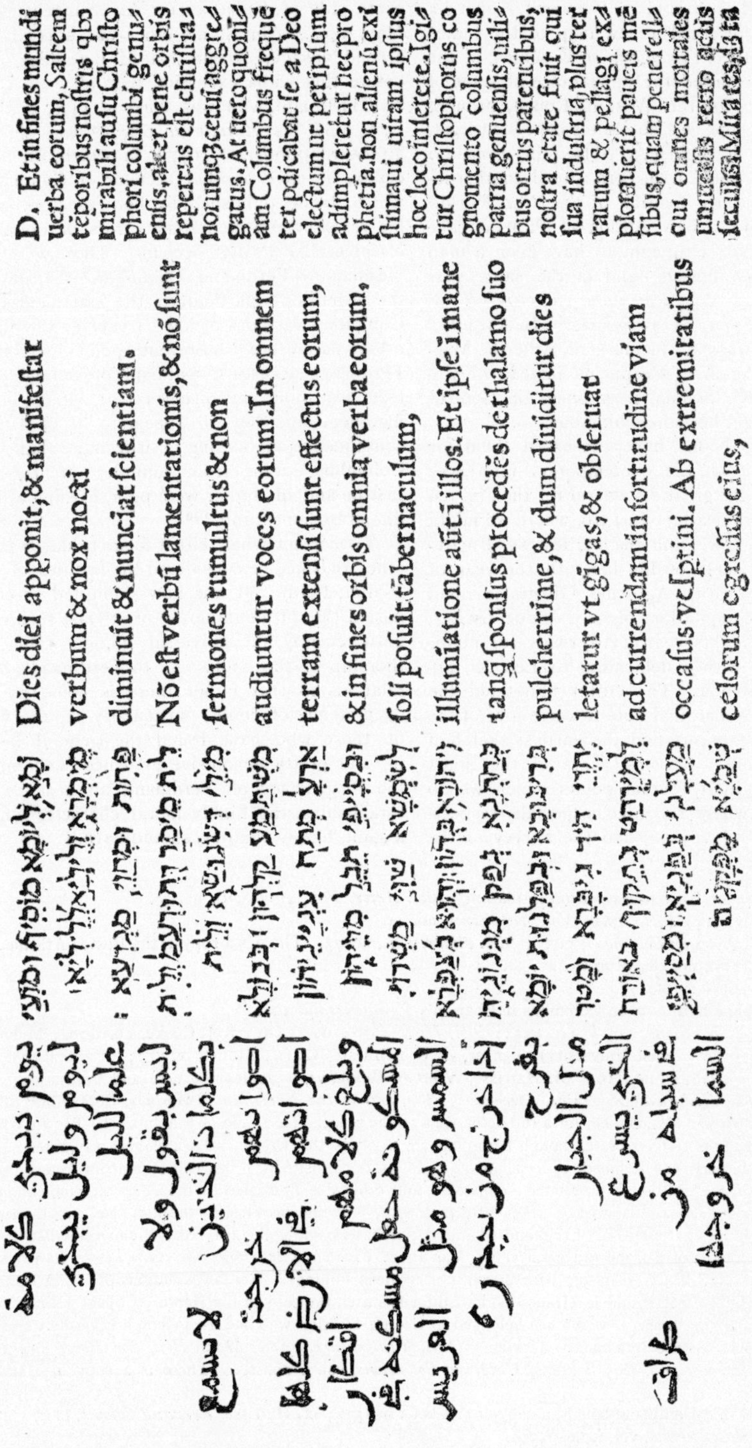

D. Et in fines mundi
uerba eorum, Saltem
téporibus nostris qb
mirabili ausu Christo
phori columbi genu-
ensis, alter pene orbis
repertus est christia-
norumqz cœtui aggre-
gatus. At uero quoni-
am Columbus frequé-
ter pdicabat se a Deo
electum ur ptipsum
adimpleretur hec pro
phetia. non alenu exi
stimaui uitam ipsius
hoc loco inferere. Igi-
tur Christophorus co
gnomento columbus
patria genuensis, uili-
bus ortus parentibus,
nostra etate fuit qui
sua industria, plus ter
rarum & pelagi exa
plorauerit paucis me
sibus, quam penerell
cui omnes mortales
unquis retro actis
seculis Mira res, &c.

Dies diei appoint, & manifestat
verbum & nox nocti
diminuit & nunciat scientiam.
Nõ est verbii lamentationis, & nõ sunt
sermones tumultus & non
audiuntur voces eorum. In omnem
terram extensi sunt effectus eorum,
& in fines orbis omniaq verba eorum,
soli posuit tabernaculum,
illumiatione aut illos. Et ipse i mane
tanq sponsus procedes de thalamo suo
pulcherrime, & dum diuiditur dies
letatur vt gigas, & obseruat
ad currendam in fortitudine viam
occasus vel ptini. Ab extremitatibus
celorum egreditur eius,

THE GIUSTINIANI PSALTER.[1]

1 Fac-simile of a portion of the page of the Giustiniani Psalter, which shows the beginning of the marginal note on Columbus.

Catholici.[1] The Stobnicza (Cracow) Appendix to Ptolemy presented a new map of the Indies in 1512; and the *Chronicon* of Eusebius, of the same date, recorded the appearance of some of the wild men of the West in Rouen, brought over by a Dieppe vessel. Some copies, at least, of Antonio de Lebrija's edition of *Prudentii opera*, printed at Lucca, 1512, afford another instance of an early mention of the New World.[2] Again, in 1513, a new edition of Ptolemy gave the world what is thought to have been a map by Columbus himself; and in the same year there was a *Supplementum supplementi* of Jacobo Philippo, of Bergomas.[3] In 1514 the *De natura locorum* (Vienna), of Albertus Magnus, points again to Vespucius instead of Columbus;[4] but Cataneo, in a poem on Genoa,[5] does not forget her son, Columbus.

These, as books have preserved them for us, are about all the contemporary references to the life of the great discoverer for the first ten years after his death.[6] In 1516, where we might least expect it, we find the earliest small gathering of the facts of his life. In the year of Columbus' death, Agostino Giustiniani had begun the compilation of a polyglot psalter, which was in this year (1516) ready for publication, and, with a dedication to Leo X., appeared in Genoa. The editor annotated the text, and, in a marginal note to verse four of the nineteenth Psalm, we find the earliest sketch of Columbus' life. Stevens[7] says of the note: "There are in it several points which we do not find elsewhere recorded, especially respecting the second voyage, and the survey of the south side of Cuba, as far as Evangelista, in May, 1494. Almost all other accounts of the second voyage, except that of Bernaldez, end before this Cuba excursion began."

Giustiniani, who was born in 1470, died in 1536, and his *Annali di Genoa*[8] was shortly afterward published (1537), in which, on folio ccxlix, he gave another account of Columbus, which, being published by his executors with his revision, repeated some errors or opinions of the earlier Psalter account. These were not pleasing to Ferdinand Columbus,[9] the son of the Admiral, — particularly the statement that Columbus was born of low parentage, — "vilibus ortus parentibus." Stevens points out how Ferdinand accuses Giustiniani of telling fourteen lies about the discoverer; "but on hunting them out, they all appear to be of trifling consequence, amounting to little more than that Columbus sprang from humble parents, and that he and his father were poor, earning a livelihood by honest toil."[10]

To correct what, either from pride or from other reasons, he considered the falsities of the Psalter, Ferdinand was now prompted to compose a Life of his father, — or at least such was, until recently, the universal opinion of his authorship of the book. As to Ferdinand's own relations to that father there is some doubt, or pretence of doubt, particularly on the part of those who have found the general belief in, and pretty conclusive evidence concerning, the illegitimacy of Ferdinand an obstacle in establishing the highly moral character which a saint, like Columbus, should have.[11]

---

[1] In the section "inventio novarum insularum," *Bibl. Amer. Vet., Additions*, no. 39.

[2] Brunet, iv. 915; *Bibl. Amer. Vet., Additions*, no. 44.

[3] Harrisse, *Notes on Columbus*, p. 57; *Bibl. Amer. Vet.*, no. 73. There is a copy in the Boston Athenæum.

[4] Carter-Brown, no. 48; Murphy, no. 32.

[5] *Bibl. Amer. Vet.*, no. 75.

[6] Cf. bibliographical note on Columbus in Charton's *Voyageurs*, iii. 190.

[7] *Historical Collections*, vol. i. no. 1,554; *Bibl. Hist.* (1870), no. 1,661; J. J. Cooke, no. 2,092; Murphy, no. 2,042 (bought by Cornell University); Panzer, vii. 63; Graesse, v. 469; Brunet, iv. 919; Rosenthal (1884); Baer, *Incunabeln* (1884), no. 116. Cf. Harrisse, *Notes on Columbus*, p. 74, for the note and translation; and other versions in *Historical Magazine*, December, 1862, and in the *Christian Examiner*, September, 1858. Also, see *Bibl. Amer. Vet.*, no. 88, for a full account; and the reduced fac-simile of title in Carter-Brown, vol. i. no. 51. The book is not very rare, though becoming so, since, as the French sale-catalogues say, referring to the note, "Cette particularité fait de ce livre un objet de haute curiosité pour les collectionneurs Américains." Harrisse says of it: "Although prohibited, confiscated, and otherwise ill-treated by the Court of Rome and the city authorities of Genoa, this work is frequently met with, — owing, perhaps, to the fact that two thousand copies were printed, of which only five hundred found purchasers, while the fifty on vellum were distributed among the sovereigns of Europe and Asia." (Cf. Van Praet, *Catalogue des livres sur vélin*, i. 8.) Its price is, however, increasing. Forty years ago Rich priced it at eighteen shillings. Recent quotations put it, in London and Paris, at £7, 100 marks, and 110 francs. The Editor has used the copy in the Harvard College Library, and in the Boston Public Library, — which last belonged to George Ticknor, who had used George Livermore's copy before he himself possessed the book. Ticknor's *Spanish Literature*, i. 188; *Mass. Hist. Soc. Proc.*, x. 431.

[8] *Bibl. Amer. Vet.*, no. 220; Stevens, *Historical Collections*, vol. i. no. 242. There is a copy in Harvard College Library.

[9] We know that Ferdinand bought a copy of this book in 1537; cf. Harrisse, *Fernand Colomb*, p. 27.

[10] *Historical Collections*, vol. i. no. 1,554.

[11] On the question of the connection of Columbus with his second companion, Donna Beatrix Enriquez who was of a respectable family in Cordova, — that there was a marriage tie has been claimed by Herrera,

Ferdinand Columbus, or Fernando Colon, was born three or four years before his father sailed on his first voyage.[1] His father's favor at Court opened the way, and in attendance upon Prince Juan and Queen Isabella he gained a good education. When Columbus went on his fourth voyage, in 1502, the boy, then thirteen years of age, accompanied his father. It is said that he made two other voyages to the New World; but Harrisse could only find proof of one. His later years were passed as a courtier, in attendance upon Charles V. on his travels, and in literary pursuits, by which he acquired a name for learning. He had the papers of his father,[2] and he is best known by the Life of Columbus which passes under his name. If it was written in Spanish, it is not known in its original form, and has not been traced since Luis Colon, the Duque de Veraguas, son of Diego, took the manuscript to Genoa about 1568. There is some uncertainty about its later history; but it appeared in 1571 at Venice in an

Italian version made by Alfonzo de Ulloa, and was entitled *Historie del S. D. Fernando Colombo; nelle quali s' ha particolare & vera relatione della vita, & de' fatti dell' Ammiraglio D. Christoforo Colombo, suo padre.* It is thought that this translation was made from an inaccurate copy of the manuscript, and moreover badly made. It begins the story of the Admiral's life with his fifty-sixth year, or thereabout; and it has been surmised that an account of his earlier years — if, indeed, the original draft contained it — was omitted, so as not to obscure, by poverty and humble station, the beginnings of a luminous career.[3] Ferdinand died at Seville, July 12, 1539,[4] and bequeathed, conditionally, his library to the Cathedral. The collection then contained about twenty thousand volumes, in print and manuscript; and it is still preserved there, though, according to Harrisse, much neglected since 1709, and reduced to about four thousand volumes. It is known as the Biblioteca Colombina.[5] Spotorno says that this

Tiraboschi, Bossi, Roselly de Lorgues, Barry, and Cadoret (*Vie de Colomb*, Paris, 1869, appendix); and that there was no such tie, by Napione (*Patria di Colombo* and Introduction to *Codice Colombo-Americano*), Spotorno, Navarrete, Humboldt, and Irving. Cf. *Historical Magazine* (August, 1867), p. 225; *Revue des questions historiques* (1879), xxv. 213; Angelo Sanguinetti's *Sull' origine di Ferdinando Colombo* (Genoa, 1876), p. 55; Giuseppe Antonio Dondero's *L'onestà di Cristoforo Colombo* (Genoa, 1877), p. 213; Harrisse, *Fernand Colomb*, p. 2; D'Avezac, in *Bulletin de la Société de Géographie* (1872), p. 19. It may be noted that Ferdinand de Galardi, in dedicating his *Traité politique* (Leyden, 1660) to Don Pedro Colon, refers to Ferdinand Colon as "Fernando Henriquez." (Stevens, *Bibl. Geog.*, no. 1,147).

The inference from Columbus' final testamentary language is certainly against the lady's chastity. In his codicil he enjoins his son Diego to provide for the respectable maintenance of the mother of Ferdinand, "for the discharge of my conscience, for it weighs heavy on my soul." Irving and others refer to this as the compunction of the last hours of the testator. De Lorgues tries to show that this codicil was made April 1, 1502 (though others claim that the document of this date was another will, not yet found), and only copied at Segovia, Aug. 25, 1505, and deposited in legal form with a notary at Valladolid, May 19, 1506, Columbus dying May 20, — the effect of all which is only to carry back, much to Columbus' credit, the compunction to an earlier date. The will (1498), but not the codicil, is given in Irving, app. xxxiv. Cancellieri, in his *Dissertazioni*, gives it imperfectly; but it is accurately given in the *Transactions* of the Genoa Academy. Cf. Harrisse (*Notes on Columbus*) p. 160; Torre's *Scritti di Colombo; Colon en Quisqueya*, Santo Domingo (1877), pp. 81, 99; *Cartas y testamento*, Madrid, 1880; Navarrete, *Coleccion*; and elsewhere.

[1] De Lorgues, on the authority of Zúñiga (*Anales eclesiásticos*, p. 496), says he was born Aug. 29, 1487, and not Aug. 15, 1488, as Navarrete and Humboldt had said. Harrisse (*Fernand Colomb*, p. 1) alleges the authority of the executor of his will for the date Aug. 15, 1488. The inscription on his supposed grave would make him born Sept. 28, 1488.

[2] Prescott (*Ferdinand and Isabella*, ii. 507) speaks of Ferdinand Columbus' "experience and opportunities, combined with uncommon literary attainments." Harrisse calculates his income from the bequest of his father, and from pensions, at about 180,000 francs of the present day. (*Fernand Colomb*, p. 29.)

[3] There has been close scrutiny of the publications of Europe in all tongues for the half century and more following the sketch of Giustiniani in 1516, till the publication of the earliest considerable account of Columbus in the Ulloa version of 1571, to gather some records of the growth or vicissitudes of the fame of the great discoverer, and of the interest felt by the European public in the progress of events in the New World. Harrisse's *Bibliotheca Americana Vetustissima*, and his *Additions* to the same, give us the completest record down to 1550, coupled with the *Carter-Brown Catalogue* for the whole period.

[4] A copy of the inscription on his tomb in Seville, with a communication by George Sumner, is printed in Major's *Select Letters of Columbus*, p. lxxxi.

[5] Cf. Edwards, *Memoirs of Libraries*, and a Memoir of Ferdinand, by Eustaquio Fernandez de Navarrete, in *Colec. de doc. inéd.*, vol. xvi. A fac-simile of the first page of the manuscript catalogue of the books, made by Ferdinand himself, is given in Harrisse's *D. Fernando Colon*, of which the annexed is the heading: —

Regestrum librorum don ferdinandi colon primi almirantis

[mdiarū filii

Luis Colon, a person of debauched character, brought this manuscript in the Spanish language to Genoa, and left it in the hands of Baliano de Fornari, from whom it passed to another patrician, Giovanni Baptista Marini, who procured Ulloa to make the Italian version in which it was first published.[1]

Somewhat of a controversial interest has been created of late years by the critiques of Henry Harrisse on Ferdinand Columbus and his Life of his father, questioning the usually accepted statements in Spotorno's introduction of the *Codice* of 1823. Harrisse undertakes to show that the manuscript was never in Don Luis' hands, and that Ferdinand could not have written it. He counts it as strange that if such a manuscript existed in Spain not a single writer in print previous to 1571 refers to it. "About ten years ago," says Henry Stevens,[2] "a society of Andalusian bibliographers was formed at Seville. Their first publication was a fierce Hispano-French attack on the authenticity of the Life of Columbus by his second son, Ferdinand, written by Henri Harrisse in French, and translated by one of the Seville bibliófilos, and adopted and published by the Society. The book [by Columbus' son] is boldly pronounced a forgery and a fraud on Ferdinand Columbus. Some fifteen reasons are given in proof of these charges, all of which, after abundant research and study, are pronounced frivolous, false, and groundless." Such is Mr. Stevens's view, colored or not by the antipathy which on more than one occasion has been shown to be reciprocal in the references of Stevens and Harrisse, one to the other, in sundry publications.[3] The views of Harrisse were also expressed in the supplemental volume of his *Bibliotheca Americana Vetustissima*, published as *Additions* in 1872. In this he says, regarding the Life of Columbus: "It was not originally written by the son of the bold navigator; and many of the circumstances it relates have to be challenged, and weighed with the utmost care and impartiality."

The authenticity of the book was ably sustained by D'Avezac before the French Academy in a paper which was printed in 1873 as *Le livre de Ferdinand Colomb: Revue critique des allégations proposées contre son authenticité*. Harrisse replied in 1875 in a pamphlet of fifty-eight pages, entitled *L'histoire de C. Colomb attribuée à son fils Fernand: Examen critique du mémoire lu par M. d'Avezac à l'Académie*, 8, 13, 22 Août, 1873. There were other disputants on the question.[4]

The catalogue of the Colombina Library as made by Ferdinand shows that it contained originally a manuscript Life of the Admiral written about 1525 by Ferdinand Perez de Oliva, who presumably had the aid of Ferdinand Columbus himself; but no trace of this Life now exists,[5] unless, as Harrisse ventures to conjecture, it may

There is a list of the books in B. Gallardo's *Ensayo de una bibliotheca de libros españoles raros*. Harrisse gives the fullest account of Ferdinand and his migrations, which can be in part traced by the inscriptions in his books of the place of their purchase; for he had the habit of so marking them. Cf. a paper on Ferdinand, by W. M. Wood, in *Once a Week*, xii. 165.

[1] Barcia says that Baliano began printing it simultaneously in Spanish, Italian, and Latin; but only the Italian seems to have been completed, or at least is the only one known to bibliographers. (*Notes on Columbus*, p. 24.) Oettinger (*Bibl. biog.*, Leipsic, 1850) is in error in giving an edition at Madrid in 1530. The 1571 Italian edition is very rare; there are copies in Harvard College, Carter-Brown, and Lenox libraries. Rich priced it in 1832 at £1 10s. Leclerc (no. 138) prices it at 200 francs. The Sobolewski copy (no. 3,756) sold in 1873 for 285 francs, was again sold in 1884 in the Court Sale, no. 77. The *Murphy Catalogue* (no. 2,881) shows a copy. This Ulloa version has since appeared somewhat altered, with several letters added, — in 1614 (Milan, priced in 1832, by Rich, at £1 10s.; recently, at 75 francs; Carter-Brown, ii. 165); in 1676 (Venice, Carter-Brown, vol. ii. no. 1,141, priced at 35 francs and 45 marks); in 1678 (Venice, Carter-Brown, vol. ii. no. 1,181, priced at 50 francs); in 1681 (Paris, Court Sale, no. 79); in 1685 (Venice, Carter-Brown, vol. ii. no. 1,310, priced at £1 8s.); and later, in 1709 (Harvard College Library), 1728, etc.; and for the last time in 1867, revised by Giulio Antimaco, published in London, though of Italian manufacture. Cancellieri cites editions of 1618 and 1672. A French translation, *La Vie de Cristofle Colomb*, was made by Cotolendi, and published in 1681 at Paris. There are copies in the Harvard College and Carter-Brown (*Catalogue*, vol. ii. no. 1,215) libraries. It is worth from $6 to $10. A new French version, "traduite et annotée par E. Muller," appeared in Paris in 1879, the editor calling the 1681 version "tronqué, incorrect, décharné, glacial." An English version appears in the chief collections of Voyages and Travels, — Churchill (ii. 479), Kerr (iii. 1), and Pinkerton (xii. 1). Barcia gave it a Spanish dress after Ulloa's, and this was printed in his *Historiadores primitivos de las Indias occidentales*, at Madrid, in 1749, being found in vol. i. pp. 1-128. (Cf. Carter-Brown, vol. iii. no. 893.)

[2] *Historical Collections* (1881), vol. i. no. 1,379.

[3] The Spanish title of Harrisse's book is *D. Fernando Colon, historiador de su padre: Ensayo crítico*. Sevilla, 1871. It was not published as originally written till the next year (1872), when it bore the title, *Fernand Colomb: sa vie, ses œuvres; Essai critique*. Paris, Tross, 1872. Cf. Arana, *Bibliog. de obras anónimas*, Santiago de Chile (1882), no. 176.

[4] Le Comte Adolphe de Circourt in the *Revue des questions historiques*, xi. 520; and *Ausland* (1873), p. 241, etc.

[5] Harrisse, *Fernand Colomb*, p. 152.

have been in some sort the basis of what now passes for the work of Ferdinand.

For a long time after the *Historie* of 1571 there was no considerable account of Columbus printed. Editions of Ptolemy, Peter Martyr, Oviedo, Grynæus, and other general books, made reference to his discoveries; but the next earliest distinct sketch appears to be that in the *Elogia virorum illustrium* of Jovius, printed in 1551 at Florence, and the Italian version made by Domenichi, printed in 1554.[1] Ramusio's third volume, in 1556, gave the story greater currency than before; but such a book as Cunningham's *Cosmographical Glasse*, in its chapter on America, utterly ignores Columbus in 1559.[2] We get what may probably be called the hearsay reports of Columbus' exploits in the *Mondo nuovo* of Benzoni, first printed at Venice in 1565. There was a brief memorial in the *Clarorum Ligurum elogia* of Ubertus Folieta, published at Rome in 1573.[3] In 1581 his voyages were commemorated in an historical poem, *Laurentii Gambaræ Brixiani de navigatione Christophori Columbi*, published at Rome.[4] Boissard, of the De Bry coterie at Frankfort in 1597, included Columbus in his *Icones virorum illustrium;*[5] and Buonfiglio Costanzo, in 1604, commemorated him in the *Historia Siciliana*, published at Venice.[6]

Meanwhile the story of Columbus' voyages was told at last with all the authority of official sanction in the *Historia general* of Herrera. This historian, or rather annalist, was born in 1549, and died in 1625;[7] and the appointment of historiographer given him by Philip II. was continued by the third and fourth monarchs of that name. There has been little disagreement as to his helpfulness to his successors. All critics place him easily first among the earlier writers; and Muñoz, Robertson, Irving, Prescott, Ticknor, and many others have united in praise of his research, candor, and justness, while they found his literary skill compromised in a measure by his chronological method. Irving found that Herrera depended so much on Las Casas that it was best in many cases to go to that earlier writer in preference;[8] and Muñoz thinks only Herrera's judicial quality preserved for him a distinct character throughout the agglutinizing process by which he constructed his book. His latest critic, Hubert H. Bancroft,[9] calls his style "bald and accurately prolix, his method slavishly chronological," with evidence everywhere in his book of "inexperience and incompetent assistance," resulting in "notes badly extracted, discrepancies, and inconsistencies." The bibliography of Herrera is well done in Sabin.[10]

Herrera had already published (1591) a monograph on the history of Portugal and the conquest (1582–1583) of the Azores, when he produced at Madrid his great work, *Historia general de los hechos de los Castellanos*, in eight decades, four of which, in two volumes, were published in 1601, and the others in 1615.[11] It has fourteen maps; and there should be bound with it, though often found separate, a ninth part, called *Descripcion de las Indias occidentales*.[12] Of the composite work, embracing the nine parts, the best edition is usually held to be one edited by Gonzales Barcia, and supplied by him with an index, which was printed in Madrid during 1727, 1728,

---

[1] Sabin, vol. vii. no. 27,478. Also in 1558, 1559.

[2] Sabin, vol. v. no. 17,971.

[3] Carter-Brown, vol. i. no. 293.

[4] Carter-Brown, vol. i. no. 340; Leclerc, nos. 226–228; J. J. Cooke, no. 575. There were other editions in 1583 and 1585; they have a map of Columbus' discoveries. Sabin, vol. vii. no. 26,500.

[5] Sabin, vol. ii. no. 6,161–6,162; Carter-Brown, vol. i. no. 509. There was a second edition, *Bibliotheca, sive thesaurus virtutis et gloriæ*, in 1628.

[6] Sabin, vol. iii. no. 9,195.

[7] He assumed his mother's name, but sometimes added his father's, — Herrera y Tordesillas. Irving (app. xxxi. to his *Life of Columbus*) says he was born in 1565.

[8] *Life of Columbus*, app. xxxi.; Herrera's account of Columbus is given in Kerr's *Voyages*, iii. 242.

[9] *Central America*, i. 317; cf. his *Chroniclers*, p. 22.

[10] *Dictionary;* also issued separately with that of Hennepin.

[11] In comparing Rich's (1832, £4 4s.) and recent prices, there does not seem to be much appreciation in the value of the book during the last fifty years for ordinary copies; but Quaritch has priced the Beckford (no. 735, copy so high as £52. There are copies in the Library of Congress, Carter-Brown, Harvard College, and Boston Public Library. Cf. *Ticknor Catalogue;* Sabin, no. 31,544; Carter-Brown, ii. 2; Murphy, 1206; Court, 169.

[12] Sabin, no. 31,539. This *Descripcion* was translated into Latin by Barlæus, and with other tracts joined to it was printed at Amsterdam, in 1622, as *Novus orbis sive descriptio Indiæ occidentalis* (Carter-Brown) vol. ii., no. 266; Sabin, no. 31,540; it is in our principal libraries, and is worth $10 or $15). It copies the maps of the Madrid edition, and is frequently cited as Colin's edition. The Latin was used in 1624 in part by De Bry, part xii. of the *Grands voyages*. (Camus, pp. 147, 160; Tiele, pp. 56, 312, who followed other engravings than Herrera's for the Incas). There was a Dutch version, *Nieuwe Werelt*, by the same publisher, in 1622 (Sabin, no. 31,542; Carter-Brown, vol. ii. no. 264), and a French (Sabin, no. 31,543; Carter-Brown, vol. ii. no. 265; Rich, 1832, £1 10s.; Quaritch, £2 12s. 6d.).

1729, and 1730, so that copies are found with all those dates, though it is commonly cited as of 1730.[1]

The principal chronicles of Spanish affairs in the seventeenth century contributed more or less to Columbus' fame ;[2] and he is commemorated in the Dutch compilation of Van den Bos, *Leven en Daden der Zeehelden*, published at Amsterdam in 1676, and in a German translation in 1681.[3]

There were a hundred years yet to pass before Robertson's *History of America* gave Columbus a prominence in the work of a historian of established fame; but this Scotch historian was forced to write without any knowledge of Columbus' own narratives.

In 1781 the earliest of the special Italian commemorations appeared at Parma, in J. Durazzo's *Elogi storici* on Columbus and Doria.[4] Chevalier de Langeac in 1782 added to his poem, *Colomb dans les fers à Ferdinand et Isabelle*, a memoir of Columbus.[5]

The earliest commemoration in the United States was in 1792, on the three hundredth anniversary of the discovery, celebrated by the Massachusetts Historical Society, when Dr. Jeremy Belknap delivered an historical discourse,[6] included later with large additions in his well-known *American Biography*. The unfinished history of Muñoz harbingered, in 1793, the revival in Europe of the study of his career. Finally, the series of modern Lives of Columbus began in 1818 with the publication at Milan of Luigi Bossi's *Vita di Cristoforo Colombo, scritta e corredata di nuove osservazioni*.[7] In 1823 the introduction by Spotorno to the *Codice*, and in 1825 the *Coleccion* of Navarrete, brought much new material to light; and the first to make use of it were Irving, in his *Life of Columbus*, 1828,[8] and Humboldt, in his *Examen critique de l'histoire de la géographie du nouveau continent*, published originally, in 1834, in a single volume; and again in five volumes, between 1836 and 1839.[9] " No one," says Ticknor,[10] " has comprehended the character of Columbus as Humboldt has, — its generosity, its enthusiasm, its far-reaching visions,

---

[1] There are copies in the Boston Athenæum, Boston Public, and Harvard College libraries (Sabin, nos. 31,541, 31,546 ; Carter-Brown, vol. iii. nos. 376, 450; Huth, vol. ii. no. 683; Leclerc, no. 278, one hundred and thirty francs ; Field, no. 689 ; ordinary copies are priced at £3 or £4; large paper at £10 or £12). A rival but inferior edition was issued at Antwerp in 1728, without maps, and with De Bry's instead of Herrera's engravings (Sabin, no. 31,545). A French version was begun at Paris in 1659, but was reissued in 1660–1670 in three volumes (Sabin, nos. 31,548–31,550 ; Field, no. 690 ; Carter-Brown, vol. ii. no. 875 ; Leclerc, no. 282, sixty francs), including only three decades. Portions were included in the Dutch collection of Van der Aa (Sabin, nos. 31,551, etc. ; Carter-Brown, iii. 111). It is also included in Hulsius, part xviii. (Carter-Brown, i. 496). The English translation of the first three decades, by Captain John Stevens, is in six volumes, London, 1725–1726 ; but a good many liberties are taken with the text (Sabin, no. 31,557 ; Carter-Brown, vol. iii. no. 355). New titles were given to the same sheets, in 1740, for what is called a second edition (Sabin, no. 31,558). " How many misstatements are attributed to Herrera which can be traced no nearer that author than Captain John Stevens's English translation? It is absolutely necessary to study this latter book to see where so many English and American authors have taken incorrect facts " (H. Stevens, *Bibliotheca Hist.*, p. xiii.).

[2] Such as the *Anales de Aragon*, 1610 ; the *Compendio historial de las chrónicas y universal historia de todos los reynos de España*, 1628 ; Zúñiga's *Annales eclesiasticos y seculares de Seville*, 1677 ; *Los reyes de Aragon, por Pedro Abarca*, 1682 ; and the *Monarquía de España, por Don Pedro Salazar de Mendoza*, 1770. The *Varones ilustres del nuevo mondo* of Pizarro y Orellana, published at Madrid in 1639, contained a Life of Columbus, as well as notices of Ojeda, Cortes, Pizarro, etc.

[3] Sabin, vol. ii. no. 6,440 ; Asher, no. 355 ; Trömel, no. 366 ; Muller (1872), no. 126.

[4] Sabin, vol. v. no. 21,418. Cf. Arana's *Bibliografía de obras anónimas*, Santiago de Chile (1882), no. 143.

[5] Sabin, vol. x. no. 38,879. Harrisse (*Notes on Columbus*, p. 190) enumerates some of the earlier and later poems, plays, sonnets, etc., wholly or incidentally illustrating the career of Columbus. Cf. also his *Fernand Colomb*, p. 131, and Larousse's *Grand dictionnaire universel*, vol. iv. The earliest mention of Columbus in English poetry is in Baptist Goodall's *Tryall of Trauell*, London, 1630.

[6] *Mass. Hist. Soc. Proc.*, i. 45 ; xii. 65.

[7] A French version, by C. M. Urano, was published at Paris in 1824 ; again in 1825. It is subjected to an examination, particularly as regards the charge of ingratitude against Ferdinand, in the French edition of Navarrete, i. 309 (Sabin, vol. ii. no. 6,464).

[8] There was a Spanish translation, made by José Garcia de Villalta, published in Madrid in 1833.

[9] In vol. iii., " De quelques faits relatifs à Colomb et à Vespuce." In vol. i. he reviews the state of knowledge on the subject in 1833. The German text, *Kritische Untersuchungen*, was printed in a translation by Jules Louis Ideler, of which the best edition is that of Berlin, 1852, edited by H. Müller. Humboldt never completed this work. The parts on the early maps, which he had intended, were later cursorily touched in his introduction to Ghillany's *Behaim*. Cf. D'Avezac's *Waltzemüller*, p. 2, and B. de Xivrey's *Des premières relations entre l'Amerique et l'Europe d'après les recherches de A. de Humboldt*, Paris, 1835, — taken from the *Revue de Paris*.

[10] *History of Spanish Literature*, i. 190.

which seemed watchful beforehand for the great scientific discovery of the sixteenth century." Prescott was warned by the popularity of Irving's narrative not to attempt to rival him; and his treatment of Columbus' career was confined to such a survey as would merely complete the picture of the reign of Ferdinand and Isabella.[1]

In 1844 there came the first intimation of a new style of biography, — a protest against Columbus' story being longer told by his natural enemies, as all who failed to recognize his pre-eminently saintly character were considered to be. There was a purpose in it to make the most possible of all his pious ejaculations, and of his intention, expressed in his letter to the Pope in 1502, to rescue the Holy City from the infidel, with his prospective army of ten thousand horse and a hundred thousand foot. The chief spokesman of this purpose has been Roselly de Lorgues. He first shadowed forth his purpose in his *La croix dans les deux mondes* in 1844. It was not till 1864 that he produced the full flower of his spirit in his *Christophe Colomb, Histoire de sa vie et de ses voyages d'après des documents authentiques tirés d'Espagne et d'Italie.*[2] This was followed, in 1874, by his *L'ambassadeur de Dieu et le Pape Pie IX*. All this, however, and much else by the abetters of the scheme of the canonization of Columbus which was urged on the Church, failed of its purpose; and the movement was suspended, for a while at least, because of an ultimate adverse determination.[3]

Of the other later lives of Columbus it remains to mention only the most considerable, or those of significant tendency.

The late Sir Arthur Helps wrote his *Spanish Conquest of America* with the aim of developing the results — political, ethnological, and economic — of the conquest, rather than the day-by-day progress of events, and with a primary regard to the rise of slavery. His *Life of Columbus* is simply certain chapters of this larger work excerpted and fitted in order.[4] Mr. Aaron Goodrich, in *A History of the so-called Christopher Columbus*, New York, 1874, makes a labored and somewhat inconsiderate effort, characterized by a certain peevish air, to prove Columbus the mere borrower of others' glories.[5]

In French, mention may be made of the Baron de Bonnefoux's *Vie de Christophe Colomb*, Paris, 1853,[6] and the Marquis de Belloy's *Christophe Colomb et la découverte du Nouveau Monde*, Paris, 1864.[7]

In German, under the impulse given by Humboldt, some fruitful labors have been given to Columbus and the early history of American discovery; but it is only necessary to mention the names of Forster,[8] Peschel,[9] and Ruge.[10]

H. PORTRAITS OF COLUMBUS. — Of Columbus there is no likeness whose claim to consideration is indisputable. We have descriptions of his person from two who knew him, — Oviedo and his own son Ferdinand; we have other

---

[1] Harrisse (*Notes on Columbus*, p. 50) speaks of Prescott as "eloquent but imaginative."

[2] The work was patronized by the Pope, and was reproduced in great luxury of ornamentation in 1879. An English abridgment and adaptation, by J. J. Barry, was republished in New York in 1869. A Dutch translation, *Leven en reizen van Columbus*, was printed at Utrecht in 1863.

[3] Some of the other contributions of this movement are these: Roselly de Lorgues, *Satan contre Christophe Colomb, ou la prétendue chute du serviteur de Dieu*, Paris, 1876; Tullio Dandolo's *I secoli di Dante e Colombo*, Milan, 1852, and his *Cristoforo Colombo, Genovese*, 1855; P. Ventura de Raulica's *Cristoforo Colombo rivendicato alla chiesa;* Eugène Cadoret, *La vie de Christophe Colomb*, Paris, 1869, — in advocacy of canonization; Le Baron van Brocken, *Des vicissitudes posthumes de Christophe Colomb, et de sa béatification possible*, Paris, 1865, — which enumerates most of the publications bearing on the grounds for canonization; Angelo Sanguineti, *La Canonizzazione di Cristoforo Colombo*, Genoa, 1875, — the same author had published a *Vita di Colombo* in 1846; *Sainteté de Christophe Colomb, résumé des mérites de ce serviteur de Dieu, traduit de l'Italien*, twenty-four pages; *Civiltà cattolica*, vol. vii.; a paper, "De l'influence de la religion dans les découvertes du XVe siècle et dans la découverte de l'Amérique," in *Etudes par des Pères de la Compagnie de Jésus*, October, 1876; Baldi, *Cristoforo Colombo glorificato dal voto dell' Episcopato Cattolico*, Genoa, 1881. A popular Catholic Life is Arthur George Knight's *Christopher Columbus*, London, 1877.

[4] There are various reviews of it indicated in Poole's *Index*, p. 29; cf. H. H. Bancroft's *Mexico*, ii. 488.

[5] A somewhat similar view is taken by Maury, in *Harpers' Monthly*, xlii. 425, 527, in "An Examination of the Claims of Columbus."

[6] From which the account of Columbus' early life is translated in Becher's *Landfall of Columbus*, pp. 1–58.

[7] An English translation, by R. S. H., appeared in Philadelphia in 1878. We regret not being able to have seen a new work by Henry Harrisse now in press: *Christophe Colomb, son origine, sa vie, ses voyages, sa famille, et ses descendants, d'après documents inédits, avec cinq tableaux généalogiques et un appendice documentaire*. [See *Postscript* following this chapter.]

[8] Fr. Forster, *Columbus, der Entdecker der Neuen Welt*, second edition, 1846.

[9] Oscar Peschel, *Geschichte des Zeitalters der Entdeckungen*, second edition, 1877.

[10] Sophus Ruge, *Die Weltanschauung des Columbus*, 1876; *Das Zeitalter der Entdeckungen*, 1883. Cf. Theodor Schott's "Columbus und seine Weltanschauung," in Virchow and Holtzendorff's *Vorträge,* xiii. 308.

NVCERINVS, HISTORICVS.

PAULUS JOVIUS.[1]

accounts from two who certainly knew his contemporaries, — Gomara and Benzoni; and in addition we possess the description given by Herrera, who had the best sources of information. From these we learn that his face was long, neither full nor thin; his cheek-bones rather high; his nose aquiline; his eyes light gray; his complexion fair, and high colored. His hair, which was of light color before thirty, became gray after that age. In the *Paesi novamente retrovati* of 1507 he is described as having a ruddy, elongated visage, and as possessing a lofty and noble stature.[2]

These are the test with which to challenge the very numerous so-called likenesses of Columbus; and it must be confessed not a single one, when you take into consideration the accessories and costume, warrants us in believing beyond dispute that we can bring before us the figure of the discoverer as he lived. Such is the opinion of Feuillet de Conches, who has produced the best critical essay on the subject yet written.[3]

---

[1] Fac-simile of cut in Reusner's *Icones*, Basle, 1589. There is another cut in *Pauli Jovii elogia virorum bellica virtute illustrium*, Basle, 1575 (copy in Harvard College Library).

[2] Harrisse, *Notes on Columbus*, p. 50.

[3] It appeared in the *Revue contemporaine*, xxiv. 484, and was drawn out by a paper on a newly discovered portrait of Columbus, which had been printed by Jomard in the *Bulletin de la Société de Géographie;* by Valentin Carderera's *Informe sobre los retratos de Cristóbal Colon*, printed by the Royal Academy of History at Madrid, in 1851, in their *Memorias*, vol. viii.; and by an article, by Isidore Löwenstern, of the Academy of Sciences at Turin, in the *Revue Archéologique*, x. 181. The paper by Jomard was the incentive of Carderera,

COLUMBUS (*after Giovio*).[1]

A vignette on the map of La Cosa, dated 1500, represents Saint Christopher bearing on his shoulders the infant Christ across a stream. This has been considered symbolical of the purpose of Columbus in his discoveries; and upholders of the movement to procure his canonization, like De Lorgues, have claimed that La Cosa represented the features of Columbus in the face of Saint Christopher. It has also been claimed that Herrera must have been of the same opinion, since the likeness given by that historian can be imagined to be an enlargement of the head on the map. This theory is hardly accepted, however, by the critics.[2]

both treatises induced the review of Löwenstern; while Feuillet de Conches fairly summed up the results. There has been no thorough account in English. A brief letter on the subject by Irving (printed in the *Life of Irving*, vol. iv.) was all there was till Professor J. D. Butler recently traced the pedigree of the Yanez picture, a copy of which was lately given by Governor Fairchild to the Historical Society of Wisconsin. Cf. Butler's paper in the *Collections* of that Society, vol. ix. p. 76 (also printed separately); and articles in *Lippincott's Magazine*, March, 1883, and *The Nation*, Nov. 16, 1882.

[1] Fac-simile of the woodcut in Paolo Giovio's *Elogia virorum bellica virtute illustrium* (Basle, 1596), p. 124. There are copies in the Boston Athenæum and Boston Public Library. It is also copied in Charton's *Voyageurs*, iii. 81, from whom Hazard (*Santo Domingo*, New York, 1873, p. 7) takes it. The 1575 edition is in Harvard College Library, and the same portrait is on p. 191. This cut is also re-engraved in Jules Verne's *La découverte de la terre*, p. 113.

[2] The vignette is given in colored fac-simile in Major's *Select Letters of Columbus*, 2d edition. Herrera's picture was reproduced in the English translation by Stevens, and has been accepted in so late a publication as Gay's *Popular History of the United States*, i. 99. Cf. also the portrait in the 1727–1730 edition of Herrera, and its equivalent in Montanus, as shown on a later page. There is a vignette portrait on the titlepage of the 1601 edition of Herrera.

Discarding the La Cosa vignette, the earliest claimant now known is an engraving published in the *Elogia virorum illustrium* (1575)[1] of Paolo Giovio (Paulus Jovius, in the Latin form). This woodcut is thought to have been copied from a picture which Jovius had placed in the gallery of notable people which he had formed in his villa at Lake Como. That collection is now scattered, and the Columbus picture cannot be traced; but that there was a portrait of the discoverer there, we know from the edition of Vasari's *Lives of the Painters* printed by Giunti at Florence (1568), wherein is a list of the pictures, which includes likenesses of Vespucius, Cortes, and Magellan, besides that of "Colombo Genovese." This indicates a single picture; but it is held by some that Jovius must have possessed two pictures, since this woodcut gives Columbus the garb of a Franciscan, while the painting in the gallery at Florence, supposed also to follow a picture belonging to Jovius, gives him a mantle. A claim has been made that the original Jovius portrait is still in existence in what is known as the Yanez picture, now in the National Library in Madrid, which was purchased of Yanez in Granada in 1763. It had originally a close-fitting tunic and mantle, which was later painted over so as to show a robe and fur collar. This external painting has been removed; and the likeness bears a certain resemblance to the woodcut and to the Florence likeness. The Yanez canvas is certainly the oldest in Spain; and the present Duque de Veraguas considers it the most authentic of all the portraits.[3] The annexed cut of it is taken from an engraving in Ruge's *Geschichte des Zeitalters der Entdeckungen* (p. 235). It bears the inscription shown in the cut.[4]

THE YANEZ COLUMBUS
(*National Library, Madrid*).[2]

The woodcut (1575) already mentioned passes as the prototype of another engraving by Aliprando Capriolo, in the *Ritratti di cento capitani illustri*, published at Rome in 1596.[5]

---

[1] The edition of Florence, 1551, has no engravings, but gives the account of Columbus on p. 171.

[2] This picture was prominently brought before the Congress of Américanistes which assembled at Madrid in 1882, and not, it seems, without exciting suspicion of a contrived piece of flattery for the Duke of Veraguas, then presiding over this same congress. Cf. Cortambert, *Nouvelle histoire des voyages*, p. 40.

[3] *Magazine of American History*, June, 1884, p. 554.

[4] Cf. *Boletin de la Sociedad geográfica de Madrid*, vol. vi. A portrait in the collection of the Marquis de Malpica is said closely to resemble it. One belonging to the Duke of Veraguas is also thought to be related to it, and is engraved in the French edition of Navarrete. It is thought Antonio del Rincon, a painter well known in Columbus' day, may have painted this Yanez canvas, on the discoverer's return from his second voyage. Carderera believed in it, and Banchero, in his edition of the *Codice Colombo Americano*, adopted it (*Magazine of American History*, i. 511). The picture now in the Wisconsin Historical Society's Rooms is copied directly from the Yanez portrait.

[5] This Capriolo cut is engraved and accepted in Carderera's *Informe*. Löwenstern fails to see how it corresponds to the written descriptions of Columbus' person. It is changed somewhat from the 1575 cut; cf. *Magasin pittoresque*, troisième année, p. 316. The two cuts, one or the other, and a mingling of the two, have given rise apparently to a variety of imitations. The head on panel preserved now, or lately, at Cuccaro, and belonging to Fidele Guglielmo Colombo, is of this type. It was engraved in Napione's *Della patria di Colombo*, Florence, 1808. The head by Crispin de Pas, in the *Effigies regum ac principum*, of an early year in the seventeenth century, is also traced to these cuts, as well as the engraving by Pieter van Opmeer in his *Opus*

The most interesting of all pictures bearing a supposed relation to the scattered collection at Lake Como is in the gallery at Florence, which is sometimes said to have been painted by Cristofano dell 'Altissimo, and before the year 1568. A copy of it was made for Thomas Jefferson in 1784, which was at Monticello in 1814; and, having been sent to Boston to be disposed of, became the property of Israel Thorndike, and was by him given to the Massachusetts Historical Society, in whose gallery it now is; and from a photograph of it the cut (p. 74) has been engraved.[1] It is perhaps the most commonly accepted likeness in these later years.[2]

After the woodcut of 1575, the next oldest engraved likeness of Columbus is the one usually called the De Bry portrait. It shows a head with a three-cornered cap, and possesses a Dutch physiognomy, — its short, broad face not corresponding with the descriptions which we find in Oviedo and the others. De Bry says that the original painting was stolen from a saloon in the Council for the Indies in Spain, and, being taken to the Netherlands, fell into his hands. He claims that it was painted from life by order of Ferdinand, the King. De Bry first used the plate in Part V. of his *Grands Voyages*, both in the Latin and German editions, published in 1595, where it is marked as engraved by Jean de Bry. It shows what seem to be two warts on the cheek,

which do not appear in later prints.[3] Feuillet de Conches describes a painting in the Versailles gallery like the De Bry, which has been engraved by

COLUMBUS (*after Capriolo*).[4]

Mercuri;[5] but it does not appear that it is claimed as the original from which De Bry worked.[6]

---

chronographicum, 1611. Landon's *Galerie historique* (Paris, 1805–1809), also shows an imitation; and another is that on the title of Cancellieri's *Notizia di Colombo*. Navarrete published a lithograph of the 1575 cut. Cf. Irving's letter. A likeness of this type is reproduced in colors, in a very pleasing way, in Roselly de Lorgues' *Christophe Colomb*, 1879, and in woodcut, equally well done, in the same work; also in J. J. Barry's adaptation of De Lorgues, New York, 1869. Another good woodcut of it is given in *Harpers' Monthly* (October, 1882), p. 729. It is also accepted in Torre's *Scritti di Colombo*.

[1] See 3 *Mass. Hist. Soc. Coll.*, vii. 285; *Proc.*, vol. ii. pp. 23, 25, 289.

[2] There are two portraits thought to have some relation with this Florentine likeness. One was formerly in the Collection d' Ambras, in the Tyrol, which was formed by a nephew of Charles V., but was in 1805 removed to the museum in Vienna. It is on panel, of small size, and has been engraved in Frankl's German poem on Columbus. The other is one whose history Isnardi, in his *Sulla patria di Colombo*, 1838, traces back for three centuries. It is now, or was lately, in the common council hall at Cogoleto.

[3] What is known as the Venetian mosaic portrait of Columbus, resembling the De Bry in the head, the hands holding a map, is engraved in *Harpers' Monthly*, liv. 1.

[4] This is a reproduction of the cut in Charton's *Voyageurs*, iii. 85. It is also copied in Carderera, and in the *Magasin pittoresque*, troisième année, p. 316.

[5] A proof-copy of this engraving is among the Tosti Engravings in the Boston Public Library.

[6] Engravings from De Bry's burin also appeared, in 1597, in Boissard's *Icones quinquaginta virorum ad vivum effictæ*; again, in the *Bibliotheca sive thesaurus virtutis et gloriæ* (Frankfort, 1628–1634), in four volumes, usually ascribed jointly to De Bry and Boissard; and, finally, in the *Bibliotheca chalcographica* (Frankfort, 1650–1664), ascribed to Boissard; but the plates are marked Jean Théodore de Bry. The De Bry type was apparent in the print in Isaac Bullart's *Académie des Sciences et des Arts*, Paris, 1682; and a few years later (1688), an aquaforte engraving by Rosaspina came out in Paul Freherus' *Théâtre des hommes célèbres*. For the later use made of this De Bry likeness, reference may be made, among others, to the works of Napione and Bossi, Durazzo's *Eulogium*, the *Historia de Mexico* by Francisco Carbajal Espinosa, published at Mexico, in 1862, tome i, J. J. Smith's *American Historical and Literary Curiosities*, sundry editions of Irving's *Life of Columbus*, and the London (1867) edition of Ferdinand Columbus' Life of

COLUMBUS (*the Jefferson copy of the Florence picture*).

Jomard, in the *Bulletin de la Société de Géogra-phie* (3d series), iii. 370, printed his "Monument

à Christophe Colomb: son portrait,"[1] in expla-nation and advocacy of a Titianesque canvas

his father. There is a photograph of it in Harrisse's *Notes on Columbus*. De Bry engraved various other pictures of Columbus, mostly of small size, — a full-length in the corner of a half-globe (part vi.); a full-length on the deck of a caravel (in part iv., re-engraved in Bossi, Charton, etc.); a small vignette portrait, together with one of Vespucius, in the Latin and German edition of part iv. (1594); the well-known picture illustrating the anecdote of the egg (part iv.). Not one of these has any claim to be other than imaginative

---

[1] There was a movement at this time (1845) to erect a monument in Genoa.

QVI RATE VELIVOLA OCCIDVOS PENETRAVIT AP IDOS
PRIMVS ET AMERICAM NOBLLITAVIT HVMVM

CHRISTOPHORVS COLVMBVS LIGVR. INDIARV PRIM' INVET A' 1492

ASTRORVM CONSVLT' ET IPSO NOBILIS AVSV
CHRISTOPHOR' TALI FRONTE COLVMB' ERAT

THE DE BRY PORTRAIT OF COLUMBUS.

which he had found at Vicenza, inscribed "Christophorus Columbus." He claimed that the features corresponded to the written descriptions of Columbus by his contemporaries

His larger likeness he reproduced in a small medallion as the title of the Herrera narrative (part xii., German and Latin, 1623–1624), together with likenesses of Vespucius, Pizarro, and Magellan. Another reminiscence of the apocryphal egg story is found in a painting, representing a man in a fur cap, holding up an egg, the face wearing a grin, which was brought forward a few years ago by Mr. Rinck, of New York, and which is described and engraved in the *Compte rendu* of the Congrès des Américanistes, 1877, ii. 375.

and accounted for the Flemish ruff, pointed beard, gold chain, and other anachronous accessories, by supposing that these had been added by a later hand. These adornments,

JOMARD'S PICTURE OF COLUMBUS.[1]

however, prevented Jomard's views gaining any countenance, though he seems to have been confident in his opinion. Irving at the time records his scepticism when Jomard sent him

a lithograph of it. Carderera and Feuillet de Conches both reject it.

A similar out-of-date ruff and mustache characterize the likeness at Madrid associated with the Duke of Berwick-Alba, in which the finery of a throne makes part of the picture. The owner had a private plate engraved from it by Rafael Esteve, a copy of which, given by the engraver to Obadiah Rich, who seems to have had faith in it, is now in the Lenox Library.[2]

A picture belonging to the Duke of Veraguas is open to similar objections, — with its beard and armor and ruff; but Muñoz adopted it for his official history, the plate being drawn by Mariano Maella.[3]

A picture of a bedizened cavalier, ascribed to Parmigiano (who was three years old when Columbus died), is preserved in the Museo Borbonico at Naples, and is, unfortunately, associated in this country with Columbus, from having been adopted by Prescott for his *Ferdinand and Isabella*,[4] and from having been copied for the American Antiquarian Society.[5] It was long since rejected by all competent critics.

A picture in the Senate chamber (or lately there) at Albany was given to the State of New York in 1784 by Mrs. Maria Farmer, a granddaughter of Governor Jacob Leisler, and was said to have been for many years in that lady's family.[6] There are many other scattered alleged likenesses of Columbus, which from the data at hand it has not been easy to link with any of those already mentioned.[7]

[1] This is a reproduction of the cut in Charton's *Voyageurs*, iii. 87.

[2] *Ticknor Catalogue*, p. 95. The medallion on the tomb in the cathedral at Havana is usually said to have been copied from this picture; but the picture sent to Havana to be used as a model is said, on better authority, to have been one belonging to the Duke of Veraguas, — perhaps the one said to be in the Consistorial Hall at Havana, which has the garb of a familiar of the Inquisition; and this is represented as the gift of that Duke (*Magazine of American History*, i. 510).

[3] It is re-engraved in the English and German translations. Carderera rejects it; but the portrait in the Archives of the Indies at Seville is said to be a copy of it; and a copy is in the Pennsylvania Academy of Arts in Philadelphia. A three-quarters length of Columbus, representing him in ruff and armor, full face, mustache and imperial, right hand on a globe, left hand holding a truncheon, called "Cristoval Colon: copiado de un Quadro origl. que se conserva en la familia," was engraved, and marked "Bart. Vazque. la Grabo, 1791."

[4] It is still unaccountably retained in the revised 1873 edition.

[5] Cf. their *Proceedings*, April, 1853.

[6] It was restored in 1850 (*Magazine of American History*, v. 446).

[7] Such are the following: (1) In full dress, with ruff and rings, said to have been painted by Sir Anthony More for Margaret of the Netherlands, and taken to England in 1590, — engraved in one of the English editions of Irving, where also has appeared an engraving of a picture by Juan de Borgoña, painted in 1519 for the Chapter-room of the Cathedral of Toledo. (2) A full-length in mail, with ruff, in the Longa or Exchange at Seville, showing a man of thirty or thirty-five years, which Irving thinks may have been taken for Diego Columbus. (3) An engraving in Fuchsius' *Metoposcopia et ophthalmoscopia*, Strasburg, 1610 (Sabin's *Dictionary*, vii. 89). (4) An engraving in N. De Clerck's *Tooneel der beroemder hertogen*, etc., Delft, 1615, — a collection of portraits, including also Cortes, Pizarro, Magellan, Montezuma, etc. (5) A

COLUMBUS. — THE HAVANA MEDALLION.[1]

The best known, probably, of the sculptured effigies of Columbus is the bust of Peschiera, full-length, engraved in Philoponus, 1621. (6) An old engraving, with pointed beard and ruff, preserved in the National Library at Paris. (7) The engraving in the *Nieuwe en onbekende Weereld* of Montanus, 1671-1673, repeated in Ogilby's *America*, and reproduced in Bos's *Leven en Daden*, and in Herrera, edition 1728. A fac-simile of it is given herewith. Cf. Ruyter's *See-Helden*, Nuremberg, 1661. (8) A copper plate, showing a man with a beard, with fur trimmings to a close-fitting vestment, one hand holding an astrolabe, the other pointing upward, — which accompanies a translation of Thevet's account of Columbus which was placed in 1821 at Genoa on the receptacle of the Columbus manuscripts.[2] The

---

[1] Reproduced from a cut in Charton's *Voyageurs*, iii. 188.

[2] A view of this receptacle of the papers, with the bust and the portfolio, is given in *Harpers' Monthly*, vol. liv., December, 1876.

artist discarded all painted portraits of Columbus, and followed the descriptions of those who had known the discoverer.[1]

The most imposing of all the memorials is the monument at Genoa erected in 1862 after a design by Freccia, and finished by Michel Canzio.[3]

COLUMBUS.[2]

I. BURIAL AND REMAINS OF COLUMBUS. — There is no mention of the death of Columbus in the Records of Valladolid. Peter Martyr, then writing his letters from that place, makes no reference to such an event. It is said that the earliest contemporary notice of his death is in an official document, twenty-seven days later, where it is affirmed that "the said Admiral is dead."[4] The story which Irving has written of the successive burials of Columbus needs to be rewritten; and positive evidence is wanting to show that his remains were placed first, as is alleged, in a vault of the Franciscans at Valladolid. The further story, as told by Irving, of Ferdinand's ordering the removal of his remains to Seville seven years later, and the erection of a monument, is not confirmed by any known evidence.[5] From the tenor of Diego's will in March, 1509, it would seem that the body of Columbus had already been carried to Seville, and that later, the coffins of his son Diego and of his brother Bartholomew were laid in Seville beside him, in the

in the appendix to the Cambridge, 1676, edition of North's *Plutarch*. (9) An old woodcut in the *Neueröffnetes Amphitheatrum*, published at Erfurt in 1723-1724 (*Brinley Catalogue*, no. 48). (10) A man with curly hair, mustache and imperial, ruff and armor, with a finger on a globe, — engraved in Cristóbal Cladera's *Investigaciones históricas, sobre los principales descubrimientos de los Españoles en el mar Oceano en el siglo XV. y principios del XVI.*, Madrid, 1794. (11) Columbus and his sons, Diego and Ferdinand, engraved in Bryan Edwards' *The History, civil and commercial, of the British Colonies in the West Indies*, 1794; again, 1801. Feuillet de Conches in his essay on the portraits calls it a pure fantasy.

[1] It is engraved in the first edition of the *Codice diplomatico Colombo-Americano*, and in the English translation of that book. It is also re-engraved in the Lenox edition of *Scyllacius*. Another bust in Genoa is given in the French edition of Navarrete. Of the bust in the Capitoline Museum at Rome — purely ideal — there is a copy in the New York Historical Society's Gallery, no. 134. The effigies on the monument at Seville, and the bust at Havana, with their costume of the latter part of the sixteenth century, present no claims for fidelity. Cf. *Magazine of American History*, i. 510.

[2] This is copied from one given in Ruge's *Geschichte des Zeitalters der Entdeckungen*, p. 234, which follows a photograph of the painting in the Ministry of Marine at Madrid.

[3] There is a model of it in the Public Library of Boston, a photograph in Harrisse's *Notes*, p. 182, and engravings in De Lorgues, Torri, etc. There is also a view of this monument in an article on Genoa, the home of Columbus, by O. M. Spencer, in *Harpers' Monthly*, vol. liv., December, 1876. The mailed figure on the Capitol steps at Washington, by Persico, is without claim to notice. There is a colossal statue at Lima, erected in 1850 by Salvatore Revelli, a marble one at Nassau (New Providence), and another at Cardeñas, Cuba.

[4] Navarrete, ii. 316.

[5] The *Informe de la Real Academia* says there is no proof of it; and of the famous inscription, —

"A Castilla y á Leon
Nuevo Mundo dió Colon," —

said to have been put on his tomb, there is no evidence that it ever was actually used, being only proposed in the *Elegías* of Castellanos, 1588.

COLUMBUS (*from Montanus*).

cuevas, or vaults of the Carthusians. Meanwhile the Cathedral in Santo Domingo was begun, — not to be completed till 1540; and in this island it had been the Admiral's wish to be buried. His family were desirous of carrying out that wish; but it seemed to require three royal orders to make good the project, and overcome objections or delays. These orders were dated June 2, 1537, Aug. 22, 1539, and Nov. 5, 1540.[1] It has been conjectured from the language of

[1] They are in the Archives at Madrid. Harrisse found one in the Archives of the Duke of Veraguas (*Los restos*, etc., p. 41). The orders are printed by Roque Cocchia, Prieto, Colmeiro, etc.

Ferdinand Columbus' will, in 1539, that the remains were still in the *cuevas*; and it is supposed that they were carried to Santo Domingo in 1541, — though, if so, there is no record of their resting-place from 1536, — when they are said, in the Convent's Records,[1] to have been

COFFER AND BONES.[2]

platform of the high altar, with the remains of his brother Don Luis on the other side, according to the tradition of the aged in this island."[5] The book from which this is extracted[6] was published in Madrid, and erred in calling Luis a brother instead of grandson, whose father, Diego, lying beside the Admiral, seems at the time to have been forgotten.[7]

Just a century later, in 1783, Moreau de Saint-Méry, prefacing his *Description topographique* of Santo Domingo,[8] sought more explicit information, and learned that, shortly before his inquiry, the floor of the chancel had been raised so as to conceal the top of the vault, which was "a case of stone" (containing the leaden coffin), on the "Gospel side of the sanctuary." This case had been discovered during the repairs, and, though "without inscription, was known from uninterrupted and invariable tradition to contain the remains of Columbus;" and the Dean of the Chapter, in certifying to this effect, speaks of the "leaden urn as a little damaged, and containing several human bones;" while he had also, some years earlier, found on "the Epistle side" of the altar a similar stone case, which, according to tradition, contained the bones of the Admiral's brother.[9]

delivered up for transportation. The earliest positive mention of their being in the Cathedral at Santo Domingo is in 1549;[3] and it is not till the next century that we find a positive statement that the remains of Diego were also removed.[4] Not till 1655 does any record say that the precise spot in the Cathedral containing the remains was known, and not till 1676 do we learn what that precise spot was, — "on the right of the altar." In 1683 we first learn of "a leaden case in the sanctuary, at the side of the

A few years later the treaty of Basle, July 22, 1795, gave to France the half of Santo Domingo still remaining to Spain; and at the cost of the Duke of Veraguas, and with the concurrence of the Chapter of the Cathedral, the Spanish General, Gabriel de Aristazabal, some-

---

1 Harrisse, *Los restos*, p. 44.

2 This follows an engraving given in John G. Shea's "Where are the Remains of Columbus?" in *Magazine of American History*, January, 1883, and separately. There are other engravings in Tejera, pp. 28, 29; and after a photograph in the *Informe de la Real Academia*, p. 197.   The case is 16⅝ × 8½ × 8⅛ inches.

3 Prieto, *Exámen*, etc., p. 18.

4 Colmeiro, p. 160.

5 Quoted in Harrisse, *Les sépultures*, etc., p. 22.

6 *Synodo Diocesan del Arzobispado di Santo Domingo*, p. 13.

7 Plans of the chancel, with the disposition of the tombs in 1540 or 1541, as now supposed, are given in Tejera, p. 10; Cocchia, p. 48, etc.

8 Published both in French and English at Philadelphia in 1796.

9 Harrisse, *Los restos*, p. 47.

what hurriedly opened a vault on the left of the altar, and, with due ceremony and notarial record,[1] took from it fragments of a leaden case and some human bones, which were unattested by any inscription found with them. The relics were placed in a gilt leaden case, and borne with military honors to Havana.[2] It is now claimed that these remains were of Diego, the son, and that the vault then opened is still empty in the Cathedral, while the genuine remains of Columbus were left undisturbed.

seem to have been suitable precautions taken to avoid occasion for imputations of deceit, and with witnesses the case was examined.[3] In it were found some bones and dust, a leaden bullet,[4] two iron screws, which fitted the holes in a small silver plate found beneath the mould in the bottom of the case.[5] This casket bore on the outside, on the front, and two ends — one letter on each surface — the letters C. C. A. On the top was an inscription here reduced : —

In 1877, in making some changes about the chancel, on the right of the altar, the workmen opened a vault, and found a leaden case containing human bones, with an inscription showing them to be those of Luis, the grandson. This led to a search on the

This inscription is supposed to mean " Discoverer of America, first Admiral." Opening the case, which in this situation presented the appearance shown in the cut on page 80, the under surface of the lid was found to bear the following legend : —

opposite, or "Gospel side" of the chancel, where they found an empty vault, supposed to be the one from which the remains were taken to Havana. Between this and the side wall of the building, and separated from the empty vault by a six-inch wall, was found another cavity, and in it a leaden case. There

This legend is translated, "Illustrious and renowned man, Christopher Columbus."[6] A fac-simile of the inscription found on the small silver plate is given on page 82, the larger of which is understood to mean " A part of the remains of the first Admiral, Don Christopher Columbus, discoverer."[7] The discovery was made

---

[1] Navarrete, ii. 365; Prieto's *Exámen*, p. 20; Roque Cocchia, p. 280 ; Harrisse, *Los restos*, app. 4.

[2] Irving's account of this transportation is in his *Life of Columbus*, app. i. Cf. letter of Duke of Veraguas (March 30, 1796) in *Magazine of American History*, i. 247. At Havana the reinterment took place with great parade An oration was delivered by Caballero, the original manuscript of which is now in the Massachusetts Historical Society's Library (cf. *Proceedings*, ii. 105, 168). Prieto (*Los restos*) prints this oration; Navarrete (vol. ii. pp. 365-381) gives extracts from the official accounts of the transfer of the remains.

[3] The Spanish consul is said to have been satisfied with the precautions. Cf. *Do existen depositadas las cenizas de Colon?* by Don José de Echeverri (Santander, 1878). There are views of the Cathedral in Hazard's *Santo Domingo*, p. 224, and elsewhere.

[4] Which some have supposed was received in Columbus' body in his early piratical days.

[5] This plate was discovered on a later examination.

[6] Both of these inscriptions are given in fac-simile in Cocchia, p. 290 ; in Tejera, p. 30 ; and in Armas, who calls it "inscripcion auténtica — escritura gótica-alemana" of the sixteenth century.

[7] Fac-similes of these are given in the *Informe de la Real Academia*, Tejera (pp. 33, 34), Prieto, Cocchia (pp. 170, 171), Shea's paper, and in Armas, who calls the inscription, "Apócrifas — escritura inglesa de la época actual."

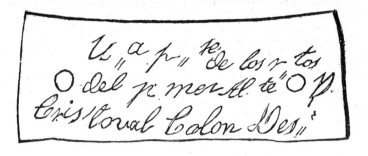

known by the Bishop, Roque Cocchia, in a pastoral letter,[1] and the news spread rapidly.[2] The Spanish King named Señor Antonio Lopez Prieto, of Havana, to go to Santo Domingo, and, with the Spanish consul, to investigate. Prieto had already printed a tract, which went through two editions, *Los restos de Colon : exámen histórico-critico*, Havana, 1877. In March, 1878, he addressed his Official Report to the Captain-general of Cuba, which was printed in two editions during the same year, as *Informe sobre los restos de Colon*. It was an attack upon the authenticity of the remains at Santo Domingo. Later in the same year, Oct. 14, 1878, Señor Manuel Colmeiro presented, in behalf of the Royal Academy of History of Madrid, a report to the King, which was printed at Madrid in 1879 as *Los restos de Colon : informe de la Real Academia de la Historia*, etc. It reinforced the views of Prieto's Report ; charged Roque Cocchia with abetting a fraud ; pointed to the A (America) of the outside inscription as a name for the New World which Spaniards at that time never used ;[3] and claimed that the remains discovered in 1877 were those of Christopher Columbus, the grandson of the Admiral, and that the inscriptions had been tampered with, or were at least much later than the date of reinterment in the Cathedral.[4] Besides Bishop Roque Cocchia, the principal upholder of the Santo Domingo theory has been Emiliano Tejera, who published his

---

[1] *Descubrimiento de los verdaderos restos de Cristóbal Colon : carta pastoral*, Santo Domingo, 1877, — reprinted in *Informe de la Real Academia*, p. 191, etc.

[2] The Bishop, in his subsequent *Los restos de Colon* (Santo Domingo, 1879), written after his honesty in the matter was impugned, and with the aim of giving a full exposition, shows, in cap. xviii. how the discovery, as he claimed it, interested the world. Various contemporaneous documents are also given in *Colon en Quisqueya, Coleccion de documentos*, etc., Santo Domingo, 1877. A movement was made to erect a monument in Santo Domingo, and some response was received from the United States. *New Jersey Historical Society's Proceedings*, v. 134 ; *Pennsylvania Magazine of History*, iii. 465.

[3] Mr. J. C. Brevoort, in "Where are the Remains of Columbus ? " in *Magazine of American History*, ii. 157, suggests that the "D. de la A." means "Dignidad de la Almirantazgo."

[4] This was a view advanced by J. I. de Armas in a Caracas newspaper, later set forth in his *Las cenizas de Cristóbal Colon suplantadas en la Catedral de Santo Domingo*, Caracas, 1881. The same view is taken by Sir Travers Twiss, in his *Christopher Columbus : A Monograph on his True Burial-place* (London, 1879), a paper which originally appeared in the *Nautical Magazine*. M. A. Baguet, in "Où sont ces restes de Colomb ? " printed in the *Bulletin de la Société d'Anvers* (1882), vi. 449, also holds that the remains are those of the grandson, Cristoval Colon. For an adverse view, see the *Informe* of the Amigos del Pais, published at Santo Domingo, 1882. Cf. also Juan Maria Asensio, *Los restos de Colon*, segunda ed., Sevile, 1881.

Los restos de Colon en Santo Domingo in 1878, and his *Los dos restos de Cristóbal Colon* in 1879, both in Santo Domingo. Henry Harrisse, under the auspices of the " Sociedad de Biblió-filos Andaluces," printed his *Los restos de Don Cristóval Colon* at Seville in 1878, and his *Les sépultures de Christophe Colomb : revue critique du premier rapport officiel publié sur ce sujet*, the next year (1879) at Paris.[1] From Italy we have Luigi Tommaso Belgrano's *Sulla recente scoperta delle ossa di Colombo* (Genoa, 1878). One of the best and most recent summaries of the subject is by John G. Shea in the *Magazine of American History*, January, 1883 ; also printed separately, and translated into Spanish. Richard Cortambert (*Nouvelle histoire des voyages*, p. 39) considers the Santo Domingo theory overcome by the evidence.

J. DATE AND PLACE OF BIRTH OF COLUMBUS, AND ACCOUNTS OF HIS FAMILY. — The year and place of Columbus' birth, and the station into which he was born, are questions of dispute. Harrisse[2] epitomizes the authorities upon the year of his nativity. Oscar Peschel reviews the opposing arguments in a paper printed in *Ausland* in 1866.[3] The whole subject was examined at greater length and with great care by D'Avezac before the Geographical Society of Paris in 1872.[4] The question is one of deductions from statements not very definite, nor wholly in accord. The extremes of the limits in dispute are about twenty years; but within this interval, assertions like those of Ramusio[5] (1430) and Charlevoix[6] (1441) may be thrown out as susceptible of no argument.[7]

In favor of the earliest date — which, with variations arising from the estimates upon fractions of years, may be placed either in 1435, 1436, or 1437 — are Navarrete, Humboldt, Ferdinand Höfer,[8] Émile Deschanel,[9] Lamartine,[10]

Irving, Bonnefoux, Roselly de Lorgues, l'Abbé Cadoret, Jurien de la Gravière,[11] Napione,[12] Cancellieri, and Cantù.[13] This view is founded upon the statement of one who had known Columbus, Andres Bernaldez, in his *Reyes católicos*, that Columbus was about seventy years old at his death, in 1506.

The other extreme — similarly varied from the fractions between 1455 and 1456 — is taken by Oscar Peschel,[14] who deduces it from a letter of Columbus dated July 7, 1503, in which he says that he was twenty-eight when he entered the service of Spain in 1484 ; and Peschel argues that this is corroborated by adding the fourteen years of his boyhood, before going to sea, to the twenty-three years of sea-life which Columbus says he had had previous to his voyage of discovery, and dating back from 1492, when he made this voyage.

A middle date — placed, according to fractional calculations, variously from 1445 to 1447 — is held by Cladera,[15] Bossi, Muñoz, Casoni,[16] Salinerio,[17] Robertson, Spotorno, Major, Sanguinetti, and Canale. The argument for this view, as presented by Major, is this : It was in 1484, and not in 1492, that this continuous sea-service, referred to by Columbus, ended ; accordingly, the thirty-seven years already mentioned should be deducted from 1484, which would point to 1447 as the year of his birth, — a statement confirmed also, as is thought, by the assertion which Columbus makes, in 1501, that it was forty years since he began, at fourteen, his sea-life. Similar reasons avail with D'Avezac, whose calculations, however, point rather to the year 1446.[18]

A similar uncertainty has been made to appear regarding the place of Columbus' birth. Outside of Genoa and dependencies, while discarding such claims as those of England,[19]

---

[1] Originally in the *Bulletin de la Société de Géographie*, October, 1878. Cf. also his paper in the *Revue critique*, Jan. 5, 1878, "Les restes mortels de Colomb."

[2] *Bibl. Amer. Vet.*, p. 3.

[3] Pages 1177–1181 : "Ueber das Geburtsjahre des Entdeckers von America."

[4] *Année véritable de la naissance de Christophe Colomb, et revue chronologique des principales époques de sa vie*, in *Bulletin de la Société de Géographie*, Juillet, 1872 ; also printed separately in 1873, pp. 64.

[5] Based on a statement in the Italian text of Peter Martyr (1534) which is not in the original Latin.

[6] Also in Prévost's *Voyages*, and in Tiraboschi's *Letteratura Italiana*.

[7] Humboldt, *Examen critique*, iii. 252.

[8] *Nouvelle biographie générale*, xi. 209.

[9] *Christophe Colomb*, Paris, 1862.

[10] *Christopher Colomb*.

[11] *Les marins du XVe et du XVIe siècle*, i. 80.

[12] *Patria di Colombo*.

[13] *Storia universale*.

[14] *Zeitalter der Entdeckungen*, p. 97 ; *Ausland*, 1866, p. 1178.

[15] *Investigaciones históricas*, p. 38.

[16] *Annali di Genova*, 1708, p. 26.

[17] *Annotationes ad Tacitum.*

[18] These various later arguments are epitomized in Ruge, *Das Zeitalter der Entdeckungen*, p. 219.

[19] Charles Malloy's *Treatise of Affairs Maritime*, 3d ed., London, 1682 ; Harrisse, *Notes on Columbus*, p. 69.

Corsica,[1] and Milan,[2] there are more defensible presentations in behalf of Placentia (Piacenza), where there was an ancestral estate of the Admiral, whose rental had been enjoyed by him and by his father ;[3] and still more urgent demands for recognition on the part of Cuccaro in Montferrat, Piedmont, the lord of whose castle was a Dominico Colombo, — pretty well proved, however, not to have been the Dominico who was father of the Admiral. It seems certain that the paternal Dominico did own land in Cuccaro, near his kinspeople, and lived there as late as 1443.[4]

In consequence of these claims, the Academy of Sciences in Genoa named a commission, in 1812, to investigate them ; and their report,[5] favoring the traditional belief in Genoa as the true spot of Columbus' birth, is given in digest in Bossi.[6] The claim of Genoa seems to be generally accepted to-day, as it was in the Admiral's time by Peter Martyr, Las Casas, Bernaldez, Giustiniani, Geraldini, Gallo, Senaraya, and Foglietto.[7] Columbus himself twice, in his will (1498), says he was born in Genoa ; and in the codicil (1506) he refers to his "beloved

country, the Republic of Genoa." Ferdinand calls his father "a Genoese."[8] Of modern writers Spotorno, in the Introduction to the *Codice diplomatico Colombo-Americano* (1823), and earlier, in his *Della origine e della patria di Colombo* (1819), has elaborated the claim, with proofs and arguments which have been accepted by Irving, Bossi, Sanguinetti, Roselly, De Lorgues, and most other biographers and writers.

There still remains the possibility of Genoa as referred to by Columbus and his contemporaries, signifying the region dependent on it, rather than the town itself ; and with this latitude recognized, there are fourteen towns, or hamlets as Harrisse names them,[9] which present their claims.[10]

Ferdinand Columbus resented Giustiniani's statement that the Admiral was of humble origin, and sought to connect his father's descent with the Colombos of an ancient line and fame ; but his disdainful recognition of such a descent is, after all, not conducive to a belief in Ferdinand's own conviction of the connection.

---

[1] Documentary proof, as it was called, has been printed in the *Revue de Paris*, where (August, 1841) it is said that the certificate of Columbus' marriage has been discovered in Corsica. Cf. Margry, *Navigations Françaises*, p. 357. The views of the Abbé Martin Casanova, that Columbus was born in Calvi in Corsica, and the act of the French President of Aug. 6, 1883, approving of the erection of a monument to Columbus in that town, have been since reviewed by Harrisse in the *Revue critique* (18 Juin, 1883), who repeats the arguments for a belief in Genoa as the birthplace, in a paper, "Christophe Colomb et la Corse," which has since been printed separately.

[2] Domingo de Valtanas, *Compendio de cosas notables de España*, Seville, 1550; *Bibl. Amer. Vet.*, no. 183.

[3] The claim is for Pradello, a village neighboring to Placentia. Cf. Campi, *Historia ecclesiastica di Piacenza*, Piacenza, 1651-1662, which contains a "discorso historico circa la nascita di Colombo," etc. ; Harrisse, *Notes on Columbus*, p. 67 ; Carter-Brown, vol. ii. no. 711.

[4] Napione, in *Mémoires de l'Académie de Turin* (1805), xii. 116, and (1823) xxvii. 73, — the first part being printed separately at Florence, in 1808, as *Della Patria di Colombo*, while he printed, in 1809, *Del primo scopritore del continente del nuovo mondo*. In the same year J. D. Lanjuinais published at Paris, in reference to Napione, his *Christophe Colomb, ou notice d'un livre Italien concernant cet illustre navigateur*. Cf. the same author's *Etudes* (Paris, 1823), for a sketch of Columbus, pp. 71-94 ; *Dissertazioni di Francesco Cancellieri sopra Colombo*, Rome, 1809; and Vicenzio Conti's historical account of Montferrat. In 1853 Luigi Colombo, a prelate of the Roman Church, who claimed descent from an uncle of the Admiral, renewed the claim in his *Patria e biografia del grande ammiraglio D. Cristoforo Colombo de' conti e signori di Cuccaro*, Roma, 1853. Cf. *Notes on Columbus*, p. 73.

[5] *Ragionamento nel quale si confirma l'opinione generale intorno al patria di Cristoforo Colombo*, in vol. iii. of the *Transactions* of the Society.

[6] A view of the alleged house and chamber in which the birth took place is given in *Harpers' Monthly*, vol. liv., December, 1876.

[7] In his *Clarorum Ligurum elogia*, where the Genoese were taunted for neglecting the fame of Columbus.

[8] See his will in Navarrete, and in Harrisse's *Fernan Colon*.

[9] *Bibl. Amer. Vet.*, pp. xix, 2.

[10] The claims of Savona have been urged the most persistently. The Admiral's father, it seems to be admitted, removed to Savona before 1469, and lived there some time ; and it is found that members of the Colombo family, even a Cristoforo Colombo, is found there in 1472 ; but it is at the same time claimed that this Cristoforo signed himself as of Genoa. The chief advocate is Belloro, in the *Corres. Astron. Géograph. du Baron de Zach*, vol. xi , whose argument is epitomized by Irving, app. v. Cf. Giovanni Tommaso Belloro, *Notizie d' atti esistenti nel publico archivio de' notaj di Savona, concernenti la famiglia di Cristoforo Colombo*, Torino, 1810, reprinted by Spotorno at Genoa in 1821. Sabin (vol. ii. no. 4,565), corrects errors of Harrisse, *Notes on Columbus*, p. 68. Other claims for these Genoese towns are brought forward, for which see Harrisse, *Notes on Columbus* ; J. R. Bartlett, in *Historical Magazine*, February, 1868, p. 100; Felice Isnardi's *Dissertazione*, 1838, and *Nuovi documenti*, 1840, etc. Caleb Cushing in his *Reminiscences of Spain*, i. 292 (Boston, 1833), gave considerable attention to the question of Columbus' nativity.

FERDINAND OF SPAIN.[1]

There seems little doubt that his father[2] was a wool-weaver or draper, and owned small landed properties, at one time or another, in or not far from Genoa;[3] and, as Harrisse infers,

[1] This follows an ancient medallion as engraved in Buckingham Smith's *Coleccion*. Cf. also the sign-manual on p. 56.

[2] Bernardo Pallastrelli's *Il suocero e la moglie di C. Colombo* (Modena, 1871; second ed., 1876), with a genealogy, gives an account of his mother's family. Cf. also *Allgemeine Zeitung*, Beilage no. 118 (1872), and *Amer. Antiq. Soc. Proc.*, October, 1873.

[3] Philip Casoni's *Annali di Genova*, Genoa, 1708.

DON BARTHOLMEO
COLON
L Adelantado.

BARTHOLOMEW COLUMBUS.[1]

it was in one of the houses on the Bisagno road, as you go from Genoa, that Columbus was perhaps born.[2]

The pedigree (p. 87) shows the alleged descent of Columbus, as a table in Spotorno's *Della origine e della patria di Colombo*, 1819, connects it with other lines, whose heirs at a later day were aroused to claim the Admiral's honors; and as the usual accounts of his immediate descendants record the transmission of his rights. After Columbus' death, his son Diego demanded the restitution of the offices and privileges [3] which had been suspended during the Admiral's later years. He got no satisfac-

---

[1] This is a fac-simile of an engraving in Herrera (Barcia's edition). There is a vignette likeness on the title of vol i., edition of 1601. Navarrete's Memoir of Bartholomew Columbus is in the *Coleccion de documentos inéditos*, vol. xvi.

[2] Harrisse, *Notes on Columbus*, p. 73. Harrisse, in his *Les Colombo de France et d'Italie, fameux marins du XVe siècle*, 1461-1492 (Paris, 1874), uses some new material from the archives of Milan, Paris, and Venice, and gathers all that he can of the Colombos; and it does not seem probable that the Admiral bore anything more than a very remote relationship to the family of the famous mariners. Major (*Select Letters*, p. xliii) has also examined the alleged connection with the French sea-leader, Caseneuve, or Colon. Cf. Desimoni's *Rassegna del nuovo libro di Enrico Harrisse: Les Colombo de France et d'Italie* (Parigi, 1874, pp. 17); and the appendices to Irving's *Columbus* (nos. iv. and vi.) and Harrisse's *Les Colombo* (no. vi).

[3] Conferred by the Convention of 1492; ratified April 23, 1497; confirmed by letter royal, March 14, 1502.

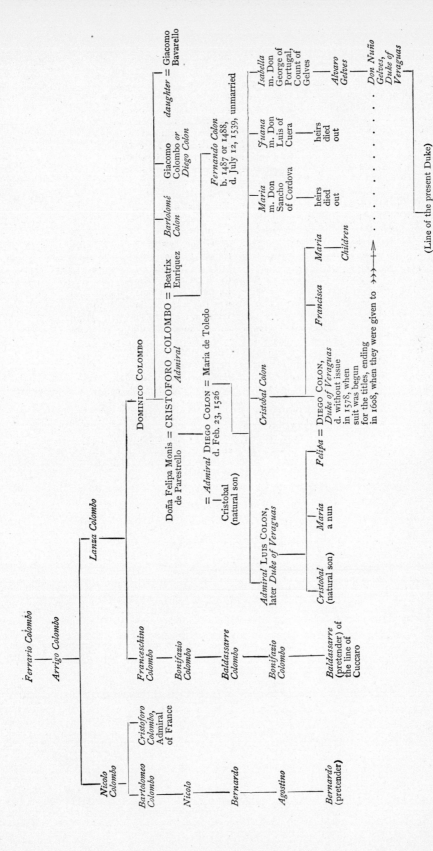

GENEALOGICAL TABLE.

tion but the privilege of contending at law with the fiscal minister of the Crown, and of giving occasion for all the latent slander about the Admiral to make itself heard. The tribunal was the Council of the Indies; the suit was begun in 1508, and lasted till 1527. The documents connected with the case are in the Archives of the Indies. The chief defence of the Crown was that the original convention was against law and public policy, and that Columbus, after all, did not discover *Terra firma*, and for such discovery alone honors of this kind should be the reward. Diego won the Council's vote; but Ferdinand, the King, hesitated to confirm their decision. Meanwhile Diego had married a niece of the Duke of Alva, the King's favorite, and got in this way a royal grant of something like vice-royal authority in the Indies, to which he went (1509) with his bride, prepared for the proper state and display. His uncles, Bartholomew and Diego, as well as Ferdinand Columbus, accompanied him. The King soon began to encroach on Diego's domain, creating new provinces out of it.[1] It does not belong to this place to trace the vexatious factions which, through Fonseca's urging, or otherwise created, Diego was forced to endure, till he returned to Spain, in 1515, to answer his accusers. When he asked of the King a share of the profits of the Darien coast, his royal master endeavored to show that Diego's father had never been on that coast. After Ferdinand's death (Jan. 23, 1516), his succes-

sor, Charles V., acknowledged the injustice of the charges against Diego, and made some amends by giving him a viceroy's functions in all places discovered by his father. He was subjected, however, to the surveillance of a supervisor to report on his conduct, upon going to his government in 1520.[2] In three years he was again recalled for examination, and in 1526 he died. Don Luis, who succeeded to his father Diego, after some years exchanged, in 1556, his rights of vice-royalty in the Indies for ten thousand gold doubloons and the title of Duque de Veraguas (with subordinate titles), and a grandeeship of the first rank;[3] the latter, however, was not confirmed till 1712.

His nephew Diego succeeded to the rights, silencing those of the daughter of Don Luis by marrying her. They had no issue; and on his death, in 1578, various claimants brought suit for the succession (as shown in the table), which was finally given, in 1608, to the grandson of Isabella, the granddaughter of Columbus. This suit led to the accumulation of a large amount of documentary evidence, which was printed.[4] The vexations did not end here, the Duke of Berwick still contesting; but a decision in 1790 confirmed the title in the present line. The revolt of the Spanish colonies threatened to deprive the Duke of Veraguas of his income; but the Spanish Government made it good by charging it upon the revenues of Cuba and Porto Rico, the source of the present Duke's support.[5]

POSTSCRIPT.

A FTER the foregoing chapter had been completed, there came to hand the first volume of *Christophe Colomb, son origine, sa vie, ses voyages, sa famille, et ses descendants, d'après des documents inédits tirés des Archives de Gênes, de* *Savone, de Séville, et de Madrid, études d'histoire critique par Henry Harrisse*, Paris, 1884.

The book is essentially a reversal of many long-established views regarding the career of Columbus. The new biographer, as has been

---

[1] Such as New Andalusia, on the Isthmus of Darien, intrusted to Ojeda; and Castilla del Oro, and the region about Veragua, committed to Nicuessa. There was a certain slight also in this last, inasmuch as Don Diego had been with the Admiral when he discovered it.

[2] The ruins of Diego Columbus' house in Santo Domingo, as they appeared in 1801, are shown in Charton's *Voyageurs*, iii. 186, and Samuel Hazard's *Santo Domingo*, p. 47; also pp. 213, 228.

[3] Papers relating to Luis Colon's renunciation of his rights as Duke of Veraguas, in 1556, are in Peralta's *Costa Rica, Nicaragua y Panamá*, Madrid, 1883, p. 162.

[4] Harrisse, *Notes on Columbus*, p. 3. Leclerc (*Bibl. Amer.*, no. 137) notes other original family documents priced at 1,000 francs.

[5] The arms granted by the Spanish sovereigns at Barcelona, May 20, 1493, seem to have been altered at a later date. As depicted by Oviedo, they are given on an earlier page. Cf. Lopez de Haro, *Nobiliario general* (Madrid, 1632), pt. ii. p. 312; Muñoz, *Historia del nuevo mondo*, p. 165; *Notes and Queries* (2d series), xii. 530; (5th series) ii. 152; *Mem. de la Real Academia de Madrid* (1852), vol. viii.; Roselly de Lorgues, *Christophe Colomb* (1856); *Documentos inéditos* (1861), xxxi. 295; *Cod. diplom. Colombo-Americano*, p. lxx; Harrisse, *Notes on Columbus*, p. 168; Charlevoix, *Isle Espagnole*, i. 61, 236, and the engraving given in Ramusio (1556), iii. 84. I am indebted to Mr. James Carson Brevoort for guidance upon this point.

shown, is not bound by any respect for the Life of the Admiral which for three hundred years has been associated with the name of Ferdinand Columbus. The grounds of his discredit of that book are again asserted; and he considers the story as given in Las Casas as much more likely to represent the prototype both of the *Historia general* of this last writer and of the *Historie* of 1571, than the mongrel production which he imagines this Italian text of Ulloa to be, and which he accounts utterly unworthy of credit by reason of the sensational perversions and additions with which it is alloyed by some irresponsible editor. This revolutionary spirit makes the critic acute, and sustains him in laborious search; but it is one which seems sometimes to imperil his judgment. He does not at times hesitate to involve Las Casas himself in the same condemnation for the use which, if we understand him, Las Casas may be supposed, equally with the author or editor of the *Historie*, to have made of their common prototype. That any received incident in Columbus' career is only traceable to the *Historie* is sufficient, with our critic, to assign it to the category of fiction.

This new Life adds to our knowledge from many sources; and such points as have been omitted or slightly developed in the preceding chapter, or are at variance with the accepted views upon which that chapter has been based, it may be well briefly to mention.

The frontispiece is a blazon of the arms of Columbus, "du cartulaire original dressé sous ses yeux à Séville en 1502," following a manuscript in the Archives of the Ministry of Foreign Affairs at Paris. The field of the quarter with the castle is red; that of the lion is silver; that of the anchors is blue; the main and islands are gold, the water blue. It may be remarked that the disposition of these islands seems to have no relation to the knowledge then existing of the Columbian Archipelago. Below is a blue bend on a gold field, with red above (see the cut, *ante*, p. 15).

In writing in his Introduction of the sources of the history of Columbus, Harrisse says that we possess sixty-four memoirs, letters, or extracts written by Columbus, of which twenty-three are preserved in his own autograph. Of these sixty-four, only the *Libro de las profecias* has not been printed entire, if we except a *Memorial que presentó Cristóbal Colon á los Reyes Catolicos sobre las cosas necesarias para abastecer las Indias* which is to be printed for the first time by Harrisse, in the appendix of his second volume. Las Casas' transcript of Columbus' *Journal* is now, he tells us, in the collection of the Duque d' Osuna at Madrid. The copy of Dr. Chanca's relation of the second voyage, used by Navarrete, and now in the Academy of History at Madrid, belonged to a collection formed

by Antonio de Aspa. The personal papers of Columbus, confided by him to his friend Gaspar Gorricio, were preserved for over a century in an iron case in the custody of monks of Las Cuevas; but they were, on the 15th of May, 1609, surrendered to Nuño Gelves, of Portugal, who had been adjudged the lawful successor of the Admiral. Such as have escaped destruction now constitute the collection of the present Duque de Veraguas; and of them Navarrete has printed seventy-eight documents. Of the papers concerning Columbus at Genoa, Harrisse finds only one anterior to his famous voyage, and that is a paper of the Father Dominico Colombo, dated July 21, 1489, of whom such facts as are known are given, including references to him in 1463 and 1468 in the records of the Bank of St. George in Genoa. Of the two letters of 1502 which Columbus addressed to the Bank, only one now exists, as far as Harrisse could learn, and that is in the Hôtel de Ville. Particularly in regard to the family of Columbus, he has made effective use of the notarial and similar records of places where Columbus and his family have lived. But use of depositions for establishing dates and relationship imposes great obligation of care in the identification of the persons named; and this with a family as numerous as the Colombos seem to have been, and given so much to the repeating of Christian names, is more than usually difficult. In discussing the evidence of the place and date of Columbus' birth (p. 137), as well as tracing his family line (pp. 160 and 166), the conclusion reached by Harrisse fixes the humble origin of the future discoverer; since he finds Columbus' kith and kin of the station of weavers, — an occupation determining their social standing as well in Genoa as in other places at that time. The table which is given on a previous page (*ante*, p. 87) shows the lines of supposable connection, as illustrating the long contest for the possession of the Admiral's honors. His father's father, it would seem, was a Giovanni Colombo (pp. 167–216), and he the son of a certain Luca Colombo. Giovanni lived in turn at Terrarossa and Quinto. Domenico, the Admiral's father, married Susanna Fontanarossa, and removed to Genoa between 1448 and 1551, living there afterward, except for the interval 1471–1484, when he is found at Savona. He died in Genoa not far from 1498. We are told (p. 29) how little the Archives of Savona yield respecting the family. Using his new notarial evidence mainly, the critic fixes the birth of Columbus about 1445 (pp. 223–241); and enforces a view expressed by him before, that Genoa as the place of Columbus' birth must be taken in the broader sense of including the dependencies of the city, in one of which he thinks Columbus was born (p. 221) in that humble station which Gallo, in his

"De navigatione Columbi," now known to us as printed in Muratori (xxiii. 301), was the first to assert. Giustiniani, in his Psalter-note, and Senarega, in his "De rebus Genuensibus" (Muratori, xxiv. 354) seem mainly to have followed Gallo on this point. There is failure (p. 81) to find confirmation of some of the details of the family as given by Casoni in his *Annali della republica di Genova* (1708, and again 1799). In relation to the lines of his descendants, there are described (pp. 49-60) nineteen different memorials, bearing date between 1590 and 1792 — and there may be others — which grew out of the litigations in which the descent of the Admiral's titles was involved.

The usual story, told in the *Historie*, of Columbus' sojourn at the University of Pavia is discredited, chiefly on the ground that Columbus himself says that from a tender age he followed the sea (but Columbus' statements are often inexact), and from the fact that in cosmography Genoa had more to teach him than Pavia. Columbus is also kept longer in Italy than the received opinion has allowed, which has sent him to Portugal about 1470; while we are now told — if his identity is unassailable — that he was in Savona as late as 1473 (pp. 253-254).

Documentary Portuguese evidence of Columbus' connection with Portugal is scant. The Archivo da Torre do Tombo at Lisbon, which Santarem searched in vain for any reference to Vespucius, seem to be equally barren of information respecting Columbus, and they only afford a few items regarding the family of the Perestrellos (p. 44).

The principal contemporary Portuguese chronicle making any reference to Columbus is Ruy de Pina's *Chronica del Rei Dom João II.*, which is contained in the *Collecção de livros ineditos de historia Portugueza*, published at Lisbon in 1792 (ii. 177), from which Garcia de Resende seems to have borrowed what appears in his *Choronica*, published at Lisbon in 1596; and this latter account is simply paraphrased in the *Decada primeira do Asia* (Lisbon, 1752) of João de Barros, who, born in 1496, was too late to have personal knowledge of earlier time of the discoveries. Vasconcellos' *Vida y acciones del Rey D. Juan al segundo* (Madrid, 1639) adds nothing.

The statement of the *Historie* again thrown out, doubt at least is raised respecting the marriage of Columbus with Philippa, daughter of Bartholomeu Perestrello; and if the critic cannot disprove such union, he seems to think that as good, if not better, evidence exists for declaring the wife of Columbus to have been the daughter of Vasco Gil Moniz, of an old family, while it was Vasco Gill's sister Isabel who married the Perestrello in question. The marriage of Columbus took place, it is claimed

there is reason to believe, not in Madeira, as Gomara and others have maintained, but in Lisbon, and not before 1474. Further, discarding the *Historie*, there is no evidence that Columbus ever lived at Porto Santo or Madeira, or that his wife was dead when he left Portugal for Spain in 1484. If this is established, we lose the story of the tie which bound him to Portugal being severed by the death of his companion; and the tale of his poring over the charts of the dead father of his wife at Porto Santo is relegated to the region of fable.

We have known that the correspondence of Toscanelli with the monk Martinez took place in 1474, and the further communication of the Italian *savant* with Columbus himself has always been supposed to have occurred soon after; but reasons are now given for pushing it forward to 1482.

The evidences of the offers which Columbus made, or caused to be made, to England, France, and Portugal, — to the latter certainly, and to the two others probably, — before he betook himself to Spain, are also reviewed. As to the embassy to Genoa, there is no trace of it in the Genoese Archives and no earlier mention of it than Ramusio's; and no Genoese authority repeats it earlier than Casoni in his *Annali di Genova*, in 1708. This is now discredited altogether. No earlier writer than Marin, in his *Storia del commercio de' Veneziani* (vol. vii. published 1800), claims that Columbus gave Venice the opportunity of embarking its fortunes with his; and the document which Pesaro claimed to have seen has never been found.

There is difficulty in fixing with precision the time of Columbus' leaving Portugal, if we reject the statements of the *Historie*, which places it in the last months of 1484. Other evidence is here presented that in the summer of that year he was in Lisbon; and no indisputable evidence exists, in the critic's judgment, of his being in Spain till May, 1487, when a largess was granted to him. Columbus' own words would imply in one place that he had taken service with the Spanish monarchs in 1485, or just before that date; and in another place that he had been in Spain as early as January, 1484, or even before, — a time when now it is claimed he is to be found in Lisbon.

The pathetic story of the visit to Rábida places that event at a period shortly after his arriving in Spain; and the *Historie* tells also of a second visit at a later day. It is now contended that the two visits were in reality one, which occurred in 1491. The principal argument to upset the *Historie* is the fact that Juan Rodriguez Cabezudo, in the lawsuit of 1513, testified that it was "about twenty-two years" since he had lent a mule to the Franciscan who accompanied Columbus away from Rábida!

With the same incredulity the critic spirits away (p. 358) the junto of Salamanca. He can find no earlier mention of it than that of Antonio de Remesal in his *Historia de la Provincia de S. Vincente de Chyapa*, published in Madrid in 1619; and accordingly asks why Las Casas, from whom Remesal borrows so much, did not know something of this junto? He counts for much that Oviedo does not mention it; and the Archives of the University at Salamanca throw no light. The common story he believes to have grown out of conferences which probably took place while the Court was at Salamanca in the winter of 1486-1487, and which were conducted by Talavera; while a later one was held at Santa Fé late in 1491, at which Cardinal Mendoza was conspicuous.

Since Alexander Geraldinus, writing in 1522, from his own acquaintance with Columbus, had made the friar Juan Perez, of Rábida, and Antonio de Marchena, who was Columbus' steadfast friend, one and the same person, it has been the custom of historians to allow that Geraldinus was right. It is now said he was in error; but the critic confesses he cannot explain how Gomara, abridging from Oviedo, changes the name of Juan Perez used by the latter to Perez de Marchena, and this before Geraldinus was printed. Columbus speaks of a second monk who had befriended him; and it has been the custom to identify this one with Diego de Deza, who, at the time when Columbus is supposed to have stood in need of his support, had already become a bishop, and was not likely, the critic thinks, to have been called a monk by Columbus. The two friendly monks in this view were the two distinct persons Juan Perez and Antonio de Marchena (p. 372).

The interposition of Cardinal Mendoza, by which Columbus secured the royal ear, has usually been placed in 1486. Oviedo seems to have been the source of subsequent writers on the point; but Oviedo does not fix the date, and the critic now undertakes to show (p. 380) that it was rather in the closing months of 1491.

Las Casas charges Talavera with opposing the projects of Columbus: we have here (p. 383) the contrary assertion; and the testimony of Peter Martyr seems to sustain this view. So again the new biographer measurably defends, on other contemporary evidence, Fonseca (p. 386) as not deserving the castigations of modern writers; and all this objurgation is considered to have been conveniently derived from the luckless *Historie* of 1571.

The close student of Columbus is not unaware of the unsteady character of much of the discoverer's own testimony on various points. His imagination was his powerful faculty; and it was as wild at times as it was powerful, and nothing could stand in the way of it. No one has emphasized the doleful story of his trials and repressions more than himself, making the whole world, except two monks, bent on producing his ignominy; and yet his biographer can pick (p. 388) from the Admiral's own admissions enough to show that during all this time he had much encouragement from high quarters. The critic is not slow to take advantage of this weakness of Columbus' character, and more than once makes him the strongest witness against himself.

It is now denied that the money advanced by Santangel was from the treasury of Aragon. On the contrary, the critic contends that the venture was from Santangel's private resources; and he dismisses peremptorily the evidence of the document which Argensola, in his *Anales de Aragon* (Saragossa, 1630), says was preserved in the archives of the treasury of Aragon. He says a friend who searched at Barcelona in 1871, among the "Archivo general de la Corona de Aragon," could not find it.

Las Casas had first told — guardedly, to be sure — the story of the Pinzons' contributing the money which enabled Columbus to assume an eighth part of the expense of the first voyage; but it is now claimed that the assistance of that family was confined to exerting its influence to get Columbus a crew. It is judged that the evidence is conclusive that the Pinzons did not take pecuniary risk in the voyage of 1492, because only their advances of this sort for the voyage of 1499 are mentioned in the royal grant respecting their arms. But such evidence is certainly inconclusive; and without the evidence of Las Casas it must remain uncertain whence Columbus got the five hundred thousand maravedis which he contributed to the cost of that momentous voyage.

The world has long glorified the story in the *Historie* of 1571 about the part which the crown jewels, and the like, played in the efforts of Isabella to assist in the furnishing of Columbus' vessels. Peter Martyr, Bernaldez, and others who took frequent occasion to sound the praises of her majesty, say nothing of it; and, as is now contended, for the good reason that there was no truth in the story, the jewels having long before been pledged in the prosecution of the war with the Moors.

It is inferred (p. 417) from Las Casas that his abridgment of Columbus' Journal was made from a copy, and not from the original (Navarrete, i. 134); and Harrisse says that from two copies of this abridgment, preserved in the collection of the Duque d' Osuna at Madrid, Varnhagen printed his text of it which is contained in his *Verdadera Guanahani*. This last text varies in some places from that in Navarrete, and Harrisse says he has collated it with the

Osuna copies without discovering any error. He thinks, however, that the *Historie* of 1571, as well as Las Casas' account, is based upon the complete text; and his discrediting of the *Historie* does not prevent him in this case saying that from it, as well as from Las Casas, a few touches of genuineness, not of importance to be sure, can be added to the narrative of the abridgment. He also points out that we should discriminate as to the reflections which Las Casas intersperses; but he seems to have no apprehension of such insertions in the *Historie* in this particular case.

The Ambrosian text of the first letter is once more reprinted (p. 419), accompanied by a French translation. In some appended notes the critic collates it with the Cosco version in different shapes, and with that of Simancas. He also suggests that this text was printed at Barcelona toward the end of March, 1493, and infers that it may have been in this form that the Genoese ambassadors took the news to Italy when they left Spain about the middle of the following month.

The closing chapter of this first volume is on the question of the landfall. The biographer discredits attempts to settle the question by nautical reasoning based on the log of Columbus, averring that the inevitable inaccuracies of such records in Columbus' time is proved by the widely different conclusions of such experienced men as Navarrete, Becher, and Fox. He relies rather on Columbus' description and on that in Las Casas. The name which the latter says was borne in his day by the island of the landfall was "Triango;" but the critic fails to find this name on any earlier map than that first made known in the *Cartas de Indias* in 1877. To this map he finds it impossible to assign an earlier date than 1541, since it discloses some reminders of the expedition of Coronado. He instances other maps in which the name in some form appears attached to an island of the Bahamas, — as in the Cabot mappemonde of 1544 (Triangula), the so-called Vallard map (Triango), that of Gutierrez in 1550 (Trriango), that of Alonso de Santa Cruz in his *Islario* of 1560 (Triangulo). Unfortunately on some of the maps Guanahani appears as well as the name which Las Casas gives. Harrisse's solution of this conjunction of names is suggested by the fact that in the Weimar map of 1527 (see sketch, *ante*, p. 43) an islet "Triango" lies just east of Guanahani, and corresponds in size and position to the "Triangula" of Cabot and the "Triangulo" of Santa Cruz. Guanahani he finds to correspond to Acklin Island, the larger of the Crooked Island group (see map, *ante*, p. 55); while the Plana Cays, shown east of it, would stand for "Triango." Columbus, with that confusion which characterizes his writings, speaks in one place of his first land being an "isleta," and in another place he calls it an "isla grande." This gives the critic ground for supposing that Columbus saw first the islet, the "Triango" of Las Casas, or the modern "Plana Cays," and that then he disembarked on the "isla grande," which was Acklin Island. So it may be that Columbus' own confused statement has misled subsequent writers. If this theory is not accepted, Fox, in selecting Samana, has, in the critic's opinion, come nearer the truth than any other.

THE EARLIEST MAPS

OF THE

SPANISH AND PORTUGUESE DISCOVERIES.

BY THE EDITOR.

THE enumeration of the cartographical sources respecting the discoveries of the earlier voyagers began with the list, "Catalogus auctorum tabularum geographicarum, quotquot ad nostram cognitionem hactenus pervenere; quibus addidimus, ubi locorum, quando et a quibus excusi sunt," which Ortelius in 1570 added to his *Theatrum orbis terrarum*, many of whose titles belong to works not now known. Of maps now existing the best-known enumerations are those in the *Jean et Sébastien Cabot* of Harrisse; the *Mapoteca Colombiana* of Uricoechea; the *Cartografia Mexicana* of Orozco y Berra, published by the Mexican Geographical Society; and Gustavo Uzielli's *Elenco descritto degli Atlanti, planisferi e carte nautiche*, originally published in 1875, but made the second volume, edited by Pietro Amat, of the new edition of the *Studi biografici e bibliografici della Società Geografica Italiana*, Rome, 1882, under the specific title of *Mappamondi, carte nautiche, portolani ed altri monumenti cartografici specialmente Italiani dei secoli XIII–XVII*.[1]

The Editor has printed in the *Harvard University Bulletin* a bibliography of Ptolemy's geography, and a calendar, with additions and annotations, of the Kohl Collection of early maps, belonging to the Department of State at Washington, both of which contributions called for enumerations of printed and manuscript maps of the early period, and included their reproductions of later years.

The development of cartography is also necessarily made a part of histories of geography like those of Santarem, Lelewel, St.-Martin, and Peschel; but their use of maps hardly made chronological lists of them a necessary part of their works. Santarem has pointed out how scantily modern writers have treated of the cartography of the Middle Ages previous to the era of Spanish discovery; and he enumerates such maps as had been described before the appearance of his work, as well as publications of the earlier ones after the Spanish discovery.[2]

---

[1] Vol. i. of the *Studi* is a chronological account of Italian travellers and voyages, beginning with Grimaldo (1120-1122), and accompanied by maps showing the routes of the principal ones. Cf. Theobald Fischer, "Ueber italienische Seekarten und Kartographen des Mittelalters," in *Zeitschrift der Gesellschaft für Erdkunde zu Berlin*, xvii. 5.

As to the work which has been done in the geographical societies of Germany, we shall have readier knowledge when Dr. Johannes Müller's *Die wissenschaftlichen Vereine und Gesellschaften Deutschlands, — Bibliographie ihrer Veröffentlichungen*, now announced in Berlin, is made public. One of the most important sale-catalogues of maps is that of the Prince Alexandre Labanoff Collection, Paris, 1823, — a list now very rare. Nos. 1-112 were given to the world, and 1480-1543 to America separately.

[2] Santarem, *Histoire de la cartographie*, etc., vol. i., preface, pp. xxxix, l, and 194. After the present volume was printed to this point, and

To what extent Columbus had studied the older maps from the time when they began to receive a certain definiteness in the fourteenth century, is not wholly clear, nor how much he knew of the charts of Marino Sanuto, of Pizignani, and of the now famous Catalan map of that period; but it is doubtless true that the maps of Bianco (1436) and Mauro (1460) were well known to him.[1] "Though these early maps and charts of the fifteenth century," says Hallam,[2] "are to us but a chaos of error and confusion, it was on them that the patient eye of Columbus had rested through long hours of meditation, while strenuous hope and unsubdued doubt were struggling in his soul."

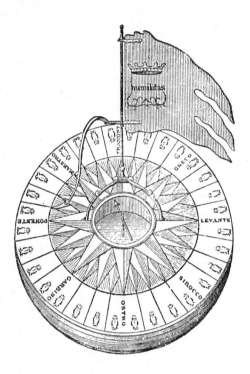

EARLY COMPASS.[5]

A principal factor in the development of map-making, as of navigation, had been the magnet. It had been brought from China to the eastern coast of Africa as early as the fourth century, and through the Arabs[3] and Crusaders it had been introduced into the Mediterranean, and was used by the Catalans and Basques in the twelfth century, a hundred years or more before Marco Polo brought to Europe his wonderful stories.[4] In that century even it had become so familiar a sight that poets used it in their metaphors. The variation of its needle was not indeed unknown long before Columbus, but its observation in mid-ocean in his day gave it a new significance. The Chinese had studied the phenomenon, and their observations upon it had followed shortly upon the introduction of the compass itself to Western knowledge; and as early as 1436 the variation of the needle was indicated on maps in connection with places of observation.[6]

after Vols. III. and IV. were in type, Mr. Arthur James Weise's *Discoveries of America to the year* 1525 was published in New York. A new draft of the Maiollo map of 1527 is about its only important feature.

[1] See an enumeration of all these earlier maps and of their reproductions in part i. of *The Kohl Collection of Early Maps*, by the present writer. Bianco's map was reproduced in 1869 at Venice, with annotations by Oscar Peschel; and Mauro's in 1866, also at Venice.

[2] *Literature of Europe*, chap. iii. sect. 4.

[3] Cf., on the instruments and marine charts of the Arabs, Codine's *La mer des Indes*, p. 74; Delambre, *Histoire de l'astronomie du moyen-âge;* Sédillot's *Les instruments astronomiques des Arabes*, etc.

[4] Major, *Prince Henry* (1868 ed.), pp. 57, 60. There is some ground for believing that the

Northmen were acquainted with the loadstone in the eleventh century. Prescott (*Ferdinand and Isabella*, 1873 ed., ii. 111) indicates the use of it by the Castilians in 1403. Cf. Santarem, *Histoire de la cartographie*, p. 280; *Journal of the Franklin Institute*, xxii. 68; *American Journal of Science*, lx. 242. Cf. the early knowledge regarding the introduction of the compass in Eden's *Peter Martyr* (1555), folio 320; and D'Avezac's *Aperçus historiques sur la boussole*, Paris, 1860, 16 pp.; also Humboldt's *Cosmos*, Eng. tr. ii. 656.

[5] This follows the engraving in Pigafetta's *Voyage* and in the work of Jurien de la Gravière. The main points were designated by the usual names of the winds, *Levante*, east; *Sirocco*, southeast, etc.

[6] For instance, the map of Bianco. The variation in Europe was always easterly after observations were first made.

The earliest placing of a magnetic pole seems due to the voyage of Nicholas of Lynn, whose narrative was presented to Edward III. of England. This account is no longer known,[1] though the title of it, *Inventio fortunata*, is preserved, with its alleged date of 1355. Cnoyen, whose treatise is not extant, is thought to have got his views about the regions of the north and about the magnetic pole from Nicholas of Lynn,[2] while he was in Norway in 1364; and it is from Cnoyen that Mercator says he got his notion of the four circumpolar islands which so long figured in maps of the Mercator and Finæus school. In the Ruysch map (1508) we have the same four polar islands, with the magnetic pole placed within an insular mountain north of Greenland. Ruysch also depended on the *Inventio fortunata*. Later, by Martin Cortes in 1545, and by Sanuto in 1588, the pole was placed farther south.[3]

Ptolemy, in the second century, accepting the generally received opinion that the world as known was much longer east and west than north and south, adopted with this theory the terms which naturally grew out of this belief, *latitude* and *longitude*, and first instituted them, it is thought, in systematic geography.[4]

Pierre d'Ailly, in his map of 1410,[5] in marking his climatic lines, had indicated the beginnings, under a revival of geographical inquiry, of a systematic notation of latitude. Several of the early Ptolemies [6] had followed, by scaling in one way and another the distance from the equator; while in the editions of 1508 and 1511 an example had been set of marking longitude. The old Arabian cartographers had used both latitude and longitude; but though there were some earlier indications of the adoption of such lines among the European map-makers, it is generally accorded that the scales of such measurements, as we understand them, came in, for both latitude and longitude, with the map which Reisch in 1503 annexed to his *Margarita philosophica*.[7]

Ptolemy had fixed his first meridian at the Fortunate Islands (Canaries), and in the new era the Spaniards, with the sanction of the Pope, had adopted the same point; though the Portuguese, as if in recognition of their own enterprise, had placed it at Madeira, — as is shown in the globes of Behaim and Schöner, and in the map of Ruysch. The difference was not great; the Ptolemean example prevailed, however, in the end.[8]

---

[1] Hakluyt, i. 122.

[2] *Journal of the American Geographical Society*, xii. 185.

[3] It is supposed to-day to be in Prince Albert Land, and to make a revolution in about five hundred years. Acosta contended that there were four lines of no variation, and Halley, in 1683, contended for four magnetic poles.

[4] Cf. notes on p. 661, *et seq.*, in Bunbury's *History of Ancient Geography*, vol. i., on the ancients' calculations of latitude and measurements for longitude. Ptolemy carried the most northern parts of the known world sixty-three degrees north, and the most southern parts sixteen degrees south, of the Equator, an extent north and south of seventy-nine degrees. Marinus of Tyre, who preceded Ptolemy, stretched the known world, north and south, over eighty-seven degrees. Marinus had also made the length of the known world 225 degrees east and west, while Ptolemy reduced it to 177 degrees; but he did not, nor did Marinus, bound it definitely in the east by an ocean, but he left its limit in that direction undetermined, as he did that of Africa in the south, which resulted in making the Indian Ocean in his conception an inland sea, with the possibility of passing by land from Southern Africa to Southern Asia, along a parallel. Marinus had been the first to place the Fortunate Islands farther west than the limits of Spain in that direction, though he put them only two and a half degrees beyond, while the meridian of Ferro is nine degrees from the most westerly part of the main.

[5] Cf. Lelewel, pl. xxviii., and Santarem, *Histoire de la cartographie*, iii. 301, and *Atlas*, pl. 15.

[6] Cf. editions of 1482, 1486, 1513, 1535.

[7] The earliest instance in a *published* Spanish map is thought to be the woodcut which in 1534 appeared at Venice in the combination of Peter Martyr and Oviedo which Ramusio is thought to have edited. This map is represented on a later page.

[8] There was a tendency in the latter part of the sixteenth century to remove the prime meridian to St. Michael's, in the Azores, for the reason that there was no variation in the needle there at that time, and in ignorance of the forces which to-day at St. Michael's make it point twenty-five degrees off the true north. As late as 1634 a congress of European mathematicians confirmed it at the west edge of the Isle de Fer (Ferro), the most westerly of the Canaries.

In respect to latitude there was not in the rude instruments of the early navigators, and under favorable conditions, the means of closely approximate accuracy. In the study which the Rev. E. F. Slafter [1] has made on the average extent of the error which we find in the records of even a later century, it appears that while a range of sixty geographical miles will probably cover such errors in all cases, when observations were made with ordinary care the average deviation will probably be found to be at least fifteen miles. The fractions of degrees were scarcely ever of much value in the computation, and the minute gradation of the instruments in use were subject to great uncertainty of record in tremulous hands. It was not the custom, moreover, to make any allowance for the dip of the horizon, for refraction or for the parallax; and when, except at the time of the equinox, dependence had to be placed upon tables of the sun's declination, the published ephemerides, made for a series of years, were the subjects of accumulated error. [2]

REGIOMONTANUS' ASTROLABE. [4]

With these impediments to accurate results, it is not surprising that even errors of considerable extent crept into the records of latitude, and long remained unchallenged. [3] Ptolemy, in A. D. 150, had placed Constantinople two degrees out of the way; and it remained so on maps for fourteen hundred years. In Columbus' time Cuba was put seven or eight degrees too far north; and under this false impression the cartography of the Antilles began.

The historic instrument for the taking of latitude was the astrolabe, which is known to have been in use by the Majorcan and Catalanian sailors in the latter part of the thirteenth century; and it is described by Raymond Lullius in his *Arte de navegar* of that time. [5] Behaim, the contemporary of Columbus, one of the explorers of the African coast, and a

[1] Edmund Farwell Slafter, *History and Causes of the Incorrect Latitudes as recorded in the Journals of the Early Writers, Navigators, and Explorers relating to the Atlantic Coast of North America* (1535–1740). Boston: Privately printed, 1882. 20 pages. Reprinted from the *N. E. Hist. and Geneal. Reg.* for April, 1882.

[2] Regiomontanus, — as Johannes Müller, of Königsberg, in Franconia, was called, from his town, — published at Nuremberg his *Ephemerides* for the interval 1475–1506; and these were what Columbus probably used. Cf. Alex. Ziegler's *Regiomontanus, ein geistiger Vorläufer des Columbus*, Dresden, 1874. Stadius, a professor of mathematics, published an almanac of this kind in 1545, and the English navigators used successive editions of this one.

[3] Cf. Kohl, *Die beiden General-Karten von Amerika*, p. 17, and Varnhagen's *Historia geral do Brazil*, i. 432.

[4] This cut follows the engravings in Ruge's *Geschichte des Zeitalters der Entdeckungen*, p. 106, and in Ghillany's *Ritter Behaim*, p. 40. Cf. Von Murr, *Memorabilia bibliothecarum Norimbergensium*, i. 9.

[5] Humboldt, *Cosmos*, Eng. tr., ii. 630, 670; Reisch's *Margarita philosophica* (1535), p. 1416; D'Avezac's *Waltzemüller*, p. 64.

pupil of Regiomontanus, had somewhat changed the old form of the astrolabe in adapting it for use on shipboard. This was in 1484 at Lisbon, and Behaim's improvement was doubtless what Columbus used. Of the form in use before Behaim we have that (said to have belonged to Regiomontanus) in the cut on page 96; and in the following cut the remodelled shape which it took after Behaim.

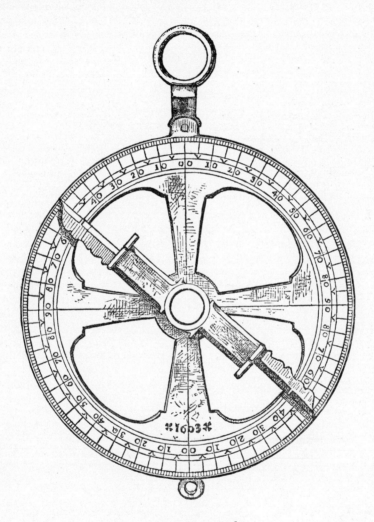

LATER ASTROLABE.[1]

[1] This cut follows an engraving (*Mag. of Amer. Hist.*, iii. 178) after a photograph of one used by Champlain, which bears the Paris maker's date of 1603. There is another cut of it in Weise's *Discoveries of America*, p. 68. Having been lost by Champlain in Canada in 1613, it was ploughed up in 1867 (see Vol. IV. p. 124; also *Canadian Monthly*, xviii. 589). The small size of the circle used in the sea-instrument to make it conveniently serviceable, necessarily op- erated to make the ninety degrees of its quarter circle too small for accuracy in fractions. On land much larger circles were sometimes used; one was erected in London in 1594 of six feet radius. The early books on navigation and voy- ages frequently gave engravings of the astrolabe; as, for instance, in Pigafetta's voyage (Magellan), and in the *Lichte der Zee-Vaert* (Amsterdam, 1623), translated as *The Light of Navigation* (Amsterdam, 1625). The treatise on navigation

An instrument which could more readily adapt itself to the swaying of the observer's body in a sea-way, soon displaced in good measure the astrolabe on shipboard. This was the cross-staff, or jackstaff, which in several modified forms for a long time served mariners as a convenient help in ascertaining the altitude of the celestial bodies. Precisely when it was first introduced is not certain ; but the earliest description of it which has been found is that of Werner in 1514. Davis, the Arctic navigator, made an improvement on it ; and his invention was called a backstaff.

While the observations of the early navigators in respect to latitude were usually accompanied by errors, which were of no considerable extent, their determinations of longitude, when attempted at all, were almost always wide of the truth,[1] — so far, indeed, that their observations helped them but little then to steer their courses, and are of small assistance now to us in following their tracks. It happened that while Columbus was at Hispaniola on his second voyage, in September, 1494, there was an eclipse of the

which became the most popular with the successors of Columbus was the work of Pedro de Medina (born about 1493), called the *Arte de navegar*, published in 1545 (reprinted in 1552 and 1561), of which there were versions in French (1554, and Lyons, 1569, with maps showing names on the coast of America for the first time), Italian (1555 with 1554, at end ; *Court Catalogue*, no. 235), German (1576), and English (1591). (Harrisse, *Bibl. Amer. Vet.*, no. 266.) Its principal rival was that of Martin Cortes, *Breve compendio de la sphera y de la arte de navegar*, published in 1551. In Columbus' time there was no book of the sort, unless that of Raymond Lullius (1294) be considered such ; and not till Enciso's *Suma de geografia* was printed, in 1519, had the new spirit instigated the making of these helpful and explanatory books. The *Suma de geografia* is usually considered the first book printed in Spanish relating to America. Enciso, who had been practising law in Santo Domingo, was with Ojeda's expedition to the mainland in 1509, and seems to have derived much from his varied experience ; and he first noticed at a later day the different levels of the tides on the two sides of the isthmus. The book is rare ; Rich in 1832 (no. 4) held it at £10 10*s*. (Cf. Harrisse, *Notes on Columbus*, 171 ; *Bibl. Amer. Vet.*, nos. 97, 153, 272, — there were later editions in 1530 and 1546, — Sabin, vol. vi. no. 22,551, etc. ; H. H. Bancroft, *Central America*, i. 329, 339 ; Carter-Brown, vol. i. no. 58, with a fac-simile of the title : *Cat. Hist. do Brazil, Bibl. Nac. do Rio de Janeiro*, no. 2.) Antonio Pigafetta in 1530 produced his *Trattato di navigazione ;* but Medina and Cortes were the true beginners of the literature of seamanship. (Cf. Brevoort's *Verrazano*, p. 116, and the list of such publications given in the *Davis Voyages*, p. 342, published by the Hakluyt Society, and the English list noted in Vol. III. p. 206, of the present *History*.) There is an examination of the state of navigation in Columbus' time in Margry's *Navigations Françaises*, p. 402, and in M. F. Navarrete's *Sobre la historia de la náutica y de las ciencias*

matemáticas, Madrid, 1846, — a work now become rare.

The rudder, in place of two paddles, one on each quarter, had come into use before this time ; but the reefing of sails seems not yet to have been practised. (Cf. *Da Gama's Voyages*, published by the Hakluyt Society, p. 242.) Columbus' record of the speed of his ship seems to have been the result of observation by the unaided eye. The log was not yet known ; the Romans had fixed a wheel to the sides of their galleys, each revolution of which threw a pebble into a tally-pot. The earliest description which we have in the new era of any device of the kind is in connection with Magellan's voyage ; for Pigafetta in his Journal (January, 1521), mentions the use of a chain at the hinder part of the ship to measure its speed. (Humboldt, *Cosmos*, Eng. tr., ii. 631 ; v. 56.) The log as we understand it is described in 1573 in Bourne's *Regiment of the Sea*, nothing indicating the use of it being found in the earlier manuals of Medina, Cortes, and Gemma Frisius. Humfrey Cole is said to have invented it. Three years later than this earliest mention, Eden, in 1576, in his translation of Taisnier's *Navigatione*, alludes to an artifice "not yet divulgate, which, placed in the pompe of a shyp, whyther the water hath recourse, and moved by the motion of the shypp, with wheels and weyghts, doth exactly shewe what space the shyp hath gone" (*Carter-Brown Catalogue*, i. no. 310),—a reminiscence of the Roman side-wheels, and a reminder of the modern patent-log. Cf. article on "Navigation" in *Encyclopædia Britannica*, ninth ed. vol. xvii.

[1] Cf. Lelewel, *Géographie du moyen-âge*, ii. 160. The rules of Gemma Frisius for discovering longitude were given in Eden's *Peter Martyr* (1555), folio 360. An earlier book was Francisco Falero's *Regimiento para observar la longitud en la mar*, 1535. Cf. E. F. de Navarrete's "El problema de la longitud en la mar," in volume 21 of the *Doc. inéditos (España) ;* and *Vasco da Gama* (Hakluyt Soc.), pp. 19, 25, 33, 43, 63, 138.

moon.[1] Columbus observed it; and his calculations placed himself five hours and a half from Seville, — an error of eighteen degrees, or an hour and a quarter too much. The error was due doubtless as much to the rudeness of his instruments as to the errors of the lunar tables then in use.[2]

The removal of the Line of Demarcation from the supposed meridian of non-variation of the needle did not prevent the phenomena of terrestrial magnetism becoming of vast importance in the dispute between the Crowns of Spain and Portugal. It characterizes the difference between the imaginative and somewhat fantastic quality of Columbus' mind and the cooler, more practical, and better administrative apprehension of Sebastian Cabot, that while each observed the phenomenon of the variation of the needle, and each imagined it a clew to some system of determining longitude, to Columbus it was associated with wild notions of a too-ample revolution of the

THE JACKSTAFF.

North Star about the true pole.[3] It was not disconnected in his mind from a fancy which gave the earth the shape of a pear; so that when he perceived on his voyage a clearing of the atmosphere, he imagined he was ascending the stem-end of the pear; where he would find the terrestrial paradise.[4] To Cabot the phenomenon had only its practical significance; and he seems to have pondered on a solution of the problem during the rest of

[1] The *Germaniæ ex variis scriptoribus perbrevis explicatio* of Bilibaldus Pirckeymerus, published in 1530, has a reference to this eclipse. Carter-Brown, vol. i. no. 96; *Murphy Catalogue*, no. 1,992. The paragraph is as follows: "Proinde compertum est ex observatione eclypsis, quæ fuit in mense Septembri anno salutis 1494. Hispaniam insulam, quatuor ferme horarum intersticio ab Hyspali, quæ Sibilia est distare, hoc est gradibus 60, qualium est circulus maximus 360, medium vero insulæ continet gradus 20 circiter in altitudine polari. Navigatur autem spacium illud communiter in diebus 35 altitudo vero continentis opposti, cui Hispani sanctæ Marthæ nomen indidere, circiter graduum est 12 Darieni vero terra et sinus de Uraca gradus quasi tenent 7½ in altitudine polari, unde longissimo tractu occidentem versus terra est, quæ vocatur Mexico et Temistitan, a qua etiam non longa remota est insula Jucatan cum aliis nuper repertis." The method of determining longitude by means of lunar tables dates back to Hipparchus.

[2] These were the calculations of Regiomontanus (Müller), who calls himself "Monteregius" in his *Tabulæ astronomice Alfonsi regis,* published at Venice in the very year (1492) of

Columbus' first voyage. (Stevens, *Bibl. Geog.,* no. 83.) At a later day the Portuguese accused the Spaniards of altering the tables then in use, so as to affect the position of the Papal line of Demarcation. Barras, quoted by Humboldt, *Cosmos,* Eng. tr. ii. 671.

Johann Stoeffler was a leading authority on the methods of defining latitude and longitude in vogue in the beginning of the new era; cf. his *Elucidatio fabricæ ususque astrolabii,* Oppenheim, 1513 (colophon 1512), and his edition of *In Procli Diadochi sphæram omnibus numeris longe absolutissimus commentarius,* Tübingen, 1534, where he names one hundred and seventy contemporary and earlier writers on the subject. (Stevens, *Bibl. Geog.,* nos. 2,633–2,634.)

[3] The polar distance of the North Star in Columbus' time was 3° 28'; and yet his calculations made it sometimes 5°, and sometimes 10°. It is to-day 1° 20' distant from the true pole. *United States Coast Survey Report,* 1880, app. xviii.

[4] Santarem, *Histoire de la cartographie,* vol. ii. p. lix. Columbus would find here the centre of the earth, as D'Ailly, Mauro, and Behaim found it at Jerusalem.

his life, if, as Humboldt supposes, the intimations of his death-bed in respect to some as yet unregistered way of discovering longitude refer to his observations on the magnetic declination.[1]

THE BACKSTAFF.

The idea of a constantly increasing declination east and west from a point of non-variation, which both Columbus and Cabot had discovered, and which increase could be reduced to a formula, was indeed partly true; except, as is now well known, the line of non-variation, instead of being a meridian, and fixed, is a curve of constantly changing proportions.[2]

The earliest variation-chart was made in 1530 by Alonzo de Santa Cruz;[3] and schemes of ascertaining longitude were at once based on the observations of these curves, as they had before been made dependent upon the supposed gradation of the change from meridian to meridian, irrespective of latitude.[4] Fifty years later (1585), Juan Jayme made a voyage with Gali from the Philippine Islands to Acapulco to test a "declinatorum" of his own invention.[5] But this was a hundred years (1698–1702) before Halley's Expedition was sent, — the first which any government fitted out to observe the forces of terrestrial magnetism;[6] and though there had been suspicions of it much earlier, it was not till 1722 that Graham got unmistakable data to prove the hourly variation of the needle.[7]

[1] *Cosmos*, Eng. tr., ii. 658. Humboldt also points out how Columbus on his second voyage had attempted to fix his longitude by the declination of the needle (Ibid., ii. 657; v. 54). Cf. a paper on Columbus and Cabot in the *Nautical Magazine*, July, 1876.

It is a fact that good luck or skill of some undiscernible sort enabled Cabot to record some remarkable approximations of longitude in an age when the wildest chance governed like attempts in others. Cabot indeed had the navigator's instinct; and the modern log-book seems to have owed its origin to his practices and the urgency with which he impressed the importance of it upon the Muscovy Company.

[2] Appendix xix. of the *Report of the United States Coast Survey* for 1880 (Washington, 1882) is a paper by Charles A. Schott of "Inquiry into the Variation of the Compass off the Bahama Islands, at the time of the Landfall of Columbus in 1492," which is accompanied by a chart, showing by comparison the lines of no-variation respectively in 1492, 1600, 1700, 1800, and 1880, as far as they can be made out from available data. In this chart the line of 1492 runs through the Azores, — bending east as it proceeds northerly, and west in its southerly extension. The no-variation line in 1882 leaves

the South American coast between the mouths of the Amazon and the Orinoco, and strikes the Carolina coast not far from Charleston. The Azores to-day are in the curve of 25° W. variation, which line leaves the west coast of Ireland, and after running through the Azores sweeps away to the St. Lawrence Gulf.

[3] Navarrete, *Noticia del cosmografo Alonzo de Santa Cruz.*

[4] Humboldt, *Cosmos*, Eng. tr., ii. 672; v. 59.

[5] *Cosmos*, v. 55.

[6] *Cosmos*, v. 59.

[7] Charts of the magnetic curves now made by the Coast Survey at Washington are capable of supplying, if other means fail, and particularly in connection with the dipping-needle, data of a ship's longitude with but inconsiderable error. The inclination or dip was not measured till 1576; and Humboldt shows how under some conditions it can be used also to determine latitude.

In 1714 the English Government, following an example earlier set by other governments, offered a reward of £20,000 to any one who would determine longitude at sea within half a degree. It was ultimately given to Harrison, a watchmaker who made an improved marine chronometer. An additional £3,000 was given

The earliest map which is distinctively associated with the views which were developing in Columbus' mind was the one which Toscanelli sent to him in 1474. It is said to have been preserved in Madrid in 1527 ;[1] and fifty-three years after Columbus' death, when Las Casas was writing his history, it was in his possession.[2] We know that this Italian geographer had reduced the circumference of the globe to nearly three quarters of its actual size, having placed China about six thousand five hundred miles west of Lisbon, and eleven thousand five hundred miles east. Japan, lying off the China coast, was put somewhere from one hundred degrees to one hundred and ten degrees west of Lisbon; and we have record that Martin Pinzon some years later (1491) saw a map in Rome which put Cipango (Japan) even nearer the European side.[3] A similar view is supposed

at the same time to the widow of Tobias Meyer, who had improved the lunar tables. It also instigated two ingenious mechanicians, who hit upon the same principle independently, and worked out its practical application, — the Philadelphian, Thomas Godfrey, in his "mariner's bow" (*Penn. Hist. Soc. Coll.*, i. 422); and the Englishman, Hadley, in his well-known quadrant.

It can hardly be claimed to-day, with all our modern appliances, that a ship's longitude can be ascertained with anything more than approximate precision. The results from dead-reckoning are to be corrected in three ways. Observations on the moon will not avoid, except by accident, errors which may amount to seven or eight miles. The difficulties of making note of Jupiter's satellites in their eclipse, under the most favorable conditions, will be sure to entail an error of a half, or even a whole, minute. This method, first tried effectively about 1700, was the earliest substantial progress which had been made; all the attempts of observation on the opposition of planets, the occultations of stars, the difference of altitude between the moon and Jupiter, and the changes in the moon's declination, having failed of satisfactory results (Humboldt, *Cosmos*, Eng. tr., ii. 671). John Werner, of Nuremberg, as early as 1514, and Gemma Frisius, in 1545, had suggested the measure of the angle between the altitude of the moon and some other heavenly body; but it was not till 1615 that it received a trial at sea, through the assiduity of Baffin. The newer method of Jupiter's satellites proved of great value in the hands of Delisle, the real founder of modern geographical science. By it he cut off three hundred leagues from the length of the Mediterranean Sea, and carried Paris two and a half degrees, and Constantinople ten degrees, farther west. Corrections for two centuries had been chiefly made in a similar removal of places. For instance, the longitude of Gibraltar had increased from 7° 50' W., as Ptolemy handed it down, to 9° 30' under Ruscelli, to 13° 30' under Mercator, and to 14° 30' under Ortelius. It is noticeable that Eratosthenes, who two hundred years and more before Christ was the librarian at Alexandria and chief of its geographical

school, though he made the length of the Mediterranean six hundred geographical miles too long, did better than Ptolemy three centuries later, and better even than moderns had done up to 1668, when this sea was elongated by nearly a third beyond its proper length. Cf. Bunbury, *History of Ancient Geography*, i. 635; Gosselin, *Géog. des Grecs*, p. 42. Sanson was the last, in 1668, to make this great error.

The method for discovering longitude which modern experience has settled upon is the noting at noon, when the weather permits a view of the sun, of the difference of a chronometer set to a known meridian. This instrument, with all its modern perfection, is liable to an error of ten or fifteen seconds in crossing the Atlantic, which may be largely corrected by a mean, derived from the use of more than one chronometer. The first proposition to convey time as a means of deciding longitude dates back to Alonzo de Santa Cruz, who had no better timekeepers than sand and water clocks (Humboldt, *Cosmos*, Eng. tr., ii. 672).

On land, care and favorable circumstances may now place an object within six or eight yards of its absolute place in relation to the meridian. Since the laying of the Atlantic cable has made it possible to use for a test a current which circles the earth in three seconds, it is significant of minute accuracy, in fixing the difference of time between Washington and Greenwich, that in the three several attempts to apply the cable current, the difference between the results has been less than $\frac{7}{100}$ of a second.

But on shipboard the variation is still great, though the last fifty years has largely reduced the error. Professor Rogers, of the Harvard College Observatory, in examining one hundred log-books of Atlantic steamships, has found an average error of three miles; and he reports as significant of the superior care of the Cunard commanders that the error in the logs of their ships was reduced to an average of a mile and a half.

[1] Lelewel, ii. 130.

[2] Humboldt, *Examen critique*, ii. 210.

[3] The breadth east and west of the Old World was marked variously, — on the Laon globe, 250°; Behaim's globe, 130°; Schöner's

BILIBALDVS PIRCHAIMERVS PATR.
Noricus, Hiftoricus.

Carminis auctor eram bonus, hiftoriæ̃₃ : fed orno
Carminis auctores hiftoriæ̃₃ magis.

M. D. XXXI.

PIRCKEYMERUS.[1]

to have been presented in the map which Bartholomew Columbus took to England in 1488;[2] but we have no trace of the chart itself.[3] It has always been supposed that in the

globe, 228°; Ruysch's map, 224°; Sylvanus' map, 220°; and the Portuguese chart of 1503, 220°.

[1] Fac-simile of a cut in Reusner's *Icones,* Strasburg, 1590, p. 42. This well-known cosmographical student was one of the collaborators of the series of the printed Ptolemies, beginning with that of 1525. There is a well-known print of Pirckeymerus by Albert Dürer, 1524, which is reproduced in the *Gazette des Beaux-Arts,* xix. 114. Cf. Friedrich Campe's *Zum Andenken Wilibald Pirkheimers, Mitglieds des Raths zu Nürnberg* (Nürnberg, 58 pp.,

with portrait), and *Wilibald Pirkheimer's Aufenthalt zu Neunhof, von ihm selbst geschildert ; nebst Beiträgen zu dem Leben und dem Nachlasse seiner Schwestern und Töchter, von Moritz Maximilian Meyer* (Nürnberg, 1828).

[2] This sea-chart was the first which had been seen in England, and almanacs at that time had only been known in London for fifteen years, with their tables for the sun's declination and the altitude of the pole-star.

[3] Cf. *Atti della Società Ligure,* 1867, p. 174; Desimoni in *Giornale Ligustico,* ii. 52. Bartholomew is also supposed to have been the

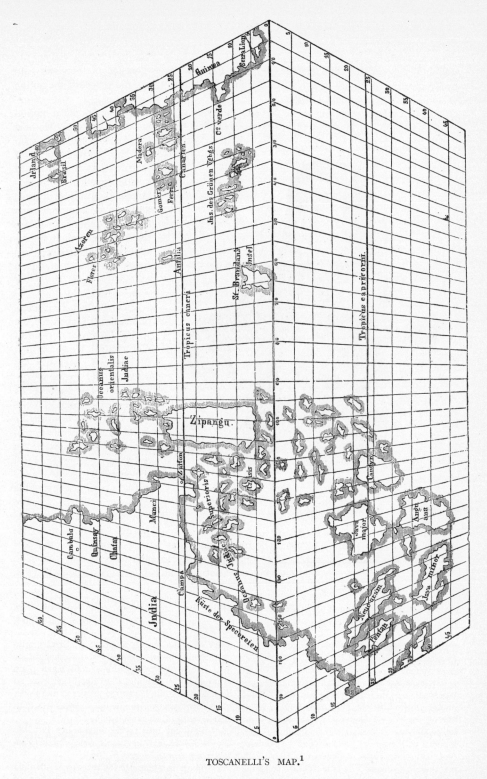

TOSCANELLI'S MAP.[1]

[1] This is a restoration of the map as given in *Das Ausland*, 1867, p. 5. The language of the original was doubtless Latin. Another restoration is given in St. Martin's *Atlas*, pl. ix.

well-known globe of Martin Behaim we get in the main an expression of the views held
by Toscanelli, Columbus, and other of Behaim's contemporaries, who espoused the notion
of India lying over against Europe.

Eratosthenes, accepting the spherical theory, had advanced the identical notion
which nearly seventeen hundred years later impelled Columbus to his voyage.   He held
the known world to span
one third of the circuit of
the globe, as Strabo did at
a later day, leaving an unknown two thirds of sea;
and "if it were not that
the vast extent of the Atlantic Sea rendered it impossible, one might even sail
from the coast of Spain
to that of India along the
same parallel." [1]

MARTIN BEHAIM.[2]

Behaim had spent much
of his life in Lisbon and the
Azores, and was a friend of
Columbus.   He had visited
Nuremberg, probably on
some family matters aris-
ing out of the death of his
mother in 1487.   While
in this his native town, he
gratified some of his towns-
people by embodying in
a globe the geographical
views which prevailed in the
maritime countries; and the
globe was finished before
Columbus had yet accom-
plished his voyage.   The
next year (1493) Behaim returned to Portugal; and after having been sent to the Low
Countries on a diplomatic mission, he was captured by English cruisers and carried to
England.   Escaping finally, and reaching the Continent, he passes from our view in 1494,
and is scarcely heard of again.

Of Columbus' maps it is probable that nothing has come down to us from his own
hand.[3]   Humboldt would fain believe that the group of islands studding a gulf which

maker of an anonymous planisphere of 1489
(Peschel, *Ueber eine alte Weltkarte*, p. 213).

[1] Strabo, i. 65.   Bunbury, *Ancient Geography*,
i. 627, says the passage is unfortunately mutilated, but the words preserved can clearly have
no other signification.   What is left to us of
Eratosthenes are fragments, which were edited
by Seidel, at Göttingen, in 1789; again and
better by Bernhardy (Berlin, 1822).   Bunbury
(vol. i. ch. xvi.) gives a sufficient survey of his
work and opinions.   The spherical shape of the
earth was so generally accepted by the learned
after the times of Aristotle and Euclid, that
when Eratosthenes in the third century, B.C.

went to some length to prove it, Strabo, who
criticised him two centuries later, thought he
had needlessly exerted himself to make plain
what nobody disputed.   Eratosthenes was so
nearly accurate in his supposed size of the globe,
that his excess over the actual size was less than
one-seventh of its great circle.

[2] This cut follows the engravings in Ghillany's *Behaim*, and in Ruge's *Geschichte des Zeitalters der Entdeckungen*, p. 105.

[3] There is a manuscript map of Hispaniola
attached to the copy of the 1511 edition of
Peter Martyr in the Colombina Library which is
sometimes ascribed to Columbus; but Harrisse

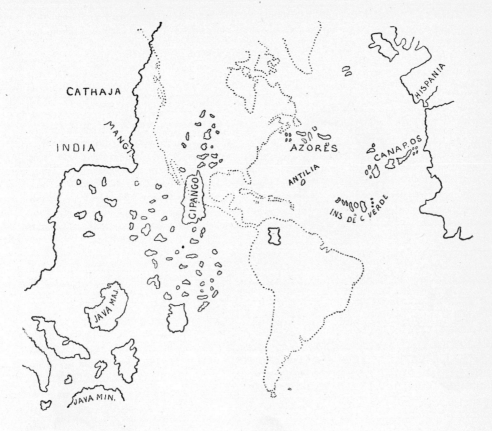

SECTION OF BEHAIM'S GLOBE.[1]

appears on a coat-of-arms granted Columbus in May, 1493, has some interest as the earliest of all cartographical records of the New World; but the early drawings of the

thinks it rather the work of his brother Bartholomew (*Bibl. Amer. Vet., Add.,* xiii.) A map of this island, with the native divisions as Columbus found them, is given in Muñoz. The earliest separate map is in the combined edition of Peter Martyr and Oviedo edited by Ramusio in Venice in 1534 (Stevens, *Bibliotheca geographica,* no. 1,778). *Le discours de la navigation de Jean et Raoul Parmentier, de Dieppe,* including a description of Santo Domingo, was edited by Ch. Schefer in Paris, 1883; a description of the "isle de Haity" from *Le grand insulaire et pilotage d'André Thevet* is given in its appendix.

[1] This globe is made of papier-maché, covered with gypsum, and over this a parchment surface received the drawing; it is twenty inches in diameter. It having fallen into decay, the Behaim family in Nuremberg caused it to be repaired in 1825. In 1847 a copy was made of it

for the Dépôt Géographique (National Library) at Paris; the original is now in the city hall at Nuremberg. The earliest known engraving of it is in J. G. Doppelmayr's *Historische Nachricht von den nürnbergischen Mathematikern und Künstlern* (1730), which preserved some names that have since become illegible (Stevens, *Historical Collection,* vol. i. no. 1,396). Other representations are given in Jomard's *Monuments de la géographie;* Ghillany's *Martin Behaim* (1853) and his *Erdglobus des Behaim und der des Schöner* (1842); C. G. von Murr's *Diplomatische Geschichte des Ritters Behaim* (1778, and later editions and translations); Cladera's *Investigaciones* (1794); Amoretti's translation of Pigafetta's *Voyage de Magellan* (Paris, 1801); Lelewel's *Moyen-âge* (pl. 40; also see vol. ii. p. 131, and *Epilogue,* p. 184); Saint-Martin's *Atlas;* Santarem's *Atlas,* pl. 61; the *Journal* of the Royal Geographical Society, vol. xviii.; Kohl's *Discovery of Maine;*

arms are by no means constant in the kind of grouping which is given to these islands.[1] Queen Isabella, writing to the Admiral, Sept. 5, 1493, asks to see the marine chart which he had made; and Columbus sent such a map with a letter.[2] We have various other

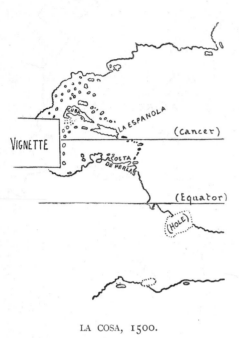

references to copies of this or similar charts of Columbus. Ojeda used such a one in following Columbus' route,[3] as he testified in the famous suit against the heirs of Columbus. Bernardo de Ibarra, in the same cause, said that he had seen the Admiral's chart, and that he had heard of copies of it being used by Ojeda, and by some others.[4] It is known that about 1498 Columbus gave one of his charts to the Pope, and one to René of Lorraine. Angelo Trivigiano, secretary of the Venetian Ambassador to Spain, in a letter dated Aug. 21, 1501, addressed to Dominico Malipiero, speaks of a map of the new discoveries which Columbus had.[5]

Three or four maps at least have come down to us which are supposed to represent in some way one or several of these drafts by Columbus. The first of these is the celebrated map of the pilot Juan de la Cosa,[6] dated in 1500, of which some account, with a heliotype fac-simile

LA COSA, 1500.

Irving's *Columbus* (some editions) ; Gay's *Popular History of the United States*, i. 103; Barnes' *Popular History of the United States; Harpers' Monthly*, vol. xlii.; H. H. Bancroft's *Central America*, i. 93. Ruge, in his *Geschichte des Zeitalters der Entdeckungen*, p. 230, reproduces the colored fac-simile in Ghillany, and shows additionally upon it the outline of America in its proper place. The sketch in the text follows this representation. Cf. papers on Behaim and his globe (besides those accompanying the engravings above indicated) in the *Journal* of the American Geographical Society (1872), iv. 432, by the Rev. Mytton Maury; in the publications of the Maryland Historical Society by Robert Dodge and John G. Morris; in the *Jahresbericht des Vereins für Erdkunde* (Dresden, 1866), p. 59. Peschel, in his *Zeitalter der Entdeckungen* (1858), p. 90, and in the new edition edited by Ruge, has a lower opinion of Behaim than is usually taken.

[1] *Cosmos*, Eng. tr., ii. 647. One of these early engravings is given on page 15.

[2] Navarrete, i. 253, 264.

[3] Navarrete, i. 5.

[4] Navarrete, iii. 587.

[5] Harrisse, *Notes on Columbus*, p. 34; Morelli's *Lettera rarissima* (Bassano, 1810), appendix. A "carta nautica" of Columbus is named

under 1501 in the *Atti della Società ligure*, 1867, p. 174, and *Giornale Ligustico*, ii. 52.

[6] Of La Cosa, who is said to have been of Basque origin, we know but little. Peter Martyr tells us that his "cardes" were esteemed, and mentions finding a map of his in 1514 in Bishop Fonseca's study. We know he was with Columbus in his expedition along the southern coast of Cuba, when the Admiral, in his folly, made his companions sign the declaration that they were on the coast of Asia. This was during Columbus' second voyage, in 1494; and Stevens (*Notes*, etc.) claims that the way in which La Cosa cuts off Cuba to the west with a line of green paint — the conventional color for " terra incognita " — indicates this possibility of connection with the main, as Ruysch's scroll does in his map. The interpretation may be correct; but it might still have been drawn an island from intimations of the natives, though Ocampo did not circumnavigate it till 1508. The natives of Guanahani distinctly told Columbus that Cuba was an island, as he relates in his Journal. Stevens also remarks how La Cosa colors, with the same green, the extension of Cuba beyond the limits of Columbus' exploration on the north coast in 1492. La Cosa, who had been with Ojeda in 1499, and with Rodrigo de Bastidas in 1501, was killed on the coast in 1509. Cf. En-

of the American part of the map, is given in another place.[1] After the death (April 27, 1852) of Walckenaer (who had bought it at a moderate cost of an ignorant dealer in second-hand articles), it was sold at public auction in Paris in the spring of 1853, when Jomard failed to secure it for the Imperial Library in Paris, and it went to Spain, where, in the naval museum at Madrid, it now is.

Of the next earliest of the American maps the story has recently been told with great fulness by Harrisse in his *Les Cortereal*, accompanied by a large colored fac-simile of the map itself, executed by Pilinski. The map was not unknown before,[2] and Harrisse had earlier described it in his *Cabots*.[3]

We know that Gaspar Cortereal[4] had already before 1500 made some explorations, during which he had discovered a mainland and some islands, but at what precise date it is impossible to determine; [5] nor can we decide upon the course he had taken, but it seems likely it was a westerly one. We know also that in this same year (1500) he made his historic voyage to the Newfoundland region,[6] coasting the neighboring shores, probably, in September and October. Then followed a second expedition from January to October of the next year (1501), — the one of which we have the account in the *Paesi novamente retrovati*, as furnished by Pasqualigo.[7] There was at this time in Lisbon one Alberto Cantino, a correspondent — with precisely what quality we know not — of Hercule d' Este, Duke of Ferrara; and to this noble personage Cantino, on the 19th of October, addressed a letter embodying what he had seen and learned of the newly returned companions of Gaspar Cortereal.[8]

The Report of Cantino instigated the Duke to ask his correspondent to procure for him a map of these explorations. Cantino procured one to be made; and inscribing it, " Carta da navigar per le Isole novam^te tr. . . . in le parte de l'India: dono Alberto Cantino Al S. Duca Hercole," he took it to Italy, and delivered it by another hand to the Duke at Ferrara. Here in the family archives it was preserved till 1592, when the reigning Duke retired to Modena, his library following him. In 1868, in accordance with an agreement between the Italian Government and the Archduke Francis of Austria, the cartographical monuments of the ducal collection were transferred to the Biblioteca Estense, where this precious map now is. The map was accompanied when it left Cantino's hands by a note

rique de Leguina's *Juan de la Cosa, estudio biográfico* (Madrid, 1877); Humboldt's *Examen critique* and his *Cosmos*, Eng. tr. ii., 639; De la Roquette, in the *Bulletin de la Société de Géographie de Paris*, Mai, 1862, p. 298; Harrisse's *Cabots*, pp. 52, 103, 156, and his *Les Cortereal*, p. 94; and the references in Vol. III. of the present *History*, p. 8.

[1] Vol. III. p. 8. The fac-simile there given follows Jomard's. Harrisse (*Notes on Columbus*, p. 40), comparing Jomard's reproduction with Humboldt's description, thinks there are omissions in it. Becher (*Landfall of Columbus*) speaks of the map as "the clumsy production of an illiterate seaman." There is also a reproduction of the American parts of the map in Weise's *Discoveries of America*, 1884.

[2] Ongania, of Venice, announced some years ago a fac-simile reproduction in his *Raccolta di mappamundi*, edited by Professor Fischer, of Kiel. It was described in 1873 by Giuseppe Boni in *Cenni storici della Reale Biblioteca Estense in Modena*, and by Gustavo Uzielli in his *Studi bibliografici e biografici*, Rome, 1875.

[3] Pages 143, 158.

[4] He was born about 1450; *Les Cortereal*, p. 36. Cf. E. do Canto's *Os Corte-Reaes* (1883), p. 28.

[5] *Les Cortereal*, p. 45.

[6] See Vol. IV. chap. i.

[7] Harrisse, *Les Cortereal*, p. 50, translates this

[8] Printed for the first time in Harrisse, *Les Cortereal*, app. xvii. From Pasqualigo and Cantino down to the time of Gomara we find no mention of these events; and Gomara, writing fifty years later, seems to confound the events of 1500 with those of 1501. Gomara also seems to have had some Portuguese charts, which we do not now know, when he says that Cortereal gave his name to some islands in the entrance of the gulf "Cuadrado" (St. Lawrence?), lying under 50° north latitude. Further than this, Gomara, as well as Ramusio, seems to have depended mainly on the Pasqualigo letter; and Herrera followed Gomara (Harrisse, *Les Cortereal*, p. 59). Harrisse can now collate, as he does (p. 65), the two narratives of Pasqualigo and Cantino for the first time, and finds Cortereal's explorations to have covered the Atlantic coast from Delaware Bay to Baffin's Bay, if not farther to the north.

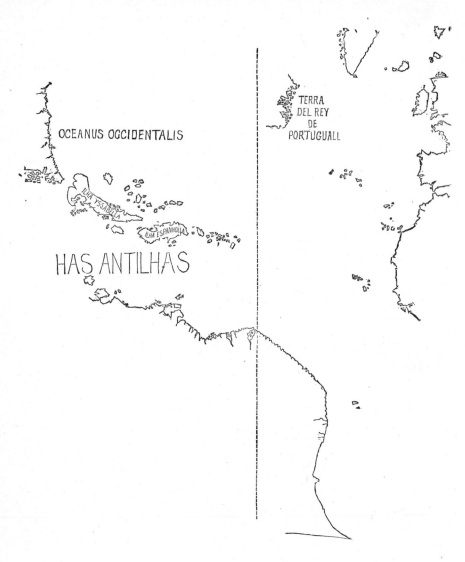

OCEANUS OCCIDENTALIS

TERRA
DEL REY
DE
PORTUGUALL

ILHA YSSABELLA

ILHA ESPANHOLLA

HAS ANTILHAS

THE CANTINO MAP.[1]

addressed to the Duke and dated at Rome, Nov. 19, 1502,[2] which fortunately for us fixes very nearly the period of the construction of the map. A much reduced sketch is annexed.

For the northern coast of South America La Cosa and Cantino's draughtsmen seem to have had different authorities. La Cosa attaches forty-five names to that coast: Cantino only twenty-nine; and only three of them are common to the two.[3] Harrisse argues from the failure of the La Cosa map to give certain intelligence of the Atlantic

---

[1] This is sketched from Harrisse's fac-simile, which is of the size of the original map. The dotted line is the Line of Demarcation, — "Este he omarco dantre castella y Portuguall," —which has been calculated by Harrisse to be at 62° 30,′ west of Paris.

[2] Harrisse, *Les Cortereal*, p. 71.

[3] Ibid., p. 96.

coast of the United States (here represented in the north and south trend of shore, north of Cuba), that there was existing in October, 1500, at least in Spanish circles, no knowledge of it,[1] but that explorations must have taken place before the summer of 1502 which afforded the knowledge embodied in this Cantino map. This coast was not visited, so far as is positively known, by any Spanish expedition previous to 1502. Besides the eight Spanish voyages of this period (not counting the problematical one of Vespucius) of which we have documentary proof, there were doubtless others of which we have intimations; but we know nothing of their discoveries, except so far as those before 1500 may be embodied in La Cosa's chart.[2] The researches of Harrisse have failed to discover in Portugal any positive trace of voyages made from that kingdom in 1501, or thereabout, records of which have been left in the Cantino map. Humboldt had intimated that in Lisbon at that time there was a knowledge of the connection of the Antilles with the northern discoveries of Cortereal by an intervening coast; but Harrisse doubts if Humboldt's authority — which seems to have been a letter of Pasqualigo sent to Venice, dated Oct. 18, 1501, found in the *Diarii* of Marino Sanuto, a manuscript preserved in Vienna — means anything more than a conjectural belief in such connection. Harrisse's conclusion is that between the close of 1500 and the summer of 1502, some navigators, of whose names and nation we are ignorant, but who were probably Spanish, explored the coast of the present United States from Pensacola to the Hudson. This Atlantic coast of Cantino terminates at about 59° north latitude, running nearly north and south from the Cape of Florida to that elevation. Away to the east in mid-ocean, and placed so far easterly as doubtless to appear on the Portuguese side of the Line of Demarcation, and covering from about fifty to fifty-nine degrees of latitude, is a large island which stands for the discoveries of Cortereal, "Terra del Rey du Portuguall;" and northeast of this is the point of Greenland apparently, with Iceland very nearly in its proper place.[3] This Cantino map, now positively fixed in 1502, establishes the earliest instance of a kind of delineation of North America which prevailed for some time. Students of this early cartography have long supposed this geographical idea to date from about this time, and have traced back the origin of what is known as "The Admiral's Map"[4] to data accumulated in the earliest years of the sixteenth century. Indeed Lelewel,[5] thirty years ago, made up what he called a Portuguese chart of 1501-1504, by combining in one draft the maps of the 1513 Ptolemy, with a hint or two from the Sylvanus map of 1511, acting on the belief that the Portuguese were the real first pursuers, or at least recorders, of explorations of the Floridian peninsula and of the coast northerly.[6]

The earliest Spanish map after that of La Cosa which has come down to us is the one which is commonly known as Peter Martyr's map. It is a woodcut measuring 11 × 7½ inches, and is usually thought to have first appeared in the *Legatio Babylonica*, or

---

[1] Some have considered that this Atlantic coast in Cantino may in reality have been Yucatan. But this peninsula was not visited earlier than 1506, if we suppose Solis and Pinzon reached it, and not earlier than 1517 if Cordova's expedition was, as is usually supposed, the first exploration. The names on this coast, twenty-two in number, are all legible but six. They resemble those on the Ptolemy maps of 1508 and 1513, and on Schöner's globe of 1520, which points to an earlier map not now known.

[2] These earliest Spanish voyages are, —
1. Columbus, Aug. 3, 1492 — March 15, 1493.
2. Columbus, Sept. 25, 1493 — June 11, 1496.
3. Columbus, May 30, 1498 — Nov. 25, 1500.
4. Alonzo de Ojeda, May 20, 1499 — June, 1500, to the Orinoco.

5. Piro Alonzo Niño and Christoval Guerra, June, 1499 — April, 1500, to Paria.
6. Vicente Yañez Pinzon, December, 1499 — September, 1500, to the Amazon.
7. Diego de Lepe, December, 1499 (?) — June, 1500, to Cape St. Augustin.
8. Rodrigo de Bastidas, October, 1500 — September, 1502, to Panama.

[3] The Greenland peninsula seems to have been seen by Cortereal in 1500 or 1501, and to be here called "Ponta d' Asia," in accordance with the prevalent view that any mainland hereabout must be Asia.

[4] See fac-simile on page 112, *post.*

[5] Plate 43 of his *Géographie du Moyen-âge.*

[6] De Costa points out that La Cosa complains of the Portuguese being in this region in 1503.

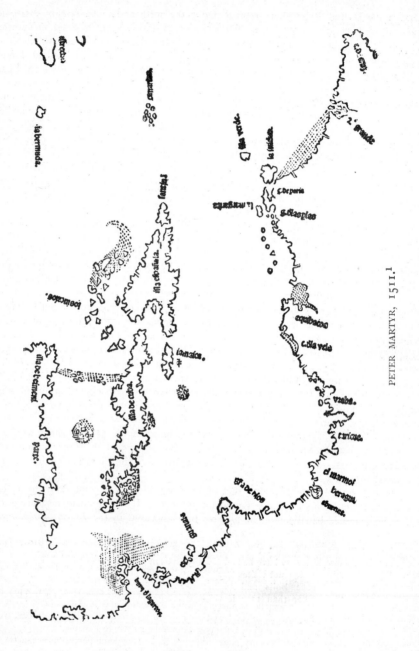

PETER MARTYR, 1511.[1]

[1] The 1511 map, here given in fac-simile after another fac-simile in the *Carter-Brown Catalogue*, has been several times reproduced, — in Stevens's *Notes*, pl. 4; J. H. Lefroy's *Memorials of the Bermudas*, London, 1877; H. A. Schumacher's *Petrus Martyr*, New York, 1879; and erroneously in H. H. Bancroft's *Central America*, i. 127. Cf. also Harrisse, *Bibl. Amer. Vet.*, no. 66; *Additions*, p. viii and no. 41; *Notes on Columbus*, p. 9; and his *Les Cortereal*, p. 113. Copies of the book are in the Carter-Brown, Lenox, Daly, and Barlow libraries. A copy (no. 1605 *) was sold in the Murphy sale. Quaritch has priced a perfect copy at £100. The map gives the earliest knowledge which we have of the Bermudas. Cf. the "Descripcion de la isla Bermuda" (1538), in Buckingham Smith's *Coleccion*, p. 92.

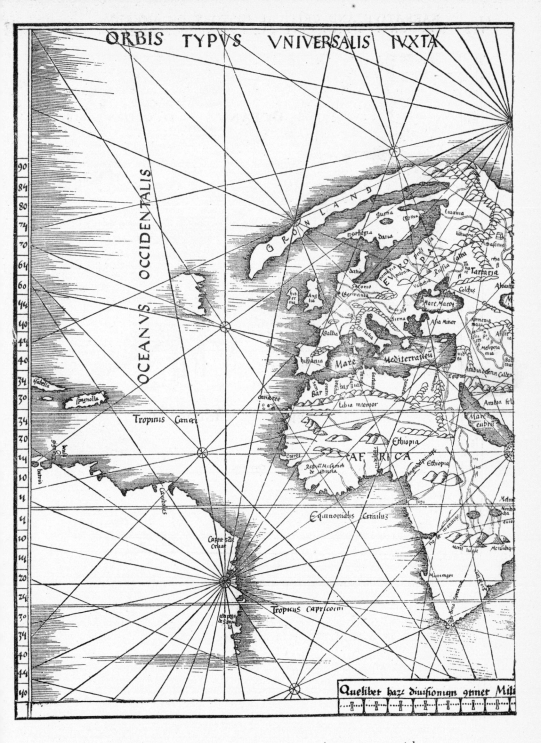

PART OF THE ORBIS TYPUS UNIVERSALIS (PTOLEMY, 1513).[1]

[1] The European prolongation of Gronland resembles that of a Portuguese map of 1490. Another reduced fac-simile is given in Ruge's *Geschichte des Zeitalters der Entdeckungen* (1881.)

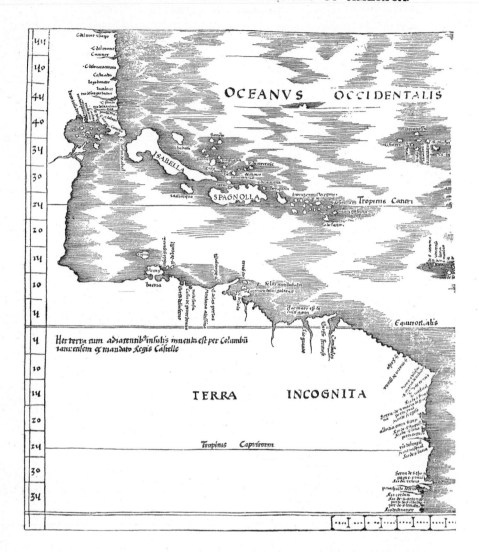

TABULA TERRE NOVE, OR THE ADMIRAL'S MAP (PTOLEMY, 1513).[1]

Martyr's first decade, at Seville, 1511; but Harrisse is inclined to believe that the map did not originally belong to Martyr's book, because three copies of it in the original vellum

These 1513 maps were reprinted in the Strasburg, 1520, edition of *Ptolemy* (copies in the Carter-Brown Library and in the *Murphy Catalogue*, no. 2,053), and were re-engraved on a reduced scale, but with more elaboration and with a few changes, for the *Ptolemies* of 1522 and 1525; and they were again the basis of those in Servetus' *Ptolemy* of 1535.

[1] Kohl remarks that the names on the South American coast (north part) are carried no farther than Ojeda went in 1499, and no farther south than Vespucius went in 1503; while the connection made of the two Americas was probably conjectural. Other fac-similes of the map are given in Varnhagen's *Premier voyage de Vespucci*, in Weise's *Discoveries of America*, p. 124; and in Stevens's *Historical and Geographical Notes*, pl. 2. Cf. Santarem (Childe's tr.), 153. Wieser, in his *Magalhães-Strasse* (Innsbruck, 1881), p. 15, mentions a manuscript note-book

which he has examined do not have the map. Quaritch [1] says that copies vary, that the leaf containing the map is an insertion, and that it is sometimes on different folios. Thus of two issues, one is called a second, because two leaves seem to have been reprinted to correct errors, and two new leaves are inserted, and a new title is printed. It is held by some that the map properly belongs to this issue. Brevoort [2] thinks that the publication of the map was distasteful to the Spanish Government (since the King this same year forbade maps being given to foreigners); and he argues that the scarcity of the book may indicate that attempts were made to suppress it. [3]

The maker of the 1513 map as we have it was Waldseemüller, or Hylacomylus, of St. Dié, in the Vosges Mountains; and Lelewel [4] gives reasons for believing that the plate had been engraved, and that copies were on sale as early as 1507. It had been engraved at the expense of Duke René II. of Lorraine, from information furnished by him to perfect some anterior chart; but the plate does not seem to have been used in any book before it appeared in this 1513 edition of Ptolemy. [5] It bears along the coast this legend: "Hec terra adjacentibus insulis inventa est per Columbū ianuensem ex mandato Regis Castelle;" and in the Address to the Reader in the Supplement appears the following sentence, in which the connection of Columbus with the map is thought to be indicated: "Charta antē marina quam Hydrographiam vocant per Admiralem [? *Columbus*] quondam serenissi. Portugalie [? *Hispaniæ*] regis Ferdinandi ceteros denique lustratores verissimis p̄agratiōibus lustrata, ministerio Renati, dum vixit, nunc pie mortui, Ducis illustris. Lotharingie liberalius prelographationi tradita est." [6]

This "Admiral's map" seems to have been closely followed in the map which Gregor Reisch annexed to his popular encyclopædia, [7] the *Margarita philosophica*, in 1515; though there is some difference in the coast-names, and the river mouths and deltas on the coast west of Cuba are left out. Stevens and others have contended that this represents Columbus' Ganges; but Varnhagen makes it stand for the Gulf of Mexico and the Mississippi,—a supposition more nearly like Reisch's interpretation, as will be seen by his distinct separation of the new lands from Asia. Reisch is, however, uncertain of their

---

of Schöner, the globe-maker, preserved in the Hof-bibliothek at Vienna, which has a sketch resembling this 1513 map. Harrisse (*Les Cortereal*, pp. 122, 126) has pointed out the correspondence of its names to the Cantino map, though the Waldseemüller map has a few names which are not on the Cantino. Again, Harrisse (*Les Cortereal*, p. 128) argues from the fact that the relations of Duke René with Portugal were cordial, while they were not so with Spain, and from the resemblance of René's map in the Ptolemy of 1513 to that of Cantino, that the missing map upon which Waldseemüller is said to have worked to produce, with René's help, the so-called "Admiral's map," was the original likewise of that of Cantino.

[1] *Catalogue* of February, 1879, pricing a copy of the book, with the map, at £100. This Quaritch copy is now owned by Mr. C. H. Kalbfleisch, of New York, and its title is different from the transcription given in Sabin, the Carter-Brown and Barlow catalogues, which would seem to indicate that the title was set up three times at least.

[2] *Verrazano*, p. 102.

[3] The editions of 1516 and 1530 have no map, and no *official* map was published in Spain till 1790. The Cabot map of 1544 is clearly

from Spanish sources, and Brevoort is inclined to think that the single copy known is the remainder after a like suppression. The Medina sketch of 1545 is too minute to have conveyed much intelligence of the Spanish knowledge, and may have been permitted.

[4] Vol. ii. p. 143.

[5] This edition will come under more particular observation in connection with Vespucius. There are copies in the Astor Library and in the libraries of Congress, of the American Antiquarian Society, and of Trinity College, Hartford (Cooke sale, no. 1,950), and in the Carter-Brown, Barlow, and Kalbfleisch collections. There was a copy in the Murphy sale, no. 2,052.

[6] Cf. Santarem in *Bulletin de la Société de Géographie de Paris* (1837), viii. 171, and in his *Recherches sur Vespuce et ses voyages*, p. 165; Wieser's *Magalhâes-Strasse*, p. 10. It will be seen that in the Latin quoted in the text there is an incongruity in making a "Ferdinand" king of Portugal at a time when no such king ruled that kingdom, but a Ferdinand did govern in Spain. The Admiral could hardly have been other than Columbus, but it is too much to say that he made the map, or even had a chief hand in it.

[7] Cf. Humboldt, *Cosmos*, Eng. tr., ii. 620, 621.

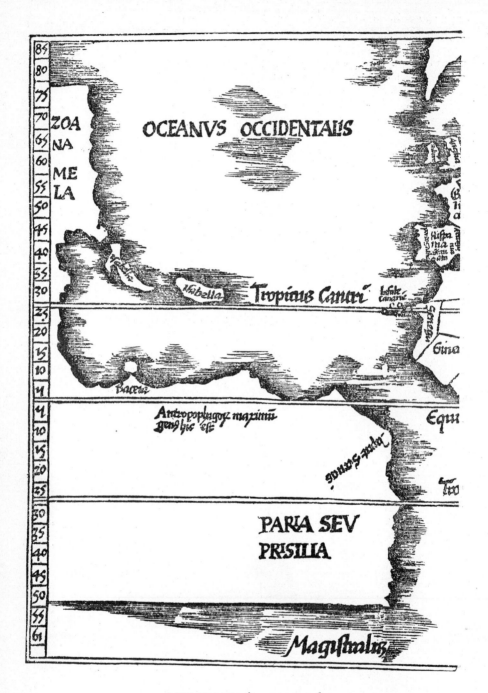

PART OF REISCH'S MAP, 1515.[1]

[1] There is another fac-simile in Stevens's *Historical and Geographical Notes*, pl. 4. An edition of Reisch appeared at Freiburg in 1503 (Murphy, no. 3,089); but in 1504 there were two editions, with a mappemonde which had no other reference to America than in the legend:

RUYSCH, 1508.[1]

western limits, which are cut off by the scale, as shown in the map; while on the other side of the same scale Cipango is set down in close proximity to it.

"Hic non terra sed mare est in quo miræ magnitudinis insulæ sed Ptolemæo fuerunt incognitæ." Some copies are dated 1505. (Murphy, no. 3,090.) A copy dated 1508, Basle, "cum additionibus novis" (Quaritch, no. 12,363; Baer's *Incunabeln*, 1884, no. 64, at 36 marks; and Murphy, no. 2,112 *) had the same map. The 1515 edition had the map above given. (Harrisse, *Bibl. Amer. Vet.*, no. 82; *Additions*, no. 45, noting a copy in the Imperial Library at Vienna. Kohl copies in his Washington Collection from one in the library at Munich.) The Basle edition of 1517 has a still different wood-cut map.

(Beckford, *Catalogue*, vol. iii. no. 1,256; Murphy, no. 2,112 **.) Not till 1535 did an edition have any reference to America in the text. (*Bibl. Amer. Vet.*, no. 208.) The latest edition is that of 1583, Basle, with a mappemonde showing America. (Leclerc, no. 2,926.) Cf. further in D'Avezac's *Waltzemüller*, p. 94; Kunstmann's *Entdeckung Amerikas*, p. 130; Stevens's *Notes*, p. 52; Kohl, *Die beiden ältesten General-Karten von America*, p. 33.

[1] A heliotype fac-simile is given in Vol. III. p. 9, where are various references and a record of other fac-similes; to which may be added

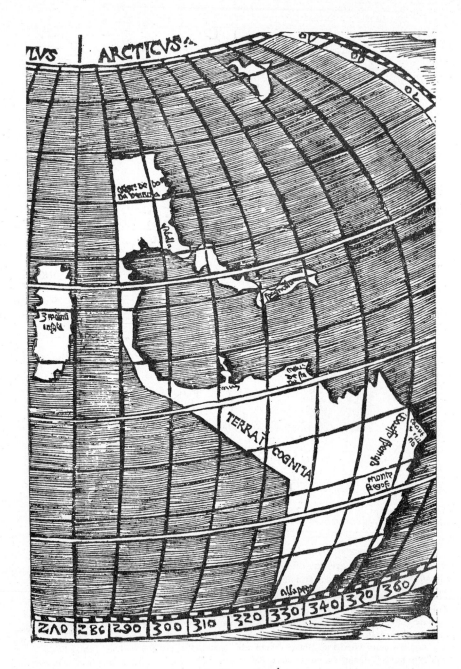

STOBNICZA, 1512.[1]

Varnhagen's *Novos estudos* (Vienna, 1874); Ruge's *Geschichte des Zeitalters der Entdeckungen*; Weise's *Discoveries of America*; and on a small scale in H. H. Bancroft's *Central America*, vol. i.

[1] It is held that this map shows the earliest attempt to represent on a plane a sphere truncated at the poles. Wieser (*Magalhaês-Strasse*, p. 11) speaks of a manuscript copy of Stobnicza's western hemisphere, made by Glareanus, which

Mathematicus.

SCHÖNER.[1]

The probability is that it was a map of this type which Bartholomew Columbus, when he visited Rome in 1505, gave to a canon of St. John Lateran, together with one of the printed accounts of his brother's voyage; and this canon gave the map to Alessandro Zorgi, "suo amico e compilatore della raccolta," as is stated in a marginal note in a copy of the *Mundus novus* in the Magliabecchian Library.[2]

Columbus is said to have had a vision before his fourth voyage, during which he saw and depicted on a map a strait between the regions north and south of the Antillian Sea. De Lorgues, with a convenient alternative for his saintly hero, says that the mistake was only in making the strait of water, when it should have been of land!

is bound with a copy of Waldseemüller's *Cosmographiæ introductio*, preserved in the University Library at Munich. Cf. Vol. III. p. 14, with references there, and Winsor's *Bibliography of Ptolemy* sub anno 1512; Harrisse, *Notes on Columbus*, p. 178, and *Bibl. Amer. Vet.*, nos. 69 and 95, and *Additions*, no. 47. The only copies of the Stobnicza *Introductio* in this country lack the maps. One in the Carter-Brown Library has it in fac-simile, and the other was sold in the Murphy sale, no. 2,075.

[1] Fac-simile of a cut in Reusner's *Icones* (Strasburg, 1590), p. 127. Cf. on Schöner's geographical labors, Doppelmayr's *Historische Nachricht von den nürnbergischen Mathematikern und Künstlern* (1730); Will und Nopitsch's *Nürnbergisches Gelehrten-Lexicon* (1757); Ghillany's *Erdglobus des Behaim und der des Schöner*; and Varnhagen's *Schöner e Apianus* (Vienna, 1872).

[2] Humboldt's *Examen critique*; Baldelli's *Il milione*; Kohl's *Lost Maps*.

SCHÖNER, 1515.[1]

We have a suspicion of this strait in another map which has been held to have had some connection with the drafts of Columbus, and that is the Ruysch map, which appeared

[1] According to Wieser (*Magalhâes-Strasse,* p. 19) this globe, which exists in copies at Weimar (of which Wieser gives the above sketch from Jomard's fac-simile of the one at Frankfort, but with some particulars added from that at Weimar) and at Frankfort (which is figured in Jomard), was made to accompany Schöner's *Luculentissima quædam terræ totius descriptio,* printed in 1515. Cf. Harrisse, *Notes on Columbus,* p. 179, and *Bibl. Amer. Vet.,* nos. 80, 81; Murphy, no. 2,233. Copies of Schöner's *Luculentis-*

sima, etc., are in the Harvard College, Carter-Brown, and Lenox libraries.

In 1523 Schöner printed another tract, *De nuper sub Castiliæ ac Portugaliæ regibus serenissimis repertis insulis ac regionibus,* descriptive of his globe, which is extremely rare. Wieser reports copies in the great libraries of Vienna and London only. Varnhagen reprinted it from the Vienna copy, at St. Petersburg in 1872 (forty copies only), under the designation, *Réimpression fidèle d'une lettre de Jean Schöner, à propos de*

SCHÖNER, 1520.[1]

son globe, écrite en 1523. The Latin is given in Wieser's *Magalhâes-Strasse*, p. 118. Johann Schoner or Schöner (for the spelling varies) was born in 1477, and died in 1547. The testimony of this globe to an early knowledge of the straits afterward made known by Magellan is examined on a later page. The notions which long prevailed respecting a large Antarctic continent are traced in Wieser's *Magalhaês-Strasse*, p. 59, and in Santarem, *Histoire de la cartographie,* ii. 277.

Cf. on the copy at Frankfort, — Vol. III. p. 215, of the present *History ;* Kohl's *General-Karten von Amerika*, p. 33, and his *Discovery of Maine*, p. 159; *Encyclopædia Britannica*, x. 681;

Von Richthofen's *China*, p. 641; *Journal* of the Royal Geographical Society, xviii. 45. On the copy at Weimar, see Humboldt, *Examen critique*, and his Introduction to Ghillany's *Ritter Behaim.*

[1] This globe, which has been distinctively known as Schöner's globe, is preserved at Nuremberg. There are representations of it in Santarem, Lelewel, Wieser, Ghillany's *Behaim,* Kohl's *Geschichte der Entdeckungsreisen zur Magellan's-Strasse* (Berlin, 1877), p. 8; H. H. Bancroft's *Central America*, i. 137; and in *Harper's Magazine*, February, 1871, and December, 1882, p. 731. The earliest engraving appeared in the *Jahresbericht der technischen Anstalten in Nürn-*

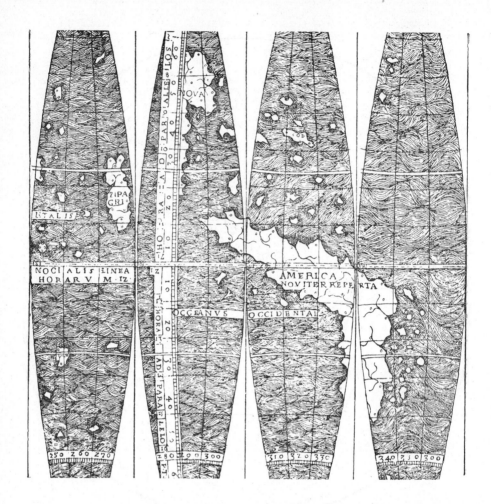

THE TROSS GORES, 1514–1519.[1]

in the Roman Ptolemy of 1508,[2] the earliest published map, unless the St. Dié map takes precedence, to show any part of the new discoveries. It seems from its resemblance to

berg für 1842, accompanied by a paper by Dr. Ghillany; and the same writer reproduced it in his *Erdglobus des Behaim und der des Schöner* (1842). The globe is signed: "Perfecit eum Bambergæ 1520, Joh. Schönerus." Cf. Von Murr, *Memorabilia bibliothecarum Noribergensium* (1786), i. 5; Humboldt, *Examen critique*, ii. 28; Winsor's *Bibliography of Ptolemy* sub anno 1522; and Vol. III. p. 214, of the present *History*.

[1] Twelve gores of a globe found in a copy of the *Cosmographiæ introductio*, published at Lugduni, 1514 (?), and engraved in a catalogue of Tross, the Paris bookseller, in 1881 (nos. xiv. 4,924). The book is now owned by Mr. C. H. Kalbfleisch, of New York. Harrisse (*Cabots*, p. 182) says the map was engraved in 1514, and

ascribes it to Louis Boulenger. (Cf. Vol. III. p. 214, of the present *History*.) There are two copies of this edition of the *Cosmographiæ introductio* in the British Museum; and D'Avezac (*Waltzemüller*, p. 123) says the date of it cannot be earlier than 1517. Harrisse says he erred in dating it 1510 in the *Bibl. Amer. Vet.*, no. 63. Cf. Winsor's *Bibliography of Ptolemy* sub anno 1522.

[2] Pope Julius II. (July 28, 1506) gave to Tosinus, the publisher, the exclusive sale of this edition for six years. It was first issued in 1507, and had six new maps, besides those of the editions of 1478 and 1490, but none of America. There are copies in the Carter-Brown Library; and noted in the *Murphy Catalogue*, no. 2,049;

the La Cosa chart to have been kept much nearer the Columbian draft than the geographer of St. Dié, with his Portuguese helps, was contented to leave it in his map. In La Cosa the vignette of St. Christopher had concealed the mystery of a westerly passage;[1] Ruysch assumes it, or at least gives no intimation of his belief in the inclosure of the Antillian Sea. Harrisse[2] has pointed out how an entirely different coast-nomenclature in the two maps points to different originals of the two map-makers. The text of this 1508 edition upon "Terra Nova" and "Santa Cruz" is by Marcus Beneventanus. There are reasons to believe that the map may have been issued separately, as well as in the book; and the copies of the map in the Barlow Collection and in Harvard College Library are perhaps of this separate issue.[3]

The distinctive features both of the La Cosa and the Ruysch drafts, of the Cantino map and of the Waldseemüller or St. Dié map of 1513, were preserved, with more or less modifications in many of the early maps. The Stobnicza map — published in an *Introductio* to Ptolemy at Cracow in 1512 — is in effect the St. Dié

MÜNSTER, 1532.[4]

map, with a western ocean in place of the edge of the plate as given in the 1513 Ptolemy, and is more like the draft of Reisch's map published three years later.

and one was recently priced by Rosenthal, of Munich, at 500 marks. It was reissued in 1508, with a description of the New World by Beneventanus, accompanied by this map of Ruysch; and of this 1508 edition there are copies in the Astor Library, the Library of Congress, of the American Geographical Society, of Yale College (Cooke sale, vol. ii. no. 1,949), and in the Carter-Brown and Kalbfleisch collections. One is noted in the Murphy sale, no. 2,050, which is now at Cornell University.

[1] H. H. Bancroft (*Central America*, p. 116) curiously intimates that the dotted line which

he gives in his engraving to mark the place of this vignette, stands for some sort of a *terra incognita!*

[2] *Les Cortereal*, p. 118.

[3] Harrisse, *Cabots*, p. 164. In his *Notes on Columbus*, p. 56, he conjectures that it sold for forty florins, if it be the same with the map of the New World which Johannes Trithemus complained in 1507 of his inability to buy for that price (*Epistolæ familiares*, 1536).

[4] There are other drawings of this map in Stevens's *Notes;* in Nordenskiöld's *Bröderna Zenos* (Stockholm, 1883); etc

The Schöner globe of 1515, often cited as the Frankfort globe ; the Schöner globe of 1520 ; the so-called Tross gores of 1514–1519 ; the map of Petrus Apianus [1] — or Bienewitz,

as he was called in his vernacular — which appeared in the *Polyhistoria* of Solinus, edited by the Italian monk Camers, and also in 1522 in the *De orbis situ* of Pomponius Mela, published by Vadianus, — all preserve the same characteristics with the St. Dié map, excepting that they show the western passage referred to in Columbus' dream, and so far unite some of the inferences from the map of Ruysch. There was a curious survival of this Cantino type, particularly as regards North America for many years yet to come, as seen in the map which Münster added to the Basle edition of the *Novus orbis* in 1532 and 1537, and in the drawing which Jomard gives [2] as from " une cassette de la Collection Trivulci, dite Cassettina all' Agemina." This last drawing is a cordiform mappemonde, very like another which accompanied Honter's *Rudimenta cosmographica* in 1542, and which was repeated in various editions to as late a period as 1590. Thus it happened that for nearly a century geographical views which the earliest navigators evolved, continued in popular books to convey the most inadequate notion of the contour of the new continent. [3]

SYLVANUS' MAP, 1511. [4]

tion with the naming of America. See *post*, p. 183.

[2] Pl. xviii.

[3] The bibliography of Honter has been traced by G. D. Teutsch in the *Archiv des Vereins für Siebenbürgische Landeskunde*, neue Folge, xiii. 137 ; and an estimate of Honter by F. Teutsch is given in Ibid., xv. 586. The earliest form of Honter's book is the *Rudimentorum cosmographiæ libri duo*, dated 1531, and published at Cracow, in a tract of thirty-two pages. It is a description of the world in verse, and touches America in the

[1] Its date was altered to 1530 when it appeared in the first complete edition of Peter Martyr's *Decades*. There are fac-similes in the *Carter-Brown Catalogue* and in Santarem's *Atlas*. It will be considered further in connec-

---

[4] The map is given in its original projection in Lelewel, pl. xlv., and on a greatly reduced scale in Daly's *Early Cartography*, p. 32. There are copies of this 1511 Ptolemy in the Lenox, Carter-Brown, Astor, Brevoort, Barlow, and Kalb-

fleisch collections. Cf. *Murphy Catalogue*, no. 2,051, for a copy now in the American Geographical Society's Library, and references in Winsor's *Bibliography of Ptolemy* sub anno 1511.

In the same year with the publication of the Peter Martyr map of 1511, an edition of Ptolemy, published at Venice and edited by Bernardus Sylvanus, contained a mappemonde on a cordiform projection, —which is said to be the first instance of the use of this method in drafting maps. What is shown of the new discoveries is brought in a distorted shape on the extreme western verge of the map; and to make the contour more intelligible, it is reduced in the sketch annexed to an ordinary plane projection. It is the earliest engraved map to give any trace of the Cortereal discoveries [1] and to indicate the Square, or St. Lawrence, Gulf. It gives a curious Latinized form to the name of the navigator himself in "Regalis Domus" (Cortereal), and restores Greenland, or Engronelant, to a peninsular connection with northwestern Europe as it had appeared in the Ptolemy of 1482.

THE LENOX GLOBE.

It will be seen that, with the exception of the vague limits of the "Regalis Domus," there was no sign of the continental line of North America in this map of Sylvanus.

chapter, "Nomina insularum oceani et maris." It is extremely rare, and the only copy to be noted is one priced by Harrassowitz (*Catalogue* of 1876, no. 2), of Leipsic, for 225 marks, and subsequently sold to Tross, of Paris. Most bibliographers give Cracow, with the date 1534 as the earliest (Sabin, no. 32,792; Muller, 1877, no. 1,456,—37.50 fl.); there was a Basle edition of the same year. (Cf. Harrisse, *Bibl. Amer. Vet.*, no. 194; Wieser, *Magalhães-Strasse*, p. 22.) Editions seem to have followed in 1540 (queried by Sabin, no. 32,793); in 1542 (if Stevens's designation of his fac-simile of the map is correct, *Notes*, pl. 3); in 1546, when the map is inscribed "Universalis cosmographia . . . Tiguri, J. H. V. E. [in monogram], 1546." (Harrisse, no. 271; Muller, 1877, no. 1,457; Carter-Brown, no. 143; Sabin, no. 32,794.) The same map, which is part of an appendix of thirteen maps, was repeated in the Tiguri edition of 1548, and there was another issue the same year at Basle. (Harrisse, no. 287; Sabin, no. 32,795; Weigel, 1877, no. 1,268.) The maps were repeated in the 1549 edition. (Sabin, no. 32,796; Carter-Brown, no. 153.) The edition at Antwerp in 1552 leaves

off the date. (Harrisse, no. 287; Weigel, no. 1,269; Murphy, no. 1,252.) It is now called, *Rvdimentorvm cosmographicorum libri III. cum tabellis geographicis elegantissimis. De uariarum rerum nomenclaturis per classes, liber I.* There was a Basle edition the same year. The maps continued to be used in the Antwerp edition of 1554, the Tiguri of 1558, and the Antwerp of 1660.

In 1561 the edition published at Basle, *De cosmographiæ rudimėntis libri VIII.*, was rather tardily furnished with new maps better corresponding to the developments of American geography. (Muller, 1877, no. 1,459.) The Tiguri publishers still, however, adhered to the old plates in their editions of 1565 (Carter-Brown, no. 257; Sabin, no. 32,797); and the same plates again reappeared in an edition, without place, published in 1570. (Muller, 1877, no. 1,457), in another of Tiguri in 1583, and in still another without place in 1590 (Murphy, no. 1,253; Muller, 1872, no. 763; Sabin, no. 32,799).

[1] Harrisse (*Les Cortereal*, p. 121) says there is no Spanish map showing these discoveries before 1534.

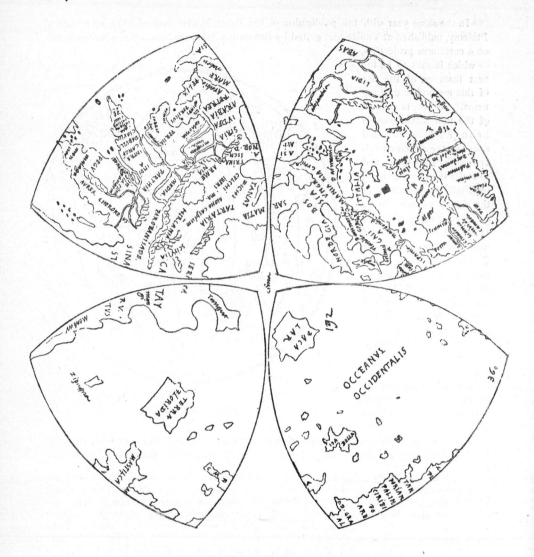

DA VINCI, NORTHERN HEMISPHERE (*original draft reduced*).

Much the same views were possessed by the maker of the undated Lenox globe, which probably is of nearly the same date, and of which a further account is given elsewhere.[1]

Another draft of a globe, likewise held to be of about the same date, shows a similar configuration, except that a squarish island stands in it for Florida and adjacent parts of the main. This is a manuscript drawing on two sheets preserved among the Queen's collections at Windsor; and since Mr. R. H. Major made it known by a communication, with accompanying fac-similes, in the *Archæologia*,[2] it has been held to be the work of Leonardo da Vinci, though this has been recently questioned.[3] If deprived of the associations of that august name, the map loses much of its attraction; but it still remains an inter-

---

[1] Vol. III. p. 212, and the present volume, page 170.

[2] Vol. xl.; also Major's *Prince Henry*, p. 388.

[3] J. P. Richter, *Literary Works of Da Vinci*, London, 1883, quoting the critic, who questions its assignment to the great Italian.

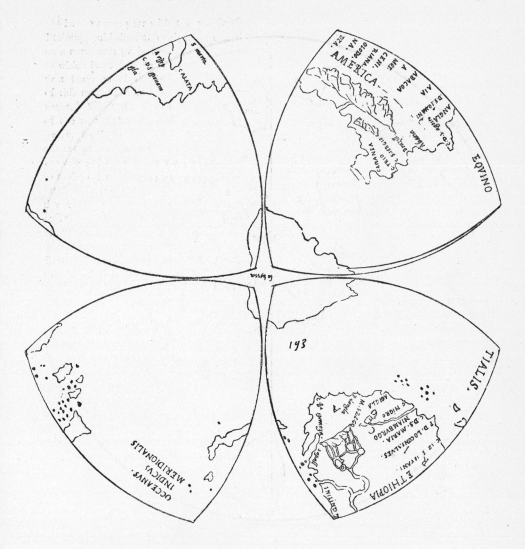

DA VINCI, SOUTHERN HEMISPHERE (*original draft reduced*).[1]

esting memorial of geographical conjecture.   It is without date, and can only be fixed in the chain of cartographical ideas by its internal evidence.   This has led Major to place it between 1512 and 1514, and Wieser to fix it at 1515–1516.[2]   A somewhat unsatisfactory map, since it shows nothing north of "Ysabella" and "Spagnollo," is that inscribed *Orbis typus universalis juxta hydrographorum traditionem exactissime depicta*, 1522, *L. F.*, which is the work of Laurentius Frisius, and appeared in the Ptolemy of 1522.[3]

---

[1] Another sketch of this hemisphere is given in *Harper's Monthly*, December, 1882, p. 733.

[2] The Portuguese portolano of about this date given in Kunstmann, pl. 4, is examined on another page.

[3] This Strasburg edition is particularly described in D'Avezac's *Waltzemüller*, p. 159.

(Cf. Harrisse's *Notes on Columbus*, 176; his *Bibl. Amer. Vet.*, no. 117; and Winsor's *Bibliography of Ptolemy's Geography* sub anno 1522.)   The maps closely resemble those of Waldseemüller in the edition of 1513; and indeed Frisius assigns them as re-engraved to Martin Ilacomylus, the Greek form of that geographer's name.   There are

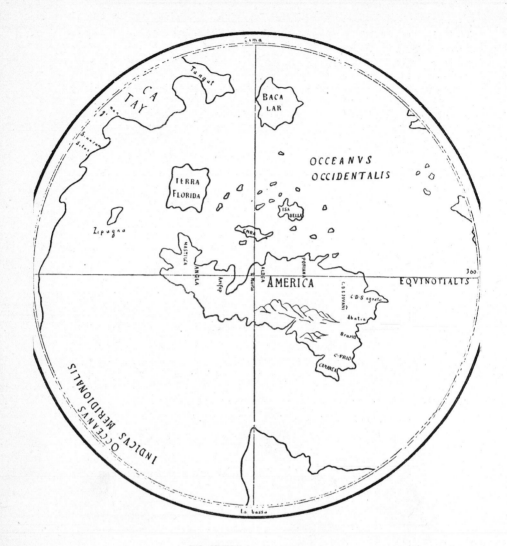

DA VINCI (*newly projected*).[1]

A new element appears in a map which is one of the charts belonging to the *Yslegung der Mer-Carthen oder Cartha Marina*, said also to be the work of Frisius, which was

copies of this 1522 Ptolemy in the Harvard College, Carter-Brown, Cornell University, and Barlow libraries, and one is noted in the *Murphy Catalogue*, no. 2,054, which is now in the Lenox Library. The map of Frisius (Lorenz Friess, as he was called in unlatinized form) was reproduced in the next Strasburg edition of 1525, of which there are copies in the Library of Congress, in the New York Historical Society, Boston Public, Baltimore Mercantile, Carter-Brown, Trinity College, and the American Antiquarian Society libraries, and in the collections of William C. Prime and Charles H. Kalbfleisch. There were two copies in the Murphy sale,

---

[1] This follows the projection as given by Wieser in his *Magalhaês-Strasse*, who dates it 1515–1516.

CARTA MARINA OF FRISIUS, 1525.

issued in 1525, in exposition of his theories of sea-charts.[1] The map is of interest as the sole instance in which North America is called a part of Africa, on the supposition that

COPPO, 1528.[2]

nos. 2,055 and 2,056, one of which is now at Cornell University. Cf. references in Winsor's *Bibliography of Ptolemy*.

This "L. F. 1522" map (see p. 175), as well as the "Admiral's map," was reproduced in the edition of 1535, edited by Servetus, of which there are copies in the Astor, the Boston Public, and the College of New Jersey libraries, and in the Carter-Brown and Barlow collections. A copy is also noted in the *Murphy Catalogue*, no. 2,057, which is now at Cornell University.

The American maps of these editions were again reproduced in the Ptolemy, published at Vienna in 1541, of which there are copies in the Carter-Brown, Brevoort, and Kalbfleisch collections. Cf. Winsor's *Bibliography of Ptolemy*.

[1] Harrisse, *Bibl. Amer. Vet.*, no. 133. The edition of 1530 has no maps (ibid., no. 158).

[2] This is drawn from a sketch given by Kohl in his manuscript, "On the Connection of the New and Old World on the Pacific Side," preserved in the American Antiquarian Society's

a continental connection by the south enclosed the "sea toward the sunset." The insular Yucatan will be observed in the annexed sketch, and what seems to be a misshapen Cuba. The land at the east seems intended for Baccalaos, judging from the latitude and the indication of fir-trees upon it. This map is one of twelve engraved sheets constituting the above-named work, which was published by Johannes Grieninger in 1530. Friess, or Frisius, who was a German mathematician, and had, as we have seen, taken part in the 1522 Ptolemy, says that he drew his information in these maps from original sources; but he does not name these sources, and Dr. Kohl thinks the maps indicate the work of Waldseemüller.

Among the last of the school of geographers who supposed North America to be an archipelago, was Pierro Coppo, who published at Venice in 1528 what has become a very rare *Portolano delli lochi maritimi ed isole der mar*.[1]

Library. There is another copy in his Washington Collection.

The map is explained by the following key: 1. Asia. 2. India. 3. Ganges. 4. Java major. 5. Cimpangi [Japan]. 6. Isola verde [Greenland?]. 7. Cuba. 8. Iamaiqua. 9. Spagnola. 10. Monde nuova [South America].

[1] There is a copy in the Grenville Collection in the British Museum. Cf. Harrisse, *Bibl. Amer. Vet.*, no. 144; Zurla, *Fra Mauro*, p. 9, and his *Marco Polo*, ii. 363. Harrisse, in his *Notes on Columbus*, p. 56, cites from Morelli's *Operette*, i. 309, a passage in which Coppo refers to Columbus.

CHAPTER II.

AMERIGO VESPUCCI.

BY SYDNEY HOWARD GAY.

AMERIGO VESPUCCI,[1] the third son of Nastugio Vespucci, a notary of Florence, and his wife Lisabetta Mini, was born on the 9th of March, 1451. The family had the respectability of wealth, acquired in trade, for one member of it in the preceding century was rich enough to endow a public hospital. Over the portal of the house, so dedicated to charity by this pious Vespucci nearly three quarters of a century before Amerigo was born, there was, says Humboldt, engraved in 1719, more than three hundred years after the founding of the hospital, an inscription declaring that here Amerigo had lived in his youth. As the monks, however, who wrote the inscription also asserted in it that he was the discoverer of America, it is quite possible that they may have been as credulous in the one case as in the other, and have accepted for fact that which was only tradition. But whether Amerigo's father, Nastugio, lived or did not live in the hospital which his father or grandfather founded, he evidently maintained the respectability of the family. Three of his sons he sent to be educated at the University of Pisa. Thenceforth they are no more heard of, except that one of them, Jerome, afterward went to Palestine, where he remained nine years, met with many losses, and endured much suffering, — all of which he related in a letter to his younger brother Amerigo. But the memory even of this Jerome — that he should have ever gone anywhere, or had any adventures worth the telling — is only preserved from oblivion because he had this brother who became the famous navigator, and whose name by a chance was given to half the globe.

Amerigo was not sent to the university. Such early education as he received came from a learned uncle, Giorgi Antonio Vespucci, a Dominican friar, who must have been a man of some influence in Florence, as it is

[1] Harrisse (*Bibl. Amer. Vet.*) gives the various ways of spelling the name by different authors as follows: "Albericus (*Madrignano, Ruchamer, Jehan Lambert*); Emeric (*Du Redouer*); Alberico or Americo (*Gomara*); Morigo (*Hojeda*); Amerrigo (*Muñoz*); Americus (*Peter Martyr*); Almerigo Florentino (*Vianello*); De Espuche, Vespuche, Despuche, Vespuccio (*Ramusio*); Vespuchy (*Christ. Columbus*)." Varnhagen uniformly calls him Amerigo Vespucci; and that is the signature to the letter written from Spain in 1492 given in the *Vita* by Bandini.

A LETTER OF VESPUCIUS TO HIS FATHER (*after a fac-simile given by Varnhagen*).[1]

[1] [Harrisse (*Bibl. Amer. Vet. Additions*, p. xxii) says that this letter was found by Bandini in the Strozzi Library, and that it is now in the collection of M. Feuillet de Conches in Paris. "This and two or three signatures added to receipts, which were brought to light by Navarrete, constitute," said Harrisse in 1872, "the

claimed for him that he was the friend and colleague of the more famous monk Savonarola. The nephew acknowledged later in life that he was not among the most diligent of his uncle's pupils; and the admission was as true as it was ingenuous, if one may judge by a letter in Latin written, when he was twenty-five years old, to his father. He excuses himself to that *spectabili et egregio viro* — as he addresses his father — for recent negligence in writing, as he hesitates to commit himself in Latin without the revision of his uncle, and he happens to be absent. Probably it was poverty of expression in that tongue, and not want of thought, which makes the letter seem the work of a boy of fifteen rather than of a young man of five and twenty. A mercantile career in preference to that of a student was, at any rate, his own choice; and in due time, though at what age precisely does not appear, a place was found for him in the great commercial house of the Princes Medici in Florence.

In Florence he remained, apparently in the service of the Medici, till 1490; for in that year he complains that his mother prevented him from going to Spain. But the delay was not long, as in January, 1492, he writes from Cadiz, where he was then engaged in trade with an associate, one Donato Nicolini, — perhaps as agents of the Medici, whose interests in Spain were large. Four years later, the name of Vespucci appears for the first time in the Spanish archives, when he was within two months of being forty-six years of age. Meanwhile he had engaged in the service of Juonato Berardi, a Florentine merchant established at Seville, who had fitted out the second expedition of Columbus in 1493.[1]

It has been conjectured that Vespucci became known at that time to Columbus, — which is not improbable if the former was so early as 1493 in the service of Berardi. But the suggestion that he went with Columbus either on his first or second expedition cannot be true, at any rate as to the second.[2] For in 1495 Berardi made a contract with the Spanish Government

only autographs of Vespucius known." Since then another fac-simile of a letter by Vespucius has been published in the *Cartas de Indias*, being a letter of Dec. 9, 1508, about goods which ought to be carried to the Antilles. Cf. *Mass. Hist. Soc. Proc.*, xvi. 318, and *Magazine of American History*, iii. 193, where it is translated, and accompanied by a fac-simile of a part of it. The signature is given on another page of the present chapter. — ED.]

[1] The facts relative to the birth, parentage, and early life of Vespucci are given by the Abbé Bandini in his *Vita e lettere di Amerigo Vespucci*, 1745, and are generally accepted by those whose own researches have been most thorough, — as Humboldt in his *Examen Critique;* Varnhagen in his *Amerigo Vespucci, son caractère, ses écrits, sa vie, et ses navigations,* and in his *Nouvelles recherches,* p. 41, where he reprints Bandini's account; and Santarem in his *Researches respecting Americus Vespucius and his Voyages,* as the

English translation is called. In relation to representatives of the family in our day, see Lester's *Vespucius,* p. 405. The newspapers within a year have said that two female descendants were living in Rome, the last male representative dying seven years ago.

[2] Humboldt says that it cannot be true of either voyage, and relies for proof upon the documentary evidence of Vespucci's presence in Spain during the absence of Columbus upon those expeditions. But he makes a curious mistake in regard to the first, which, we think, has never been noticed. Columbus sailed on his first voyage in August, 1492, and returned in March, 1493. Humboldt asserts that Vespucci could not have been with him, because the letter written from Cadiz and jointly signed by him and Donato Nicolini was dated Jan. 30, 1493. But Humboldt has unaccountably mistaken the date of that letter; it was not 1493, but 1492, seven months before Columbus sailed on his

to furnish a fleet of ships for an expedition westward which he did not live to complete. Its fulfilment was intrusted to Vespucci; and it appears in the public accounts that a sum of money was paid to him from the Treasury of the State in January, 1496. Columbus was then absent on his second voyage, begun in September, 1493, from which he did not return till June, 1496.

In the interval between the spring of 1495 and the summer of 1497 any adventurer was permitted by Spain, regardless of the agreement made with Columbus, to go upon voyages of commerce or discovery to that New India to which his genius and courage had led the way. "Now," wrote Columbus, "there is not a man, down to the very tailors, who does not beg to be allowed to become a discoverer." The greed of the King; the envy of the navigators who before 1492 had laughed at the theories of Columbus; the hatred of powerful Churchmen, more bitter now than ever, because those theories which they had denounced as heresy had proved to be true, — all these influences were against him, and had combined to rob the unhappy Admiral, even before he had returned from his second voyage, of the honor and the riches which he thought would rightfully become his own. Ships now could go and come in safety over that wide waste of waters which even children could remember had been looked upon as a "Sea of Darkness," rolling westward into never-ending space, whence there was no return to the voyager mad enough to trust to its treacherous currents. It was no longer guarded by perpetual Night, by monsters hideous and terrible, and by a constant wind that blew ever toward the west. But ships came safely back, bringing, not much, but enough of gold and pearls to seem an earnest of the promise of the marvellous wealth of India that must soon be so easily and so quickly reached; with the curious trappings of a picturesque barbarism; the soft skins and gorgeous feathers of unknown beasts and birds; the woods of a new beauty in grain and vein and colors; the aromatic herbs of subtle virtue that would stir the blood beneath the ribs of Death; and with all these precious things the captive men and women, of curious complexion and unknown speech, whose people were given as a prey to the stranger by God and the Pope. Every rough sailor of these returning ships was greeted as a hero when to the gaping, wide-eyed crowd he told of his adventures in that land of perpetual summer, where the untilled virgin soil brought forth its fruits, and the harvest never failed; where life was without care or toil, sickness or poverty; where he who would might gather wealth as he would idly pick up pebbles on a beach. These were the sober realities of the times; and there were few so poor in spirit or so lacking in imagination as not to desire to share in the possession of these new Indies. It was not long, indeed, before a reaction came; when disappointed adventurers

first voyage. The *alibi*, therefore, is not proved. There is indeed no positive proof that Vespucci was not on that voyage; but, on the other hand, there is nothing known of that period of his life to suggest that he was; and, moreover, the strong negative evidence is — unusually strong in his case — that he never claimed to have sailed with Columbus.

returned in poverty, and sat in rags at the gates of the palace to beg relief of the King. And when the sons of Columbus, who were pages in the Court of the Queen, passed by, "they shouted to the very heavens, saying: 'Look at the sons of the Admiral of Mosquitoland! — of that man who has discovered the lands of deceit and disappointment, — a place of sepulchre and wretchedness to Spanish hidalgos!'"[1]

From his second voyage Columbus returned in the summer of 1496; and meeting his enemies with the courage and energy which never failed him, he induced the King and Queen to revoke, in June of the next year, the decree of two years before. Meanwhile he made preparations for his third voyage, on which he sailed from San Lucar on the 30th of May, 1498. Two months later he came in sight of the island he named Trinidad; and entering the Gulf of Paria, into which empties the Orinoco by several mouths, he sailed along the coast of the mainland. He had reached the continent, not of Asia, as he supposed, but of the western hemisphere. None of the four voyages of the great discoverer is so illustrative of his peculiar faith, his religious fervor, and the strength of his imagination as this third voyage; and none, in that respect, is so interesting. The report of it which he sent home in a letter, with a map, to the King and Queen has a direct relation to the supposed first voyage of Amerigo Vespucci.

As he approached the coast, Columbus wrote,[2] he heard "in the dead of night an awful roaring;" and he saw "the sea rolling from west to east like a mountain as high as the ship, and approaching little by little; on the top of this rolling sea came a mighty wave roaring with a frightful noise." When he entered the Gulf, and saw how it was filled by the flow of the great river, he believed that he had witnessed far out at sea the mighty struggle at the meeting of the fresh with the salt water. The river, he was persuaded, must be rushing down from the summit of the earth, where the Lord had planted the earthly Paradise, in the midst whereof was a fountain whence flowed the four great rivers of the world, — the Ganges, the Tigris, the Euphrates, and the Nile. He did not quite agree with those earlier philosophers who believed that the earth was a perfect sphere; but rather that it was like "the form of a pear, which is very round except where the stalk grows, at which part it is most prominent; or like a round ball, upon one part of which is a prominence like a woman's nipple, this protrusion being the highest and nearest the sky, situated under the equinoctial line, and at the eastern extremity of this sea." "I call that the eastern extremity," he adds, "where the land and the islands end."

Now had come to him at last in the observations and experience of this voyage the confirmation of his faith. That "eastern extremity of the sea

---

[1] *The History of the Life and Actions of Admiral Christopher Colon.* By his son, Don Ferdinand Colon. [For the story of this book, see the previous chapter. — ED.]

[2] *Select Letters of Christopher Columbus, with* other *Original Documents relating to his Four Voyages to the New World.* Translated and edited by R. H. Major, Esq., of the British Museum, London. Printed for the Hakluyt Society, 1847.

where the lands and the islands end" he had reached, he thought, at the islands of Trinidad, of Margarita, and of Cubagua, and at the coast of the Gulf of Paria, into which poured this great river rushing down from the pinnacle of the globe. For he had observed, as he sailed westward from a certain line in the ocean, that "the ships went on rising smoothly towards the sky." Some of the older astronomers, he said, believed that the Arctic pole was "the highest point of the world, and nearest to the heavens;" and others that this was true of the Antarctic. Though all were wrong as to the exact locality of that elevation, it was plain that they held a common faith that somewhere there was a point of exaltation, if only it could be found, where the earth approached the sky more nearly than anywhere else. But it had not occurred to any of them that possibly the blessed spot which the first rays of the sun lit up in crimson and in gold on the morning of creation, because it was the topmost height of the globe, and because it was in the east, might be under the equinoctial line; and it had not occurred to them, because this eastern extremity of the world, which it had pleased God he should now discover, had hitherto been unknown to civilized man.

Every observation and incident of this voyage gave to Columbus proof of the correctness of his theory. The farther south he had gone along the African coast, the blacker and more barbarous he had found the people, the more intense the heat, and the more arid the soil. For many days they had sailed under an atmosphere so heated and oppressive that he doubted if his ships would not fall to pieces and their crews perish, if they did not speedily escape into some more temperate region. He had remarked in former voyages that at a hundred leagues west of the Azores there was a north-and-south line, to cross which was to find an immediate and grateful change in the skies above, in the waters beneath, and in the reviving temperature of the air. The course of the ships was altered directly westward, that this line might be reached, and the perils escaped which surrounded him and his people. It was when the line was crossed that he observed how his ships were gently ascending toward the skies. Not only were the expected changes experienced, but the North Star was seen at a new altitude; the needle of the compass varied a point, and the farther they sailed the more it turned to the northwest. However the wind blew, the sea was always smooth; and when the Island of Trinidad and the shores of the continent were reached, they entered a climate of exceeding mildness, where the fields and the foliage were "remarkably fresh and green, and as beautiful as the gardens of Valencia in April." The people who crowded to the shore "in countless numbers" to gaze at these strange visitors were "very graceful in form, tall, and elegant in their movements, wearing their hair very long and smooth." They were, moreover, of a whiter skin than any the Admiral had heretofore seen "in any of the Indies," and were "shrewd, intelligent, and courageous."

The more he saw and the more he reflected, the more convinced he was that this country was "the most elevated in the world, and the nearest to the sky." Where else could this majestic river, that rushed eagerly to this mighty struggle with the sea, come from, but from that loftiest peak of the globe, in the midst whereof was the inexhaustible fountain of the four great rivers of the earth? The faith or the fanaticism — whichever one may please to call it — of the devout cosmographer was never for an instant shadowed by a doubt. The human learning of all time had taught him that the shorter way to India must be across that western ocean which, he was persuaded, covered only one third of the globe and separated the western coast of Europe from the eastern coast of Asia. When it was taken for granted that his first voyage had proved this geographical theory to be the true one, then he could only understand that as in each successive voyage he had gone farther, so he was only getting nearer and nearer to the heart of the empire of the Great Khan.

But to the aid of human knowledge came a higher faith; he was divinely led. In writing of this third voyage to Dona Juana de la Torres, a lady of the Court and a companion to the Queen, he said: "God made me the messenger of the new heaven and the new earth of which he spoke in the Apocalypse by Saint John, after having spoken of it by the mouth of Isaiah; and he showed me the spot where to find it."[1] The end of the world he believed was at hand; by which he meant, perhaps, only the world of heathenism and unbelief. In his letter to the sovereigns he said that "it was clearly predicted concerning these lands by the mouth of the prophet Isaiah in many places in Scripture, that from Spain the holy name of God was to be spread abroad." Amazing and even fantastic as his conclusions were when they came from the religious side of his nature, they were to him irrefragable, because they were so severely logical. He was the chosen instrument of the divine purpose, because it was to him that the way had been made straight and plain to the glorious East, where God had planted in the beginning the earthly Paradise, in which he had placed man, where man had first sinned, and where ere long was to break the promised dawn of the new heaven and the new earth.

The northern continent of the New World was discovered by the Cabots a year before the southern mainland was reached by Columbus. Possibly this northern voyage may have suggested to the geographers of England

---

[1] The very name he bore had a divine significance, according to the fanciful interpretation of his son, Don Ferdinand Colon. For as the name Christopher, or Christophorus, — the Christ-bearer, — was bestowed upon the Saint who carried the Christ over deep waters at his own great peril, so had it fallen upon him, who was destined to discover a new world, "that those Indian nations might become citizens and inhabitants of the Church triumphant in heaven." Nor less appropriate was the family name of Columbus, or Colomba, — a dove, — for him who showed "those people, who knew him not, which was God's beloved Son, as the Holy Ghost did in the figure of a dove at Saint John's baptism; and because he also carried the olive-branch and oil of baptism over the waters of the ocean like Noah's dove, to denote the peace and union of these people with the Church, after they had been shut up in the ark of darkness and confusion." Saint Christopher carrying Christ, appears as a vignette on Cosa's chart.

a new theory, as yet, so far as we know, not thought of in Spain and Portugal, — that a hemisphere was to be circumnavigated, and a passage found
among thousands of leagues of islands, or else through some great continent hitherto unknown, — except to a few forgotten Northmen of five
hundred years earlier, — before India could be reached by sailing westward.
In speaking of this voyage long afterward, Sebastian Cabot said: "I began
to saile toward the northwest, not thinking to find any other land than that
of Cathay, and from thence turne toward India; but after certaine dayes
I found that the land ranne towards the North, which was to mee a great
displeasure."[1] This may have been the afterthought of his old age, when
the belief that the new Indies were the outlying boundaries of the old was
generally discarded. He had forgotten, as the same narrative shows, —
unless the year be a misprint, — the exact date of that voyage, saying that
it "was, as farre as I remember, in the yeare 1496, in the beginning of
Summer." This was a year too soon. But if the statement be accepted as
literally true that he was disappointed in finding, not Cathay and India,
as he had hoped, but another land, then not only the honor of the discovery of the western continent belongs to his father and to him, — or
rather to the father alone, for the son was still a boy, — but the further
distinction of knowing what they had discovered; while Columbus never
awoke from the delusion that he had touched the confines of India.

A discussion of the several interesting questions relating to the voyages
of the Cabots belongs to another chapter;[2] but assuming here that the
voyage of the "Mathew" from Bristol, England, in the summer of 1497,
is beyond controversy, the precedence of the Cabots over Columbus in the
discovery of the continent may be taken for granted. There is other
ample evidence besides his curious letters to show that the latter was on
the coast of South America in the summer of 1498, just thirteen months
and one week after the Cabots made the *terra primum visa*, whether on the
coast of Nova Scotia, Labrador, or possibly Newfoundland.[3] Not that this
detracts in any degree, however slight, from the great name of Columbus
as the discoverer of the New World. Of him Sebastian Cabot was mindful
to say, in conversation with the Pope's envoy in Spain, — just quoted from
in the preceding paragraph, — that "when newes were brought that Don
Christopher Colonus, Genoese, had discovered the coasts of India, whereof
was great talke in all the Court of King Henry the 7, who then raigned,
insomuch that all men with great admiration affirmed it to be a thing more
divine than humane to saile by the West into the Easte, where spices
growe, by a map that was never knowen before, — by this fame and report
there increased in my heart a great flame of desire to attempt some notable

---

[1] *A Discourse of Sebastian Cabot touching his
Discovery, etc.* Translated from Ramusio (1550)
by Hakluyt for his *Principal Navigations, Voyages, and Discoveries of the English Nation*, 1589,
and in later editions.

[2] [See Vol. III. chap. i. — ED.]
[3] For the distinction which possibly Cabot
meant to convey between *terra* and *insula*, see
Biddle's *Memoir of Sebastian Cabot* (London
1831), p. 54.

thing." However notable the thing might be, it could be only secondary to that achievement of Columbus which Cabot looked upon as "more divine than human;" but whether in the first sight of the mainland which all hoped to find beyond the islands already visited, Vespucci did not take precedence both of the Cabots and of Columbus, has been a disputed question for nearly four hundred years; and it will probably never be considered as satisfactorily settled, should it continue in dispute for four hundred years longer.

The question is, whether Vespucci made four voyages to that half of the world which was ever after to bear his name,[1] and whether those voyages were really made at the time it is said they were. The most essential point, however, is that of the date of the first voyage: for if that which is asserted to be the true date be correct, the first discoverer of the western continent was neither the Cabots nor Columbus, but Vespucci; and his name was properly enough bestowed upon it. "In the year 1497," says an ancient and authentic Bristol manuscript,[2] "the 24th June, on St. John's day, was Newfoundland found by Bristol men [the Cabots] in a ship called the 'Mathew.'" On his third voyage, in 1498, Columbus says: "We saw land [Trinidad] at noon of Tuesday the 31st of July." In a letter, written no doubt by Vespucci, he says: "We sailed from the port of Cadiz on the 10th of May, 1497;"[3] and after leaving the Canaries, where the four ships of the expedition remained a few days to take in their final supplies of wood, water, and provisions, they came, he continues, "at the end of twenty-seven days, upon a coast which we thought to be that of a continent." Of these dates the first two mentioned are unquestionably authentic. If that last given were equally so, there would be an end of all controversy upon the subject; for it would prove that Vespucci's discovery of the continent preceded that of the Cabots, though only by a week or two, while it must have been earlier than that of Columbus by about fourteen months.

It should first of all be noted that the sole authority for a voyage made by Vespucci in 1497 is Vespucci himself. All contemporary history, other than his own letters, is absolutely silent in regard to such a voyage, whether it be history in printed books, or in the archives of those kingdoms of Europe where the precious documents touching the earlier expeditions to the New World were deposited. Santarem, in his *Researches*, goes even farther than this; for he declares that even the name of Vespucci is not to be found in the Royal Archives of Portugal, covering the period from 1495 to 1503, and including more than a hundred thousand documents relating to voyages of discovery; that he is not mentioned in the Diplo-

[1] Humboldt (*Examen critique*, vol. iv.), supported by the authority of Professor Von der Hugen, of the University of Berlin, shows that the Italian name Amerigo is derived from the German Amalrich or Amelrich, which, under the various forms of Amalric, Amalrih, Amilrich, Amulrich, was spread through Europe by the Goths and other Northern invaders.

[2] [See Vol. III. p. 53. — ED.]

[3] On the 20th of May, according to one edition of the letter, — that published by Hylacomylus at St-Dié.

matic Records of Portugal, which treat of the relations of that kingdom with Spain and Italy, when one of the duties of ambassadors was to keep their Governments advised of all new discoveries; and that among the many valuable manuscripts belonging to the Royal Library at Paris, he, M. Santarem, sought in vain for any allusion to Vespucci. But these assertions have little influence over those who do not agree with Santarem that Vespucci was an impostor. The evidence is overwhelming that he belonged to some of the expeditions sent out at that period to the south-west; and if he was so obscure as not to be recognized in any contemporary notices of those voyages, then it could be maintained with some plausibility that he might have made an earlier voyage about which nothing was known. And this would seem the more probable when it was remembered that the time (1497) of this alleged expedition was within that interval when "the very tailors," as Columbus said, might go, without let or hindrance, in search of riches and renown in the new-found world. Many, no doubt, took advantage of this freedom of navigation whose names and exploits are quite unknown to history.

Nevertheless, the fact of the obscurity of Vespucci at that period is not without great weight, though Santarem fails in his attempt to prove too much by it. Columbus believed when, on his second voyage, he coasted the southern shore of Cuba, that he had touched the continent of Asia. The extension of that continent he supposed, from indications given by the natives, and accepted by him as confirming a foregone conclusion, would be found farther south; and for that reason he took that course on his third voyage. "The land where the spices grow" was now the aim of all Spanish energy and enterprise; and it is not likely that this theory of the Admiral was not

AUTOGRAPH OF VESPUCIUS, 1508.[1]

well understood among the merchants and navigators who took an intelligent as well as an intense interest in all that he had done and in all that he said. Is it probable, then, that nobody should know of the sailing of four ships from Cadiz for farther and more important discoveries in the direc-

[1] [This is the conclusion of a letter of Vespucius, printed and given in fac-simile in the *Cartas de Indias*. — ED.]

VESPUCIUS.[1]

†tion pointed out by Columbus? Or, if their departure was secret, can there be a rational doubt that the return, with intelligence so important

[1] [After a picture in the Massachusetts Historical Society's Gallery (no. 253), which is a copy of the best-known portrait of Vespucius. It is claimed for it that it was painted from life by Bronzino, and that it had been preserved in the family of Vespucius till it was committed, in 1845, to Charles Edwards Lester, United States consul at Genoa. It is engraved in Lester and Foster's *Life and Voyages of Americus Vespucius* (New York, 1846), and described on p. 414 of that book. Cf. also Sparks's statement in *Mass. Hist. Soc. Proc.*, iv. 117. It has been also engraved in Canovai among the Italian authorities, and was first, I think, in this country, produced in Philadelphia, in 1815, in Delaplaine's *Repository of the Lives and Portraits of distinguished American characters*, and later in various other places. The likeness of Vespucius in the Royal

and generally interesting, would have been talked about in all the ports of Spain, and the man who brought it have become instantly famous?

But as no account of the voyage appeared till years afterward, and then in a letter from Vespucci himself; and as, meanwhile, for most of those years the absence of his name from contemporary records shows that no celebrity whatever was attached to it, — the logical conclusion is, not only that the voyage was unknown, but that it was unknown because it was never made. Moreover, if it was ever made it could not have been unknown, if we may trust Vespucci's own statement. For in his letter — not written till 1504, and not published in full till 1507 — he said that this expedition was sent out by order of King Ferdinand; that he, Vespucci, went upon it by royal command; and that after his return he made a report of it to the King. The expedition, therefore, was clearly not one of those which, in the interval between the summers of 1495 and 1497, so often referred to, escaped all public record; and as there cannot be found any recognition of such an enterprise at that date either in contemporaneous history or State documents, what other conclusion can be accepted as rational and without prejudice, than that no such voyage so commanded was made at that time?

VESPUCIUS.[1]

There seems to be no escape from this evidence, though it is so purely negative and circumstantial. But Humboldt, relying upon the researches

Gallery at Naples, painted by Parmigianino, is supposed to be the one originally in the possession of the Cardinal Alexander Farnese (*Bulletin de la Société de Géographie de Paris*, iii. 370, by Jomard). That artist was but eleven years old at the death of Vespucius, and could not have painted Vespucius from life. A copy in 1853 was placed in the gallery of the American Antiquarian Society (*Proceedings*, April, 1853, p. 15; Paine's *Portraits and Busts*, etc., no. 28). C. W. Peale's copy of the likeness in the gallery of the Grand Duke of Tuscany is in the collection belonging to the Pennsylvania Historical Society (*Catalogue*, 1872, no. 148). There is also a portrait in the gallery of the New York Historical Society (*Catalogue*, no. 131), but the origin of it is not named. De Bry gives vignette portraits in parts iv., vi., and xii. of his *Grands Voyages*. See Bandini's *Vita e lettere di Vespucci*, chap. vii. for an account of the various likenesses. — ED.]

[1] [A sketch of an old engraving as given in the *Allgem. geog. Ephemeriden* (Weimar, 1807), vol. xxiii. There are other engravings of it in Jules Verne's *Découverte de la terre*, and elsewhere. — ED.]

VESPUCIUS.[1]

of the Spanish historian Muñoz, and upon those gathered by Navarrete
in his *Coleccion de los viages y descubrimientos*, presents the proof of an *alibi*

1 [A fac-simile of the engraving in *Montanus*, copied in *Ogilby*, p. 60. — Ed.]

for Vespucci. As has been already said on a previous page, the fact is unquestioned that Vespucci, who had been a resident of Spain for some time, became in 1495 a member of the commercial house of Juanoto Berardi, at Seville, and that in January of the next year, as the public accounts show, he was paid a sum of money relative to a contract with Government which Berardi did not live to complete. The presumption is that he would not soon absent himself from his post of duty, where new and onerous responsibilities had been imposed upon him by the recent death of the senior partner of the house with which he was connected. But at any rate he is found there in the spring of 1497, Muñoz having ascertained that fact from the official records of expenses incurred in fitting out the ships for western expeditions, still preserved at Seville. Those records show that from the middle of April, 1497, to the end of May, 1498, Vespucci was busily engaged at Seville and San Lucar in the equipment of the fleet with which Columbus sailed on his third voyage. The *alibi*, therefore, is complete. Vespucci could not have been absent from Spain from May, 1497, to October, 1498, — the period of his alleged first voyage.

All this seems incontrovertible, and should be accepted as conclusive till fresh researches among the archives of that age shall show, if that be possible, that those hitherto made have been either misunderstood or are incomplete. Assuming the negative to be proved, then, as to the alleged date of Vespucci's first voyage, the positive evidence, on the other hand, is ample and unquestioned, that Columbus sailed from San Lucar on his third voyage on the 30th of May, 1498, and two months later reached the western continent about the Gulf of Paria.

Was Vespucci then a charlatan? Was he guilty of acts so base as a falsification of dates, and narratives of pretended voyages, that he might secure for himself the fame that belonged to another, — that other, moreover, being his friend? There are reasons for believing this to be quite true of him; and other reasons for not believing it at all. There is not, to begin with, a scrap of original manuscript of his bearing on this point known to exist; it is not even positively known in what tongue his letters were written; and anything, therefore, like absolute proof as to what he said he did or did not do, is clearly impossible. The case has to be tried upon circumstantial evidence and as one of moral probabilities; and the verdict must needs differ according to the varying intelligence and disposition of different juries.

He made, or he claimed to have made, — assuming the letters attributed to him to be his, — four voyages, of each of which he wrote a narrative. According to the dates given in these letters, he twice sailed from Spain by order of Ferdinand, — in May, 1497, and in May, 1499; and twice from Portugal, in the service of King Emanuel, — in May, 1501, and in May, 1503. He was absent, as we learn from the same letters, about seventeen months on the first voyage, about sixteen each on the second and third, and on the fourth eleven months. If he went to sea, then, for the first time in May,

1497, and the last voyage ended, as the narrative says, in June, 1504, the whole period of his seafaring life was eighty-four months, of which sixty were passed at sea, and twenty-four, at reasonable intervals, on shore. As the dates of departure and of return are carefully given, obviously the period from May, 1497, to June, 1504, must be allowed for the four expeditions. But here we come upon an insurmountable obstacle. If to the first voyage of 1497 the wrong date was given, — if, that is, the actual first voyage was that of 1499, which Vespucci calls his second, — then he could not have gone upon four expeditions. From May, 1499, to June, 1504, is a period of sixty months; and as the aggregate length he gives to the assumed four voyages is sixty months, they could not have been made in that time, as that would have compelled him to be at sea the whole five years, with no interval of return to Spain or Portugal to refit, — which is manifestly absurd.

The solution of the difficulty relied upon by Humboldt and others seems, therefore, insufficient; it is not explained by assuming that the date 1497 in the narrative of the first voyage was the careless blunder of the translator, copyist, or printer of Vespucci's original letter. It is not an error if there were four voyages; for as the date of the last one is undisputed, the date of 1497 for the first one must remain to give time enough for the whole. But that there were four voyages does not depend solely upon the date given to the first one. That there were four — " quatuor navigationes " — is asserted repeatedly by Vespucci in the different letters. In the relation of the first one, wherein is given this troublesome date which has so vexed the souls of scholars, he says at some length that as he had seen on these " twice two " voyages so many strange things, differing so much from the manners and customs of his own country, he had written a little book, not yet published, to be called " Four Expeditions, or Four Voyages," in which he had related, to the best of his ability, about all he had seen.[1] If, then, the date 1497 is to be explained away as the result of carelessness or accident, — even admitting that such an explanation would explain, — what is to be done with this passage? It cannot, like a single numeral — a 7 for a 9 — be attributed to chance; and it becomes necessary, therefore, to regard it as an interpolation contrived to sustain a clumsy falsification of date.

It has also been conjectured that two of the letters have been misapprehended; that Vespucci meant one as only a continuation of the other in a description of a single voyage, or if intended as two letters, they were meant to describe the same voyage. The early editors, it has been suggested, supposing that each letter described a separate voyage, forged or

[1] " Et quoniam in meis hisce bis geminis navigationibus, tam varia diversaque, ac tam a nostris rebus, et modis differentia perspexi, idcirco libellum quempiam, quem Quatuor diætas sive quatuor navigationes appello, conscribere paravi, conscripsique; in quo maiorem rerum a me visarum partem distincte satis juxta ingenioi mei tenuitatem collegi: verumtamen non adhuc publicavi." From the *Cosmographiæ introductio* of Hylacomylus (Martin Waldseemüller). St.-Dié, 1507. Repeated in essentially the same words in other editions of the letter.

changed the dates in accordance with that supposition. If there were no other objection to this theory, it is untenable if what has just been said be true. The duration of each voyage, the aggregate length of the whole, and the distinct and careful assertion that there were four of them, require that there should be one prior to that which Vespucci calls his second.

All this leads, according to our present knowledge of the facts, inevitably to this conclusion, — whether Vespucci himself wrote, or others wrote for him, these letters, their very consistency of dates and of circumstantial assertion show them to have been deliberately composed to establish a falsehood. For the researches of Muñoz and of Navarrete, as is said above, prove that Vespucci could not have sailed from Spain on his first voyage on the 10th or 20th of May, 1497; for from the middle of April of that year to the end of May, 1498, he was busily employed at Seville and San Lucar in fitting out the fleet for the third expedition of Columbus.

There is other evidence, negative indeed, but hardly less conclusive, that this assumed voyage of 1497 was never made. In 1512 Don Diego Columbus brought an action against the Crown of Spain to recover, as the heir of his father, Christopher Columbus, the government and a portion of the revenues of certain provinces on the continent of America. The defence was that those countries were not discovered by Columbus, and the claim, therefore, was not valid. It is not to be supposed that the Crown was negligent in the search for testimony to sustain its own cause, for nearly a hundred witnesses were examined. But no evidence was offered to prove that Vespucci — whose nephew was present at the trial — visited in 1497 the Terra Firma which the plaintiff maintained his father discovered in 1498. On the other hand, Alonzo de Ojeda, an eminent navigator, declared that he was sent on an expedition in 1499 to the coast of Paria next after it was discovered by the Admiral (Columbus); and that "in this voyage which this said witness made, he took with him Juan de la Cosa and Morigo Vespuche [Amerigo Vespucci] and other pilots."[1] When asked how he knew that Columbus had made the discovery at the time named, his reply was that he knew it because the Bishop Fonseca had supplied him with that map which the Admiral had sent home in his letter to the King and Queen. The act of the Bishop was a dishonorable one, and intended as an injury to Columbus; and to this purpose Ojeda further lent himself by stopping at Hispaniola on the return from his voyage, and by exciting there a revolt against the authority of the Admiral in that island. Perhaps the bitter animosity of those years had been buried in the grave of the great navigator, together with the chains which had hung always in his chamber as a memento of the royal ingratitude; but even in that case it is not likely that Ojeda would have lost such an opportunity to justify, in some degree,

[1] In the original: *En este viage que este dicho testigo hizo trujo consigo a Juan de la Cosa, piloto, e Morigo Vespuche, e otros pilotos.* The testimony of other pilots confirmed that of Ojeda. The records of this trial are preserved among the archives at Seville, and were examined by Muñoz, and also by Washington Irving in his studies for the *Life of Columbus.* See also *ante*, p. 88.

his own conduct by declaring, if he knew it to be so, that Columbus was not the first discoverer of the continent. It is of course possible, but it is certainly not probable, that he should not have heard from Vespucci that this was his second visit to the Gulf of Paria, if that were the fact, and that his first visit was a year before that of Columbus, whose chart Ojeda was using to direct his course through seas with which Vespucci was familiar. This reasonable reflection is dwelt upon by Humboldt, Irving, and others; and it comes with peculiar force to the careful reader of the letters of Vespucci, for he was never in the least inclined to hide his light under a bushel.

The originals of the letters, as has already been said, are not, so far as is known, in existence; it is even uncertain whether they were written in Latin, Italian, Spanish, or Portuguese. Nor has the book which Vespucci said he had prepared — "The Four Voyages" — ever been found; but Humboldt believed that the collected narrative first published at St.-Dié in 1507, in the *Cosmographiæ introductio* of Hylacomylus, was made up of extracts from that book. This St.-Dié edition was in Latin, translated, the editor says, from the French.[1] There is in the British Museum a rare work of four pages, published also in 1507, the author of which was Walter Lud. This Lud was the secretary of the Duke of Lorraine, a canon of the St.-Dié Cathedral, and the founder of the school or college, where he had set up a printing-press on which was printed the *Cosmographiæ introductio*. From this little book it is learned that the Vespucci letters were sent from Portugal to the Duke of Lorraine in French, and that they were translated into Latin by another canon of the St.-Dié Cathedral, one Jean Basin de Sandacourt, at the request of Lud.[2]

Vespucci's last two voyages were made, so his letters assert, in the service of the King of Portugal. The narrative of the first of these — the third of the four voyages — appeared at different times, at several places, and were addressed to more than one person, prior to the publication of the St.-Dié edition of all the letters addressed to René II., the Duke of Lorraine. This fact has added to the confusion and doubt; for each of these copies sent to different persons was a translation, presumably from some common original. One copy of them was addressed to Pietro Soderini, Gonfaloniere of Florence, whom Vespucci claimed as an old friend and school-fellow under the instruction of his uncle, Giorgi Antonio Vespucci; another was sent to Lorenzo di Pier Francesco de' Medici, — Vespucci's early employer, — both appearing prior to that addressed in the collected edition of St.-Dié addressed to the Duke of Lorraine. Of the earlier editions there was one published, according to Humboldt, in Latin, in 1504, at Augs-

---

[1] The title of this work is *Cosmographiæ introductio cum quibusdam geometriæ ac astronomiæ principiis ad eam rem necessariis. Insuper quatuor Americi Vespucii navigationes.* The name of the editor, Martinus Hylacomylus, is not given in the first edition, but appears in a later,

VOL. II. — 19.

published at Strasburg in 1509. [See *post*, p. 167. — ED.]

[2] See Major's *Henry the Navigator*, p. 383. The title of Lud's four-leaved book is *Speculi orbis succinctiss. sed neque pœnitenda neque inelegans declaratio et canon.*

burg and also at Paris; another in German, in 1505, at Strasburg, and in 1506 at Leipsic; and still another in Italian at Vicenza, in the collection called *Paesi novamente*, simultaneously with the St.-Dié edition of 1507. These in later years were followed by a number of other editions. While they agree as to general statement, they differ in many particulars, and especially in regard to dates. These, however, are often mere typographical blunders or errors of copyists, not unusual at that era, and always fruitful of controversy. But upon one point, it is to be observed, there is no difference among them; the voyage of 1501 — the first from Portugal — is always the third of the four voyages of Vespucci. This disposes, as Humboldt points out, of the charge that Vespucci waited till after the death of Columbus, in 1506, before he ventured to assert publicly that he had made two voyages by order of the King of Spain prior to entering the service of the King of Portugal.

To induce him to leave Spain and come to Portugal, Vespucci says, in the letter addressed to Pietro Soderini, that the King sent to him one Giuliano Bartholomeo del Giocondo, then a resident of Lisbon. Jocundus (the latinized pseudonym of Giocondo) is named as the translator of the Augsburg edition of 1504, addressed to Lorenzo de' Medici. This Jocundus, Humboldt thinks, was Giuliano Giocondo. But Major, in his *Henry the Navigator,* says that the translation was made, not by Giuliano Giocondo, but by his kinsman Giovanni Giocondo, of Verona. His authority for this statement is apparently Walter Lud's *Speculum.* Varnhagen thinks it possible that the work may have been done by one Mathias Ringman, — of whom more presently. Varnhagen says also, in another place, that the translator of the Italian version — published in the *Paesi novamente* at Vicenza in 1507 — unwittingly betrayed that he lied (*son mensonge*) when he said that he followed a Spanish copy; for while he failed to comprehend the use of the word Jocundus, he showed that it was before him in the Latin copy, as he rendered *Jocundus interpres* — Jocundus the translator — as *el iocondo interprete*, the agreeable translator. This is only one example of the confusion in which the subject is involved.

It was due, however, to the *Cosmographiæ introductio* of St.-Dié, in which the letters appeared as a sort of appendix, that the name of America, from Amerigo, was given to the western hemisphere. But how it happened that the *Quatuor navigationes* should have been first published in that little town in the Vosges mountains; and what the relation was between Vespucci and René II., the Duke of Lorraine, — are among the perplexing questions in regard to the letters that have been discussed at great length. Major finds in the fact, or assumed fact, that Fra Giovanno Giocondo was the translator of the narrative of the third voyage, the first published, in 1504, an important link in the chain of evidence by which he explains the St.-Dié puzzle. This Giocondo was about that time at Paris as the architect of the bridge of Notre Dame. A young student, Mathias Ringman, from Alsace, was also there at that period; and Major supposes he may have become acquainted with Giocondo, who inspired him with great admiration for Vespucci. It is certain, at any rate, that Ringman, whose literary pseudonym was Philesius Vogesina, — that is, Philesius of the Vosges, — on his return to his native province edited the Strasburg edition (1505) of Giocondo's translation, appending to it some verses written by himself in praise of Vespucci and his achievements.

In the rare book already referred to, the *Speculum* of Walter Lud, it is said of this Strasburg edition that "the booksellers carry about a certain epigram of our Philesius in a little book of Vespucci's translated from Italian into Latin by Giocondo, of Verona, the architect of Venice." Doubtless Ringman is here spoken of as "our Philesius," because he had become identified with Lud's college, where he was the professor of Latin. It seems almost certain, therefore, that the interest at St.-Dié in Vespucci's voyages was inspired by Ringman, whether his enthusiasm was first aroused by his friendship with Giocondo at Paris, or whether, as Varnhagen supposes, it was the result of a visit or two to Italy. The latter question is not of much moment, except as a speculation; and certainly it is not a straining of probabilities to doubt if Ringman would have taken for his Strasburg edition of 1505 the Giocondo translation, as Lud says he did, if he had himself translated, as Varnhagen supposes, the Augsburg edition of 1504.

Lud also asserts in the *Speculum* that the French copy of the *Quatuor navigationes* which was used at St.-Dié came from Portugal. Major supposes that Ringman's enthusiasm may have led to correspondence with Vespucci, who was in Portugal till 1505, and that he caused his letters to be put into French and sent to Ringman at his request. The narrative of the third voyage in its several editions must have already given some renown to Vespucci. Here were other narratives of other voyages by the same navigator. The clever and enterprising young professors, eager for the dissemination of knowledge, and not unmindful, possibly, of the credit of their college, brought out the letters as a part of the *Cosmographiæ introductio* by Hylacomylus — Martin Waldzeemüller — the teacher of geography, and the proof-reader to their new press. Their prince, René II., was known as a patron of learning; and it is more likely that they should have prefixed his name to the letters than that Vespucci should have done so. Their zeal undoubtedly was greater than their knowledge; for had they known more of the discoveries of the previous fifteen years they would have hesitated to give to the new continent the name of one who would be thereby raised thenceforth from comparative, though honorable, obscurity to dishonorable distinction. That Vespucci himself, however, was responsible for this there is no positive evidence; and were it not for the difficulty of explaining his constant insistence of the completion of four voyages, it might be possible to find some plausible explanation of the confusion of the St.-Dié book.

In that book are these words: " And the fourth part of the world having been discovered by Americus, it may be called Amerige; that is, the land of

Americus or America."[1] And again: "Now truly, as these regions are more widely explored, and another fourth part is discovered, by Americus Ves- putius, as may be learned from the following letters, I see no reason why it should not be justly called Amerigen, — that is, the land of Americus, or America, from Americus, its discoverer, a man of acute intellect; inasmuch as both Europe and Asia have chosen their names from the feminine form." [2]

It was discovered, less than half a century ago, through the diligent researches of Humboldt, that this professor of geography at St.-Dié, Hyla- comylus, was thus the inventor, so to speak, of this word America.   That it came at last to be received as the designation of the western continent was due, perhaps, very much to the absence of any suggestion of any other dis- tinctive name that seemed appropriate and was generally acceptable.   Rare as the little work, the *Cosmographiæ introductio*, now is, it was probably well known at the time of the publication of its several editions; as the central position of St.-Dié — between France, Germany, and Italy — gave to the book, as Humboldt thought, a wide circulation, impressing the word Amer- ica upon the learned world.   The name, however, came very slowly into use, appearing only occasionally in some book, till in 1522 it gained a more permanent place on a mappemonde in the *Geographia* of Ptolemy.   From that time it appeared frequently upon other maps, and by the middle of the century became generally recognized outside of Spain, at least, as the established continental name.   But the effect of its suggestion was more immediate upon the fame of Vespucci.   While the learned understood that the great captain of that time was Christopher Columbus, the name of Amerigo was often united with his as deserving of at least the second place, and sometimes even of the first.   The celebrity which Hylacomylus bestowed upon him was accepted for performance by those who were ignorant of the exact truth; and those who knew better did not give themselves the trouble to correct the error.

In each of Vespucci's voyages he probably held a subordinate posi- tion.   His place may sometimes have been that of a pilot,[3] or as the com- mander of a single ship, or attached to the fleet, as Herrera [4] says he was in Ojeda's expedition (1499), " as merchant, being skilful in cosmography and navigation."   Vespucci himself does not in so many words assert that he

[1] " *Et quarta orbis pars quam quis Americus invenit, Amerigen quasi Americi terram, sive Americam nuncupare licet.*"

[2] " *Nunc vero et hæc partes sunt latius lustratæ, et alia quarta Pars per Americum Vesputium, ut in sequentibus audietur, inventa est, quam non video cur quis iure vetet ab America inventore, sagacis ingenii viro, Amerigen quasi Americi ter- ram sive Americam dicendum, cum et Europa et Asia a mulieribus sua sortitæ sint nomina.*" *Hyla- comylus.*

[3] [Vespucci himself says that his mission was "per ajutare a discoprire."   An astronomer was an important officer of all these early expeditions. Isabella urged Columbus not to go without one on his second voyage; and in his narrative of his fourth voyage, Columbus contends that there is but one infallible method of making a ship's reckoning, that employed by astronomers. Cf. Humboldt, *Cosmos*, Eng. tr., ii. 671. — ED.]

[4] Herrera, — of whom Robertson says that " of all Spanish writers he furnishes the fullest and most authentic information upon American discoveries" — accuses Vespucci of " false- hoods" in pretending to have visited the Gulf of Paria before Columbus.

was in command of the expeditions upon which he sailed, while he occasionally alludes, though usually in terms of contempt, to those whose authority was above his own. Once he speaks of Columbus, and then almost parenthetically, as the discoverer merely of the Island of Hispaniola; but of other of his achievements, or of those of other eminent navigators, he has nothing to say. In reply to such criticisms of his letters it has been urged on his behalf that they were written for intimate friends, as familiar narratives of personal experiences, and not meant to be, in any broad sense, historical. But the deception was as absolute as if it had been deliberately contrived; and, whether intentional or not, was never by act or word corrected, though Vespucci lived for five years after the appearance of the letters from the St.-Dié press.

But whatever can be or may be said in extenuation of Vespucci, or however strong the reasons for supposing that for whatever was reprehensible in the matter he was innocent and the St.-Dié professors alone responsible, there nevertheless remains the one thing unexplained and inexplicable, — his own repeated assertion that he made four voyages. Humboldt supposes that the narrative of the first, so called, of these four voyages, beginning in May, 1497, was made up of that on which Vespucci certainly sailed with Ojeda, starting in May, 1499. The points of resemblance are so many and so striking as to seem not only conclusive, but to preclude any other theory. If this be true, then it follows that the narrative of the voyage of 1497 was simply a forgery, whosoever was responsible for it; and if a forgery, then Vespucci was not the discoverer of the western continent, and an historical renown was given to his name to which he was not entitled.

The second of the assumed four voyages Humboldt supposes to be the first voyage of Vincente Yañez Pinzon, — hesitating, however, between that and the voyage of Diego de Lepe: the former sailing with four ships in December, 1499, and returning in September, 1500; the latter with two ships, in January, 1500, and returning in June. Vespucci says that he had two ships; that he sailed in May, 1499, and returned in June or September of the next year. It is of the first voyage of 1497 that he says he had four ships. As on that assumed voyage there are many incidents identical with those related of Ojeda's voyage of 1499, so here there are strong points of resemblance between Vespucci's supposed second voyage and that of Pinzon. In both cases, however, there are irreconcilable differences, which Humboldt does not attempt to disguise; while at the same time they indicate either dishonesty on the part of Vespucci in his letters, or that those letters were tampered with by others, either ignorantly or with dishonest intent, to which Vespucci afterward tacitly assented.

It would be hypercritical to insist upon a strict adherence to the dates of the several voyages, and then to decide that the voyages were impossible because the dates are irreconcilable. The figures are sometimes obviously mere blunders; as, for example, the assertion in the St.-Dié edition that the second voyage was begun in May, 1489, when it had been already said that the first voyage was made in 1497. But there are statements of facts, nevertheless, which it is necessary to reconcile with dates; and when this is impossible, a doubt of truthfulness is so far justifiable. Thus in the relation of the second voyage Vespucci asserts, or is made to assert, that on the 23d of August, 1499, he saw while at sea a conjunction of Mars and the Moon. That phenomenon did occur at that time, as Humboldt learned from the Ephemeris; and if it was observed by Vespucci at sea, that could not have been upon a voyage with Pinzon, who did not sail till (December, 1499) four months after the conjunction of the planets. But here, moreover, arises another difficulty: Vespucci's second voyage, in which he observed this conjunction, could not have been made with Ojeda, and must have been made with Pinzon, if on other points the narrative be accepted; for it was upon that voyage that Vespucci says he sailed several degrees south of the equinoctial line to the mouth of the Amazon, — which Pinzon did do, and Ojeda did not. These and other similar discrepancies have led naturally to the suspicion that the incidents of more than one expedition were used, with more or less discrimination, but with little regard to chronology, for the composition of a plausible narrative of two voyages made in the service of Spain. One blunder, detected by Navarrete in this so-called second voyage, it is quite incredible that Vespucci could have committed; for according to the course pursued and the distance sailed, his ships would have been navigated over nearly three hundred leagues of dry land into the interior of the continent. No critical temerity is required to see in such a blunder the carelessness of a copyist or a compositor.

It was of the first voyage from Lisbon — the third of the *Quatuor navigationes* — that, as has been already said, a narrative was first published in a letter addressed to Lorenzo de' Medici. This was illustrated with diagrams of some of the constellations of the southern hemisphere; and the repute it gave to the writer led the way to his subsequent fame. What Vespucci's position was in the expedition is not known; but that it was still a subordinate one is evident from his own words, as he speaks of a commander, though only to find fault with him, and without giving his name. The object of the expedition was to discover the western passage to the Spice Islands of the East (Melcha, Melacca, Malaccha, according to the varying texts of different editions of the letter); and though the passage was not found, the voyage was, like Cabot's, one of the boldest and most important of the age. But it is also, of all Vespucci's voyages, real or assumed, that which has been most disputed. Navarrete, however, after a careful examination of all the evidence that touches the question, comes to the conclusion that such an expedition, on which Vespucci may have gone in some subordinate position, was really sent out in 1501 by the King of Portugal; and Humboldt concurs in this opinion.

The Terra de Vera Cruz, or Brazil, as it was afterward named, was visited successively for the first time, from January to April, 1500, by Pinzon, De Lepe, De Mendoza, and Cabral. But the expedition to which Vespucci was attached explored the coast from the fifth parallel of southern latitude, three degrees north of Cape St. Augustin, — first discovered and so named by Pinzon, — as far south, perhaps, as about the thirty-eighth parallel of latitude. They had sailed along the coast for about seven hundred leagues; and so beautiful was the country, so luxuriant its vegetation, so salubrious its climate, where men did not die till they were a hundred and fifty years old, that Vespucci was persuaded — as Columbus, only three years before, had said of the region drained by the Orinoco — that the earthly Paradise was not far off. Gold, the natives said, was abundant in the interior; but as the visitors found none, it was determined at last to continue the voyage in another direction, leaving behind them this coast, of what seemed to Vespucci a continent, along which they had sailed from the middle of August to the middle of February. Starting now on the 15th of February from the mainland, they steered southeast, till they reached, on the 3d of April, the fifty-second degree of latitude. They had sailed through stormy seas, driven by violent gales, running away from daylight into nights of fifteen hours in length, and encountering a severity of cold unknown in Southern Europe, and quite beyond their power of endurance. A new land at length was seen; but it only needed a few hours of observation of its dangerous, rocky, and ice-bound coast to satisfy them that it was a barren, uninhabited, and uninhabitable region. This, Varnhagen suggests most reasonably, was the Island of Georgia, rediscovered by Captain Cook nearly three centuries afterward.

The return to Lisbon was in September, 1502. By order of the King, Vespucci sailed again in May, 1503, from Lisbon on a second voyage, — the fourth of his *Quatuor navigationes*. The object, as before, was to find a western passage to the Moluccas; for it was the trade of India, not new discoveries in the western continent, upon which the mind of the King was bent. There were six ships in this new expedition; and it is generally agreed that as Gonzalo Coelho sailed from Lisbon in May, 1503, by order of Emanuel, in command of six ships, Vespucci probably held a subordinate position in that fleet. He does not name Coelho, but he refers to a superior officer as an obstinate and presumptuous man, who by his bad management wrecked the flag-ship. Vespucci may have been put in command of two of the ships by the King; with two, at any rate, he became separated, in the course of the voyage, from his commodore, and with them returned to Lisbon in June of the next year. The rest of the fleet Vespucci reported as lost through the pride and folly of the commander; and it was thus, he said, that God punished arrogance. But Vespucci either misunderstood the divine will or misjudged his commander, for the other ships soon after returned in safety.

The southernmost point reached by him on this voyage was the eighteenth degree of southern latitude. At this point, somewhere about Cape Frio, he built a fort, and left in it the crew of one of the two vessels which had been shipwrecked. The precise spot of this settlement is uncertain; but as it was planted by Vespucci, and as it was the first colony of Europeans in that part of the New World, there was an evident and just propriety in bestowing the derivative — America — of his name upon the country, which at first was known as "The Land of the True Cross," and afterward as "Brazil." The name of Brazil was retained when the wider application — America — was given to the whole continent.

Soon after his return from this, the last of the *Navigationes* of which he himself, so far as is known, gave any account, he went back, in 1505, to Spain. It is conjectured that he made other voyages; but whether he did or did not, no absolute evidence has ever been found.[1] We know almost nothing of him up to that time except what is told by himself. When he ceased writing of his own exploits, then also the exploits ceased so far as can be learned from contemporary authors, who hitherto also had been silent about him. In 1508 (March 22) Ferdinand of Spain appointed him pilot-major of the kingdom,[2] — an office of dignity and importance, which probably he retained till he died (Feb. 22, 1512). His fame was largely posthumous; but a hemisphere is his monument. If not among the greatest of the world's great men, he is among the happiest of those on whom good fortune has bestowed renown.

S. H. Gay

---

[1] [Varnhagen thinks there is reason to believe, from the letter of Vianello, that Vespucius made a voyage in 1505 to the northern coast of South America, when he tracked the shore from the point of departure on his second voyage as far as Darien; and he is further of the opinion, from passages in the letters of Francesco Corner, that Vespucius made still a final voyage with La Cosa to the coast of Darien (*Postface* in *Nouvelles recherches*, p. 56). Harrisse (*Bibl. Amer. Vet., Additions*, p. xxvii) gives reasons, from letters discovered by Rawdon Brown at Venice, for believing that Vespucius made a voyage in 1508. — Ed.]

[2] Cf. Navarrete, iii. 297, for the instructions of the King.

CRITICAL AND BIBLIOGRAPHICAL

NOTES ON VESPUCIUS

AND THE

NAMING OF AMERICA.

BY THE EDITOR.

WHILE Vespucius never once clearly affirms that he discovered the main, such an inference may be drawn from what he says. Peter Martyr gives no date at all for the voyage of Pinzon and Solis to the Honduras coast, which was later claimed by Oviedo and Gomara to have preceded that of Columbus to the main. Navarrete has pointed out the varied inconsistencies of the Vespucius narrative,[1] as well as the changes of the dates of the setting out and the return, as given in the various editions.[2] All of them give a period of twenty-nine months for a voyage which Vespucius says only took eighteen, — a difficulty Canovai and others have tried to get over by changing the date of return to 1498; and some such change was necessary to enable Vespucius to be in Spain to start again with Ojeda in May, 1499. Humboldt further instances a great variety of obvious typographical errors in the publications of that day, — as, for instance, where Oviedo says Columbus made his first voyage in 1491.[3] But, as shown in the preceding narrative, an allowance for errors of the press is not sufficient. In regard to the proof of an *alibi* which Humboldt brought forward from documents said to have been collected by Muñoz from the archives of the Casa de la Contratacion, it is unfortunate that Muñoz himself did not complete that part of his work which was to pertain to Vespucius,

and that the documents as he collated them have not been published. In the absence of such textual demonstration, the inference which Humboldt drew from Navarrete's representations of those documents has been denied by Varnhagen; and H. H. Bancroft in his *Central America* (i. 99, 102, 106) does not deem the proof complete.[4]

Vespucius' own story for what he calls his second voyage (1499) is that he sailed from Cadiz shortly after the middle of May, 1499. The subsequent dates of his being on the coast are conflicting; but it would appear that he reached Spain on his return in June or September, 1500. We have, of course, his narrative of this voyage in the collective letter to Soderini;[5] but there is also an independent narrative, published by Bandini (p. 64) in 1745, said to have been written July 18, 1500, and printed from a manuscript preserved in the Riccardiana at Florence.[6] The testimony of Ojeda that Vespucius was his companion in the voyage of 1499–1500 seems to need the qualification that he was with him for a part, and not for the whole, of the voyage; and it has been advanced that Vespucius left Ojeda at Hispaniola, and, returning to Spain, sailed again with Pinzon in December, 1499, — thus attempting to account for the combination of events which seem to connect Vespucius with the voyages of both these navigators.

---

1 "Noticias exactas de Americo Vespucio," in his *Coleccion*, iii. 315. The narrative in English will be found in Lester's *Life of Vespucius*, pp. 112–139.

2 May 10, 20, 1497, and Oct. 1, 15, 18, 1499.

3 Cf. *Examen critique*, iv. 150, 151, 273–282; v. 111, 112, 197–202; *Cosmos*, Eng. tr., ii. 678.

4 Humboldt, *Examen critique*, iv. 50, 267, 268, 272; Harrisse, *Bibl. Amer. Vet.*, no. 57; Navarrete, iii. 317.

5 This part is given in English in Lester, p. 175.

6 It is translated in Lester, pp. 151–173; cf. Canovai, p. 50.

It is noteworthy that Oviedo, who sought to interpret Peter Martyr as showing that Solis and Pinzon had preceded Columbus to the main, makes no mention of Vespucius. There is no mention of him in what Beneventano furnished to the Ptolemy of 1508. Castanheda does not allude to him, nor does Barreiros in his *De Ophira regione* (Coimbra, 1560), nor Galvano in his *Descobrimientos*, nor Pedro Magalhaes de Gandavo in his account of Santa Cruz (1576).[1]

But it was not all forgetfulness as time went on. The currency to his fame which had been given by the *De orbe antarctica*, by the *Paesi novamente*, by the *Cosmographiæ introductio*, as well as by the *Mundus novus* and the publications which reflected these, was helped on in 1510 by the Roman archæologist Francesco Albertini in his *Opusculum de mirabilibus Urbis Romæ*, who finds Florence, and not Genoa, to have sent forth the discoverer of the New World.[2]

Two years later (1512) an edition of Pomponius Mela which Cocleus edited, probably at Nuremberg, contained, in a marginal note to a passage on the "Zona incognita," the following words : " Verus Americus Vesputius iam nostro seculo | novū illū mundū invenissefert Portugalie Castilieq. regū navibus," etc. Pighius in 1520 had spoken of the magnitude of the region discovered by Vespucius, which had gained it the appellation of a new world.[3] The references in Glareanus, Apian, Phrysius, and Münster show familiarity with his fame by the leading cosmographical writers of the time. Natale Conti, in his *Universæ historiæ sui temporis libri XXX* (1545–1581), brought him within the range of his memory.[4] In 1590 Myritius, in his *Opusculum geographicum*, the last dying flicker, as it was, of a belief in the Asian connection of the New World,[5] repeats the oft-told story, — "De Brasilia, terrâ ignis, de meridionali parte Africæ ab Alberico Vesputio inventa."

In the next century the story is still kept up by the Florentine, Francesco Bocchi, in his *Libri duo elogiorum* (1607),[6] and by another Florentine, Raffael Gualterotti, in a poem, *L' America* (1611),[7] — not to name many others.[8]

But all this fame was not unclouded, and it failed of reflection in some quarters at least. The contemporary Portuguese pilots and cosmographers give no record of Vespucius' eminence as a nautical geometrician. The Portuguese annalist Damião de Goes makes no mention of him. Neither Peter Martyr nor Benzoni allows him to have preceded Columbus. Sebastian Cabot, as early as 1515, questioned if any faith could be placed in the voyage of 1497 "which Americus says he made." It is well known that Las Casas more than intimated the chance of his being an impostor; nor do we deduce from the way that his countrymen, Guicciardini[9] and Segni, speak of him, that their faith in the prior claim in his behalf was stable.

An important contestant appeared in Herrera in 1601,[10] who openly charged Vespucius with falsifying his dates and changing the date of 1499 to 1497; Herrera probably followed Las Casas' manuscripts which he had.[11] The allegation fell in with the prevalent indignation that somebody, rather than a blind fortune, had deprived Columbus of the naming of the New World; and Herrera helped this belief by stating positively that the voyage of Pinzon and Solis, which had been depended upon to antedate Columbus, had taken place as late as 1506.

In the last century Angelo Maria Bandini attempted to stay this tide of reproach in the *Vita e lettere di Amerigo Vespucci, gentiluomo fiorentino*, which was printed at Florence in 1745.[12] It was too manifestly an unbounded panegyric to enlist the sympathy of scholars. More atten-

---

[1] These instances are cited by Santarem. Cf. Ternaux's *Collection*, vol. ii.

[2] Harrisse, *Bibl. Amer. Vet.*, no. 64; Humboldt, *Examen critique*, v. 209. There were other editions of Albertini in 1519 and 1520, as well as his *De Roma prisca* of 1523, repeating the credit of the first discovery in language which Muller says that Harrisse does not give correctly. Cf. *Bibl. Amer. Vet.*, nos. 96, 103, 106; *Additions*, 56, 74; Muller, *Books on America* (1872), no. 17.

[3] *Bibl. Amer. Vet.*, no. 107.

[4] Editions at Venice in 1572 and 1589 (Sabin, vol. iv. no. 16,161).

[5] Cf. Vol. IV. p. 96.

[6] Sabin, vol. ii. no. 6,102.

[7] Carter-Brown, ii. 114. It was reprinted at Florence in 1859, and at Milan in 1865.

[8] Santarem enumerates various others; cf. Childe's translation, p. 34 etc. Bandini (*Vita e lettere di Vespucci*, cap. vii.) also enumerates the early references.

[9] Though Guicciardini died in 1540, his *Historia d' Italia* (1494–1532) did not appear at Florence till 1564, and again at Venice in 1580. Segni, who told the history of Florence from 1527 to 1555, and died in 1559, was also late in appearing.

[10] Dec. i. lib. iv. cap. 2 ; lib. vii. c. 5.

[11] Robertson based his disbelief largely upon Herrera (*History of America*, note xxii.).

[12] Carter-Brown, vol. iii. no. 793; Murphy, no. 142; Leclerc, no. 2,473. There was a German translation in 1748 (Carter-Brown, iii. 866; Sabin, vol. i. no. 3,150), with annotations, which gave occasion to a paper by Caleb Cushing in the *North American Review*, xii. 318.

tion was aroused[1] by an address, with equal adulation, which Stanislao Canovai delivered to the Academy at Cortona in 1788, and which was printed at once as *Elogio di Amerigo Vespucci*, and various times afterward, with more or less change, till it appeared to revive anew the antagonism of scholars, in 1817.[2] Muñoz had promised to disclose the impostures of Vespucius, but his uncompleted task fell to Santarem, who found a sympathizer in Navarrete; and Santarem's labored depreciation of Vespucius first appeared in Navarrete's *Coleccion*,[3] where Canovai's arguments are examined at length, with studied refutations of some points hardly worth the labor. This paper was later expanded, as explained in another place.

He claims that one hundred thousand documents in the Royal Archives of Portugal, and the register of maps which belonged to King Emmanuel, make no mention of Vespucius,[4] and that there is no register of the letters-patent which Vespucius claimed to have received. Nor is there any mention in several hundred other contemporary manuscripts preserved in the great library at Paris, and in other collections, which Santarem says he has examined.[5]

An admirer of Vespucius, and the most prominent advocate of a belief in the disputed voyage of 1497, is Francisco Adolpho de Varnhagen, the Baron de Porto Seguro. As early as 1839, in notes to his *Diario* of Lopez de Souza, he began a long series of publications in order to counteract the depreciation of Vespucius by Ayres de Cazal, Navarrete, and Santarem. In 1854, in his *Historia geral do Brazil*, he had combated Humboldt's opinion that it was Pinzon with whom Vespucius had sailed on his second voyage, and had contended for Ojeda. Varnhagen not only accepts the statements of the St.-Dié publications regarding that voyage, but undertakes to track the explorer's course. In his *Amerigo Vespucci, son caractère*, etc., he gives a map marking the various voyages of the Florentine.[6] For the voyage of 1497 he makes him strike a little south of west from the Canaries; but leaving his course a blank from the mid-Atlantic, he resumes it at Cape Gracias a Dios on the point of Honduras,[7] and follows it by the coast thence to the Chesapeake, when he passes by Bermuda,[8] and reaches Seville. In this he departs from all previous theories of the landfall, which had placed the contact on the coast of Paria. He takes a view of the Ruysch map[9] of 1508 different from that of any other commentator, in holding the smaller land terminated with a scroll to be not Cuba, but a part of the main westerly, visited by Vespucius in this 1497 voyage; and recently Harrisse, in his *Cortereal*,[10] argues that the descriptions of Vespucius in this disputed voyage

---

[1] Santarem reviews this literary warfare of 1788–1789 (Childe's translation, p. 140).

[2] Sabin (*Dictionary*, iii. 312) gives the following contributions of Canovai: (1) *Difensa d' Amerigo Vespuccio*, Florence, 1796 (15 pp). (2) *Dissertazione sopra il primo viaggio d' Amerigo Vespucci alle Indie occidentali*, Florence, 1809. (3) *Elogio d' Amerigo Vespucci . . . con una dissertazione giustificativa*, Florence, 1788; con illustrazioni ed aggiunte [Cortona], 1789; no place, 1790, Florence, 1798. (4) *Esame critico del primo viaggio d' Amerigo Vespucci al nuovo mondo*, Florence, 1811. Cf. Il Marquis Gino Capponi, *Osservazioni sull' esame critico del primo viaggio d' Amerigo Vespucci al nuovo mondo*, Florence, 1811. Leclerc, no. 400; copy in Harvard College Library. (5) *Lettera allo Stampat. Sig. P. Allegrini a nome dell' autore dell' elogio prem. di Am. Vespucci*, Florence, 1789. (6) *Monumenti relativi al giudizio pronunziato dall' Accademia Etrusca di Cortona di un Elogio d' Amerigo Vespucci*, Florence, 1787. (7) *Viaggi d' Amerigo Vespucci con la vita, l' elogio e la dissertazione giustificativa*, Florence, 1817; again, 1832. There was an English version of the *Elogio* printed at New Haven in 1852. Canovai rejects some documents which Bandini accepted; as, for instance, the letter in Da Gama, of which there is a version in Lester, p. 313. Cf. also Varnhagen, *Amerigo Vespucci*, pp. 67, 69, where it is reprinted.

[3] Irving got his cue from this, and calls the voyage of 1497 pure invention. The documents which Navarrete gives are epitomized in Lester, p. 395, and reprinted in Varnhagen's *Nouvelles recherches*, p. 26.

[4] Childe's translation, p. 24.

[5] Childe's translation, pp. 65, 66.

[6] There is another laying down of his course in a map published with a volume not seldom quoted in the present work, and which may be well described here: *Studi biografici e bibliografici sulla storia della geografia in Italia publicati in occasione del III° Congresso Geografico Internazionale, Edizione seconda*, Rome, 1882. Vol. i. contains *Biografia dei viaggiatori Italiani, colla bibliografia delle loro opere per Pietro Amat di San Filippo*. The special title of vol. ii. is *Mappamondi, carte nautiche, portolani ed altri monumenti cartografici specialmente Italiani dei secoli XIII–XVII, per Gustavo Uzielli e Pietro Amat di San Filippo*.

[7] He gives his reasons for this landfall in his *Le premier voyage*, p. 5.

[8] We have no positive notice of Bermuda being seen earlier than the record of the Peter Martyr map of 1511.

[9] See Vol. III. p. 8, and the present volume, p. 115.

[10] Where (p. 106) he announced his intention to discuss at some future time the voyages of Vespucius, and to bring forward, "selon notre habitude," some new documentary evidence. He has since given the proposed title: *Americ Vespuce, sa Correspondance, 1483–1491; soixante-huit lettres inédites tirées du portefeuille des Médicis*, with annotations.

correspond more nearly with the Cantino map [1] than with any other. Harrisse also asks if Waldseemüller did not have such a map as Cantino's before him; and if the map of Vespucius, which Peter Martyr says Fonseca had, may not have been the same?

Varnhagen, as might be expected in such an advocate, turns every undated incident in Vespucius' favor if he can. He believes that the white-bearded men who the natives said preceded the Spaniards were Vespucius and his companions. A letter of Vianello, dated Dec. 28, 1506, which Humboldt quotes as mentioning an early voyage in which La Cosa took part, but hesitates to assign to any particular year, Varnhagen eagerly makes applicable to the voyage of 1497.[2] The records of the Casa de la Contratacion which seem to be an impediment to a belief in the voyage, he makes to have reference, not to the ships of Columbus, but to those of Vespucius' own command. Varnhagen's efforts to elucidate the career of Vespucius have been eager, if not in all respects conclusive.[3]

We get upon much firmer ground when we come to the consideration of the voyage of 1501, — the first for Portugal, and the third of Vespucius' so-called four voyages. It seems clear that this voyage was ordered by the Portuguese Government to follow up the chance discovery of the Brazil coast by Cabral in 1500, of which that navigator had sent word back by a messenger vessel. When the new exploring fleet sailed is a matter of uncertainty, for the accounts differ, — the Dutch edition of the account putting it as early as May 1, 1501, while one account places it as late as June 10.[4] When the fleet reached the Cape de Verde Islands, it found there Cabral's vessels on the return voyage; and what Vespucius here learned from Cabral he embodied in a letter, dated June 4, 1501, which is printed by Baldelli in his *Il Milione di Marco Polo*, from a manuscript preserved in the Riccardiana Collection.[5] Some time in August — for the exact day is in dispute — he struck the coast of South America, and coursed southward, — returning to Lisbon Sept. 7, 1502.[6]

Vespucius now wrote an account of it, addressed to Lorenzo Piero Francesco de Medici,[7] in which he proposed a designation of the new regions, "novum mundum appellare licet." Such is the Latin phraseology, for the original Italian text is lost.[8] Within the next two years numer-

---

[1] See p. 108.

[2] This Vianello document was printed by Ferraro in his *Relazione* in 1875.

[3] His publications on the subject of Vespucius are as follows: (1) *Vespuce et son premier voyage, ou notice d'une découverte et exploration du Golfe du Méxique et des côtes des États-Unis en 1497 et 1498, avec le texte de trois notes de la main de Colomb*, Paris, 1858. This had originally appeared from the same type in *Bulletin de la Société de Géographie de Paris*, January and February, 1858; and a summary of it in English will be found in the *Historical Magazine*, iv. 98, together with a letter from Varnhagen to Buckingham Smith. (2) *Examen de quelques points de l'Histoire géographique du Brésil, — second voyage de Vespuce*, Paris, 1858. (3) *Amerigo Vespucci, son caractère, ses écrits, sa vie, et ses navigations*, Lima, 1865. (4) *Le premier voyage de Amerigo Vespucci définitivement expliqué dans ses détails*, Vienna, 1869. (5) *Nouvelles recherches sur les derniers voyages du navigateur florentin, et le reste des documents et éclaircissements sur lui*, Vienna, 1869. (6) *Postface auxtrois livraisons sur Amerigo Vespucci* Vienna, 1870. This is also given as pages 55–57 of the *Nouvelles recherches*, though it is not included in its contents table. (7) *Ainda Amerigo Vespucci, novos estudos e achegas, especialmente em favor da interpretação dada à sua 1ª viagem, em 1497–1498, ás Costas do Yucatan*, Vienna, 1874, eight pages, with fac-similes of part of Ruysch's map. Cf. *Cat. Hist. Brazil, Bibl. nac. do R. de Janeiro*, no. 839. (8) *Cartas de Amerigo Vespucci*, in the *Rev. do Inst. Hist.*, i. 5.

[4] Cf. Harrisse, *Bibl. Amer. Vet.*, p. 61.

[5] It is reprinted in Varnhagen, *Amerigo Vespucci*, p. 78. The manuscript is not in Vespucius' hand (*Bulletin de la Société de Géographie de Paris*, April, 1858). Varnhagen is not satisfied of its genuineness.

[6] Cf. Humboldt, *Examen critique*, v. 1, 34; Major, *Prince Henry*, p. 375; Navarrete, iii. 46, 262; Ramusio, i. 139; Grynæus, p. 122; Galvano, p. 98. Santarem, in his iconoclastic spirit, will not allow that Vespucius went on this voyage, or on that with Coelho in 1503, — holding that the one with Ojeda and La Cosa is the only indisputable voyage which Vespucius made (Childe's translation, p. 145), though, as Navarrete also admits, he may have been on these or other voyages in a subordinate capacity. Santarem cites Lafitau, Barras, and Osorius as ignoring any such voyage by Vespucius. Vespucius says he could still see the Great Bear constellation when at 32° south; but Humboldt points out that it is not visible beyond 26° south latitude.

[7] This was a cousin of Lorenzo the Magnificent; he was born in 1463, and died in 1503. Cf. Ranke's letter in Humboldt's *Examen critique*, and translated in Lester's *Life and Voyages of Vespucius*, p. 401. Varnhagen has an "Étude bibliographique" on this 1503 letter in his *Amerigo Vespucci, son caractère*, etc., p. 9.

[8] Varnhagen is confident (*Postface* in *Nouvelles recherches*, p. 56) that Vespucius was aware that he had found a new continent, and thought it no longer Asia, and that the letter of Vespucius, on which Humboldt based the statement of Vespucius' dying in the belief that only Asia had been found, is a forgery.

ous issues of Giocondo's Latin text were printed, only two of which are dated, — one at Augsburg in 1504, the other at Strasburg in 1505; and, with a few exceptions, they all, by their published title, gave currency to the designation of *Mundus novus*. The earliest of these editions is usually thought to be one *Alberic' vespucci' laurē-tio petri francisci de medicis Salutem plurimā dicit*, of which a fac-simile of the title is annexed, and which bears the imprint of Jehan Lambert.[1] It is a small plaquette of six leaves; and there are copies in the Lenox and Carter-Brown collections. D'Avezac, and Harrisse, in his later opinion (*Additions*, p. 19), agree in supposing this the first edition. The dated (1504) Augsburg edition, *Mundus novus*, is called "extraordinarily rare" by Grenville, who had a copy, now in the British Museum. On the reverse of the fourth and last leaf we read : " Magister Jo-hānes otmar : vindelice impressit Auguste An-no millesimo quingentesimo quarto." There are copies in the Lenox and Carter-Brown libraries.[2] An edition, *Mundus novus*, whose four unnumbered leaves, forty lines to the full page, correspond wholly with this last issue, except that for the dated colophon the words LAUS DEO are substituted, was put at first by Harrisse[3] at the head of the list, with this title.

There is a copy in the Lenox Library, which has another issue, *Mundus novus*, also in black-letter, forty-two lines to the page;[4] still another, *Mundus novus*, forty lines to the page;[5]

and another, with the words *Mundus novus* in Roman, of eight leaves, thirty lines to the page.[6] At this point in his enumeration Harrisse placed originally the Jehan Lambert issue (mentioned

---

1 *Bibl. Amer. Vet.*, no. 26 ; D'Avezac, *Waltzemüller*, p. 74 ; Carter-Brown, i. 26 ; Sunderland, vol. v. no. 12,919 ; Brunet, vol. v. col. 1,155 ; *Bibliotheca Grenvilliana*, p. 766.

2 *Bibl. Amer. Vet.*, no. 31 ; Carter-Brown, i. 21 ; Ternaux, no. 6 ; *Bibliotheca Grenvilliana*, p. 766 ; Brunet, vol. v. col. 1,154 ; Huth, p. 1525. A copy was sold in the Hamilton sale (1884) for £47, and subsequently held by Quaritch at £55. The *Court Catalogue* (no. 369) shows a duplicate from the Munich Library. Harrassowitz, *Rarissima Americana* (91 in 1882), no. 1, priced a copy at 1,250 marks.

3 *Bibl. Amer. Vet.*, no. 22.

4 *Bibl. Amer. Vet.*, no. 23 ; Carter-Brown, i. 22 ; *Bibliotheca Grenvilliana*, p. 766 ; Court, no. 368 ; Quaritch (no. 321, title 12,489) held a copy at £100.

5 *Bibl. Amer. Vet.*, no. 24.

6 *Bibl. Amer. Vet.*, no. 25 ; *Bibliotheca Grenvilliana*, ii. 766 ; Huth, v. 1525.

above), and after it a *Mundus novus* printed in Paris by Denys Roce, of which only a fragment (five leaves) exists, sold in the Libri sale in London, 1865, and now in the British Museum.[1]

Another Paris edition, *Mundus novus*, printed by Gilles de Gourmont, eight leaves, thirty-one lines to the page, is, according to Harrisse,[2] known only in a copy in the Lenox Library; but D'Avezac refers to a copy in the National Library in Paris.[3]

Another *Mundus novus* is supposed by Harrisse to have been printed somewhere in the lower Rhineland, and to bear the mark of Wm. Vorsterman, of Antwerp, on the last leaf, merely to give it currency in the Netherlands. It has four leaves, and forty-four lines to the full page. There are copies in the Lenox and Harvard College libraries.[4] The *Serapeum* for January, 1861, describes a *Mundus novus* as preserved in the Mercantile Library at Hamburg, — a plaquette of four leaves, with

FIRST PAGE OF MUNDUS NOVUS.[5]

[1] *Bibl. Amer. Vet.*, no. 27.

[2] *Bibl. Amer. Vet.*, no. 28.

[3] Cf. also Libri (*Catalogue* of 1859); Brunet, vol. v. col. 1,155; Harrisse, *Notes on Columbus*, p. 30. " La petite édition de la lettre de Vespuce à Médicis sur son troisième voyage, imprimée à Paris chez Gilles de Gourmont, vendue à Londres en 1859 au prix de £32 10s., et placée dans la riche collection de M. James Lenox de New York, n'existe plus dans le volume à la fin duquel elle était reliée à la Bibliothèque Mazarine." D'Avezac: *Waltzemüller*, p. 5.

[4] *Bibl. Amer. Vet.*, no. 29; Huth, v. 1525; Humboldt, *Examen critique*, v. 7, describing a copy in the Göttingen Library; *Bibliophile Belge*, v. 302.

[5] Harrisse, no. 29. Cf. Navarrete, *Opúsculos* i. 99.

forty-five lines to the page, — which seems to differ from all others.[1] Later, in his *Additions* (1872), Harrisse described other issues of the *Novus mundus* which do not seem to be identical with those mentioned in his *Bibliotheca Americana Vetustissima.* One of these — *Mūdus novus*, printed in a very small gothic letter, four leaves — he found in the Biblioteca Cosatenense at Rome.[2] The other has for the leading title, *Epistola Albericii: de novo mundo*, — a plaquette of four leaves, forty-eight lines to the page, with map and woodcut.[3]

This letter of Vespucius was again issued at Strasburg in 1505, with the title *Be [De] ora antarctica*, as shown in the annexed fac-simile; and joined with this text, in the little six-leaved tract, was a letter of Philesius to Bruno, and some Latin verses by Philesius; and in this form we have it probably for the last time in that language.[4] This Philesius we shall encounter again later.

It was this Latin rendering by Giocondo, the architect, as Harrisse thinks,[5] upon which the Italian text of the *Paesi novamente* was founded. Varnhagen in his *Amerigo Vespucci, son caractère* (p. 13), prints side by side this Italian and the Latin text, marking different readings in the latter. In this same year (1505) the first German edition was issued at Nuremberg, though it is undated: *Von der new gefundē Region die wol*

ein welt genennt mag werden durch den cristenlichen Künig von Portugall wunnderbarlich erfunden.[6] The colophon shows that this German version was made from a copy of the Latin text

---

[1] *Bibl. Amer. Vet.*, no. 30; Carter-Brown, i. 23. A copy was (no. 233) in a sale at Sotheby's, London, Feb. 22, 1883. It seems probable that no. 14 of Harrisse's *Additions*, corresponding to copies in the Lenox, Trivulziana, and Marciana libraries, is identical with this.

[2] Harrisse, *Additions*, p. 12, where its first page is said to have thirty-three lines; but the *Court Catalogue* (no. 367), describing what seems to be the same, says it has forty-two lines, and suggests that it was printed at Cologne about 1503.

[3] *Additions*, p. 13, describing a copy in the British Museum. Varnhagen (*Amerigo Vespucci*, Lima, 1865, p. 9) describes another copy which he had seen.

[4] *Bibl. Amer. Vet.*, no. 39; Carter-Brown, vol. i. no. 24; Brunet, vol. v. col. 1,155; Court, no. 370; Huth, v. 1526; D'Avezac, *Waltzemüller*, p. 91. Tross, of Paris, in 1872, issued a vellum fac-simile reprint in ten copies. Murphy, no. 2,615; Court, no. 371.

[5] *Bibl. Amer. Vet.*, *Additions*, p. 36.

[6] This title is followed on the same page by a large cut of the King of Portugal with sceptre and shield. The little plaquette has six folios, small quarto (*Bibl. Amer. Vet.*, no. 33). A fac-simile edition was made by Pilinski at Paris (twenty-five copies), in 1861. Cf. Carter-Brown, vol. i. no. 25, with fac-simile of title; Murphy, no. 2,616; Huth, v. 1525; O'Callaghan, no. 2,328; Cooke, no. 2,519. There is a copy of this fac-simile, which brings about $5 or $6, in the Boston Public Library. Cf. also Panzer, *Annalen, Suppl.*, no. 561 *bis*, and Weller, *Repertorium*, no. 335.

Von der neü gefunden Region die wol
ein welt genent mag werden/durch den Cristenlichen künig
von portigal/wunderbarlich erfunden.

TITLE OF THE DRESDEN COPY.[1]

brought from Paris in May, 1505: *Ausz latein ist dist missiue in Teütsch gezogē ausz dem exemplar das von Parisz kam ym maien monet nach Christi geburt, Funfftzenhundert vnnd Fünffjar. Gedruckt vn Nüremburg durch Wolffgang Hueber.* The full page of this edition has thirty-seven lines.

Another edition, issued the same year (1505), shows a slight change in the title, *Von der neü*

gefunden Region so wol ein welt genempt mag werden, durch den Christelichen künig, von Portigal wunderbarlich erfunden. This is followed by the same cut of the King, and has a similar colophon. Its full page contains thirty-three lines.[2]

Still another edition of the same year and publisher shows thirty-five lines to the page, and above the same cut the title reads: *Von der neu*

1 This follows the fac-simile given in Ruge's *Geschichte des Zeitalters der Entdeckungen*, p. 333, of an edition in the Royal Library at Dresden.

2 There is a copy in the Carter-Brown Collection (*Catalogue*, vol. i. no. 586). It seems to be Harrisse's no. 37, where a copy in the British Museum is described.

Albericus Vespuccius Laurentio Petri

Francisci de medicis vil gruß.

In vergangen tagen hab ich dir eben weyt geschryben von
meiner widerfart von den neuen lantschafften die ich mit
Clasen versamneter schyffen mit schwerem kosten von ge
bot des durchleuchtigisten Künigs von portigal durchsucht ha
ben vnd funden/Die man mag die neuen welt nennen/So bey vn
sern vorfarn vettern dauon keyn wissen gewesen/vnd allen den die
solichs hörn aller ding ein neus sey/Sünder auch das alle meinüg
vnser eltern über trysst so doch der metteyl der selben spricht/das
vber die gleichmitnechtige lynien genant Equinoctialis/vnd ge
gen mittag keyn wonung der leutten/sunder alleyn das groß mer
inhalten/Das sy nennen das attlandisch mer/Vn ob yemand der
selben wonungen daselbs sein geredt so hab sy doch aus vil sach
das do wonhafftig land vn ertrich sey widerredt/Aber das solich
ir maynung falsch vnnd der warheit wider sey in alle weg hat diß
mein letzte schiffung beweist/So ich in den selben gegnunge gege
mittag menschliche inwonung finden hab mit vil volcks vnd vil
thieren bewert/dan vnser Europa oder Asiam oder Affricam/vn
so vil mer gefunden temperierten lufft schon vnd lauter mer vnnd
lustiger dan in eynicher andern lantschafft die wir wissen/Als dir
hernach sehen vnnd verstan würst/so ich kürtz die obern ding be
schryben vnd die ding so vermerckens vnnd gedegnuß aller wirbi
gest vnnd von mir gesehen oder gehört in dieser neuen welt synd/
Als hernach gezeygt würt.

FROM THE DRESDEN COPY.[1]

gefunden Region die wol ein welt genent mag wer-
den durch den Cristenlichen künig von portigal
wunderbarlich erfunden. This is the copy described in the *Carter-Brown Catalogue* (vol. i.
no. 26), and seems to correspond to the copy in
the Dresden Library, of which fac-similes of the
title and its reverse are given herewith.[2]

Harrisse[3] cites a copy in the British Museum
(Grenville), which has thirty-five lines to the
page, with the title: *Vonderneüw gefunden Re-*

gion, etc. It is without date and place; but
Harrisse sets it under 1505, as he does another issue, *Von der Neüwen gefundē Region,* of
which he found a copy in the Royal Library at
Munich,[4] and still another, *Von den Nawen Insu-*
len unnd Landen, printed at Leipsic.[5]

In 1506 there were two editions, — one published at Strasburg,[6] *Von den Nüwe Insulē und*
landen (eight leaves); and the other at Leipsic,
Von den newen Insulen und Landen (six leaves).[7]

[1] This follows the fac-simile given in Ruge's *Geschichte des Zeitalters der Entdeckungen,* p. 334, of the
reverse of title of a copy preserved in the Royal Library at Dresden.

[2] Harrisse (*Bibl. Amer. Vet.*) says he describes his no. 38 from the Carter-Brown and Lenox copies; but
the colophon as he gives it does not correspond with the *Carter-Brown Catalogue,* nor with the Dresden copy
as described by Ruge. Cf. also Panzer, *Annalen,* vol. i. p. 271, no. 561; Humboldt, *Examen critique,* v. 6.

[3] *Bibl. Amer. Vet.,* no. 34.

[4] *Bibl. Amer. Vet., Additions,* no. 21.

[5] *Bibl. Amer. Vet., Additions,* no. 20, following Weller's *Repertorium,* no. 320.

[6] *Bibl. Amer. Vet.,* no. 40; there is a copy in the Lenox Library.

[7] *Bibl. Amer. Vet.,* no. 41; Heber, vol. vi. no. 3,846; Rich, no. 1; Humboldt, *Examen critique,* iv. 160.

In 1508 there was, according to Brunet,[1] a Strasburg edition, *Von den Neüwen Insulen und Landen.* There was also a Dutch edition, *Van der nieuwer werelt,* etc., printed at Antwerp by Jan van Doesborgh, which was first made known by Muller, of Amsterdam, through his *Books on America* (1872, no. 24). It is a little quarto tract of eight leaves, without date, printed in gothic type, thirty and thirty-one lines to the page, with various woodcuts. It came from an "insignificant library," — that of the architect Bosschaert,[2] — sold in 1871 in Antwerp, and was bound up with three other tracts of the first ten years of the sixteenth century. It cost Muller 830 florins, and subsequently passed into the Carter-Brown Library, and still remains unique. Muller had placed it between 1506 and 1509; but Mr. Bartlett, in the *Carter-Brown Catalogue* (vol. i. no. 38), assigns it to 1508. Muller had also given a fac-simile of the first page; but only the cut on that page is reproduced in the *Carter-Brown Catalogue* (i. 46), as well as a cut showing a group of four Indians, which is on the reverse of the last leaf. Mr. Carter-Brown printed a fac-simile edition (twenty-five copies) in 1874 for private distribution.[3]

That portion of the Latin letter which Vespucius addressed to Soderini on his four voyages differs from the text connected with Giocondo's name, and will be found in the various versions of the *Paesi novamente* and in Grynæus, as well as in Ramusio (i. 128), Bandini (p. 100), and Canovai in Italian, and in English in Kerr's *Voyages* (vol. iii., 1812, p. 342) and in Lester (p. 223). There are also German versions in Voss, *Alleraelteste Nachricht von den neuen Welt* (Berlin, 1722), and in Spanish in Navarrete's *Coleccion* (iii. 190).

There is another text, the "Relazione," published by Francesco Bartolozzi in 1789,[4] after it had long remained in manuscript; it also is addressed to the same Lorenzo.[5] If the original account as written by Vespucius himself was in Portuguese and addressed to King Manoel, it is lost.[6]

Of the Vespucius-Coelho voyage we have only the account which is given in connection with the other three, in which Vespucius gives May 10 as the date of sailing; but Coelho is known to have started June 10, with six ships. Varnhagen has identified the harbor, where he left the shipwrecked crew, with Port Frio.[7] Returning, they reached Lisbon June 18 (or 28), and on the 4th of the following September Vespucius dated his account.[8]

If we draw a line from Nancy to Strasburg as the longer side of a triangle, its apex to the south will fall among the Vosges, where in a secluded valley lies the town of St.-Dié. What we see there to-day of man's work is scarcely a century and a half old; for the place was burned in 1756, and shortly after rebuilt. In the early part of the sixteenth century St.-Dié was in the dominion of Duke René of Lorraine. It had its cathedral and a seminary of learning (under the patronage of the Duke), and a printing-press had been set up there. The reigning prince, as an enlightened friend of erudition, had drawn to his college a number of learned men; and Pico de Mirandola, in addressing a letter to the editor of the Ptolemy of 1513, expressed surprise that so scholarly a body of men existed in so obscure a place. Who were these scholars?

The chief agent of the Duke in the matter seems to have been his secretary, Walter Lud or Ludd, or Gualterus Ludovicus, as his name was latinized. The preceding narrative has indicated his position in this learned community,[9] and has cited the little tractate of four leaves by him, the importance of which was first discovered, about twenty years ago, by Henry Stevens,[10]

---

[1] Vol. v. col. 1156; *Bibl. Amer. Vet.,* no. 50.

[2] *Bulletin de la Société de Géographie d'Anvers,* 1877, p. 349.

[3] There is a copy of this fac-simile in the Boston Public Library [G. 302, 22]. Cf. *Historical Magazine,* xxi. 111.

[4] *Ricerche istorico-critiche circa alle scoperte d'Amerigo Vespucci con l' aggiunta di una relazione del medesimo fin ora inedita* (Florence, 1789), p. 168. He followed, not an original, but a copy found in the Biblioteca Strozziana. This text is reprinted in Varnhagen's *Amerigo Vespucci,* p. 83.

[5] Cf. the *Relazione delle scoperte fatte da C. Colombo, da A. Vespucci,* etc., following a manuscript in the Ferrara Library, edited by Professor Ferraro, and published at Bologna in 1875 as no. 144 of the series *Scelta di curiosità letterarie inedite e rare dal secolo XIII al XVII.*

[6] Lucas Rem's *Tagebuch aus den Jahren 1494-1542. Beitrag zur Handelsgeschichte der Stadt Augsburg. Mitgetheilt mit Bemerkungen und einem Anhange von noch ungedruckten Briefen und Berichten über die Entdeckung des newen Seeweges nach Amerika und Ost-Indien, von B. Greiff.* Augsburg, 1861. This privately printed book in a "kurtzer Bericht aus der neuen Welt, 1501," is said to contain an account of a voyage of Vespucius, probably this one (Muller, *Books on America,* 1877, no. 2,727).

[7] *Hist. geral do Brazil* (1854), p. 427. Cf. Navarrete, iii. 281, 294; Bandini, p. 57; Peschel, *Erdkunde* (1877), p. 275; Callender's *Voyages to Terra Australis* (1866), vol. i.; Ramusio, i. 130, 141.

[8] That portion of it relating to this voyage is given in English in Lester, p. 238.

[9] N. F. Gravier in his *Histoire de Saint-Dié,* published at Épinal in 1836, p. 202, depicts the character of Lud and the influence of his press. Lud died at St.-Dié in 1527, at the age of seventy-nine.

[10] Cf. his *Notes,* etc., p. 35.

and of which the only copies at present known are in the British Museum and the Imperial Library at Vienna.[1] From this tiny *Speculum*, as we shall see, we learn some important particulars. Just over the line of Lorraine, and within the limits of Alsace, there was born and had lived a certain Mathias Ringmann or Ringman. In these early years of the century (1504) he was a student in Paris among the pupils of a certain Dr. John Faber, — to be in other ways, as we shall see, connected with the development of the little story now in progress. In Paris at the same time, and engaged in building the Notre Dame bridge, was the Veronese architect Fra Giovanni Giocondo. Major thinks there is great reason for believing that the young Alsatian student formed the acquaintance of the Italian architect, and was thus brought to entertain that enthusiasm for Vespucius which Giocondo, as a countryman of the navigator, seems to have imparted to his young friend. At least the little that is known positively seems to indicate this transmission of admiration.

We must next revert to what Vespucius himself was doing to afford material for this increase of his fame. On his return from his last voyage he had prepared an account at full length of his experiences in the New World, "that coming generations might remember him." No such ample document, however, is now known. There was at this time (1504) living in Florence a man of fifty-four, Piero Soderini, who two years before, had been made perpetual Gonfaloniere of the city. He had been a schoolmate of Vespucius; and to him, dating from Lisbon, Sept. 4, 1504, the navigator addressed an account of what he called his four voyages, abstracted as is supposed from the larger narra-

tive. The original text of this abstract is also missing, unless we believe, with Varnhagen, that the text which he gives in his *Amerigo Vespucci, son caractère*, etc. (p. 34), printed at Lima in 1865, is such, which he supposes to have been published at Florence in 1505-1506, since a printed copy of an Italian text, undated, had been bought by him in Havana (1863) in the same covers with another tract of 1506.[2] Other commentators have not placed this Italian tract so early. It has not usually been placed before 1510.[3] Dr. Court put it before 1512. Harrisse gave it the date of 1516 because he had found it bound with another tract of that date; but in his *Additions*, p. xxv, he acknowledges the reasons inconclusive. Major contends that there is no reason to believe that any known Italian text antedates the Latin, yet to be mentioned. This Italian text is called *Lettera di Amerigo Vespucci delle isole nuovamente trovate in quattro suoi viaggi . . . Data in Lisbona a di 4 di Septembre, 1504.* It is a small quarto of sixteen leaves.[4]

Varnhagen does not question that the early Italian print is the better text, differing as it does from Bassin's Latin; and he follows it by preference in all his arguments. He complains that Bandini and Canovai reprinted it with many errors.

Ramusio in his first volume had reprinted that part of it which covers the third and fourth voyage; and it had also been given in French in the collection of Jean Temporal at Lyons in 1556, known otherwise as Jean Leon's (Leo Africanus) *Historiale description de l'Afrique*, with a preface by Ramusio.[5]

It is Major's belief that the original text of the abstract intended for Soderini was written in a sort of composite Spanish-Italian dialect, such as an Italian long in the service of

---

[1] Varnhagen's *Le premier voyage*, p. 1.

[2] Varnhagen, *Amerigo Vespucci, son caractère*, etc., p. 28; D'Avezac's *Waltzemüller*, p. 46; Harrisse, *Bibl. Amer. Vet.*, *Additions*, p. xxiv.

[3] Napione puts it in this year in his *Del primo scopritore*, Florence, 1809.

[4] Harrisse (*Bibl. Amer. Vet.*, no. 87) describes it from a copy in the British Museum which is noted in the *Grenville Catalogue*, p. 764, no. 6,535. D'Avezac, in 1867, noted, besides the Grenville copy, one belonging to the Marquis Gino Capponi at Florence, and Varnhagen's (*Waltzemüller*, p. 45; Peignot, *Répertoire*, p. 139; Heber, vol. vi. no. 3,848; Napione, *Del primo scopritore del nuovo mondo*, 1809, p. 107; Ebert, *Dictionary*, no. 27,542; Ternaux, no. 5). Harrisse in 1872 (*Bibl. Amer. Vet.*, *Additions*, p. xxiv), added a fourth copy, belonging to the Palatina in Florence (Biblioteca Nazionale), and thinks there may have been formerly a duplicate in that collection, which Napione describes. The copy described by Peignot may have been the same with the Heber and Grenville copies; and the Florence copy mentioned by Harrisse in his *Ferdinand Colomb*, p. 11, may also be one of those already mentioned. The copy which Brunet later described in his *Supplément* passed into the Court Collection (no. 366); and when that splendid library was sold, in 1884, this copy was considered its gem, and was bought by Quaritch for £524, but is now owned by Mr. Chas. H. Kalbfleisch, of New York. The copies known to Varnhagen in 1865 were — one which had belonged to Baccio Valori, used by Bandini; one which belonged to Gaetano Poggiale, described by Napione; the Grenville copy; and his own, which had formerly belonged to the Libreria de Nuestra Señora de las Cuevas de la Cartuja in Seville. The same text was printed in 1745 in Bandini's *Vita e lettere di Amerigo Vespucci*, and in 1817 in Canovai's *Viaggi d' Americo Vespucci*, where it is interjected among other matter, voyage by voyage.

[5] There was also a French edition at Antwerp the same year, and it was reprinted in Paris in 1830. There were editions in Latin at Antwerp in 1556, at Tiguri in 1559, and an Elzevir edition in 1632 (Carter-Brown, vol. i. no. 211).

the Iberian nations might acquire,[1] and that a copy of it coming into the possession of Vespucius' countryman, Giocondo, in Paris, it was by that architect translated into French, and at Ringmann's suggestion addressed to René and intrusted to Ringmann to convey to the Duke, of whom the Alsatian felt proud, as an enlightened sovereign whose dominions were within easy reach of his own home. Major also suggests that the preliminary parts of the narrative, referring to the school-day acquaintance of Vespucius with the person whom he addressed, while it was true of Soderini,[2] was not so of René; but, being retained, has given rise to confusion.[3] Lud tells us only that the letters were sent from Portugal to René in French, and Waldseemüller says that they were translated from the Italian to the French, but without telling us whence they came.

We know, at all events, that Ringmann returned to the Vosges country, and was invited to become professor of Latin in the new college, where he taught thereafter, and that he had become known, as was the fashion, under the Latin name of Philesius, whose verses have already been referred to. The narrative of Vespucius, whether Ringmann brought it from Paris, or however it came, was not turned from the French into Latin by him,[4] but, as Lud informs us, by another canon of the Cathedral, Jean Bassin de Sandacourt, or Johannes Basinus Sandacurius, as he appears in Lud's Latin.

Just before this, in 1504, there had joined the college, as teacher of geography, another young man who had classicized his name, and was known as Hylacomylus. It was left, as has been mentioned, for Humboldt (*Examen critique*, iv. 99) to identify him as Martin Waltzemüller, — who however preferred to write it Waldseemüller.

It was a project among this St.-Dié coterie to edit Ptolemy,[5] and illustrate his cosmographical views, just as another coterie at Vienna were engaged then and later in studying the complemental theories of Pomponius Mela. Waldseemüller, as the teacher of geography, naturally assumed control of this undertaking; and the Duke himself so far encouraged the scheme as to order the engraving of a map to accompany the exposition of the new discoveries, — the same which is now known as the Admiral's map.[6]

In pursuance of these studies Waldseemüller had prepared a little cosmographical treatise, and this it was now determined to print at the College Press at St.-Dié. Nothing could better accompany it than the Latin translation of the Four Voyages of Vespucius and some verses by Philesius; for Ringmann, as we have seen, was a verse-maker, and had a local fame as a Latin poet. Accordingly, unless Varnhagen's theory is true, which most critics are not inclined to accept, these letters of Vespucius first got into print, not in their original Italian, but in a little Latin quarto of Waldseemüller, printed in this obscure nook of the Vosges. Under the title of *Cosmographiæ introductio*, this appeared twice, if not oftener, in 1507.[7]

To establish the sequence of the editions of the *Cosmographiæ introductio* in 1507 [8] is a bibliographical task of some difficulty, and experts are at variance. D'Avezac (*Waltzemüller*, p. 112) makes four editions in 1507, and establishes a test for distinguishing them by taking the first line of the title, together with the date of the colophon; those of May corresponding to the 25th of April, and those of September to the 29th of August: —

1. *Cosmographiæ introdu — vij kl' Maij.*
2. *Cosmographiæ introductio — vij kl' Maij.*

---

[1] Cf. Varnhagen, *Le premier voyage*, p. 1.

[2] Bandini, p. xxv; Bartolozzi, *Recherche*, p. 67.

[3] Santarem dismisses the claim that Vespucius was the intimate of either the first or second Duke René. Cf. Childe's translation, p. 57, and H. Lepage's *Le Duc René II. et Améric Vespuce*, Nancy, 1875. Irving (*Columbus*, app. ix.) doubts the view which Major has contended for.

[4] Varnhagen, ignorant of Lud, labors to make it clear that Ringmann must have been the translator (*Amerigo Vespucci*, p. 30); he learned his error later.

[5] See the chapters of Bunbury in his *History of Ancient Geography*, vol. ii., and the articles by De Morgan in Smith's *Dictionary of Ancient Biography*, and by Malte-Brun in the *Biographie universelle*.

[6] See Vol. IV. p. 35, and this volume, p. 112.

[7] Cf. D'Avezac, *Waltzemüller*, p. 8; Lelewel, *Moyen-âge*, p. 142; N. F. Gravier, *Histoire de la ville de Saint-Dié*, Épinal, 1836. The full title of D'Avezac's work is *Martin Hylacomylus Waltzemüller, ses ouvrages et ses collaborateurs. Voyage d'exploration et de découvertes à travers quelques épîtres dédicatoires, préfaces, et opuscules du commencement du XVIᵉ siècle: notes, causeries, et digressions bibliographiques et autres par un Géographe Bibliophile* (Extrait des *Annales des Voyages*, 1866). Paris, 1867, pp. x. 176, 8vo. D'Avezac, as a learned writer in historical geography, has put his successors under obligations. See an enumeration of his writings in Sabin, vol. i. nos. 2,492, etc., and in Leclerc, no. 164, etc., and the notice in the *Proceedings* of the American Antiquarian Society, April, 1876. He published in the *Bulletin de la Société de Géographie de Paris*, 1858, and also separately, a valuable paper, *Les voyages de Améric Vespuce au compte de l'Espagne et les mesures itinéraires employées par les marins Espagnols et Portugais des XVᵉ et XVIᵉ siècles* (188 pp.).

[8] They bear the press-mark of the St.-Dié Association, which is given in fac-simile in Brunet, vol. ii. no. 316. It is also in the *Carter-Brown Catalogue*, i. 33, and in the *Murphy Catalogue*, p. 94.

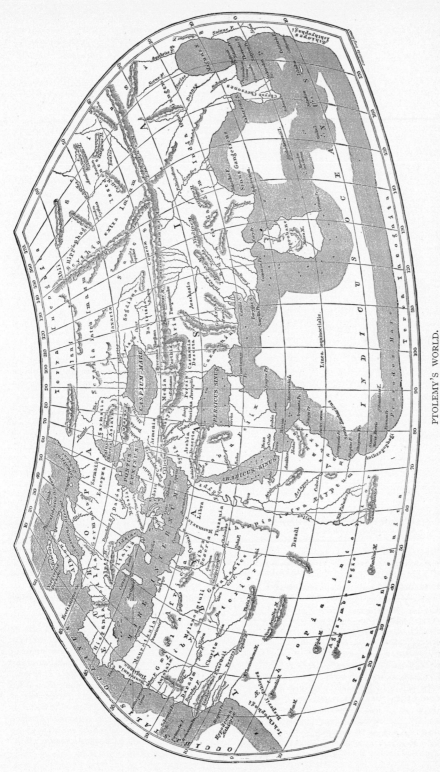

PTOLEMY'S WORLD.

(*Reduced after map in Bunbury's Ancient Geography, London, 1879, vol. ii.*)

3. *Cosmographiæ — iiij kl' Septembris.*

4. *Cosmographiæ introdu — iiij kl' Septembris.*

The late Henry C. Murphy [1] maintained that nos. 1 and 4 in this enumeration are simply made up from nos. 2 and 3 (the original May and September editions), to which a new title, — the same in each case, — with the substitution of other leaves for the originals of leaves 1, 2, 5, and 6, — also the same in each case, — was given. Harrisse, however, dissents, and thinks D'Avezac's no. 1 a genuine first edition. The only copy of it known [2] was picked up on a Paris quay for a franc by the geographer Eyriès, which was sold at his death, in 1846, for 160 francs, and again at the Nicholas Yéméniz sale (Lyons, no. 2,676), in 1867, for 2,000 francs. It is now in the Lenox Library.[3]

Of the second of D'Avezac's types there are several copies known. Harrisse [4] names the copies in the Lenox, Murphy,[5] and Carter-Brown [6] collections. There is a record of other copies in the National Library at Rio Janeiro,[7] in the Royal Library at Berlin,[8] in the Huth Collection [9] in London, and in the Mazarine Library in Paris, — a copy which D'Avezac [10] calls "irréprochable." Tross held a copy in 1872 for 1,500 francs. Waldseemüller's name does not appear in these early May issues, which are little quartos of fifty-two leaves, twenty-seven lines to the full page, with an inscription of twelve lines, in Roman type, on the back of the folding sheet of a skeleton globe.[11]

On the 29th of August (iiij kl' Septembris) it was reissued, still without Waldseemüller's name, of the same size, and fifty-two leaves; but the folding sheet bears on the reverse an inscription in fifteen lines. The ordinary title is D'Avezac's no. 3. Harrisse [12] mentions the Lenox and Carter-Brown [13] copies; but there are others in Harvard College Library (formerly the Cooke copy, no. 625, besides an imperfect copy which belonged to Charles Sumner), in Charles Deane's Collection, and in the Barlow Library. The Murphy Library had a copy (no. 680) in

its catalogue, and the house of John Wiley's Sons advertised a copy in New York in 1883 for $350.

There are records of copies in Europe, — in the Imperial Library at Vienna, in the National Library at Paris, and in the Huth Collection (*Catalogue*, i. 356) in London. D'Avezac (*Waltzemüller*, pp. 54, 55) describes a copy which belonged to Yéméniz, of Lyons. Brockhaus advertised one in 1861 (Trömel, no. 1). Another was sold in Paris for 2,000 francs in 1867. There was another in the Sobolewski sale (no. 3,769), and one in the Court Catalogue (no. 92). Leclerc, 1878 (no. 599), has advertised one for 500 francs, Harrassowitz, 1881, (no. 309) one for 1,000 marks, and Rosenthal, of Munich, in 1884 (no. 30) held one at 3,000 marks. One is also shown in the *Catalogue of the Reserved and Most Valuable Portion of the Libri Collection* (no. 15).

The latter portion of the book, embracing the *Quattuor Americi Vesputii navigationes*, seems to have been issued also separately, and is still occasionally found.[14]

What seems to have been a composite edition, corresponding to D'Avezac's fourth, made up, as Harrisse thinks (*Bibl. Amer. Vet.*, no. 47), of the introductory part of D'Avezac's first and the voyages of his third edition, is also found, though very rarely. There is a copy in the Lenox Library of this description, and another, described by Harrisse, in the Mazarine Library in Paris.[15]

It was in this precious little quarto of 1507, whose complicated issues we have endeavored to trace, that, in the introductory portion, Waldseemüller, anonymously to the world, but doubtless with the privity of his fellow-collegians, proposed in two passages, already quoted, but here presented in fac-simile, to stand sponsor for the new-named western world; and with what result we shall see.

It was a strange sensation to name a new continent, or even a hitherto unknown part of

---

[1] *Carter-Brown Catalogue*, i. 35; Harrisse, *Bibl. Amer. Vet., Additions*, no. 24.

[2] D'Avezac, *Waltzemüller*, p. 28.

[3] *Bibl. Amer. Vet.*, no. 44; *Additions*, no. 24; D'Avezac, *Waltzemüller*, p. 31. It is said that an imperfect copy in the Mazarine Library corresponds as far as it goes. D'Avezac says the Vatican copy, mentioned by Napione and Foscarini, cannot be found.

[4] *Bibl. Amer. Vet.*, no. 45.

[5] *Catalogue*, no. 679, bought (1884) by President White of Cornell University.

[6] *Catalogue*, vol. i. no. 28.

[7] *Cat. Hist. Brazil, Bibl. Nac. do Rio de Janeiro*, no. 825.

[8] Described by Humboldt.

[9] *Catalogue*, i. 356.

[10] *Waltzemüller*, p. 52, etc.

[11] Cf. Brunet, ii. 317; Ternaux, no. 10.

[12] *Bibl. Amer. Vet.*, no. 46; *Additions*, no. 24.

[13] *Catalogue*, i. 29. It was Ternaux's copy, no. 10.

[14] *Bibl. Amer. Vet., Additions*, no. 25; Leclerc, no. 600 (100 francs); D'Avezac, *Waltzemüller*, p. 58.

[15] Cf. D'Avezac, *Waltzemüller*, p. 111, and Orozco y Berra's *Cartografia Mexicana* (Mexico, 1871), p. 19.

COSMOGRAPHIAE
INTRODVCTIO
CVM QVIBVS
DAM GEOME
TRIAE
AC
ASTRONO
MIAE PRINCIPIIS AD
EAM REM NECESSARIIS

Insuper quattuor Americi
Vespucij nauigationes.

Vniuersalis Cosmographiæ descriptio tam
in solido ꝗ plano / eis etiam insertis
quæ Ptholomeo ignota a nu
peris reperta sunt.

DISTHYCON

Cum deus astra regat / & terræ climata Cæsar
Nec tellus / nec eis sydera maius habent.

TITLE OF THE SEPTEMBER EDITION, 1507.[1]

an old one. There was again the same uncertainty of continental lines as when Europe had been named[2] by the ancients, for there was now only the vaguest notion of what there was to be named. Columbus had already died in the belief that he had only touched the eastern limits of Asia. There is no good reason to believe that Vespucius himself was of a different mind.[3] So insignificant a gain to Europe had men come to believe these new islands, compared with the regions of wealth and spices with which Vasco da Gama and Cabral had opened trade by the African route, that the advocate and deluded finder of the western route had died obscurely, with scarcely a record being made of his departure. A few islands and their savage inhabi-

---

1 This is the third edition of D'Avezac's enumeration.

2 How Europe, which on a modern map would seem to be but one continent with Asia, became one of three great continents known to the ancients, is manifest from the world as it was conceived by Eratosthenes in the third century. In his map the Caspian Sea was a gulf indented from the Northern Ocean, so that only a small land-connection existed between Asia and Europe, spanned by the Caucasus Mountains, with the Euxine on the west and the Caspian on the east; just as the isthmus at the head of the Arabian Gulf also joined Libya, or Africa, to Asia. Cf. Bunbury's *History of Ancient Geography*, i. 660.

3 Humboldt, *Examen critique*, v. 182; but Varnhagen thinks Humboldt was mistaken so far as Vespucius was concerned.

RVDIMENTA

quę oppoſitu vel contra denotat. Atcʒ in ſexto cli
mate Antarcticū verſus/ & pars extrema Affricæ
nuper reperta & Zamziber/laua minor/ & Seula
inſulę/ & quarta orbis pars(quam quia Americus
inuenit Amerigen/ quaſi Americi terrā/ſiue Ame-
cam nuncupare licet)ſitæ ſunt. De quibus Auſtrali
bus climatibus hæc Pomponij Mellę Geographi
verba intelligenda ſunt/ vbi ait. Zone habitabiles
paria agunt anni tempora/verum non pariter An-
tichthones alteram/nos alteram incolimus. Illius ſi-
tus ob ardore intercedētis plage incognitus/ huius
dicendus eſt. Vbi animaduertendum eſt quod cli-
matum quodcʒ alios cʒ aliud plerumcʒ fœtus pro-
ducat/cum diuerſę ſunt naturæ/ & alia atcʒ alia ſy-
derum virtute moderentur. Vnde Virgilins.

Ame-
rige
Pōpo:
Melę

Virgil.

FROM THE COSMOGRAPHIÆ INTRODUCTIO.[1]

Iaʒ
Ame-
rico

Nunc vero & heę partes ſunt latius luſtratæ/ &
alia quarta pars per Americū Veſputium(vt in ſe-
quentibus audietur)inuenta eſt:quā non video cur
quis iure vetet ab Americo inuentore ſagacis inge
nij viro Amerigen quaſi Americi terram/ſiue Ame
ricam dicendam:cum & Europa & Aſia a mulieribus ſua ſortita ſint nomina. Eius ſitū & gentis mores ex bis binis Americi nauigationibus quę ſequū
tur liquide intelligi datur.

FROM THE COSMOGRAPHIÆ INTRODUCTIO.[2]

tants had scarcely answered the expectation of
those who had pictured from Marco Polo the
golden glories of Cathay.

To Columbus himself the new-found regions
were only "insulæ Indiæ super Gangem,"—
India east of the Ganges; and the "Indies"

[1] That part of the page (sig. C) of the September edition (1507) which has the reference to America and Vespucius.

[2] That part of the page of the 1507 (September) edition in which the name of America is proposed for the New World.

which he supposed he had found, and for whose native races the Asiatic name was borrowed and continues to abide, remained the Spanish designation of their possessions therein, though distinguished in time by the expletive *West* Indies.[1] It never occurred to the discoverers themselves to give a new name to regions which they sometimes designated generically as *Mundus Novus* or *Alter Orbis;* but it is doubtful as Humboldt says, if they intended by such designation any further description than that the parts discovered were newly found, just as Strabo, Mela, Cadamosto and others had used similar designations.[2] It was at a much later day, and when the continental character of the New World was long established, that some Spaniard suggested *Colonia*, or *Columbiana;* and another, anxious to commemorate the sovereigns of Castile and Leon, futilely coined the cumbrous designation of *Fer-Isabelica*.[3] When Columbus and others had followed a long stretch of the northern coast of South America without finding a break, and when the volume of water pouring through the mouths of the Orinoco betokened to his mind a vast interior, it began to be suspected that the main coast of Asia had been found; and the designation of *Tierra firme* was naturally attached to the whole region, of which Paria and the Pearl coast were distinguishable parts. This designation of Firm Land was gradually localized as explorations extended, and covered what later was known as Castilla del Oro; and began to comprehend in the time of Purchas,[4] for instance, all that extent of coast from Paria to Costa Rica.[5]

When Cabral in 1500 sighted the shores of Brazil, he gave the name of *Terra Sanctæ Crucis* to the new-found region, — the land of the Holy Cross; and this name continued for some time to mark as much as was then known of what we now call South America, and we find it in such early delineations as the Lenox globe and the map of Sylvanus in 1511.[6] It will be remembered that in 1502, after what is called his third voyage, Vespucius had simply named the same region *Mundus Novus.*

Thus in 1507 there was no general concurrence in the designations which had been bestowed on these new islands and coasts; and the only unbroken line which had then been discovered was that stretching from Honduras well down the eastern coast of South America, if Vespucius' statement of having gone to the thirty-second degree of southern latitude was to be believed. After the exploration of this coast, — thanks to the skill of Vespucius in sounding his own exploits and giving them an attractive setting out,[7] aided, probably, by that fortuitous dispensation of fortune which sometimes awards fame where it is hardly deserved, — it had come to pass that the name of Vespucius had, in common report, become better associated than that of Columbus with the magnitude of the new discoveries. It was not so strange then as it appears now that the Florentine, rather than the Genoese, was selected for such continental commemoration. All this happened to some degree irrespective of the question of priority in touching Tierra Firme, as turning upon the truth or falsity of the date 1497 assigned to the first of the voyages of Vespucius.

The proposing of a name was easy; the acceptance of it was not so certain. The little tract had appeared without any responsible voucher. The press-mark of St.-Dié was not a powerful stamp. The community was obscure, and it had been invested with what influence it possessed by the association of Duke René with it.

This did not last long. The Duke died in 1508, and his death put a stop to the projected edition of Ptolemy and broke up the little press; so that next year (1509), when Waldseemüller planned a new edition of the *Cosmographiæ introductio*, it was necessary to commit it to Grüninger in Strasburg to print. In this edition Waldseemüller first signed his own name to the preface. Copies of this issue are somewhat less rare than those of 1507. It is a little tract of thirty-two leaves, some copies having fourteen, others fifteen, lines on the back of the folding sheet.[8] The Lenox Library has examples of each. There are other copies in the Carter-

---

[1] As early as 1519, for instance, by Enciso in his *Suma de geographia.*

[2] *Examen critique*, i. 181; v. 182.

[3] Suggested by Pizarro y Orellano in 1639; cf. Navarrete, French tr., ii. 282.

[4] *Pilgrimes*, iv. 1433.

[5] Bancroft, *Central America*, i. 291.

[6] See p. 122.

[7] Humboldt (*Cosmos*, Eng. tr., ii. 420) particularly instances his descriptions of the coast of Brazil. For fifteen hundred years, as Humboldt points out (p. 660), naturalists had known no mention, except that of Adulis, of snow in the tropical regions, when Vespucius in 1500 saw the snowy mountains of Santa Marta. Humboldt (again in his *Cosmos*, Eng. tr., ii. 664, 667), according Vespucius higher literary acquirements than the other early navigators had possessed, speaks of his extolling not ungracefully the glowing richness of the light and picturesque grouping and strange aspect of the constellations that circle the Southern Pole, which is surrounded by so few stars, — and tells how effectively he quoted Dante at the sight of the four stars, which were not yet for several years to be called the Southern Cross. Irving speaks of Vespucius' narrative as "spirited."

[8] Harrisse, no. 60; Brunet, ii. 319.

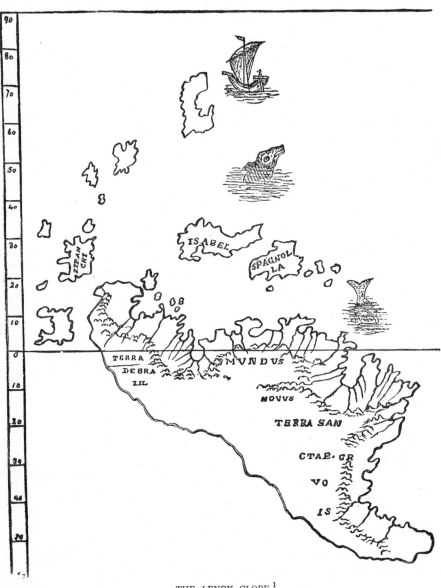

THE LENOX GLOBE.[1]

Brown (*Catalogue*, vol. i. no. 40), Barlow, and Harvard College libraries. Another is in the Force Collection, Library of Congress, and one was sold in the Murphy sale (no. 681). The copy which belonged to Ferdinand Columbus is still preserved in Seville; but its annotations do not signify that the statements in it respecting Vespucius' discoveries attracted his attention.[2] It was this edition which Navarrete used when he made a Spanish version for

---

[1] A section of the drawing given by Dr. De Costa in his monograph on the globe, showing the American parts reduced to a plane projection, and presenting the name of *Terra Sanctæ Crucis*. There is another sketch on p. 123.

[2] Harrisse, *Fernand Colomb*, p. 145.

his *Coleccion* (iii. 183) D'Avezac used a copy in the Mazarine Library; and other copies are noted in the Huth (i. 356) and Sunderland (*Catalogue*, vol. v. no. 12,920) collections. The account of the voyages in this edition was also printed separately in German as *Diss buchlin saget wie die zwē . . . herrē*, etc.[1]

While the Strasburg press was emitting this 1509 edition it was also printing the sheets of another little tract, the anonymous *Globus mundi*,[2] of which a fac-simile of the title is annexed, in which it will be perceived the bit of the New World shown is called "Newe welt," and not America, though "America lately discovered" is the designation given in the text. The credit of the discovery is given unreservedly to Vespucius, and Columbus is not mentioned.[3]

The breaking up of the press was a serious blow to the little community at St.-Dié. Ringmann, in the full faith of completing the edition of Ptolemy which they had in view, had brought from Italy a Greek manuscript of the old geographer; but the poet was soon to follow his patron, for, having retired to Schlestadt, his native town, he died there in 1511 at the early age of twenty-nine. The Ptolemy project, however, did not fail. Its production was transferred to Strasburg; and there, in 1513, it appeared, including the series of maps associated ever since with the name of Hylacomylus, and showing evidences in the text of the use which had been made of Ringmann's Greek manuscript.

We look to this book in vain for any attempt to follow up the conferring of the name of Vespucius on the New World. The two maps which it contains, showing the recent discoveries,

are given in fac-simile on pages 111 and 112. In one the large region which stands for South America has no designation; in the other there is supposed to be some relation to Columbus' own map, while it bears a legend which gives to Columbus unequivocally the credit of the dis-

Cosmographie intro
ductio:cum quibusdam Geome
trie ac Astronomie princi
piis ad eam rem
necessariis.

Insuper quattuor Americi Ve
spucij navigationes.

Universalis Cosmographie descriptio
tam in solido qͣ plano/eis etiam
insertis que Ptholomeo
ignota/a nuperis
reperta sunt.

Cum deus astra regat/et terre climata Cesar
Nec tellus/nec eis sydera maius babent.

TITLE OF THE 1509 (STRASBURG) EDITION.

covery of the New World. It has been contended of late that the earliest cartographical application of the name is on two globes preserved in the collection of the Freiherr von Hauslab, in Vienna, one of which (printed) Varnhagen in his paper on Apianus and Schöner puts under 1509, and the other (manuscript) under 1513. Weiser in his *Magalhães-Strasse* (p. 27)

---

[1] *Bibl. Amer. Vet.*, no. 62; *Additions*, no. 31; Huth, v. 1,526; Varnhagen, *Amerigo Vespucci*, p. 31. Cf. Navarrete, *Opúsculos*, i. 94.

[2] Equally intended, as Varnhagen (*Le premier voyage*, p. 36), thinks to be accompanied by the Latin of the *Quattuor navigationes*.

[3] This little black-letter quarto contains fourteen unnumbered leaves, and the woodcut on the title is repeated on Bii, *verso*, E, *recto*, and Eiiii, *verso*. There are five other woodcuts, one of which is repeated three times. Harrisse (*Bibl. Amer. Vet.*, no. 61; also p. 462) reports only the Harvard College copy, which was received from Obadiah Rich in 1830. There are other entries of this tract in Panzer, vi. 44, no. 149, under Argentorati (Strasburg), referring to the *Crevenna Catalogue*, ii. 117; Sabin, vii. 286; *Grenville Catalogue*, p. 480; Graesse, iii. 94; Henry Stevens's *Historical Nuggets*, no. 1,252, pricing a copy in 1862 at £10 10s.; Harrassowitz (81, no. 48), pricing one at 1,000 marks; Huth, ii. 602; Court, no. 145; *Bibliotheca Thottiana*, v. 219; and Humboldt refers to it in his *Examen critique*, vi. 142, and in his introduction to Ghillany's *Behaim*, p. 8, note. Cf. also D'Avezac's *Waltzemüller*, p. 114; Major's *Prince Henry the Navigator*, p. 387, and his paper in the *Archæologia*, vol. xl.; Harrisse, *Notes on Columbus*, p. 173. D'Avezac used a copy in the Mazarine Library. A German translation, printed also by Grüninger at Strasburg, appeared under the title, *Der Welt Kugel*, etc. (*Bibl. Amer. Vet.*, *Additions*, no. 32.) Varnhagen (*Le premier voyage*, p. 36) thinks this German text the original one.

Globus mundi

Declaratio siue descriptio mundi

et totius orbis terrarum, globulo rotundo comparati vt spera soli
da. Qua cuiuis etiã mediocriter docto ad oculũ videre licet an,
tipodes esse, quoꝛ pedes nostris oppositi sunt. Et qualiter in vna,
quaꝗ orbis parte homines vitam agere queunt salutarē, sole sin,
gula terrę loca illustrante: que tamen terra in vacuo aere pendere
videtur: solo dei nutu sustẽtata, alijsꝗ permultis de quarta orbis
terrarũ parte nuperab Americo reperta,

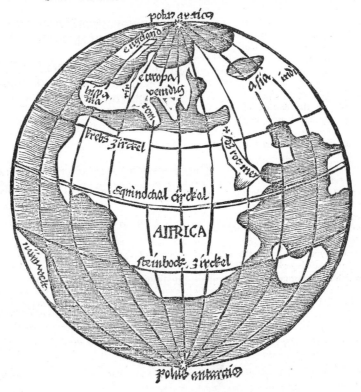

TITLE OF THE 1509 (STRASBURG) EDITION.

doubts these dates.[1] The application of the new name, America, we also find not far from this time, say between 1512 and 1515, in a manuscript mappemonde (see p. 125) which Major, when he described it in the *Archæologia* (xl. p. 1), unhesitatingly ascribed to Leonardo da Vinci, thinking that he could trace certain relations between Da Vinci and Vespucius. This map bears distinctly the name *America* on the South American continent. Its connection with Da Vinci is now denied.

Not far from the same time a certain undated edition of the *Cosmographiæ introductio* appeared at Lyons, though no place is given. Of this

[1] Cf. Harrisse, *Cabots*, 182; D'Avezac, *Allocution à la Société de Géographie de Paris*, Oct. 20, 1871, p. 16; and his *Waltzemüller*, p. 116.

edition there are two copies in the British Museum, and others in the Lenox and Barlow collections; but they all lack a map,[1] which is found in a copy first brought to public attention by the bookseller Tross, of Paris, in 1881,[2] and which is now owned by Mr. C. H. Kalbfleisch, of New York. Its date is uncertain. Harrisse (*Bibl. Amer. Vet.*, no. 63) placed it first in 1510, but later (*Cabots*, p. 182) he dated it about 1514, as Tross had already done. D'Avezac (*Waltzemüller*, p. 123) thinks it could not have been earlier than 1517.[3]

The chief interest of this map to us is the fact that it bears the words "America noviter reperta" on what stands for South America; and there is fair ground for supposing that it antedates all other printed maps yet known which bear this name.

At not far from the same time, fixed in this instance certainly in 1515, we find *America* on the earliest known globe of Schöner.[4] Probably printed to accompany this globe, is a rare little tract, issued the same year (1515) at Nuremberg, under the title of *Luculentissima quædā terræ totius descriptio*. In this Schöner speaks of a "fourth part of the globe, named after its discoverer, Americus Vespucius, a man of sagacious mind, who found it in 1497," adopting the controverted date.[5]

Meanwhile the fame of Vespucius was prospering with the Vienna coterie. One of them, Georg Tanstetter, sometimes called Collimitius, was editing the *De natura locorum librum* of Albertus Magnus; and apparently after the book was printed he made with type a marginal note, to cite the profession of Vespucius that he had reached to fifty degrees south, as showing that

there was habitable land so far towards the Southern Pole.[6]

Joachim Watt, or Vadianus, as he was called in his editorial Latin, had in 1515 adopted the new name of America, and repeated it in 1518, when he reproduced his letter in his edition of Pomponius Mela, as explained on another page.[7] Apian had been employed to make the mappe-monde for it, which was to show the new discoveries. The map seems not to have been finished in time; but when it appeared, two years later (1520), in the new edition of Solinus, by Camers, though it bore the name of America on the southern main, it still preserved the legend in connection therewith which awarded the discovery to Columbus.[8] Watt now quarrelled with Camers, for they had worked jointly, and their two books are usually found in one cover, with Apian's map between them. Returning to St. Gall, Vadianus practised there as a physician, and re-issued his Mela at Basle in 1522, dedicating it to that Dr. Faber who had been the teacher of Ringmann in Paris eighteen years before.[9]

In 1522 Lorenz Friess, or Laurentius Phrysius, another of Duke René's coterie, a correspondent of Vespucius, published a new edition of Ptolemy at the Grüninger press in Strasburg, in which the fame of Columbus and Vespucius is kept up in the usual equalizing way. The preface, by Thomas Ancuparius, sounds the praises of the Florentine, ascribing to him the discovery "of what we to-day call America;" the Admiral's map, *Tabula Terre Nove*,[10] which Waldseemüller had published in the 1513 edition, is once more reproduced, with other of the maps of that edition, re-engraved on a reduced

1 See this Vol. p. 120.

2 No. 4,924 of his *Catalogue*, no. xiv. of that year.

3 This Latin text of Bassin was also printed at Venice in 1537 (*Bibl. Amer. Vet.*, *Additions*, no. 156; Leclerc, no. 2,517). Humboldt (*Examen critique*, iv. 102, 114) and others have been misled by a similarity of title in supposing that there were other editions of the *Cosmographiæ introductio* published at Ingoldstadt in 1529, 1532, and at Venice in 1535, 1541, 1551, and 1554. This book, however, is only an abridgment of Apian's *Cosmographia*, which was originally printed at Landshut in 1524. Cf. Huth, i. 357; Leclerc, no. 156; D'Avezac, *Waltzemüller*, p. 124. The Bassin version of the voyages was later the basis of the accounts, either at length or abridged, or in versions in other languages, in the *Paesi novamente* and its translations; in the *Novus orbis* of 1532 (it is here given as addressed to René, King of Sicily and Jerusalem), and later, in Ramusio's *Viaggi*, vol. i. (1550); in Eden's *Treatyse of the Newe India* (1553); in the *Historiale description de l'Afrique* of Leo Africanus (1556), — cf. *Carter-Brown Catalogue*, i. 211, 229; in De Bry, first and second parts of the *Grands voyages*, and third and fourth of the *Petits voyages*, not to name other of the older collections; and among later ones in Bandini, *Vita e lettere di Vespucci* (pp. 1, 33, 46, 57), and in the *Collecção de noticias para a historia e geografia das nações ultramarinas* (1812), published by the Royal Academy of Lisbon. Varnhagen reprints the Latin text in his *Amerigo Vespucci*, p. 34.

4 Depicted on p. 118. Cf. Wieser, *Magalhães-Strasse*, pp. 26, 27.

5 *Bibl. Amer. Vet.*, p. 142.

6 The original edition appeared at Vienna in 1514; but it was reprinted at Strasburg in 1515. Cf. Sabin, vol. i. no. 671; *Bibl. Amer. Vet.*, nos. 76, 77, 78; Stevens, *Bibliotheca geographica*, 70; Carter-Brown, vol. i. no. 48.

7 See the following section of the present chapter.

8 See a fac-simile of this part of the map in the chapter on Magellan.

9 Stevens, *Bibliotheca historica* (1870), no. 1,272; *Bibliotheca geographica*, no. 1,824.

10 See p. 112.

scale. The usual legend, crediting the discovery to Columbus, is shown in a section of the map, which is given in another place.[1] Phrysius acknowledges that the maps are essentially Waldseemüller's, though they have some changes and additions; but he adds a new mappemonde of his own, putting the name America on the great southern main, — the first time of its appearing in any map of the Ptolemy series. A fac-simile is annexed.

There is thus far absolutely no proof that any one disputed the essential facts of the discovery by Columbus of the outlying islands of Asia, as the belief went, or denied him the credit of giving a new world to the crowns of Aragon and Castile, whether that were Asia or not. The maps which have come down to us, so far as they record anything, invariably give Columbus the credit. The detractors and panegyrists of Vespucius have asserted in turn that he was privy to the doings at St.-Dié and Strasburg, and that he was not; but proof is lacking for either proposition. No one can dispute, however, that he was dead before his name was applied to the new discoveries on any published map.

If indeed the date of 1497, as given by the St.-Dié publication, was correct, there might have been ground for adjudging his explorations of the mainland to have antedated those of Columbus; but the conclusion is irresistible that either the Spanish authorities did not know that such a claim had been made, or they deemed the date an error of the press; since to rely upon the claim would have helped them in their conflict with the heirs of Columbus, which began the year following the publication of that claim, or in 1508, and continued to vex all concerned till 1527; and during all that time Vespucius, as has been mentioned, is not named in the records of the proceedings. It is equally hard to believe that Ferdinand Columbus would have passed by a claim derogating from the fame of his father, if it had come to him as a positive assertion. That he knew of the St.-Dié tract we have direct evidence in his possession of a copy of it. That it did not trouble him we know also with as much confidence as negative testimony can impart; for we have no knowledge of his noticing it, but instead the

positive assertion of a contemporary that he did not notice it.

The claim for Vespucius, however, was soon to be set up. In 1527 Las Casas began, if we may believe Quintana, the writing of his *Historia*.[2] It is not easy, however, to fix precisely the year when he tells us that the belief had become current of Vespucius being really the first to set his foot on the main. "Amerigo," he tells us further,[3] "is said to have placed the name of America on maps,[4] thus sinfully failing toward the Admiral. If he purposely gave currency to this belief in his first setting foot on the main, it was a great wickedness; and if it was not done intentionally, it looks like it." Las Casas still makes allowances, and fails of positive accusation, when again he speaks of "the injustice of Amerigo, or the injustice perhaps those who printed the *Quattuor navigationes* appear to have committed toward the Admiral;" and once more when he says that "foreign writers call the country America: it ought to be called Columba." But he grows more positive as he goes on, when he wonders how Ferdinand Columbus, who had, as he says, Vespucius' account, could have found nothing in it of deceit and injustice to object to.

Who were these "foreign writers?" Stobnicza, of Cracow, in the *Introductio in Claudii Ptholomei cosmographiā*, which he published in 1512, said: "Et ne soli Ptolomeo laborassem, curavi etiam notas facere quasdam partes terre ipsi ptolomeo alijsque vetustioribus ignotas que Amerii vespucij lustratione ad nostram noticiam puenere." Upon the reverse of folio v., in the chapter "De meridianis," occurs: "Similiter in occasu ultra africam & europam magna pars terre quam ab Americo eius reptore Americam vocant vulgo autem novus mundus dicitur." Upon the reverse of folio vii. in the chapter "De partibus terre" is this: "Non solū aūt pdicte tres ptes nunc sunt lacius lustrate, verum & alia quata pars ab Americo vesputio sagacis ingenii viro inventa est, quam ab ipso Americo eius inventore Amerigem q̄si a americi terram sive americā appellari volunt cuius latitudo est sub tota torrida zona," etc. These expressions were repeated in the second edition in 1519. Apian in 1524 had accepted the name in his *Cosmographicus liber*, as he had in an uncertain way, in 1522, in two editions, one

---

[1] See chapter on Magellan.

[2] Helps, however, cannot trace him at work upon it before 1552, and he had not finished it in 1561; and for three centuries yet to come it was to remain in manuscript.

[3] Book i. cap. 140.

[4] Harrisse (*Fernand Colomb*, p. 30), says: "The absence of nautical charts and planispheres, not only in the Colombina, but in all the muniment offices of Spain, is a signal disappointment. There is one chart which above all we need, — made by Vespucius, and which, in 1518, was in the collection of the Infanta Ferdinand, brother of Charles V." A copy of Valsequa's chart of 1439 which belonged to Vespucius, being marked "Questa ampla pelle di geographia fù pagata da Amerigo Vespucci cxxx ducati di oro di marco," was, according to Harrisse (*Bibl. Amer. Vet. Add.*, p. xxiii), in existence in Majorca as late as 1838.

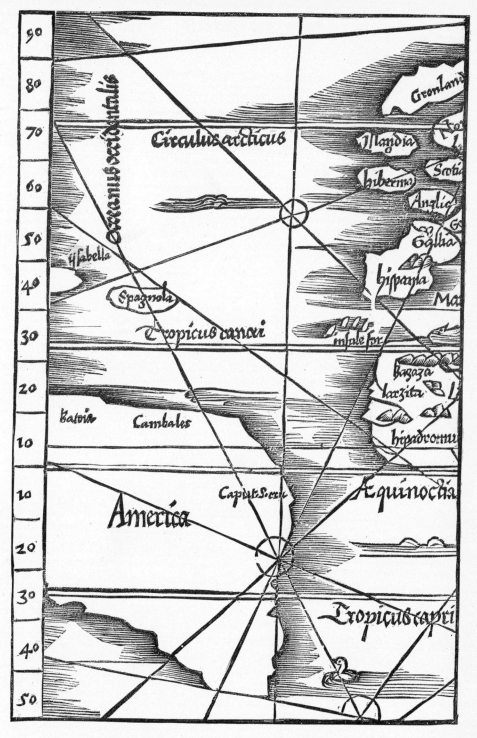

LAURENTIUS FRISIUS, IN THE PTOLEMY OF 1522 (*westerly part.*)

printed at Ratisbon, the other without place, of the tract, *Declaratio et usus typi cosmographici,* illustrative of his map.[1]

Glareanus in 1529 spoke of the land to the west "quam Americam vocant," though he couples the names of Columbus and Vespucius in speaking of its discovery. Apian and Gemma Phrysius in their *Cosmographia* of the same year recognize the new name;[2] and Phrysius again in his *De principiis astronomiæ,* first published at Antwerp in 1530, gave a chapter (no. xxx.) to "America," and repeated it in later editions.[3] Münster in the *Novus orbis* of 1532 finds that the extended coast of South America "takes the name of America from Americus, who discovered it."[4] We find the name again in the *Epitome trium terræ partium* of Vadianus, published at Tiguri in 1534,[5] and in Honter's *Rudimentorum cosmographiæ libri,* published at Basle in the same year. When the Spanish sea-manual, Medina's *Arte de navegar,* was published in Italian at Venice in 1544, it had a chart with America on it; and the *De sphæra* of Cornelius Valerius (Antwerp, 1561) says this fourth part of the world took its name from Americus.

Thus it was manifest that popular belief, outside of Spain, at least,[6] was, as Las Casas affirms, working at last into false channels. Of course the time would come when Vespucius, wrongfully or rightfully, would be charged with promoting this belief. He was already dead, and could not repel the insinuation. In 1533 this charge came for the first time in print, so far as we now know, and from one who had taken his part in spreading the error. It has already been mentioned how Schöner, in his globe of 1515, and in the little book which explained that globe, had accepted the name from the coterie of the Vosges. He still used the name in 1520

in another globe.[7] Now in 1533, in his *Opusculum geographicum ex diversorum libris ac cartis summa cura & diligentia collectum, accomodatum ad recenter elaboratum ab eodem globum decriptionis terrenæ. Ioachimi Camerarii. Ex urbe Norica, . . . Anno XXXIII,*[8] he unreservedly charged Vespucius with fixing his own name upon that region of India Superior which he believed to be an island.[9]

In 1535, in a new edition of Ptolemy, Servetus repeated the map of the New World from the editions of 1522 and 1525 which helped to give further currency to the name of America; but he checks his readers in his text by saying that those are misled who call the continent America, since Vespucius never touched it till long after Columbus had.[10] This cautious statement did not save Servetus from the disdainful comment of Gomara (1551), who accuses that editor of Ptolemy of attempting to blacken the name of the Florentine.

It was but an easy process for a euphonious name, once accepted for a large part of the new discoveries, gradually to be extended until it covered them all. The discovery of the South Sea by Balboa in 1513 rendered it certain that there was a country of unmistakably continental extent lying south of the field of Columbus' observations, which, though it might prove to be connected with Asia by the Isthmus of Panama, was still worthy of an independent designation.[11] We have seen how the Land of the Holy Cross, Paria, and all other names gave way in recognition of the one man who had best satisfied Europe that this region had a continental extent. If it be admitted even that Vespucius was in any way privy to the bestowal of his name upon it, there was at first no purpose to enlarge the application of such name beyond this well-recognized coast. That the name went beyond

---

[1] The letters AM appear upon the representation of the New World contained in it.

[2] Cf. on Gemma Frisius' additions to Apianus' *Cosmographia,* published in Spanish from the Latin in 1548, what Navarrete says in his *Opúsculos,* ii. 76.

[3] Antwerp, 1544, cap. xxx. "America ab inventore Amerio [*sic*] Vesputio nomen habet;" Antwerp, 1548, adds "alii Bresiliam vocât;" Paris, 1548, cap. xxx., "de America," and cap. xxxi. "de insulis apud Americam;" Paris, 1556, etc. Cf. Harrisse, *Bibl. Amer. Vet.,* nos. 156, 252, 279; *Additions,* nos. 92, 168.

[4] "Quam ab Americo primo inventore Americam vocant."

[5] "Insularum America cognominata obtenditur."

[6] Sir Thomas More in his *Utopia* (which it will be remembered was an island on which Vespucius is represented as leaving one of his companions), as published in the 1551 edition at London, speaks of the general repute of Vespucius' account, — "Those iiii voyages that be nowe in printe and abrode in euery mannes handes." Cf. *Carter-Brown Catalogue,* vol. i. no. 162. William Cuningham, in his *Cosmographical Glasse* (London, 1559), ignores Columbus, and gives Vespucius the credit of finding "America" in June, 1497 (Ibid., no. 228).

[7] See p. 119.

[8] *Bibl. Amer. Vet.,* no. 178; Carter-Brown, vol. i. no. 106; Charles Deane's paper on Schöner in the *Amer. Antiq. Soc. Proc.,* October, 1883.

[9] *Examen critique,* v. 174. Here is a contemporary's evidence that Vespucius supposed the new coasts to be Asia.

[10] "Tota itaque quod aiunt aberrant cœlo qui hanc continentem Americâ nuncupari contendunt, cum Americus multo post Columbû eandê terram adieret, nec cum Hispanis ille, sed cum Portugallensibus, ut suas merces commutaret, èo se contulito." It was repeated in the edition of 1541.

[11] Pedro de Ledesma, Columbus' pilot in his third voyage, deposed in 1513 that he considered Paria a part of Asia (Navarrete, iii. 539).

AME

BACCALEARUM
REGIO

INS. CORTEREALIS

ISLAND
INS
OLIM
THYLE

HISPANIA MAJOR
CAPTA ANNO
1530

ANDROBON

☐CORBO
☐FLORES

HEPTAPOLIS

☐GRACIOSA

FAIALO ☐ TERCERA
☐ S.MICHAEL
EL PICO

BARMUDA
SIVE
GARCA

☐ S.MARIA

ACORES INS

ESPIRITO
SANTO
FL.DEL

FLORIDA

GUANAO

PORTUS Sᵗ ☐
MADERA ☐

HISPANIA
NOVA

CUBA

INS FORTUNATE

YUCATANA
COSUMELA

IAMAICA

HISPANIOLA

NUNC CANARIE

CAMERCANE
INSULE

HESPERIDESO NUNC
INS DE ANTON

TRINITATIS INS

PARIA

S.PAULI

PERU
NOVA CASTILIA

C.S.CRUCIS

C.S.AUGUSTIN.

COSCO

RICA
A MULTIS HODIE NOVA
INDIA DICTA

MARE PACIFICUM

FRETUM PATHAGONICUM
SIVE MAGELLANICUM

MERCATOR, 1541.[1]

[1] This is the configuration of Mercator's gores (for a globe) reduced to Mercator's subsequently-devised projection.

that coast came of one of those shaping tenden-
cies which are without control. "It was," as
Humboldt says,[1] "accident, and not fraud and
dissensions, which deprived the continent of
America of the name of Columbus." It was
in 1541, and by Mercator in his printed gores
for a globe, that in a cartographical record
we first find the name *America* extended to
cover the entire continent; for he places the
letters AME at Baccalaos, and completed the
name with RICA at the La Plata.[2] Thus
the injustice was made perpetual; and there
seems no greater instance of the instability
of truth in the world's history. Such monstrous perversion could but incite an indignation which needed a victim, — and it found him
in Vespucius. The intimation of Schöner was
magnified in time by everybody, and the unfortunate date of 1497, as well as the altogether
doubtful aspect of his *Quattuor navigationes*,
helped on the accusation. Vespucius stood in
every cyclopædia and history as the personifi-
cation of baseness and arrogance;[3] and his
treacherous return for the kindness which Columbus did him in February, 1505, when he gave
him a letter of recommendation to his son
Diego,[4] at a time when the Florentine stood in
need of such assistance, was often made to point
a moral. The most emphatic of these accusers,
working up his case with every subsidiary help,
has been the Viscount Santarem. He will not
admit the possibility of Vespucius' ignorance
of the movement at St.-Dié. "We are led to
the conclusion," he says, in summing up, "that
the name given to the new continent after the
death of Columbus was the result of a precon-
ceived plan against his memory, either design-
edly and with malice aforethought, or by the
secret influence of an extensive patronage of

foreign merchants residing at Seville and elsewhere, dependent on Vespucius as naval con-
tractor."[5]

It was not till Humboldt approached the
subject in the fourth and fifth volumes of his
*Examen critique de l'histoire et de la géographie du
nouveau monde* that the great injustice to Vespucius on account of the greater injustice to
Columbus began to be apparent. No one but
Santarem, since Humboldt's time, has attempted
to rehabilitate the old arguments. Those who
are cautious had said before that he might
pardonably have given his name to the long
coast-line which he had tracked, but that he was
not responsible for its ultimate expansion.[6] But
Humboldt's opinion at once prevailed, and he reviewed and confirmed them in his *Cosmos*.[7] Humboldt's views are convincingly and elaborately
enforced; but the busy reader may like to know
they are well epitomized by Wiesener in a paper,
" Améric Vespuce et Christophe Colomb : la véritable origine du nom d'Amérique," which was
published in the *Revue des questions historiques*
(1866), i. 225–252, and translated into English
in the *Catholic World* (1867), v. 611.

The best English authority on this question
is Mr. R. H. Major, who has examined it
with both thoroughness and condensation of
statement in his paper on the Da Vinci map in
the *Archæologia*, vol. xl., in his *Prince Henry
the Navigator* (pp. 367–380),[8] and in his *Discoveries of Prince Henry*, chap. xiv. Harrisse
in his *Bibl. Amer. Vet.*, pp. 65, 94, enumerates
the contestants on the question; and Varnhagen,
who is never unjust to Columbus, traces in a
summary way the progress in the acceptance of
the name of America in his *Nouvelles recherches
sur les derniers voyages du navigateur Florentin*.
In German, Oscar Peṣchel in his *Geschichte des*

---

[1] *Cosmos*, Eng. tr., ii. 676.

[2] Wieser, *Der Portulan des Königs Philipp*, vol. ii. Vienna, 1876.

[3] See instances cited by Prof. J. D. Butler, *Transactions* of the Wisconsin Academy of Sciences, vol. ii.
(1873, 1874). There was an attempt made in 1845, by some within the New York Historical Society, to render
tardy justice to the memory of Columbus by taking his name, in the form of Columbia, as a national designation
of the United States; but it necessarily failed (*Mass. Hist. Soc. Proc.*, ii. 315). "Allegania" was an alternative suggestion made at the same time.

[4] This letter is preserved in the Archives of the Duke of Veraguas. It has been often printed. Harrisse,
Notes on Columbus, p. 149.

[5] Vizconde de Santarem (Manoel Francisco de Barros y Sousa), *Researches respecting Americus Vespucius
and his Voyages.* Translated by E.V. Childe (Boston, 1850), 221 pp. 16mo. This is a translation of the *Recherches
historiques, critiques et bibliographiques sur Améric Vespuce et ses voyages*, which was published in Paris in
1842. Santarem had before this sought to discredit the voyages claimed for Vespucius in 1501 and 1503, and
had communicated a memoir on the subject to Navarrete's *Coleccion*. He also published a paper in the *Bulletin
de la Société de Géographie de Paris* in October, 1833, and added to his statements in subsequent numbers
(October, 1835 ; September, 1836; February and September, 1837). These various contributions were combined and annotated in the *Recherches*, etc., already mentioned. Cf. his *Memoria e investigaciones históricas
sobre los viajes de Américo Vespucio*, in the *Recueil complet de traités*, vi. 304. There is a biography of Vespucius, with an appendix of " Pruebas é ilustraciones " in the *Coleccion de Opúsculos* of Navarrete, published
(1848) at Madrid, after his death.

[6] Such, for instance, was Caleb Cushing's opinion in his *Reminiscences of Spain*, ii. 234.

[7] Eng. tr., ii. 680.

[8] These chapters are reprinted in Sabin's *American Bibliopolist*, 1870–1871.

Zeitalters der Entdeckungen (book ii. chap. 13) has examined the matter with a scholar's instincts. The subject was followed by M. Schoetter in a paper read at the Congrès des Américanistes at Luxemburg in 1877; but it is not apparent from the abstract of the paper in the *Proceedings* of that session (p. 357) that any new light was thrown upon the matter.

Professor Jules Marcou would drive the subject beyond the bounds of any personal associations by establishing the origin of the name in the native designation (Americ, Amerrique, Amerique) of a range of mountains in Central America;[1] and Mr. T. H. Lambert, in the *Bulletin* of the American Geographical Society (no. 1 of 1883), asks us to find the origin in the name given by the Peruvians to their country, — neither of which theories has received or is likely to receive any considerable acceptance.[2]

[1] His theory was advanced in a paper on "The Origin of the Name America" in the *Atlantic Monthly* (March, 1875), xxxv. 291, and in "Sur l'origine du nom d'Amérique," in the *Bulletin de la Société de Géographie de Paris*, June, 1875. He again advanced his theory in the *New York Nation*, April 10, 1884, to which the editors replied that it was "fatally ingenious," — a courteous rejoinder, quite in contrast with that of H. H. Bancroft in his *Central America* (i. 291), who charges the Professor with "seeking fame through foolishness" and his theory. Marcou's argument in part depends upon the fact, as he claims, that Vespucius' name was properly Albericus or Alberico, and he disputes the genuineness of autographs which make it Amerigo; but nothing was more common in those days than variety, for one cause or another, in the fashioning of names. We find the Florentine's name variously written, — Amerigo, Merigo, Almerico, Alberico, Alberigo; and Vespucci, Vespucy, Vespuchi, Vespuchy, Vesputio, Vespulsius, Despuchi, Espuchi; or in Latin Vespucius, Vespuccius, and Vesputius.

[2] The Germans have written more or less to connect themselves with the name as with the naming, — deducing Amerigo or Americus from the Old German Emmerich. Cf. Von der Hagen, *Jahrbuch der Berliner Gesellschaft für Deutsche Sprache*, 1835; *Notes and Queries*, 1856; *Historical Magazine*, January, 1857, p. 24; Dr. Theodor Vetter in *New York Nation*, March 20, 1884; Humboldt, *Examen critique*, iv. 52.

APIANUS (*from* REUSNER'S *Icones*, 1590, p. 175).

THE BIBLIOGRAPHY

OF

POMPONIUS MELA, SOLINUS, VADIANUS, AND APIANUS.

BY THE EDITOR.

OF Pomponius Mela we know little beyond the fact that he was born in Spain, not far from Gibraltar, and that he wrote, as seems probable, his popular geographical treatise in the year 43 A. D.[1] The *editio princeps* of this treatise was printed in 1471 at Milan, it is supposed, by Antonius Zarotus, under the title *Cosmographia*. It was a small quarto of fifty-

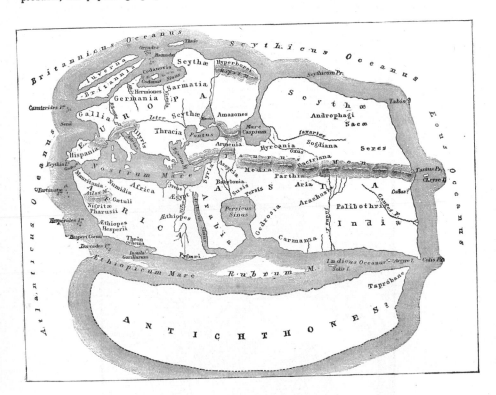

POMPONIUS MELA'S WORLD.[2]

1 Bunbury, *History of Ancient Geography*, ii. 352–368.
2 Reduced after map in Bunbury's *Ancient Geography* (London, 1879), ii. 368.

IOACHIMVS VADIANVS MEDI.
cus, & Poëta.

Phœbicultor eram, medicæ ſtudioſus & artis,
Ac medicæ: Galli Conſul in vrbe bonus.

M; D. LI.

VADIANUS.[1]

nine leaves. Two copies have been sold lately. The Sunderland copy (no. 10,117) brought £11 5s., and has since been held by Quaritch at £15 15s. Another copy was no. 897 in part iii. of the *Beckford Catalogue*. In 1478 there was an edition, *De situ orbis*, at Venice (Sunderland, no. 10,118) ; and in 1482 another edition, *Cosmographia geographica*, was also published at Venice (Leclerc, no. 456 ; Murphy, no. 2,003 ; D'Avezac, *Géographes Grecs et Latins*, p. 13). It was called *Cosmographia* in the edition of 1498 (*Bibl. Amer. Vet., Additions*, no. 8 ;

Huth, iv. 1166) ; *De orbis situ* in that of Venice, 1502 ; *De totius orbis descriptione* in the Paris edition of 1507, edited by Geofroy Tory (A. J. Bernard's *Geofroy Tory, premier imprimeur royal*, Paris, 1865, p. 81 ; Carter-Brown, i. 32 ; Muller, 1872, no. 2,318 ; 1877, no. 2,062).

In 1512 the text of Mela came under new influences. Henry Stevens (*Bibliotheca geographica*, p. 210) and others have pointed out how a circle of geographical students at this time were making Vienna a centre of interest by their interpretation of the views of Mela and

1 Fac-simile of a cut in Reusner's *Icones* (Strasburg, 1590), p. 162.

of Solinus, a writer of the third century, whose *Polyhistor* is a description of the world known to the ancients. Within this knot of cosmographers, John Camers undertook the editing of Mela; and his edition, *De situ orbis*, was printed by Jean Singrein at Vienna in 1512, though it bears neither place nor date (Stevens, *Bibliotheca geographica*, no. 1,825; D'Avezac, *Géographes Grecs et Latins*, p. 14; Leclerc, no. 457; Sunderland, no. 10,119). Another Mela of the same year (1512) is known to have been printed by Weissenburger, presumably at Nuremberg, and edited by Johannes Cocleius as *Cosmographia Pomponii Mele: authoris nitidissimi tribus libris digesta: . . . compendio Johannis Coclei Norici adaucta quo geographie principia generaliter comprehēduntur* (Weigel, 1877, no. 227; there is a copy in Charles Deane's library). In 1517 Mela made a part of the collection of Antonie Francino at Florence, which was reissued in 1519 and 1526 (D'Avezac, p. 16; Sunderland, nos. 10,121, 10,122).

Meanwhile another student, Joachim Watt, a native of St. Gall, in Switzerland, now about thirty years old, who had been a student of Camers, and who is better known by the latinized form of his name, Vadianus, had, in November, 1514, addressed a letter to Rudolfus Agricola, in which he adopted the suggestion first made by Waldseemüller that the fore-name of Vespucius should be applied to that part of the New World which we now call Brazil. This letter was printed at Vienna (1515) in a little tract, — *Habes, Lector, hoc libello, Rudolphi Agricolæ Junioris Rheti ad Jochimum Vadianum epistolam*, — now become very rare. It contains also the letter of Agricola, Sept. 1, 1514, which drew out the response of Vadianus dated October 16, — Agricola on his part referring to the work on Mela which was then occupying Vadianus (a copy owned by Stevens, *Bibliotheca geographica*, no. 2,799, passed into the Huth Library, *Catalogue*, v. 1506. Harrassowitz has since priced a copy, *Catalogue*, List 61, no. 57, at 280 marks).

The *De situ orbis* of Mela, as edited by Vadianus, came out finally in 1518, and contained one of the two letters, — that of Vadianus himself; and it is in this reproduction that writers have usually referred to its text (Harrisse, *Bibl. Amer. Vet.*, no. 92; Murphy, no. 2,004; Leclerc, no. 458; Sunderland, no. 10,120; Graesse, v. 401; Carter-Brown, i. 55). Camers also issued at the same time an edition uniform with the Aldine imprint of Solinus; and this and the Mela are often found bound together. Two years later (1520) copies of the two usually have bound up between them the famous cordiform map of Apian (Petrus Apianus, in the Latin form; Bienewitz, in his vernacular). This for a long time was considered the earliest engraved map to show the name of America, which ap-

peared, as the annexed fac-simile shows, on the representation of South America. There may be some question if the map equally belongs to the Mela and to the Solinus, for the two in this edition are usually bound together; yet in a few copies of this double book, as in the Cranmer copy in the British Museum, and in the Huth copy (*Catalogue*, iv. 1372), there is a map for each book. There are copies of the Solinus in the Carter-Brown, Lenox, Harvard College, Boston Public, and American Antiquarian Society libraries (cf. Harrisse, *Notes on Columbus*, p. 175; *Bibl. Amer. Vet.*, no. 108; Murphy, no. 2,338; Trübner, 1876, £15 15*s.*; Weigel, 1877, 240 marks; Calvary, 1883, 250 marks; Leclerc, 1881, no. 2,686, 500 francs; Ellis & White, 1877, £25). The inscription on the map reads: "Tipus orbis universalis juxta Ptolomei cosmographi traditionem et Americii Vespucii aliosque lustrationes a Petro Apiano Leysnico elucbrat. An. Do. M. D. XX." Harrisse (*Bibl. Amer. Vet.*, *Additions*, no. 68) cites from Varnhagen's *Postface aux trois livraisons sur Vespucci*, a little tract of eight leaves, which is said to be an exposition of the map to accompany it, called *Declaratio et usus typi cosmographici*, Ratisbon, 1522. The map was again used in the first complete edition of Peter Martyr's *Decades*, when the date was changed to "M. D. XXX" (Carter-Brown, i. 94; *Bibl. Amer. Vet.*, no. 154; Kunstmann, *Entdeckung Amerikas*, p. 134; Kohl, *Die beiden ältesten General-Karten von Amerika*, p. 33; Uricoechea, *Mapoteca Colombiana*, no. 4). Vadianus meanwhile had quarrelled with Camers, and had returned to St. Gall, and now re-edited his *Mela*, and published it at Basle in 1522 (*Bibl. Amer. Vet.*, no. 112; Murphy, no. 2,004 **; Carter-Brown, i. 590; Leclerc, no. 459).

In 1524 Apianus published the first edition of his cosmographical studies, — a book that for near a century, under various revisions, maintained a high reputation. The *Cosmographicus liber* was published at Landshut in 1524, — a thin quarto with two diagrams showing the New World, in one of which the designation is "Ameri" for an island; in the other, "America." Bibliographers differ as to collation, some giving fifty-two, and others sixty leaves; and there are evidently different editions of the same year. The book is usually priced at £5 or £6. Cf. Harrisse, *Notes on Columbus*, p. 174; *Bibl. Amer. Vet.*, no. 127, and *Additions*, p. 87; Carter-Brown, i. 78; Huth, i. 39; Murphy, no. 93; Sabin, no. 1,738. There is an account of Apianus (born 1495; died 1551 or 1552) in Clement's *Bibliographie curieuse* (Göttingen, 1750–1760). It is in chapter iv. of part ii. of the *Cosmographicus liber* that America is mentioned; but there is no intimation of Columbus having discovered it. Where " Isabella aut

PART OF APIANUS'S MAP, 1520.[1]

'Cuba" is spoken of, is thought to be the earliest instance of conferring the latter name on
that island.

In 1529 a pupil of Apianus, Gemma Frisius,
annotated his master's work, when it was published at Antwerp, while an abridgment, *Cos-*

---

[1] There are fac-similes of the entire map in the *Carter-Brown Catalogue*, i. 69, and in Santarem's *Atlas :*
and on a much reduced scale in Daly's *Early Cartography.* Cf. Varnhagen's *Jo: Schöner e P. Apianus :*

mographiæ introductio, was printed the same year (1529) at Ingoldstadt (Sabin, no. 1,739; Court, no. 21; *Bibl. Amer. Vet.*, nos. 148, 149, and *Additions*, no. 88. There is a copy of the abridgment in Harvard College Library).

The third edition of *Mela, cum commentariis Vadiani* appeared at Paris in 1530, but without maps (cf. Carter-Brown, i. 97; Muller, 1877, no. 2,063; *Bibl. Amer. Vet.*, no. 157); and again in 1532 (Sunderland, no. 10,124; Harrassowitz, list 61, no. 60).

It is not necessary to follow, other than synoptically, the various subsequent editions of these three representative books, with brief indications of the changes that they assumed to comport with the now rapidly advancing knowledge of the New World.

1533. Apianus, full or abridged, in Latin, at Venice, at Freiburg, at Antwerp, at Ingoldstadt, at Paris (Carter-Brown, i. 591; *Bibl. Amer. Vet.*, nos. 179, 202, and *Additions*, no. 100; Sabin, nos. 1,742, 1,757. Some copies have 1532 in the colophon). Apianus printed this year at Ingoldstadt various tracts in Latin and German on the instruments used in observations for latitude and longitude (Stevens, *Bibliotheca geographica*, no. 173, etc). Vadianus, in his *Epitome trium terræ partium*, published at Tiguri, described America as a part of Asia (Weigel, 1877, no. 1,574). He dated his preface at St. Gall, "VII. Kallen. August, M. D. XXXIII."

1534. Apianus in Latin at Venice (*Bibl. Amer. Vet., Additions*, no. 106). The *Epitome* of Vadianus in folio, published at Tiguri, with a map, "Typus cosmographicus universalis, Tiguri, anno M. D. XXXIIII," which resembles somewhat that of Finæus, representing the New World as an island approaching the shape of South America. The Carter-Brown copy has no map (cf. Huth, v. 1508; Leclerc, no. 586, 130 francs; Carter-Brown, i. 112; Weigel, 1877, no. 1,576; *Bibl. Amer. Vet.*, no. 189). An edition in octavo, without date, is held to be of the same year. It is usually said to have no map; but Quaritch (no. 12,475) has advertised a copy for £4, — "the only copy he had ever seen containing the map." The *Huth Catalogue*, v. 1508, shows a copy with twelve wood-cut maps of two leaves each, and four single leaves of maps and globes. The part pertaining to America in this edition is pages 544–564,

"Insulæ Oceani præcipuæ," which is considered to belong to the Asiatic continent (cf. Stevens, 1870, no. 2,179; Muller, 1872, no. 1,551; 1877, no. 3,293; Weigel, 1877, no. 1,575).

1535. Apianus, in Latin, at Venice (Sabin, no. 1,743; *Bibl. Amer. Vet.*, no. 202). Vadianus, in Latin, at Antwerp. (*Bibl. Amer. Vet.*, 209; Huth, v. 1508; Court, no. 360).

1536. An edition of Mela, *De situ orbis*, without place and date, was printed at Basle, in small octavo, with the corrections of Olive and Barbaro. Cf. D'Avezac, *Géographes Grecs et Latins*, p. 20; Sunderland, no. 10,123; Weigel (1877), p. 99.

1537. The first Dutch edition of Apianus, *De cosmographie rā Pe Apianus*, Antwerp, with woodcut of globe on the title. The first of two small maps shows America. It contains a description of Peru. Cf. Carter-Brown, i. 121; Muller (1875), no. 2,314.

1538. Mela and Solinus, printed by Henri Petri at Basle with large and small maps, one representing the New World to the east of Asia as "Terra incognita." Cf. Harrassowitz (1882), no. 91, p. 2, 60 marks; D'Avezac, p. 21.

1539. An edition of Mela, *De orbis situ*, at Paris (Sunderland, no. 10,124). Apianus's *Cosmographia per Gemmam Phrysium restituta*, in small quarto, was published at Antwerp by A. Berckman. A globe on the titlepage shows the Old World. It has no other map (Carter-Brown, i. 124; Sabin, no. 1,744; *Bibl. Amer. Vet.*, nos. 229, 230).

1540. An edition of Mela, issued at Paris, has the Orontius Finæus map of 1531, with the type of the Dedication changed. The Harvard College copy and one given in Harrassowitz' *Catalogue* (81), no. 55, show no map. Cf. Leclerc, no. 460, 200 francs; Harrisse, *Bibl. Amer. Vet.*, no. 230, *Additions*, nos. 126, 127, 460; Court, no. 283; Rosenthal (1884), no. 51, at 150 marks. An edition of Apianus in Latin at Antwerp, without map; but Lelewel (*Moyen-âge*, pl. 46) gives a map purporting to follow one in this edition of Apianus. Cf. Carter-Brown, i. 125; *Bibl. Amer. Vet.*, no. 230; Sabin, no. 1,745.

1541. Editions of Apianus in Latin at Venice and at Nuremberg. Cf. *Bibl. Amer. Vet.*, nos. 235, 236; Sabin, nos. 1,746, 1,747.

1543. Mela and Solinus at Basle (D'Avezac, p. 21).

Influencia de um e outro e de varios de seus contemporaneos na adopção do nome America; primeiros globos e primeiros mappas-mundi com este nome; globo de Waltzeemüller, e plaquette acerca do de Schöner, Vienna, 1872, privately printed, 61 pp., 100 copies (*Murphy Catalogue*, no. 2,231; Quaritch prices it at about £1). A recent account of the history of the Vienna presses, *Wiens Buchdrucker-geschichte* (1883), by Anton Mayer, refers to the edition of Solinus of 1520 (vol. i. pp. 38, 41), and to the editions of Pomponius Mela, edited by Vadianus, giving a fac-simile of the title (p. 39) in one case.

Santarem gives twenty-five editions of Ptolemy between 1511 and 1584 which do not bear the name of America, and three (1522, 1541, and 1552) which have it. Cf. *Bulletin de la Société de Géographie de Paris* (1837), vol. viii.

ASTROLOGVS PETRVS APIANVS BINVITIZIVS

QVOD COELOS PANDIS, RADIO QVOD SIDERA PINGIS
GERMANVS MERITO DICERIS ARCHIMEDES.

APIANUS.[1]

1544. An edition of Apianus in French at Antwerp, with a map, which was used in various later editions. Cf. Sabin, no. 1,752; Carter-Brown, i. 592; *Bibl. Amer. Vet.*, no. 253.

1545. Apianus, in Latin, at Antwerp, with the same map as in the 1544 French edition. Cf. Carter-Brown, i. 135; *Bibl. Amer. Vet.*, no. 262; Muller (1875), no. 2,365 (1877), no. 158; Sabin, no. 1,748.

---

[1] This follows a fac-simile of an old cut given in the *Carter-Brown Catalogue*, i. 294.

1548. Apianus in Spanish, *Cosmographia augmentada por Gemma Frisio*, at Antwerp, with the same folding map. Cf. *Bibl. Amer. Vet.*, no. 283; Sabin, no. 1,753; Carter-Brown, i. 147; Dufosse, no. 10,201, 45 francs; Quaritch (1878), no. 104, £6 6s.; *Cat. hist. Brazil, Bibl. Nac. do Rio de Janeiro*, no. 3. Apianus in Italian at Antwerp, *Libro de la cosmographia de Pedro Apiano*, with the same map. The *Epitome* of Vadianus, published at Tiguri, with double maps engraved on wood, contains one, dated 1546, showing America, which is reproduced in Santarem's *Atlas*. Cf. Carter-Brown, i. 151; *Bibl. Amer. Vet.*, nos. 170, 464, *Additions*, no. 104.

1550. Apianus in Latin at Antwerp, with map at folio 30, with additions by Frisius; and folios 30–48, on America (cf. Carter-Brown, i. 154; *Bibl. Amer. Vet.*, no. 298; Murphy, no. 94; Sabin, no. 1,749; Muller, 1875, no. 2,366). Some bibliographers report Latin editions of this year at Amsterdam and Basle.

1551. Editions of Apianus at Paris, in Latin and French, with a folding map and two smaller ones, — a reprint of the Antwerp edition of 1550. The language of the maps is French in both editions (Court, no. 20). Clement (*Bibliothèque curieuse*, i. 404) gives 1553 as the date of the colophon. An edition of Mela and Solinus (D'Avezac, p. 21).

1553. Editions of Apianus in Latin at Antwerp and Paris, and in Dutch at Antwerp, with mappemonde and two small maps. Cf. Carter-Brown, i. 174, 594. Some copies have 1551 in the colophon, as does that belonging to Jules Marcou, of Cambridge. There is a copy of the Paris edition in the Boston Public Library, no. 2,285, 58.

1554. An abridged edition of Apianus, *Cosmographiæ introductio*, Venice. A copy in Harvard College Library.

1556. An edition of Mela, at Paris (Sunderland, no. 10,125).

1557. An edition of Mela, as edited by Vadianus, at Basle (D'Avezac, p. 21).

1561. A Dutch edition of Apianus, at Antwerp, without map. Cf. Carter-Brown, i. 597; Sabin, no. 1,754.

1564. An octavo edition of Vadianus' *Mela* (D'Avezac, p. 21). A Latin edition of Apianus at Antwerp, with mappemonde.

1574. Latin editions of Apianus at Antwerp and Cologne, with a folding mappemonde (Carter-Brown, i. 296, 297; Sabin, no. 1,750).

1575. Spanish and Italian texts of Apianus published at Antwerp, with mappemonde, and descriptions of the New World taken from Gomara and Girava. Cf. Carter-Brown, i. 302; Sabin, no. 1,756; Clement, *Bibliothèque curieuse*, i. 405.

1576. Mela, as edited by Vadianus (D'Avezac, p. 21). With the *Polyhistor* of Solinus, published at Basle. The Harvard College copy has no map of America. Cf. Graesse, v. 402.

1577. Henri Estienne's collection in quarto, containing Mela (D'Avezac, p. 24).

1581. Apianus in French, at Antwerp, with a folding mappemonde (p. 72). The part on America is pp. 155–187 (Murphy, no. 95).

1582. An edition of Mela edited by A. Schottus, published at Antwerp, with map by Ortelius (Sunderland, no. 10,126).

1584. The *Cosmographia* of Apianus and Frisius, called by Clement (*Bibliothèque curieuse*, i. 404) the best edition, published at Antwerp by Bellero, in two issues, a change in the title distinguishing them. It has the same map with the 1564 and 1574 editions, and the section on "Insulæ Americæ" begins on p. 157. Cf. Carter-Brown, i. 354, no map mentioned; Sabin, no. 1,751.

1585. An edition of Mela in English, translated by Arthur Golding, published at London as *The Worke of Pomponius Mela, the Cosmographer, concerning the Situation of the World*. The preface is dated Feb. 6, 1584, in which Golding promises versions of Solinus and Thevet. There is a copy in the Library of the Massachusetts Historical Society.

1592. A Dutch edition of Apianus, published at Antwerp (Sabin, no. 1,755).

1595. An edition of Mela, as edited by Vadianus, published at Basle (D'Avezac, p. 21).

1598. A Dutch edition of Apianus, published at Amsterdam, with folding map. Cf. Carter-Brown, i. 521; Muller (1877), no. 164.

1605. Mathias Bonhomme published an edition of Mela and Solinus (D'Avezac, p. 21).

1609. A Dutch edition of Apianus, printed at Antwerp, with mappemonde (Carter-Brown, ii. 76; Sabin, no. 1,755). Bonhomme's edition of Mela and Solinus, reissued (D'Avezac, p. 21).

1615, etc. Numerous editions of Mela appeared subsequently: 1615 (Vadianus), Basle, 1619, 1625, 1626, 1635; at Madrid, 1642, 1644, in Spanish; Leyden, 1646, in Latin; and under different editors, 1658, 1685, and 1700, and often later.

CHAPTER III.

THE COMPANIONS OF COLUMBUS.

BY EDWARD CHANNING, PH.D.,

Instructor in History in Harvard College.

IN 1498 the news of the discovery of Paria and the pearl fisheries reached Spain; and during the next year a number of expeditions was fitted out at private expense for trade and exploration. The first to set sail was commanded by Alonso de Ojeda, the quondam captor of Caonabo, who, with Juan de la Cosa — a mariner scarcely inferior in his own estimation to the Admiral himself — and with Morigo Vespuche, as Ojeda calls him, left the Bay of Cadiz toward the end of May, 1499. Ojeda, provided with a copy of the track-chart sent home by Columbus, easily found his way to the coast of South America, a few degrees north of the equator. Thence he coasted northward by the mouth of the Rio Dulce (Essequibo) into the Gulf of Paria, which he left by the Boca del Drago. He then passed to the Isla Margarita and the northern shores of Tierra Firme, along which he sailed until he came to a deep gulf into which opened a large lagoon. The gulf he called the Golfo de Venecia (Venezuela), from the fancied resemblance of a village on its shores to the Queen of the Adriatic; while to the lagoon, now known as the Lake of Maracáibo, he gave the name of S. Bartoloméo. From this gulf he sailed westward by the land of Coquibacoa to the Cabo de la Vela, whence he took his departure for home, where, after many adventures, he arrived in the summer of the following year.

Close in his track sailed Cristóbal Guerra and Pedro Alonso Niño, who arrived off the coast of Paria a few days after Ojeda had left it. Still following him, they traded along the coast as far west as Caucheto, and tarried at the neighboring islands, especially Margarita, until their little vessel of fifty tons was well loaded; when they sailed for Spain, where they arrived in April, 1500, "so laden with pearls that they were in maner with every mariner as common as chaffe."

About four months before Guerra's return, Vicente Yañez Pinzon, the former captain of the "Niña," sailed from Palos with four vessels; and, pursuing a southerly course, was the first of Europeans to cross the equator

on the American side of the Atlantic.   He sighted the coast of the New
World in eight degrees south latitude, near a cape to which he gave the
name of Santa Maria de la Consolacion (S. Augustin).   There he landed;
but met with no vestiges of human beings, except some footprints of gigantic size.   After taking possession of the country with all proper forms, he
reimbarked; and proceeding northward and westward, discovered and partially explored the delta of an immense river, which he called the Paricura,
and which, after being known as the Marañon or Orellana, now appears on

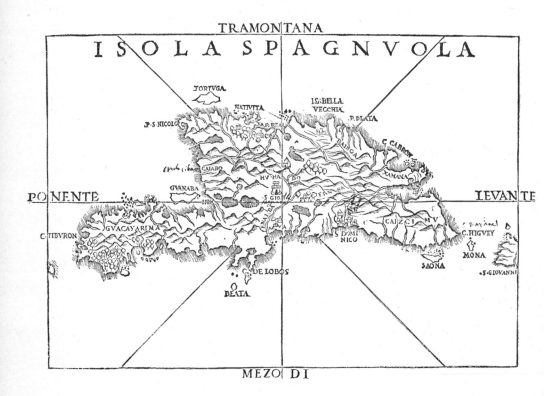

HISPANIOLA.[1]

the maps as the Amazon.   Thence, by the Gulf of Paria, Española (Hispaniola), and the Bahamas, he returned to Spain, where he arrived in the
latter part of September, 1500.[2]

Diego de Lepe left Palos not long after Vicente Yañez, and reached the
coast of the New World to the south of the Cabo de S. Augustin, to which
he gave the name of *Rostro hermoso;* and doubling it, he ran along the coast

---

[1] A reduced fac-simile of the map (1556) in
Ramusio, iii. 44, following that which originally
appeared in the Venice edition of Peter Martyr
and Oviedo, 1534.

[2] [Cf. the section on the "Historical chorography of South America" in which the gradual
development of the outline of that continent is
traced. — ED.]

to the Gulf of Paria, whence he returned to Palos. In October, 1500, Rodrigo de Bastidas and Juan de la Cosa sailed from the bay of Cadiz for the Golfo de Venecia (Venezuela), which they entered and explored. Thence, stopping occasionally to trade with the natives, they coasted the shores of Tierra Firme, by the Cabo de la Vela, the province of Santa Marta, the mouths of the Rio Grande de la Magdalena, the port of Cartagena, the river of Cenú, and the Punta Caribana, to the Gulf of Urabá (Darien), which they explored with some care. They were unsuccessful in their search for a strait to the west; and after sailing along the coast of Veragua to Nombre de Dios, they started on the return voyage. But the ravages of the *broma* (teredo) rendering their ships leaky, they were forced into a harbor of Española, where the vessels, after the most valuable portions of the cargo had been removed, went to the bottom. Bastidas was seized by order of Bobadilla, then governor of Española, for alleged illicit traffic with the natives, and sent to Spain for trial, where he arrived in September, 1502. He was soon after acquitted on the charges brought against him.

Alonso de Ojeda had reported the presence of Englishmen on the coast of Tierra Firme; and, partly to forestall any occupation of the country by them, he had been given permission to explore, settle, and govern, at his own expense, the province of Coquibacoa. He associated with him Juan de Vergara and Garcia de Ocampo, who provided the funds required, and went with the expedition which left Cadiz in January, 1502. They reached, without any serious mishap, the Gulf of Paria, where they beached and cleaned their vessels, and encountered the natives. Thence through the Boca del Drago they traded from port to port, until they came to an irrigated land, which the natives called Curiana, but to which Ojeda gave the name of Valfermoso. At this place they seized whatever they could which might be of service in the infant settlement, and then proceeded westward; while Vergara went to Jamaica for provisions, with orders to rejoin the fleet at S. Bartoloméo (Maracáibo), or at the Cabo de la Vela. After visiting the Island of Curazao (Curaçoa) Ojeda arrived at Coquibacoa, and finally decided to settle at a place which he called Santa Cruz, — probably the Bahia Honda of the present day. Vergara soon arrived; but the supply of food was inadequate, and the hostility of the natives made foraging a matter of great difficulty and danger. To add to their discomfort, quarrels broke out between the leaders, and Ojeda was seized by his two partners and carried to Española, where he arrived in September, 1502. He was eventually set at liberty, while his goods were restored by the King's command. The expedition, however, was a complete failure.

This second unprofitable voyage of Ojeda seems to have dampened the ardor of the navigators and their friends at home; and although Navarrete regards it as certain that Juan de la Cosa sailed to Urabá as chief in command in 1504–1506, and that Ojeda made a voyage in the direction of Tierra Firme in the beginning of 1505, it was not until after the successful voyage of La Cosa in 1507–1508, that the work of colonization was again

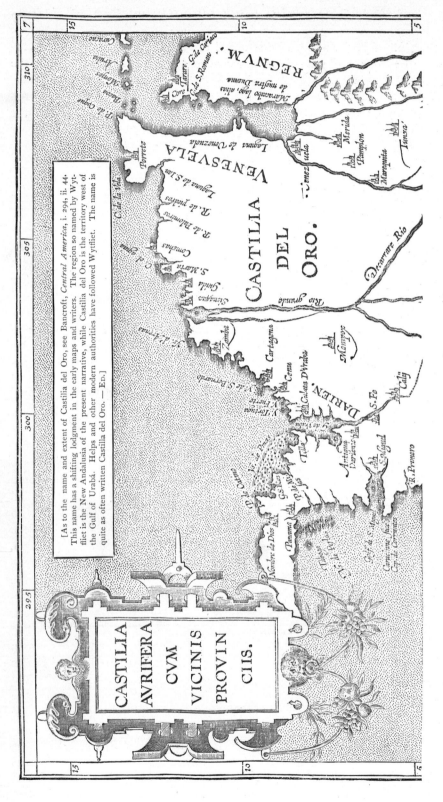

[As to the name and extent of Castilia del Oro, see Bancroft, *Central America*, i. 294, ii. 44. This name has a shifting lodgment in the early maps and writers. The region so named by Wytfliet is the New Andalusia of the present narrative, while Castilia del Oro is the territory west of the Gulf of Urabá. Helps and other modern authorities have followed Wytfliet. The name is quite as often written Castilla del Oro. — ED.]

CASTILIA DEL ORO, 1597 (*after Wytfliet*).

taken up with vigor.[1] Two men offered themselves as leaders in this enterprise; and, as it was impossible to decide between them, they were both commissioned to settle and govern for four years the mainland from the Cabo de la Vela to the Cabo Gracias á Dios, while the Gulf of Urabá (Darien) was to be the boundary between their respective governments. To Alonso de Ojeda was given the eastern province, or Nueva Andaluçia, while Diego de Nicuesa was the destined governor of the western province, then for the first time named Castilla del Oro. The fertile Island of Jamaica was intended to serve as a granary to the two governors; and to them were also granted many other privileges,— as, for instance, freedom from taxation, and, more important still, the right for each to take from Española four hundred settlers and two hundred miners.

Nicuesa and Ojeda met at Santo Domingo, whither they had gone to complete their preparations, and became involved in a boundary dispute. Each claimed the province of Darien[1] as within his jurisdiction. It was finally agreed, however, that the river of Darien should be the boundary line. With regard to Jamaica, the new admiral, Diego Columbus, prevented all disputes by sending Juan de Esquivel to hold it for him. Diego further contributed to the failure of the enterprise by preventing the governors from taking the colonists from Española, to which they were entitled by their licenses. At last, however, on Nov. 12, 1509, Ojeda, with Juan de la Cosa and three hundred men, left Santo Domingo; and five days later entered the harbor of Cartagena, where he landed, and had a disastrous engagement with the natives. These used their poisoned arrows to such good purpose that sixty-nine Spaniards, Juan de la Cosa among them, were killed. Nicuesa arrived in the harbor soon after; and the two commanders, joining forces, drove the natives back, and recovered the body of La Cosa, which they found swollen and disfigured by poison, and suspended from a tree. The two fleets then separated; Nicuesa standing over to the shore of Castilla del Oro, while Ojeda coasted the western shore of the Gulf of Urabá, and settled at a place to which he gave the name of San Sebastian. Here they built a fort, and ravaged the surrounding country in search of gold, slaves, and food; but here again the natives, who used poisoned arrows, kept the Spaniards within their fort, where starvation soon stared them in the face. Ojeda despatched a ship to Española for provisions and recruits; and no help coming, went himself in a vessel which had been brought to San Sebastian by a certain piratical Talavera. Ojeda was wrecked on Cuba; but after terrible suffering reached Santo Domingo, only to find that his lieutenant, Enciso, had sailed some time before with all that was necessary for the relief of the colony. The future movements of Ojeda are

---

[1] It should be remembered that Columbus on his fourth voyage had sailed along the coast from Cape Honduras to Nombre de Dios, and that Vicente Yañez Pinzon and Juan Diaz de Solis, coasting the shores of the Gulf of Honduras, had sailed within sight of Yucatan in 1506; and there-fore that in 1508 the coast-line was well known from the Cabo de S. Augustin to Honduras.

[2] [This name in the early narratives and maps appears as Tarena, Tariene, or Darien, with a great variety of the latter form. Cf. Bancroft, *Central America*, i. 326. — ED.]

CARTAGENA.[1]

[1] [This view of the town of Cartagena at a somewhat later day is a fac-simile of a cut in Montanus, and has some of the doubt attached to all of his pictures. — ED.]

not known. He testified in the trial of Talavera and his companions, who were hanged in 1511; and in 1513 and 1515 his depositions were taken in the suit brought by the King's attorney against the heirs of Columbus. Broken in spirit and ruined in fortune, he never returned to his colony.

Martin Fernandez de Enciso, a wealthy lawyer (*bachiller*) of Santo Domingo, had been appointed by Ojeda *alcalde mayor* of Nueva Andaluçia, and had been left behind to follow his chief with stores and recruits. On his way to San Sebastian he stopped at Cartagena; found no difficulty in making friends with the natives who had opposed Ojeda so stoutly; and while awaiting there the completion of some repairs on a boat, was surprised by the appearance of a brigantine containing the remnant of the San Sebastian colony. When Ojeda had sailed with Talavera he had left Pizarro, the future conqueror of Peru, in command, with orders to hold the place for fifty days, and then, if succor had not arrived, to make the best of his way to Santo Domingo. Pizarro had waited more than fifty days, until the colonists had dwindled to a number not too large for the two little vessels at his disposal. In these they had then left the place. But soon after clearing the harbor one of his brigantines, struck by a fish, had gone down with all on board; and it had been with much difficulty that the other had been navigated to Cartagena. Enciso, commander now that Ojeda and La Cosa were gone, determined to return to San Sebastian; but, while rounding the Punta Caribana, the large vessel laden with the stores went on the rocks and became a total loss, the crew barely escaping with their lives. They were now in as bad a plight as before; and decided, at the suggestion of Vasco Nuñez de Balbóa, to cross the Gulf of Urabá to a country where the natives did not use poisoned arrows, and where, therefore, foraging would not be so dangerous as at San Sebastian.[1] The removal to the other side of the gulf was safely carried out, and the natives driven from their village. The Spaniards settled themselves here, and called the place Santa Maria del Antigua del Darien. Provisions and gold were found in abundance; but Enciso, declaring it unlawful for private persons to trade with the natives for gold, was deposed; for, as Vasco Nuñez said, the new settlement was within the jurisdiction of Nicuesa, and therefore no obedience whatever was due to Enciso. A municipal form of government was then instituted, with Vasco Nuñez and Zamudio as *alcaldes*, and Valdivia as *regidor*. But the Antigua settlers were no more disposed to obey their chosen magistrates than they had been to give obedience to him who had been appointed to rule over them, and they soon became divided into factions. At this juncture arrived Rodrigo Enriquez de Colmenares, whom Nicuesa had left at Española to follow him with recruits and provisions. Colmenares easily persuaded the settlers at Antigua to put themselves under

---

[1] This Vasco Nuñez was a bankrupt farmer of Española who went with Bastidas on his voyage to the Gulf of Urabá, and had been so carefully concealed aboard Enciso's ship that the officers sent to apprehend absconding debtors had failed to discover him.

the government of Nicuesa; and then, accompanied by two agents from Darien, sailed away in search of his chief. Nicuesa, after aiding Ojeda at Cartagena, had sailed for Castilla del Oro; but while coasting its shores had become separated from the rest of his fleet, and had been wrecked off the mouth of a large river. He had rejoined the rest of his expedition after the most terrible suffering. Nicuesa had suspected Lope de Olano, his second in command, of lukewarmness in going to his relief, and had put him in chains. In this condition he was found by the agents from Antigua, to one of whom it appears that Olano was related. This, and the punishment with which Nicuesa threatened those at Antigua who had traded for gold, impelled the agents to return with all speed to oppose his reception; and, therefore, when he arrived off Antigua he was told to go back. Attempting to sustain himself on land, he was seized, put on a worn-out vessel, and bid to make the best of his way to Española. He sailed from Antigua in March, 1511, and was never heard of again.

After his departure the quarrels between the two factions broke out again, and were appeased only by the sending of Enciso and Zamudio to Spain to present their respective cases at Court. They sailed for Española in a vessel commanded by the *regidor* Valdivia (a firm friend of Vasco Nuñez), who went well provided with gold to secure the favor and protection of the new admiral, Diego Columbus, and of Pasamonte, the King's treasurer at Santo Domingo, for himself and Vasco Nuñez. While Valdivia was absent on this mission, Vasco Nuñez explored the surrounding country and won the good-will of the natives. It was on one of these expeditions that the son of a chief, seeing the greed of the Spaniards for gold, told them of the shores of a sea which lay to the southward of the mountains, where there were kings who possessed enormous quantities of the highly coveted metal. Valdivia, who brought a commission from the Admiral to Vasco Nuñez (commonly called Balbóa) as governor of Antigua, was immediately sent back with a large sum of money, carrying the news of a sea to be discovered. Valdivia was wrecked on the southern coast of Yucatan, where, with all but two of his crew, he was sacrificed and eaten by the natives. After some time had elapsed with no news from Española, Vasco Nuñez, fearing that Valdivia had proved a treacherous friend, despatched two emissaries — Colmenares and Caicedo — to Spain to lay the state of affairs at Darien before the King.

Not long after their departure a vessel arrived from Española, commanded by Serrano, with food, recruits, and a commission from Pasamonte to Vasco Nuñez as governor. But Serrano also brought a letter from Zamudio, giving an account of his experience in Spain, where he had found the King more disposed to consider favorably the complaints of Enciso than the justifications which he himself offered. Indeed, it seems that Zamudio, who barely escaped arrest, wrote that it was probable that Vasco Nuñez would be summoned to Spain to give an account of himself. Upon the receipt of this unpleasant letter, Vasco Nuñez determined to discover the new sea of

El Adelantado BASCO NUÑES de
xeres que descubrió la mar del Sur.

BALBÓA.[1]

which there was report, and thus to atone for his shortcomings with respect
to Enciso and Nicuesa.

To this end he left Antigua on the 1st of September, 1513; and proceeding by the way of the country of Careta, on the evening of September 24
encamped on the side of a mountain from whose topmost peak his native
guide declared the other sea could be discerned. Early in the morning
of the next day, Sept. 25, 1513, the sixty-seven Spaniards ascended
the mountain; and Vasco Nuñez de Balbóa, going somewhat in advance,
found himself—first of civilized men—gazing upon the new-found sea,
which he called *Mar del Sur* (South Sea), in distinction to the *Mar del*

[1] [Fac-simile of an engraving in Herrera, edition of 1728.—ED.]

Norte, or the sea on the northern side of the isthmus, although it is known to us by the name of Pacific, which Magellan later gave to it.   Of this ocean and all lands bordering upon it he took possession for his royal master and mistress, and then descended toward its shores.   The sea itself was hard to reach, and it was not until three days later that a detachment under Alonso Martin discovered the beach; when Alonso Martin, jumping into a convenient canoe, pushed forth, while he called upon his comrades to bear witness that he was the first European to sail upon the southern sea.   On the 29th of September Vasco Nuñez reached the water; and marching boldly into it, again claimed it for the King and Queen of Castile and Aragon.   It was an arm of the ocean which he had found.   According to the Spanish custom, he bestowed upon it the name of the patron saint of that particular day, and as the Gulf of San Miguel it is still known to us.   After a short voyage in some canoes, in the course of which Vasco Nuñez came near drowning, he collected an immense amount of tribute from the neighboring chiefs, and then took up his homeward march, arriving at Antigua without serious accident in the latter part of January, 1514.   When we consider the small force at his command and the almost overpowering difficulties of the route, — to say nothing of hostile natives, — this march of Vasco Nuñez de Balbóa is among the most wonderful exploits of which we have trustworthy information.

But this achievement did not bring him the indemnity and honors for which he hoped.   A new governor, appointed July 27, 1513, — notwithstanding the news which Colmenares and Caicedo had carried with them of the existence of a sea, — had sailed before Pedro de Arbolancha, bearing the news of the discovery, could arrive in Spain, inasmuch as he did not even leave Antigua until March, 1514.   This new governor was Pedro Arias de Avila, better known as Pedrárias, though sometimes called by English writers Dávila.   Pedrárias, dubbed *El Galan* and *El Justador* in his youth, and *Furor Domini* in his later years, has been given a hard character by all historians.   This is perfectly natural, for, like all other Spanish governors, he cruelly oppressed the natives, and thus won the dislike of Las Casas; while Oviedo, who usually differs as much as possible from Las Casas, hated Pedrárias for other reasons.   Pedrárias' treatment of Vasco Nuñez, in whose career there was that dramatic element so captivating, was scant at least of favor.   But, on the other hand, it must be remembered that Pedrárias occupied an office from which Nicuesa and Enciso had been driven, and he ruled a community which had required the utmost vigilance on the part of Vasco Nuñez to hold in check.

With Pedrárias went a goodly company, among whom may be mentioned Hernando de Soto, Diego de Almagro, and Benalcazar, who, with Pizarro, already in Antigua, were to push discovery and conquest along the shores of the Mar del Sur.   There also went in the same company that Bernal Diaz del Castillo who was to be one of the future conquistadores of Mexico and the rude but charming relater of that conquest; and Pascual de Andagoya, who, while inferior to Benalcazar as a ruler and to Bernal Diaz as a narrator, was yet a very important character. The lawyer Enciso returned among them to the scene of his former disappointment as *alguazil mayor;* and, lastly, let us mention Gonzalo Fernandez de Oviedo y Valdés, who accompanied the expedition as *escriban general* and *veedor.* Pedrárias sailed from San Lucar on the 12th of April, 1514, and arrived safely in the harbor of Antigua on the 29th of June. The survivors of the companies of Ojeda and Nicuesa, and of the reinforcements brought thither at different times, numbered in all but four hundred and fifty souls; and they could have offered little opposition to the fifteen hundred accompanying Pedrárias, if they had so desired. But no attempt was made to prevent his landing; and as soon as Pedrárias felt himself fairly installed, an inquiry was instituted into the previous acts of Vasco Nuñez. This trial, or *residencia,* was conducted by Espinosa, the new *alcalde mayor.* There is no doubt but that Enciso tried hard to bring the murder of Nicuesa, for such it was, home to Vasco Nuñez. The efforts of Quivedo, the recently appointed bishop of Santa Maria de la Antigua é Castilla del Oro, and of Isabel del Bobadilla, the new governor's wife, who had been won over in some unknown way, secured the acquittal of Vasco Nuñez on all criminal charges. In the innumerable civil suits, however, which were brought against him by Enciso and by all others who felt grieved, he was mulcted in a large amount.

This affair off his hands, Pedrárias set about executing his supplementary instructions, which were to connect the north and south seas by a chain of posts. He sent out three expeditions, which, besides exploration, were to forage for food, since the supply in Antigua was very small. The stores brought by the fleet had been in a great measure spoiled on the voyage, and the provisions at Antigua which Vasco Nuñez' foresight had provided, while ample for his little band, were entirely inadequate to the support of the augmented colony. The leaders of these expeditions — with the exception of Enciso, who went to Cenú, whence he was speedily driven — acted in a most inhuman fashion; and the good feeling which had subsisted between Vasco Nuñez and the natives was changed to the most bitter hatred. To use Vasco Nunez' own words: "For where the Indians were like sheep, they have become like fierce lions, and have acquired so much daring, that formerly they were accustomed to come out to the paths with presents to the Christians, now they come out and they kill them; and this has been on account of the bad things which the captains who went out on the incursions have done to them." He especially blamed Ayora and Morales, who commanded two of the earliest expeditions. Ayora escaped with his ill-gotten wealth to Spain, where he died before he could be brought to justice.

Morales, following the route of Vasco Nuñez across the isthmus, arrived on the other side, and sailed to the Pearl Islands, which Vasco Nuñez had seen in the distance. Here he obtained an immense booty; and thence, crossing to the southern side of the Gulf of San Miguel, he endeavored to return to Darien by the way of Birú and the River Atrato. But he was speedily driven back; and was so hard pressed by the natives throughout his homeward march that he and his companions barely escaped with their treasure and their lives. It was about this time that Vasco Nuñez went for a second time in search of the golden temple of Dabaibe and suffered defeat, with the loss of Luis Carillo, his second in command, and many of his men; while another attempt on Cenú, this time by Becerra, ended in the death of that commander and of all but one of his companions. In 1515, however, a force commanded by Gonzalo de Badajos crossed the isthmus and discovered the rich country lying on the Gulf of Parita. Badajos accumulated an enormous amount of gold, which he was obliged to abandon when he sought safety in ignominious flight.

These repeated disasters in the direction of Cenú nettled old Pedrárias, and he resolved to go himself in command of an expedition and chastise the natives. He was speedily defeated; but, instead of returning immediately to Antigua, he sailed over to Veragua and founded the town of Acla (Bones of Men), as the northern termination of a road across the isthmus. He then sent Gaspar Espinosa across the isthmus to found a town on the other side. Espinosa on his way met the fleeing Badajos; but being better prepared, and a more able commander, he recovered the abandoned treasure and founded the old town of Panamá; while a detachment under Hurtado, which he sent along the coast toward the west, discovered the Gulf of San Lucar (Nicoya).

As we have seen, Vasco Nuñez' account of the discovery of the South Sea reached Spain too late to prevent the sailing of Pedrárias; but the King nevertheless placed reliance in him, and appointed him *adelantado*, or lieutenant, to prosecute discoveries along the shores of the southern sea, and also made him governor of the provinces of Panamá and Coyba. This commission had reached Antigua before the departure of Espinosa; but Pedrárias withheld it for reasons of his own. And before he delivered it there arrived from Cuba a vessel commanded by a friend of Vasco Nuñez, — a certain Garabito, — who by making known his arrival to Vasco Nuñez and not to Pedrárias, aroused the latter's suspicions. Accordingly, Vasco Nuñez was seized and placed in confinement. After a while, however, upon his promising to marry one of Pedrárias' daughters, who at the time was in Spain, they became reconciled, and Vasco Nuñez was given his commission, and immediately began preparation for a voyage on the South Sea. As it seemed impossible to obtain a sufficient amount of the proper kind of timber on the other side the isthmus, enough to build a few small vessels was carried over the mountains. When the men began to work it, they found it worm-eaten; and a new supply was procured, which was almost immediately washed away by a sudden rise of the Rio Balsas, on whose banks they had established their ship-yard. At last, however, two little vessels were built and navigated to the Islas de las Perlas, whence Vasco Nuñez made a short and unsuccessful cruise to the southward. But before he went a second time

he sent Garabito and other emissaries to Acla to discover whether Pedrárias
had been superseded.   It seems to have been arranged that when these
men arrived near Acla one of their number should go secretly to the house
of Vasco Nuñez there and obtain the required information.   If a new
governor had arrived they were to return to the southern side of the
isthmus, and Vasco Nuñez would put himself and his little fleet out of the
new governor's reach, trusting in some grand discovery to atone for his
disloyalty.   Pedrárias was still governor ; but Garabito proved a false friend,
and told Pedrárias that Vasco Nuñez had no idea of marrying his daughter :
on the contrary, he intended to sail away with his native mistress (with
whom Garabito was in love) and found for himself a government on the
shores of the Mar del Sur.   Pedrárias was furious, and enticed Vasco Nuñez
to Acla, where this new charge of treason, added to the former one of the
murder of Nicuesa, secured his conviction by the *alcalde mayor* Espinosa,
and on the very next day he and his four companions were executed.   This
was in 1517.

In 1519 Pedrárias removed the seat of government from Antigua to
Panamá, which was made a city in 1521, while Antigua was not long after
abandoned.   In 1519 Espinosa coasted northward and westward, in Vasco
Nuñez' vessels, as far as the Gulf of Culebras ; and in 1522 Pascual de Andagoya penetrated the country of Birú for twenty leagues or more, when ill
health compelled his return to Panamá.   He brought wonderful accounts
of an Inca empire which was said to exist somewhere along the coast to
the south.[1]

In 1519 a pilot, Andrés Niño by name, who had been with Vasco Nuñez
on his last cruise, interested Gil Gonzalez de Avila, then *contador* of Española, in the subject of exploration along the coast of the South Sea.
Gonzalez agreed to go as commander-in-chief, accompanying Niño in the
vessels which Vasco Nuñez had built.   The necessary orders from the King
were easily obtained, and they sailed for Antigua, where they arrived safely ;
but Pedrárias refused to deliver the vessels.   Gil Gonzalez, nothing daunted,
took in pieces the ships by which he had come from Spain, transported the
most important parts of them across the isthmus, and built new vessels.
These, however, were lost before reaching Panamá ; but the crews arrived
there in safety, and Pedrárias, when brought face to face with the commander, could not refuse to obey the King's orders.   Thus, after many
delays, Gil Gonzalez and Andrés Niño sailed from the Islas de las Perlas
on the 21st of January, 1522.   After they had gone a hundred leagues or
more, it was found necessary to beach and repair the vessels.   This was
done by Niño, while Gil Gonzalez, with one hundred men and four horses,
pushed along the shore, and, after many hairbreadth escapes, rejoined
the fleet, which under Niño had been repaired and brought around by water.
The meeting was at a gulf named by them Sanct Viçente ; but it proved

[1] [See the chapter on Peru. — Ed.]

to be the San Lucar of Hurtado, and the Nicoya of the present day. After a short time passed in recuperation, the two detachments again separated. Niño with the vessels coasted the shore at least as far as the Bay of Fonseca, and thence returned to the Gulf of Nicoya. Here he was soon rejoined by the land party; which, after leaving the gulf, had penetrated inland to the Lake of Nicaragua. They explored the surrounding country sufficiently to discover the outlet of the lake, which led to the north, and not to the south, as had been hoped. They had but one severe fight with the natives, accumulated vast sums of gold, and baptized many thousand converts. With their treasure they returned in safety to Panamá on the 25th of June, 1523, after an absence of nearly a year and a half.

At Panamá Gil Gonzalez found an enemy worse than the natives of Nicaragua in the person of Pedrárias, whose cupidity was aroused by the sight of the gold. But crossing the isthmus, he escaped from Nombre de Dios just as Pedrárias was on the point of arresting him, and steered for Española, where his actions were approved by the Hieronimite Fathers, who authorized him to return and explore the country. This he endeavored to do by the way of the outlet of the Lake of Nicaragua, by which route he would avoid placing himself in the power of Pedrárias. He unfortunately reached the Honduras coast too far north, and marched inland only to be met by a rival party of Spaniards under Hernando de Soto. It seemed that as soon as possible after Gil Gonzalez' departure from Nombre de Dios, Pedrárias had despatched a strong force under Francisco Hernandez de Córdoba to take possession of and hold the coveted territory for him. Córdoba, hearing from the natives of Spaniards advancing from the north, had sent De Soto to intercept them. Gil Gonzalez defeated this detachment; but not being in sufficient force to meet Córdoba, he retreated to the northern shore, where he found Cristóbal de Olid, who had been sent by Cortés to occupy Honduras in his interest. Olid proved a traitor to Cortés, and soon captured not only Gil Gonzalez, but Francisco de las Casas, who had been sent by Cortés to seize him. Las Casas, who was a man of daring, assassinated Olid, with the help of Gil Gonzalez. The latter was then sent to make what terms he could with Cortés as to a joint occupation of the country.[1] But Gil Gonzalez fell into the hands of the enemies of the Conqueror of Mexico, and was sent to Spain to answer, among other things, for the murder of Olid. He reached Seville in 1526; but, completely overwhelmed by his repeated disasters, died soon after.

Córdoba, who had thrown off allegiance to Pedrárias, was executed. Pedrárias himself was turned out of his government of Darien by Pedro de los Rios, and took refuge in the governorship of Nicaragua, and died quietly at Leon in 1530, at the advanced age of nearly ninety years.

[1] [Cf. the chapter on Cortés. — ED.]

In 1492 Christopher Columbus had discovered Cuba, which he called Juana; and two years later he had partially explored the Island of Jamaica, whither he had been driven on his fourth voyage, and compelled to stay from June, 1503, to June, 1504. In 1508 this lesser island had been granted to Ojeda and Nicuesa as a storehouse from which to draw supplies in case of need. But, as we have seen, the Admiral of the Indies at that time, Diego Columbus, son of the great Admiral, had sent Juan de Esquivel with sixty men to seize the island and hold it for him against all comers. Esquivel founded the town of Sevilla Nueva — later Sevilla d' Oro — on the shores of the harbor where Columbus had stayed so long; and thus the island was settled.

Although Cuba had been discovered in 1492, nothing had been done toward its exploration till 1508, when Ovando, at that time governor of Española, sent Sebastian de Ocampo to determine whether it was an island or not. Columbus, it will be remembered, did not, or would not, believe it insular, though the Indians whom he brought from Guanahani had told him it was; and it had suited his purpose to make his companions swear that they believed it a peninsula of Asia. Ocampo settled the question by circumnavigating it from north to south; and, after another delay, Diego Columbus in 1511 sent Diego Velasquez, a wealthy planter of Española, to conquer and settle the island, which at that time was called Fernandina. Velasquez, assisted by thirty men under Pamphilo de Narvaez from Jamaica, had no difficulty in doing this; and his task being accomplished, he threw off his allegiance to the Admiral. Settlers were attracted to Cuba from all sides. With the rest came one hundred, Bernal Diaz among them, from Antigua. But Velasquez had distributed the natives among his followers with such a lavish hand that these men were unable to get any slaves for themselves, and in this predicament agreed with Francisco Hernandez de Córdoba[1] to go on a slave-catching expedition to some neighboring islands. Velasquez probably contributed a small vessel to the two vessels which were fitted out by the others. With them went Anton Alaminos as pilot. Sailing from Havana in February, 1517, they doubled the Cabo de S. Anton, and steered toward the west and south. Storms and currents drove them from their course, and it was not until twenty-one days had passed after leaving S. Anton that they sighted some small islands. Running toward the coast, they espied inland a city, the size of which so impressed them that they called it *El gran Cairo*. Soon after some natives came on board, who, to their inquiries as to what land it was, answered " Conex Catoche; " and accordingly they named it the Punta de Catoche. At this place, having landed, they were enticed into an ambush, and many Spaniards were killed. From this inhospitable shore they sailed to the west, along the northern coast of Yucatan, and in two weeks arrived at a village which they named S. Lázaro, but to which the native name of Campeche has clung. There

[1] Not the Córdoba of Nicaragua.

HAVANA.[1]

1 [This cut of the chief Cuban seaport represents it at a somewhat later day, and is a fac-simile from the cut in Montanus. — ED.]

the natives were hostile. So they sailed on for six days more, when they arrived off a village called Pontonchan, now known, however, as Champoton. As they were short of water they landed at this place, and in a fight which followed, fifty-seven Spaniards were killed and five were drowned. Nevertheless the survivors continued their voyage for three days longer, when they came to a river with three mouths, one of which, the Estero de los Lagartos, they entered. There they burned one of their vessels; and, having obtained a supply of water, sailed for Cuba. The reports which they gave of the riches of the newly discovered country so excited the greed of Velasquez that he fitted out a fleet of four vessels, the command of which he gave to his nephew, Juan de Grijalva. Anton Alaminos again went as pilot, and Pedro de Alvarado was captain of one of the ships. They left the Cabo de S. Anton on the 1st of May, 1518, and three days later sighted the Island of Cozumel, which they called Santa Cruz. From this island they sailed along the southern coast of Yucatan, which they thought an island, and which they named Santa Maria de los Remedios. They came finally to a shallow bay, still known by the name which they gave it, Bahia de la Ascension. But the prospect not looking very promising in this direction, they doubled on their track, and in due season arrived at S. Lázaro (Campeche), or, more probably, perhaps, at Champoton, where they had their first hostile encounter with the natives. But, being better provided with artillery and cotton armor than was Francisco Hernandez, Grijalva and his men maintained their ground and secured a much-needed supply of water. Thence following the shore, they soon came to an anchorage, which they at first called Puerto Deseado. On further investigation the pilot Alaminos declared that it was not a harbor, but the mouth of a strait between the island of Santa Maria de los Remedios (Yucatan) and another island, which they called Nueva España, but which afterward proved to be the mainland of Mexico. They named this strait the Boca de Términos. After recuperating there, they coasted toward the north by the mouths of many rivers, among others the Rio de Grijalva (Tabasco), until they came to an island on which they found a temple, where the native priests were wont to sacrifice human beings. To this island they gave the name of Isla de los Sacrificios; while another, a little to the north, they called S. Juan de Ulúa. The sheet of water between this island and the mainland afforded good anchorage, and to-day is known as the harbor of Vera Cruz. There Grijalva stayed some time, trading with the inhabitants, not of the islands merely, but of the mainland. To this he was beckoned by the waving of white flags, and he found himself much honored when he landed. After sending Pedro de Alvarado, with what gold had been obtained, to Cuba in a caravel which needed repairs, Grijalva proceeded on his voyage; but when he had arrived at some point between the Bahia de Tanguijo and the Rio Panuco, the pilot Alaminos declared it madness to go farther. So the fleet turned back, and, after more trading along the coast, they arrived safely at Matanzas in October of the same year. Velasquez, when he saw the spoil gathered on this expedition, was much vexed that Grijalva had not broken his instructions and founded a settlement. A new expedition was immediately prepared, the command of which was given to Hernan Cortés.[1] As for Grijalva, he took service under Pedrárias, and perished with Hurtado in Nicaragua.

———————◆———————

CRITICAL ESSAY ON THE SOURCES OF INFORMATION.

THE best account of the voyages and expeditions of the companions of Columbus, with the exception of those relating immediately to the settlement of Darien and the exploration of the western coast of the isthmus, is Navarrete's *Viages menores*.[2] This historian[3] had extraordinary opportunities in this field; and a nautical education contributed to his power of weighing evidence with regard to maritime affairs. No part of Navarrete has been translated into English, unless the first portion of Washington Irving's *Companions of Columbus* may be so regarded. The best account of these voyages in English, however, is Sir Arthur Helps's *Spanish Conquest in America*,[4] which, although defective in form, is readable, and, so far as it goes, trustworthy. This work deals not merely with the *Viages menores*, but also with the settlement of Darien; as, too, does Irving's *Companions*.

The first voyage of Ojeda rests mainly on the answers to the questions propounded by the *fiscal real* in the suit brought against Diego, the son of Columbus, in which the endeavor was made to show that Ojeda, and not Columbus, discovered the pearl coasts. But this claim on the part of the King's attorney was unsuccessful; for Ojeda himself expressly stated in his deposition, taken in Santo Domingo in 1513, that he was the first man who went to Tierra-Firme *after* the Admiral, and that he knew that the Admiral had been there because he saw the chart[5] which the Admiral had sent home. This lawsuit is so important in relation to these minor voyages that Navarrete printed much of the testimony then taken, with some notes of his own, at the end of his third volume.[6] Among the witnesses were Ojeda, Bastidas, Vicente Yañez Pinzon, Garcia Hernandez a "*físico*," who had accompanied Vicente Yañez on his first voyage, the pilots Ledesma, Andrés de Morales, Juan Rodriguez, and many other mariners who had sailed with the different commanders. Their testimony was taken with regard to the third voyage of Columbus (second question); the voyage of Guerra and Niño (third and fourth questions); Ojeda's first voyage (fifth question); Bastidas (sixth question); Vicente Yañez (seventh question); Lepe (eighth question); etc. Taken altogether, this evidence is the best authority for what was done or was not done on these early voyages.[7]

---

[1] [From this point the story is continued in the chapter on Cortés. — ED.]

[2] *Coleccion de los viages y déscubrimientos, que hicieron por mar los Españoles desde fines del siglio XV.*, por Don Martin Fernandez de Navarrete. The third volume of this series constitutes the *Viages menores, y los de Vespucio; Poblaciones en el Darien, suplemento al tomo II*, Madrid, 1829. [Cf. the Introduction to the present volume. — ED.]

[3] Cf. *Biblioteca marítima española*, ii. 436–438; H. H. Bancroft, *Central America*, i. 198. [Cf. Introduction to the present volume. — ED.]

[4] [Cf. the chapters on Columbus, Las Casas, and Pizarro. — ED.]

[5] Navarrete, iii. 5, *note* 1, and 539, 544; Humboldt, *Examen critique*, i. 88, *note*.

[6] *Coleccion*, iii. 538–615.

[7] Besides this original material, something concerning this first voyage of Ojeda is contained in Oviedo, i. 76, and ii. 132; Las Casas, ii. 389-434 (all references to Oviedo and Las Casas in this chapter are to the editions issued by the *Real Academia*); Herrera, dec. i. lib. 4, chaps. i.–iv.; Navarrete, *Coleccion*, iii. 4–11, 167, 543–545; Humboldt, *Examen critique*, i. 313, and iv. 195, 220; Helps, *Spanish Conquest*, i. 263, 280, ii. 106; Irving, *Companions*, pp. 9–27; Bancroft, *Central America*, i. 111, 118, 308; Ruge, *Geschichte des Zeitalters der Entdeckungen*, p. 322. There

The only things worth noting in the voyage of Guerra and Niño are the smallness of the vessel (fifty tons),[1] and the enormous pecuniary return. One of the voyagers,[2] very possibly Niño himself,[3] wrote an account of the voyage, which was translated into Italian, and published as chapters cx. and cxi. of the *Paesi novamente retrovati*. It was then translated into Latin, and inserted by Grynæus in the *Novus orbis*.[4]

A contemporary account of the voyage of Vicente Yañez Pinzon was printed in the *Paesi novamente*,[5] by whom written is not known. Varnhagen has attempted to show that the cape near which Vicente Yañez landed was not the Cabo de S. Augustin, but some point much farther north.[6] For a time the point was raised that Vicente Yañez arrived on the coast after Cabral; but that was plainly impossible, as he undoubtedly sighted the American coast before Cabral left Portugal.[7] As to the landfall itself, both Navarrete and Humboldt place it in about eight degrees south latitude; and they base their argument on the answers to the seventh question of the *fiscal real* in the celebrated lawsuit, in which Vicente Yañez said that it was true that he discovered from " El cabo de Consolacion que es en la parte de Portugal é agora se llama cabo de S. Augustin." [8] In this he was corroborated by the other witnesses.[9] The voyage was unsuccessful in a pecuniary point of view. Two vessels were lost at the Bahamas, whither Vicente Yañez had gone in quest of slaves. After his return to Spain it was only through the interposition of the King that he was able to save a small portion of his property from the clutches of the merchants who had fitted out the fleet.[10]

The voyage of Diego de Lepe rests entirely on the evidence given in the Columbus lawsuit,[11] from which it also appears that he drew a map for Fonseca on which the coast of the New World was delineated trending toward the south and west from Rostro Hermoso (Cabo de S. Augustin). Little is known of the further movements of Diego de Lepe, who, according to Morales, died in Portugal before 1515.[12] Navarrete printed nothing relating to him of a later date than November, 1500;[13] but in the *Documentos inéditos*

---

is also a notice of Ojeda by Navarrete in his *Opúsculos*, i. 113.

[1] [On this see note on p. 7 of the present volume. — ED.]

[2] Navarrete, *Coleccion*, iii. 12, note 1.

[3] *Biblioteca marítima española*, ii. 525.

[4] Page 117, ed. 1532. For other references to this voyage, see Peter Martyr (dec. i. chap. viii.), whose account is based on the above; Herrera, dec. i. lib. 4, chap. v.; Navarrete, *Coleccion*, iii. 11–18, 540–542; Humboldt, *Examen critique*, iv. 220; Bancroft, *Central America*, i. 111; Irving, *Companions*, pp. 28–32.

[5] Chapters cxii. and cxiii. In Latin in Grynæus, p. 119, edition of 1532.

[6] Varnhagen, *Examen de quelques points de l'histoire géographique du Brésil*, pp. 19–24; Varnhagen, *Historia geral do Brazil* (2d ed.), i. 78–80.

[7] Cf. Navarrete, *Coleccion*, iii. 19, *note*. Humboldt (*Examen critique*, i. 313) says that Vicente Yañez saw the coast forty-eight days before Cabral left Lisbon. As to the exact date of Vicente Yañez' landfall, the *Paesi novamente* (chap. cxii.) gives it as January 20, while Peter Martyr (dec. i. chap. ix.), who usually follows the *Paesi novamente*, in his description of this and of the Guerra and Niño voyages gives it as " Septimo kalendas Februarii," or January 26. But the difference is unimportant. [Cf. further the section on the " Historical Chorography

of South America," in which the question is further examined. — ED.]

[8] Navarrete, iii. 547 *et seq.*

[9] See also Navarrete, *Notice chronologique*, in *Quatre voyages*, i. 349, and Humboldt, Introduction to Ghillany's *Behaim*, p. 2, where he says, in the description of the La Cosa map, that Cabo de S. Augustin, whose position is very accurately laid down on that map, was first called Rostro Hermoso, Cabo Sta. Maria de la Consolacion, and Cabo Sta. Cruz. In this he is probably correct; for if Vicente Yañez or Lepe did not discover it, how did La Cosa know where to place it ? — unless he revised his map after 1500. This is not likely, as the map contains no hint of the discoveries made during his third voyage undertaken with Rodrigo de Bastidas in 1500–1502. Cf. Stevens, *Notes*, p. 33, note.

[10] Cf. two *Real provisions* of date Dec. 5, 1500, in Navarrete, iii. 82, 83; and see also a *Capitulacion* and *Asiento* of date Sept. 5, 1501, in *Documentos inéditos*, xxx. 535. Other references to this voyage are, — Herrera, dec. i. lib. 4, chap. vi.; Navarrete, iii. 18–23; Humboldt, *Examen critique*, iv. 221; Bancroft, *Central America*, i. 112; and Irving, *Companions*, pp. 33–41.

[11] Navarrete, *Coleccion*, iii. 552–555.

[12] Ibid., iii. 552.

[13] Ibid., iii. 80, 81.

are documents which would seem to show that he was preparing for a voyage in the beginning of 1502.[1]

Juan de la Cosa returned with Ojeda in the middle of June, 1500, and he sailed with Bastidas in the following October. The intervening time he probably spent in working on the map which bears the legend "Juan de la Cosa la fizo en Puerto de Sta. Maria en año de 1500." This is the earliest existing chart made by one of the navigators of the fifteenth century, the track-chart sent home by Columbus in 1498,[2] and the Lepe map, being lost. Humboldt was especially qualified to appreciate the clearness and accuracy of this La Cosa map by the knowledge of the geography of Spanish America which he gained during a long sojourn in that part of the world;[3] and this same knowledge gives especial value to whatever he says in the *Examen critique*[4] concerning the voyages herein described. Of Juan de la Cosa's knowledge of the geography of the northern coast of South America there can be little doubt, especially when it is borne in mind that he made no less than six voyages to that part of the world,[5] only two of which, however, preceded the date which he gives to his map. A comparison of La Cosa's map with the chart of 1527 usually, but probably erroneously, ascribed to Ferdinand Columbus, and with that of 1529 by Ribero, gives a clearer idea than the chronicles themselves do, of the discoveries of the early navigators.[6]

Like all these early minor voyages, that of Rodrigo Bastidas rests mainly on the testimony given in the lawsuit already referred to.[7] Navarrete in his *Viages menores* stated that Ojeda procured a license from Bishop Fonseca, who had been empowered to give such licenses. No document, however, of the kind has been produced with regard to Ojeda or any of these commanders before the time of Bastidas, whose *Asiento que hizo con SS. MM. Católicas* of June 5, 1500, has been printed.[8] As already related, the ravages of the teredo drove Bastidas into a harbor of Española, where he was forced to abandon his vessels and march to Santo Domingo. He divided his men into three bands, who saved themselves from starvation by exchanging for food some of the ornaments which they had procured on the coast of Tierra-Firme. This innocent traffic was declared illegal by Bobadilla, who sent Bastidas to Spain for trial. But two years later, on Jan. 29, 1504, their Majesties ordered his goods to be restored to him, and commanded that all

---

[1] *Capitulacion*, etc., Sept. 14, 1501 (*Documentos inéditos*, xxxi. 5); *Cédulas*, November, 1501 (*Documentos inéditos*, xxxi. 100, 102); another *cédula* of January, 1502 (*Documentos inéditos*, xxxi. 119). See also Herrera, dec. i. lib. 4, chap. vii.; Navarrete, iii. 23, 594; Humboldt, *Examen critique*, i. 314, iv. 221; Bancroft, *Central America*, i. 113; and Irving, *Companions*, p. 42.

[2] Navarrete, *Coleccion*, iii. 5, and *note*, and p. 539; Humboldt, *Examen critique*, i. 88, and *note*. [Cf. the section in the present volume on "The Early Maps of the Spanish and Portuguese Discoveries," *ante*, p. 106. — ED.]

[3] Cf. *Voyage aux régions équinoxiales du nouveau continent fait en 1799, 1800, 1801, 1802, 1803, et 1804, par Alexandre de Humboldt et A. Bonpland, rédigé par Alexandre de Humboldt, avec un atlas géographique et physique* (8 vols.), Paris, 1816–1832. Translated into English by Helen Maria Williams, and published as *Personal Narrative of Travels to the Equinoctial Regions*, etc. (7 vols.), London, 1818–1829. There is another translation, with the same title, by Thomassina Ross (7 vols.), London,

1818–1829, of which a three-volume edition was brought out in 1852.

[4] *Examen critique de l'histoire de la géographie du nouveau continent*, etc., par A. de Humboldt, Paris, 1836–1839. This was first published in *Voyage de Humboldt et Bonpland*. Cf. *Bibliography of Humboldt*, vol. iii.

[5] (1) With Columbus — September, 1493 to June, 1496. (2) With Ojeda — May, 1499 to June, 1500. (3) With Bastidas — October, 1500 to September, 1502. (4) In command — 1504 to 1506. (5) In command — 1507 to 1508. (6) With Ojeda — 1509. Cf. Humboldt, *Examen critique*, v. 163; also Navarrete, *Biblioteca maritima española*, ii. 208.

[6] [See further on the La Cosa map, Vol. III. of the present *History*, p. 8, and the present volume, p. 106, where fac-similes and sketches are given. — ED.]

[7] Answers to the sixth question (*Coleccion*, iii. 545), reviewed by the editor on pp. 591 and 592 of the same volume.

[8] *Documentos inéditos*, ii. 362. It was partially translated in Bancroft, *Central America*, i. 186, *note*.

further proceedings should be abandoned.[1] They also granted him a pension of fifty thousand maravedis, to be paid from the revenues "de los Golfos de Huraba e Barú;"[2] while Juan de la Cosa was not only pensioned in a similar fashion, but also made *alguacil mayor* of the Gulf of Urabá.[3] With the exception of a slave-catching voyage to Urabá in 1504, Bastidas lived quietly as a farmer in Española until 1520, when he led an expedition to settle the province of Santa Marta, and was there killed by his lieutenant.   After his death his family, seeking to receive compensation for his services and losses, drew up an *Informacion de los servicios del adelantado Rodrigo de Bastidas;*[4] and eight years later presented another.[5] From this material it is possible to construct a clear and connected account of this voyage, especially when supplemented by Oviedo and Las Casas.[6]

This was the first voyage which really came within the scope of Hubert H. Bancroft's *Central America;* and therefore he has described it at some length.[7] This book is a vast and invaluable mine of information, to be extracted only after much labor and trouble, owing to a faulty table of contents, and the absence of side-notes or dates to the pages; and there is at present no index.   The text is illustrated with a mass of descriptive and bibliographical notes which are really the feature of the work, and give it its encyclopedic value.   Considering its range and character, the book has surprisingly few errors of any kind; and indeed the only thing which prevents our placing implicit reliance on it is Mr. Bancroft's assertion[8] that "very little of the manuscript as it comes to me, whether in the form of rough material or more finished chapters, is the work of one person alone;" while we are not given the means of attaching responsibility where it belongs, as regards both the character of the investigation and the literary form which is presented.   As to the ultimate authorship of the text itself, we are only assured[9] that "at least one half of the manuscript has been written by my own hand."[10]

The second voyage of Alonso de Ojeda rests entirely on some documents which Navarrete printed in the third volume of his *Coleccion*, and upon which he founded his account of the voyage.[11] The first, in point of time, is a *cédula* of June 8, 1501, continuing a license of July, 1500, to explore and govern the Isla de Coquivacoa.[12] Two days later, on June 10, 1501, a formal commission as governor was given to Ojeda,[13] and the articles of association were executed by him and his partners, Vergara and Ocampo, on the 5th of July.[14] An *escribano*, Juan de Guevara by name, was appointed in the beginning of September of the same year.   The fleet was a long time in fitting out, and it was not till the next spring that Ojeda issued his orders and instructions to the commanders of the other vessels and to the pilots.[15] These are of great importance, as giving the names of the places which he had visited on his first voyage.   The attempt at colonization ended disastrously, and Ojeda found himself at Santo Domingo as the defendant in a suit brought against him by his associates.   Navarrete used the evidence given in this suit in his account; but he printed only the *ejecutoria*, in which the King and Queen ordered that Ojeda should be set at liberty, and that his goods should be restored to him.[16] The

---

1 Navarrete, *Coleccion*, ii. 416.

2 *Documentos inéditos*, xxxi. 230.

3 *Título* (1502, April 3), *Documentos inéditos*, xxxi. 129.

4 *Documentos inéditos*, ii. 366.

5 Ibid., xxxvii. 459.

6 Oviedo, i. 76, and ii. 334; Las Casas, iii. 10.   Something may also be found in Herrera, dec. i. lib. 4, chap. xiv., and in Navarrete, *Coleccion*, iii. 25; Quintana, *Obras completas* in *Biblioteca de autores Españoles*, xix. 281; Humboldt, *Examen critique*, i. 360, iv. 224; Helps, i. 281; and Irving, *Companions*, p. 43-45.

7 Vol. i. pp. 114, 183-194.

8 Cf. *Early American Chroniclers*, p. 44.

9 *Chroniclers*, p. 44.

10 [There is a further estimate in another part of the present work. — ED.]

11 *Coleccion*, pp. 28, 168, 591; see also Humboldt, *Examen critique*, i. 360, and iv. 226; and Irving, *Companions*, pp. 46-53.

12 *Coleccion*, iii. 85.

13 Ibid., iii. 89.

14 Ibid., iii. 91.

15 Ibid., iii. 103, 105-107.

16 Ibid., ii. 420-436.

position of the irrigated land [1] which he called Valfermoso is difficult to determine; but it certainly was not the Curiana of the present day, which is identical with the Curiana of Guerra and Niño.[2]

Martin Fernandez de Enciso — the *bachiller Enciso* — "first came to the Indies with Bastidas," says Bancroft,[3] and practised law to such good purpose that he accumulated two thousand castellanos, — equivalent to ten thousand in our day.[4] This he contributed toward the expenses of the Nueva Andalucia colony, of which he was made *alcalde mayor*. But he was unfortunate in that office, as we have seen, and was sent to Spain, whence he returned in 1513 with Pedrárias as *alguacil mayor*. In 1514 he led an expedition to Cenú, to which Irving erroneously gives an earlier date.[5] From 1514 to 1519 nothing is known of Enciso's movements; but in the latter year he published the *Suma de geografía que trata de todas las partidas y provincias del mundo, en especial de las Indias*, which contains much bearing on this period. What became of the author is not known.

The trading voyages to Tierra-Firme between Ojeda's two attempts at colonization have no geographical importance; and, indeed, their very existence depends on a few documents which were unearthed from the Archives of the Indies by the indefatigable labors of Muñoz, Navarrete, and the editors of the *Coleccion de documentos inéditos relativos al descubrimiento, conquista y organizacion de las antiguas posesiones Españolas de América y Oceanía*.[6] Of these trading voyages first comes the cruise of Juan de la Cosa, or Juan Vizcaino, as he was sometimes called, whose intention to embark upon it is inferred from a letter from the Queen to the royal officers,[7] and an *asiento* bearing date Feb. 14, 1504.[8] Nothing is known of the voyage itself, except that Navarrete, on the authority of a *cédula* which he did not print, gives the amount of money received by the Crown as its share of the profits.[9]

The voyage which Ojeda is supposed to have made in 1505 rests on a still weaker foundation, as there is nothing with regard to it except a *cédula*, bearing date Sept. 21, 1505,[10] concerning certain valuables which may have been procured on this voyage or on the first ill-fated attempt at colonization. That it was contemplated is ascertained from a *Cédula para que Alfonso Doxeda sea Gobernador de la Costa de Ququebacóa e Huraba*,[11] etc. The document, dated Sept. 21, 1504, is followed by two of the same date referring to Ojeda's financial troubles. Is it not possible that the above-mentioned document of Sept. 21, 1505, belongs with them? The agreement (*asiento*) of Sept. 30, 1504, confirmed in March of the next year, is in the same volume, while an order to the Governor of Española not to interfere with the luckless Ojeda was printed by Navarrete (iii. 111), who has said all that can be said concerning the expedition in his *Noticia biográfica*.[12]

The voyage of Juan de la Cosa with Martin de los Reyes and Juan Correa rests entirely on the assertion of Navarrete that they returned in 1508, because it was stated (where, he does not say) that the proceeds of the voyage were so many hundred

---

[1] *Tierra de riego*, Navarrete, *Coleccion*, iii. 32.

[2] Navarrete, iii. 32, *note* 3. In this note he mentions Enciso's *Suma de geografía* as an authority.

[3] *Central America*, i. 339, *note*.

[4] Navarrete, *Biblioteca marítima española*, ii. 432; but see also Bancroft, *Central America*, i. 192, *note*.

[5] Irving, *Companions*, pp. 126–129. See *Memorial que dió el bachiller Enciso de lo ejecutado por el en defensa de los Reales derechos en la materia de los indios*, in *Documentos inéditos*, i. 441. This document contains, pp. 442–444, the celebrated *requerimiento* which Pedrárias was ordered to read to the natives before he seized their lands. A translation is in Bancroft, *Central America*, i.

397, *note*. It may also be found in Oviedo, iii. 28. Bancroft in the above note also indicates the depositary of the *requerimiento* drawn up for the use of Ojeda and Nicuesa. With regard to this Cenú expedition, see also Enciso, *Suma de geografía*, p. 56.

[6] Cited in this chapter as *Documentos inéditos*. [See further on this collection in the Introduction to the present volume. — ED.]

[7] Navarrete, *Coleccion*, iii. 109; and see also *Biblioteca marítima española*, ii. 210, 211.

[8] *Documentos inéditos*, xxxi. 220.

[9] Navarrete, *Coleccion*, iii. 161.

[10] *Documentos inéditos*, xxxi. 360.

[11] Ibid., xxxi. 250.

[12] *Coleccion*, iii. 169.

thousand maravedis.[1] Concerning the discovery of Yucatan by Vicente Yañez Pinzon, there is no original material;[2] but here again evidence of preparation for a voyage can be found in an *asiento y capytulacion* of April 24, 1505, in the *Documentos inéditos* (xxxi. 309).

After this time the history of Tierra-Firme is much better known; for it is with the colonies sent out under Ojeda and Nicuesa in 1509 that the *Historia general* of Oviedo becomes a standard authority. Gonzalo Fernandez de Oviedo y Valdés was born in Madrid in 1478, and in 1490 he entered the household of the Duke of Villahermoso. Later he served under Prince Juan and the King of Naples until 1507, when he entered the service of the King and Queen of Spain. In 1513 he was appointed *escribano*, and later (upon the death of Caicedo, who, it will be remembered, was one of the agents Vasco Nuñez had sent to Spain to announce the existence of an unknown sea) *veedor de las fundaciones d' oro* to the expedition which under Pedrárias was sent to Tierra-Firme in that year. Oviedo did not approve of the course pursued by that worthy, and returned to Spain in 1515 to inform the new King, Charles I. (Emperor Charles V.) of the true condition of affairs in the Indies. He brought about many important reforms, secured for himself the office of perpetual *regidor* of Antigua, — *escribano general* of the province, receiver of the fines of the *cámara*,[3] — and cargoes and goods forfeited for smuggling were also bestowed upon him. His *veeduría* was extended so as to include all Tierra-Firme; and when the news of the execution of Vasco Nuñez arrived at Court, he was ordered to take charge of his goods and those of his associates. Oviedo, provided with so many offices and with an order commanding all governors to furnish him with a true account of their doings, returned to Antigua soon after the new governor, Lope de Sosa, who had been appointed, upon his representations, to succeed Pedrárias. But unfortunately for him Lope de Sosa died in the harbor of Antigua (1520), and Oviedo was left face to face with Pedrárias. It was not long before they quarrelled as to the policy of removing the seat of government of the province from Antigua to Panamá, which Oviedo did not approve. Pedrárias craftily made him his lieutenant at Antigua, in which office Oviedo conducted himself so honestly that he incurred the hatred of all the evil-disposed colonists of that town, and was forced to resign. He also complained of Pedrárias before the new *alcalde mayor*, and was glad to go to Spain as the representative of Antigua. On his way he stopped at Cuba and Santo Domingo, where he saw Velasquez and Diego Columbus; with the latter he sailed for home. There he used his opportunities so well that he procured, in 1523, the appointment of Pedro de los Rios as Pedrárias' successor, and for himself the governorship of Cartagena; and after publishing his *Sumario* he returned to Castilla del Oro, where he remained until 1530, when he returned to Spain, resigned his *veeduría*, and some time after received the appointment of *Cronista general de Indias*. In 1532 he was again in Santo Domingo, and in 1533 he was appointed *alcaid* of the fortress there. But the remainder of his life was passed in literary pursuits, and he died in Valladolid in 1557 at the age of seventy-nine. From this account it can easily be seen that whatever he wrote with regard to the affairs of Tierra-Firme must be received with caution, as he was far from being an impartial observer.[4]

The first document with regard to the final and successful settlement of Tierra-Firme is the *cédula* of June 9, 1508, in which Diego de Nicuesa and Alonso de Ojeda were commissioned governors of Veragua and Urabá for four years.[5] Juan de la Cosa was

[1] *Coleccion*, iii. 162.

[2] Navarrete, *Coleccion*, iii. 46; Humboldt, *Examen critique*, iv. 228; Herrera, dec. i. lib. 6, chap. xvii.

[3] "Collector of penalties." Cf. Bancroft, *Central America*, i. 473.

[4] [The bibliographical history of Oviedo's writings is given in the note following the chapter on Las Casas. Harrisse, who gives a chapter on Oviedo in his *Christophe Colomb*, p. 97, points out how rarely he refers to original documents. — ED.]

[5] *Real cédula por la cual, con referencia á lo capitulado con Diego de Nicuesa y Alonso de Hojeda, y al nombramiento de ámbos por cuatro años para gobernadores de Veragua el primero y de Urabá et segundo, debiendo ser Teniente suyo Juan de la Cosa, se ratifica el nombramiento á Hojeda*

confirmed in his office of *alguacil mayor de Urabá* on the seventeenth of the same month;[1] and the Governor of Española was directed to give him a house for his wife and children, together with a sufficient number of Indians.[2]

As we have seen, the two governors were prevented by Diego Columbus from taking the well-to-do class of colonists from Española upon which they had counted. This statement is made on the authority of Nicuesa's lieutenant, Rodrigo de Colmenares, who afterward deserted Nicuesa at Antigua, and went to Spain in 1512 in company with Caicedo to report the existence of a new sea. While there, either on this or a later visit, he presented a memorial to the King *sobre el desgraciado suceso de Diego de Nicuesa.*[3] The allegations of Colmenares are borne out by two *cédulas* of Feb. 28, 1510;[4] while a *cédula* of June 15, 1510, declared that the Gulf of Urabá belonged to the province which had been assigned to Ojeda.[5] Nicuesa was informed of this decision in a *cédula* of the same date.[6] There are four more *cédulas* of July 25, 1511, in two of which the Admiral Diego Columbus and the treasurer Pasamonte are ordered to assist the unhappy governors, while the other two were written to inform those governors that such orders had been sent.[7] The fate of neither of them, however, is certain. The judges of appeal in Española were ordered to inquire into the crimes, *délits*, and excesses of Ojeda, Talavera, and companions.[8] Talavera and his associates were hanged in Jamaica in 1511, and Ojeda's deposition was taken in 1513, and again in 1515 in Santo Domingo, in the celebrated lawsuit; but beyond this his further movements are not accurately known.[9] As for Nicuesa, he too underwent shipwreck and starvation; and when at last fortune seemed about to smile upon him, he was cruelly cast out by the mutinous settlers at Darien; and although a story was current that he had been wrecked on Cuba and had there left inscribed on a tree, "Here died the unfortunate Nicuesa," yet the best opinion is that he and his seventeen faithful followers perished at sea. [10]

The only complete biography of Vasco Nuñez de Balbóa is that of Don Manuel José Quintana,[11] who had access to the then unpublished portion of Oviedo, and to documents many of which are possibly not yet published. His *Vida*,[12] therefore, is very useful in filling gaps in the account of the expeditions from Antigua both before and after the coming of Pedrárias. There is no account by an eye-witness of the expeditions undertaken by Vasco Nuñez before 1514; and the only approach to such a document is the

---

(June 9, 1508), Navarrete, *Coleccion*, iii. 116; in the original spelling, and bearing date May 9, 1508, in *Documentos inéditos*, xxxii. 25. The "*capitulado*" mentioned in the above title is in *Documentos inéditos*, xxxii. 29-43, and is followed by the *Real cédula para Xoan de la Cossa sea capitan e gobernador por Alhonso Doxeda; e en las partes donde esthobiere el dicho Doxeda su Lugar Thiniente* (June 9, 1508); and see also *Capitulacion que se toma con Diego de Nicuesa y Alonso de Ojeda* (June 9, 1508), *Documentos inéditos*, xxii. 13.

[1] Navarrete, *Coleccion*, iii. 118; *Documentos inéditos*, xxxii. 46; and see also Ibid., p. 52.

[2] *Cédula, Documentos inéditos*, xxxii. 51.

[3] Navarrete, *Coleccion*, iii. 386 and note; probably presented in 1516. Cf. *Biblioteca marítima española*, ii. 666.

[4] *Documentos inéditos*, xxxi. 529, 533.

[5] Ibid., xxxii. 101.

[6] Ibid., xxxii. 103.

[7] Ibid., xxxii. 231, 236, 240, 257.

[8] See document of October 5, 1511, in Navarrete, *Coleccion*, iii. 120, and of Oct. 6, 1511, in *Documentos inéditos*, xxxii. 284.

[9] Other references are Oviedo, ii. 421; Las Casas, iii. 289-311; Peter Martyr, dec. ii. chap. i.; Herrera, dec. i. lib. 7, chaps. vii., xi., xiv.-xvi., and lib. 8, iii.-v.; Navarrete, *Coleccion*, iii. 170; Quintana, *U. S.*, pp. 281, 301; Helps, i. 287-296; Bancroft, *Central America*, i. 289-301; Irving, *Companions*, pp. 54-102.

[10] See, however, on the career of Nicuesa after leaving Cartagena the following authorities: Oviedo, ii. 465-477; Las Casas, iii. 329-347; Peter Martyr, dec. ii. chaps. ii.-iii.; Herrera, dec. i. lib. 7, chap. xvi., and lib. 8, chaps. i.-iii. and viii.; *Vidas de Españoles célebres* in vol. xix. of *Biblioteca de autores Españoles, obras completas del Excímo Sr. D. Manuel José Quintana*, p. 283; Helps, i. 303-317; Bancroft, *Central America*, i. 289-308, and 336, *note*; Irving, *Companions*, pp. 103-117, 138-146.

[11] Cf. Navarrete, *Biblioteca marítima española*, ii. 409.

[12] Quintana, *U. S.*, pp. 281-300.

letter which Vasco Nuñez wrote to the King on Jan. 20, 1513.[1] The writer of this letter came to the Indies with Bastidas in 1500 ; and after the unhappy ending of that voyage settled in Española. But he was not suited to the placid life of a planter, and becoming involved in debt, was glad to escape from his creditors in Enciso's ship. It was by his advice that the San Sebastian colony was transferred to the other side of the Gulf of Urabá ; and when there his shrewdness had discovered a way of getting rid of Enciso. The exact part he played in the murder of Nicuesa is not clear ; but it is certain, as Bancroft points out, that his connection with that nefarious act was the lever by which his enemies finally accomplished his overthrow. It can be thus easily understood that the censures which he passes on Enciso and Nicuesa must be received with caution. Still, we should not forget that Vasco Nuñez succeeded where they failed. He was a man of little or no education, and portions of this letter are almost untranslatable. Nevertheless, Clements R. Markham has given an English rendering in the Introduction to his translation of Andagoya's *Relacion*.[2] Among the other accounts,[3] that of Herrera is very full, and, so far as it can be compared with accessible documents, sufficiently accurate.

There is no real discrepancy in the various narratives, except with regard to the date of the discovery of the Pacific, which Peter Martyr says took place on the 26th of September, while all the other authorities have the 25th ; Oviedo going so far as to give the very hour when the new waters first dawned on Balbóa's sight.[4]

There is no lack of original material concerning the government of Pedrárias. First come his commission [5] (July 27, 1513) and instructions [6] (Aug. 2, 1513), which Navarrete has printed, together with the letter written by the King on receipt of the reports of Vasco Nuñez' grand discovery.[7] The date of this paper is not given ; but there has recently been printed [8] a letter from the King to Vasco Nuñez of Aug. 19, 1514. In this note the monarch states that he has heard of the discovery of the new sea through Pasamonte, although he had not then seen Arbolancha. Pasamonte had probably written in Vasco Nuñez' favor ; for the King adds that he has written to Pedrárias that he (Vasco Nuñez) should be well treated. It is possible that this is the letter above mentioned, a portion only of which is printed in Navarrete.

The date of the expedition to Dabaibe, in which so many men were lost, is not certain ; but Vasco Nuñez saw the necessity of putting forward a defence, which he did in a letter to the King on the 16th of October, 1515.[9] In this letter, besides describing the really insuperable obstacles in the way of a successful expedition in that direction, — in which the lack of food, owing to the ravages of the locusts, bears a prominent part, — he attacks Pedrárias and his government very severely.

The doings of Arbolancha in Spain are not known. There is a letter of the King to Pedrárias, dated Sept. 27, 1514, appointing Vasco Nuñez *adelantado* of the coast region

[1] Navarrete, *Coleccion*, iii. 358–375.

[2] *Narrative . . . of Pascual de Andagoya*, translated by C. R. Markham for the Hakluyt Society, 1865, Introduction, pp. iii, xix.

[3] Oviedo, iii. 4-21 ; Las Casas, iii. 312-328, iv. 66-134 ; Peter Martyr, dec. ii. chaps. iii.-vi., dec. iii. chap. i. ; Herrera, dec. i. lib. 9 and 10, with the exception of chap. vii. of book 10, which relates to Pedrárias, and of a few other chapters with regard to the affairs of Velasquez, etc. ; Galvano, Hakluyt Society ed., p. 124 ; Helps, i. 321-352, and chap. iv. of his *Pizarro* ; Bancroft, *Central America*, i. 129, 133, 330-385, 438 ; and *Mexico*, iii. 558 ; Irving, *Companions*, pp. 136-212 and 254-276 ; Ruge, *Geschichte des Zeitalters der Entdeckungen*, p. 347.

[4] Cf. Bancroft, *Central America*, i. 364, *note*. Irving unluckily followed Peter Martyr, as Bancroft shows. [Humboldt is inclined to magnify the significance of the information which Columbus in his third voyage got, as looking to a knowledge, by the Spaniards, of the south sea as early as 1503. Cf. his *Relation historique du voyage aux régions équinoxiales*, iii. 703, 705, 713 ; *Cosmos*, Eng. tr. (Bohn), ii. 642 ; *Views of Nature* (Bohn), p. 432. — ED.]

[5] *Coleccion*, iii. 337-342.

[6] Ibid., iii. 342-355.

[7] Ibid., iii. 355.

[8] *Documentos inéditos*, xxxvii. 282.

[9] Ibid., ii. 526 ; Navarrete, *Coleccion*, iii. 375. Cf. Navarrete's *nota* on the credibility of Vasco Nuñez in Ibid., p. 385. Portions of this letter have been translated by Markham in the notes to pages 1 and 10 of Andagoya's *Narrative*, published by the Hakluyt Society.

which he had discovered.[1] We have several letters of the King to Pedrárias, to the new *adelantado*, and to other officers, on November 23 and 27.[2]

The next document of importance is the narrative of Espinosa's expedition, written by himself. It is printed in the *Documentos inéditos* (vol. ii. pp. 467–522), with some corrections by the editors ; but it may be found in the original spelling, and without such corrections, in another volume of that series,[3] where the date of 1514 is most erroneously assigned to it.

The *licenciate* Gaspar de Espinosa came to Tierra-Firme with Pedrárias as *alcalde mayor*. Soon after his arrival at Antigua he held the *residencia* of Vasco Nuñez, and then is not heard of again until he is found in command of this expedition. He founded Panamá (for the first time) and returned to Antigua, whence he followed Pedrárias to Acla to try Vasco Nuñez for treason. He unwillingly convicted him, but recommended mercy. After the great explorer's death he cruised in his vessels to the coast of Nicaragua ; and later he played an important part in the conquest of Peru, and died at Cuzco while endeavoring to accommodate the differences between Pizarro and Almagro. The only other document of his which I have found is a *Relacion e proceso* concerning the voyage of 1519.[4]

There are a few other documents bearing on the history of Tierra-Firme ;[5] but the best and most complete contemporary account of this period[6] was written by Pascual de Andagoya, who came to Antigua with Pedrárias. Andagoya was with Vasco Nuñez on his last voyage, accompanied Espinosa on both his expeditions, and led a force into Birú in 1522. After his return from that expedition he lived in Panamá until 1529, when Pedro de los Rios banished him from the isthmus. After a few years spent in Santo Domingo he returned to Panamá as lieutenant to the new governor, Barrionuevo, and acted as agent to Pizarro and the other conquerors of Peru until 1536, when his *residencia* was held with much rigor by the *licenciate* Pedro Vasquez, and he was sent to Spain. In 1539 he returned as *adelantado* and governor of Castilla Nueva, as the province bordering on the *Mar del Sur* from the Gulf of San Miguel to the San Juan River was then called. But the remainder of his life was one succession of disappointments, and he died some time after 1545.[7]

From this brief biography it will be seen that Andagoya's earlier career was successful, and that he was on friendly terms with Pedrárias, Espinosa, and Vasco Nuñez. He was therefore, so far as we are concerned, an impartial witness of the events which he describes ; and his testimony is therefore more to be relied on than that of Oviedo, who was absent from Tierra-Firme a great part of the time, and who was besides inimical to Pedrárias. Otherwise Oviedo's account is the better ; for the sequence of events is difficult, if not impossible, to unravel from Andagoya.

---

[1] Cf. Sabin, *Dictionary*, vol. xiii. no. 56,338 ; also vol. x. no. 41,604.

[2] Letter from the King to Pedrárias, Sept. 23, 1514 (*Documentos inéditos*, xxxvii. 285) ; to Alonso de la Fuente, nuestro Thesoréro de Castilla del Oro, same date (*Doc. in.*, p. 287) ; to other officials (*Doc. in.*, p. 289) ; to Vasco Nuñez (*Doc. in.*, p. 290). See also some extracts printed in the same volume, pp. 193–197.

[3] *Documentos inéditos*, xxxvii. 5–75.

[4] Ibid., xx. 5–119.

[5] *Carta de Alonso de la Puente* [*thesoréro* of Tierra-Firme] *y Diego Marquez*, 1516 (*Documentos inéditos*, ii. 538) ; *Carta al Mr. de Zevres el lycenciado Çuaço*, 1518 (*Documentos inéditos*, i. 304). *Alonso de Çuaço*, or *Zuazo*, was *juez de Residencia en Santo Domingo*. Cf. *Documentos inéditos*, i. 292, *note*.

[6] *Relacion de los sucesos de Pedrárias Dávila en las provincias de Tierra firme ó Castilla del oro, y de lo occurido en el descubrimiento de la mar del Sur y costas del Perú y Nicaragua, escrita por el Adelantado Pascual de Andagoya*, in Navarrete, *Coleccion*, iii. 393–456. The portion bearing on the events described in this chapter ends at page 419. This has been translated and edited with notes, a map, and introduction by Clements R. Markham, in a volume published by the Hakluyt Society, London, 1865. [Cf. chapter on Peru, and the paper on Andagoya by Navarrete in his *Opúsculos*, i. 137. — ED.]

[7] Cf. Navarrete, *Noticia biográfica del Adelantado Pascual de Andagoya, Coleccion*, iii. 457 ; also *Biblioteca marítima española*, ii. 519 ; and Markham's translation of Andagoya's *Relacion*, pp. xx.–xxx.

The second chronicler of the Indies, Antonio de Herrera y Tordesillas, who published the first two volumes of his *Historia general* in 1601,[1] drew upon himself the wrath of a descendant of Pedrárias, Don Francisco Arias Dávila, Conde de Puñonrostro, who petitioned for redress. *Memorials, relaciones,* and *refutaciones* were given on both sides until September, 1603, when the matter was referred to "Xil Ramirez de Arellano, del Consexo de Su Maxestad e Su Fiscal." This umpire decided in effect[2] that Herrera had gone too far, and that the acrimony of some of the passages objected to should be mitigated. The papers which passed in this discussion, after remaining for a long time buried in the Archives of the Indies, have been printed in the thirty-seventh volume of *Documentos inéditos,*[3] and are without doubt one of the most valuable sets among the papers in that collection. Among them are many letters from the King to the royal officials which throw much light on the history of that time. There is nothing in them, however, to remove the unfavorable opinion of Pedrárias which the execution of Vasco Nuñez aroused; for although there can be little doubt that Vasco Nuñez meditated technical treason, yet conviction for treason by the *alcalde mayor* would not have justified execution without appeal, especially when the fair-minded judge, Gaspar Espinosa, recommended mercy. This is perfectly clear; but the mind of Pedrárias, who presented the facts from his point of view, in the *Testimónio de mandamiénto de Pedrárias Dávila mandando proscesar a Vasco Nuñez de Balbóa,*[4] had been poisoned by the jealous Garabito.

The convicted traitors were executed without delay or appeal of any kind being given them. The general opinion is that this execution took place in 1517, and that date has been adopted in this chapter; but in the second volume of *Documentos inéditos* (p. 556), there is a *Peticion presentada por Hernando de Arguello, á nombre de Vasco Nuñez de Balbóa, sobre que se le prorrogue el término que se le habia dado para la construccion de unos navíos,* etc., which was granted, for eight months, on the 13th day of January, 1518 (*en treze de Enero de quiniéntos é diez é ocho años*). This document is signed by Pedrárias Dávila, Alonso de la Puente, and Diego Marquez; and it is properly attested by Martin Salte, *escribáno.* Argüello was the principal financial supporter of Vasco Nuñez in the South Sea enterprise, and was executed in the evening of the same day on which his chief suffered.[5]

The first fifty-seven pages of the fourteenth volume of the *Documentos inéditos* are taken up with the affairs of Gil Gonzalez Dávila. The first is an *asiénto* with the pilot Niño, by which he was given permission to discover and explore for one thousand leagues to the westward from Panamá. Gil Gonzalez was to go in command of the fleet,[6] composed of the vessels built by Vasco Nuñez, which Pedrárias was ordered to deliver to the new adventurers, but which he refused to do until Gil Gonzalez made the demand in person.[7]

A full statement of the equipments and cost of fitting out the fleet in Spain is given in *Documentos inéditos* (vol. xiv. pp. 8–20), and is exceedingly interesting as showing what the Spaniards thought essential to the outfit of an exploring expedition. What was

[1] [See the bibliography of Herrera on p. 67, *ante.* — ED.]

[2] *Documentos inéditos,* xxxvii. 311.

[3] See also Oviedo, iii. 21–51, 83 *et seq.;* Las Casas, iv. 135–244; Peter Martyr, dec. ii. chap. vii. dec. iii. chaps. i.–iii., v., vi., and x., and dec. v. chap. ix.; Herrera, dec. ii. lib. 1, 2, 3, dec. iii. lib. 4. 5, 8, 9, and 10 *passim;* Quintana, *U. S.,* p. 294; Helps, i. 353–388; Bancroft, *Central America,* i. 386–431; Irving, *Companions,* pp. 212–276.

[4] *Documentos inéditos,* xxxvii. 215–231.

[5] Oviedo, iii. 56; Las Casas, iv. 230–244; Peter Martyr, dec. iv. chap. ix.; Herrera, dec. ii.

lib. 2, chaps. xiii., xv., and xxi.; Quintana, *U. S.,* pp. 298–299; Helps, i. 389–411; Bancroft, *Central America,* i. 432–459; Irving, *Companions,* pp. 259–276. Cf. Manuel M. De Peralta, *Costa Rica, Nicaragua y Panamá en el siglo XVI.* (Madrid, 1883), pp. ix, 707, for documents relating to Pedrárias in Costa Rica and Nicaragua, and p. 83 for Diego Machuca de Zuazo's letter to the Emperor, written from Granada, May 30, 1531, referring to the death of Pedrárias.

[6] *Documentos inéditos,* xiv. 5, partly translated in Bancroft, *Central America,* i. 480, *note.*

[7] Bancroft, *Central America,* i. 481, *note.*

actually accomplished in the way of sailing, marching, and baptizing is fully set forth in *Relacion de las leguas que el capitan Gil Gonzalez Dávila anduvo á pié por tierra por la costa de la mar del Sur, y de los caciques y indios que descubrió y se babtizaron, y del oro que dieron para Sus Magestades* (1522).[1]

The latter part of the career of Gil Gonzalez is described in the *Informacion sobre la llegada de Gil Gonzalez Dávila y Cristóbal de Olid á las Higueras* (Oct. 8, 1524) [2] and in the succeeding documents, especially a *Traslado testimoniado de una cédula del Emperador Carlos V. . . . entre los capitanes Gil Gonzalez Dávila y Cristóbal Dolid* (Nov. 20, 1525).[3] The *Relacion* of Andagoya[4] contains a narrative of the expedition from a different point of view. Besides these papers, Bancroft found a document in the Squier Collection,[5] which he cites as *Carta de Gil Gonzalez Dávila el Rey* (March, 1524). This letter contains a great deal of detailed information, of which Bancroft has made good use in his account of that adventurer.[6]

There is no documentary evidence with regard to the settlement of Jamaica by Juan de Esquivel, or of the circumnavigation of Cuba by Sebastian de Ocampo ; and there are but slight allusions to them in the "chroniclers."[7] There is not much to be found concerning the settlement of Cuba, except the accounts given by the early chroniclers. I should place Oviedo (vol. i. p. 494) first, although he got his knowledge second hand from the account given by Las Casas ; while the story of this actual observer is necessarily tinged by the peculiar views — peculiar for the nation and epoch — which he held in later life with regard to the enslavement of the natives.[8]

With the voyage of Córdoba to Yucatan, Navarrete[9] again becomes useful, although he printed no new evidence. The voyage, therefore, rests upon the accounts given in the standard books,[10] upon the *Historia verdadera* of Bernal Diaz, the *Vida de Cortés* in Icazbalceta (i. 338), and a few documents recently dragged from the recesses of the Indian Archives.

Bernal Diaz del Castillo came to Tierra-Firme with Pedrárias ; but, discouraged with the outlook there, he and about one hundred companions found their way to Cuba, attracted thither by the inducements held out by Velasquez. But there again he was doomed to disappointment, and served under Córdoba, Grijalva, and Cortés. After the conquest of Mexico he settled in Guatemala. Whatever may be the exaggerations in the latter part of his *Historia verdadera*,[11] there is no reason why Bernal Diaz should

---

[1] *Documentos inéditos*, xiv. 20.

[2] Ibid., xiv. 25.

[3] Ibid., xiv. 47.

[4] Navarrete, *Coleccion*, iii. 413–418; Markham's translation, pp. 31–38; see also Oviedo, iii. 65 *et seq.* ; Las Casas, v. 200 *et seq.* ; Peter Martyr, dec. vi. chaps. ii.–viii. ; Herrera, dec. ii. lib. 3, chap. xv. and lib. 4 etc., dec. iii. lib. 4, chaps. v. and vi. ; Helps, iii. 69–76.

[5] Cf. Bancroft, *Central America*, i. 483, *note*. [See the Introduction to the present volume. — ED.]

[6] *Central America*, i. 478–492, 512–521, and 527–538. This letter, which is dated at Santo Domingo (March 6, 1524), has since been printed in Peralta's *Costa Rica, Nicaragua y Panamá en el Siglo XVI.* (Madrid, 1883), p. 3, where is also (p. 27) his *Itinerario*, beginning "21 de Enero de 1522."

[7] For Esquivel and Jamaica, see Herrera, dec. i. lib. 8, chap. v.; Navarrete, *Coleccion*, iii. 171. For Ocampo's voyage, Oviedo, i. 495;

Las Casas, iii. 210; Herrera, dec. i. lib. 7, chap. i.; Stevens's *Notes*, p. 35; Helps, i. 415, and ii. 165.

[8] See also Herrera, dec. i. lib. 9, chaps. iv., vii., and xv.; also lib. 10, chap. viii.; Helps, i. 415–432, and *Vida de Cortés* in Icazbalceta, *Coleccion . . . para la historia de México*, i. 319–337. [There is a little contemporary account of the conquest of Cuba in the Lenox Library, *Provinciæ . . . noviter reperta in ultima navigatione*, which seems to be a Latin version of a Spanish original now lost (*Bibl. Amer. Vet.* no. 101). On the death of Velasquez, see *Magazine of American History*, i. 622, 692. — ED.]

[9] *Coleccion*, iii. 53.

[10] Oviedo, i. 497; Las Casas, iv. 348–363; Peter Martyr, dec. iv. chap. i.; Herrera, dec. ii. lib. 2, chap. xvii.; Navarrete, *Coleccion*, iii. 53; Cogolludo, *Historia de Yucatan*, 3; Prescott, *Mexico*, i. 222; Helps, ii. 211–217; Bancroft, *Central America*, i. 132, and *Mexico*, i. 5–11.

[11] [Cf. the chapter on Cortés. — ED.]

not have wished to tell the truth as to the voyages of Córdoba and Grijalva, with one or two exceptions, to be hereafter noted.

Prescott, in his *Conquest of Mexico* (vol. i. p. 222), says that Córdoba sailed for one of the neighboring Bahamas, but that storms drove him far out of his course, etc. Bancroft[1] has effectually disposed of this error. But is it not a curious fact that Bernal Diaz and Oviedo should give the length of the voyage from Cape St. Anton to the sighting of the islands off Yucatan as from six to twenty-one days? Oviedo was probably nearer the mark, as it is very likely that the old soldier had forgotten the exact circumstances of the voyage; for it must be borne in mind that he did not write his book until long after the events which it chronicles. As to the object of the expedition, it was undoubtedly undertaken for the purpose of procuring slaves, and very possibly Velasquez contributed a small vessel to the two fitted out by the other adventurers;[2] but the claim set forth by the descendants of Velasquez, that he sent four fleets *at his own cost — La una con un F. H. de Córdoba*[3] — is preposterous.

The voyage of Juan de Grijalva was much better chronicled; for with regard to it there are in existence three accounts written by eye-witnesses. The first is that of Bernal Diaz,[4] which is minute, and generally accurate; but it is not unlikely that in his envy at the praise accorded to Cortés, he may have exaggerated the virtues of Grijalva. The latter also wrote an account of the expedition, which is embodied in Oviedo,[5] together with corrections suggested by Velasquez, whom Oviedo saw in 1523.

But before these I should place the *Itinerario* of Juan Diaz, a priest who accompanied the expedition.[6] The original is lost; but an Italian version is known, which was printed with the *Itinerario de Varthemà* at Venice, in 1520.[7] This edition was apparently unknown to Navarrete, who gives 1522 as the date of its appearance in Italian, in which he is followed by Ternaux-Compans and Prescott.

Notwithstanding this mass of original material, it is not easy to construct a connected narrative of this voyage, for Oviedo sometimes contradicts himself; Bernal Diaz had undoubtedly forgotten the exact dates, which he nevertheless attempts to give in too many cases; Juan Diaz, owing partly to the numerous translations and changes incidental thereto, is sometimes unintelligible; and Las Casas,[8] who had good facilities for getting at the exact truth, is often very vague and difficult to follow.

[1] *History of Mexico*, i. 7, *note* 4.

[2] Bancroft, *Mexico*, i. 5, 6, *notes*.

[3] *Memorial del negocio de D. Antonio Velasquez de Bazan*, etc., *Documentos Inéditos*, x. 80–86; this extract is on p. 82.

[4] *Historia verdadera*, chaps. viii.–xiv.

[5] *Historia general*, i. 502–537.

[6] As to the identity of Juan Diaz, see note to Bernal Diaz, *Historia verdadera*, ed. of 1632, folio 6; Oviedo, i. 502; Herrera, dec. ii. lib. 31, chap. i. As to his future career, see Bancroft, *Mexico*, ii. 158 and *note* 5. The full title of this account of Juan Diaz is: *Itinerario del armata del Re catholico in India verso la isola de Iuchathan del anno M.D.XVIII. alla qual fu presidente & capitan generale Ioan de Grisalva: el qual e facto per el capellano maggior de dicta armata a sua altezza*.

[7] [A copy of this, which belonged to Ferdinand Columbus, is in the Cathedral Library at Seville. The book is so scarce that Muñoz used a manuscript copy; and from Muñoz' manuscript the one used by Prescott was copied. Maisonneuve (1882 *Catalogue*, no. 2,980) has recently priced a copy at 600 francs. There is a copy

in the Carter-Brown Library (*Catalogue*, vol. i. no. 65), and was sold the present year in the Court sale (no. 362). It was reprinted in 1522, 1526 (Murphy, no, 2,580), and 1535, — the last priced by Maisonneuve (no. 2,981) at 400 francs. Cf. Harrisse, *Bibl. Amer. Vet.*, nos. 98, 114, 137, 205, and *Additions*, no. 59. The *Carter-Brown Catalogue* (i. 119) puts a Venice edition, without date, under 1536. Ternaux gives a French translation in his *Relations et mémoires*, vol. x. Icazbalceta has given a Spanish version from the Italian, together with the Italian text, in his *Coleccion de documentos para la historia de México*, i. 281; also see his introduction, p. xv. He points out the errors of Ternaux's version. Cf. Bandelier's "Bibliography of Yucatan" in *Amer. Antiq. Soc. Proc.* (October, 1880), p. 82. Harrisse in his *Bibl. Amer. Vet., Additions*, no. 60, cites a *Lettera mãdata della insula de Cuba*, 1520, which he says differs from the account of Juan Diaz. — ED.]

[8] Las Casas, iv. 421–449. Other references to this voyage are, — Peter Martyr, dec. iv. chaps. iii. and iv.; Herrera, dec. ii. lib. 3, chaps. i., ii., ix., x., and xi.; Navarrete, *Coleccion*,

EL CAPITAN JUAN
de GRIJALVA de
Cuellar

JUAN DE GRIJALVA.[1]

In addition to this material, the *Décadas abreviadas de los descubrimientos, conquistas, fundaciones y otras cosas notables, acaecidas en las Indias occidentales desde 1492 á 1640,* has been of considerable service. This paper was found in manuscript form, without date or signature, in the Biblioteca Nacional by the editors of the *Documentos inéditos*, and printed by them in their eighth volume (pp. 5–52). It is not accurate throughout; but it gives the dates and order of events in many cases so clearly, that it is a document of some importance.

Edward Channing

iii. 55; Cogolludo, *Historia de Yucathan*, p. 8; Brasseur de Bourbourg, iv. 50; Helps, ii. 217; Bancroft, *Central America*, i. 132; and *Mexico*, pp. 15–35.

[1] Fac-simile of an engraving in Herrera, i. 312. Cf. also the Mexican edition of Prescott, and Carbajal Espinosa's *Historia de México*, i. 64.

THE EARLY CARTOGRAPHY

OF THE

GULF OF MEXICO AND ADJACENT PARTS.

BY THE EDITOR.

IN a previous section on the early maps of the Spanish and Portuguese discoveries the Editor has traced the development of the geography of the Gulf of Mexico with the group of the Antilles and the neighboring coasts, beginning with the delineation of La Cosa in 1500. He has indicated in the same section the influence of the explorations of Columbus and his companions in shaping the geographical ideas of the early years of the sixteenth century. Balbóa's discovery in 1513 was followed by the failure to find any passage to the west in the latitude of the Antilles; but the

THE PACIFIC, 1518.

disappointment was not sufficient to remove the idea of such a passage from the minds of certain geographers for some years to come. The less visionary among them hesitated to embrace the notion, however, and we observe a willingness to be confined by something like definite knowledge in the maker of a map of the Pacific which is preserved in the Military Library at Weimar. This map shows Cordova's discoveries about Yucatan (1517), but has no indication of the islands which Magellan discovered (1520) in the Pacific; accordingly, Kohl places it in 1518. Balbóa's discovery is noted in the sea which was seen by the Castilians.[1]

[1] This map has seemingly some relation to a map, preserved in the Propaganda at Rome, of which mention is made by Thomassy, *Les papes géographes*, p. 133.

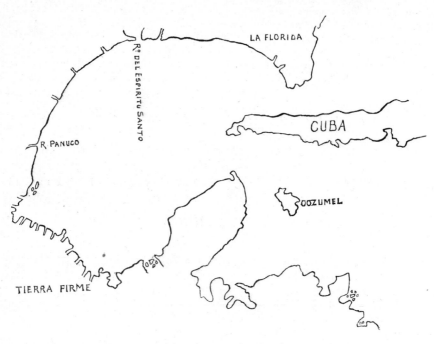

GULF OF MEXICO, 1520.[1]

A sketch of a map found by Navarrete in the Spanish archives, and given by him in his *Coleccion*, vol. iii., as "Las Costas de Tierra-Firme y las tierras nuevas," probably embodies the results of Pinedo's expedition to the northern shores of the

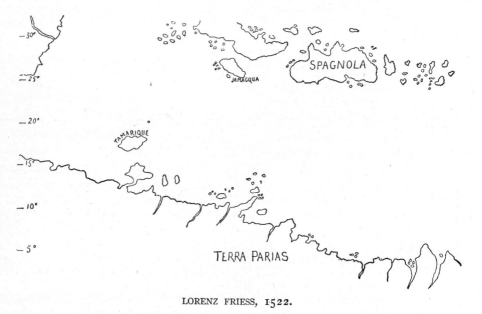

LORENZ FRIESS, 1522.

[1] This map is also given in Weise's *Discoveries of America*, p. 278.

Gulf in 1519. This was the map sent to Spain by Garay, the governor of Jamaica. What seems to be the mouth of the Mississippi will be noted as the "Rio del Espiritu Santo." The surprisingly accurate draft of the shores of the Gulf which

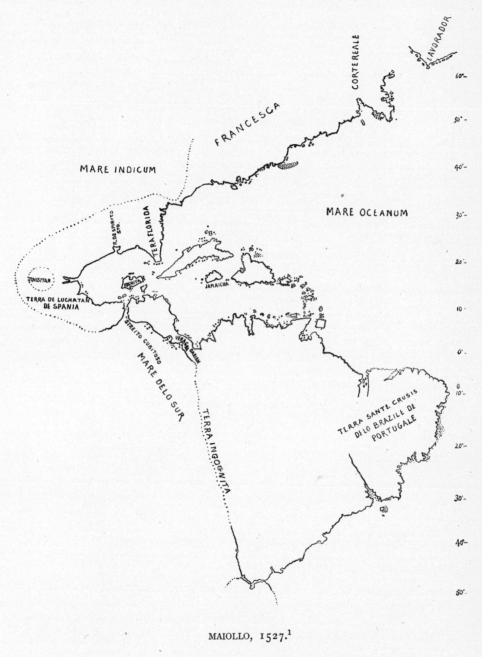

MAIOLLO, 1527.[1]

[1] Sketch of the map in the Ambrosian Library, of which the part north of Florida is given on a larger scale, after Desimoni's sketch, with coast names, in the present *History*, Vol. IV. pp. 28, 39. The present sketch follows a facsimile given in Weise's *Discoveries of America*.

Cortés sent to Europe was published in 1524, and is given to the reader on another page.[1]

There is a sketch of the northern shore of South America and the " Insule Canibalorum sive Antiglie " which was made by Lorenz Friess (Laurentius Frisius) in 1522. The outline, which is given herewith, represents one of the sheets of twelve woodcut maps which were not published till 1530 — under the title *Carta marina navigatoria Portugalensium*.   Friess does not mention whence he got his material, which seems to be of an earlier date than the time of using it ; and Kohl suspects it came from Waldseemüller.   South America is marked " Das nüw Erfunde land."

In the Maiollo map of 1527 we find two distinct features, — the strait, connecting with the Pacific, which Cortés had been so anxious to find ; and the insular Yucatan pushed farther than usual into the Gulf.   The notion that Yucatan was an island is said to have arisen from a misconception of the meaning of the designation which the Indians applied to the country.[2] The Portuguese Portulano of 1514–1518[3] had made Yucatan a peninsula ; but four years later Grijalva had been instructed to sail round it, and Cortés in his map of 1520 had left an intervening channel.[4] We see the uncertainty which prevailed

NUÑO GARCIA DE TORENO, 1527.

among cartographers regarding this question in the peninsular character which Yucatan has in the map of 1520,[5] as resulting from Pinedo's search ; in the seeming hesitancy of the Toreno map,[6] and in the unmistakable insularity of the Friess,[7] Verrazano,[8] and Ribero[9] charts. The decision of the latter royal hydrographer governed a school of mapmakers for some years, and a similar strait of greater or less width separates it from the main in the Finæus map of 1531,[10] the Lenox woodcut of 1534,[11] the Ulpius globe of 1542,[12] not to name others ; though the peninsular notion still prevailed with some of the cartographers.[13]

A map which shows the extent of the explorations on the Pacific from Balbóa's time till Gonzales and others reached the country about the Isthmus of Tehuantepec, is that of

---

[1] See notes following chap. vi.

[2] Yucatan seems to have been first named, or its name at least was first recorded, as Yuncatan by Bartholomew Columbus (*Bibl. Amer. Vet.*, p. 471). There are various theories regarding the origin of the name. Cf. Bancroft, *Mexico*, i. 11, 12 ; Prescott, *Mexico*, i. 223. A new Government map of Yucatan was published in 1878 (*Magazine of American History*, vol. iii. p. 295).

[3] As given by Kunstmann. See Vol. IV. p. 36 of the present work.

[4] See notes following chap. vi.

[5] See *ante*, p. 218.

[6] See *ante*, p. 43.

[7] See *ante*, p. 127.

[8] See Vol. IV. p. 26.

[9] See *post*, p. 221.

[10] See Vol. III. p. 11.

[11] See *post*, p. 223.

[12] See Vol. IV. p. 42.

[13] Cf. Bancroft, *Mexico*, i. 21 ; Valentini in *Magazine of American History*, iii. 295, who supposes that the land usually thought to be an incomplete Cuba in Ruysch's map of 1508 (p. 115, *ante*) is really Yucatan, based on the results of the so-called first voyage of Vespucius, and that its seven Latin names correspond to a part of the nineteen Portuguese names which are given on the western shore of the so-called Admiral's map of the Ptolemy of 1513 (p. 112, *ante*).   Peschel (*Geschichte der Erdkunde*, 1865, p. 235) also suggests that this map is the work of Vespucius.

1527, which was formerly ascribed to Ferdinand Columbus, but has been shown by Harrisse to be more likely the work of Nuño Garcia de Toreno. The map, which is of the world, and of which but a small section is given herewith, is called *Carta universal en que se contiene todo lo que del mundo se a descubierto hasta aora; hizola un cosmographo de su magestad anno M. D. XXVII en Sevilla.* Its outline of the two Americas is shown in a sketch given on an earlier page.[1] The original is preserved in the Grand-Ducal Library at Weimar.

A map of similar character, dated two years later, is one which is the work of Diego Ribero, a Portuguese in the service of Spain, who had been the royal cosmogra-

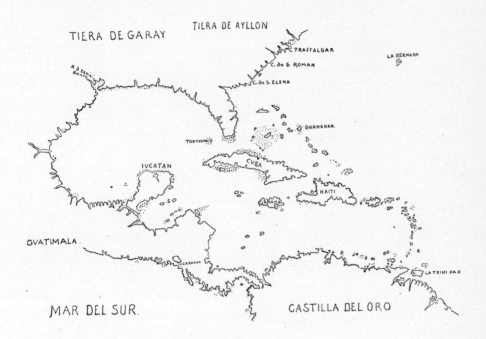

RIBERO, 1529.

pher since 1523, — an office which he was to hold till his death, ten years later, in 1533. There are two early copies of this map, of which a small section is herewith given; both are on parchment, and are preserved respectively at Weimar and Rome, though Thomassy[2] says there is a third copy. The Roman copy is in the Archivio del Collegio di Propaganda, and is said to have belonged to Cardinal Borgia. The North American sections of the map have been several times reproduced in connection with discussions of the voyages of Gomez and Verrazano.[3] The entire American continent was first engraved by M. C. Sprengel in 1795, after a copy then in Büttner's library at Jena, when it was appended to a German translation of Muñoz, with a memoir upon it which was also printed separately as *Ueber Ribero's älteste Welt-karte.* The map is entitled *Carta universal en que*

[1] Page 43. The best reproduction of it is in Kohl's *Die beiden ältesten General-Karten von Amerika;* and there is another fac-simile in Santarem's *Atlas,* no. xiv. Cf. Humboldt, *Examen critique,* ii. 184, and his preface to Ghillany's *Behaim;* Harrisse, *Cabots,* pp. 69, 172; Murr,

Memorabilia bibliothecarum (Nuremberg, 1786), ii. 97; Lindenau, *Correspondance de Zach* (October, 1810); Lelewel, *Géographie du moyen-âge,* ii. 110; 110; *Ocean Highways* (1872).

[2] *Les papes géographes,* p. 118.

[3] See Vol. IV. p. 38.

se contiene todo lo que del mundo se ha descubierto fasta agora : Hizola Diego Ribero cosmographo de su magestad : año de 1529. *La Qual se divide en dos partes conforme á la capitulaçion que hizieron los catholicos Reyes de España, y el Rey don Juan de portugal en la Villa* [*citta*] *de Tordesillas : Año de* 1494, — thus recording the Spanish understanding, as the map of 1527 did, of the line of demarcation. The Propaganda copy has " en Sevilla " after the date. The most serviceable of the modern reproductions of the American parts is that given by Kohl in his *Die beiden ältesten General-Karten von Amerika*, though several other drafts are open to the student in Santarem's *Atlas* (pl. xxv.), Lelewel's *Moyen-âge* (pl. xli.), Ruge's *Geschichte des Zeitalters der Entdeckungen*, and Bancroft's *Central America* (i. 146).[1]

These two maps of 1527 and 1529 established a type of the American coasts which prevailed for some time. One such map is that of which a fac-simile is given in the *Cartas de Indias*, called " Carta de las Antillas, seno Mejicano y costas de tierra-firme, y de la America setentrional," which seems, however, to have been made later than 1541.[2] Another is preserved in the Ducal Library at Wolfenbüttel, of which Harrisse makes mention in his *Cabots*, p. 185. A significant map of this type, commonly cited as the *Atlas de Philippe II., dédié à Charles Quint*, is more correctly defined in the title given to a photographic reproduction,[3] *Portulano de Charles Quint donné à Philippe II., accompagné d'une notice par MM. F. Spitzer et Ch. Wiener*, Paris, 1875. The map is not dated ; but the development of the coasts of Florida, California, Peru, and of Magellan's Straits, with the absence of the coast-line of Chili, which had been tracked in 1536, has led to the belief that it represents investigations of a period not long before 1540. The original draft first attracted attention when exhibited in 1875 at the Geographical Congress in Paris, and shortly after it was the subject of several printed papers.[4] Major is inclined to think it the work of Baptista Agnese, and Wieser is of the same opinion ; while for the American parts it is contended that the Italian geographer — for the language of the map is Italian — followed the maps of 1527 and 1529.

What would seem to be the earliest engraved map of this type exists, so far as is known, in but a single copy, now in the Lenox Library. It is a woodcut, measuring 21 × 17 inches, and is entitled *La carta uniuersale della terra firma & Isole delle Indie occidētali, cio è del mondo nuouo fatta per dichiaratione delli libri delle Indie, cauata da due carte da nauicare fatte in Sibilia da li piloti della Maiesta Cesarea,* — the maps referred to being those of 1527 and 1529, as is supposed. Harrisse, however, claims that this Venice cut preceded the map of 1527, and was probably the work of the same chartmaker. Stevens holds that it followed both of these maps, and should be dated 1534 ; while Harrisse would place it before Peter Martyr's death in September, 1526. According to Brevoort and Harrisse,[5] the map was issued to accompany the conglomerate work of Martyr and Oviedo, *Summario de la generale historia de l'Indie occidentali*, which was printed in three parts at Venice in 1534.[6] Murphy, in his *Verrazzano* (p. 125), quotes the colophon of the Oviedo part of the book as evidence of the origin of the map, which translated stands thus : " Printed at Venice in the month of December, 1534. For the explanation of these books there has been made a universal map of the countries of

<hr/>

[1] Cf. Humboldt, *Examen critique*, iii. 184; *Gazetta letteraria universale* (May, 1796), p. 468; Santarem in *Bulletin de la Société de Géographie* (1847), vii. 310, and in his *Recherches sur la découverte des pays au-delà du Cap-Bojador*, pp. xxiii and 125; Murr, *Histoire diplomatique de Behaim*, p. 26; Lelewel, *Géographie du moyen-âge*, ii. 166.

[2] See *ante*, p. 92.

[3] One hundred copies issued.

[4] Dr. J. Chavanne in *Mittheilungen der k. k. geographischen Gesellschaft in Wien* (1875),

p. 485; A. Steinhauser in Ibid., p. 588; *Petermann's Mittheilungen* (1876), p. 52; Malte-Brun in the *Bulletin de la Société de Géographie de Paris* (1876), p. 625; Dr. Franz Wieser's " Der Portulan des Infanten und nachmaligen Königs Philipp II. von Spanien," printed in the *Sitzungsberichte der philosophisch-historischen Classe der kaiserlichen Akademie der Wissenschaften in Wien*, lxxxii. 541 (March, 1876), and also printed separately.

[5] *Cabots*, p. 168.

[6] See Vol. III. p. 19.

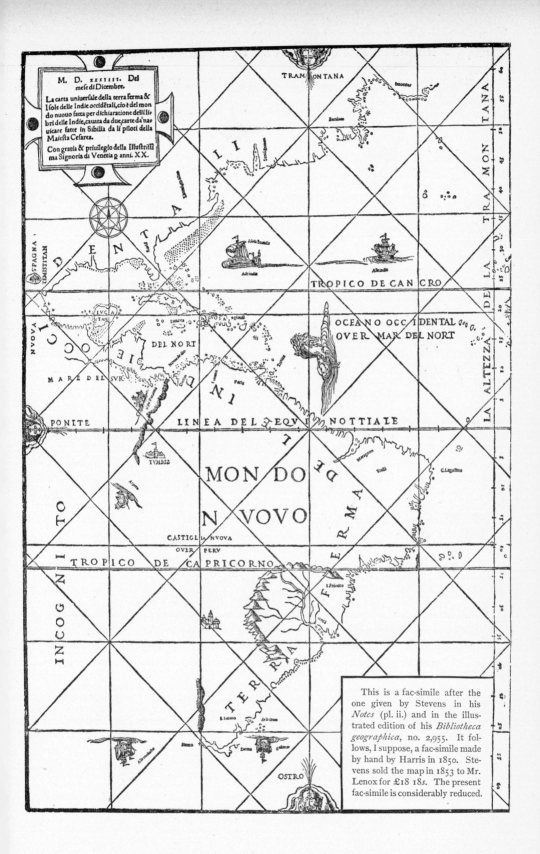

This is a fac-simile after the one given by Stevens in his *Notes* (pl. ii.) and in the illustrated edition of his *Bibliotheca geographica*, no. 2,955. It follows, I suppose, a fac-simile made by hand by Harris in 1850. Stevens sold the map in 1853 to Mr. Lenox for £18 18s. The present fac-simile is considerably reduced.

all the West Indies, together with a special map [Hispaniola] taken from two marine charts of the Spaniards, one of which belonged to Don Pietro Martire, councillor of the Royal Council of said Indies, and was made by the pilot and master of marine charts, Niño Garzia de Loreno [*sic*] in Seville ; the other was made also by a pilot of his Majesty, the Emperor, in Seville." Quaritch [1] says that an advertisement at the end of the *secundo libro* of Xeres, *Conquista del Peru* (Venice, 1534), shows that the map in the first edition of Peter Martyr's *Decades* was made by Nuño Garcia de Toreno in Seville; but the statement is questionable. Harrisse refers to a map of Toreno preserved in the Royal Library at Turin, dated 1522, in which he is called " piloto y maestro de cartas de nauegar de su Magestad." The American part of this last chart is unfortunately missing.[2]

Harrisse calls this Lenox woodcut the earliest known chart of Spanish origin which is crossed by lines of latitude and longitude, and thinks it marks a type adopted by the Spanish cosmographers a little after the return of Del Cano from his voyage of circumnavigation and the coming of Andagoya from Panama in 1522, with additions based on the tidings which Gomez brought to Seville in December, 1525, from his voyage farther north.

It is not worth while to reproduce here various maps of this time, all showing more or less resemblance to the common type of this central portion of the New World. Such

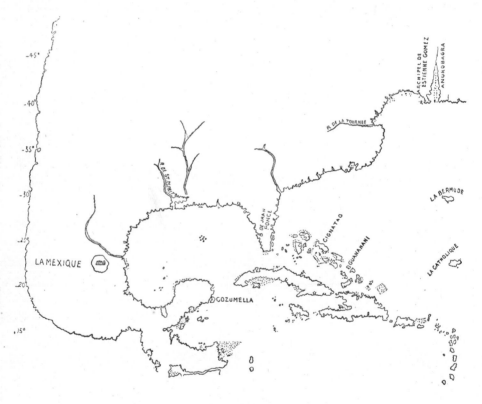

AN EARLY FRENCH MAP.

[1] *Catalogue*, no. 349, p. 1277.

[2] Cf. Vincenzo Promis, *Memoriale di Diego Colombo con nota sulla bolla di Alessandro VI.* (Torino, 1869), p. 11 ; Heinrich Wuttke, "Zur Geschichte der Erdkunde in der letzten Hälfte des Mittelalters," in the *Jahresbericht des Vereins für Erdkunde in Dresden* (1870), vol. vi. and vii. p. 61, etc. ; Wieser, *Der Portulan*, etc., p. 15.

are the maps of Verrazano [1] and of Thorne,[2] the draft of the Sloane manuscript,[3] the cordi-form map of Orontius Finæus,[4] one given by Kunstmann,[5] and the whole series of the Agnese type.[6]

There is a French map, which was found by Jomard in the possession of a noble family in France, which Kohl supposes to be drawn in part from Ribero. A sketch is annexed as of " An Early French Map." The absence of the Gulf of California and of all

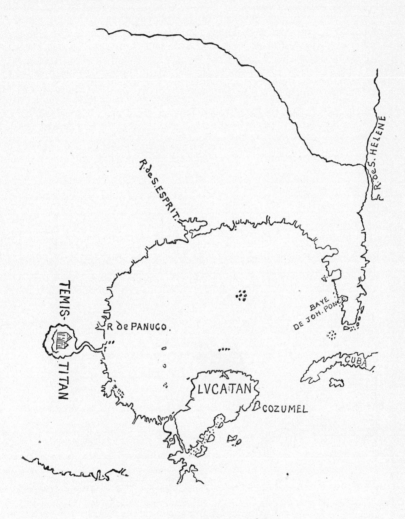

GULF OF MEXICO, 1536.

traces of De Soto's expedition leads Kohl to date it before 1533. Jomard placed the date later; but as the map has no record of the expeditions of Ribault and Laudonnière, it would appear to be earlier than 1554.[7]

[1] Vol. IV. p. 26.
[2] Vol. III. p. 17.
[3] See *post*, p. 432.
[4] Vol. III. p. 11.
[5] Vol. IV. p. 46.

[6] Vol. IV. p. 40.
[7] Kohl, ignorant of the Peter Martyr map of 1511 (see p. 110), mistakes in considering that the map must be assigned to a date later than 1530, for the reason that the Bermudas are shown in it.

There is a large manuscript map in the British Museum which seems to have been made by a Frenchman from Spanish sources, judging from the mixture and corruption of the languages used in it. In one inscription there is mention of "the disembarkation of the Governor;" and this, together with the details of the harbors on the west coast of Florida, where Narvaez went, leads Kohl to suppose the map to have been drawn from that commander's reports. The sketch, which is annexed and marked "Gulf of Mexico, 1536," follows Kohl's delineation in his Washington collection.[1]

We can further trace the geographical history of the Antilles in the Münster map of 1540,[2] in the Mercator gores of 1541,[3] and in the Ulpius globe of 1542.[4] In this last year (1542) we find in the Rotz *Idrography*, preserved in the British Museum, a map which

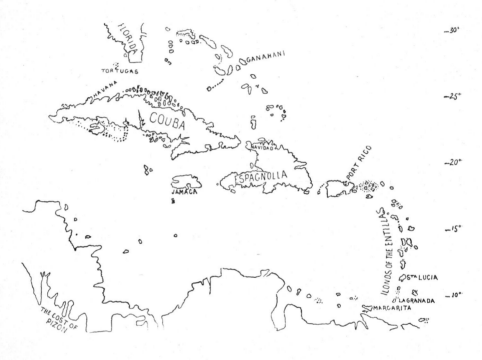

ROTZ, 1542.

records the latitudes about three degrees too high for the larger islands, and about two degrees too low for the more southern ones, making the distance between Florida and Trinidad too great by five degrees. The map is marked "The Indis of Occident quhas the Spaniards doeth occupy." The sketch here given follows Kohl's copy.[5] Rotz seems to have worked from antecedent Portuguese charts ; and in the well-known Cabot map of 1544, of which a section is annexed, as well as in the Medina map of 1545,[6] we doubtless have the results reached by the Spanish hydrographers. The "Carta marina" of the Italian Ptolemy of 1548,[7] as well as the manuscript atlas of Nicholas Vallard (1547), now in the Sir Thomas Phillipps Collection, may be traced ultimately to the same

[1] This may be the map referred to by R. H. Schomburgk in his *Barbadoes* (London, 1848), as being in the British Museum, to which it was restored in 1790, after having been in the possession of Edward Harley and Sir Joseph Banks.

[2] See Vol. IV. p. 41.

[3] See *ante*, p. 177.

[4] See Vol. IV. p. 42.

[5] Cf. Schomburgk's *Barbadoes*, p. 256.

[6] See "Hist. Chorography of S. America."

[7] See Vol. IV. p. 43, and fac-simile given in "Hist. Chorography of South America."

source; and the story goes respecting the latter that a Spanish bishop, Don Miguel de Silva, brought out of Spain and into France the originals upon which it was founded. These originals, it would appear, also served Homem in 1558 in the elaborate manuscript map, now preserved in the British Museum, of which a sketch (in part) is annexed (p. 229).

The maps of the middle of the century which did most to fix popularly the geography of the New World were probably the Bellero map of 1554,[1] which was so current in

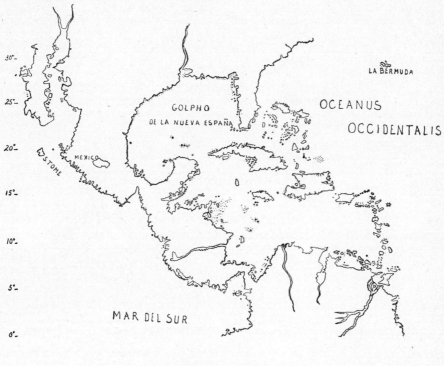

CABOT, 1544.[2]

Antwerp publications of about that time, and the hemisphere of Ramusio (1556) which accompanied the third volume of his *Viaggi*, and of which a fac-simile is annexed. There is a variety of delineations to be traced out for the Antilles through the sequence of the better-known maps of the next following years, which the curious student may find in the maps of the Riccardi Palace,[3] the Nancy globe,[4] the Martines map of 155-,[5] that of Forlani in 1560,[6] the map of Ruscelli in the Ptolemy of 1561, besides those by Zalterius (1566),[7] Des Liens (1566),[8] Diegus (1568),[9] Mercator (1569),[10] Ortelius (1570),[11] and Porcacchi (1572).[12] Of the map of Martines, in 1578, which is in a manuscript atlas preserved in

[1] See "Hist. Chorography of S. America."
[2] Sketch of a section of the so-called Sebastian Cabot Mappemonde in the National Library at Paris, following a photographic reproduction belonging to Harvard College Library. There is a rude draft of the Antilles by Allfonsce of this same year.
[3] Figured in the *Jahrbuch des Vereins für Erdkunde in Dresden*, 1870.

[4] See *post*, p. 433.
[5] See *post*, p. 450.
[6] See *post*, p. 438.
[7] See Vol. IV. p. 93.
[8] See Vol. IV. p. 79.
[9] See *post*, p. 449.
[10] See Vol. IV. pp. 94, 373.
[11] See Vol. IV. p. 95.
[12] See Vol. IV. p. 96.

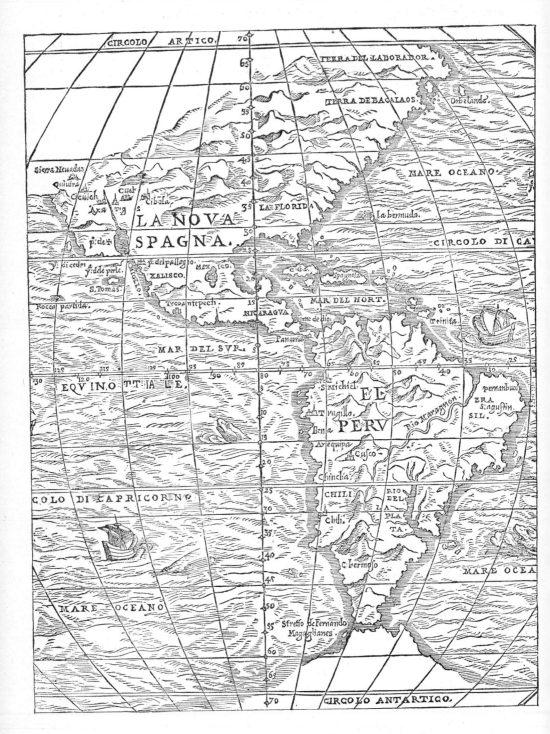

RAMUSIO, 1556.[1]

1 H. H. Bancroft, *Northwest Coast*, i. 49, sketches this map, but errs in saying the shape of the California peninsula was no copied in later maps. Cf. map in Best's *Frobisher* (1578).

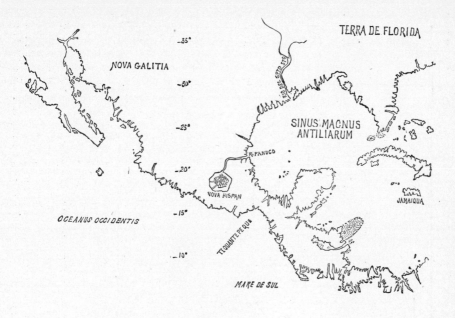

HOMEM, 1558.

the British Museum, Kohl says its parallels of latitude are more nearly correct than on any earlier map, while its meridians of longitude are expanded far too much.[1]

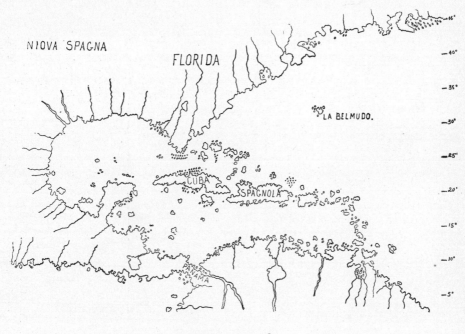

MARTINES, 1578.

[1] Cf. Vol. IV. p. 97.

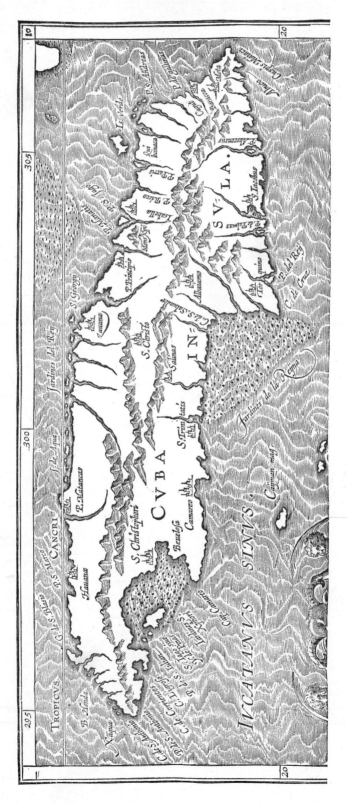

CUBA (after Wytfliet, 1597).[1]

1 The earliest map of Cuba is that in the La Cosa Chart, which is reproduced, among other places, in Ramon de la Sagra's *Histoire physique et politique de l'île de Cuba*, 1842–1843, which contains also the chart of Guillaure Testu. There are other early maps of Cuba — besides those in maps of the Antilles already mentioned in the present section — in Porcacchi, 1572 (pp. 81, 88), in the Ortelius of 1592, and in the Mercator atlases. The bibliography of Cuba is given in Bachiler's *Apuntes para la historia de la isla de Cuba*, Havana, 1861. For the cartography, cf. the *Mapoteca Columbiana* of Uricoechea, London, 1860, p. 53. Of the several maps of the Antilles toward the end of the century, it may be sufficient to name the detailed map of the West Indies in the Ortelius of 1584, the Hakluyt-Martyr map of 1587, the map of Thomas Hood in Kunstmann, the De Bry map of 1596, as well as the maps of the first distinctively American atlas, — that of Wytfliet in 1597.

CHAPTER IV.

ANCIENT FLORIDA.

BY JOHN GILMARY SHEA, LL.D.

THE credit of being the first to explore our Atlantic coast has not yet been positively awarded by critical historians. Ramusio preserves the report of a person whom he does not name, which asserts that Sebastian Cabot claimed for his father and himself, in the summer of 1497, to have run down the whole coast, from Cape Breton to the latitude of Cuba; but the most recent and experienced writer on Cabot treats the claim as unfounded.[1]

The somewhat sceptical scholars of our day have shown little inclination to adopt the theory of Francisco Adolpho de Varnhagen, that Americus Vespucius on his first voyage reached Honduras in 1497, and during the ensuing year ran along the northern shore of the Gulf of Mexico, doubled the Florida cape, and then sailed northward along our Atlantic coast to the Gulf of St. Lawrence, where he built a vessel and sailed to Cadiz.[2]

Although Columbus made his first landfall on one of the Bahamas, and Cuba was soon after occupied, no definite knowledge seems to have been obtained of the great mainland so near them. There is nothing in narrative or map to betray any suspicion of its existence prior to the year 1502, when a map executed in Lisbon at the order of Cantino, an Italian merchant, for Hercules d' Este, shows a mainland north of Cuba, terminating near that island in a peninsula resembling Florida. The tract of land thus shown has names of capes and rivers, but they can be referred to no known exploration. To some this has seemed to be but a confused idea of Cuba as mainland;[3] by others it is regarded as a vague idea of Yucatan. But Harrisse in his *Corte-Real*, where he reproduces the map, maintains that

---

[1] Harrisse, *Jean et Sebastien Cabot, leur origine et leurs voyages* (Paris, 1882), pp. 97–104. The Cabot claim appears in Peter Martyr, *Decades* (Basle, 1533), dec. iii. lib. 6, folio 55; Ramusio, *Viaggi* (1550–1553), tom. i. folio 414; Jacob Ziegler, *Opera varia* (Argentorati, 1532), folio xcii. [Cf. the present *History* Vol. III. chap. i., where it is shown that the person not named by Ramusio was Gian Giacomo Bardolo. — ED.]

[2] *Historical Magazine*, 1860, p. 98. Varnhagen ascribes the names of the Cantino and subsequent Ptolemy maps to Vespucius. The name Paria near Florida seems certainly to have come from this source. [The question of this disputed voyage is examined in chapter ii. of the present volume. — ED.]

[3] James Carson Brevoort, *Verrazano the Navigator*, p. 72.

" between the end of 1500 and the summer of 1502 navigators, whose name and nationality are unknown, but whom we presume to be Spaniards, discovered, explored, and named the part of the shore of the United States which from the vicinity of Pensacola Bay runs along the Gulf of Mexico to the Cape of Florida, and, turning it, runs northward along the Atlantic coast to about the mouth of the Chesapeake or Hudson." [1]

But leaving these three claims in the realm of conjecture and doubt, we come to a period of more certain knowledge.

The Lucayos of the Bahamas seem to have talked of a great land of Bimini not far from them. The Spaniards repeated the story; and in the edition of Peter Martyr's *Decades* published in 1511 is a map on which a large island appears, named " Illa de Beimeni, parte." [2]

Discovery had taken a more southerly route; no known Spanish vessel had passed through the Bahama channel or skirted the coast. But some ideas must have prevailed, picked up from natives of the islands, or adventurous pilots who had ventured farther than their instructions authorized. Stories of an island north of Hispaniola, with a fountain whose waters conferred perpetual youth, had reached Peter Martyr in Spain, for in the same edition of his *Decades* he alludes to the legends.

John Ponce de Leon, who had accompanied Columbus on his second voyage, and had since played his part bravely amid the greatest vicissitudes, resolved to explore and conquer Bimini. He had friends at Court, and seems to have been a personal favorite of the King, who expressed a wish for his advancement. [3] The patent he solicited was based on that originally issued to Columbus; but the King laughingly said, that it was one thing to grant boundless power when nothing was expected to come of it, and very different to do so when success was almost certain. Yet on the 23d of February, 1512, a royal grant empowered John Ponce de Leon " to proceed to discover and settle the Island of Bimini." [4] The patent was subject to the condition that the island had not been already discovered. He was required to make the exploration within three years, liberty being granted to him to touch at any island or mainland not subject to the King of Portugal. If he succeeded in his expedition he was to be governor of Bimini for life, with the title of *adelantado*. [5]

The veteran immediately purchased a vessel, in order to go to Spain and make preparations for the conquest of Bimini. But the authorities in Porto Rico seized his vessel; and the King, finding his services necessary

[1] Harrisse, *Les Corte-Real et leurs voyages au Nouveau Monde*, pp. 111, 151. [The Cantino map is sketched on p. 108. — ED.]

[2] *P. Martyris Angli Mediolanensis opera. Hispali Corumberger*, 1511. [A fac-simile of this map in given on p. 110. — ED.]

[3] King to Ceron and Diaz, Aug. 12, 1512.

[4] Las Casas was certainly mistaken in saying that Ponce de Leon gave the name Bimini to Florida; the name was in print before it appears in connection with him, and is in his first patent before he discovered or named Florida (Las Casas, *Historia de las Indias*, lib. ii. chap. xx., iii. p. 460.

[5] *Capitulacion que el Rey concedió á Joan Ponce de Leon para que vaya al descubrimiento de la ysla de Bemini. Fecha en Burgos a xxiij de hebrero de Dxij aº.*

in controlling the Indians, sent orders to the Council of the Indies to defer the Bimini expedition, and gave Ponce de Leon command of the fort in Porto Rico.[1]

Thus delayed in the royal service, Ponce de Leon was unable to obtain vessels or supplies till the following year. He at last set sail from the port of San German in Porto Rico in March, 1513,[2] with three caravels, taking as pilot Anton de Alaminos, a native of Palos who had as a boy accompanied Columbus, and who was long to associate his own name with explorations of the Gulf of Mexico. They first steered northeast by north, and soon made the Caicos, Yaguna, Amaguayo, and Manigua. After refitting at Guanahani, Ponce de Leon bore northwest; and on Easter Sunday (March 27) discovered the mainland, along which he ran till the 2d of April, when he anchored in 30° 8' and landed. On the 8th he took possession in the name of the King of Spain, and named the country — which the Lucayos called Cancio — Florida, from Pascua Florida, the Spanish name for Easter Sunday.

The vessels then turned southward, following the coast till the 20th, when Ponce landed near Abayoa, a cluster of Indian huts. On attempting to sail again, he met such violent currents that his vessels could make no headway, and were forced to anchor, except one of the caravels, which was driven out of sight. On landing at this point Ponce found the Indians so hostile that he was obliged to repel their attacks by force. He named a river Rio de la Cruz; and, doubling Cape Corrientes on the 8th of May, sailed on till he reached a chain of islands, to which he gave the name of the Martyrs. On one of these he obtained wood and water, and careened a caravel. The Indians were very thievish, endeavoring to steal the anchors or cut the cables, so as to seize the ships. He next discovered and named the Tortugas. After doubling the cape, he ran up the western shore of Florida to a bay, in 27° 30', which for centuries afterward bore the name of Juan Ponce. There are indications that before he turned back he may have followed the coast till it trended westward. After discovering Bahama he is said to have despatched one caravel from Guanima under John Perez de Ortubia, with Anton de Alaminos, to search for Bimini, while he himself returned to Porto Rico, which he reached September 21. He was soon followed by Ortubia, who, it is said, had been successful in his search for Bimini.

Although Ponce de Leon had thus explored the Florida coast, and added greatly to the knowledge of the Bahama group, his discoveries are not noted in the editions of Ptolemy which appeared in the next decade, and which retained the names of the Cantino map. The Ribeiro map (1529) gives the Martyrs and Tortugas, and on the mainland Canico, — apparently

[1] Letter of the King to Ceron and Diaz, Aug. 12, 1512; the King to Ponce de Leon, and letter of the King, Dec. 10, 1512, to the officials in the Indies.

[2] The King, writing to the authorities in Española July 4, 1513, says: "Alegrome de la ida de Juan Ponce á Biminy; tened cuidado de proveerle i avisadme de todo."

Cancio, the Lucayan name of Florida. In the so-called Leonardo da Vinci's Mappemonde, Florida appears as an island in a vast ocean that rolls on to Japan.[1]

Elated with his success, John Ponce de Leon soon after sailed to Spain; and, obtaining an audience of the King, — it is said through the influence of his old master, Pero Nuñez de Guzman, Grand Comendador of Calatrava, — gave the monarch a description of the attractive land which he had discovered. He solicited a new patent for its conquest and settlement; and on the 27th of September, 1514, the King empowered him to go and settle "the Island of Brimini and the Island Florida" which he had discovered under the royal orders. He was to effect this in three years from the delivery of the *asiento;* but as he had been employed in His Majesty's service, it was extended so that this term was to date from the day he set sail for his new province. After reducing the Caribs, he was empowered to take of the vessels and men employed in that service whatever he chose in order to conquer and settle Florida. The natives were to be summoned to submit to the Catholic Faith and the authority of Spain, and they were not to be attacked or captured if they submitted. Provision was made as to the revenues of the new province, and orders were sent to the viceroy, Don Diego Columbus, to carry out the royal wishes.[2]

The Carib war was not, however, terminated as promptly as the King and his officers desired. Time passed, and adventurers in unauthorized expeditions to Florida rendered the Indians hostile.[3] It was not till 1521 that Ponce de Leon was able to give serious thought to a new expedition. His early hopes seem to have faded, and with them the energy and impulsiveness of his youth. He had settled his daughters in marriage, and, free from domestic cares, offered himself simply to continue to serve the King as he had done for years. Writing to Charles V. from Porto Rico on the 10th of February, 1521, he says: —

"Among my services I discovered, at my own cost and charge, the Island Florida and others in its district, which are not mentioned as being small and useless; and now I return to that island, if it please God's will, to settle it, being enabled to carry a number of people with which I shall be able to do so, that the name of Christ may be praised there, and Your Majesty served with the fruit that land produces. And I also intend to explore the coast of said island further, and see whether it is an island, or

---

[1] *Memoir on a Mappemonde by Leonardo da Vinci* communicated to the Society of Antiquaries by R. H. Major, who makes its date between 1513 and 1519, — probably 1514. The *Ptolemy* printed at Basle 1552 lays down Terra Florida and Ins. Tortucarum, and the map in Girava's *Cosmography* shows Florida and Bacalaos; but the B. de Joan Ponce appears in *La geografia di Clavdio Ptolomeo Alessandrino,* Venice, 1548. [A fac-simile of the sketch accredited to Da Vinci is given on p. 126. — ED.]

[2] *Asiento y capitulacion que se hizo demas con Joan Ponce de Leon sobre la ysla Binini y la ysla Florida,* in the volume of *Asientos y capitulaciones* (1508–1574), Royal Archives at Seville, in *Coleccion de documentos inéditos,* xxii. pp. 33–38.

[3] *Cédula* to the Jeronymite Fathers, July 22, 1517 (*Coleccion de documentos inéditos,* xi. 295–296). One of these surreptitious voyages was made by Anton de Alaminos as pilot (Ibid., pp. 435–438). [See *ante,* p. 201, for the voyage of Alaminos. — ED.]

El Adelantado IUAN PONCE *Des= cubridor de la Florida.*

PONCE DE LEON.[1]

whether it connects with the land where Diego Velasquez is, or any other; and I shall endeavor to learn all I can. I shall set out to pursue my voyage hence in five or six days."[2]

As he wrote to the Cardinal of Tortosa, he had expended all his substance in the King's service; and if he asked favors now it was "not to treasure up or to pass this miserable life, but to serve His Majesty with them and his person and all he had, and settle the land that he had discovered."[3]

[1] Fac-simile of an engraving in Herrera, edition of 1728.

[2] Ponce de Leon to Charles V., Porto Rico, Feb. 10, 1521.

[3] Extracted from a letter of Ponce de Leon to the Cardinal of Tortosa (who was afterward Pope Adrian VI.), dated at Porto Rico, February 10, 1521.

He went prepared to settle, carrying clergymen for the colonists, friars to found Indian missions, and horses, cattle, sheep, and swine. Where precisely he made the Florida coast we do not know; but it is stated that on attempting to erect dwellings for his colonists he was attacked by the natives, who showed great hostility. Ponce himself, while leading his men against his assailants, received so dangerous an arrow wound, that, after losing many of his settlers by sickness and at the hands of the Indians, he abandoned the attempt to plant a colony in Florida, which had so long been the object of his hopes; and taking all on board his vessels, he sailed to Cuba. There he lingered in pain, and died of his wound.[1]

John Ponce de Leon closed his long and gallant career without solving the problem whether Florida was an island or part of the northern continent. Meanwhile others, following in the path he had opened, were contributing to a more definite knowledge. Thus Diego Miruelo, a pilot, sailed from Cuba in 1516 on a trading cruise; and running up the western shore of the Floridian peninsula, discovered a bay which long bore his name on Spanish maps, and was apparently Pensacola. Here he found the Indians friendly, and exchanged his store of glass and steel trinkets for silver and gold. Then, satisfied with his cruise, and without making any attempt to explore the coast, he returned to Cuba.[2]

The next year Francis Hernandez de Cordova[3] sent from Cuba on the 8th of February two ships and a brigantine, carrying one hundred and ten men, with a less humane motive than Miruelo's; for Oviedo assures us that his object was to capture on the Lucayos, or Bahama Islands, a cargo of Indians to sell as slaves. His object was defeated by storms; and the vessels, driven from their course, reached Yucatan, near Cape Catoche, which he named. The Indians here were as hostile as the elements; and Hernandez, after several sharp engagements with the natives, in which almost every man was wounded, was sailing back, when storms again drove his vessels from their course. Unable to make the Island of Cuba, Alaminos, the pilot of the expedition, ran into a bay on the Florida coast, where he had been with Ponce de Leon on his first expedition. While a party which had landed were procuring water, they were attacked with the utmost fury by the Indians, who, swarming down in crowds, assailed those still in the boats. In this engagement twenty-two of the Indians were killed, six of the Spaniards in the landing party were wounded, — including Bernal Diaz, who records the event in his History, — and four of those in the boats, among the number Anton de Alaminos, the pilot. The only man in the expedition who had come away from Yucatan unwounded, a soldier named Berrio, was acting as sentry on shore, and fell into the

---

[1] Herrera, dec. iii. book i, chap. xiv.; Oviedo, lib. 36, chap. i. pp. 621-623; Barcia, *Ensaio cronologico*, pp. 5, 6.

[2] Oviedo (edition of Amador de los Rios, ii. 143), gives in his *Derrotero*, "la bahia que llaman de Miruelos" as west of Apalache Bay. See Barcia's *Ensaio cronológico*, p. 2.

[3] [The Córdoba of chap. iii., *ante*. — ED.]

hands of the Indians. The commander himself, Hernandez de Cordova, reached Cuba only to die of his wounds.

This ill-starred expedition led to two other projects of settlement and conquest. Diego Velasquez, governor of Cuba, the friend and host of Hernandez, obtained a grant, which was referred to by Ponce de Leon in his final letter to the King, and which resulted in the conquest of Mexico; [1] and Francis de Garay, governor of Jamaica, persuaded by Alaminos to enter upon an exploration of the mainland, obtained permission in due form from the priors of the Order of St. Jerome, then governors of the Indies, and in 1519 despatched four caravels, well equipped, with a good number of men, and directed by good pilots, to discover some strait in the mainland, — then the great object of search.

Alonzo Alvarez de Pineda, the commander of the expedition, reached the coast within the limits of the grant of Ponce de Leon, and endeavored to sail eastward so as to pass beyond and continue the exploration. Unable, from headwinds, to turn the Cape of Florida, he sailed westward as far as the River Pánuco, which owes its name to him. Here he encountered Cortés and his forces, who claimed the country by actual possession.

The voyage lasted eight or nine months, and possession was duly taken for the King at various points on the coast. Sailing eastward again, Garay's lieutenant discovered a river of very great volume, evidently the Mississippi.[2] Here he found a considerable Indian town, and remained forty days trading with the natives and careening his vessels. He ran up the river, and found it so thickly inhabited that in a space of six leagues he counted no fewer than forty Indian hamlets on the two banks.

According to their report, the land abounded in gold, as the natives wore gold ornaments in their noses and ears and on other parts of the body. The adventurers told, too, of tribes of giants and of pigmies; but declared the natives to have been friendly, and well disposed to receive the Christian Faith.

Wild as these statements of Pineda's followers were, the voyage settled conclusively the geography of the northern shore of the Gulf, as it proved that there was no strait there by which ships could reach Asia. Florida was no longer to be regarded as an island, but part of a vast continent. The province discovered for Garay received the name of Amichel.

Garay applied for a patent authorizing him to conquer and settle the new territory, and one was issued at Burgos in 1521. By its tenor Christopher de Tapia, who had been appointed governor of the territory discovered by Velasquez, was commissioned to fix limits between Amichel and the discoveries of Velasquez on the west and those of Ponce de Leon on the east. On the map given in Navarrete,[3] Amichel extends apparently from Cape Roxo to Pensacola Bay.

---

[1] [See chap. vi. of the present volume. — ED.]

[2] The great river might be supposed to be the Rio Grande; but its volume is scarcely sufficient to justify the supposition, while the Missis-sippi is indicated on the map of his province with its name R. del Espiritu Santo, evidently given by Garay.

[3] [See *ante*, p. 218. — ED.]

After sending his report and application to the King, and without await-ing any further authority, Garay seems to have deemed it prudent to secure a footing in the territory; and in 1520 sent four caravels under Diego de Camargo to occupy some post near Pánuco. The expedition was ill man-aged. One of the vessels ran into a settlement established by Cortés and made a formal demand of Cortés himself for a line of demarcation, claim-ing the country for Garay. Cortés seized some of the men who landed, and learned all Camargo's plans. That commander, with the rest of his force, attempted to begin a settlement at Pánuco; but the territory afforded no food, and the party were soon in such straits that, unable to wait for two vessels which Garay was sending to their aid, Camargo despatched a caravel to Vera Cruz to beg for supplies.[1]

In 1523 Garay equipped a powerful fleet and force to conquer and settle Amichel. He sailed from Jamaica at the end of June with the famous John de Grijalva, discoverer of Yucatan, as his lieutenant. His force com-prised thirteen vessels, bearing one hundred and thirty-six cavalry and eight hundred and forty infantry, with a supply of field-pieces. He reached Rio de las Palmas on the 25th of July, and prepared to begin a settlement; but his troops, alarmed at the unpromising nature of the country, insisted on proceeding southward. Garay yielded, and sailed to Pánuco, where he learned that Cortés had already founded the town of San Esteban del Puerto. Four of his vessels were lost on the coast, and one in the port. He himself, with the rest of his force, surrendered to Cortés. He died in Mexico, while still planning a settlement at Rio de las Palmas; but with his death the province of Amichel passed out of existence.

Thus the discoveries of Ponce de Leon and of Garay, with those of Miruelos, made known, by ten years' effort, the coast-line from the Rio Grande to the St. John's in Florida.

The next explorations were intended to ascertain the nature of our Atlantic coast north of the St. John's.

In 1520 Lucas Vasquez de Ayllon, one of the auditors of the Island of St. Domingo, though possessed of wealth, honors, and domestic felicity, aspired to the glory of discovering some new land, and making it the seat of a prosperous colony. Having secured the necessary license, he despatched a caravel under the command of Francisco Gordillo, with directions to sail northward through the Bahamas, and thence strike the shore of the continent. Gordillo set out on his exploration, and near the Island of Lucayoneque, one of the Lucayuelos, descried another caravel. His pilot, Alonzo Fernandez Sotil, proceeded toward it in a boat, and soon recognized it as a caravel commanded by a kinsman of his, Pedro de Quexos, fitted out in part, though not avowedly, by Juan Ortiz de Matienzo, an auditor associated with Ayllon in the judiciary. This caravel was return-ing from an unsuccessful cruise among the Bahamas for Caribs, — the object

---

[1] [See chapter vi. of the present volume. — ED.]

of the expedition being to capture Indians in order to sell them as slaves. On ascertaining the object of Gordillo's voyage, Quexos proposed that they should continue the exploration together. After a sail of eight or nine days, in which they ran little more than a hundred leagues, they reached the coast of the continent at the mouth of a considerable river, to which they gave the name of St. John the Baptist, from the fact that they touched the coast on the day set apart to honor the Precursor of Christ. The year was 1521, and the point reached was, according to the estimate of the explorers, in latitude 33° 30′.[1]

Boats put off from the caravels and landed some twenty men on the shore; and while the ships endeavored to enter the river, these men were surrounded by Indians, whose good-will they gained by presents.[2]

Some days later, Gordillo formally took possession of the country in the name of Ayllon, and of his associate Diego Caballero, and of the King, as Quexos did also in the name of his employers on Sunday, June 30, 1521. Crosses were cut on the trunks of trees to mark the Spanish occupancy.[3]

Although Ayllon had charged Gordillo to cultivate friendly relations with the Indians of any new land he might discover,[4] Gordillo joined with Quexos in seizing some seventy of the natives, with whom they sailed away, without any attempt to make an exploration of the coast.

On the return of the vessel to Santo Domingo, Ayllon condemned his captain's act; and the matter was brought before a commission, presided over by Diego Columbus, for the consideration of some important affairs. The Indians were declared free, and it was ordered that they should be restored to their native land at the earliest possible moment. Meanwhile they were to remain in the hands of Ayllon and Matienzo.

The latter made no attempt to pursue the discovery; but Ayllon, adhering to his original purpose, proceeded to Spain with Francisco, — one of the Indians, who told of a giant king and many provinces,[5] — and on the 12th of June, 1523, obtained a royal *cédula*.[6] Under this he was to send out vessels in 1524, to run eight hundred leagues along the coast, or till he reached lands already discovered; and if he discovered any strait leading to the west, he was to explore it. No one was to settle within the limits explored by him the first year, or within two hundred leagues beyond the extreme points reached by him north and south; the occupancy of the territory was to be effected within four years; and as the conversion of the natives was one of the main objects, their enslavement was forbidden, and Ayllon was required to take out religious men of some Order to instruct them in the doctrines of Christianity. He obtained a second *cédula* to demand from Matienzo the Indians in his hands in order to restore them to their native country.[7]

---

[1] Testimony of Pedro de Quexos; Act of taking possession by Quexos.

[2] Testimony of Pedro de Quexos.

[3] Act of possession; Testimony of Aldana.

[4] Answer of Ayllon to Matienzo.

[5] Navarrete, *Coleccion*, iii. 69.

[6] Ibid., p. 153.

[7] *Cédula*, June 12, 1523.

On his return to the West Indies, Ayllon was called on the King's service to Porto Rico; and finding it impossible to pursue his discovery, the time for carrying out the *asiento* was, by a *cédula* of March 23, 1524, extended to the year 1525.[1]

To secure his rights under the *asiento*, he despatched two caravels under Pedro de Quexos to the newly discovered land early in 1525. They regained the good-will of the natives and explored the coast for two hundred and fifty leagues, setting up stone crosses with the name of Charles V. and the date of the act of taking possession. They returned to Santo Domingo in July, 1525, bringing one or two Indians from each province, who might be trained to act as interpreters.[2]

Meanwhile Matienzo began legal proceedings to vacate the *asiento* granted by the King to Ayllon, on the ground that it was obtained surreptitiously, and in fraud of his own rights as joint discoverer. His witnesses failed to show that his caravel had any license to make a voyage of exploration, or that he took any steps to follow up the discovery made; but the suit embarrassed Ayllon, who was fitting out four vessels to sail in 1526, in order to colonize the territory granted to him. The armada from Spain was greatly delayed; and as he expected by it a store of artillery and muskets, as well as other requisites, he was at great loss. At last, however, he sailed from Puerto de la Plata with three large vessels, — a caravel, a breton, and a brigantine, — early in June, 1526.[3] As missionaries he took the famous Dominican, Antonio de Montesinos, the first to denounce Indian slavery, with Father Antonio de Cervantes and Brother Pedro de Estrada, of the same Order. The ships carried six hundred persons of both sexes, including clergymen and physicians, besides one hundred horses.

They reached the coast, not at the San Juan Bautista, but at another river, at 33° 40', says Navarrete, to which they gave the name of Jordan.[4] Their first misfortune was the loss of the brigantine; but Ayllon immediately set to work to replace it, and built a small vessel such as was called a *gavarra*, — the first instance of ship-building on our coast. Francisco, his Indian guide, deserted him; and parties sent to explore the interior brought back such unfavorable accounts that Ayllon resolved to seek a more fertile district. That he sailed northward there can be little doubt; his original *asiento* required him to run eight hundred leagues along the coast, and he, as well as Gomez, was to seek a strait or estuary leading to the Spice Islands. The Chesapeake was a body of water which it would be imperative on him to explore, as possibly the passage sought. The soil of the country bordering on the bay, superior to that of the sandy region south of it, would seem better suited for purposes of a settlement. He at last

[1] *Cédula* given at Burgos.

[2] Interrogatories of Ayllon; Testimony of Quexos.

[3] Testimony of Alonzo Despinosa Cervantes and of Father Antonio de Cervantes, O.S.D., in 1561. The date is clearly fixed after May 26, and before June 9, as Ayllon testified on the former day, and on the latter his procurator appeared for him. Navarrete is wrong in making him sail about the middle of July (*Coleccion*, iii. 72).

[4] If Ayllon really reached the Jordan, this was the Wateree.

reached Guandape, and began the settlement of San Miguel, where the English in the next century founded Jamestown.[1]

Here he found only a few scattered Indian dwellings of the communal system, long buildings, formed of pine posts at the side, and covered with branches, capable of holding, in their length of more than a hundred feet, a vast number of families. Ayllon selected the most favorable spot on the bank, though most of the land was low and swampy. Then the Spaniards began to erect houses for their shelter, the negro slaves — first introduced here — doing the heaviest portion of the toil. Before the colonists were housed, winter came on. Men perished of cold on the caravel " Catalina," and on one of the other vessels a man's legs were frozen so that the flesh fell off. Sickness broke out among the colonists, and many died. Ayllon himself had sunk under the pestilential fevers, and expired on St. Luke's Day, Oct. 18, 1526.

He made his nephew, John Ramirez, then in Porto Rico, his successor as head of the colony, committing the temporary administration to Francis Gomez. Troubles soon began. Gines Doncel and Pedro de Bazan, at the head of some malcontents, seized and confined Gomez and the *alcaldes*, and began a career of tyranny. The Indians were provoked to hostility, and killed several of the settlers; the negroes, cruelly oppressed, fired the house of Doncel. Then two settlers, Oliveros and Monasterio, demanded the release of the lawful authorities. Swords were drawn; Bazan was wounded and taken, Doncel fled, but was discovered near his blazing house. Gomez and his subordinates, restored to power, tried and convicted Bazan, who was put to death.

Such were the stormy beginnings of Spanish rule in Virginia. It is not to be wondered at that with one consent the colonists soon resolved to abandon San Miguel de Guandape. The body of Ayllon was placed on board a tender, and they set sail; but it was not destined to reach a port and receive the obsequies due his rank. The little craft foundered; and of the five hundred who sailed from Santo Domingo only one hundred and fifty returned to that island.

Contemporaneous with the explorations made by and under Ayllon was an expedition in a single vessel sent out by the Spanish Government in 1524 under Stephen Gomez, a Portuguese navigator who had sailed under Magallanes, but had returned in a somewhat mutinous manner. He took part in a congress of Spanish and Portuguese pilots held at Badajoz to consider the probability of finding a strait or channel north of Florida by which vessels might reach the Moluccas. To test the question practically, Charles V. ordered Gomez to sail to the coast of Bacallaos, or Newfoundland and Labrador, and examine the coast carefully, in order to ascertain whether any such channel existed. Gomez fitted out a caravel at Corunna, in northern Spain, apparently in the autumn of 1524, and sailed across.

[1] [See Vol. III. p. 130. — Ed.]

After examining the Labrador coast, he turned southward and leisurely explored the whole coast from Cape Race to Florida, from which he steered to Santiago de Cuba, and thence to Corunna, entering that port after ten months' absence. He failed to discover the desired channel, and no account in detail of his voyage is known; but the map of Ribeiro,[1] drawn up in 1529, records his discoveries, and on its coast-line gives names which were undoubtedly bestowed by him, confirming the statement that he sailed southerly. From this map and the descriptions of the coast in Spanish writers soon after, in which descriptions mention is made of his discoveries, we can see that he noted and named in his own fashion what we now know as Massachusetts Bay, Cape Cod, Narragansett Bay, the Connecticut, Hudson, and Delaware rivers.

This voyage completed the exploration of our coast from the Rio Grande to the Bay of Fundy; yet Sebastian Cabot in 1536 declared that it was still uncertain whether a single continent stretched from the Mississippi to Newfoundland.[2]

The success of Cortés filled the Spanish mind with visions of empires in the north rivalling that of Mexico, which but awaited the courage of valiant men to conquer.

Panfilo de Narvaez, after being defeated by Cortés, whom he was sent to supersede,[3] solicited of Charles V. a patent under which he might conquer and colonize the country on the Gulf of Mexico, from Rio de Palmas to Florida. A grant was made, under which he was required to found two or more towns and erect two fortresses. He received the title of *adelantado*, and was empowered to enslave all Indians who, after being summoned in due form, would not submit to the Spanish King and the Christian Faith. In an official document he styles himself Governor of Florida, Rio de Palmas, and Espiritu Santo, — the Mississippi.[4]

Narvaez collected an armament suited to the project, and sailed from San Lucar de Barrameda, June 17, 1527, in a fleet of five ships carrying six hundred persons, with mechanics and laborers, as well as secular priests, and five Franciscan friars, the superior being Father Juan Xuarez. On the coast of Cuba his fleet was caught by a hurricane, and one vessel perished. After refitting and acquiring other vessels, Narvaez sailed from Cuba in March with four vessels and a brigantine, taking four hundred men and eighty horses, his pilot being Diego Miruelo, of a family which had acquired experience on that coast.

The destination was the Rio de Palmas; but his pilot proved incompetent, and his fleet moved slowly along the southern coast of Cuba, doubled Cape San Antonio, and was standing in for Havana when it was

---

1 See *ante*, p. 221; and references to reproductions, on p. 222.

2 Duro, *Informe relativo a los pormenores de descubrimiento del Nuevo Mundo*, Madrid, 1883.

p. 266, where Cabot's testimony in the Colon. Pinzon suit is given.

3 [See chapter vi. of this volume — Ed.]

4 *Coleccion de documentos inéditos*, xii. 86.

driven by a storm on the Florida coast at a bay which he called Bahia de la Cruz, and which the map of Sebastian Cabot identifies with Apalache Bay.[1] Here Narvaez landed a part of his force (April 15), sending his brigantine to look for a port or the way to Pánuco, — much vaunted by the pilots, — and if unsuccessful to return to Cuba for a vessel that had remained there.   He was so misled by his pilots that though he was near or on the Florida peninsula, he supposed himself not far from the rivers Pánuco and Palmas.   Under this impression he landed most of his men, and directed his vessels, with about one hundred souls remaining on them, to follow the coast while he marched inland.   No steps were taken to insure their meeting at the harbor proposed as a rendezvous, or to enable the brigantine and the other ship to follow the party on land.   On the 19th of April Narvaez struck inland in a northward or northeasterly direction; and having learned a little of the country, moved on with three hundred men, forty of them mounted. On the 15th of the following month they reached a river with a strong current, which they crossed some distance from the sea.   Cabeza de Vaca, sent at his own urgent request to find a harbor, returned with no encouraging tidings; and the expedition plodded on till, on the 25th of June, they reached Apalache, — an Indian town of which they had heard magnificent accounts. It proved to be a mere hamlet of forty wretched cabins.

The sufferings of Narvaez' men were great; the country was poverty-stricken; there was no wealthy province to conquer, no fertile lands for settlement.   Aute (a harbor) was said to be nine days' march to the southward; and to this, after nearly a month spent at Apalache, the disheartened Spaniards turned their course, following the Magdalena River.   On the 31st of July they reached the coast at a bay which Narvaez styled Bahia de Cavallos; and seeing no signs of his vessels, he set to work to build boats in which to escape from the country.   The horses were killed for food; and making forges, the Spaniards wrought their stirrups, spurs, and other iron articles into saws, axes, and nails.   Ropes were made of the manes and tails of the horses and such fibres as they could find; their shirts were used for sailcloth.   By the 20th of September five boats, each twenty-two cubits long, were completed, and two days afterward the survivors embarked, forty-eight or nine being crowded into each frail structure.   Not one of the whole number had any knowledge of navigation or of the coast.

Running between Santa Rosa Island and the mainland, they coasted along for thirty days, landing where possible to obtain food or water, but generally finding the natives fierce and hostile.   On the 31st of October they came to a broad river pouring into the Gulf such a volume of water that it freshened the brine so that they were able to drink it; but

---

[1] "Aqui desembarco Panfilo de Narvaez." Mappemonde of Sebastian Cabot in Jomard. This map has always been supposed to be based on Spanish sources; but owing to the strict prohibition of publication in Spain, it was probably printed elsewhere, "in Brussels or Amsterdam, or some such place," as Gayangos thinks. It is seemingly engraved on wood (Smith's *Relation of Alvar Nuñez Cabeça de Vaca*, p. 56); or at least some have thought so.

the current was too much for their clumsy craft.   The boat commanded by Narvaez was lost, and never heard of; that containing Father Xuarez and the other friars was driven ashore bottom upward; the three remaining boats were thrown on the coast of western Louisiana or eastern Texas. The crews barely escaped with life, and found themselves at the mercy of cruel and treacherous savages, who lived on or near Malhado Island, and drew a precarious living from shellfish and minor animals, prickly-pears and the like.   They were consequently not as far west as the bison range, which reached the coast certainly at Matagorda Bay.[1]   Here several of the wretched Spaniards fell victims to the cruelty of the Indians or to disease and starvation, till Alvar Nuñez Cabeza de Vaca, the treasurer of the expedition, escaping from six years' captivity among the Mariames, reached the Avavares, farther inland, with two companions, Castillo and Dorantes, and a negro slave.   After spending eight months with them, he penetrated to the Arbadaos, where the mesquite is first found, near the Rio Grande; and skirting the San Saba Mountains, came to the bison plains and the hunter nations; then keeping westward through tribes that lived in houses of earth and knew the use of cotton and mined the turquoise, he finally came upon some Spanish explorers on the River Petatlan; and thus on the 1st of April, 1536, with hearts full of joy and gratitude, the four men entered the town of San Miguel in Sinaloa.

The vessels of Narvaez, not finding the alleged port of the pilots, returned to the harbor where they had landed him, and were there joined by the two vessels from Cuba; but though they remained nearly a year, cruising along the coast of the Gulf, they never encountered the slightest trace of the unfortunate Narvaez or his wretched followers.   They added nothing apparently to the knowledge of the coast already acquired; for no report is extant, and no map alludes to any discovery by them.

Thus ended an expedition undertaken with rashness and ignorance, and memorable only from the almost marvellous adventures of Cabeza de Vaca and his comrades, and the expeditions by land which were prompted by his narrative.

The wealth of Mexico and Peru had inflamed the imagination of Spanish adventurers; and though no tidings had been received of Narvaez, others were ready to risk all they had, and life itself, in the hope of finding some wealthy province in the heart of the northern continent.   The next to try his fortune was one who had played his part in the conquest of Peru.

Hernando de Soto, the son of an esquire of Xerez de Badajoz, was eager to rival Cortés and Pizarro.   In 1537 he solicited a grant of the province from Rio de las Palmas to Florida, as ceded to Narvaez, as well as

---

[1] Compare Cabeza de Vaca's account, Oviedo, lib. 35, chap. i.–vii., pp. 582–618; and the French accounts of La Salle's expedition, — Joutel and Anastase Douay in Le Clercq, *Établissement de la Foi*, for the animals and plants of the district.

of the province discovered by Ayllon; and the King at Valladolid, on the 20th of April, issued a concession to him, appointing him to the government of the Island of Cuba, and requiring him in person to conquer and occupy Florida within a year, erect fortresses, and carry over at least five hundred men as settlers to hold the country. The division of the gold, pearls, and other valuables of the conquered caciques was regulated, and provision made for the maintenance of the Christian religion and of an hospital in the territory.

The air of mystery assumed by Cabeza de Vaca as to the countries that he had seen, served to inflame the imagination of men in Spain; and Soto found many ready to give their persons and their means to his expedition. Nobles of Castile in rich slashed silk dresses mingled with old warriors in well-tried coats of mail. He sailed from San Lucar in April, 1538, amid the fanfaron of trumpets and the roar of cannon, with six hundred as high-born and well-trained men as ever went forth from Spain to win fame and fortune in the New World. They reached Cuba safely, and Soto was received with all honor. More prudent than Narvaez, Soto twice despatched Juan de Añasco, in a caravel with two pinnaces, to seek a suitable harbor for the fleet, before trusting all the vessels on the coast.[1]

Encouraged by the reports of this reconnoitring, Soto, leaving his wife in Cuba, sailed from Havana in May, 1539, and made a bay on the Florida coast ten leagues west of the Bay of Juan Ponce. To this he gave the name of Espiritu Santo, because he reached it on the Feast of Pentecost, which fell that year on the 25th of May.[2] On the 30th he began to land his army near a town ruled by a chief named Uçita. Soto's whole force was composed of five hundred and seventy men, and two hundred and twenty-three horses, in five ships, two caravels, and two pinnaces. He took formal possession of the country in the name of the King of Spain on the 3d of June, and prepared to explore and subject the wealthy realms which he supposed to lie before him. Though the chief at his landing-place was friendly, he found that all the surrounding tribes were so hostile that they began to attack those who welcomed him.

Ortiz, a Spaniard belonging to Narvaez' expedition, who in his long years of captivity had become as naked and as savage as were the Indians, soon joined Soto.[3] He was joyfully received; though his knowledge of the country was limited, his services were of vital necessity, for the Indians secured by Añasco, and on whom Soto relied as guides and interpreters, deserted at the first opportunity.

Soto had been trained in a bad school; he had no respect for the lives or rights of the Indians. As Oviedo, a man of experience among the

[1] *Relaçam verdadeira* (Evora, 1557), chaps. i.–vi., continued in Smith's translation, pp. 1–21; in Hakluyt's Supplementary Volume (London, 1812), pp. 695–712; and in Force's *Tracts.* Rangel in Oviedo, book xvii. chap. xxii. p. 546.

[2] Biedma's *Relacion* in Smith's *Coleccion*, and his *Soto*, p. 231; *Coleccion de documentos inéditos*, iii. 414–441.

[3] Cf. Buckingham Smith on "The Captivity of Ortis," in the appendix to his *Letter on De Soto.*

conquistadores, says: "This governor was very fond of this sport of kill-ing Indians."[1]

The plan of his march showed his disregard of the rights of the natives. At each place he demanded of the cacique, or head chief, corn for his men and horses, and Indians of both sexes to carry his baggage and do the menial work in his camp. After obtaining these supplies, he compelled the chief to accompany his army till he reached another tribe whose chief he could treat in the same way; but though the first chief was then released, few of the people of the tribe which he ruled, and who had been carried off by Soto, were so fortunate as ever to be allowed to return to their homes.

On the 15th of July Soto, sending back his largest ships to Cuba, moved to the northeast to make his toilsome way amid the lakes and streams and everglades of Florida. Before long his soldiers began to suffer from hunger, and were glad to eat water-cresses, shoots of Indian corn, and pal-metto, in order to sustain life; for native villages were few and scattered, and afforded little corn for the plunderers. The natives were met only as foe-men, harassing his march. At Caliquen the Indians, to rescue their chief, whom Soto was carrying to the next town, made a furious onslaught on the Spaniards; but were driven to the swamps, and nearly all killed or taken. Their dauntless spirit was, however, unbroken. The survivors, though chained as slaves, rose on their masters; and seizing any weapon within their reach, fought desperately, one of them endeavoring to throttle Soto himself. Two hundred survived this gallant attempt, only to be slaughtered by the Indian allies of the Spanish commander. Soto fought his way westward step by step so slowly that at the end of three months, Oct. 30, 1539, he had only reached Agile, — a town in the province of Apalache. Añasco, sent out from this point to explore, discovered the port where Narvaez had embarked, — the remains of his forges and the bones of his horses attesting the fact. Soto despatched him to Tampa Bay. Añasco with a party marched the distance in ten days; and sending two caravels to Cuba, brought to Soto in the remaining vessels the detachment left at his landing-place. Before he reached his commander the Indians had burned the town of Anaica Apalache, of which Soto had taken possession.[2]

A good port, that of Pensacola, had been discovered to the westward; but Soto, crediting an Indian tale of the rich realm of Yupaha in the north-east, left his winter quarters March 3, 1540, and advanced in that direc-tion through tribes showing greater civilization. A month later he reached the Altamaha, receiving from the more friendly natives corn and game. This was not sufficient to save the Spaniards from much suffering, and they treated the Indians with their wonted cruelty.[3]

---

[1] Oviedo, i. 547.
[2] *Relaçam verdadeira*, chap. xi.; Smith's *Soto*, pp. 43–44; Biedma, Ibid., 234.
[3] Oviedo, i. 554–557.

At last Soto, after a march of four hundred and thirty leagues, much of it through uninhabited land, reached the province ruled by the chieftainess of Cofitachiqui. On the 1st of May she went forth to meet the Spanish explorer in a palanquin or litter; and crossing the river in a canopied canoe, she approached Soto, and after presenting him the gifts of shawls and skins brought by her retinue, she took off her necklace of pearls and placed it around the neck of Soto. Yet her courtesy and generosity did not save her from soon being led about on foot as a prisoner. The country around her chief town, which Jones identifies with Silver Bluff, on the Savannah, below Augusta,[1] tempted the followers of Soto, who wished to settle there, as from it Cuba could be readily reached. But the commander would attempt no settlement till he had discovered some rich kingdom that would rival Peru; and chagrined at his failure, refused even to send tidings of his operations to Cuba. At Silver Bluff he came upon traces of an earlier Spanish march. A dirk and a rosary were brought to him, which were supposed, on good grounds, to have come from the expedition of Ayllon.

Poring over the cosmography of Alonzo de Chaves, Soto and the officers of his expedition concluded that a river, crossed on the 26th of May, was the Espiritu Santo, or Mississippi. A seven days' march, still in the chieftainess's realm, brought them to Chelaque, the country of the Cherokees, poor in maize; then, over mountain ridges, a northerly march brought them to Xualla, two hundred and fifty leagues from Silver Bluff. At the close of May they were in Guaxule, where the chieftainess regained her freedom. It was a town of three hundred houses, near the mountains, in a well-watered and pleasant land, probably at the site of Coosawattie Old Town. The chief gave Soto maize, and also three hundred dogs for the maintenance of his men.

Marching onward, Soto next came to Canasagua, in all probability on a river even now called the Connasauga, flowing through an attractive land of mulberries, persimmons, and walnuts. Here they found stores of bear oil and walnut oil and honey. Marching down this stream and the Oostanaula, into which it flows, to Chiaha, on an island opposite the mouth of the Etowa, in the district of the pearl-bearing mussel-streams, Soto was received in amity; and the cacique had some of the shellfish taken and pearls extracted in the presence of his guest. The Spaniards encamped under the trees near the town, leaving the inhabitants in quiet possession of their homes. Here, on the spot apparently now occupied by Rome, they rested for a month. A detachment sent to discover a reputed gold-producing province returned with no tidings to encourage the adventurers; and on the 28th of June Soto, with his men and steeds refreshed, resumed his march, having obtained men to bear his baggage, though his demand of thirty women as slaves was refused.[2]

---

[1] *Relaçam verdadeira*, chap. xii.–xv.; Biedma, *Relacion;* Smith's *Soto*, pp. 49–68, 236–241; Rangel in Oviedo, *Historia General*, i. 562.

[2] Oviedo, i. 563.

Chisca, to which he sent two men to explore for gold, proved to be in a rugged mountain land; and the buffalo robe which they brought back was more curious than encouraging. Soto therefore left the territory of the Cherokees, and took the direction of Coça, probably on the Coosa river. The cacique of that place, warned doubtless by the rumors which must have spread through all the land of the danger of thwarting the fierce strangers, furnished supplies at several points on the route to his town, and as Soto approached it, came out on a litter attired in a fur robe and plumed headpiece to make a full surrender. The Spaniards occupied the town and took possession of all the Indian stores of corn and beans, the neighboring woods adding persimmons and grapes. This town was one hundred and ninety leagues west of Xualla, and lay on the east bank of the Coosa, between the mouths of the Talladega and Tallasehatchee, as Pickett, the historian of Alabama, determines. Soto held the chief of Coça virtually as a prisoner; but when he demanded porters to bear the baggage of his men, most of the Indians fled. The Spanish commander then seized every Indian he could find, and put him in irons.

After remaining at Coça for twenty-five days, Soto marched to Ullibahali, a strongly palisaded town, situated, as we may conjecture, on Hatchet Creek. This place submitted, giving men as porters and women as slaves. Leaving this town on the 2d of September, he marched to Tallise, in a land teeming with corn, whose people proved equally docile.[1] This submission was perhaps only to gain time, and draw the invaders into a disadvantageous position.

Actahachi, the gigantic chief of Tastaluza, sixty leagues south of Coça, which was Soto's next station, received him with a pomp such as the Spaniards had not yet witnessed. The cacique was seated on cushions on a raised platform, with his chiefs in a circle around him; an umbrella of buckskin, stained red and white, was held over him. The curveting steeds and the armor of the Spaniards raised no look of curiosity on his stern countenance, and he calmly awaited Soto's approach. Not till he found himself detained as a prisoner would he promise to furnish the Spaniards with porters and supplies of provisions at Mauila[2] to enable Soto to continue his march. He then sent orders to his vassal, the chief of Mauila, to have them in readiness.

As the Spaniards, accompanied by Actahachi, descended the Alabama, passing by the strong town of Piache, the cacique of Mauila came to meet them with friendly greetings, attended by a number of his subjects playing upon their native musical instruments, and proffering fur robes and service; but the demeanor of the people was so haughty that Luis de Moscoso urged Soto not to enter the town. The *adelantado* persisted; and riding in with seven or eight of his guard and four horsemen, sat down with the cacique

---

[1] *Relaçam verdadeira*, chap. xv.–xvi.; Biedma, *Relacion*; Smith's *Soto*, pp. 66-77, 240-242; Rangel in Oviedo, i. 563-566.

[2] It is variously written also *Mavila* and *Mavilla*.

and the chief of Tastaluza, whom, according to custom, he had brought to this place. The latter asked leave to return to his own town; when Soto refused, he rose, pretending a wish to confer with some chiefs, and entered a house where some armed Indians were concealed. He refused to come out when summoned; and a chief who was ordered to carry a message to the cacique, but refused, was cut down by Gallego with a sword. Then the Indians, pouring out from the houses, sent volleys of arrows at Soto and his party. Soto ran toward his men, but fell two or three times; and though he reached his main force, five of his men were killed, and he himself, as well as all the rest, was severely wounded. The chained Indian porters, who bore the baggage and treasures of Soto's force, had set down their loads just outside the palisade. When the party of Soto had been driven out, the men of Mauila sent all these into the town, took off their fetters, and gave them weapons. Some of the military equipments of the Spaniards fell into the hands of the Indians, and several of Soto's followers, who had like him entered the town, among them a friar and an ecclesiastic, remained as prisoners.

The Indians, sending off their caciques, and apparently their women, prepared to defend the town; but Soto, arranging his military array into four detachments, surrounded it, and made an assault on the gates, where the natives gathered to withstand them. By feigning flight Soto drew them out; and by a sudden charge routed them, and gaining an entrance for his men, set fire to the houses. This was not effected without loss, as the Spaniards were several times repulsed by the Indians. When they at last fought their way into the town, the Indians endeavored to escape. Finding that impossible, as the gates were held, the men of Mauila fought desperately, and died by the sword, or plunged into the blazing houses to perish there.

The battle of Mauila was one of the bloodiest ever fought on our soil between white and red men in the earlier days. The *Adelantado* had twenty of his men killed, and one hundred and fifty wounded; of his horses twelve were killed and seventy wounded. The Indian loss was estimated by the Portuguese chronicler of the expedition at twenty-five hundred, and by Rangel at three thousand. At nightfall Biedma tells us that only three Indians remained alive, two of whom were killed fighting; the last hung himself from a tree in the palisade with his bowstring.[1] The Gentleman of Elvas states Soto's whole loss up to his leaving Mauila to have been one hundred and two by disease, accident, and Indian fighting. Divine worship had been apparently offered in the camp regularly up to this time; but in the flames of Mauila perished all the chalices and vestments of the clergy, as well as the bread-irons and their store of wheat-flour and wine, so that Mass ceased from this time.[2]

---

[1] *Relaçam verdadeira*, chs. xvii.–xix.; Biedma, *Relacion;* Smith's *Soto*, pp. 80–90, 242–245.

[2] See Smith's *Soto*, p. 90; Rangel in Oviedo, i. 569. The requiems said years afterward to have been chanted over Soto's body are therefore imaginary. No Mass, whether of requiem or other, could have been said or sung after the battle of Mauila.

Soto here ascertained that Francisco Maldonado was with vessels at the port of Ichuse (or Ochuse) only six days' march from him, awaiting his orders. He was too proud to return to Cuba with his force reduced in numbers, without their baggage, or any trophy from the lands he had visited. He would not even send any tidings to Cuba, but concealed from his men the knowledge which had been brought to him by Ortiz, the rescued follower of Narvaez.

Stubborn in his pride, Soto, on the 14th of November, marched north-ward; and traversing the land of Pafallaya (now Clarke, Marengo, and Greene counties), passed the town of Taliepatua and reached Cabusto, identified by Pickett with the site of the modern town of Erie, on the Black Warrior. Here a series of battles with the natives occurred; but Soto fought his way through hostile tribes to the little town of Chicaça, with its two hundred houses clustered on a hill, probably on the western bank of the Yazoo, which he reached in a snow-storm on the 17th of December. The cacique Micu-lasa received Soto graciously, and the Spanish commander won him by sending part of his force to attack Sacchuma, a hostile town. Having thus propitiated this powerful chief, Soto remained here till March; when, being ready to advance on his expedition in search of some wealthy province, he demanded porters of the cacique. The wily chief amused the invader with promises for several days, and then suddenly attacked the town from four sides, at a very early hour in the morning, dashing into the place and set-ting fire to the houses. The Spaniards, taken by surprise, were assailed as they came out to put on their armor and mount their horses. Soto and one other alone succeeded in getting into the saddle; but Soto himself, after killing one Indian with his spear, was thrown, his girths giving way.

The Indians drew off with the loss of this one man, having killed eleven Spaniards, many of their horses, and having greatly reduced their herd of swine. In the conflagration of the town, Soto's force lost most of their remaining clothing, with many of their weapons and saddles. They at once set to work to supply the loss. The woods gave ash to make sad-dles and lances; forges were set up to temper the swords and make such arms as they could; while the tall grass was woven into mats to serve as blankets or cloaks.

They needed their arms indeed; for on the 15th of March the enemy, in three divisions, advanced to attack the camp. Soto met them with as many squadrons, and routed them with loss.

When Soto at last took up his march on the 25th of April, the sturdy Alibamo, or Alimamu, or Limamu, barred his way with a palisade manned by the painted warriors of the tribe. Soto carried it at the cost of the lives of seven or eight of his men, and twenty-five or six wounded; only to find that the Indians had made the palisade not to protect any stores, but simply to cope with the invaders.[1]

---

[1] *Relaçam verdadeira*, chap. xx.–xxi.; Biedma,   Rangel in Oviedo, *Historia General*, chap. xxviii. *Relacion;* Smith's *Soto*, pp. 91–100, 246–248;   pp. 571–573.

At Quizquiz, or Quizqui, near the banks of the Mississippi, Soto surprised the place and captured all the women; but released them to obtain
canoes to cross the river. As the Indians failed to keep their promise, Soto
encamped in a plain and spent nearly a month building four large boats,
each capable of carrying sixty or seventy men and five or six horses. The
opposite shore was held by hostile Indians; and bands of finely formed
warriors constantly came down in canoes, as if ready to engage them, but
always drawing off.

The Spaniards finally crossed the river at the lowest Chickasaw Bluff,
all wondering at the mighty turbid stream, with its fish, strange to
their eyes, and the trees, uprooted on the banks far above, that came
floating down.[1] Soto marched northward to Little Prairie in quest of
Pacaha and Chisca, provinces reported to abound in gold. After planting a cross on St. John's Day[2] at Casqui, where the bisons' heads above
the entrances to the huts reminded them of Spain, he entered Pacaha
June 29, as Oviedo says. These towns were the best they had seen
since they left Cofitachiqui. Pacaha furnished them with a booty which
they prized highly,—a fine store of skins of animals, and native blankets
woven probably of bark. These enabled the men to make clothing,
of which many had long been in sore want. The people gradually
returned, and the cacique received Soto in friendly guise, giving him
his two sisters as wives.

While the army rested here nearly a month, expeditions were sent in
various directions. One, marching eight days to the northwest through a
land of swamps and ponds, reached the prairies, the land of Caluça, where
Indians lived in portable houses of mats, with frames so light that a man
could easily carry them.[3]

Despairing of finding his long-sought El Dorado in that direction, Soto
marched south and then southwest, in all a hundred and ten leagues, to
Quiguate, a town on a branch of the Mississippi. It was the largest they
had yet seen. The Indians abandoned it; but one half the houses were
sufficient to shelter the whole of Soto's force.

On the first of September the expedition reached Coligua,—a populous
town in a valley among the mountains, near which vast herds of bison roamed.
Then crossing the river again,[4] Soto's jaded and decreasing force marched
onward. Cayas, with its salt river and fertile maize-lands, was reached; and
then the Spaniards came to Tulla, where the Indians attacked them, fighting
from their housetops to the last. The cacique at last yielded, and came weeping with great sobs to make his submission.

Marching southeast, Soto reached Quipana; and crossing the mountains
eastward, wintered in the province of Viranque, or Autiamque, or Utianque,

[1] *Relaçam verdadeira*, chap. xxii.; Biedma,
Relacion, in Smith, *Soto*, pp. 101–105, 249–250;
Hakluyt; Rangel in Oviedo.

[2] Oviedo, p. 573.

[3] *Relaçam verdadeira*, chap. xxiii., xxiv.;

Biedma, *Relacion*, in Smith's *Soto*, pp. 106–
117, 250–252; Hakluyt; Rangel in Oviedo.
Compare *Relacion* of Coronado's expedition in
Smith's *Coleccion*, p. 153.

[4] Rangel in Oviedo, i. 576.

El Adelantado Hernando de Soto,

SOTO.[1]

on a branch of the Mississippi, apparently the Washita.[2] The sufferings of the Spaniards during a long and severe winter were terrible, and Ortiz, their interpreter, succumbed to his hardships and died. Even the proud spirit of Soto yielded to his disappointments and toil. Two hundred and fifty of his splendid force had left their bones to whiten along the path which he had followed.   He determined at last to push to the shores of the Gulf, and there build two brigantines, in order to send to Cuba and to New Spain for aid.

[1] Fac-simile of an engraving in Herrera (1728), iv. 21.

[2] Oviedo, p. 577. Here, unfortunately, his abridgment of Rangel ends. The contents of two subsequent chapters are given, but not the text.

Passing through Ayays and the well-peopled land of Nilco, Soto went with the cacique of Guachoyanque to his well-palisaded town on the banks of the Mississippi, at the mouth of the Red River, arriving there on Sunday, April 17, 1542. Here he fell ill of the fever; difficulties beset him on every side, and he sank under the strain. Appointing Luis de Moscoço as his successor in command, he died on the 21st of May. The *Adelantado* of Cuba and Florida, who had hoped to gather the wealth of nations, left as his property five Indian slaves, three horses, and a herd of swine. His body, kept for some days in a house, was interred in the town; but as fears were entertained that the Indians might dig up the corpse, it was taken, wrapped in blankets loaded with sand, and sunk in the Mississippi.[1]

AUTOGRAPH OF SOTO.

Muscoço's first plan was to march westward to Mexico. But after advancing to the province of Xacatin, the survivors of the expedition lost all hope; and returning to the Mississippi, wintered on its banks. There building two large boats, they embarked in them and in canoes. Hostile Indians pursued them, and twelve men were drowned, their canoes being run down by the enemy's *periaguas*. The survivors reached the Gulf and coasted along to Pánuco.[2]

The expedition of Soto added very little to the knowledge of the continent, as no steps were taken to note the topography of the country or the language of the various tribes. Diego Maldonado and Gomez Arias, seeking Soto, explored the coast from the vicinity of the Mississippi nearly to Newfoundland; but their reports are unknown.

Notwithstanding the disastrous result of Soto's expedition, and the conclusive proof it afforded that the country bordering on the Gulf of

[1] *Relaçam verdad.*, chaps. xxv.–xxx.; Biedma, *Relacion*, in Smith's *Soto*, pp. 118–149, 252–257.

[2] *Relaçam verdad.*, chaps. xxxi.–xlii.; Biedma, *Relacion*, in Smith's *Soto*, pp. 150–196, 257–261.

Mexico contained no rich kingdom and afforded little inducement for settlements, other commanders were ready to undertake the conquest of Florida. Among these was Don Antonio de Mendoza, the viceroy of New Spain, who sought, by offers of rank and honors, to enlist some of the survivors of Soto's march in a new campaign. In a more mercantile spirit, Julian de Samano and Pedro de Ahumada applied to the Spanish monarch for a patent, promising to make a good use of the privileges granted them, and to treat the Indians well. They hoped to buy furs and pearls, and carry on a trade in them till mines of gold and silver were found. The Court, however, refused to permit the grant.[1]

ANTONIO DE MENDOZA,
Viceroy of New Spain.

Yet as a matter of policy it became necessary for Spain to occupy Florida. This the Court felt; and when Cartier was preparing for his voyage to the northern part of the continent,[2] Spanish spies followed his movements and reported all to their Government. In Spain it was decided that Cartier's occupation of the frozen land, for which he was equipping his vessels, could not in any way militate against the interests of the Catholic monarch; but it was decided that any settlement attempted in Florida must on some pretext be crushed out.[3] Florida from its position afforded a basis for assailing the fleets which bore from Vera Cruz the treasures of the Indies; and the hurricanes of the tropics had already strewn the Florida coast with the fragments of Spanish wrecks. In 1545 a vessel laden with silver and precious commodities perished on that coast, and two hundred persons reached land, only to fall by the hands of the Indians.[4]

The next Spanish attempt to occupy Florida was not unmixed with romance; and its tragic close invests it with peculiar interest. The Dominicans, led by Father Antonio de Montesinos and Las Casas, — who had by this time become Bishop of Chiapa, — were active in condemning the cruelties of their countrymen to the natives of the New World; and the atrocities perpetrated by Soto in his disastrous march gave new themes for their indignant denunciations.[5]

One Dominican went further. Father Luis Cancer de Barbastro, when the Indians of a province had so steadily defied the Spaniards and prevented their entrance that it was styled "Tierra de Guerra," succeeded by mild and gentle means in winning the whole Indian population, so that the province obtained the name of "Vera Paz," or True Peace. In 1546 this

[1] Barcia, *Ensaio cronológico*, p. 24; Gomara, *Hist. gen.*, lib. i. c. 45.

[2] Cf. Vol. IV. chap. 2.

[3] Documents printed in Smith's *Coleccion*, pp. 103-118.

[4] Barcia, *Ensaio cronológico*, p. 24.

[5] Las Casas, *Destruccion de las Indias. De las provincias de la Tierra Firme por la parte que se llama la Florida*, — a chapter written partly before and partly after Moscoço's arrival in Mexico. [See the chapter on Las Casas, following the present one. — ED.]

energetic man conceived the idea of attempting the peaceful conquest of Florida. Father Gregory de Beteta and other influential members of his Order seconded his views. The next year he went to Spain and laid his project before the Court, where it was favorably received. He returned to Mexico with a royal order that all Floridians held in slavery, carried thither by the survivors of Soto's expedition, should be confided to Father Cancer to be taken back to their own land. The order proved ineffectual. Father Cancer then sailed from Vera Cruz in 1549 in the "Santa Maria del Enzina," without arms or soldiers, taking Father Beteta, Father Diego de Tolosa, Father John Garcia, and others to conduct the mission. At Havana he obtained Magdalen, a woman who had been brought from Florida, and who had become a Christian. The vessel then steered for Florida, and reaching the coast, at about 28°, on the eve of Ascension Day, ran northward, but soon sailed back. The missionaries and their interpreter landed, and found some of the Indians fishing, who proved friendly. Father Diego, a mission coadjutor, and a sailor, resolved to remain with the natives, and went off to their cabins. Cancer and his companions awaited their return; but they never appeared again. For some days the Spaniards on the ship endeavored to enter into friendly relations with the Indians, and on Corpus Christi Fathers Cancer and Garcia landed and said Mass on shore. At last a Spaniard named John Muñoz, who had been a prisoner among the Indians, managed to reach the ship; and from him they learned that the missionary and his companions had been killed by the treacherous natives almost immediately after reaching their cabins. He had not witnessed their murder, but declared that he had seen the missionary's scalp. Magdalen, however, came to the shore and assured the missionaries that their comrade was alive and well.

It had thus become a serious matter what course to pursue. The vessel was too heavy to enter the shallow bays, the provisions were nearly exhausted, water could not be had, and the ship's people were clamoring to return to Mexico. The missionaries, all except Father Cancer, desired to abandon the projected settlement, but he still believed that by presents and kindness to the Indians he could safely remain. His companions in vain endeavored to dissuade him. On Tuesday, June 25, he was pulled in a boat near the shore. He leaped into the water and waded towards the land. Though urged to return, he persevered. Kneeling for a few minutes on the beach, he advanced till he met the Indians. The sailors in the boat saw one Indian pull off his hat, and another strike him down with a club. One cry escaped his lips. A crowd of Indians streamed down to the shore and with arrows drove off the boat. Lingering for awhile, the vessel sailed back to Vera Cruz, after five lives had thus rashly been sacrificed.[1]

[1] The best account of this affair is a "Relacion de la Florida para el Illmo Señor Visorrei de la Na España la qual trajo Fray Grego de Beteta," in Smith's *Coleccion*, pp. 190-202. The first part is by Cancer himself, the conclusion by Beteta. There are also extant "Requirimentos y respuestas que pasaron en la Nao Sa Maria de la Encina," and the Minutes of dis-

On the arrival of the tidings of this tragic close of Cancer's mission a congress was convened by Maximilian, King of Bohemia, then regent in Spain; and the advocates of the peace policy in regard to the Indians lost much of the influence which they had obtained in the royal councils.[1]

The wreck of the fleet, with rich cargoes of silver, gold, and other precious commodities, on the northern shore of the Gulf of Mexico in 1553, when several hundred persons perished, and the sufferings of the surviving passengers, among whom were several Dominicans, in their attempt to reach the settlements; and the wreck of Farfan's fleet on the Atlantic coast near Santa Elena in December, 1554, — showed the necessity of having posts on that dangerous coast of Florida, in order to save life and treasure.[2]

The Council of the Indies advised Philip II. to confide the conquest and settlement of Florida to Don Luis de Velasco, viceroy of New Spain, who was anxious to undertake the task. The Catholic monarch had previously rejected the projects of Zurita and Samano; but the high character of Velasco induced him to confide the task to the viceroy of Mexico. The step was a gain for the humanitarian party; and the King, on giving his approval, directed that Dominican friars should be selected to accompany the colonists, in order to minister to them and convert the Indians. Don Luis de Velasco had directed the government in Mexico since November, 1550, with remarkable prudence and ability. The natives found in him such an earnest, capable, and unwavering protector that he is styled in history the Father of the Indians.

The plans adopted by this excellent governor for the occupation of Florida were in full harmony with the Dominican views. In the treatment of the Indians he anticipated the just and equitable methods which give Calvert, Williams, and Penn so enviable a place in American annals.[3]

The occupation was not to be one of conquest, and all intercourse with the Indians was to be on the basis of natural equity. His first step was prompted by his characteristic prudence.[4] In September, 1558, he despatched Guido de Labazares, with three vessels and a sufficient force, to explore the whole Florida coast, and select the best port he found for the projected settlement. Labazares, on his return after an investigation of

cussions between the missionaries, and the Captain's order to his pilot and sailors. There is a somewhat detailed sketch of Cancer's life in Davila Padilla's *Historia de la fundacion de la Provincia de Santiago de México*, 1596, chapters liv.–lvii., and a brief notice in Touron, *Histoire de l'Amérique*, vi. 81. Cf. Herrera, dec. viii. lib. 5, p. 112; Gomara, c. xlv.; Barcia, *Ensaio cronológico*, pp. 25–26.

[1] Barcia, *Ensaio cronológico*, p. 26.

[2] Barcia, *Ensaio cronológico*, pp. 28–29. "Don Luis Velasco a los officiales de Sevilla," Mexico, November, 1554. Farfan to same, Jan. 3, 1555. The vessels were wrecked at Cape Santa Elena, 9° N. Villafañe was sent to rescue the sur-

vivors. Davila Padilla gives details in his sketches of Fathers Diego de la Cruz, Juan de Mena, Juan Ferrer, and Marcos de Mena.

[3] "The Viceroy has treated this matter in a most Christian way, with much wisdom and counsel, insisting strenuously on their understanding that they do not go to conquer those nations, nor do what has been done in the discovery of the Indies, but to settle, and by good example, with good works and with presents, to bring them to a knowledge of our holy Faith and Catholic truth." — FATHER PEDRO DE FERIA, *Letter of March* 3, 1559.

[4] Alaman, *Disertaciones históricas*, vol. iii., apendice, p. 11.

several months, reported in favor of Pensacola Bay, which he named Feli-
pina; and he describes its entrance between a long island and a point
of land. The country was well wooded, game and fish abounded, and
the Indian fields showed that Indian corn and vegetables could be raised
successfully.[1] On the return of Labazares in December, preparations were
made for the expedition, which was placed under the command of Don
Tristan de Luna y Arellano. The force consisted of fifteen hundred soldiers
and settlers, under six captains of cavalry and six of infantry, some of whom
had been at Coça, and were consequently well acquainted with the country
where it was intended to form the settlement. The Dominicans selected
were Fathers Pedro de Feria, as vicar-provincial of Florida, Dominic of
the Annunciation, Dominic de Salazar, John Maçuelas, Dominic of Saint
Dominic, and a lay brother. The object being to settle, provisions for a
whole year were prepared, and ammunition to meet all their wants.

The colonists, thus well fitted for their undertaking, sailed from Vera
Cruz on the 11th of June, 1559; and by the first of the following month
were off the bay in Florida to which Miruelo had given his name. Although
Labazares had recommended Pensacola Bay, Tristan de Luna seems to have
been induced by his pilots to give the preference to the Bay of Ichuse; and
he sailed west in search of it, but passed it, and entered Pensacola Bay.
Finding that he had gone too far, Luna sailed back ten leagues east to
Ichuse, which must have been Santa Rosa Bay. Here he anchored his
fleet, and despatched the factor Luis Daza, with a galleon, to Vera Cruz to
announce his safe arrival. He fitted two other vessels to proceed to Spain,
awaiting the return of two exploring parties; he then prepared to land his
colonists and stores.[2] Meanwhile he sent a detachment of one hundred men
under captains Alvaro Nyeto and Gonzalo Sanchez, accompanied by one of
the missionaries, to explore the country and ascertain the disposition of the
Indians. The exploring parties returned after three weeks, having found
only one hamlet, in the midst of an uninhabited country.[3] Before Luna
had unloaded his vessels, they were struck, during the night of September
19,[4] by a terrible hurricane, which lasted twenty-four hours, destroying five
ships, a galleon and a bark, and carrying one caravel and its cargo into a
grove some distance on land. Many of the people perished, and most of
the stores intended for the maintenance of the colony were ruined or lost.

The river, entering the Bay of Ichuse, proved to be very difficult of
navigation, and it watered a sparsely-peopled country. Another detach-

[1] *Declaracion de Guido de Bazares de la Jornada que hizo á descubrir las puertos y vaias qͤ hai
en la costa de la Florida*, Feb. 1, 1559. A poor
translation of this document is given in French
in Ternaux' *Voyages*, vol. x., and a still worse
one in English in French's *Historical Collections
of Louisiana*, etc., new series, ii. 236.

[2] *Relacion de Dn Luis de Velasco a S. M.
Mexico*, Sept. 24, 1559. This was written after

receiving, on the 9th, the letters sent by Tristan
de Luna on the galleon. It is given in B. Smith's
Coleccion, p. 10. See Davila Padilla, *Historia de
la fundacion de la Provincia de Santiago de México*
(Madrid, 1596), chaps. lviii.–lix., pp. 231–234.
Ichuse in some documents is written Ochuse.

[3] *Testimony of Cristóval Velasquez.*

[4] Davila Padilla (p. 236) says August 20;
but it was evidently September.

ment,[1] sent apparently to the northwest, after a forty days' march through uncultivated country, reached a large river, apparently the Escambia, and followed its banks to Nanipacna, a deserted town of eighty houses. Explorations in various directions found no other signs of Indian occupation. The natives at last returned and became friendly.

Finding his original site unfavorable, Tristan de Luna, after exhausting the relief-supplies sent him, and being himself prostrated by a fever in which he became delirious, left Juan de Jaramillo at the port with fifty men and negro slaves, and proceeded[2] with the rest of his company, nearly a thousand souls, to Nanipacna, some by land, and some ascending the river in their lighter craft. To this town he gave the name of Santa Cruz. The stores of Indian corn, beans, and other vegetables left by the Indians were soon consumed by the Spaniards, who were forced to live on acorns or any herbs they could gather.

The Viceroy, on hearing of their sufferings, sent two vessels to their relief in November, promising more ample aid in the spring. The provisions they obtained saved them from starvation during the winter, but in the spring their condition became as desperate as ever. No attempt seems to have been made to cultivate the Indian fields, or to raise anything for their own support.[3]

In hope of obtaining provisions from Coça, Jaramillo sent his sergeant-major with six captains and two hundred soldiers, accompanied by Father Dominic de Salazar and Dominic of the Annunciation, to that province. On the march the men were forced to eat straps, harnesses, and the leather coverings of their shields; some died of starvation, while others were poisoned by herbs which they ate. A chestnut wood proved a godsend, and a fifty days' march brought them to Olibahali (Hatchet Creek), where the friendly natives ministered to their wants.[4]

About the beginning of July they reached Coça, on the Coosa River, then a town of thirty houses, near which were seven other towns of the same tribe. Entering into friendly intercourse with these Indians, the Spaniards obtained food for themselves and their jaded horses. After resting here for three months, the Spaniards, to gain the good-will of the Coosas, agreed to aid them in a campaign against the Napochies, — a nation near the Ochechiton,[5] the Espiritu Santo, or Mississippi. These were in all probability the Natchez. The Coosas and their Spanish allies defeated this tribe, and compelled them to pay tribute, as of old, to the Coosas. Their town,

[1] *Letter of Velasco*, Oct. 25, 1559, citing a letter of Tristan de Luna. Said by Montalvan and Velasquez to have been one hundred and fifty men, horse and foot, under Mateo de Sauce, the sergeant-major, and Captain Christopher de Arellano, accompanied by Fathers Annunciation and Salazar (*Testimony of Miguel Sanchez Serrano*). He remained three months at Ichuse before he heard from Ypacana; and though urged to go there, lingered five or six months more.

[2] *Letter of Tristan de Luna to the King*, Sept. 24, 1559, in *Coleccion de documentos inéditos*, xii. 280–283.

[3] *Letter of Velasco to Luna*, Oct. 25, 1559; Davila Padilla, book i. chap. lxi. pp. 242–244.

[4] Barcia, *Ensaio cronológico*, pp. 33–34; Davila Padilla, book i. chap. lxii., pp. 245–246.

[5] Ochechiton, like Mississippi, means great river, — from *okhina*, river; *chito*, great (Byington's *Choctaw Definer*, pp. 79, 97).

saved with difficulty from the flames, gave the Spaniards a supply of corn. On their return to Coça, the sergeant-major sent to report to Tristan de Luna; but his messengers found no Spaniard at Nanipacna, save one hanging from a tree. Tristan de Luna, supposing his men lost, had gone down to Ochuse Bay, leaving directions on a tree, and a buried letter.[1] Father Feria and some others had sailed for Havana, and all were eager to leave the country.[2] Tristan de Luna was reluctant to abandon the projected settlement, and wished to proceed to Coça with all the survivors of his force. His sickness had left him so capricious and severe, that he seemed actually insane. The supplies promised in the spring had not arrived in September, though four ships left Vera Cruz toward the end of June. Parties sent out by land and water found the fields on the Escambia and Mobile[3] forsaken by the Indians, who had laid waste their towns and removed their provisions. In this desperate state George Ceron, the *maestro de campo*, opposed the Governor's plan,[4] and a large part of the force rallied around him. When Tristan de Luna issued a proclamation ordering the march, there was an open mutiny, and the Governor condemned the whole of the insurgents to death. Of course he could not attempt to execute so many, but he did hang one who deserted. The mutineers secretly sent word to Coça, and in November the party from that province with the two missionaries arrived at Pensacola Bay.[5] Don Tristan's detachment was also recalled from the original landing, and the whole force united. The dissensions continued till the missionaries, amid the solemnities of Holy Week, by appealing to the religious feelings of the commander and Ceron, effected a reconciliation.[6]

At this juncture Angel de Villafañe's fleet entered the harbor of Ichuse. He announced to the people that he was on his way to Santa Elena, which Tristan de Luna had made an ineffectual effort to reach. All who chose were at liberty to accompany him. The desire to evacuate the country where they had suffered so severely was universal. None expressed a wish to remain; and Tristan de Luna, seeing himself utterly abandoned, embarked for Havana with a few servants. Villafañe then took on board all except a detachment of fifty or sixty men who were left at Ichuse under Captain Biedma, with orders to remain five or six months; at the expiration of which time they were to sail away also, in case no instructions came.

Villafañe, with the "San Juan" and three other vessels and about two hundred men, put into Havana; but there many of the men deserted, and several officers refused to proceed.[7]

---

[1] Testimony of soldiers.

[2] Davila Padilla, book i. chap. lxiii.–lxvi. pp. 247–265.

[3] These I take to be the Rio Manipacna and Rio Tome.

[4] Ceron, *Respuesta*, Sept. 16, 1560. Velasco, *Letter, Aug. 20–Sept.* 3, 1560; Davila Padilla, book i. p. 268.

[5] Davila Padilla, p. 270. The labors of Cancer and of Feria and his companions are treated briefly in the *Relacion de la fundacion de la Provincia de Santiago*, 1567. Cf. *Coleccion de documentos inéditos*, v. 447.

[6] Barcia, *Ensaio cronológico*, pp. 34–41; Davila Padilla, pp. 271–277.

[7] *Testimony of Velasquez and Miguel Sanchez Serrano*. The expedition sent out by Tristan de Luna to occupy Santa Elena was composed of three vessels, bearing one hundred men. The vessels were scattered in a storm, and ran

With Gonzalo Gayon as pilot, Villafañe reached Santa Elena — now Port Royal Sound — May 27, 1561, and took possession in the name of the King of Spain. Finding no soil adapted for cultivation, and no port suitable for planting a settlement, he kept along the coast, doubled Cape Roman, and landing on the 2d of June, went inland till he reached the Santee, where he again took formal possession. On the 8th he was near the Jordan or Pedee; but a storm drove off one of his vessels. With the rest he continued his survey of the coast till he doubled Cape Hatteras. There, on the 14th of June, his caravel well-nigh foundered, and his two smaller vessels undoubtedly perished. He is said to have abandoned the exploration of the coast here, although apparently it was his vessel, with the Dominican Fathers, which about this time visited Axacan, on the Chesapeake, and took off a brother of the chief.[1]

Villafañe then sailed to Santo Domingo, and Florida was abandoned. In fact, on the 23d of September the King declared that no further attempt was to be made to colonize that country, either in the Gulf or at Santa Elena, alleging that there was no ground to fear that the French would set foot in that land or take possession of it; and the royal order cites the opinion of Pedro Menendez against any attempt to form settlements on either coast.[2]

As if to show the fallacy of their judgment and their forecast, the French (and what was worse, from the Spanish point of view, French Calvinists) in the next year, under Ribault, took possession of Port Royal, — the very Santa Elena which Villafañe considered unfitted for colonization. Here they founded Charlesfort and a settlement, entering Port Royal less than three months after the Spanish officers convened in Mexico had united in condemning the country.

Pedro Menendez de Aviles had, as we have seen, been general of the fleet to New Spain in 1560, and on his return received instructions to examine the Atlantic coast north of the very spot where the French thus soon after settled. In 1561 he again commanded the fleet; but on his homeward voyage a terrible storm scattered the vessels near the Bermudas, and one vessel, on which his only son and many of his kinsmen had embarked, disappeared. With the rest of his ships he reached Spain,

[1] Testimonio de Francisco de Aguilar, escrivano que fue en la jornada á la Florida con Angel de Villafañe Relacion del reconocimiento que hizo el Capitan General Angel de Villafañe de la costa de la Florida, y posesion que tomó . . . desde 33° hasta 35°. Testimony of Montalvan, Velasquez, Serrano, etc. The Indian, however, may have been found among a still more southerly tribe.

to Mexico and Cuba. After that Pedro Menendez, who was in command of a fleet sailing from Vera Cruz, was ordered to run along the Atlantic coast for a hundred leagues above Santa Elena. Letter of Velasco, Sept. 3, 1560; Testimony of Montalvan.

[2] A council held in Mexico of persons who had been in Florida agreed that the royal order was based on accurate information (Parecer que da S. M. el conséjo de la Nueva España, March 12, 1562). Tristan de Luna sailed to Spain, and in a brief, manly letter solicited of the King an investigation into his conduct, professing his readiness to submit to any punishment if he was deemed deserving of it (Memorial que dió al Rey Don Tristan de Luna y Arellano dandole cuenta del suceso de la jornada de la Florida).

filled with anxiety, eager only to fit out vessels to seek his son, who, he believed, had been driven on the Florida coast, and was probably a prisoner in the hands of the Indians. At this critical moment, however, charges were brought against him; and he, with his brother, was arrested and detained in prison for two years, unable to bring the case to trial, or to obtain his release on bail.

When Menendez at last succeeded in obtaining an audience of the King, he solicited, in 1564, permission to proceed with two vessels to Bermuda and Florida to seek his son, and then retire to his home, which he had not seen for eighteen years. Philip II. at last consented; but required him to make a thorough coast-survey of Florida, so as to prepare charts that would prevent the wrecks which had arisen from ignorance of the real character of the sea-line. Menendez replied that his Majesty could confer no higher boon upon him for his long and successful services on the seas than to authorize him to conquer and settle Florida.

Nothing could be in greater accordance with the royal views than to commit to the energy of Menendez [1] the task which so many others had undertaken in vain. A patent, or *asiento*, was issued March 20, 1565, by the provisions of which Menendez was required to sail in May with ten vessels, carrying arms and supplies, and five hundred men, one hundred to be capable of cultivating the soil. He was to take provisions to maintain the whole force for a year, and was to conquer and settle Florida within three years; explore and map the coast, transport settlers, a certain number of whom were to be married; maintain twelve members of religious Orders as missionaries, besides four of the Society of Jesus; and to introduce horses, black cattle, sheep, and swine for the two or three distinct settlements he was required to found at his own expense.[2] The King gave only the use of the galleon "San Pelayo," and bestowed upon Menendez the title of *Adelantado* of Florida, a personal grant of twenty-five leagues square, with the title of Marquis, and the office of Governor and Captain-General of Florida.

While Menendez was gathering, among his kindred in Asturias and Biscay, men and means to fulfil his part of the undertaking, the Court of Spain became aware for the first time that the Protestants of France had quietly planted a colony on that very Florida coast. Menendez was immediately summoned in haste to Court; and orders were issued to furnish him in America three vessels fully equipped, and an expeditionary force of two hundred cavalry and four hundred infantry. Menendez urged, on the contrary, that he should be sent on at once with some light vessels to attack the French; or, if that was not feasible, to occupy a neighboring port and

---

[1] There is a copperplate engraving of "Pedro Menendez de Aviles, Natural de Avilés en Asturias, Comendador de la orden de Santiago, Conquistador de la Florida, nombrado Gral de la Armada contra Jnglaterra. Murió en Santander A° 1574, á los 55, de edad." Drawn by Josef Camaron, engraved by Franco de Paula Marte, 1791 (7⅛ × 11⅜ inches). Mr. Parkman engraved the head for his *France in the New World*, and Dr. Shea used the plate in his *Charlevoix*.

[2] *Coleccion de documentos inéditos*, xxii. 242.

fortify it, while awaiting reinforcements. The Government, by successive orders, increased the Florida armament, so that Menendez finally sailed from Cadiz, June 29, with the galleon " San Pelayo " and other vessels to the number of nineteen, carrying more than fifteen hundred persons, including farmers and mechanics of all kinds.

The light in which Spaniards, especially those connected with commerce and colonies, regarded the Protestants of France was simply that of pirates. French cruisers, often making their Protestantism a pretext for their actions, scoured the seas, capturing Spanish and Portuguese vessels, and committing the greatest atrocities. In 1555 Jacques Sorie surprised Havana, plundered it, and gave it to the flames, butchering the prisoners who fell into his hands. In 1559 Megander pillaged Porto Rico, and John de la Roche plundered the ships and settlements near Carthagena.[1]

It seems strange, however, that neither in Spain nor in America was it known that this dreaded and hated community, the Huguenots of France, had actually, in 1562, begun a settlement at the very harbor of Santa Elena where Villafañe had taken possession in the name of the Spanish monarch a year before. Some of the French settlers revolted, and very naturally went off to cruise against the Spaniards, and with success; but the ill-managed colony of Charlesfort on Port Royal Sound had terminated its brief existence without drawing down the vengeance of Spain.

When the tidings of a French occupancy of Florida startled the Spanish Court, a second attempt of the Huguenots at settlement had been made, — this time at the mouth of St. John's River, where Fort Caroline was a direct menace to the rich Spanish fleets, offering a safe refuge to cruisers, which in the name of a pure gospel could sally out to plunder and to slay. Yet that settlement, thus provoking the fiercest hostility of Spain, was ill-managed. It was, in fact, sinking, like its predecessor, from the unfitness of its members to make the teeming earth yield them its fruits for their maintenance. René Laudonnière, the commandant, after receiving some temporary relief from the English corsair Hawkins,[2] and learning that the Spaniards meditated hostilities, was about to burn his fort and abandon the country, when John Ribault arrived as commandant, with supplies and colonists, as well as orders to maintain the post. His instructions from Coligny clearly intended that he should attack the Spaniards.[3]

[1] " They burned it [Havana], with all the town and church, and put to death all the inhabitants they found, and the rest fled to the mountains; so that nothing remained in the town that was not burned, and there was not an inhabitant left alive or dwelling there" (*Memorial de Pedro Menendez de Aviles á S.M. sobre los agravios . . . que recivio de los oficiales de la casa de contratacion*, 1564). Menendez was personally cognizant, as he sent a vessel and men from his fleet to help restore the place.

[2] [Laudonnière's account of this relief is translated in the *Hawkins Voyages* (p. 65), pub-lished by the Hakluyt Society. A project of the English for a settlement on the Florida coast (1563), under Stukely, came to nought. Cf. Doyle's *English in America*, p. 55. — ED.]

[3] " En fermant ceste lettre i'ay eu certain aduis, comme dom Petro Melandes se part d'Espagne, pour aller à la coste de la Nouvelle Frãce; vous regarderez n'endurer qu'il n'entrepreine sur nous non plus qu'il veut que nous n'entreprenions sur eux." As Mr. Parkman remarks, "Ribault interpreted this into a command to attack the Spaniards." — *Pioneers of France in the New World.*

The two bitter antagonists, each stimulated by his superiors, were thus racing across the Atlantic, each endeavoring to outstrip the other, so as to be able first to assume the offensive. The struggle was to be a deadly one, for on neither side were there any of the ordinary restraints; it was to be a warfare without mercy.

After leaving the Canaries, Menendez' fleet was scattered by storms. One vessel put back; the flagship and another were driven in one direction, five vessels in another. These, after encountering another storm, finally reached Porto Rico on the 9th of August, and found the flagship and its tender there.[1]

The other ships from Biscay and Asturias had not arrived; but Menendez, fearing that Ribault might outstrip him, resolved to proceed, though his vessels needed repairs from the injuries sustained in the storm. If he was to crush Fort Caroline, he felt that it must be done before the French post was reinforced; if not, all the force at his disposal would be insufficient to assume the offensive. He made the coast of Florida near Cape Cañaveral on the 25th of August; and soon after, by landing a party, ascertained from the natives that the French post was to the northward. Following the coast in that direction, he discovered, on the 28th, a harbor which seemed to possess advantages, and to which he gave the name of the great Bishop of Hippo, Augustine, who is honored on that day. Sailing on cautiously, he came in sight of the mouth of the St. John's River about two o'clock in the afternoon of the 4th of September. The ten days he had lost creeping along the coast were fatal to his project, for there lay the four vessels of Ribault, the flagship and its consort flinging to the breeze the colors of France.

Menendez' officers in council were in favor of running back to Santo Domingo till the whole force was united and ready to assume the offensive; but Menendez inspired them with his own intrepidity, and resolved to attack at once. A tremendous thunderstorm prevented operations till ten at night, when he bore down on the French, and ran his ship, the "Pelayo," between the two larger vessels of Ribault. To his hail who they were and what they were doing there, the reply was that John Ribault was their captain-general, and that they came to the country by order of the King of France; and the French in return asked what ships they were, and who commanded them. To quote his own words, "I replied to them that I was Peter Menendez, that I came by command of the King of Spain to this coast and land to burn and hang the French Lutherans found in it, and that in the morning I would board his ships to know whether he belonged to that sect; because if he did, I could not avoid executing on them the justice which his Majesty commanded. They replied that this was not right, and that I might go without awaiting the morning."

[1] *Relacion de Mazauegos. Relacion de lo sub-cedido en la Habana cerca de la entrada de los Franceses.* Smith, *Coleccion,* p. 202. *Relacion de los robos que corsarios franceses han hecho* 1559–1571. *Relacion de los navios que robaron franceses los años de* 1559 y 1560.

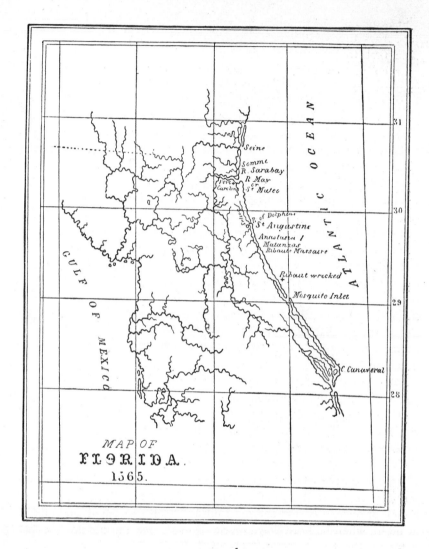

FLORIDA.[1]

As Menendez manœuvred to **get** a favorable position, the French vessels cut their cables and stood out to sea. The Spaniards gave chase, rapidly firing five cannon at Ribault's flagship, — which Menendez supposed that he injured badly, as boats put off to the other vessels. Finding that the French outsailed him, Menendez put back, intending to land soldiers on an island at the mouth of the river and fortify a position which would command the entrance; but as he reached the St. John's he saw three French vessels coming out, ready for action.

[1] [This sketch-map of the scene of the operations of the Spanish and the French follows one given by Fairbanks in his *History* of *St. Augustine.* Other modern maps, giving the old localities, are found in Parkman, Gaffarel, etc. — ED.]

His project was thus defeated; and too wily to be caught at a disadvantage by the returning French vessels, Menendez bore away to the
harbor of St. Augustine, which he estimated at eight leagues from the

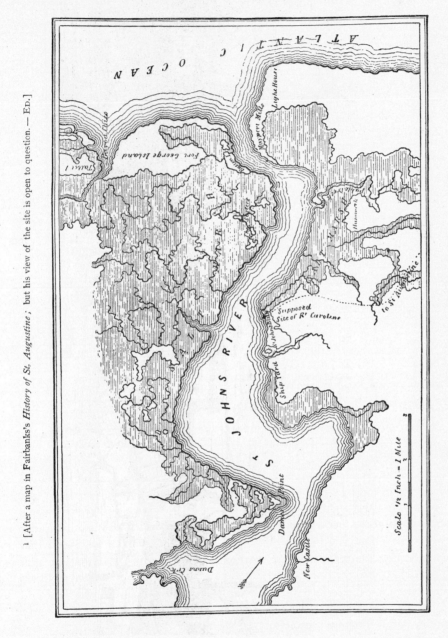

[1] [After a map in Fairbanks's *History of St. Augustine*; but his view of the site is open to question. — ED.]

SITE OF FORT CAROLINE.[1]

French by sea, and six by land. Here he proceeded to found the oldest city in the present territory of the United States. Two hundred
mail-clad soldiers, commanded by Captain John de San Vicente and

ST. AUGUSTINE.[1]

[1] [This view of Pagus Hispanorum, as given in Montanus and Ogilby, represents the town founded by Menendez at a somewhat later period, if it is wholly truthful of any period. The same view was better engraved at Leide by Vander Aa. — ED.]

SPANISH VESSELS.
(*From the* PAGUS HISPANORUM *in Montanus.*)

Captain Patiño, landed on the 6th of September, 1565. The Indians were friendly, and readily gave the settlers the large house of one of the caciques which stood near the shore of the river. Around this an intrenchment was traced; and a ditch was soon dug, and earthworks thrown up, with such implements as they had at hand, for the vessel bearing their tools had not yet arrived.

The next day three of the smaller vessels ran into the harbor, and from them three hundred more of the soldiers disembarked, as well as those who had come to settle in the country, — men, women, and children. Artillery and munitions for the fort were also landed. The eighth being a holiday in the Catholic Church, — the Nativity of the Blessed Virgin, — was celebrated with due solemnity. Mass was offered for the first time at a spot ever after held in veneration, and where in time arose the primitive shrine of Nuestra Señora de la Leche. Then the work of debarkation was resumed; one hundred more persons landed; and great guns, precious

THE BUILDING OF FORT CAROLINE.
(Lemoyne, in De Bry.)

stores of provisions, and munitions were brought to the new fort.   Amid
all this bustle and activity the Spaniards were startled by the appearance

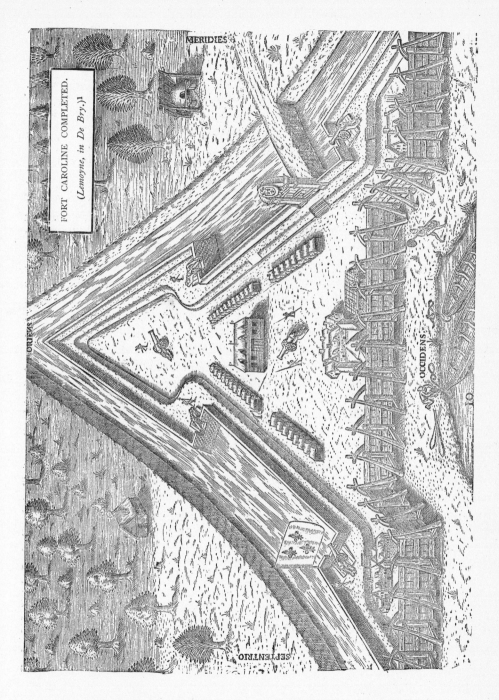

FORT CAROLINE COMPLETED. (Lemoyne, in De Bry.)[1]

[1] [Two pictures of Fort Caroline accompany the *Brevis narratio* of Lemoyne, — one the beginning of work upon it, and the other the completed structure, "a more finished fortification than could possibly have been constructed, but to be taken as a correct outline," as Fairbanks (p. 54) presumes. The engraving of the completed fort is reproduced in Fairbanks's *St. Augustine*, Stevens's *Georgia*, etc. Another and better view of it, called "Arx Carolina —Charles-

of two large French vessels[1] in the offing, evidently ready for action. It was no part of Menendez' plan to engage them, and he waited till, about three in the afternoon, they bore away for the St. John's. Then he prepared to land in person. As his boat left the vessel with banners unfurled, amid the thunder of cannon and the sounds of warlike music, Mendoza Grajales, the first priest of St. Augustine, bearing a cross, went down at the head of those on shore to meet the *adelantado*, all chanting the Te Deum. Menendez proceeded at once with his attendants to the cross, which he kissed on bended knee.

Formal possession of the land was then taken in the name of Philip H., King of Spain. The captains of the troops and the officers of the new colony came forward to take the oath to Peter Menendez de Aviles as governor, captain-general, and *adelantado* of Florida and its coasts under the patents of the Spanish King. Crowds of friendly Indians, with their chieftains, gathered around.

From them the Spanish commander learned that his position was admirably taken, as he could, at a short distance, strike the river on which the French lay, and descend it to assail them. Here then he resolved to make his position as strong as possible, till the rest of his armament arrived. His galleon "San Pelayo," too large to enter the port, rode without, in danger from the sudden storms that visit the coast, and from the French. Putting on board some French prisoners whom he had captured in a boat, he despatched her and another vessel to Santo Domingo. He organized his force by appointing officers, — a lieutenant and a sergeant-major, and ten captains. The necessity of horses to operate rapidly induced him to send two of his lighter vessels to Havana to seek them there; and by this conveyance he addressed to Philip II. his first letter from Florida.[2]

The masts of his vessels could scarcely have vanished from the eyes of the Spanish force, when the French vessels appeared once more, and nearly captured Menendez himself in the harbor, where he was carrying to the shore, in the smaller vessels that he had retained, some artillery and munitions from the galleons. He escaped, however, though the French were so near that they called on him to surrender. And he ascribed his deliverance rather to prayer than to human skill; for, fierce seaman as he was, he was a man of deep and practical religious feeling, which influenced all his actions.

Menendez' position was now one of danger. The force at his command was not large, and the French evidently felt strong enough, and were determined to attack him. He had acknowledged his inability to cope with them

fort sur Floride," was engraved at Leide by Vander Aa, but it is a question if it be truthful. No traces of the fort have ever been recorded by subsequent observers, but Fairbanks places it near a place called St. John's Bluff, as shown in the accompanying map. Others have placed it on the Bell River (an estuary of the St. Mary's River), at a place called Battle Bluff. Cf. Carroll's *Hist. Coll.*, i. p. xxxvi. — ED.]

[1] One was commanded by Captain Cossette (*Basanier*, p. 105).

[2] Letter of Menendez to the King, dated Province of Florida, Sept. 11, 1565. Mendoza Grajales, *Relacion de la jornada de P° Menendez*, 1565.

on the ocean, and could not have felt very sanguine of being able to defend the slight breastworks that had been thrown up at St. Augustine.

Fortune favored him. Ribault, after so earnestly determining to assume the offensive, fatally hesitated. Within two days a tremendous hurricane, which the practised eye of Menendez had anticipated, burst on the coast. The French were, he believed, still hovering near, on the look-out for his larger vessels, and he knew that with such a norther their peril was extreme. It was, moreover, certain that they could not, for a time at least, make the St. John's, even if they rode out the storm.

· This gave him a temporary superiority, and he resolved to seize his opportunity. Summoning his officers to a council of war, he laid before them his plan of marching at once to attack Fort Caroline, from which the French had evidently drawn a part of their force, and probably their most effective men. The officers generally, as well as the two clergymen in the settlement, opposed his project as rash; but Menendez was determined. Five hundred men — three hundred armed with arquebuses, the rest with pikes and targets — were ordered to march, each one carrying rations of biscuit and wine. Menendez, at their head, bore his load like the rest. They marched out of the fort on the 16th of September, guided by two caciques who had been hostile to the French, and by a Frenchman who had been two years in the fort. The route proved one of great difficulty; the rain poured in torrents, swelling the streams and flooding the lowlands, so that the men were most of the time knee-deep in water. Many loitered, and, falling back, made their way to St. Augustine. Others showed a mutinous disposition, and loudly expressed their contempt for their sailor-general.

On the 29th, at the close of the day, he was within a short distance of the French fort, and halted to rest so as to storm it in the morning. At daybreak the Spaniards knelt in prayer; then, bearing twenty scaling-ladders, Menendez advanced, his sturdy Asturians and Biscayans in the van. Day broke as, in a heavy rain, they reached a height from which their French guide told them they could see the fort, washed by the river. Menendez advanced, and saw some houses and the St. John's; but from his position could not discover the fort. He would have gone farther; but the Maese de Campo and Captain Ochoa pushed on till they reached the houses, and reconnoitred the fort, where not a soul seemed astir. As they returned they were hailed by a French sentinel, who took them for countrymen. Ochoa sprang upon him, striking him on the head with his sheathed sword, while the Maese de Campo stabbed him. He uttered a cry; but was threatened with death, bound, and taken back. The cry had excited Menendez, who, supposing that his officers had been killed, called out: "Santiago! at them! God helps us! Victory! The French are slaughtered! Don Pedro de Valdes, the Maese de Campo, is in the fort, and has taken it!"

The men, supposing that the officers were in advance with part of the force, rushed on till they came up with the returning officers, who, taking in the situation, despatched the sentry and led the men to the attack. Two Frenchmen, who rushed out in their shirts, were cut down. Others outside the fort seeing the danger, gave the alarm; and a man at the principal gate threw it open to ascertain what the trouble was. Valdes, ready to scale the fort, saw the advantage, sprang on the man and cut him down, then rushed into the fort, followed by the fleetest of the Spanish detachment. In a moment two captains had simultaneously planted their colors on the walls, and the trumpets sounded for victory.

The French, taken utterly by surprise, made no defence; about fifty, dashing over the walls of the fort, took to the woods, almost naked, and unarmed, or endeavored in boats and by swimming to reach the vessels in the stream. When Menendez came up with the main body, his men were slaughtering the French as they ran shrieking through the fort, or came forward declaring that they surrendered. The women, and children under the age of fifteen, were, by orders of the commander, spared. Laudonnière, the younger Ribault, Lemoyne, and the carpenter Le Challeux, whose accounts have reached us, were among those who escaped.

Menendez had carried the fort without one of his men being killed or wounded. The number of the French thus unsparingly put to the sword is stated by Menendez himself as one hundred and thirty-two, with ten of the fugitives who were butchered the next day. Mendoza Grajales corroborates this estimate. Fifty were spared, and about as many escaped to the vessels; and some, doubtless, perished in the woods.

The slaughter was too terrible to need depicting in darker colors; but in time it was declared that Menendez hung many, with an insulting label: " I do not this to Frenchmen, but to Heretics." The Spanish accounts, written with too strong a conviction of the propriety of their course to seek any subterfuge, make no allusion to any such act; and the earliest French accounts are silent in regard to it. The charge first occurs in a statement written with an evident design to rouse public indignation in France, and not, therefore, to be deemed absolutely accurate.

No quarter was given, for the French were regarded as pirates; and as the French cruisers gave none, these, who were considered as of the same class, received none.

The booty acquired was great. A brigantine and a galiot fell into the hands of the Spaniards, with a vessel that had grounded. Another vessel lay near the fort, and Spanish accounts claim to have sunk it with the cannon of the fort, while the French declare they scuttled it. Two other vessels lay at the mouth of the river, watching for the Spaniards, whose attack was expected from the sea, and not from the land side. Besides these vessels and their contents, the Spaniards gained in the fort artillery and small-arms, supplies of flour and bread, horses, asses, sheep, and hogs.[1]

[1] Letter of Menendez to the King, Oct. 15, *de documentos inéditos* (edited by Pacheco, etc.), 1565; Mendoza Grajales, *Relacion* in *Coleccion* iii. 441–479.

Such was the first struggle on our soil between civilized men; it was brief, sanguinary, merciless.

Menendez named the captured fort San Mateo, from its capture on the feast of St. Matthew (September 21). He set up the arms of Spain, and selected a site for a church, which he ordered to be built at once. Then, leaving Gonçalo de Villaroel in command, with a garrison of three hundred men, he prepared to march back to St. Augustine with about one hundred, who composed the rest of the force which had remained with him till he reached Caroline. But of them all he found only thirty-five able or willing to undertake the march; and with these he set out, deeming his presence necessary at St. Augustine. Before long, one of the party pushed on to announce his coming.

The Spaniards there had learned of the disaster which had befallen Ribault's fleet from a Frenchman who was the sole survivor of one small vessel that had been driven ashore, its crew escaping a watery death only to perish by the hands of the Indians. The vessel was secured and brought to St. Augustine. The same day, September 23, a man was seen running toward the fort, uttering loud shouts. The priest, Mendoza Grajales, ran out to learn the tidings he bore. The soldier threw his arms around him, crying: " Victory! Victory! the French fort is ours!" He was soon recounting to his countrymen the story of the storming of Caroline. Toward nightfall the *adelantado* himself, with his little party, was seen approaching. Mendoza in surplice, bearing a crucifix, went forth to meet him. Menendez knelt to kiss the cross, and his men imitated his example; then they entered the fort in procession, chanting the Te Deum.[1]

Menendez despatched some light boats with supplies to San Mateo; but the fort there took fire a few days after its capture, and was almost entirely destroyed, with much of the booty. He sent other light craft to Santo Domingo with prisoners, and others still to patrol the coast and seek any signs of the galleon " San Pelayo," or of the French. Then he turned his whole attention to work on his fort and town, so as to be in readiness to withstand any attack from Ribault if the French commander should return and prove to be in a condition to assail him while his forces were divided. He also cultivated friendly intercourse with the neighboring chiefs whom he found hostile to the French and their allies.

On the 28th, some of the Indians came to report by signs that the French were six leagues distant, that they had lost their ships, and that they had reached the shore by swimming. They had halted at a stream which they could not cross, — evidently Matanzas inlet. Menendez sent out a boat, and followed in another with some of his officers and Mendoza, one of the clergymen. He overtook his party, and they encamped near the inlet, but out of sight. On the opposite side, the light of the camp-fires marked the spot occupied by the French. The next day, seeing Menendez, a sailor swam over, and stated that he had been sent to say that they were survivors

[1] Mendoza Grajales, *Relacion.*

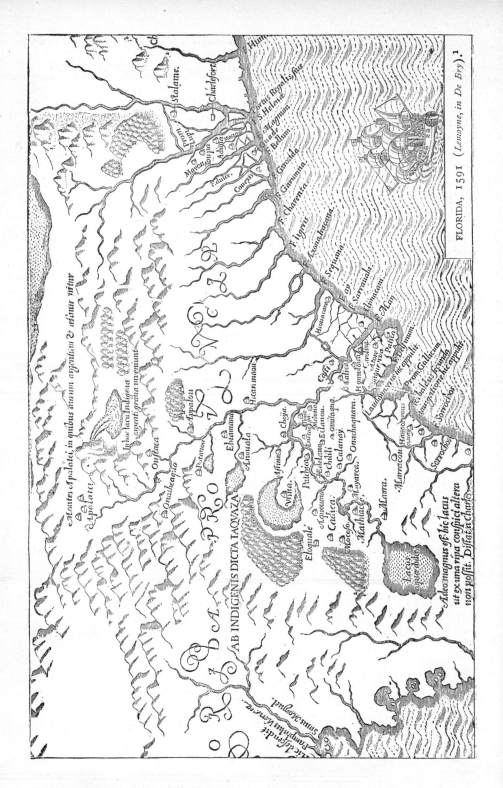

FLORIDA, 1591 (Lemoyne, in De Bry).[1]

[1] [This is the only cartographical result of   in Gaffarel's *Floride Française*, and in Shipp's
the French occupation. It is also reproduced   *De Soto and Florida*. It was literally copied

of some of Ribault's vessels which had been wrecked; that many of their people had been drowned, others killed or captured by the Indians; and that the rest, to the number of one hundred and forty, asked permission and aid to reach their fort, some distance up the coast. Menendez told him that he had captured the fort and put all to the sword. Then, after asking whether they were Catholics or Lutherans, and receiving the reply, the Spaniard sent the sailor to his companions, to say that if they did not give up their arms and surrender, he would put them all to the sword. On this an officer came over to endeavor to secure better terms, or to be allowed to remain till vessels could be obtained to take them to France; but Menendez was inexorable. The officer pleaded that the lives of the French should be spared; but Menendez, according to Mendoza, replied, " that he would not give them such a pledge, but that they should bring their arms and their persons, and that he should do with them according to his will; because if he spared their lives he wished them to be grateful to him for it, and if he put them to death they should not complain that he had broken his word." Solis de Meras, another clergyman, brother-in-law of Menendez, and in St. Augustine at the time, in his account states that Menendez said, "That if they wished to lay down their colors and their arms, and throw themselves on his mercy, they could do so, that he might do with them what God should give him the grace to do; or that they could do as they chose: for other truce or friendship could not be made with him; " and that he rejected an offer of ransom which they made.

Menendez himself more briefly writes: " I replied that they might surrender me their arms and put themselves under my pleasure, that I might do with them what our Lord might ordain; and from this resolution I do not and will not depart, unless our Lord God inspired me otherwise." The words held out hopes that were delusive; but the French, hemmed in by the sea and by savages, saw no alternative. They crossed, laid down their arms, and were bound, by order of Menendez, — ostensibly to conduct them to the fort. Sixteen, chiefly Breton sailors, who professed to be Catholics, were spared; the rest, one hundred and eleven in all, were put to death in cold blood, — as ruthlessly as the French, ten years before, had despatched their prisoners amid the smoking ruins of Havana, and, like them, in the name of religion.[1]

by Hondius in 1607, and not so well in the Mercator-Hondius *Atlas* of 1633. Lescarbot followed it; but in his 1618 edition altered for the worse the course of the St. John's River; and so did De Laet. Cf. Kohl, *Maps in Hakluyt*, p. 48, and Brinton, *Floridian Peninsula*, p. 80, who says (p. 86) that De Laet was the first to confine the name Florida to the peninsula; but Thevet seems nearly to do so in the map in his *Cosmographia*, which he based on Ortelius, a part of which is given in fac-simile in Weise's *Discoveries of America*, p. 304; and

it seems also to be the case in the earlier Mercator gores of 1541. The map accompanying Charlevoix' narrative will be found in his *Nouvelle France*, i. 24, and in Shea's translation of it, i. 133. — ED.]

[1] Jacques de Sorie, in 1555, at Havana, after pledging his word to spare the lives of the Spaniards who surrendered, put them and his Portuguese prisoners to death; negroes he hung up and shot while still alive (*Relacion de Diego de Mazauegos, MS.*; Letter of Bishop Sarmiento in *Coleccion de documentos inéditos*, v. 555).

Ribault himself, who was advancing by the same fatal route, was ignorant alike of the fall of Caroline and of the slaughter of the survivors of the advanced party; he too hoped to reach Laudonnière. Some days after the cruel treatment of the first band he reached the inlet, whose name to this day is a monument of the bloody work, — Matanzas.

The news of the appearance of this second French party reached Menendez on the 10th of October, — at the same time almost as that of the destruction of Fort San Mateo and its contents by fire, and while writing a despatch to the King, unfolding his plan for colonizing and holding Florida, by means of a series of forts at the Chesapeake, Port Royal, the Martyrs, and the Bay of Juan Ponce de Leon. He marched to the inlet with one hundred and fifty men. The French were on the opposite side, some making a rude raft. Both parties sounded drum and trumpet, and flung their standards to the breeze, drawing up in line of battle. Menendez then ordered his men to sit down and breakfast. Upon this, Ribault raised a white flag, and one of his men was soon swimming across. He returned with an Indian canoe that lay at the shore, and took over La Caille, an officer. Approaching Menendez, the French officer announced that the force was that of John Ribault, viceroy for the French king, three hundred and fifty men in all, who had been wrecked on the coast, and was now endeavoring to reach Fort Caroline. He soon learned how vain was the attempt. The fate of the fort and of its garrison, and the stark bodies of the preceding party, convinced him that those whom he represented must prepare to meet a similar fate. He requested Menendez to send an officer to Ribault to arrange terms of surrender; but the reply was that the French commander was free to cross with a few of his men, if he wished a conference.

When this was reported to him, the unfortunate Ribault made an effort in person to save his men. He was courteously received by Menendez, but, like his lieutenant, saw that the case was hopeless. According to Solis de Meras, Ribault offered a ransom of one hundred and fifty thousand ducats for himself and one part of his men; another part, embracing many wealthy nobles, preferring to treat separately. Menendez declined the offer, expressing his regret at being compelled to forego the money, which he needed. His terms were as enigmatical as before. He declared, so he himself tells us, "that they must lay down their arms and colors and put themselves under my pleasure; that I should do with their persons as I chose, and that there was nothing else to be done or concluded with me."

Priests, especially those of religious Orders, met no mercy at the hands of the French cruisers at this period, the most atrocious case being that of the Portuguese Jesuit Father Ignatius Azevedo, captured by the French on his way to Brazil with thirty-nine missionary companions, all of whom were put to death, in 1570. In all my reading, I find no case where the French in Spanish waters then gave quarter to Spaniards, except in hope of large ransom. Two of the vessels found at Caroline were Spanish, loaded with sugar and hides, captured near Yaguana by the French, who threw all the crew overboard; and Gourgues, on reaching Florida, had two barks, evidently captured from the Spaniards, as to the fate of whose occupants his eulogists observe a discreet silence.

Ribault returned to his camp and held a council with his officers. Some were inclined to throw themselves on the mercy of Menendez; but the majority refused to surrender. The next morning Ribault came over with seventy officers and men, who decided to surrender and trust to the mercy of the merciless. The rest had turned southward, preferring to face new perils rather than be butchered.

The French commander gave up the banner of France and that of Coligny, with the colors of his force, his own fine set of armor, and his seal of office. As he and his comrades were bound, he intoned one of the Psalms; and after its concluding words added: "We are of earth, and to earth we must return; twenty years more or less is all but as a tale that is told." Then he bade Menendez do his will. Two young nobles, and a few men whom Menendez could make useful, he spared; the rest were at once despatched.[1]

The French who declined to surrender retreated unpursued to Cañaveral, where they threw up a log fort and began to build a vessel in order to escape from Florida. Menendez, recalling some of the men who remained at San Mateo, set out against them with one hundred and fifty men, three vessels following the shore with one hundred men to support his force. On the 8th of November apparently, he reached the fort. The French abandoned it and fled; but on promise that their lives should be spared, one hundred and fifty surrendered. Menendez kept his word. He destroyed their fort and vessel; and leaving a detachment of two hundred under Captain Juan Velez de Medrano to build Fort Santa Lucia de Cañaveral in a more favorable spot, he sailed to Havana. Finding some of his vessels there, he cruised in search of corsairs — chiefly French and English — who were said to be in great force off the coast of Santo Domingo, and who had actually captured one of his caravels; he was afraid that young Ribault might have joined them, and that he would attack the Spanish posts in Florida.[2] But encountering a vessel, Menendez learned that the King had sent him reinforcements, which he resolved to await, obtaining supplies from Campechy for his forts, as the Governor of Havana refused to furnish any.

The Spaniards in the three Florida posts were ill-prepared for even a Florida winter, and one hundred died for want of proper clothing and food. Captain San Vicente and other malcontents excited disaffection, so that

[1] This is the Spanish account of Solis de Meras. Lemoyne, who escaped from Caroline, gives an account based on the statement of a Dieppe sailor who made his way to the Indians, and though taken by the Spaniards, fell at last into French hands. Challeux, the carpenter of Caroline, and another account derived from Christophe le Breton, one of those spared by Menendez, maintain that Menendez promised La Caille, under oath and in writing, to spare their lives if they surrendered. This seems utterly improbable; for Menendez from first to last held to his original declaration, "*el que fuere herege morira.*" Lemoyne is so incorrect as to make this last slaughter take place at Caroline.

[2] Menendez to the King, — writing from Matanzas, Dec. 5, 1565; and again from Havana, Dec. 12, 1565. Barcia, *Ensaio cronológico,* p. 91.

mutinies broke out, and the insurgents seized vessels and deserted. Fort San Mateo was left with only twenty-one persons in it.

In February, 1566, Menendez explored the Tortugas and the adjacent coast, seeking some trace of the vessel in which his son had been lost. His search was fruitless; but he established friendly relations with the cacique Carlos, and rescued several Spanish prisoners from that cruel chief, who annually sacrificed one of them.

Meanwhile the French fugitives excited the Indians who were friendly to them to attack the Spanish posts; and it was no longer safe for the settlers to stir beyond the works at San Mateo and St. Augustine. Captain Martin de Ochoa, one of the bravest and most faithful officers, was slain at San Mateo; and Captain Diego de Hevia and several others were cut off at St. Augustine. Emboldened by success, the Indians invested the latter fort, and not only sent showers of arrows into it, but by means of blazing arrows set fire to the palmetto thatching of the storehouses. The Spaniards in vain endeavored to extinguish the flames; the building was consumed, with all their munitions, cloth, linen, and even the colors of the *adelantado* and the troops. This encouraged the Indians, who despatched every Spaniard they could reach.

Menendez reached St. Augustine, March 20, to find it on the brink of ruin. Even his presence and the force at his command could not bring the mutineers to obedience. He was obliged to allow Captain San Vicente and many others to embark in a vessel. Of the men whom at great labor and expense he had brought to Florida, full five hundred deserted. After their departure he restored order; and, proceeding to San Mateo, relieved that place. His next step was to enter into friendly relations with the chief of Guale, and to begin a fort of stockades, earth, and fascines at Port Royal which he called San Felipe. Here he left one hundred and ten men under Stephen de las Alas. From this point the adventurous Captain Pardo, in 1566 and the following year, explored the country, penetrating to the silver region of the Cherokees, and visiting towns reached by De Soto from Cofitachiqui to Tascaluza.[1]

Returning to St. Augustine, Menendez transferred the fort to its present position, to be nearer the ship landing and less exposed to the Indians. All the posts suffered from want of food; and even for the soldiers in the King's pay the *adelantado* could obtain no rations from Havana, although he went there in person. He obtained means to purchase the necessary provisions only by pledging his own personal effects.

Before his return there came a fleet of seventeen vessels, bearing fifteen hundred men, with arms, munitions, and supplies, under Sancho de Arciniega. Relief was immediately sent to San Mateo and to Santa Elena, where most

---

[1] Juan de la Vandera, *Memoir*, — in English in *Historical Magazine*, 1860, pp. 230–232, with notes by J. G. Shea, from the original in *Coleccion de documentos inéditos*, iv. 560–566, and in Buckingham Smith's *Coleccion*. There is also a version in B. F. French's *Historical Collections of Louisiana and Florida* (1875), p. 289.

of the soldiers had mutinied, and had put Stephen de las Alas in irons, and sailed away. Menendez divided part of his reinforcements among his three posts, and then with light vessels ascended the St. John's. He endeavored to enter into negotiations with the caciques Otina and Macoya; but those chiefs, fearing that he had come to demand reparation for the attacks on the Spaniards, fled at his approach. He ascended the river till he found the stream narrow, and hostile Indians lining the banks. On his downward voyage Otinà, after making conditions, received the *adelantado*, who came ashore with only a few attendants. The chief was surrounded by three hundred warriors; but showed no hostility, and agreed to become friendly to the Spaniards.

On his return Menendez despatched a captain with thirty soldiers and two Dominican friars to establish a post on Chesapeake Bay; they were accompanied by Don Luis Velasco, brother of the chief of Axacan, who had been taken from that country apparently by Villafañe, and who had been baptized in Mexico. Instead, however, of carrying out his plans, the party persuaded the captain of the vessel to sail to Spain.

Two Jesuit Fathers also came to found missions among the Indians; but one of them, Father Martinez, landing on the coast, was killed by the Indians; and the survivor, Father Rogel, with a lay brother, by the direction of Menendez began to study the language of the chief Carlos, in order to found a mission in his tribe. To facilitate this, Menendez sent Captain Reynoso to establish a post in that part of Florida.[1]

News having arrived that the French were preparing to attack Florida, and their depredations in the Antilles having increased, Menendez sailed to Porto Rico, and cruised about for a time, endeavoring to meet some of the corsairs. But he was unable to come up with any; and after visiting Carlos and Tequeste, where missions were now established, he returned to St. Augustine. His efforts, individually and through his lieutenants, to gain the native chiefs had been to some extent successful; Saturiba was the only cacique who held aloof. He finally agreed to meet Menendez at the mouth of the St. John's; but, as the Spanish commander soon learned, the cacique had a large force in ambush, with the object of cutting him and his men off when they landed. Finding war necessary, Menendez then sent four detachments, each of seventy men, against Saturiba; but he fled, and the Spaniards returned after skirmishes with small bands, in which they killed thirty Indians.

Leaving his posts well defended and supplied, Menendez sailed to Spain; and landing near Coruña, visited his home at Aviles to see his wife and family, from whom he had been separated twenty years. He then proceeded to Valladolid, where, on the 20th of July, he was received with honor by the King.

---

[1] Letter of Menendez, October 15, 1566, in Alcazar, *Chrono. historia de la Compañía de Jesus en la provincia de Toledo* (Madrid, 1710), vol. ii. dec. iii. año vi. cap. iii., translated by Dr. D. G. Brinton in the *Historical Magazine*, 1861, p. 292.

During his absence a French attack, such as he had expected, was made on Florida. Fearing this, he had endeavored to obtain forces and supplies for his colony; but was detained, fretting and chafing at the delays and formalities of the *Casa de Contratacion* in Seville.[1]

An expedition, comprising one small and two large vessels, was fitted out at Bordeaux by Dominic de Gourgues, with a commission to capture slaves at Benin. De Gourgues sailed Aug. 22, 1567, and at Cape Blanco had a skirmish with some negro chiefs, secured the harbor, and sailed off with a cargo of slaves. With these he ran to the Spanish West Indies, and disposed of them at Dominica, Porto Rico, and Santo Domingo, finding Spaniards ready to treat with him. At Puerto de la Plata, in the last island, he met a ready confederate in Zaballos, who was accustomed to trade with the French pirates. Zaballos bought slaves and goods from him, and furnished him a pilot for the Florida coast. Puerto de la Plata had been a refuge for some of the deserters from Florida, and could afford definite information. Here probably the idea of Gourgues' Florida expedition originated; though, according to the bombastic French account, it was only off the Island of Cuba that De Gourgues revealed his design. He reached the mouth of the St. John's, where the French narratives place two forts that are utterly unknown in Spanish documents, and which were probably only batteries to cover the entrance. Saluted here as Spanish, the French vessels passed on, and anchored off the mouth of the St. Mary's, — the Tacatacuru of the Indians. By means of a Frenchman, a refugee among the Indians, Gourgues easily induced Saturiba, smarting under the recent Spanish attack, to join him in a campaign against San Mateo. The first redoubt was quickly taken; and the French, crossing in boats, their allies swimming, captured the second, and then moved on Fort San Mateo itself. The French account makes sixty men issue from each of what it calls forts, each party to be cut off by the French, and then makes all of each party of sixty to fall by the hands of the French and Indians, except fifteen or thereabout kept for an ignominious death.

Gourgues carried off the artillery of the fort and redoubts; but before he could transport the rest of his booty to the vessels, a train left by the Spaniards in the fort was accidentally fired by an Indian who was cooking fish; the magazine blew up, with all in it. Gourgues hanged the prisoners who fell into his hands at San Mateo, and descending the river, hanged thirty more at the mouth, setting up an inscription: "Not as to Spaniards, but as to Traitors, Robbers, and Murderers." Returning to his vessels, he hoisted sail on the 3d of May, and early in June entered the harbor of La Rochelle. His loss, which is not explained, is said to have been his smallest vessel, five gentlemen and some soldiers killed.[2]

---

[1] Barcia, *Ensaio cronológico*, p. 133.

[2] *La Reprise de la Floride*, etc. Garibay says briefly that they went to Florida and destroyed and carried off the artillery of San Mateo, and then menaced Havana (*Sucesos de la Isla d̀ Santo Domingo*).

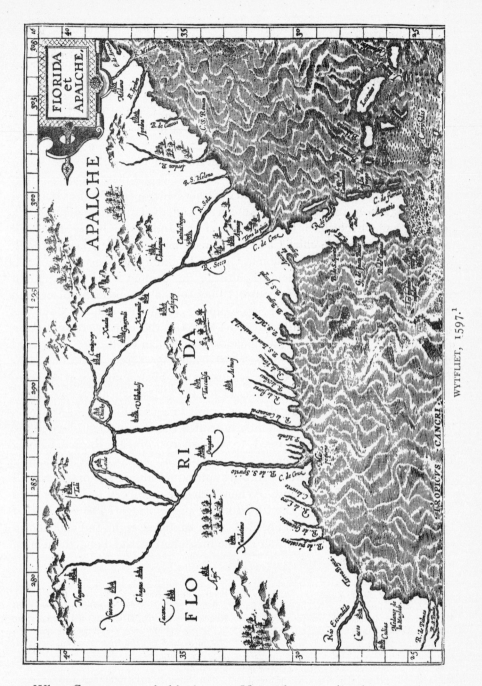

WYTFLIET, 1597.[1]

When Gourgues made his descent, Menendez was already at sea, having
sailed from San Lucar on the 13th of March, with abundant supplies and

[1] [Cf. the "Florida et Apalche" in Acosta, German edition, Cologne, 1598 (also in 1605); that of Hieronymus Chaves, given in Ortelius, 1592; and later the maps of the French cartographer Sanson, showing the coast from Texas to Carolina. — ED.]

reinforcements, as well as additional missionaries for the Indians, under Father John Baptist Segura as vice-provincial. After relieving his posts in Florida and placing a hundred and fifty men at San Mateo, he proceeded to Cuba, of which he had been appointed governor. To strengthen his colony, he solicited permission to colonize the Rio Pánuco; but the authorities in Mexico opposed his project, and it failed. The Mississippi, then known as the Espiritu Santo, was supposed to flow from the neighborhood of Santa Elena, and was depended on as a means of communication.[1] The next year the *adelantado* sent a hundred and ninety-three persons to San Felipe, and eighty to St. Augustine. Father Rogel then began missions among the Indians around Port Royal; Father Sedeño and Brother Baez began similar labors on Guale (now Amelia) Island, the latter soon compiling a grammar and catechism in the language of the Indians. Others attempted to bring the intractable chief Carlos and his tribe within the Christian fold. Rogel drew Indians to his mission at Orista; he put up houses and a church, and endeavored to induce them to cultivate the ground. But their natural fickleness would not submit to control; they soon abandoned the place, and the missionary returned to Fort San Felipe. A school for Indian boys was opened in Havana, and youths from the tribes of the coast were sent there in the hope of making them the nucleus of an Indian civilization. In 1570 Menendez, carrying out his project of occupying Chesapeake Bay, sent Father Segura with several other Jesuits to establish a mission at Axacan, the country of the Indian known as Don Luis Velasco, who accompanied missionaries, promising to do all in his power to secure for them a welcome from his tribe. The vessel evidently ascended the Potomac and landed the mission party, who then crossed to the shores of the Rappahannock. They were received with seeming friendship, and erected a rude chapel; but the Indians soon showed a hostile spirit, and ultimately massacred all the party except an Indian boy. When Menendez returned to Florida from Spain in 1572, he sailed to the Chesapeake, and endeavored to secure Don Luis and his brother; but they fled. He captured eight Indians known to have taken part in the murder of the missionaries, and hanged them at the yard-arm of his vessel.[2]

---

[1] *Parecer que da á S. M. la Audiencia de Nueva España*, Jan. 19, 1569. The fort at San Mateo was not immediately restored; a new fort, San Pedro, was established at Tacatacuru (*Coleccion de documentos inéditos*, xii. 307–308). Stephen de las Alas in 1570 withdrew the garrisons, except fifty men in each fort, — a step which led to official investigation (Ibid., xii. 309, etc.).

[2] Barcia, *Ensaio cronológico*, pp. 137–146. For the Jesuit mission in Florida, see Alegambe, *Mortes illustres*, pp. 44, etc.; Tanner, *Societas militans*, pp. 447–451; Letter of Rogel, Dec. 9, 1570, in the *Chrono. historia de la Compañia de Jesus en la Provincia de Toledo*, by Alcazar (Madrid, 1710), ii. 145, translated by Dr. D. G.

Brinton in the *Historical Magazine*, 1861, p. 327, and chap. v. of his *Floridian Peninsula;* Letter of Rogel, Dec. 2, 1569, MS.; one of Dec. 11, 1569, in *Coleccion de documentos inéditos*, xii. 301; one of Quiros and Segura from Axacan, Sept. 12, 1570; Sacchini, *Historia Societatis Jesu*, part iii., pp. 86, etc.

[Dr. Shea, in 1846, published a paper in the *United States Catholic Magazine*, v. 604 (translated into German in *Die Katolische Kirche in den V. S. von Nordamerika*, Regensburg, 1864, pp. 202–209), on the Segura mission; and another in 1859 in the *Historical Magazine*, iii. 268, on the Spanish in the Chesapeake from 1566 to 1573; and his account of a temporary Spanish

From this time Menendez gave little personal attention to the affairs of Florida, being elsewhere engaged by the King; and he died at Santander, in Spain, Sept. 17, 1574, when about to take command of an immense fleet which Philip II. was preparing. With his death Florida, where his nephew Pedro Menendez Marquez [1] had acted as governor, languished. Indian hostilities increased, San Felipe was invested, abandoned, and burned, and soon after the Governor himself was slain.[2] St. Augustine was finally burned by Drake.

CRITICAL ESSAY ON THE SOURCES OF INFORMATION.

OUR account of the voyages of Ponce de Leon is mainly from the *cédulas* to him and official correspondence, correcting Herrera,[3] who is supposed by some to have had the explorer's diary, now lost. Oviedo [4] mentions Bimini [5] as forty leagues from Guanahani. The modern edition [6] of Oviedo is vague and incorrect; and gives Ponce de Leon two caravels, but has no details. Gomara [7] is no less vague. Girava records the discovery, but dates it in 1512.[8] As early as 1519 the statement is found that the Bay of Juan Ponce had been visited by Alaminos, while accompanying Ponce de Leon,[9] — which must refer to this expedition of 1513. The "Traza de las costas" given by Navarrete (and reproduced by Buckingham Smith),[10] with the Garay patent of 1521, would seem to make Apalache Bay the western limit of the discoveries of Ponce de Leon, of whose expedition and of Alaminos's no report is known. Peter Martyr [11] alludes to it, but only incidentally, when treating of Diego Velasquez. Barcia, in his *Ensayo cronológico*,[12] writing specially on Florida, seems to have had neither of the patents of

settlement on the Rappahannock in 1570 is given in Beach's *Indian Miscellany*, or the "Log Chapel on the Rappahannock" in the *Catholic World*, March, 1875. Cf. present *History*, Vol. III. p. 167, and a paper on the "Early Indian History of the Susquehanna," by A. L. Guss, in the *Historical Register ; Notes and Queries relating to the Interior of Pennsylvania*, 1883, p. 115 *et seq.* De Witt Clinton, in a Memoir on the Antiquities of the Western Parts of New York, published at Albany in 1820, expressed an opinion that traces of Spanish penetration as far as Onondaga County, N. Y., were discoverable; but he omitted this statement in his second edition. Cf. Sabin, vol. iv. no. 13,718. — ED.]

[1] This officer, Fairbanks, in his misunderstanding of Spanish and Spanish authorities, transforms into Marquis of Menendez!

[2] Barcia, *Ensayo cronológico*, pp. 146–151.

[3] *Historia general de las Indias* (ed. 1601), dec. i. lib. ix. cap. 10–12, p. 303 (313).

[4] *Historia general* (1535), part i. lib. xix. cap. 15, p. clxii.

[5] [The Peter-Martyr map (1511) represents a land called Bimini ("illa de Beimeni" — see *ante* p. 110) in the relative position of Florida. The fountain of perpetual youth, the search

for which was a part of the motive of many of these early expeditions, was often supposed to exist in Bimini; but official documents make no allusion to the idle story. Dr. D. G. Brinton (*Floridian Peninsula*, p. 99) has collected the varying statements as to the position of this fountain. — ED.]

[6] Oviedo, Madrid (1850), lib. xvi. cap. 11, vol. i. p. 482.

[7] *Primera y segunda parte de la historia general de las Indias* (1553), cap. 45, folio xxiii.

[8] *Dos libros de cosmografia* (Milan, 1556), p. 192.

[9] Bernal Diaz, *Historia verdadera* (1632).

[10] *Cabeça de Vaca*, Washington, 1851. [It is also sketched *ante*, p. 218. — ED.]

[11] *De insulis nuper inventis* (Cologne, 1574), p. 349.

[12] *Ensayo cronológico para la historia general de la Florida, por Don Gabriel de Cardenas y Cano* [anagram for Don Andres Gonzales Barcia], Madrid, 1723. [He includes under the word "Florida" the adjacent islands as well as the main. Joseph de Salazars' *Crisis del ensayo cronológico* (1725) is merely a literary review of Barcia's rhetorical defects. Cf. Brinton's *Floridian Peninsula*, p. 51. — ED.]

Ponce de Leon, and no reports; and he places the discovery in 1512 instead of 1513.[1] Navarrete[2] simply follows Herrera.

In the unfortunate expedition of Cordova Bernal Diaz was an actor, and gives us a witness's testimony;[3] and it is made the subject of evidence in the suit in 1536 between the Pinzon and Colon families.[4] The general historians treat it in course.[5]

The main authority for the first voyage of Garay is the royal letters patent,[6] the documents which are given by Navarrete[7] and in the *Documentos inéditos*,[8] as well as the accounts given in Peter Martyr,[9] Gomara,[10] and Herrera.[11]

Of the pioneer expedition which Camargo conducted for Garay to make settlement of Amichel, and of its encounter with Cortés, we have the effect which the first tidings of it produced on the mind of the Conqueror of Mexico in his second letter of Oct. 30, 1520; while in his third letter he made representations of the wrongs done to the Indians by Garay's people, and of his own determination to protect the chiefs who had submitted to him.[12] For the untoward ending of Garay's main expedition, Cortés is still a principal dependence in his fourth letter;[13] and the official records of his proceedings against Garay in October, 1523, with a letter of Garay dated November 8, and evidently addressed to Cortés, are to be found in the *Documentos inéditos*,[14] while Peter Martyr,[15] Oviedo,[16] and Herrera[17] are the chief general authorities. Garay's renewed effort under his personal leadership is marked out in three several petitions which he made for authority to colonize the new country.[18]

---

[1] Barcia, in the *Introduccion a el Ensayo cronológico*, pp. 26, 27, discusses the date of Ponce de Leon's discovery. He refutes Remesal, Ayeta, and Moreri, who gave 1510, and adopts the date 1512 as given by the "safest historians," declaring that Ponce de Leon went to Spain in 1513. The date 1512 was adopted by Hakluyt, George Bancroft, and Irving; but after Peschel in his *Geschichte des Zeitalters der Entdeckungen* called attention to the fact that Easter Sunday in 1512 did not fall on March 27, the date given by Herrera, without mentioning the year, but that it did fall on that day in 1513, Kohl (*Discovery of Maine*, p. 240), George Bancroft, in later editions, and others adopted 1513, without any positive evidence. But 1512 is nevertheless clung to by Gravier in his "Route du Mississippi" (*Congrès des Américanistes*, 1878, i. 238), by Shipp in his *De Soto and Florida*, and by H. H. Bancroft in his *Central America* (vol. i. p. 128). Mr. Deane, in a note to Hakluyt's use of 1512 in the *Westerne Planting* (p. 230), says the mistake probably occurred "by not noting the variation which prevailed in the mode of reckoning time." The documents cited in chapter iv. settle the point. The *Capitulacion* under which Ponce de Leon sailed, was issued at Burgos, Feb. 23, 1512. He could not possibly by March 27 have returned to Porto Rico, equipped a vessel, and reached Florida. The letters of the King to Ceron and Diaz, in August and December 1512, show that Ponce de Leon, after returning to Porto Rico, was prevented from sailing, and was otherwise employed. The letter written by the King to the authorities in Española, July 4, 1513, shows that he had received from them information that Ponce de Leon had sailed in that year.

[2] *Coleccion* (*Viages menores*), iii. 50–53.

[3] *Historia verdadera* (1632), cap. vi. p. 4, verso.

[4] Duro, *Colon y Pinzon*, p. 268.

[5] Oviedo (ed. Amador de los Rios), lib. xxi. cap. 7, vol. ii. p. 139; Herrera, *Historia general*, dec. ii. p. 63; Navarrete, *Coleccion*, iii. 53; Barcia, *Ensayo cronológico*, p. 3; Peter Martyr, dec. iv. cap. 1; Torquemada, i. 350; Gomara, folio 9; Icazbalceta, *Coleccion*, i. 338.

[6] *Real cédula dando facultâd á Francisco de Garay para poblar la provincia de Amichel en la costa firme*, Burgos, 1521.

[7] *Coleccion*, iii. 147–153.

[8] *Coleccion de documentos inéditos*, ii. 558–567.

[9] *Decades*, dec. v. cap. 1.

[10] In his *Historia*.

[11] *Historia*, dec. ii. lib. x, cap. 18.

[12] [Cf. the bibliography of these letters in chap. vi. The notes in Brinton's *Floridian Peninsula* are a good guide to the study of the various Indian tribes of the peninsula at this time. — ED.]

[13] [Cf. chap. vi. of the present volume. — ED.]

[14] Vol. xxvi. pp. 77–135.

[15] Epis. June 20, 1524, in *Opus epistolarum*, pp. 471–476.

[16] *Historia*, lib. xxxiii. cap. 2, p. 263.

[17] *Historia*, dec. iii. lib. v. cap. 5. Cf. also Barcia, *Ensayo cronológico*, p. 8, and Galvano (Hakluyt Society's ed.), pp. 133, 153.

[18] *Coleccion de documentos inéditos*, x. 40–47; and the "testimonio de la capitulacion" in vol. xiv. pp. 503–516.

Of the preliminary expedition on the Atlantic coast of Gordillo and the subsequent attempt of his chief, Ayllon, to settle in Virginia, there is a fund of testimony in the papers of the suit which Matienzo instituted against Ayllon, and of which the greater part is still unprinted; but a few papers, like the complaint of Matienzo and some testimony taken by Ayllon when about to sail himself, can be found in the *Documentos inéditos*.[1] As regards the joint explorations of the vessels of Gordillo and Quexos, the testimony of the latter helps us, as well as his act of taking possession, which puts the proceeding in 1521; though some of Ayllon's witnesses give 1520 as the date. Both parties unite in calling the river which they reached the San Juan Bautista, and the *cédula* to Ayllon places it in thirty-five degrees. Navarrete in saying they touched at Chicora and Gualdape confounds the

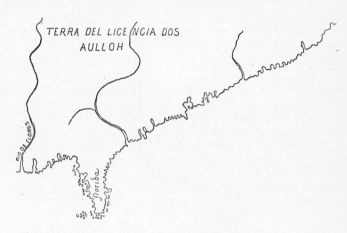

AYLLON'S EXPLORATIONS.[2]

first and third voyages; and was clearly ignorant of the three distinct expeditions;[3] and Herrera is wrong in calling the river the Jordan,[4] — named, as he says, after the captain or pilot of one of the vessels, — since no such person was on either vessel, and no such name appears in the testimony: the true Jordan was the Wateree (Guatari).[5] That it was the intention of Ayllon to make the expedition one of slave-catching, would seem to be abundantly disproved by his condemnation of the commander's act.[6]

Ayllon, according to Spanish writers, after reaching the coast in his own voyage, in 1526, took a northerly course. Herrera[7] says he attempted to colonize north of Cape Trafalgar (Hatteras); and the *piloto mayor* of Florida, Ecija, who at a later day, in 1609, was sent to find out what the English were doing, says positively that Ayllon had fixed his settlement at Guandape. Since by his office Ecija must have had in his possession the early charts of his people, and must have made the locality a matter of special study, his assertion has far greater weight than that

[1] Vol. xxxiv. pp. 563-567; xxxv. 547-562.

[2] [This sketch follows Dr. Kohl's copy of a map in a manuscript atlas in the British Museum (no. 9,814), without date; but it seems to be a record of the explorations (1520) of Ayllon, whose name is corrupted on the map. The map bears near the main inscription the figure of a Chinaman and an elephant, — tokens of the current belief in the Asiatic connections of North America. Cf. Brinton's *Floridian Peninsula*, p. 82, 99, on the "Traza de costas de Tierra Ferme y de las Tierras Nuevas," accompanying the royal grant to Garay in 1521, being the chart of Cristóbal de Tobia, given in the third volume of Navarrete's *Coleccion*, and sketched on another page of the present volume (*ante*, p. 218) in a section on "The Early Cartography of the Gulf of Mexico and adjacent Parts," where some light is thrown on contemporary knowledge of the Florida coast. — ED.]

[3] Vol. iii. p. 69. His conjectures and those of modern writers (Stevens, *Notes*, p. 48), accordingly require no examination. As the documents of the first voyage name both 33° 30' and 35° as the landfall, conjecture is idle.

[4] Dec. ii. lib. xi. cap. 6. This statement is adopted by many writers since.

[5] Pedro M. Marquez to the King, Dec. 12, 1586.

[6] Gomara, *Historia*, cap. xlii.; Herrera, *Historia*, dec. iii. lib. v. cap. 5.

[7] Vol. ii. lib. xxi. cap. 8 and 9.

of any historian writing in Spain merely from documents.[1] It is also the opinion of Navarrete [2] that Ayllon's course must have been north.

Oviedo [3] does not define the region of this settlement more closely than to say that it was under thirty-three degrees, adding that it is not laid down on any map. The Oydores of Santo Domingo, in a letter to the King in 1528,[4] only briefly report the expedition, and refer for particulars to Father Antonio Montesinos.[5]

The authorities for the voyage of Gomez are set forth in another volume.[6]

Upon the expedition of Narvaez, and particularly upon the part taken in it by Cabeza de Vaca, the principal authority is the narrative of the latter published at Zamora in 1542

AUTOGRAPH OF NARVAEZ
(*From Buckingham Smith*).

as *La relacion que dio Aluar Nuñez Cabeça de Vaca de lo acaescido en las Indias en la armada donde yua por gouernador Pãphilo de narbaez.*[7] It was reprinted at Valladolid in 1555, in an edition usually quoted as *La relacion y comentarios* [8] *del governador Aluar Nuñez Cabeça de Vaca de lo acaescido en las dos jornadas que hizo á los Indios.*[9] This edition was reprinted under the title of *Naufragios de Alvar Nuñez Cabeza de Vaca*, by Barcia (1749) in his *Historiadores primitivos,*[10] accompanied by an "exámen apologético de la historia" by Antonio Ardoino, which is a defence of Cabeza

de Vaca against the aspersions of Honorius Philoponus,[11] who charges Cabeza de Vaca with claiming to have performed miracles.

The *Relacion*, translated into Italian from the first edition, was included by Ramusio

[1] Ecija, *Relacion del viage* (June–September, 1609).

[2] Vol. iii. pp. 72-73. Recent American writers have taken another view. Cf. Brevoort, *Verrazano*, p. 70; Murphy, *Verrazzano*, p. 123.

[3] *Historia*, lib. xxxvii. cap. 1-4, in vol. iii. pp. 624-633.

[4] *Documentos inéditos*, iii. 347.

[5] Galvano (Hakluyt Society's ed., p. 144) gives the current account of his day.

[6] Cf. Vol. IV. p. 28. The *capitulacion* is given in the *Documentos inéditos*, xxii. 74.

[7] [Harrisse, *Bibl. Amer. Vet.*, no. 239; Sabin, vol. iii. no. 9,767. There is a copy in the Lenox Library. Cf. the *Relacion* as given in the *Documentos inéditos*, vol. xiv. pp. 265-279, and the "Capitulacion que se tomó con Panfilo de Narvaez" in vol. xxii. p. 224. There is some diversity of opinion as to the trustworthiness of this narrative; cf. Helps, *Spanish Conquest*, iv. 397, and Brinton's *Floridian Peninsula*, p. 17. "Cabeça has left an artless account of his recollections of the journey; but his memory sometimes

called up incidents out of their place, so that his narrative is confused." — BANCROFT: *History of the United States*, revised edition, vol. i. p. 31. — ED.]

[8] The *Comentarios* added to this edition were by Pero Hernandez, and relate to Cabeza de Vaca's career in South America.

[9] [There are copies of this edition in the Carter-Brown (*Catalogue*, vol. i. no. 197) and Harvard College libraries; cf. Sabin, vol. iii. no. 9,768. Copies were sold in the Murphy (no. 441), Brinley (no. 4,360 at $34), and Beckford (*Catalogue*, vol. iii. no. 183) sales. Rich (no. 28) priced a copy in 1832 at £4 4s. Leclerc (no. 2,487) in 1878 prices a copy at 1,500 francs; and sales have been reported at £21, £25, £39 10s., and £42. — ED.]

[10] [Vol. i. no. 6. Cf. Carter-Brown, iii. 893; Field, *Indian Bibliography*, no. 79. — ED.]

[11] [*Nova typis transacta navigatio Novi Orbis*, 1621. Ardoino's *Exámen apologético* was first published separately in 1736 (*Carter-Brown, iii. 545*). — ED.]

in his *Collection*[1] in 1556. A French version was given by Ternaux in 1837.[2] The earliest English rendering, or rather paraphrase, is that in Purchas;[3] but a more important version was made by the late Buckingham Smith, and printed (100 copies) at the expense of Mr. George W. Riggs, of Washington, in 1851, for private circulation.[4] A second edition was undertaken by Mr. Smith, embodying the results of investigations in Spain, with a revision of the translation and considerable additional annotation;

AUTOGRAPH OF CABEZA DE VACA
(*From Buckingham Smith*).

but the completion of the work of carrying it through the press, owing to Mr. Smith's death,[5] devolved upon others, who found his mass of undigested notes not very intelligible. It appeared in an edition of one hundred copies in 1871.[6] In these successive editions Mr. Smith gave different theories regarding the route pursued by Cabeza de Vaca in his nine years journey.[7]

The documents[8] which Mr. Smith adds to this new edition convey but little information beyond what can be gathered from Cabeza de Vaca himself. He adds, however, engravings of Father Juan Xuarez and Brother Juan Palos, after portraits preserved in Mexico of the twelve Franciscans who were first sent to that country.[9]

[1] Vol. iii. pp. 310–330.

[2] Following the 1555 edition, and published in his *Voyages*, at Paris.

[3] Vol. iv. pp. 1499–1556.

[4] [*Menzies Catalogue*, no. 315; Field, *Indian Bibliography*, nos. 227–229. — ED.]

[5] [Cf. Field, *Indian Bibliog.*, no. 364., — ED.]

[6] Printed by Munsell at Albany, at the charge of the late Henry C. Murphy. [Dr. Shea added to it a memoir of Mr. Smith, and Mr. T. W. Field a memoir of Cabeza de Vaca. — ED.]

[7] [The writing of his narrative, not during but after the completion of his journey, does not conduce to making the statements of the wanderer very explicit, and different interpretations of his itinerary can easily be made. In 1851 Mr. Smith made him cross the Mississippi within the southern boundary of Tennessee, and so to pass along the Arkansas and Canadian rivers to New Mexico, crossing the Rio Grande in the neighborhood of thirty-two degrees. In his second edition he tracks the traveller nearer the Gulf of Mexico, and makes him cross the Rio Grande near the mouth of the Conchos River in Texas, which he follows to the great mountain chain, and then crosses it. Mr. Bartlett, the editor of the *Carter-Brown Catalogue* (see vol. i. p. 188), who has himself tracked both routes, is

not able to decide between them. Davis, in his *Conquest of New Mexico*, also follows Cabeza de Vaca's route. H. H. Bancroft (*North Mexican States*, i. 63) finds no ground for the northern route, and gives (p. 67) a map of what he supposes to be the route. There is also a map in Paul Chaix' *Bassin du Mississipi au seizième siècle*. Cf. also L. Bradford Prince's *New Mexico* (1883), p. 89. — ED.] The buffalo and mesquite afford a tangible means of fixing the limits of his route.

[8] Including the petition of Narvaez to the King and the royal memoranda from the originals at Seville (p. 207), the instructions to the factor (p. 211), the instructions to Cabeza de Vaca (p. 218), and the summons to be made by Narvaez (p. 215). Cf. French's *Historical Collections of Louisiana*, second series, ii. 153; *Historical Magazine*, April, 1862, and January and August, 1867.

[9] Smith's *Cabeça de Vaca*, p. 100; Torquemada (*Monarquia Indiana*, 1723, iii. 437–447) gives Lives of these friars. Barcia says Xuarez was made a bishop; but Cabeza de Vaca never calls him bishop, but simply commissary, and the portrait at Vera Cruz has no episcopal emblems. Torquemada in his sketch of Xuarez makes no allusion to his being made a bishop,

Some additional facts respecting this expedition are derived at second hand from a letter which Cabeza de Vaca and Dorantes wrote after their arrival in Mexico to the *Audiencia* of Hispaniola, which is not now known, but of which the substance is professedly given by Oviedo.[1]

The Bahia de la Cruz of Narvaez' landing, made identical with Apalache Bay by Cabot, is likely to have been by him correctly identified, as the point could be fixed by the pilots who returned with the ships to Cuba, and would naturally be recorded on the charts.[2] Smith[3] believed it to be Tampa Bay. The *Relacion* describes the bay as one whose head could be seen from the mouth; though its author seems in another place to make it seven or eight leagues deep.[4] Narvaez and his party evidently thought they were nearer Panuco, and had no idea they were so near Havana. Had they been at Tampa Bay, or on a coast running north and south, they can scarcely be supposed to have been so egregiously mistaken.[5] If Tampa was his landing place, it is necessary to consider the bay where he subsequently built his boats as Apalache Bay.[6] Charlevoix[7] identifies it with Apalache Bay, and Siguenza y Gongora finds it in Pensacola.[8]

Of the expedition of Soto we have good and on the whole satisfactory records. The Concession made by the Spanish King of the government of Cuba and of the conquest of Florida is preserved to us.[9] There are three contemporary narratives of the progress of the march. The first and best was printed in 1557 at Evora as the *Relaçam verdadeira dos trabalhos q̃ ho gouernador dõ Fernãdo de Souto e certos fidalgos portugueses passarom no descobrimẽto da provincia da Frolida. Agora nouamente feita per hũ fidalgo Deluas.*[10] It is usually cited in English as the "Narrative of the Gentleman of Elvas,"

and the name is not found in any list of bishops. We owe to Mr. Smith another contribution to the history of this region and this time, in a *Coleccion de varios documentos para la historia de la Florida y tierras adyacentes,* — only vol. i. of the contemplated work appearing at Madrid in 1857. It contained thirty-three important papers from 1516 to 1569, and five from 1618 to 1794; they are for the most part from the Simancas Archives. This volume has a portrait of Ferdinand V., which is reproduced *ante*, p. 85. Various manuscripts of Mr. Smith are now in the cabinet of the New York Historical Society.

[1] Oviedo's account is translated in the *Historical Magazine*, xii. 141, 204, 267, 347. [H. H. Bancroft (*No. Mexican States*, i. 62) says that the collation of this account in Oviedo (vol. iii. pp. 582–618) with the other is very imperfectly done by Smith. He refers also to careful notes on it given by Davis in his *Spanish Conquest of New Mexico*, pp. 20–108. Bancroft (pp. 62, 63) gives various other references to accounts, at second hand, of this expedition. Cf. also L. P. Fisher's paper in the *Overland Monthly*, x. 514. Galvano's summarized account will be found in the Hakluyt Society's edition, p. 170. — ED.]

[2] Bancroft, *United States*, i. 27.

[3] *Cabeça de Vaca*, p. 58; cf. Fairbanks's *Florida*, chap. ii.

[4] *Cabeça de Vaca*, pp. 20, 204.

[5] [Tampa is the point selected by H. H. Bancroft (*No. Mexican States*, i. 60); cf. Brinton's note on the varying names of Tampa (*Floridian Peninsula*, p. 113). — ED.]

[6] B. Smith's *De Soto*, pp. 47, 234.

[7] *Nouvelle France*, iii. 473.

[8] Barcia, p. 308. The Magdalena may be the Apalachicola, on which in the last century Spanish maps laid down Echete; cf. Leroz, *Geographia de la America* (1758).

[9] The manuscript is in the Hydrographic Bureau at Madrid. The Lisbon Academy printed it in their (1844) edition of the Elvas narrative. Cf. Smith's *Soto*, pp. 266–272; *Historical Magazine*, v. 42; *Documentos inéditos*, xxii. 534. [It is dated April 20, 1537. In the following August Cabeza de Vaca reached Spain, to find that Soto had already secured the government of Florida; and was thence turned to seek the government of La Plata. It was probably before the tidings of Narvaez' expedition reached Spain that Soto wrote the letter regarding a grant he wished in Peru, which country he had left on the outbreak of the civil broils. This letter was communicated to the *Historical Magazine* (July, 1858, vol. ii. pp. 193–223) by Buckingham Smith, with a facsimile of the signature, given on an earlier page (*ante*, p. 253). — ED.]

[10] [Rich in 1832 (no. 34) cited a copy at £31 10s., which at that time he believed to be unique, and the identical one referred to by Pinelo as being in the library of the Duque de Sessa. There is a copy in the Grenville Collection, British Museum, and another is in the Lenox Library (B. Smith's *Letter of De Soto*, p. 66). It was reprinted at Lisbon in 1844 by the Royal Academy at Lisbon (Murphy, no. 1,004; Carter-Brown, vol. i. no. 596). Sparks says of it: "There is much show of exactness in regard to dates; but the account was evidently drawn up

since Hakluyt first translated it, and reprinted it in 1609 at London as *Virginia richly valued by the Description of the Mainland of Florida, her next Neighbor.*[1] It appeared again in 1611 as *The worthye and famous Historie of the Travailles, Discovery, and Conquest of Terra Florida*, and was included in the supplement to the 1809 edition of the Collection of Hakluyt. It was also reprinted from the 1611 edition in 1851 by the Hakluyt Society as *Discovery and Conquest of Florida*,[2] edited by William B. Rye, and is included in Force's *Tracts* (vol. iv.) and in French's *Historical Collections of Louisiana* (vol. ii. pp. 111–220). It is abridged by Purchas in his *Pilgrimes*.[3]

Another and briefer original Spanish account is the *Relacion del suceso de la jornada que hizo Hernando de Soto* of Luys Hernandez de Biedma, which long remained in manuscript in the Archivo General de Indias at Seville,[5] and was first published in a French

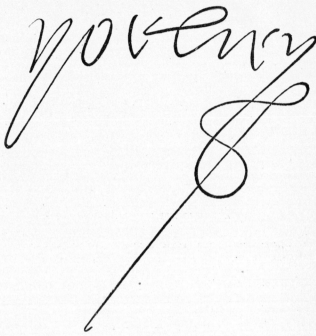

YO EL REY.[4]

for the most part from memory, being vague in its descriptions and indefinite as to localities, distances, and other points." Field says it ranks second only to the Relation of Cabeza de Vaca as an early authority on the Indians of this region. There was a French edition by Citri de la Guette in 1685, which is supposed to have afforded a text for the English translation of 1686 entitled *A Relation of the Conquest of Florida by the Spaniards* (see Field's *Indian Bibliography*, nos. 325, 340). These editions are in Harvard College Library. Cf. Sabin, *Dictionary*, vi. 488, 491, 492; Stevens, *Historical Collections*, i. 844; Field, *Indian Bibliography*, no. 1,274; Carter-Brown, vol. iii. nos. 1,324, 1,329; Arana, *Bibliografía de obras anónimas* (Santiago de Chile, 1882), no. 200. The Gentleman of Elvas is supposed by some to be Alvaro Fernandez; but it is a matter of much doubt (cf. Brinton's *Floridian Peninsula*, p. 20). There is a Dutch version in Gottfried and Vander Aa's *Zee- und Landreizen* (1727), vol. vii. (Carter-Brown, iii. 117). — ED.]

[1] [Carter-Brown, vol. ii. no. 86; Murphy, no. 1,118. Rich (no. 110) priced it in 1832 at £2 2s. — ED.]

[2] Field, *Indian Bibliography*, no. 1,338.

[3] [It is also in Vander Aa's *Versameling* (Leyden, 1706). The *Relaçam* of the Gentleman of Elvas has, with the text of Garcilasso de la Vega and other of the accredited narratives of that day, contributed to the fiction which, being published under the sober title of *Histoire naturelle et morale des Iles Antilles* (Rotterdam, 1658), passed for a long time as unimpeached history. The names of César de Rochefort and Louis de Poincy are connected with it as successive signers of the introductory matter. There were other editions of it in 1665, 1667, and 1681, with a title-edition in 1716. An English version, entitled *History of the Caribby Islands*, was printed in London in 1666. Cf. Duyckinck, *Cyclopædia of American Literature*, supplement, p. 12; Leclerc, nos. 1,332–1,335, 2,134–2,137. — ED.]

[4] [The sign-manual of Charles V. to the *Asiento y Capitulacion* granted to De Soto, 1537, as given by B. Smith in his *Coleccion*, p. 146. — ED.]

[5] [A copy of the original Spanish manuscript is in the Lenox Library. — ED.]

version by Ternaux in 1841;[1] and from this William B. Rye translated it for the Hakluyt Society.[2] Finally, the original Spanish text, "Relación de la Isla de la Florida," was published by Buckingham Smith in 1857 in his *Coleccion de varios documentos para ·la historia de la Florida.*[3]

AUTOGRAPH OF BIEDMA.[4]

In 1866 Mr. Smith published translations of the narratives of the Gentleman of Elvas and of Biedma, in the fifth volume (125 copies) of the Bradford Club Series under the title of *Narratives of the Career of Hernando de Soto in the Conquest of Florida, as told by a Knight of Elvas, and in a Relation* [presented 1544] *by Luys Hernandez de Biedma.*

The third of the original accounts is the *Florida del Ynca* of Garcilasso de la Vega, published at Lisbon in 1605,[5] which he wrote forty years after Soto's death, professedly to do his memory justice.[6] The spirit of exaggeration which prevails throughout the volume has deprived it of esteem as an historical authority, though Theodore Irving[7] and others have accepted it. It is based upon conversations with a noble Spaniard who had accompanied Soto as a volunteer, and upon the written but illiterate reports of two common soldiers, — Alonzo de Carmona, of Priego, and Juan Coles, of Zabra.[8] Herrera largely embodied it in his *Historia general.*

---

[1] *Recueil des pièces sur la Floride.*

[2] In the volume already cited, including Hakluyt's version of the Elvas narrative. It is abridged in French's *Historical Collections of Louisiana,* apparently from the same source.

[3] Pages 47–64. Irving describes it as "the confused statement of an illiterate soldier." Cf. *Documentos inéditos,* iii. 414.

[4] From the *Coleccion,* p. 64, of Buckingham Smith.

[5] [Carter-Brown, vol. ii. no. 42; Sunderland, vol. v. no. 12,815; Leclerc, no. 881, at 350 francs; Field, *Indian Bibliography* no. 587; Brinley, no. 4,353. Rich (no. 102) priced it in 1832 at £2 2s. — ED.]

[6] [Brinton (*Floridian Peninsula,* p. 23) thinks Garcilasso had never seen the Elvas narrative; but Sparks (*Marquette,* in *American Biography,* vol. x.) intimates that it was Garcilasso's only written source. — ED.]

[7] [Theodore Irving, *The Conquest of Florida by Hernando de Soto,* New York, 1851. The first edition appeared in 1835, and there were editions printed in London in 1835 and 1850. The book is a clever popularizing of the original sources, with main dependence on Garcilasso (cf. Field, *Indian Bibliography,* no. 765), whom its author believes he can better trust, especially as regards the purposes of De Soto, wherein he differs most

from the Gentleman of Elvas. Irving's championship of the Inca has not been unchallenged; cf. Rye's Introduction to the Hakluyt Society's volume. The Inca's account is more than twice as long as that of the Gentleman of Elvas, while Biedma's is very brief, — a dozen pages or so. Davis (*Conquest of New Mexico,* p. 25) is in error in saying that Garcilasso accompanied De Soto. — ED.]

[8] [There was an amended edition published by Barcia at Madrid in 1723 (Carter-Brown, iii. 328; Leclerc, no. 882, at 25 francs); again in 1803; and a French version by Pierre Richelet, *Histoire de la conquête de la Floride,* was published in 1670, 1709, 1711, 1731, 1735, and 1737 (Carter-Brown, vol. ii. no. 1,050; vol. iii. nos. 132, 470; O'Callaghan Catalogue, no. 965). A German translation by H. L. Meier, *Geschichte der Eroberung von Florida,* was printed at Zelle in 1753 (Carter-Brown, vol. iii. no. 997) with many notes, and again at Nordhausen in 1785. The only English version is that embodied in Bernard Shipp's *History of Hernando de Soto and Florida* (p. 229, etc.), — a stout octavo, published in Philadelphia in 1881. Shipp uses, not the original, but Richelet's version, the Lisle edition of 1711, and prints it with very few notes. His book covers the expeditions to North America between 1512 and 1568, taking Florida in its con-

Still another account of the expedition is the official Report which Rodrigo Ranjel, the secretary of Soto, based upon his Diary kept on the march. It was written after reaching Mexico, whence he transmitted it to the Spanish Government. It remained unpublished in that part of Oviedo's *History* which was preserved in manuscript till Amador de los Rios issued his edition of Oviedo in 1851. Oviedo seems to have begun to give the text of Ranjel as he found it; but later in the progress of the story he abridges it greatly, and two chapters at least are missing, which must have given the wanderings of Soto from Autiamque, with his death, and the adventures of the survivors under Mosçoso. The original text of Ranjel is not known.

These independent narratives of the Gentlemen of Elvas, Biedma, and Ranjel, as well as those used by Garcilasso de la Vega, agree remarkably, not only in the main narrative as to course and events, but also as to the names of the places.

There is also a letter of Soto, dated July 9, 1539, describing his voyage and landing, which was published by Buckingham Smith in 1854 at Washington,[1] following a transcript (in the Lenox Library) of a document in the Archives at Simancas, and attested by Muñoz. It is addressed to the municipality of Santiago de Cuba, and was first made known in Ternaux's *Recueil des pièces sur la Floride.* B. F. French gave the first English version of it in his *Historical Collections of Louisiana,* part ii. pp. 89–93 (1850).[2]

The route of De Soto is, of course, a question for a variety of views.[3] We have in the preceding narrative followed for the track through Georgia a paper read by Colonel Charles C. Jones, Jr., before the Georgia Historical Society, and printed in Savannah in 1880,[4] and for that through Alabama the data given by Pickett in his *History of Alabama,*[5] whose local knowledge adds weight to his opinion.[6] As to the point of De Soto's crossing the

tinental sense; but as De Soto is his main hero, he follows him through his Peruvian career. Shipp's method is to give large extracts from the most accessible early writers, with linking abstracts, making his book one mainly of compilation. — ED.]

[1] *Letter of Hernando de Soto, and Memoir of Hernando de Escalante Fontaneda.* [The transcript of the Fontaneda Memoir is marked by Muñoz "as a very good account, although it is by a man who did not understand the art of writing, and therefore many sentences are incomplete. On the margin of the original [at Simancas] are points made by the hand of Herrera, who doubtless drew on this for that part [of his *Historia general*] about the River Jordan which he says was sought by Ponce de Leon." This memoir on Florida and its natives was written in Spain about 1575. It is also given in English in French's *Historical Collection of Louisiana* (1875), p. 235, from the French of Ternaux; cf. Brinton's *Floridian Peninsula,* p. 26. The Editor appends various notes and a comparative statement of the authorities relative to the landing of De Soto and his subsequent movements, and adds a list of the original authorities on De Soto's expedition and a map of a part of the Floridian peninsula. The authorities are also reviewed by Rye in the Introduction to the Hakluyt Society's volume. Smith also printed the will of De Soto in the *Hist. Mag.* (May, 1861), v. 134. — ED.]

[2] [A memorial of Alonzo Vasquez (1560), asking for privileges in Florida, and giving evidences of his services under De Soto, is trans-

lated in the *Historical Magazine* (September, 1860), iv. 257. — ED.]

[3] [Buckingham Smith has considered the question of De Soto's landing in a paper, "Espiritu Santo," appended to his *Letter of De Soto* (Washington, 1854), p. 51. — ED.]

[4] [Colonel Jones epitomizes the march through Georgia in chap. ii. of his *History of Georgia* (Boston, 1883). In the *Annual Report* of the Smithsonian Institution, 1881, p. 619, he figures and describes two silver crosses which were taken in 1832 from an Indian mound in Murray County, Georgia, at a spot where he believed De Soto to have encamped (June, 1540), and which he inclines to associate with that explorer. Stevens (*History of Georgia,* i. 26) thinks but little positive knowledge can be made out regarding De Soto's route. — ED.]

[5] [Pages 25–41. Pickett in 1849 printed the first chapter of his proposed work in a tract called, *Invasion of the Territory of Alabama by One Thousand Spaniards under Ferdinand de Soto in* 1540 (Montgomery, 1849). Pickett says he got confirmatory information respecting the route from Indian traditions among the Creeks. — ED.]

[6] "We are satisfied that the Mauvila, the scene of Soto's bloody fight, was upon the north bank of the Alabama, at a place now called Choctaw Bluff, in the County of Clarke, about twenty-five miles above the confluence of the Alabama and Tombigbee" (Pickett, i. 27). The name of this town is written "Mauilla" by the Gentleman of Elvas, "Mavilla" by Biedma, but "Mabile"

Mississippi, there is a very general agreement on the lowest Chickasaw Bluff.[1] We are without the means, in any of the original sources, to determine beyond dispute the most

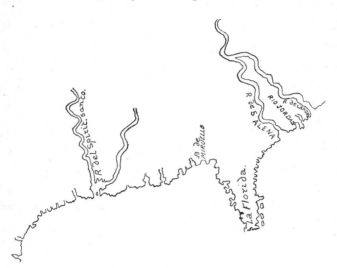

THE MISSISSIPPI, SIXTEENTH CENTURY.[2]

northerly point reached by Soto. He had evidently approached, but had learned nothing of, the Missouri River. Almost at the same time that Soto, with the naked, starving remnant of his army, was at Pacaha, another Spanish force under Vasquez de Coronado, well handled and perfectly equipped, must in July and August, 1541, have been encamped so near that an Indian runner in a few days might have carried tidings between them. Coronado actually heard of his countryman, and sent him a letter; but his messenger failed to find Soto's party.[3] But, strangely enough, the cruel, useless expedition of Soto finds ample space in history, while the well-managed march of Coronado's careful exploration finds scant mention.[4] No greater contrast exists in our history than that between these two campaigns.

A sufficient indication has been given, in the notes of the preceding narrative, of the sources of information concerning the futile attempts of the Spaniards at colonization on the Atlantic coast up to the time of the occupation of Port Royal by Ribault in 1562. Of the consequent bloody struggle between the Spanish Catholics and the French Huguenots there are original sources on both sides.

by Ranjel. The *u* and *v* were interchangeable letters in Spanish printing, and readily changed to *b*. (Irving, second edition, p. 261).

[1] Bancroft, *United States*, i. 51; Pickett, *Alabama*, vol. i.; Martin's *Louisiana*, i. 12; Nuttall's *Travels into Arkansas* (1819), p. 248; Fairbanks's *History of Florida*, chap. v.; Ellicott's *Journal*, p. 125; Belknap, *American Biography*, i. 192. [Whether this passage of the Mississippi makes De Soto its discoverer, or whether Cabeza de Vaca's account of his wandering is to be interpreted as bringing him, first of Europeans, to its banks, when on the 30th of October, 1528, he crossed one of its mouths, is a question in dispute, even if we do not accept the view that Alonzo de Pineda found its mouth in 1519 and called it Rio del Espiritu Santo (Navarrete, iii. 64). The arguments pro and con are examined by Rye in the Hakluyt Society's volume. Cf., besides the authorities above named, French's *Historical Collections of Louisiana*; Sparks's *Marquette*;

Gayarré's *Louisiana*; Theodore Irving's *Conquest of Florida*; Gravier's *La Salle*, chap. i., and his "Route du Mississipi" in *Congrès des Américanistes* (1877), vol. i.; De Bow's *Commercial Review*, 1849 and 1850; *Southern Literary Messenger*, December, 1848; *North American Review*, July, 1847. — ED.]

[2] [This sketch is from a copy in the Kohl Washington Collection, after a manuscript atlas in the Bodleian. It is without date, but seemingly of about the middle of the sixteenth century. The "B. de Miruello" seems to commemorate a pilot of Ponce de Leon's day. The sketch of the Atlantic coast made by Chaves in 1536 is preserved to us only in the description given by Oviedo, of which an English version will be found in the *Historical Magazine*, x. 371. — ED.]

[3] Jaramillo, in Smith's *Coleccion*, p. 160.

[4] [See chap. vii. on "Early Explorations of New Mexico." — ED.]

On the Spanish part we have the *Cartas escritas al rey* of Pedro Menendez (Sept. 11, Oct. 15, and Dec. 5, 1565), which are preserved in the Archives at Seville, and have been used by Parkman,[1] and the *Memoria del buen suceso i buen viage* of the chaplain of the expedition, Francisco Lopez de Mendoza Grajales.[2] Barcia's *Ensayo cronológico* is the most comprehensive of the Spanish accounts, and he gives a large part of the *Memorial de las jornadas* of Solis de Meras, a brother-in-law of Menendez. It has never been printed separately; but Charlevoix used Barcia's extract, and it is translated from Barcia in French's *Historical Collections of Louisiana and Florida* (vol. ii. p. 216). Barcia seems also to have had access to the papers of Menendez,[3] and to have received this Journal of Solis directly from his family.

On the French side, for the first expedition of Ribault in 1562 we have the very scarce text of the *Histoire de l'expédition Française en Floride*, published in London in 1563, which Hakluyt refers to as being in print "in French and English" when he wrote his *Westerne Planting*.[4] Sparks [5] could not find that it was ever published in French; nor was Winter Jones aware of the existence of this 1563 edition when he prepared for the Hakluyt Society an issue of Hakluyt's *Divers Voyages* (1582), in which that collector had included an English version of it as *The True and Last Discoverie of Florida, translated into Englishe by one Thomas Hackit*, being the same text which appeared separately in 1563 as the *Whole and True Discovery of Terra Florida*.[6]

At Paris in 1586 appeared a volume, dedicated to Sir Walter Raleigh, entitled, *L'histoire notable de la Floride, . . . contenant les trois voyages faits en icelle par certains capitaines et pilotes François descrits par le Capitaine Laudonnière, . . . à laquelle a esté adjousté un quatriesme voyage fait par le Capitaine Gourgues, Mise en lumiere par M. Basanier.* This was a comprehensive account, or rather compilation, of the four several French expeditions, — 1562, 1564, 1565, 1567, — covering the letters of Laudonnière for the first three, and an anonymous account, perhaps by the editor Basanier, of the fourth. Hakluyt, who had induced the French publication, gave the whole an English dress in his *Notable History*, *translated by R. H.*, printed in London in 1587,[7] and again in his *Principall Navigations*, vol. iii., the text of which is also to be found in the later edition and in French's *Historical Collections of Louisiana and Florida* (1869), i. 165.[8]

---

[1] *Pioneers of France in the New World*; cf. Gaffarel, *La Floride Française*, p. 341.

[2] There is a French version in Ternaux' *Recueil de la Floride*, and an English one in French's *Historical Collections of Louisiana and Florida* (1875), ii. 190. The original is somewhat diffuse, but is minute upon interesting points.

[3] Cf. Sparks, *Ribault*, p. 155; Field, *Indian Bibliography*, p. 20. Fairbanks in his *History of St. Augustine* tells the story, mainly from the Spanish side.

[4] Edited by Charles Deane for the Maine Historical Society, pp. 20, 195, 213.

[5] *Life of Ribault*, p. 147.

[6] [This original English edition (a tract of 42 pages) is extremely scarce. There is a copy in the British Museum, from which Rich had transcripts made, one of which is now in Harvard College Library, and another is in the Carter-Brown Collection (cf. Rich, 1832, no. 40; Carter-Brown, i. 244). The text, as in the *Divers Voyages*, is reprinted in French's *Historical Collections of Louisiana and Florida* (1875), p. 159. Ribault supposed that in determining to cross the ocean in a direct westerly course, he was the first to make such an attempt, not knowing that Verrazano had already done so. Cf. Brevoort, *Verrazano*, p. 110; Hakluyt, *Divers Voyages*, edition by J. W. Jones, p. 95. See also Vol. III. p. 172. — ED.]

[7] [This is the rarest of Hakluyt's publications, the only copy known in America being in the Lenox Library (Sabin, vol. x. no. 39,236) — ED.]

[8] [Brinton, *Floridian Peninsula*, p. 39. The original French text was reprinted in Paris in 1853 in the *Bibliothèque Elzévirienne;* and this edition is worth about 30 francs (Field, *Indian Bibliography*, no. 97; Sabin, vol. x. no. (39,235). The edition of 1586 was priced by Rich in 1832 at £5 5s., and has been sold of late years for $250, £63, and 1,500 francs. Cf. Leclerc, no. 2,662; Sabin, vol. x. no. 39,234; Carter-Brown, i. 366; Court, nos. 27, 28; Murphy, no. 1,442; Brinley, vol. iii. no. 4,357; Field, *Indian Bibliography*, p. 24. Gaffarel in his *La Floride Française* (p. 347) gives the first letter entire, and parts of the second and third, following the 1586 edition. — ED.]

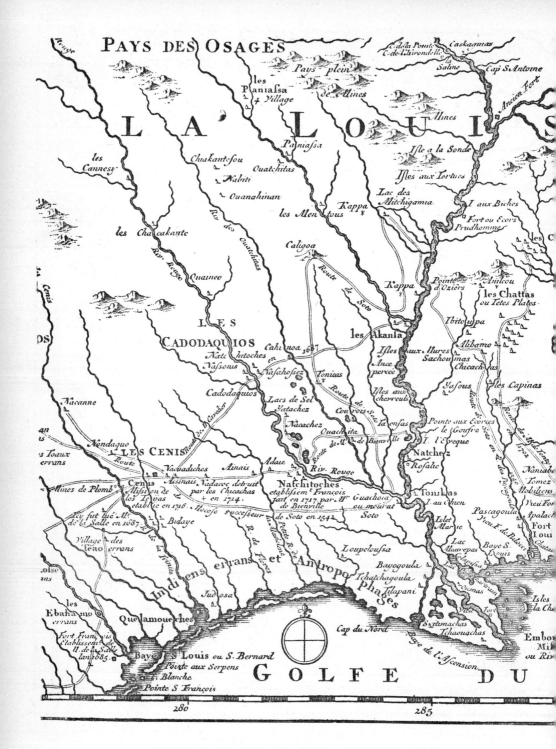

ROUTE OF DE SOTO (*after Delisle*), — WESTERLY PART.[1]

[1] [This map of Delisle, issued originally at Paris, is given in the Amsterdam (1707) edition of Garcilasso de la Vega's *Histoire des Incas et de* *la conquête de la Floride*, vol. ii; cf. *Voyages au nord*, vol. v., and Delisle's *Atlas nouveau*. The map is also reproduced in French's *Historical*

ROUTE OF DE SOTO (*after Delisle*),—EASTERLY PART.

Collections of Louisiana, and Gravier's *La Salle*
(1870). Other maps of the route are given by
Rye, McCulloch, and Irving; by J. C. Brevoort

in Smith's *Narratives of Hernando de Soto*, and in
Paul Chaix' *Bassin du Mississipi au seizième siècle*.
Besides the references already noted, the ques-

Jacques Lemoyne de Morgues, an artist accompanying Laudonnière, wrote some years later an account, and made maps and drawings, with notes describing them. De Bry made a visit to London in 1587 to see Lemoyne, who was then in Raleigh's service; but Lemoyne resisted all persuasions to part with his papers.[1] After Lemoyne's death De Bry bought them of his widow (1588), and published them in 1591, in the second part of his *Grands voyages*, as *Brevis narratio*.[2]

One Nicolas le Challeux, or Challus, a carpenter, a man of sixty, who was an eye-witness of the events at Fort Caroline, and who for the experiences of Ribault's party took the statements of Dieppe sailors and of Christopher le Breton, published a simple narrative at Dieppe in 1566 under the title of *Discours de l'histoire de la Floride*, which was issued twice, — once with fifty-four, and a second time with sixty-two, pages,[3] and the same year reprinted, with some variations, at Lyons as *Histoire mémorable du dernier voyage fait par le Capitaine Iean Ribaut en l'an MDLXV* (pp. 56).[4]

tion of his route has been discussed, to a greater or less extent, in Charlevoix' *Nouvelle France ;* in Warden's *Chronologie historique de l'Amérique*, where the views of the geographer Homann are cited ; in Albert Gallatin's "Synopsis of the Indian Tribes" in the *Archæologia Americana*, vol. ii. ; in Nuttall's *Travels in Arkansas* (1819 and 1821); in Williams's *Florida* (New York, 1837); in McCulloch's *Antiquarian Researches in America* (Baltimore, 1829) ; in Schoolcraft's *Indian Tribes*, vol. iii. ; in Paul Chaix' *Bassin du Mississipi au seizième siècle ;* in J. W. Monette's *Valley of the Mississippi* (1846) ; in Pickett's *Alabama;* in Gayarré's *Louisiana ;* in Martin's *Louisiana ;* in *Historical Magazine*, v. 8 ; in *Knickerbocker Magazine*, lxiii. 457; in *Sharpe's Magazine*, xlii. 265 ; and in Lambert A. Wilmer's *Life of De Soto* (1858). Although Dr. Belknap in his *American Biography* (1794, vol. i. p. 189), had sought to establish a few points of De Soto's march, the earliest attempt to track his steps closely was made by Alexander Meek, in a paper published at Tuscaloosa in 1839 in *The Southron*, and reprinted as "The Pilgrimage of De Soto," in his *Romantic Passages in Southwestern History* (Mobile, 1857), p. 213. Irving, in the revised edition of his *Conquest of Florida*, depended largely upon the assistance of Fairbanks and Smith, and agrees mainly with Meek and Pickett. In his appendix he epitomizes the indications of the route according to Garcilasso and the Portuguese gentleman. Rye collates the statements of McCulloch and Monette regarding the route beyond the Mississippi, and infers that the identifying of the localities is almost impossible. Chaix (*Bassin du Mississipi*) also traces this part. — ED.]

[1] Cf. Stevens *Bibliotheca historica* (1870,) p. 224 ; Brinton, *Floridian Peninsula*, p. 32.

[2] *Brevis narratio eorum quæ in Florida Americæ proviĭa Gallis acciderunt, secunda in illam Navigatione, duce Renato de Laudoñiere classis Præfecto: anno MDLXIIII. Quæ est secunda pars Americæ. Additæ figuræ et Incolarum eicones ibidem ad vivŭ expressæ, brevis*

etiam declaratio religionis, rituum, vivendique ratione ipsorum. Auctore Iacobo Le Moyne, cui cognomen de Morgues, Laudoñierum in ea Navigatione Sequnto. [There was a second edition of the Latin (1609) and two editions in German (1591 and 1603), with the same plates. Cf. Carter-Brown, vol. i. nos. 399, 414 ; Court, no. 243 ; Brinley, vol. iii. no. 4,359. The original Latin of 1591 is also found separately, with its own pagination, and is usually in this condition priced at about 100 francs. It is supposed to have preceded the issue as a part of De Bry (Dufossé, 1878, nos. 3,691, 3,692).

The engravings were reproduced in heliotypes ; and with the text translated by Frederick B. Perkins, it was published in Boston in 1875 as the *Narrative of Le Moyne, an Artist who accompanied the French Expedition to Florida under Laudonnière*, 1564. These engravings have been in part reproduced several times since their issue, as in the *Magazin pittoresque*, in *L'univers pittoresque*, in Pickett's *Alabama*, etc. — ED.]

[3] Sabin, vol. x. no. 39,631–32 ; Carter-Brown, i. 262.

[4] [Sabin, vol. x. no. 39,634 ; Carter-Brown, vol. i. no. 263. An English translation, following the Lyons text, was issued in London in 1566 as *A True and Perfect Description of the Last Voyage of Ribaut*, of which only two copies are reported by Sabin, — one in the Carter-Brown Library (vol. i. no. 264), and the other in the British Museum. This same Lyons text was included in Ternaux' *Reçueil de pièces sur la Floride* and in Gaffarel's *La Floride Française*, p. 457 (cf. also pp. 337–339), and it is in part given in Cimber and Danjon's *Archives curieuses de l'histoire de France* (Paris, 1835), vi. 200. The original Dieppe text was reprinted at Rouen in 1872 for the Société Rouennaise de Bibliophiles, and edited by Gravier under the title: *Deuxième voyage du Dieppois Jean Ribaut à la Floride en* 1565, *précédé d'une notice historique et bibliographique.* Cf. Brinton, *Floridian Peninsula*, p. 30. — ED.]

It is thought that Thevet in his *Cosmographie universelle* (1575) may have had access to Laudonnière's papers; and some details from Thevet are embodied in what is mainly a translation of Le Challeux, the *De Gallorum expeditione in Floridam anno MDLXV brevis historia*, which was added (p. 427) by Urbain Chauveton, or Calveton, to the Latin edition of Benzoni, — *Novæ novi orbis historiæ tres libri*, printed at Geneva in 1578 and 1581,[1] and reproduced under different titles in the French versions, published likewise at Geneva in 1579, 1588, and 1589.[2] There is a separate issue of it from the 1579 edition.[3]

It was not long before exaggerated statements were circulated, based upon the representations made in *Une requête au roi* (Charles IX.) of the widows and orphans of the victims of Menendez, in which the number of the slain is reported at the impossible figure of nine hundred.[4]

Respecting the expedition of De Gourgues there are no Spanish accounts whatever, Barcia[5] merely taking in the main the French narrative, — in which, says Parkman, " it must be admitted there is a savor of romance."[6] That Gourgues was merely a slaver is evident from this full French account. Garibay notes his attempt to capture at least one Spanish vessel; and he certainly had on reaching Florida two barks, which he must have captured on his way. Basanier and many who follow him suppress entirely the slaver episode in this voyage. All the De Gourgues narratives ignore entirely the existence of St. Augustine, and make the three pretended forts on the St. John to have been of stone; and Prévost, to heighten the picture, invents the story of the flaying of Ribault, of which there is no trace in the earlier French accounts.

There are two French narratives. One of them, *La reprinse de la Floride*, exists, according to Gaffarel,[7] in five different manuscript texts.[8] The other French narrative

---

[1] [O'Callaghan, no. 463; Rich (1832), no. 60. There was an edition at Cologne in 1612 (Stevens, *Nuggets*, no. 2,300; Carter-Brown, ii. 123). Sparks (*Life of Ribault*, p. 152) reports a *De navigatione Gallorum in terram Floridam* in connection with an Antwerp (1568) edition of Levinus Apollonius. It also appears in the same connection in the joint German edition of Benzoni, Peter Martyr, and Levinus printed at Basle in 1582 (Carter-Brown, vol. i. no. 344). It may have been merely a translation of Challeux or Ribault (Brinton, *Floridian Peninsula*, p. 36) — ED.].

[2] Murphy, nos. 564, 2,853.

[3] Sabin, vol. x. no. 39,630; Carter-Brown, vol. i. no. 330; Dufossé, no. 4,211.

[4] This petition is known as the *Epistola supplicatoria*, and is embodied in the original text in Chauveton's French edition of Benzoni. It is also given in Cimber and Danjon's *Archives curieuses*, vi. 232, and in Gaffarel's *Floride Française*, p. 477; and in Latin in De Bry, parts ii. and vi. (cf. Sparks's *Ribault*, appendix). [There are other contemporary accounts or illustrations in the "Lettres et papiers d'état du Sieur de Forquevaulx," for the most part unprinted, and preserved in the Bibliothèque Nationale in Paris, which were used by Du Prat in his *Histoire d'Élisabeth de Valois* (1859), and some of which are printed in Gaffarel, p. 409. The nearly contemporary accounts of Popellinière in his *Trois mondes* (1582) and in the

VOL. II. — 38.

Histoire universelle of De Thou, represent the French current belief. The volume of Ternaux' *Voyages* known as *Recueil de pièces sur la Floride inédites*, contains, among eleven documents, one called *Coppie d'une lettre venant de la Floride*, ... *ensemble le plan et portraict du fort que les François y ont faict* (1564), which is reprinted in Gaffarel and in French's *Historical Collections of Louisiana and Florida*, vol. iii. This tract, with a plan of the fort on the sixth leaf, *recto*, was originally printed at Paris in 1565 (Carter-Brown, i. 256). None of the reprints give the engravings. It was seemingly written in the summer of 1564, and is the earliest account which was printed. — ED.]

[5] *Ensayo cronológico.*

[6] [Parkman, however, inclines to believe that Barcia's acceptance is a kind of admission of its "broad basis of truth." — ED.]

[7] Page 340. Cf. *Manuscrits de la Bibliothèque du Roi*, iv. 72.

[8] [They are: *a.* Preserved in the Château de Vayres, belonging to M. de Bony, which is presumably that given as belonging to the Gourgues family, of which a copy, owned by Bancroft, was used by Parkman. It was printed at Mont-de-Marsan, 1851, 63 pages.

b. In the Bibliothèque Nationale, no. 1,886. Printed by Ternaux-Compans in his *Recueil*, etc., p. 301, and by Gaffarel, p. 483, collated with the other manuscripts and translated into English in French's *Historical Collections of Louisiana and*

is the last paper in the compilation of Basanier, already mentioned. Brinton [1] is inclined to believe that it is not an epitome of the *Reprinse*, but that it was written by Basanier himself from the floating accounts of his day, or from some unknown relater. Charlevoix mentions a manuscript in the possession of the De Gourgues family; but it is not clear which of these papers it was.

The story of the Huguenot colony passed naturally into the historical records of the seventeenth century; [2] but it got more special treatment in the next century, when Charlevoix issued his *Nouvelle France*.[3] The most considerable treatments of the present century have been by Jared Sparks in his *Life of Ribault*,[4] by Francis Parkman in his *Pioneers of France in the New World*,[5] and by Paul Gaffarel in his *Histoire de la Floride Française*.[6] The story has also necessarily passed into local and general histories of this period in America, and into the accounts of the Huguenots as a sect.[7]

John Gilmary Shea

Florida, ii. 267. This copy bears the name of Robert Prévost; but whether as author or copyist is not clear, says Parkman (p. 142).

c. In the Bibliothèque Nationale, no. 2,145. Printed at Bordeaux in 1867 by Ph. Tamizey de Larroque, with preface and notes, and giving also the text marked *e* below.

d. In the Bibliothèque Nationale, no. 3,384. Printed by Taschereau in the *Revue rétrospective* (1835), ii. 321.

e. In the Bibliothèque Nationale, no. 6,124. See *c* above.

The account in the *Histoire notable* is called an abridgment by Sparks, and of this abridgment there is a Latin version in De Bry, part ii., — *De quarta Gallorum in Floridam navigatione sub Gourguesio.* See other abridgments in Popellinière, *Histoire des trois mondes* (1582), Lescarbot, and Charlevoix.

[1] *Floridian Peninsula*, p. 35.

[2] Such as Wytfliet's *Histoire des Indes;* D'Aubigné's *Histoire universelle* (1626); De Laet's *Novus orbis*, book iv.; Lescarbot's *Nouvelle France;* Champlain's *Voyages;* Brantôme's *Grands capitaines François* (also in his *Œuvres*). Faillon (*Colonie Française*, i. 543) bases his account on Lescarbot.

[3] Cf. Shea's edition with notes, where (vol. i.

p. 71) Charlevoix characterizes the contemporary sources; and he points out how the Abbé du Fresnoy, in his *Méthode pour étudier la géographie*, falls into some errors.

[4] *American Biography*, vol. vii. (new series).

[5] Boston, 1865. Mr. Parkman had already printed parts of this in the *Atlantic Monthly*, xii. 225, 536, and xiv. 530.

[6] Paris, 1875. He gives (p. 517) a succinct chronology of events.

[7] Cf., for instance, Bancroft's *United States*, chap. ii.; Gay's *Popular History of the United States*, chap. viii.; Warburton's *Conquest of Canada*, app. xvi.; Conway Robinson's *Discoveries in the West*, ii. chap. xvii. *et seq;* Kohl's *Discovery of Maine;* Fairbanks's *Florida;* Brinton's *Floridian Peninsula*, — among American writers; and among the French, — Guérin, *Les navigateurs Français* (1846); Ferland, *Canada;* Martin, *Histoire de France;* Haag, *La France protestante;* Poussielgue, "Quatre mois en Floride," in *Le tour du monde*, 1869-1870; and the Lives of Coligny by Tessier, Besant, and Laborde. There are other references in Gaffarel, p. 344.

There is a curious article, "Dominique de Gourgues, the Avenger of the Huguenots in Florida, a Catholic," in the *Catholic World*, xxi. 701.

CHAPTER V.

LAS CASAS, AND THE RELATIONS OF THE SPANIARDS TO THE INDIANS.

BY GEORGE EDWARD ELLIS,

Vice-President of the Massachusetts Historical Society.

WHEN the great apostle of the new faith, on his voyage from Asia to Europe, was shipwrecked on a Mediterranean island, " the barbarous people" showed him and his company " no little kindness." On first acquaintance with their chief visitor they hastily judged him to be a murderer, whom, though he had escaped the sea, yet vengeance would not suffer to live. But afterward " they changed their minds, and said that he was a god." [1] The same extreme revulsion of feeling and judgment was wrought in the minds of the natives of this New World when the ocean-tossed voyagers from the old continent first landed on these shores, bringing the parted representatives of humanity on this globe into mutual acquaintance and intercourse. Only in this latter case the change of feeling and judgment was inverted. The simple natives of the fair western island regarded their mysterious visitors as superhuman beings; further knowledge of them proved them to be " murderers," rapacious, cruel, and inhuman, — fit subjects for a dire vengeance.

In these softer times of ours the subject of the present chapter might well be passed silently, denied a revival, and left in the pitiful oblivion which covers so many of the distressing horrors of " man's inhumanity to man." But, happily for the writer and for the reader, the title of the chapter is a double one, and embraces two themes. The painful narrative to be rehearsed is to be relieved by a tribute of admiring and reverential homage to a saintly man of signal virtues and heroic services, one of the grandest and most august characters in the world's history. Many of the obscure and a few of the dismal elements and incidents of long-passed times, in the rehearsal of them on fresh pages, are to a degree relieved by new light thrown upon them, by the detection and exposure of errors, and by

---

[1] *The Acts of the Apostles*, xxviii. 2–6.

readjustments of truth.   Gladly would a writer on the subject before us avail himself of any such means to reduce or to qualify its repulsiveness. But advancing time, with the assertion of the higher instincts of humanity which have sharpened regrets and reproaches for all the enormities of the past, has not furnished any abatements for the faithful dealing with this subject other than that just presented.

It is a fact worthy of a pause for thought, that in no single instance since the discovery of our islands and continent by Europeans — to say nothing about the times before it — has any new race of men come to the knowledge of travellers, explorers, and visitors from the realms of so-called civilization, when the conditions were so fair and favorable in the first introduction and acquaintance between the parties as in that between Columbus and the natives of the sea-girt isle of Hispaniola.   Not even in the sweetest idealizings of romance is there a more fascinating picture than that which he draws of those unsophisticated children of Nature, their gentleness, docility, and friendliness.   They were not hideous or repulsive, as barbarians; they did not revolt the sight, like many of the African tribes, like Bushmen, Feejeans, or Hottentots; they presented no caricaturings of humanity, as giants or dwarfs, as Amazons or Esquimaux; their naked bodies were not mutilated, gashed, or painted; they uttered no yells or shrieks, with mad and threatening gestures.   They were attractive in person, well formed, winning and gentle, and trustful; they were lithe and soft of skin, and their hospitality was spontaneous, generous, and genial.   Tribes of more warlike and less gracious nature proved to exist on some of the islands, about the isthmus and the continental regions of the early invasion; but the first introduction and intercourse of the representatives of the parted continents set before the Europeans a race of their fellow-creatures with whom they might have lived and dealt in peace and love.

And what shall we say of the new-comers, the Spaniards, — the subjects of the proudest of monarchies, the representatives of the age of chivalry; gentlemen, nobles, disciples of the one Holy Catholic Church, and soldiers of the Cross of Christ?   What sort of men were they, what was their errand, and what impress did they leave upon the scenes so fair before their coming, and upon those children of Nature whom they found so innocent and loving, and by whom they were at first gazed upon with awe and reverence as gods?

In only one score of the threescore years embraced in our present subject the Spaniards had sown desolation, havoc, and misery in and around their track.   They had depopulated some of the best-peopled of the islands, and renewed them with victims deported from others.   They had inflicted upon hundreds of thousands of the natives all the forms and agonies of fiendish cruelty, driving them to self-starvation and suicide as a way of mercy and release from an utterly wretched existence.   They had come to be viewed by their victims as fiends of hate, malignity, and all dark and cruel desperation and mercilessness in passion.   The hell which they denounced upon their victims was shorn of its worst terror by the assurance that these tormentors were not to be there.

Only what is needful for the truth of history is to be told here, while shocking details are to be passed by. And as the rehearsal is made to set forth in relief the nobleness, grandeur of soul, and heroism of a man whose nearly a century of years was spent in holy rebuke, protest, exposure, and attempted redress of this work of iniquity, a reader may avert his gaze from the narration of the iniquity and fix it upon the character and career of the " Apostle to the Indians."

There was something phenomenal and monstrous, something so aimless, reckless, wanton, unprovoked, utterly ruinous even for themselves, in that course of riot and atrocity pursued by the Spaniards, which leads us — while palliation and excuse are out of the question — to seek some physical or moral explanation of it. This has generally been found in referring to the training of Spanish nature in inhumanity, cruelty, contempt of human life, and obduracy of feeling, through many centuries of ruthless warfare. It was in the very year of the discovery of America that the Spaniards, in the conquest of Granada, had finished their eight centuries of continuous war for wresting their proud country from the invading Moors. This war had made every Spaniard a fighter, and every infidel an enemy exempted from all tolerance and mercy. Treachery, defiance of pledges and treaties, brutalities, and all wild and reckless stratagems, had educated the champions of the Cross and faith in what were to them but the accomplishments of the soldier and the fidelity of the believer. Even in the immunities covenanted to the subject-Moors, of tolerance in their old home and creed, the ingenuities of their implacable foes found the means of new devices for oppression and outrage. The Holy Office of the Inquisition, with all its cavernous secrets and fiendish processes, dates also from the same period, and gave its fearful consecration to all the most direful passions.

With that training in inhumanity and cruelty which the Spanish adventurers brought to these shores, we must take into view that towering, overmastering rapacity and greed which were to glut themselves upon the spoils of mines, precious stones, and pearls. The rich soil, with the lightest tillage, would have yielded its splendid crops for man and beast. Flocks would have multiplied and found their own sustenance for the whole year without any storage in garner, barn, or granary. A rewarding commerce would have enriched merchants on either side of well-traversed ocean pathways. But not the slightest thought or recognition was given during the first half-century of the invasion to any such enterprise as is suggested by the terms colonization, the occupancy of soil for husbandry and domestication. Spanish pride, indolence, thriftlessness regarded every form of manual labor as a demeaning humiliation. There was no peasantry among the new-comers. The humblest of them in birth, rank, and means was a gentleman; his hands could not hold a spade or a rake, or guide the plough. The horse and the hound were the only beasts on his inventory of values. Sudden and vast enrichment by the treasures of gold wrung from the natives, first in their fragmentary ornaments, and then by compulsory toil from the mines which would yield it in heaps, were the lure and passion of the invaders. The natives, before they could reach any conception of the Divine Being of the Catholic creed, soon came to the understanding of the real object of their worship: as a cacique plainly set forth to a group of his trembling subjects, when, holding up a piece of gold, he said, "This is the Spaniards' god." A sordid passion, with its overmastery of all the sentiments of humanity, would inflame the nerves and intensify all the brutal propensities which are but masked in men of a low range of development even under the restraints of social and civil life. We must allow for the utter recklessness and frenzy of their full indulgence under the fervors of hot climes, in the loosening of all domestic and neighborly obligations, in the homelessness of exile and the mad freedom of adventure. Under the fretting discomforts and restraints of the ocean-passage hither, the imagination of these rapacious treasure-seekers fed itself on visions of wild license of arbitrary power over simple victims, and of heaps of treasure to be soon carried back to Spain to make a long revel in self-indulgence for the rest of life.

"Cruelties" was the comprehensive term under which Las Casas gathered all the enormities and barbarities, of which he was a witness for half a century, as perpetrated on the successive scenes invaded by his countrymen on the islands and the main of the New World. He had seen thousands of the natives crowded together, naked and helpless, for slaughter, like sheep in a park or meadow. He had seen them wasted at the extremities by torturing fires, till, after hours of agony, they turned their dying gaze, rather in amazed dread than in rage, upon their tormentors. Mutilations of hands, feet, ears, and noses surrounded him with ghastly spectacles of all the processes of death without disease. One may well leave all details to the imagination; and may do this all the more willingly that even the imagination will fail to fill and fashion the reality of the horror.

Previous to the successful ventures on the western ocean, the Portuguese had been resolutely pursuing the work of discovery by pushing their daring enterprise farther and farther down the coast of Africa, till they at last turned the Cape.[1] The deportation of the natives and their sale as slaves at once became first an incidental reward, and then the leading aim of craving adventurers. It was but natural that the Spaniards should turn their success in other regions to the same account. Heathen lands and heathen people belonged by Papal donation to the soldiers of the Cross; they were the heritage of the Church. The plea of conversion answered equally for conquest and subjugation of the natives on their own soil, and for transporting them to the scenes and sharers of a pure and saving faith.

[1] [See Chapter I. — ED.]

A brief summary of the acts and incidents in the first enslavement of the natives may here be set down. Columbus took with him to Spain, on his first return, nine natives. While on his second voyage he sent to Spain, in January, 1494, by a return vessel, a considerable number, described as Caribs, "from the Cannibal Islands," for "slaves." They were to be taught Castilian, to serve as interpreters for the work of "conversion" when restored to their native shores. Columbus pleads that it will benefit them by the saving of their souls, while the capture and enslaving of them will give the Spaniards consequence as evidence of power. Was this even a plausible excuse, and were the victims really cannibals? The sovereigns seemed to approve the act, but intimated that the "cannibals" might be converted at home, without the trouble of transportation. But Columbus enlarged and generalized sweepingly upon his scheme, afterward adding to it a secular advantage, suggesting that as many as possible of these cannibals should be caught for the sake of their souls, and then sold in Spain in payment for cargoes of live stock, provisions, and goods, which were much needed in the islands. The monarchs for a while suspended their decision of this matter. But the abominable traffic was steadily catching new agents and victims, and the slave-trade became a leading motive for advancing the rage for further discoveries. The Portuguese were driving the work eastward, while the Spaniards were keenly following it westward. In February, 1495, Columbus sent back four ships, whose chief lading was slaves. From that time began the horrors attending the crowding of human cargoes with scant food and water, with filth and disease, and the daily throwing over into the sea those who were privileged to die. Yet more victims were taken by Columbus when he was again in Spain in June, 1496, to circumvent his enemies. Being here again in 1498, he had no positive prohibition against continuing the traffic. A distinction was soon recognized, and allowed even by the humane and pious Isabella. Captives taken in war against the Spaniards might be brought to Spain and kept in slavery; but natives who had been seized for the purpose of enslaving them, she indignantly ordered should be restored to freedom. This wrong, as well as that of the *repartimiento* system, in the distribution of natives to Spanish masters as laborers, was slightly held in check by this lovable lady during her life. She died while Columbus was in Spain, Nov. 26, 1504. Columbus died at Valladolid, May 20, 1506. The ill that he had done lived after him, to qualify the splendor of his nobleness, grandeur, and constancy.

And here we may bring upon the scene that one, the only Spaniard who stands out luminously, in the heroism and glory of true sanctity, amid these gory scenes, himself a true soldier of Christ.

Bartholomew Las Casas was born at Seville in 1474. Llorente — a faithful biographer, and able editor and expositor of his writings, of whom farther on we are to say much more — asserts that the family was French in its origin, the true name being Casuas; which appears, indeed, as an alias on the titlepage of some of his writings published by the apostle in his lifetime.[1]

Antoine Las Casas, the father of Bartholomew, was a soldier in the marine service of Spain. We find no reference to him as being either in sympathy or otherwise with the absorbing aim which ennobled the career of his son. He accompanied Columbus on his first western voyage in 1492, and returned with him to Spain in 1493.

During the absence of the father on this voyage the son, at the age of eighteen, was completing his studies at Salamanca. In May, 1498,[2] at the age of about twenty-four, he went to the Indies with his father, in employment under Columbus, and returned to Cadiz, Nov. 25, 1500. In an address to the Emperor in 1542, Bartholomew reminded him that Columbus had given liberty to each of several of his fellow-voyagers to take to Spain a single native of the islands for personal service, and that a youth among those so transported had been intrusted to him. Perhaps under these favoring circumstances this was the occasion of first engaging the sympathies of Las Casas for the race to whose redemption he was to consecrate his life. Isabella, however, was highly indignant at this outrage upon the natives, and under pain of death to the culprits ordered the victims to be restored to their country. It would seem that they were all carried back in 1500 under the Commander Bobadilla, and among them the young Indian who had been in the service of Bartholomew. One loves to imagine that in some of the wide wanderings of the latter, amid the scenes of the New World, he may again have met with this first specimen of a heathen race who had been under intimate relations with himself, and who had undoubtedly been baptized.

We shall find farther on that the grievous charge was brought against Las Casas, when he had drawn upon himself bitter animosities, that he was the first to propose the transportation of negro slaves to the islands, in 1517. It is enough to say here, in anticipation, that Governor Ovando, in 1500, received permission to carry thither negro slaves "who had been born under Christian Powers." The first so carried were born in Seville

---

[1] Llorente adds that he had a personal acquaintance with a branch of the family at Calahorra, his own birthplace, and that the first of the family went to Spain, under Ferdinand III., to fight against the Moors of Andalusia. He also traces a connection between this soldier and Las Cases, the chamberlain of Napoleon, one of his councillors and companions at St. Helena, through a Charles Las Casas, one of the Spanish seigneurs who accompanied Blanche of Castile when she went to France, in 1200, to espouse Louis VIII.

[2] There is a variance in the dates assigned by historians for the visits of both Las Casas and his father to the Indians. Irving, following Navarrete, says that Antoine returned to Se- ville in 1498, having become rich (*Columbus* iii. 415). He also says that Llorente is incorrect in asserting that Bartholomew in his twenty-fourth year accompanied Columbus in his third voyage, in 1498, returning with him in 1500, as the young man was then at his studies at Salamanca. Irving says Bartholomew first went to Hispaniola with Ovando in 1502, at the age of about twenty-eight. I have allowed the dates to stand in the text as given by Llorente, assigning the earlier year for the first voyage of Las Casas to the New World as best according with the references in writings by his own pen to the period of his acquaintance with the scenes which he describes.

of parents brought from Africa, and obtained through the Portuguese traffickers.

On May 9, 1502, Las Casas embarked for the second time with Columbus, reaching San Domingo on June 29. In 1510 he was ordained priest by the first Bishop of Hispaniola, and was the first ecclesiastic ordained in the so-called Indies to say there his virgin Mass. This was regarded as a great occasion, and was attended by crowds; though a story is told, hardly credible, that there was then not a drop of wine to be obtained in the colony. The first Dominican monks, under their Bishop, Cordova, reached the islands in 1510. As we shall find, the Dominicans were from the first, and always, firm friends, approvers, and helpers of Las Casas in his hard conflict for asserting the rights of humanity for the outraged natives. The fact presents us with one of the strange anomalies in history, — that the founders and prime agents of the Inquisition in Europe should be the champions of the heathen in the New World.

The monks in sympathy with the ardent zeal of Las Casas began to preach vehemently against the atrocious wrongs which were inflicted upon the wretched natives, and he was sent as curate to a village in Cuba. The Franciscans, who had preceded the Dominicans, had since 1502 effected nothing in opposition to these wrongs. Utterly futile were the orders which came continually from the monarchs against overworking and oppressing the natives, as their delicate constitutions, unused to bodily toil, easily sank under its exactions. The injunctions against enslaving them were positive. Exception was made only in the case of the Caribs, as reputed cannibals, and the then increasing number of imported negro slaves, who were supposed to be better capable of hard endurance. Las Casas was a witness and a most keen and sensitive observer of the inflictions — lashings and other torturing atrocities — by which his fellow-countrymen, as if goaded by a demoniac spirit, treated these simple and quailing children of Nature, as if they were organized without sensitiveness of nerve, fibre, or understanding, requiring of them tasks utterly beyond their strength, bending them to the earth with crushing burdens, harnessing them to loads which they could not drag, and with fiendish sport and malice hacking off their hands and feet, and mutilating their bodies in ways which will not bear a description. It was when he accompanied the expedition under Velasquez for the occupation of Cuba, that he first drew the most jealous and antagonistic opposition and animosity upon himself, as standing between the natives and his own countrymen, who in their sordidness, rapacity, and cruelty seemed to have extinguished in themselves every instinct of humanity and every sentiment of religion. Here too was first brought into marked observation his wonderful power over the natives in winning their confidence and attachment, as they were ever after docile under his advice, and learned to look to him as their true friend. We pause to contemplate this wonderful and most engaging character, as, after filling his eye and thought with the shocking scenes in which his countrymen — in name the disciples of Jesus and loyal members of his Church — perpetrated such enormities against beings in their own likeness, he began his incessant tracking of the ocean pathways in his voyages to lay his remonstrances and appeals before successive monarchs. Beginning this service in his earliest manhood, he was to labor in it with unabated zeal till his death, with unimpaired faculties, at the age of ninety-two. He calls himself "the Clerigo." He was soon to win and worthily to bear the title of "Universal Protector of the Indians." Truly was he a remarkable and conspicuous personage, — unique, as rather the anomaly than the product of his age and land, his race and fellowship. His character impresses us alike by its loveliness and its ruggedness, its tenderness and its vigor, its melting sympathy and its robust energies. His mental and moral endowments were of the strongest and the richest, and his spiritual insight and fervor well-nigh etherealized him. His gifts and abilities gave him a rich versatility in capacity and resource. He was immensely in advance of his age, so as to be actually in antagonism with it. He was free alike from its prejudices, its limitations, and many of its superstitions, as well as from its barbarities. He was single-hearted, courageous, fervent, and persistent, bold and daring as a venturesome voyager over new seas and mysterious depths of virgin wildernesses, missionary, scholar, theologian, acute logician, historian, curious observer of Nature, the peer of Saint Paul in wisdom and zeal. Charles V. coming to the throne at the age of sixteen, when Las Casas was about forty, was at once won to him by profound respect and strong attachment, as had been the case with Charles's grandfather Ferdinand, whom Las Casas survived fifty years, while he outlived Columbus sixty years.

The Clerigo. found his remonstrances and appeals to his own nominally Christian fellow-countrymen wholly ineffectual in restraining or even mitigating the oppressions and cruelties inflicted upon the wretched natives. There was something phenomenal, as has been said, in the license yielded to the ingenuity of Spanish barbarity. It combined all the devices of inquisitorial torturing with the indulgence of the bestial ferocities of the bull-fight. At times it seemed as if the heartless oppressors were seeking only for a brutal mirth in inventing games in which their victims should writhe and yell as for their amusement. Then, as opportunity suggested or served, a scheme of the most cunning treachery and malice would turn an occasion of revelry or feasting, to which the natives had been invited or been beguiled by their tormentors, into a riot of fury and massacre. The utter aimlessness and recklessness of most of these horrid enormities impress the reader in these days as simply the indulgence of a wanton spirit in giving free license in human passions to those mocking employments of grinning devils in the old church paintings as they inflict retributions on the damned spirits in hell. The forked weapons, the raging flames, and the hideous demoniac delights exhibited in paintings, with which the eyes of the Spaniards were so familiar, found their all-too-faithful counterparts in the tropical zones and valleys of our virgin islands. The only pretences offered, not for justifying but for inflicting such wanton barbarities on the natives, were such as these, — that they refused to make known or to guide their oppressors to rich mines, or to work beyond their powers of endurance, or to bear intolerable burdens, or to furnish food which they had not to give. Touching and harrowing it is to read of many instances in which the simple diplomacy of the natives prompted them to neglect the little labor of husbandry required to supply their own wants, in order that the invaders might with themselves be brought to starvation. Whenever the Clerigo accompanied a body of Spaniards on the way to an Indian village, he always made an effort to keep the two people apart by night and by day, and he employed himself busily in baptizing infants and little children. He could never be too quick in this service, as these subjects of his zeal were the victims of the indiscriminate slaughter. The only consolation which this tender-hearted yet heroic missionary could find, as his share in the enterprise of his people, was in keeping the reckoning on his tablets of the number of those born under the common heathen doom whom he had snatched, by a holy drop, from the jaws of hell.

Baffled in all his nearly solitary endeavors to check the direful havoc and wreck of poor humanity on the scenes which were made so gory and hateful, Las Casas returned again to Spain in 1515, buoyed by resolve and hope that his dark revelations and bold remonstrances would draw forth something more effective from the sovereign. He was privileged by free and sympathizing interviews with Ferdinand at Placentia. But any hope of success here was soon crushed by the monarch's death. Las Casas was intending to go at once to Flanders to plead with the new King, Charles I., afterward Emperor, but was delayed by sympathetic friends found in Cardinal Ximenes and Adrian, the Regents.

It may seem strange and unaccountable that Las Casas should have encountered near the Court of a benignant sovereign a most malignant opposition to all his endeavors from first to last in securing the simply humane objects of his mission. But in fact he was withstood as resolutely at home as abroad, and often by a more wily and calculating policy. He found enemies and effective thwarters of his influence and advice in the order of the Jeronymites. Of the grounds and methods of their harmful activity, as well as of some of the more ostensible and plausible of the motives and alleged reasons which made him personal enemies both in Spain and in the Indies, we must speak with some detail farther on. It may be well here to follow him summarily in his frequent alternation between his missionary fields and his homeward voyages, to ply his invigorated zeal with new and intenser earnestness from his fuller experiences of the woes and outrages which he sought to redress. With some, though insufficient, assurances of regal authority in support of his cause, he re-embarked for the Indies, Nov. 11, 1516, and reached Hispaniola in December, fortified with the personal title of the "Universal Protector of the Indians." He sailed again

for Spain, May 7, 1517. His plainness of speech had in the interval increased the animosity and the efforts to thwart him of the local authorities
on the islands, and had even induced coldness and lack of aid among his
Dominican friends. He had many public and private hearings in Spain,
stirring up against himself various plottings and new enemies. In each of
these homeward visits Las Casas of course brought with him revelations
and specific details of new accumulations of iniquity against the natives;
and with a better understanding of himself, and also of all the intrigues and
interests warring against him, his honest soul assured him that he must at
last win some triumph in his most righteous cause. So he heaped the
charges and multiplied the disclosures which gave such vehemence and
eloquence to his pleadings. Having during each of his home visits met
some form of misrepresentation or falsehood, he would re-embark, furnished
as he hoped with some new agency and authority against the evil-doers.
But his enemies were as ingenious and as active as himself. Perhaps the
same vessel or fleet which carried him to the islands, with orders intended
to advance his influence, would bear fellow-passengers with documents or
means to thwart all his reinforced mission. He left Spain again in 1520,
only to cast himself on a new sea of troubles soon inducing him to return.
His sixth voyage carried him this time to the mainland in Mexico, in 1537.
He was in Spain once more in 1539. While waiting here for the return of
the Emperor, he composed six of his many essays upon his one unchan-
ging theme, all glowing with his righteous indignation, and proffering wise
and plain advice to the monarch. Yet again he crossed the now familiar
ocean to America, in 1544, it being his seventh western voyage, and returned
for the seventh and last time to Spain in 1547. Here were fourteen sea-
voyages, with their perils, privations, and lack of the common appliances and
comforts shared in these days by the rudest mariners. These voyages
were interspersed by countless trips and ventures amid the western islands
and the main, involving twofold, and a larger variety of harassments and
risks, with quakings, hurricanes, and reefs, exposures in open skiffs, and the
privilege of making one's own charts. But one year short of fifty in the
count out of his lengthened life were spent by this man of noble ardor, of
dauntless soul, and of loving heart in a cause which never brought to him
the joy of an accomplished aim.

    Las Casas shared, with a few other men of the most fervent and self-
sacrificing religious zeal, an experience of the deepest inward conviction,
following upon, not originally prompting to, the full consecration of his
life to his devoutest aim. Though he had been ordained to the priesthood
in 1510, he was afterward made to realize that he had not then been the
subject of that profound experience known in the formulas of piety as true
conversion. He dates this personal experience, carrying him to a deeper
devotional consciousness than he had previously realized, to the influence
over him of a faithful lay friend, Pedro de la Renteria, with whom he became intimate in 1514. To the devout conversation, advice, and example

of this intimate companion he ascribed his better-informed apprehension of the radical influences which wrought out the whole system of wrong inflicted upon the natives. Las Casas himself, like all the other Spaniards, had a company of Indian servants, who were in effect slaves; and he put them to work, the benefit of which accrued to himself. A form of servitude which exceeded all the conditions of plantation slavery had been instituted by Columbus under the system of so-called *repartimientos*. It was founded on the assumption that the Spanish monarch had an absolute proprietary right over the natives, and could make disposals and allotments of their services to his Christian subjects, the numbers being proportioned to the rank, standing, and means of individuals, the meanest Spaniard being entitled to share in the distribution of these servitors. This allowance made over to men of the lowest grade of intelligence, character, and humanity, the absolute and irresponsible power over the life and death of the natives intrusted to the disposal of masters. Under it were perpetrated cruelties against which there were no availing remonstrances, and for which there was no redress. The domestic cattle of civilized men are to be envied above the human beings who were held under the system of *repartimientos*, — tasked, scourged, tormented, and hunted with bloodhounds, if they sank under toils and inflictions beyond their delicate constitutions, or sought refuge in flight.

The slavery which afterward existed in the British Colonies and in these United States had scarce a feature in common with that which originated with the Spanish invaders. Las Casas thinks that Ferdinand lived and died without having had anything like a full apprehension of the enormities of the system. This, however, was not because efforts were lacking to inform him of these enormities, or to engage his sovereign intervention to modify and restrain, if not positively to prohibit, them. As we shall see, the system was so rooted in the greed and rapacity of the first adventurers here, who were goaded by passion for power and wealth, that foreign authority was thwarted in every attempt to overrule it. The most favored advisers of Ferdinand endeavored at first to keep him in ignorance of the system, and then, as he obtained partial information about it, to lead him to believe that it was vitally indispensable to conversion, to colonization, and to remunerative trade. The Dominican missionaries had, as early as 1501, informed the monarch of the savage cruelties which the system imposed. All that they effected was to induce Ferdinand to refer the matter to a council of jurists and theologians. Some of these were even alleged to have personal interests in the system of *repartimientos;* but at any rate they were under the influence and sway of its most selfish supporters. As the result of their conference, they persuaded the monarch that the system was absolutely necessary, — as, first, the Spaniards themselves were incapable of bodily labor under a debilitating climate; and second, that the close and dependent relation under which the natives were thus brought to their masters could alone insure the possibility of their conversion to the true faith. Ferdinand was so far won over to the allowance of the wrong as to issue an ordinance in its favor; while he sought to limit, restrain, and qualify it by injunctions which, of course, were futile in their dictation, for operating at a distance, in islands where sordid personal interests were all on the side of a defiance of them.

The Clerigo affirms that his own conscience was more startlingly aroused to a full sense of the wrongs and iniquities of the system of the *repartimientos* by his religious friend Renteria. He had previously, of course, so far as he was himself made the master or guardian in this relation of any number of the natives, brought his humanity and his ardor for justice into full exercise. But he was quickened by his friend to the duty of private and also of bold public protest against the system, and most plainly to offenders in proportion to the number of the victims which they enthralled and to the cruelty inflicted upon them. It was not his wont to allow any timidity or personal regards or temporizing calculations to compel his silence or to moderate his rebukes. His infirmity rather led him to excess in impatience and passion in his remonstrances. His bold and denunciatory preaching — though it appears that in this, and, as we shall note, on other occasions of speech and writing, he restrained himself from using the name of conspicuous offenders — caused an intense consternation and excitement. His clerical character barely saved him from personal violence. He found his hearers obdurate, and utterly beyond the sway of his protests and appeals. Again, therefore, he turned his face toward Spain, sustained by the fond assurance that he could so engage the King's intervention by his disclosures and rehearsals, that the royal authority should at this time be effectually exerted against a giant iniquity. This was his homeward errand in 1515. That even his presence and speech had had some restraining influence in Cuba, is signified by the fact that after his withdrawal and during his absence all the wrongs and miseries of which the natives, wholly impotent to resist, were the victims, ran into wilder license. The Spaniards kept bloodhounds in training and in hunger, to scour the woods and thickets and wilderness depths for the despairing fugitives. Whole families of the natives took refuge in voluntary and preferred self-destruction.

Two Dominicans of like mind with Las Casas accompanied him on his errand. Pedro de Cordova, prelate of the Dominicans, was his stanch friend. The Clerigo reached Seville in the autumn of 1515, and at once addressed himself to Ferdinand. He found the monarch old and ailing. The most able and malignant opponent with whose support, enlisted upon the side of the wrong and of the wrongdoers, Las Casas had to contend, was the Bishop of Burgos, Fonseca, whose influence had sway in the Council for the Indies.[1] After the King's death, Jan. 23, 1516, Las Casas

---

[1] The administration of affairs in the Western colonies of Spain was committed by Ferdinand, in 1511, to a body composed chiefly of clergy and jurists, called "The Council for the Indies." Its powers originally conferred by Ferdinand were afterward greatly enlarged by Charles

enjoyed the countenance, and had hope of the effectual aid, of the two Regents, previously mentioned, during the minority of Charles, the heir to the throne. The earnestness and persistency of the Clerigo so far availed as to obtain for him instructions to be carried to those in authority in the islands for qualifying the *repartimiento* system, and with penalties for the oppressions under it. Some Jeronymites were selected to accompany him on his return, as if to reinforce the objects of his mission, and to insure the efficacy of the title conferred upon him as the "Protector of the Indians." The Jeronymites, however, had been corrupted by the cunning and intrigues of the wily and exasperated enemies of Las Casas, who effected in secrecy what they could not or dared not attempt publicly against the courageous Clerigo and his purposes backed by authority. Already alienated during the voyage, they reached San Domingo in December, 1516. Perhaps candor may induce the suggestion that while the Jeronymites, from motives of prudence, temporized and qualified their activity in their errand, Las Casas was heady and unforbearing in his uncompromising demand for instant redress of wrong. At any rate he was wholly foiled in the exercise of his delegated authority; and so, with a fire in his blood which allowed no peace to his spirit, he was again in Spain in July, 1517. Here he found Cardinal Ximenes, his friendly patron, near to death. He was, however, encouraged with the hope and promise of patronage from high quarters. For a season his cause presented a favorable aspect. He had become sadly assured that upon the Spaniards in the islands, whose hearts and consciences were smothered by their greed and inhumanity, no influence, not even that of ghostly terrorism, which was tried in the refusal of the sacraments, would be of the least avail. His only resource was to engage what force there might be in the piety and humanity of the Church at

V. These powers were full and supreme, and any information, petition, appeal, or matter of business concerning the Indies, though it had been first brought before the monarch, was referred by him for adjudication to the Council. This body had an almost absolute sway alike in matters civil and ecclesiastical, with supreme authority over all appointments and all concerns of government and trade. It was therefore in the power of the Council to overrule or qualify in many ways the will or purpose or measures of the sovereigns, which were really in favor of right or justice or humane proceedings in the affairs of the colonies. For it naturally came about that some of its members were personally and selfishly interested in the abuses and iniquities which it was their rightful function and their duty to withstand. At the head of the Council was a dignitary whose well-known character and qualities were utterly unfavorable for the rightful discharge of his high trust. This was Juan Rodriguez de Fonseca, successively Bishop of Badajoz, Valencia, and Burgos, and constituted "Patriarch of the Indies." He had full control of colonial affairs for thirty years, till near his death in 1547. He bore the repute among his associates of extreme worldliness and ambition, with none of the graces and virtues becoming the priestly office, the duties of which engaged but little of his time or regard. It is evident also that he was of an unscrupulous and malignant disposition. He was inimical to Columbus and Cortés from the start. He tried to hinder, and succeeded in delaying and embarrassing, the second westward voyage of the great admiral. (Irving's *Columbus*, iii.; Appendix XXXIV.) He was a bitter opponent of Las Casas, even resorting to taunting insults of the apostle, and either openly or crookedly thwarting him in every stage and effort of his patient importunities to secure the intervention of the sovereigns in the protection of the natives. The explanation of this enmity is found in the fact that Fonseca himself was the owner of a *repartimiento* in Hispaniola, with a large number of native slaves.

home, in the sense of justice among high civil dignitaries, and in such sympathetic aid as he might draw from his countrymen who had no interest in the mining or the commerce sustained by the impositions upon the natives. The young King had wise councillors, and they made with him some good plans for means of relieving the natives from severities in their tasks of labor, from cruel inflictions in working the mines, and from exorbitant taxes exacting of them produce and commodities enormously exceeding their possible resources, however willing they might be in yielding. It was at this time and under its emergency, that Las Casas unfortunately gave something more than his assent, even his countenance and advice, to a proposition the effect of which was to root in pure and free soil an enormity whose harvesting and increase were a sum of woes. He certainly did advise that each Spaniard, resident in Hispaniola, should be allowed to import a dozen negro slaves. He did this, as he afterward affirmed and confessed, under the lure of a deep mist and delusion. So painful was the remorse which he then experienced for his folly and error, that he avows that he would part with all he had in the world to redress it. He says that when he gave this advice he had not at all been aware of the outrages perpetrated by the Portuguese dealers in entrapping these wretched Africans. Besides this, he had been promised by the colonists that if they might be allowed to have negroes, whose constitutions were stronger for endurance, they would give up the feeble natives. We may therefore acquit Las Casas in his confessed sin of ignorance and willing compromise in an alternative of wrongs. But he is wholly guiltless of a charge which has been brought 'against him, founded upon this admitted error, of having been the first to propose and to secure the introduction of African slavery into the New World. As has already been said, the wrong had been perpetrated many years before Las Casas had any agency in it by deed or word. While the young King was still in Flanders negro slaves had been sent by his permission to Hispaniola. The number was limited to a thousand for each of the four principal islands. As there was a monopoly set up in the sale of these doleful victims, the price of them was speedily and greatly enhanced.[1]

Las Casas devised and initiated a scheme for the emigration of laboring men from Spain. Thwarted in this purpose, he formed a plan for a colony where restrictions were to be enforced to guard against the worst abuses. Fifty Spaniards, intended to be carefully selected with regard to character and habits, and distinguished by a semi-clerical garb and mode of life, were his next device for introducing some more tolerable conditions of

---

[1] There is an extended Note on Las Casas in Appendix XXVIII. of Irving's *Columbus*. That author most effectively vindicates Las Casas from having first advised and been instrumental in the introduction of African slavery in the New World, giving the dates and the advisers and agents connected with that wrong previous to any word on the subject from Las Casas. The devoted missionary had been brought to acquiesce in the measure on the plausible plea stated in the text, acting from the purest spirit of benevolence, though under an erroneous judgment. Cardinal Ximenes had from the first opposed the project.

work and thrift in the islands.   Ridicule was brought to bear, with all sorts of intrigues and tricks, to baffle this scheme.   But the Clerigo persevered in meeting all the obstructions thrown in his way, and sailed for San Domingo in July, 1520.   He established his little Utopian colony at Cumana; but misadventures befel it, and it came to a melancholy end.   It seemed for a season as if the tried and patient Clerigo was at last driven to complete disheartenment.   Wearied and exhausted, he took refuge in a Dominican convent in San Domingo, receiving the tonsure in 1522.   Here he was in retirement for eight years, occupying himself in studying and writing, of which we have many results.   During this interval the work of depopulation and devastation was ruinously advancing under Cortés, Alvarado, and Pizarro, in Mexico, Guatemala, and Peru.   There is some uncertainty about an alleged presence of Las Casas at the Court in Spain in 1530. But he was in Mexico in 1531, in Nicaragua in 1534, and in Spain again in 1539, in behalf of a promising work undertaken in Tuzulutlan, from which all lay Spaniards were to be excluded.   Having accomplished, as he hoped, the object of his visit, he would have returned at once to the American main; but was detained by the Council of the Indies as the person best able and most trustworthy to give them certain information which they desired.   It was at this period that he wrote his remarkable work, *The Destruction of the Indies*.   This bold and daring product of his pen and of the righteous indignation which had heretofore found expression from his eloquent and fervid speech, will soon be examined in detail.   It may be said now that this work, afterward so widely circulated and translated into all the languages of Europe, — perhaps with some reductions from the original, — was not at first allowed to be published, but was submitted to the Emperor and his ministers.   As the shocking revelations made in this book state in round numbers the victims of the Spaniards in different places, it is at once observable that there are over-statements and exaggerations.   This, however, applies only to the numbers, not at all to the acts of barbarity and iniquity.[1]   The book was published twelve years after it was written, and was dedicated to Philip, the heir to the throne.

[1] As will appear farther on in these pages, Las Casas stands justly chargeable with enormous exaggerations of the number or estimate of the victims of Spanish cruelty.   But I have not met with a single case in any contemporary writer, nor in the challengers and opponents of his pleadings at the Court of Spain, in which his hideous portrayal of the forms and methods of that cruelty, its dreadful and revolting tortures and mutilations, have been brought under question.   Mr. Prescott's fascinating volumes have been often and sometimes very sharply censured, because in the glow of romance, chivalric daring, and heroic adventure in which he sets the achievements of the Spanish "Conquerors" of the New World he would seem to be somewhat lenient to their barbarities.

In the second of his admirable works he refers as follows to this stricture upon him: "To American and English readers, acknowledging so different a moral standard from that of the sixteenth century, I may possibly be thought too indulgent to the errors of the Conquerors;" and he urges that while he has "not hesitated to expose in their strongest colors the excesses of the Conquerors, I have given them the benefit of such mitigating reflections as might be suggested by the circumstances and the period in which they lived" (Preface to the *Conquest of Mexico*).

It is true that scattered over all the ably-wrought pages of Mr. Prescott's volumes are expressions of the sternest judgment and the most indignant condemnation passed upon the

It may be as well here to complete the summary of the career of Las Casas. While detained by the Council he was engaged in the advice and oversight of a new code of laws for the government of the colonies and the colonists. Up to this time he had crossed the ocean to the islands or the main twelve times, and had journeyed to Germany four times to confer with the Emperor. He was offered the bishopric of Cusco, in Toledo, but was not thus to be withdrawn from his foreign mission. In order, however, to secure authority to enforce the new laws, he accepted the foreign bishopric of Chiapa, was consecrated at Seville in 1544, embarked on July 4, with forty-four monks, and arrived at Hispaniola. He bore the aversion and hate which his presence everywhere provoked, was faithful to the monastic habits, and though so abstemious as to deny himself meat, he kept the vigor of his body. He resolutely forbade absolution to be given to Spaniards holding slaves contrary to the provisions of the new laws. Resigning his bishopric, he returned to Spain for the last time in 1547, — engaging in his bold controversy with Sepulveda, to be soon rehearsed. He resided chiefly in the Dominican College at Valladolid. In 1564, in his ninetieth year, he wrote a work on Peru. On a visit to Madrid in the service of the Indians, after a short illness, he died in July, 1566, at the age of ninety-two, and was buried in the convent of "Our Lady of Atocha."

The most resolute and effective opponents which Las Casas found at the Spanish Court were Oviedo and Sepulveda, representatives of two different classes of those who from different motives and by different methods stood between him and the King. Oviedo had held high offices under Government both in Spain and in various places in the New World. He wrote a history of the Indies, which Las Casas said was as full of lies almost as of pages. He also had large interests in the mines and in the enslaving of the natives. Sepulveda[1] was distinguished as a scholar and an author.

most signal enormities of these incarnate spoilers, who made a sport of their barbarity. But those who have most severely censured the author upon the matter now in view have done so under the conviction that cruelty unprovoked and unrelieved was so awfully dark and prevailing a feature in every stage and incident of the Spanish advance in America, that no glamour of adventure or chivalric deeds can in the least lighten or redeem it. The underlying ground of variance is in the objection to the use of the terms "Conquest" and "Conquerors," as burdened with the relation of such a pitiful struggle between the overmastering power of the invaders and the abject helplessness of their victims.

As I am writing this note, my eye falls upon the following extract from a private letter written in 1847 by that eminent and highly revered divine, Dr. Orville Dewey, and just now put into print: "I have been reading Prescott's *Peru*. What a fine accomplishment there is about it! And yet there is something wanting to me in the moral nerve. History should teach men how to estimate characters; it should be a teacher of morals; and I think it should make us *shudder* at the names of Cortez and Pizarro. But Prescott does not; he seems to have a kind of sympathy with these inhuman and perfidious adventurers, as if they were his heroes. It is too bad to talk of them as the soldiers of Christ; if it were said of the Devil, they would have better fitted the character" (*Autobiography and Letters of Orville Dewey, D.D.* p. 190).

[1] Juan Ginez de Sepulveda, distinguished both as a theologian and an historian, was born near Cordova in 1490, and died in 1573. He was of a noble but impoverished family. He availed himself of his opportunities for obtaining the best education of his time in the universities of Spain and Italy, and acquired an

Las Casas charges that his pen and influence were engaged in the interest of parties who had committed some of the greatest ravages, and who had personal advantages at stake. Sepulveda in his opposition to the Clerigo makes two points or "Conclusions," — 1. That the Spaniards had a right to subjugate and require the submission of the Indians, because of their superior wisdom and prudence; and that, therefore, the Indians were bound to submit and acquiesce. 2. That in case of their refusal to do so they might justly be constrained by force of arms. It was the proceeding on these assumptions that, as Las Casas pleaded, had led to the entire depopulation of vast territories. With high professions of loyalty Sepulveda urged that his motive in writing was simply to justify the absolute title of the King of Spain to the Indies. In offering his book to the Royal Council he importunately solicited its publication; and as this was repeatedly refused, he engaged the urgency of his friends to bring it about. Las Casas, well knowing what mischief it would work, strongly opposed the publication. The Council, regarding the matter as purely theological, referred Sepulveda's treatise for a thorough examination to the universities of Salamanca and Alcala. They pronounced it unsound in doctrine and unfit to be printed. Sepulveda then secretly sent it to Rome, and through his friend, the Bishop of Segovia, procured it to be printed. The Emperor prohibited its circulation in Spain, and caused the copies of it to be seized.

Las Casas resolved to refute this dangerous treatise, and Sepulveda was personally cited to a dispute, which was continued through five days. As a result, the King's confessor, Dominic de Soto, an eminent divine,

eminent reputation as a scholar and a disputant, — not, however, for any elevation of principles or nobleness of thought. In 1536 he was appointed by Charles V. his historiographer, and put in charge of his son Philip. Living at Court, he had the repute of being crooked and unscrupulous, his influence not being given on the side of rectitude and progressive views. His writings concerning men and public affairs give evidence of the faults imputed to him. He was vehement, intolerant, and dogmatic He justified the most extreme absolutism in the exercise of the royal prerogative, and the lawfulness and even the expediency of aggressive wars simply for the glory of the State. Melchior Cano and Antonio Ramirez, as well as Las Casas, entered into antagonism and controversy with his avowed principles. One of his works, entitled *Democrates Secundus, seu de justis belli causis*, may be pronounced almost brutal in the license which it allowed in the stratagems and vengefulness of warfare. It was condemned by the universities of Alcala and Salamanca. He was a voluminous author of works of history, philosophy, and theology, and was admitted to be a fine and able writer. Erasmus pronounced him the Spanish Livy. The disputation between him and Las Casas took place before Charles in 1550. The monarch was very much under his influence, and seems to some extent to have sided with him in some of his views and principles. Sepulveda was one of the very few persons whom the monarch admitted to interviews and intimacy in his retirement to the Monastery at Yuste.

It was this formidable opponent — a personal enemy also in jealousy and malignity — whom Las Casas confronted with such boldness and earnestness of protest before the Court and Council. It was evidently the aim of Sepulveda to involve the advocate of the Indians in some disloyal or heretical questioning of the prerogatives of monarch or pope. It seemed at one time as if the noble pleader for equity and humanity would come under the clutch of the Holy Office, then exercising its new-born vigor upon all who could be brought under inquisition for constructive or latent heretical proclivities. For Las Casas, though true to his priestly vows, made frequent and bold utterances of what certainly, in his time, were advanced views and principles.

was asked to give a summary of the case.   This he did in substance as follows : —

"The prime point is whether the Emperor may justly make war on the Indians before the Faith has been preached to them, and whether after being subdued by arms they will be in any condition to receive the light of the Gospel, more tractable, more docile to good impressions, and ready to give up their errors.   The issue between the disputants was, that Sepulveda maintained that war was not only lawful and allowable, but necessary ; while Las Casas insisted upon the direct contrary, — that war was wholly unjust, and offered invincible obstacles to conversion.   Sepulveda presented four arguments on his side : 1. The enormous wickedness and criminality of the Indians, their idolatry, and their sins against nature.   2. Their ignorance and barbarity needed the mastery of the intelligent and polite Spaniards.   3. The work of conversion would be facilitated after subjugation.   4. That the Indians treat each other with great cruelty, and offer human sacrifices to false gods.   Sepulveda fortifies these arguments by examples and authorities from Scripture, and by the views of doctors and canonists, — all proceeding upon the assumed exceeding wickedness of the Indians. In citing *Deuteronomy* xx. 10–16, he interprets 'far-off cities' as those of a different religion.   Las Casas replies that it was not simply as idolaters that the seven nations in Canaan were to be destroyed, — as the same fate, on that score, might have been visited upon all the inhabitants of the earth, except Israel,— but as intruders upon the Promised Land.   The early Christian emperors, beginning with Constantine, did not make their wars as against idolaters, but for political reasons.   He cites the Fathers as giving testimony to the effect of a good example and against violent measures.   The Indians under the light of Nature are sincere, but are blinded in offering sacrifices. They are not like the worst kind of barbarians, to be hunted as beasts; they have princes, cities, laws, and arts.   It is wholly unjust, impolitic, and futile to wage war against them as simply barbarians.   The Moors of Africa had been Christians in the time of Augustine, and had been perverted, and so might rightfully be reclaimed."

The Royal Council, after listening to the dispute and the summary of its points, asked Las Casas to draw up a paper on the question whether they might lawfully enslave the Indians, or were bound to set free all who were reduced to bondage.   He replied that the law of God does not justify war against any people for the sake of making them Christians; so the whole course of treatment of the Indians had been wrong from the start.   The Indians were harmless; they had never had the knowledge or the proffer of Christianity: so they had never fallen away, like the Moors of Africa, Constantinople, and Jerusalem.   No sovereign prince had authorized the Spaniards to make war.   The Spaniards cannot pretend that their reason for making war was because of the cruelty of the Indians to each other. The slaughter of them was indiscriminate and universal.   They were enslaved and branded with the King's arms.   The monarch never authorized these execrable artifices and shocking atrocities, a long catalogue of which is specified.

The Clerigo then warms into an earnest dissertation on natural and Christian equity.   He quotes some beautiful sentences from the will of Isabella, enjoining her own humanity on her husband and daughter. He makes a strong point of the fact that Isabella first, and then a council of divines and lawyers at Burgos, and Charles himself in 1523, had declared that all the inhabitants of the New World had been born free. Only Las Casas' earnestness, his pure and persistent purpose, relieve of weariness his reiteration of the same truths and appeals to the King. He insists over and over again that the delegating of any portion of the King's own personal authority to any Spaniard resident in the New World, or even to the Council of the Indies, opens the door to every form and degree of abuse, and that he must strictly reserve all jurisdiction and control to himself.

In a second treatise, which Las Casas addressed to Charles V., he states at length the practical measures needful for arresting the wrongs and disasters consequent upon the enslaving of the Indians. Of the twenty methods specified, the most important is that the King should not part with the least portion of his sovereign prerogative. He meets the objection artfully raised by Sepulveda, that if the King thus retains all authority to himself he may lose the vast domain to his crown, and that the Spaniards will be forced to return to Europe and give up the work of Gospel conversion.

Las Casas wrote six memorials or argumentative treatises addressed to the sovereigns on the one same theme. The sameness of the information and appeals in them is varied only by the increasing boldness of the writer in exposing iniquities, and by the warmer earnestness of his demand for the royal interposition. His sixth treatise is a most bold and searching exposition of the limits of the royal power over newly discovered territory, and within the kingdoms and over the natural rights of the natives. A copy of this paper was obtained by a German ambassador in Spain, and published at Spire, in Latin, in 1571. It is evident that for a considerable period after the composition — and, so to speak, the publication — of these successive protests and appeals of the Clerigo, only a very limited circulation was gained by them. Artful efforts were made, first to suppress them, and then to confine the knowledge of the facts contained in them to as narrow a range as possible. His enemies availed themselves of their utmost ingenuity and cunning to nullify his influence. Sometimes he was ridiculed as a crazy enthusiast, — a visionary monomaniac upon an exaggerated delusion of his own fancy. Again, he would be gravely and threateningly denounced as an enemy to Church and State, because he imperilled the vast interests of Spain in her colonies.

The principal and most important work from the pen of Las Casas, on which his many subsequent writings are based and substantially developed, bears (in English) the following title: *A Relation of the First Voyages and Discoveries made by the Spaniards in America. With an Account of their Unparalleled Cruelties on the Indians, in the Destruction of above Forty Millions of People; together with the Propositions offered to the King of Spain to prevent the further Ruin of the West Indies. By Don Bartholomew de las Casas, Bishop of Chiapa, who was an Eye-witness of their Cruelties.* It was composed in Spanish, and finished at Valencia, Dec. 8, 1542, near the beginning of the reign of Philip II., to whom it is dedicated. This was about fifty years after the discovery of America; and during the greater part of the period Las Casas had lived as an observer of the scenes and events which he describes. He makes Hispaniola his starting-point, as the navigators usually first touched there. The reader will at once be struck by the exaggeration, the effect of a high-wrought and inflamed imagination, so evident in the words of the title, which set the number of the victims of Spanish cruelty at forty millions. Of this weakness of Las Casas in over-estimate and exaggeration of numbers, we shall have to take special notice by and by. It is enough to say here that his license in this direction is confined to this one point, and is by no means to be viewed as discrediting his integrity, fidelity, and accuracy in other parts of his testimony. He certainly had been deeply impressed with the density of the population in some of the islands, for he says: " It seems as if Providence had amassed together the greatest part of mankind in this region of the earth." He tells us that his motives for writing and publishing his exposure of iniquities were, — the call made upon him by pious and Christian people thus to enlist the sympathies and efforts of the good to redress the wrong; and his sincere attachment to his King and Master, lest God should avenge the wrong on his kingdom. For this purpose he has followed the Court with his pleadings, and will not cease his remonstrances and appeals. At the time of completing his work savage cruelties were prevailing over all the parts of America which had been opened, slightly restrained for the time in Mexico, through the stern intervention of the King. An addition to his work in 1546 recognized many new ordinances and decrees made by his Majesty at Barcelona since 1542, and signed at Madrid in 1543. But nevertheless a new field for oppression and wickedness had been opened in Peru, with exasperations from civil war and rebellion among the natives; while the Spaniards on most frivolous pretexts defied the orders of the King, pretending to wait for his answers to their pleas in self-justification. The period was one in which the rapacity of the invaders was both inflamed and gratified by abundance of spoil, which sharpened the avarice of the earlier claimants, and drew to them fresh adventurers.

Las Casas gives a very winning description of the natives under his observation and in his ever-kindly and sympathetic relations with them. He says they are simple, humble, patient, guileless, submissive, weak, and effeminate; incapable of toil or labor, short-lived, succumbing to slight illnesses; as frugal and abstemious as hermits; inquisitive about the Catholic religion, and docile disciples. They were lambs who had encountered tigers, wolves, and lions. During the lifetime of Las Casas Cuba had been rendered desolate and a desert; then St. John and Jamaica; and in all thirty islands had come to the same fate. A system of deportation from one island to another had been devised to obtain new supplies of slaves. The Clerigo deliberately charges that in forty years the number of victims counted

to fifty millions.   Enslaving was but a protracted method of killing, — all in
the greed for gold and pearls.   The sight of a fragment of the precious metal
in the hands of a native was the occasion for demanding more of him, as if
he had hidden treasure, or for his guiding the Spaniards to some real or
imagined mines.   Las Casas follows his details and examples of iniquity
through the islands in succession, then through the provinces of Nicaragua,
New Spain, Guatemala, Pannco, Jalisco, Yucatan, St. Martha, Carthagena,
the Pearl Coast, Trinidad, the River Yuya-pari, Venezuela, Florida, La Plata,
and Peru, — being in all seventeen localities, — repeating the similar facts,
hardly with variations.   Against the Spaniards with their horses, lances,
swords, and bloodhounds, the natives could oppose only their light spears and
poisoned arrows.   The victims would seek refuge in caves and mountain fastnesses, and if approached would kill themselves, as the easiest escape from
wanton tortures.   Las Casas says : " I one day saw four or five persons, of the
highest rank, in Hispaniola, burned by a slow fire."   Occasionally, he tells us,
a maddened Indian would kill a Spaniard, and then his death would be
avenged by the massacre of a score or a hundred natives.   Immediately
upon the knowledge of the death of Isabella, in 1504, as if her humanity
had been some restraint, the barbarous proceedings were greatly intensified.
The Spaniards made the most reckless waste of the food of the natives.
Las Casas says : " One Spaniard will consume in a day the food of three
Indian families of ten persons each for a month."   He avows that when he
wrote there were scarce two hundred natives left in St. John and Jamaica,
where there had once been six hundred thousand.   For reasons of caution
or prudence — we can hardly say from fear, for never was there a more
courageous champion — Las Casas suppresses the names of the greatest
offenders.   The following are specimens of his method : " Three merciless
tyrants have invaded Florida, one after another, since 1510."   " A Spanish
commander with a great number of soldiers entered Peru," etc.   " In the
year 1514 a merciless governor, destitute of the least sentiment of pity or
humanity, a cruel instrument of the wrath of God, pierced into the continent."
" The fore-mentioned governor," etc.   " The captain whose lot it was to
travel into Guatemala did a world of mischief there."   " The first bishop
that was sent into America imitated the conduct of the covetous governors
in enslaving and spoiling."   " They call the countries they have got by their
unjust and cruel wars their conquests."   " No tongue is capable of describing to the life all the horrid villanies perpetrated by these bloody-minded
men.   They seemed to be the declared enemies of mankind."   The more
generous the presents in treasures which were made by some timid cacique
to his spoilers, the more brutally was he dealt with, in the hope of extorting
what he was suspected of having concealed.   Las Casas stakes his veracity
on the assertion : " I saw with my own eyes above six thousand children die
in three or four months."

To reinforce his own statements the Clerigo quotes letters from high
authorities.   One is a protest which the Bishop of St. Martha wrote in 1541

to the King of Spain, saying that "the Spaniards live there like devils, rather than Christians, violating all the laws of God and man."   Another is from Mark de Xlicia, a Franciscan friar, to the King, the General of his Order, who came with the first Spaniards into Peru, testifying from his eyesight to all enormities, in mutilations, cutting off the noses, ears, and hands of the natives, burning and tortures, and keeping famished dogs to chase them.

Las Casas follows up his direful catalogue of horrors into the "New Kingdom of Grenada," in 1536, which he says received its name from the native place of "the captain that first set his foot in it."   Those whom he took with him into Peru were "very profligate and extremely cruel men, without scruple or remorse, long accustomed to all sorts of wickedness." The second "governor," enraged that his predecessor had got the first share of the plunder, though enough was left for spoil, turned informer, and made an exposure of his atrocities in complaints to the Council of the Indies, in documents which "are yet to be seen."   The spoils were prodigious quantities of gold and precious stones, especially emeralds.   The "governor" seized and imprisoned the cacique, or inca, Bogata, requiring him to send for and gather up all the gold within his reach ; and after heaps of it had been brought, put him to horrid torture in order to extort more.

There were published at Madeira certain "Laws and Constitutions" made by the King at Barcelona, in 1542, under the influence of Las Casas, as the result of a council at Valladolid.   Strict orders to put a stop to the iniquitous proceedings were circumvented by agents sent in the interest of the authors of the outrages.   The Clerigo petitioned the King to constitute all the natives his free subjects, with no delegated lordship over them, and enjoined upon him "to take an oath on the Holy Gospels, for himself and his successors, to this effect, and to put it in his will, solemnly witnessed." He insists that this is the only course to prevent the absolute extermination of the natives.   He adds that the Spaniards in their covetousness combine to keep out priests and monks, not the slightest attempt being made to convert the natives, though the work would be easy, and they themselves crave it.   "The Spaniards have no more regard to their salvation than if their souls and bodies died together, and were incapable of eternal rewards or punishments."   Yet he admits that it would hardly be reasonable to expect these efforts for conversion of the heathen from men who are themselves heathen, and so ignorant and brutish that they "do not know even the number of the commandments."   "As for your Majesty," the Clerigo says, with a keen thrust, "the Indians think you are the most cruel and impious prince in the world, while they see the cruelty and impiety your subjects so insolently commit, and they verily believe your Majesty lives upon nothing but human flesh and blood."   He positively denies the imputations alleged to justify cruelty, — that the Indians indulged in abominable lusts against nature, and were cannibals.   As for their idolatry, that is a sin against God, for Him, not for man, to punish.   The monarchs, he insists, had been most artfully imposed upon in allowing the deportation of natives from the Lucay Islands to supply the havoc made in Hispaniola. The Clerigo goes into the most minute details, with specifications and reiterations of horrors, ascribing them to the delegated authority exercised by petty officers, under the higher ones successively intrusted with power. There is a holy fervor of eloquence in his remonstrances and appeals to his Majesty to keep the sole power in his own hands, as he reminds him that fearful retributive judgments from God may be visited upon his own kingdom. The Council of the Indies, he says, had desired him to write to the monarch about the exact nature of the right of the kings of Spain to the Indies; and he intimates that the zeal which he had shown in exposing iniquities under those whom the King had put in authority in the New World had been maliciously turned into a charge that he had questioned the royal title to those regions. As will appear, Las Casas, under the leadings of that intelligent search for the fundamentals of truth and righteousness which a quickened conscience had prompted, found his way to the principles of equity on this subject.

He had, therefore, previously sent to the King thirty well-defined and carefully stated " Propositions," which he regards as so self-evident that he makes no attempt to argue or prove them. His enemies have in view to cover up their iniquities by misleading the King. Therefore, for conscience' sake, and under a sense of obligation to God, he sets himself to a sacred task. Little foreseeing that his life and labor were to be protracted till he had nearly doubled his years, he says that, finding himself " growing old, being advanced to the fiftieth year of his age," and " from a full acquaintance with America," his testimony shall be true and clear.

His subtle enemies plead against him that the King has a right to establish himself in America by force of arms, however ruthless the process, — quoting the examples of Nimrod, Alexander, the old Romans, and the Turks. They allege also that the Spaniards have more prudence and wisdom than other peoples, and that their country is nearest to the Indies. He therefore announces his purpose to put himself directly before the King, and stand for his " Propositions," which he sends in advance in writing, suggesting that if it be his Majesty's pleasure, they be translated into Latin and published in that language, as well as in Spanish.

The " Propositions" may be stated in substance as follows; they were keenly studied and searched by those who were anxious to detect flaws or heresies in them : —

1. The Pope derives from Christ authority and power extending over all men, believers or infidels, in matters pertaining to salvation and eternal life. But these should be exercised differently over infidels and those who have had a chance to be believers.

2. This prerogative of the Pope puts him under a solemn obligation to propagate the Gospel, and to offer it to all infidels who will not oppose it.

3. The Pope is obliged to send capable ministers for this work.

4. Christian princes are his most proper and able helpers in it.

5. The Pope may exhort and even oblige Christian princes to this work, by authority and money, to remove obstructions and to send true workers.

6. The Pope and princes should act in accord and harmony.

7. The Pope may distribute infidel provinces among Christian princes for this work.

8. In this distribution should be had in view the instruction, conversion, and interests of the infidels themselves, not the increase of honors, titles, riches, and territories of the princes.

9. Any incidental advantage which princes may thus gain is allowable; but temporal ends should be wholly subordinate, the paramount objects being the extending of the Church, the propagation of the Faith, and the service of God.

10. The lawful native kings and rulers of infidel countries have a right to the obedience of their subjects, to make laws, etc., and ought not to be deprived, expelled, or violently dealt with.

11. To transgress this rule involves injustice and every form of wrong.

12. Neither these native rulers nor their subjects should be deprived of their lands for their idolatry, or any other sin.

13. No tribunal or judge in the world has a right to molest these infidels for idolatry or any other sins, however enormous, while still infidels, and before they have voluntarily received baptism, unless they directly oppose, refuse, and resist the publication of the Gospel.

14. Pope Alexander VI., under whom the discovery was made, was indispensably obliged to choose a Christian prince to whom to commit these solemn obligations of the Gospel.

15. Ferdinand and Isabella had especial claims and advantages for this intrustment by the Pope above all other Catholic princes, because they had with noble efforts driven out the infidels and Mohammedans from the land of their ancestors, and because they sent at their own charge Columbus, the great discoverer, whom they named the chief admiral.

16. As the Pope did right in this assignment, so he has power to revoke it, to transfer the country to some other prince, and to forbid, on pain of excommunication, any rival prince to send missionaries.

17. The kings of Castile and Leon have thus come lawfully to jurisdiction over the Indies.

18. This obliges the native kings of the Indies to submit to the jurisdiction of the kings of Spain.

19. Those native kings, having freely and voluntarily received the Faith and baptism, are bound (as they were not before) to acknowledge this sovereignty of the kings of Spain.

20. The kings of Spain are bound by the law of God to choose and send fit missionaries to exhort, convert, and do everything for this cause.

21. They have the same power and jurisdiction over these infidels before their conversion as the Pope has, and share his obligations to convert them.

22. The means for establishing the Faith in the Indies should be the same as those by which Christ introduced his religion into the world, — mild, peaceable, and charitable; humility; good examples of a holy and regular way of living, especially over such docile and easy subjects; and presents bestowed to win them.

23. Attempts by force of arms are impious, like those of Mahometans, Romans, Turks, and Moors : they are tyrannical, and unworthy of Christians, calling out blasphemies ; and they have already made the Indians believe that our God is the most unmerciful and cruel of all Gods.

24. The Indians will naturally oppose the invasion of their country by a title of conquest, and so will resist the work of conversion.

25. The kings of Spain have from the first given and reiterated their orders against war and the ill-treatment of the Indians.   If any officers have shown commissions and warrants for such practices, they have been forged or deceptive.

26. So all wars and conquests which have been made have been unjust and tyrannical, and in effect null ; as is proved by proceedings on record in the Council against such tyrants and other culprits, who are amenable to judgment.

27. The kings of Spain are bound to reinforce and establish those Indian laws and customs which are good — and such are most of them — and to abolish the bad ; thus upholding good manners and civil policy.   The Gospel is the method for effecting this.

28. The Devil could not have done more mischief than the Spaniards have done in distributing and spoiling the countries, in their rapacity and tyranny ; subjecting the natives to cruel tasks, treating them like beasts, and persecuting those especially who apply to the monks for instruction.

29. The distribution of the Indians among the Spaniards as slaves is wholly contrary to all the royal orders given by Isabella successively to Columbus, Bobadilla, and De Lares.   Columbus gave three hundred Indians to Spaniards who had done the most service to the Crown, and took but one for his own use.   The Queen ordered all except that one to be sent back.   What would she have said to the present iniquities ? The King is reminded that his frequent journeys and absences have prevented his fully informing himself of these facts.

30. From all these considerations it follows that all conquests, acquisitions, usurpations, and appropriations by officers and private persons have no legality, as contrary to the orders of the Spanish monarchs.

Here certainly is an admirable and cogent statement of the principles of equity and righteousness, as based upon natural laws and certified and fortified by the great verities and sanctions supposed to be held in reverence by professed Christians.   Las Casas, in taking for his starting-point the Pope's supreme and inclusive right over half the globe, just brought to the knowledge of civilized men, seems to make a monstrous assumption, only greater than that of the Spanish kings' holding under and deriving dominion from him.   But we may well pardon this assumption to so loyal a disciple of the Church, when we consider how nobly he held this Papal right as conditioned and limited, involving lofty duties, and balanced by an obligation to confer inestimable blessings.   He had ever before him the contrast between fair scenes of luxurious Nature, ministering to the easy happiness of a gentle race of delicate and short-lived beings akin to himself, and the ruthless passions, lusts, and savagery of his own countrymen and fellow-Christians.   We can well account for the opposition and thwarting of his efforts amid these scenes, but may need a further explanation of the resistance and ill-success which he encountered when pleading his cause before monarchs and great councillors at home, whose sympathies seem to have been generally on his side. He often stood wholly alone in scenes where these ravaging cruelties had full sweep, — alone in the humane sensitiveness with which he regarded them; alone in freedom from the mastering passions of greed and rapacity which excited them; and alone in realizing the appalling contrast between the spirit of blood and rapine which prompted them, and the spirit of that Gospel, the assumed championship of which at these ends of the earth was the blasphemous pretence of these murderers. Those ruthless tyrants, who here treated hundreds and thousands of the natives subject to them worse than even brutes from which useful service is expected, would not, of course, have the front to offer on the spot the pretence set up for them by their abetters at the Spanish Court, — that they were thus drawing the natives to them for their conversion; they laughed at the Clerigo when they did not openly thwart him.

Las Casas had many powerful and embittered opponents, and by the use of various means and artifices they were able to put impediments in his way, to qualify and avert what would seem to be the natural effects of his ardent appeals and shocking disclosures, and to keep him through his protracted life in what looked like a hopeless struggle against giant iniquities. Nor is it necessary that we go deeper than the obvious surface of the story to find the reasons for the opposition and discomfiture which he encountered. It may be that all those who opposed him or who would not co-operate with him were not personally interested in the iniquities which he exposed and sought to redress. Something may need to be said by and by concerning alleged faults of temper, over-ardor of zeal and over-statement, and wild exaggeration attributed to this bold apostle of righteousness. But that the substance of all his charges, and the specifications of inhumanity, cruelty, and atrocity which he set forth in detail, and with hardly enough diversity to vary his narrative, is faithful to the soberest truth, cannot be questioned. He spoke and wrote of what he had seen and known. He had looked upon sights of shocking and enormous iniquity and barbarity, over every scene which he had visited in his unresting travel. His sleep by night had been broken by the piteous shrieks of the wretched victims of slow tortures.

Much help may be derived by a reader towards a fuller appreciation of the character and life-work of Las Casas from the biography of him and the translation and editing of his principal writings by his ardent admirer, Llorente.[1] This writer refers to a previous abridged translation of the works

---

[1] Juan Antonio Llorente, eminent as a writer and historian, both in Spanish and French, was born near Calahorra, Aragon, in 1756, and died at Madrid in 1823. He received the tonsure when fourteen years of age, and was ordained priest at Saragossa in 1779. He was of a vigorous, inquisitive, and liberal spirit, giving free range to his mind, and turning his wide study and deep investigations to the account of his enlargement and emancipation from the limitations of his age and associates. He tells us that in 1784 he had abandoned all ultramontane doctrines, and all the ingenuities and perplexities of scholasticism. His liberalism ran into rational-

of Las Casas, published in Paris in 1642. His own edition in French, in 1822, is more full, though somewhat condensed and reconstructed. He remarks justly upon the prolixity of Las Casas, his long periods, his repetitions, his pedantic quotations from Scripture and the Latin authors, as the results of his peripatetic training. His translator and editor credits to the magnanimity and nobleness of nature of Las Casas the omission of the names of great offenders in connection with the terrible wrongs done by them. This reserve of Las Casas has been already referred to. But Llorente, in seventeen critical notes, answering to the same number of divisions in the *Relation* of Las Casas, supplies the names of the leading criminals; and he also gives in a necrology the shocking or tragic elements and the dates of the death of these "men of blood." He adds to the "Remedies" which Las Casas had suggested to Charles V. the whole additional series of measures proposed up to 1572. Llorente says that, admitting that the starting-point in the Thirty Propositions of Las Casas,—namely, the assumption of the Papal prerogative as to new-discovered territory,—was in his day "incontestable," it is now recognized as a falsity. He furnishes an essay of his own upon the right and wrong of the claim; and he adds to that of Las Casas a treatise on the limits of the sovereign power of the King. Paw first, and then Raynal and Robertson, had brought the charge against Las Casas of having first introduced African slavery into the New World. As we have seen, the charge was false. Gregoire, bishop of Blois, read an *Apologie* before the Institute of France in 1801, in vindication of the Clerigo. This *Apologie* is given at length by Llorente. He adds, from manuscripts in the Royal Library of Paris, two inedited treatises of Las Casas, written in 1555–1564, — one against a project for perpetuating the *commanderies* in the New World; the other on the necessity of restoring the crown of Peru to the Inca Titus.[1]

ism. His secret or more or less avowed alienation from the prejudices and obligations of the priestly order, while it by no means made his position a singular or even an embarrassing one under the influences and surroundings of his time, does at least leave us perplexed to account for the confidence with which functions and high ecclesiastical trusts were committed to and exercised by him. He was even made Secretary-General of the Inquisition, and was thus put in charge of the enormous mass of records, with all their dark secrets, belonging to its whole history and processes. This charge he retained for a time after the Inquisition was abolished in 1809. It was thus by a singular felicity of opportunity that those terrible archives should have been in the care, and subject to the free and intelligent use, of a man best qualified of all others to tell the world their contents, and afterward prompted and at liberty to do so from subsequent changes in his own opinions and relations. To this the world

is indebted for a *History of the Inquisition*, the fidelity and sufficiency of which satisfy all candid judgments. He was restive in spirit, provoked strong opposition, and was thus finally deprived of his office. After performing a variety of services not clerical, and moving from place to place, he went to Paris, where, in 1817–1818, he courageously published the above-mentioned *History*. He was interdicted the exercise of clerical functions. In 1822, the same year in which he published his Biography and French translation of the principal works of Las Casas, he published also his *Political Portraits of the Popes*. For this he was ordered to quit Paris, —a deep disappointment to him, causing chagrin and heavy depression. He found refuge in Madrid, where he died in the following year.

[1] Mr. Ticknor, however, says that these two treatises "are not absolutely proved" to be by Las Casas. — *History of Spanish Literature*, i. 566.

Llorente says it is not strange that the apostle Las Casas, like other great and noble men, met with enemies and detractors. Some assailed him through prejudice, others merely from levity, and without reflection. Four principal reproaches have been brought against him : —

1. He is charged with gross exaggeration in his writings, as by the Spanish writers Camporicanes, Nuix, and Muñoz, and of course by those interested in excusing the work of conquest and devastation, who cannot justify themselves without impeaching Las Casas as an impostor. His sufficient vindication from this charge may be found in a mass of legal documents in the Archives, in the Records of the Council for the Indies, and in Government processes against wrong-doers. Herrera, who had seen these documents, says: "Las Casas was worthy of all confidence, and in no particular has failed to present the truth." Torquemada, having personally sought for evidence in America, says the same. Las Casas, when challenged on this point, boldly affirmed: "There were once more natives in Hispaniola than in all Spain," and that Cuba, Jamaica, and forty other islands, with parts of Terra Firma, had all been wrecked and made desolate. He insists over and over again that his estimates are within the truth.

2. Another charge was of imprudence in his ill-considered proceedings with the Indians. Allowance is to be made on the score of his zeal, his extreme ardor and vehemence, — an offset to the apathy and hard-heartedness of those around him. He was in a position in which he could do nothing for the Indians if he kept silence. He witnessed the reckless and defiant disobedience of the positive instructions of the King by his own high officers.

3. The third charge was of *inconsistency* in condemning the enslaving of Indians, and favoring that of negroes. This has already been disposed of.

4. The final charge was that he was consumed by ambition. Only a single writer had the effrontery to ascribe to Las Casas the desperate purpose of seizing upon the sovereignty of a thousand leagues of territory. The whole foundation of the charge was his attempt to plant a particular colony in the province of Cumana, near St. Martha, on Terra Firma. So far from claiming sovereignty for himself, he even denied the right of the King to bestow such sovereignty.

He was, says Llorente, blameless; there is no stain upon his great virtues. Indeed, not only Spain, but all nations, owe him a debt for his opposition to despotism, and for his setting limits to royal power in the age of Charles V. and the Inquisition.

Then follows Llorente's translation into French of Las Casas' Memoir on the *Cruelties practised on the Indians*, with the Dedicatory Letter addressed to Philip II., 1552. The Spaniards at Hispaniola and elsewhere forgot that they were men, and treated the innocent creatures around them for forty-two years as if they were famished wolves, tigers, and lions. So that in Hispaniola, where once were three millions, there remained not more than two hundred. Cuba, Porto Rico, and Jamaica had been wholly depopulated. On more than sixty Lucayan islands, on the smallest of which were once five hundred thousand natives, Las Casas says, "my own eyes" have seen but eleven.

These appalling enumerations of the victims of Spanish cruelty during half a century from the first coming of the invaders to the islands and main of America, are set before the reader in the figures and estimates of Las Casas. Of course the instant judgment of the reader will be that there is obvious and gross exaggeration in them. It remains to this day a debated and wholly undecided question among archæologists, historians, and explorers best able to deal with it, as to the number of natives on island and continent when America was opened to knowledge. There are no facts within our use for any other mode of dealing with the question than by estimates, conjectures, and inferences. A reasonable view is that the southern islands were far more thickly peopled than the main, vast regions of which, when first penetrated by the whites, were found to be perfect solitudes. The general tendency now with those who have pursued any thorough investigations relating to the above question, is greatly to reduce the number of the aborigines below the guesses and the once-accepted estimates. Nor does it concern us much to attempt any argument as to the obvious over-estimates made by Las Casas, or to decide whether they came from his imagination or fervor of spirit, or whether, as showing himself incredible in these rash and wild enumerations, he brings his veracity and trustworthiness under grave doubts in other matters.

Las Casas says that near the Island of San Juan are thirty others without a single Indian. More than two thousand leagues of territory are wholly deserted. On the continent ten kingdoms, "each larger than Spain," with Aragon and Portugal, are an immense solitude, human life being annihilated there. He estimates the number of men, women, and children who have been slaughtered at more than fifteen millions. Generally they were tormented, no effort having been made to convert them. In vain did the natives, helpless with their feeble weapons, hide their women and children in the mountains. When, maddened by desperation, they killed a single Spaniard, vengeance was taken by the score. The Clerigo, as if following the strictest process of arithmetic, gives the number of victims in each of many places, only with variations and aggravations. He asserts that in Cuba, in three or four months, he had seen more than seven thousand children perish of famine, their parents having been driven off to the mines. He adds that the worst of the cruelties in Hispaniola did not take place till after the death of Isabella, and that efforts were made to conceal from her such as did occur, as she continued to demand right and mercy. She had done her utmost to suppress the system of *repartimientos*, by which the natives were distributed as slaves to masters.

An inference helpful to an approximate estimate of the numbers and extent of the depopulation of the first series of islands seized on by the

Spaniards, might be drawn from the vast numbers of natives deported from other groups of islands to replace the waste and to restore laborers. Geographers have somewhat arbitrarily distinguished the West Indies into three main groupings of islands, — the Lucayan, or Bahamas, of fourteen large and a vast number of small islands, extending, from opposite the coast of Florida, some seven hundred and fifty miles oceanward; the Greater Antilles, embracing Cuba, San Domingo, Porto Rico, Jamaica, etc., running, from opposite the Gulf of Mexico, from farther westward than the other groups; and the Lesser Antilles, or Carribean, or Windward Islands.   The last-named, from their repute of cannibalism, were from the first coming of the Spaniards regarded as fair subjects for spoil, violence, and devastation.   After ruin had done its work in the Greater Antilles, recourse was had to the Lucayan Islands.   By the foulest and meanest stratagems for enticing away the natives of these fair scenes, they were deported in vast numbers to Cuba and elsewhere as slaves.   It was estimated that in five years Ovando had beguiled and carried off forty thousand natives of the Lucayan Islands to Hispaniola.

The amiable and highly honored historian, Mr. Prescott, says in general, of the numerical estimates of Las Casas, that " the good Bishop's arithmetic came more from his heart than his head." [1]

From the fullest examination which I have been able to make, by the comparison of authorities and incidental facts, while I should most frankly admit that Las Casas gave even a wild indulgence to his dismay and his indignation in his figures, I should conclude that he had positive knowledge, from actual eyesight and observation, of every form and shape, as well as instance and aggregation, of the cruelties and enormities which aroused his lifelong efforts.   Besides the means and methods used to discredit the statements and to thwart the appeals of Las Casas at the Court, a very insidious attempt for vindicating, palliating, and even justifying the acts of violence and cruelty which he alleged against the Spaniards in the islands and on the main, was in the charge that their victims were horribly addicted to cannibalism and the offering of human sacrifices.   The number estimated of the latter as slaughtered, especially on great royal occasions, is appalling, and the rites described are hideous.   It seems impossible for us now, from so many dubious and conflicting authorities, to reach any trustworthy knowledge on this subject.   For instance, in Anahuac, Mexico, the annual number of human sacrifices, as stated by different writers, varies from twenty to fifty thousand.   Sepulveda in his contest with Las Casas was bound to

[1] *Conquest of Mexico*, i. 80, *n.*   Of his *Short Account of the Destruction of the Indies*, this historian says : " However good the motives of its author, we may regret that the book was ever written. . . . The author lent a willing ear to every tale of violence and rapine, and magnified the amount to a degree which borders on the ridiculous.   The wild extravagance of his numer- ical estimates is of itself sufficient to shake confidence in the accuracy of his statements generally.   Yet the naked truth was too startling in itself to demand the aid of exaggeration." The historian truly says of himself, in his Preface to the work quoted : " I have not hesitated to expose in their strongest colors the excesses of the conquerors."

make the most of this dismal story, and said that no one of the authorities estimated the number of the victims at less than twenty thousand. Las Casas replied that this was the estimate of brigands, who wished thus to win tolerance for their own slaughterings, and that the actual number of annual victims did not exceed twenty.[1] It was a hard recourse for Christians to seek palliation for their cruelties in noting or exaggerating the superstitious and hideous rites of heathens!

It is certain, however, that this plea of cannibalism was most effectively used, from the first vague reports which Columbus took back to Spain of its prevalence, at least in the Carribean Islands, to overcome the earliest humane protests against the slaughter of the natives and their deportation for slaves. In the all-too hideous engravings presented in the volumes in all the tongues of Europe exposing the cruelties of the Spanish invaders, are found revolting delineations of the Indian shambles, where portions of human bodies, subjected to a fiendish butchery, are exposed for sale. Las Casas nowhere denies positively the existence of this shocking barbarism. One might well infer, however, from his pages that he was at least incredulous as to its prevalence; and to him it would only have heightened his constraining sense of the solemn duty of professed Christians to bring the power of the missionary, rather than the maddened violence of destruction, to bear upon the poor victims of so awful a sin. Nor does the evidence within our reach suffice to prove the prevalence, to the astounding extent alleged by the opponents of Las Casas, of monstrous and bestial crimes against nature practised among the natives. Perhaps a parallel between the general morality respectively existing in the license and vices of the invaders and the children of Nature as presented to us by Columbus, as well as by Las Casas, would not leave matter for boasting to the Europeans. Mr. Prescott enters into an elaborate examination of a subject of frequent discussion by American historians and archæologists, — who have adopted different conclusions upon it, — as to whether venereal diseases had prevalence among the peoples of the New World before it was opened to the intercourse of foreigners. I have not noticed in anything written by Las Casas that he brings any charge on this score against his countrymen. Quite recent exhumations made by our archæologists have seemingly set the question at rest, by revealing in the bones of our prehistoric races the evidences of the prevalence of such diseases.

Sufficient means, in hints and incidental statements, have been furnished in the preceding pages from which the reader may draw his own estimate, as appreciative and judicious as he may be able to make it, of the character of Las Casas as a man and as a missionary of Christ. A labored analysis or an indiscriminating eulogium of that character is wholly uncalled for, and would be a work of supererogation. His heart and mind, his soul and body, his life, with all of opportunity which it offered, were consecrated;

VOL. II. — 42.   [1] Llorente, i. 365, 386.

his foibles and faults were of the most trivial sort, never leading to injury for others, and scarcely working any harm for himself.

It is a well-proved and a gladdening truth, that one who stands for the championship of any single principle involving the rights of humanity will be•led by a kindled vision or a gleam of advanced wisdom to commit himself to the assumption of some great, comprehensive, illuminating verity covering a far wider field than that which he personally occupies. Thus Las Casas' assertion of the common rights of humanity for the heathen natives expanded into a bold denial of the fundamental claims of ecclesiasticism. It was the hope and aim of his opponents and enemies to drive him to a committal of himself to some position which might be charged with at least constructive heresy, through some implication or inference from the basis of his pleadings that he brought under question the authority of the Papacy. Fonseca and Sepulveda were both bent upon forcing him into that perilous attitude towards the supreme ecclesiastical power. To appreciate fully how nearly Las Casas was thought to trespass on the verge of a heresy which might even have cost him his life, but would certainly have nullified his personal influence, we must recognize the full force of the one overmastering assumption, under which the Pope and the Spanish sovereigns claimed for themselves supreme dominion over territory and people in the New World. As a new world, or a disclosure on the earth's surface of vast realms before unknown to dwellers on the old continents, its discovery would carry with it the right of absolute ownership and of rule over all its inhabitants. It was, of course, to be "conquered" and held in subjection. The earth, created by God, had been made the kingdom of Jesus Christ, who assigned it to the charge and administration of his vicegerent, the Pope. All the continents and islands of the earth which were not Christendom were heathendom. It mattered not what state of civilization or barbarism, or what form or substance of religion, might be found in any new-discovered country. The Papal claim was to be asserted there, if with any need of explanation, for courtesy's sake, certainly without any apology or vindication. Could Las Casas be inveigled into any denial or hesitating allowance of this assumption? He was on his guard, but he stood manfully for the condition, the supreme obligation, which alone could give warrant to it. The papal and the royal claims were sound and good; they were indeed absolute. But the tenure of possession and authority in heathendom, if it were to be claimed through the Gospel and the Church, looked quite beyond the control of territory and the lordship over heathen natives, princes, and people, — it was simply to prompt the work and to facilitate, while it positively enjoined the duty of, conversion, — the bringing of heathen natives through baptism and instruction into the fold of Christ. Fonseca and Sepulveda were baffled by the Clerigo as he calmly and firmly told the monarchs that their prerogative, though lawful in itself, was fettered by this obligation. In asserting this just condition, Las Casas effectually disabled his opponents.

The following are the closing sentences of the Reply of Las Casas to Sepulveda : —

"The damages and the loss which have befallen the Crown of Castile and Leon will be visited also upon the whole of Spain, because the tyranny wrought by these desolations, murders, and slaughters is so monstrous that the blind may see it, the deaf may hear it, the dumb may rehearse it, and the wise judge and condemn it after our very short life.   I invoke all the hierarchies and choirs of angels, all the saints of the Celestial Court, all the inhabitants of the globe, and chiefly all those who may live after me, for witnesses that I free my conscience of all that has transpired ; and that I have fully exposed to his Majesty all these woes ; and that if he leaves to Spaniards the tyranny and government of the Indies, all of them will be destroyed and without inhabitants, — as we see that Hispaniola now is, and the other islands and parts of the continent for more than three thousand leagues, without occupants.   For these reasons God will punish Spain and all her people with an inevitable severity.   So may it be ! "

It is grateful to be assured of the fact that during the years of his last retirement in Spain, till the close of his life at so venerable an age, Las Casas enjoyed a pension sufficient for his comfortable subsistence.   Allowing only a pittance of it for his own frugal support, he devoted it mostly to works of charity.   His pen and voice and time were still given to asserting and defending the rights of the natives, not only as human beings, but as free of all mastery by others.   Though his noble zeal had made him enemies, and he had appeared to have failed in his heroic protests and appeals, he had the gratification of knowing before his death that restraining measures, sterner edicts, more faithful and humane officials, and in general a more wise and righteous policy, had abated the rage of cruelty in the New World. But still the sad reflection came to qualify even this satisfaction, that the Spaniards were brought to realize the rights of humanity by learning that their cruelty had wrought to their own serious loss in depopulating the most fertile regions and fastening upon them the hate of the remnants of the people.   The reader of the most recent histories, even of the years of the first quarter of this century, relating to the Spanish missions in the pueblos of Mexico and California, will note how some of the features of the old *repartimiento* system, first introduced among the Greater Antilles, survived in the farm-lands and among the peons and converts of the missionaries.

CRITICAL ESSAY ON THE SOURCES OF INFORMATION.

THE subject of this chapter is so nearly exclusively concerned with the personal history, the agency, and the missionary work of Las Casas, both in the New World and at the Court of Spain, that we are rather to welcome than to regret the fact that he is almost our sole authority for the statements and incidents with which we have had to deal. Giving due allowance to what has already been sufficiently recognized as his intensity of spirit, his wildness of imagination, and his enormous overstatement in his enumeration of the victims of Spanish cruelty, he must be regarded as the best authority we could have for the use which he serves to us.[1]   Free as he was from all selfish and sinister motives, even the daring assurance with which he speaks out before the monarch and his councillors, and prints on his titlepages the round numbers of these victims, prompts us to give full credit to his testimony on other matters, even if we substitute thousands in place of millions.   As to the forms and aggravations of the cruel methods in which the Spaniards

LAS CASAS.

[1] [Helps (*Spanish Conquest*) says : " Las Casas may be thoroughly trusted whenever he is speaking of things of which he had competent knowledge."   Ticknor (*Spanish Literature*, ii. 31) calls him "a prejudiced witness, but on a point of fact within his own knowledge one to be believed."   H. H. Bancroft (*Early American Chroniclers*, p. 20; also *Central America*, i. 274, 309; ii. 337) speaks of the exaggeration which the zeal of Las Casas leads him into ; but with due abatement therefor, he considers him "a keen and valuable observer, guided by practical sagacity, and endowed with a certain genius." — Ed.]

dealt with the natives, the recklessness and ingenuity of the work of depopulation, — which was as naturally the consequence of the enslaving of the Indians as of their indiscriminate slaughter, — Las Casas' revelations seem to have passed unchallenged by even his most virulent enemies.

Sepulveda may be received by us as the representative alike in spirit and in argument of the opposition to Las Casas. He was an acute and able disputant, and would readily have availed himself of any weak points in the positions of the apostle. It is observable that, instead of assailing even the vehement and exaggerated charges alleged by Las Casas against the Spanish marauders for their cruelty, he rather spends his force upon the maintenance of the abstract rights of Christian champions over the heathen and their territory. The Papal and the Royal prerogatives were, in his view, of such supreme and sweeping account in the controversy, as to cover all the incidental consequences of establishing them. He seemed to argue that heathens and heathenism invited and justified conquest by any method, however ruthless; that the rights of the Papacy and of Christian monarchs would be perilled by allowing any regards of sentiment or humanity to stand in the way of their assertion; and that even the sacred duty of conversion was to be deferred till war and tyranny had obtained the absolute mastery over the natives.

The eight years spent by Las Casas in retirement in the Dominican convent at San Domingo were used by him in study and meditation. His writings prove, in their references and quotations from the classics, as well as from Scripture, that his range was wide, and that his mind was invigorated by this training.

In 1552–1553, at Seville, Las Casas printed a series of nine tracts, which are the principal source of our information in relation to his allegations against the Spanish oppressors of the Indians. It is only necessary

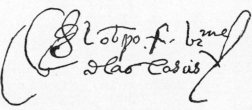

AUTOGRAPH OF LAS CASAS.

to refer the reader to the bibliographies [1] for the full titles of these tracts, of which we simply quote enough for their identification, while we cite them in the order in which they seem to have been composed, following in this the extensive Note which Field has given in his *Indian Bibliography* : —

1. *Breuissima relacion de la destruycion de las Indias* . . . *año* 1552; 50 unnumbered leaves.

The series of tracts is usually cited by this title, which is that of the first tract,[2] for there is no general printed designation of the collection. Four folios appended to this, but always reckoned as a distinct tract, are called, —

[1] Sabin's *Works of Las Casas*, and his *Dictionary*, iii. 388–402, and x. 88–91; Field's *Indian Bibliography*; *Carter-Brown Catalogue*; Harrisse's *Notes on Columbus*, pp. 18–24; the *Huth Catalogue*; *Brunet's Manuel*, etc.

[2] [Field says it was written in 1540, and submitted to the Emperor in MS.; but in the shape in which it was printed it seems to have been written in 1541–1542. Cf. Field, *Indian Bibliography*, nos. 860, 870; Sabin, *Works of Las Casas*, no. 1; *Carter-Brown Catalogue*, i. 164; Ticknor, *Spanish Literature*, ii. 38; and *Catalogue*, p. 62. The work has nineteen sections on as many provinces, ending with a summary for the year 1546. This separate tract was reprinted in the original Spanish in London, in 1812, and again in Philadelphia, in 1821, for the Mexican market, with an introductory essay on Las Casas. Stevens, *Bibliotheca historica*, 1105; cf. also *Coleccion de documentos inéditos (España)*, vol. vii.

The *Cancionero spiritual*, printed at Mexico in 1546, is not assigned to *Bartholomew* Las Casas in Ticknor's *Spanish Literature*, iii. 44, but it is in Gayangos and Vedia's Spanish translation of Ticknor. Cf. also Sabin, vol. x. no. 39,122; Harrisse, *Bib. Am. Vet.*, *Additions*, No. 159. — ED.]

TITLE OF FIRST TRACT.

2. *Lo que se sigue es vn pedoço de vna carta,* etc. It records the observations of a Spanish traveller upon the enormities practised on the natives.[1]

3. *Entre los remedios . . . para reformaciō de las Indias;* 1552; 53 unnumbered leaves. It gives the eighth of the proposed remedies, assigning twenty reasons against the enslaving of the natives.[2]

4. *Aqui se cōtienē vnos auisos y reglas para los confessores,* etc; 1552; 16 unnumbered leaves. It gives the rules for the confessors of his bishopric of Chiapa to deny the offices of the Church to such as held *repartimientos.*[3]

5. *Aqui se contiene vna disputa . . . entre el obispo . . . y el doctor Gines de Sepulveda;* 1552; 61 unnumbered leaves. This strong enunciation of Las Casas' convictions grew out of his controversy with Sepulveda.[4] It contains, first, a summary by Domingo de Soto of the differences between the two disputants; second, the arguments of Sepulveda; and third, the replies of Las Casas, — twelve in all.

6. *Este es vn tratado . . . sobre la materia de los Yndios, que se han hecho en ellas esclauos;* 1552; 36 unnumbered leaves. This contains reasons and judicial authorities on the question of the restitution of the natives to freedom.[5]

7. *Aqui se cōtienē treynta proposiciones . . .;* 1552; 10 leaves. These are the Propositions, mentioned on a preceding page, as Las Casas' reply to those who objected to the rigor of his rules for his confessors.[6]

8. *Principia quedā ex quibus procedendum,* etc; 1552; 10 leaves. This gives the principles on which he conducts his defence of the rights of the natives.[7]

9. *Tratado cōprobatorio del imperio soberano,* etc.; 80 unnumbered leaves. The title-date is 1552, but that in the colophon is 1553. The purpose is "to prove the sovereign empire and universal dominion by which the kings of Castile and Leon hold the West Indies."[8]

Complete sets of these tracts have become very rare, though it is not uncommon to find, in current catalogues, single copies of some of those less scarce.[9]

---

[1] [Field does not give it a date; but Sabin says it was written in 1552. Cf. Field, nos. 860, 870, *note;* Sabin, no. 2; Carter-Brown, i. 165; *Ticknor Catalogue,* p. 62. — ED.]

[2] [Field says it was written "soon after" no. 1; Sabin places it in 1543. Cf. Field, no. 862, 870, *note;* Carter-Brown, i. 166; Sabin, 3; Stevens, *Bibl. Geog.,* no. 595; *Ticknor Catalogue,* p. 62. — ED.]

[3] [Sabin says it was written in America in 1546–1547. Field, nos. 863, 870, *note;* Carter-Brown, i. 167; Sabin, no. 6. — ED.]

[4] [There seems, according to Field (nos. 864, 865), to have been two distinct editions in 1552, as he deduces from his own copy and from a different one belonging to Mr. Brevoort, there being thirty-three variations in the two. Quaritch has noted (no. 11,855, priced at £6 6s.) a copy likewise in Gothic letter, but with different woodcut initials, which he places about 1570. Cf. Field, p. 217; Carter-Brown, i. 168; Sabin, no. 8; *Ticknor Catalogue,* p. 62.

The initial work of Sepulveda, *Democrates Secundus,* defending the rights of the Crown over the natives, was not published, though he printed his *Apologia pro libro de justis belli causis,* Rome, 1550 (two copies of which are known), of which there was a later edition in 1602; and some of his views may be found in it. Cf.

Ticknor, *Spanish Literature,* ii. 37; Harrisse, *Notes on Columbus,* p. 24, and *Bib. Amer. Vet.,* no. 303; and the general histories of Bancroft, Helps, and Prescott. The *Carter-Brown Catalogue,* no. 173, shows a MS. copy of Sepulveda's book. It is also in Sepulveda's *Opera,* Cologne, 1602, p. 423; Carter-Brown, vol. ii. no. 15. — ED.]

[5] [Sabin dates it in 1543. Cf. Field, nos. 866, 870, *note;* Sabin, no. 4; Carter-Brown, i. 170. — ED.]

[6] [Sabin says it was written in Spain in 1548. Cf. Field, nos. 867, 870, *note;* Sabin, no. 7; Carter-Brown, i. 171. — ED.]

[7] [Field, nos. 868, 870, *note;* Sabin, no. 9; Carter-Brown, i. 169. — ED.]

[8] [This is the longest and one of the rarest of the series. Sabin says it was written about 1543. There were two editions of the same date, having respectively 80 and 84 leaves; but it is uncertain which is the earlier, though Field supposes the fewer pages to indicate the first. Field, nos. 869, 870, *note;* Sabin, no. 5; Carter-Brown, i. 172. — ED.]

[9] [It is only of late years that the entire series has been described. De Bure gives only five of the tracts; Dibdin enumerates but seven; and Llorente in his edition omits three, as was done in the edition of 1646. Rich in 1832 priced a

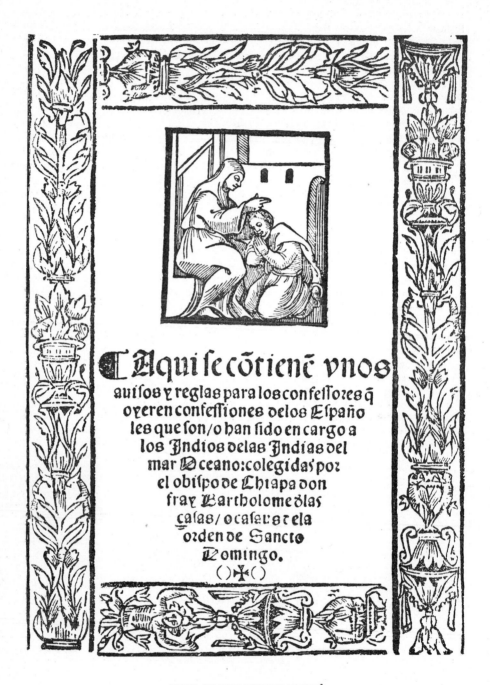

TITLE OF THE FOURTH TRACT.[1]

[1] [From the copy in Harvard College Library. — ED.]

In 1571, five years after Las Casas' death, what is sometimes called a tenth part was printed at Frankfort, under the title of *Explicatio questionis utrum Reges vel Principes jure aliquo . . . Cives ac subditos a regia corona alienare?* This further showing of the arguments of Las Casas is even rarer than its predecessors.[1] Its authorship, without much reason, has been sometimes denied.[2] It is translated, however, in Llorente's edition, as is also a letter of Las Casas which he wrote in 1555 to the Archbishop of Toledo, protesting against the contemplated sale of *Encomiendas* in perpetuity, which, being communicated to the King, led to the prohibition of the plan.

In 1854 Henry Stevens printed, in a style corresponding to that of the tracts of 1552, a series of six papers from original manuscripts in his possession, interesting as contributions to the history of Las Casas and his work;[3] and there is also a letter of Las Casas in the volume a few years since printed by the Spanish Government as *Cartas de Indias*. There is an enumeration of thirteen other treatises, noted as still in manuscript, which is to be found in Sabin's *Dictionary* or in his separate *Works of Las Casas;* but Mr. Field is inclined for one reason or another to reduce the number to five, in addition to the two which were published by Llorente.[4] There are also two manuscripts recorded in the *Carter-Brown Catalogue*.[5]

set at £12 12s. A full set is now worth from $100 to $150; but Leclerc (nos. 327, 2,556) has recently priced a set of seven at 700 francs, and a full set at 1,000 francs. An English dealer has lately held one at £42. Quaritch has held four parts at £10, and a complete set at £40. Single tracts are usually priced at from £1 to £5. Recent sales have been shown in the Sunderland (no. 2,459, 9 parts); Field (no. 1,267); Cooke (vol. iii. no. 369, 7 parts); Stevens, *Hist. Coll.* (no. 311, 8 parts); Pinart (no. 536); and Murphy (no. 487) catalogues. The set in the Carter-Brown Library belonged to Ternaux; that belonging to Mr. Brevoort came from the Maximilian Library. The Lenox Library and Mr. Barlow's Collection have sets. There are also sets in the Grenville and Huth collections.

The 1646 reprint, above referred to, has sometimes a collective title, *Las Obras*, etc., but most copies, like the Harvard College copy, lack it. As the titles of the separate tracts (printed in this edition in Roman) retained the original 1552 dates, this reprint is often called a spurious edition. It is usually priced at from $15 to $30. Cf. Sabin, no. 13; Field, p. 216; Quaritch, no. 11,856; Carter-Brown, i. 173; ii. 584; Stevens, *Hist. Coll.*, i. 312; Cooke, iii. 370. Some of the Tracts are included in the *Obras escogidas de filósofos*, etc. Madrid, 1873. — Ed.]

[1] [Field, no. 870, and *note;* Sabin, no. 11; the Carter-Brown Collection lacks it. It was reprinted at Tübingen, and again at Jena, in 1678. It has never been reprinted in Spain, says Stevens (*Bibl. Hist.*, no. 1,096). — Ed.]

[2] ["Not absolutely proved to be his," says Ticknor (*Spanish Literature*, ii. 37). — Ed.]

[3] [There were a hundred copies of these printed. They are:—

1. *Memorial de Don Diego Colon sobre la conversion de las gentes de las Yndias.* With an Epistle to Dr. Reinhold Pauli. It is Diego Colon's favorable comment on Las Casas's

VOL. II. — 43.

scheme of civilizing the Indians, written at King Charles's request. Cf. Stevens, *Hist. Coll.*, i. 881.

2. *Carta*, dated 1520, and addressed to the Chancellor of Charles, in which Las Casas urges his scheme of colonization of the Indians. Mr. Stevens dedicates it to Arthur Helps in a letter. Cf. Stevens, *Hist. Coll.*, i. 882; the manuscript is described in his *Bibl. Geog.*, no. 598.

3. *Paresçer o determinaciõ de los señores theologos de Salamanca*, dated July 1, 1541. This is the response of the Faculty of Salamanca to the question put to them by Charles V., if the baptized natives could be made slaves. Mr. Stevens dedicates the tract to Sir Thomas Phillipps. Cf. Stevens, *Hist. Coll.* i. 883.

4. *Carta de Hernando Cortés.* Mr. Stevens, in his Dedication to Leopold von Ranke, supposes this to have been written in 1541-1542. It is Cortes' reply to the Emperor's request for his opinions regarding *Encomiendas*, etc., in Mexico. Cf. Stevens, *Hist. Coll.*, i. 884.

5. *Carta de Las Casas*, dated Oct. 22, 1545, with an abstract in English in the Dedication to Colonel Peter Force. It is addressed to the Audiencia in Honduras, and sets forth the wrongs of the natives. Cf. Stevens, *Hist. Coll.*, i. 885. The manuscript is now in the Huth Collection, *Catalogue*, v. 1,681.

6. *Carta de Las Casas* to the Dominican Fathers of Guatemala, protesting against the sale of the reversion of the *Encomiendas*. Mr. Stevens supposes this to have been written in 1554, in his Dedication to Sir Frederick Madden. Cf. Stevens, *Hist. Coll.*, i. 886. A set of these tracts is worth about $25. The set in the Cooke Sale (vol. iii. no. 375) is now in Harvard College Library; another set is shown in the *Murphy Catalogue*, no. 488, and there is one in the Boston Public Library. — Ed.]

[4] Field, p. 219.

[5] Vol. i. p. 160.

TITLE OF THE SEVENTH TRACT.[1]

[1] [From a copy in Harvard College Library. — ED.]

The most labored of Las Casas' books was his *Historia de las Indias*, — the original manuscript of which is still preserved, according to Helps, in the library of the Academy of History at Madrid.[1] Las Casas began this work while in his convent in 1527,[2] and seems to have worked upon it, without finishing it, up to 1561. It has all the fervor and vigor of his nature ; and so far as it is the result of his own observation, its character is unimpeachable. It is in large part, as Helps has remarked, autobiographic ; but it does.

LAS CASAS' INDORSEMENT ON THE MANUSCRIPT OF HIS "HISTORIA."[3]

[1] [Harrisse, *Notes on Columbus*, says volumes i. and ii. are in the Academy ; but volume iii. is in the Royal Library. Cf., however, the "Advertencia preliminar" of the Madrid (1875) edition of the *Historia* on this point, as well as regards the various copies of the manuscript existing in Madrid. — ED.]

[2] [Such is Quintana's statement ; but Helps failed to verify it, and says he could only fix the dates 1552, 1560, 1561 as those of any part of the writing. *Life of Las Casas*, p. 175. — ED.]

[3] [This is slightly reduced from the facsimile given in vol. iii. of the 1875 (Madrid) edition of the *Historia*. — ED.]

not bring the story down later than 1520. Its style is characteristically rambling and awkward, and more or less confused with extraneous learning, the result of his convent studies, and interjected with his usual bursts of a somewhat tiresome indignation. Outside of his own knowledge he had large resources in documents, of which we have no present knowledge. He seems to have had a prescience of the feelings in his countrymen which would long keep the manuscript from the printing-office, for he left instructions at his death that no one should use it for forty years. The injunction did not prevent Herrera having access to it; and when this latter historian published his book in 1601, the world got a large part of Las Casas' work, — much of it copied by Herrera *verbatim*, — but extracted in such a way that Las Casas could have none of his proper effect in ameliorating the condition of the Indians and exposing the cruelty of their oppression. In this way Las Casas remained too long eclipsed, as Irving says, by his copyist. Notwithstanding the publication of the book was prohibited, various manuscript copies got abroad, and every reputable historian of the Spanish rule has made use of Las Casas' labors.[1] Finally, the Royal Academy of History at Madrid undertook the revision of the manuscript; but that body was deterred from putting their revision on the press by the sentiments, which Spanish scholars had always felt, adverse to making public so intense an arraignment of their countrymen.[2] At last, however, in 1875–1876, the Academy finally printed it in five volumes.[3] The *Historia* was of course not included, nor were two of the tracts of the issues of 1552 (nos. 4 and 8) embraced, in the edition of Las Casas' *Obras* which Llorente issued in Paris in 1822 in the original Spanish, and also in the same year in a French translation, *Œuvres de Las Casas*.[4] This work is dedicated " Au modèle des virtues héréditaires, A. M. le Comte de las Casas." Sufficient recognition has been made in the preceding narrative of this work of Llorente. As a Spaniard by birth, and a scholar well read in the historical literature of his own country, as one trained and exercised in the priestly office, though he had become more or less of a heretic, and as a most ardent admirer of the virtues and the heroic services of the great Apostle to the Indians, he had the attainments, qualifications, and motives for discharging with ability and fidelity the biographical and editorial task which he undertook. It is evident from his pages that he devoted conscientious labor in investigation, and a purpose of strict impartiality to its discharge. He is not an undiscriminating eulogist of Las Casas, but he penetrates with a true sympathetic admiration to the noble unselfishness and the sublime constancy of this sole champion of righteousness against powerful forces of iniquity.

The number of versions of all or of part of the series of the 1552 tracts into other languages strikingly indicates the interest which they created and the effect which they produced throughout Europe. None of the nations showed more eagerness to make

---

[1] [I trace no copy earlier than one Rich had made. Prescott had one, which was probably burned in Boston (1872). Helps used another. There are other copies in the Library of Congress, in the Lenox Library, and in H. H. Bancroft's Collection. — Ed.]

[2] [Harrisse, *Bibl. Amer. Vet.*, p. 119, says the purpose of the Academy at one time was to annotate the manuscript, so as to show Las Casas in a new light, using contemporary writers. — Ed.]

[3] [It is worth from $30 to $40. It is called *Historia de las Indias, ahora por primera vez dada á luz por el Marqués de la Fuensanta del Valle y José Sancho Rayon*. It contains, beginning in vol. v. at p. 237, the *Apologética historia* which Las Casas had written to defend the Indians against aspersions upon their lives and character. This latter work was not included in

another edition of the *Historia* printed at Mexico in two volumes in 1877–1878. Cf. Vigel, *Biblioteca Mexicana*. Parts of the *Apologética* are given in Kingsborough's *Mexico*, vol. viii. Cf. on the *Historia*, Irving's *Columbus*, App.; Helps's *Spanish Conquest* (Am. ed.), i. 23, and *Life of Las Casas*, p. 175; Ticknor, *Spanish Literature*, ii. 39; Humboldt's *Cosmos* (Eng. tr.), ii. 679; H. H. Bancroft, *Central America*, i. 309; Prescott's *Mexico*, i. 378; Quintana's *Vidas*, iii. 507. — Ed.]

[4] [Llorente's version is not always strictly faithful, being in parts condensed and paraphrastic. Cf. Field, no. 889; Ticknor, *Spanish Literature*, ii. 38, and *Catalogue*, p. 62; Sabin, nos. 14, 50; H. H. Bancroft, *Central America*, i. 309. This edition, besides a life of Las Casas, contains a necrology of the Conquerors, and other annotations by the editor. — Ed.]

public these accusations against the Spaniards by one of their own number, than the Flemings and Dutch. The earliest of all the translations, and one of the rarest of these publications, is the version of the first tract, with parts of others, which appeared in the dialect of Brabant, in 1578, — the precursor of a long series of such testimonies, used to incite the Netherlanders against the Spanish rule.[1] The French came next with their *Tyrannies et cruautéz des Espagnols*, published at Antwerp in 1579, in which the translator, Jacques de Miggrode, softened the horrors of the story with a due regard for his Spanish neighbors.[2] A somewhat bolder venture was a new version, not from the originals, but from the Dutch translation, and set out with all the horrors of De Bry's seventeen engravings, which was supplied to the French market with an Amsterdam imprint in 1620. It is a distorted patchwork of parts of the three of the 1552 tracts.[3] In a brief preface, the translator says that the part relating to the Indies is derived from the original, printed at Seville by Sebastian Trugillo in 1552, the writer "being Las Casas, who seems to be a holy man and a Catholic." There were still other French versions, printed both in France and in Holland.[4] The earliest English translation is a version signed by M. M. S., entitled *The Spanish Colonie, or Briefe Chronicle of the Acts and Gestes of the Spaniardes in the West Indies, called the Newe Worlde, for the Space of XL. Yeeres*, issued in London in 1583.[5] The best-known of the English versions is *The Tears of the Indians*, "made English by J. P.," and printed in London in 1656.[6] "J. P." is John Phillips, a nephew of John Milton. His little book, which contains a terse translation of Las Casas's "Cruelty," etc., without his controversy with Sepulveda, is dedicated to Oliver Cromwell. It is prefaced by a glowing appeal "To all true Englishmen," which rehearses the proud position they hold in history for religion, liberty, and human rights, and denounces the Spaniards as

[1] [This earliest version is a tract of 70 leaves, printed probably at Brussels, and called *Seer cort Verhael vande destructie van d' Indien*. Cf. Sabin, no. 23; Carter-Brown, i. 320; Stevens, *Bibl. Hist.*, no. 1,097. The whole series is reviewed in Tiele's *Mémoire bibliographique* (who gives twenty-one editions) and in Sabin's *Works of Las Casas* (taken from his *Dictionary*); and many of them are noted in the *Carter-Brown Catalogue* and in Muller's *Books on America*, 1872 and 1877. This 1578 edition was reissued in 1579 with a new title, *Spieghel der Spaenscher Tirannije*, which in some form continued to be the title of subsequent editions, which were issued in 1596, 1607, 1609, 1610, 1612 (two), 1620 (two), 1621, 1627 (?), 1634, 1638, 1663, 1664, etc. Several of these editions give De Bry's engravings. sometimes in reverse. A popular chap-book, printed about 1730, is made up from Las Casas and other sources. — ED.]

[2] [This included the first, second, and sixth of the tracts of 1552. In 1582 there was a new edition of the *Tyrannies*, etc., printed at Paris; but some copies seem to have had a changed title, *Histoire admirable des horribles insolences*, etc. It was again reissued with the original title at Rouen in 1630. Cf. Field, 873, 874; Sabin, nos. 41, 42, 43, 45; Rich (1832); Stevens, *Bibl. Hist.*, no. 1,098; Leclerc, nos. 334, 2,558; Carter-Brown, i. 329, 345, 347; O'Callaghan, no. 1,336; a London catalogue (A. R. Smith, 1874) notes an edition of the *Histoire admirable des horribles Insolences, Cruautez et tyrraines exercées par les Espagnols*, etc., Lyons, 1594. — ED.]

[3] [Sabin, no. 44; Leclerc, no. 335; Field, no. 876; Carter-Brown, ii. 236; O'Callaghan, no. 1,337. It is a rare book, and is sometimes quoted at £15 or thereabout. It is called *Le miroir de la tyrannie Espagnole.* — ED.]

[4] [One printed at Lyons in 1642 is called *Histoire des Indes occidentales*, which Graesse says follows a Paris edition of 1635. Cf. Field, pp. 222, 223; Carter-Brown, ii. 498; Sabin, no. 46; Muller (1877), no. 1797. Rich says this translation was made by the Abbé de Bellegarde, who tempered the rougher parts, as his predecessors had done. The text is much abbreviated from Las Casas, using, however, only a part of his tracts. This version was reissued, according to Graesse, in 1692; but most bibliographers cite as the same with it, *La découverte des Indes occidentales*, Paris, 1697 and 1701, and the *Relation des voyages . . . dans les Indes occidentales*, Amsterdam, 1698. Cf. Sabin, nos. 47, 48, 49; Carter-Brown, ii. 1,510, 1,527; O'Callaghan, nos. 1,340, 1,342. — ED.]

[5] [It is a tract of sixty-four leaves in Gothic letter, and is very rare, prices being quoted at £20 and more. Cf. Sabin, no. 61; Carter-Brown, i. 351; Stevens, *Bibl. Geog.*, 596, *Huth Catalogue*, i. 271. Cf. William Lightfoote's *Complaints of England*, London, 1587, for English opinion at this time on the Spanish excesses (Sabin, vol. x. no. 41,050), and the *Foreign Quarterly Review* (1841), ii. 102. — ED.]

[6] [Field, p. 877; Carter-Brown, ii. 804; Sabin, no. 60. The first tract is translated in Purchas's *Pilgrimes*, iv. 1,569. — ED.]

"a Proud, Deceitful, Cruel, and Treacherous Nation, whose chiefest Aim hath been the Conquest of this Land," etc., closing with a call upon them to aid the Protector in the threatened contest for the West Indies.

While Phillips places the number of the slaughtered Indians at twenty millions, these are reckoned at forty millions by the editor of another English version, based upon the French *Tyrannies et cruautéz*, which was printed at London, in 1699, as *A Relation of the First Voyages and Discoveries made by the Spaniards in America*.[1] The earliest German edition appeared, in 1597, as *Newe Welt: warhafftige Anzeigung der Hispanier grewlichen . . . Tyranney*.[2] The Latin edition appeared at Frankfort, in 1598, as *Narratio regionum Indicarvm per Hispanos qvosdam deuastatarum verissima*.[3] This Latin translation has a brief introduction, mainly a quotation from Lipsius, commenting on these atrocities. The version is spirited and faithful, covering the narrative of Las Casas and his discussion with Sepulveda. The engravings by De Bry are ghastly and revolting, and present all too faithfully the shocking enormities related in the text. It is a fearful parody of deception and truth which introduces a hooded friar as holding a crucifix before the eyes of one under torment by fire or mutilation. We can scarcely regret that the circumstances under which the indiscriminate slaughter was waged but rarely allowed of this desecration of a sacred symbol. The artist has overdrawn his subjects in delineating heaps of richly wrought and chased vessels as brought by the hounded victims to appease their tormentors.

To close this list of translations, it is only necessary to refer to the sundry ways in which Las Casas was helped to create an influence in Italy, the Italian text in these publications usually accompanying the Spanish.[4]

George E. Ellis.

[1] [Some copies read, *Account of the First Voyages*, etc. Cf. Field, no. 880; Carter-Brown, vol. ii. no. 1,556; Sabin, no. 63; Stevens, *Bibl. Geog.*, no. 603; and *Prince Library Catalogue*, p. 34. Another English edition, London, 1689, is called *Popery truly display'd in its Bloody Colours*. Cf. Carter-Brown, vol. ii. no. 1,374; Sabin, no. 62. Another London book of 1740. *Old England for Ever*, is often called a Las Casas, but it is not his. Field, no. 888. — ED.]

[2] [Sabin, no. 51; Carter-Brown, i. 510; Stevens, *Hist. Coll.*, i. 319. It has no place. Muller calls a *Warhafftiger Bericht* of 1599, with no place, the earliest German edition, with De Bry's, engravings, — which were also in the Oppenheim edition of 1613, *Warhafftiger und gründlicher Bericht*, etc. Cf. Sabin, no. 54; Carter-Brown, ii. 146. A similar title belongs to a Frankfort edition of 1597 (based on the Antwerp French edition of 1579), which is noted in Sabin, no. 52, and in *Bib. Grenvilliana*, ii. 828, and was accompanied by a volume of plates (Sabin, no, 53).

There seem to be two varieties of the German edition of 1665, *Umbständige warhafftige Beschreibung der Indianischen Ländern*. Cf. Carter-Brown, ii. 957; Sabin, no. 55; Field, no. 882. Sabin (no. 56) also notes a 1790 and other editions. — ED.]

[3] [It followed the French edition of 1579, and was reissued at Oppenheim in 1614. Cf. Field, p. 871; Carter-Brown, i. 453, 524; ii. 164; Sabin, nos. 57, 58.

The Heidelberg edition of 1664, *Regionum Indicarum per Hispanos olim devastatarum descriptio*, omits the sixteen pages of preliminary matter of the early editions; and the plates, judging from the Harvard College and other copies, show wear. Sabin, no. 59; Carter-Brown, ii. 944. — ED.]

[4] [As in the *Istoria ò brevissima relatione*, Venice, 1626, 1630, and 1643, a version of the first tract of 1552, made by Castellani. It was later included in Marmocchi's *Raccolta di viaggi*. Cf. Sabin, nos. 16, 17, 18; Carter-Brown, ii. 311, 360, 514; Leclerc, no. 331; Field, no 885; Stevens, *Hist. Coll.*, i. 315; *Bibl. Hist.*, no. 1,100. The sixth tract was translated as *Il supplice schiavo Indiano*, and published at Venice in 1635, 1636, and 1657. Cf. Carter-Brown, ii. 434, 816; Field, no. 886; Sabin, nos. 20, 21. It was reissued in 1640 as *La libertà pretesa*. Sabin, no. 19; Field, no. 887; Carter-Brown, ii. 473. The eighth and ninth tracts appeared as *Conquista dell' Indie occidentali*, Venice, 1645. Cf. Field, no. 884; Sabin, no. 22; Carter-Brown, ii. 566. — ED.]

EDITORIAL NOTE.

THE most important distinctive lives of Las Casas are those of Llorente, prefixed to his edition of Las Casas' *Œuvres;* that which Quintana (born, 1772; died, 1857) gives in his *Vidas de Españoles célebres,* vol. iii., published at Madrid in 1833, and reprinted, with Quintana's *Obras,* in the *Biblioteca de autores Españoles* in 1852; and the *Vida y escritos de Las Casas* of A. M. Fabié, published at Madrid in 1879, in two volumes, with a large number of unpublished documents, making vols. 70 and 71 of the *Documentos inéditos (España).* The life which was constructed mainly by the son of Arthur Helps out of *The Spanish Conquest in America* by the father, is the most considerable account in English. The larger work was written in a spirit readily appreciative of the character of Las Casas, and he is made such a centre of interest in it as easily to favor the excision of parts of it to form the lesser book. This was hardly possible with the broader connections established between Las Casas and his times which accompany the portrayal of his career in the works of Prescott and H. H. Bancroft. The great friend of the Indian is mainly, however, to be drawn from his own writings.

Las Casas was by no means alone in his advocacy of the rights of the natives, as Harrisse (*Bibl. Am. Vet. Add.,* p. 119) has pointed out; naming Julian Garces, Francis of Vittoria, Diego de Avendaño, Alonzo de Noreña, and even Queen Isabel herself, as evinced by her will (in Dormer, *Discursos varios,* p. 381). The fame of Las Casas was steadfastly upheld by Remesal in his *Historia de Chyapa,* etc., 1619 (cf. Bancroft, *Central America,* ii. 339); and the great apostle found a successor in his labors in Juan de Palafox y Mendoça, whose appeal to the King, printed about 1650, and called *Virtudes del Indio, é naturaleza y costumbres de los Indios de Nueva España,* has become very rare. (Cf. Carter-Brown, vol. ii. no. 691.) Brasseur de Bourbourg, in the fourth volume of his *Nations civilisées du Mexique,* set forth in all their enormity the barbarities of the Spanish conquerors; but he seeks to avoid all imputations of exaggeration by shunning the evidence drawn from Las Casas.

The opponents of Las Casas — who became in due time the best-hated man in the Spanish colonies — were neither few nor powerless, as the thwarting of Las Casas' plans constantly showed. The Fray Toribio Motolinia took issue with Las Casas, and Ramirez, in his Life of Motolinia contained in Icazbalceta's *Coleccion,* undertakes to show (p. lvii) the difference between them. Cf. B. Smith's *Coleccion,* p. 67.

The most conspicuous of his fellow-observers, who reached conclusions constantly quite at variance with Las Casas, was Gonzalo Fernandez de Oviedo y Valdes, — to give his full name, though Oviedo is the one by which he is usually cited. Oviedo was but a few years younger than Las Casas. He had seen Columbus' triumph at Barcelona, and had come to America with Pedrarias ten years after Las Casas, and spent thirty-four of the next forty years in the New World, holding part of the time the office of inspector of the gold-smeltings at Darien, and latterly living at Hispaniola. He is thought to have begun his historical studies as early as 1520, and he published his first book, usually called the *Sumario,* in 1526, on his return from his second voyage. It is a description of the West Indies and its natives. Returning to Spain in 1530, he was after a while made the official chronicler of the Indies, and in 1535 began the publication of his

great *Historia de las Indias.* On this chief labor Ticknor (*Spanish Literature,* ii. 33) traces him at work certainly as late as 1548, and he may have added to it down to 1555. He had the royal direction to demand of the various governors whatever document and aid he might need as he went on. Ticknor calls him the first authorized chronicler of the New World, — "an office," he adds, "which was at one time better paid than any other similar office in the kingdom, and was held at different times by Herrera, Tamayo, Solis, and other writers of distinction, and ceased (he believed) with the creation of the Academy of History." Oviedo was a correspondent of Ramusio, and found the acquaintance helpful. He knew Cortes, and exchanged letters with him. Ticknor, after speaking of the scope of the *Historia* as taxing the powers of Oviedo beyond their strength, still accounts the work of great value as a vast repository of facts, and not wholly without merit as a composition. In the

TITLE OF OVIEDO, 1526, REDUCED.

estimates commonly made of Oviedo there is allowed him but scant scholarship, little power of discrimination, — as shown in his giving at times as much weight to hearsay evidence as to established testimony, — a curious and shrewd insight, which sometimes, with his industry, leads him to a better balance of authorities than might be expected from his deficient judgment. His resources of material were uncommon; but his use of them is generally tedious, with a tendency to wander from his theme. Ternaux sees in him the prejudices of his times, — and these were not certainly very friendly to the natives. Las Casas could no more endure him than he could bear with the average *conquistador*. The bishop charges the historian with constantly bearing false witness against the Indians, and with lying on every page. Oviedo died at Valladolid in 1557. (Cf. Prescott's *Mexico*, ii. 283; Irving's *Columbus*, App. xxviii.; H. H. Bancroft, *Chroniclers*, p. 20, and *Central America*, i. 309, 463–467.)

The bibliography of Oviedo deserves to be traced. His initial publication, *De la natural hystoria de las Indias*, was printed at Toledo in 1526, — not in 1525, as the Real Academia says in their reprint, nor 1528, as Ticknor gives it. It is often cited as Oviedo's *Sumario*, since that is the first word of the secondary title. (Cf. Sabin, *Dictionary*, vol. xiv. no. 57,987; Harrisse, *Notes on Columbus*, p. 12; and *Bibl. Amer. Vet.*, no. 139; Ternaux, no. 35; Rich, 1832, no. 6, £12 12s.; Carter-Brown, i. 89.) There are also copies in the Library of Congress and Harvard College. The Spanish text is included in Barcia's *Historiadores primitivos* and in Vedia's *Hist. prim. de Indias*, 1858, vol. i. It is in large part translated into English in Eden's *Decades of the New World*, 1555 (chap. 18), and this version is condensed in Purchas's *Pilgrimes*, iv. 5. There is an Italian version in Ramusio's *Viaggi*, iii. 44.

The publication of Oviedo's great work, which is quite different from the 1526 book, was begun at Seville, in 1535, under the title of *Historia general de las Indias*. In this he gave the first

nineteen books, and ten chapters of book 50. At the end is a *carta missiva*, to which the author usually attached his own signature, and that annexed is taken (slightly reduced) from the copy in Harvard College Library. (Cf. Sabin, vol. xiv. no. 57,988; Harrisse, *Bibl. Am. Vet.*, no. 207; Murphy, nos. 1886–87; Carter-Brown, i. 114, with fac-simile of title.) Ramusio translated these nineteen books. In 1547, what purports to be a summary, but is in fact a version, of Xeres

ARMS OF OVIEDO.[1]

by Jacques Gohory, appeared in Paris as *L'histoire de la terre neuve du Péru en l'Inde occidentale*. (Cf. *Bib. Am. Vet.*, no. 264; Ternaux, no. 52; Sabin, vol. xiv. no. 57,994.)

In 1547 a new edition of the Spanish, somewhat increased, appeared at Salamanca as *Coronica de las Indias; la hystoria general de las Indias agora nueuamente impressa, corregida, y emendada*. Sometimes it is found in the same cover with the *Peru* of Xeres, and then the title varies a little. The book is rare and costly. Rich, in 1832 (no. 17), priced it at £10 10s.; it has been sold recently at the Sunderland sale

---

[1] Reduced from the cut at the end of the edition of Oviedo, 1535.

for £61, and in the library of an old admiral (1883, no. 340) for £40; Quaritch has priced it at £63, and Maisonneuve (Leclerc, no. 432), at 1,000 francs. There is a copy in Harvard College Library. (Cf. Sabin, vol. xiv. no. 57,989; Carter-Brown, i. 145; *Bibl. Am. Vet.*, no. 278; *Additions*, no. 163; and Murphy, no. 1885.)

A full French translation of ten books, made by Jean Poleur, appeared in Paris under the set is worth about $20. See further, Brunet, iv, 299; Ternaux, no. 46; Panzer, vii. 124; Stevens, *Nuggets*, ii. 2,067.) Ternaux had already, in 1840, published in French, as a *Histoire de Nicaragua* (in his second series, vol. iii.) thirteen chapters of book xlii.

There was an Italian traveller in the Spanish provinces between 1541 and 1556 who, while he thought that Las Casas mistook his vocation in

ciecia real de Cefar z la de.Ⓐ.Ⓢ.reueredoiſſima z deſſos ſeñozes del cóſejo mas ſin eſ crupulo eſtuuieſſen: z los vezinos de aĝllas partes mas ſeguros z pacificamēte biuieſ ſemos a glozia z alabáça de jeſu chziſto:el qual la reuerendiſſima z illuſtriſſima perſoナ na y eſtado de.Ⓐ.Ⓢ largos tiempos pzoſpere ĝ ſu ſanto ſeruicio.De ſeuilla a trezēta diaas del meſ de Setiembze:de.ⒶⒹ.o.z trezēta z cinco años.

title of *Histoire naturelle et génèralle des Indes*, without out the translator's name in 1555, and with it in 1556. (Cf. Sabin, vol. xiv. no. 57,992–93; Ternaux, no. 47; Carter-Brown, iii. 214; Beckford, iii. 342; Murphy, no. 1884; Leclerc, no. 434, 130 francs, and no. 2,888, 350 francs; Quaritch, no. 12,313, £7 10s.) There is a copy in Harvard College Library.

The twentieth book, *Libro xx de la segunda parte de la general historia de las Indias* appeared for the first time and separately at Valladolid in 1557; the death of the author while his book was in press prevented the continuance of its pnblication. (Cf. Rich, 1832, no. 34, £6 6s.; Sabin, vol. xiv. no. 57,991; Carter-Brown, i. 219.)

The fate of the remaining parts of the manuscript was for a while uncertain. Rich, in 1832, said that books xxi. to xxviii., which were in the printer's hands at Oviedo's death, were not recovered, while he knew of manuscript copies of books xxix. to xlviii. in several collections. Irving says he found a copy of the unprinted parts in the Colombina Library at Seville. Harrisse (*Notes on Columbus* and *Bibl. Am. Vet.*, no. 207) says the manuscript was scattered, but was brought together again after some vicissitudes. Another statement places it in the Casa de la Contratacion after Oviedo's death; whence it was transferred to the Convent of Monserrat. Meanwhile sundry manuscript copies were taken. (Cf. *Notes on Columbus*, p. 17.) In 1775 the publication of it was ordered by Government; but it was not till 1851–1855 that the Real Academia de la Historia at Madrid issued the fifty books, complete in four volumes folio, under the editing of José Amador de los Rios, who added to the publication several maps, a bibliography, and the best Life of Oviedo yet written. (Cf. Sabin, vol. xiv. no. 57,990; the

attempting to administer a colony, bears evidence to the atrocities which Las Casas so persistently magnified. This wanderer was a Milanese, Girolamo Benzoni, who at the early age of twenty-two had started on his American travels. He did not altogether succeed in ingratiating himself with the Spaniards whom he encountered, and perhaps his discontent colored somewhat his views. He was not much of a scholar, yielded not a little to credulity, and picked up mere gossip indeed, but of a kind which gives us much light as to the conditions both of the Europeans and natives. (Cf. Field, *Indian Bibliography*, no. 117; Bancroft, *Central America*, ii. 232; Admiral Smith's Introduction to the Hakluyt Society edition.) After his return he prepared and published — prefixing his own likeness, as shown here in fac-simile — the results of his observations in his *Historia del Mondo Nuovo*, which was issued at Venice in 1565. It became a popular book, and spread through Europe not only in the original Italian, but in French and Latin versions. In Spanish it never became current; for though it so greatly concerns that people, no one of them ventured to give it the help of a translation into their vernacular; and as he had not said much in praise of their American career, it is not altogether strange.

The bibliography of the book merits explanation. It is treated at length in Sabin's *Dictionary*, vol. ii. no. 4,791, and in the *Studi biog. e bibliog. della Società Geografica Italiana*, i. 293 (1882). The original Italian edition, *La Historia del Mondo Nuovo, laqual tratta dell' Isole & Mari nuovamente ritrovati, & delle nuove Citta da lui proprio vedute, per acqua & per terra in quattordeci anni*, was published at Venice in 1565. There are copies in Harvard College, Cornell University, and the Carter-Brown libraries. Cf. Rich (1832), no. 43 — £1 1s. 0d.; Leclerc (1878), no. 59 — 120 francs; A. R. Smith (1874), £2 2s. 0d.; Brinley, no. 10; Carter-Brown, i. 253; Huth, i. 132; Field, *Indian Bibliography*, no. 117; Sparks, no. 240; Stevens (1870), no. 171. A second Italian edition — *Nuovamente ristampata . . . con la giunta d'alcune cose notabile dell' Isole di Canaria* — was issued at Venice in 1572. Cf. Rich (1832), no. 49, £1 1s. 0d.; Carter-Brown, i. 289; Stevens, no. 172; Muller (1877), no. 285; Sunderland, no. 1,213; H. C. Murphy, no. 2,838; Huth, i. 132; J. J. Cooke, nos. 219, 220.

The first Latin edition *Novæ Novi Orbis Historiæ*, translated by Urban Chauveton (who added an account of the French expedition to Florida), was published at Geneva in 1578; followed by a second in 1581; a third in 1586, with Lery's book on Brazil added; others in 1590 (no place); 1598 and 1600 (Geneva); (Coloniæ Allobrogum), 1612, with three other tracts; and at Hamburg in 1648. Besides these the Latin version appeared in De Bry, parts iv., v., and vi., printed at Frankfort in 1592, 1593, 1594, 1595, and at Oppenheim in 1617. Cf. Carter-Brown, i. 318, 338, 365; ii. 123, 629; Stevens, *Nuggets* 2,300; *Bibl. Hist.*, no. 173-174; Muller (1872), nos. 78, 79; (1877), 287; Sunderland, no. 1,214; Cooke, nos. 218, 222; Pinart, no. 97; Huth, i. 132; Field, p. 119. There are copies of the 1578 edition in the Boston Public and Harvard College libraries.

The French editions were issued at Geneva in 1579 and 1589. The notes are different from those of the Latin editions; and there are no notes to book iii., as in the Latin. Cf. Carter-Brown, i. 326; Cooke, no. 221; Court, no. 32.

There are two German versions. The first was by Nicholas Höniger, and was printed at Basle, in 1579, as *Der Newenn Weldt*. It was reissued, with tracts of Peter Martyr and others, in 1582. The version of Abel Scherdigers was issued at Helmstadt in 1590, 1591, again at Frankfort in 1595, and at Wittenberg in 1606. There were in addition some later imprints, besides those included in De Bry and in Saegh-

man's *Voyagien*. Cf. Rich, no. 61; Carter-Brown, i. 344, 388, ii. 44, 917; Muller (1872), nos. 80, 1880, (1877), 286.

The first Dutch edition appeared at Haarlem in 1610; there was an abridged issue at Amsterdam in 1663. Cf. Tiele, nos. 276, 277; Muller (1872), nos. 81, 82; Carter-Brown, ii. 97.

Purchas gave an abstract in English; but there was no complete English version till Admiral Smith's was published by the Hakluyt Society in 1857. This has fac-similes of the cuts of the 1572 edition; and De Bry also followed the early cuts.

In 1542 and 1543 Las Casas largely influenced the royal decrees relating to the treatment of the Indians, which were signed by the monarch, Nov. 20, 1542, and June 4, 1543, and printed at Alcala in 1543 as *Leyes y Ordenanças*. This book stands as the earliest printed ordinances for the New World, and is rare. Rich in 1832 (no. 13) priced it at £21. (Cf. *Bib. Am. Vet.*, no. 247; Carter-Brown, vol. i. no. 130; Sabin, vol. x. p. 320.) There were later editions at Madrid in 1585,[1] and at Valladolid in 1603. Henry Stevens, in 1878, issued a fac-simile edition made by Harris after a vellum copy in the Grenville Collection, accompanied by a translation, with an historical and bibliographical introduction.

The earliest compilation of general laws for the Indies, entitled *Provisiones, cedulas, instrucciones de su Magestad*, was printed in Mexico in 1563. This is also very rare; Rich priced it in

---

[1] In Harvard College Library, with also the *Ordenanzas reales del Conseio de las Indias*, of the same date.

1832 at £16 16s. It was the work of Vasco de Puga, and Helps calls it "the earliest summary of Spanish colonial law." The Carter-Brown copy (*Catalogue*, i. 242) was sent to England for Mr. Helps's use, there being no copy in that country, so far as known.

The next collection was *Provisiones, cédulas,* etc., arranged by Diego de Encinas, and was printed at Madrid in 1596. The work early became scarce, and Rich priced it at £5 5s. in 1832 (no. 81). It is in Harvard College and the Carter-Brown Library (*Catalogue*, vol. i. no. 502). The bibliography of the general laws, particularly of later collections, is sketched in Bancroft's *Central America*, i. 285, and *Mexico*, iii. 550; and in chap. xxvii. of this same volume the reader will find an examination of the administration and judicial system of the Spaniards in the New World;[1] and he must go chiefly to Bancroft (*Central America*, i. 255, 257, 261, 285; *Mexico*, ii. 130, 516, 563, etc.) and Helps (*Spanish Conquest* and *Life of Las Casas*) for aid in tracing the sources of the subject of the legal protection sought to be afforded to the natives, and the attempted regulation of the slavery which they endured. Helps carefully defines the meaning and working of the *encomienda* system, which gave in effect a property value to the subjection of the natives to the Conquerors. Cf. *Spanish Conquest* (Am. ed.), iii. 113, 128, 157, 212.

[1] There are convenient explanations and references respecting the functions of the Casa de la Contratacion, the Council of the Indies, the Process of the Audiencia, and the duties of an Alcalde, in Bancroft's *Central America*, vol. i. pp. 270, 280, 282, 297, 330.

CHAPTER VI.

CORTÉS AND HIS COMPANIONS.

BY JUSTIN WINSOR,
The Editor.

GRIJALVA had returned in 1518 to Cuba from his Western expedition,[1] flushed with pride and expectant of reward. It was his fate, however, to be pushed aside unceremoniously, while another was sent to follow up his discoveries. Before Grijalva had returned, the plan was formed; and Hernando Cortés distanced his competitors in suing for the leadership of the new expedition. Cortés was at this time the *alcalde* of Santiago in Cuba, and about thirty-three years old, — a man agile in mind, and of a frame well compacted for endurance; with a temper to please, and also to be pleased, if you would but wait on his wishes. He had some money, which Velasquez de Cuellar, the Governor, needed; he knew how to decoy the intimates of the Governor, and bait them with promises: and so the appointment of Cortés came, but not altogether willingly, from Velasquez.

Cortés was born in Spain,[2] of humble, respectable stock. Too considerable animal spirits had made him an unprofitable student at Salamanca, though he brought away a little Latin and a lean store of other learning. A passion for the fairer sex and some military ardor, dampened with scant income all the while, characterized the following years; till finally, in 1504, he sailed on one of the fleets for the New World. Here he soon showed his quality by participating in the suppression of an Indian revolt. This got him a small official station, and he varied the monotony of life with love intrigues and touches of military bravado. In 1511, when Diego Columbus sent Velasquez on an expedition to Cuba, Cortés joined it as the commander's executive officer. A certain adroitness turned a quarrel which he had with Velasquez (out of which grew his marriage with a fair Catalina) to his advantage with the Governor, who made him in the end the *alcalde* of Santiago, — a dignity which mining and stock-raising luckily enabled the adventurer to support. He was in this condition when all schemes worked happily, and Velasquez was induced to commission him commander-in-chief of the new expedition. The Governor gave him

---

[1] See chap. iii. p. 203, *ante.*   [2] At Medellin, in Estremadura, in 1485.

El Adelantado DON DIEGO VELASQUES de Cuellar Autor del descrubrimiento de nueva España.

VELASQUEZ.[1]

instructions on the 23d of October, 1518. Cortés understood, it turned out, that these were to be followed when necessary and disregarded when desirable. There seemed, indeed, to have been no purpose to confine the business of the expedition to exploration, as the instructions set forth.[2] Cortés put all his substance into ships and outfits. He inveigled his friends into helping him. Velasquez converted what Government resources he could to the purpose of the expedition, while at the same time he seems to have cunningly sold to Cortés his own merchandise at exorbitant prices.

---

[1] Fac-simile of an engraving in Herrera, i. 298. It is lithographed in Cabajal's *México*, ii. 21.

[2] They are given in Pacheco's *Coleccion*, xii. 225, Prescott's *Mexico*, app. i., and elsewhere. Cf. H. H. Bancroft, *Mexico*, i. 55.

Twenty thousand ducats apparently went into somebody's pockets to get the expedition well started.[1] Three hundred men, including some of position, joined him. The Governor's jester, instigated, as is supposed, by Velasquez' relatives, threw out a hint that Cortés was only preparing to proclaim his independence when he reached the new domain. The thought worried the Governor, and seems in part to have broken the spell of the admiration which he entertained for Cortés; yet not so much so but he could turn a cold shoulder to Grijalva when he arrived with his ships, as happened at this juncture.

Cortés could not afford to dally; and secret orders having been given for all to be in readiness on the evening of the 17th of November, on the next morning the fleet sailed.[2] There were six vessels composing it, and a seventh later joined them. At Trinidad (Cuba) his force was largely augmented with recruits from Grijalva's men. Here messengers arrived from Velasquez, ordering the authorities to depose Cortés and put another in command. Cortés had, however, too strongly environed himself; and he simply took one of the messengers into his service, and sent back the other with due protestations of respect. Then he sailed to San Cristóbal (Havana), sending a force overland to pick up horses. The flagship met a mishap on the way, but arrived at last. Cortés landed and displayed his pomp. Letters from Velasquez still followed him, but no one dared to arrest him. He again sailed. His fleet had now increased to twelve vessels, the largest measuring one hundred tons; his men were over six hundred, and among them only thirteen bore firelocks; his artillery consisted of ten guns and four falconets. Two hundred natives, men and women, were taken as slaves. Sixteen horses were stowed away on or below deck.[3] This was the force that a few days later, at Guaguanico, Cortés passed in review, while he regaled his men with a specious harangue, steeped in a corsair's piety. On the 18th of February they steered boldly away on the mission which was to become famous.

Looking around upon his officers, Cortés could discover, later if not then, that he had some stanch lieutenants. There was Pedro de Alvarado, who had already shown his somewhat impetuous quality while serving under Grijalva. There was Francisco de Montejo, a good administrator as well as a brave soldier. Names not yet forgotten in the story of the Conquest were those of Alonso de Avila, Cristóbal de Olid, and the youngest of all, Gonzalo de Sandoval, who was inseparable from his white stallion Motilla. Then there were Velasquez de Leon, Diego de Ordaz, and others less known to fame.

The straggling vessels gathered again at Cozumel Island, near the point of Yucatan. Cortés sent an expedition to discover and ransom some

[1] There is much conflict of testimony on the respective share of Cortés and Velasquez in equipping the expedition. H. H. Bancroft (*Mexico*, i. 57) collates the authorities.

[2] Prescott makes Cortés sail clandestinely;

Bancroft makes his departure a hurried but open one; and this is Helps's view of the authorities.

[3] The authorities are not in unison about all these figures. Cf. H. H. Bancroft, *Mexico*, i. 70.

Christians who were in the interior, as he heard.   The mission failed; but a single one of the wanderers, by some other course, found the Spaniards, and was welcomed as an interpreter.   This man reported that he and another were the sole survivors of a ship's company wrecked on the coast eight years before.

Early in March the fleet started to skirt the Yucatan shore, and Cortés had his first fight with the natives at Tabasco, — a conflict brought on for no reason but that the town would not supply provisions.   The stock-

CANNON OF CORTÉS' TIME.[1]

ade was forced, and the place formally occupied.   A more signal victory was required; and the Spaniards, getting on shore their horses and artillery, encountered the savage hordes and dispersed them, — aided, as the veracious story goes, by a spectral horseman who shone upon the field.   The native king only secured immunity from further assaults by large presents.   The Spaniards then re-embarked, and next cast anchor at San Juan de Ulloa.

[1] As represented in a cut by Israel van Mecken, which is here reduced from a fac-simile in A. O. Essenwein's *Kulturhistorischer Bilder Atlas*, ii., *Mittelalter* (Leipsic, 1883), pl. cxv.   It will be observed that the pieces have no trunnions, and are supported in a kind of trough. They were breech-loaders by means of chambers, three of which, with handles, are seen (in the cut) lying on the ground, and one is in place, in the gun on the right.   In the Naval Museum at Annapolis there are guns captured in the Mexican war, that are supposed to be the ones used by Cortés.   A search of the records of the Ordnance Department at Washington, instituted for me by Commodore Sicard, at the suggestion of Prof. Charles E. Munroe of the Naval Academy, has not, however, revealed any documentary evidence; but a paper in the *Army and Navy Journal*, Nov. 22, 1884, p. 325, shows such guns to have been captured by Lieutenant Wyse in the "Darien."   The guns at Annapolis are provided with like chambers, as seen in photographs kindly sent to me.   Similar chambers are now, or were recently, used in firing salutes on the Queen's birthday in St. James's Park.   Cf. Stanley's *De Gama's Voyages* (Hakluyt Society), p. 227.

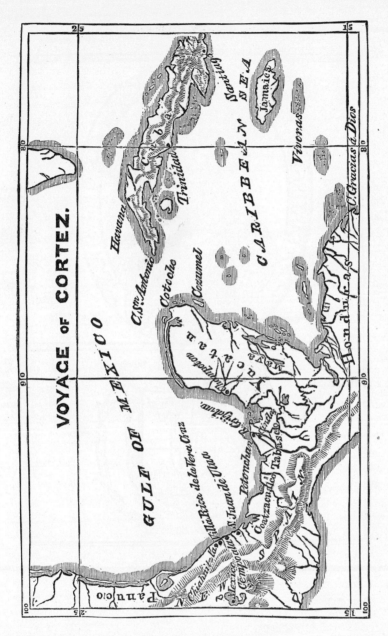

VOYAGE of CORTEZ.

Meanwhile the rumors of the descent of the Spaniards on the coast had certainly hurried to Montezuma at his capital; and his people doubtless rehearsed some of the many portents which are said to have been regarded.[1] We read also of new temples erected, and immense sacrifices of war-captives made, to propitiate the deities and avert the dangers which these

[1] See the long note comparing some of these accounts in H. H. Bancroft's *Mexico*, i. 102, etc.

[2] This is a reproduction of the map in Arthur Helps's *Spanish Conquest*, ii. 236.

CORTÉS AND HIS ARMS.[1]

portents and forebodings for years past had indicated to the believing. The men of Grijalva had already some months earlier been taken to be similar woful visitants, and one of Montezuma's officers had visited Grijalva's vessel, and made report of the wonders to the Mexican monarch.

[1] Copied from a cut in Gabriel Lasso de la Vega's *Cortés valeroso*, — a poem published at Madrid in 1588. There is a copy in Harvard College Library; cf. Carter-Brown, i. 377. The same cut is also used in the edition published in 1594, then called *Mexicana*.

Studied offices of propitiation had been ordered, when word came back that the ship of the bearded men had vanished.

The coming of Cortés was but a dreaded return. While his ship lay at Juan de Ulloa, two canoes came from the main, and their occupants climbed to his deck. No one could understand them. The rescued Spaniard who had been counted on as an interpreter was at a loss. At last a female slave, Marina by name, taken at Tabasco, solved the difficulty. She could understand this same Spaniard, and knew also Aztec.[1] Through this double interpretation Cortés now learned that the mission of his visitors was one of welcome and inquiry. After the usual interchange of gifts, Cortés sent word to the cacique that he would soon confer with him. He then landed a force, established a camp, and began to barter with the natives. To a chief, who soon arrived, Cortés announced his intention to seek the presence of Montezuma and to deliver

GABRIEL LASSO DE LA VEGA.[2]

the gifts and messages with which he was charged as the ambassador of his sovereign. Accordingly, bearing such presents as Cortés cared to send forward, native messengers were sent to Montezuma to tell tales of the sights they had seen,—the prancing horses and the belching cannon. The Mexican king sought to appease the eagerness of the new-comers by returning large stores of fabrics and gold, wishing them to be satisfied and to depart. The gold was not a happy gift to produce such an end.

Meanwhile Cortés, by his craft, quieted a rising faction of the party of Velasquez which demanded to be led back to Cuba. He did this by seeming to acquiesce in the demand of his followers in laying the foundations of a town and constituting its people a municipality competent to choose a representative of the royal authority. This done, Cortés resigned his commission from Velasquez, and was at once invested with supreme

---

[1] Marina did more. She impressed Cortés, who found her otherwise convenient for a few years; and after she had borne him children, married her to one of his captains. What purports to be a likeness of her is given in Cabajal's *México*, ii. 64.

[2] Fac-simile of the portrait in *Cortés valeroso*.

power by the new municipality. The scheme which Velasquez had suspected was thus brought to fruition. Whoever resisted the new captain was conquered by force, persuasion, tact, or magnetism; and Cortés became as popular as he was irresistible.

At this point messengers presented themselves from tribes not far off who were unwilling subjects of the Aztec power. The presence of possible allies was a propitious circumstance, and Cortés proceeded to cultivate the friendship of these tribes. He moved his camp day by day along the shore, inuring his men to marches, while the fleet sailed in company. They reached a large city, and were regaled. Each chief told of the tyranny of Montezuma, and the eyes of Cortés glistened. The Spaniards went on to another town, slaves being provided to bear their burdens. Here they found tax-gatherers of Montezuma collecting tribute. Emboldened by Cortés' glance, his hosts seized the Aztec emissaries and delivered them to the Spaniards. Cortés now played a double game. He propitiated the servants of Montezuma by secretly releasing them, and added to his allies by enjoining every tribe he could reach to resist the Aztec collectors of tribute.

The wandering municipality, as represented in this piratical army, at last stopped at a harbor where a town (La Villa Rica de Vera Cruz) sprang up, and became the base of future operations.[1]

Montezuma and his advisers, angered by the reports of the revolt of his subjects, had organized a force to proceed against them, when the tax-gatherers whom Cortés had released arrived and told the story of Cortés' gentleness and sympathy. It was enough; the rebellion needed no such active encounter. The troops were not sent, and messengers were despatched to Cortés, assuring the Spanish leader that Montezuma forbore to chastise the entertainers of the white strangers. Cortés now produced other of the tax-gatherers whom he had been holding, and they and the new embassy went back to Montezuma more impressed than before; while the neighboring people wondered at the deference paid by Montezuma's lieutenants to the Spaniards. It was no small gain for Cortés to have instigated the equal wonder of two mutually inimical factions.

The Spanish leader took occasion to increase his prestige by despatching expeditions hither and thither. Then he learned of efforts made by Velasquez to supplant him. To confirm his rule against the Cuban Governor he needed the royal sanction; and the best way to get that was to despatch a vessel with messages to the Emperor, and give him earnest of what he might yet expect in piles of gold thrown at his feet. So the flagship sailed for Spain; and in her in command and to conduct his suit

[1] Prescott (*Mexico*, revised edition, i. 345) points out how this site was abandoned later for one farther south, where the town was called Vera Cruz Vieja; and again, early in the seventeenth century, the name and town were transferred to another point still farther south, — Nueva Vera Cruz. These changes have caused some confusion in the maps of Lorenzana and others. Cf. the maps in Prescott and H. H. Bancroft.

CORTÉS.[1]

before the throne, Cortés sent faithful servitors, such as had influence at court, to outwit the emissaries of Velasquez. Sailing in July, touching at Cuba long enough to raise the anger of Velasquez, but not long enough for him to catch them, these followers of Cortés reached Spain in October, and found the agents of Velasquez ready for them. Their vessel was seized, and the royal ear was held by Bishop Fonseca and other friends of the

[1] After a picture on panel in the Massachusetts Historical Society's gallery. It is described in the *Catalogue of the Cabinet* of that Society as "Restored by Henry Sargent about 1831, and again by George Howorth about 1855." Cf. *Proceedings*, i. 446, where it is said to have been given by the family of the late Dr. Foster, of Brighton, who received it by inheritance from a Huguenot family who brought it to New England after the Revocation of the Edict of Nantes.

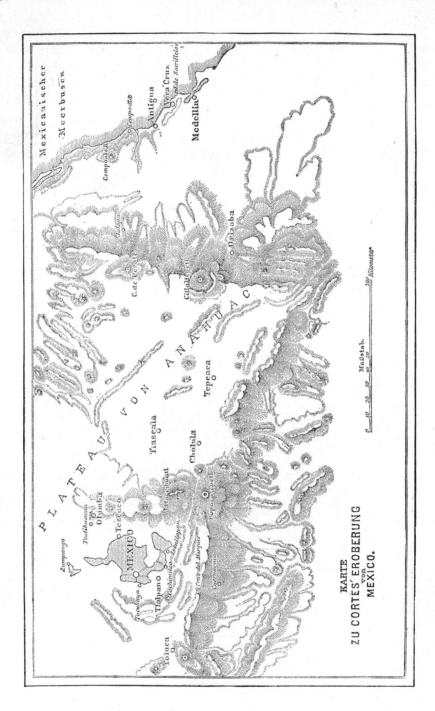

THE MARCH OF CORTÉS ON MEXICO.[1]

Cuban Governor; yet not so effectually but that the duplicate letters of Cortés' messengers were put into the Emperor's hand, and the train of natives paraded before him.

Now came the famous resolve of Cortés. He would band his heterogeneous folk together — adherents of Cortés and of Velasquez — in one common cause and danger. So he adroitly led them to be partners in the deed which he stealthily planned.[1] Hulk after hulk of the apparently worm-eaten vessels of the fleet sank in the harbor, until there was no flotilla left upon which any could desert him. The march to Mexico was now assured. The force with which to accomplish this consisted of about four hundred and fifty Spaniards, six or seven light guns, fifteen horses, and a swarm of Indian slaves and attendants. A body of the Totonacs accompanied them.[2] Two or three days brought them into the higher plain and its enlivening vegetation. When they reached the dependencies of Montezuma, they found orders had been given to extend to them every courtesy. They soon reached the Anahuac plateau, which reminded them not a little of Spain itself. They passed from cacique to cacique, some of whom groaned under the yoke of the Aztec; but not one dared do more than orders from Montezuma dictated. Then the invaders approached the territory of an independent people, those of Tlascala, who had walled their country against neighboring enemies. A fight took place at the frontiers, in which the Spaniards lost two horses. They forced passes against great odds, but again lost a horse or two, — which was a perceptible diminution of their power to terrify. The accounts speak of immense hordes of the Tlascalans, which historians now take with allowances, great or small. Cortés spread what alarm he could by burning villages and capturing the country people. His greatest obstacle soon appeared in the compacted army of Tlascalans arrayed in his front. The conflict which ensued was for a while doubtful. Every horse was hurt, and sixty Spaniards were wounded; but the result was the retreat of the Tlascalans. Divining that the Spanish power was derived from the sun, the enemy planned a night attack; but Cortés suspected it, and assaulted them in their own ambush.

Cortés now had an opportunity to display his double-facedness and his wiles. He received embassies both from Montezuma and from the senate of the Tlascalans. He cajoled each, and played off his friendship for the one in cementing an alliance with the other. But to Tlascala and Mexico he would go, so he told them. The Tlascalans were not averse, for they

---

or New Spain, are not infrequent. Cf. Blaeu's *Atlas*, De Bry, several issued by Vander Aa, of Amsterdam, the Brussels edition (1704) of Solis, Lorenzana's *Cortés* (1770), and various others.

[1] There is some discrepancy in the authorities here as regards the openness or stealth of the act of destroying the fleet. See the authorities collated in Prescott, *Mexico*, new edition, i. 369, 370.

[2] The estimates of numbers in all the operations throughout the Conquest differ widely, sometimes very widely, according to different authorities. The student will find much of the collation of these opposing statements done for him in the notes of Prescott and Bancroft.

FERDINANDO CORTES
CAVATO DA VN ORIGINALE FATTO IÑAZI
CHEI SI PORTASSI ALLA CONQVISTA DEL MESSICO

CORTÉS.[1]

thought it boded no good to the Aztecs if he could be bound to themselves. Montezuma dreaded the contact, and tried to intimidate the
strangers by tales of the horrible difficulties of the journey.

[1] Fac-simile of an engraving on copper in the edition of Solis printed at Venice in 1715, p. 29. It is inscribed : "Cavato da vn originale fatto iñazi chei si portassi alla Conqvista del Messico."

MONTEZUMA.[1]

[1] This cut of the "Rex ultimus Mexica-
norum" is a fac-simile from Montanus and
Ogilby, p. 253. The source of the likeness is
VOL. II. — 46.

not apparent, and the picture seems questionable. Prescott, in his second volume, gives a
likeness, which belonged to the descendants of

Presently the army took up its march for Tlascala, where they were royally received, and wives in abundance were bestowed upon the leaders. Next they passed to Cholula, which was subject to the Aztecs; and here the Spaniards were received with as much welcome as could be expected to be bestowed on strangers with the hostile Tlascalans in their train. The scant welcome covered treachery, and Cortés met it boldly. Murder and plunder impressed the Cholulans with his power, and gave some sweet revenge to his allies. Through the wiles of Cortés a seeming reconciliation at last was effected between these neighboring enemies. But the massacre of Cholula was not a pastime, the treachery of Montezuma not forgotten; and the march was again resumed, about six thousand native allies of one tribe and another following the army. The passage of a defile brought the broad Valley of Mexico into view; and Montezuma, awed by the coming host, sent a courtier to personate him and to prevail upon Cortés to avoid the city. The trick and the plea were futile. On to one of the aquatic cities of the Mexican lakes the Spaniards went, and were received in great state by a vassal lord of Montezuma, who now invited the Spanish leader to the Aztec city. On they went. Town after town received them; and finally, just without his city, Montezuma, in all his finery and pomp, met the Spanish visitors, bade them welcome, and committed them to an escort which he had provided. It was the 8th of November, 1519. Later in his own palace, in the quarters which had been assigned to Cortés, and on several occasions, the two indulged in reciprocal courtesies and watched each other. Cortés was not without fear, and his allies warned him of Aztec treachery. His way to check foul designs was the bold one of seizing Montezuma and holding him as a hostage; and he did so under pretence of honoring him. A chieftain who had attacked a party of the Spaniards by orders of Montezuma some time before, was executed in front of the palace. Montezuma himself was subjected for a while to chains. Expeditions were sent out with impunity to search for gold mines; others explored the coast for harbors. A new governor was sent back to Villa Rica, and he sent up shipwrights; so it was not long before Cortés commanded a flotilla on the city lakes, and the captive king was regaled with aquatic sports.

---

the Aztec king, the Counts of Miravalle. It is claimed to have been painted by an artist, Maldonado, who accompanied Cortés; but, on the other hand, some have represented it as an ideal portrait painted after the Conquest. Prescott (vol. ii. p. 72) makes up his description of Montezuma from various early authorities, — Diaz, Zuazo (MS.), Ixtlilxochitl, Gomara, Oviedo, Acosta, Sahagun, Toribio, etc., particularizing the references. H. H. Bancroft (*Mexico*, i. 285) also depicts him from the early sources. He is made of an age from forty to fifty-four by different writers; but the younger period is thought by most to be nearest. Bancroft refers to the prints in Th. Armin's *Das alte Mexico* (Leipsic, 1865) as representing a coarse Aztec warrior, and the native picture in Carbajal Espinosa's *Historia de México* (Mexico, 1862) as purely conventional. The same writer thinks the colored portrait, "peint par ordre de Cortes," in Linati's *Costûmes et mœurs de Mexique* (Brussels) conforms to the descriptions; while that in Clavigero's *Storia antica del Messico* (1780) is too small to be satisfactory. The line of Montezuma's descendants is traced in Prescott, *Mexico*, ii. 339, iii. 446, and in Bancroft, *Mexico*, i. 459. Cf. also the portrait of Montezuma, "d'après Sandoval," given in Charton's *Voyageurs*, iii. 393, and that in Cumplido's Mexican edition of Prescott's *Mexico*, vol. iii.

MONTEZUMA.[1]

[1] Fac-simile of the copper plate in the Venice edition of Solis' *Conquista* (1715) inscribed "Cavato dall' originale venvto dal' Messico al Ser^{mo} G. D. di Toscana."

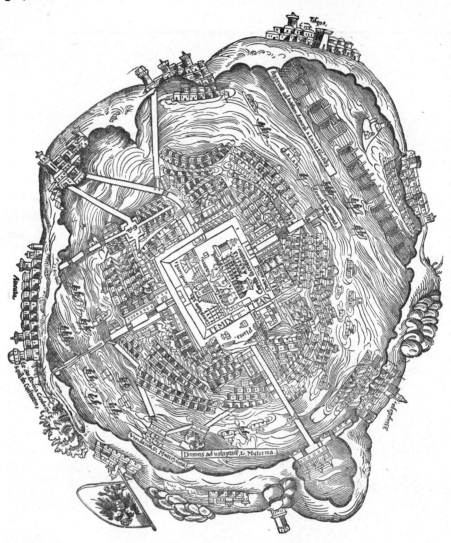

MEXICO BEFORE THE CONQUEST.[1]

Then came symptoms of conspiracy among the native nobles, with the
object of overthrowing the insolent strangers; and Cacama, a nephew
of Montezuma and a chief among them, indulged the hope of seizing the

[1] This is reduced from the cut in Henry Stevens's *American Bibliographer*, p. 86, which in
turn is reproduced from the edition of Cortés'
letters published at Nuremberg in 1524. Bancroft in his *Mexico* (vol. i. p. 280) gives a greatly
reduced sketch of the same plan, and adds to
it a description and references to the various
sources of our information regarding the Aztec
town; and this may be compared with the same
author's *Native Races*, ii. 560. Helps describes
the city in his *Spanish Conquest* (New York
ed., ii. 277, 423), where he thinks that the early
chroniclers failed to make clear the full number of the causeways connecting the town with
the main, and traversing the lake. Prescott
describes it in his *Mexico* (Kirk's ed., ii. 101),
and discredits the plan given in Bullock's *Mexico* as one prepared by Montezuma for Cortés.
This last plan is also given in Carbajal's *Historia de México* (1862), ii. 221. The nearly equal

throne itself. Montezuma protested to his people that his durance was directed by the gods, and counselled caution. When this did not suffice, he gave orders, at the instigation of Cortés, to seize Cacama, who was brought to Mexico and placed in irons. The will of Cortés effected other displacements of the rural chiefs; and the allegiance of Montezuma to the Spanish sovereign became very soon as sure and abject as forms could make it.

Tribute was ordered, and trains bore into the city wealth from all the provinces, — to be the cause of heart-burnings and quarrels in the hour of distribution. The Aztec king and the priests were compelled to order the removal of idols from their temples, and to see the cross and altar erected in their places.

Meanwhile the difficulties of Cortés were increasing. The desecration of the idols had strengthened the party of revolt, and Montezuma was powerless to quiet them. He warned the Spaniards of their danger. Cortés, to dispel apprehension, sent men to the coast with the ostensible purpose of building ships for departure. It was but a trick, however, to gain time; for he was now expecting a response to his letters sent to Spain, and he hoped for supplies and a royal commission which might enable him to draw reinforcements from Cuba.

The renegade leader, however, had little knowledge of what was planning at this very moment in that island. Velasquez de Cuellar, acting under a sufficient commission, had organized an expedition to pursue Cortés, and had given the command of it to Panfilo de Narvaez. The friends of Cortés and those who dreaded a fratricidal war joined in representations to the *audiencia,* which sent Lucas Vasquez de Aillon to prevent an outbreak. The fleet under Narvaez left Cuba, Aillon on board, with instructions to reach a peaceable agreement with Cortés; but this failing, they were to seek other regions. In April, 1520, after some mishaps, the fleet, which had been the largest ever seen in those waters, anchored at San Juan de Ulloa, where they got stories of the great success of Cortés from some deserters of one of his exploring parties. On the other hand, these same deserters, learning from Narvaez the strength and purpose of the new-comers, — for the restraint of Aillon proved ineffectual, — communicated with the neighboring caciques; and the news was not slow in travelling to

---

distance on all sides at which the shores of the lake stand from the town is characteristic of this earliest of the plans (1524); and in this particular it is followed in various plans and bird's-eye views of the town of the sixteenth century, and in some of a later date. The Aztec town had been founded in 1325, and had been more commonly called Tenochtitlan, which the Spaniards turned into Temixtitan and Tenustitan, the term Mexico being properly applied to one of the principal wards of the city. The two names were first sometimes joined, as Temixtitlan-Mexico (1555); but in the end the more pronounceable part survived, and the rest was lost. Cf. Bancroft, *Mexico,* i. 12–14, with references. The correspondence of sites in the present city as compared with those of the Aztec time and of the conquerors, is examined in Alaman's *Discertaciones sobre la historia de la república Méjicana* (Mexico, 1844–1849), ii. 202, 246; Carbajal Espinosa's *Historia de México,* ii. 226, and by Ramirez in the Mexican edition of Prescott. Cf. Ant. du Pinet's *Descriptions de plusieurs villes et forteresses,* Lyon, 1564.

El Adelantado Don **PEDRO** *de* **ALVARADO**
de Badajoz,[1]

Montezuma, who heard it not long after the mock submission of Cortés and the despatching of the ship-builders to the coast. Narvaez next tried, in vain, to swerve Velasquez de Leon from his fidelity to Cortés, — for this officer was exploring with a party in the neighborhood of the coast. San-doval, in command at Villa Rica, learned Narvaez' purposes from spies; and when messengers came to demand the surrender of the town, an altercation ensued, and the chief messengers were seized and sent to Cortés. The Conqueror received them kindly, and, overcoming their aversion, he sent them back to Narvaez with letters and gifts calculated

[1] Fac-simile of an engraving in Herrera, ii. 274. For appearance and other portraits, see Bancroft, *Mexico*, i. 75. One of a sinister aspect often engraved, but which Ramirez distrusts, is given in Cabajal's *México*, ii. 341; in the *Proceso de residencia contra Pedro de Alvarado* (Mexico, 1847); and in Cumplido's Mexican edition of Prescott's *Mexico*, vol. iii.

to conciliate. While many under Narvaez were affected, the new leader remained stubborn, seized Aillon, who was endeavoring to mediate, and sent him on shipboard with orders to sail for Cuba. Thus the arrogance of Narvaez was greatly helping Cortés in his not very welcome environment.

Cortés now boldly divided his force; and leaving Alvarado behind with perhaps one hundred and forty men, — for the accounts differ,[1] — and taking half that number with him, beside native guides and carriers, marched to confront Narvaez. Velasquez de Leon with his force joined him on the way, and a little later Sandoval brought further reinforcements; so that Cortés had now a detachment of nearly three hundred men. Cortés had prudently furnished them long native lances, with which to meet Narvaez' cavalry, for his own horsemen were very few. Adroitness on the part of Cortés and a show of gold had their effect upon messengers who, with one demand and another, were sent to him by Narvaez. Velasquez was sent by Cortés to the enemy's camp; but the chief gain to Cortés from this manœuvre was a more intimate knowledge of the army and purpose of Narvaez. He then resolved to attack the intruder, — who, however, became aware of the intention of Cortés, but, under the stress of a storm, unaccountably relaxed his precautions. Cortés took advantage of this carelessness; and attacking boldly by night, carried everything before him, and captured the rival leader. The loss was but small to either side. The followers of the invader now became adherents of Cortés, and were a powerful aid in his future movements.[2] The same good fortune had given him possession of the invader's fleet.

AUTOGRAPH OF PEDRO DE ALVARADO.[3]

Meanwhile there were stirring times with Alvarado in Mexico. The Aztecs prepared to celebrate a high religious festival. Alvarado learned, or pretended to learn, that the disaffected native chiefs were planning to rise upon the Spaniards at its close. So he anticipated their scheme by attacking them while at their worship and unarmed. Six hundred or more

[1] H. H. Bancroft (*Mexico*, i. 378) and Prescott (new edition vol. ii., p. 231) collate the authorities.

[2] There are a variety of views as to the force Cortés now commanded; cf. H. H. Bancroft, *Mexico*, i. 424.

[3] Copied from a fac-simile in Cabajal's *México*, ii. 686.

of the leading men were thus slain. The multitude without the temple were infuriated, and the Spaniards regained their quarters, not without difficulty, Alvarado himself being wounded. Behind their defences they managed to resist attack till succor came.

Cortés, who had learned of the events, was advancing, attaching to himself the peoples who were inimical to the Aztecs; but as he got within the Aztec influence he found more sullenness than favor. When he entered Mexico he was not resisted. The city seemed almost abandoned as his force made their way to the Spanish fort and entered its gates.

As a means of getting supplies, Cortés ordered the release of a brother of Montezuma, who at once used his liberty to plan an insurrection. An attack on the Spanish quarters followed, which Cortés sought to repel by sorties; but they gained little. The siege was so roughly pressed that Cortés urged Montezuma to present himself on the parapet and check the fierceness of the assault. The captive put on his robes of state and addressed the multitude; but he only became the target of their missiles, and was struck down by a stone.[1] The condition of the Spaniards soon became perilous in the extreme. A parley with the chief of the Aztecs was of no avail; and Cortés resolved to cut his way along the shortest causeway from the city, to the mainland bordering the lake. In this he failed. Meanwhile a part of his force were endeavoring to secure the summit of a neighboring pyramid, from which the Mexicans had annoyed the garrison of the fort. Cortés joined in this attack, and it was successful. The defenders of the temples on its summit were all killed or hurled from the height, and Cortés was master of the spot.

Events followed quickly in this June of 1520. There was evidently a strong will in command of the Mexicans. The brother of Montezuma was a doughtier foe than the King had been. The temporary success on the pyramid had not diminished the anxiety of Cortés. Montezuma was now dying on his hands. The King had not recovered from the injuries which his own people had inflicted, and sinking spirits completed the work of the mob. On the 30th of June he died, at the age of forty-one, having been on the throne since 1503.[2] Cortés had hoped for some turn of fortune from this event; but none came. He was more than ever convinced of the necessity of evacuating the city. Another sortie had failed as before; and the passage of the causeway was again planned for the evening of that day.[3] The order of march, as arranged, included the whole Spanish force and about six thousand allies. Pontoons of a rough description were contrived for bridging the chasms in the causeway. As many jewels and gold as would not encumber them were taken, together

---

[1] Prescott (*Mexico*, new ed., ii. 309) collates the diverse accounts.

[2] It must be mentioned that the Spaniards have been accused of murdering Montezuma. Bancroft (*Mexico*, i. 464) collates the different views of the authorities. Cortes sent the body out of the fort. Indignities were offered it; but some of the imperial party got possession of it, and buried it with such honor as the times permitted.

[3] There are difficulties about the exact date; cf. H. H. Bancroft, *Mexico*, i. 472.

with such prisoners of distinction as remained to them, besides the sick and wounded.

A drizzling rain favored their retreat; but the Mexicans were finally aroused, and attacked their rear. A hundred or more Spaniards were cut off, and retreated to the fort, where they surrendered a few days later, and were sacrificed. The rest, after losses and much tribulation, reached the mainland. Nothing but the failure of the Mexicans to pursue the Spaniards, weakened as they were, saved Cortés from annihilation. The Aztecs were too busy with their successes; for forty Spaniards, not to speak of numerous allies, had been taken, and were to be immolated; and rites were to be performed over their own dead.

Cortés the next

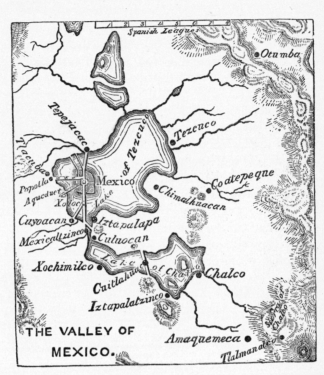

HELPS'S MAP.[1]

morning was marshalling the sorry crowd which was left of his army, when a new attack was threatened. His twelve hundred and fifty Spaniards and six thousand allies had been reduced respectively to five hundred and two thousand;[2] and he was glad to make a temple, which was hard by, a place of refuge and defence. Here he had an opportunity to count his losses. His cannon and prisoners were all gone. Some of his bravest officers did not respond to his call. He could count but twenty-four of

[1] This is the map given by Helps in his *Spanish Conquest.* One of the differences in the variety of maps which have been offered of the Valley of Mexico, to illustrate the conquest by Cortés, consists in the number and direction of the causeways. The description and the remains of the structures themselves have not sufficed to make investigators of one mind respecting them. Prescott (Kirk's ed., vol. ii.) does not represent so many causeways as Helps does. The map in Bancroft (vol. i. p. 583) is still different in this respect. There is also a plan of the city and surrounding country in Cabajal's *México* (vol. ii. p. 538); and two others have been elsewhere given in the present volume (pp. 364, 379).

[2] Bancroft (*Mexico*, i. 488) collates the various authorities; so does Prescott (*Mexico*, new ed., ii. 364) of the losses of this famous *triste Noche.*

his three or four score of horses. After dark he resumed his march. His pursuers still worried him, and hunger weakened his men. He lost several horses at one point, and was himself badly wounded. Reaching a plain on the 7th of July, the Spaniards confronted a large force drawn up against them. Cortés had but seven muskets left, and no powder; so he trusted to pike and sabre. With these he rushed upon them; but the swarm of the enemy was too great. At last, however, making a dash with some horsemen at the native commander, who was recognized by his state and banner, the Mexican was hurled prostrate and killed, and the trophy captured. The spell

TREE OF TRISTE NOCHE.[1]

was broken, and the little band of Spaniards and their allies hounded the craven enemy in every direction. This victory at Otumba (Otompan) was complete and astounding.

The march was resumed; and not till within the Tlascalan borders was there any respite and rest. In the capital of his allies Cortés breathed freer. He learned, however, of misfortunes to detached parties of Spaniards which had been sent out from Villa Rica. He soon got some small supplies of ammunition and men from that seaport. Amid all this, Cortés himself succumbed to a fever from his wounds, and barely escaped death.

Meantime Cuitlahuatzin, the successful brother of Montezuma, had been crowned in Mexico, where a military rule (improved by what the Spaniards had taught them) was established. The new monarch sent ambassadors to try to win the Tlascalans from their fidelity to Cortés; but the scheme failed, and Cortés got renewed strength in the fast purpose of his allies.

---

[1] This cut is borrowed from *Harper's Magazine*, January, 1874, p. 172, and represents the remains of the tree under which Cortés and his followers gathered after that eventful night. There is another view of this tree in *Tour du monde*, 1862, p. 277.

CHARLES V.[1]

His prompt and defiant ambition again overcame the discontents among his own men, and induced him to take the field once more against the Tepeacans, enemies of the Tlascalans, who lived near by. It took about a month to subdue the whole province. Other strongholds of Aztec influence fell one by one. The prestige of the Spanish arms was rapidly re-established, and the Aztec forces went down before them here and there in detachments. New arrivals on the coast pronounced for Cortés, and two hundred men and twenty horses soon joined his army. The small-pox, which the Spaniards had introduced, speedily worked more disaster than the Spaniards, as it spread through the country; and among the victims of it was the new monarch of the Aztecs, leaving the throne open to the succession of Quauhtemotzin, a nephew and son-in-law of Montezuma.

On the 30th of October, 1520, Cortés addressed his second letter to the Emperor Charles V. He and his adherents craved confirmation for his

---

[1] Fac-simile of a woodcut of Charles V. in *Pauli Jovii elogia virorum bellica virtute illustrium*, Basle, 1575, p. 365, and 1596, p. 240.

acts, and reinforcements.   Other letters were despatched to Hispaniola and Jamaica for recruits and supplies.   Some misfortunes prevented the prompt sailing of the vessel for Spain, and Cortés was enabled to join a supplemental letter to the Emperor.   The vessels also carried away some of the disaffected, whom Cortés was not sorry to lose, now that others had joined him.

Meanwhile Cortés had established among the Tepeacans a post of observation named Segura; and from this centre Sandoval made a successful incursion among the Aztec dependencies.   Cortés himself was again at Tlascala, settling the succession of its government; for the small-pox

AUTOGRAPH OF CHARLES V.

had carried off Maxixcatzin, the firm friend of the Spaniards.   Here Cortés set carpenters to work constructing brigantines, which he intended to carry to Tezcuco, on the Lake of Mexico, where it was now his purpose to establish the base of future operations against the Aztec capital.   The opportune arrival of a ship at Villa Rica with supplies and materials of war was very helpful to him.

Cortés first animated all by a review of his forces, and then went forward with the advance toward Tezcuco.   He encountered little opposition, and entered the town to find the inhabitants divided in their fears and sympathies.   Many had fled toward Mexico, including the ruler who had supplanted the one given them by Cortés and Montezuma.   Under the instigation of Cortés a new one was chosen whom he could trust.

Cortés began his approach to Mexico by attacking and capturing, with great loss to the inhabitants, one of the lake towns; but the enemy, cutting a dike and flooding the place, forced the retirement of the invaders, who fell back to Tezcuco.   Enough had been accomplished to cause many of

El Invictiſſimo Emperador CARLOS
Quirito Reÿ natural de Castilla
ÿ de Leon etc.

CHARLES V.[1]

the districts dependent on the Aztecs to send in embassies of submission;
and Cortés found that he was daily gaining ground. Sandoval was sent
back to Tlascala to convoy the now completed brigantines, which were
borne in pieces on the shoulders of eight thousand carriers. Pending the
launching of the fleet, Cortés conducted a reconnoissance round the north
end of the lakes to the scene of his sorrowful night evacuation, hoping for
an interview with an Aztec chief. In this, however, he failed, and returned
to Tezcuco. Then followed some successful fighting on the line of com-

[1] Fac-simile of an engraving in Herrera, iii.
84. Cf. the full-length likeness given in Cumplido's Mexican edition of Prescott's *Mexico*, vol.
iii., and various other portraits of the Emperor.

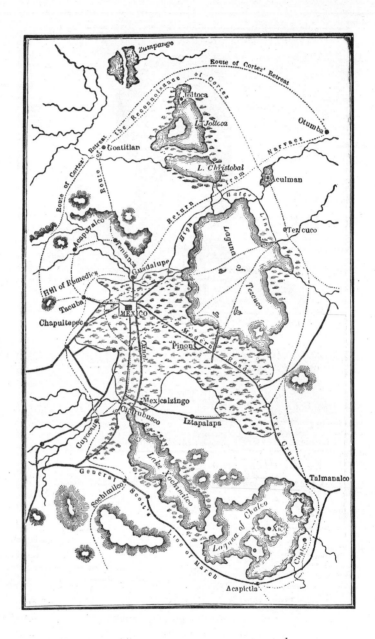

TOPOGRAPHY OF THE MEXICAN VALLEY.[1]

munication with the coast, which enabled Cortés to bring up safely some
important munitions, besides two hundred soldiers, who had lately reached
Villa Rica from the islands whither he had sent for help the previous

[1] This is the map given in Wilson's *New
Conquest of Mexico*, p. 390, in which he makes
the present topography represent that of Cortés'
time, in opposition to the usual view that at the
period of the Conquest the waters of the lake
covered the parts here represented as marsh.

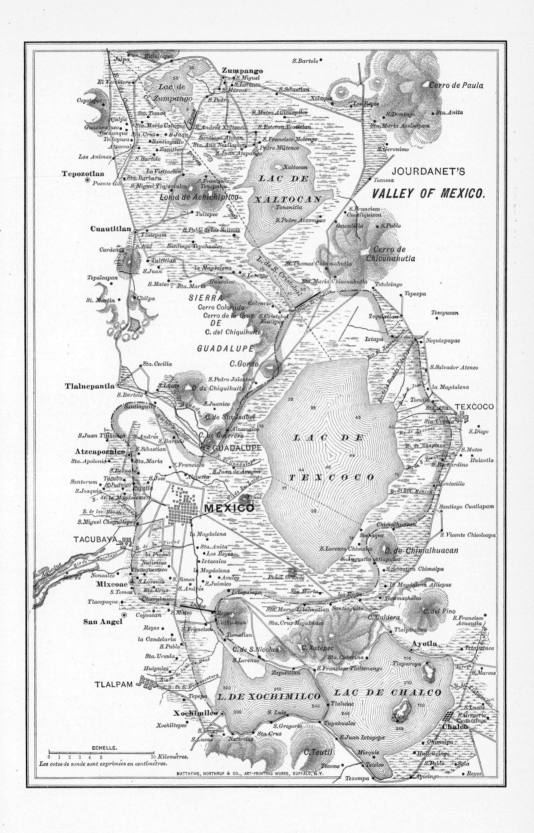

JOURDANET'S

VALLEY OF MEXICO.

autumn. The Spanish leader now conducted another reconnoissance into the southern borders of the Mexican Valley, — a movement which overcame much opposition, — and selected Coyohuacan as a base of operations on that side against the Aztec city. After this he returned to Tezcuco, and was put to the necessity of quelling an insurrection, in which his own death had been planned.

At last the brigantines were launched. At the command of Cortés the allies mustered. On the 28th of April, 1521, the Spanish general counted his own countrymen, and found he had over nine hundred in all, including eighty-seven horsemen. He had three heavy guns, and fifteen smaller ones, which were mostly in the fleet. Cortés kept immediate charge of the brigantines, and allotted the main divisions of the army to Alvarado, Olid, and Sandoval. The land forces proceeded to occupy the approaches which

The waters of Tezcuco are at present seven or eight feet (Prescott says four feet) below the level of the city, and Wilson contends that they did not in Cortés' time much exceed in extent their present limits; and it is one of his arguments against Cortés' representations of deep water about the causeways that such a level of the lake would have put the town of Tezcuco six or seven feet under water. Wilson gives his views on this point at length in his *New Conquest*, pp. 452–460. The map will be seen also to show the line of General Scott's approach to the city in 1847. (Cf. Prof. Henry Coppée on the "Coincidences of the Conquests of Mexico, 1520–1847," in the *Journal of the Military Service Institution*, March, 1884.) The modern city of Mexico lies remote by several miles from the banks of the lake which represents to-day the water commonly held to have surrounded the town in the days of the Conquest. The question of the shrinking of the lagunes is examined in Orozco y Berra's *Mémoire pour la carte hydrographique de la Vallée de Mexico*, and by Jourdanet in his *Influence de la pression de l'air sur la vie de l'homme*, p. 486. A colored map prepared for this latter book was also introduced by Jourdanet in his edition of *Sahagun* (1880), where (p. xxviii) he again examines the question. From that map the one here presented **was** taken, and the marsh surrounding "Lac de Texcoco" marks the supposed limits of the lake in Montezuma's time. Jourdanet's map is called, "Carte hydrographique de la Vallée de Mexico d'après les travaux de la Commission de la Vallée en 1862, avec addition des anciennes limites du Lac de Texcoco."

Humboldt in his *Essai politique sur la Nouvelle Espagne*, while studying this problem of the original bounds of the water, gives a map defining them as traced in 1804–1807; and this is reproduced in John Black's translation of Humboldt's *Personal Essay on the Kingdom of New Spain*, third edition, London, 1822. Humboldt gives accounts of earlier attempts to map the valley with something like accuracy, as was the case with the Lopez map of 1785. Siguenza's map of the sixteenth century, though false, has successively supplied, through the publication of it which Alzate made in 1786, the geographical data of many more modern maps. Cf. the map in Cumplido's edition of Prescott's *Mexico* (1846), vol. iii., and the enumeration of maps of the valley given in Orozco y Berra's *Cartografia Mexicana*, pp. 315–316.

A map of Mexico and the lake also appeared in *Le petit atlas maritime* (Paris, 1764); and this is given in fac-simile in the *Proceedings of the American Philosophical Society*, xxi. 616, in connection with a translation of the *Codex Ramirez* by Henry Phillips, Jr.

There is reason to believe that the decrease in the waters had begun to be perceptible in the time of Cortés; and Humboldt traces the present subsidence to the destruction of neighboring forests. Bernal Diaz makes record of the changes observable within his recollection, and he wrote his account fifty years after the Conquest.

The geographers of the eighteenth century often made the waters of the valley flow into the Pacific. The map in the 1704 edition of Solis shows this; so do the maps of Bower and other English cartographers, as well as the map from Herrera on a later page (p. 392).

The inundations to which the city has been subjected (the most serious of which was in 1629), and the works planned for its protection from such devastations are the subject of a rare book by Cepeda and Carillo, *Relacion universal del sitio en que esta fundada la ciudad de México* (Mexico, 1637). Copies are found complete and incomplete. Cf. Carter-Brown, ii. 441; Leclerc, no. 1,095, complete, 400 francs, and no. 1,096, incomplete, 200 francs; Quaritch, incomplete, £10.

the reconnoissances had indicated, — Alvarado at Tlacopan, Olid at Coyo-huacan, on the westerly shores of the lake, and, later, Sandoval at Iztapa-lapan, on the eastern side. Each of these places commanded the entrance to causeways leading to the city. The land forces were no sooner in posi-tion than Cortés appeared with his fleet. The Aztecs attacked the brigan-tines with several hundred canoes; but Cortés easily overcame all, and established his naval supremacy. He then turned to assist Olid and Alva-rado, who were advancing along their respective causeways; and the strong-hold, Xoloc, at the junction of the causeway, was easily carried. Here the besiegers maintained themselves with an occasional fight, while Sandoval was sent to occupy Tepeyacac, which commanded the outer end of the northern causeway. This completed the investment. A simultaneous attack was now made from the three camps. The force from Xoloc alone succeeded in entering the city; but the advantage gained was lost, and Cortés, who was with this column, drew his forces back to camp. His success, however, was enough to impress the surrounding people, who were watching the signs; and various messengers came and offered the submission of their people to the Spaniards. The attacks were renewed on subsequent days; and little by little the torch was applied, and the habitable part of the town grew less and less. The lake towns as they submitted furnished flotillas, which aided the brigantines much in their incursions into the canals of the town. For a while the Mexicans maintained night commu-nication across the lake for supplies; but the brigantines at last stopped this precarious traffic.

Alvarado on his side had made little progress; but the market of Tlatelulco was nearer him, and that was a point within the city which it was desirable to reach and fortify. Sandoval was joined to Alvarado, who increased the vigor of his assault, while Cortés again attacked on the other side. The movement failed, and the Mexicans were greatly encour-aged. The Spaniards, from their camps, saw by the blaze of the illumina-tions on the temple tops the sacrifice of their companions who had been captured in the fight. The bonds that kept the native allies in subjection were becoming, under these reverses, more sensibly loosened day by day, and Cortés spared several detachments from his weakened force to raid in various directions to preserve the prestige of the Spanish power.

The attack was now resumed on a different plan. The fighting-men led the way and kept the Mexicans at bay; while the native auxiliaries razed every building as they went, leaving no cover for the Aztec marauders. The demolition extended gradually to the line of Alvarado's approach, and communication was opened with him. This leader was now approach-ing the great market-place, Tlatelulco. By renewed efforts he gained it, only to lose it; but the next day he succeeded better, and formed a junction with Cortés. Not more than an eighth part of the city was now in the hands of its inhabitants; and here pestilence and famine were the Spaniards' prompt allies. Still the Aztec King, Quauhtemotzin, scorned to

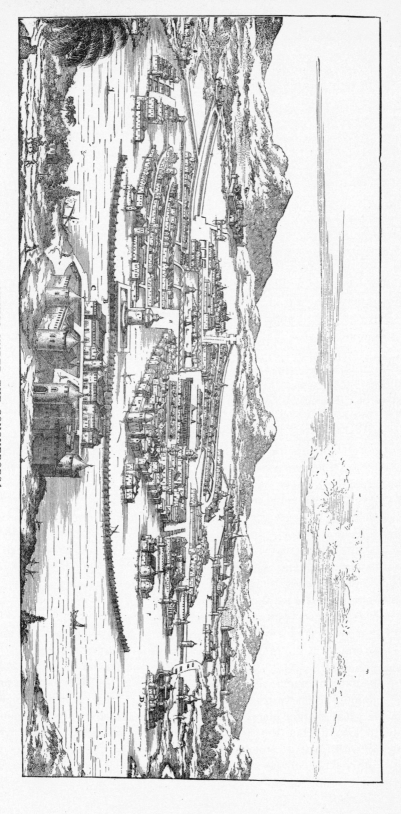

MEXICO UNDER THE CONQUERORS.[1]

1 This is the engraving given in the *Nieuwe Weereld* (1670) of Montanus, which was repeated in Ogilby's *America*, and is familiar from reproductions elsewhere. It may

yield; and the slaughter went on from day to day, till finally, on the 13th of August, 1521, the end came. The royal Aztec was captured, trying to escape in a boat; and there was no one left to fight. Of the thousand Spaniards who had done the work about a tenth had succumbed; and probably something like the same proportion among the many thousand allies. The Mexican loss must have been far greater, perhaps several times greater.[1] The Spaniards were no sooner in possession than quarrels began over the booty. Far less was found than was hoped for, and torture was applied, with no success, to discover the hiding-places. The captive prince was not spared this indignity. Cortés was accused of appropriating an undue share of what was found, and hot feelings for a while prevailed.

The conquest now had to be maintained by the occupation of the country; and the question was debated whether to build the new capital on the ruins of Mexico, or to establish it at Tezcuco or Coyohuacan. Cortés preferred the prestige of the traditional site, and so the new Spanish town rose on the ruins of the Aztec capital; the Spanish quarter being formed about the square of Tenochtitlan (known in the early books usually as Temixtitan), which was separated by a wide canal from the Indian settlement clustered about Tlatelulco. Two additional causeways were constructed, and the Aztec aqueduct was restored. Inducements were offered to neighboring tribes to settle in the city, and districts were assigned to them.

be traced back as a sketch to the much less elaborate one given by Bordone in his *Libro* of 1528, later called his *Isolario*, which was accompanied by one of the earliest descriptions by a writer not a conqueror. Bancroft (*Mexico*, ii. 14) gives a small outline engraving of a similar picture, and recapitulates the authorities on the rebuilding of the city by Cortés. The Cathedral, however, was not begun till 1573, and was over sixty years in building (Ibid., iii. 173).

One of the most interesting of the early accounts, accompanied as it was with a plan of the town and lake, made part of the narrative of the "Anonymous Conqueror." This picture has been reproduced by Icazbalceta in his *Coleccion* (i. 390) from the engraving in Ramusio, whence we derive our only knowledge of this anonymous writer. The Ramusio plan is also given on the next page.

The plate used in the 1572 edition of Porcacchi (p. 105) served for many successive editions. Another plan of the same year showing an oval lake surrounding the town, is found in Braun and Hogenberg's *Civitates orbis terrarum* (Cologne, 1572), and of later dates, and the French edition, *Théâtre des cités du monde* (Brussels, 1574), i. 59. A similar outline characterizes the small woodcut (6 × 6 inches) which is found in Münster's *Cosmographia* (1598), p. dccccxiiii.

Later views and plans appeared in Gottfriedt's *Newe Welt* (1655); in Solis's *Conquista*

(1704), p. 261, reproduced in the English edition of 1724; in La Croix' *Algemeene Weereld Beschryving* (1705); in Herrera (edition of 1728), p. 399; in Clavigero (1780), giving the lake and the town (copied in Verne's *Découverte de la Terre*, p. 248), and also a map of Anahuac, both reproduced in the London (1787) and Philadelphia (1817) editions, as well as in the Spanish edition published at Mexico in 1844; in Solis, edition of 1783 (Madrid), where the lake is given an indefinite extension; in Keating's edition of Bernal Diaz, besides engraved plates by the Dutch publisher Vander Aa.

The account of Mexico in 1554 written by Francisco Cervantes Salazar, and republished with annotations by Icazbalceta in 1875 (Carter-Brown, i. 595) is helpful in this study of the ancient town. Cf. "Mexico et ses environs en 1554," by L. Massbieau, in the *Revue de géographie*, October, 1878.

A descriptive book, *Sitio, naturaleza y propriedades de la ciudad de México*, by Dr. Diego Cisneros, published at Mexico in 1618, is become very rare. Rich in 1832 priced a copy at £6 6s., — a great sum for those days (Sabin, vol. iv. no. 13,146; Carter-Brown, ii. 199).

[1] The figures usually given are enormous, and often greatly vary with the different authorities. In this as in other cases where numbers are mentioned, Prescott and Bancroft collate the several reckonings which have been recorded.

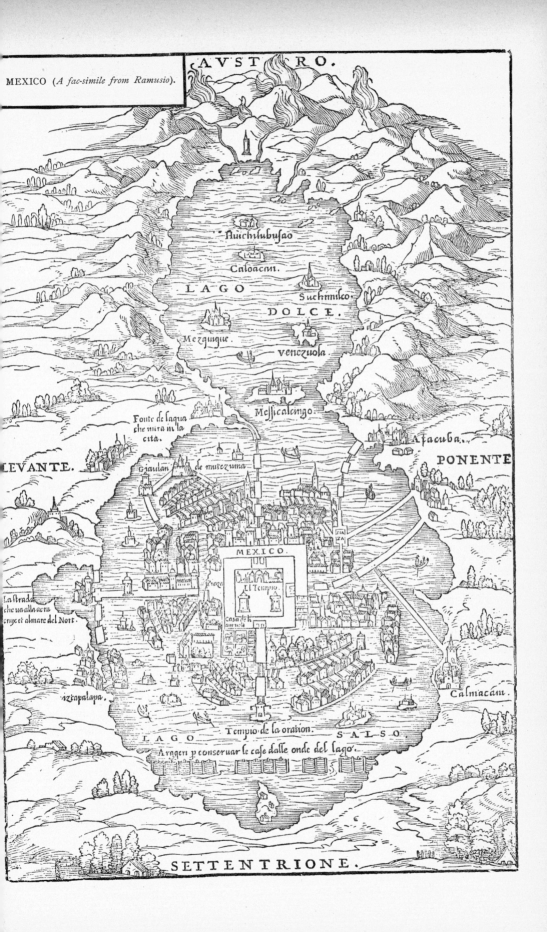

MEXICO (*A fac-simile from Ramusio*).

Thus were hewers of wood and drawers of water abundantly secured. But Mexico never regained with the natives the dominance which the Aztecs had given it. Its population was smaller, and a similar decadence marked the fate of the other chief towns; Spanish rule and disease checked their growth. Even Tezcuco and Tlascala soon learned what it was to be the dependents of the conquerors.

Cortés speedily decided upon further conquests. The Aztec tribute-rolls told him of the comparative wealth of the provinces, and the turbulent spirits among his men were best controlled in campaigns. He needed powder, so he sent some bold men to the crater of Popocatepetl to get sulphur. They secured it, but did not repeat the experiment. Cortés also needed cannon. The Aztecs had no iron, but sufficient copper; and finding a tin mine, his craftsmen made a gun-metal, which soon increased his artillery to a hundred pieces.

Expeditions were now despatched hither and thither, and province after province succumbed. Other regions sent in their princes and chief men with gifts and words of submission. The reports which came back of the great southern sea opened new visions; and Cortés sent expeditions to find ports and build vessels; and thus Zacalula grew up. Revolts here and there followed the Spanish occupancy, but they were all promptly suppressed.

While all this was going on, Cortés had to face a new enemy. Fonseca, as patron of Velasquez, had taken occasion in the absence of the Emperor, attending to the affairs of his German domain, to order Cristóbal de Tapia from Hispaniola to take command in New Spain and to investigate the doings of Cortés. He arrived in December, 1521, with a single vessel at Villa Rica, and was guardedly received by Gonzalo de Alvarado, there in command. Tapia now despatched a messenger to Cortés, who replied with many blandishments, and sent Sandoval and others as a council to confer with Tapia, taking care to have among its members a majority of his most loyal adherents.

They met Dec. 12, 1521, and the conference lasted till Jan. 6, 1522. It resulted in a determination to hold the orders borne by Tapia in abeyance till the Emperor himself could be heard. Tapia protested in vain, and was quickly hustled out of the country. He was not long gone when new orders for him arrived, — this time under the sign-manual of the Emperor himself. This increased the perplexity; but Cortés won the messenger in his golden fashion. Shortly afterwards the same messenger set off for Spain, carrying back the letters with him. These occurrences did not escape notice throughout the country, and Cortés was put to the necessity of extreme measures to restore his prestige; while in his letter to the Emperor he threw the responsibility of his action upon the council, who felt it necessary, he alleged, to take the course they did to make good the gains which had already been effected for the Emperor. In a spirit of conciliation, however, Cortés released Narvaez, who had been confined

CORTÉS.[1]

[1] Fac-simile of a woodcut in *Pauli Jovii elogia virorum bellica virtute illustrium* (Basle, 1575), p. 348, and 1596, p. 229, called a portrait of Cortés.

The autograph follows one given by Prescott, revised ed., vol. iii. Autographs of his proper name, and of his title, Marques del Valle, are given in Cumplido's edition of Prescott, vol. iii. An original autograph was noted for sale in Stevens (*Bibliotheca geographica*, no. 760), which is given in fac-simile in some of the illustrated copies of that catalogue. Prescott (vol. i. p. 447) mentions a banner, preserved in Mexico, though in rags, which Cortés is said to have borne in the Conquest. But compare Wilson's *New Conquest*, p. 369.

at Villa Rica; and so in due time another enemy found his way to Spain, and joined the cabal against the Conqueror of Mexico.

In the spring (1522) Cortés was cheered by a report from the *Audiencia* of Santo Domingo, confirming his acts and promising intercession with the Emperor. To support this intercession, Cortés despatched to Spain some friends with his third letter, dated at Coyohuacan May 15, 1522. These agents carried also a large store of propitiatory treasure. Two of the vessels, which held most of it, were captured by French corsairs,[1] and the Spanish gains enriched the coffers of Francis I. rather than those of Charles V. The despatches of Cortés, however, reached their destination, though Fonseca and the friends of Velasquez had conspired to prevent their delivery, and had even appropriated some part of the treasure which a third vessel had securely landed. Thus there were charges and counter-charges, and Charles summoned a council to investigate. Cortés won. Velasquez, Fonseca, and Narvaez were all humiliated in seeing their great rival made, by royal command, governor and captain-general of New Spain.

Meanwhile Cortés, hearing of a proposed expedition under Garay to take possession of the region north of Villa Rica, conducted a force himself to seize, in advance, that province known as Pánuco, and to subjugate the Huastecs who dwelt there. This was done. The plunder proved small; but this disappointment was forgotten in the news which now, for the first time, reached Cortés of his late success in Spain. The whole country was jubilant over the recognition of his merit; and opportunely came embassies from Guatemala bringing costlier tributes than the Spaniards had ever seen before. This turned their attention to the south. There was apprehension that the Spaniards who were already at Panamá might sooner reach these rich regions, and might earlier find the looked-for passage from the Gulf to the south sea. To anticipate them, no time could be lost. So Alvarado, Olid, and Sandoval were given commands to push explorations and conquests southward and on either shore. Before the expeditions started, news came that Garay, arriving from Jamaica, had landed with a force at Pánuco to seize that region in the interests of the Velasquez faction. The mustered forces were at once combined under Cortés' own lead, and marched against Garay, — Alvarado in advance. Before Cortés was ready to start, he was relieved from the necessity of going in person by the receipt of a royal order from Spain confirming him in the possession of Pánuco and forbidding Garay to occupy any of Cortés' possessions. This order was hurriedly despatched to Alvarado; but it did not reach him till he had made some captives of the intruders. Garay readily assented to lead his forces farther north if restitution should be made to him of the captives and munitions which Alvarado had taken. This was not so easily done, for plunder in hand was doubly rich, and Garay's own men preferred to enlist with Cortés. To compose matters

---

[1] Their chief was Juan Florin, who has been identified by some with Verrazano.

Garay went ·to Mexico, where Cortés received him with ostentatious kindness, and promised him assistance in his northern conquests. In the midst of Cortés' hospitality his guest sickened and died, and was buried with pomp.

While Garay was in Mexico, his men at Pánuco, resenting the control of Garay's son, who had been left in charge of them, committed such ravages on the country that the natives rose on them, and were so rapidly annihilating them that Alvarado, who had left, was sent back to check the outbreak. He encountered much opposition; but conquered as usual, and punished afterward the chief ringleaders with abundant cruelty. Such of Garay's men as would, joined the forces of Cortés, while the rest were sent back to Jamaica.

The thoughts of Cortés were now turned to his plan of southern exploration, and early in December Alvarado was on his way to Guatemala.[1] Desperate fighting and the old success attended Cortés' lieutenant, and the Quiché army displayed their valor in vain in battle after battle. It was the old story of cavalry and arquebusiers. As Alvarado approached Utatlan, the Quiché capital, he learned of a plot to entrap him in the city, which was to be burned about his ears. By a counterplot he seized the Quiché nobles, and burned them and their city. By the aid of the Cakchiquels he devastated the surrounding country. Into the territory of this friendly people he next marched, and was received royally by King Sinacam in his city of Patinamit (Guatemala), and was soon engaged with him in an attack on his neighbors, the Zutugils, who had lately abetted an insurrection among Sinacam's vassals. Alvarado beat them, of course, and established a fortified post among them after they had submitted, as gracefully as they could. With Quichés and Cakchiquels now in his train, Alvarado still went on, burned towns and routed the country's defenders, till, the rainy season coming on, he withdrew his crusaders and took up his quarters once more at Patinamit, late in July, 1524. From this place he sent despatches to Cortés, who forwarded two hundred more Spanish soldiers for further campaigns.

The Spanish extortions produced the usual results. The Cakchiquels turned under the abuse, deserted their city, and prepared for a campaign. The Spaniards found them abler foes than any yet encountered. The Cakchiquels devastated the country on which Alvarado depended for supplies, and the Spaniards found themselves reduced to great straits. It was only after receiving reinforcements sent by Cortés that Alvarado was enabled to push his conquests farther, and possess himself of the redoubtable fortress of Mixco and successfully invade the Valley of Zacatepec.

The expedition to Honduras was intrusted to Cristóbal de Olid, and started about a month after Alvarado's to Guatemala. Olid was given a

---

[1] H. H. Bancroft (*Central Mexico*, i. 626) collates as usual the various estimates of Alvarado's force.

fleet; and a part of his instructions was to search for a passage to the great south sea. He sailed from the port now known as Vera Cruz on the 11th of January, 1524, and directed his course for Havana, where he was to find munitions and horses, for the purchase of which agents had already been sent thither by Cortés. While in Cuba the blandishments of Velasquez had worked upon Olid's vanity, and when he sailed for Honduras he was harboring thoughts of defection. Not long after he landed he openly

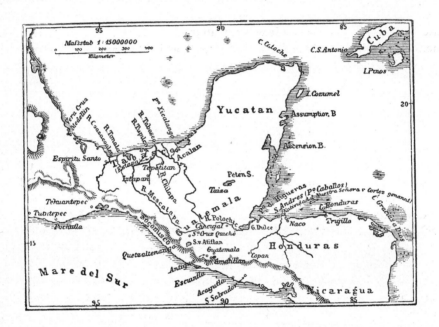

GUATEMALA AND HONDURAS.[1]

announced them, and gained the adherence of most of his men. Cortés, who had been warned from Cuba of Olid's purpose, sent some vessels after him, which were wrecked. Thus Casas, their commander, and his men fell into Olid's hands. After an interval, an opportunity offering, the captive leader conspired to kill Olid. He wounded and secured him, brought him to a form of trial, and cut off his head. Leaving a lieutenant to conduct further progress, Casas started to go to Mexico and make report to Cortés.

Meanwhile, with a prescience of the mischief brewing, and impelled by his restless nature, Cortés had determined to march overland to Honduras; and in the latter part of October, 1524, he set out. He started with great state; but the difficulties of the way made his train a sorry sight as they struggled through morass after morass, stopped by river after river, which they were under the necessity of fording or bridging. All the while their

1 Following the map given in Ruge's *Zeitalter der Entdeckungen*, p. 391. Cf. map in Fan-shawe's *Yucatan*.

provisions grew less and less.   To add to the difficulties, some Mexican chief-tains, who had been taken along as hostages for the security of Mexico, had conspired to kill Cortés, and then to march with their followers back to Mex-ico as deliverers.   The plot was discovered, and the leaders were executed.[1] Some of the towns passed by the army had been deserted by their inhabi-tants, without leaving any provisions behind.   Guides which they secured ran away.   On they went, however, hardly in a condition to confront Olid, should he appear, and they were now approaching his province.   At last some Spaniards were met, who told them of Casas' success; and the hopes of Cortés rose.   He found the settlers at Nito, who had been decimated by malaria, now engaged in constructing a vessel in which to depart.   His com-ing cheered them; and a ship opportunely appearing in the harbor with pro-visions, Cortés purchased her and her lading.   He then took steps to move the settlement to a more salubrious spot.   Using the newly acquired vessel, he explored the neighboring waters, hoping to find the passage to the south sea; and making some land expeditions, he captured several pueblos, and learned, from a native of the Pacific coast whom he fell in with, that Alvarado was conducting his campaign not far away.   Finally, he passed on to Trujillo, where he found the colony of Olid's former adherents, and confirmed the dispositions which Casas had made, while he sent vessels to Cuba and Jamaica for supplies.

At this juncture Cortés got bad news from Mexico.   Cabal and anti-cabal among those left in charge of the government were having their effect.   When a report reached them of the death of Cortés and the loss of his army, it was the signal for the bad spirits to rise, seize the govern-ment, and apportion the estates of the absentees.   The most steadfast friend of Cortés — Zuazo — was sent off to Cuba, whence he got the news to Cortés by letter.   After some hesitation and much saying of Masses, Cortés appointed a governor for the Honduras colony; and sending Sandoval with his forces overland, he embarked himself to go by sea. Various mishaps caused his ship to put back several times.   Discouraged at last, and believing there was a divine purpose in keeping him in Honduras for further conquest, he determined to remain a while, and sent messengers instead to Mexico.   Runners were also sent after Sandoval to bring him back.

Cortés now turned his attention to the neighboring provinces; and one after another he brought them into subjection, or gained their respect by interfering to protect them from other parties of marauding Spaniards. He had already planned conquests farther south, and Sandoval had received orders to march, when a messenger from Mexico brought the exhortations of his friends for his return to that city.   Taking a small force with him, including Sandoval, he embarked in April, 1526.   After being tempest-

---

[1] There is some doubt whether the alleged plot was not, after all, a fiction to cover the getting rid of burdensome personages. H. H.

Bancroft (*Central America*, i. 555) collates the various views, but it does not seem that any unassailable conclusion can be reached.

tossed and driven to Cuba, he landed late in May near Vera Cruz, and proceeded in triumph to his capital.

Cortés' messenger from Honduras had arrived in good time, and had animated his steadfast adherents, who succeeded very soon in overthrowing the usurper Salazar and restoring the Cortés government. Then followed the request for Cortés' return, and in due time his arrival. The natives vied with each other in the consideration which they showed to Malinche, as Cortés was universally called by them. Safe in their good wishes, Cortés moved by easy stages toward Mexico. Everybody was astir with shout and banner as he entered the city itself. He devoted himself at once to re-establishing the government and correcting abuses.

Meanwhile the enemies of Cortés at Madrid had so impressed the Emperor that he ordered a judge, Luis Ponce de Leon, to proceed to Mexico and investigate the charges against the Governor, and to hold power during the suspension of Cortés' commission. Cortés received him loyally, and the transfer of authority was duly made, — Cortés still retaining the position of captain-general. Before any charges against Cortés could be heard, Ponce sickened and died, July 20, 1526; and his authority descended to Marcos de Aguilar, whom he had named as successor. He too died in a short time; and Cortés had to resist the appeals of his friends, who wished him to reassume the governorship and quiet the commotions which these sudden changes were producing. Meanwhile the enemies of Cortés were actively intriguing in Spain, and Estrada received a royal decree to assume alone the government, which with two others he had been exercising since the death of Aguilar. The patience of Cortés and his adherents was again put to a test when the new ruler directed the exile of Cortés from the city. Estrada soon saw his mistake, and made advances for a reconciliation, which Cortés accepted.

But new developments were taking place on the coast. The Emperor had taken Pánuco out of Cortés' jurisdiction by appointing Nuño de Guzman to govern it, with orders to support Ponce if Cortés should resist that royal agent. Guzman did not arrive on the coast till May 20, 1527, when he soon, by his acts, indicated his adherence to the Velasquez party, and a disposition to encroach upon the bounds of New Spain. He was forced to deal with Cortés as captain-general; and letters far from conciliatory in character passed from Guzman to the authorities in Mexico. Estrada had found it necessary to ask Cortés to conduct a campaign against his ambitious neighbor; but Cortés felt that he could do more for himself and New Spain in the Old, and so prepared to leave the country and escape from the urgency of those of his partisans who were constantly trying to embroil him with Estrada. A letter from the new President of the Council of the Indies urging his coming, helped much to the determination. He collected what he could of treasure, fabric, and implement to show the richness of the country. A great variety of animals,.

representatives of the various subjugated peoples, and a showy train of dependents, among them such conspicuous characters as Sandoval and Tapia, with native princes and chieftains, accompanied him on board the vessels.

Cortés, meanwhile, was ignorant of what further mischief his enemies had done in Spain. The Emperor had appointed a commission (*audiencia*) to examine the affairs of New Spain, and had placed Guzman at the head. It had full power to assume the government and regulate the administration. In December, 1528, and January, 1529, all the members assembled at Mexico. The jealous and grasping quality of their rule was soon apparent. The absence of Cortés in Spain threatened the continuance of their power; for reports had reached Mexico of the enthusiasm which attended his arrival in Spain. They accordingly despatched messengers to the Spanish court renewing the charges against Cortés, and setting forth the danger of his return to Mexico. Alvarado and other friends of Cortés protested in vain, and had to look on and see, under one pretext or another, all sorts of taxes and burdens laid upon the estates of the absent hero. He was also indicted in legal form for every vice and crime that any one might choose to charge him with; and the indictments stood against him for many years.

AUTOGRAPH OF SANDOVAL.[1]

Guzman was soon aware of the smouldering hatred which the rule of himself and his associate had created; and he must have had suspicions of the representations of his rapacity and cruelty which were reaching Madrid from his opponents. To cover all iniquities with the splendor of conquest, he gathered a formidable army and marched to invade the province of Jalisco.

[1] After a fac-simile in Cabajal, *México*, ii. 686.

CONZALO de SANDOVAL
de Medellin,
Capitan Valeroso,

SANDOVAL.[1]

Cortés, with his following, had landed at Palos late in 1528, and was under the necessity, a few days later, of laying the body of Sandoval — worn out with the Honduras campaign — in the vaults of La Rabida. It was a sad duty for Cortés, burdened with the grief that his young lieutenant could not share with him the honors now in store, as he made his progress to Toledo, where the Court then was. He was received with unaccustomed honor and royal condescensions, — only the prelude to substantial grants of territory in New Spain, which he was asked to particularize and describe. He was furthermore honored with the station and title of Marqués del Valle de Oajaca. He was confirmed as captain-general; but his reinstatement as governor was deferred till the reports of the new commission in New Spain should be received. He was, however,

---

[1] Fac-simile of an engraving in Herrera, ii. 32. It is dressed up in Cabajal's *México*, ii. 254.

Don HERNANDO CORTES
Marquez de Valle.
natural de Medellin

CORTÉS.[1]

assured of liberty to make discoveries in the south sea, and to act as governor of all islands and parts he might discover westward.

The wife of Cortés, whom he had left in Cuba, had joined him in Mexico after the conquest, and had been received with becoming state. Her early decease, after a loftier alliance would have become helpful to his ambition,

---

[1] Fac-simile of an engraving in Herrera, ii. 1. There is also a portrait which hangs, or did hang, in the series of Viceroys in the Museo at Mexico. This was engraved for Don Antonio Uguina, of Madrid; and from his engraving the picture given second by Prescott is copied. Engravings of a picture ascribed to Titian are given in Townsend's translation of Solis (London, 1724) and in the Madrid edition of Solis (1783). Cf. H. H. Bancroft, *Mexico*, i. 39, *note*. The Spanish translation of Clavigero, published in Mexico in 1844, has a portrait; and one "after Velasquez" is given in Laborde's *Voyage pittoresque*, vol. iv., and in Jules Verne's *Découverte de la Terre*.

A small copper-plate representing Cortés in armor, with an uplifted finger and a full beard (accompanied by a brief sketch of his career) is given in *Select Lives collected out of A. Thevet, Englished by I. S.* (Cambridge, 1676), which is a section of a volume, *Prosopographia* (Cambridge, 1676), an English translation of Thevet's Collection of Lives. The copper may be the same used in the French original.

CORTÉS' ARMOR.[1]

had naturally raised a suspicion among Cortés' traducers that her death had been prematurely hastened. He had now honors sufficient for any match among the rank of grandees; and a few days after he was ennobled he was married, as had been earlier planned, to the daughter of the late Conde de Aguilar and niece of the Duque de Béjar, — both houses of royal extraction.

[1] Copied from an engraving (in Ruge's *Das Zeitalter der Entdeckungen*, p. 405) of the original in the Museum at Madrid. Wilson refers to some plate armor in the Museum at Mexico, which he, of course, thinks apocryphal (*New Conquest*, p. 444).

Cortés now prepared to return to Mexico with his new titles. He learned that the Emperor had appointed a new *audiencia* to proceed thither, and it promised him better justice than he had got from the other. The Emperor was not, however, satisfied as yet that the presence of Cortés in Mexico was advisable at the present juncture, and he ordered him to stay; but the decree was too late, and Cortés, with a great retinue, had already departed. He landed at Vera Cruz, in advance of the new judge, July 15, 1530.

His reception was as joyous as it had been four years before; and though an order had reached him forbidding his approach within ten leagues of Mexico till the new *audiencia* should arrive, the support of his retinue compelled him to proceed to Tezcuco, where he awaited its coming, while he was put in the interim to not a little hazard and inconvenience by the efforts of the Guzman government to deprive him of sustenance and limit his intercourse with the natives.

Near the end of the year the new Government arrived, — or all but its president, Fuenleal, for he was the Bishop of Santo Domingo, whom the others had been ordered to take on board their vessel on the way; but stress of weather had prevented their doing this. The Bishop did not join them till September. In Mexico they took possession

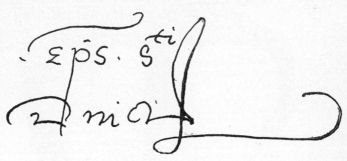

AUTOGRAPH OF FUENLEAL
(*Episcopus Sancti Dominici*).

of Cortés' house, which they had been instructed to appropriate at an appraisement.

The former Government was at once put on trial, and judgment was in most cases rendered against them, so that their property did not suffice to meet the fines imposed. Cortés got a due share of what they were made to disgorge, in restitution of his own losses through them. Innumerable reforms were instituted, and the natives received greater protection than ever before.

Guzman, meanwhile, was on his expedition toward the Pacific coast, conducting his rapacious and brutal conquest of Nueva Galicia. He refused to obey the call of the new *audiencia*, while he despatched messengers to Mexico to protect, if possible, his interests. By them also he forwarded his own statement of his case to the Emperor. Cortés, vexed at Guzman's anticipation of his own intended discoveries toward the Pacific, sent a lieutenant to confront him; but Guzman was wily enough to circumvent

MEXICO AND ACAPULCO.[1]

the lieutenant, seized him, and packed him off to Mexico with scorn and
assurance. It was his last hour of triumph. His force soon dwindled;
his adherents deserted him; his misdeeds had left him no friends; and he
at last deserted the remnant of his army, and starting for Pánuco, turned

---

[1] Fac-simile of a map in Herrera, i. 408.

aside to Mexico on the way. He found in the city a new *régime*. Antonio de Mendoza had been sent out as viceroy, and to succeed Fuenleal at the same time as president of the *audiencia*. He had arrived at Vera Cruz in October, 1535. His rule was temperate and cautious. Negroes, who had been imported into the country in large numbers as slaves, plotted an insurrection: but the Viceroy suppressed it; and if there was native complicity in the attempt, it was not proved. The Viceroy had received from his predecessors a source of trial and confusion in the disputed relations which existed between the civil rulers and the Captain-General. There were endless disputes with the second *audiencia*, and disagreements continued to exist with the Viceroy, about the respective limits of the powers of the two as derived from the Emperor.

Cortés had been at great expense in endeavoring to prosecute discovery in the Pacific, and he had the vexation of seeing his efforts continually embarrassed by the new powers. Previous to his departure for Spain he had despatched vessels from Tehuantepec to the Moluccas to open traffic with the Asiatic Indies; but the first *audiencia* had prevented the despatch of a succoring expedition which Cortés had planned. On his return to New Spain the Captain-General had begun the construction of new vessels both at Tehuantepec and at Acapulco; but the second *audiencia* interfered with his employment of Indians to carry his material to the coast. He however contrived to despatch two vessels up the coast under Hurtado de Mendoza, which left in May, 1532. They had reached the coast to the north, where Guzman was marauding, who was glad of the opportunity of thwarting the purpose of his rival. He refused the vessels the refuge of a harbor, and they were subsequently lost. Cortés now resolved to give his personal attention to these sea explorations, and proceeding to Tehuantepec, he superintended the construction of two vessels, which finally left port Oct. 29, 1533. They discovered Lower California. Afterward one of the vessels was separated from the other, and fell in distress into the hands of Guzman while making a harbor on the coast. The other ship reached Tehuantepec. Cortés appealed to the *audiencia*, who meted equal justice in ordering Guzman to surrender the vessel, and in commanding Cortés to desist from further exploration. An appeal to the Emperor effected little, for it seems probable that the *audiencia* knew what support it had at court. Cortés next resolved to act on his own responsibility and take command in person of a third expedition. So, in the winter of 1534–1535, he sent some vessels up the coast, and led a land force in the same direction. Guzman fled before him. Cortés joined his fleet at the port where Guzman had seized his ship on the earlier voyage, and embarked. Crossing to the California peninsula, he began the settlement of a colony on its eastern shore. He left the settlers there, and returned to Acapulco to send forward additional supplies and recruits. At this juncture the new Viceroy had reached Mexico; and it was not long before he began to entertain schemes of despatching fleets of discovery, and Cortés found a new rival in his plans.

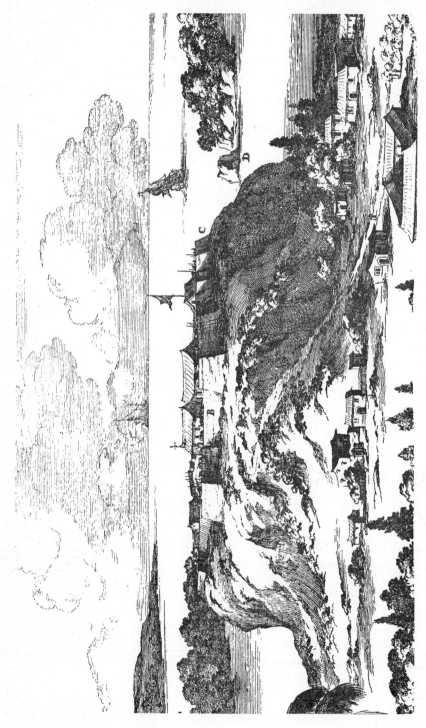

ACAPULCO.[1]

[1] Part of a view of Acapulco as given in Montanus and Ogilby, p. 261, showing the topog- raphy, but representing the later fort and build- ings. The same picture, on a larger scale, was

The Captain-General got the start of his rival, and sent out a new expedition from Acapulco under Francisco de Ulloa; but the Viceroy gave orders to prevent other vessels following, and his officers seized one already at sea, which chanced to put into one of the upper ports. Cortés could endure such thraldom no longer, and early in 1540 he left again for Spain to plead his interests with the Emperor. He never saw the land of his conquest again.

CORTÉS.[1]

We left Guzman for a while in Mexico, where Mendoza not unkindly received him, as one who hated Cortés as much or more than he did. Guzman was bent on escaping, and had ordered a vessel to be ready on the coast. He was a little too late, however. The Emperor had sent a judge to call him to account, and Guzman suddenly found this evil genius was in Mexico. The judge put him under arrest and marched

published by Vander Aa at Amsterdam. A plan of the harbor is given in Bancroft's *Mexico*, iii. 25. The place had no considerable importance as a Spanish settlement till 1550 (Ibid., ii. 420). Cf. the view in Gay's *Popular History of the United States*, ii. 586.

[1] This follows a sketch of the picture, in the Hospital of Jesus at Mexico, which is given in Charton's *Voyageurs*, iii. 359. Prescott gives an engraving after a copy then in his own possession. The picture in the Hospital is also said to be a copy of one taken in Spain a few years before the death of Cortés, during his last visit. The original is not known to exist. The present descendants of the Conqueror, the family of the Duke of Monteleone in Italy, have only a copy of the one at Mexico. Another copy, made during General Scott's occupation of the city, is in the gallery of the Pennsylvania Historical Society (*Catalogue*, no. 130). The upper part

him to prison. A trial was begun; but it dragged along, and Guzman sent an appeal forward to the Council for the Indies, in which he charged Cortés with promoting his persecution. He was in the end remanded to Spain, where he lingered out a despised life for a few years, with a gleam of satisfaction, perhaps, in finding, some time after, that Cortés too had found a longer stay in New Spain unprofitable.

CORTÉS MEDAL.[1]

Cortés had reached Spain in the early part of 1540, and had been received with honor by the Court; but when he began to press for a judgment that might restore his losses and rehabilitate him in his self-respect, he found nothing but refusal and procrastination. He asked to return to Mexico, but found he could not. With a reckless aim he joined an expedition against Algiers; but the ship on which he embarked was wrecked, and he only saved himself by swimming, losing the choicest of his Mexican jewels, which he carried on his person. Then again he memorialized the Emperor for a hearing and award, but was disregarded. Later he once more appealed, but was still unheard. Again he asked permission to return to New Spain. This time it was granted; but before he could make the final preparations, he sank under his burdens, and at a village near Seville Cortés died on the 2d of December, 1547, in his sixty-second year.[2]

---

of the figure is reproduced in Carbajal's *Historia de México*, ii. 12; and it is also given entire in Cumplido's edition of Prescott's *Mexico*, vol. iii.

[1] This follows the engraving in Ruge's *Das Zeitalter der Entdeckungen* (p. 361) of a specimen in the Royal Cabinet at Berlin. The original is of the same size.

[2] The remains of Cortés have rested uneasily. They were buried at Seville; but in 1562 his son removed them to New Spain and placed them in a monastery at Tezcuco. In 1629 they were carried with pomp to Mexico to the church of St. Francis; and again, in 1794, they were transferred to the Hospital of Jesus (Prescott, *Mexico*, iii. 465), where a monument with a bust was placed over them. In 1823, when a patriotic zeal was turned into the wildness of a mob,

the tomb was threatened, and some soberer citizens secretly removed the monument and sent it (and later the remains) clandestinely to his descendant, the Duke of Monteleone, in Palermo, where they are supposed now to be, if the story of this secret shipment is true (Prescott, *Mexico*, iii. 335; Harrisse, *Bibl. Amer. Vet.*, pp. 219, 220; Bancroft, *Mexico*, iii. 479, 480). Testimony regarding the earlier interment and exhumation is given in the *Coleccion de documentos inéditos* (*España*), xxii. 563. Cf. B. Murphy on "The Tomb of Cortés" in the *Catholic World*, xxxiii. 24.

For an account of the family and descendants of Cortés, see Bancroft, ii. 480; Prescott, iii. 336. The latter traces what little is known of the later life of Marina (vol. iii. p. 279).

CRITICAL ESSAY ON THE DOCUMENTARY SOURCES OF MEXICAN HISTORY.

MR. H. H. BANCROFT, in speaking of the facilities which writers of Spanish American history now have in excess of those enjoyed by the historian of thirty years ago, claims that in documentary evidence there are twenty papers for his use in print to-day for one then.[1] These are found in part in the great *Coleccion* of Pacheco and others mentioned in the Introduction. The Mexican writer Joaquin Garcia Icazbalceta (born 1825) made a most important contribution in the two volumes of a *Coleccion de documentos para la historia de México* which passes by his name and which appeared respectively in 1858 and 1866.[2] He found in Mexico few of the papers which he printed, obtaining them chiefly from Spain. Of great interest among those which he gives is the *Itinerario* of Grijalva, both in the Italian and Spanish text.[3] Of Cortés himself there are in this publication various letters not earlier made public. The quarrel between him and Velasquez is illustrated by other papers. Here also we find what is mentioned elsewhere as " De rebus gestis Cortesii " printed as a "Vida de Cortés," and attributed to C. Calvet de Estrella. The recital of the so-called " Anonymous Conqueror," held by some to be Francisco de Terrazas, is translated from Ramusio (the original Spanish is not known), with a fac-simile of the plan of Mexico.[4] There is also the letter from the army of Cortés to the Emperor; and in the second volume various other papers interesting in connection with Cortés' career, including the memorial of Luis de Cárdenas, etc. Two other papers have been recognized as important. One of these in the first volume is the *Historia de los Indios de Nueva España* of Fray Toribio Motolinia, accompanied by a Life of the Father by Ramirez, with a gathering of bibliographical detail. Toribio de Benavente — Motolinia was a name which he took from a description of him by the natives — had come over with the Franciscans in 1523. He was a devoted, self-sacrificing missionary; but he proved that his work did not quiet all the passions, for he became a violent opponent of Las Casas' views and measures.[5] His labors took him the length and breadth of the land; his assiduity acquired for him a large knowledge of the Aztec tongue and beliefs; and his work, besides describing institutions of this people, tells of the success and methods secured or adopted by himself and his companions in effecting their conversion to the faith of the conquerors. Robertson used a manuscript copy of the work, and Obadiah Rich procured a copy for Prescott, who ventured the assertion, when he wrote, that it had so little of popular interest that it would never probably be printed.[6]

---

[1] Those pertaining to Cortés in vols. i.–iv. of the *Documentos inéditos* (*España*) had already appeared. Harrisse, *Bibl. Amer. Vet.*, pp. 213-215, enumerates the manuscripts which had been collected by Prescott. Clavigero had given accounts of the collections in the Vatican, at Vienna, and of those of Boturini, etc.

[2] Sabin, vol. xx. no. 34,153. In the Introduction to both volumes Icazbalceta discusses learnedly the authorship of the various papers, and makes note of considerable bibliographical

detail. The edition was three hundred copies, with twelve on large paper.

[3] Vol. i. 281; see also *ante*, p. 215.

[4] Vol. i. 368. This plan is given on an earlier page. Cf. Bancroft, *Early American Chroniclers*, p. 15.

[5] See chap. v. p. 343.

[6] *Mexico*, ii. 96. A part of it was printed in the *Documentos inéditos* as " Ritos antiquos . . . de las Indias." Cf. Kingsborough, vol. ix.

Bancroft[1] calls the *Relacion* of Andrés de Tápia one of the most valuable documents of the early parts of the Conquest. It ends with the capture of Narvaez; recounting the antecedent events, however, with "uneven completeness." It is written warmly in the interests of Cortés. Icazbalceta got what seemed to be the original from the Library of the Academy of History in Madrid, and printed it in his second volume (p. 554). It was not known to Prescott, who quotes it at second hand in Gomara.[2]

The next most important collection is that published in Mexico from 1852 to 1857,[3] under the general title of *Documentos para la historia de México*. This collection of four series, reckoned variously in nineteen or twenty-one volumes, is chiefly derived from Mexican sources, and is largely illustrative of the history of northwestern Mexico, and in general concerns Mexican history of a period posterior to the Conquest.

There have been two important series of documents published and in part unearthed by José Fernando Ramirez, who became Minister of State under Maximilian. The first of these is the testimony at the examination of the charges which were brought against Pedro de Alvarado, and some of those made in respect to Nuño de Guzman, — *Procesos de residencia*,[4] which was published in Mexico in 1847;[5] the other set of documents pertain to the trial of Cortés himself. Such of these as were found in the Mexican Archives were edited by Ignacio L. Rayon under the title of *Archivo Mexicano; Documentos para la historia de México*, and published in the city of Mexico in 1852–1853, in two volumes. At a later day (1867–1868) Ramirez discovered in the Spanish Archives other considerable portions of the same trial, and these have been printed in the *Coleccion de documentos inéditos de las Indias*, vols. xxvi.–xxix.

The records of the municipality of Mexico date from March 8, 1524, and chronicle for a long time the sessions as held in Cortés' house; and are particularly interesting, as Bancroft says,[6] after 1524, when we no longer have Cortés' own letters to follow, down to 1529. Harrisse has told us what he found in the repositories of Italy, particularly at Venice, among the letters sent to the Senate during this period by the Venetian ambassadors at Madrid.[7] Three volumes have so far been published of a *Coleccion de documentos para la historia de Costa-Rica* at San José de Costa-Rica, under the editing of León Fernández, which have been drawn from the Archives of the Indies and from the repositories in Guatemala. A few letters of Alvarado and other letters of the Conquest period are found in the *Coleccion de documentos antiguous de Guatemala* published at Guatemala in 1857.[8]

No more voluminous contributor to the monographic and documentary history of Mexico can be named than Carlos Maria de Bustamante. There will be occasion in other connections to dwell upon particular publications, and some others are of little interest to us at present, referring to periods as late as the present century. Bustamante was a Spaniard, but he threw himself with characteristic energy into a heated advo-

---

[1] *Mexico*, i. 405.

[2] Prescott, *Mexico*, ii. 147.

[3] Sabin, vol. ix. nos. 34,154–34,156; Quaritch, *Ramirez Collection* (1880), no. 89, priced it at £40.

[4] This institution is clearly defined by Helps, iii. 141. Cf. Bancroft, *Central America*, i. 250.

[5] Prescott, *Mexico*, ii. 272; Bancroft, *Mexico*, ii. 373; *Murphy Catalogue*, no. 2,092; *Pinart-Brasseur Catalogue*, no. 770. The book has a portrait of Alvarado, and is enriched with notes by Ramirez. The manuscript of the charges against Alvarado was discovered in 1846 among some supposed waste-papers in the Mexican Archives which the licentiate, Ignacio Rayon, was then examining (Bancroft, *Central America*, ii. 104).

[6] *Mexico*, ii. 9. Bancroft says he uses a copy made from one which escaped the fire that destroyed so much in 1692, and which belonged to the Maximilian Collection. Quaritch offered, a few years since, as from the Ramirez Collection, for £175, the Acts of the Municipality of Mexico, 1524–1564, in six manuscript volumes. Bancroft (*Mexico*, iii. 508, etc.), enumerates the sources of a later period.

[7] *Bibl. Amer. Vet., Additions*, p. xxxiv.

[8] There appeared in 1882, in two volumes, in the *Biblioteca de los Americanistas*, a *Historia de Guatemala ó recordación Florida escrita el siglo XVII por él Capitán D. Francisco Antonio de Fuentes y Guzman . . . publica por primera vez con notas é ilustraciones D. Justo Zaragoza*.

racy of national Mexican feelings; and this warmly partisan exhibition of himself did much toward rendering the gathering of his scattered writings very difficult, in view of the enemies whom he made and of their ability to suppress obnoxious publications when they came into power. Most of these works date from 1812 to 1850, and when collected make nearly or quite fifty volumes, though frequently bound in fewer.[1] The completest list, however, is probably that included in the enumeration of authorities prefixed by Bancroft to his *Central America* and *Mexico*, which shows not only the printed works of Bustamante, but also the autograph originals, — which, Bancroft says, contain much not in the published works.[2] Indeed, these lists show an extremely full equipment of the manuscript documentary stores relating to the whole period of Mexican history,[3] including a copy of the *Archivo general de México*, as well as much from the catalogues of José Maria Andrade and José Fernando Ramirez, records of the early Mexican councils, and much else of an ecclesiastical and missionary character not yet put in print.[4]

[1] Quaritch in his *Catalogue*, no. 321, *sub* 11,807, shows a collection of forty-seven for £50, apparently the Ramirez Collection. Cf. Sabin, vol. iii. no. 9,567, etc.

[2] *Mexico*, vol. i. p. viii.

[3] Indeed, the footnotes of Prescott are meagre by comparison. The enumeration of the manuscript sources on the Conquest given in Charton's *Voyageurs*, iii. 420, shows what provision of this sort was most to be depended on thirty years ago. There is a set of nine folios in Harvard College Library, gathered by Lord Kingsborough, called *Documentos para el historia de México y Peru*. It includes some manuscripts; but they are all largely, perhaps wholly, of a later period than the Conquest.

[4] Quaritch, who in his *Catalogue* of 1870 (no. 259, *sub* 376) advertised for £105 the original manuscripts of three at least of these councils (1555, 1565, 1585), intimates that they never were returned into the Ecclesiastical Archives after Lorenzana had used them in preparing an edition of the Proceedings of these Councils, which he published in 1769 and 1770, — *Concilios provinciales de México*, — though in the third, and perhaps in the first, he had translated apparently his text from the Latin published versions. Bancroft describes these manuscripts in his *Mexico*, ii. 685. The Acts of the First Council had been printed (1556) before Lorenzana; but the book was suppressed, and the Acts of the Third Council had been printed in 1622 in Mexico, and in 1725 at Paris. The Acts of the Third also appeared in 1859 at Mexico with other documents. The readiest source for the English reader of the history of the measures for the conversion of the Indians and for the relation of the Church to the civil authorities in New Spain are sundry chapters (viii., xix., etc.) in Bancroft's *Central America*, and others (ix., xix., xxxi., xxxii.) in his *Mexico*. (Cf. references in Harrisse, *Bibl. Amer. Vet.*, p. 209.) The leading Spanish authorities are Torobio Motolinia, Mendieta, and Torquemada, all characterized elsewhere. Alonso Fernandez' *Historia eclesiástica de nuestros tiempos*

(Toledo, 1611) is full in elucidation of the lives of the friars and of their study of the native tongues. (Cf. Rich, 1832, £2 2s.; Quaritch, 1870, £5; Bancroft, *Mexico*, ii. 190.) Gil Gonzales Davila's *Teatro eclesiástico de la primitiva Iglesia de las Indias* (Madrid, 1649–1655) is more important and rarer (Quaritch, 1870, £8 8s.; Rosenthal, Munich, 1884, for 150 marks; Bancroft, *Mexico*, ii. 189). Of Las Casas and his efforts, see the preceding chapter in the present volume.

The Orders of friars are made the subject of special treatment in Bancroft's *Mexico*. The Franciscans were the earliest to arrive, coming, in response to the wish of Cortés, in 1524. There are various histories of their labors, — Francisco Gonzaga's *De origine seraphicæ religionis Franciscanæ*, Rome, 1587 (Carter-Brown, i. 372); sections of Torquemada and the fourth part of Vetancour's *Teatro Mexicano*, Mexico, 1697–1698; Francisco Vasquez' *Chronica . . . de Guatemala*, 1714; Espinosa's *Chronica apostolica*, 1746 (Sabin, vi. 239; Carter-Brown, iii. 827), etc. Of the Dominicans we have Antonio de Remesal's *Historia de la S. Vincent de Chyapa*, Madrid, 1619 (Bancroft, *Central America*, ii. 339, 736), and Davilla Padilla's *Santiago de México*, mentioned in the text. Of the Augustinian friars there is Juan de Grijalva's *Cronica*, Mexico, 1624. Of the books on the Jesuits who came late (1571, etc.), there is a note in Bancroft's *Mexico*, iii. 447, showing as of chief importance Francisco de Florencia's *Compañia de Jesus* (Mexico, 1694), while the subject was taken up under the same title by Francisco Javier Aleque, who told the story of their missions from 1566 in Florida to 1765. The manuscript of this work was not printed till Bustamante edited it in 1841.

The legend or belief in our Lady of Guadalupe gives a picturesque and significant coloring to the history of missions in Mexico, since from the day of her apparition the native worship, it is said, steadily declined. It is briefly thus: In 1531 a native who had received a baptismal name of Juan Diego, passing a hill neighboring

Of particular value for the documents which it includes is the *Historia de la fundacion y discurso de la provincia de Santiago de México, de la orden de predicadores, por las vidas de sus varones insignes y casos notables de Nueva España*, published in Madrid in 1596.[1] The author, Davilla Padilla, was born in Mexico in 1562 of good stock; he became a Dominican in 1579, and died in 1604. His opportunities for gathering material were good, and he has amassed a useful store of information regarding the contact of the Spanish and the Indians, and the evidences of the national traits of the natives. His book has another interest, in that we find in it the earliest mention of the establishment of a press in Mexico.[2]

to the city of Mexico, was confronted by a radiant being who announced herself as the Virgin Mary, and who said that she wished a church to be built on the spot. The native's story, as he told it to the Bishop, was discredited, until some persons sent to follow the Indian saw him disappear unaccountably from sight.

It was now thought that witchcraft more than a heavenly interposition was the cause, until, again confronting the apparition, Diego was bidden to take some roses which the Lady had handled and carry them in his mantle to the Bishop, who would recognize them as a sign. When the garment was unrolled, the figure of the Virgin was found painted in its folds, and the sign was accepted. A shrine was soon erected, as the Lady had wished; and here the holy effigy was sacredly guarded, until it found a resting-place in what is thought to be the richest church in Mexico, erected between 1695 and 1709; and there it still is. It has been at times subjected to some ecclesiastical scrutiny, and there have been some sceptics and cavillers. Cf. Bancroft, *Mexico*, ii. 407, and authorities there cited. Lorenzana in his *Cartas pastorales* (1770) has given a minute account of the painting (Carter-Brown, vol. iii. no. 1,749; Sabin, vol. xii. no. 56,199; and the *Coleccion de obras pertenecientes a la milagrosa aparicion de Nuestra Señora de Guadalupe*).

[1] Carter-Brown, i. 496; Bancroft, *Mexico*, iii. 723. There is a copy in Harvard College Library. There were later editions at Brussels in 1625 (Carter-Brown, ii. 300; Stevens, *Historical Collection*, i. 177), and again at Valladolid in 1634 as *Varia historia de la Nueva España y Florida, segunda impresion* (Carter-Brown, ii. 412).

[2] We read in the 1596 edition (p. 670) that one Juan Pablos was the first printer in Mexico, who printed, as early as 1535, a religious manual of Saint John Climachus. The book, however, is not now known (Sabin, vi. 229), and there is no indisputable evidence of its former existence; though a similar story is told by Alonzo Fernandez in his *Historia eclesiástica* (Toledo, 1611), and by Gil Gonzales Davila in his *Teatro eclesiástico* (Madrid, 1649), — who gives, however, the date as 1532. The *Teatro* is of further interest for the map of the diocese of Michoacan and

for the arms of the different dioceses. It is in two volumes, and is worth from thirty to forty dollars.

The subject of early printing in Mexico has been investigated by Icazbalceta in the *Diccionario universal de historia y de geografia*, v. 961 (published in Mexico in 1854), where he gives a list of Mexican imprints prior to 1600 (Carter-Brown, i. 129, 130). A similar list is given in connection with an examination of the subject by Harrisse in his *Bibl. Amer. Vet.*, no. 232. Mr. John Russell Bartlett gives another list (1540 to 1600) in the *Carter-Brown Catalogue*, i. 131, and offers other essays on the subject in the *Historical Magazine*, November, 1858, and February, 1865, and again in the new edition of Thomas's *History of Printing* (Worcester, 1875), i. 365, appendix.

The earliest remaining example of the first Mexican press which we have is a fragmentary copy of the *Manual de adultos* of Cristóbal Cabrera, which was originally discovered in the Library of Toledo, whence it disappeared, to be again discovered by Gayangos on a London bookstall in 1870. It is supposed to have consisted of thirty-eight leaves, and the printed date of Dec. 13, 1540, is given on one of the leaves which remain (*Bibl. Amer. Vet.*, no. 232; *Additions*, no. 123, with fac-similes, of which a part is given in the *Carter-Brown Catalogue*, i. 131). Harrisse, perhaps, is in error, as Quaritch affirms (*Ramirez Collection*, 1880, no. 339), in assigning the same date, 1540, to an edition of the *Doctrina Christiana* found by him at Toledo; and there seem to have been one or two other books issued by Cromberger (*Catalogue Andrade*, nos. 2,366, 2,367, 2,369, 2,477) before we come to an acknowledged edition of the *Doctrina Cristiana* — which for a long time was held to be the earliest Mexican imprint — with the date of 1544. It is a small volume of sixty pages, "impressa en México, en casa de Juan Cromberger" (Rich, 1832, no. 14; Sabin, vol. iv. no. 16,777; Carter-Brown, i. 134, with fac-similes of title; *Bookworm*, 1867, p. 114; Quaritch, no. 321, *sub* 12,551). Of the same date is Dionisio Richel's *Compendio breve que tracta a' la manera de como se hã de hazer las processiones*, also printed, as the earlier one was, by command of Bishop Zumarraga, this time with a distinct date, — "Año de M. D.

One of the earliest of the modern collections of documents and early monographs is the *Historiadores primitivos de las Indias occidentales* of Andres Gonzales de Barcia Carballido y Zuniga (known usually as Barcia), published at Madrid in 1749 in three volumes folio, and enriched with the editor's notes. The sections were published separately; and it was not till after the editor's death (1743) that they were grouped and put out collectively with the above distinctive title. In this form the collection is rare, and it has been stated that not over one or two hundred copies were so gathered.[1]

First among all documents respecting the Conquest are the letters sent by Cortés himself to the Emperor; and of these a somewhat detailed bibliographical account is given in the Notes following this Essay, as well as an examination of the corrective value of certain other contemporaneous and later writers.

Justin Winsor

xliiij." A copy which belonged to the Emperor Maximilian was sold in the Andrade sale (no. 2,667), and again in the Brinley sale (no. 5,317). Quaritch priced Ramirez' copy in 1880 at £52.

The lists above referred to show eight separate issues of the Mexican press before 1545. Icazbalceta puts, under 1548, the *Doctrina en Mexicano* as the earliest instance known of a book printed in the native tongue. Up to 1563, with the exception of a few vocabularies and grammars of the languages of the country, of the less than forty books which are known to us, nearly all are of a theological or devotional character. In that year (1663) Vasco de Puga's Collection of Laws — *Provisiones, cédulas, instrucciones de su*

Majestad — was printed (Quaritch, *Ramirez Collection*, 1880, no. 236, £30). Falkenstein in his *Geschichte der Buchdruckerkunst* (Leipsic, 1840) has alleged, following Pinelo and others, that a Collection of Laws — *Ordinationes legumque collectiones* — was printed in 1649; but the existence of such a book is denied. Cf. Thomas, *History of Printing*, i. 372; Harrisse, *Bibl. Amer. Vet.*, no. 288.

[1] Quaritch, *Ramirez Collection* (1880), no. 28, £15; Sabin, vol. I. no. 3,349; Carter-Brown, iii. 893; Rich, *Bibl. Nova Amer.* (1835), p. 95; Stevens, *Bibliotheca historica*, no. 126; Leclerc, no. 50, — 400 francs; Field, *Indian Bibliography*, no. 79.

NOTES.

A. THE LETTERS OF CORTÉS. — I. *The Lost First Letter, July* 10, 1519. The series of letters which Cortés sent to the Emperor is supposed to have begun with one dated at Vera Cruz in July, 1519, which is now lost, but which Barcia and Wilson suppose to have been suppressed by the Council of the Indies at the request of Narvaez. There are contemporaneous references to show that it once existed. Cortés himself mentions it in his second letter, and Bernal Diaz implies that it was not shown by Cortés to his companions. Gomara mentions it, and is thought to give its purport in brief. Thinking that Charles V. may have carried it to Germany, Robertson caused the Vienna Archives to be searched, but without avail; though it has been the belief that this letter existed there at one time, and another sent with it is known to be in those Archives. Prescott caused thorough examinations of the repositories of London, Paris, and Madrid to be made, — equally without result.

Fortunately the same vessel took two other letters, one of which we have. This was addressed by the *justicia y regimiento* of La Villa Rica de la Vera Cruz, and was dated July 10, 1519. It was discovered, by Robertson's agency, in the Imperial Library at Vienna. It rehearses the discoveries of Córdoba and Grijalva, and sustains the views of Cortés, who charged Velasquez with being incompetent and dishonest. This letter is sometimes counted as the first of the series; for though it was not written by Cortés, he is thought to have inspired it.[1]

The other letter is known only through the use of it which contemporary writers made. It was from some of the leading companions in arms of Cortés, who, while they praised their commander, had something to say of others not quite to the satisfaction of Cortés. The Conqueror, it is intimated, intrigued to prevent its reaching the Emperor, — which may account for its loss. Las Casas and Tapia both mention it.[2]

Beside the account given in Gomara of Cortés' early life and his doings in the New World up to the time of his leaving Cuba in 1519, there is a contemporary narrative, quite in Cortés' interest, of unknown authorship, which was found by Muñoz at Simancas.[3] The Latin version is called "De rebus gestis Ferdinandi Cortesii;" but it is called "Vida de Hernan Cortés" in the Spanish rendering which is given by Icazbalceta in his *Coleccion de documentos*, i. 309–357.[4]

A publication of Peter Martyr at Basle in 1521 is often taken as a substitute for the lost first epistle of Cortés. This is the *De nuper sub-*

---

[1] Navarrete first printed it in his *Coleccion*, i. 421; it was included also in Vedia's *Historiadores primitivos de Indias* (Madrid, 1852); and Gayangos, in his *Cartas de Hernan Cortés* (Paris, 1866) does not hesitate to let it stand for the first letter, while he also annotates it. It is likewise printed in the *Biblioteca de autores Españoles*, vol. xxii., and by Alaman in his *Disertaciones sobre la historia de la República Mejicana*, vol. i., appendix, with a sketch of the expedition. Cf. Prescott's *Mexico*, i. 360, iii. 428; H. H. Bancroft's *Mexico*, i. 169.

[2] Bancroft, *Mexico*, i. 170. It is supposed that still a third letter went at the same time, which is now known to us. Three letters of this time were found in 1866 among some old account-books in a library sold in Austria. Two of them proved to be written in Spain upon the news of Cortés' discoveries, while one was written by a companion of Cortés shortly after the landing on the Mexican coast, but is not seemingly an original, for it is written in German, and the heading runs: *Newzeit wie unnsers aller-gnadigistn hern des Romischn und hyspaenischn Koningsleut Ain Costliche Newe Lanndschafft habn gefundn*, and bears date June 28, 1519. There are some contradictions in it to the received accounts; but these are less important than the mistake of a modern French translator, who was not aware of the application of the name of Yucatan, at that time, to a long extent of coast, and who supposed the letters referred to Grijalva's expedition. The original text, with a modern German and French version, appears in a small edition (thirty copies) which Frederic Muller, of Amsterdam, printed from the original manuscript (cf. his *Books on America*, 1872, no. 1,144; 1877, no. 2,296, priced at 120 florins) under the title of *Trois lettres sur la découverte de Yucatan*, Amsterdam, 1871 (Carter-Brown, vol. i. no. 66; Muller, *Books on America*, 1877, no. 2,296; C. H. Berendt in *American Bibliopolist*, July and August, 1872; Murphy, no. 2,795).

One of the news-sheets of the time, circulated in Europe, is preserved in the Royal Library at Berlin. A photo-lithographic fac-simile was published (one hundred copies) at Berlin in 1873. It is called: *Newe Zeittung. von dem lande. das die Sponier funden haben ym* 1521. *iare genant Iucatan.* It is a small quarto in gothic type, of four unnumbered leaves, with a woodcut. Cf. *Bibl. Amer. Vet.*, no. 70, with fac-simile of title; Carter-Brown, i. 69; Muller (1877), no. 3,593; Sobolewski, no. 4,153.

[3] Prescott used a copy taken from Muñoz' transcript.

[4] Cf. Prescott, *Mexico*, i. 262; Bancroft, *Mexico*, i. 72.

D. Carolo repertis insulis . . . Petri Martyris enchiridion, which gives a narrative of the expeditions of Grijalva and Cortés, as a sort of supplement to what Peter Martyr had written on the affairs of the Indies in his Three Decades. It was afterward included in his Basle edition of 1533 and in the Paris Extraict of 1532.[1]

Harrisse[2] points out an allusion to the expedition of Cortés and a description of those of Córdoba and Grijalva, in Ein Auszug ettlicher Sendbrieff . . . von wegen einer new gefunden Inseln, published at Nuremberg in March, 1520;[3] and Harrisse supposes the information is derived from Peter Martyr.[4] Bancroft[5] points out a mere reference in a publication of 1522, — Translationuss hispanischer Sprach, etc.

II. The Second Letter, Oct. 30, 1520. We possess four early editions of this, — two Spanish (1, 2) and one Latin (3), and one Italian (4).

1. The earliest Spanish edition was published at Seville Nov. 8, 1522, as Carta de relaciõ, having twenty-eight leaves, in gothic type.[6]

2. The second Spanish edition, Carta de relacion, was printed at Saragossa in 1524. It is in gothic letter, twenty-eight leaves, and has a cut of Cortés before Charles V. and his Court, of which a reduced fac-simile is herewith given.[7]

[1] Cf. Stevens, Bibliotheca historica (1870), p. 103; Historical Collections, i. 342; and the section on "Early Descriptions of America" in the present work.

[2] Bibl. Amer. Vet., no. 179.

[3] Sabin, vi. 126; Carter-Brown, i. 63.

[4] Bibl. Amer. Vet., no. 105.

[5] Mexico, i. 547.

[6] Cf. Harrisse Bibl. Amer. Vet., no. 118; Carter-Brown, i. 71; Brunet, ii. 310; Sabin, vol. iv. no. 16,933; Folsom, introduction to his edition. The Lenox and Barlow libraries have most, if not all, of the various early editions of the Cortés letters.

[7] Cf. Sabin, vol. iv. no. 16,934, Carter-Brown, i. 73; Brunet, ii. 311; Bibliotheca Grenvilliana, p. 84, Bibl. Amer. Vet., no. 120; Heber, vol. vii. no. 1,884; Ternaux, no. 27.

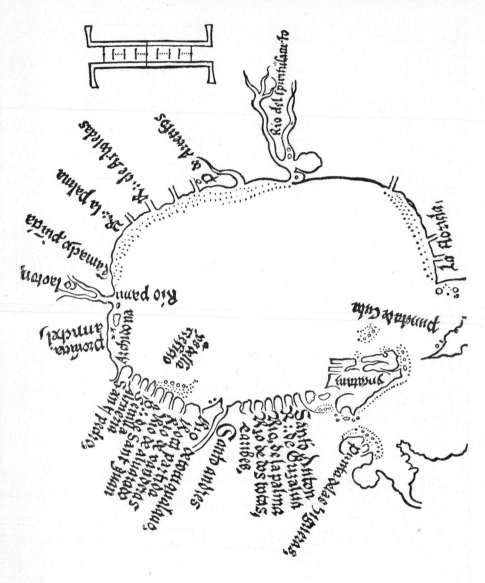

CORTÉS' GULF OF MEXICO.[1]

3. The first Latin edition was published in folio at Nuremberg, in August, 1524, in roman type, with marginal notes in gothic, and was entitled: *Præclara Ferdinādi Cortesii de noua maris Oceani Hypania narratio.* It was the work of Pierre Savorgnanus.[2]

[1] This fac-simile follows the reproduction given by Stevens in his *American Bibliographer,* p. 86, and in his *Notes,* etc., pl. iv. Dr. Kohl published in the *Zeitschrift für allgemeine Erdkunde,* neue Folge, vol. xv., a paper on the "Aelteste Geschichte der Entdeckung und Erforschung des Golfs von Mexico durch die Spanier von 1492 bis 1543." Cf. also Oscar Peschel's *Zeitalter der Entdeckungen* (1858), chap. vii., and Ruge's *Geschichte des Zeitalters der Entdeckungen,* p. 355.

[2] Cf. Carter-Brown, i. 81; *Bibl. Amer. Vet.,* nos. 118, 125; Brunet, ii. 312; *Bibliotheca Grenvilliana,* p. 166; Huth, i. 353; C. Fiske Harris, *Catalogue,* no. 896; *Cooke Catalogue,* vol. iii. no. 623; Sunderland, vol. ii. no. 3,479; Sabin, vol. iv. no. 16,947; Panzer, vii. 466; Menzel, *Bibl. Hist.,* part i. p. 269; Ternaux,

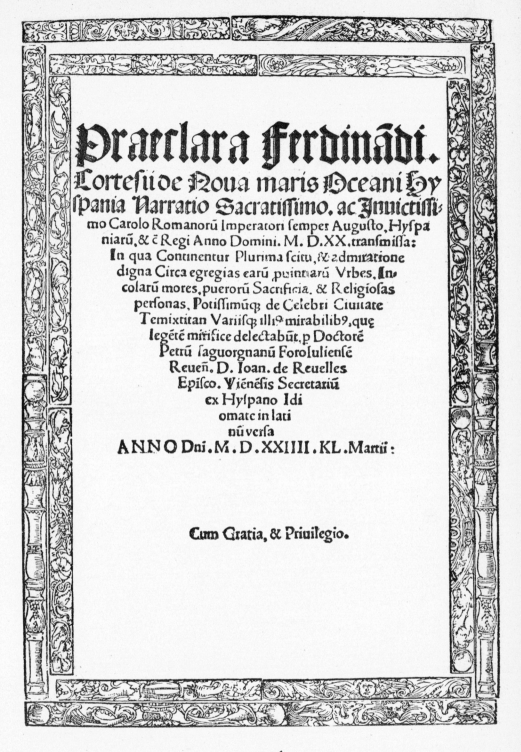

Praeclara Ferdinādi.

Cortefii de Noua maris Oceani Hy
spania Narratio Sacratissimo. ac Inuictissi
mo Carolo Romanorū Imperatori semper Augusto, Hyspa
niarū, & c̄ Regi Anno Domini. M. D.XX. transmissa:
In qua Continentur Plurima scitu, & admiratione
digna Circa egregias earū puintuarū Vrbes. In
colarū mores, puerorū Sacrificia. & Religiosas
personas. Potissimūcʒ de Celebri Ciuitate
Temixtitan Variiscʒ illiꝰ mirabilibꝰ, quę
legēte mirifice delectabūt. p Doctorē
Petrū saguorgnanū Foroſulienſē
Reuen̄. D. Ioan. de Reuelles
Episco. Viēnēsis Secretariū
ex Hyspano Idi
omate in lati
nū versa
ANNO Dni. M. D.XXIIII. KL. Martii :

Cum Gratia, & Priuilegio.

TITLE OF THE LATIN CORTÉS, 1524. — REDUCED.

p. 32; Heber, vol. vi. no. 2,415 and ix. 910; Murphy Catalogue, no. 676; Stevens, *American Bibliographer*,
p. 85.   The book, when it contains the large folding plan of Mexico and the map of the Gulf of Mexico, is
worth about $100.   The plan and map are missing from the copy in the Boston Public Library.   [D. 3101.
56, no. 1].

ARMS, ON THE REVERSE OF TITLE, OF THE LATIN CORTÉS, 1524.

CLEMENT VII.[1]

4. The Italian edition, *La preclara narratione di Ferdinando Cortese della Nuova Hispagna del Mare Oceano . . . per Nicolo Liburnio con fidelta . . . tradotta*, was printed at Venice in 1524. It follows the Latin version of Savorgnanus, and includes also the third letter.

This edition has a new engraving of the map in the Nuremberg edition, though Quaritch and others have doubted if such a map belongs to it. Leclerc (no. 151) chronicles copies with and without the map.[2] An abstract of the second letter in Italian, *Noue de le Isole et Terra Ferma*

[1] Fac-simile of a cut in the Latin Cortés of 1524. It was this Pope who was so delighted with the Indian jugglers sent to Rome by Cortés. The Conqueror also made His Holiness other more substantial supplications for his favor, which resulted in Cortés receiving plenary indulgence for his and his companions' sins (Prescott, iii. 299).

[2] Cf. Brunet, ii. 312, and *Supplément*, col. 320; Carter-Brown, i. 82, which shows a map with inscriptions in Italian; *Bibl. Amer. Vet.*, no. 129; Pinart, no. 262; Sabin, vol. iv. no. 16,951; Panzer, vol. viii. no. 1,248; Court, nos. 90, 91; Heber, vol. vi. no. 1,002, and x. 848; Walckenaer, no. 4,187. There are copies

nouamente trouate, had already appeared two years earlier, in 1522, at Milan.[1]

There were other contemporary abstracts of this letter. Sigmund Grimm, of Augsburg, is said to be the author of one, published about 1522 or 1523, called *Ein schöne newe Zeytung, so kayserlich Mayestet auss India yetz newlich zükommen seind.* It is cited in Harrisse and the *Bibliotheca Grenvilliana ;* and Ternaux (no. 5) is thought to err in assigning the date of 1520 to it, as if printed in Augsburg. Of about the same date is another described by Sabin (vol. iv. no. 16,952) as printed at Antwerp, and called *Tressacree Imperiale et Catholique Mageste . . . eust nouvelles des marches ysles et terre ferme occeanes.* This seems to be based, according to Brunet, *Supplément*, vol. i. col. 320), on the first and second letters, beginning with the departure, in 1519, from Vera Cruz, and ending with the death of Montezuma.[2]

The second letter forms part of various collected editions, as follows : —

In Spanish. Bancroft (*Mexico*, i. 543) notes the second and third letters as being published in the Spanish *Thesóro de virtudes* in 1543.

Barcia's *Historiadores primitivos* (1749) ; also edited by Enrique de Vedia, Madrid, 1852–1853.

Historia de Nueva España, escrita por su esclarecido Conquistador Hernan Cortés, aumentada con otros documentos y notas por Don Francisco Antonio Lorenzana, arzobispo de México, Mexico, 1770. This important work, embracing the second, third, and fourth letters, has a large view of the great temple of Mexico, a map of New Spain,[3] and thirty-one plates of a hieroglyphic register of the tributaries of Montezuma,—the same later reproduced in better style by Kingsborough. Lorenzana was born in 1722, and rising through the gradations of his Church, and earning a good name as Bishop of Puebla, was made Archbishop of Toledo shortly after he had published the book now under consideration. Pius VI. made him a cardinal in 1789, and he

died in Rome in 1804. Icazbalceta was not able to ascertain whether the Bishop had before him the original editions of the letters or Barcia's reprint ; but he added to the value of his text by numerous annotations. In 1828 an imperfect reprint of this book, " á la ortografía moderna," was produced in New York for the Mexican market, by Manuel del Mar, under the title of *Historia de Méjico*,[4] to which a life of Cortés, by R. C. Sands, was added.[5] Icazbalceta notes some of the imperfections of this edition in his *Coleccion*, vol. i. p. xxxv.[6]

Cartas y relaciones al Emperador Carlos V., colegidas é ilustradas por P. de Gayangos,

Paris, 1866. Besides the Cortés letters, this distinguished scholar included in this book various other contemporary documents relating to the Conquest, embracing letters sent to Cortés' lieutenants ; and he also added an important introduction. He included the fifth letter for the first time in the series, and drew upon the archives of Vienna and Simancas with advantage.[7]

The letters were again included in the *Biblioteca histórica de la Iberia* published at Mexico in 1870.

In Latin. The second and third letters, with the account of Peter Martyr, were issued at Cologne in 1532, with the title *De insulis nuper inventis*, etc., as shown in the annexed facsimile of the title, with its portrait of Charles V. and the escutcheons of Spanish towns and provinces.[8]

In French. Harrisse (*Bibl. Amer. Vet., Additions*, no. 73) notes a French rendering of a

with another colophon (*Bibl. Amer. Vet.*, no. 130), connecting two printers with it,—Lexona and Sabio. F. S. Ellis, London, 1884 (no. 60), priced a copy at £52 10*s.*, and Dufossé (no. 14,184) at 200 francs.

[1] Cf. Sabin, vol. iv. no. 16,950, and xiii. 56,052 ; *Bibl. Amer. Vet.*, no. 119; *Bibliotheca Grenvilliana*, p. 166.

[2] It is very rare, but Tross, of Paris, had a copy in his hands in 1866.

[3] Annexed herewith in fac-simile.

[4] Cf. Arana, *Bibliografía de obras anónimas* (1882) no. 244.

[5] Cf. the notice of Cortés in R. C. Sands's *Writings*, vol. i.

[6] The original edition of Lorenzana is usually priced at $10 to $20. Cf. Sabin, vol. iv. nos. 16,938, 16,939, and vol. x. p. 462 ; H. H. Bancroft, *Mexico*, iii. 378 (with a sketch of Lorenzana) ; Brunet, *Supplément*, i. 321 ; Carter-Brown ; vol. iii. no. 1,750 ; Leclerc, no. 155 ; Sobolewski, no. 3,767 ; F. S. Ellis (1884), £2 2*s.*

[7] Sabin, vol. iv. no. 16,942. Bancroft (*Mexico*, i. 549), speaking of Gayangos' edition, says : " Although a few of Lorenzana's blunders find correction, others are committed ; and the notes of the archbishop are adopted without credit and without the necessary amendment of date, etc., — which often makes them absurd."

[8] The book is variously priced from $20 to $60. Cf. *Bibl. Amer. Vet.*, no. 168 ; Carter-Brown, vol. i. no. 100 ; *Bibliotheca Grenvilliana*, p. 167 ; Leclerc, no. 152 ; Sunderland, no. 3,480 ; Pinart, no. 261 ; O'Callaghan, no. 683 ; Sabin, vol. iv. nos. 16,947–16,949. There were also Latin versions in the *Novus orbis* of Grynæus, 1555 and 1616.

DE INSVLIS NV

PER INVENTIS FERDINANDI CORTESII
ad Carolum V. Rom. Imperatorem Narrationes, cum alio
quodam Petri Martyris ad Clementem VII. Pon-
tificem Maximum consimilis argumenti
libello.

¶ His accesserunt Epistolæ duæ, de felicissimo apud Indos
Euangelij incremento, quas superioribus hisce diebus qui-
dam fratres Mino. ab India in Hispaniam transmiserunt.

¶ Item Epitome de inuentis nuper Indiæ populis idololatris
ad fidem Christi, atq; adeo ad Ecclesiam Catholicam conuer-
tendis, Autore R. P. F. Nicolao Herborn, regularis obser-
uantiæ, ordinis Minorum Generali Commissario
Cismontano.

¶ Venduntur in pingui Gallina.
Anno M. D. XXXII.

text, seemingly made up of the first and second letters, and probably following a Spanish original, now lost, which was printed at Antwerp in 1523.[1] This second letter is also epitomized in the French *Extraict ou recueil des isles nouvellement trouvées* of Peter Martyr, printed at Paris in 1532, and in Bellegarde's *Histoire universelle des voyages* (Amsterdam, 1708), vol. i.

The principal French translation is one based on Lorenzana, abridging that edition somewhat, and numbering the letters erroneously first, second, and third. It was published at Paris in 1778, 1779, etc., under the title *Correspondance de Fernand Cortes avec l'Empereur Charles Quint*, and was translated by the Vicomte de Flavigny.[2] The text of Flavigny's second letter is included in Charton's *Voyageurs*, iii. 368–420. There were also editions of Flavigny printed in Switzerland and at Frankfort.

In German. A translation of the second and third letters, made by Andrew Diether and Birck, was published at Augsburg in 1550 as *Cortesi von dem Newen Hispanien.* After the second letter, which constitutes part i., the beginning of part ii. is borrowed from Peter Martyr, which is followed by the third letter of Cortés; and this is succeeded in turn, on folios 51–60, by letters from Venezuela about the settlements there (1534–1540), and one from Oviedo written at San Domingo in 1543. There are matters which are not contained in any of the Spanish or Latin editions.[3]

The second, third, and fourth letters — translated by J. J. Stapfer, who supplied a meritorious introduction and an appendix — were printed at Heidelberg in 1779 as *Eroberung von Mexico*, and again at Berne in 1793.[4] Another German version, by Karl Wilhelm Koppe, — *Drei Berichte des General-Kapitäns Cortes an Karl V.*, — with an introduction and notes, was published at Berlin in 1834. It has the tribute-registers and map of New Spain, as in Lorenzana's edition.[5]

In Dutch and Flemish. Harrisse (*Bibl. Amer. Vet., Additions*, no. 72) notes a tract of thirty leaves, in gothic letter, called *De Contreyen vanden Eylanden*, etc., which was printed in Antwerp in 1523 (with a French counterpart at the same time), and which seems to have been based on the first and second letters, combined in a Spanish original not now known. There is a copy in the National Library at Paris. There was a Dutch version, or epitome, in the Dutch edition of Grynæus, 1563, and a Flemish version appeared in Ablyn's *Nieuwe Weerelt*, at Antwerp, 1563. There was another Dutch rendering in Gottfried and Vander Aa's *Zee-en landreizen* (1727)[6] and in the *Brieven van Ferdinand Cortes*, Amsterdam, 1780.[7]

In Italian. In the third volume of Ramusio.

In English. Alsop translated from Flavigny the second letter, in the *Portfolio*, Philadelphia, 1817. George Folsom, in 1843, translated from Lorenzana's text the second, third, and fourth letters, which he published as *Despatches written during the Conquest*, adding an introduction and notes, which in part are borrowed from Lorenzana.[8] Willes in his edition of Eden, as early as 1577, had given an abridgment in his *History of Travayle*.[9] (See Vol. III. p. 204.)

III. *The Third Letter, covering the interval, Oct.* 30, 1520, *to May* 15, 1522. It is called *Carta tercera de relaciō*, and was printed (thirty leaves) at Seville in 1523.[10]

The next year, 1524, a Latin edition (*Tertia narratio*) appeared at Nuremberg in connection with the Latin of the second letter of that date.[11] This version was also made by Savorgnanus, and was reprinted in the *Novus orbis* of 1555.[12]

This third letter appeared also in collective editions, as explained under the head of the second letter. This letter was accompanied by

---

[1] The only copy known is noted in Tross's *Catalogue*, 1866, no. 2,881. It is in Roman letter, sixteen leaves.

[2] Cf. Sabin, vol. iv. no. 16,953.

[3] Cf. *Bibl. Amer. Vet.*, no. 297; Ternaux, p. 57; Trömel, p. 14; Brunet, ii. 312; Stevens, *Nuggets*, i. 188; O'Callaghan, no. 989; Sobolewski, no. 3,766; J. J. Cooke, iii. 624 (copy now in Harvard College Library). It is usually priced at £2 or £3. Dufossé (1884, no. 14,185) held a copy at 100 francs.

[4] Cf. Sabin, vol. iv. no. 16,958.

[5] Cf. Sabin, vol. iv. no. 16,959.

[6] Cf. Carter-Brown, iii. 113.

[7] Cf. Sabin, vol. iv. no. 16,962.

[8] Cf. Sabin, vol. iv. 16,964.

[9] Cf. on the second letter, Prescott, *Mexico*, Kirk's ed., ii. 425.

[10] Cf. Rich, (1832) no. 5, — £10 10s.; Stevens, *American Bibliographer*, p. 84; *Bibliotheca Grenvilliana*, p. 166; Panzer, vii. 122; Heber, vol. vii. no. 1,884; Ternaux, no. 26; Brunet, ii. 311; *Bibl. Amer. Vet.*, no. 121; Carter-Brown, i. 74; Sabin, vol. iv. no. 16,935.

[11] Priced by F. S. Ellis (1884) at £18 18s.

[12] Cf. Carter-Brown, i. 83; Ternaux, no. 33; *Bibl. Amer. Vet.*, no. 126; *Bibliotheca Grenvilliana*, p. 167; Brunet, ii. 312; Sabin, vol. iv. no. 16,948; Stevens, *American Bibliographer*, p. 87. There is a copy of the 1524 edition in the Boston Public Library. [D. 3101. 56, no. 2].

what is known as the "secret letter," which was first printed in the *Documentos inéditos*, i. 11, in Kingsborough, vol. viii., and in Gayangos' edition of the letters.

IV. *The Fourth Letter, covering the interval, May,* 1522, *to October,* 1524. There were two Spanish editions (*a, b*).

a. La quarta relacion (Toledo, 1525), in gothic letter, twenty-one leaves.[1]

b. La quarta relaciõ (Valencia, 1526), in gothic type, twenty-six leaves.[2]

This letter was accompanied by reports to Cortés from Alvarado and Godoy, and these are also included in Barcia, Ramusio, etc.

A secret letter (dated October 15) of Cortés to the Emperor, — *Esta es una carta que Hernando Cortés escrivio al Emperador,* — sent with this fourth letter, is at Simancas. It was printed by Icazbalceta in 1855 (Mexico, sixty copies),[3] who reprinted it in his *Coleccion*, i. 470. Gayangos, in 1866, printed it in his edition (p. 325) from a copy which Muñoz had made. Icazbalceta again printed it sumptuously, " en caracteres góticos del siglo XVI.," at Mexico in 1865 (seventy copies).[4] This letter also appears in collections mentioned under the second letter. It was in this letter that Cortés explained to the Emperor his purpose of finding the supposed strait which led from the Atlantic to the south sea.

V. *The fifth letter, dated Sept.* 3, 1526. It pertains to the famous expedition to Honduras.[5] It is called *Carta quinta de relacion,* and was discovered through Robertson's instrumentality, but not printed at length till it appeared in the *Coleccion de documentos inéditos (España),* iv. 8–167, with other "relaciones" on this expedition. George Folsom reprinted it in New York in 1848 as "carta sexta . . . publicada ahora por primera vez " by mistake for "carta quinta."[6] It was translated and annotated by Gayangos for the Hakluyt Society in 1868.[7] Gayangos had already included it in his edition of the *Cartas,* 1866, and it had also been printed by Vedia in Ribadeneyras' *Biblioteca de autores Españoles* (1852), vol. xxii., and later in the *Biblioteca histórica de la Iberia* (1870). Extracts in English are given in the appendix of Prescott's *Mexico,* vol. iii. Mr. Kirk, the editor of Prescott, doubts if the copy in the Imperial Library at Vienna is the original, because it has no date. A copy at Madrid, purporting to be made from the original by Alonzo Diaz, is dated Sept. 3, 1526,[8] and is preferred by Gayangos, who collated its text with that of the Vienna Library. Various other less important letters of Cortés have been printed from time to time.[9]

In estimating the letters of Cortés as historical material, the soldierly qualities of them impressed Prescott, and Helps is struck with their directness so strongly that he is not willing to believe in the prevarications or deceits of any part of them. H. H. Bancroft,[10] on the contrary, discovers in them "calculated misstatements, both direct and negative." It is well known that Bernal Diaz and Pedro de Alvarado made complaints of their leader's too great willingness to ignore all others but himself.[11]

[1] Cf. Sabin, vol. iv. no. 16,936; Carter-Brown, i. 85; Brunet, ii. 311; *Bibl. Amer. Vet.,* no. 135; *Bibliotheca Grenvilliana,* p. 166.

[2] The only copy known is that in the Carter-Brown Library (*Catalogue,* no. 88). Cf. Sabin, vol. iv. no. 16,937; *Bibl. Amer. Vet.,* no. 138; Stevens, *American Bibliographer,* p. 85; Brunet, ii. 312; Panzer, x. 28; Heber, vol. vii. no. 1,884; *Bibliotheca Grenvilliana,* p. 166; Ternaux, no. 34.

[3] Sabin, vol. iv. no. 16,940.

[4] Cf. Sabin, vol. iv. no. 16,941; Carter-Brown, i. 84; Court, no. 89; Prescott, *Mexico,* iii. 248.

[5] A letter about the Olid rebellion is lost; Helps, iii. 37.

[6] Cf. Sabin, vol. iv. no. 16,943.

[7] Cf. H. Vattemare in *Revue contemporaine,* 1870, vii. 532.

[8] Prescott's *Mexico,* iii. 266. Cf. references on this expedition to Honduras in H. H. Bancroft's *Central America,* i. 537, 567, 582; ii. 144; and his *Native Races,* iv. 79. This Honduras expedition is also the subject of one of Ixtlilxochitl's *Relaciones,* printed in Kingsborough's ninth volume.

[9] *Cartas al Emperador* (Sept. 11, 1526, Oct. 10, 1530), in *Documentos inéditos (España),* i. 14, 31, and in Kingsborough's *Mexico,* vol. viii.; *Memorial al Emperador* (1539) in *Documentos inéditos,* iv. 201. Cf. also Purchas, v. 858, and Ramusio, iii. 187. His *Última y sentidisima carta,* Feb. 3, 1544, is given in *Documentos inéditos,* i. 41, and in Prescott's *Mexico,* Kirk's ed., iii. 460. Other letters of Cortés are in the Pacheco *Coleccion* and in that of Icazbalceta. The twelfth volume of the *Biblioteca histórica de la Iberia* (Mexico, 1871), with the special title of *Escritos sueltos de Cortés,* gives nearly fifty documents. Icazbalceta, in the introduction of vol. i. p. xxxvii. of his *Coleccion,* gives a list of the *escritos sueltos* of Cortés in connection with a full bibliography of the series of *Cartas,* with corrections, derived largely from Harrisse, in vol. ii. p. lxiii.

[10] *Mexico,* i. 549, 696. "Ever ready with a lie when it suited his purpose; but he was far too wise a man needlessly to waste so useful an agent." — *Early American Chroniclers,* p. 16.

[11] Harrisse (*Bibl. Amer. Vet.*) gives numerous references on Cortés. It is somewhat singular that there is no mention of him in the *Novus orbis* of 1532, and none in De Bry. Mr. Brevoort prepared the article on Cortés in Sabin's *Dictionary.*

B. THREE CONTEMPORARY WRITERS, — GOMARA, BERNAL DIAZ, AND SAHAGUN. — Fortunately we have various other narratives to qualify or confirm the recitals of the leader.

In 1540, when he was thirty years old, Francisco Lopez Gomara became the chaplain and secretary of Cortés. In undertaking an historical record in which his patron played a leading part, he might be suspected to write somewhat as an adulator; and so Las Casas, Diaz, and many others have claimed that he did, and Muñoz asserts that Gomara believed his authorities too easily.[1] That the Spanish Government made a show of suppressing his book soon after it was published, and kept the edict in their records till 1729, is rather in favor of his honest chronicling. Gomara had good claims for consideration in a learned training, a literary taste, and in the possession of facilities which his relations with Cortés threw in his way; and we find him indispensable, if for no other reason, because he had access to documentary evidence which has since disappeared. His questionable reputation for bias has not prevented Herrera and other later historians placing great dependence on him, and a native writer of the beginning of the seventeenth century, Chimalpain, has translated Gomara, adding some illustrations for the Indian records.[2]

Gomara's book is in effect two distinct ones, though called at first two parts of a *Historia general de las Indias*. Of these the second part — *La conquista de México* — appeared earliest, at Saragossa in 1552, and is given to the Conquest of Mexico, while the first part, more particularly relating to the subjugation of Peru, appeared in 1553.[3] What usually passes for a second edition appeared at Medina del Campo, also in 1553;[4] and it was again reprinted at Saragossa in 1554, this time as two distinct works, — one, *Cronica de la Nueva España con la conquista de México;* and the other, *La historia general de las Indias y Nuevo Mundo*.[5] The same year (1554) saw several editions in Spanish at Antwerp, with different publishers.[6] An Italian edition followed in 1555-1556, for one titlepage, *Historia del . . . capitano Don Ferdinando Cortés*, is dated 1556, and a second, *Historia de México*, has 1555, — both at Rome.[7] Other editions, more or less complete, are noted as published in Venice

---

[1] Ticknor, *Spanish Literature*, ii. 30; Prescott's *Mexico*, i. 474, and *Peru*, ii. 304, 457; H. H. Bancroft, *Central America*, i. 314, his *Mexico*, and his *Early American Chroniclers*, p. 21.

[2] There are curious stories about this book, in which there is not entire accord with one another. The fact seems to be that Bustamante got hold of the manuscript, and supposed it an original work of Chimalpain, and announced it for publication in a Spanish dress, as translated from the Nahuatl, under the title of *Historia de las conquistas de Hernando Cortés*, under which name it appeared in two volumes in Mexico in 1826 (*Ticknor Catalogue*, p. 207). Bandelier and others referring to it have supposed it to be what the title represented (*Amer. Antiq. Soc. Proc.*, new series, i. 84; cf. *Bibl. Amer. Vet.*, p. 204); but it is printed in Spanish nevertheless, and is nothing more than a translation of Gomara. Bustamante in his preface does not satisfy the reader's curiosity, and this Mexican editor's conduct in the matter has been the subject of apology and suspicion. Cf. Quaritch's *Catalogues*, nos. 11,807, 12,043, 17,632; H. H. Bancroft, *Central America*, i. 315; Sabin, vii. no. 27,753. Quaritch adds that Bustamante's text seems rather like a modern improvement of Gomara than a retranslation, and that a manuscript apparently different and called Chimalpain's history was sold in the Abbé Fischer's sale in 1869.

[3] It is a small folio, and has become extremely rare, owing, perhaps, in part to the attempted suppression of it. Quaritch in 1883 priced a copy at £75. It should have two maps, one of the Indies, the other of the Old World (Ternaux, no. 61; Carter-Brown, nos. 177, 178; Sunderland, vol. iii. no. 7,575; *Library of an Elizabethan Admiral*, 1883, no. 338; Leclerc, no. 2,779; Rich (1832), no. 23, £10 10s.; Sabin, vol. vii. no. 27,724; Murphy, no. 1,062).

[4] Carter-Brown, vol. i. nos. 179, 180; Sabin, vol. vii. no. 27,725; Leclerc, 800 francs. Mr. J. C. Brevoort has a copy. Sabin (no. 27,726) notes a *Conquista de México* (Madrid, 1553) which he has not seen, but describes it at second hand as having the royal arms where the Medina edition has the arms of Cortés, and intimates that this last may have been the cause of the alleged suppression.

[5] Carter-Brown, vol. i. nos. 187, 188, with a fac-simile of the title of the former; and on p. 169 is noted another Saragossa edition of 1555. Sabin, vol. vii. nos. 27,727, 27,728.

[6] *Historia de México*, Juan Steelsio, and again Juan Bellero (with his map); *La historia general de las Indias*, Steelsio. These are in Harvard College Library. Sabin (vol. vii. nos. 27,729-27,732) notes of these Antwerp editions, — *Historia general*, Nucio, Steelsio, and Bellero; *Historia de México*, Bellero, Lacio, Steelsio; and *Conquista de México*, Nucio. The *Carter-Brown Catalogue* (nos. 189-193) shows the *Historia de México* with the Steelsio and Bellero imprints, and copies of the *Historia general* with the imprints of Bellero and Martin Nucio. Quaritch prices the Bellero *México* at £5 5s. Rich priced it in 1832 at £3 3s. There is a Steelsio *México* in the Boston Public Library. Cf. *Huth Catalogue*, ii. 605; Murphy, nos. 1,057-1,059; Court, nos. 146, etc. Of the later Spanish texts, that in Barcia's *Historiadores primitivos* (1748-1749) is mutilated; the best is that in the *Biblioteca de autores Españoles*, published at Madrid in 1852.

[7] Such, at least, is the condition of the copy in Harvard College Library; while the two titles are attached to different copies in the *Carter-Brown Catalogue*, vol. i. nos. 199, 210. The *México* is also in the Boston Athenæum. Cf. *O'Callaghan Catalogue*, no. 989. Sabin (vol. vii. nos. 27,734-27,735) says the 1555 title is a

HISPANIA VICTRIX.

PRIMERA Y SEGVNDA PAR
te de la hiſtoria general de las Indias có todo el deſcu-
brimiento, y coſas notables que han acaeſcido dende que ſe ganaron haſta el año
de 1551. Coolaconquiſta de Mexico, y dela nueua Eſpaña.

En Medina del Campo, por Guillermo de Millis. 1553

cancelled one. Mr. Brevoort possesses a *Historia generale delle Indie occidentali* (Rome, 1556), which he calls
a translation of part i. Cf. Sabin, vol. vii. no. 27,736 ; Carter-Brown, vol. i. no. 200. F. S. Ellis (1884, no.
111) prices a copy at £2 2s. Sabin (no. 27,737) also notes a Gomara, as published in 1557 at Venice, as the
second part of a history, of which Cieza de Leon's was the first part.

in 1560, 1564, 1565, 1566, 1570, 1573, 1576, and 1599.[1] The earliest French edition appeared at Paris in 1568 and 1569, for the two dates and two imprints seem to belong to one issue; and its text — a not very creditable translation by Fumée — was reproduced in the editions of 1577, 1578, 1580, and with some additions in 1584, 1587, 1588, and 1597.[2] The earliest edition in English omits much. It is called *The Pleasant Historie of the Conquest of the Weast India, now called New Spayne, atchieved by the worthy Prince Hernando Cortes, Marques of the valley of Huaxacac, most delectable to reade, translated out of the Spanishe tongue by T[homas] N[icholas]*, published by Henry Bynneman in 1578.[3] Gomara himself warned his readers against undertaking a Latin version, as he had one in hand himself; but it was never printed.[4]

Gomara had, no doubt, obscured the merits of the captains of Cortés in telling the story of that leader's career. Instigated largely by this, and confirmed in his purpose, one of the partakers in the glories and hardships of the Conquest was impelled to tell the story anew, in the light of the observation which fell to a subordinate. He was not perhaps so much jealous of the fame of Cortés as he was hurt at the neglect by Gomara of those whose support had made the fame of Cortés possible. This was Bernal Diaz del Castillo, and his book is known as the *Historia verdadera de la conquista de la Nueva España*, which was not printed till 1632 at Madrid, nor had it been written till half a century after the Conquest, during which interval the name of Cortés had gathered its historic prestige.

Diaz had begun the writing of it in 1568 at Santiago in Guatemala, when, as he tells us,

only five of the original companions of Cortés remained alive.[5] It is rudely, or rather simply, written, as one might expect. The author has none of the practised arts of condensation; and Prescott[6] well defines the story as long-winded and gossiping, but of great importance. It is indeed inestimable, as the record of the actor in more than a hundred of the fights which marked the progress of the Conquest. The untutored air of the recital impressed Robertson and Southey with confidence in its statements, and the reader does not fail to be conscious of a minute rendering of the life which made up those eventful days. His criticism of Cortés himself does not, by any means, prevent his giving him great praise; and, as Prescott says,[7] he censures his leader, but he does not allow any one else to do the same. The lapse of time before Diaz set about his literary task did not seem to abate his zeal or check his memory; but it does not fail, however, to diminish our own confidence a good deal. Prescott[8] contends that the better the acquaintance with Diaz' narrative, the less is the trust which one is inclined to put in it.[9] The Spanish text which we possess is taken, it is said, directly from the original manuscript, which had slumbered in private hands till Father Alonso Rémon found it, or a copy of it, in Spain,

[1] Carter-Brown, vol. i. nos. 232, 233, 250, 306, 541; Sabin, vol. vii. nos. 27,739–27,745. The *Historia general* was published in Venice in 1565 as the second part of a *Historie dell' Indie*, of which Cieza de Leon's *Historie del Peru* was the first part, and Gomara's *Conquista di Messico* (1566) was the third. This Italian translation was made by Lucio Mauro. The three parts are in Harvard College Library and in the Boston Public Library (Sabin, vol. vii. no. 27,738).

[2] Carter-Brown, vol. i. nos. 273, 274, 314, 324, 334, 357, 371, 375; Sabin, vol. vii. nos. 27,746–27,750; Murphy, nos. 1,059*, 1,061; O'Callaghan, no. 990. F. S. Ellis (1884, no. 108) prices the 1569 edition at £10 10s. The 1578 and 1588 editions are in Harvard College Library, — the latter is called *Voyages et conquestes du Capitaine Ferdinand Courtois*. Cf. Sabin, vol. iv. no. 16,955. Harrisse says that Oviedo, as well as Gomara, was used in this production. There were later French texts in 1604, 1605, and 1606. Cf. Carter-Brown, vol. ii. nos. 34, 46; Rich (1832), no. 104; Sabin (vol. vii. no. 27,749) also says of the 1606 edition that pp. 67–198 are additional to the 1578 edition.

[3] Carter-Brown, vol. i. no. 323; Menzies, no. 814; Crowninshield, no. 285; Rich (1832), no. 58; Brinley, no. 5,309; Murphy, no. 1,060. There are copies of this and of the 1596 reprint in Harvard College Library; and of the 1578 edition in the Massachusetts Historical Society's Library and in Mr. Deane's Collection; cf. Vol. III. pp. 27, 204. An abridgment of Gomara had already been given in 1555 by Eden in his *Decades*, and in 1577 in Eden's *History of Travayle*; and his account was later followed by Hakluyt.

[4] The bibliography of Gomara in Sabin (vol. vii. p. 395) was compiled by Mr. Brevoort. The *Carter-Brown Catalogue* (vol. i. p. 169) gives a list of editions; cf. Leclerc, no. 243, etc.

[5] Bancroft (*Mexico*, ii. 339) gives references for tracing the Conquerors and their descendants.

[6] *Mexico*, ii. 146; cf. H. H. Bancroft, *Early Chroniclers*, p. 14.

[7] Ibid., ii. 459.

[8] Ibid., i. 473.

[9] Bancroft speaks of the account's "exceeding completeness, its many new facts, and varied version" (*Mexico*, i. 697).

and obtained a decree to print it,[1] about fifty years after Diaz' death, which occurred in 1593, or thereabouts.

The nearest approach among contemporaries to a survey of the story of the Conquest from the Aztec side is that given by the Franciscan, Sahagun, in connection with his great work on the condition of the Mexican peoples prior to the coming of the Spaniards. Sahagun came to Mexico in 1529. He lived in the new land for over sixty years, and acquired a proficiency in the native tongue hardly surpassed by any other of the Spaniards. He brought to the new field something besides the iconoclastic frenzy that led so many of his countrymen to destroy what they could of the literature and arts of the Aztecs, — so necessary in illustration of their pagan life and rites. This zealous and pious monk turned aside from seeking the preferments of his class to study the motives, lives, and thoughts of the Aztec peoples. He got from them their hieroglyphics; these in turn were translated into the language of their speech, but expressed in the Roman character; and the whole subjected more than once to the revising of such of the natives as had, in his day, been educated in the Spanish schools.[2] Thirty years were given to this kind of preparation; and when he had got his work written out in Mexican, the General of his Order seized it, and some years elapsed before a restitution of it was made. Sahagun had got to be eighty years old when, with his manuscript restored to him, he set about re-writing it, with the Mexican text in one column and the Spanish in another. The two huge volumes of this script found their way to Spain, and were lost sight of till Muñoz discovered them in the convent of Tolosa in Navarre, not wholly unimpaired by the vicissitudes to which they had been subjected.

[1] Scherzer (in his edition of Ximenes' *Las historias del origen de los Indios de esta provincia de Guatemala*, 1857) says that the text as published is very incorrect, and adds that the original manuscript is in the city library at Guatemala. Brasseur says he has seen it there. It is said to have a memorandum to show that it was finished in 1605 at Guatemala. We have no certain knowledge of Diaz' death to confirm the impression that he could have lived to the improbable age which this implies. (Cf. *Magazine of American History*, i. 129, 328–329.) There are two editions of it, in different type, which have the seal of authenticity. One was dated in 1632; the other, known as the second edition, is without date, and has an additional chapter (numbered wrongly ccxxii.) concerning the portents among the Mexicans which preceded the coming of the Spaniards. It is explained that this was omitted in the first edition as not falling within the personal observation of Diaz. (Cf. Sabin, vol. vi. nos. 19,978, 19,979; Carter-Brown, ii. 387; Murphy, no. 790; Court, nos. 106, 107; Leclerc, no. 1,115. Rich priced it in his day at $10; it now usually brings about $30.) There are later editions of the Spanish text, — one issued at Mexico in 1794–1795, in four small volumes (Sabin, vol. vi. no. 19,980; Leclerc, no. 1,117, 40 francs); a second, Paris, 1837 (Sabin, vol. vi. no. 19,981); and another, published in 1854, in two quarto volumes, with annotations from the Cortés letters, etc. It is also contained in Vedia's edition of the *Historiadores primitivos*, vol. ii. There are three German editions, one published at Hamburg in 1848, with a preface by Karl Ritter, and others bearing date at Bonn, 1838 and 1843 (Sabin, vi. no. 19,986–19,987). There are two English versions, — one by Maurice Keating, published at London in 1800 (with a large map of the Lake of Mexico), which was reprinted at Salem, Mass., in 1803 (Sabin, vol. vi. nos. 19,984–19,985). Mr. Deane points out how Keating, without any explanation, transfers from chap. xviii. and other parts of the text sundry passages to a preface. A second English translation, —*Memoirs of Diaz*,— by John Ingram Lockhart, was published in London in 1844 (Sabin, vol. vi. no. 19,983), and is also included in Kerr's *Voyages*, vols. iii. and iv. Munsell issued an abridged English translation by Arthur Prynne at Albany in 1839 (Sabin, vol. vi. no. 19,982). The best annotated of the modern issues is a French translation by D. Jourdanet, *Histoire véridique de la conquête de la Nouvelle Espagne*, Paris, 1876. In the following year a second edition was issued, accompanied by a study on the human sacrifices of the Aztecs, and enriched with notes, a bibliography, and a chapter from Sahagun on the vices of the Mexicans. It also contained a modern map of Mexico, showing the marches of Cortés; the map of the valley, indicating the contraction of the lake (the same as used by Jourdanet in other works), and a reproduction of a map of the lake illustrating the operations of Cortés, which follows a map given in the Mexican edition of Clavigero. A list of the *Conquistadores* gives three hundred and seventy-seven names, which are distinguished apart as constituting the followers of Cortés, Camargo, Salcedo, Garay, Narvaez, and Ponçe de Leon. This list is borrowed from the *Diccionario universal de historia y de geografía, . . . especialmente sobre la república Mexicana*, 1853–1856. (Cf. *Norton's Literary Gazette*, Jan. 15, 1835, and *Revue des questions historiques*, xxiii. 249.) This *Diccionario* was published at Mexico, in 1853–1856, in ten volumes, based on a similar work printed in Spain, but augmented in respect to Mexican matters by various creditable collaborators, while vols. viii., ix., and x. are entirely given to Mexico, and more particularly edited by Manuel Orozco y Berra. The work is worth about 400 francs. The *Cartas de Indias* (Madrid, 1877) contained a few unpublished letters of Bernal Diaz.

[2] Sahagun's study of the Aztec tongue was a productive one. Biondelli published at Milan in 1858, from a manuscript by Sahagun, an *Evangelarium epistolarium et lectionarium Aztecum sive Mexicanum, ex antiquo codice Mexicano nuper reperto;* and Quaritch in 1880 (*Catalogue*, p. 46, no. 261, etc.) advertised various other manuscripts of his *Sermones in Mexicano*, etc. Jourdanet in his edition (p. x.) translates the opinion of Sahagun given by his contemporary and fellow-Franciscan, Fray Geronimo Mendieta, in his *Historia eclesiastica Indiana* (Mexico, 1860) p. 633. There is a likeness of Sahagun in Cumplido's edition of Prescott's *Mexico*, published at Mexico in 1846, vol. iii.

The Nahuatl text, which made part of it, is still missing.[1]

It was not long afterward (1829–1830) printed by Cárlos María Bustamante in three volumes as *Historia general de las cosas de Nueva España*,[2] to which was added, as a fourth volume, also published separately, *Historia de la conquista de México*, containing what is usually cited as the twelfth book of Sahagun. In this, as in the other parts, he used a copy which Muñoz had made,

the Muñoz text, and has made, according to Simeon, fewer errors in transcribing the Nahuatl words than Bustamante, and has also given a purer Spanish text. Bustamante again printed, in 1840, another text of this twelfth book, after a manuscript belonging to the Conde de Cortina, appending notes by Clavigero and others, with an additional chapter.[4] The Mexican editor claimed that this was the earlier text; but Prescott denies it. Torquemada is thought to have used, but without due acknowledgment, still another text, which is less modified than the others in expressions regarding the Conquerors. The peculiar value of Sahagun's narrative hardly lies in its completeness, proportions, or even trustworthiness as an historical record. "His accuracy as regards any historical fact is not to be relied on," says Helps.[5] Brevoort calls the work of interest mainly for its records of persons and places not found elsewhere.[6] Prescott thinks that this twelfth book is the most honest record which the natives have left us, as Sahagun embodies the stories and views prevalent among the descendants of the victims of the Conquest. "This portion of the work," he says, "was re-written by Sahagun at a later period of his life, and considerable changes were made in it; yet it may be doubted if the reformed version reflects the traditions of the country as faithfully as the original draft."[7] This new draft was made by Sahagun in 1585, thirty years after the original writing, for the purpose, as he says, of adding some things which had been omitted, and leaving out others. Prescott could not find, in comparing this later draft with the earlier, that its author had mitigated any of the statements which, as he first wrote them, bore so hard on his countrymen. The same historian

and which is the earlier draft of the text as Sahagun formed it. It begins with a recital of the omens which preceded the coming of Grijalva, and ends with the fall of the city; and it is written, as he says, from the evidence, in large part, of the eye-witnesses, particularly on the Aztec side, though mixed, somewhat confusedly, with recollections from old Spanish soldiers. Harrisse[3] speaks of this edition as "castrated in such a way as to require, for a perfect understanding of this dry but important book, the reading of the parts published in vols. v. and vi. of Kingsborough." The text, as given in Kingsborough's *Mexico*, began to appear about a year later, that edition only giving, in the first instance, book vi., which relates to the customs of the Aztecs before the Conquest; but in a later volume he reproduced the whole of the work without comment. Kingsborough had also used

---

[1] A part of the original manuscript of Sahagun was exhibited, says Brinton (*Aboriginal American Authors*, p. 27), at the Congrès des Américanistes at Madrid in 1881.

[2] Field, *Indian Bibliography*, no. 1,348. Stevens (*Historical Collections*, vol. i., no. 1,573) mentions a copy of this edition, which has notes and collations with the original manuscript made by Don J. F. Ramirez. Cf. *Ticknor Catalogue*, p. 316.

[3] *Bibl. Amer. Vet.*, no. 208.

[4] The book was called: *La aparicion de N^{tra}. Señora de Guadalupe de México, comprobada con la refutacion del argumento negativo que presenta Muñoz, fundandose en el testimonio del P. Fr. Bernardino Sahagun; ó sea: Historia original de este escritor, que altera la publicada en 1829 en el equivocado concepto de ser la unica y original de dicho autor. Publicala, precediendo una disertacion sobre la aparicion guadalupana, y con notas sobre la conquista de México.* Cf. *Ticknor Catalogue*, p. 46.

[5] *Spanish Conquest*, ii. 346.

[6] *Magazine of American History* (November, 1881) p. 378. Cf. other estimates in H. H. Bancroft's *Mexico*, i. 493, 696; *Native Races*, iii. 231–236; *Early Chroniclers*, pp. 19, 20. Bernal Diaz and Sahagun are contrasted by Jourdanet in the introduction to his edition of the latter. Cf. also Jourdanet's edition of Bernal Diaz and the article on Sahagun by Ferdinand Denis in the *Revue des Deux Mondes*.

[7] Prescott's *Mexico*, Kirk's ed. ii. 38.

thinks there is but little difference in the intrinsic value of the two drafts.[1]

The best annotated edition of Sahagun is a French translation, published in Paris in 1880 as *Histoire générale des choses de la Nouvelle Espagne*, seemingly from the Kingsborough text, which is more friendly to the Spaniards than the first of Bustamante. The joint editors are Denis Jourdanet and Remi Siméon, the latter, as a Nahuatl scholar, taking charge of those portions of the text which fell within his linguistic range, and each affording a valuable introduction in their respective studies.[2]

C. Other Early Accounts. — The *Voyages, Relations, et Mémoires* of Ternaux-Compans (Paris, 1837–1840) offer the readiest source of some of the most significant of the documents and monographs pertaining to early Mexican history. Two of the volumes [3] gather some of the minor documents. Another volume [4] is given to Zurita's "Rapport sur les différentes classes des chefs de la Nouvelle Espagne." Three others [5] contain an account of the cruelties practised by the Spaniards at the Conquest, and the history of the ancient kings of Tezcuco, — both the work of Ferdinando d'Alva Ixtlilxochitl.[6] The former work, not correctly printed, and called, somewhat arbitrarily, *Horribles crueldades de los Conquistadores de México*, was first published by Bustamante, in 1829, as a supplement to Sahagun. The manuscript (which was no. 13 of a number of *Noticias*, or *Relaciones históricas*, by this native writer) had been for a while after the writer's death (about 1648) preserved in the library of the Jesuit College in Mexico, and had thence passed to the archivo-general of the State. It bears the certificate of a notary, in 1608, that it had been compared with the Aztec records and found to be correct. The original work contained several *Relaciones*, but only the one (no. 13) relating to the Conquest was published by Bustamante and Ternaux.[7]

The other work of Ixtlilxochitl was first printed (after Veytia's copy) in Spanish by Kingsborough, in his ninth volume, before Ternaux, who used another copy, included it in his collection under the title of *Histoire des Chichimeque ou des anciens Rois de Tezcuco*. This is the only work of Ixtlilxochitl which has been printed entire. According to Clavigero, these treatises were written at the instance of the Spanish viceroy; and as a descendant of the royal line of Tezcuco (the great great-grandson, it is said, of the king of like name) their author had great advantages, with perhaps great predispositions to laudation, though he is credited with extreme carefulness in his statements; [8] and Prescott affirms that he has been followed with confidence by such as have had access to his writings. Ixtlilxochitl informs us that he has derived his material from such remains of his ancestral documents as were left to him. He seems also to have used Gomara and other accessible authorities. He lived in the early part of the seventeenth century, and as interpreter of the viceroy maintained a respectable social position when many of his royal line were in the humblest service. His *Relaciones* are hardly regular historical compositions, since they lack independent and compact form; but his *Historia Chichimeca* is the best of them, and is more depended upon by Prescott than the others are. There is a certain charm in his simplicity, his picturesqueness, and honesty; and readers accept these qualities often in full recompense for his credulity and want of discrimination, — and perhaps for a certain servility to the Spanish masters, for whose bounty he could press the claims of a line of vassals of his own blood.[9]

D. Native Writers. — The pious vandalism of the bishops of Mexico and Yucatan, which doomed to destruction so much of the native records of days antecedent to the Conquest,[10] fortunately was not so ruthlessly exercised later, when native writers gathered up what they could, and told the story of their people's downfall, either in the language of the country or in an acquired Spanish.[11] Brasseur

---

[1] Prescott, *Mexico*, iii. 214.

[2] Mr. Brevoort reviewed this edition in the *Magazine of American History*.

[3] Vols. x. and xvi. In one of these is the *Chronica Compendiosissima* of Amandus (Antwerp, 1534), which contains the letters of Peter of Ghent, or De Mura, — *Recueil des pièces relatives à la Conquête du Mexique*, pp. 193–203. Cf. Sabin, vol. i. no. 994.

[4] Vol. xi. Zurita is also given in Spanish in the *Coleccion de documentos inéditos*, vol. ii. (1865), but less perfectly than in Ternaux. The document was written about 1560.

[5] Vols. viii., xii., xiii.

[6] Field, *Indian Bibliography*, nos. 1540–1541.   [7] Ibid., no. 767.

[8] Ibid., no. 766; Sabin, vol. ix. p. 168. Cf. Brinton, *Aboriginal American Authors*, p. 15.

[9] Prescott, *Mexico*, vol. i. pp. 163, 174, 206, 207; vol. iii. p. 105; and H. H. Bancroft, *Mexico*, vol. i. pp. 339, 697; vol. ii. p. 24; Kingsborough, vol. ix.

[10] Brinton, *Aboriginal American Literature*, p. 24.

[11] Icazbalceta, in his *Apuntes para un Catálogo de Escritores en lenguas indigenas de America* (Mexico 1866), gives a summary of the native literature preserved to us. Cf. Brinton's *Aboriginal American Authors*, p. 14, etc., on natives who acquired reputation as writers of Spanish.

de Bourbourg, in the introduction to his *Nations civilisées du Mexique* (Paris, 1857–1859), enumerates the manuscript sources to which he had access,[1] largely pertaining to the period anterior to the Spaniards, but also in part covering the history of the Conquest, which in his fourth volume[2] he narrates mainly from the native point of view, while he illustrates the Indian life under its contact with the Spanish rule.

Brasseur was fortunate in having access to the Aubin Collection of manuscripts,[3] which had originally been formed between 1736 and 1745 by the Chevalier Lorenzo Boturini Benaduci; and that collector in 1746 gave a catalogue of them at the end of his *Idea de una nueva historia general de la America septentrional*, published at Madrid in that year.[4]   Unfortunately, the labors of this devoted archæologist incurred the jealousy of the Spanish Government, and his library was more or less scattered; but to him we owe a large part of what we find in the collections of Bustamante, Kingsborough, and Ternaux. Mariano Veytia[5] was his executor, and had the advantages of Boturini's collections in his own *Historia Antigua de Mejico*.[6]   Boturini's catalogue, however, shows us that much has disappeared, which we may regret. Such is the *Cronica* of Tlaxcala, by Juan Ventura Zapata y Mendoza, which brought the story down to 1689, which Brinton hopes may yet be discovered in Spain.[7] One important work is saved, — that of Camargo.

Muñoz Camargo was born in Mexico just after the Conquest, and was connected by marriage with leading native families, and attained high official position in Tlaxcala, whose history he wrote, beginning its composition in 1576, and finishing it in 1585. He had collected much material. Ternaux[8] printed a French translation of a mutilated text; but it has never been printed in the condition, fragmentary though it be, in which it was recovered by Boturini. Prescott says the original manuscript was long preserved in a convent in Mexico, where Torquemada used it. It was later taken to Spain, when it found its way into the Muñoz Collection in the Academy of History at Madrid, whence Prescott got his copy. This last historian speaks of the work as supplying much curious and authentic information respecting the social and religious condition of the Aztecs. Camargo tells fully the story of the Conquest, but he deals out his applause and sympathy to the conquerors and the conquered with equal readiness.[9]

Other manuscripts have not yet been edited. Chimalpain's *Cronica Mexicana*, in the Nahuatl tongue, which covers the interval from A. D. 1068 to 1597, is one of these. Another Nahuatl manuscript in Boturini's list is an anonymous history of Culhuacan and Mexico. An imperfect translation of this into Spanish, by Galicia, has been made in Mexico. Brasseur copied it, and called it the *Codex Chimalpopoca*.[10] In 1879 the Museo Nacional at Mexico began to print it in their *Anales* (vol. ii.), adding a new version by Mendoza and Solis, under the title of *Anales de Cuauhtitlan*.[11]

Bancroft's list, prefixed to his *Mexico*, makes mention of most of these native Mexican sources. Of principal use among them may be mentioned Fernando de Alvaro Tezozomoc's *Cronica Mexicana*, or *Histoire du Mexique*, written in 1598, and published in 1853, in Paris, by Ternaux-Compans.[12]

---

[1] Vol. i. p. lxxiv; and on p. lxxviii he gives accounts of various manuscripts, chiefly copies, owned by himself. He also traces the rise of his interest in American studies, while official position in later years gave him unusual facilities for research. His conclusions and arguments are often questioned by careful students. Cf. Bandelier, in *Amer. Antiq. Soc. Proc.*, October, 1880, p. 93.

[2] In the introduction to this volume Brasseur reviews the native writers on the Conquest. Bancroft (*Mexico*, vol. i. p. 493, vol. ii. p. 488) thinks he hardly does Cortés justice, and is prone to accept without discrimination the native accounts, to the discredit of those of the conquerors. Brasseur gives abundant references; and since the publication of the *Pinart-Brasseur Catalogue*, we have a compact enumeration of his own library.

[3] He enumerates a few of the treasures, vol. i. p. lxxvi.

[4] The list is not found in all copies. *Murphy Catalogue*, p. 300. F. S. Ellis (London, 1884) prices a copy at £2 2s.

[5] Born at Puebla 1710; died 1780.

[6] Published in three volumes in Mexico in 1836. Edited by C. F. Ortega. Cf. Prescott, *Mexico*, book i. chap. i. Veytia also edited from Boturini's collection, and published with notes at Mexico in 1826, *Tezcuco en los ultimos tiempos de sus antiguos reyes* (*Murphy Catalogue*, no. 428).

[7] *Aboriginal American Authors*, p. 26, where are notices of other manuscripts on Tlaxcalan history.

[8] Cf. *Nouvelles Annales des Voyages* (1845), vol. ii. p. 129, etc.

[9] Prescott, *Mexico*, vol. ii. p. 286; Bancroft, *Mexico*, vol. i. p. 200.

[10] *Pinart-Brasseur Catalogue*, no. 237.

[11] Brinton's *Aboriginal American Authors*, p. 26.   Mr. A. F. Bandelier is said to be preparing an edition of it.

[12] Cf. *Nouvelles Annales des Voyages*, 1844–1849. Ternaux's translation is much questioned. Cf. also Kingsborough, vol. ix., and the *Biblioteca Mexicana* of Vigel, with notes by Orozco y Berra.

Brinton has published in the first volume of his library of *Aboriginal American Literature* (1882, p. 189) the chronicle of Chac-xulub-chen, written in the Maya in 1562, which throws light on the methods of the Spanish Conquest.

There was a native account, by Don Gabriel Castañeda, of the conquest of the Chichimecs by the Viceroy Antonio de Mendoza in 1541; but Brinton[1] says all trace of it is lost since it was reported to be in the Convent of Ildefonso in Mexico.

Perhaps the most important native contribution to the history of Guatemala is Francisco Ernandez Arana Xahila's *Memorial de Tecpan Atitlan*, written in 1581 and later in the dialect of Cakchiquel, and bringing the history of a distinguished branch of the Cakchiquels down to 1562, from which point it is continued by Francisco Gebuta Queh. Brasseur de Bourbourg loosely rendered it, and from this paraphrase a Spanish version has been printed in Guatemala; but the original has never been printed. Brinton (in his *Aboriginal American Authors*, p. 32) says he has a copy; and another

is in Europe. It is of great importance as giving the native accounts of the conquest of Guatemala.[2] An ardent advocacy of the natives was also shown in the *Historia de las Indias de Nueva España* of the Padre Diego Duran, which was edited by Ramirez, so far as the first volume goes, in 1867, when it was published in Mexico with an atlas of plates after the manuscript; but this publication is said not to present all the drawings of the original manuscript. The overthrow of Maximilian prevented the completion of the publication. The incoming Republican government seized what had been printed, so that the fruit of Ramirez's labor is now scarce. Quaritch priced the editor's own copy at £8 10s. The editor had polished the style of the original somewhat, and made other changes, which excited some disgust in the purists; and this action on his part may have had something to do with the proceedings of the new Government. Ramirez claimed descent from the Aztecs, and this may account for much of his stern judgment respecting Cortés.[3] The story in this first volume is only brought down to the reign of Montezuma. The

---

[1] *Aboriginal American Authors*, p. 28.

[2] Bancroft, *Central America*, vol. i. p. 686. Bandelier has given a partial list of the authorities on the conquest of Guatemala in the *Amer. Antiq. Soc. Proc.*, October, 1880; and Bancroft (*Central America*, vol. i. p. 703, vol. ii. p. 736) characterizes the principal sources. Helps (end of book xv. of his *Spanish Conquest*) complained of the difficulty in getting information of the Guatemala affairs; but Bancroft makes use of all the varied published collections of documents on Spanish-American history, which contain so much on Guatemala; and to his hands, fortunately, came also all the papers of the late E. G. Squier. A *Coleccion de Documentos Antiguos de Guatemala*, published in 1857, has been mentioned elsewhere, as well as the *Proceso* against Alvarado, so rich in helpful material. The general historians must all be put under requisition in studying this theme,— Oviedo, Gomara, Diaz, Las Casas, Ixtlilxochitl, and Herrera, not to name others. Antonio de Remesal's is the oldest of the special works, and was written on the spot. His *Historia de Chyapa* is a Dominican's view; and being a partisan, he needs more or less to be confirmed. A Franciscan friar, Francisco Vasquez, published a *Chronica de la Provincia del Santissimo Nombre de Jesus de Guatemala* in 1714, a promised second volume never appearing. He magnified the petty doings of his brother friars; but enough of historical interest crept into his book, together with citations from records no longer existing, to make it valuable. He tilts against Remesal, while he constantly uses his book; and the antagonism of the Franciscans and Dominicans misguides him sometimes, when borrowing from his rival. He lauds the conquerors, and he suffers the charges of cruelty to be made out but in a few cases (Bancroft, *Central America*, vol. ii. pp. 142, 736). The *Historia de Guatemala* of Francisco Antonio de Fuentes y Guzman is quoted by Bancroft from a manuscript copy (*Central America*, vol. ii. p. 736), but it has since been printed in Madrid in 1882–1883, in two volumes, with annotations by Justo Zaragoza, as one of the series *Biblioteca de los Americanistes*. Bancroft thinks he has many errors and that he is far from trustworthy, wherever his partiality for the conquerors is brought into play. The chief modern historian of Guatemala is Domingo Juarros, who was born in that city in 1752, and died in 1820. His *Compendio de la historia de la Ciudad de Guatemala* was published there, the first volume in 1808 and the second in 1818; and both were republished in 1857. It was published in English in London in 1823, with omissions and inaccuracies,— according to Bancroft. The story of the Conquest is told in the second volume. Except so far as he followed Fuentes, in his partiality for the conquerors, Juarros' treatment of his subject is fair; and his industry and facilities make him learned in its details. Bancroft (*Central America*, vol. ii. pp. 142, 737) remarks on his omission to mention the letters of Alvarado, and doubts, accordingly, if Juarros could have known of them.

Of the despatches which Alvarado sent to Cortés, we know only two. Bandelier (*American Antiquarian Society's Proceedings*, October, 1880) says that Squier had copies of them all; but Bancroft (*Central America*, vol. i. p. 666), who says he has all of Squier's papers, makes no mention of any beyond the two, — of April 11 and July 28, 1524, — which are in print in connection with Cortés' fourth letter, in Ramusio's version, except such as are of late date (1534–1541), of which he has copies, as his list shows (Cf. also Ternaux, vol. x., and Barcia, vol. i. p. 157). Ternaux is said to have translated from Ramusio. Oviedo uses them largely, word for word. Herrera is supposed to have used a manuscript History of the Conquest of Guatemala by Gonzalo de Alvarado.

[3] Prescott, *Mexico*, vol. ii. p. 165.

manuscript is preserved in the royal library at Madrid.[1] Duran was a half-breed, his mother being of Tezcuco. He became a Dominican; but a slender constitution kept him from the missionary field, and he passed a monastic life of literary labors. He had finished in 1579 the later parts of his work treating of the Mexican divinities, calendars, and festivals; and then, reverting to the portions which came first in the manuscript, he tells the story of Mexican history rather clumsily, but with a certain native force and insight, down to the period of the Honduras expedition. The manuscript of Duran passed, after his death in 1588, to Juan Tovar, and from him, perhaps with the representations that Tovar (or Tobar) was its author, to José de Acosta, who represents Tovar as the author, and who had then prepared, while in Peru, his *De Natura Novi Orbis*.

E. The Earlier Historians. — José de Acosta was born about 1540 in Spain; but at fourteen he joined the Jesuits. He grew learned, and in 1571 he went to Peru, in which country he spent fifteen years, becoming the provincial of his Order. He tarried two other years in Mexico — where he saw Tovar — and in the islands. He then returned to Spain laden with manuscripts and information, became a royal favorite, held other offices, and died as rector of Salamanca in 1600,[2] having published in his books on the New World the most popular and perhaps most satisfactory account of it up to that time; while his theological works give evidence, as Markham says, of great learning.

Acosta's first publication appeared at Salamanca in 1588 and 1589, and was in effect two essays, though they are usually found under one cover (they had separate titles, but were continuously paged), *De natura Novi Orbis libri duo, et de promulgatione evangelii apud barbaros, . . . libri sex.* In the former he describes the physical features of the country, and in the latter he told the story of the conversion of the Indians.[3] Acosta now translated the two books of the *De natura* into Spanish, and added five other books. The work was thus made to form a general cosmographical treatise, with particular reference to the New World; and included an account of the religion and government of the Indians of Peru and Mexico. He also gave a brief recital of the Conquest. In this extended form, and under the title of *Historia natvral y moral de las Indias, en qve se tratan las cosas notables del cielo, y elementos, metales, plantas, y animales dellas; y los ritos, y ceremonias, leyes, y govierno, y guerras de los Indios,* it was published at Seville in 1590.[4]

Two other accounts of this period deserve notice. One is by Joan Suarez de Peralta, who

<hr/>

[1] A copy is in the Force Collection, Library of Congress, and another in Mr. Bancroft's, from whose *Mexico*, vol. i. p. 461, we gather some of these statements.

[2] Cf. Backer, *Bibliothèque des écrivains de la Compagnie de Jésus;* Markham's introduction to his edition of Acosta in the Hakluyt Society's publications.

[3] The original edition of the *De natura* is scarce. Rich priced it at £1 1s. fifty years ago; Leclerc, no. 2,639, at 150 francs (cf. also Carter-Brown, i. 379; Sabin, i. 111, — for a full account of successive editions; Sunderland, i. 23). It was reprinted at Salamanca in 1595, and at Cologne in 1596. The latter edition can usually be bought for $3 or $4. Cf. Field, no. 9; Stevens, *Bibliotheca Historica,* no. 9; Murphy, no. 11, etc.

[4] Rich priced it in 1832 at £1 10s.; ordinary copies are now worth about £2 or £3, but fine copies in superior binding have reached £12 12s. (Cf. Leclerc, no. 5 — 200 francs; Sunderland, i. 24; J. A. Allen, *Bibliography of Cetacea,* p. 24, — where this and other early books on America are recorded with the utmost care.) Other Spanish editions are Helmstadt, 1590 (Bartlett); Seville, 1591 (Brunet, Backer); Barcelona, 1591 (Carter-Brown, i. 478; Leclerc, no. 7); Madrid, 1608 (Carter-Brown, ii. 61; Leclerc, no. 8) and 1610 (Sabin); Lyons, 1670; and Madrid, 1792, called the best edition, with a notice of Acosta.

The French editions followed rapidly: Paris, by R. Regnault, 1597 (Brunet, Markham); 1598 (Leclerc, no. 10 — 100 francs; Dufossé, 125 francs, 140 francs, 160 francs); 1600 (Leclerc, no. 11; Bishop Huet's copy in the Bibliothèque Nationale at Paris has notes which are printed by Camus in his book on De Bry); 1606 (Leclerc, nos. 12, 13); 1616 (Carter-Brown, ii. 177; Leclerc, no. 2,639 — 50 francs); 1617 (Leclerc, no. 14); 1619 (Sabin); 1621 (Rich). An Italian version, made by Gallucci, was printed at Venice in 1596 (Leclerc, no. 15).

There were more liberties taken with it in German. It was called *Geographische und historische Beschreibung der America,* when printed at Cologne in 1598, with thirty maps, as detailed in the *Carter-Brown Catalogue,* i. 520. Antonio (*Biblioteca Hispana Nova*) gives the date 1599. At Cologne again in 1600 it is called *New Welt* (Carter-Brown, i. 548), and at Wesel, in 1605, *America oder West India,* which is partly the same as the preceding (Carter-Brown, ii. 31). Antonio gives an edition in 1617.

The Dutch translation, following the 1591 Seville edition, was made by Linschoten, and printed at Haarlem in 1598 (Leclerc, no. 16); and again, with woodcuts, in 1624 (Carter-Brown, ii. 287; Murphy, no. 9). It is also in Vander Aa's collection, 1727. It was from the Dutch version that it was turned (by Gothard Arthus for De Bry in his *Great Voyages,* part ix.) into German, in 1601; and into Latin, in 1602 and 1603.

The first English translation did not appear till 1604, at London, as *The naturall and morall historie of the East und West Indies. Intreating of the remarkable things of Heaven, of the Elements, Mettalls, Plants,*

was born in Mexico in 1536, and wrote a *Tratado del descubrimiento de las Yndias y su conquista*, which is preserved in manuscript in the library at Toledo in Spain. It is not full, however, on the Conquest; but is more definite for the period from 1565 to 1589. It was printed at Madrid in 1878, in the *Noticias históricas de la Nueva España publicadas con la protection del ministerio de fomento por Don Justo Zaragoza*. The other is Henrico Martinez' *Repertorio de los Tiempos y historia natural de la Nueva España*, published at Mexico in 1606. It covers the Mexican annals from 1520 to 1590.[1]

One of the earliest to depend largely on the native chroniclers was Juan de Torquemada, in his *Monarquía Indiana*. This author was born in Spain, but came young to Mexico; and was a priest of the Franciscan habit, who finally became (1614–1617) the provincial of that Order. He had assiduously labored to collect all that

he could find regarding the history of the people among whom he was thrown; and his efforts were increased when, in 1609, he received orders to prepare his labors for publication. His book is esteemed for the help it affords in understanding these people. Ternaux calls it the most complete narrative which we possess of the ancient history of Mexico. He took the history, as the native writers had instructed him, of the period before the Conquest, and derived from them and his own observation much respecting the kind of life which the conquerors found prevailing in the country. In his account of the Conquest, which constitutes the fourth book in vol. i., Torquemada seems to depend largely on Herrera, though he does not neglect Sahagun and the native writers. Clavigero tells us that Torquemada for fifty years had known the language of the natives, and spent twenty years or more in arranging his history.

---

and Beasts which are proper to that Country; Together with the Manners, Ceremonies, Lawes, Governements, and Warres of the Indians. Written in Spanish by Ioseph Acosta, and translated into English by E[dward] G[rimston]*. Rich priced it fifty years ago at £1 16s.; it is usually priced now at from four to eight guineas (cf. Carter-Brown, ii. 21; Field, no. 8; Menzies, no. 4; Murphy, no. 8). It was reprinted, with corrections of the version, and edited by C. R. Markham for the Hakluyt Society in 1880.

[1] This is extremely rare. Quaritch, who said in 1879 that only three copies had turned up in London in thirty years, prices an imperfect copy at £5. (*Catalogue*, no. 326 *sub* no. 17,635.)

It is worth while to note how events in the New World, during the early part of the sixteenth century, were considered in their relation to European history. Cf. for instance, Ulloa's *Vita dell' imperator Carlo V.* (Rome, 1562), and such chronicles as the *Anales de Aragon*, first and second parts. Harrisse (*Bibl. Amer. Vet.* and *Additions*), and the *Carter-Brown Catalogue* (vol. i.) will lead the student to this examination, in their enumeration of books only incidentally connected with America. To take but a few as representative:

Maffeius, *Commentariorum urbanorum libri*, Basle, 1530, with its chapter on "loca nuper reperta." (Harrisse, *Additions*, no. 93; edition of 1544, *Bibl. Amer. Vet.* no. 257, and *Additions*, no. 146. Fabricius cites an edition as early as 1526.)

Laurentius Frisius, *Der Cartha Marina*, Strasburg, 1530. (Harrisse, *Bibl. Amer. Vet.*, no. 151; *Additions*, no. 90.)

Gemma Phrysius, *De Principiis Astronomiæ et Cosmographicæ*, with its cap. xxix., "De insulis nuper inventis." (Harrisse, *Bibl. Amer. Vet.*, *Additions*, no. 92.) There are later editions in 1544 (*Bibl. Amer. Vet.*, no. 252), 1548; also Paris, in French, 1557, etc.

Sebastian Franck, *Weltbuch*, Tübingen, 1533–1534, in which popular book of its day a separate chapter is given to America. The book in this first edition is rare, and is sometimes dated 1533, and again 1534. (Cf. Harrisse, *Bibl. Amer. Vet.*, nos. 174, 197; Sabin, vi. 570; Carter-Brown, i. 111; Muller, 1877, no. 1,151; H. H. Bancroft, *Mexico*, i. 250.) There was another edition in 1542 (*Bibl. Amer. Vet.*, no. 238; Stevens, *Bibliotheca Historica*, no. 738), and later in Dutch and German, in 1558, 1567, 1595, etc. (Leclerc, nos. 212, 217, etc.).

George Rithaymer, *De orbis terrarum*, Nuremberg, 1538, with its "De terris et insulis nuper repertis" (*Bibl. Amer. Vet.*, *Additions*, no. 119).

Achilles P. Gassarum, *Historiarum et chronicarum mundi epitomes libellus*, Venice, 1538, with its "insulæ in oceano antiquioribus ignotæ."

Ocampo, *Chronica general de España*, 1543, who, in mentioning the discovery of the New World, forgets to name Columbus (*Bibl. Amer. Vet.*, no. 242; Sabin, vol. xiii.).

Guillaume Postel, *De orbis terræ concordia*, Basle, about 1544 (*Bibl. Amer. Vet.*, *Additions*, no. 145).

John Dryander, *Cosmographiæ introductio*, 1544 (*Bibl. Amer. Vet.*, *Additions*, no. 147).

Biondo, *De ventis et navigatione*, Venice, 1546, with cap. xxv. on the New World (*Bibl. Amer. Vet.*, no. 274).

Professor J. R. Seeley, in his *Expansion of England* (p. 78), has pointed out how events in the New World did not begin to react upon European politics, till the attacks of Drake and the English upon the Spanish West Indies instigated the Spanish Armada, and made territorial aggrandizement in the New World as much a force in the conduct of politics in Europe as the Reformation had been. The power of the great religious revolution gradually declined before the increasing commercial interests arising out of trade with the New World.

He also tells us of the use which Torquemada made of the manuscripts which he found in the colleges of Mexico, of the writings of Ixtlilxochitl, Camargo, and of the history of Cholula by another writer of native origin, Juan Batista Pomar. Another book of considerable use to him was the work of a warm eulogist of the natives, if not himself of their blood; and this was the *Historia Eclesiástica Indiana*, a work written by Gerónimo de Mendieta near the end of the sixteenth century. Mendieta was in Mexico from 1554 to 1571,[1] and his work, finished in 1596, after having remained for two hundred years in manuscript, was printed and annotated by Icazbalceta at Mexico, in 1870.[2]

The *Monarquía Indiana*, in which these and other writers were so freely employed as to be engrafted in parts almost bodily, was first printed in three volumes at Madrid in 1615; but before this the Inquisition had struck out from its pages some curious chapters, particularly, says Rich, one comparing the migration of the Toltecs to that of the Israelites. The colophon of this edition shows the date of 1614.[3] It is said that most of it was lost in a shipwreck, and this accounts, doubtless, for its rarity. The original manuscript, however, being preserved, it served Barcia well in editing a reprint in 1723, published at Madrid, which is now considered the standard edition.[4] Torquemada doubtless derived something of his skill in the native tongue from his master, Fray Joan Baptista, who had the reputation of being the most learned scholar of the Mexican language in his time.[5]

The *Teatro Mexicano* of Augustin de Vetancurt, published at Mexico in 1697–1698,[6] is the next general chronicle after Torquemada. Vetancourt, also, was a Franciscan, born in Mexico in 1620, and died in 1700. He had the literary fecundity of his class; but the most important of his works is the one already named; and in the third part of the first volume we find his

history of the Conquest. He seldom goes behind his predecessor, and Torquemada must stand sponsor for much of his recital.

F. MODERN HISTORIANS. — The well-known work of Solis (*Historia de la Conquista de México*,[7] published at Madrid in 1684) is the conspicuous precursor of a long series of histories of the Conquest, written without personal knowledge of the actors in this extraordinary event. Solis ended his narrative with the fall of the city, the author's death preventing any further progress, though it is said he had gathered further materials; but they are not known to exist. A work by Ignacio Salazar y Olarte, continuing the narrative down to the death of Cortés, is called a second part, and was published at Cordova in 1743, under the title of *Historia de la conquista de México, poblacion y progressos de la América septentrional conocida por el nombre de Nueva España*. This continuation was reprinted at Madrid in 1786, and in the opinion of Bancroft[8] abounds "in all the faults of the superficial and florid composition of Solis."

Solis, who was born at Alcala in 1610, was educated at Salamanca, and had acquired a great reputation in letters, when he attracted the attention of the Court, and was appointed historiographer of the Indies. Some time afterward (1667) he entered the Church, at fifty-six; but to earn his salary as official chronicler, — which was small enough at best, — he turned, with a good deal of the poetic and artistic instinct which his previous training had developed, to tell the story of the Conquest, with a skill which no one before had employed upon the theme. The result was a work which, "to an extraordinary degree," as Ticknor[9] says, took on "the air of an historical epic, so exactly are all its parts and episodes modelled into a harmonious whole, whose catastrophe is the fall of the great Mexican Empire." The book was a striking contrast to the chronicling spirit of all preced-

---

[1] Bancroft, *Mexico*, ii. 667. He died in 1604.

[2] Sabin, vol. xii. no. 47,812. Icazbalceta showed Torquemada's debt to Mendieta by collations. (Bancroft, *Mexico*, ii. 668.) No author later than Torquemada cites it. Barcia was not able to find it, and it was considered as hopelessly lost. In 1860 its editor was informed that the manuscript had been found among the papers left by D. Bartolomé José Gallardo. Later it was purchased by D. José M. Andrade, and given to Icazbalceta, at whose expense it has been published (*Boston Public Library Catalogue*).

[3] Carter-Brown, ii. 176; Sunderland, vol. v. no. 12,536. Some of the bibliographies give the date 1613, and the place Seville. Cf. further on Torquemada, Bancroft, *Mexico*, ii. 786; *Early American Chroniclers*, p. 23; Prescott, *Mexico*, i. 53.

[4] Carter-Brown, iii. 339; Leclerc, no. 370; Field, no. 1,557; Court, no. 354. It is in three volumes. Kingsborough in his eighth volume gives some extracts from Torquemada.

[5] Baptista published various devotional treatises in both Spanish and Mexican, some of which, like his *Compassionario* of 1599, are extremely rare. Cf. Leclerc, no. 2,306; Quaritch, *The Ramirez Collection*, 1880, nos. 25, 26.

[6] Again in four volumes, Mexico, 1870–1871. Cf. Bancroft, *Mexico*, iii. 507.

[7] Carter-Brown, vol. ii. no. 1,300.

[8] *Mexico*, i. 187.

[9] *Spanish Literature*, vol. iii. no. 196.

DON ANTONIO
DE SOLIS.

SOLIS.[1]

ing recitals. The world soon saw — though the sale of the book was not large at once, and the author died very poor two years later (1686) — that the strange story had been given its highest setting. Solis gives no notes; and one needs to know the literature of the subject, to

---

[1] Fac-simile of engraving in his *Historia*, published at Venice in 1715. There are other likenesses in the Madrid (1783) edition, and in Cumplido's Mexican edition of Prescott's *Mexico*, vol. iii.

track him to his authorities. If this is done, however, it appears that his investigation was far from deep, and that with original material within his reach he rarely or never used it, but took the record at second hand. Robertson, who had to depend on him more or less, was aware of this, and judged him less solicitous of discovering truth than of glorifying the splendor of deeds. This panegyrical strain in the book has lowered its reputation, particularly among foreign critics, who fail to share the enthusiasm which Solis expresses for Cortés. We may call his bitter denunciations of the natives bigotry or pious zeal; but Ticknor accounts for it by saying that Solis "refused to see the fierce and marvellous contest except from the steps of the altar where he had been consecrated." The religion and national pride of the Spaniards have not made this quality detract in the least from the estimation in which the book has long been held; but all that they say of the charm and purity of its style, despite something of tiresomeness in its even flow, is shared by the most conspicuous of foreign critics, like Prescott and Ticknor. Rich, who had opportunities for knowing, bears evidence to the estimation in Spain of those qualities which have insured the fame of Solis.[1]

The story was not told again with the dignity of a classic, — except so far as Herrera composed it, — till Robertson, in his *History of America*, recounted it. He used the printed sources with great fidelity; but he was denied a chance to examine the rich manuscript material which was open to Solis, and which Robertson would doubtless have used more abundantly. In a Note (xcvii.) he enumerates his chief authorities, and they are only the letters of Cortés and the story as told by Gomara, Bernal Diaz, Peter Martyr, Solis, and Herrera.[2] Of Solis, Robertson says he knows no author in any language whose literary fame has risen so far beyond his real merits. He calls him "destitute of that patient industry in research which conducts to the knowledge of truth, and a stranger to that impartiality which weighs evidence with cool attention. . . . Though he sometimes quotes the despatches of Cortés, he seems not to have consulted them; and though he sets out with some censure on Gomara, he frequently prefers his authority — the most doubtful of any — to that of the other contemporary historians." Robertson judged that Herrera furnished the fullest and most accurate information, and that if his work had not in its chronological order been so perplexed, disconnected, and obscure, Herrera might justly have been ranked among the most eminent historians of his country. William Smyth, in the twenty-first section of his *Lectures on Modern History*, in an account which is there given of the main sources of information respecting the Conquest, as they were accessible forty or fifty years ago, awards high praise — certainly not undeserved for his time — to Robertson. Southey accused Robertson of unduly depreciating the character and civilization

---

[1] Cf., for accounts and estimates, Ticknor, *Spanish Literature*, vol. iii. no. 196; Prescott, *Mexico*, vol. iii. p. 208; Bancroft, *Mexico*, vol. i. pp. 186, 697; *Early Chroniclers*, p. 22. Editions of Solis became, in time, numerous in various languages. Most of them may be found noted in the following list: —

In Spanish. Barcelona, 1691, accompanied by a Life of Solis, by Don Juan de Goyeneche, Madrid, 1704, a good edition; Brussels, 1704, with numerous plates; Madrid, 1732, two columns, without plates; Brussels, 1741, with Goyeneche's Life; Madrid, 1748, said to have been corrected by the author's manuscript; Barcelona, 1756; Madrid, 1758; Madrid, 1763; Barcelona, 1771; Madrid, 1776; Madrid, 1780; Madrid, 1783–1784, — a beautiful edition, called by Stirling "the triumph of the press of Sancha" (cf. Ticknor Catalogue, p. 335; Carter-Brown, vol. ii. no. 1,300); Barcelona, 1789; Madrid, 1791, 1798, 1819, 1822; Paris, 1827; Madrid, 1828, 1829, 1838; Barcelona, 1840; Paris, 1858, with notes. Sabin (vol. iv. nos. 16,944–16,945) gives abridged editions, — Barcelona, 1846, and Mexico, 1853. An edition, London, 1809, is "Corregida por Augustin Luis Josse," and is included in the *Biblioteca de autores españoles*, in 1853.

In French. The earliest translation was made by Bon André de Citri et de la Guette, and appeared with two different imprints in Paris in 1691 in quarto (Carter-Brown, vol. ii. 1427–1428). Other editions followed, — La Haye, 1692, in 12mo; Paris, 1704, with folding map and engravings reduced from the Spanish editions; Paris, 1714, with plates; Paris, 1730, 1759, 1774, 1777, 1844, etc.; and a new version by Philippe de Toulza, with annotations, published in Paris in 1868.

In Italian. The early version was published at Florence in 1699, with portraits of Solis, Cortés, and Montezuma (Carter-Brown, vol. ii. no. 1,577). An edition at Venice in 1704 is without plates; but another, in 1715, is embellished. There was another at Venice in 1733.

In Danish. Copenhagen, 1747 (Carter-Brown, vol. iii. no. 859).

In English. Thomas Townsend's English version was published in London in 1724, and was reissued, revised by R. Hooke in 1753, both having a portrait of Cortés, by Vertue, copied "after a head by Titian," with other folding plates based on those of the Spanish editions (Carter-Brown, vol. iii. nos. 350, 588; Field, *Indian Bibliography*, nos. 1,464, 1,465). There were later editions in 1753.

It was when he was twenty-eight years old, that Prescott took his first lesson in Spanish history in reading Solis, at Ticknor's recommendation.

[2] The story as the English had had it up to this time — except so far as they learned it in translations of Solis — may be found in Burke's *European Settlements in America*, 1765, part i. pp. 1–166.

of the Mexicans; and others have held the opinion that he had a 'tendency to palliate the crimes of the invaders. Robertson, in his later editions, replied to such strictures, and held that Clavigero and others had differed from him chiefly in confiding in the improbable narratives and fanciful conjectures of Torquemada and Boturini.

Francisco Saverio Clavigero was a Jesuit, who had long resided in Mexico, being born at Vera Cruz in 1731; but when expelled with his Order, he took up his abode in Italy in 1767. He had the facilities and the occasion for going more into detail than Robertson. His *Storia antica del Messico cavata da' migliori storici spagnuoli, e da' manoscritti; e dalle pitture antiche degl' Indiani: divisa in dieci libri, e corredata di carte geografiche, e di varie figure: e dissertazioni sulla terra, sugli animali, e sugli abitatori del Messico,*[1] was published in four volumes at Cesena in 1780–1781. He gives the names of thirty-nine Indian and Spanish writers who had written upon the theme, and has something to say of the Mexican historical paintings which he had examined. H. H. Bancroft esteems him a leading authority,[2] and says he rearranged the material in a masterly manner, and invested it with a philosophic spirit, altogether superior to anything presented till Prescott's time.[3] It is in his third volume that Clavigero particularly treats of the Conquest, having been employed on the earlier chronicles and the manners and customs of the people in the first and second, while the fourth volume is made up of particular dissertations. Clavigero was not without learning. He had passed three years at the Jesuit College at Tepozotlan, and had taught as a master in various branches. At Bologna, where he latterly lived, he founded an academy; and here he died in 1787, leaving behind him a *Storia della California*, published at Venice in 1789.[4]

Fifteen years ago it was the opinion of Henry Stevens,[5] that all other books which have been elaborated since on the same subject, instead of superseding Clavigero's, have tended rather to magnify its importance.[6]

The most conspicuous treatment of the subject, in the minds of the elders of the present generation, is doubtless that of Prescott, who published his *Conquest of Mexico* in 1843, dividing it into three distinct parts, — the first showing a survey of the Aztec civilization; the second depicting the Conquest; while the final period brought down the life of Cortés to his death. Charton[7] speaks of Solis as a work "auquel le livre de Prescott a porté un dernier coup." Prescott was at great expense and care in amassing much manuscript material never before used, chiefly in copies, which Rich and others had procured for him, and he is somewhat minute in his citations from them. They have since been in large part printed, and doubtless very much more is at present accessible in type to the student than was in Prescott's day.[8]

Prescott was of good New England stock, settled in Essex County, Massachusetts, where (in Salem) he was born in 1796. His father removed to Boston in 1808, and became a judge of one of the courts. A mischance at Harvard, in a student's frolic, deprived young Prescott of the use of one eye; and the other became in time permanently affected. Thus he subsequently labored at his historical studies under great disadvantage,[9] and only under favorable circumstances and for short periods could he read for himself. In this way he became dependent upon the assistance of secretaries, though he generally wrote his early drafts by the aid of a noctograph. From 1826 to 1837 he was engaged on his *Ferdinand and Isabella*, and this naturally led him to the study of his Mexican and Peruvian themes; and Irving, who had embarked on

---

[1] Sabin, vol. iv. no. 13,518. It was written in Spanish, but translated into Italian for publication. A Spanish version, *Historia Antigua de Mégico*, made by Joaquin de Mora, was printed in London in 1826, and reprinted in Mexico in 1844 (Leclerc, nos. 1,103, 1,104, 2,712). A German translation, *Geschichte von Mexico*, was issued at Leipsic in 1789–1790, with notes. This version is not made from the original Italian, but from an English translation printed in London in 1787 as *The History of Mexico*, translated by Charles Cullen. It was reprinted in London in 1807, and in Philadelphia in 1817 (Field, *Indian Bibliography*, p. 326).

[2] *Early American Chronicles*, p. 24.

[3] Bancroft, *Mexico*, i. 697; also Prescott, *Mexico*, i. 53.

[4] Bancroft, *Mexico*, i. 700; Leclerc, no. 846.

[5] *Bibliotheca Historica*, no. 377.

[6] There is a portrait of Clavigero in Cumplido's edition of Prescott's *Mexico* (1846), vol. iii.

[7] *Voyageurs*, iii. 422.

[8] Mr. H. H. Bancroft (*Mexico*, vol. i, p. 7, *note*), however, charges his predecessor with parading his acquisition of this then unprinted material, and with neglecting the more trustworthy and more accessible chroniclers. He also speaks (*Mexico*, i. 701) of an amiable weakness in Prescott which sacrificed truth to effect, and to a style which he calls "magnificent," and to a "philosophic flow of thought," — the latter trait in Prescott being one of his weakest; nor is his style what rhetoricians would call "magnificent."

[9] Mr. R. A. Wilson makes more of it than is warranted, in affirming that "Prescott's inability to make a personal research" deprives us of the advantage of his integrity and personal character (*New Conquest of Mexico*, p. 312).

WILLIAM H. PRESCOTT.[1]

them as a literary field, generously abandoned his pursuit to the new and rising historian.[2] The *Conquest of Mexico* appeared in 1843,[3] and has long remained a charming book, as fruitful in

[1] This cut follows an engraving in mezzotint in the *Eclectic Magazine* (1858), and shows him using his noctograph. The likeness was thought by his wife and sister (Mrs. Dexter) to be the best ever made, as Mr. Arthur Dexter informs me. See other likenesses in Ticknor's *Life of Prescott; Mass. Hist. Soc. Proc.,* iv. 167; and *N. E. Hist. and Geneal. Reg.* (1868), p. 226.

[2] Ticknor's *Prescott*, quarto edition, pp. 167-172.

[3] It was soon afterward reprinted in London and in Paris.

authority as the material then accessible could make it.

In the Preface to his *Mexico* Mr. Prescott tells of his success in getting unpublished material, showing how a more courteous indulgence was shown to him than Robertson had enjoyed. By favor of the Academy of History in Madrid he got many copies of the manuscripts of Muñoz and of Vargas y Ponçe, and he enjoyed the kind offices of Navarrete in gathering this material. He mentions that, touching the kindred themes of Mexico and Peru, he thus obtained the bulk of eight thousand folio pages. From Mexico itself he gathered other appliances, and these largely through the care of Alaman, the minister of foreign affairs, and of Calderon de la Barca, the minister to Mexico from Spain. He also acknowledges the courtesy of the descendants of Cortés in opening their family archives; that of Sir Thomas Phillipps, whose manuscript stores have become so famous, and the kindness of Ternaux-Compans.

To Mr. John Foster Kirk, who had been Prescott's secretary, the preparation of new editions of Prescott's works was intrusted, and in this series the *Mexico* was republished in 1874. Kirk was enabled, as Prescott himself had been in preparing for it, to make use of the notes which Ramirez had added to the Spanish translation by Joaquin Navarro, published in Mexico in 1844, and of those of Lúcas Alaman, attached to another version, published also in Mexico.[1]

Almost coincident with the death of Prescott, was published by a chance Mr. Robert Anderson Wilson's *New History of the Conquest of Mexico*.[2] Its views were not unexpected, and indeed Prescott had been in correspondence[3] with the author. His book was rather an extravagant argument than a history, and was aimed to prove the utter untrustworthiness of the ordinary chroniclers of the Conquest, charging the conquerors with exaggerating and even creating the fabric of the Aztec civilization, to enhance the effect which the overthrow of so much splendor would have in Europe. To this end he pushes Cortés aside as engrafting fable on truth for such a purpose, dismisses rather wildly Bernal Diaz as a myth, and declares the picture-writings to be Spanish fabrications. This view was not new, except in its excess of zeal. Albert Gallatin had held a similar belief.[4] Lewis Cass had already seriously questioned, in the *North American Review*, October, 1840, the consistency of the Spanish historians. A previous work by Mr. Wilson had already, indeed, announced his views, though less emphatically. This book had appeared in three successive editions, — as *Mexico and its Religion* (New York, 1855); then as *Mexico, its Peasants and its Priests* (1856); and finally as *Mexico, Central America, and California*.

It was easy to accuse Wilson of ignorance and want of candor, — for he had laid himself open too clearly to this charge, — and Mr. Prescott's friend, Mr. George Ticknor, arraigned him in the *Mass. Hist. Soc. Proc.*, April, 1859.[5]

---

[1] Cf. the collation of criticisms on the *Mexico*, given by Allibone in his *Dictionary of Authors*, and by Poole in his *Index to Periodical Literature*. Archbishop Spalding, in his *Miscellanea*, chapters xiii. and xiv., gives the Catholic view of his labors; and Ticknor, in his *Life of Prescott*, prints various letters from Hallam, Sismondi, and others, giving their prompt expressions regarding the book. In chapters xiii., xiv., and xv. of this book the reader may trace Prescott through the progress of the work, not so satisfactorily as one might wish however, for in his diaries and letters the historian failed often to give the engaging qualities of his own character. It is said that Carlyle, when applied to for letters of Prescott which might be used by Ticknor in his Life of the historian, somewhat rudely replied that he had never received any from Prescott worth preserving. Prescott's library is, unfortunately, scattered. He gave some part of it to Harvard College, including such manuscripts as he had used in his *Ferdinand and Isabella;* and some years after his death a large part of it was sold at public auction. It was then found that, with a freedom which caused some observation, the marks of his ownership had been removed from his books. Many of his manuscripts and his noctograph were then sold, perhaps through inadvertence, for the family subsequently reclaimed what they could. The noctograph and some of the manuscripts are now in the cabinet of the Massachusetts Historical Society (cf. *Proceedings*, vol. xiii. p. 66), and other manuscripts are in the Boston Public Library (*Bulletin of Boston Public Library*, iv. 122). A long letter to Dr. George E. Ellis, written in 1857, and describing his use of the noctograph, is in the same volume (*Proceedings*, vol. xiii. p. 246). The estimate in which Prescott was held by his associates of that Society may be seen in the records of the meeting at which his death was commemorated, in 1859 (*Proceedings*, iv. 167, 266). There is a eulogy of Prescott by George Bancroft in the *Historical Magazine*, iii. 69. Cf. references in Poole's *Index*, p. 1047.

[2] Philadelphia and London, 1859.

[3] This correspondence was civil, to say the least. Bancroft (*Mexico*, i. 205), with a rudeness of his own, calls Wilson "a fool and a knave."

[4] *American Ethnological Society Transactions*, vol. i.

[5] Also in *Boston Daily Courier*, May 3, 1859. Cf. *Mass. Hist. Soc. Proc.* v. 101; *Atlantic Monthly*, April and May, 1859, by John Foster Kirk; Allibone's *Dictionary*, vol. ii. p. 1669. L. A. Wilmer, in his *Life of De Soto* (1859) is another who accuses Prescott of accepting exaggerated statements. Cf. J. D. Washburn on the failure of Wilson's arguments to convince, in *Amer. Antiq. Soc. Proc.*, October 21, 1879, p. 18.

He reminded Wilson that he ought to have known that Don Enrique de Vedia, who had published an edition of Bernal Diaz in 1853, had cited Fuentes y Guzman, whose manuscript history of Guatemala was before that editor, as referring in it to the manuscript of Bernal Diaz (his great-grandfather), which was then in existence, — a verity and no myth. Further than this, Brasseur de Bourbourg, who chanced then to be in Boston, bore testimony that he had seen and used the autograph manuscript of Bernal Diaz in the archives of Guatemala.

In regard to the credibility of the accounts which Prescott depends upon, his editor,[1] Mr. Kirk, has not neglected to cite the language of Mr. E. B. Tylor, in his *Anahuac*,[2] where he says, respecting his own researches on the spot, that what he saw of Mexico tended generally to confirm Prescott's History, and but seldom to make his statements appear improbable. The impeachment of the authorities, which Wilson attacks, is to be successful, if at all, by other processes than those he employs.

Meanwhile Arthur Helps,[3] in tracing the rise of negro slavery and the founding of colonial government in Spanish America, had published his *Conquerors of the New World and their Bondsmen* (London, 1848–1852), — a somewhat speculative essay, which, with enlargement of purpose and more detail, resulted in 1855–1861 in the publication of his *Spanish Conquest in America*, reprinted in New York in 1867. He gives a glowing account of the Aztec civilization, and, excerpting the chapters on the Conquest, he added some new details of the private life of Cortés, and published it separately in 1871 as an account of that leader, which is attractive as a biography, if not comprehensive as a history of the Conquest. "Every page affords evidence of historic lore," says Field, "and almost every sentence glows with the warmth of his philanthropy."[4] Helps has himself told the object and method of his book, and it is a different sort of historical treatment

from all the others which we are passing in review. "To bring before the reader, not conquest only, but the results of conquest; the mode of colonial government which ultimately prevailed; the extirpation of native races, the introduction of other races, the growth of slavery, and the settlement of the *encomiendas* on which all Indian society depended, — has been the object of this history."[5]

Among the later works not in English we need not be detained long. The two most noteworthy in French are the *Histoire des nations civilisées du Mexique* of Brasseur de Bourbourg, more especially mentioned on another page, and Michel Chevalier's *Mexique avant et pendant la Conquête*, published at Paris in 1845.[6] In German, Theodor Arnim's *Das Alte Mexico und die eroberung Neu Spaniens durch Cortes*, Leipsic, 1865, is a reputable book.[7] In Spanish, beside the *Vida de Cortés* given by Icazbalceta in his *Coleccion*, vol. i. p. 309, there is the important work of Lúcas Alaman, the *Disertaciones sobre la Historia de la República Mejicana*, published at Mexico in three volumes in 1844–1849, which is a sort of introduction to his *Historia de Méjico*, in five volumes, published in 1849–1852.[8] He added not a little in his appendixes from the archives of Simancas, and the latter book is considered the best of the histories in Spanish. In 1862 Francisco Carbajal Espinosa's *Historia de México*, bringing the story down from the earliest times, was begun in Mexico. Bancroft calls it pretentious, and mostly borrowed from Clavigero.[9]

Returning to the English tongue, in which the story of Mexico has been so signally told more than once from the time of Robertson, we find still the amplest contribution in the *History of Mexico*, a part of the extended series of the *History of the Pacific States*, published under the superintendence of Hubert H. Bancroft. Of Bancroft and these books mention is made in another place. The *Mexico* partakes equally of the merits and demerits attaching to

---

[1] Edition of 1874, ii. 110.

[2] Page 147.

[3] Born about 1817, and knighted in 1872.

[4] *Indian Bibliography*, no. 682.

[5] Cf. H. H. Bancroft, *Mexico*, ii. 488.

[6] Cf. *Revue des deux mondes*, 1845, vol. xi. p. 197. The book was later translated into English. He also published in 1863 and in 1864 *Le Mexique ancien et moderne*, which was also given in an English translation in London in 1864. Cf. *British Quarterly Review*, xl. 360.

[7] Ruge, in his *Geschichte des Zeitalters der Entdeckungen*, tells the story with the latest knowledge.

[8] Both books command good prices, ranging from $25 to $50 each.

[9] *Mexico*, i. 697; ii. 788, — where he speaks of N. de Zamacois' *Historia de Méjico*, Barcelona, 1877-1880, in eleven volumes, as " blundering ; " and Mora's *Méjico y sus Revoluciones*, Paris, 1836, in three volumes, as "hasty." Bancroft's conclusion regarding what Mexico itself has contributed to the history of the Conquest is " that no complete account of real value has been written." Andrés Cavo's *Tres siglos de México* (Mexico, 1836-1838, in three volumes) is but scant on the period of the Conquest (Bancroft, *Mexico*, iii. 508). It was reprinted in 1852, with notes and additions by Bustamante, and as part of the *Biblioteca Nacional y Extranjera*, and again at Jalapa in 1860.

his books and their method. It places the student under more obligations than any of the histories of the Conquest which have gone before, though one tires of the strained and purely extraneous classical allusions, — which seem to have been affected by his staff, or by some one on it, during the progress of this particular book of the series.

G. YUCATAN. — With the subsequent subjugation of Yucatan Cortés had nothing to do. Francisco de Montejo had been with Grijalva when he landed at Cozumel on the Yucatan coast, and with Cortés when he touched at the same island on his way to Mexico. After the fall of the Aztecs, Montejo was the envoy whom Cortés sent to Spain, and while there the Emperor commissioned him (Nov. 17, 1526) to conduct a force for the settlement of the peninsula. Early in 1527 Montejo left Spain with Alonso de Avila as second in command. For twenty years and more the conquest went on, with varying success. At one time not a Spaniard was left in the country. No revolts of the natives occurred after 1547, when the conquest may be considered as complete. The story is told with sufficient fulness in Bancroft's *Mexico*.[1] The main sources of our information are the narrative of Bernal Diaz, embodying the reports of eye-witnesses, and the histories of Oviedo and Herrera. Bancroft[2] gives various incidental references. The more special authorities, however, are the *Historia de Yucathan* of Diego Lopez Cogolludo, published at Madrid in 1688,[3] who knew how to use miracles for his reader's sake, and who had the opportunity of consulting most that had been written, and all that had been printed up to his time. He closes his narrative in 1665.[4] The Bishop of Yucatan, Diego de Landa, in his *Relation des choses de Yucatan*, as the French translation terms it, has left us the only contemporary Spanish document of the period of the Conquest. The book is of more interest in respect to the Maya civilization than as to the progress of the Spanish domination. It was not printed till it was edited by Bras-

seur de Bourbourg, with an introduction, and published in Paris in 1864.[5]

Landa was born in 1524, and was one of the first of his Order to come to Yucatan, where he finally became Bishop of Mérida in 1572, and died in 1579. Among the books commonly referred to for the later period is the first part (the second was never published) of Juan de Villagutierre Sotomayor's *Historia de la Conquista de la provincia de el Itza*, etc., Madrid, 1701. It deals somewhat more with the spiritual and the military conquests, but writers find it important.[6]

The latest English history of the peninsula is that by Charles St. J. Fancourt, *History of Yucatan*, London, 1854;[7] but a more extended, if less agreeable, book is Ancona's *Historia de Yucatan desde la época mas remota hasta nuestros dias*, published at Mérida in four volumes in 1878–1880. It gives references which will be found useful.[8]

H. BIBLIOGRAPHY OF MEXICO. — The earliest special bibliography of Mexico of any moment is that which, under the title of *Catalogo de sa museo historico Indiano*, is appended to Boturini Benaduci's *Idea de una nueva historia general de la America septentrional* (Madrid, 1746), which was the result of eight years' investigations into the history of Mexico. He includes a list of books, maps, and manuscripts, of which the last remnants in 1853 were in the Museo Nacional in Mexico.[9] Of the list of New Spain authors by Eguiara y Eguren, only a small part was published in 1755 as *Bibliotheca Mexicana*.[10] It was intended to cover all authors born in New Spain; but though he lived to arrange the work through the letter J, only A, B, and C were published. All titles are translated into Latin. Its incompleteness renders the bibliographical parts of Maneiro's *De Vitis Mexicanorum* (1791) more necessary, and makes Beristain's *Bibliotheca Hispano-Americano Septentrional*,[11] of three volumes, published at Mexico in 1816, 1819, and 1821, of more importance than it would otherwise be. Beristain, also, only partly finished his work; but a nephew

---

[1] Vol. ii. chaps. xxi. and xxx., p. 648.

[2] *Mexico*, ii. 455–456.

[3] Carter-Brown, vol. ii. no. 1,350.

[4] Rich, 1832, no. 422; Bancroft, *Mexico*, ii. 650. It was reprinted at Mérida in 1842, and again in 1867.

[5] Leclerc, nos. 1,172, 2,289. *Amer. Antiq. Soc. Proc.*, October, 1880, p. 85, where will be found Bandelier's partial bibliography of Yucatan.

[6] Cf. Field, 1605; *Amer. Antiq. Soc. Proc.*, October, 1880, p. 89. The book is not so rare as it is sometimes claimed; Quaritch usually prices copies at from £2 to £5.

[7] Field, p. 522.

[8] The *Registro Yucateco*, a periodical devoted to local historical study, and published in Mérida, only lived for two years, 1845–1846.

[9] Cf. Sabin, vol. ii. no. 6,834, and references. There is a copy of Boturini Benaduci in Harvard College Library. A portrait of him is given in Cumplido's edition of Prescott's *Mexico*, vol. iii.

[10] It is rare. Quaritch in 1880 priced Ramirez' copy at £12. It was printed, "Mexici in Ædibus Authoris."

[11] Trübner, *Bibliographical Guide*, p. xiii.

completed the publication. It has become rare; and its merits are not great, though its notices number 3,687.

Of more use to the student of the earlier history, however, is the list which Clavigero gives in his *Storia del Messico* published in 1780. A Jesuit, and a collector, having a book-lover's keen scent, he surpassed all writers on the theme who had preceded him, in amassing the necessary stores for his special use. Since his day the field has been surveyed more systematically both by the general and special bibliographers. The student of early Spanish-Mexican history will of course not forget the help which he can get from general bibliographers like Brunet, from the *Dictionary* of Sabin, the works of Ternaux and Harrisse, the *Carter-Brown Catalogue*, not to speak of other important library catalogues.

The sale catalogues are not without assistance. Principal among them are the collections which had been formed by the Emperor Maximilian of Mexico, — which was sold in Leipsic in 1869 as the collection of José Maria Andrade,[1] — and the *Bibliotheca Mexicana* formed by José Fernando Ramirez, which was sold in London in 1880.[2]

All other special collections on Mexico have doubtless been surpassed by that which has been formed in San Francisco by Mr. Hubert Howe Bancroft, as a component part of his library pertaining to the western slope of America. Lists of such titles have been prefixed to his histories of *Central America* and of *Mexico*, and are to be supplemented by others as his extended work goes on. He has explained, in his preface to his *Mexico* (p. viii), the wealth of his manuscript stores; and it is his custom, as it was Prescott's, to append to his chapters, and sometimes to passages of the text, considerable accounts, with some bibliographical detail, of the authorities with which he deals.[3] Helps, though referring to his authorities, makes no such extended references to them.[4]

[1] It contained nearly fourteen hundred entries about Mexico, or its press. Another collection, gathered by a gentleman attached to Maximilian's court, was sold in Paris in 1868; and still another, partly the accumulation of Père Augustin Fischer, the confessor of Maximilian, was dispersed in London in 1869 as a *Biblioteca Mejicana*. Cf. Jackson's *Bibliographies Géographiques*, p. 223.

[2] Many of these afterwards appeared in B. Quaritch's *Rough List*, no. 46, 1880. The principal part of a sale which included the libraries of Pinart and Brasseur de Bourbourg (January and February, 1884) also pertained to Mexico and the Spanish possessions.

[3] Cf. for instance his *Native Races*, iv. 565; *Central America*, i. 195; *Mexico*, i. 694, ii. 487, 784; *Early Chroniclers*, p. 19, etc. It is understood that his habit has been to employ readers to excerpt and abstract from books, and make references. These slips are put in paper bags according to topic. Such of these memoranda as are not worked into the notes of the pertinent chapter are usually massed in a concluding note.

[4] The general bibliographies of American history are examined in a separate section of the present work and elsewhere in the present chapter something has been said of the bibliographical side of various other phases of the Mexican theme. Mr. A. F. Bandelier has given a partial bibliography of Yucatan and Central America, touching Mexico, however, only incidentally, in the *Amer. Antiq. Soc. Proc.*, October, 1880. Harrisse, in his *Bibl. Amer. Vet.*, p. 212, has given a partial list of the poems and plays founded upon the Conquest. Others will be found in the *Chronological List of Historical Fiction* published by the Boston Public Library. Among the poems are Gabriel Lasso de la Vega's *Cortés Valeroso*, 1588, republished as *Mexicana* in 1594 (Maisonneuve, no. 2,825 — 200 francs); Saavedra Guzman's *El Peregrino indiano*, Madrid, 1599 (Rich, 1832, no. 86, £4 4s.); Balbuena's *El Bernardo*, a conglomerate heroic poem (Madrid, 1624), which gives one book to the Conquest by Cortés (Leclerc, no. 48 — 100 francs); Boesnier's *Le Mexique Conquis*, Paris, 1752; Escoiquiz, *México Conquistada*, 1798; Roux de Rochelle, *Ferdinand Cortez*; P. du Roure, *La Conquête du Mexique.*

Among the plays, — Dryden's *Indian Emperor* (Cortés and Montezuma); Lope de Vega's *Marquez del Valle;* Fernand de Zarate's *Conquista de México;* Canizares, *El Pleyto de Fernan Cortes;* F. del Rey, *Hernand Cortez en Tabasco;* Piron, *Cortes;* Malcolm MacDonald, *Guatemozin* (Philadelphia, 1878), etc.

DISCOVERIES

ON THE

PACIFIC COAST OF NORTH AMERICA.

BY THE EDITOR.

THE cartographical history of the Pacific coast of North America is one of shadowy and unstable surmise long continued.[1] The views of Columbus and his companions, as best shown in the La Cosa and Ruysch maps,[2] precluded, for a considerable time after the coming of Europeans, the possibility of the very existence of such a coast; since their Asiatic theory of the new-found lands maintained with more or less modification a fitful existence for a full century after Columbus. In many of the earliest maps the question was avoided by cutting off the westerly extension of the new continent by the edge of the sheet;[3] but the confession of that belief was still made sometimes in other ways, as when, in the Portuguese *portolano*, which is placed between 1516 and 1520, Mahometan flags are placed on the coasts of Venezuela and Nicaragua.[4]

In 1526 a rare book of the monk Franciscus, *De orbis situ ac descriptione Francisci epistola*,[5] contained a map which represented South America as a huge island disjoined from the Asiatic coast by a strait in the neighborhood of Tehuantepec, with the legend, "Hoc orbis hemisphærium cedit regi Hispaniæ."[6] A few years later we find two other maps showing this Asiatic connection, — one of which, the Orontius Finæus globe, is well known, and is the earliest engraved map showing a return to the ideas of Columbus. It appeared in the Paris edition of the *Novus Orbis* of Simon Grynæus, in 1532,[7] and was made the previous year. It is formed on a cordiform projection, and is entitled " Nova et integra universi orbis descriptio." It is more easily understood by a reference to Mr.

[1] Dr. Kohl's studies on the course of geographical discovery along the Pacific coast were never published. He printed an abstract in the *United States Coast Survey Report*, 1855, pp. 374, 375. A manuscript memoir by him on the subject is in the library of the American Antiquarian Society (*Proceedings*, 23 Apr. 1872, pp. 7, 26) at Worcester. So great advances in this field have since been made that it probably never will be printed. There is a chronological statement of explorations up the Pacific coast in Duflot de Mofras' *Exploration du territoire de l'Orégon* (Paris, 1844), vol. i. chap. iv.; but H. H. Bancroft's *Pacific States*, particularly his *North-west Coast*, vol. i., embodies the fullest information on this subject. In the enumeration of maps in the present paper, many omissions are made purposely, and some doubtless from want of knowledge. It is intended only to give a sufficient number to mark the varying progress of geographical ideas.

[2] See *ante*, pp. 106, 115.

[3] Cf. maps *ante*, on pp. 108, 112, 114, 127.

[4] This map is preserved in the Royal Library at Munich, and is portrayed in Kunstmann's *Atlas*, pl. iv., and in Stevens's *Notes*, pl. v. Cf. Kohl, *Discovery of Maine* (for a part), no. 10; and Harrisse's *Cabots*, p. 167.

[5] Harrisse, *Bibl. Amer. Vet.*, no 131.

[6] A sketch of the map is given by Lelewel, pl. xlvi.

[7] The *Novus Orbis* (Paris) has sometimes another map; but Harrisse says the Finæus one is the proper one. *Bibl. Amer. Vet.*, nos. 172, 173.

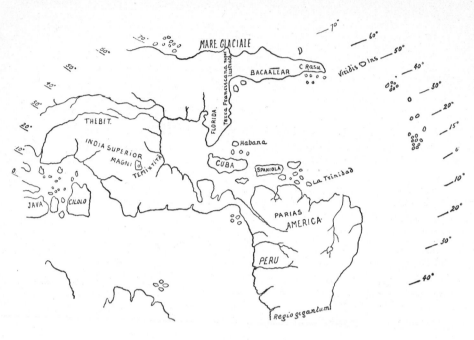

SLOANE MANUSCRIPTS, 1530.[1]

Brevoort's reduction of it to Mercator's projection, as shown in another volume.[2]   The same map, with a change in the inserted type dedication, appeared in the Pomponius Mela

RUSCELLI, 1544.[5]

of 1540,[3] and it is said also to be found much later in the *Geografia* of Lafreri published at Rome, 1554–1572.

The other of the two maps already referred to belongs to a manuscript, *De Principiis Astronomie*, preserved in the British Museum among the Sloane manuscripts.[4]   It closely resembles the Finæus map.   The authorities place it about 1530, or a little later.   In 1533, in his *Opusculum Geographicum*, Schöner maintained that the city of Mexico was the Quinsay of Marco Polo ; and about the same time Francis I., in commissioning Cartier for his explorations, calls the St. Lawrence valley a part of Asia.

What is known as the Nancy Globe preserved the same idea, as will be seen by the sketch of it annexed, which follows an engraving published in the *Compte Rendu* of the

---

[1] This follows a drawing in Kohl's Washington Collection.

[2] Vol. III. p. 11.   This reduction, there made from Stevens's *Notes*, pl. iv., is copied on a reduced scale in Bancroft's *Central America*, vol. i. p. 149.   Stevens also gives a fac-simile of the original, and a greatly reduced reproduction is given in Daly's *Early Cartography*.   Its names,

as Harrisse has pointed out (*Cabots*, p. 182), are similar to the two Weimar charts of 1527 and 1529.   The bibliography of this Paris Grynæus is examined elsewhere.

[3] *Bibl. Amer. Vet., Additions*, no. 127.

[4] *Brit. Mus. Cat. of Maps*, 1844, p. 22.

[5] This follows a sketch given by Dr. Kohl in his *Discovery of Maine*, pl. xv., which is also

THE NANCY GLOBE.

Congrès des Américanistes.[1] The same view is maintained in a manuscript map of Ruscelli, the Italian geographer, preserved in the British Museum. Perhaps the earliest instance of a connection of America and Europe, such as Ruscelli here imagines, is the map of "Schondia," which Ziegler the Bavarian published in his composite work at Strasburg in 1532,[2] in which it will be observed he makes "Bacallaos" a part of Greenland, preserving the old notion prevailing before Columbus, as shown in the maps of the latter part of the fifteenth century, that Greenland was in fact a prolongation of northwestern Europe, as Ziegler indicates at the top of his map, the western half of which only is here reproduced. In this feature, as in others, there is a resemblance in these maps of Ziegler and Ruscelli to two maps by Jacopo Gastaldi, "le coryphée des géographes de péninsule

copied in Bancroft's *Central America*, vol. i. p. 148. Cf. Lelewel, p. 170; Peschel, *Geschichte der Erdkunde* (1865), p. 371.

VOL. II. — 55.

[1] Vol. for 1877, p. 359. Cf. the present History, Vol. I. p. 214; II. 81.
[2] See Vol. III. p. 18.

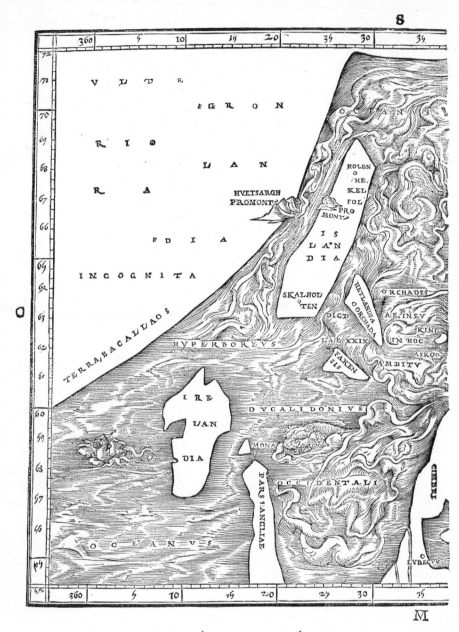

ZIEGLER'S SCHONDIA, 1532.[1]

italique," as Lelewel[2] calls him. These maps appeared in the first Italian edition of Ptolemy, published at Venice in 1548.[3] The first (no. 59), inscribed "Dell' universale

[1] This is a fac-simile made from Mr. Charles Deane's (formerly the Murphy) copy. Cf. Dr. A. Breusing's *Leitfaden durch das Wiegenalter der Kartographie bis zum Jahre* 1600, Frankfurt a. M., 1883, p. 11.

[2] *Epilogue*, p. 219.

[3] This edition was in small octavo, with sixty maps, engraved on metal, of which there are seven of interest to students of American cartography. They are of South America (no. 54),

nuova," is an elliptical projection of the globe, showing a union of America and Asia, somewhat different in character of contour from that represented in the other (no. 60), a " Carta Marina Universale," of which an outline sketch is annexed. This same map was

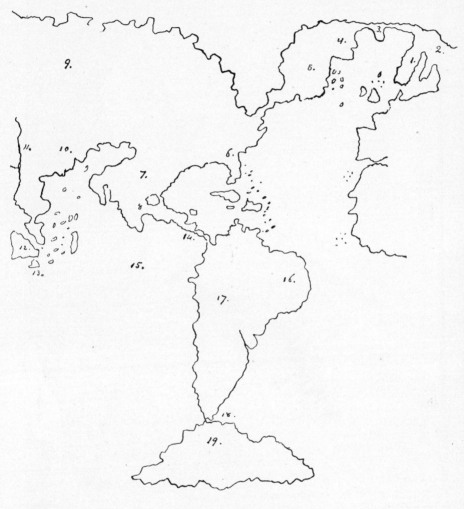

CARTA MARINA, 1548.[1]

New Spain (no. 55), "Terra nova Bacalaos" or Florida to Labrador (no. 56), Cuba (no. 57), and Hispaniola (no. 58). The copies in America which have fallen under the Editor's observation are those in the Library of Congress, in the Astor and Carter-Brown libraries, and in the collections of Mr. Barlow and Mr. Kalbfleisch in New York, and of Prof. Jules Marcou in Cambridge. There was one in the Murphy Collection, no. 2,067. It is worth from $15 to $25. Cf. on Gastaldi's maps, Zurla's *Marco Polo* ii. 368; the *Notizie di Jacopo Gastaldi*, Torino, 1881;

Castellani's *Catalogo delle più rare opere geografiche*, Rome, 1876, and other references in Winsor's *Bibliography of Ptolemy*, sub anno 1548; and Vol. IV. p. 40 of the present History.

[1] The key is as follows: 1. Norvegia. 2. Laponia. 3. Gronlandia. 4. Tierra del Labrador. 5. Tierra del Bacalaos. 6. La Florida. 7. Nueva Hispania. 8. Mexico. 9. India Superior. 10. La China. 11. Ganges. 12. Samatra. 13. Java. 14. Panama. 15. Mar del Sur. 16. El Brasil. 17. El Peru. 18. Strecho de Fernande Magalhaes. 19. Tierra del Fuego. This map is also repro-

VOPELLIO, 1556.
(Reduction of western half.)

adopted (as no. 2) by Ruscelli in the edition of Ptolemy which he published at Venice in 1561,[1] though in the "Orbis descriptio" (no. 1) of that edition Ruscelli hesitates to accept

duced in Nordenskiöld's *Bröderna Zenos*, Stockholm, 1883.

[1] This edition is in small quarto and contains six American maps: no. 1, "Orbis De-

the Asiatic theory, and indicates a "littus incognitum," as Gastaldi did in the map which he made for Ramusio in 1550.

scriptio;" no. 2, "Carta Marina;" no. 3, a reproduction of the Zeni map; no. 4, "Schonlandia" (Greenland region, etc.); no. 5, South America; no. 6, New Spain; no. 7, "Tierra nueva," or eastern coast of North America; no. 8, Brazil; no. 9, Cuba; no. 10, Hispaniola. These maps were repeated in the 1562, 1564, and 1574 editions of Ptolemy. The copies in

Wuttke [1] has pointed out two maps preserved in the Palazzo Riccardi at Florence, which belong to about the year 1550, and show a similar Asiatic connection.[2] The map of Gaspar Vopellius, or Vopellio (1556), also extended the California coast to the Ganges.   It appeared in connection with Girava's *Dos Libros de Cosmographia*, Milan, 1556,[3] but when a new titlepage was given to the same sheets in 1570, it is doubtful if the map was retained, though Sabin says it should have the map.[4]   The Italian cartographer, Paulo de Furlani, made a map in 1560, which according to Kohl is preserved in the British Museum.   It depicts Chinamen and elephants in the region of the Mississippi Valley.   From Kohl's sketch, preserved in his manuscript in the library of the American Antiquarian Society, the annexed outline is drawn.   Furlani is reported to have received it from a

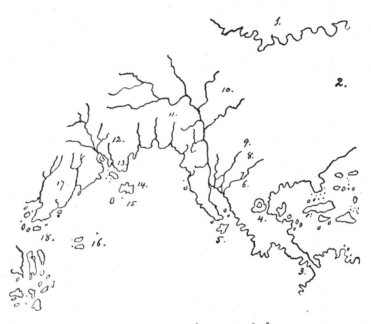

PAULO DE FURLANI'S MAP, 1560.[5]

America of these editions known to the Editor are in the following libraries : Library of Congress, 1561, 1562, 1574; Boston Public Library, 1561; Harvard College Library, 1562; Carter-Brown Library, 1561, 1562, 1564, 1574; Philadelphia Library, 1574; Astor Library, 1574; S. L. M. Barlow's, 1562, 1564; James Carson Brevoort's, 1562; J. Hammond Trumbull's, 1561; Trinity College (Hartford), 1574; C. C. Baldwin's (Cleveland) 1561; Murphy Catalogue, 1561, 1562, 1574, — the last two bought by President A. D. White of Cornell University.   These editions of Ptolemy's *Geographica* are described, and their American maps compared with the works of other contemporary cartographers, in Winsor's *Bibliog. of Ptolemy's Geography* (1884).

[1] *Jahresbericht des Vereins für Erdkunde in Dresden*, 1870, pages 62 ; plates vi., vii., ix.

[2] These and other maps of the Palazzo are noted in *Studi biografici e bibliografici della società geografica italiana*, Rome, 1882, ii. 169, 172.

[3] *Carter-Brown Catalogue*, i. 209; Leclerc, *Bibliotheca Americana*, no. 240; *Murphy Catalogue*, no. 1,047.   The map is very rare.   Henry Stevens published a fac-simile made by Harris. This and a fac-simile of the title of the book are annexed.   Cf. Orozco y Berra, *Cartografia Mexicana*, 37.

[4] Sabin, *Dictionary of books relating to America*, vii. 27,504; Stevens, *Historical Collections*, i. 2,413 (books sold in London, July, 1881).   The Harvard College copy lacks the map.   Mr. Brevoort's copy has the map, and that gentleman thinks it belongs to this edition as well as to the other.

[5] The key is this : 1. Oceano settentrionale. 2. Canada. 3. panaman. 4. Mexico. 5. s. tomas. 6. Nova Ispania.   7. Cipola.   8. Le sete cita. 9. Topira. 10. tontontean. 11. Zangar. 12. Tebet. 13. Quisai.   14. Cimpaga.   15. Golfo di Tonza. 16. Ys. de las ladrones. 17. mangi. 18. mar de la china.

Spanish nobleman, Don Diego Hermano, of Toledo.[1] The connection with Asia is again adhered to in Johannes Myritius's *Opusculum geographicum*, where the map is dated 1587, though the book was published at Ingolstadt in 1590.[2] Just at this time Livio Sanuto, in his *Geografia distinta* (Venice, 1588), was disputing the Asiatic theory on the ground that the Mexicans would not have shown surprise at horses in Cortés' time, if they had formerly been inhabitants of a continent like Asia, where horses are common. Perhaps the latest use of the type of map shown in the "Carta Marina" of 1548 was just a half century later, in 1598, in an edition of Ortelius, *Il Theatro del mondo*, published at Brescia. The belief still lingered for many years yet in some quarters; and Thomas Morton in 1636 showed that in New England it was not yet decided whether the continent of America did not border upon the country of the Tartars.[3] Indeed, the last trace of the assumption was not blown away till Behring in 1728 passed from the Pacific to the Arctic seas.

Such is in brief the history of the inception and decline of the belief in the prolongation of Asia over against Spain, as Toscanelli had supposed in 1474, and as had been suspected by geographers at intervals since the time of Eratosthenes.[4] The beginning of the decline of such belief is traced to the movements of Cortés. Balboa in 1513 by his discovery of the South Sea, later to be called the Pacific Ocean,[5] had established the continental form of South America, whose limits southward were fixed by Magellan in 1520; but it was left for Cortés to begin the exploration to the north which Behring consummated.

After the Congress of Badajos had resolved to effect a search for a passage through the American barrier to the South Sea, the news of such a determination was not long in reaching Cortés in Mexico, and we know from his fourth letter, dated Oct. 15, 1524, that it had already reached him, and that he had decided to take part in the quest himself by despatching an expedition towards the Baccalaos on the hither side; while he strove also to connect with the discoveries of Magellan on the side of the South Sea.[6] Cortés had already been led in part by the reports of Balboa's discovery, and in part by the tidings which were constantly reaching him of a great sea in the direction of Tehuantepec, to establish a foothold on its coast, as the base for future maritime operations. So his explorers had found a fit spot in Zacatula, and thither he had sent colonists and shipwrights to establish a town and build a fleet,[7] the Emperor meanwhile urging him speedily to use the vessels in a search for the coveted strait, which would open a shorter passage than Magellan had found to the Spice Islands.[8] But Cortés' attention was soon distracted by his Honduras expedition, and nothing was done till he returned from that march, when he wrote to the Emperor, Sept. 3, 1526, offering to conduct his newly built fleet to the

---

[1] The Catalogue of the British Museum puts under 1562 a map by Furlani called *Univerales Descrittione di tutta la Terra cognosciuta da Paulo di Forlani*. A "carta nautica" of the same cartographer, now in the Bibliothèque Nationale at Paris, is figured in Santarem's *Atlas*. (Cf. *Bulletin de la Société de Géographie*, 1839; and *Studi biografici e bibliografici*, ii. p. 142). Thomassy in his *Papes géographes*, p. 118, mentions a Furlani (engraved) map of 1565, published at Venice, and says it closely resembles the Gastaldi type. Another, of 1570, is contained in Lafreri's *Tavole moderne di geografia*, Rome and Venice, 1554–1572 (cf. Manno and Promis, *Notizie di Gastaldi*, 1881, p. 19; Harrisse, *Cabots*, p. 237). Furlani, in 1574, as we shall see, had dissevered America and Asia. As to Diego Hermano, cf. Willes' *History of Trauvayle* (London, 1577) fol. 232, *verso*.

[2] There are copies in the Library of Con-gress and in the Carter-Brown Library. Dufossé recently priced it at 25 francs.

[3] Morton's *New English Canaan*, Adams's edition, p. 126.

[4] See *ante*, p. 104.

[5] Magellan and his companions seem to have given the latter name, according to Pigafetta, and Galvano and others soon adopted the name. (Cf. Bancroft, *Central America*, vol. i. pp. 135, 136, 373; and the present volume, *ante*, p. 196).

[6] Brevoort (*Verrazano*, p. 80) suspects that the Vopellio map of 1556 represents the geographical views of Cortés at this time. Mr. Brevoort has a copy of this rare map. See *ante*, p. 436, for fac-simile.

[7] Cf. collation of references in Bancroft, *No. Mexican States*, i. 18; *Northwest Coast*, i. 13.

[8] Pacheco, *Coleccion de documentos inéditos*, xxiii. 366.

Moluccas. But two other fleets were already on the way thither, — one under Garcia de Loaysa which left Spain in August, 1525, and the other under Sebastian Cabot, who stopped on the way at La Plata, had left in April, 1526. So Cortés finally received orders

THE PACIFIC, 1513.[1]

to join with his fleet that of Loaysa, who had indeed died on his voyage, and of his vessels only one had reached the Moluccas. Another, however, had sought a harbor not far

[1] Kohl gives this old Portuguese chart of the Pacific in his Washington Collection, after an original preserved in the military archives at Munich, which was, as he thinks possible, made by some pilot accompanying Antonio da Miranda de Azevedo, who conducted a Portuguese fleet to the Moluccas in 1513 to join the earlier expedition (1511) under D'Abreu and Serraõ. A legend at Maluca marks these islands as the place "where the cloves grow," while the group south of them is indicated as the place "where nutmegs grow." The coast on the right must stand for the notion then prevailing of the main of America, which was barring the Spanish progress from the east.

Of the early maps of the Moluccas, there is one by Baptista Agnese in his *portolano* of 1536, preserved in the British Museum; one by Diego

from Zacatula, and had brought Cortés partial tidings at least of the mishaps of Loaysa's undertaking.[1] What information the rescued crew could give was made use of, and Cortés, bearing the whole expense, for a reimbursement of which he long sued the home Government, sent out his first expedition on the Pacific, under the command of his cousin Alvaro de Saavedra Ceron, armed with letters for Cabot, whose delay at La Plata was not suspected, and with missives for sundry native potentates of the Spice Islands and that region.[2]

After an experimental trip up the coast, in July, 1527,[3] two larger vessels and a brigantine set sail Oct. 31, 1527. But mishap was in store. Saavedra alone reached the Moluccas, the two other vessels disappearing forever. He found there a remnant of Loaysa's party, and, loading his ship with cloves, started to return, but died midway, when the crew headed their ship again for the Moluccas, where they fell at last into Portuguese prisons, only eight of them finally reaching Spain in 1534.

It will be remembered that the Portuguese, following in the track of Vasco da Gama, had pushed on beyond the great peninsula of India, and had reached the Moluccas in 1511, where they satisfied themselves, if their longitude was substantially correct, that there was a long space intervening yet before they would confront the Spaniards, pursuing their westerly route. It was not quite so certain, however, whether the line of papal demarcation, which had finally been pushed into the mid-ocean westerly from the Azores, would on this opposite side of the globe give these islands to Spain or to themselves. The voyage of Magellan, as we shall see, seemed to bring the solution near; and if we may believe Scotto, the Genoese geographer, at about the same date (1520) the Portuguese had crossed the Pacific easterly and struck our northwest coast.[4] The mishaps of Loaysa and Saavedra, as well as a new understanding between the rival crowns of the Iberian peninsula, closed the question rather abruptly through a sale in 1529 — the treaty of Saragossa — by Spain, for 350,000 ducats, to Portugal of all her rights to the Moluccas under the bull of demarcation.[5]

Cortés, on his return from Spain (1530), resolved to push his discoveries farther up the coast. The Spaniards had now occupied Tehuantepec, Acapulco, and Zacatula on the sea, and other Spaniards were also to be found at Culiacan, just within the Gulf of California on its eastern shore. The political revolutions in Cortés' absence had caused the suspension of work on a new fleet, and Cortés was obliged to order the construction of another; and the keels of two were laid at Tehuantepec, and two others at Acapulco. In the early part of 1532 they were launched, and in May or June two ships started under Hurtado de Mendoza, with instructions which are preserved to us. It is a matter of doubt just how far he went,[6] and both vessels were lost. Nuño de Guzman, who held the region to the north,[7] obstructed their purpose by closing his harbors to them and refusing succor; and Cortés was thus made to feel the deadliness of his rivalry. The conqueror now himself repaired to Tehuantepec, and superintended in person, working with his men, the construction of two other ships. These, the "San Lazaro" and "Concepcion," under Diego Becerra, left port on the 29th of October, 1533, and being blown to sea, they first saw land in the latitude of 29° 30' north on the 18th of December, when, coasting south and east, they developed the lower parts of the Californian peninsula. Mutiny, and attacks of

Homem in a similar atlas, dated 1558, likewise in the Museum; and one of 1568, by J. Martines. Copies of these are all included in Kohl's Washington Collection.

[1] Bancroft, *Mexico*, ii. 258.

[2] These are given in Navarrete, v. 442. Cf. other references in Bancroft, *Mexico*, ii. 258, where his statements are at variance with those in his *Central America*, i. 143.

[3] *Documentos inéditos*, xiv. 65, where a report describes this preliminary expedition.

[4] In 1524 Francisco Cortés in his expedition

to the Jalisco coast heard from the natives of a wooden house stranded there many years earlier, which may possibly refer to an early Portuguese voyage. H. H. Bancroft, *North Mexican States*, i. 15.

[5] Prescott, *Ferdinand and Isabella*, ii. 180, and references.

[6] Cf. Bancroft, *North Mexican States*, vol. i. chap. iii., on this voyage, with full references.

[7] Cf. Bancroft, *North Mexican States*, vol. i. chap. ii., with references; p. 29, on Guzman's expedition, and a map of it, p. 31.

the natives, during one of which the chief pilot Ximenes was killed, were the hapless accompaniments of the undertaking, and during stress of weather the vessels were separated. The "San Lazaro" finally returned to Acapulco, but the "Concepcion" struggled in a crippled condition into a port within Guzman's province, where the ship was seized. A quarrel ensued before the *Audiencia*, Cortés seeking to recover his vessel; but he prospered little in his suit, and was driven to undertake another expedition under his own personal lead. Sending three armed vessels up the coast to Chiametla, where Guzman had seized the "Concepcion," Cortés went overland himself, accompanied by a force which Guzman found it convenient to avoid. Here he joined his vessels and sailed away with a part of his land forces to the west; and on the 1st of May, 1535, he landed at the Bay of Santa Cruz, where Ximenes had been killed. What parts of the lower portion of the Californian peninsula Cortés now coasted we know from his map, preserved in the Spanish Archives,[1] which accompanied the account of his taking possession of the new land of Santa Cruz, "discovered by Cortés, May 3, 1535," as the paper reads. The point of occupation seems to have been the modern La Paz, called by him Santa Cruz. The notary's account of the act of possession goes on to say,[2] —

"On the third day of May, in the year of our Lord 1535, on the said day, it may be at the hour of noon, be the same less or more, the very illustrious Lord don Hernando Cortés, Marquis of the Valley of Guaxaca, Captain-general of New Spain and of the Southern Sea for his Majesty, etc., arrived in a port and bay of a country newly discovered in the same Southern Sea, with a ship and armament of the said Lord Marquis, at which said port his Lordship arrived with ships and men, and landed on the earth with his people and horses; and standing on the shore of the sea there, in presence of me Martin de Castro, notary of their Majesties and notary of the Administration of the said Lord Marquis, and in presence of the required witnesses, the said Lord Marquis spoke aloud and said that he, in the name of His Majesty, and in virtue of his royal provision, and in fulfilment of His Majesty's instructions regarding discovery in the said Southern Sea, had discovered with his ship and armament the said land, and that he had come with his armament and people to take possession of it."

Finding his men and horses insufficient for the purposes of the colony which he intended to establish, Cortés despatched orders to the main for assistance, and, pending its arrival, coursed up the easterly side of the gulf, and opportunely fell in with one of his vessels, much superior to his own brigantine. So he transferred his flag, and, returning to Santa Cruz, brought relief to an already famishing colony.

News reaching him of the appointment of Mendoza as viceroy, Cortés felt he had greater stake in Mexico, and hurriedly returned.[3] Not despairing of better success in another trial, and spurred on by indications that the new viceroy would try to anticipate him, he got other vessels, and, putting Francisco de Ulloa in charge, despatched them (July 8, 1539) before Guzman's plan for their detention could be put into execution. Ulloa proceeded up the gulf nearly to its head, and satisfied himself that no practicable water passage, at least, could bring him to the ocean in that direction, as Cortés had supposed.[4] Ulloa now turned south, and following the easterly coast of the peninsula rounded its extremity, and coursed it northerly to about 28° north latitude, without finding any cut-off on that side. So he argued for its connection with the main.[5] And here

---

[1] The Rev. Edward E. Hale procured a copy of this when in Spain in 1883, and from his copy the annexed wood-cut is made. Cf. Gomara, folio 117; Herrera, Decade viii. lib. viii. cap. ix. and x. Bancroft (*Central America*, i. 150) writes without knowledge of this map.

[2] The Spanish is printed in Navarrete, iv. 190.

[3] This expedition of Cortés is not without difficulties in reconciling authorities and tracing the fate of the colonists which he sought

to plant at Santa Cruz. Bancroft has examined the various accounts (*North Mexican States*, i. 52, etc.).

[4] Cortés had called California an island as early as 1524, in a report to the Emperor, deducing his belief from native reports. De Laet in 1633 mentions having seen early Spanish maps showing it of insular shape.

[5] Cf. Prescott's *Mexico*, iii. 322; Bancroft's *Mexico*, ii. 425; *Central America*, i. 152, and *North Mexican States*, i. 79, with references. The

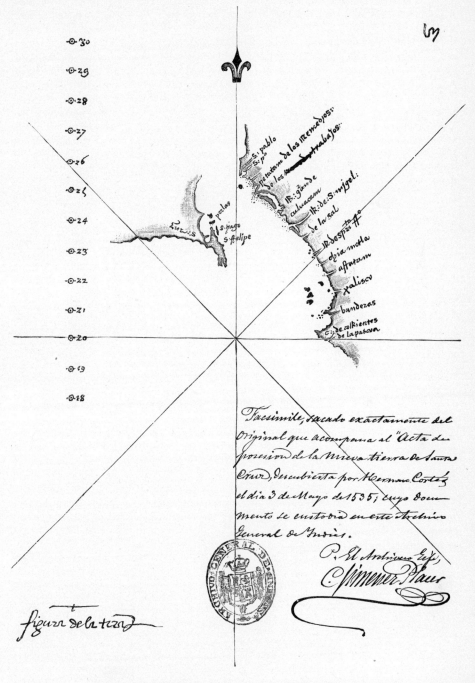

Cortés' connection with discoveries on the Pacific ends ; for Mendoza, who had visions of his own, thwarted him in all subsequent attempts, till finally Cortés himself went to Spain. The name which his captains gave to the gulf, the Sea of Cortés, failed to abide. It grew to be generally called the Red Sea, out of some fancied resemblance, as Wytfliet says, to the Red Sea of the Old World. This appellation was supplanted in turn by the name of California, which, it is contended, was given to the peninsula by Cortés himself.[1]

The oldest map which we were supposed to possess of these explorations about the gulf,[2] before Dr. Hale brought the one, already mentioned, from Spain, was that of Castillo, of which a fac-simile is herewith given as published by Lorenzana in 1770, at Mexico, in his *Historia de Nueva España.* Castillo was the pilot of the expedition, sent by Mendoza to co-operate by sea with the famous expedition of Coronado,[3] and which the viceroy put under the command of Hernando d'Alarcon. The fleet, sailing in May, 1540, reached the head of the gulf, and Alarcon ascended the Colorado in boats ; but Marcou[4] thinks he could not have gone up to the great cañon, which however he must have reached if his supposed latitude of 36° is correct. He failed to open communication with Coronado, but buried some letters under a cross, which one of that leader's lieutenants subsequently found.[5]

accounts are not wholly reconcilable. It would seem probable that Ulloa's own ship was never heard from. Ramusio gives a full account (vol. iii. p. 340) by one of the companions of Ulloa, on another ship.

[1] At least so says Herrera (Stevens's edition, vi. 305). Castañeda defers the naming till Alarcon's expedition. Cabrillo in 1542 used the name as of well-known application. The origin of the name has been a cause of dispute. Professor Jules Marcou is in error in stating that the name was first applied by Bernal Diaz to a bay on the coast, and so was made to include the whole region. He claims that it was simply a designation used by Cortés to distinguish a land which we now know to be the hottest in the two Americas, — Tierra California, derived from "calida fornax," fiery furnace. (Cf. *Annual Report of the Survey west of the hundredth Parallel,* by George M. Wheeler, 1876, p. 386; and *Annual Report of the Chief of Engineers,* U.S.A., 1878, appendix, also printed separately as *Notes upon the First Discoveries of California and the Origin of its Name,* by Jules Marcou, Washington, 1878.) Bancroft (*California,* i. 65, 66) points out a variety of equivalent derivations which have been suggested. The name was first traced in 1862, by Edward E. Hale, to a romance published, it is supposed, in 1510, — *Las Sergas de Esplandian,* by Garcia Ordoñez de Montalvo, which might easily enough have been a popular book with the Spanish followers of Cortés. There were later editions in 1519, 1521, 1525, and 1526. In this romance Esplandian, emperor of the Greeks, the imaginary son of the imaginary Amadis, defends Constantinople against the infidels of the East. A pagan queen of Amazons brings an army of Amazons to the succor of the infidels. This imaginary queen is named Calafia, and her kingdom is called "California," — a name possibly derived from "Calif," which, to the readers of such a book, would

be associated with the East. California in the romance is represented as an island rich with gold and diamonds and pearls. The language of the writer is this : —

"Know that on the right hand of the Indies there is an island called California, very close to the side of the Terrestrial Paradise; and it was peopled by black women, without any man among them, for they lived in the fashion of Amazons. They were of strong and hardy bodies, of ardent courage and great force. Their island was the strongest in all the world, with its steep cliffs and rocky shores. Their arms were all of gold, and so was the harness of the wild beasts which they tamed to ride ; for in the whole island there was no metal but gold. They lived in caves wrought out of the rock with much labor. They had many ships, with which they sailed out to other countries to obtain booty."

That this name, as an omen of wealth, struck the fancy of Cortés is the theory of Dr. Hale, who adds "that as a western pioneer now gives the name of 'Eden' to his new home, so Cortés called his new discovery 'California.'" (Cf. Hale in *Amer. Antiq. Soc. Proc.,* April 30, 1862; in *Historical Magazine,* vi. 312, Oct. 1862; in *His Level Best,* p. 234; and in *Atlantic Monthly,* xiii. 265; J. Archibald in *Overland Monthly,* ii. 437, Prof. J. D. Whitney in article "California" in *Encyclopædia Britannica.*) Bancroft (*North Mexican States,* vol. i. p. 82; and *California,* vol. i. p. 64) points out how the earliest use of the name known to us was in Preciado's narrative (Ramusio, vol. iii. p. 343) of Ulloa's voyage; and that there is no evidence of its use by Cortés himself. It was applied then to the bay or its neighborhood, which had been called Santa Cruz or La Paz.

[2] Kohl, *Maps in Hakluyt,* p. 58.

[3] Cf. *post,* chap. vii.

[4] *Notes,* etc., p. 4.

[5] We have Alarcon's narrative in Ramusio, iii. 363; Herrera, Dec. vi. p. 208; Hakluyt, iii.

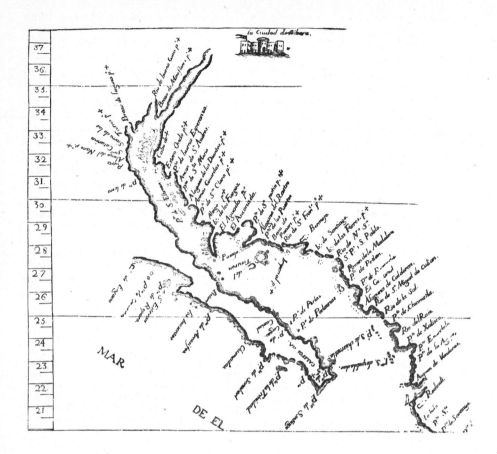

CASTILLO'S MAP, 1541.[1]

In 1542 and 1543 an expedition which started under Juan Rodriguez Cabrillo, a Portuguese in the Spanish service, explored the coast as far as 44° north,[2] reaching that
point by coasting from 33°, where he struck the land. He made a port which he calls
San Miguel, which Bancroft is inclined to believe is San Diego; but the accounts are too
confused to track him confidently,[3] and it is probable that Cabrillo's own vessel did
not get above 38°, for Cabrillo himself died Jan. 3, 1543, his chief pilot, Ferrelo (or
Ferrer), continuing the explorations.[4] Bancroft does not think that the pilot passed
north of Cape Mendocino in 40° 26'.

425, 505; Ternaux-Compans' *Voyages*, etc., ix.
299. Bancroft (*North Mexican States*, vol. i.
p. 93) gives various references. An intended
second expedition under Alarcon, with a co-operating fleet to follow the outer coast of the peninsula, failed of execution. The instructions
given in 1541 to Alarcon for his voyage on the
California coast, by order of Mendoza, are given
in B. Smith's *Coleccion*, p. 1.

[1] This map is marked "Domingo del Castillo, piloto me fecit en Mexico, año del naci-
miento de N. S. Jesu Christo de M. D. XLI."

Bancroft, *Central America*, vol. i. p. 153, gives
a sketch of this map, and again in *North Mexican States*, i. 81; but he carries the outer coast
of the peninsula too far to the west.

[2] These are the ship's figures; but it is
thought their reckoning was one or two degrees
too high.

[3] Attempts have been made. Cf. Bancroft,
California, i. 70; *Northwest Coast*, i. 38.

[4] The source of our information for this voyage is a *Relacion* (June 27, 1542, to April 14,
1543) printed in Pacheco's *Coleccion de docu-

Thus from the time when Balboa discovered the South Sea, the Spanish had taken thirty years to develop the coast northerly, to the latitude of Oregon. In this distance they had found nothing of the Straits of Anian, which, if Humboldt[1] is correct, had begun to take form in people's minds ever since Cortereal, in 1500, had supposed Hudson's Straits to be the easterly entrance of a westerly passage.[2]

There seems to have been a general agreement among cartographers for some years yet to consider the newly discovered California as a peninsula, growing out of the concurrent testimony of those who, subsequent to Cortés' own expedition, had tracked both the gulf and the outer coast. The Portuguese map given by Kunstmann[3] shows it as such, though the map cannot be so early as that geographer places its anterior limit (1530), since the development of the gulf could not have been made earlier than 1535, unless by chance there were explorations from the Moluccas, of which we have no record. The map in this part bears a close resemblance to a manuscript chart in the British Museum, placed about 1536, and it seems probable that this is the approximate date of that in Kunstmann. The California peninsula is shown in much the same way in a map which Major ascribes to Baptista Agnese, and places under 1539.[4] It belongs (pl. iv.) to what has been sometimes spoken of as an atlas of Philip II. inscribed to Charles V., but in fact it was given to Philip by Charles.[5] Its essential features were almost exactly

mentos inéditos, xiv. 165; and very little is added from other sources, given in Bancroft, *North Mexican States,* i. 133. Buckingham Smith gave the *Relacion* earlier in his *Coleccion de varios Documentos para la historia de la Florida y Tierras adyacentes* (Madrid, 1857, vol. i. p. 173). A translation is contained in Wheeler's *United States Geological Survey,* vol. vii., with notes, and an earlier English version by Alexander S. Taylor was published in San Francisco in 1853, as *The First Voyage to the Coast of California.* Cf. also Bancroft's *California,* i. 69; *Northwest Coast,* i. 137. It is thought that Juan Paez was the author of the original, which is preserved among the Simancas papers at Seville. Herrera seems to have used it, omitting much and adding somewhat, thus making the narrative which, till the original was printed, supplied the staple source to most writers on the subject. In 1802 Navarrete summarized the story from this *Relacion* in vol. xv. of his *Documentos inéditos.* Bancroft (vol. i. p. 81) cites numerous unimportant references.

[1] *Nouvelle Espagne* (i. 330), where, as well as in other of the later writers, it is said the name "Anian" came from one of Cortereal's companions. But see H. H. Bancroft, *Northwest Coast,* vol. i. pp. 36, 55, 56, where he conjectures that the name is a confused reminiscence at a later day of the name of *Anus* Cortereal, mentioned by Hakluyt in 1582.

[2] There was at one time a current belief in the story of a Dutch vessel being driven through such a strait to the Pacific, passing the great city of Quivira, which had been founded by the Aztecs after they had been driven from Mexico by the Spaniards. Then there are similar stories told by Menendez (1554) and associated with Urdaneta's name (cf. Bancroft, *Northwest*

Coast, vol. i. p. 51); and at a later day other like stories often prevailed. The early maps place the "Regnum Anian" and "Quivira" on our northwestern coast. Bancroft (*Northwest Coast,* vol. i. pp. 45, 49) thinks Gomara responsible for transferring Quivira from the plains to the coast. See Editorial Note at the end of chap. vii.

It is sometimes said (see Bancroft, *Northwest Coast,* vol. i. p. 55) that the belief in the Straits of Anian sprang from a misinterpretation of a passage in Marco Polo; but Bancroft (p. 53) cannot trace the name back of 1574, as he finds it in one of the French (Antwerp) editions of Ortelius of that year. Ortelius had used the name, however, in his edition of 1570, but only as a copier, in this as in other respects, of Mercator, in his great map of 1569, as Bancroft seems to suspect. Porcacchi (1572), Furlani or Forlani (1574), and others put the name on the Asian side of the strait, where it is probable that it originally appeared. Bancroft (p. 81) is in error in saying that the name "Anian" was "for the first time" applied to the north and south passage between America and Asia, as distinct from the east and west passage across the continent, in the "Mercator Atlas of 1595;" for such an application is apparent in the map of Zalterius (1566), Mercator (1569), Porcacchi (1572), Forlani (1574), Best's Frobisher (1578), — not to name others.

[3] Sketched in this History, Vol. IV. p. 46.

[4] Harrisse (*Cabots,* p. 193) places it about 1542.

[5] It is described by Malte Brun in the *Bulletin de la Société de Géographie,* 1876, p. 625; and an edition of a hundred copies of a photographic reproduction, edited by Frédéric Spitzer, was issued in Paris in 1875. There

reproduced in a draft of the New World (preserved in the British Museum) assigned to about 1540, and held to be the work of the Portuguese hydrographer Homem. Apian[1] and

Münster[2] in 1540, and Mercator in 1541,[3] while boldly delineating a coast which extends farther north than Cabrillo had reached in 1542, wholly ignore this important feature. Not so, however, Sebastian Cabot in his famous Mappemonde of 1544, as will be seen by the annexed sketch. The idea of Münster, as embodied in his edition of Ptolemy in 1540,[4] already referred to, was continued without essential change in the Basle edition of Ptolemy in 1545.[5] In 1548 the " carta marina " of Gastaldi, as shown on a previous page,[6] clearly defined the peninsula, while merging

HOMEM, ABOUT 1540.[7]

is a copy of the last in Harvard College Library. A similar peninsula is shown in plate xiv. of the same atlas.

[1] Repeated in 1545.

[2] See Vol. IV. p. 41.

[3] See *ante*, p. 177.

[4] This edition, issued at Basle, had twenty modern maps designed by Münster, two of which have American interest : —

a. Typus universalis, — an elliptical map, showing America on the left, but with a part of Mexico (Temistitan) carried to the right of the map, with a strait — " per hoc fretū iter patet ad molucas " — separating America from India superior on the northwest.

b. Novæ insulæ, — the map reproduced in Vol. IV. p. 41.

There are copies of this 1540 edition of Ptolemy in the Astor Library, in the collections of Mr. Barlow, Mr. Deane, and President White of Cornell, while one is noted in the Murphy Catalogue, no. 2,058, which is now in the library of the American Geographical Society. This edition was issued the next year with the date changed to 1541. Cf. Winsor's *Bibliography of Ptolemy.* The same maps were also used in the Basle edition of 1542, with borders surrounding them, some of which were designs, perhaps, of Holbein. There are copies of this edition in the Astor Library, and in the collections of Brevoort, Barlow, and J. H. Trumbull, of Hartford. The *Murphy Catalogue* shows another, no. 2,066.

[5] The "Typus universalis " of this edition, much the same as in the edition of 1540, was re-engraved for the Basle edition of 1552, with a few changes of names : " Islandia," for instance, which is on the isthmus connecting " Bacalhos " with Norway, is left out, and so is " Thyle " on Iceland, which is now called " Island." This last engraving was repeated in Münster's *Cosmographia* in 1554.

There are copies of the Ptolemy of 1545 in the libraries of Congress and of Harvard College, and in the Carter-Brown Collection. One is also owned by J. R. Webster, of East Milton, Mass., and another is shown in the *Murphy Catalogue,* no. 2,078.

Copies of the 1552 edition are in the libraries of Congress, of New York State, and of Cornell University. The Sobolewski copy is now in the collection of Prof. J. D. Whitney, Cambridge, Mass. Dr. O'Callaghan's copy was sold in New York, in December, 1882; the Murphy copy is no. 2,065 of the *Murphy Catalogue.*

The maps were again reproduced in the Ptolemy of 1555.

[6] *Ante,* p. 435.

[7] This follows Kohl's drawing, of which a portion is also given in his *Discovery of Maine,* p. 298. It is evidently of a later date than another of his in which the west coast is left indefinite, and which is assigned to about 1530. In the present map he apparently em-

the coast line above into that of Asia. The peninsula was also definitely marked in several of the maps preserved in the Riccardi palace at Florence, which are supposed to be of about the middle of the sixteenth century.[1]

In the map of Juan Freire, 1546, we have a development of the coast northward from the peninsula, for which it is not easy to account; and the map is peculiar in other respects.

CABOT, 1544.[2]

The annexed sketch of it follows Kohl's drawing of an old *portolano*, which he took from the original while it was in the possession of Santarem. Freire, who was a Portuguese hydrographer, calls it a map of the Antipodes, a country discovered by Columbus, the Genoese. It will be observed that about the upper lake we have the name "Bimini regio," applied to Florida after the discovery of Ponce de Leon, because of the supposition that the fountain of youth existed thereabout. The coasts on both sides of the gulf are described as the discovery of Cortés. There seems to be internal evidence that Freire was acquainted with the reports of Ulloa and Alarcon, and the chart of Castillo; but it is not so clear whence he got the material for his draft of the more westerly portions of the coast, which, it will be observed, are given much too great a westerly trend. The names upon it do not indicate any use of Cabrillo's reports; though from an inscription upon this upper coast Freire credits its discovery to the Spaniards, under

bodied Cabot's discoveries in the La Plata, but had not heard of Orellana's exploration of the Amazon in 1542; though he had got news of it when he made his map of 1558. A marked peculiarity of the map is the prolongation of northwestern Europe as "Terra Nova," which probably means Greenland, — a view entertained before Columbus.

[1] Plates vi., vii., ix., as shown in the *Jahrbuch des Vereins für Erdkunde in Dresden*, 1870.

[2] Sketched from a photograph of the original mappemonde in the great library at Paris.

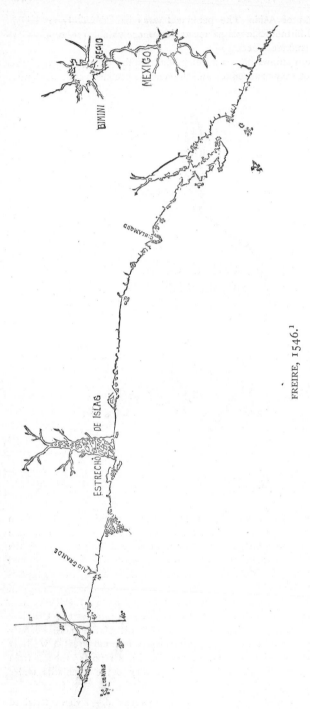

FREIRE, 1546.[1]

orders from the emperor, conducted by one Villalobos. Kohl could not find any mention of such an explorer, but conjectured he was perhaps the one who before Cabrillo, as Herrera mentions, had named a river somewhere near 30° north latitude " Rio de Nuestra Señora," and which Cabrillo sought. Kohl also observes that though the coast line is continuous, there are places upon it marked " land not seen," with notes of its being again seen west of such places; and from this he argues that the expedition went up and not down the coast. It not unlikely had some connection with the fleet which Ruy Lopez de Villalobos conducted under Mendoza's orders, in November, 1542, across the Pacific to the islands on the Asiatic coast.[2]

In 1554 Agnese again depicts the gulf, but does not venture upon drawing the coast above the peninsula, which in turn in the Vopellio map of 1556,[3] and in that in Ramusio the same year,[4] is made much broader, the gulf indenting more nearly at a right angle. The Homem map of 1558, preserved in the British Museum, returns to the more distinctive peninsula,[5] though it is again somewhat broadened in the Martines map of about the same date, which also is of interest as establish-

[1] This is sketched from a drawing in the Kohl Collection at Washington.

[2] Bancroft, *North Mexican States*, i. 137.

[3] See *ante*, p. 436.

[4] See *ante*, p. 228.

[5] This map of Homem is given on another page. His delineation of the gulf seems to be like Castillo's, and is carried two degrees too

ing a type of map for the shores of the northern Pacific, and for prefiguring Behring's Straits, which we shall later frequently meet. Mention has already been made of the Furlani map of 1560 for its Asiatic connections, while it still clearly defined the California peninsula.[1] The Ruscelli map in the Ptolemy of 1561 again preserves the peninsula, while marking the more northerly coasts with a dotted line, in its general map of the New World; but the "Mar Vermeio" in its map of "Nueva Hispania" is the type of the gulf given in the 1548 edition. The Martines type again appears in the Zaltieri map of 1566, which is thought to be the earliest engraved map to show the Straits of Anian.[2]

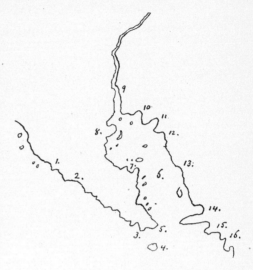

PTOLEMY, 1548.[4]

The manuscript map of Diegus (Homem) of 1568, in the Royal Library in Dresden, gives the peninsula, but turns the more northerly coast abruptly to the east, connecting it with the archipelago, which stands for the St. Lawrence in his map of 1558.[3]

The great Mappemonde of Mercator, published at Duisburg in 1569, in which he introduced his new projection,[5] as will be seen by the annexed sketch,[6] keeps to the Martines type; and while it depicts the Straits of Anian, it renders uncertain, by interposing a vignette, the passage by the north from the Atlantic to the Pacific.[7] The next year Ortelius followed the same type in his *Theatrum orbis terrarum*, — the prototype of the modern atlas.[8]

A similar western coast[9] is defined by Porcacchi, in his *L' isole piu famose del mondo*, issued at Venice in 1572.[10]

---

far north as in that draft; but Castillo's names are wanting in Homem, who lays down the peninsula better, following, as Kohl conjectures, Ulloa's charts. He marks the coast above 33° as unknown, showing that he had no intelligence of Cabrillo's voyage.

[1] See *ante*, p. 438.

[2] See *post*, p. 451.

[3] See Vol. IV. p. 92. The 1568 map is a part of an *Atlante maritimo,* of which a full-size colored fac-simile of the part showing the Moluccas is given in Ruge's *Geschichte des Zeitalters der Entdeckungen.* It is a parchment collection of twenty-seven maps showing the Portuguese possessions in the two Indies. Cf. *Katalog der Handschriften der Kais. Off. Bibl. zu Dresden,* 1882, vol. i. p. 369.

[4] Key: 1. Basos. 2. Ancoras. 3. p°. balenas. 4. S. Tomas. 5. C : + 6. Mar Vermeio. 7. b : canoas. 8. p°. secōdido. 9. R. tontonteanc. 10. p°. tabursa. 11. puercos. 12. s. franc°. 13. b : de s. + 14. Vandras. 15. Ciguata. 16. s. tiago.

VOL. II. — 57.

[5] See Vol. IV. p. 369; and the note, *post,* p. 470.

[6] See p. 452.

[7] There is a full-size fac-simile in Jomard's *Monuments de la Géographie,* pl. xxi., but it omits the legends given in the tablets; in Lelewel, vol. i. pl. v.; also cf. vol. i. p. xcviii, and vol. ii. pp 181, 225; and, much reduced from Jomard, in Daly's *Early Cartography,* p. 38.

[8] Cf. Vol III. p. 34; Vol. IV. p. 372; and the note, *post,* p. 471.

[9] See the map, *post,* p. 453.

[10] There are copies of this first edition in the Harvard College, Boston Public, Astor, and Carter-Brown libraries, and in the Brevoort Collection. It should have thirty small copperplate maps, inserted in the text. Cf. *Carter-Brown Catalogue,* vol. i. no. 292; Stevens, *Historical Collections,* vol. i. no. 648; *O'Callaghan Catalogue,* no. 1,866 (now Harvard College copy); Court, no. 284; Rich, *Catalogue* (1832), nos. 51, 55, etc.

Two of its maps show America, but only

The peninsula of California, but nothing north of it, is again delineated in a Spanish mappemonde of 1573, shown in Lelewel.[1] The Mercator type is followed in the maps which are dated 1574, but which appeared in the *Theatri orbis terrarum enchiridion* of Philippus Gallæus, published at Antwerp in 1585.[2] In the same year the Italian cartographer Furlani, or Forlani, showed how he had advanced from the views which he held in 1560, in a map of the north-

MARTINES, 155 − (?).[3]

and ii. p. 114. He says it was taken from Spain to Warsaw, and has disappeared.

[2] It has two maps, varying somewhat, "Typus orbis terrarum" and "Americæ sive novi orbis nuova descriptio," — the work of Hugo Favolius. Cf. Leclerc, no. 206; Muller (1877), no. 1,198. The text is in verse.

one gives the western coast, while both have the exaggerated continental Tierra del Fuego. The map sketched in the text is given in fac-simile in Stevens's *Notes*. Both maps were repeated in the 1576 edition (Venice, with 1575 in the colophon). This edition shows forty-seven maps; and pp. 157-184 (third book) treat of America. Besides a map of the world it has a "carta da navigar" (p. 198), maps of Cuba and other islands, and a plan of Mexico and its lake. There are copies in the Boston Public and Harvard College libraries, Mr. Deane's Collection, etc. Cf. Stevens, *Historical Collections*, vol. i. no. 82; Carter-Brown, vol. i. no. 309; Muller (1872), no. 1,255.

Another edition was issued at Venice in 1590. Cf. *Boston Public Library Catalogue*, no. 6271.14, Carter-Brown, i. 393; Murphy, no. 2,010. Later editions were issued at Venice in 1604 (forty-eight maps); in 1605 (Carter-Brown, ii. 40); and in 1620 (Carter-Brown, ii. 241; Cooke, no. 2,858, now in Harvard College Library), which was published at Padua, and had maps of North America (p. 161), Spagnolla (p. 165), Cuba (p. 172), Jamaica (p. 175), Moluccas (p. 189), and a mappemonde (p. 193). The last edition we have noted was issued at Venice in 1686, with the maps on separate leaves, and not in the text as previously.

[1] Plate vi. He describes it in vol. i. p. ci,

[3] This sketch follows a copy by Kohl (Washington Collection) of the general map of the world, contained in a manuscript vellum atlas in the British Museum (no. 9,814), from the collection of the Duke de Cassano Serra. It is elaborately executed with miniatures and figures. The language of the map is chiefly Italian, with some Spanish traces. Kohl believes it to be the work of Joannes Martines, the same whose atlas of 1578 is also in the Museum, and whose general map (1578) agrees in latitudes and other particulars with this. The present one lacks degrees of longitude, which the 1578 map has, as well as the name "America," wanting also in this. Kohl places it not long after the middle of the sixteenth century. In the *Catalogue of Manuscript Maps*, i. 29, the atlas of 1578 is mentioned as containing the following numbers relating to America: 1. The world. 2. The two hemispheres. 3. The world in gores. 10. West coast of America. 11. Coast of Mexico. 12-13. South America. 14. Gulf of Mexico. 15. Part of the east coast of North America.

In the Museum manuscripts, no. 22,018, is a *portolano* by Martines, dated 1579; and another, of date 1582, is entered in the 1844 edition of the *Catalogue of Manuscript Maps*, i. 31. Kohl's Washington Collection includes two Martines maps of 1578.

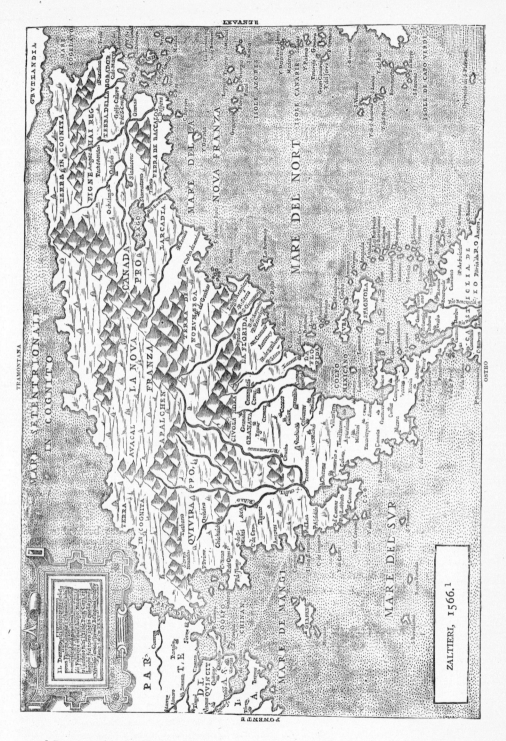

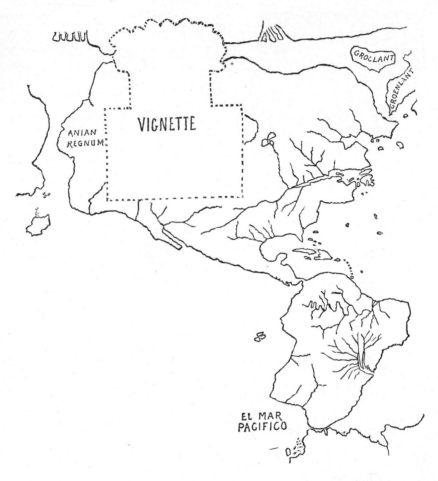

MERCATOR, 1569.

ern Pacific, which is annexed.[1] It is the earliest map in which Japan has been noted as having its greatest length east and west; for Ortelius and others always give it an extension on the line of the meridian.

Sir Humphrey Gilbert's map in 1576 gives the straits, but he puts "Anian" on the Asiatic side, and does not indicate the Gulf of California, unless a forked bay in 35° stands for it.[2] The map in Best's Frobisher makes the Straits of Anian connect with "Frobisher's straightes" to give a through passage from ocean to ocean, and depicts a distorted California peninsula.[3]

Mention has already been made on a previous page of a Martines map of 1578. It has a similar configuration to that already shown as probably the earliest instance of its type. Of the explorations of Francis Drake in 1579 we have no cartographical record, except as it may be embodied in the globe of Molineaux, preserved in the Middle Temple, London, which is dated 1592, and in the map of the same cartographer, dated

[1] See p. 454.
[2] Cf. the map, as given in Vol. III. p. 203. Bancroft (Northwest Coast, vol. i. p. 58) epito-

mizes Gilbert's arguments for a passage. Willes gives reasons in Hakluyt, vol. iii. p. 24.
[3] See fac-simile in Vol. III. p. 102.

PORCACCHI, 1572.

1600.[1] Molineaux seemingly made use of the results of Cabrillo's voyage, as indicated by the Spanish names placed along the coast.   It was one of the results of Drake's voyage that the coast line of upper California took a more northerly trend.   The map of Dr. Dee (1580) evidently embodied the views of the Spanish hydrographers.[2]

[1] Cf. the sketch of the California coast from this last in Vol. III. p. 80.

The question of the harbor in which Drake refitted his ship for his return voyage by Cape of Good Hope has been examined in another place (Vol. III. pp. 74, 80).   Since that volume was printed, H. H. Bancroft has published vol. i. of his *History of California*; and after giving a variety of references on Drake's voyage (p. 82) he proceeds to examine the question anew, expressing his own opinion decidedly against San Francisco, and believing it can never be settled whether Bodega or the harbor under Point Reyes (Drake's Bay of the modern maps) was the harbor; though on another page (p. 158) he thinks the spot was Drake's Bay, and in a volume previously issued (*Central America*, vol. ii. p. 419) he had given a decided opinion in favor of it. In his discussion of the question, he claims that Dr. Hale and most other investigators have not been aware that the harbor behind Point Reyes was discovered in 1595 by Cermeñon (p. 96), and then named San Francisco; and that it is this old San Francisco, visited by Viscaino in 1603, and sought by Portolá in 1769, when this latter navigator stumbled on the Golden Gate, which is the San Francisco of the old geographers and cartographers, and not the magnificent harbor now known by that name (p. 157).   He adds that the tradition among the Spaniards of the coast has been more in favor of Bodega than of Drake's Bay; while the modern San Francisco has never been thought of by them.   Beyond emphasizing the distinction between the old and new San Francisco, Mr. Bancroft has brought no new influence upon the solution of the question. He makes a point of a Pacific sea-manual of Admiral Cabrera Bueno, published at Manilla in 1734 as *Navegacion Especulation*, being used to set this point clear for the first time in English, when one of his assistants wrote a paper in the *Overland Monthly* in 1874.   The book is not very scarce; Quaritch advertised a copy in 1879 for £4.   Bancroft (p. 106) seems to use an edition of 1792, though he puts the 1734 edition in his list of authorities.   Various documents from the Spanish Archives relating to Drake's exploits in the Pacific have been published (since Vol. III. was printed) in Peralta's *Costa Rica, Nicaragua y Panamá en el siglo XVI*, Madrid, 1883, p. 569, etc.

[2] See the sketch in Vol. IV. p. 98.

In 1582 Popellinière [1] repeated the views of Mercator and Ortelius ; but in England Michael Lok in this same year began to indicate the incoming of more erroneous views. [2] The California gulf is carried north to 45°, where a narrow strip separates it from a vague northern sea, the western extension of the sea of Verrazano.

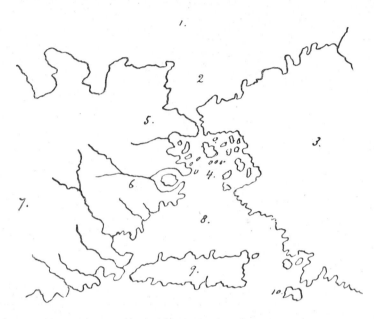

MAP OF PAULO DE FURLANI, 1574. [3]

After the Spaniards had succeeded, in opposition to the Portuguese, in establishing a regular commerce between Acapulco and Manilla (Philippine Islands), the trade-winds conduced to bring upper California into better knowledge. The easterly trades carried their outward-bound vessels directly west ; but they compelled them to make a détour northward on their return, by which they also utilized the same Japanese current which brought the Chinese to Fusang [4] many centuries before. An expedition which Don Luis de Velasco had sent in 1564, by direction of Philip II., accompanied by Andres de Urdaneta, who had been in those seas before with Loaysa in 1525, had succeeded in making a permanent occupation of the Philippines for Spain in 1564. It became now important to find a practicable return route, and under Urdaneta's counsel it was determined to try to find it by the north. One of the galleons deserted, and bearing northerly struck the California coast near Cape Mendocino, and arrived safe at Acapulco three months before Urdaneta

---

[1] Cf. Sabin, vol. x. p. 75; Court, 185, 186; Carter-Brown, vol. i. p. 292; Huth, iv. 1,169; Stevens's *Historical Collections*, vol. i. no. 135, and Vol. III. of the present History, p. 37, for other mention of Popellinière's *Les Trois Mondes*. The third world is the great Antarctic continent so common in maps of this time.

[2] Lok's map from Hakluyt's *Divers Voyages* is given in fac-simile in Vol. III. p. 40 and Vol. IV. p. 44. There is a sketch of it in Bancroft, *North Mexican States*, vol. i. p. 151, and in his *Northwest Coast*, vol. i. p. 65.

[3] Furlani is said to have received this map from a Spaniard, Don Diego Hermano de Toledo, in 1574. The sketch is made from the drawing in Kohl's manuscript in the American Antiquarian Society Library. The key is as follows : 1. Mare incognito. 2. Stretto di Anian. 3. Quivir. 4. Golfo di Anian. 5. Anian regnum. 6. Quisau. 7. Mangi Prov. 8. Mare de Mangi. 9. Isola di Giapan. 10. Y. de Cedri.

[4] The question of Fusang, which Kohl believes to be Japan, is discussed in Vol. I.

himself had proved the value of his theory.   The latter's course was to skirt the coast of Japan till under 38°, when he steered southerly; and after a hard voyage, in which he saw no land and most of his crew died, he reached Acapulco in October.[1] Other voyages were made in succeeding years, but the next of which we have particular account was that of Francisco Gali, who, returning from Macao in 1584, struck the California coast in 37° 30', and marked a track which other navigators later followed.[2]

The map (1587) in Hakluyt's Paris edition of Peter Martyr conformed more nearly to the Mercator type ;[3] and Hakluyt, as well as Lok, records Drake's discovery, both of them putting it, however, in 1580.

With the year 1588 is associated a controversy over what purports to be a memoir setting forth the passage of the ship of a Spanish navigator, Lorenzo Ferrer de Maldonado, from the Atlantic to the Pacific, through a strait a quarter of a league wide. The passage took him as high as 75°; but he reached the Pacific under the sixtieth parallel.   The

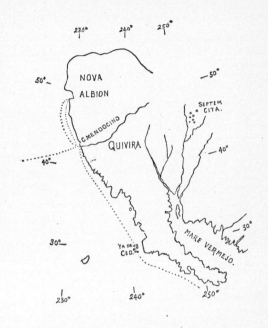

FROM MOLINEAUX'S GLOBE, 1592.[4]

opening was identified by him with the long-sought Straits of Anian.   The belief in this story had at one time some strong advocates, but later geographical discoveries have of course pushed it into the limbo of forgotten things ; for it seems hardly possible to identify, as was done by Amoretti, the narrow passage of Maldonado, under 60°, with that which Behring discovered, sixteen leagues wide, under 65°.[5]

[1] Peschel, *Geschichte der Erdkunde*, 1865, pp. 322, 395 ; J. C. Brevoort in *Magazine of American History*, vol. i. p. 250; Burney, *Voyages*, vol. i., and Bancroft, *North Mexican States*, vol. i. p. 139, where there are references and collections of authorities.

[2] Gali's letter is in Hakluyt, vol. iii. p. 526, copied from Linschoten. Cf. inscription on the Molineaux map of 1600 in this History, Vol. III. p. 80, and Bancroft, *California*, vol. i. p. 94. The map which Gali is thought to have made is not now known (Kohl, *Maps in Hakluyt*, 61).   Bancroft says that Gali's mention of Cape Mendocino is the earliest, but it is not definitely known by whom that prominent point was first named.

[3] This map is sketched in Vol. III. p. 42.

[4] This is sketched from a draught in the Kohl Collection.   Cf. Vol. III. pp. 196, 212. The dotted line indicates the track of Drake. There has been much controversy over the latitude of Drake's extreme northing, fixed, as

it will be seen in this map, at about 48°, which is the statement of the *World Encompassed*, and by the *Famous Voyage*, at 43°. The two sides were espoused warmly and respectively by Greenhow in his *Oregon and California*, and by Travers Twiss in his *Oregon Question*, during the dispute between the United States and Great Britain about the Oregon boundary. Bancroft (*Northwest Coast*, vol. i. p. 144), who presents the testimony, is inclined to the lower latitude.

[5] It is claimed that Maldonado presented his memoir in 1609 to the Council of the Indies, and asked for a reward for the discovery ; and there are two manuscripts purporting to be the original memoir. One, of which trace is found in 1672, 1738, 1775, 1781 (copied by Muñoz), and printed in 1788, was still existing, it is claimed, in 1789, and was reviewed in 1790 by the French geographer Buache, who endeavored to establish its authenticity; and it is translated, with maps, in Barrow's *Chronologi*

In 1592 we have the alleged voyage of De Fuca, of which he spoke in 1596, in Venice, to Michael Lok, who told Purchas; and he in turn included it in his *Pilgrims*.[1] He told

Lok that he had been captured and plundered on the California coast by Cavendish,[2] — a statement which some have thought confirmed by Cavendish's own avowal of his taking a pilot on that coast, — and that at the north he had entered a strait a hundred miles wide, under 47° and 48°, which had a pinnacle rock at the entrance; and that within the strait he had found the coast trending northeast, bordering a sea upon which he had sailed for twenty days. This story, despite its exaggerations, and though discarded formerly, has gained some credence with later investigators; and the application of his name to the passage which leads to Puget Sound seems to have been the result of a vague and

SPANISH GALLEON.[3]

cal History of Voyages, etc. Another manuscript was found in the Ambrosian library in 1811, and was published at Milan as *Viaggio dal mare Atlantico al Pacifico*, translated from a Spanish manuscript (Stevens, *Bibliotheca geographica*, no. 1,746), and again in French at Plaisance in 1812. The editor was Charles Amoretti, who added a discourse, expressing his belief in it, together with a circumpolar map marking Maldonado's track. (Harvard College Library, no. 4331.2.) This book was reviewed by Barrow in the *Quarterly Review*, October, 1816. Cf. Burney's *Voyages*, vol. v. p. 167. A memoir by the Chevalier Lapie, with another map of the "Mer polaire," is printed in the *Nouvelles Annales des Voyages*, vol. xi. (1821). Bancroft (*Northwest Coast*, i. 98) reproduces Lapie's map. Navarrete searched the Spanish Archives for confirmation of this memoir, — a search not in vain, inasmuch as it led to the discovery of the documents with which he illustrated the history of Columbus; and he also gave his view of the question in

vol. xv. of his *Coleccion de documentos inéditos* in the volume specially called *Examen historico-critico de los Viages y Descubrimientos apócrifos del capitan Lorenzo Ferrer Maldonado, de Juan de Fuca y del almirante Bartolomé de Fonte: memoria comenzada por D. M. F. de Navarrete, y arreglada y concluida por D. Eustaquio Fernandez de Navarrete*. Bancroft calls it an elaboration of the voyage of the *Sutil y Méxicana*. (Cf. Arcana, *Bibliographia de obras anonimas*, 1882, no. 408.) Goldson in his *Memoir on the Straits of Anian* places confidence in the Maldonado memoir. Cf. Bancroft (*Northwest Coast*, vol. i. p. 92), who recapitulates the story and cites the examiners of it, *pro* and *con*, and gives (p. 96) Maldonado's map of the strait.

[1] Vol. iii. p. 849.

[2] On Cavendish's Pacific Explorations. See Vol. III., chap. ii.

[3] A fac-simile of the sketch given in Jurien de la Gravière's *Les marins du XVe et du XVIe siècle*.

general concurrence, in the belief of some at least, that this passage must be identified with the strait which De Fuca claimed to have passed.[1]

With the close of the sixteenth century, the maps became numerous, and are mostly of the Mercator type. Such are those of Cornelius de Judæis in 1589 and in 1593,[2] the draughts of 1587 and 1589 included in the Ortelius of 1592,[3] the map of 1593 in the *Historiarum indicarum libri XVI.* of Maffeius,[4] and those of Plancius [5] and De Bry.[6] The type is varied a little in the 1592 globe of Molineaux, as already shown, and in the 1587 map of Myritius we have the Asiatic connection of the upper coast as before mentioned; but in the Ptolemy of 1597 the contour of Mercator is still essentially followed.[7] In this same year (1597) the earliest distinctively American atlas was published in the *Descriptionis Ptolemaicæ Augmentum* of Cornelius Wytfliet, of which an account is given in another place.[8] Fac-similes of the maps of the Gulf of California and of the New World are annexed, to indicate the full extent of geographical knowledge then current with the best cartographers. The Mercator type for the two Americas and the great Antarctic Continent common to most maps of this period are the distinguishing features of the new hemisphere. The same characteristics pertain also to the mappemondes in the original Dutch edition of Linschoten's *Itinerario*, published in two editions at Amsterdam in 1596,[9] in Münster's *Cosmographia*, 1598, and in the Brescia edition (1598) of Ortelius.

[1] Greenhow in his *Oregon* contends for a certain basis of truth in De Fuca's story. Cf. Navarrete in the *Coleccion de documentos inéditos*, vol. xv., and Bancroft (*North Mexican States*, vol. i. p. 146, and *Northwest Coast*, vol. i. pp. 71-80), who pronounces it pure fiction, and in a long note gives the writers *pro* and *con*.

[2] In his *Speculum Orbis Terræ.* Cf. Muller, (1872), no. 1,437, and Vol. IV. p. 97 of this History. This map of 1593 gives to the lake which empties into the Arctic Ocean the name "Conibas,"— an application of the name that Bancroft (*Northwest Coast*, vol. i. p. 84) finds no earlier instance of than that in Wytfliet in 1597.

[3] *Mapoteca Colombiana* of Uricoechea, nos. 16, 17, and 18.

[4] Copy in Harvard College Library. Cf. *Mapoteca Colombiana*, no. 19.

[5] The map of Plancius was first drafted — according to Blundeville — in 1592, and is dated 1594 in the Dutch Linschoten of 1596, where it was republished. It was re-engraved, but not credited to Plancius, in the Latin Linschoten of 1599. The English Linschoten of 1598 has a map, re-engraved from Ortelius, which is given in the Hakluyt of 1589.

[6] *Mapoteca Colombiana*, nos. 20 and 21. Cf. this History, Vol. IV. p. 99.

[7] Cf. nos. 2, 28, 29, 32, 34, 35. This 1597 edition of Ptolemy was issued at Cologne, under the editing of Jean Antonio Magini, a Paduan, born in 1556. (Cf. Lelewel, *Epilogue*, 219.) The maps showing America are,—

No. 2. A folding map of the two spheres, drawn by Hieronymus Porro from the map which Rumoldus Mercator based on his father's work.

Nos. 28 and 32. Asia, showing the opposite American shores.

Nos. 34-35. America, of the Mercator type, but less accurate than Ortelius. There are copies of this edition in the library of the Massachusetts Historical Society, and in Mr. Brevoort's collection. (Walckenaer, no. 2,257; Stevens, *Nuggets*, no. 2,259; Graesse, vol. v. p. 502.)

This same edition is sometimes found with the imprint of Arnheim, and copies of this are in the Library of Congress and in the Carter-Brown Collection. (Cf. Carter-Brown, vol. i. no. 514; Graesse, v. 502.)

An edition in Italian, 1598 (with 1597 in the colophon), embodying the works of Magini and Porro, was published at Venice; and there are copies of this in the Library of Congress and in the Philadelphia Library; also in the collections of J. Carson Brevoort, President White of Cornell University, and C. C. Baldwin, of Cleveland.

The text of Ruscelli, edited by Rosaccio, was printed at Venice in 1599, giving three maps of the world and nine special American maps. There is a copy of this edition in the Carter-Brown Library, and one was sold in the Murphy sale (no. 2,077). The Magini text was again printed at Cologne in 1608, and of this there are copies in the Harvard College and Carter-Brown libraries.

[8] Cf. Vol. IV. p. 369.

[9] This and the other maps were repeated in the six Dutch editions, in the second and third French, and in the original Latin edition. The third Dutch edition, in three parts, is the rarest of the editions in that language; the first part being without date, while the second and third are dated respectively 1604 and 1605. The fourth Dutch edition is dated 1614, the fifth 1623 (a reprint of the 1614), the sixth

FROM WYTFLIET, 1597.[1]

In 1600 Metullus in his *America sive novus orbis*, published at Cologne, simply followed Wytfliet.[2] From the map of Molineaux, likewise of 1600, a sketch of the California

1644 (a reprint of the 1623). Cf. Tiele, *Biblio-graphie sur les journaux des navigateurs*, nos. 80, 82, 86, 88, 90; Carter-Brown, vol. i. no. 503, vol. ii. no. 547; Stevens, *Bibliotheca historica*,

---

[1] Bancroft (*North Mexican States*, vol. i. p. 152) sketches this map; it is also in his *Northwest Coast*, vol. i. p. 82.

[2] Sabin, xii. 48,170.

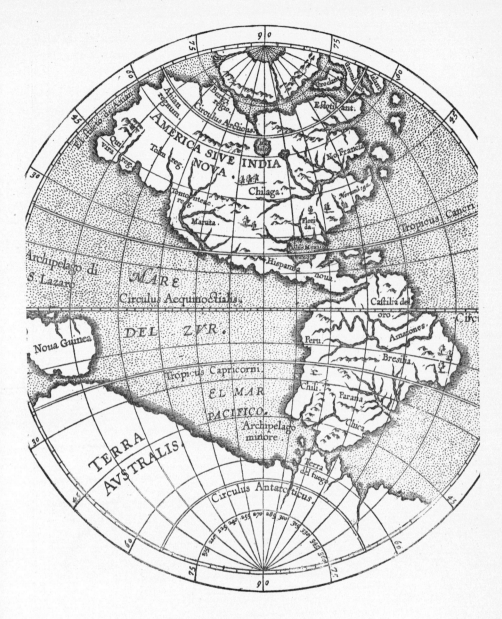

WYTFLIET, 1597.

peninsula is given elsewhere.[1] A contour of the coast more like that of the Molineaux globe figured on a preceding page belongs to the map given in the Herrera of 1601, but it

no. 1,148; Muller, *Books on America*, 1872, nos. 2,185, 2,188, 2,190; and 1877, nos. 1,880, 1,882 1,883, 1,884.

The English translation by Wolfe (1598) is mentioned in Vol. III. p. 206. It was so rare in 1832 that Rich priced it at £8 8s.; and yet

---

also introduces views which held to a much wider separation of the shores of the north Pacific than had been maintained by the school of Mercator.[1]

An important voyage in both furthering and confusing the knowledge of the California coast was that of Sebastian Viscaino.[2] This navigator, it is sometimes said, had been in a Manilla galleon which Cavendish had captured near Cape St. Lucas in 1587, when the English freebooter burned the vessel and landed her crew.[3] He is known to have had much opportunity for acquiring familiarity with the coast; and in 1597 he had conducted an expedition to the coast of the California peninsula which had failed of success.[4]

In 1602 (May 5) he was again despatched from Acapulco with three vessels, for the same purpose of discovering some harbor up the coast which returning vessels from the Philippines could enter for safety or repairs, and of finding the mysterious strait which led to the Atlantic. He was absent ten months.[5] He himself went up to 42°, but one of

---

Crowninshield bought his copy in 1844 at a Boston auction for $10.50. The Roxburgh copy had brought £10 15s., and the Jadis copy the same. Smith, the London dealer, in 1874 advertised one for £7 15s. 6d. The Menzies copy (no. 1,254) brought $104. There was a copy sold in the Beckford sale, 1883, no. 1,813, and another in the Murphy sale, no. 1,498.

The first Latin edition, *Navigatio ac Itinerarium*, was printed in 1599, its first part being translated, with some omissions, from the Dutch, and the description of America being omitted from the second part. It was reissued with a new title in 1614, — an edition very rare; but there are copies in the Lenox and Carter-Brown libraries. Cf. Carter-Brown, vol. i. no. 542, vol. ii. no. 167; Leclerc, no. 360 — 150 francs; Murphy, no. 1,499; Tiele, no. 81; Muller, 1872, no. 2,196; 1877, nos. 1,890, 1,891; and Rosenthal (Munich, 1883) — 100 marks.

The earliest French edition, *Histoire de la Navigation*, etc., bears two different imprints of Amsterdam, 1610, though it is thought to have been printed by De Bry at Frankfort. A second is dated Amsterdam, 1619 (part i. being after the French edition of 1610, and parts ii. and iii. being translated from the Dutch). It has usually appended to it a *Description de l'Amérique* (Amsterdam, 1619), pp. 88 and map. America is also described in the *Beschryvinge van verscheyde landen* (Amsterdam, 1619), included in the Saegman Collection (Carter-Brown, vol. ii. no. 1,024). A third French edition, "augmentée," but a reprint of the 1619 edition, appeared at Amsterdam in 1638. Cf. Carter-Brown, vol. ii. nos. 104, 105, 214, 454; Leclerc, 362 (1610 edition) — 130 francs; Trömel, no. 58; Tiele, nos. 83, 87, 89; Muller (1872), no. 2,193 (1877), nos. 1,887, 1,888, 1,889; Field, *Indian Bibliography*, no. 941; Leclerc, no. 2,845 (1638 edition) — 250 francs; Rich, 1832 (1638 edition), no. 219 — £1 10s.; Murphy, nos. 2,977, 2,978; Quaritch (1638 edition) — £8 10s.

There are copies of the editions of 1596, 1598, and 1599 in Mr. Deane's collection. The

Dutch editions are rarely in good condition; this is said to be on account of the general use made of them as sea-manuals. The Latin and German texts in De Bry are not much prized. (Camus, p. 189; Tiele, p. 90.) Sabin (*Dictionary*, vol. x. p. 375) gives the bibliography of Linschoten. His life is portrayed in Van Kampen's *Levens van beroëmde Nederlanders*, Haarlem, 1838–1840. He was with Barentz on his first and second Arctic voyages. Cf. *Voyagie ofte Schipvaert by Noorden*, 1601; again, 1624; Tiele, no. 155; Murphy, no. 1,497; Muller, 1872, no. 2,064, and 1877, no. 1,893. His voyages are included in *Verscheyde Oost-Indische Voyagien*, Amsterdam, *circa* 1663.

[1] This Herrera map was reproduced in the 1622 edition, and so late as 1723 in Torquemada, with a few changes. The Herrera of 1601 has the following American maps: —

Page 2. The two Americas.
Page 7. The West India Islands.
Page 21. The Audiencia of New Spain.
Page 33. The Audiencia of Guatemala.
Page 38. South America.
Page 47. Audiencia of Quito.
Page 63. The Chile coast.

Jefferys, in his *Northwest Passage*, gives a fac-simile of the American hemisphere.

The Quadus map of 1600, showing the California peninsula, is sketched in Vol. IV. p. 101.

The Japanese map, showing the west coast, which Kaempfer gave to Hans Sloane, and which figures so much in the controversy of the last century over the "mer de l'ouest," is supposed to have been drawn between 1580 and 1600.

[2] Biscayer he is sometimes called.

[3] Greenhow, *Oregon and California*, 89; Bancroft doubts Viscaino's presence (*North Mexican States*, i. 148).

[4] Torquemada gives the chief information on this voyage. Bancroft (*North Mexican States*, i. 151) cites other writers.

[5] Our knowledge of this expedition comes largely from the account of a Carmelite priest, Antonio de la Ascension, who accompanied it,

his vessels under Martin Aguilar proceeded to 43°, where he reported that he found the entrance of a river or strait, not far from Cape Blanco ; [1] and for a long period afterwards the entrance and Aguilar's name stood together on the maps.[2] Buache, in his *Considérations géographiques et physiques,* says that it was the reports brought back from this expedition, describing an easterly trend of the coast above the 43°, which gave rise to the notion that the waters of the Gulf of California found a passage to the ocean in two ways, making an island of the peninsula. The official recorder of the expedition (Ascension) is known to have held this view. We shall see how fixed this impression later became.

Meanwhile the peninsular shape was still maintained in the map in Botero's *Relaciones Universales del mundo,* published at Valladolid in 1603 ; in the Spanish map of 1604, made at Florence by Mathieu Neron Pecciolen (engraved for Buache in 1754) ; in that of Cespedes' *Regimiento de Navigacion* (1606), and in that published in connection with Ferdinand de Quir's narrative in the *Detectionis Freti* (1613) of Hudson's voyage.[3]

A map of Jodocus Hondius of about this time first gave indication of the growing uncertainty which led finally to a prevailing error regarding the head of the gulf. The map was inscribed "Vera totius expeditionis nauticæ Descriptio D. Franc. Draci," etc., and illustrated Hondius's edition of Drake and Cavendish's voyages, and has been reproduced in the Hakluyt Society's edition of *The World Encompassed.* The gulf is made to divide about an island at its northern end, producing two arms whose prolongation is left undecided. The circumpolar map of Hondius which appeared in Pontanus's *Amsterdam* in 1611, and is given in fac-simile in Asher's *Henry Hudson,* shows the Straits of Anian, but nothing more. Another Hondius map in the Mercator of 1613 turns the coast easterly, where the Straits of Anian separate it from Asia. The same atlas of 1613 contains also the America of Michael Mercator, which is of the usual Gerard Mercator type, with the enclosed northern sea contracted to narrow limits and called "Mare dulce." A similar western coast is drawn in the America of Johannes Oliva of Marseilles, preserved in the British Museum.[4]

In Kasper van Baerle's edition of Herrera, published at Amsterdam in 1622, we get — as far as has been observed — the earliest [5] insularizing of the California peninsula, and this only by a narrow thread of water connecting a large gulf below and a smaller one above. And even this attempt was neutralized by a second map in the same book, in which these two gulfs were not made to mingle their waters. A bolder and less equivocal severing of the peninsula followed in the maps of two English geographers. The first of these is the

and whose report, presented in the Biblioteca Nacional at Madrid, is printed in Pacheco's *Coleccion de documentos,* viii. 539. Torquemada used it, and so did Venegas in his *Noticia de la California* (Madrid, 1757 ; English edition, London, 1759 ; French edition, Paris, 1767 ; German, 1769). Cf. on Venegas, Carter-Brown, vol. iii. nos. 1,172, 1,239, 1,601, 1,710 Field, *Indian Bibliography,* nos. 1,599, 1,600 ; Bancroft, *North Mexican States,* i. 281. An abridged narrative from Lorenzana is given in the *Boletin* of the Mexican Geographical Society, vol. v., 1857. Navarrete adds some other documents in his *Coleccion,* xv. Bancroft (*North Mexican States,* i. 154-155, and *California,* i. 98) enumerates other sources ; as does J. C. Brevoort in the *Magazine of American History,* i. 124.

[1] Bancroft does not believe that he went beyond the Oregon line (42°), and considers his Cape Blanco to be the modern St. George (*History of California,* i. 104 ; *Northwest Coast,* i. 84).

[2] Bancroft, *Mexico,* iii. 3 ; *California,* ii. 97 ; *North Mexican States,* i. 153. A sketch of Viscaino's map from Cape Mendocino south is given in this History, Vol. III. p. 75. The map was published, as reduced from the thirty-six original sheets by Navarrete, in the *Atlas para el viage de las goletas Sutil y Méxicana al reconocimiento del Estrecho de Juan de Fuca* (1802). Cf. Navarrete, xv. ; Greenhow's *Northwest Coast* (1840), p. 131 ; Burney's *South Sea Voyages* (1806), vol. ii. (with the map) ; and Bancroft, *North Mexican States,* i. 156 ; *California,* i. 97, and *Northwest Coast,* i. 101, 146.

[3] This is reproduced in Charton's *Voyageurs,* iv. 184, 185.

[4] There is a draught of it in the Kohl Collection. Cf. *Catalogue of Manuscript Maps in the British Museum* (1844), i. 33.

[5] Bancroft (*Northwest Coast,* i. 101) refers to the suspicions of Father Ascension in 1603, of Oñate in 1604, and of Nicolas de Cardona in or about 1617, that California was an island ; but

map of Master Briggs.[1] In this the island stretches from 23° to 44°, showing Cape Blanco, with Cape Mendocino and " Po. S^r. Francisco Draco" south of it, the latter in about 38°. The map bears the following legend : " California, sometymes supposed to be part of y° Westerne continent ; but since by a Spanish charte taken by ye Hollanders it is found to be a goodly Ilande, the length of the west shoare beeing about 500 leagues from Cape Mendocino to the south cape thereof called Cape St. Lucas, as appeareth both by that Spanish Chart, and by the relation of Francis Gaule [Gali], whereas in the ordinarie charts it is sett downe to be 1700 leagues." [2] The other was that given in John Speed's *Prospect*, which contains one of the maps of Abraham Goos of Amsterdam, " described and enlarged by I. S. Ano. 1626." This carries up the outer coast of the island beyond the " Po[rto] Sir Francisco Dr[ake]" and Cape Mendocino. The coast of the main opposite the northern end of the island ceases to be defined, and is continued northerly with a dotted line, while the western shore of Hudson's Bay is also left undetermined.[3] De Laet, however, in 1630 still kept to the peninsula, placing " Nova Albion" above it.[4] In 1636 W. Saltonstall's English translation of Hondius's Mercator presents an island, with the now somewhat common break in the main coast opposite its northern end. This gap is closed up, however, in another map in the same volume.[5]

The map in Pierre D'Avity's *Le Monde* [6] makes California a peninsula, with the river St. Lawrence rising close to it, and flowing very near also to Hudson's Bay in its easterly passage.

The circumstantial story of Bartolemé de Fonte, whose exploits are placed in 1640, at one time commanded a certain degree of confidence, and made strange work with the carto-graphical ideas of the upper part of the Pacific coast. It is now believed that the story was coined by James Petiver, one of the contributors to the *Monthly Miscellany, or Memoirs for the Curious*, published in London in April and June, 1708, in which first appeared what purported to be a translation of a letter of a certain Admiral De Fonte.[7] In this a Spanish navigator — whose name was possibly suggested by a veritable De Fonta who was exploring Tierra del Fuego in 1649 — was made to depart from Callao, April 3, 1640, and proceed up the coast to 53°, above which he navigated a net-work of interior waters, and encountered a ship from Boston which had entered these regions from the Atlantic side.[8] To this

there was on their part no cartographical expression of the idea.

[1] In Purchas's *Pilgrims*, iii. 853, in 1625. This map is sketched in Bancroft's *North Mexican States*, i. 169.

[2] This Spanish chart here referred to is not identified, though Delisle credits it — according to Bancroft (*Northwest Coast*, i. 103) — to Jann-son's *Monde Maritime*. If by this is meant Jannson's *Orbis Maritimus*, it was not till 1657 that Jannson added this volume to his edition of the *Mercator-Hondius Atlas*. Carpenter's *Geography* (Oxford, 1625) repeats Purchas's story, and many have followed it since. In Heylin and Ogilby, the story goes that some people on the coast in 1620 were carried in by the current, and found themselves in the gulf. The Spanish chart may have been the source of the map in the Amsterdam *Herrera* of 1622.

[3] Bancroft (*Northwest Coast*, i. 104) sketches a similar map which appeared in 1624 at Amster-dam in Inga's *West Indische Spieghel*. Muller, *Books on America*, 1872, no. 805 ; 1877, no. 1,561.

[4] It was repeated in later editions. Bancroft uses no earlier edition than that of 1633. The edition of 1625 did not contain the map of 1630.

[5] In 1636 a report was made by the Spanish on the probable inter-oceanic communication by way of the Gulf of California. Cf. *Documentos inéditos*, xv. 215 ; Bancroft, *Northwest Coast*, i. 107.

[6] Paris, 1637, five volumes, folio. Bancroft gives his map in his *Northwest Coast*, i. 107.

[7] Arthur Dobbs reprinted it in his *Countries adjoining to Hudson's Bay*, in 1744, — according to Bancroft.

[8] He is particular to describe this ship as owned by Major Gibbons, who was on board, and as commanded by one Shapley. Major Edward Gibbons was a well-known merchant of Boston at this time, and the story seems first to have attracted the notice of the local antiquaries of that city, when Dr. Franklin brought it to the attention of Thomas Prince ; and upon Prince reporting to him evidence favorable to the exist-ence of such persons at that time, Franklin ad-dressed a letter to Dr. Pringle, in which he considers the story " an abridgment and a trans-lation, and bad in both respects ; " and he adds, " If a fiction, it is plainly not an English one ; but it has none of the features of fiction." (Cf. Sabin's *American Bibliopolist*, February, 1870.

archipelago, as it seemed, he gave the name of St. Lazarus ; and to a river, leading from a lake with an island in it, he applied that of Velasco ; and these names, curiously, appear in the fanciful maps which were made by Delisle and Buache in elucidation of the voyage in which they expressed not a little faith, though the Spanish antiquaries early declared that their archives contained no record of the voyage.[1]

The Dutch, under De Vries, in 1643 had pushed up from Japan, and discovered, as they thought, an island, "Jesso," separated from land on the west by a water which they called the "Detroit de Vries," and on the American side by a channel which had an uncertain extension to the north, and might after all be the long-sought Straits of Anian.[2] The idea of an interjacent land in the north Pacific between America and Asia is also said to have grown out of the report of a Portuguese navigator, Don João da Gama, who claimed to have seen such a land in sailing from China to New Spain. It long maintained a fleeting existence on the maps.[3]

p. 65.) Dr. Snow examined it in his *History of Boston* (p. 89), and expressed his disbelief in it. Caleb Cushing in the *North American Review* (January, 1839) expressed the opinion that the account was worthy of investigation; which induced Mr. James Savage to examine it in detail, who in the same periodical (April, 1839, p. 559) set it at rest by at least negative proof, as well as by establishing an *alibi* for Gibbons at the date assigned. It may be remarked that among the English there was no general belief in a practicable western passage at this time, and the directors of the East India Company had given up the hope of it after Baffin's return in 1616.

[1] It was very easy for the credulous to identify the Archipelago of St. Lazarus with the Charlotte Islands. The map of Delisle and Buache, published in Paris in 1752 in *Nouvelles Cartes des Découvertes de l'Amiral de Fonte*, endeavors to reconcile the voyages of De Fuca and De Fonte. The map is reproduced in Bancroft's *Northwest Coast*, i. 128. Under 45° there are two straits entering a huge inland "mer de l'ouest," the southerly of which is supposed to be the one found by Aguilar in 1603, and the northerly that of De Fuca in 1592. Under 60° is the St. Lazarus Archipelago, and thridding the adjacent main are the bays, straits, lakes, and rivers which connect the Pacific with Hudson's Bay. The next year (1753) Vaugondy, in some *Observations critiques*, opposed Delisle's theory; and the opposing memoirs were printed in Spanish, with a refutation of Delisle by Buriel, in Venegas' *California*, in 1757. Some years later the English geographer Jefferys attacked the problem in maps appended to Dragg's *Great Probability of a Northwest Passage*, which was printed in London in 1768. Jefferys made the connection with Baffin's Bay, and bounded an island — in which he revived the old Chinese legend by calling it Fusang — by De Fuca's Straits on the south and De Fonte's Archipelago on the north. Foster, in 1786, and Clavigero, in 1798, repudiated the story ; but it appealed sufficiently to Burney to induce him to include it in his *Chronological History of Voyages*

to the South Seas, vol. iii. (1813). William Goldson, in his *Passage between the Atlantic and Pacific, in two Memoirs on the Straits of Anian and the Discoveries of De Fonte* (Portsmouth, England, 1793), supposed that De Fonte got into the Great Slave Lake ! Navarrete has examined the question in his *Documentos inéditos*, xv., as he had done at less length in his *Sutil y Méxicana* in 1802, expressing his disbelief; and so does Bancroft in his *Northwest Coast*, i. 115, who cites additionally (p. 119) La Harpe, *Abrégé des Voyages* (1816), vol. xvi., and Lapie, *Nouvelles Annales des Voyages* (1821), vol. xi., as believing the story. A "Chart for the better understanding of De Font's letter" appeared in *An Account of a Voyage for the Discovery of a Northwest Passage*, by Theodore Swaine Drage (clerk of the "California"), London, 1749, vol. ii.

[2] *Recueil de Voyages au Nord*, Amsterdam, 1732, vol. iv.; Coxe's *Discoveries of the Russians in the North Pacific*, 1803.

[3] Sanson adopted it, and it is laid down in Van Loon's *Zee Atlas* of 1661, where, in the chart "Nova Granada en l'Eylandt California," it is marked as the thither shore of the Straits of Anian, and called "Terra incognita," — and Van Loon had the best reputation of the hydrographers of his day. The map published by Thevenot in 1663 also gives it.

Nicolas Sanson died in 1667, and two years later (1669), his son Guillaume reissued his father's map, still with the island and the interjacent land, which in Blome's map, published in his *Description* (1670), and professedly following Sanson, is marked "Conibas." Later, in 1691, we have another Sanson map; but though the straits still bound easterly the "Terre de Jesso," they are without name, and open easterly into a limitless "mer glaciale." Hennepin at a later day put a special draught of it in the margin of his large map (1697), where it has something of continental proportions, stretching through forty degrees of longitude, north of the thirty-eighth parallel; and from Hennepin Campanius copied it (1702) in his *Nya Swerige*, p. 10, as shown herewith (p. 464).

Two maps of Petrus Koerius, dated 1646, in Speed's *Prospect* (1668), indicate what variable moods geographers could assume in the same year. In one we have an island and a determinate coast line running north to the straits; in the other we have a peninsula with two different trends of the coast north of it in half-shading. We owe to an expatriated Englishman a more precise nomenclature for the western coast than we had had previous to the appearance of his maps in 1646; and the original manuscript drawings preserved at Munich are said by Dr. Hale to be richer still in names.[1] This is the *Arcano del mare* of Robert Dudley. He was born in Surrey in 1573, and whether the natural or legitimate son of the Earl of Leicester depends on the proof of the secret marriage of that nobleman with Lady Sheffield. An adventurous spirit kept him away from the enjoyment of Kenilworth, which he inherited, and he was drawn nearer to the associations of the sea by marrying a sister of Cavendish. He was among the many Englishmen who tried their daring on the Spanish main. He married a second wife, a daughter of Sir Thomas Leigh, whom he abandoned, partly to be rid of a stepmother; and out of chagrin at his failure to secure the dukedom of Northumberland, which had been in abeyance since the execution of his grandfather, Lady Jane Grey's adherent, he sold Kenilworth to young Prince Henry, and left England in company with a daughter of Sir Robert Southwell. He now gave himself up to practical seamanship and the study of hydrography. The grand-duke of Tuscany gave him employment, and he drained a morass to enable Leghorn to become a beautiful city. Under authority of Ferdinand II., he assumed the title of Duke of Northumberland, which was recognized

It is also delineated in 1700 in the map of the Dutchman, Lugtenberg. The idea was not in 1728, had mapped out the Asiatic shore of this region.

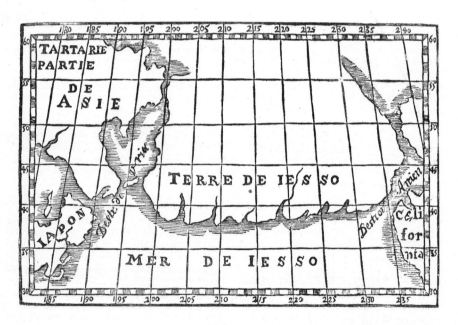

TERRE DE IESSO.

totally given up till Cook's map of his explorations in 1777–1778 appeared, which was the first to give to the peninsula of Alaska and the Aleutian islands a delineation of approximate accuracy; and this was fifty years after Behring,

[1] *Amer. Antiq. Soc. Proc.*, October, 1873; and *Memorial History of Boston*, i. 59. Kohl's Washington Collection has several draughts from the charts at Munich. An earlier edition (1630) of the *Arcano del Mare* is sometimes mentioned.

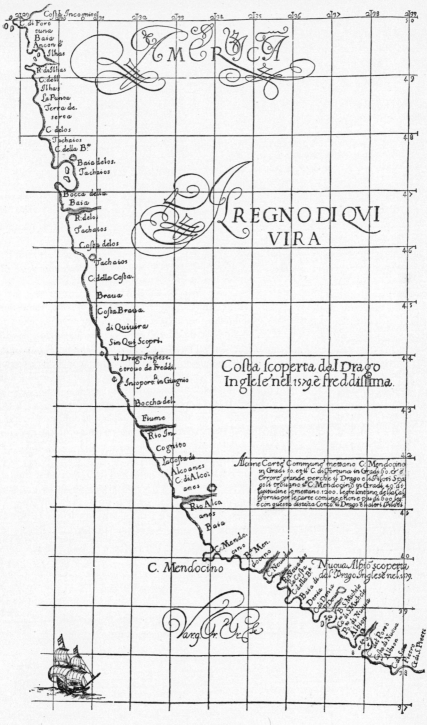

DUDLEY, 1646.

throughout the empire. He died in 1639.[1] The *Arcano* has thirty-three American maps ; but the Munich manuscript shows thirteen more. One of the Pacific coast, which records Drake's explorations, is annexed ; but with Dudley's text [2] there is another showing the coast from Cape Mendocino south, which puts under thirty degrees north a "golfo profondo" of undefined inland limits, with " I di Cedros " off its mouth. The bay with the anchor and soundings just north of thirty degrees, called in the fac-simile " Pto di Nouova Albion," corresponding, it would seem, to San Francisco, is still seen in this other chart, with a more explicit inscription, — " Po : dell nuovo Albion scoperto dal' Drago Cno Inglese."

In 1649, in Texeira's chart, there is laid down for the first time a sketch of the coast near the Straits of Anian, which is marked as seen by João da Gama, and extends easterly from Jesso, in the latitude of 50°. Gama's land lived for some time in the charts.[3]

We have another of Speed's maps, five years later (1651), which appears in the 1676 edition of his *Prospect*, in which that geographer is somewhat confused. He makes California an island, with a break in the coast line of the main opposite its northern extremity, and its northwest point he calls " C. Mendocino," while " Pt. Sir Francisco Draco " is placed south of it; but rather confusedly another Cape Mendocino projects from the main coast considerably further to the north.[4] A map of Visscher in 1652 [5] reverts, however, to the anterior notions of Mercator ; but when in 1655 Wright, an Englishman, adopted Mercator's projection, and first made it really serviceable for navigation, in his *Certain Errors in Navigation*, he gave an insular shape to California.

The French geographer Nicolas Sanson [6] introduced a new notion in 1656. California was made an island with " Pto de Francisco Draco " on the west side, somewhat south of the northern cape of it. On the main the coast in the same latitude is made to form a projection to the north called " Agubela de Cato," without any extension of the shore farther northward. The map in Petavius's (Petau's) *History of the World* (London, 1659) carries the coast up, but leaves a gap opposite the northern end of the insular California. The atlas of Van Loon (1661) converts the gap into the Straits of Anian, and puts a " terra incognita " north of it. Danckerts of Amsterdam in the same year (1661), and Du Val in various maps of about this time make it an island. The map of 1663, which appeared in Heylin's *Cosmographie*,[7] gives the insular California, and a dotted line for the main coast northward, with three alternative directions. A map of the Sanson type is given in Blome's *Description of the World*, 1670. Ogilby's map in 1671 makes it an island,[8] following Montanus's *Nieuwe Weereld*.

Hennepin had in his 1683 map made California a peninsula, and in that of 1697 he still preserved the gulf-like character of the waters east of it ; but the same plate in the 1698 edition is altered to make an island, as it still is in the edition of 1704. The French geographer Jaillot, in 1694, also conformed to the insular theory, as did Corolus Allard in his well-known Dutch atlas. Campanius, copying Hennepin, speaks of California as

[1] See Vols. III. and IV., index; George Adlard's *Amye Robsart and Leicester*, 1870; *Warwickshire Historical Collections ;* Dugdale's *Warwickshire*, p. 166.

[2] Vol. i. lib. ii. p. 19. The other maps are numbered xxxi., xxxii., and xxxiii. A second edition, " Corretta e accresciuta secondo l' originale des medesimo Duca, che si conserva nella libreria del Convento de Firenze della Pace," appeared at Florence in 1661.

[3] Sanson put it in his atlas made in 1667 ; Delisle rejected it in 1714; Bowen adhered to it in 1747.

[4] It is worth while to note Virginia Farrer's map of Virginia, given in Vol. III. p. 465, for the strange belief which with some people prevailed in England in 1651, that the Pacific coast was at the foot of the western slope of the Alleghanies, — a belief which was represented in 1625 by Master Briggs in Purchas (vol. iii. p. 852), where he speaks of the south sea "on the other side of the mountains beyond our falls, which openeth a free and fair passage to China."

[5] " Autore, N. I. Piscator."

[6] Born 1600; died 1667.

[7] 1669, and later editions. Bancroft (*Northwest Coast*, i. 115) is led to believe that Heylin copied this map in 1701 from Hacke's *Collection of Voyages* (1699), thirty years after he had published his own map in 1669.

[8] It is copied in Bancroft, *Northwest Coast*, i. 110.

the largest island "which the Spaniards possess in America. From California the land extends itself [he says] to that part of Asia which is called Terra de Jesso, or Terra Esonis. The passage is only through the Straits of Anian, which hitherto has remained unknown, and therefore is not to be found in any map or chart," — all of which shows something of Campanius's unacquaintance with what had been surmised, at least, in cartography. All this while Blaeu in his maps was illustrating the dissolving geographical opinions of his time. In 1659 he had drawn California as an island; in 1662 as a peninsula; and once more, in 1670, as an island. Coronelli in 1680, and Franquelin in his great manuscript map of 1684 had both represented it as an island.[1]

In 1698 the English geographer Edward Wells, in his *New Sett of Maps*, showed a little commendable doubt in marking the inlet just north of the island as "the supposed Straits of Anian," — a caution which Delisle in 1700, with a hesitancy worthy of the careful hydrographer that he was destined to become, still further exemplified. While restoring California to its peninsular character, he indicated the possibility of its being otherwise by the unfinished limitations of the surrounding waters.[2] Dampier in 1699, in chronicling the incidents of the voyage with which he was connected, made it an island.[3]

In 1701 one would have supposed the question of the insularity of California would have been helped at least by the explorations overland of Father Kino the Jesuit which were begun in 1698. His map, based rather upon shrewd conjecture than upon geographical discovery, and showing the peninsular form of the land, was published in the *Lettres Édifiantes*, vol. v., in 1705.[4] In 1705 the map in Harris's *Collection of Voyages* preserves the insular character of California.[5] In 1715 Delisle[6] expressed himself as undecided between the two theories respecting California,[7] but in 1717 he gave the weight of his great name[8] to an imagined but indefinite great gulf north of the California peninsula, which held for a while a place in the geography of his time as the "Mer de l'ouest." Homann, of Nuremberg, in 1719 marked the entrance of it, while he kept to the insular character of the land to the south; as did Seutter in his *Atlas Geographicus* published at Augsburg in 1720. Daniel Coxe in his *Carolana* had a sufficient stock of credulity — if he was not a "liar," as Bancroft calls him[9] — in working up some wondrous stories of interior lakes emptying into the South Sea.[10] In 1727 the English cartographer Moll converted the same inlet into the inevitable Straits of Anian. The maps in such popular books as Shelvocke's *Voyages* (1726)[11] and Anson's *Voyages* (1748), as did

[1] It is also an island in Coronelli's globe of 1683. Cf. Marcou's *Notes*, p. 5.

[2] Marcou's *Notes*, p. 5.

[3] *New Voyage round the World*. The map is sketched in Bancroft's *North Mexican States*, vol. i. p. 195; cf. his *Northwest Coast*, vol. i. pp. 112, 119, for other data.

[4] It was re-engraved in Paris in 1754 by the geographer Buache, and later in the margin of a map of North America published by Sayer of London. It is given in fac-simile in Jules Marcou's paper on the first discoverers of California, appended to the *Annual Report of the Chief of Engineers, U. S. A.*, 1878, and is also sketched in Bancroft's *North Mexican States*, vol. i. p. 499. Cf. his *Northwest Coast*, vol. i. pp. 113, 115, 120, where it is shown that Kino never convinced all his companions that the accepted island was in fact a peninsula. One of his associates, Luis Velarde (*Documentos para la historia de México*, ser. iv. vol. i. p. 344), opposed his views. The view is advanced by

E. L. Berthoud in the *Kansas City Review* (June, 1883), that a large area between the head of the gulf and the ocean, now below the sea level, was at one time covered with water, and that the island theory was in some way connected with this condition, which is believed to have continued as recently as the sixteenth and seventeenth centuries.

[5] This map is reproduced in Bancroft, *Northwest Coast*, vol. i. p. 114; as well as a map of Vander Aa (1707) on page 115.

[6] *Recueil des Voyages au Nord*, vol. iii. p. 268.

[7] Bancroft cites Travers Twiss (*Oregon Question*, 1846) as quoting a map of Delisle in 1722, making it a peninsula.

[8] Cf. Saint-Martin, *Histoire de la géographie* p. 423.

[9] *Northwest Coast*, vol. i. p. 123.

[10] Cf. something of the sort in Dobbs's map of 1744, given in Bancroft, *Northw. Coast*, i. 123.

[11] Shelvocke says he accepted current views, unable to decide himself.

sundry maps issued by Vander Aa of Amsterdam, still told the mass of readers of the island of California ; as had Bruzen la Martinière in his *Introduction à l'histoire* (1735), and Salmon (using Moll's map of 1736) in his *History of America.*

Meanwhile, without knowing it because of the fogs, Behring, in 1728, had pushed through the straits now known by his name into the Arctic Seas, and had returned along the Asiatic shore in continued ignorance of his accomplishment. It was not till 1732 that another Russian expedition was driven over to the Alaskan shore ; and in 1738 and 1741 Behring proved the close proximity of the two continents, and made demonstration of their severance.

At this time also the English were making renewed efforts from the side of Hudson's Bay to reach the Pacific ; and Arthur Dobbs, in his *Countries adjoining to Hudson's Bay* (1744), gives a variety of reasons for supposing a passage in that direction, showing possible solutions of the problem in an accompanying map.[1]

The Spaniards, who were before long to be spurred on to other efforts by the reports of Russian expeditions, were reviving now, through the 1728 edition of Herrera, more confidence in the peninsular character of California ; though Mota Padilla in his *Nueva Galicia*, in 1742, still thought it an island.

The French map-maker Bellin, in his cartographical illustrations for Charlevoix in 1743, also fell into the new belief; as did Consag the Jesuit, in a map which he made in 1746.[2]

The leading English geographer Bowen in 1747 was advocating the same view, and defining the more northerly parts as " undiscovered." In 1748 Henry Ellis published his *Voyage to Hudson's Bay*, — made in 1746–1747, and mentions a story that a high or low tide made California an island or a peninsula, and was inclined to believe in a practicable northwest passage.[3] In 1750 Robert de Vaugondy, while preserving the peninsula, made a westerly entrance to the north of it, which he marks as the discovery of Martin d'Aguilar. The lingering suspicion of the northerly connection of the California Gulf with the ocean had now nearly vanished ; and the peninsula which had been an island under Cortés, then for near a century connected with the main, and then again for more than a century in many minds an island again, was at last defined in its proper geographical relations.[4]

The coast line long remained, however, shadowy in the higher latitudes. Buriel, in his editorial notes to Venegas's *California*, in 1757, confessed that nothing was known. The French geographers, the younger Delisle and Buache,[5] published at this time various solutions of the problem of straits and interior seas, associated with the claims of Maldonado, De Fuca, and De Fonte ; and others were found to adopt, while others rejected, some of their very fanciful reconciling of conflicting and visionary evidences, in which the " Mer de l'ouest " holds a conspicuous position.[6] The English map-maker Jefferys at-

---

[1] Reproduced in Bancroft, *Northwest Coast*, vol. i. p. 123.

[2] It is in the Kohl Collection, and is sketched in Bancroft's *North Mexican States*, vol. i. p. 463; *Northwest Coast*, vol. i. pp. 125, 126.

[3] Bancroft (*Northwest Coast*, vol. i. pp. 126, 129) thinks his book more complete than any earlier one on the subject. As late as 1755 Hermann Moll, the English cartographer, kept the *island* in his map.

[4] Bancroft (*Northwest Coast*, vol. i. pp. 127, 128) thinks that a theory, started in 1751 by Captain Salvador, and reasserted in 1774 by Captain Anza, that the Colorado sent off a branch which found its way to the sea above the peninsula, was the last flicker of the belief in the insularity of California.

[5] Delisle was born in 1688 and died in 1747 ;

Buache lived from 1700 to 1773. Other cartographical solutions of the same data are found in William Doyle's *Account of the British Dominions beyond the Atlantic* (London, 1770), and in the *Mémoires sur la situation des pays septentrionaux*, by Samuel Éngel, published at Lausanne in 1765. Engel's maps were repeated in a German translation of his book published in 1772, and in his *Extraits raisonés des Voyages faits dans les parties septentrionales de l'Asie et de l'Amérique*, also published at Lausanne in 1779.

[6] Buache's " Mer de l'ouest " was re-engraved in J. B. Laborde's *Mer du Sud* (Paris, 1791), as well as a map of Maldonado's explorations. Cf. Samuel Engel's *Extraits raisonés des Voyages faits dans les parties septentrionales* (Lausanne, 1765 and 1779), and Dobbs's *Northwest Passage* (1754).

the same epoch (1753) was far less complex in his supposition, and confined himself to a single "river which connects with Lake Winnepeg." A map of 1760, " par les Srs Sanson, rectifiée par Sr Robert," also indicates a like westerly entrance; and Jefferys again in 1762, while he grows a little more determinate in coast lines, more explicitly fixes the passage as one that Juan de Fuca had entered in 1592.[1] The *Atlas Moderne*, which was published at Paris, also in 1762, in more than one map, the work of Janvier, still clung to the varieties presented by Delisle ten years before, and which Delisle himself the next year (1763) again brought forward. In 1768 Jefferys made a map [2] to illustrate the De Fonte narrative; but after 1775 he made several studies of the coast, and among other services reproduced the map which the Russian Academy had published, and which was a somewhat cautious draught of bits of the coast line here and there, indicating different landfalls, with a dotted connection between them.[3] One of Jefferys's own maps (1775) carries the coast north with indications of entrances, but without attempting to connect them with any interior water-sheds. Going north from New Albion we then find on his map the passage of D'Aguilar in 1603; then that of De Fuca, "where in 1592 he pretends he went through to the North Sea;" then the "Fousang" coast, visited by the Spaniards in 1774; then Delisle's landfall in 1741; Behring's the same year; while the coast stops at Mount St. Elias. In his 1776 map Jefferys gives another scheme. "Alaschka" is now an island athwart the water, dividing America from Asia, with Behring's Straits at its western end; while the American main is made up of what was seen by Spangenberg in 1728, with a general northeasterly trend higher up, laid down according to the Japanese reports. The Spaniards were also at this time pushing up among the islands beyond the Oregon coast.[4] In 1774 Don Juan Perez went to Nootka Sound, as is supposed, and called it San Lorenzo.[5] In 1775 another Spanish expedition discovered the Columbia River.[6] Janvier in 1782 published a map [7] still perpetuating the great sea of the west, which Buache and others had delineated thirty years before. The English in 1776 transferred their endeavors from Hudson's Bay to the Pacific coast, and Captain James Cook was despatched to strike the coast in the latitude of Drake's New Albion, and proceed north in search of a passage eastward.[8] Carver the traveller had already, in 1766–1768, got certain notions of the coast from Indian stories, as he heard them in the interior, and embodied them with current beliefs in a map of his own, which made a part of his *Travels through the interior parts of North America*, published in 1778. In this he fixed the name of Oregon for the supposed great river of the west, which remained in the end attached to the region which it was believed

---

[1] Jefferys also published at this time (2d ed. in 1764) *Voyages from Asia to America, for completing the discoveries of the Northwest Coast, with summary of voyages of the Russians in the Frozen sea, tr. from the high Dutch of S. Muller* [should be G. F. Muller], *with 3 maps*: (1) *Part of Japanese map* [this is sketched in Bancroft, *Northwest Coast*, i. p. 130]. (2) *Delisle and Buache's fictitious map*. (3) *New Discoveries of Russians and French*.

Muller's book was also published in French at Amsterdam in 1766. Cf. also William Coxe's *Account of the Russian discoveries between Asia and America* (2d ed. rev.), *London*, 1780, and later editions in 1787 and 1803; also, see Robertson's *America*, note 43.

[2] Sketched in Bancroft, *Northwest Coast*, vol. i. p. 131.

[3] Bancroft (*Northwest Coast*, vol. i. p. 124) gives a Russian map of 1741, which he says he copied from the original in the Russian archives.

[4] There is in the department of State at Washington a volume of copies from manuscripts in the hydrographic office at Madrid, attested by Navarrete, and probably procured by Greenhow at the time of the Oregon question. It is called *Viages de los Españoles a la costa norveste de la America en los años de* 1774–1775–1779, 1788 *y* 1790. My attention was drawn to them by Theodore F. Dwight, Esq., of that department.

[5] The details of this and subsequent explorations are given with references in Bancroft's *Northwest Coast*, vol. i. p. 151 *et seq.* Such voyages will be only briefly indicated in the rest of the present paper.

[6] Malaspina with a Spanish Commission in 1791, and later Galiano and Valdés, explored the coast, and their results were published in 1802. Cf. Navarrete, *Sutil y Mexicana*.

[7] It is sketched by Bancroft, *Northwest Coast*, vol. i. p. 135.

[8] Bancroft (*Northwest Coast*, vol. i. p. 169) reproduces a part of his map.

to water.[1] In 1786 the Frenchman La Pérouse was on the coast.[2] In 1789 the English and Spanish meeting on the coast, the English commander was seized. This action led to a diplomatic fence, the result of which was the surrender of Nootka to the English.

Meanwhile a Boston ship, the " Columbia," commanded by Captain Kendrick, in company with the " Washington " (Captain Gray), was on a voyage, which was the first American attempt to sail around the globe.[3] They entered and named the Columbia River ; and meeting Vancouver, the intelligence was communicated to him. When the English commander occupied Nootka, the last vestige of uncertainty regarding the salient features of the coast may be said to have disappeared under his surveys. Before they were published, George Foster issued in 1791 his map of the northwest coast, in which the Straits of Juan de Fuca were placed below 40°, by which Captain Gray is supposed to have entered, on his way to an open sea, coming out again in 55°, through what we now know as the Dixon entrance, to the north of Queen Charlotte's Island; the American navigator having threaded, as was supposed, a great northern archipelago. Vancouver's own map finally cleared the remaining confusion, and the migratory Straits of Juan de Fuca were at last fixed as the channel south of Vancouver's Island which led to Puget Sound.[4]

NOTES.

MERCATOR'S PROJECTION. — It was no new thing to convert the spherical representation of the earth into a plane on the cylindrical

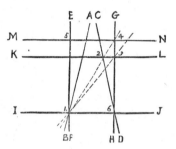

principle, for it had been done in the fourteenth century; but no one had devised any method by which it could be used for a sea-chart, since the parallelizing of the meridians altered the direction of point from point. Mercator seems to have reasoned out a plan in this wise : A B and C D are two meridians drawing together as they approach the pole. If they are made parallel, as in E F and G H, the point 2 is moved to 3, which is in a different direction from 1, in the parallel of latitude, I J. If the line of direction from 1 to 2 is prolonged till it strikes the perpendicular meridian G H at 4, the original direction is preserved, and the parallel K L can then be moved to become M N; thus prolonging the distance from 1 to 5, and from 6 to 4, to counteract the effect on direction by perpendicularizing the meridians. To do this accurately involved a law which could be applicable to all parallels and meridians ; and that law Mercator seems only to have reached approximately. But the idea once conveyed, it was seized by Edward Wright in England in 1590, who evolved the law, and published it with a map, the first engraved on the new system, in his *Certain Errors of Navigation*, London, 1599. Mead, in his *Construction of Maps* (1717), examined all previous systems of projections ; but contended that Varenius in Latin, and his follower Newton in English, had not done the subject justice. There have been some national controversies over the

[1] Bancroft (*Northwest Coast*, vol. i. p. 133) reproduces his map.

[2] Bancroft (Ibid., i. 176) reproduces a part of his map.

[3] Cf. *Memorial History of Boston*, vol. iv. p. 208 ; *Historical Magazine*, vol. xviii. p. 155 ; *Harper's Magazine*, December, 1882 ; Bulfinch, *Oregon and El Dorado*, p. 3. The report on the claims of the heirs of Kendrick and Gray, for allowance for the rights established by them for the U. S. Government, is printed in the *Historical Magazine*, September, 1870. A medal struck on occasion of this voyage is engraved in Bulfinch. Cf. also *American Journal of Numismatics*, vi. 33, 63 ; vii. 7 ; *Coin-Collectors Journal*, vi. 46 ; *Magazine of American History*, v. 140. The fullest account yet given of this expedition is in Bancroft's *Northwest Coast*, i. 185 *et seq.* He had the help of a journal kept on one of the ships.

[4] Bancroft's *Northwest Coast*, vol. i., must be consulted for these later and for subsequent exploring and trading voyages.

claims of the German Mercator and the English Wright; but D'Avezac, in his "Coup d'Œil historique sur la projection des cartes de géographie," printed in the *Bulletin de la Société de Géographie*, 1863 (also separately), defends Mercator's claims to be considered the originator of the projection; and he (pp. 283–285) gives references to writers on the subject, who are also noted in Van Raemdonck's *Mercator*, p. 120.

The claim which Van Raemdonck had made in his *Gérard Mercator, sa vie et ses œuvres*, — that the great geographer was a Fleming, — was controverted by Dr. Breusing in his *Gerhard Kremer, gen. Mercator, der Deutsche Geograph*, 1869, and in an article (supposed to be his) in the *Mittheilungen aus Justus Perthes' Geographischer Anstalt*, 1869, vol. xi. p. 438, where the German birth of Mercator is contended for. To this Van Raemdonck replied in his *Gérard de Cremer, ou Mercator, Géographe Flamand*, published at St. Nicholas in 1870. The controversy rose from the project, in 1869, to erect a monument to Mercator at Duisburg. Cf. also Bertrand in the *Journal des Savants*, February, 1870.

ORTELIUS. — Ortelius was born in 1527, and died in 1598, aged seventy-one years. He was a rich man, and had visited England in his researches. Stevens says in his *Bibliotheca historica* p. 133 : "A thorough study of Ortelius is of the last importance. . . . He was a bibliographer, a cartographer, and an antiquary, as well as a good mathematician and geographer; and what is of infinite importance to us now, he gave his authorities." Cf. also "La Généalogie du Géographe Abraham Ortelius," by Génard in the *Bulletin de la Société Géographique d'Anvers*, v. 315; and Felix Van Hulst's *Life of Ortelius*, second edition, Liege, 1846, with a portrait, which can also be found in the 1580, 1584, and perhaps other editions of his own *Theatrum*. There is also a brief notice, by M. de Macedo, of his geographical works in *Annales des Voyages*, vol. ii. pp. 184–192. Thomassy (*Les Papes géographes*, p. 65) has pointed out how Ortelius fell into some errors, from ignorance of Ruscelli's maps, in the 1561 edition of Ptolemy. The engraver of his early editions was Francis Hagenberg, and of his later ones, Ferdinand Orsenius and Ambroise Orsenius. He prefixed to his book a list of the authorities, from whose labors he had constructed his own maps. It is a most useful list for the students of the map-making of the sixteenth century. It has not a single Spanish title, which indicates how closely the Council for the Indies had kept their archives from the unofficial cartographers. The titles given are wholly of the sixteenth century, not many anterior to 1528, and mostly of the latter half of the century, indeed after 1560; and

they are about one hundred and fifty in all. The list includes some maps which Ortelius had not seen; and some, to which in his text he refers, are not included in the list. There are some maps among them of which modern inquiry has found no trace. Stevens, in unearthing Walter Lud, turned to the list and found him there as Gualterus Ludovicus. (See *ante*, p. 162.)

Ortelius supplied some titles which he had omitted, — including some earlier than 1528, — as well as added others produced in the interval, when, in 1592, he republished the list in its revised state. Lelewel has arranged the names in a classified way in his *Géographie du moyen âge*, vol. ii. pp. 185, 210, and on p. 217 has given us an account of the work of Ortelius. Cf. also Lelewel, vol. v. p. 214; Sabin, vol. xiv. p. 61.

The original edition of the *Theatrum* was issued at Antwerp, in Latin, and had fifty-three maps; it was again published the same year with some changes. There are copies in Mr. Brevoort's Jules Marcou's collections, and in the Carter-Brown, Harvard College, and Astor libraries. Stevens, in his illustrated *Bibliotheca geographica*, no. 2,077, gives a fac-simile of the title. Cf. also *Huth Catalogue*, vol. iii. p. 1068; *Carter-Brown Catalogue*, vol. i. no. 278; and Muller, *Books on America* (1877), no. 2,380.

The third Latin edition appeared the next year (1571) at Antwerp, with the same maps, as did the first edition with Dutch text, likewise with the same maps. Stevens, *Bibliotheca historica*, no. 1,473, thinks the Dutch is the original text.

To these several editions a supplement or additamentum, with eighteen new maps (none, however, relating to America), was added in 1573. Sabin's *Dictionary*; Brockhaus, *Americana* (1861), no. 28. Muller, *Books on America* (1877), no. 2,381.

The same year (1573, though the colophon reads "Antorff, 1572") the first German edition appeared, but in Roman type, and with a somewhat rough linguistic flavor. It had sixty-nine maps, and included the map of America. Koehler, of Leipsic, priced a copy in 1883 at 100 marks. The Latin (Antwerp) edition of this year (1573), "nova editio aliquot iconibus aucta," seems also to have the same peculiarity of an earlier year (1572) in the colophon. *Huth Catalogue*, vol. iii. p. 1068). Copies of all these editions seem to vary in the number of the maps. (*Library of Congress Catalogue*; *Carter-Brown Catalogue*, and the catalogues of Quaritch, Weigel, and others.) In 1574 some of the Antwerp issues have a French text, with maps corresponding to the German edition.

There are copies of the 1575 edition in the libraries of Congress, Harvard College, and the Boston Athenæum; and the four maps of interest in American cartography may be described from the Harvard College copy. They are reproductions of the maps of the 1570 edition.

a. Mappemonde. North America has a perfected outline much as in the Mercator map, with "Anian regnum" at the northwest. North America is marked, as by Wytfliet, "America sive India nova;" but the geography of the Arctic and northeastern parts is quite different from Wytfliet. Groclant and Groenland have another relative position, and take a general trend east and west; while in Wytfliet it is north and south. Northern Labrador is called Estotilant; while Frisland and Drogeo, islands to the south and east of it, are other reminders of the Zeni chart. This same map was reissued in the 1584 edition; and again, new cut, with a few changes, and dated 1587, it reappeared in the 1597 edition.

b. The two Americas. Anian and Quivira are on the northwest coast of North America. Tolm and Tototeac are northeast of the Gulf of California, and mark the region where the St. Lawrence rises, flowing, without lakes, to the gulf, with Terra Corterealis on the north and Norumbega on the south. Estotilant is apparently north of Hudson's Straits, and off its point is Icaria (another Zeni locality), with Frislant south of it. Newfoundland is cut into two large islands, with Baccalaos, a small island off its eastern coast. South America has the false projection (from Mercator) on its southwestern coast in place of Ruscelli's uncertain limits at that point. This projecting coast continued for some time to disfigure the outline of that continent in the maps. This map also reappeared in the 1584 edition.

c. Scandia, or the Scandinavian regions, and the North Atlantic show Greenland, Groclant, Island, Frisland, Drogeo, and Estotilant on a large scale, but in much the same relation to one another as in the map *a.* East of Greenland, and separated from it by a strait, is a circumpolar land which has these words: "Pygmei hic habitant." The general disposition of the parts of this map resembles Mercator's, and it was several times repeated, as in the editions of Ortelius of 1584 and 1592; and it was re-engraved in Münster's *Cosmographia* of 1595, and in the Cologne-Arnheim Ptolemy of 1597.

d. Indiæ orientalis. It shows Japan, an island midway in a sea separating Mangi (Asia) on the west from "Americæ sive Indie occidentalis pars" on the east. This map also reappeared in the 1584 edition, and may be compared with those of the Wytfliet series.

In 1577 an epitome of Ortelius by Heyn, with a Dutch text and seventy-two maps, appeared at Antwerp.

In 1580 the German text, entirely rewritten, appeared at Antorff, with a portrait of Ortelius and twenty-four new maps (constituting the third supplement), with a new general map of America. Among the new maps was one of New Spain, dated 1579, containing, it is reckoned, about a thousand names; another showing Florida, Northern Mexico, and the West India Islands; and a third on one sheet showing Peru, Florida, and Guastecan Regio.

The Latin edition of 1584, with a further increase of maps, is in Harvard College Library. In 1587 there was a French text issued, the mappemonde of which is reproduced in Vivien de St. Martin's *Histoire de la géographie.* This text in the 1588 edition is called "revue, corrigé et augmentée pour la troisième fois." This French text is wholly independent of, and not a translation of, the Latin and German. The maps are at this time usually ninety-four in number. In 1589 there was Marchetti's edition at Brescia and a Latin one at Antwerp. In 1591 there was a fresh supplement of twenty-one maps. In 1592 the Antwerp edition was the last one superintended by Ortelius himself. The map of the New World was re-engraved, and the maps number in full copies two hundred and one, usually colored; there is a copy in Harvard College Library. In 1593 there was an Italian text, and other Latin editions in 1595 and 1596, a copy of the last being in Harvard College Library. This completes the story of the popularity of Ortelius down to the publication of Wytfliet, when American cartography obtained its special exponent.

A few later editions may mark the continued popularity of the work of Ortelius, and of those who followed upon his path: —

Il theatro del mondo, Brescia (1598), one hundred maps, of which three are American.

A French text at Antwerp (1598), with one hundred and nineteen maps, including the same American maps as in the 1587 edition, except that of the world and of America at large.

Peeter Heyn's *Miroir du monde,* Amsterdam (1598), with eighty woodcut maps, — an epitome of Ortelius.

After Ortelius's death, the first Latin edition in 1601, at Antwerp (111 maps), had his final corrections; other issues followed in 1603, 1609 (115 maps), 1612, 1624, with an epitome by Crignet in 1602 (123 maps); and an epitome in English in 1610. An Italian text by Pigafetta appeared in 1612 and 1697.

Lelewel (*Géographie du moyen âge,* vol. ii. pp. 181, 185, and *Epilogue,* p. 214) has somewhat carefully examined the intricate subject of the make-up of editions of Ortelius; but the truth probably is, that there was much independent grouping of particular copies which obscures the bibliography.

CHAPTER VII.

EARLY EXPLORATIONS OF NEW MEXICO.

BY HENRY W. HAYNES.

Archæological Institute of America.

A T the time of the Spanish conquest of Mexico there were living, some
fifteen hundred miles to the north of the city so named, in the upper
valley of the Rio del Norte, and upon some of the eastern affluents of the
Colorado of the West, certain native tribes, who had attained to a degree
of culture superior to that of any people in North America, with the exception of the semi-civilized Aztec and Maya races. These were the Sedentary or Pueblo Indians, — village communities dwelling together in large
buildings constructed of stone or adobe, — whose home lay principally
within the present limits of New Mexico and Arizona, although extending
somewhat into southwestern Colorado and southeastern Utah. The first
rumors of the existence of this people which had reached the ears of the
Spaniards grew out of a tale told to Nuño de Guzman in 1530, when
he was at the head of the Royal Audience then governing New Spain.[1]
He had an Indian slave, called by the Spaniards Tejos, who represented
himself to be a son of a trader in feathers, such as were used by the natives
for head-dresses. Tejos said that it was his father's habit to travel about,
exchanging his wares for silver and gold, which were abundant in certain
regions. Once or twice he had accompanied his father on these journeys,
and then he had seen cities large enough to be compared with Mexico.
They were seven in number, and entire streets in them were occupied by
jewellers. To reach them it was necessary to travel northward forty days'
journey through a desert region lying between the two seas.

Guzman placed confidence in this narrative; and collecting a force of
four hundred Spaniards and twenty thousand Indians, he set out from
Mexico in search of this country. It was believed to be only about six
hundred miles distant, and already the name of *The Land of the Seven
Cities* had been given to it. There were also other strange stories current,
that had been told to Cortés a few years before, about a region called Ciguatan, lying somewhere in the north, near to which was an island inhabited

---

[1] *Relation de Castañeda,* in Ternaux-Compans, *Voyages,* etc., ix. i.

solely by Amazons. In this, also, there was said to be gold in abundance; and it was quite as much the hope of finding the Island of the Amazons, with its gold, that inspired Guzman's expedition, as of gaining access to the treasures of The Seven Cities. But on his march confirmatory reports about these cities kept reaching him; and eventually the expedition succeeded in penetrating to Ciguatan, and even as far within the province of Culiacan, the extreme limit of Spanish discovery, as to Colombo. Nevertheless, they did not find the Island of the Amazons, and The Seven Cities kept receding farther toward the north.[1] Meanwhile one of his captains made a reconnoissance some seventy leagues in an easterly direction without any satisfactory result. At last, the difficulties of an advance through a wild country and amid pathless mountains brought the expedition to a halt, which soon dampened the ardor of the soldiers, who grew clamorous to return to Mexico. But in the mean time news had reached Guzman that Cortés was once more there, clothed with new titles and authority, and he did not dare to brave the anger which his hostile proceedings during Cortés' absence were sure to have provoked. Accordingly he retraced his steps no farther than to Compostella and Guadalaxara, where he remained, and established the colonies from which was formed the province known afterwards as New Gallicia.[2] Not long after, he was deposed from his authority as governor of this province by direct commands from Spain; and Antonio de Mendoza, who had now been created Viceroy of New Spain, appointed Francisco Vasquez de Coronado to the vacant post.

Meanwhile the Indian Tejos had died, and the mysterious Seven Cities would have remained only a name, if the interest in them had not been revived by a remarkable occurrence. This was the arrival in the province of Culiacan, in 1536, of Antonio Nuñez Cabeza de Vaca, with three companions. They were the sole survivors of the numerous company who had followed Pamphilo de Narvaez, in 1527, to the shores of Florida. During nine years of almost incredible perils and hardships, after traversing in their wanderings all the great unknown region lying north of the Gulf of Mexico, they had at last reached the shores of the southern sea. They brought back accounts of having fallen in with civilized peoples, dwelling in permanent habitations, where were "populous towns with very large houses."[3] The story of their strange adventures is told elsewhere in more detail,[4] so that here it suffices to put on record simply that they were the first Europeans to tread the soil of New Mexico. As soon as they reached Mexico, the intelligence of their discoveries was communicated to the Viceroy Mendoza, by whom it was at once transmitted to Coronado, the new governor of New Gallicia. He was a gentleman of good family, from Salamanca, but long established in Mexico, where he had married a

---

[1] *Segunda relacion de Nuño de Guzman*, in Icazbalceta, *Coll. de Docs.*, ii. 303; *Quarta relacion*, in Ibid., p. 475; *García de Lopez' Relacion*, in Pacheco's *Coll. Doc. Inéd.*, tom. xiv. pp. 455–460.

[2] [See *ante*, p. 391. — ED.]

[3] *Relacion de Cabeça de Vaca*, translated by Buckingham Smith (chap. xxxi. p. 167).

[4] [See *ante*, p. 243 in Dr. J. G. Shea's chapter on "Ancient Florida." — ED.]

daughter of Alonzo d'Estrada, former governor of that place, who was generally believed to be a natural son of Ferdinand the Catholic. Coronado at this time was occupied in travelling through New Spain; but he repaired immediately to his province to investigate the reports, taking with him one of Cabeza de Vaca's companions, a negro named Stephen, and also three Franciscan monks, missionaries to the natives. After a brief interval a proposition was made to one of these monks, Fray Marcos de Nizza (of Nice), to undertake a preliminary exploration of the country. He was selected for this task on account of his character and attainments, and because of the experience he had acquired in Peru, under Alvarado. Elaborate instructions were sent to him by the Viceroy, which seem inspired by a spirit of humanity as well as intelligence.[1] He was told that the expedition was to be undertaken for the spread of the holy Catholic faith, and that he must exhort the Spaniards to treat the natives with kindness, and threaten them with the Viceroy's displeasure if this command should be disobeyed. The natives were to be informed of the Emperor's indignation at the cruelties that had been inflicted upon them, and to be assured that they should no longer be enslaved or removed from their homes. He was ordered to take the negro Stephen as his guide, and cautioned against giving any ground of offence to the natives. He was to take special note of their numbers and manner of life, and whether they were at peace or war among themselves. He was also to observe particularly the nature of the country, the fertility of the soil, and the character of its products; to learn what wild animals were to be found there, and whether there were any rivers, great or small. He was to search for precious stones and metals, and if possible to bring back specimens of them; and to make inquiry whether the natives had any knowledge of a neighboring sea. If he should succeed in reaching the southern sea, he was to leave an account of his discoveries buried at the foot of some conspicuous tree marked with a cross, and to do the same thing at the mouths of all rivers, so that any future maritime expedition might be instructed to be on the lookout for such a sign. Especially was he ordered to send back constant reports as to the route he had taken, and how he was received; and if he should discover any great city, he was to return immediately to give private information about it. Finally, he was told to take possession of the new country in the name of the Emperor, and to make the natives understand that they must submit themselves to him.

In accordance with these instructions, Fray Marcos set out from S. Miguel de Culiacan on the 7th of March, 1539, with Fray Honoratus for a companion, and the negro Stephen for a guide. The monks were not greatly pleased with this man, on account of his avaricious and sensual nature; but they hoped to reap some benefit from his ability to communicate with the natives, several of whom, who had been brought away from their homes by Cabeza de Vaca, but who had been redeemed and set free by the Viceroy, also accompanied the party. There was, besides, a much larger company of

---

[1] Ternaux-Compans, ix. 249.

natives from the neighboring regions, who were induced to join the expedition on account of the favorable representations made to them by those whom the Viceroy had freed.

Fray Marcos, upon his return, made a formal report of all his doings; [1] and to this we must look for the first definite information in regard to the early exploration and history of the region with which we are now concerned, since Cabeza de Vaca's narrative is too confused to furnish any sure indications of locality, and he has even been charged by Castañeda with "representing things very differently from what he had found them in reality." [2]   The monk relates how they reached Petatlan, after having met with great kindness from the natives on their way; and while resting there for three days Fray Honoratus fell ill, and was obliged to be left behind. He himself continued his journey for some thirty leagues, still finding the natives most friendly, and even willing to share with him their supply of food, although it was but scanty, owing to no rain having fallen for three years.   On his way he was met by some inhabitants of the island, which had previously been visited by Cortés, by whom he was assured that it was indeed an island, and not a continent as some had supposed.   Still other people came to visit him from a larger island, but more distant, who informed him that there were still thirty islands more, but that they were only poorly supplied with food. [3]   These Indians wore shells suspended from their necks, like those in which pearls are found; and when a pearl was shown to them, they said they had an abundance of them, although the friar admits that he himself did not see any.   After this his route lay for four days through a desert, during which he was accompanied by the Indians from the islands and the inhabitants of the villages through which he had passed. Finally he came to a people who were astonished to see him, as they had no intercourse with the people on the other side of the desert, and had no knowledge whatsoever of Europeans.   Nevertheless, they received him kindly, and supplied him with food, and endeavored to touch his garments, calling him "a man sent from heaven."   In return, he endeavored, as best he might by means of interpreters, to teach them about "God in heaven, and his Majesty upon earth."   Upon being asked if they knew of any country more populous and civilized than their own, they replied that four or five days' journey into the interior, in a great plain at the foot of the mountains, there were many large cities, inhabited by a people who wore garments made of cotton.   When specimens of different metals were shown to them, they selected the gold, and said that this people had their common dishes made of this material, and wore balls of it suspended from their ears and noses, and even used "thin plates of it to scrape off their sweat."   However, as this plain was quite remote from the sea, and as it was his purpose

[1] *A relation of the Rev. Frier Marco de Nica touching his discovery of the kingdom of Cevola or Cibola* in Hakluyt's *Voyages*, etc., iii. 438 (edition of 1810).

[2] Castañeda, *Relation*, p. 9.

[3] [See *ante*, p. 431, "Discoveries on the Pacific Coast of North America," for the explorations up that coast by Cortés. — ED.]

never to be far away from it during his journeyings, the monk decided to defer the exploration of this country until his return.

Meanwhile Fray Marcos continued to travel for three days through the territories of the same tribe, until he arrived at a town of moderate size, called Vacapa, situated in a fertile region about forty leagues from the sea.[1] Here he rested for several days, while three exploring parties were despatched to the coast with directions to bring back some of the natives dwelling there as well as upon the neighboring islands, in order that he might obtain more definite information about those regions. The negro was ordered to advance in a northerly direction fifty or sixty leagues, and to send back a report of what he should discover. In four days' time a messenger came from him bringing news of "a country the finest in the world;" and with him came an Indian, who professed to have visited it, and who reported that it was a thirty days' journey from the place where Stephen then was to the first city of this province. The name of this province was Cibola,[2] and it contained seven great cities, all under the rule of one lord. The houses were built of stone and lime; some of them were three stories high, and had their doorways ornamented with turquoises, of which there was an abundance in that country; beyond this, there were still other provinces all greater than that of The Seven Cities. This tale was all the more readily credited by the monk, as the man appeared to be "of good understanding." Nevertheless, he deferred his departure until the exploring parties should return from the coast. After a short time they came back, bringing with them some of the dwellers upon the coast and on two of the islands, who reported that there were thirty-four islands in all, near to one another; but that all, as well as the main land, were deficient in food supplies. They said that the islanders held intercourse with each other by means of rafts, and that the coast stretched due north. On the same day there came to Vacapa, to visit the monk, three Indians who had their faces, hands, and breasts painted. They said that they dwelt in the eastern country, in the neighborhood of Cibola, and they confirmed all the reports in regard to it.

As fresh messengers had now come from Stephen, urging the monk to hasten his departure, he sent the natives of the coast back to their homes and resumed his journey, taking with him two of the islanders—who begged to accompany him for several days—and the painted Indians. In three days' time he arrived among the people who had given the negro his information about Cibola. They confirmed all that had been said about it; and they also told about three other great kingdoms, called Marata, Acus, and Totonteac. They said they were in the habit of going to these countries to labor in the fields, and that they received in payment turquoises and skins of cattle. All the people there wore turquoises in

---

[1] Mr. A. F. Bandelier puts this place "in southern Arizona, somewhat west from Tucson." *Historical Introduction to Studies among the Sedentary Indians of New Mexico*, p. 8.

[2] This word was borrowed by the Spaniards from the native languages, and applied by them to the Bison. [As early as 1542 Rotz drew pictures of this animal on his maps. — ED.]

their ears and noses, and were clad in long cotton robes reaching to their feet, with a girdle of turquoises around the waist. Over these cotton garments they wore mantles made of skins, which were considered to be the clothing best suited to the country. They gave the monk several of these skins, which were said to come from Cibola, and which proved to be as well dressed and tanned as those prepared by the most highly civilized people. The people here treated him with very great kindness, and brought the sick to him to be healed, and endeavored to touch his garments as he recited the Gospels over them. The next day he continued his journey, still attended by the painted Indians, and arrived at another village, where the same scenes were repeated. He was told that Stephen had gone on four or five days' journey, accompanied by many of the natives, and that he had left word for Fray Marcos to hasten forward. As this appeared to be the finest country he had found thus far, he proceeded to erect two crosses, and to take formal possession of it in the name of the Emperor, in accordance with his instructions. He then continued on his journey for five days more, passing through one village after another, everywhere treated with great kindness, and receiving presents of turquoises and of skins, until at last he was told that he was on the point of coming to a desert region. To cross this would be five days' march; but he was assured that provisions would be transported for him, and places provided in which he could sleep. This all turned out as had been promised, and he then reached a populous valley, where the people all wore turquoises in greater profusion than ever, and talked about Cibola as familiarly as did the Spaniards about Mexico or Quito. They said that in it all the products of civilization could be procured, and they explained the method by which the houses were constructed of several stories.

Up to this point the coast had continued to run due north; but here, in the latitude of 35°, Fray Marcos found, from personal examination, that it began to trend westward. For five days he journeyed through this fertile and well-watered valley, finding villages in it at every half-league, when there met him a native of Cibola, who had fled hither from the governor of that place. He was a man advanced in years, and of good appearance and capacity; and from him were obtained even more definite and detailed accounts of Cibola and the neighboring kingdoms, their condition and mode of government; and he begged to be allowed to return home in the friar's company, in order to obtain pardon through his intercession. The monk pursued his way for three days more through this rich and populous valley, when he was informed that soon another desert stretch, fifteen long days' march in extent, would begin. Accordingly, as he had now travelled one hundred and twelve leagues from the place where he had first learned of this new country, he determined to rest here a short time. He was told that Stephen had taken along with him more than three hundred men as his escort, and to carry provisions across the desert; and he was advised to do likewise, as the natives all expected to return laden with riches. But

Fray Marcos declined; and selecting only thirty of the principal men, and the necessary porters, he entered upon the desert in the month of May, and travelled for twelve days, finding at all the halting-places the cabins which had been occupied by Stephen and other travellers. Of a sudden an Indian came in sight, covered with dust and sweat, with grief and terror stamped upon his countenance. He had been one of Stephen's party, and was the son of one of the chiefs who were escorting the friar. This was the tale he told: On the day before Stephen's arrival at Cibola, according to his custom, he sent forward messengers to announce his approach. These carried his staff of office, made of a gourd, to which was attached a string of bells and two feathers, one white and one red, which signified that he had come with peaceful intentions and to heal the sick. But when this was delivered to the governor, he angrily dashed it to the ground, saying he knew the strangers, and forbade their entering the city, upon pain of death. This message was brought back to Stephen, who nevertheless continued on, but was prevented from entering the city. He was conducted to a large house outside the walls, where everything was taken from him; and the whole party passed the night without food or drink. The following morning, while the narrator had gone to the river which flowed near by, to quench his thirst, suddenly he saw Stephen in full flight, pursued by the people of Cibola, who were slaying all of his companions; whereupon he hid himself under the bank, and finally succeeded in escaping across the desert. When they heard this pitiful story, the Indians began to wail, and the monk to tremble for his own life; but he says he was troubled still more at the thought of not being able to bring back information about this important country. Nevertheless, he proceeded to cut the cords of some of his packages, from which he had as yet given nothing away, and to distribute all the contents among the chief men, bidding them fear nothing, but continue on with him still farther; which they did, until they came within a day's journey of Cibola. Here there met them two more of Stephen's Indian companions, still bleeding from their wounds, who told the same story about his death and the destruction of his company, supposing that they alone had escaped, by hiding themselves under the heaps of those who had been slain by flights of arrows.[1]

The monk goes on to relate that he tried to comfort the weeping natives, by telling them that God would punish the people of Cibola, and the Em-

[1] Castañeda, however, relates the circumstances of Stephen's death somewhat differently, stating that the negro and his party, on their arrival at Cibola, were shut up in a house outside the city, while for three days the chiefs continued to question him about the object of his coming. When told that he was a messenger from two white men, who had been sent by a powerful prince to instruct them in heavenly things, they would not believe that a black man could possibly have come from a land of white men, and they suspected him of being the spy of some nation that wished to subjugate them. Moreover, the negro had the assurance to demand from them their property and their women; upon which they resolved to put him to death, without, however, harming any of those with him, all of whom, with the exception of a few boys, were sent back, to the number of sixty. (*Relation*, p. 12.) This latter statement, as well as that in relation to the libidinous practices of the negro, are confirmed by Coronado. *Relation;* Hakluyt's *Collection of Voyages* (*Principall Navigations*), iii. 454.

peror would send an army to chastise them; but they refused to believe him, saying no power could resist that of Cibola. He thereupon distributed everything he had left among them to appease them, and endeavored to persuade some of them to go nearer the city, in order to make sure of the fate of the party; and upon their refusal, he said that he should at all events endeavor to obtain a sight of Cibola. Seeing his determination, two of the chiefs consented to accompany him; and they came to a hill, from which they could look down upon the city. It is situated in a plain, he says, and seemed to be handsomer and more important than any city he had yet seen, and even larger than Mexico. The houses were built of stone, and were of several stories, as the natives had told him, and with flat roofs; and upon his expressing his admiration of it, his companions said that it was the smallest of The Seven Cities, and that Totonteac, one of the neighboring towns, was still larger and finer. With the help of the Indians he proceeded to raise a great pile of stones, upon which he planted a cross as large as he was able to make, and in the name of the Viceroy and Governor of New Spain, on behalf of the Emperor, he took possession of the Land of the Seven Cities, and the realms of Totonteac, Acus, and Marata; and to the whole country he gave the name of the New Kingdom of St. Francis. Upon retracing his steps across the desert, he failed to receive as friendly a reception as before, for all the people were in tears for the loss of their murdered relatives; so that he became alarmed, and hastened through the valley so rapidly that in three days' time he had crossed the second desert. From this point he made a detour in the direction of the country lying to the East, about which he had been told on his first coming. Without venturing to penetrate into it, he contented himself with observing the approaches, when he found seven small villages in a verdant valley, but in the distance he could see the smoke of a fine city. He was informed that the country was very rich in gold, but that the inhabitants refused all intercourse with strangers. Nevertheless, he planted two more crosses here, and took formal possession of the country. From this point he retraced his steps as speedily as possible to Compostella, where he rejoined Coronado, and sent immediate notice of his return to the Viceroy.

While Fray Marcos had been absent upon his journey, Coronado had himself been occupied in searching for a province lying somewhere to the north of his own dominions, called Topira. After a toilsome march through a mountain region this was reached, and proved to be entirely different from what it had been reported; and he had just returned from this fruitless expedition, when the monk arrived. So glowing were the accounts he gave of what he had himself seen and what the natives had told him, as well as of the wealth to be found in the islands of the southern seas, that Coronado determined to take the monk at once with himself to Mexico and lay the matter before the Viceroy. There, on the 2d of September, 1539, according to the notaries' attest, Fray Marcos presented a report in writing to Mendoza, by whom it was transmitted to the Emperor Charles V., accompanied by a letter from himself containing a brief narrative of the previous attempts that had been made for the exploration of the country.[1]

In a very short time Coronado began to proclaim openly what hitherto he had only whispered in strictest confidence to his most intimate friends, — that the marvellous Seven Cities had been discovered which Nuño de Guzman had sought for in vain; and he proceeded forthwith to make preparations and to collect a military force for their conquest. Meanwhile the Franciscans chose Fray Marcos for their general; and soon all the pulpits of that Order were resounding to such good purpose, that before long an army of three hundred Spaniards and eight hundred Indians of New Spain had been collected. So many gentlemen of noble birth volunteered for this service that the Viceroy was much embarrassed in selecting officers; but at last he decided upon the principal ones, and appointed Coronado, as was only his due, general-in-chief. Compostella, the capital of New Gallicia, was named as the place of rendezvous for the army; and in the mean time Hernando Alarcon received instructions to sail along the coast of the southern sea in order to accompany the march of the expedition. He was directed to transport the heavy stores and to keep up communications by means of the rivers that empty into it. This part of the plan, however, failed of success, as Coronado's line of march soon led him to a distance from the coast.[2]

AUTOGRAPH OF CORONADO.

In the last days of February, 1540, the Viceroy himself came to Compostella, and from there he accompanied the army for two days on its

---

[1] Ternaux-Compans, ix. 283, 290.

[2] Alarcon set sail on the 9th of May, 1540, and by penetrating to the upper extremity of the Gulf of California, proved that California was not an island, as had been supposed. He made two attempts to ascend the Colorado in boats, and planted a cross at the highest point he reached, burying at its foot a writing, which, as will be seen, was subsequently found by Melchior Diaz. His report of this voyage, containing valuable information in regard to the natives, can be found in Hakluyt, *Voyages*, iii. 505 (ed. 1810); translated from Ramusio, *Navigationi*, iii. 363 (ed. 1565). There is a French translation in

Ternaux-Compans, ix. 299. This information about California is supplemented by the narrative of the voyage made two years later by Juan Rodriguez Cabrillo along the Pacific shore of the peninsula, and up the northwest coast probably as far as the southern border of Oregon. It was printed in Buckingham Smith's *Coleccion*, p. 173; and subsequently in Pacheco's *Documentos inéditos*, tom. xiv. p. 165. A translation by Mr. R. S. Evans, with valuable notes by Mr. H. W. Henshaw, is given in vol. vii. (Archæology) of *United States Geological Survey west of the one hundredth Meridian*. [See also the present volume, p. 443. — ED.]

march. But soon the difficulties of the route began to tell upon the inex-
perienced cavaliers, who were obliged each to carry his own provisions and
baggage, so that when they had reached Chiametla, they were compelled
to halt for several days in order to procure a supply of food. In doing
this a collision with the natives occurred, in which one of the superior
officers was slain; and in revenge, all who were *believed* to be inhabitants
of the village where it happened were hanged. Soon after this, dissatis-
faction began to manifest itself among the troops, which was heightened
by the discouraging reports which were spread on the return of Melchior
Diaz and his party, whom Coronado had sent by Mendoza's orders on
a reconnoitring expedition during his own absence in Mexico. They had
penetrated two hundred leagues beyond Culiacan, as far as the edge of the
desert, and they gave very different accounts from those of Fray Marcos.
Very few inhabitants were seen, except in two or three little villages of
some thirty huts, and everywhere was a great scarcity of provisions; while
the mountainous nature of the country rendered it almost impassable.[1]
The friar, however, strove to encourage their drooping spirits, promising
them that they should not return empty handed; and the march was continued to Culiacan, where the expedition was received with great hospitality by the Spanish colonists. Here Coronado left the main body of the
army under the command of Tristan d'Arellano, with orders to follow him
in a fortnight, while he himself set out on the 22d of April, 1540, with
fifty horse and a few foot-soldiers and the monks who did not choose to
be left behind. In somewhat more than a month's time he came to the last
inhabited place on the borders of the desert, having everywhere met with
a friendly reception from the natives. At an intervening village, in the
valley which Cabeza de Vaca had called Corazones, he had halted, and
despatched messengers to the sea-coast, which was five days' journey
distant, and learned that a vessel had been seen passing by. The place
which he had now reached bore the name of Chichilticalli, or The Red
House, and it proved to be something very different from what Fray
Marcos had reported. Instead of a populous town at a distance of five
leagues from the sea, he found merely a single ruinous, roofless structure, at least ten days' journey from the coast. Nevertheless, it bore
the appearance of having once been a fortified work which had been constructed out of red earth by a civilized people, but had been destroyed
in former times by some barbarous enemy.[2] Here Coronado entered upon
the desert, and proceeding in a northeasterly direction he came in a fort-

[1] Extracts from a report sent back by Melchior Diaz while on this journey are given in a
letter from Mendoza to the Emperor Charles
V., dated April 17, 1540, in Ternaux-Compans,
ix. 290.

[2] Chichiltic-calli, or Red House, is generally
supposed to be the ruined structure, called
Casa Grande, in southern Arizona, near Florence, a little south of the river Gila, and not far
from the Southern Pacific Railroad. But Mr.
A. F. Bandelier, after a thorough topographical
exploration of the regions, is inclined to place
it considerably to the southeast of this point,
upon the river Arivaypa, in the vicinity of Fort
Grant. [This question is further examined in
Vol. I. of the present History. — ED.]

night's time to a river, to which the name of the Vermejo was given, on account of its turbid waters. This was only eight leagues distant from Cibola, where they arrived on the following day, sometime early in July, having only escaped by the general's prudence from falling into an ambuscade of hostile natives.[1]

Cibola turned out to be even a greater disappointment than the Red House, and many were the maledictions showered upon the monk by the soldiers. Instead of the great city which he had reported, it proved to be only a little village of not more than two hundred inhabitants, situated upon a rocky eminence, and difficult of access.[2] From its resemblance in situation, Coronado gave the name of Granada to the village; and he states that the name Cibola properly belonged to the whole district containing seven towns, and not to any particular place. As the natives continued to manifest a hostile disposition, and the army was almost famished from lack of food, it was resolved to attempt to carry it at once by assault, in order to get at the abundance of provisions stored there. But the inhabitants made such a stout resistance with missiles and showers of stones, that it would have gone hard with the Spaniards if it had not been for the protection of their armor. As it was, Coronado himself was twice felled to the earth, and his life was only saved by the devotion of one of his officers, who shielded him with his own body. However, in less than an hour's time the place was captured, though several of the horses of the Spaniards were killed, and a few of the assailants wounded. But when once possession of this strong point was secured, the whole district was speedily reduced to submission.

Here Coronado awaited the arrival of the main body of his army before attempting to penetrate farther into the country; and from this place he transmitted to the Viceroy, under date of Aug. 3, 1540, a report of what he had already accomplished, in which his disappointment about the character of the region through which he had journeyed was very plainly expressed, as well as his entire disbelief in the truth of the reports which Fray Marcos had brought back respecting the rich and powerful kingdoms lying at a distance. He shows that he had discovered the inherent defect of the country by laying particular stress upon the "great want of pasture;" and says that he had learned that "what the Indians worship is

---

[1] Jaramillo has given a very full itinerary of this march, describing with great particularity the nature of the country and the streams crossed (Ternaux-Compans, ix. 365–369). When the results of the latest explorations of Mr. A. F. Bandelier in this region are published by the Archæological Institute of America, there is good reason to hope for an exact identification of most if not all these localities, which at present is impossible. There can be little doubt, however, that the Vermejo is the Colorado Chiquito.

[2] In the *Proceedings* of the American Antiquarian Society for October, 1881, I have given in detail the reasons for identifying Cibola with the region of the present Zuñi pueblos. Mr. Frank H. Cushing has made the important discovery that this tribe has preserved the tradition of the coming of Fray Marcos, and of the killing of the negro Stephen, whom they call "the black Mexican," at the ruined pueblo called Quaquima. They claim also to have a tradition of the visit of Coronado, and even of Cabeza de Vaca.

water, for it causeth their corn to grow and maintaineth their life." [1]   With
this despatch he sent specimens of the garments worn by the natives and
of their weapons, and also "two cloths painted with the beasts of the
country;" he also reports that the natives possessed a certain amount of
gold and silver, but that he could not discover whence they procured it.

While waiting at Cibola the arrival of the main body of the army,
Coronado sent out a small party under Pedro de Tobar to explore a province lying some twenty leagues or more to the northwest, called Tusayan,[2]
where there were said to be seven cities, with houses built like those of
Cibola, and inhabited by a warlike people.   Tobar succeeded in approaching close to the first of these without being observed, as the natives now
seldom ventured far from their houses on account of the fear inspired by
the rumors spread abroad that Cibola had been captured by a fierce people
mounted upon animals that devoured human flesh.   However, as soon as
the Spaniards were discovered, the natives showed a bold front, advancing
to meet them in good order, and well armed.   Drawing a line in the sand,
they forbade the Spaniards crossing it, and wounded the horse of a soldier
who ventured to leap over it; whereupon a friar named Juan de Padilla,
who had been a soldier in his youth, urged the captain to make an onslaught
upon them, and the natives were soon put to flight and many of them
slain.   In a short time all this province gave in its submission, and peaceable relations were once more established.   The natives brought as gifts
to the Spaniards turquoises, tanned skins, maize, and other provisions,
and especially cotton stuffs, which were regarded by them as the choicest
present, since it did not grow in their own country.   They also gave information about a large river lying farther to the west, on whose banks, at
some days' journey down the stream, there dwelt a race of very large men.
Tobar returned to Cibola with this report, and Coronado immediately
despatched a second exploring party to verify it, under García Lopez de
Cardenas.   These were well received on their way by the people of
Tusayan, who supplied them with guides and provisions for the journey.
For twenty days their march lay through a desert, at the end of which they
came to the banks of a river which seemed to them to be elevated "three
or four leagues in the air."   So steep were these banks that it was impossible
to descend to the water, which appeared so far away as to seem to be
only an arm's-length in width, and yet their guides assured them that it
was over half a league broad.   Although it was summer time, it was quite
cold, and the country was covered with a growth of stunted pines.   For
three days they followed the bank in search of a passage; and some volunteers who made the attempt returned with the report that they had only
been able to accomplish a third of the descent, and that rocks which had
seemed scarcely as high as a man, were found to be loftier than the towers

[1] Coronado's relation as given in English in
Hakluyt, *Collection of Voyages*, etc., iii. 453 (reprint, London, 1810).

[2] Tusayan can be clearly identified as the site
of the present Moqui villages.   Bandelier, *Historical Introduction*, p. 15.

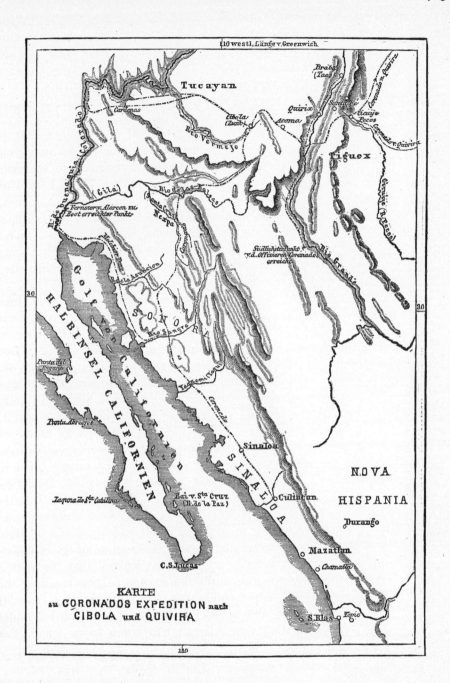

CORONADO'S EXPEDITION.[1]

[1] The map given in Ruge's *Das Zeitalter der Entdeckungen*, p. 417. With slight corrections, this is as accurate as our present information permits. Melchior Diaz penetrated farther north, and crossed the Colorado. Tiguex should be placed west of the Rio Grande, between Acoma and Quirex. The Rio "Sangra" is probably a mistake for "Sonora."

of Seville Cathedral.   For three or four days more they continued on; but at length they were forced to return by want of water, which they had been obliged to seek for every night a league or two back from the river, and retraced their steps to Cibola.[1]

In the mean time the main body of the army, which had been left at Culiacan under the command of Tristan d'Arellano, with orders to follow Coronado in a fortnight, set out, and slowly advancing reached at length Cabeza de Vaca's province of Corazones.   Here it was thought best to attempt to establish a colony; but owing to the difficulty of procuring a sufficient supply of food, it was subsequently transferred to the spot in the valley of the river which is now called Sonora.   From here Don Roderigo Maldonado was despatched down the river in the hope of finding Alarcon's vessels.   He returned without having accomplished his purpose, but brought back with him a native of huge stature, and reported that a nation of still larger men dwelt farther down the coast.   The whole army now transferred itself across the river to the new colony, and there waited for further orders from Coronado.

About the middle of September, 1540,[2] Melchior Diaz and Juan Gallegos arrived from Cibola with instructions for the army to proceed thither at once.   Gallegos continued on to Mexico, carrying to the Viceroy an account of the discoveries; and with him went Fray Marcos, who dared not remain any longer with the army, so incensed were they with him for his gross misrepresentations.   Diaz was ordered to remain at the new colony in the capacity of governor, and to seek to put himself in communication with Alarcon's vessels.   Immediately the army took up its march for Cibola, but Arellano remained behind.   As soon as they had departed, Diaz set out to explore the sea-coast, leaving Diego d'Alcarraz in command in his stead, who turned out to be very poorly fitted to exercise authority, so that disorders and mutinies broke out.   Diaz himself, after marching one hundred and fifty leagues in a southwesterly direction (as Castañeda reports),[3] struck the Tizon at some distance from its mouth, at a place where it was at least half a league wide.   Here he found a race of huge men dwelling together in large numbers in underground cabins roofed with straw, from whom he learned that the vessels had been seen three days' march down the stream.   Upon reaching the spot indicated, which the natives told him was fifteen leagues from its mouth, he came upon a tree with an inscription upon it, and buried under it he found a writing stating that Alarcon had come so far,[4] and after

[1] It is plain that this river was the Colorado; the description of the Grand Cañon cannot fail to be recognized. Bandelier, *Historical Introduction*, p. 15. The name by which it was called was the Tizon, the Spanish word for "firebrand," which the natives dwelling upon its banks were reported to be in the habit of carrying upon their winter journeyings. Castañeda, p. 50.

[2] Castañeda, *Relation*, p. 48; Ibid., p. 46, "Middle of October."

[3] Davis (*Spanish Conquest*, p. 160) suggests that he should have written "northwest." The anonymous Relacion (Pacheco's *Documentos Inéditos*, tom. xiv. p. 321) states that he travelled "westward."

[4] [See *ante*, p. 443, in the section of "Discoveries on the Pacific Coast." — ED.]

waiting there awhile had returned to New Spain. It also contained the information that this supposed south sea was actually a gulf which separated the mainland from what had been called the Island of California. With the intention of exploring this peninsula, Diaz proceeded up the river five or six days' march in the hope of finding a ford, and at length attempted to cross by means of rafts. The natives, whose assistance he had called in to help construct them, proved treacherous, and laid a plot to attack the Spaniards on both banks of the river, while a portion were in the act of crossing. When this was detected, they made their assault boldly, but were speedily put to flight. Diaz then continued his journey along the coast, which took here a southeasterly direction, until he reached a volcanic region where farther progress became impossible. While retracing his steps, he met with an accident which put an end to his life; but the rest of his party returned to Sonora in safety.

While Diaz was making these explorations, the main body of the army had continued on to Chichilticalli without having encountered any other peril than being severely poisoned from having eaten preserved fruits that had been given to them by the natives. Castañeda records their falling in with a flock of large mountain sheep, which ran so swiftly that they could not be captured. When within a day's march of Cibola they were overtaken by a terrible storm, accompanied by a heavy snow-fall, which caused the Spaniards great suffering, and nearly cost the lives of their Indian allies, natives of a warm country. But on arriving they found comfortable quarters provided by Coronado, and the whole force was now reunited, with the exception of a detachment which had been sent upon an expedition in an entirely different direction.

A party of natives had come to Cibola from a village called Cicuyé, situated some seventy leagues away toward the east, under a chief to whom the Spaniards gave the name of Bigotes, from the long mustache he wore. They proffered their friendly services to the strangers and invited them to visit their country, at the same time making them presents of tanned bison-skins. One of them had the figure of this animal painted on his body, which gave the Spaniards their first knowledge of its appearance. Coronado made them in return presents of glass beads and bells, and ordered Hernando d'Alvarado to take twenty men with him and explore that region, and after eighty days to return and report what he had discovered. After five days' travel Alvarado came to a village called Acuco, situated on a precipitous cliff so high that an arquebus-ball could scarcely reach the top. The only approach to it was by an artificial stairway cut in the rock, of more than three hundred steps, and for the last eighteen feet there were only holes into which to insert the toes.[1] By showing a bold front,

---

[1] The identity of Acuco with the modern pueblo of Acoma is perfectly established. See the plates and description in Lieutenant Abert's report, *Senate Executive Documents*, no. 41, 30*th* *Congress*, 1*st Session*, p. 470. Jaramillo is evidently wrong in naming this place Tutahaco, p. 370. Hernando d' Alvarado in his Report calls it Coco.

friendly relations were established with the inhabitants of this formidable stronghold, who numbered some two hundred fighting men, and a large supply of provisions was received from them.   Three days' march farther brought them to a province called Tiguex, containing twelve villages situated on the banks of a great river.[1]   The presence in the party of Bigotes, who was a renowned warrior well known in all that region, conciliated the favor of the people of Tiguex; and the country pleased Alvarado so much, that he sent a messenger to Coronado to persuade him to make it his winter quarters.[2]   Continuing his journey, in five days more he reached Cicuyé, which he found to be a strongly fortified village of four-story terraced houses, built around a large square.   It was also protected by a low stone wall, and was capable of putting five hundred warriors into the field.[3]

THE BUFFALO (*after Thevet*).[5]

Here they were welcomed with great demonstrations of friendship, and received many gifts of turquoises, which were abundant in that country.[4]   While resting here for several days they fell in with an Indian slave, — a native of the region lying toward Florida, which De Soto afterward explored, — who told them marvellous tales about the stores of gold and silver to be found in the great cities of his own country.   This man they named " the Turk," from his resemblance to men of that nation; and such implicit credence did they place in his stories, that after penetrating a little way into the plains under his guidance, — where for the first time they saw the bisons, with whose skins they had become familiar, — they retraced their steps in order to bring this information to Coronado.   On reaching Tiguex, Alvarado found Cardenas there, who had

---

[1] Davis (*The Spanish Conquest of New Mexico*, p. 185, note) places Tiguex on the banks of the Rio Puerco; and General Simpson (*Coronado's March*, p. 335), on the Rio Grande, below the Puerco.   But Mr. Bandelier (*Historical Introduction*, pp. 20–22), from documentary evidence, places it higher up the Rio Grande, in the vicinity of Bernalillo; corresponding perfectly with the "central point" which Castañeda declared it to be (p. 182).

[2] Alvarado's report of this expedition can be found in Buckingham Smith's *Coleccion de documentos*, p. 65; Pacheco's *Documentos Inéditos*, tom. iii. p. 511.   He says, " Partimos de Granada veinte y nueve de Agosto de 40, la via de Coco."

[3] General J. H. Simpson, *Coronado's March*, p. 335, has identified Cicuyé with Old Pecos. Additional arguments in support of this opinion may be found in Bandelier's *Visit to the Aboriginal Ruins in the Valley of Pecos*, p. 113.

[4] The turquoise mines of Cerillos, in the Sandia Mountains, are about twenty miles west of Pecos.   Bandelier's *Visit*, pp. 39, 115.

[5] [This is one of the earliest engravings — if not the earliest — of the buffalo, occurring on folio 144 *verso*, of Thevet's *Les Singularitez de la France Antarctique*, Antwerp, 1558.   Davis (*Spanish Conquest of New Mexico*, p. 67) says Cabeza de Vaca is the earliest to mention the buffalo. — ED.]

been sent on by the General, in accordance with his advice, to prepare winter quarters for the army now on its march from Sonora. Alvarado accordingly decided to remain in that province and wait for the coming of the army; but in making their preparations for its comfort the Spaniards showed very little consideration for the natives, forcing them to abandon one of their villages, taking only the clothes that they were wearing.

SKETCH OF THE BUFFALO.[1]

By this time Arellano had arrived at Cibola, coming from Sonora; and to him Coronado once more intrusted the command of the main force, with instructions for it to rest twenty days at Cibola, and then to proceed direct to Tiguex. He himself, having heard of a province containing eight towns called Tutahaco, took a party of his hardiest men and set out to explore it. On his way thither, which took the direction of the route to Tiguex, for two days and a half they were without water, and were forced to seek for it in a chain of snow-covered mountains. After eight days' march they reached this place, and there they heard of other villages situated still farther down the river. The people were found to be a friendly race, dwelling in buildings constructed of earth, like those at Tiguex, which province Coronado reached by following up the course of the river.[2]

On his arrival there he found Alvarado and the Turk, who repeated his story about the marvellous wealth to be found in his country, adding many fanciful embellishments, — which were the more readily believed, as he was able to distinguish copper from gold. He pretended that the people of Cicuyé had taken some gold bracelets from him when they

---

[1] [By the kindness of the Rev. Edward E. Hale, D. D., a tracing by him from a sketch made about 1599 by order of Oñate, and by his Sergeant-Major Vincente de Galdivia Mendoza, is here copied. The original is inscribed, "Trasunto de como son las Bacos de Gibola." See *ante*, p. 477, note. — ED.]

[2] Bandelier (*Historical Introduction*, p. 22) places Tutahaco in the vicinity of Isleta, on the Rio Grande, in opposition to Davis's opinion

(*Spanish Conquest*, p. 180) that it was at Laguna. Coronado subsequently sent an officer southward to explore the country, who reached a place some eighty leagues distant, where the river disappeared in the earth, and on his way discovered four other villages. (Castañeda, p. 140.) These, Bandelier places near Socorro. (*Ibid.*, p. 24.) General Simpson (*Coronado's March*, p. 323, note) discusses the question of the disappearance of the river.

made him prisoner, and Coronado accordingly sent Alvarado back to Cicuyé to reclaim them. The people there received him again in a friendly way, but denied all knowledge of the gold bracelets, and declared the Turk to be a liar. Upon this, Alvarado threw the chief men of the town and Bigotes into chains and brought them to Tiguex, where they were kept prisoners more than six months, to the great grief and indignation of the natives, who endeavored in vain to rescue them. This affair did much to discredit the Spaniards in the estimation of the natives, whom their subsequent harsh treatment soon stirred up to active resistance.

After the twenty days had expired, Arellano and the army started for Tiguex, passing on their way the rock of Acuco, which many of the Spaniards ascended to enjoy the view, — but with great difficulty, although the native women accomplished it easily, carrying their water-jars. They had rested, after their first day's march, at the finest town in all the province, where were private houses seven stories high. Here it began to snow. It was now early in December (1540), and for ten days of their journey the snow fell every night. But there was wood in plenty for their fires, and they did not suffer, even finding the snow a protection. But when they reached the village in the province of Tiguex, where their winter quarters had been prepared, they forgot all their past toils in listening to the delusive fables told them by the Turk. The whole province, however, was found to be in a state of revolt, occasioned by the severity of exactions imposed by Coronado in his anxiety for the comfort of his men, together with the brutality of officers and soldiers alike in carrying out his orders. The General had made requisition for three hundred pieces of cloth; and without allowing time for the natives to allot their several proportions to the different villages to complete the amount, the soldiers stripped the garments off whomsoever they met, without regard to rank or condition, and had added to the injury by offering violence to the women. The people of one of the villages had slain one of the Indian allies and driven off several of the horses, where-upon Coronado had sent Cardenas with the greater part of the force to attack it; and only after more than twenty-four hours of hard fighting, and when many of the Spaniards had been wounded by arrows, were the defenders at last forced to surrender by a device of the Indian allies, who drove a mine into the lower portion of the houses, and filled them with the smoke of burning combustibles. By an act of base treachery they were put to death after having been promised quarter; and at once the report was spread far and wide that the Spaniards were violators of their solemn engagements.

It was just at the time of the capture of this village that the main body of the army arrived; and then the snow began to fall and continued to do so for two months, so that it was impossible to undertake any new enter-prise. Attempts were made, however, to conciliate the natives; but they refused to place any confidence in the representations made to them.

Force was thereupon resorted to; and Cardenas, after an ineffectual attempt upon one of the villages, came near losing his life by treachery before the principal town of Tiguex, to which Coronado finally determined to lay regular siege. This lasted for fifty days, during which the besieged suffered greatly from want of water; and finally, in attempting to escape by night they were discovered, and a great many of them were driven into the river and perished. The Spaniards themselves suffered considerably, more than twenty being wounded by arrows, several of whom died from bad medical treatment. Two of the officers perished, — one killed in battle, the other taken prisoner and carried into the town.[1]

During the siege Coronado himself made a brief visit to Cicuyé, for the purpose of examining the country and restoring to his home the chieftain whom Alvarado had brought away. At this time he promised to set Bigotes also at liberty, when he should pass by the place on his way to the rich countries which the Turk had told about. This delighted the people, and he returned to the camp before Tiguex, leaving them in a very friendly state of mind toward him.

About this time there arrived messengers from Alcarraz and the colony at Sonora, bringing information of the death of Melchior Diaz, and of the disorderly condition prevailing there. Coronado immediately despatched Tobar to take command at that place, and to escort the messengers whom he sent to the Viceroy to report what had already been accomplished and the marvellous information received from the Turk. Tobar soon found himself involved in hostilities with the natives, and lost seventeen of his men by their poisoned arrows. Not feeling himself sufficiently secure at Sonora, he transferred the colony to the valley of Suya, forty leagues nearer to Cibola; and not long afterward he received orders from Coronado to rejoin the army with the best of his force.

When the siege was over, an expedition was sent out to receive the submission of the people of Chia, a large town situated four leagues west of the river, in whose charge were left four bronze cannon which were in a bad condition. Another expedition was equally successful in a province of seven villages called Quirex.[2]

For four months the river had been closed by ice strong enough to bear a horse; but now it had melted, and Coronado prepared to start for the lands called Quivira, Arche, and the country of the Guyas, which the Turk declared abounded to a greater or less degree with gold and silver. Many of the Spaniards, however, began to have their suspicions about these fine stories.

The army left Tiguex, April 23, 1541,[3] for Cicuyé, twenty-five leagues distant; and with them went Bigotes, who was set at liberty on arriving

<hr/>

[1] Castañeda (*Relation*, p. 101) says the siege terminated at the close of 1542; but it is clear, from the course of the narrative, that it must have been early in 1541.

[2] All the authorities agree in identifying Chia with the modern pueblo of Cia, or Silla, and in placing Quirex in the Queres district of Cochití, Santo Domingo, etc.

[3] Letter of Coronado to the Emperor Charles the Fifth; Ternaux-Compans, vol. ix. p. 356. Castañeda (*Relation*, p. 113) says it was on May 5.

there, to the great joy of his countrymen. Provisions in abundance were supplied by them, besides a guide, named Xabe, a native of Quivira, who confirmed to some extent the stories of the Turk. On quitting Cicuyé they immediately entered the mountains, and after four days' march came to a broad river over which they were forced to build a bridge, which occupied four days more.[1] From here they journeyed in a direction north-northeast over the plains, and in a few days fell in with immense herds of bisons. At first there were only bulls, but some days later they came upon the cows and calves; and at this time, after seventeen days' march, they came upon a band of nomads called Querechos, busy in the pursuit of the animals. This people dwelt in tents made of tanned bison-skins stretched around poles planted in the earth and fastened above and below. They possessed large packs of dogs, by whom the tents were transported, and obtained their whole sustenance by hunting the bison. Castañeda relates that on one occasion he saw an arrow driven completely through the body of one of these animals. The Querechos were intelligent and perfectly fearless, but friendly; and by signs they confirmed what the Turk had said, adding that to the eastward was a large river whose banks were thickly inhabited, and that the nearest village was called Haxa. Two days' march farther on, the same tribe was again met, and they said that the villages lay still more to the east.

As the Turk now represented that Haxa was only two days' march distant, Diego Lopez was sent in advance, with ten light-armed men, to explore it; while the army, continuing on in the same direction, fell in with an innumerable quantity of bisons, and lost several horses in chasing them. Lopez, after marching twenty leagues without seeing anything but the sky and the bisons, was at last brought back by the friendly natives; and his ill success contributed still more to discredit the Turk. One of the force, a native of Quivira named Sopete, had given quite different information about the route; and Coronado therefore sent out another exploring party under Rodrigo Maldonado, who came to a village in a great ravine, where a blind old man gave them to understand by signs that a long while before he had seen four of their countrymen: these were believed to be Cabeza de Vaca and his companions.[2] This people were very friendly, and gave to the Spaniards a great quantity of tanned skins and other objects, including a tent as large as a house. Forthwith a messenger was despatched to bring the whole body of the soldiers to this spot, who, on arriving, proceeded at once to divide the skins among themselves, to the great chagrin of the natives, who had supposed that they would only bless the skins, as Cabeza de Vaca had done, and then return them. While the army was resting here there came a terrible storm, in which hailstones fell of such enormous size as would have done great mischief if it had

---

[1] General J. H. Simpson (*Coronado's March*, p. 336) has given the reasons for regarding this river as the Gallinas, which is a tributary of the Pecos.

[2] Jaramillo (*Relation* p. 374) says that this was "much nearer New Spain;" but Castañeda (*Relation*, p. 120) makes them to have passed by this very village.

been encountered in the open plain. A party sent out to reconnoitre came upon another wandering tribe, called Teyas, who conducted the army for three days' march to their town, which was called Cona. This people were hostile to the Querechos, and had their faces and bodies painted; and from them guides were procured, who were not permitted to have any communication with the Turk. These confirmed what Sopete had said, that Quivira lay some forty days' march in a northerly direction; and they led the way to another great valley, a league broad, watered by a little stream, where were vines and fruit-trees in abundance; and here the army rested some time. As it had now become evident that the Turk had deceived them, and as their supply of food began to run short, Coronado called a council of war, at which it was decided that he should take thirty of the bravest and best mounted horsemen and push on in search of Quivira, and that the rest of the army should return to Tiguex, under the command of Arellano. This decision, however, was not well received by the soldiers, who besought their General not to leave them, declaring that they were ready to die with him. But Coronado would not yield to their wishes, and set out with his party, promising to send back word in eight days if they might rejoin him.

The army waited fifteen days, during which they killed a large number of bisons; but several of their number lost the way and were never found, although cannon were fired and every means taken to recover them. Then messengers arrived repeating the order to return to Tiguex, and they quitted the valley for the country of the Teyas. This nomadic people knew the region perfectly, and supplied them with guides, by whom they were conducted back in twenty-five days to the river of Cicuyé, which they struck more than thirty leagues below where they had built the bridge, passing on their way great salt marshes. The guides told them that the river flowed toward the east, and fell into the river of Tiguex more than twenty days' journey away. From this point they marched up the river to Cicuyé, where they were no longer well received by the inhabitants, who refused to furnish them with provisions. Accordingly they returned to Tiguex, arriving about the middle of July, 1541.

In the mean time Coronado, after marching in a northerly direction over the plains for thirty days, came to a large river, which was named for Saints Peter and Paul. All this time he and his men had lived entirely upon the flesh of bisons, and often had only their milk to drink. Sopete said there were villages farther down the river; and accordingly he followed the northern bank for three days or more in a northeasterly direction, until he came to one situated upon a branch of the great river. Journeying for four or five days more, he reached in succession six or seven other villages similarly situated, until he arrived at one which he was told was called Quivira.[1] Here he heard of other villages still farther

---

[1] In his *Letter to Charles V.* (p. 358), Coronado states that having marched forty-two days after parting from the main body of his force, he arrived at Quivira in about sixty-seven days

distant on the banks of a yet larger river called Teucarea. Great was
Coronado's disappointment at finding that Quivira, instead of being as he
had been informed a city of stone houses of many stories, consisted only of
a collection of straw-built huts, and that its people were the most barbarous
of any that he had hitherto encountered. They ate their meat raw, like the
Querechos and the Teyas, and were clad in tanned bison-skins, not having
any cotton; but they cultivated maize. The Turk, who had for some time
been conducted in chains with the rear-guard, was now interrogated as
to his motives in so misrepresenting the nature of the country, and misleading the Spaniards. He replied that his own country lay beyond
Quivira, and that the people of Cibola had begged him to lead the
strangers astray upon the plains, so that they might perish by famine,
as it was supposed that they relied upon maize for their food, and did not
know how to chase the bison. One night he endeavored to stir up the
people of Quivira to massacre the Spaniards; but being put upon their
guard, the Spaniards strangled him, to the great delight of Sopete. No
gold or silver was found in the country; but one of the chiefs wore a plate
of copper suspended from his neck, by which he set great store. Coronado
says that Quivira was nine hundred and fifty leagues distant from Mexico,
and was situated in latitude 40°. The soil was rich and black, watered by
many streams, and bore an abundance of grapes and plums.[1] Here he
remained for twenty-five days, sending out exploring parties in all directions, who found great difficulty in communicating with the natives, owing
to the diversity of languages spoken by them, and the want of interpreters.
It was now the latter part of July,[2] and it was time to start to rejoin the
army at Tiguex. So, after collecting a supply of maize for the journey,
and erecting a cross with an inscription saying that Coronado had been

(p. 359). This gives twenty-five days for accomplishing the distance to the point of separation, instead of thirty-seven, as stated by
Castañeda (*Relation*, pp. 127, 134), who estimates that they had travelled two hundred and
fifty leagues from Tiguex, marching six or seven
leagues a day, as measured by counting their
steps.

[1] *Letter to Charles V.*, p. 360. There is a
great difference of opinion as to the situation
of Quivira. The earlier writers, Gallatin,
Squier, Kern, Abert, and even Davis, have
fallen into the error of fixing it at Gran Quivira,
about one hundred miles directly south of Santa
Fé, where are to be seen the ruins of a Franciscan Mission founded subsequently to 1629.
See *Diary of an excursion to the ruins of Abo,
Quarra, and Gran Quivira, in New Mexico*, 1853,
by Major J. H. Carleton (Smithsonian Report,
1854, p. 296). General Simpson, however,
(*Coronado's March*, p. 339) argues against this
view, and maintains that Coronado "reached
the fortieth degree of latitude, or what is now

the boundary line between the States of Kansas
and Nebraska, well on toward the Missouri
River." Judge Savage believes that he crossed
the plains of Kansas and came out at a point
much farther west, upon the Platte River.
Proceedings of American Antiquarian Society,
April, 1881, p. 240. Prince (*History of New
Mexico*, p. 141) thinks that "Coronado traversed
parts of the Indian Territory and Kansas, and
finally stopped on the borders of the Missouri,
somewhere between Kansas City and Council
Bluffs." Judge Prince, who is President of the
Hist. Society of New Mexico, adds that it would
be impossible from what Castañeda tells us, to
determine the position of Quivira with certainty.
Bandelier (*Historical Introduction*, p. 25) is not
satisfied that he reached as far northeast as
General Simpson states, and believes that he
moved more in a circle.

[2] Jaramillo (*Relation*, p. 377) says "it was
about the middle of August;" but according
to Castañeda (*Relation*, p. 141), Coronado got
back to Tiguex in August.

there, he procured fresh guides, leaving Sopete in his home, and returned by the route he had come, as far as to the river named for Saints Peter and Paul. At that point, bending more towards the west, they reached the country where they had first fallen in with the Querechos, and had been turned from the direct course by the Turk; and in forty days they reached Cicuyé.

In the mean time, Arellano and the main portion of the force had been making preparations for passing the winter at Tiguex, and had been despatching parties in different directions to procure supplies of provisions. One under Francisco de Barrio-Nuevo was sent in a northerly direction up the river and visited two provinces, of which one, called Hemez, contained seven villages; the other, named Yuque-Yunque, two fine ones on the bank of the river, and four others strongly fortified and difficult of access in the mountains.[1] Twenty leagues farther up the river was a large and powerful village called Braba, to which the Spaniards gave the name of Valladolid. It was built on both banks of a deep and rapid stream, which was crossed by a bridge of well-squared pine timber; and contained large rooms that could be heated, supported by huge pillars, superior to anything of the kind that had been seen in the country.[2] Another expedition was sent down the river, as has been already related.

By this time some apprehension began to be felt for Coronado's safety, as the time fixed for his return had expired and nothing had yet been heard from him. Accordingly Arellano started with a small party in search of him, and at Cicuyé he was attacked by the inhabitants, with whom he kept up a contest for four days. Tidings then came from the General; and, contenting himself with guarding the passes, Arellano waited there for his arrival. Coronado soon succeeded in re-establishing friendly relations, and continued on immediately to Tiguex. As soon as he reached that place he set about in earnest to pacify the whole province, and to persuade the inhabitants to return to their homes. The most strenuous exertions were made to procure a supply of clothing for the troops, who were in great distress for it, and to provide in every way for their comfort; so that Castañeda says, "Never was Spanish general in the Indies more beloved or better obeyed than he." In the spring he promised his men that they should start again in search of the unknown countries, about which the Turk had set their imaginations on fire. The greater part were firm in the conviction that the natives were familiar with gold, despite their assurances to the contrary, and that they should find it in abundance. But it is plain from Coronado's report that he did not share in this belief; and the sequel proved that others agreed with him. The region of Tiguex

---

[1] Hemez evidently is the Jemez pueblos; and Yuque-Yunque has been identified as the Tehua pueblos, Santa Clara, San Ildefonso, etc., north of Santa Fé. Bandelier, *Historical Introduction*, p. 23.

[2] General J. H. Simpson (*Coronado's March*, p. 339) has identified Braba with the celebrated pueblo of Taos, where such a stubborn resistance was made to the American arms in 1847. Of this, Gregg, in his *Commerce of the Prairies*, had given a description corresponding perfectly with that of Castañeda's *Relation*, p. 139.

he found far too cold and too distant from the sea to make it a desirable situation for a colony.

About this time Tobar arrived with the reinforcements which, as we have seen, he had been ordered to bring from the valley of Suya. He had taken only the best soldiers, leaving many discontented and mutinous ones behind; and these arrived in the full expectation of finding the General already established in the rich countries about which the marvellous reports had reached them. But their disappointment was somewhat consoled when they learned that in the spring the whole army would start in the search of them. Tobar had brought despatches from the Viceroy, and private letters, — among them one informing Cardenas that he had fallen heir to his elder brother's estate. Cardenas accordingly obtained leave to return to Mexico, and several others went with him. Castañeda says that many more would have been glad to do so, if they had not been restrained by fear of being accused of cowardice. This shows the divided feeling that prevailed. And soon trouble arose between the General, who studied only the welfare of the whole army, and certain of the officers, who selfishly looked more after the interests of their own men; so that some already began to talk of abandoning the expedition and returning to New Spain.

When the winter was over, Coronado ordered preparations to be made to start for Quivira, on the way to the unknown countries. But fate had ordained a different termination for his enterprise. On a holiday, while he was amusing himself by tilting at the ring with Maldonado, Coronado's saddle-girths broke, and he fell to the ground, where he received a blow on the head from Maldonado's horse, which nearly cost him his life. A long illness followed, during which Cardenas suddenly returned in haste from Suya, with the news that he had found that post broken up and the inhabitants massacred. It seems that the discontented element left behind by Tobar, — pretending that they had been abandoned, and that the route for New Spain had left them on one side, — had deserted Alcarraz and the sick men under his charge, and had fled to Culiacan. Upon this the natives became insubordinate, and one night made an attack upon the enfeebled force with poisoned arrows, killing a number of them. The rest escaped on foot to Corazones, whose people, always friendly to the Spaniards, aided them on their way to Culiacan, where they, as well as the mutineers, were found by Gallegos not long afterward, when he arrived there with reinforcements.

The news of this calamity was so afflicting to Coronado that he grew worse, or, as Castañeda intimates, feigned to do so, as he had allowed himself to give way to the influence of superstitious terrors. In his youth the prediction had been made that he would become lord of a distant land, and that he would lose his life there by a fall. This now seemed to him to be in the way of accomplishment, and he longed to return to die with his wife and children. The surgeon had kept him informed of the discontent that prevailed among a portion of his force, and he accordingly took secret counsel with certain of the officers, in which it was agreed that they should persuade their men to present a petition, praying that they might be allowed to return to New Spain. A council of war was then held, at which the conclusion was reached that the country was neither sufficiently rich nor populous to make it worth the holding. Coronado thereupon issued the necessary orders for the return march. Some of the officers, however, repented of their decision, and asked the General to give them sixty picked men, with which to maintain themselves until reinforcements should be sent by the Viceroy; or for him to take that number of men for his escort, and leave the command of the expedition to some other person. But the army would not listen to either of these propositions, as they had no inclination to make the trial of any new commander. The consequence was that the zeal and affection of some of the officers for their chief disappeared, though that of the men still held firm.

It was in the early part of April, 1542, that the army began its return march to New Spain. Two of the missionaries remained behind, in the hope of making proselytes of the natives. One of them, a lay brother named Luis, remained at Cicuyé; the other, Juan de Padilla, who had led the charge at Tusayan, continued on to Quivira with some native converts; where, in the words of Castañeda, he speedily "received the martyr's crown." To better insure the safety of the priests, Coronado ordered his men to set at liberty their native slaves, and then started for Cibola. On the journey thither the horses, which thus far had kept in excellent condition, began to die in great numbers. The army accordingly rested a while there before entering upon the desert lying between that place and Chichilticalli; and some Christianized Indians from Mexico remained behind at Cibola, where they were found by Antonio de Espejo, forty-one years afterward, in 1583.[1]

The crossing of the desert was uneventful, and two days after they reached Chichilticalli, Gallegos arrived there from the Viceroy with reinforcements of men and munitions of war. Great was his dismay at finding the army on its way back, and all the splendid visions dissipated that the Turk had conjured up. Those of the officers who had offered to remain and hold the country until the Viceroy's commands should be received, now renewed their proposition; but the soldiers refused to return, and clamored to be led back to New Spain. Coronado found himself powerless to constrain them, even if he possessed the inclination to do so; nor was his authority sufficient to enable him to inflict any punishment upon the deserters who had abandoned Alcarraz at Suya. During the march, Castañeda says that Coronado kept up the fiction of being ill, and only allowed his intimates access to his person. The natives, seeing that the country was being abandoned by the Spaniards, kept up a succession of hostile encounters, in which several of the force perished. As provisions began to fail,

---

[1] *Carta, April* 23, 1584, *Documentos inéditos,* tom. xv. p. 180; Hakluyt, *Voyages,* etc. iii. 462 (edition of 1810).

the army hastened on to Petatlan, thirty leagues from Culiacan, the seat of Coronado's government. All the bonds of discipline had now become relaxed, and even his authority there as governor was not sufficient to reinforce it; but by begging his friends to use their influence with the men, he was able to bring about one hundred of the force back with himself to Mexico. Here he was received but coolly by the Viceroy, Mendoza; his reputation was gone, and soon after he was deprived of his position as Governor of New Gallicia.

Such was the end of an expedition which, as General Simpson says, "for extent in distance travelled, duration in time, and the multiplicity of its co-operating expeditions, equalled, if it did not exceed, any land expedition that has been undertaken in modern times."[1]

CRITICAL ESSAY ON THE SOURCES OF INFORMATION.

THE original sources of information in regard to the early Spanish explorations of New Mexico have been made available for students within the last thirty years by the publication of several collections of documents, preserved either in Mexico or in the Archivo de Indias, at Seville, or in the great national repository at Simancas. The first to appear was the one entitled *Documentos para la historia de Mejico*, published by order of the Mexican Government between 1853 and 1857.[2] This is distributed into four series, of which the third and the fourth contain important historical material bearing upon this subject. Next came the well-selected *Coleccion de varios documentos para la historia de la Florida y tierras adyacentes*, undertaken by the late Buckingham Smith, of which, however, only the first volume appeared in Madrid, in 1857.[3] Then Joaquin Garcia Icazbalceta, the accomplished translator of Prescott's *Conquest of Peru*, published in Mexico a valuable *Coleccion de documentos para la historia de México*, in two volumes, the first in 1858 and the second in 1866.[4] But by far the most important of all is the great *Coleccion de documentos inéditos relativos al descubrimiento, conquista y colonizacion de las posesiones Españolas en América y Oceanía, sacados en su mayor parte del real Archivo de Indias.* Forty volumes of this indispensable repertory have already appeared at Madrid, between 1864 and 1884, edited by Joaquin Francesco Pacheco and other scholars.[5] A most essential service, however, had been rendered to the students of early American history at a still earlier date by the publication of Henri Ternaux-Compans' admirable series of *Voyages, relations, et mémoires originaux pour servir à l'histoire de la découverte de l'Amérique, publiés pour la première fois en Français*, of which twenty parts appeared in Paris between 1837 and 1841.[6] Prior to this our knowledge had been mainly restricted to Italian translations of original narratives published by Giovanni Battista Ramusio in the third volume of his *Navigationi et Viaggi*, Venice, 1556 (reprinted in 1565 and subsequently); of most of which Richard Hakluyt has given an English version in the third volume of his *Voyages, nauigations, traffiques, and discoueries*, London, 1600 (reprinted in 1810).

[1] *Coronado's March*, p. 324.
[2] [See *ante*, p. 397. — ED.]
[3] [See *ante*, p. 290. — ED.]
[4] [See *ante*, p. 397. — ED.]
[5] [See Introduction, *ante*, p. vii. The latest volumes read on the titlepage: *Coleccion de documentos inéditos relativos al descubrimiento, conquista y organizacion de las antiguas posesiones españolas de América y Oceanía sacados de los Archivos del reino y muy especialmente del de Indias. Competentemente autorizada.* — ED.]
[6] [See Introduction, *ante*, p. vi. — ED.]

The different expeditions, in their chronological order, may now be studied in the following original authorities : —

An account of the expedition of Nuño Beltran de Guzman to Ciguatan is contained in the *Primera (segunda) (tercera) (quarta) relacion anonima de la jornada que hizo Nuño de Guzman à la Nueva Galicia*, in Icazbalceta's *Coleccion*, vol. ii. pp. 288–306; 439–483. Other narratives can be found in Pacheco's *Documentos Inéditos*, tom. xiv., pp. 347–373, and 411–463; tom. xvi., pp. 363–375. De Guzman first conquered and then colonized Sinaloa, and even penetrated into Sonora, thus preparing the way for the subsequent explorations. Very little information, however, about New Mexico is to be obtained from any of these narratives.

Alvar Nuñez Cabeza de Vaca published his remarkable story at Zamora in 1542, under the title : *La relacion que dio Aluar Nuñez Cabeça de Vaca de lo acaescido en las Indias en la armada donde yua por gouernador Páphilo de Narbaez, desde el año de veynte y siete hasta el año de treynta y seys que boluio a Sevilla con tres de su compañia.*[1] Notwithstanding the vivid interest that will always attach to this thrilling story of adventure and suffering, the indications given in it of the routes by which he journeyed, and of the places and peoples he visited, are practically of far too vague a character to enable them to be satisfactorily identified,[2] even if we feel warranted in placing implicit confidence in the author's veracity.

The original report by Fray Marcos de Nizza (of Nice) of his *Descubrimiento de las Siete Ciudades*, can be found in Pacheco's *Documentos inéditos*, tom. iii. p. 329; and the instructions received by him from the Viceroy Mendoza are given on p. 325 of the same volume. An Italian translation of the report is contained in Ramusio, *Navigationi*, vol. iii. p. 356 (ed. of 1565) ; and from this was made the English version in Hakluyt, *Voyages*, vol. iii. p. 438 (ed. of 1810). But on comparing both Ramusio's and Hakluyt's versions with the original, not only will it be found that in many places they are mere paraphrases, but that frequently additional particulars have been foisted into the text. Especially noticeable are the many exaggerated statements in regard to the quantities of gold and of precious stones seen by the monk during his journey, or about which stories are told to him by the natives, for which there is not a vestige of authority to be found in the original. Fray Marcos claims to have related what he himself saw or what was told to him ; but it is evident not only that he was prone to lend a credulous ear to whatever fictions might be imposed upon him, but that he grossly misrepresented what he had himself seen. This is directly charged upon him by those who followed in his footsteps under Coronado, and who suffered grievously by reason of his falsifications ; so that he was even compelled to flee to Mexico to escape the consequences of their just indignation. We think that he fairly deserves the epithet of "the lying monk," which has been bestowed upon him, in spite of the air of probability which pervades the greater part of his narrative. But it must in justice be said, however, that he appears rather to have been carried away by religious enthusiasm than actuated by any personal or mercenary considerations ; and with the hope of being able to convert the natives to Christianity, he invested them and their surroundings with the glow of his own imagination. Still, this need not militate against the truth of his statements in regard to the distances he travelled, or the physical characteristics of the regions through which his route lay; so that his narrative will always be important for the students of the topography, if not of the ethnology, of New Mexico at the period of its discovery.

Ternaux-Compans (*Voyages, etc.*, vol. ix. p. 256) has made a most faithful French translation, from copies of the originals at Simancas, of Fray Marcos's report, and of the letter from Mendoza to the Emperor Charles V., which accompanied it, as well as of the instructions received by the Friar from Mendoza.

The story of Coronado's romantic expedition in search of " The Seven Cities of Cibola " has been told with more or less of detail by four different persons who took part in it.

---

[1] [For bibliography of this *Relacion* see *ante*, p. 286. — ED.]   [2] [See *ante*, p. 287. — ED.]

We have also three of his own letters and despatches narrating his earlier proceedings. Of these, the first is a brief one, written to the Viceroy Mendoza, dated Culiacan, March 8, 1539, transmitting a report received from Fray Marcos while upon his journey. An English version of this can be found in Hakluyt, *Voyages*, vol. iii. p. 434 (ed. of 1810), translated from Ramusio, *Navigationi*, vol. iii. p. 395 (ed. of 1565) ; and a French translation, in Ternaux-Compans, vol. ix. p. 349. Next comes a short letter to the Viceroy dated April 10, 1539, in which he tells about the preparations for his ineffectual expedition to Topira ; Hakluyt, p. 352 ; Ramusio, p. 435 ; Ternaux-Compans, p. 352. Of much greater importance, however, is the full report transmitted by him to Mendoza from Cibola (or Granada, as he called it), August 3, 1540, setting forth everything that had occurred between that date and April 22, when he had started. An Italian version of this is given by Ramusio, *Navigationi*, vol. iii. p. 359 (ed. of 1565) ; *Relatione de Francisco Vazquez de Coronado del viagio alle dette setta cita.* An English translation can be found in Hakluyt, *Voyages*, vol. iii. p. 446 (ed. of 1810). Finally, there is the letter which he wrote to the Emperor Charles V., from Tiguex, after his return from Quivira, in which is related the course of events from April 23, 1541, up to October 20 of the same year. This can be found in Pacheco's *Documentos inéditos*, tom. iii. p. 363 ; and it has been repeated in tom. xiii. p. 261. A French translation of it is given in the *Voyages* of Ternaux-Compans, vol. ix. p. 355.

The four narratives by other pens are —

1. An anonymous *Relacion del suceso de la jornada que Francisco Vazquez hizo en el descubrimiento de Cibola*, contained in Buckingham Smith's *Coleccion de varios documentos*, p. 147. This was afterwards printed in Pacheco's *Documentos inéditos*, tom. xiv. p. 318, but with the erroneous date of 1531, instead of 1541.

2. A second anonymous account, entitled *Traslado de las nuevas y noticias que dieron sobre el descobrimiento de una Cibdad que llamaron de Cibola, situada en la Tierra Nueva*, can also be found in *Documentos inéditos*, tom. xix. p. 529, with the same error in the date.

3. Of much greater value is the *Relacion que dió el Capitan Joan Jaramillo, de la jornada que hizo à la tierra nueva de la que fué General Francisco Vazquez de Coronado;* of which a French translation was first published by Ternaux-Compans, in his *Voyages*, etc., vol. ix. p. 364. The original was afterwards printed in Buckingham Smith's *Coleccion*, p. 155, and subsequently in Pacheco's *Documentos inéditos*, tom. xiv. p. 304, but under the erroneous date of 1537. It is a straightforward, soldierly narrative, well written, and with many picturesque details, and it contains an unusual amount of topographical information ; so that it is of great value in establishing the route followed by the expedition, and in identifying the various localities.

4. But if our knowledge of the expedition had been confined to the authorities thus far indicated, we should have had a very imperfect idea both of its events and of its results. In 1838 Ternaux-Compans published a translation into French of a quarto manuscript, of 157 leaves, which he had found in the Uguina Collection, at Paris, under the title *Relation du Voyage de Cibola enterpris in* 1540 ; *ou l'on traite de toutes les peuplades qui habitent cette contrée, de leurs mœurs et coutumes, par Pédro de Castañeda de Nagera* (*Voyages*, vol. ix. p. 1). Nothing has been discovered in relation to this writer except what is contained in his own account. He states that he "wrote his narrative in the city of Culiacan, where he was living in the midst of misery and dangers, as the whole country was in a state of insurrection" (p. 233). The volume bears the indorsement, " Finished copying at Seville, Oct. 26, 1596." As his name is not mentioned in the list of officers which he has given, it is supposed that he was only a private soldier. The work shows that he was a man of considerable education, but it is evidently the production of a novice in the art of literary composition. It is an attempt at a methodical narrative, divided into three parts, but it is quite difficult to follow in it the order of events. In the first part he treats of the incidents of the expedition, and of the army and its officers ; the second contains a description of the provinces, villages, and mountains that were discovered, of the religion

and customs of the inhabitants, and of the animals, fruits, and vegetables to be found ; and in the last part he tells about the return of the army, and explains the reasons for abandoning the attempt at colonization. As he wrote more than twenty years after the events he has described, he sometimes signifies his inability to remember precisely the number of miles travelled, or of the days during which they journeyed. He has even fallen into the error of making the day on which the expedition entered Campostello, Shrove Tuesday, 1541 (p. 24), although he gives the correct date, 1540, in the *Dedicatory Epistle* (p. xiv). Throughout his entire narrative, whenever he gives the date of the year, it is always one too large, as can be seen on pp. 101, 137, and 213. He professes to have written for the purpose of correcting the many misrepresentations and fables that had sprung up in regard to the country they had discovered, and the character of the people, and the nature of the animals to be found there. Castañeda impresses the reader as a religious, humane, and candid man, who cannot fail to win his confidence in the truth of the events he relates. He does not hesitate to expose and to comment upon the cruel and rapacious acts of his own countrymen ; and he does full justice both to the natural amiability and to the valor of the natives. His various observations show him to have been a man of sagacity and good judgment. Mr. Bandelier vouches for the remarkable accuracy of his description of the country, although the distances generally are estimated one third too great (*Historical Introduction to Studies among the Sedentary Indians of New Mexico*, p. 22). The Castañeda MS. is now in the Lenox library.

These are all the original sources of knowledge in regard to the earliest attempts at exploration in New Mexico by the Spaniards, and especially respecting Coronado's expedition to the Seven Cities of Cibola. The historians of Mexico, from Gomara down, while adding no new information to that detailed by Castañeda, are in agreement with him as to the general facts.

Renewed attention was directed to Coronado's expedition and to the probable locality of Cibola by the publication of the reports contained in the *Notes of a Military Reconnoissance made by Lieut.-Colonel William H. Emory, in 1846–1847, with the advance guard of the army of the West*, during the war between the United States and Mexico,[1] and the *Report of Lieutenant J. W. Abert of his examination of New Mexico*. Colonel Emory, in a letter to Hon. Albert Gallatin, dated Oct. 8, 1847, made the statement that he had met with "an Indian race living in four-story houses, built upon rocky promontories, inaccessible to a savage foe, cultivating the soil, and answering the description of the seven cities of Coronado, except in their present insignificance in size and population, and the fact that the towns, though near each other, are not in a (continuous) valley six leagues long, but on different branches of the same stream" (p. 133). He had in mind the villages in the vicinity of Ciboletta, Laguna, etc., on the Rio San Jose, a tributary of the Rio Grande del Norte, about ninety miles east of the present Zuñi pueblo. This opinion was corroborated by Lieutenant Abert (p. 491). Mr. Gallatin thereupon proceeded to prepare for the *Transactions of the American Ethnological Society* (vol. ii. p. liii, 1848) an elaborate essay on the *Ancient semi-civilization of New Mexico, Rio Gila, and its vicinity*, in which large use was made of these military reports, and to which was prefixed a map compiled by Mr. E. G. Squier. In November of the same year Mr. Squier contributed to the *American Review* an article on *New Mexico and California. The ancient monuments and the aboriginal semi-civilized nations of New Mexico and California, with an abstract of the early Spanish explorations and conquests in those regions, particularly those falling within the territory of the United States*. Mr. Gallatin came to the conclusion that the seven cities "appear to have been near the sources of a tributary of the great Colorado, and not of the Rio del Norte" (p. lxxii) ; but he inclined to the opinion that they had been destroyed by the Apaches (p. xciv). Mr. Squier identified Cibola with Zuñi ; but there are inconsistencies to be found between his map and statements contained in his article. In that same year Lieutenant J. H.

---

[1] Senate Executive Documents, No. 41, 30th Congress, 1st Session, 1848.

Simpson, in his *Journal of a Military Reconnoissance from Santa Fé to the Navajo Country*,[1] gave a detailed description of Zuñi, which he considered to be the site of Cibola.

The explorations carried on in New Mexico and Arizona, from 1853 to 1856, during the search for a suitable route for the Pacific Railroad, took Lieutenant A. W. Whipple and Professor W. W. Turner over the same ground, and they both came to a similar conclusion (*Pacific Railroad Reports*, vol. iii. pp. 68, 104). But in 1857 Mr. H. M. Breckenridge published at Pittsburg a brief narrative of the *Early discoveries by Spaniards in New Mexico, containing an account of the castles of Cibola and the present appearance of their ruins*, in which he maintained that Cibola was the well-known ruin called Casa Grande, on the river Gila.   Mr. R. H. Kern, however, upheld the Zuñi theory in his map, prepared in 1854 to accompany Schoolcraft's *History of the Indian Tribes of North America* (vol. iv. p. 33) ; and Mr. Schoolcraft himself adopted the same view (vol. vi. p. 70, 1857).

In the year 1869 important additions were made to our knowledge of the early history of New Mexico, and especially of Coronado's expedition.   Mr. W. H. H. Davis, who had held an official position in that Territory, and in 1856 had published an interesting study of it under the title of *El Gringo*, gave to the world the first history of *The Spanish Conquest of New Mexico*, Doylestown, Penn.   In the same year Brevet Brigadier General Simpson, who had had his attention directed to the question twenty years previously, prepared for the *Annual Report of the Regents of the Smithsonian Institution for* 1869 a thorough study, accompanied by a map, of *Coronado's March in search of the "Seven Cities of Cibola," and discussion of their probable location*.[2]   In April of the same year there appeared in the *North American Review* an article by the late Mr. Lewis H. Morgan, entitled *The Seven Cities of Cibola*, in which that eminent archæologist made an elaborate argument in favor of the identification of that site with the remarkable group of ruined stone structures, discovered not long before in the valley of the Rio Chaco, one of the affluents of the Colorado, about one hundred miles to the northeast of Zuñi.   On this point, however, both Mr. Davis (p. 119) and General Simpson have pronounced in favor of Zuñi, and General Simpson has even undertaken to answer Mr. Morgan's arguments in detail (p. 232).   Mr. Morgan, nevertheless, still held to his opinion in his *Study of the houses of the American Aborigines*, p. 46 (*First annual report of the Archæological Institute of America*, 1880) expanded into the *House and House-life of the American Aborigines* (Geographical and Geological Survey of the Rocky Mountain region, in charge of J. W. Powell, vol. iv., 1881, pp. 167–170).

The Spanish Conquest of New Mexico, by Mr. Davis, is a valuable contribution to history, in which faithful and diligent use has been made of the original authorities and of unpublished documents ; and it is the only full and connected narrative that has yet appeared of the series of events which it relates.   The important episode to which General Simpson confines his attention is treated in abundant detail, and great acuteness and local knowledge are displayed in the discussion of the route followed by Coronado. It is likely to remain always the leading authority upon this subject.

In his elaborate work upon *The Native Races of the Pacific States*, Mr. H. H. Bancroft adopted the Zuñi theory as to the site of Cibola (vol. iv. p. 674), repeated in his *History of the Pacific States* (vol. x. p. 85).[3]   This is also the opinion maintained by Mr. A. F. Bandelier in his *Historical Introduction to Studies among the Sedentary Indians of New Mexico*, p. 12 (*Papers of the Archæological Institute of America.*

[1] Senate Executive Documents, No. 64, 31st Congress, 1st Session, 1850.

[2] Cf. also *Journal of the American Geographical Society*, vol. v. p. 194, and *Geographical Magazine* (1874), vol. i. p. 86.

[3] This is his *North Mexican States*, vol. i. pp. 27, 71–76, 82–87, which is at present his chief treatment of the subject.   He touches it incidentally in his *Central America*, vol. i. p. 153 ; *Mexico*, vol. ii. pp. 293, 465–470 ; *California*, vol. i. p. 8 ; *Northwest Coast*, vol. i. pp. 44–46 ; but he promises more detailed treatment in his volumes on *New Mexico and Arizona*, which are yet to be published.

American series, no. 1, Boston, 1881). This is a very careful and thorough investigation of the whole subject of the geography of New Mexico and of the tribal relations of its inhabitants.

At a meeting, however, of the American Antiquarian Society in April, 1881, Rev. E. E. Hale read a paper entitled *Coronado's Discovery of the Seven Cities*, in which he expressed himself as inclined to abandon his previously maintained opinion[1] in favor of the Zuñi identification, on account of certain newly discovered evidence set forth in an accompanying letter from Lieutenant J. G. Bourke, who argued that the Moqui pueblos better satisfy the conditions of the question. To this the present writer replied in a communication at the following October meeting of the society, under the title *What is the true site of " The Seven Cities of Cibola" visited by Coronado in* 1540? In this all the different opinions are discussed and the Zuñi theory upheld.

The same view is supported by Mr. L. Bradford Prince, late Chief-Justice of New Mexico, in his *Historical Sketches of New Mexico from the earliest records to the American occupation*, 1883 (p. 115). This modest little volume is the first attempt yet made to write a continuous history of the Territory down to the year 1847. It is a useful and in the main a trustworthy compendium. But in the chapter upon Coronado he has followed Castañeda's erroneous dates, as Davis also has done before him, and he has fallen into a few other mistakes.[2]

Henry W. Haynes

EDITORIAL NOTE.

IN the *Don Diego de Peñalosa y su descubrimiento del reino de Quivira* of Cesário Fernández Duro, published at Madrid in 1882, there is an enumeration (pp. 123–144) of the expeditions organized in New Spain for exploration towards the north. The following list, with the chief sources of information, is taken from this book:

1523. Francisco de Garay to Pánuco. *Documentos inéditos* (Pacheco), xxvi. 77.

1526. Garay and Nuño de Guzman to Pánuco, *MS.* in Archivo de Indias.

1530. Nuño de Guzman to New Galicia. *Doc. inéd.* (Pacheco) xiv. 411; also xiii. and xvi. (see chap. vi. of the present History, *ante*, p. 441 and chap. vii. p. 499).

1531. Coronado to Cibola. *Doc. inéd.* (Pacheco), xiv. 318; xix. 529. (See chap. vii.)

1533. Diego de Guzman to Sinaloa, *Doc. inéd.* (Navarrete); B. Smith's *Coleccion*, 94.

1536. Cabeça de Vaca. *Doc. inéd.* (Pacheco), xiv. (See chap. iv.)

1537. Coronado to Amatepeque. *Muñoz's MSS.* in Madrid Acad. of Hist. lxxxi., fol. 34.

1539. Fray Marcos de Nizza to Cibola. *Muñoz MSS.; Ramusio; Ternaux-Compans; Doc. inéd.* (Pacheco), iii. 325, 351.

1539. Coronado to Cibola. (See chap. vii.)

1539. Hernando de Soto. (See chap. iv.)

1540. Melchior Diaz. (See chap. vii.)

1540. Hernando de Alvarado and Juan de Padilla to the South Sea. *Doc. inéd.* (Pacheco), iii. 511; B. Smith, 65. (See chap. vii.)

1540. Gomez Ariaz and Diego Maldonado along Gulf of Mexico. Garcilasso de la Vega, *La Florida del Inca.*

1541. Coronado to Tiguex. *Doc. inéd.* (Pacheco), iii. 363; xiii. 261. (See chap. vii.)

1548. Juan de Tolosa, one of the captains serving under Cortés.

---

[1] See *Amer. Antiq. Soc. Proc.*, October, 1857, and October, 1878.

[2] No attempt is made to establish a theory in another recent compendium, Shipp's *De Soto and Florida* ch. vii.

1554. Francisco de Ibarra to Copala, New Biscay, etc. *Doc. inéd.* (Pacheco), xiv. 463.

1558. Guido de Lavazares to Pánuco and Florida.

1559. Tristán de Arellano to the Coast of Florida, and river Espiritu Santo. *Doc. inéd.* (Pacheco), iv. 136, xiii. 280.

1563. Diego Ibarra to Copala. *Doc. inéd.* (Pacheco), xiv. 553.

1566. Juan Pardo to Florida. *Doc. inéd.* (Pacheco), iv. 560.

1568. Francisco Cano to New Mexico, *Doc. inéd.* (Pacheco), xix. 535.

1569. Juan de Orozco on New Gallicia, with map. *Doc. inéd.* (Pacheco), ii. 561.

1575. Juan de Miranda on the Country. *Doc. inéd.* (Pacheco), xvi. 563.

1581. Francisco Sanchez Chamuscado to New Mexico and Cibola.

1581. Fray Francisco Ruiz among the Indians.

1582. To New Mexico. *Cartas de Indias,* 230.

1582. Antonio de Espejo to New Mexico. Juan Gonzáles de Mendoza's *Historia del Reino de China,* Madrid, 1589; De Laet's *Novus Orbis.*

1583. Cristóbal Martín to New Mexico. *Doc. inéd.* (Pacheco), xvi. 277.

1584. Antonio de Espejo's continued discoveries. *Doc. inéd.* (Pacheco), xv. 151.

1589. Juan Battista de Lomas Colmenares agrees to settle New Mexico. *Doc. inéd.* (Pacheco), xv. 54.

1590. Gaspar Castaño de Sosa, Governor of New Leon, to New Mexico. *Doc. inéd.* (Pacheco), iv. 283; xv. 191.

1596. Sebastian Viscaino on the Coast.

1598. Juan de Oñate to New Mexico. Bustamante, *Los Tres Siglos de México; Doc. inéd.* (Pacheco), xvi. 88, 306, 316–320. Of his expedition to the Pueblo of Acomo, Luis Tribaldo of Toledo sent an account to Hakluyt in 1603, and extracts from it are published in De Laet's *Novus Orbis.*

1599. Juan de Humaña to Quivira.

Others are noted from 1600 to 1783. Captain George M. Wheeler, U. S. Geological Survey, is preparing a Chronology of the Voyages and Explorations to the West Coast and the interior of North America between 1500 and 1800.

The alleged expedition of Peñalosa to Quivira is placed about 1662. The accounts of it depend on a *Relacion del descubrimiento del Pais y Ciudad de Quivira echo por D. Diego Dionisio de Peñalosa, escrita por el Padre Fr. Nicolas de Freytas* (1684). In 1882 there were two annotated renderings of this narrative, — one by Duro, mentioned at the beginning of this note, who discredits the journal and gives other documents on the same theme; the other, an English version, was issued under the title, *The expedition of Don Diego Dionisio de Peñalosa, from Santa Fé to the river Mischipi and Quivira in 1662, as described by Father Nicholas de Freytas. With an account of Peñalosa's projects to aid the French to conquer the mining country in Northern Mexico; and his connection with Cavelier de la Salle. By John Gilmary Shea,* New York, 1882.

Dr. Shea in this volume claims that Quivira was north of the Missouri, while it has generally been placed south of that river. He also derives from this narrative an opinion, contrary to the one ordinarily received, namely, that La Salle was carried, against his will, beyond the mouths of the Mississippi in his expedition of 1682; for he judges his over-shooting the mouths was intentional, in order to land where he could better co-operate with Peñalosa in wresting the mines in New Mexico from the Spaniards.

CHAPTER VIII.

PIZARRO, AND THE CONQUEST AND SETTLEMENT OF PERU AND CHILI.

BY CLEMENTS R. MARKHAM, F.R.S.

Honorary Secretary of the Hakluyt Society.

WHEN the Isthmus of Darien was discovered by Vasco Nuñez de Balbóa, during the six years between 1511 and 1517, there can be little doubt that tidings, perhaps only in the form of vague rumors, were received of the greatness and the riches of the Empire of the Yncas. The speech which the son of the Cacique Comogre is said to have made to the gold-seeking followers of the discoverer of the South Sea most probably had reference to Peru; and still more certainly, when the Cacique of Tumaco told Vasco Nuñez of the country far to the south which abounded in gold, and moulded the figure of a llama in clay, he gave tidings of the land of the Yncas. There was a chief in the territory to the south of the Gulf of San Miguel, on the Pacific coast, named Biru, and this country was visited by Gaspar de Morales and Francisco Pizarro in 1515. For the next ten years Biru was the most southern land known to the Spaniards; and the consequence was that the unknown regions farther south, including the rumored empire abounding in gold, came to be designated as *Biru*, or Peru. It was thus that the land of the Yncas got the name of Peru from the Spaniards, some years before it was actually discovered.[1]

Pedro Arias de Avila, the governor of the mainland called Castilla del Oro, founded the city of Panamá. He went there from the Pearl Islands, in the vessels which had been built by his victim Vasco Nuñez, while Gaspar de Espinosa, the *Alcalde Mayor*, led the rest of the colony by land. The city was founded in 1519. The governor divided the land among four hundred settlers from Darien. Among them were Pascual de Andagoya, Hernando Luque (a priest), Francisco Pizarro, and Diego de Almagro. Nombre de Dios, on the Atlantic side of the isthmus, was settled towards

---

[1] [Cf. Markham's *Royal Commentary of G. de la Vega*, vol. i. chap. iv. Kohl says that the name "Peru" first occurs in Ribero's map (1529), and that his delineations of the coast of Peru were made probably after Pizarro's first reports. — ED.]

the end of the same year by a captain named Diego Alviles, in obedience to orders from Pedro Arias.[1]

In the year 1522 Pascual de Andagoya, who had come out to Darien with Pedro Arias in 1514 and was a cavalier of good family from the province of Alava, was appointed inspector-general of the Indians on the isthmus. He made a journey to a district called Chuchama, south of the Gulf of San Miguel, where the chief told him that a certain people from a province called Biru, farther south, came to make war upon them in canoes at every full moon. Andagoya sent to Panamá for reinforcements, in order to comply with the prayer of the people of Chuchama that he would defend them, as well as to discover what there was farther south. Having received an addition to his forces, he set out with the chief of Chuchama, and in six days arrived at the province called Biru. It had already been visited by Morales and Pizarro. After capturing their principal stronghold, several chiefs of Biru made their submission to Andagoya. From these people he collected information respecting the great empire of the Yncas, and he then descended a river and continued the examination of the coast in a small vessel which had followed him from Chuchama. But he was attacked by a severe illness caused by having been capsized in a canoe, and then kept for several hours in his wet clothes. He therefore returned to Panamá, to report the knowledge he had acquired, giving up his intention of conducting discovery to the southward in person. It was fully three years before Andagoya had so far recovered as to be able to ride on horseback.

The governor, Pedro Arias, therefore requested Andagoya to hand over the enterprise to three partners who formed a company at Panamá. These were Pizarro, Almagro, and Luque.

Francisco Pizarro was born about the year 1470 [2] in the province of Estremadura, and was the illegitimate son of Gonzalo Pizarro, a soldier who had served under the Great Captain in Italy. He had arrived at Darien in the expedition of Alonzo de Ojeda in 1509. During fifteen years he had been diligently serving as a brave, steady, much-enduring man-at-arms; and on two or three occasions he found himself in important and responsible positions. In 1524 he was a citizen of Panamá with very limited means, but endowed with indomitable energy and perseverance, and fifty-four years of age. Diego Almagro is said to have been a foundling. At all events his parentage is unknown. He had probably served for some years on the isthmus, but his name does not occur until he entered into this partnership. Almagro is described as a man of short stature, with a very plain face, and was at least as old as Pizarro. He was hasty in temper, but generous and warm-hearted, and his fine qualities attracted to

---

[1] Nombre de Dios was abandoned on account of its unhealthy situation, in the reign of Philip II., and Puerto Bello then became the chief port on the Atlantic side.

[2] [Authorities do not agree on the date of his birth, placing it between the years 1470 and 1478. Prescott, i. 204. Harrisse, *Bibl. Amer. Vet.*, p. 317. — ED.]

him many faithfully attached adherents. Luque had been schoolmaster at Darien, and was now the principal parochial clergyman at Panamá, holding valuable property on the adjacent island of Taboga, and in an influential position in the colony.

Pizarro was to command the expedition; Almagro was to keep open communications with Panamá and bring supplies; while Luque acted as agent, and obtained the needful funds.

One of the small vessels which had been built for Vasco Nuñez was obtained, and a force of eighty men (one hundred and twelve, according to Xeres) and four horses was collected. Pizarro prepared to sail with this single vessel and two canoes, having received all the information and instructions that Andagoya could give him, and taking with him the interpreters brought from Biru by that officer. It was arranged that large trees near the sea-shore should be blazed, as guides to the course taken by Pizarro, when his partner Almagro should follow with supplies.

Pizarro sailed from Panamá Nov. 14, 1524, and after enduring terrible sufferings on the coast of Biru, including famine, and losing twenty-seven of his men, he went back to Chuchama, and sent the treasurer Nicolas de Ribera to Panamá with the gold which he had collected. Meanwhile Almagro had followed in another vessel with provisions, and went on the traces of his companion by means of the trees that had been marked, until he reached the Rio San Juan in 4° north. Finding no further traces of Pizarro he returned, having lost an eye in an encounter with natives. He also lost upwards of seventy men; [1] but he obtained some gold.

After this failure it was more difficult to obtain money and recruits for a second attempt. Fortunately, the *Alcalde Mayor*, who was impressed with the promising character of the undertaking, came forward with the necessary funds, which he advanced through the agency of Luque. Gaspar de Espinosa thus became one of the partners. The agreement between the partners was signed March 10, 1526. Luque signed as the agent of Espinosa. Pizarro and Almagro could neither read nor write. One Juan de Pares signed on the part of Pizarro, and Alvaro del Quiro for Almagro.

The second expedition sailed in 1526. It consisted of two vessels commanded by Pizarro and Almagro respectively, with a very able and gallant sailor named Bartolomé Ruiz, of Moguer, as pilot. There were one hundred and sixty men all told. The adventurers made direct for the river of San Juan, the farthest point reached by Almagro during the previous voyage. Here Pizarro landed with his troops. Almagro returned to Panamá in one vessel, for recruits and provisions, while Ruiz proceeded on a voyage of discovery to the southward in the other.

Ruiz made a remarkable voyage, having rounded Cape Passado and reached 1° south. He was thus the first European to cross the equator

[1] [His followers probably numbered about a hundred. Herrera places them as low as eighty; Father Naharro, at one hundred and twenty-nine. Prescott, i. 211. — ED.]

on the Pacific Ocean. He also fell in with a raft under sail, which belonged to Tumbez in Peru, and thus obtained several curious specimens

NATIVE RAFTS.

of Ynca art, and some additional information. Almagro made a prosperous voyage back to Panamá, and returned with supplies.

Pizarro had been left on a forest-covered, fever-haunted coast, which has changed very little from that day to this. Hoping to find a better country inland, he undertook long marches through the tangled forest; but many of his men perished, and his party returned to the coast, suffering from disease and famine. In this sorry plight the all-enduring Pizarro was found, when Almagro and Ruiz returned.

Almagro had found a new governor installed at Panamá. Pedro de los Rios had superseded Pedro Arias, who was transferred to Nicaragua, where he died in 1532. With the new governor's sanction, about eighty recruits were collected, and with these and a fresh supply of stores Almagro returned to the Rio de San Juan.

The two partners then embarked, and under the guidance of the pilot Ruiz they advanced along the coast as far as Atacames. They were now in the province of Quito, a part of the Ynca empire. Here were large towns, much ground under cultivation, and a formidable array of well-armed troops to oppose their depredations. It was evident that the Spanish force was too weak to make a successful settlement. Pizarro proposed a return; Almagro opposed him, and there was a violent quarrel, which was outwardly reconciled, leaving a permanent feeling of suppressed jealousy and ill-will on both sides. Finally it was resolved that Pizarro and part of the force should remain on the island of Gallo, which had been discovered by Ruiz in 1° 57' north, while Almagro should return once more for recruits. The arrangements caused much discontent. The men complained that they were being left to starve. Some wrote letters home to Panamá,

---

[1] [This is Benzoni's sketch of the rafts and boats used by the native on the Pacific coast of the northern parts of South America. Edition of 1572, p. 165. — ED.]

full of complaints, which were seized by Almagro.   One, however, named Saravia, concealed a note in a large ball of cotton sent as a present to the governor's wife.   It contained the following lines : —

"Pues Señor Gobernador,
 Mírelo bien por entero,
 Que allá va el recogedor,
 Y acá queda el carnicero." [1]

Pizarro, soon after Almagro's departure, sent off the other ship with the most mutinous of his followers.   But the governor, Los Rios, was much incensed at the result of the expedition.   He refused to

[1] Helps translates them : —

"My good Lord Governor,
 Have pity on our woes ;
 For here remains the butcher,
 To Panamá the salesman goes."

Prescott (*Peru*, vol. i. p. 257) has thus rendered them into English : —

"Look out, Señor Governor,
 For the drover while he's near;
 Since he goes home to get the sheep
 For the butcher, who stays here."

[2] [This map and map No. 2 show the modern geography. The development of the cartography of Peru may be traced in Ramusio (1556) in the map of the parts of the world newly discovered; in Ortelius (1584 and 1592) and De Bry, part iii. (1592, a map of South America corrected in 1624); in Wytfliet, 1597 (see map on a later page) ; in Van Baerle's edition of Herrera (1622) ; in Sanson, with the course of the Amazon (1656); in Dudley's *Arcano del mare* (carta xxviii. 1647), for the coast; in Vander Aa (1679), and in Boudouin's translation of Garcilasso de la Vega, published at Amsterdam in 1737. Markham, in his *Reports on the Discovery of Peru*, gives a map showing the marches of Francisco and Hernando Pizarro, May, 1532, to May, 1533. Other maps are given

SKETCH MAP OF THE CONQUEST OF PERU, NO. I.[2]

by Prescott, H. H. Bancroft, and Helps. The best, however, is in Markham's *Travels of Cieza de Leon.* — ED.]

give any further countenance to the enterprise, and sent two vessels, under the command of Don Pedro Tafur, of Cordova, to Gallo, with orders to take every Spaniard off the island and bring them back to Panamá. Meanwhile Pizarro and his people were suffering from famine and disease, and from the incessant rains. Nearly all had lost every feeling of desire for hazardous adventures. They longed only to be relieved from their sufferings, and hailed the arrival of Tafur with unconcealed joy.

Then it was that Pizarro displayed that heroic resolution which has made the famous act of himself and his sixteen companions immortal. The story is differently told. Herrera says that Tafur stationed himself in one part of the vessel, and drawing a line, placed Pizarro and his soldiers on the other side of it. He then told those who wished to return to Panamá to come over to him, and those who would remain, to stay on Pizarro's side of the line. But Garcilasso de la Vega tells us that when Pizarro saw his men electing to return in the ship, he drew his sword and made a long line with the point along the sand. Then, turning to his men, he said, " Gentlemen ! This line signifies labor, hunger, thirst, fatigue, wounds, sickness, and every other kind of danger that must be encountered in this conquest until life is ended. Let those who have the courage to meet and overcome the dangers of this heroic achievement cross the line, in token of their resolution, and as a testimony that they will be my faithful companions. And let those who feel unworthy, return to Panamá ; for I do not wish to put force upon any man. I trust in God that, for his greater honor and glory, his Eternal Majesty will help those who remain with me, though they be few, and that we shall not miss those who forsake us." Of the two accounts, that of Garcilasso is probably nearer the truth, because it is unlikely that the embarkation would have taken place before the election was made. It would naturally be made on the beach, before going on board. Most of the authorities give the number of those who crossed the line at thirteen. Xeres, Pizarro's secretary, says there were sixteen. Herrera gives the names of thirteen heroic men, Garcilasso supplying the remaining three ; and they deserve to be held in memory.[1]

[1] (a) Bartolomé Ruiz, of Moguer, the pilot.

(b) Pedro de Candia, a Greek, who had charge of Pizarro's artillery, consisting of two falconets ; an able and experienced officer. After the death of Pizarro he joined the younger Almagro, who, suspecting him of treachery, ran him through at the battle of Chupas. He left a half-caste son, who was at school at Cusco with Garcilasso de la Vega.

(c) Cristóval de Peralta, a native of Baeza, in Andalusia. He was one of the first citizens of Lima when that city was founded, — in 1535.

(d) Alonzo Briceño, a native of Benavente. He was at the division of Atahualpa's ransom, and received the share of a cavalry captain.

(e) Nicolas de Ribera, the treasurer, was one of the first citizens of Lima in 1535. He passed through all the stormy period of the civil wars in Peru. He deserted from Gonzalo Pizarro to the side of the president, Gasca, and was afterwards captain of the Guard of the Royal Seal. He is said to have founded the port of San Gallan, the modern Pisco. Ribera was born at Olvera, in Andalusia, of good family. He eventually settled near Cusco, and died, leaving children to inherit his estates.

(f) Juan de la Torre, a native of Benavente, in Old Castile. He was a stanch adherent of Gonzalo Pizarro, and was at the battle of Anaquito, where he showed ferocious enmity against the ill-fated viceroy, Blasco Nuñez de Vela. He married a daughter of an Indian chief near Puerto Viejo, and acquired great wealth. After the battle of Sacsahuana, in 1548, he was hanged by

Nothing could shake the resolution of Pizarro. He would not return until he had achieved greatness, and he found sixteen good men and true to stand by him in his great need. They removed from Gallo to the island of Gorgona, where there was some game and better water; while the others returned with Tafur to Panamá.

The governor looked upon Pizarro's conduct as an act of madness, and refused all succor; but at length yielding to the entreaties of Luque and Almagro, he allowed one vessel to be sent to Gorgona, with strict orders to return in six months. So a small vessel was fitted out under the command of the pilot Ruiz, and after seven weary months the little forlorn hope at Gorgona descried the white sail, and joyfully welcomed their friends with a supply of food and stores. Full of hope, Pizarro and his gallant friends embarked; and the expert Ruiz, guided by information obtained from the Peruvian sailors on the raft, made direct for the Gulf of Guayaquil, performing the voyage in twenty days. The year 1527 was now well advanced. Anchoring off the island of Santa Clara, they stood across to the town of Tumbez on the following day. Here they saw the undoubted signs of a great civilization, betokening the existence of a powerful empire. Their impressions were confirmed by a subsequent cruise along the Peruvian coast as far as Santa, in 9° south latitude. They learned enough to justify a return to Panamá with the report of a great discovery, the importance of which would justify an application to the Spanish Government for some valuable concession to Pizarro and his partners. Pizarro took with him, from Tumbez, a lad who was to act as interpreter, — called Felipillo by the Spaniards, — and also a few llamas. He then made the best of his

order of the president, Gasca. He was a citizen of Arequipa, and left descendants there.

(*g*) Francisco de Cuellar, a native of Cuellar; but nothing more is known of him.

(*h*) Alonzo de Molina, a native of Ubeda. He afterwards landed at Tumbez, where it was arranged that he should remain until Pizarro's return; but he died in the interval.

(*i*) Domingo de Soria Luce, a native of the Basque Provinces, probably of Guipuzcoa; but nothing more is known of him.

(*j*) Pedro Alcon. He afterwards landed on the coast of Peru, fell in love with a Peruvian lady, and refused to come on board again. So the pilot Ruiz was obliged to knock him down with an oar, and he was put in irons on the lower deck. Nothing more is known of him.

(*k*) Garcia de Jerez (or Jaren). He appears to have made a statement on the subject of the heroism of Pizarro and his companions, Aug. 3, 1529, at Panamá. *Documentos inéditos, tom.* xxvi. p. 260, quoted by Helps, vol. iii. p. 446.

(*l*) Anton de Carrion. Nothing further is known of him.

(*m*) Martin de Paz. Nothing further is known of him.

(*n*) Diego de Truxillo (Alonzo, according to Zarate). He was afterwards personally known to Garcilasso at Cusco. He appears to have written an account of the discovery of Peru, which is still in manuscript. *Antonio,* ii. 645; also, *Leon Pinelo.*

(*o*) Alonzo Ribera (or Geronimo) was settled at Lima, where he had children.

(*p*) Francisco Rodriguez de Villa Fuerte was the first to cross the line drawn by Pizarro. He was afterwards a citizen of Cusco, having been present at the siege by the Ynca Manco, and at the battle of Salinas. Garcilasso knew him, and once rode with him from Cusco to Quispicanchi, when he recounted many reminiscences of his stirring life. He was still living at Cusco in 1560, a rich and influential citizen. [Mr. Markham has given the number as sixteen in his *Reports on the Discovery of Peru*, p. 8, together with his reasons for it, which do not commend themselves, however, to Kirk, the editor of Prescott (*History of the Conquest of Peru*, edition of 1879, i. 303). Helps dismisses the story of the line as the melodramatic effort of a second-rate imagination. Cf. also Markham's *Travels of Cieza de Leon,* p. 419. — ED.]

way back to Panamá; and it was agreed that he should proceed to Spain and make a direct application to the Crown for authority to undertake the conquest of the empire of the Yncas. In the spring of 1528, after having collected the necessary funds with much difficulty, Pizarro set out for Spain, accompanied by Pedro de Candia. Luque and Almagro waited at Panamá for the result.

Francisco Pizarro was well received by the Emperor Charles V. in an interview at Toledo; but the sovereign set out for Italy immediately afterwards, and subsequent arrangements were made with the Government of the queen-mother. The capitulation was signed on the 26th of July, 1529. Pizarro was appointed captain-general and *adelantado*, and was decorated with the order of Santiago. He was also granted a coat-of-arms, and thirteen out of the sixteen who crossed the line at Gallo were ennobled by name. Almagro was made governor of Tumbez, and afterwards received the title of marshal. Luque was to be bishop of Tumbez, and protector of the Indians. Ruiz received the title of grand pilot of the South Sea. Candia was appointed commander of the artillery. Pizarro visited Estremadura, and from his home took back with

EMBARKING.[1]

him to Peru his four brothers. Hernando, the eldest and only legitimate son of his father, was a big tall man, with thick lips and very red nose, brave and proud, with an uncompromising temper, and ruthlessly cruel. Juan and Gonzalo were illegitimate, like Francisco, and Francisco Martin de Alcantara was a uterine brother. His young cousin Pedro Pizarro, the future historian, then only fifteen, went out as the conqueror's page; Fray Vicente de Valverde, a fanatical Dominican, also went out; and Pizarro set sail from San Lucar on the 19th of January, 1530. On arriving at Panamá, he was upbraided by Almagro for not having attended fairly to his (Almagro's) interests, while careful to secure everything for himself. From that time the old partners were never really friends, and there was

---

1 [Fac-simile of a cut made to do duty in various connections in Antwerp publications of the last half of the sixteenth century. It is copied in this case from fol. 23 of *De Wonderlijcke ende warachtighe Historie* (Zarate), published by Willem Silvius in 1573. — ED.]

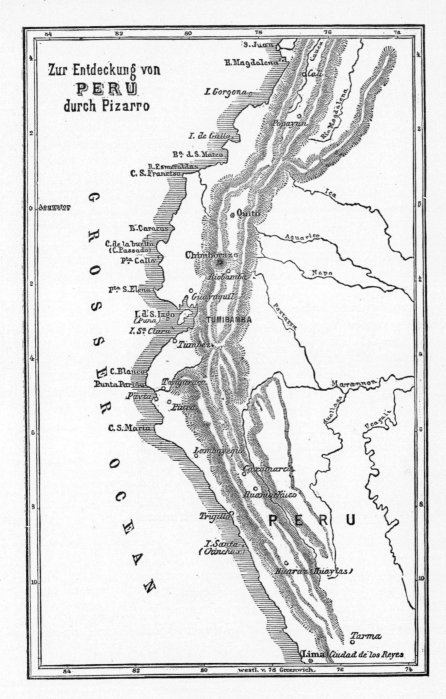

PIZARRO'S DISCOVERIES.[1]

[1] [The map given in Ruge's *Zeitalter der Entdeckungen*, p. 436. — ED.]
VOL. II. — 65.

ill-concealed enmity between Almagro and Hernando Pizarro. Meanwhile preparations for the expedition were busily proceeded with at Panamá; and, as on former occasions, Almagro was to follow with supplies and reinforcements.

Pizarro sailed from Panamá on the 28th of December, 1531, with three small vessels carrying one hundred and eighty-three men and thirty-seven horses. In thirteen days he arrived at the bay of San Mateo, where he landed the horses and soldiers to march along the shore, sending back the ships to get more men and horses at Panamá and Nicaragua. They returned with twenty-six horses and thirty more men. With this force Pizarro continued his march along the sea-coast, which was well peopled; and on arriving at the bay of Guayaquil, he crossed over in the ships to the island of Puna. Here a devastating war was waged with the unfortunate natives, and from Puna the conqueror proceeded again in his ships to the Peruvian town of Tumbez. The country was in a state of confusion, owing to a long and desolating war of succession between Huascar and Atahualpa, the two sons of the great Ynca Huayna Capac, and

NATIVE HUTS IN TREES.[1]

was thus an easy prey to the invaders. Huascar had been defeated and made prisoner by the generals of his brother, and Atahualpa was on his way from Quito to Cusco, the capital of the empire, to enjoy the fruits of his victory. He was reported to be at Caxamarca, on the eastern side of the mountains; and Pizarro, with his small force, set out from Tumbez on the 18th of May, 1532.

The coast of Peru is a rainless region of desert, crossed at intervals by fertile valleys which follow the courses of the streams from the Andes to the sea. Parallel with this coast region, to the eastward, is the *sierra*, or mountainous country of the *cordilleras* of the Andes, the cradle and centre of the civilized tribes of Peru. Still farther to the eastward are the great rivers and vast forests or *montaña* of the basin of the Amazons.[2] Thus the length

[1] [Benzoni's sketch of the native habitations on the coast towards Peru. Edition of 1572, p. 161. — ED.]　　　　　　[2] See the section on " El Dorado," *post*.

EL INGA ATAHUALPA ULTIMO REY.
del Peru.

ATAHUALPA.[1]

of Peru is divided into three very different and distinctly marked regions, —
the coast, the *sierra*, and the *montaña*.

The first part of Pizarro's march was southward from Tumbez, in the
rainless coast region. After crossing a vast desert he came to Tangarara,
in the fertile valleys of the Chira, where he founded the city of San Miguel,
the site of which was afterwards removed to the valley of Piura. The

[1] [From Herrera (1728), vol. iii. p. 5. Quaritch
in 1870 (*Catalogue*, 259, no. 651) held at £105 the
original oil paintings from which the likenesses
of thirteen Incas in Herrera's *Hechos de los Castellanos* were engraved, in 1599, with an extra
one of Atahualpa, which was not given in Herrera. The previous thirteen are given in small
marginal engravings in the border of the frontispiece of Herrera's fifth and sixth Decades, and
copied in the edition of Barcia, who throws discredit on the engravings which De Bry had given.
These last are reproduced in Tschudi's *Antique-
dades Peruanas*. Cf. *Catalogue of Gallery of the
New York Historical Society*, No. 378. — ED.]

accountant Antonio Navarro and the royal treasurer Riquelme were left in command at San Miguel, and Pizarro resumed his march in search of the Ynca Atahualpa on the 24th of September, 1532. He detached the gallant cavalier, Hernando de Soto, into the *sierra* of Huancabamba, to reconnoitre, and pacify the country. De Soto rejoined the main body after an absence of about ten days. The brother of Atahualpa, named Titu Atauchi, arrived as an envoy, with presents, and a message to the effect that the Ynca desired friendship with the strangers.

Crossing the vast desert of Sechura, Pizarro reached the fertile valley of Motupe, and marched thence to the foot of the *cordilleras* in the valley of the Jequetepeque. Here he rested for a day or two, to arrange the order for the ascent. He took with him forty horses and sixty foot, instructing Hernando de Soto to follow him with the main body and the baggage. News arrived that the Ynca Atahualpa had reached the neighborhood of Caxamarca about three days before, and that he desired peace. Pizarro pressed forward, crossed the *cordillera*, and on Friday, the 15th of November, 1532, he entered Caxamarca with his whole force. Here he found excellent accommodation in the large masonry buildings, and was well satisfied with the strategic position. Atahualpa was established in a large camp outside, where Hernando de Soto had an interview with him. Atahualpa announced his intention of visiting the Christian commander, and Pizarro arranged and perpetrated a black act of treachery. He kept all his men under arms. The Ynca, suspecting nothing, came into the great square of Cusco in grand regal procession. He was suddenly attacked and made prisoner, and his people were massacred.

ATAHUALPA.[1]

¹ [Fac-simile of the copper-plate in the English edition of Thevet's *Pourtraitures and Lives* appended to North's *Plutarch*, Cambridge, England, 1676, p. 66. A somewhat famous picture by a Peruvian artist, Monteros, representing the Spanish soldiers hustling the wailing women out of the hall while the funeral rites over Atahualpa were in progress, is heliotyped in the second volume of Hutchinson's *Two Years in Peru.* — ED.]

The Ynca offered a ransom, which he described as gold enough to fill a room twenty-two feet long and seventeen wide, to a height equal to a man's stature and a half. He undertook to do this in two months, and sent orders for the collection of golden vases and ornaments in all parts of the empire.[1] Soon the treasure began to arrive, while Atahualpa was deceived by false promises; and he beguiled his captivity by acquiring Spanish and learning to play at chess and cards.

Meanwhile Pizarro sent an expedition under his brother Hernando, to visit the famous temple of Pachacamac on the coast; and three soldiers were also despatched to Cusco, the capital of the empire, to hurry forward the treasure. They set out in February, 1533, but behaved with so much imprudence and insolence at Cusco as to endanger their own lives and the success of their mission. Pizarro therefore ordered two officers of distinction, Hernando de Soto and Pedro del Barco, to follow them and remedy the mischief which they were doing. On Easter eve, being the 14th of April, 1533, Almagro arrived at Caxamarca with a reinforcement of one hundred and fifty Spaniards and eighty-four horses.

On the 3d of May it was ordered that the gold already arrived should be melted down for distribution; but another large instalment came on the 14th of June. An immense quantity consisted of slabs, with holes at the corners, which had been torn off the walls of temples and palaces; and there were vessels and ornaments of all shapes and sizes. After the royal fifth had been deducted, the rest was divided among the conquerors. The total sum of 4,605,670 ducats would be equal to about £3,500,000 of modern money.[2] After the partition of the treasure, the murder of the Ynca was seriously proposed as a measure of good policy. The crime was committed by order of Pizarro, and with the concurrence of Almagro and the friar Valverde.[3] It was expected that the sovereign's death would be followed by the dispersion of his army, and the submission of the people. This judicial murder was committed in the square of Caxamarca on the 29th of August, 1533. Hernando de Soto was absent at the time, and on his return he expressed the warmest indignation. Several other honorable

---

[1] [Accounts of the space to be filled differ. Cf. Prescott's *Peru*, i. 422; Humboldt's *Views of Nature* (Bohn's ed.), 410, 430. — ED.]

[2] [Prescott (*History of the Conquest of Peru*, i. 453) enters into an explanation of his conversion of the money of Ferdinand and Isabella's time into modern equivalents, and cites an essay on this point by Clemencin in vol vi. of the Memoirs of the Royal Academy of History at Madrid. — ED.]

[3] [Atahualpa was hurriedly tried on the charge of assassinating Huascar and conspiring against the Spaniards. Oviedo speaks of the "villany" of the transaction. Cf. Prescott, *History of the Conquest of Peru*, vol. i. p. 467. Pizarro's secretary, Xeres, palliates the crime as being committed upon "the greatest butcher that the world ever saw."

Prescott (*Peru*, ii. 473, 480) prints several of the contemporary accounts of the seizure and execution of Atahualpa. He says that Garcilasso de la Vega "has indulged in the romantic strain to an unpardonable extent in his account of the capture; . . . yet his version has something in it so pleasing to the imagination, that it has ever found favor with the majority of readers. The English student might have met with a sufficient corrective in the criticism of the sagacious and sceptical Robertson." There are the usual stories of a comet at the time of the death of the Ynca. Cf. Humboldt, *Views of Nature*, pp. 411, 429. — ED.]

El Adelantado Don DIEGO *de* ALMAGRO
Capitan Liberaliſsimo.

DIEGO DE ALMAGRO.[1]

cavaliers protested against the execution.   Their names are even more worthy of being remembered than those of the heroic sixteen who crossed the line on the sea-shore at Gallo.[2]

[1] [From Herrera (1728) vol. ii. p. 285. An original manuscript letter of Almagro, Jan. 1, 1535, addressed to the Emperor, and asking for a province beyond Pizarro's, is noted in Stevens, *Bibliotheca geographica*, no. 109. — ED.]

[2] They are as follows : —

(*a*) Hernando de Soto, the explorer of Florida and discoverer of the Mississippi.

(*b*) Francisco de Chaves, a native of Truxillo. He was murdered at Lima, in 1541, in attempting

to defend the staircase against the assassins of Pizarro.   Zarate says that when he died he was the most important personage in Peru, next to Pizarro.

(*c*) Diego de Chaves, brother of Francisco, whose wife, Maria de Escobar, introduced the cultivation of wheat into Peru.

(*d*) Francisco de Fuentes, in the list of those who shared the ransom.

(*e*) Pedro de Ayala.

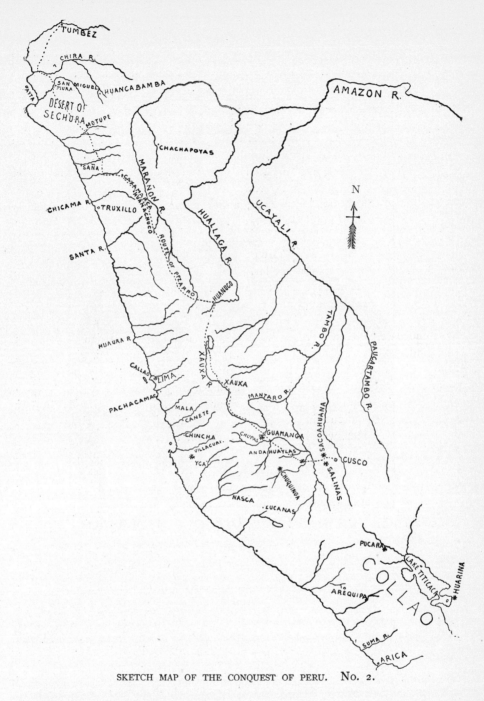

SKETCH MAP OF THE CONQUEST OF PERU. No. 2.

Pizarro at first set up a son of Atahualpa as his successor; but the boy died within two months. A more important matter was the despatch of the treasure to Spain, with tidings of the conquest. The first ship, laden with

(*f*) Diego de Mora, afterwards settled at Truxillo on the coast of Peru. The president, Gasca made him a captain of cavalry, and he was subsequently corregidor of Lima.

(*g*) Francisco Moscoso.

(*h*) Hernando de Haro, taken prisoner by the Ynca Titu Atauchi, but treated kindly.

(*i*) Pedro de Mendoza, in the list of those who shared the ransom.

(*j*) Juan de Rada, a stanch follower of

Peruvian gold, arrived at Seville on the 5th of December, 1534. The second ship followed in January, having on board, besides the treasure, Hernando Pizarro, the conqueror's brother. The excitement caused by these arrivals was intense; and there was an eager desire among adventurers, both of high and low degree, to become settlers in this land of promise.

In September Pizarro began his march from Caxamarca to Cusco, the capital of the empire, with five hundred Spaniards and about one hundred and fifty horses. The artilleryman Candia had charge of two falconets. The march was along the lofty valleys and over the passes of the *sierra*, by Huamachuco, Huánuco, Xauxa, and Huamanga. The rear-guard was attacked by Titu Atauchi, brother of Atahualpa, with six thousand men; and eight Spaniards were taken prisoners, among them Francisco de Chaves and Hernando de Haro, who had protested against the murder of the Ynca Atahualpa, and Sancho de Cuellar, who had been clerk to the court at the mock trial. They were taken to Caxamarca, which had been abandoned by the Spaniards. Chaves and Haro were treated with the greatest kindness. Cuellar was strangled on the spot where Atahualpa was put to death. Hernando de Soto and Almagro led the van of the Spanish army, and they had to fight a well-contested battle beyond the Apurimac, with a native army led by one of the generals of Atahualpa. Leaving a garrison at Xauxa, Pizarro followed more leisurely; and on forming a junction with Almagro on the great plain of Sacsahuana, near Cusco, he perpetrated another great crime. Challcuchima, one of Atahualpa's ablest generals, who had been taken prisoner, was burned alive. Soon afterward the Ynca Manco, son of Huayna Capac, and the rightful heir to the sovereignty, arrived at the Spanish camp to make his submission and claim protection. His rights were recognized; and on the 15th of November, 1533, the conqueror Pizarro entered the city of Cusco in company with the rightful sovereign. The Ynca Manco was inaugurated with the usual ceremonies and rejoicings; but in March, 1534, his beloved city of Cusco was converted into a Spanish town, and a municipality was established. The palaces and spacious halls were appropriated as churches and private houses of the conquerors. The Dominicans received the great Temple of the Sun as their monastery; and Friar Valverde, who became the first bishop of Cusco, in 1538, took the spacious palace of the Ynca Uira-ccocha, in the great square, for his cathedral.

It was not long before the fame of the riches of Peru brought more conquerors to seek for a share of the spoils. In March, 1534, Pedro de Alvarado, one of the conquerors of Mexico, landed at Puerto Viejo, close

Almagro. He accompanied his chief on his expedition to Chili, and avenged his death by the assassination of Pizarro.

(*k*) Alonzo de Avila.

(*l*) Blas de Atienza was the second man who ever embarked on the Pacific, when he served under Vasco Nuñez de Balbóa in 1513.

He settled at Truxillo; and his daughter Inez accompanied Pedro de Ursua in 1560 in his ill-fated expedition to discover El Dorado. His son Blas was a friar, who published a book called *Relacion de los Religiosos*, at Lima, in 1617.

[Cf. also note in Markham's *Reports on the Discovery of Peru*, p. 104. — ED.]

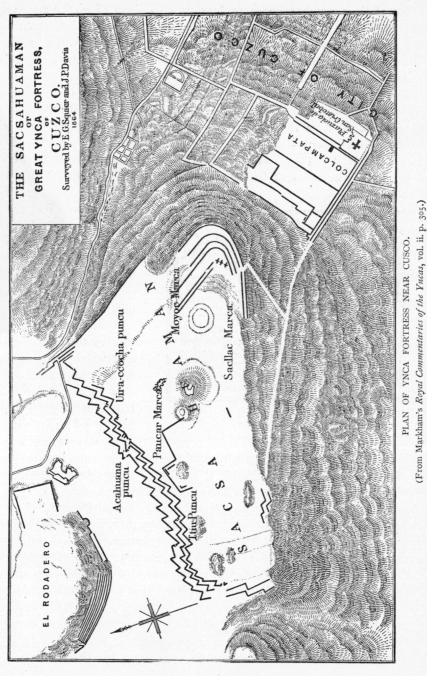

THE SACSAHUAMAN or GREAT YNCA FORTRESS, of CUZCO. Surveyed by E.G.Squier and J.P.Davis 1864

PLAN OF YNCA FORTRESS NEAR CUSCO.

(From Markham's *Royal Commentaries of the Yncas*, vol. ii. p. 305.)

to the equator, with five hundred Spaniards, half of whom were mounted. Among them was the noble cavalier Garcilasso de la Vega, father of the future historian. After suffering dreadful hardships in passing through the forests of the coast, the adventurers reached Riobamba, with a loss of one fourth of their number. Pizarro, leaving a garrison of ninety men under his brother Juan at Cusco, proceeded to the sea-coast, where he had an interview with Alvarado at Pachacamac. It was agreed that Alvarado should return to his government of Guatemala, while many of his surviving followers attached themselves to the fortunes of Pizarro.

The conqueror now resolved to fix the principal seat of his government within a short distance of some convenient seaport. He finally selected a site in the valley of the Rimac, six miles from the shores of the Pacific Ocean. Here Pizarro founded the city of Lima on the festival of Epiphany, the 6th of January, 1535. It was called "Ciudad de los Reyes" (the city of the kings) in honor of Charles V. and his mother Juana, and also in memory of the day.

BUILDING OF A TOWN.[1]

The city was laid out on a regular plan, which has been little altered down to the present time, with broad streets, at right angles, and a spacious square near the centre, one side of which was to be occupied by the cathedral and another by the palace. Pizarro appointed municipal officers, collected laborers, and with great energy pushed on the work of building.

Hernando Pizarro, arriving with such welcome treasure, was very graciously received in Spain. Charles V. confirmed all his brother's previous grants, and created him a marquis;[2] while Almagro, with the title of marshal, was empowered to discover and occupy territory for two hundred leagues, beginning from the southern boundary of Pizarro's government. Hernando himself was created a knight of Santiago, and was authorized to enlist recruits, and equip a fleet for his return to Peru. The return of Hernando was the signal for the breaking out of a feud between the old partners. Almagro and his friends declared that Cusco itself was to the south of the boundary assigned to the territory of Pizarro. The conqueror hurried from his work of building at Lima to Cusco, and made a solemn reconciliation with Almagro, by a written agreement dated June 12, 1535. Almagro was induced to undertake an expedition for the discovery and

[1] [Fac-simile of a cut made to do duty in various Antwerp imprints on Peru of the latter half of the sixteenth century. It is copied in this case from folio eighteen (reverse) of *De Wonderlijcke ende Warachtighe Historie* (Zarate), published by Willem Silvius, 1573. — ED.]

[2] There is no record, however, that a special designation for the marquisate was ever granted to Pizarro. It is therefore an error to call him Marquis of Atabillos, as he is sometimes designated. He signed himself simply the Marquis Pizarro.

Gabriel de Rojas General de la Artilleria,

GABRIEL DE ROJAS.[1]

conquest of Chili. He was accompanied by a large army of Indians, led by two Yncas of the blood royal; and he had with him about two hundred Spaniards. He set out from Cusco in the autumn. Pizarro then returned to the coast, to push forward the building of Lima, and to found the cities of Truxillo (1535), Chachapoyas (1536), Huamanga (1539), and Arequipa (1540). Hernando Pizarro, on his return, was sent to join his brothers Juan and Gonzalo at Cusco, and to take command of that city and fortress.

[1] [Fac-simile of an engraving in Herrera, vol. iv. p. 260. He was one of the distinguished cavaliers of the Conquest, to whom Muñoz — erroneously, as Prescott thinks — assigned the authorship of the *Relacion primera* of Onde-gardo. He was distinguished at the defence of Cusco, when that town was besieged by the Indians. Later, as governor of Cusco for Alma-gro, he had charge of Gonzalo Pizarro while he was held a prisoner, and had, later still, com-mand of the artillery under Gasca. He died at Charcas. — ED.]

The Spaniards had already begun to look upon the natives as their slaves, and the young Ynca Manco was not only treated with neglect, but exposed to every kind of humiliating insult. He escaped from Cusco, and put himself at the head of a great army of his subjects in the valley of Yucay. This was a signal; and immediately the whole country was in revolt against the invaders. Juan Pizarro was driven back into Cusco, and the city was closely besieged by the armies of the Ynca from February, 1536. The besiegers succeeded in setting the thatched roofs of the halls and palaces on fire, and the Spanish garrison was reduced to the greatest straits. The Yncas had occupied the fortress which commands the town, and Juan Pizarro was killed in an attempt to carry it by storm. Finally Hernando Pizarro himself captured the fortress, after a heroic defence by the Ynca garrison. Still the close siege of the city continued, and the garrison was reduced to the last straits by famine. Month after month passed away without tidings. At last the season for planting arrived, and in August the Ynca was obliged to raise the siege.

SKETCH MAP OF THE CONQUEST OF CHILI.

Chili, the long strip of land along the west coast of South America, to the south of Peru, had been conquered by the Yncas as far as the river Maule. Beyond that limit were the indomitable tribes of Araucanian Indians. Bounded on one side by the *cordillera* of the Andes, and on the other by the sea, the country enjoys a temperate climate, suited for the cultivation of wheat and the rearing of cattle. It can be approached from Peru either by traversing the great desert of Atacama on the coast, or by marching over the snowy plateaus and rocky passes of the Andes. Almagro chose the latter route. The Indian auxiliaries, led by Paullu, the brother of Ynca Manco, and by the Uillac Umu, or high-priest, marched first, carrying provisions and making arrangements for their supply, taking the road through the Collao

and Charcas (the modern republic of Bolivia). The Indian contingent
was followed by one hundred Spaniards under Don Juan Saavedra; and
this advanced party waited at Paria, in the south of Charcas, for the main
body. This was commanded by Don Rodrigo Orgoñez, a native of Oropesa, who had served under the constable Bourbon at the sack of Rome.
He was a brave and experienced commander, ever faithful to his chief,
the marshal Almagro. The whole force, when united in the distant valley
of Jujuy, consisted of five hundred Spaniards, with two hundred horses.
The march across the Andes to Coquimbo, in Chili, during the winter of
1536, was a time of intense suffering and hardship bravely endured; but
it was stained by the most revolting cruelties to the people of Charcas
and Jujuy.

Almagro advanced from Coquimbo to the southward, and his Peruvian
contingent suffered a defeat from an army of Promauca Indians. He was
reinforced by Orgoñez and Juan Rada, another faithful adherent, who
brought with them the royal order appointing Almagro to be *adelantado*,
or governor, of New Toledo, which was to extend two hundred leagues from
the southern limit of Pizarro's government of New Castile. The explorers
now desired to return and occupy this new government, which they claimed
to include the city of Cusco itself. Almagro had arranged that three small
vessels should sail from Callao, the port of Lima, for the Chilian coast, with
provisions. Only one ever sailed, named the " Santiaguillo," having a cargo
of food, clothing, and horse-shoes. She arrived in a port on the coast
of Chili; and when the tidings reached Almagro, he sent the gallant Juan
de Saavedra, the leader of his vanguard, with thirty horsemen, to communicate with her. Saavedra found the little vessel anchored in a bay surrounded by rugged hills covered with an undergrowth of shrubs, and having
a distant view of the snowy *cordillera*. In some way it reminded him of
his distant Spanish home. Saavedra was a native of the village of Valparaiso, near Cuenca, in Castile. He named the bay, where the principal
seaport of Chili was destined to be established, Valparaiso. This was in
September, 1536. Landing the much-needed supplies, Saavedra rejoined
his chief, and the expedition of Almagro began its painful return journey
by the desert of Atacama. On arriving at Arequipa, Almagro first heard
of the great insurrection of the Yncas. Marching rapidly to Cusco, his
lieutenant, Orgoñez, defeated the Ynca Manco in the valley of Yucay; and
Almagro entered the ancient city, claiming to be its lawful governor.

The royal grant had given Pizarro all the territory for two hundred and
seventy leagues southward from the river of Santiago, in 1° 20' north, and
to Almagro two hundred leagues extending from Pizarro's southern limit.
Herrera says that there were seventeen and one half leagues in a degree.
This would bring Pizarro's boundary as far south as 14° 50', and would
leave Cusco (13° 30' 55" south) well within it. But neither the latitudes of
the river Santiago nor of Cusco had been fixed, and the question was open
to dispute.

Almagro seized upon Cusco on the 8th of April, 1537, and placed the brothers Hernando and Gonzalo Pizarro, who had defended the place against the Yncas, in confinement. News then came that a large body of men under Alonzo de Alvarado, sent by the governor Pizarro from Lima, was approaching Cusco. Alvarado, with about five hundred men, had advanced as far as the river Abancay, where he was surprised and defeated by Orgoñez on the 12th of July, 1537. Meanwhile some reinforcements were arriving at Lima, in reply to the appeals of Pizarro for help against the native insurrection.

The ecclesiastic Luque had died; but the other partner who advanced the money for the original expedition, the licentiate Gaspar de Espinosa, still lived; and he now joined Pizarro at Lima, with a force of two hundred and fifty men. Cortés also despatched a vessel with supplies and military stores from Mexico.

The Marquis — as Pizarro was now styled — sent an embassy to Almagro at Cusco, under the licentiate Espinosa, in the hope of settling the dispute amicably. Almagro, elated by his successes, was in no mood for moderating his demands; and, unfortunately, Espinosa died very suddenly in the midst of the negotiation. It was broken off; and Almagro declared his intention of retaining Cusco and marching to the coast, in order to establish for himself a seaport. Orgoñez had again defeated the Ynca Manco, dispersed his army, and forced him to take refuge, with his family and little court, in the mountainous fastness of Vilcabamba. Leaving Gonzalo Pizarro in prison at Cusco, Almagro marched to the valley of Chincha, on the sea-coast, taking Hernando Pizarro with him. At Chincha he began to lay out a city, to be called Almagro, which was to rival Lima, one hundred miles to the northward. Chincha is nearly in the same latitude as Cusco.

While he was at Chincha, Almagro received news that Gonzalo Pizarro and Alonzo de Alvarado had escaped from their Cusco prison, and reached the camp of the marquis, near Lima. After some correspondence, it was agreed that a friar named Francisco de Bobadilla should arbitrate, and that Pizarro and Almagro should have a personal interview in the little town of Mala, near the coast, between Lima and Chincha. The meeting took place on the 13th of November, 1537. There was a furious altercation. They parted in anger; indeed Almagro, fearing treachery, rode off very hastily. A cavalier of Pizarro's party had hummed two lines of an old song in his hearing, —

"Tiempo es el cavallero,
Tiempo es de andar de aqui."

It was the last time the old partners ever saw each other. The friar's award was that a skilful pilot should be sent to fix the latitude of the river of Santiago, and that meanwhile Almagro should deliver up Cusco, and Hernando Pizarro should be set at liberty. But in order to secure the safety of his brother, the marquis made the concession that Almagro should hold Cusco until the boundaries were fixed.   Hernando was then allowed to leave the camp of Almagro.

But the marquis had no intention of allowing his rival to retain Cusco. Too old to take the field himself, he intrusted the command of his army to his brother Hernando.   His rival was also broken down by age and infirmities, and Rodrigo de Orgoñez became the actual commander of Almagro's forces.   He retreated by short marches towards Cusco, the old marshal being carried in a litter, and requiring long intervals of rest.   The marquis led his army down the coast to Yca, where he took leave of it, and returned to Lima.   His brother Hernando then proceeded still farther along the coast to Nasca, and ascended the *cordilleras* by way of Lucanas, reaching the neighborhood of Cusco in April, 1538.   Almagro had arrived at Cusco ten days before.

Orgoñez took up a position at a place called Salinas, about three miles from Cusco, with a force of five hundred men and about two hundred horses.   His artillery consisted of six falconets, which, with the cavalry, he stationed on the flanks of his infantry.   On Saturday, the 26th of April, 1538 (or the 6th, the day of Saint Lazarus, according to Garcilasso), Hernando Pizarro began the attack.   The infantry was led by his brother Gonzalo, and by Pedro de Valdivia, the future governor of Chili. Crowds of Indians watched the battle, and rejoiced to see their oppressors destroying one another.   The cavalry charged at full gallop, the infantry fought desperately; but Orgoñez was killed, and after an hour the fortune of the day turned against the marshal.   His soldiers fled to Cusco, followed by the victorious party, and Almagro himself was put in chains and confined in the same prison where he had put the Pizarros.   His young son Diego, — by an Indian girl of Panamá, — to whom the old man was devotedly attached, was sent at once to the camp of the marquis at Lima, in charge of Alcantara, the half-brother of the Pizarros.   Hernando then prepared a long string of accusations against his defeated foe, obtained his condemnation, and caused him to be garroted in the prison.   Almagro was buried in the church of La Merced at Cusco, in July, 1538.

The Marquis Francisco Pizarro received the young Almagro with kindness, and sent him to Lima, ordering him to be treated as his son.   The governor himself remained for some time at Xauxa, and then proceeded to Cusco, where he confiscated the property of Almagro's followers.   He sent his brother Gonzalo to conquer the people of Charcas.   In 1539 Hernando Pizarro set out for Spain; but the friends of Almagro were before him. He was coldly received, and eventually committed to prison for his conduct at Cusco, and lingered in captivity for upwards of twenty years.

Pizarro returned to Lima, and despatched numerous expeditions in various directions for discovery and conquest.   Gomez de Alvarado was intrusted with the settlement of Huánuco; Francisco de Chaves, of Conchucos; Vergara and Mercadillo were to explore Bracamoras and Chachapoyas; and Pedro de Candia was to settle the Collao. Gonzalo Pizarro himself undertook an expedition to the land of cinnamon, — the forest-covered region to the eastward of Quito. Leaving Pedro de Puelles in command at Quito, Gonzalo entered the forests with three hundred and fifty Spaniards and four thousand Indians on Christmas Day, 1539. The hardships and sufferings of these dauntless explorers have seldom been equalled by any body of men on record. Descending the rivers Coca and Napo, Gonzalo intrusted the command of a small vessel to Francisco de Orellana to go on in advance and seek for supplies. But Orellana deserted his starving comrades, discovered the whole course of the river Amazon, and returned to Spain. Out of the three hundred and fifty Spaniards that started, fifty deserted with Orellana, two hundred and ten died of hunger and disease, and the miserable remnant eventually returned to Quito with their intrepid leader, Gonzalo Pizarro, in June, 1542.

The marquis had also resolved to renew the attempt to conquer Chili, which had been abandoned by Almagro. A cavalier had actually been sent out from Spain, named Pedro Sanchez de Hoz, to undertake this service. The marquis associated with him a commander on whose judgment, resolution, and fidelity he could better rely. Pedro de Valdivia was a native of Serena in Estremadura. He had seen much service in Italy; was at the taking of Milan and at the battle of Pavia. He had arrived in Peru in 1535, having been sent from Mexico by Hernando Cortés when the governor of Peru appealed for help to resist the Ynca revolt. He did important service for the Pizarros at the battle of Salinas.

Having collected one hundred and fifty soldiers at Cusco, Valdivia began his march for Chili in March, 1540. His camp-master was Pedro Gomez; his standard-bearer, Pedro de Mayor; his chief of the staff, Alonso Monroy. Francisco de Aguirre and Jeronimo de Alderete were his captains of cavalry; Francisco de Villagran led the arquebusiers, and Rodrigo de Quiroga the pikemen. Two priests, named Bartolomé Rodrigo and Gonzalo Marmolejo, accompanied the expedition. Before starting, Valdivia went to the cathedral of Cusco, and swore, in presence of Bishop Valverde, that the first church he built should be dedicated to Our Lady of the Assumption, the patroness of Cusco, and that the first city he founded should be named Santiago, after the patron of Spain. Valdivia marched by way of the desert of Atacama, and at the very outset he made an agreement with Sanchez de Hoz that the sole command should rest with himself.

Valdivia had for a guide the friar Antonio Rondon, who had accompanied Almagro's expedition; and with his aid he overcame all the difficulties of the march, and safely reached Copiapo in Chili. Advancing by Huasco and Coquimbo, he defeated a large army of natives in the valley of Chili or Aconcagua, and eventually selected a site for the foundation of a new city on the banks of the river Mapocho, in the territory of the Cacique Huelen-Guala. The foundation of the church, dedicated

Pedro de Valdibia Governador de Chile.

PEDRO DE VALDIVIA.[1]

to the Assumption, in accordance with the vow made at Cusco, was laid on the 12th of February, 1541. The plan of the city was laid out, and it received the name of Santiago. The officers of the municipality were elected on the 7th of March, to remain in office for one year.

It was not long before the natives of Chili took up arms to oppose the intruders. Valdivia marched against a large body, leaving Monroy in command at Santiago. But another force of Indians attacked the city itself, with desperate valor, during fifteen days, killing four Spaniards and twenty-three horses, and setting fire to the houses. Valdivia hastily returned; and although the whole country was in insurrection, Monroy

1 [From Herrera (1728), iv. 200. — ED.]

nobly volunteered to make his way to Peru and return with reinforcements and supplies.   He set out Jan. 28, 1542.   Valdivia began to cultivate the land near Santiago, and to sow wheat, in the hope of raising crops; and on the hill of Santa Lucia he constructed a fort where provisions and valuables could be stored.   But the little colony continued to suffer much from scarcity of provisions.   Monroy, hiding in the woods during the day and travelling at night, escaped from Chili and reached Cusco in safety.   He

VALDIVIA.[1]

succeeded in getting a small vessel sent from the port of Arequipa to Valparaiso, while he himself returned by the desert of Atacama, reaching Santiago in December, 1543.   Valdivia was now able to assume the offensive, and the armed Indians retired to a distance from Santiago.

The chief pilot of Panamá, an experienced Genoese seaman named Juan Bautista Pastene, with Juan Calderon de la Barca, was ordered to undertake a voyage of discovery along the coast of Chili at about the same time.   He sailed from Callao in July, 1544, and arrived at the port of Valparaiso in August, in his little vessel the " San Pablo."   Here he was

[1] [Fac-simile of a part of a copperplate, which appears in Ovalle's *Historica Relacion de Chile,* Rome, 1648. — ED.]

visited by Valdivia, who confirmed the name of Valparaiso and officially declared it to be the port of Santiago. Valdivia proclaimed the foundation of the town of Valparaiso on the 3d of September, 1544, and appointed Pastene his lieutenant in command of the Chilian seas. The two little vessels "San Pedro" and "Santiaguillo" then took some men-at-arms on board, and proceeded on a voyage of discovery to the southward on the 4th of September. Pastene went as far as 41° south, discovering a

PASTENE.[1]

harbor which was named Valdivia, the mouths of several rivers, the island of Mocha and the Bay of Penco. He returned to Valparaiso on the 30th of September, and reported his success to the governor, who now had two hundred Spaniards at Santiago, besides women and children. In the same year Valdivia sent a captain named Bohan to found a town in the valley of Coquimbo, to serve as a refuge and resting-place on the road between Santiago and Peru. It was named La Serena, after the native place of Valdivia. The "San Pedro" was sent to Coquimbo to be caulked and otherwise repaired. The governor then undertook an expedition to the south, crossed the river Maule, defeated a large body of Indians at a

---

[1] [Fac-simile of part of a copperplate in Ovalle's *Hist. Rela. de Chile*, Rome, 1648.—ED.]

EL MARQUEZ DON FRANCISCO PISARRO
de Truxillo.

PIZARRO.[1]

place called Quilacara, and advanced as far as the banks of the river Bio-bio, returning to Santiago, after an absence of forty days, in March, 1546. Pastene had made another voyage to Callao, taking with him the gallant Alonso Monroy, who died on the passage. He returned to Valparaiso,

[1] [Fac-simile of engraving in Herrera, vol. ii. p. 280. De Bry (part vi.) gives a small medallion likeness. Cf. Verne's *La Découverte de la Terre*. Prescott (vol. i.) gives an engraving after a painting in the series of the line of the viceroys, preserved at that time in the viceregal palace at Lima. It gives the conqueror in civic costume, with cap and cloak, and a letter in one hand and a glove in the other. A colored representation of the royal standard borne by Pizarro is given in *El General San Martin*, Buenos Ayres, 1863. They continue to show, or did exhibit till recently, a body claimed to be that of Pizarro, in the cathedral at Lima. (Hutchinson's *Two Years in Peru*, vol. i. p. 309.) — ED.]

PIZARRO.[1]

[1] [Fac-simile of the engraving as given in Montanus and Ogilby. — ED.]

with a melancholy account of the disturbed state of Peru, Dec. 1, 1547; and Valdivia determined, after much deliberation, to take up arms against Gonzalo Pizarro, as a loyal servant of the Spanish Crown. He went on board Pastene's ship, made sail Dec. 10, 1547, and arrived at Callao, the port of Lima. He had founded a new colony, and left it securely established in Chili.

During the seven years of Valdivia's absence in Chili, stirring events had occurred in the land of the Yncas. The marquis returned to Lima, where he was busily engaged in the work of building, and in administering the affairs of his vast command. Many of the ruined followers of Almagro were there also, driven to desperation by the confiscation of their property. They were called, in derision, the " men of Chili." Pizarro treated them with contemptuous indifference, and expelled the young Almagro from his house.

The most conspicuous of the malcontents was Juan de Rada; and he matured a plot for the assassination of the governor. On the 26th of June, 1541, the conspirators, headed by Rada, ran across the great square during the dinner hour, and entered the court of Pizarro's house.[1] The marquis had just dined, and his brother Martin de Alcantara, the judge Velasquez, Francisco de Chaves, and others were with him. Being unarmed, several of those present, on hearing the outcry, let themselves down into a garden from the corridor, and escaped. Chaves went out on the stairs, where he was murdered by the conspirators, who were running up. The marquis had thrown off his robe, put on a cuirass, and seized a spear. He was past seventy. His brother, a cavalier named Gomez de Luna, and two pages were with him. The assassins numbered nineteen strong men. Pizarro fought valiantly, until Rada thrust one of his companions on the spear and rushed in. Alcantara, Luna, and the two pages were despatched. Pizarro continued to defend himself until a wound in the throat brought him to the ground. He made the sign of the cross on the floor, and kissed it. He then breathed his last. The conspirators rushed into the street shouting, " The tyrant is dead! " The houses of the governor and his secretary were pillaged. Juan de Rada coerced the municipality and proclaimed Diego Almagro, the young half-caste lad, governor of Peru. The body of Pizarro was buried in the cathedral, by stealth, and at night.

But the colonists did not immediately submit to the new rule. Alvarez de Holguin, one of Pizarro's captains, held Cusco with a small force, and Alonzo de Alvarado opposed the conspiracy in the north of Peru. The bishop Valverde, of Cusco, and the judge Velasquez were allowed to embark at Callao in November, 1541; but they fell into the hands of the Indians on the island of Puna, in the Gulf of Guayaquil, and were both killed.

---

[1] [A view of the house of Francisco Pizarro, in Hutchinson's *Two Years in Peru*, vol. i. p. as it is now or was recently existing, is shown 311. — ED.]

El Licenciado Vaca de Castro Governador del Peru.

VACA DE CASTRO.[1]

The followers of Almagro the lad, as he was called, determined to march from Lima in the direction of Cusco, so as to get between Alvarado and Holguin. At Xauxa the youthful adventurer had the misfortune to lose his most trusty adherent. Juan de Rada died of fever. The two most influential of his supporters who remained were Cristóval de Sotelo and Garcia de Alvarado, — and they had quarrelled with one another. Their delays enabled Holguin to pass to the north, and unite his forces with Alvarado's. Almagro then established himself at Cusco, where Sotelo was murdered by his rival Alvarado; and the latter was put to death by the young Almagro, who assumed the direction of his own affairs. He was barely twenty-two years of age.

1 [From Herrera (1728), vol. iv. p. 1. — ED.]

The Emperor Charles V., long before the death of Pizarro, had decided upon sending out a royal judge to act as the old conqueror's coadjutor and adviser, especially with regard to the treatment of the Indians. For this delicate post the emperor's choice fell upon Dr. Don Cristóval Vaca de Castro, a Judge of the Audience of Valladolid. After a long voyage the new judge had landed at Buenaventura, a town recently founded by Pascual de Andagoya, near that river San Juan where Pizarro had waited in such dire distress during his first voyage. He had a royal order to assume the post of governor of Peru in the event of Pizarro's death; and on arriving at Popayan he received tidings of the assassination. He then proclaimed his commission as governor, and advanced southwards, by way of Quito, along the Peruvian coast. At Huara he was joined by Alvarado and Holguin with their forces. He entered Lima, and then proceeded, by way of Xauxa, in search of the assassins. Young Almagro had a force of five hundred Spaniards, with two hundred horses; and he had a park of artillery consisting of sixteen pieces under the direction of the veteran Pedro de Candia. With this force he left Cusco in July, 1542. Vaca de Castro marched in great haste to Guamanga, in order to secure that important post before Almagro could reach it from Cusco. The rebels, as they must be called, took a route along the skirts of the *cordillera*, until they reached an elevated plateau called Chupas, above and a little to the south of the newly built town of Guamanga. Their object appears to have been to cut off the communications of Vaca de Castro with the coast. In order to approach them, it was necessary for the royal army to evacuate Guamanga, and ascend a very steep slope to the terrace-like plateau where Almagro's army was posted. It was the 16th of September, 1542, and the ascent from Guamanga must have occupied the greater part of the day. The army of Vaca de Castro was marshalled by the veteran Francisco de Carbajal, an old soldier who had seen forty years' service in Italy before he crossed the Atlantic. Carbajal led the troops into action with such skill that they were protected by intervening ground until they were close to the enemy; and when Almagro's artillery opened fire on them, the guns were so elevated as to do no execution. This led young Almagro to suspect Pedro de Candia of treachery, and he there and then ran the old gunner through the body, and pointed one of the guns himself with good effect. The royal army now began to suffer severely from the better-directed artillery fire. Then the opposing bodies of cavalry charged, while Carbajal led a desperate attack with the infantry, and captured Almagro's guns. Holguin fell dead; Alvarado was driven back, and young Almagro behaved with heroic valor. Yet when night closed in, the army of Vaca de Castro was completely victorious, and five hundred were left dead on the field. It was a desperately contested action. Almagro fled to Cusco with a few followers, where he was arrested by the magistrates. Vaca de Castro followed closely, and on arriving in the city he condemned the lad to death. Almagro suffered in the great square, and was buried by the side of his father in the church of La Merced.

Vaca de Castro assumed the administration of affairs in Peru as royal governor.   In the same year the Dominican Friar Geronimo de Loaysa, a native of Talavera, became bishop of Lima.   He was promoted to the rank of archbishop in 1545.   Another Dominican, Juan de Solano, succeeded Valverde as bishop of Cusco in 1543.   Gonzalo Pizarro, when he returned from his terrible expedition in the forests east of Cusco, was induced by the governor to retire peaceably to his estates in Charcas.   The efforts of Vaca de Castro as an administrator were directed to regulating the employment of the natives, and to improving communications.

When the good Bartolomé Las Casas returned to Spain, in 1538, he published his famous work on the destruction of the native race of America. He protested against the Indians being given to the Spaniards in *encomienda*, or vassalage for personal service.[1]   At last the emperor appointed a committee consisting of churchmen and lawyers of the highest position, to sit at Valladolid in 1542, and to consider the whole subject.   The result was the promulgation of what were called the "New Laws."

I. After the death of the conquerors, the *repartimientos* of Indians, given to them in *encomienda*, were not to pass to their heirs, but be placed directly under the king. Officers of his majesty were to renounce the *repartimientos* at once.

II. All *encomenderos* in Peru who had been engaged in the factious wars between the Pizarros and Almagros were to be deprived.

III. Personal service of the Indians was to be entirely abolished.

Blasco Nuñez Vela was appointed viceroy of Peru to enforce the "New Laws," assisted by a court of justice, of which he was president, called the *Audiencia* of Lima.   There were four other judges, called *oidores*, or auditors, named Cepeda, Zarate, Alvarez, and Tejada.   The viceroy and his colleagues embarked at San Lucar on the 3d of November, 1543.   Leaving the judges sick at Panamá, the viceroy landed at Tumbez on the 4th of March, 1544, with great magnificence, and proceeded by land to Lima, proclaiming the "New Laws" as he advanced.   The Spanish conquerors were thrown into a state of dismay and exasperation.   They entreated Gonzalo Pizarro to leave his retirement and protect their interests, and when he entered Cusco he was hailed as procurator-general of Peru.   He seized the artillery at Guamanga, and assembled a force of four hundred men, while old Francisco de Carbajal, the hero of the battle of Chupas, became his lieutenant.

The viceroy was a headstrong, violent man, without judgment or capacity for affairs.   His first act after entering Lima was to imprison the late governor, Vaca de Castro.   The principal citizens entreated him not to enforce the "New Laws" with imprudent haste.   But he would listen to no arguments; and when the auditors arrived from Panamá, he quarrelled with them, and acted in defiance of their protests.   At last the auditors ventured

---

[1] [See chap. v. — ED.]

upon the bold step of arresting the viceroy in his palace, and placing him in confinement. He was sent to the island of San Lorenzo, and a government was formed with the auditor Cepeda as president, who suspended the "New Laws" until further instructions could be received from Spain. The auditor Alvarez was commissioned to embark on board a vessel with the viceroy, and take him to Panamá.

Meanwhile Gonzalo Pizarro was approaching Lima by rapid marches, and he entered the capital on the 28th of October, 1544, at the head of twelve hundred Spaniards and several thousand Indians dragging the artillery, which had formed the special strength of young Almagro. The *Audiencia* submitted; the judges administered the oaths, and Gonzalo was declared governor and captain-general of Peru. At the same time Vaca de Castro persuaded the captain of a vessel on board of which he was confined in Callao Bay to get under way and convey him to Panamá. Accusations were brought against him in Spain, and he was kept in prison for twelve years, but was eventually acquitted and reinstated.

As soon as the ship conveying the viceroy to Panamá was at sea, the judge Alvarez liberated him. He landed at Tumbez in October, 1544, denounced Gonzalo Pizarro and the judge Cepeda as traitors, and called upon all loyal subjects to support him. Volunteers arrived, and Blasco Nuñez raised his standard at San Miguel de Piura. Gonzalo Pizarro assembled a rival force at Truxillo; but the viceroy retreated before him towards Quito, Carbajal pressing closely on his rear. The retreat was almost a rout. Passing through Quito, the viceroy took refuge at Pasto, within the jurisdiction of Sebastian Benalcazar, the governor of Popayan. Early in January, 1546, having received reinforcements, Blasco Nuñez ventured to advance once more towards Quito. Gonzalo Pizarro took up a strong position outside; but the viceroy, now accompanied by Benalcazar, made a detour and entered Quito. On the 18th of January, 1546, the viceroy led his followers to the plains of Anaquito, near the town, where his enemy was posted, seven hundred strong. The battle was not long doubtful. Alvarez the judge was mortally wounded. Benalcazar was left for dead on the field. The viceroy was unhorsed and wounded, and while lying on the ground his head was struck off by order of Pedro de Puelles, Pizarro's governor of Quito. The slaughter was terrific. Cruel old Carbajal never showed any mercy, and no quarter was given. Benalcazar, when he recovered, was allowed to return to Popayan; and Gonzalo Pizarro attended as chief mourner at the funeral of the viceroy in the cathedral of Quito.

Leaving a garrison at Quito, under Puelles, Gonzalo began his journey southwards in July, 1546, and entered Lima in triumph. The only resistance throughout Peru was from an officer in Charcas named Diego Centeno, a native of Ciudad Rodrigo, who had come to Peru in 1534 with Pedro Alvarado. He declared in favor of the viceroy at Chucuito; but Alonzo Toro, who had been left in command at Cusco by Gonzalo Pizarro, marched against him, and he fled into the fastnesses of Chichas, in the far south.

GASCA.[1]

Pizarro was undisputed master of Peru, and his lieutenant Carbajal retired to Charcas to work the silver mines.

News of the revolt had reached Spain, and the licentiate Pedro de la Gasca, an astute and very able ecclesiastic, was appointed to proceed to Peru, and mediate between the viceroy and the malcontents. He received very full powers, with large discretion, and was entitled president of the *Audiencia*. He was very ugly, with a dwarfish body and exceedingly long, ungainly legs. The president sailed from Spain on the 26th of May, 1546, and received the news of the viceroy's death on his arrival at the isthmus. He brought out with him the announcement of the revocation of the "New Laws," owing to the dangerous spirit of discontent they had caused through-

[1] [This follows the engraving given by Prescott (*History of the Conquest of Peru*) of the portrait hanging in the sacristy of Saint Mary Magdalene at Valladolid, — an inscription on which says that Gasca died in 1567 at the age of seventy-one. — ED.]

El Licenciado
Pedro de la
Gasca

PEDRO DE LA GASCA.[1]

out the Indies.   They were withdrawn by a decree dated at Malines on the 20th of October, 1545.

The president arrived at Panamá on the 11th of August, 1546, where he found the fleet of Gonzalo Pizarro, under the command of Pedro de Hinojosa. Soon afterward Lorenzo de Aldana arrived as an envoy from Pizarro, but was induced to submit to the president's authority.   Hinojosa followed the example, and thus Gasca gained possession of the fleet.   When the offer of pardon reached Lima, Gonzalo was advised by his lieutenant Carbajal to accept the terms; but the auditor Cepeda, who had turned against the viceroy and administered the oaths of office to a rebel, felt that there could be no pardon for him.   The mad ambition of Pizarro induced him to listen to Cepeda rather than to Carbajal, and he finally rejected the offer of pardon; but many of his old followers deserted him.

[1] [From Herrera (1728), vol. iv. p. 215. — ED.]

Lorenzo de Aldana was despatched from Panamá, with several vessels, in February, 1547, and arrived in Callao Bay; while Diego Centeno once more rose in the south, and began to collect troops. Gonzalo Pizarro resolved to abandon Lima and march to Arequipa with only five hundred men, so numerous had been the desertions from his ranks. Aldana then entered the capital, while Gasca himself sailed from Panamá on the 10th of April, 1547, landing at Tumbez on the 13th of June. He advanced to Xauxa, and great numbers flocked to his standard. Pedro de Valdivia, the governor of Chili, had landed at Callao, and overtook the president, on his march towards Cusco, at Andahuaylas.

Gonzalo Pizarro, despairing of being able to make head against the president Gasca with all the prestige of royal approval on his side, had determined to retreat into Chili. But he feared to leave Centeno hanging on his rear, and thought it necessary first to disperse his forces. Centeno occupied a position near Huarina, at the south-eastern angle of Lake Titicaca, upwards of twelve thousand feet above the level of the sea. Pizarro's troops advanced to the attack over an open plain. He had about four hundred and eighty men, the strength of his army being in his infantry armed with arquebuses, and disciplined under the direct supervision of Carbajal. Centeno had a larger force, and was accompanied by Solano, the bishop of Cusco. Carbajal waited for the attack of the enemy, and then poured a deadly volley into their ranks. Centeno's footmen broke and fled; but his cavalry defeated Pizarro, and would have won the day, if they too had not been repelled and broken by the admirable steadiness of Carbajal's arquebusiers. As it was, Pizarro's victory was complete, and three hundred and fifty of Centeno's followers were killed. All fugitives taken by Carbajal were put to death without mercy.

The doomed Pizarro now abandoned all idea of retreating into Chili. He marched in triumph to Cusco, while the president Gasca approached by leisurely marches, gathering reinforcements by the way. With him were the bishops of Lima and Cusco, the marshal Alonzo de Alvarado, the veteran Hinojosa, Pascual de Andagoya the first adventurer in search of Peru, Valdivia the governor of Chili, Centeno, escaped from Huarina, Cieza de Leon the future historian, and many others well known to fame. The president's army crossed the river Apurimac, and advanced to the plain of Sacsahuana, near Cusco, whither Gonzalo Pizarro came out to meet him. On the morning of the 9th of April, 1548, the commanders of both armies made ready for battle. But soon there were symptoms of desertion on Pizarro's side. An important cavalier, Garcilasso de la Vega, galloped across to the army of Gasca. He was followed by the treacherous auditor Cepeda. Soldiers began to follow in small parties. Old Carbajal was humming two lines of an old song, —

> "Estos mis cabellicos madre,
> Dos á dos me los lleva el ayre."

Then desertions took place by companies and squadrons. Pizarro sorrow-fully took his way to the royal camp and gave himself up. Carbajal was seized by the soldiers. He was hanged and quartered the following day, and soon afterwards Gonzalo Pizarro was executed in presence of the army.

The president entered Cusco on the 12th of April, and began a bloody assize. Scarcely a day passed without followers of Gonzalo Pizarro being hanged, flogged, or sent in large batches to the galleys. Two priests were executed. A canon of Quito, who was tutor to Gonzalo Pizarro's little son, was hanged for writing a book called *De bello justo*. At length, sated with blood, the president left Cusco on the 11th of July with Archbishop Loaysa, and went to a small village called Huayna-rimac in the neigh-borhood. He retired into this seclusion to escape the importunities of his partisans. Here he proceeded to arrange the distribution of *encomiendas*, or grants of lands and Indians, among his followers. He allowed a tenth of the Indians to be employed on forced labor in the mines, thus reversing the humane legislation advocated by Las Casas. Having completed his work, the president sent the archbishop to announce his awards at Cusco, and they caused a howl of rage and disappointed greed. Gasca himself went down to Lima by the unfrequented route of Nasca, and when a positive order from the emperor arrived, that all personal service among the Indians should be abolished, he suspended its publication until he was safe out of Peru. In January, 1550, the president Gasca sailed for Panamá, leaving the country in the greatest confusion, and all the most difficult administrative points to be solved by his successors. The municipality of Lima wrote a complaint to the emperor, representing the untimely depar-ture of the president. His abilities and his services have been much over-stated. He himself is the witness to his own revolting cruelties at Cusco.

Gasca left the government of Peru, with none of the difficulties settled, in the hands of the auditors or judges of the royal *Audiencia*, of which Don Andres de Cianca was president. His colleagues were Melchor Bravo de Sarabia, Hernando de Santillan, and Pedro Maldonado. The judges were in charge of the executive from January, 1550, to the 23d of Septem-ber, 1551, when Don Antonio de Mendoza arrived from Mexico as viceroy. They had taken steps to organize a systematic plan for the instruction of the natives, under the auspices of Archbishop Loaysa, Friar Thomas de San Martin, and the indefatigable friar Domingo de Santo Tomas, the first Quichua scholar. They worked harmoniously under the viceroy Mendoza, who was a statesman of high rank and great experience. He promulgated the royal order against the enforced personal service of Indians, antici-pating serious discontents and troubles, which he was resolved to meet and overcome. But his premature death at Lima, on the 21st of July, 1552, left the country once more in the hands of the judges, who had to meet a storm which would sorely test their administrative abilities.

The ringleader of the malcontents was a cavalier of good family named Francisco Hernandez Giron. Born at Caceres, in Estremadura, he crossed the Atlantic in 1535, and joined the unfortunate viceroy Blasco Nuñez de Vela at Quito, fighting under his banner in the fatal battle of Anaquito. He also did good service in the army of President Gasca, and was in the left wing at the rout of Sacsahuana. Gasca had assigned the plain of Sacsahuana to him, as his *repartimiento;* but he grumbled loudly, and all the malcontents looked upon him as their leader. The promulgation of the abolition of personal service was received with a howl of execration among the conquerors, who looked forward to the accumulation of wealth by the use of forced labor in the silver mines. Troubles broke out in Charcas, and Giron resolved to raise the standard of revolt at Cusco.

The 12th of November, 1553, was the wedding day of Don Alonzo de Loaysa, a nephew of the archbishop, who married a young lady named Maria de Castilla. The *corregidor* of Cusco and most of the leading citizens were at the supper. Suddenly Giron presented himself in cuirass and helmet, with his sword drawn, and a crowd of conspirators behind him. The street was occupied by a body of cavalry under his lieutenant, Tomas Vasquez. The guests sprang from their seats, but Giron told them not to fear, as he only wished to arrest the *corregidor*. He and the others then put out the lights and drew their swords. The *corregidor* took refuge with the ladies in the drawing-room, and shut the doors. Two guests were stabbed. Many escaped by the windows and climbed a wall at the back of the house. The *corregidor* and other officials were seized and imprisoned. Giron issued a proclamation declaring that the conquerors would not be robbed of the fruits of their labors. He soon had a respectable force under his command; but most of the leading citizens fled to Lima. The rebel declared that his object was the public good, and to induce the king to listen to the prayers of his subjects. The *Audiencia* was called upon to restore matters to the state they were in at the time of Gasca's departure. Tomas Vasquez was sent to Arequipa, and Guamanga also declared in favor of Giron.

The governing judges were in great perplexity at Lima. After some hesitation they put the archbishop Loaysa in command of their army, with the judge Bravo de Saravia as his colleague. The marshal Alonzo de Alvarado was in upper Peru, and he also got some loyal cavaliers round him, and assembled a small force. Giron entered Guamanga Jan. 27, 1554, where he was joined by Tomas Vasquez, from Arequipa; and he then marched down to the coast. The judges encamped at Até, outside Lima, with five hundred arquebusiers, four hundred and fifty pikemen, three hundred cavalry, and fourteen field-pieces. Giron arrived at Pachacamac on the shores of the Pacific, and the judges advanced to Surco. But instead of boldly attacking, the rebels turned their backs and marched southwards along the coast to Yca, followed by a detachment under an officer named Meneses. Giron turned, and defeated his pursuers at Villacuri, in the desert between Pisco and Yca, but continued his retreat to Nasca. He had lost a great opportunity.

El Mariscal
Alonso de
ALVARADO

ALONZO DE ALVARADO.[1]

The royal army advanced to Chincha; but the archbishop quarrelled with Bravo de Saravia, and where so many commanded, and none were military men, efficient operations were impossible. Meanwhile Alvarado had assembled an army for the judges, of seven hundred men, the rendezvous being La Paz in upper Peru. With this force he entered Cusco on the 30th of March, 1554, and continued his march in search of Giron, who remained at Nasca, on the coast, until the 8th of May. On that day the rebels once more ascended the wild passes of the *cordillera* to Lucanas, and were soon in the neighborhood of Alvarado's army, which now numbered eleven hundred men. The rebels encamped at Chuquinga, in the wildest part of the Andes, on a mountain terrace by the side of a deep ravine, with the river Abancay in front. The marshal Alvarado was on the other side of the ravine, and was advised not to attack, but to

---

[1] [Fac-simile of engraving in Herrera, iii. 235. — ED.]

harass the retreat of Giron.   But on the 21st of May, under every possible disadvantage, he ordered the river to be forded, and an attack to be made.   The river was crossed, but the men could not form on the other side in the face of an active enemy.   They fell back, and the retreat was soon converted into a rout.   Alvarado was wounded, but contrived to escape with Lorenzo de Aldana and the learned Polo de Ondegardo who accompanied him, leaving seventy dead on the field, and two hundred and eighty wounded.

Giron entered Cusco in triumph.   The judges, on receiving news of the disastrous battle of Chuquinga, decided that their army should advance to Xauxa, and eventually towards Cusco.   The *Audiencia* now consisted of Dr. Melchor Bravo de Saravia, Hernando de Santillan, Diego Gonzalez Altamirano, and Martin Mercado.   Altamirano was to remain in charge of the government at Lima, while the other judges marched with the army, preceded by their officer Pablo de Meneses with the royal standard.   In July, 1554, the three judges, Saravia, Santillan, and Mercado reached Guamanga, and in August they entered Cusco, having met with no opposition.   Giron had retreated to Pucara, near Lake Titicaca, a very strong position consisting of a lofty rock rising out of the plain.   The royal army encamped in front of the rock, and the judges sent promises of pardon to all who would return to their allegiance.   Giron hoped that the royal army would attack him, repeating the error at Chuquinga; but the judges had resolved to play a waiting game.   A night attack led by Giron was repulsed.   Then desertions began, Tomas Vasquez setting the example.   The unfortunate rebel could trust no one.   He feared treachery.   He bade a heartrending farewell to his noble-minded wife, Doña Mencia, leaving her to the care of the judge Saravia.   He rode away in the dead of night, almost alone, and Pucara was surrendered.   Meneses was sent in chase of Giron, who was captured near Xauxa.   He was brought to Lima, Dec. 6, 1554, and beheaded.   His head was put in an iron cage, and nailed up by the side of those of Gonzalo Pizarro and Carbajal.   Ten years afterward a friend of his wife secretly took all three down, and they were buried in a convent.   Doña Mencia, the widow of Giron, founded the first nunnery in Lima, — that of " La Encarnacion," — and died there as abbess.

Thus the judges succeeded in putting down this formidable insurrection, and were able to hand over the country, in a state of outward tranquillity, to the great viceroy who now came out to establish order in Peru.

Don Andrea Hurtado de Mendoza, Marquis of Cañete, was nominated by Charles V., at Brussels, to be viceroy of Peru for six years.   He came out with the intention of checking with a firm hand the turbulence of the military adventurers who were swarming over the country.   Writing to the emperor before he sailed, May 9, 1555, he said that there were eight thousand Spaniards in Peru, of whom four hundred and eighty-nine held *repartimientos*, and about one thousand were employed officially or otherwise. A large portion desired to live in idleness. He proposed to employ them on expeditions into unknown regions, and he submitted that no more Spaniards ought to be allowed to come to Peru without good cause assigned. In a letter to his daughter, the governess Juana, the emperor approved the policy sketched out by the new viceroy.

The Marquis of Cañete landed at Payta, and travelling by land, entered Lima on the 29th of June, 1556. He assumed office with unprecedented state and solemnity. He was fully resolved to put down sedition once and for all. He ordered that no Spaniard should leave his town without permission of the authorities, and for good cause. As regards the *Audiencia*, he reported to the emperor that the judges were hostile to each other, and that they lived in such discord that all peace was hopeless. He spoke favorably of two, and requested that the others might be recalled. He also reported that the *corregidors* maintained quantities of idle soldiers waiting for opportunities of mischief. He estimated the number of the idlers at three thousand, and said that the peace of the country was endangered by the immorality, license, and excesses of these men. The viceroy kept all the artillery in the country under his own eye, ordering guns to be seized and brought to him wherever they could be found; and he formed a permanent guard of four hundred arquebusiers. He then sent for a number of settlers, of turbulent antecedents, who came to Lima joyfully, expecting that they were about to receive *repartimientos*. But he disarmed them, shipped them at Callao, and sent them out of the country. Among these banished men were included the most notorious disturbers of the peace in the late civil wars. Altogether thirty-seven were sent to Spain. Tomas Vasquez and Juan Piedrahita, the chief supporters of Giron, were beheaded, and the *corregidors* were authorized to seize and execute any turbulent or dangerous persons within their jurisdictions. These were very strong measures, but they were necessary. The intolerable anarchy under which Peru had groaned for so many years was thus stamped out. Moderate *encomiendas* were then granted to deserving officers.

While the turbulence and cruelty of the Spanish conquerors were checked with relentless severity, the policy of the Marquis of Cañete towards the people and their ancient rulers was liberal and conciliatory. In both courses of action there was wisdom. After the siege of Cusco, the Ynca Manco, with his family and chief nobles, had taken refuge in the mountain fastness of Vilcabamba, and there he met his death in 1553, after a disastrous reign of twenty years. He was succeeded by his son Sayri Tupac, who continued in his secluded hiding-place. The viceroy thought it important, for the tranquillity of the country and the peace of mind of the Indians, that the descendant of their ancient kings should be induced to reside among the Spaniards. The negotiation was intrusted to the Ynca's aunt, a princess who had married a Spanish cavalier, and to Juan de Betanzos, an excellent Quichua scholar. It was settled that the Ynca should receive the *encomienda* forfeited by Giron (the valley of Yucay near Cusco, where he was to reside), together with a large pension. All was finally arranged, and on the 6th of January, 1558, the Ynca entered Lima, and was most cordially received by the viceroy. From that time he resided in the valley of Yucay, surrounded by his family and courtiers, until his death in 1560.

Several of the Spanish conquerors had married Ynca ladies of the blood royal, and a number of half-caste youths were growing up in the principal cities of Peru, who formed links between the Yncas and their conquerors. There was a school at Cusco where they were educated, and the Ynca Garcilasso de la Vega records many anecdotes of his early days, and enumerates the names of most of his school-fellows. The Marquis of Cañete also founded schools at Lima and Truxillo, and took great pains to supply the Indians with parochial clergy of good conduct, who were strictly prohibited from trading. In 1558 the *curacas*, or native chiefs, who had proved their rights by descent before the *Audiencia*, were allowed to exercise jurisdiction as magistrates.

The Marquis of Cañete founded the towns of Cuenca in the province of Quito, of Santa on the coast to the north of Lima, and of Cañete in a rich and fertile valley to the south. He also established the hospital of San Andres at Lima, and built the first bridge over the Rimac. Very great activity was shown in the introduction of useful plants and domestic animals. Vines were sent out from Spain and the Canaries, and a harvest of grapes was reaped near Cusco in 1555. Wheat was first reaped in the valley of Cañete by a lady named Maria de Escobar, and olives were planted in 1560. Other fruit trees and garden vegetables soon followed.

The king, Philip II., determined to supersede this able viceroy in 1560, appointing a young nobleman named Diego Lopez de Zuñiga y Velasco, Conde de Nieva, in his place. But the Marquis of Cañete died at Lima before his successor arrived, on the 30th of March, 1561, having governed nearly five years. He was buried in the church of San Francisco, but his bones were afterwards taken to Spain and deposited with those of his ancestors at Cuenca. The Conde de Nieva entered Lima on the 27th of April, — a month after the death of the marquis. He was a handsome young cavalier, of loose morals, and fond of every sort of pleasure. There is very little doubt that he lost his life owing to a powerful husband's jealousy. He was set upon in the street, after leaving the lady's house, in the dead of night. He was found dead on the 20th of February, 1564, and the matter was hushed up to prevent scandal. The judges of the *Audiencia* took charge of the government until the arrival of a successor.

During this period the Chilian colony was holding its own, with difficulty, against the indomitable Araucanian Indians. After the rout of Sacsahuana, the governor Valdivia took his leave of the president Gasca, and embarked at Arica on the 21st of January, 1549, with two hundred men. His lieutenant, Francisco de Villagra, had ruled at Santiago in his absence, vigilantly thwarting a plot of Alonzo de Hoz, whom he executed, and suppressing a revolt of the Indians of Coquimbo and Copiapo. He met Valdivia on his landing at Valparaiso and accompanied him to the capital. The first expedition of the governor, after his return, was undertaken with a view to establishing Spanish influence in the south of Chili. In January, 1550, with two hundred men, he crossed the Biobio, and intrenched himself in the valley of the Penco, where he founded the town of Concepcion, repuls-

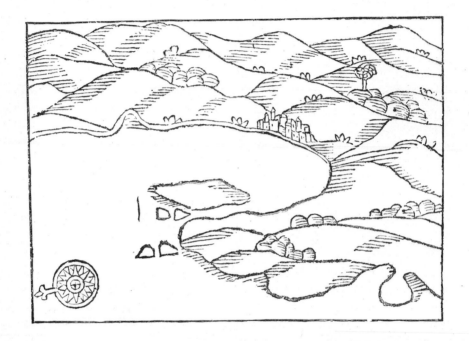

CONCEPTION BAY.[1]

ing an attack from a large army of Indians with great slaughter. In the following year he founded the towns of Imperial and Valdivia still farther south.

The Araucanians now flew to arms in defence of their fatherland, at the call of their aged chief, Colo-colo. A younger but equally brave leader, named Caupolican, was elected *toqui*, or general, of the army; and they began operations by attempting to destroy a Spanish fort at Tucapel. Valdivia hurried from Concepcion, at the head of fifty cavalry, and attacked the Araucanian host. The governor had with him a young Indian lad of eighteen, named Lautaro, as groom. There was great slaughter among the Araucanians, and they were beginning to give way, when all the best feelings of Lautaro were aroused at the sight of his countrymen in peril. On

---

[1] [Fac-simile of a cut in Ovalle's *Historica Relacion de Chile*, Rome, 1648. — ED.]

the instant he felt the glow of ardent patriotism. He went over to the enemy, exhorted them to rally, and led them once more to the attack. The Spanish force was annihilated, and the governor was taken prisoner. Led before the *toqui*, young Lautaro interceded for his master, and the generous Caupolican listened favorably; but the savage chief Leucaton protested, and felled Valdivia by a deadly blow with a club on the back of the head. This disaster took place on the last day of December, 1553. Don Pedro de Valdivia was in his fifty-sixth year, and by his conquest and settlement of Chili he won a place in history side by side with Cortés and Pizarro. He was childless.

Francisco de Villagra succeeded his old chief as governor of Chili, and made preparations to repair the disaster. Lautaro became the second leader of his countrymen, under Caupolican. Their tactics were to allow the Spaniards to penetrate into their country as far as they pleased, but to cut off supplies, and harass their retreat. Thus Villagra easily marched from Arauco to Tucapel; but he was attacked by an immense army under Lautaro, which stopped his retreat, and he suffered such severe loss in the battle of Mariguanu that the town of Concepcion was abandoned in November, 1555. There was hard fighting again in 1556, in defence of the garrisons at Imperial and Valdivia. Early in the following year Lautaro was intrenched with an army on the banks of the Mataquito, when he was surprised at dawn by Villagra. He made a gallant defence, but was killed; and six hundred warriors fell with him. Thus died one of the noblest patriots of the American race.

In the same year the viceroy, Marquis of Cañete, appointed his son, Don Garcia Hurtado de Mendoza, a youth barely twenty-two years of age, to be governor of Chili. His cavalry, under Luis de Toledo, marched by land over the desert of Atacama, while the young governor embarked at Callao, and sailed for Chili with three vessels conveying seven hundred infantry. Among the officers was Don Alonso de Ercilla, whose epic poem records the events of this famous war. Don Garcia landed at Coquimbo on the 25th of April, 1557, and the cavalry arrived on the following day. After having assumed the government at Santiago, and ungratefully dismissed Villagra, to secure the tranquillity of his own rule, he continued the interminable war. His first operation was to occupy the island of Quiriquina, off Talcahuano, and to build the fort of Pinto on the west side of the valley of the Penco. Here he was attacked by Caupolican with a great army. There were marvellous individual acts of bravery on both sides; Don Garcia himself was wounded, and two thousand Araucanians were slain. The governor then crossed the river Biobio and fought another great battle, Caupolican retreating with heavy loss. Don Garcia disgraced his victory by hanging twelve captive chiefs, including the heroic Galvarino. Penetrating far to the south, the town of Osorno was founded beyond Valdivia, and the archipelago of Chiloe was discovered. During the governor's absence in the far south, the *toqui* Caupolican

GARCIA HURTADO DE MENDOZA.[1]

[1] [Fac-simile of a copperplate in Ovalle's *Historica Relacion de Chile*, Rome, 1648. — ED.]

was betrayed into the hands of Alonso de Reinosa, the captain in command at Tucapel, who put him to a horrible death by impalement.

There was now a brief interval of peace.   Don Garcia had brought with him to Chili the good licentiate Gonzalez Marmolejo, afterwards first bishop of Santiago, who prepared rules for the humane treatment of the peaceful natives.   Only a sixth were allowed to be employed at the mines; no one was to work who was under eighteen or over fifty; no laborer was to be forced to work on feast days, and all were to be paid and supplied with food. On the 5th of February, 1561, Don Garcia Hurtado de Mendoza embarked at Valparaiso and left Chili, being succeeded by Francisco de Villagra, the old companion in arms of Valdivia.   Villagra died in 1563, and was succeeded by Rodrigo de Quiroga.   In 1563 the bishopric of

PERUVIANS WORSHIPPING THE SUN.[1]

Santiago was founded, and in 1565 the royal *Audiencia* of Chili was instituted, with Dr. Melchor Bravo de Saravia as its first president.   Its seat was fixed in the city of Concepcion.

We must now return to the course of events in Peru.   The scandalous death of the viceroy Conde de Nieva seems to have induced the king to choose his successor from among men learned in the law rather than from the nobility, and to drop the title of viceroy.   Lope Garcia de Castro had been a judge of the *Audiencia* of Valladolid, and afterwards a member of the council of the Indies.   He was appointed governor and captain-general of Peru, and president of the *Audiencia* of Lima, where he made his public entry Sept. 22, 1564.   To avoid scandal, the belief had been encouraged that the Conde de Nieva had been murdered in bed.   But everybody knew that he had been struck to the ground by several stout negroes with bags full of sand; that the blows had been continued until life was extinct; and that after the murder people came out of the house of the Zarates, and carried the body to the palace.   The culprit was Don Rodrigo Manrique de Lara, a powerful citizen of proud lineage, who had discovered love

[1] [After the sketch in Benzoni, edition of 1572, p. 168. — ED.]

passages between his young wife and her near relative the viceroy. But the judges thought there would be grave scandal if the delinquent was brought to justice, and the new governor took the same view. The affair was hushed up.

Lope de Castro established a mint, imposed the *almojarifazgo*, or customs dues, and organized the work at the newly-discovered quicksilver mines of Huancavelica, and at the silver mines. In 1567 the Jesuits arrived in Peru, and in the same year the second council of Lima was convoked by Archbishop Loaysa, the governor assisting as representative of the king. The first council was in 1552. At the second the decisions of the council of Trent were accepted, and the parochial arrangements were made; while the governor proceeded with the work of fixing the divisions of land among the Indians, and marking out the country into *corregimientos*, or provinces, under *corregidors*. In 1567 Castro despatched an expedition from Callao, under the command of his nephew, Alvaro de Mendaña, who discovered the Solomon Islands. Lope Garcia de Castro governed Peru for five years, handing over his charge to his successor, in 1569, to return to Spain and resume his seat at the council board of the Indies.

Don Francisco de Toledo, second son of the third Count of Oropesa, was the king's major-domo, and was advanced in years when he was selected to succeed the licentiate Lope de Castro. In his case the title of viceroy was revived, and was retained by his successors until the independence. Landing at Payta, the viceroy Toledo travelled along the coast, closely observing the condition both of Spaniards and Indians; and he then made up his mind to visit every province within his government. He made his public entrance into Lima on the 26th of November, 1569.

Toledo was assisted by statesmen of great ability and experience, who warmly sympathized with the aboriginal races, and were anxious for their welfare. Chief among his advisers was the licentiate Polo de Ondegardo, who had now been several years in Peru, had filled important administrative posts, — especially as *corregidor* of Charcas and of Cusco, — and had studied the system of the government and civilization of the Yncas with minute attention, especially as regards the tenures of land, and always with a view to securing justice to the natives. The licentiate Juan Matienzo was another upright and learned minister who had studied the indigenous civilization and the requirements of colonial policy with great care; while in affairs relating to religion and the instruction of the people, the viceroy consulted the accomplished Jesuit author, José de Acosta.

But the conduct of Toledo with regard to the Ynca royal family was dictated by a narrow view of political expediency, and was alike unwise and iniquitous. He reversed the generous and enlightened policy of the Marquis of Cañete. After the death of Sayri Tupac, the Ynca court had again retired into the mountain fastnesses of Vilcabamba, where the late Ynca's two brothers, Titu Cusi Yupanqui and Tupac Amaru, resided with many native chiefs and followers.   When the new viceroy arrived at Cusco, in January, 1571, the Ynca Titu Cusi sent an embassy to him, and requested that ministers of religion might be sent to Vilcabamba. Accordingly, the friar Diego Ortiz arrived at the Ynca court; but almost immediately afterward Titu Cusi sickened and died, and the superstitious people, believing that it was the work of the friar, put him to death.   The youthful Tupac Amaru was then proclaimed Ynca, as successor to his brother.   This gave the viceroy the pretext he sought.   He despatched a strong force into Vilcabamba, under the command of Martin Garcia Loyola, who was married to an Ynca princess, the daughter of Sayri Tupac.   Loyola penetrated into Vilcabamba, and took young Tupac Amaru prisoner on the 4th of October, 1571.   He was brought to Cusco and confined in a palace, under the shadow of the great fortress, which until now had belonged to the family of his uncle, the Ynca Paullu.   But the viceroy had seized it as a strong position to be held by Spanish troops under his uncle Don Luis de Toledo.   There was a trial for the murder of the friar; several chiefs were sentenced to be strangled, and Tupac Amaru, who was perfectly innocent and against whom there was no evidence, was to be beheaded.

The young sovereign was instructed for several days by two monks who were excellent Quichua scholars, and who spoke the language with grace and elegance.   He was then taken to a scaffold, which had been erected in the great square.   The open spaces and the hills above the town were covered with dense crowds of people.   When the executioner produced his knife, there was such a shout of grief and horror that the Spaniards were amazed, and there were few of them with a dry eye.   The boy was perfectly calm.   He raised his right arm, and there was profound silence. He spoke a few simple words of resignation, and the scene was so heart-rending that the hardest of the conquerors lost self-control.   Led by the bishop and the heads of the monasteries, they rushed to the house of the viceroy and threw themselves on their knees, praying for mercy and entreating him to send the Ynca to Spain to be judged by the king. Toledo was a laborious administrator, but his heart was harder than the nether millstone.   He sent off the chief Alguazil, of Cusco, to cause the sentence to be executed without delay.   The crime was perpetrated amid deafening shouts of grief and horror, while the great bell of the cathedral was tolled.   The body was taken to the palace of the Ynca's mother, and was afterward interred in the principal chapel of the cathedral, after a solemn service performed by the bishop and the chapter.   Toledo caused the head to be cut off and stuck on a pike beside the scaffold; but such vast crowds came to worship before it every day, that it was taken down and interred with the body.

The judicial murder of Tupac Amaru was part of a settled policy. Toledo intended to crush out all remains of reverence and loyalty for the ancient family among the people.   He confiscated the property of

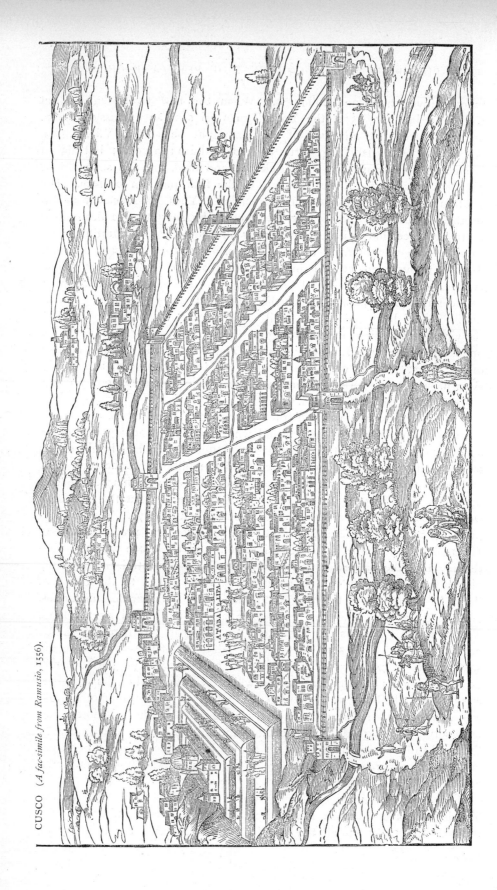

CUSCO (*A fac-simile from Ramusio*, 1556).

TEMPLE OF CUSCO.[1]

[1] [Fac-simile of the engraving as given in Montanus and in Ogilby. Garcilasso de la Vega describes Cusco soon after the Conquest, and explains the distribution of buildings which was

the Yncas, deprived them of most of the privileges they had hitherto been allowed to retain, and even banished the numerous half-caste children of Spaniards by Ynca princesses.

At the same time he labored diligently to formulate and establish a colonial policy and system of government on the ruins of the civilization of the Yncas.

The instructions of the kings of Spain, through their council of the Indies, were remarkable for beneficence and liberality in all that concerned the natives. Strict orders were given for their instruction and kind treatment, and special officers were appointed for their protection. But at the same time there were incessant demands for increased supplies of treasure from the mines. It was like the orders of the directors of the East India Company to Warren Hastings, — justice to the natives, but more money. The two orders were incompatible. In spite of their beneficent rules and good intentions, the Spanish kings must share the guilt of their colonial officers, as regards the treatment of the natives. It is right, however, that the names of those conquerors should be recorded who displayed feelings of sympathy and kindness for their Indian vassals. Lorenzo de Aldana, who took a prominent and important part in the civil wars, died at Arequipa in 1556, and left all his property to the Indians whom he had received in *repartimiento*, for the payment of their tribute in future years. Marcio Sierra de Leguizamo described the happy condition of the people when the Spaniards arrived, and in his will expressed deep contrition at having taken part in their destruction. Garcilasso de la Vega was ever kind and considerate to his Indian vassals. Cieza de Leon in his writings[1] shows the warmest sympathy for the Ynca people. There were, however, too many of the first conquerors of a different stamp.

The viceroy Toledo wisely based his legislation on the system of the Yncas. His elaborate code, called the *Libro de Tasas*, was the text-book for all future viceroys. He fixed the amount of tribute to be paid by the

made among the conquerors. A plan of the ancient and modern city, showing the conquerors' houses, is given in Markham's *Royal Commentaries of De la Vega*, vol. ii., and in the *Journal of the Royal Geographical Society*, 1871, p. 281. A plan of the ancient and modern town, by E. G. Squier, is given in that author's *Peru, Land of the Incas* (New York), 1877, p. 428. The house of Pizarro is delineated in Charton's *Voyageurs*, vol. iii. p. 367; and the remains of the palace of the first Inca, in Squier's *Land of the Incas*, p. 451.

Cieza de Leon says: "Cusco was grand and stately; it must have been founded by a people of great intelligence." (Markham's edition. *Travels*, pp. 322, 327.)

Early plans or views of Cusco are given in Ramusio, vol. iii. p. 412 (see *ante*, p. 554); in Münster's *Cosmographia*, 1572 and 1598; in Braun and Hogenberg's *Civitates orbis terrarum*; in De Bry, part vi., and in Herrera (1728), vol. iii. p. 161. There is a large woodcut map of Cusco, in Ant. du Pinet's *Plantz, Pourtraitz et Descriptions de plusieurs Villes*, etc., Lyons, 1564.

Vander Aa published a view at Leyden, and another is in Rycaut's translation of Garcilasso de la Vega, p. 12. Accounts of the modern town are given by Markham, Squier, and others, and there is a view of it in *Tour du Monde*, 1863, p. 265. — ED.]

[1] For the writings of Cieza de Leon, see the "Critical Essay," *post*.

Indians, wholly exempting all males under the age of eighteen, and over that of fifty. He recognized the positions of hereditary nobles or *curacas*, assigning them magisterial functions, and the duty of collecting the tribute and paying it to the Spanish *corregidors*. He enacted that one seventh part of the population of every village should be subject to the *mita*, or forced labor in mines or factories; at the same time fixing the distance they might be taken from their homes, and the payment they were to receive. It was the abuse of the *mita* system, and the habitual infraction of the rules established by Toledo, which caused all the subsequent misery and the depopulation of the country. Humane treatment of the people was incompatible with the annual despatch of vast treasure to Spain. Toledo also fixed the tenures of land, organized local government by *corregidors*, and specified the duties of all officials, in his voluminous code of ordinances.

In the days of this viceroy the Inquisition was introduced into Peru, but the natives were exempted from its penalties as catechumens. Heretical Europeans or Creoles were alone exposed to its terrible jurisdiction. The first *auto da fé* took place at Lima on November 19, 1573, when a crazy old hermit, suspected of Lutheranism, was burned. Another was celebrated with great pomp on the 13th of April, 1578, the viceroy and judges of the *Audiencia* being present in a covered stand on the great square of Lima. There were sixteen victims to suffer various punishments, but none were put to death.

During the government of Toledo, in 1579, Sir Francis Drake appeared on the coast of Peru,[1] and in the following year the viceroy despatched an important surveying expedition to the Straits of Magellan under Sarmiento. After a long and eventful period of office, extending over upwards of twelve years, Don Francisco de Toledo returned to Spain. He was coldly received by Philip II., who said that he had not been sent to Peru to kill kings, and dismissed him. He was a hard-hearted man, but a conscientious and able administrator, and a devoted public servant.

Don Martin Henriquez, second son of the Marquis of Alcanizes, was then viceroy of Mexico, whence he was removed to Peru as successor to Toledo. He entered Lima on the 28th of September, 1581. He worked assiduously to carry out the ordinances of his able predecessor in all branches of administration; but his career was cut short by death after holding office for eighteen months. He died on the 15th of March, 1583, and was buried in the church of San Francisco. In 1582 he had founded the college of San Martin, to be under the rule of Jesuits, and on the 15th of August of the same year the second council of Lima assembled under the presidency of the archbishop.

Loaysa, the first archbishop of Lima, died in 1575, and the see was vacant for six years. Toribio de Mogrovejo was consecrated at Seville in 1586, and entered Lima May 24, 1581, at the age of forty-three. He at

---

[1] [See Vol. III. p. 66 — ED.]

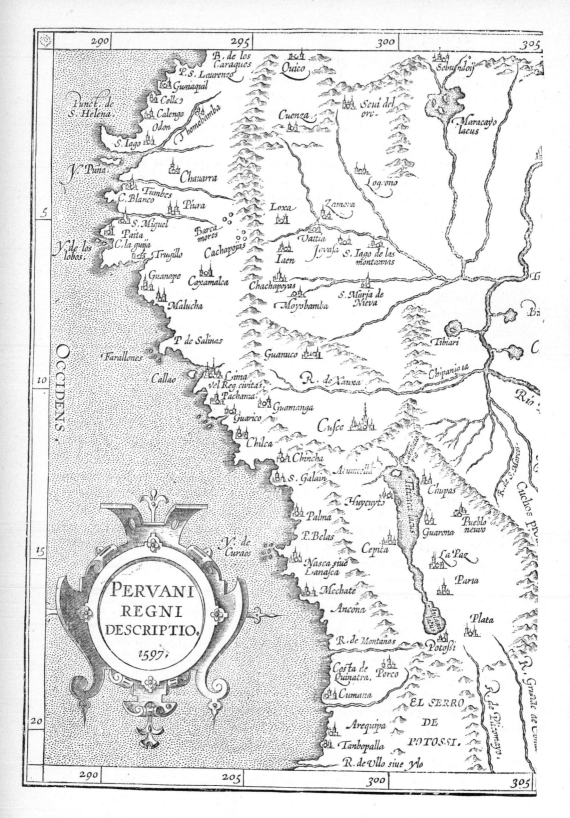

PERU (after Wytfliet, 1597).

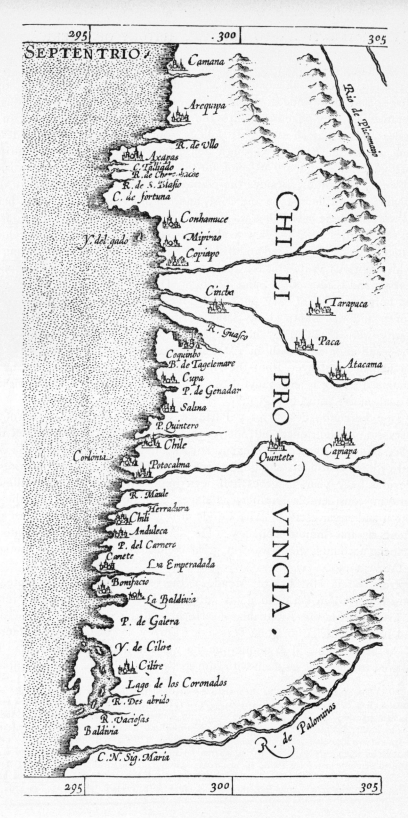

SEPTENTRIO ?

Camana

Arequipa

R. de Ullo
Axapas
C. Tajliado
R. de Chere-bache
R. de S. Blasio
C. de fortuna

Conhamuce

Y. del gado
Mipirao
Copiapo

Cincha

Tarapaca

R. Guasco
Paca

Coquinbo
B. de Tagelemare
Atacama
Cupa
P. de Genadar

Salina

P. Quintero

Chile
Quintete
Capiapa
Cordonia
Potocalma

R. Maule
Herradura
Chili
Anduleca
P. del Carnero
Canete
La Emperadada

Bonifacio

La Baldiuia

P. de Galera

Y. de Cilire
Cilire
Lago de los Coronados
R. Des abrido
R. Vaciosas
Baldiuia

C. N. Sig. Maria

CHILI
PRO
VINCIA.

Rio de Pliomaio

R. de Palominos

CHILI (after Wytfliet, 1597).

once began the study of the Quichua language, to prepare for his tours of inspection. He had a mule, but generally travelled on foot, stopping in villages and at wayside huts, instructing, catechising, and administering the sacraments. He penetrated into the most inaccessible fastnesses of the Andes and visited all the coast valleys, journeying over burning deserts, along snowy heights, and through dense forests, year after year untiringly. He founded the seminary at Lima, for the education of priests, which is now known by his name. Besides the council of 1582, he celebrated two other provincial councils in 1592 and 1601, and ten diocesan synods. The principal work of these assemblies was to draw up catechisms and questions for the use of priests, with a view to the extirpation of idolatry, and to regulate parochial work. The good archbishop died at Saña on the coast, during one of his laborious visitations, on the 23d of March, 1606. He was canonized in 1680, and is revered as Saint Toribio. During his archiepiscopate a girl was born at Lima, of very poor and honest Spanish parents, named Rosa Flores, and was baptized by Saint Toribio in 1586. Her goodness and charity were equalled by her surpassing beauty, which she dedicated to God; and after her death, in 1617, a conclave of theologians decided that she had never strayed from the right path in thought or deed. She was canonized in 1671, and Santa Rosa is the patron saint of Lima, with her festival on the 30th of August.[1]

Don Fernando de Torres y Portugal, Conde de Villar Don Pardo, the successor of Henriquez, did not reach Lima until the 20th of November, 1586. He endeavored to prevent abuses in taking Indians for the *mita*, and ordered that none should be sent to unsuitable climates. During the previous forty years negroes had been imported into the coast valleys of Peru in considerable numbers as slaves, and supplied labor for the rich cotton and sugar estates. The Conde de Villar was an old man, with good intentions but limited capacity. He allowed abuses to creep into the financial accounts, which were in great confusion when he was superseded in the year 1590.

Don Garcia Hurtado de Mendoza, the fourth marquis of Cañete, had already served in Peru, when his father was viceroy, and had won renown in his war with the Araucanians. He had also seen service in Germany and Italy. Married to Doña Teresa de Castro y de la Cueva, granddaughter of the proud Duke of Albuquerque, he was the first viceroy who had been allowed to take a vice-queen with him to Peru, and he was also accompanied

---

[1] [A life of Santa Rosa, by Léonard de Hansen, was printed at Rome in 1664. A Spanish translation, *La bienaventurada Rosa*, etc., by Father Iacinto de Parra, was published at Madrid in 1668. It is enlarged upon the original from documents gathered to induce the Pope to canonize her. De Parra, in his *Rosa Laureada* (Madrid, 1670), gives an account of the movement to effect her canonization; and an account of the solemnities on the occasion of its consummation is printed in the *Mercure de France* (1671). A Spanish translation of Hansen, by Antonio de Lorea, was issued at Madrid in 1671; and a Portuguese version appeared at Lisbon in 1669 and 1674. Another Life, by Acuña, bishop of Caracas, was printed at Rome in 1665. A metrical *Vida de Santa Rosa*, by Oviedo y Herrera has the imprint of Madrid, 1711. (Cf. Leclerc, 1705, 1754-56, 1784, 1812 1813.) — Ed.]

by her brother, the gallant and chivalrous Don Beltran de Castro y Cueva, as commander of the forces.   On the 6th of January, 1590, the new viceroy made his solemn entry into Lima, in a magnificent procession of richly adorned Indian nobles, arquebusiers and pikemen, gentlemen of the household, judges of the *Audiencia*, professors and students of the University of San Marcos, and kings-at-arms.   The marquis came out with the usual injunctions to enforce the kindly treatment of Indians, but he received urgent demands from the king for more and more money.   In 1591 he imposed the *alcabala*, or duties on sales in markets, and on coca.   He was obliged to send increasing numbers of victims to the silver mines, and to the quicksilver mines of Huancavelica.   He made numerous ordinances for the regulation of industries and of markets, the suppression of gambling, and the punishment of fugitive slaves.   He founded the college of San Felipe and San Marcos at Lima in 1592.   He despatched an important expedition under Mandaña, which discovered the Marquesas Islands.   He was an active and intelligent ruler; but all the good he attempted to do was counterbalanced by the calls for treasure from Spain.   He sent home 1,500,000 ducats, besides value in jewels and plate.

After having governed Peru for six years and a half, the Marquis of Cañete begged to be allowed to return home.   He was succeeded by Don Luis de Velasco, Marquis of Salinas, who came from Mexico, where he had been the viceroy.   The Marquis of Salinas entered Lima on the 24th of July, 1596, and governed Peru until the end of 1604.

Chili had been comparatively quiet under the immediate successors of Don Garcia Hurtado de Mendoza, although the war with the Araucanians had never actually ceased.   In 1583 Philip II. selected a military officer of great experience and approved valor as governor of Chili.   Don Alonso de Sotomayor left Spain for Buenos Ayres with seven hundred men, and made the journey across the Pampas and over the pass of Uspallata, reaching Santiago on the 22d of September, 1583.   He and his brother Luis carried on a desultory war against the Araucanians for several years. During 1588 the attacks of the Indians were led by an intrepid heroine named Janequeo, who was resolved to avenge the death of her husband. The governor was superseded in 1592 and proceeded to Callao, where he commanded a ship, under Don Beltran de Cueva, in the fleet which attacked and captured Sir Richard Hawkins and his ship.   Sotomayor then returned to Spain.

The new governor of Chili was Don Martin Garcia Oñez de Loyola, the same cavalier who married an Ynca princess, and captured young Tupac Amaru.   He was a Basque, of the province of Guipuzcoa, and a near relative of Saint Ignatius.   He arrived at Valparaiso, with four hundred soldiers and abundant supplies of warlike stores, on the 23d of September, 1592, reaching Santiago on the 6th of October.   The Araucanians had elected the aged chief Paillamacu as their *toqui*, with two younger warriors named

Pelantaru and Millacalquin as his lieutenants. Believing the subjugation of Araucaria to be practicable, the new governor traversed the country between Imperial and Villarica during the year 1597, but failed to discover his astute foes. In the spring of 1598 Loyola was at Imperial, where he received a letter from his wife, the Ynca princess Doña Beatriz Coya, urging him to retreat to Concepcion, as the Araucanians were rising.

SOTOMAYOR.[1]

He set out for Angol, accompanied by only sixty officers, on the 21st of November, 1598, and stopped for the night in the valley of Curalaba. When all were wrapped in sleep, the tents were attacked by five hundred native warriors, and the governor was killed, with all his companions. His widow, the Ynca princess, went to Spain with a young daughter, who was given in marriage by Philip III. to Juan Henriquez de Borja, heir of the house of Gandia, and was at the same time created Marquesa de Oropesa.

The death of the governor was a signal for a general rising. Within forty-eight hours there were thirty thousand Araucanian warriors in the

[1] [Fac-similie of a part of a copperplate in Ovalle's *Historica Relacion de Chili.* Rome, 1648. — ED.]

field under the *toqui* Paillamacu.   All the Spanish towns south of the river Biobio were taken and destroyed, the invasion was hurled back beyond Concepcion, and the Spaniards were placed on the defensive.

The seventeenth century opened in Peru with a period of peace, during which the system of government elaborated by the viceroy Toledo was to be worked out to its consequences, — and in Chili, with the prospect of a prolonged contest and an impoverished treasury.   In both countries the future of the native races was melancholy and without hope.

———•———

CRITICAL ESSAY ON THE SOURCES OF INFORMATION.

THE king of Spain instituted the office of historiographer of the Indies, and that post was held for upwards of half a century by the learned Antonio de Herrera, who died in 1625.   All the official reports and correspondence were placed in his hands, and he had the use of a great deal of material which is now lost ; so that he is indispensable as an authority.[1]   His great work, *Historia General de las Indias Occidentales*, covers the whole ground from 1492 to 1554, and is divided into eight decades, in strict chronological order. The history of the conquest of Peru and of the subsequent civil wars is recorded with reference to chronological order as bearing on events in other parts of the Indies, and not connectedly.   The work first appeared in 1601 and 1615, in five folio volumes, and was republished in 1730.   The English version by Stevens, in six octavo volumes (1725), is worthless.   The episode relating to the descent of the river Amazon by Francisco de Orellana (*Herrera*, dec. vi. lib. ix.), was translated by Clements R. Markham, C. B., and printed for the Hakluyt Society in 1859 as a part of the volume called *Expeditions into the Valley of the Amazons.*

Francisco Lopez de Gomara was another compiler, who never personally visited Peru, and is best known for his history of the conquest of Mexico.   His narrative of the conquest of Peru forms an important part of his work entitled *Historia de las Indias.*   Although he was a contemporary, and had peculiarly good opportunities for obtaining trustworthy information, he was careless in his statements, and is an unsafe authority.[2]

Gonzalo Fernandez de Oviedo y Valdés, born in 1478 of an old Asturian family, was an eye-witness of the events on the isthmus which directly led to the discovery of Peru.   He went out with the governor Pedro Arias in 1513, and was at Panamá when Pizarro and Almagro were fitting out their first expedition.   He afterwards resided for many years in Hispaniola, and at his death, in 1557, he was chronicler of the Indies, the predecessor of Herrera.   He was devoted to historical composition, interspersing his narrative with anecdotes and personal reminiscences ; but most of his works long remained in manuscript. His two chapters on the conquest of Peru cover the ground from the landing of Pizarro to the return of Almagro from Chili.[3]

[1] [See Introduction (p. i) and p. 67. — ED.]
[2] [Cf. the chapter on Cortés.— ED.]
[3] [The bibliography of Oviedo is traced in a note following the chapter on Las Casas. Prescott has measured him as an authority in his *Peru* (Kirk's edition, vol. ii. p. 305).   Helps speaks of his history as a "mass of confusion and irrelevancy ; but at the same time," he adds, " it is a most valuable mine of facts."   A paper, appended to the combined edition of Peter Martyr and Oviedo published at Venice in 1534, seems to have been enlarged upon a tract *La Conquista del Peru*, published at Seville in 1534 (*Bibl. Amer. Vet.* p. 199), and is thought to bear some relation to the "Relatione d'un Capitano Spagnuolo" given in Ramusio, vol. iii. (*Bibliotheca Grenvilliana*, vol. ii. p. 536 ; Sabin, xvi, no. 61,097). — ED.]

It is, however, a relief to escape from compilers, and to be able to read the narratives of the actual actors in the events they describe.   The first adventurer who attempted to discover Peru was the *adelantado* Pascual de Andagoya, and he has recorded the story of his failures.   Born of a good stock in the province of Alava, Pascual went out to Darien when very young, with the governor Pedro Arias, in 1514.   After the failure of his first attempt he was in Panamá for some years, and in 1540 received the government of the country round the Rio San Juan, the scene of Pizarro's early sufferings.   Here he founded the town of Buenaventura ; but having got into a dispute with Benalcazar respecting the boundaries of their jurisdictions, Andagoya returned to Spain, where he remained five years.   He accompanied the president Gasca to Peru, and died at Cusco on the 18th of June, 1548.   He had broken his leg, but was recovering, when fever supervened, which carried him off.   Gasca reported that his death was mourned by all, because he was such a good man, and so zealous in the service of his country.   The historian Oviedo, who knew him well in the early days of the Darien colony, speaks of Andagoya as a noble-minded and virtuous person. He was a man of some education ; and his humane treatment of the Indians entitles his name to honorable mention.   His interesting narrative long remained in manuscript at Seville, but it was at length published by Navarrete.[1]   An English translation,[2] by Clements R. Markham, C. B., with notes and an introduction, was printed for the Hakluyt Society in 1865.[3]

Francisco de Xeres, the secretary of Pizarro, wrote his account of the early days of the conquest of Peru on the spot, by order (March, 1533) of his master.   He left Spain with Pizarro in January, 1530, returned to Seville with the first instalment of gold from Caxamarca in July, 1534 ; and his narrative, which embraces the period between these dates, was printed at Seville in the same year.[4]   This edition and that of 1547, printed somewhat carelessly at Salamanca, are extremely rare.[5]   The third and best-known edition was published at Madrid in 1749 in the Barcia Collection, *Historiadores primitivos de las Indias*.   Italian editions appeared in 1535,[6] and in 1556 in Ramusio ;[7] and a French version was published at Paris by M. Ternaux-Compans in 1837.[8]   An English translation, with notes and an introduction by Clements R. Markham, C. B., was printed for the Hakluyt Society in 1872.   There is a freshness and reality in the story told by Xeres, owing to his having been an eye-witness of all the events he describes, which the more elaborate accounts of compilers cannot

---

[1] *Coleccion de viages y descubrimientos,* vol. iii. no. vii. p. 393.

[2] [*Narrative of the Proceedings of Pedrárias Davilla, and of the Discovery of the South Sea and Coasts of Peru,* etc. — ED.]

[3] [Oviedo traces Andagoya's career in vol. iv. p. 126. Cf. Bancroft's *Central America,* vol. i. p. 503; Helps, vol. iii. p. 426; and the notice in Pacheco, *Coleccion de documentos inéditos,* vol. xxxix. p. 552. — ED.]

[4] [*Verdadera relacion de la Conquista del Peru.* There is a copy in the Lenox Library. Cf. *Bibl. Amer. Vet.,* no. 198. — ED.]

[5] [There are copies in the Lenox and Carter-Brown libraries. Quaritch in 1873 priced it at £35. Cf. *Bibl. Amer. Vet.,* p. 277 ; Ternaux, no. 54; Carter-Brown, vol. i. no. 146. It is sometimes bound with Oviedo's *Coronica,* and F. S. Ellis (1882, no. 221) prices the combined edition at £105. The *Huth Catalogue,* vol. v. p. 1628, shows an edition, *Conquista del Peru,* black-letter, without place or date, which Harrisse thinks preceded this 1547 edition. The Huth copy is the only one known. — ED.]

[6] [This Italian version (Venetian dialect) was made by Domingo de Gazlelu, and appeared at Venice ; and a fac-simile of the title is given herewith showing the arms of the emperor. Rich (no. 11) in 1832 priced it at £1 4s. ; Quaritch of late years has held it at £5 and £7 ; F. S. Ellis (1884) at £12, 12s. ; and Leclerc (no. 2,998) at 750 francs. There are copies in the Lenox, Harvard College, and Carter-Brown (*Catalogue,* vol. i. no. 116) libraries. It was reprinted at Milan the same year in an inferior manner, and a copy of this edition is in the British Museum. Cf. *Bibl. Amer. Vet.,* nos. 200, 201 ; *Bibliotheca Grenvilliana,* p. 818; Huth, p. 1628; Court, no. 376. What is said to be a translation of this Italian version into French, *L'histoire de la terre neuve du Peru,* Paris, 1545, signed I. G. (Jacques Gohory), purports to be an extract from Oviedo's *Historia.* Cf. *Bibl. Amer. Vet.,* no. 264; *Court Catalogue,* no. 175. — ED.]

[7] [Vol. iii. p. 378. — ED.]

[8] [*Voyages,* etc., vol. iv. This edition is worth about eight francs. A German edition is recorded as made by Külb at Stuttgard in 1843. — ED.]

LIBRO PRI

MO DE LA CONQVISTA
del PERV & prouincia del Cuzco
de le Indie occidentali.

Con gratia & priuilegio per anni X

TITLE OF XERES. VENICE, 1535.

impart.   Xeres has increased the value of his book by inserting the narrative of Miguel Astete, who accompanied Hernando Pizarro on his expedition to Pachacamac.

Hernando Pizarro wrote a letter to the royal *Audiencia* of Santo Domingo, which goes over the same ground as the narratives of Xeres and Astete, but is of course much briefer.   It is peculiarly valuable as containing the observations of the man of highest rank in the expedition who was able to write.[1]   The letter is dated November, 1533, and was written on his way to Spain with the treasure.   Oviedo gives it in his *Historia General*,[2] and it is printed by Quintana in his *Vidas de Españoles celebres*.[3]   It was translated into English by Clements R. Markham, C. B., and printed for the Hakluyt Society in 1872 in the volume of *Reports on the Discovery of Peru*.

Pedro Sancho, the notary, wrote a note of the distribution of the ransom of Atahualpa, with a list of the conquerors and the amount each received.   It is contained in the inedited work of Francisco Lopez de Caravantes, and was reprinted by Quintana in his *Vidas de Españoles celebres*.   An English translation by Clements R. Markham, C. B., was printed for the Hakluyt Society in 1872, in the volume already cited.   See also *Ramusio*, vol. iii. p. 414, for an Italian version, in which form it was used by Robertson and Prescott.[4]

Vicente de Valverde, the Dominican friar who accompanied Pizarro in the conquest of Peru and took part in the imprisonment and murder of Atahualpa, was made bishop of Cusco in 1536.   On his way to Spain, in 1541, he landed on the island of Puna, in the Bay of Guayaquil, was seized by the natives, and put to death with his brother-in-law and twenty-six other Spaniards.   He wrote a detailed *Carta-relacion* on the affairs of Peru, which is still inedited.   He also addressed letters to the emperor Charles V., which contain original information of great value.   A copy of one, dated Cusco, April 2, 1539, was among Sir Thomas Phillipps's collection of manuscripts.   It is frequently quoted by Helps.

Pedro Pizarro, a cousin of the conqueror, went out as his page in 1530, when only fifteen.   He was an eye-witness of all the events of the Conquest, and of the subsequent civil wars, having retired to Arequipa after the assassination of his patron.   Here he probably wrote his *Relaciones del Descubrimiento y Conquista de los Reynos del Peru*, finished in 1571.   It is a plain, unadorned statement of facts, but of the highest value as an authority. It remained in manuscript for centuries, but was at length printed in the *Coleccion de documentos inéditos para la historia de Espana*, v. 201–388.[5]

The death-struggle between the Pizarros and the old marshal Almagro is fully told in the above general histories; but light is also thrown upon the story from other directions. Among the manuscripts in the National Library at Madrid[6] there is an autobiography by a young scapegrace of noble birth named Alonzo Enriquez de Guzman, comprising a period from 1518 to 1543, from his nineteenth to his forty-fourth year.   The early part reminds one of the adventures of Gil Blas ; but in 1534 he went to Peru, and was a principal actor in the events which took place between the departure of Almagro for Chili in 1535 and

---

[1] [Prescott says (*Peru*, vol. i. p. 385) : "Allowing for the partialities incident to a chief actor in the scenes he describes, no authority can rank higher." — ED.]

[2] Chap. xv. lib. 43.

[3] Paris, 1845, p. 180.

[4] [Harrisse, *Bibl. Amer. Vet., Additions*, no. 109, notes, but not *de visu*, a plaquette enumerating the treasure sent to Spain by Pizarro in 1534.   F. S. Ellis (1884, no. 235) priced at £21 a second copy of the tract mentioned by Harrisse (no. 108) as known only in a copy in a private library in New York, entitled *Copey etlicher brieff so auss Hispania Kummen seindt*, 1535, which purports to be translated through the French from the Spanish.   Ellis pronounces it a version of Harrisse's no. 109, the only copy known of which was, as he says, lost in a binder's shop.   Cf. the *Libro ultimo de le Indie occidentale intitulato nova Castiglia, e del Conquisto del Peru*, published at Rome, May, 1535 (Sunderland, vol. i. no. 265).   For the effect of Peruvian gold on prices in Europe, see Brevoort's *Verrazano*, p. iii. — ED.]

[5] [It would seem to have been used by Herrera.   Navarrete communicated a copy to Prescott, who characterizes it in his *Conquest of Peru*, ii. 72. — ED.]

[6] *Papeles Manuscripts Originales y Ineditos*, G. 127.

his execution in 1538. Don Alonzo seems to have quarrelled with Hernando Pizarro during the siege of Cusco, and warmly espoused the cause of Almagro, who made him one of his executors. The latter portion of the autobiography, including a long letter to the emperor on the conduct of Hernando Pizarro, is very interesting, while the frankness of Don Alonzo's confessions as regards his own motives is most entertaining. *The Life and Acts of Don Alonzo Enriquez de Guzman* was translated and edited by Clements R. Markham, C. B., and printed by the Hakluyt Society in 1862. It had up to this time escaped notice.

The last years of the marquis Pizarro were occupied in laying out and building the capital of Peru, and we are indebted to the researches of the learned Peruvian, Don Manuel Gonzalez de la Rosa, for having discovered the most detailed account of the founding and early history of Lima among the manuscripts in the Biblioteca Colombina at Seville. The *Historia de la Fundacion de Lima* was written by the Jesuit Bernabé Cobo between 1610 and 1629, and was first printed under the superintendence of Dr. De la Rosa in the *Revista Peruana*.[1]

The story of the murder of Pizarro is told in the general histories, and there are some additional particulars in Montesinos. A very laudatory life of the marquis, which, how-ever, contains the results of original research, is contained in the *Varones Ilustres del Nuevo Mundo*, by Fernando Pizarro y Orellana (Madrid, 1639). This work also contains Lives of Pizarro's brothers and of Almagro.[2]

But by far the best life of Pizarro, both as regards literary merit and conscientious research, is contained in the *Vidas de Españoles Celebres* by Don Manuel Josef Quintana.[3] Quintana also gives the texts of the original agreement (1526) between Pizarro, Almagro, and Luque, and of the capitulation (July 26, 1529, at Toledo) between Queen Juana and Pizarro. These documents are also given by Prescott in the Appendix to the second volume of his *Conquest of Peru*.[4]

After the assassination of Pizarro, the licentiate Vaca de Castro, having defeated the younger Almagro, succeeded as governor of Peru, and the history of his rule is told in his own letters. The first is to the emperor, reporting his arrival at Santo Domingo, and is very brief. The second, also to the emperor, is from Quito, and announces the assassi-nation of Pizarro and the rebellion of Almagro the lad. The third is addressed to the emperor from Cusco, after the battle of Chupas, and is a straightforward statement of his proceedings. The fourth is a long letter from Cusco to his wife on private affairs. There is also a long letter on the revolt of young Almagro and the battle of Chupas from the municipality of Cusco to the emperor. These letters are included in the great official volume of *Cartas de Indias* published at Madrid in 1877, pp. 463–521. The *Vida y elojio del licenciado Vaca de Castro, Gobernador del Peru*, was written by Antonio de Herrera, the chronicler of the Indies.[5]

A good historian accompanied the ill-fated viceroy Blasco Nuñez de Vela to Lima. Augustin de Zarate was comptroller of accounts for Castile, and was sent out with the first viceroy to examine into the financial affairs of Peru. He collected notes and materials during his residence at Lima, and began the compilation of a history from the dis-covery by Pizarro to the departure of Gasca, when he returned to Spain. He had access to the best official sources of information, and his work is not without value ; but he was strongly prejudiced, and his style is tedious and inelegant. He assigns as the reason for not having begun his narrative in Peru, that Carbajal had threatened any one who should

---

[1] Lima, 1880.

[2] [The author of the *Varones* was a grand-son of the daughter of Francisco Pizarro (cf. Carter-Brown, ii. 465). H. H. Bancroft, *Central America*, ii. 273. — ED.]

[3] [It was published at Madrid in 1807, 1830, 1833, and at Paris in 1845. — ED.]

[4] [Harrisse (*Bibl. Am. Vet.*, 132) quotes from Asher's *Catalogue*, 1865, a *Lettere di Pietro Arias*, 1525, without place, which he supposes to refer to the first expedition of Almagro, Pizarro, and Luque. — ED.]

[5] [Cf. the notice of Herrera with references, given in the Introduction. — ED.]

attempt to record his exploits. In the earlier portions he relied on the testimony of the actors still living; but for the later part he was himself a spectator and actor. He had not intended to publish it in his lifetime; but the commendation of the emperor, to whom it was shown, induced him to depart from his purpose. The original manuscript of Zarate is or was preserved at Simancas; and Muñoz has disclosed how the printed volume differs considerably from it, in suppressing things too frankly stated, and in taking on a literary flavor not in the draft. Muñoz supposed that Florian d' Ocampo performed this critical office in passing the book through the press.[1] His *Historia del Descubrimiento y Conquista de la Provincia del Peru* was printed at Antwerp in 1555,[2] and a folio edition appeared at Seville in 1577;[3] but the best edition of Zarate is in the Barcia Collection, vol. iii. It was included in 1853 in the *Biblioteca de Autores Españoles*, vol. xxvi.[4]

A more important narrative of the civil war, which ended with the death of the viceroy Blasco Nuñez, was written by Pedro de Cieza de Leon, and has been recently published. Cieza de Leon landed in South America when he was barely fifteen, in the year 1534, and during his military service he conceived a strong desire to write an account of the strange things that were to be seen in the new world. " Oftentimes," he wrote, " when the other soldiers were reposing, I was tiring myself by writing. Neither fatigue, nor the ruggedness of the country, nor the mountains and rivers, nor intolerable hunger and suffering have ever been sufficient to obstruct my two duties; namely, writing, and following my flag and my captain without fault." In 1547 he joined the president Gasca, and was present at the final rout of Gonzalo Pizarro. He was many years in Peru, and he is certainly one of the most important authorities on Ynca history and civilization, whether we consider his peculiar advantages in collecting information, or his character as a conscientious historian. He lived to complete a great work, but unfortunately only a small portion of it has seen the light. The first and second parts of the Chronicle of Cieza de Leon have been published, but they relate to Ynca civilization and are discussed in a chapter in the first volume of the present work. The third part, treating of the discovery and conquest of Peru by Pizarro, is inedited, though the manuscript is believed to have been preserved. Part IV. was divided into five books relating the history of the civil wars of the conquerors. Only the third book has been published in the *Biblioteca Hispano-Ultramarina*. It was very ably edited by Don Márcos Jiménez de la Espada (Madrid, 1877), and is entitled *La Guerra de Quito*. The volume begins with the departure of the viceroy Blasco Nuñez de Vela from Spain, and consists of fifty-three chapters in the first part, the concluding portion forming a subsequent volume.[5]

The proceedings of the president, Pedro de la Gasca, were recorded by himself in very full reports to the Council of the Indies, which almost amount to official diaries. The first, dated at Santa Marta on his way out, July 12, 1546, has been published in the

---

[1] [Prescott, ii. 494. — ED.]

[2] [There is a copy in the Carter-Brown Library (*Catalogue*, no. 207). Quaritch priced it in 1879 at £9. — ED.]

[3] [There is a copy in the Carter-Brown Collection (no. 316); and others were sold in the Brinley (no. 5,346) and Murphy (no. 2,808) sales, as well as in the Sunderland (no. 13,521) and the Old Admiral's sales (no. 329) in England. Quaritch priced a copy at £16 10s. in 1883, — a rapid advance on earlier sales, but exceeded in 1884 by F. S. Ellis (£21). Leclerc (giving the date 1557) priced it in 1878 at 400 francs (no. 1,862). — ED.]

[4] [Zarate was early translated into other languages. An Italian version appeared at Venice in 1563, translated by Alfonzo Ulloa (Carter-Brown, i. 246; Leclerc, 1865 — 100 francs; Stevens — £3 3s.). Muller (*Books on America* (1872), nos. 1,231, etc.) enumerates five Dutch editions, the earliest edited by Willem Silvius, Antwerp, 1564 (the Carter-Brown copy is dated 1563, *Catalogue*, no. 245). In 1573 a new title and preface were put to the sheets of this edition. In 1596, 1598, and 1623 there were editions at Amsterdam. There were French versions published at Amsterdam in 1700, 1717, 1718, 1719, and at Paris in 1706, 1716, 1742, 1752-54, 1830. An English translation, made by T. Nicholas, was published at London in 1581 (Carter-Brown, vol. i. p. 285; Murphy, 2,213). Ellis priced a copy in 1884 at £28. — ED.]

[5] [For a detailed bibliography of the manuscripts and editions of Cieza de Leon, with various references, see the Editorial Note following this chapter. — ED.]

official volume of *Cartas de Indias* (Madrid, 1877). Other published correspondence throws light on the astute proceedings of the president while he was at Panamá. His instructions to Lorenzo de Aldana, his letters to Gonzalo Pizarro, and the detailed report of his agent Paniagua have been published in the *Revista de Lima*, 1880. His report to the Council of the Indies, when on his way to attack Gonzalo Pizarro at Cusco (dated Andahuaylas, March 7, 1548), has not been edited. But the Chilian historian Don Diego Barros Arana has published[1] the long despatch from Gasca to the Council, dated at Cusco, May 7, 1548, in which he describes the rout of Sacsahuana, the executions of Gonzalo Pizarro and Carbajal, and the subsequent bloody assize at Cusco. The document frequently quoted by Prescott (in book v. chap. iii. of his history)[2] as *Relacion del Licenciado Gasca MS.* is an abridged and mutilated copy of this despatch of May 7, 1548, from the Muñoz Collection,[3] and is preserved at Simancas. The sentence pronounced on Gonzalo Pizarro is published in the *Revista Peruana* (1880), from the original manuscript of Zarate's Chronicle.[4] Gasca continues his narrative in the despatches to the Council, dated at Lima, Sept. 25 and Nov. 26, 1548, which are also published by Barros Arana.[5] There are six other despatches of the president from Lima, dated in 1549, in the *Cartas de Indias*. The invaluable papers of the president Gasca are not in the Archives at Seville, but have been preserved by his family.[6]

But the best-known historian of the period during which the president Gasca was in Peru was Diego Fernandez de Palencia, usually called "el Palentino," from the place of his birth. He went out to Peru, served in the army which was raised to put down the rebellion of Giron, and having collected materials for a history, he was appointed chronicler of Peru by the viceroy Marquis of Cañete. Fernandez first wrote the history of the rebellion of Giron, in the suppression of which he was personally engaged; and afterwards he undertook to write a similar account of the rebellion of Gonzalo Pizarro and the administration of Gasca. Fernandez is a very painstaking writer, and no history of the time enters so fully into detail; yet it is pleasantly written, and the graver narrative is frequently relieved by anecdotes of personal adventures, and by amusing incidents. He is however a thorough-going partisan, and can see no redeeming feature in a rebellion, nothing but evil in the acts of rebels. His book is called *Primera y Secunda Parte de la Historia del Peru, que se mando escrebir á Diego Fernandez, vecino de la ciudad de Palencia.* It was published at Seville in 1571 (folio; primera parte, pp. 142; segunda parte, pp. 130). This is the only edition.[7]

The first part of the work of the Ynca Garcilasso de la Vega relates to the history and civilization of the Yncas, and is discussed in the first volume of the present work. But the second part is a general history of the discovery of Peru, and of the civil wars down to the termination of the administration of the viceroy Toledo in Peru, and to the death of the governor Loyola in Chili. Like the first part, the second is rather a commentary than a history, for the Ynca quotes largely from other writers, especially from the

[1] [In his *Proceso de Pedro de Valdivia i otros documentos inéditos concernientes a este conquistador, reunidos i anotados por Diego Barros Arana,* Santiago de Chile (1873), 8o pp. 392. — ED.]

[2] [The Philadelphia edition, 1879, vol. ii. p. 406. — ED.]

[3] The historiographer Juan Bautista Muñoz intended to have written an exhaustive history of America, but he only completed one volume. He however made copies of documents from the Seville Archives in 1782 and 1783, which form one hundred and fifty volumes. They are now in various libraries, but the greater part belongs to the Real Academia de la historia de Madrid. [See the Introduction to the present volume, p. iii. — ED.]

[4] Prescott's copy (in his Appendix, vol. ii. p. 471) unfortunately contains various inaccuracies.

[5] *Ubi supra.*

[6] [Helps speaks of these family papers as in the possession of the Counts of Cancelada, and he used copies which were procured for him by Gayangos. *Spanish Conquest*, New York edition, iv. 227. — ED.]

[7] [Rich (no. 48) priced this edition in 1832 at £5 5s.; Leclerc (no. 1,733) in 1878 at 800 francs. The Council of the Indies is said to have tried to check its circulation. A copy is in the Carter-Brown (i. 282) Collection; and another was sold in the Court sale recently (no. 128). — ED.]

Palentino, always carefully indicating the quotations and naming the authors. But his memory was well stored with anecdotes that he had heard when a boy ; and with these he enlivens the narrative, while often a recollection of the personal appearance or of some peculiarity of the historical character whose deeds he is recording enables him to give a finishing touch to a picture. His father was a conqueror and an actor in most of the chief events of the time ;[1] his mother, an Ynca princess, and born in the city of Cusco ; so the future author had special advantages for storing up information. He was born in 1539, but a few years after the conquest and one year after the death of Almagro. He passed his school days at Cusco, with many other half-caste sons of the conquerors, and went to Spain in 1560, dying at Cordova in 1616. The first part of his great work on Peru originally appeared at Lisbon in 1609, the second part at Cordova in 1617. The second and best edition of the two parts appeared at Madrid in 1723. The English translation of Sir Paul Rycaut (1688) is worthless, and there has never been a complete English version of the second part, which is entitled *Historia General del Peru*. The episode of the expedition of Gonzalo Pizarro to the land of cinnamon (part ii. lib. iii.) was translated by Clements R. Markham, C.B., and printed for the Hakluyt Society in 1859.[2]

The licentiate Fernando Montesinos is an authority of some reputation, but chiefly valuable for his studies of native lore. He was altogether upwards of fifteen years in Peru. He was there a century after the conquest. His *Memorias Antiguas Historiales* exclusively relate to Ynca history; but his *Annales* contain a history of the conquest and of subsequent events, and include some original documents, and a few anecdotes which are not to be found elsewhere.[3]

The authorities for the final settlement of Peru, after the crushing of the spirit of revolt by the Marquis of Cañete, are a good deal scattered. A learned account of the life and administration of Andres Marquis of Cañete himself will be found in the admirable *Diccionario Histórico-Biografico del Peru* by General Mendiburu, published at Lima in 1880 ; which also contains a Life of his successor, the licentiate Lope Garcia de Castro.

The viceroy Don Francisco de Toledo has left a deeper mark on the history of Peru by his *Libro de Tasas* and *Ordenanzas* relating to mines and the treatment of Indians. The transactions with reference to the judicial murder of Tupac Amaru and the persecution of the Ynca family are briefly related by Garcilasso de la Vega ; but there is a much more detailed account in the *Coronica Moralizada del Orden de San Augustin en el Peru* by Fray Antonio de la Calancha, published at Barcelona in 1638.[4] Calancha also gives the remorseful will of Mancio Sierra de Leguizamo, whose life-story is fully related by Don José Rosendo Gutierrez in the *Revista Peruana* (tomo ii. 1880).

The story of the capture and execution of Tupac Amaru by the viceroy Toledo is told in very full detail by Baltasar d'Ocampo, who was an eye-witness. His narrative has all the charm of honest truthfulness ; and yet the incidents, thus simply related, are as interesting as the most ingeniously constructed romance. Unfortunately the story, as told by

---

[1] [A view of what is called the house of Garcilasso de la Vega is given in Squier's *Peru, Land of the Incas*, p. 449. — ED.]

[2] [A detailed bibliographical note of Garcilasso de la Vega's works on Peru is given in Note B, following the present chapter. — ED.]

[3] [Prescott, who had copies of both manuscripts, speaks of the opportunities which Montesinos enjoyed in his official visits to Peru, of having access to repositories, and of making an inspection of the country. He adds that a comparison of his narrative with other contemporary accounts leads one sometimes to distrust him. "His writings seem to me," he says, "entitled to little praise, either for the accuracy of their statements or the sagacity of their reflections." — ED.]

[4] [Cf. Rich, no. 226 £2 10s.; Sabin, vol. iii. no. 9,870; Carter-Brown, vol. ii. no. 450; Dufossé, no. 11,818, — 2,180 francs. A second part was printed at Lima in 1653 by Cordova y Salinas, the same who published a Life of Francisco Solano, the apostle of Peru, at Lima in 1630, which appeared, augmented by Alonzo de Mendieta, at Madrid in 1643 (Leclerc, nos. 1,714, 1,731. — ED.]

Ocampo (*Descripcion de la Provincia de San Francisco de Villcapampa*), has never been printed.   It is among the manuscripts of the British Museum.[1]

Polo de Ondegardo, the learned lawyer, was the principal adviser of the viceroy Toledo.   He arrived in Peru before the president Gasca, and held the important posts of *corregidor* of Potosi and of Cusco.   He had a profound knowledge of the Ynca system of government, and his two *Relaciones*,[2] addressed to the Marquis of Cañete and the Conde de Nieva, discuss the land tenures, colonial policy, and social legislation of the natives.   His labors were all undertaken with a view to adapting the best parts of the Ynca system to the new polity to be instituted by the Spanish conquerors; and his numerous suggestions, from this standpoint, are wise and judicious.   A feeling of sympathy for the Indians, and the evidence of a warm desire for their welfare pervade all his writings.   There is another rough draft of a report by Polo de Ondegardo, a manuscript in the National Library at Madrid,[3] which contains much information respecting the administrative system of the Yncas; and here, also, he occasionally points out the way in which native legislation might usefully be imitated by the conquerors.   This report of Polo de Ondegardo was translated by Clements R. Markham, C.B., and printed for the Hakluyt Society in 1873 in the volume called *Rites and Laws of the Incas*.   It is believed that Polo de Ondegardo died at Potosi in about the year 1580.

The other adviser of the viceroy Toledo was a man of a very different character, a hard, relentless politician, indifferent alike to the feelings and the physical well-being of the conquered people.   Judge Matienzo wrote a work in two parts on the condition of the people, the *mita*, or forced labor, the tribute, the mining laws, and on the duties of the several grades of Spanish officials.   The *Gobierno de el Peru* of Matienzo is a manuscript in the British Museum.[4]

The whole body of ordinances and regulations relating to the aboriginal people and their treatment by the conquerors is fully explained and discussed by Dr. Don Juan de Solorzano, a profoundly learned jurist, and member of the Council of the Indies, in his *Politica Indiana* (Madrid, 1648).   The history of *encomiendas* in Peru is well and ably discussed by Enrique Torres Saldamando in the *Revista Peruana* (vol. ii. 1880).[5]

The second Marquis of Cañete, who was viceroy of Peru in the last decade of the sixteenth century, was best known for his conduct of the Araucanian war, when, as a young man, he was governor of Chili.   That famous war formed the subject of the epic poem of Alonzo de Ercilla, the warrior-poet.   Born at Bermeo on the shores of the Bay of Biscay, where the house of his ancestors is still standing, Ercilla began life as a page to the prince of Spain, and volunteered to go out and serve against the Araucanians, when news arrived of an outbreak and the death of Valdivia.   Born in 1533, he was only twenty-one when he set out for Chili under the command of the youthful governor Garcia Hurtado de Mendoza. Ercilla was present at seven regular battles, and suffered much from hardships during the harassing campaigns.   He returned to Spain in 1562, after an absence of eight years.   His *Araucana*[6] is a versified history of the war, in which he describes all the events in their

---

[1] Additional Manuscripts, 17, 585.

[2] [These are dated 1561 and 1570.   The originals are in the Escurial; copies are at Simancas.   A copy, made for Kingsborough, became Prescott's, who records his estimate of it (*Peru*, vol. i. p. 181).   It is said that Herrera made use of Ondegardo's manuscript. — ED.]

[3] Quarto on parchment, B. 135.

[4] Additional Manuscripts, 5,469.

[5] [Cf. notes to chap. on Las Casas. — ED.]

[6] [The first edition, of only fifteen cantos, was printed at Madrid in 1569.   This was enlarged with a second part when issued at Antwerp in 1575; again at Madrid, in 1578; and at Lisbon, in 1581–88.   A third part was printed at Ma-

drid in 1589, and at Antwerp in 1597; and the three parts, with a general title, appeared at Madrid in 1590, — the first complete edition as Ercilla wrote it.   Two parts were again issued at Antwerp in 1586; and other editions appeared at Barcelona in 1592, and at Perpignan in 1596. A fourth and a fifth part were added by Osorio after Ercilla's death, and appeared at Salamanca, 1597, and at Barcelona, 1598.   There were later complete editions at Madrid, 1633, 1776, 1828; at Lyons, 1821; and at Paris, 1824 and 1840.   Cf. Sabin, vol. vi. no. 22,718; Ticknor, *Spanish Literature*, ii. 465; Hallam, *Literature of Europe*, ii. 284; Sismondi, *Literature of South of Europe*, ii. 271. — ED.]

order, enumerates the contending chiefs, with a few lines to denote the character or special characteristic of each, and is minutely accurate even in his geographical details.   He tells us that much of the poem was composed in the country, and that by the light of the camp-fires at night he wrote down what had occurred during the day.   Ticknor looks upon the *Araucana* as an historical rather than an epic poem ;[1] and he considers the descriptive powers of Ercillo — except in relation to natural scenery — to be remarkable, the speeches he puts in the mouths of Araucanian chiefs often excellent, and his characters to be drawn with force and distinctness.   Pedro de Oña, in his *Arauco Domado*,[2] praises the governor, Hurtado de Mendoza, the future Marquis of Cañete ; and Lope de Vega made his Araucanian war the subject of one of his plays.

The Life of the viceroy Marquis of Cañete (Garcia) was written by Don Cristóval Suarez de Figueroa, a man of some literary fame in his day.   When the marquis returned from Peru broken in health, he was treated with neglect and ingratitude; nor had he received full justice from Ercilla for his youthful exploits, — at least so thought his heirs when he died in 1599; and they applied to Suarez de Figueroa to undertake his biography, placing all the viceroy's family and official papers in the author's hands.   The result was the *Hechos de Don Garcia Hurtado de Mendoza, cuarto Marques de Cañete*, which was printed in 1613.[3]   It was reprinted in the *Coleccion de Historiadores de Chile*, — a work published in seven volumes at Santiago in 1864, edited by Don Diego Barros Arana.   This work contains a very full account of the administration of the marquis while he was viceroy of Peru.

Pedro de Valdivia has written his own history of his conquest and settlement of Chili, in his letters to the emperor, Charles V.   They are preserved in the Archives at Seville among the documents sent from Simancas, and have been published by Claudio Gaye in his *Historia de Chile* (Paris, 1846), and also in the first volume of the *Coleccion de Historiadores de Chile* (Santiago, 1864).   The first of Valdivia's despatches is dated from La Serena, Sept. 4, 1545, and the second from Lima, June 15, 1548.   In the third he reports fully on the state of affairs in Chili, and refers to his own previous career.   It is dated from Concepcion, Oct. 15, 1550.   There are two others, dated Concepcion, Sept. 25, 1551, and Santiago, Oct. 26, 1552, which are short, and not so interesting.

Some discontented soldiers brought a series of fifty-seven accusations against Valdivia, which were considered by the president Gasca at Lima in October, 1548, — the result being acquittal.   The *Acta de Accusacion* was published at Santiago in 1873 by Barros Arana, together with Valdivia's defence and several other important historical documents. That accomplished Chilian historian has also edited a very interesting letter from Pedro de Valdivia to Hernando Pizarro, dated at La Serena on the 4th of September, 1545, which fell into the hands of the president Gasca, and remained among his papers ; and when he was at Seville in 1859, he discovered one more unimportant letter from the Chilian conqueror to Charles V., dated at Santiago, July 9, 1549.   The first book of the records of the Santiago municipality, called the *Libro Becerro*, embraces the years from 1541 to 1557. It has been published in the first volume of the *Coleccion de Historiadores de Chile*, etc. (Santiago, 1861), and contains the appointment of Valdivia as governor of Chili, the founding of Santiago, with the nomination of the first municipal officers, ordinances for mines, and other important entries.

There is thus ample original material for the opening chapter of the history of Chili. Moreover, the first connected work on the subject was written by one of the early conquerors.   Gongora Marmolejo served under Valdivia, and was an eye-witness of all the stirring events of the time.   His history begins at the discovery of Chili, in 1536, and

---

[1] ["A military journal done into rhyme," as Prescott calls it, — *History of the Conquest of Peru*, ii. 108. — ED.]

[2] [Published at Lima, 1596. Cf Ticknor,

Spanish Literature, ii. 469 ; Sabin, vol. xiv. no. 57,300 ; Carter-Brown, vol. i. no. 506. — ED.]

[3] [This was reissued in 1616. Rich, no. 143 — £1 4*s*. — ED.]

is brought down to the year 1575. Written in Santiago, it is addressed to the president of the Council of the Indies; and though the style is confused, and often obscure, the narrative has the merit of impartiality, and supplies many interesting details. It also has annexed documents, including a letter from Gonzalo Pizarro to Valdivia giving an account of events in Peru, down to the death of Blasco Nuñez de Vela. The *Historia de Chile* of Gongora Marmolejo remained in manuscript in the Biblioteca de Salazar (H. 45) until it was edited by Don Pascual de Gayangos, in 1850, for the fourth volume of the *Memorial Histórico Español*. It has since been published in the *Coleccion de Historiadores de Chile*.

The story of the surprise and death of the governor, Martin Garcia de Loyola, and of the subsequent formidable rising of the Araucanians in 1598, was written in the form of a poem by Captain Fernando Alvarez de Toledo. The work has no literary merit, and is only valuable as an historical narrative. The manuscript is in the National Library at Madrid, and it was published by Don Diego Barros Arana, in the *Collection d'Ouvrages inédits ou rares sur L'Amérique* (Paris, 1861). An interesting modern account of the death of the governor Loyola, entitled *La sorpresa de Curalava*, was written by the accomplished Chilian, Miguel Luis Amunátegui, and published as one of his *Naraciones Históricas* (Santiago, 1876).[1]

The history of Chili, which follows Marmolejo in point of time, is by Cordova y Figueroa, a native of the country, and a descendant of Juan de Negrete, one of the followers of Valdivia. Cordova y Figueroa was born at Concepcion in 1692, served with credit in a war with the Araucanians, and is believed to have written the history between 1740 and 1745. Beginning with the expedition of Almagro, it comes down to the year 1717, and is the most complete history that had been written up to that date. The manuscript was in the National Library at Madrid, and a copy was made for the Chilian government, under the auspices of Don Francisco S. Astaburriaga, who was then minister to Spain. It was published in the *Coleccion de Historiadores de Chile*.

In this review of works on the conquest and first settlement of Peru and Chili, those which refer only to the history and civilization of the Yncas, or to geography and natural history, have been omitted, as they receive notice in the chapter on ancient Peru in the first volume of this History.

Clements R. Markham

---◆---

EDITORIAL NOTES.

A. CIEZA DE LEON.— It does not seem desirable to divide the bibliographical record of Cieza de Leon between the present and the first volume. His work was separated into four parts, — the *first* relating to the geography and description of Peru; the *second*, to the period of the Incas; the *third*, to the Spanish Conquest; the *fourth*, to the civil wars of the conquerors. The fate of each part has been distinct.

Part I. Prescott (*Peru*, vol. ii. p. 306) speaks of this as more properly an itinerary or geography of Peru, presenting the country in its moral and physical relations as it appeared to the eye of the conquerors; and not many of them, it is probable, were so impressed as Cieza de Leon was with the grandeur of the *cordilleras*. This, as *Parte primera de la chronica del Peru*, was published in folio at Seville, in 1553. In

1 [The *Descubrimiento i Conquista de Chile* of Miguel Luis Amunátegui, published at Santiago de Chile in 1862, was a work presented to the University of Chili in 1861. — ED.]

Rich's time (183.) it was worth £5 5s.[1] It was reprinted the next year (1554) at Antwerp in two distinct editions. One, *La chronica del Peru*, in duodecimo, has the imprint of Nucio; the other, likewise in duodecimo, is printed in an inferior manner, and sometimes has the name of Bellero, and sometimes that of Steelsio, as publisher. This last edition has the larger title, *Parte primera de la chronica del Peru*, etc., and was the one used by Prescott, and followed by Markham in the translation, *Travels of Cieza de Leon*, published by the Hakluyt Society in 1864.[2]

In 1555 an Italian translation, *La prima parte de la cronica del . . . Peru*, appeared at Rome, made by Agostino Cravaliz, or Augustino di Gravalis.[3] A second edition — *La prima parte dell' istorie del Peru* — appeared the next year (1556) at Rome, and is found with the names of two different publishers.[4]

At Venice, in 1560, appeared the *Cronica del gran regno del Peru*. This makes a work of which the first volume is a reprint of Gravaliz' version of Cieza, and volumes ii. and iii. contain an Italian version of Gomara in continuation offered by the same publisher, Ziletti, under the title, *La seconda, terza parte delle historie dell India*.[5]

The English translation of Stevens (*The Seventeen Years' Travels of Peter de Cieza through the mighty Kingdom of Peru and the large Provinces of Cartagena and Popayan in South America, from the City of Panama on the Isthmus to the Frontiers of Chile*) was printed at London in 1709, and appeared both separately and as a part of his collection of *Voyages*. It gives only ninety-four of the one hundred and nineteen chapters.

Part II. Rich, though he had heard of this part, supposed it to have disappeared; and it is spoken of as missing by Markham in 1864, and by Harrisse in his *Bibl. Amer. Vet.* (p. 319). The manuscript of it was meanwhile in the Escurial, preserved in a bad copy made about the middle or end of the sixteenth century; but it is deficient in chapters i. and ii. and in part of chapter iii. Another manuscript copy not well done is in the Academy of History at Madrid.

Lord Kingsborough had a copy, and from this Rich had a fifth copy made, which was used by Prescott; but it does not appear that any of these students suspected it to be the second part of Cieza de Leon. Prescott, supposing it to be written *by* the president of the Council of the Indies, Sarmiento, instead of *for* that officer, ascribed it to him; but Kirk, Prescott's editor (*Peru*, vol. ii. p. 308), has recognized its identity, which Dr. Manuel Gonzales de la Rosa established when he edited the Escurial manuscript in 1873. This edition, though wholly printed in London, has not been made public. Following another transcript, and correcting the spelling, etc., Márcos Jiménez de la Espada printed it at Madrid in 1880 as vol. v. of the *Biblioteca Hispano-Ultramarina*. An English translation of it was made by Mr. Markham, and published by the Hakluyt Society in 1883.

Part III. Markham reports that Espada says that this part is in existence, but inaccessible.

Part IV. Espada is cited as asserting that books i. and ii. of this part are in existence, but inaccessible.

A manuscript of book iii. is in the Royal Library at Madrid, in handwriting of the middle of the sixteenth century. It covers the period from the appointment of Blasco Nuñez as viceroy in 1543 to a period just previous to Gasca's departure from Panamá for Peru in 1547. A copy of this manuscript, belonging to Uguina, passed to Ternaux, thence to Rich, who sold it for £600 to Mr. Lenox; and it is now in the Lenox Library.

It has since been included under Espada's editing in the *Biblioteca Hispano-Ultramarina*, and was published at Madrid in 1877 as *Tercero libro de las Guerras Civiles del Peru*.[6]

Books iv. (war of Huarina) and v. (war of Xaquixaguana), and two appended commentaries on events from the founding of the *Audiencia* to the departure of the president, and on events extending to the arrival of the viceroy Mendoza, are not known to exist, though Cieza refers to them as written. These would complete the fourth part, and end the work.

---

[1] Cf. Rich, no. 24; Carter-Brown, vol. i. no. 176; Murphy, no. 462; Sunderland, vol. iii. no. 7,575; Sabin, vol. iv. no. 13,044.

[2] Cf. Rich, nos. 26, 27 — £1 1s. and £1 10s.; Sabin, 13,045–13,046; Cooke, no. 523; Carter-Brown vol. i, nos. 185, 186; Court, no. 63; Ternaux, no. 66; Brinley, no. 5,345; Leclerc, no. 1,706, — 200 francs; Quaritch, £5 and £10; F. S. Ellis (1884) £7 10s. The latest Spanish edition, *Crónica del Peru*, constitutes vol. xxvi. of the *Biblioteca de Autores Españoles*, published at Madrid in 1852.

[3] Sabin, no. 13,047; Carter-Brown, vol. i. no. 198.

[4] There are copies in the Lenox and Carter-Brown (vol. i. no. 208) libraries. Cf. Sabin, nos. 13,048–13,049; Leclerc, no. 1,707; Tröwel, no. 19.

[5] There are copies in the Boston Public, Lenox, and Carter-Brown (vol. i. nos. 231, 249, 254) libraries. A set is worth about $20. (Sabin, nos. 13,050–13,052; Field, 314, 315; Rich, no. 39 — 10s.; Court, no. 64: Leclerc, no. 1,708; Sobolewski, 3,744; Dufossé, no. 8,978.) Some copies are dated 1564, and dates between 1560 and 1564 are on the second and third volumes (Sabin, no. 13,053). These three parts were again reprinted at Venice in 1576 (Sabin, no. 13,054; Leclerc, no. 1,709; Cooke, no. 524).

[6] Cf. Leclerc, nos. 2,503, 2,672; *Coleccion de documentos inéditos* (*España*) vol. lxviii.

What we know of Cieza is mainly derived from himself and the brief notice in Antonio's *Bibliotheca Hispana Nova* (Madrid, 1788). The writer of the foregoing chapter gives an account of Cieza's career, as well as it could be made out, in his translation of the *Travels;* but he supplements that story in the introduction to his version of Part II.

B. GARCILASSO DE LA VEGA. — The *Primera parte de los Commentarios reales* seems to have been printed — according to the colophon at Lisbon — in 1608, but to have been published in 1609. It has incidental notices of Spanish-American history, though concerned mainly with chronicles of the Incas.[1]

The second part, called *Historia General del Peru*, was printed at Cordova in 1616, though most copies are dated 1617. The titles of the two dates slightly vary. This volume is of larger size than that of 1609.[2]

The two parts were reprinted by Barcia at Madrid in 1722–1723.[3] There have been later editions of the Spanish at Madrid in 1800, and in 1829, in four volumes, as a part of a series; *Conquista del Nuevo Mondo*, in nine volumes, which embraced also Solis's Mexico, Garcilasso de la Vega's Florida, and the Florida of Cardenas y Cano.

Rycaut's English *Royal Commentaries of Peru* (London, 1688) was priced by Rich (no. 420) in 1832 at £1 4s., and is not worth more now.[4] Markham's English version of the first part was issued in two volumes by the Hakluyt Society in 1869–1871.

The French version (by J. Baudoin) of the first part was printed at Paris in 1633 as *Le Commentaire Royal*,[5] and of the second part as *Histoire des Guerres Civiles* in 1650, and again in 1658 and 1672,[6] and at Amsterdam in 1706.[7] A French version of the first part was also printed at Amsterdam in 1715,[8] and joined with

the book on Florida; another French edition appeared at Amsterdam in 1737.[9] A new translation of this first part, made by Dalibard, was printed in Paris in 1744.[10] Baudoin's version of both parts was reissued in Paris in 1830.[11] There was a German translation in 1798.

An account of Garcilasso de la Vega and his ancestry is given by Markham in the introduction to his version of the *Royal Commentaries of the Yncas*. Another account is in the *Documentos inéditos (España)*, vol. xvi.[12]

The estimate held of him by Robertson has been largely shared among the older of the modern writers, who seem to think that Garcilasso added little to what he borrowed from others, though we find some traces in him of authorities now lost. The later writers are more generous in their praise of him. Prescott quotes him more than twice as often as he cites any other of the contemporary sources. (Cf. his *Peru*, vol. i. p. 289.)

Helps says that "with the exception of Bernal Diaz and Las Casas, there is not perhaps any historical writer of that period, on the subject of the Indies, whose loss would be more felt than that of Garcilasso de la Vega."

C. MEMORANDA. — An early voyage to the coast is supposed to be indicated in an Italian tract of 1521, mentioned in the catalogue of the Biblioteca Colombina. It is not now known, except in what is supposed to be a German version.[13] The first tidings (March 15, 1533) which Europe got of Pizarro's success came from a letter which was addressed to the emperor, probably in Spanish, though we have no copy of it in that tongue; but it is preserved in Italian, *Copia delle lettere del prefetto della India, la Nuova Spagna detta*, a plaquette of two leaves, of which there is a copy in the Lenox Library. It is supposed to have been printed at Venice.[14] This version is also included in the

---

[1] Rich priced it in 1832 at £1 10s., and Leclerc in 1878 (no. 1,740) at 100 francs. There are copies in the Carter-Brown (vol. ii. no. 96), Boston Public, and Harvard College libraries; and others were sold in the Murphy (no. 2,589) and O'Callaghan (no. 963) collections. Cf. Sunderland, vol. ii. no. 5,358; vol. v. no. 12,814; Ticknor, *Spanish Literature*, vol. iii. p. 146.

[2] There are copies in the Boston Public, Harvard College, and Carter-Brown (vol. ii. nos. 183, 197) libraries. Rich priced it in 1832 at £1 10s.; Leclerc (no. 1,741) in 1878 at 100 francs. Cf. Murphy, no. 2,590; Huth, vol. ii. p. 574.

[3] Leclerc, no. 1,742; Carter-Brown, vol. iii. nos. 327–329; Field, 589.

[4] Cf. Prescott's *Peru*, vol. i. p. 294; Field, 592.

[5] Carter-Brown, vol. ii. no. 405; Leclerc, no. 1,745.

[6] Ibid., vol. ii. nos. 700, 842; Leclerc, no. 1,744.

[7] Ibid., vol. iii. no. 82.

[8] Ibid., vol. iii. no. 205.

[9] Ibid., vol. iii. no. 561; Field, no. 591.

[10] Leclerc, no. 1,746; Carter-Brown, vol. iii. no. 768.

[11] Ibid., no. 1,747.

[12] Cf. Ticknor, *Spanish Literature*, vol. iii. p. 188.

[13] *Bibl. Amer. Vet.*, no. 102; *Additions*, no. 65.

[14] *Bibl. Amer. Vet.*, no. 193; *Bibliotheca Grenvilliana*, p. 537; *Bibliotheca Heberiana*, vol. i. no. 1,961.

Libro di Benedetto (Venice, 1534). A German translation was printed at Nuremberg, February, 1534, as *Newe Zeitung aus Hispanien,* of four leaves.[1] A French issue, *Nouvelles certaines des isles du Peru,* dated 1534, is in the British Museum.[2] Ticknor[3] cites Gayangos' references to a tractate of four leaves, *La Conquista del Peru,* which he found in the British Museum.[4]

It is not very clear to what city reference is made in a plaquette, *Letera de la nobil cipta, novamente ritrouvata alle Indie . . . data in Peru adi. xxv de novembre, de MDXXXIIII.* An edition of the next year (1535) is "data in Zhaual."[5] Marco Guazzo's *Historie di tutte le cose degne di memoria qual del anno MDXXIIII.,* etc., published at Venice in 1540, gives another early account.[6] It was repeated in the edition of 1545 and 1546.

The *De Peruviæ regionis, inter novi orbis provincias celeberrimæ inventione* of Levinus Apollonius of Ghent was published at Antwerp in 1565, 1566, 1567, for copies with these respective dates are found;[7] though Sabin thinks Rich and Ternaux are in error in assigning an edition to 1565. It covers events from the discovery to the time of Gasca and the death of Gonzalo Pizarro.[8] It also appeared as a third part to the German translation of Benzoni (Basle 1582).

Ternaux-Compans in his *Voyages* has preserved in a French version several early chronicles of minor importance. Such is Miguel Carello Balbóa's *Histoire du Peru* (in vol. xvii.), the work of one who went to Bogota in 1566, and finished his work at Quito in 1586. It rehearses the story of the Inca rule, not always agreeing with Garcilasso, and only touches the Spanish Conquest as it had proceeded before the murder of Atahualpa.[9] Another work is the *Histoire du Pérou* of Father Anello Oliva, a Jesuit, who was born at Naples in 1593, came to Peru as a Jesuit in 1597, and died at Lima

in 1642. It was apparently written before 1631; but what Ternaux affords us is only the first of the four books which constitute the completed work.[10] Juan de Velasco's *Histoire de Quito,* a work of a later day but based on the early sources, makes volumes xviii. and xix. of Ternaux's collection.

Alonso de Ovalle's historical account of Chili was issued at Rome in 1646, in Italian, as *Historica Relatione del Regno di Cile,* and the same year at the same place in Spanish, as *Histórica Relacion del Reyne de Chile.* Six of the eight books are given in English in Churchill's *Voyages* (1732), and in Pinkerton.[11]

Among the minor documentary sources there is much of interest to be found in the *Documentos inéditos (España),* vols. v., xiii., xxvi., xlix., l., and li.

The Ministerio de Fomento of Peru printed at Madrid in 1881 the first volumes — edited by Jiménez de la Espada — of *Relaciones geográficas de Indias.* The editor supplied a learned introduction, and the volume contained twelve documents of the sixteenth century, which were then published for the first time;[12] and they contribute to our knowledge of the condition of the country during that period.

There are other documents covering the whole course of Peruvian history in the collection of *Documentos históricos del Peru en las epocas del coloniage despues de la conquista y de la independencia hasta a presente, colectados y arreglados por el coronel Manuel Odriozola,* the first volume of which was published at Lima about twenty-five years ago (1863).

Harrisse (*Bibl. Amer. Vet.,* pp. 320–322) enumerates many copies of manuscripts preserved in New York and Boston, some of which have since been printed. There is record of other manuscripts in New York in the *Magazine of American History,* i. 254.

The *Varias relaciones del Peru y Chile y Conquista de la isla de Santa Catalina,* 1535-

---

[1] *Bibl. Amer. Vet.,* no. 195; *Libri* [Catalogue (reserved part), no. 32. There is a copy in the Lenox Library.

[2] *Bibl. Amer. Vet.,* no. 196; *Bibliotheca Grenvilliana,* p. 537.

[3] *Spanish Literature,* ii. 40.

[4] Cf. Sabin, vol. xiii. no. 54,945.

[5] Cf. Carter-Brown, i. nos. 111, 113; *Bibl. Amer. Vet.,* nos. 191, 206; Leclerc, nos. 2,839, at 1,200 francs.

[6] *Bibl. Amer. Vet., Additions,* nos. 124, 153, 157.

[7] Leclerc, no. 1,689.

[8] Cf. Rich, no. 44 — £1 4s.; Carter-Brown, i. 268; Quaritch, £3 3s.; Sunderland, vol. iv. no. 9,515; Sabin, vol. i. no. 1,761; Huth, i. 41; Cohn (1884), no. 113, at 75 marks. The *Catalogue de M. A. Chaumette des Fossé's,* Paris, 1842, is mainly of books pertaining to Peru.

[9] Field, *Indian Bibliography,* no. 67.

[10] Leclerc, no. 1,808.

[11] Rich, no. 253 — £3 3s.; Sabin, vol. xiv. no. 57,971, 57,972; Carter-Brown, ii. 592; Quaritch, £6 6s.; Sunderland (1883), £5; Rosenthal (1884), 60 marks.

[12] Leclerc, no. 3,029.

PRESCOTT'S LIBRARY.

1658 (Madrid, 1879) [1] constitutes vol. xiii. of *Coleccion de libros raros ó curiosos,* which includes anonymous manuscripts in "Relacion del sitio del Cusco, 1537-1539," in the "Rebelion de Giron, 1553," and in some others of the seventeenth century. Vol. xvi. of the same *Coleccion* is edited by Jiménes de la Espada, and is entitled *Memorias antiguas historiales y políticas del Perú, por D. Fernando Montesinos, seguidas de las Informaciones acerca del señorío de los Incas, hechas por mandado de D. Francisco de Toledo, virey del Perú* [1570-1572]. *Madrid,* 1882. An account of the original which this edition of the work of Montesinos follows is given in the preface. The editor criticises the translation by Henri Ternaux-Compans in his Mémoires historiques sur l'ancien Pérou (forming part of his *Voyages*), Paris, 1840.[2]

Leclerc in 1878 [3] offered for 2,500 francs an unprinted manuscript containing the military Lives of Pedro Alvarez de Holguin and Martin de Almendral (Almendras), consisting of depositions respecting their services by eye-witnesses, taken in pursuance of a claim by their families for the possession of titles and property, their ancestors having been among the conquerors.

The most conspicuous writers upon Peruvian history in English are Prescott, Helps, and Markham,—the first two as the historians of the Conquest, and the third as an annotator of the original sources and an elucidator of controverted points. Prescott's *Conquest of Peru* was published in 1843. He had been fortunate enough to secure copies from the manuscript stores which Muñoz had gathered, and Navarrete allowed his collections to be gleaned for the American's use. He did not fail of the sympathy and support of Ternaux and of Gayangos. The ingenious and active assistance of Obadiah Rich secured him a good share of the manuscripts of the Kingsborough Collection when that was scattered. The *Conquest of Peru* was promptly translated into Spanish, and published at Madrid in 1847-1848; and again in a version supposed to have been made by Icazbalceta. It was printed at Mexico in 1849. A French translation was introduced to the world by Amédée Pichot, and the English on the continent were soon able to read it in their own tongue under a Paris imprint. The Dutch and German people were not long without versions in their vernaculars. Since Mr. Prescott's death the revision, which the American reader was long kept from (owing to the obstructions to textual improvements imposed

[1] Leclerc, no. 2,928.   [2] *Boston Public Library Catalogue.*   [3] *Bibliotheca Americana,* no. 1,687.

VOL. II. — 73.

by the practice of stereotyping), was made by Mr. Kirk, who had been Prescott's secretary; and the new edition, with that gentleman's elucidatory and corrective notes, appeared at Philadelphia in 1874.

As was the case with the hero of Mexico, the chapters in Helps's *Spanish Conquest* on the conqueror of Peru have, since the publication of that book, been extracted and fitted newly together under the title of *The Life of Pizarro, with some account of his Associates in the Conquest of Peru,* published in London in 1869. Pizarro is not, under Helps's brush, the abhorrent figure of some other historians. "He is always calm, polite, dignified," he says. "He was not one of the least admirable of the conquerors."

Mr. Markham, referring to a visit which he made to Prescott, says: "He it was who encouraged me to undertake my Peruvian investigations and to persevere in them. To his kindly advice and assistance I owe more than I can say, and to him is due, in no small degree, the value of anything I have since been able to do in furtherance of Peruvian research." The first fruit of Mr. Markham's study was his *Cusco and Lima* in 1856. Three years later (1859) he was sent by the British Government to superintend the collection of cinchona plants and seeds (quinine) in Peru, and to introduce them into India. In pursuit of this mission, he formed the acquaintance with the country which was made public in his *Travels in Peru and India* in 1862. In 1880 he epitomized his great knowledge in a useful little handbook on *Peru,* which was published in London in the series of *Foreign Countries and British Colonies.* His greatest aid to the historian has come, however, from the annotations given by him to numerous volumes of the Hakluyt Society, which he has edited, and in his communications to the *Journal of the Royal Geographical Society.*

The Peruvian story is but an incidental feature of Hubert H. Bancroft's *Central America,* where Alvarado's report of May 12, 1535, and other documents which fell into that author's hands with the Squier manuscripts afford in part the basis of his narrative, vol. ii. chap. vii. Bancroft accounts Pizarro himself the most detestable man in the Indies after Pedrárias. He collates the authorities on many disputed points, and is a valuable assistant, particularly for the relations of operations on the isthmus to those in Peru,—such as the efforts of Gonzalo Pizarro to make the isthmus the frontier of his Peruvian government, and Gasca's method of breaking through it. In his chapter on "Mines and Mining" in his *Mexico* (vol. iii.) he incidentally recapitulates the story of the wealth which was extracted from Peru.

The dignified and well-balanced story as told in Robertson's *America* (book vi.) is not without use to-day, and his judgment upon authorities (note cxxv.) is usually sound. He has of course fallen behind that sufficiency which Dr. Smyth found in him, when he gave his *Lectures on Modern History* (lecture xxi.). The latter writer reflected an opinion not yet outgrown when he says that " Pizarro was, after all, a vulgar conqueror, and is from the first detested, though he seizes upon our respect, and retains it in defiance of ourselves, from the powerful and decisive nature of his courage and of his understanding."

The latest English summarized view of the Conquest will be found in R. G. Watson's *Spanish and Portuguese South America during the Colonial Period* (London, 1884). The author lived in South America about twenty years ago, in various parts, as a diplomatic agent of the English government.

THE

AMAZON AND ELDORADO.

BY THE EDITOR.

IN 1528, in order to follow up the explorations of Ojeda and others on the coast of Venezuela the Emperor had agreed with the great German mercantile house of the Velsers to protect a colony to be sent by them to found cities and to mine on this northern coast.[1] This was the origin of the expedition led by Ambrosio de Alfinger to find a fabulous golden city, of which reports of one kind and another pervaded the Spanish settlements along the coast. It was in 1530 that Alfinger started inland. This march produced the usual story of perfidy and cruelty practised upon the natives, and of attack and misery experienced by the invaders. Alfinger died on the way, and after two years (in 1532) what was left of his followers found their way back to the coast.

Meanwhile an expedition inland had started under Diego Ordaz in 1531, by way of the Orinoco ; but it had failed, its leader being made the victim of a mutiny. One of his officers, Martinez, being expelled from the force for misbehavior, wandered away until he fell into the hands of people who blindfolded him and led him a great way to a city, where the bandage was removed from his eyes. Here they led him for a day and night through its streets till they came to the palace of Inga their Emperor, with whom being handsomely entertained he stayed eight months, when, being allowed to return, he came down the Orinoco to Trinidad, and thence to Porto Rico, where, when dying, he told this tale of Manoa, as he called the city. He was the first, the story goes, to apply the name of Eldorado to the alluring kingdom in the depths of the continent. This is the pretended story as Raleigh sixty years later learned from a manuscript which Berreo the Governor of Trinidad showed to him.[2]

Again, the Germans made another attempt to penetrate the country and its mystery. George of Spires, under the imperial sanction, coming from Spain with four hundred men, started inland from Coro in 1534. He succeeded in penetrating about fifteen hundred miles, and returned with the survivors in 1538.

A lieutenant had played him false. Nicolaus Federmann[3] had been disappointed in not getting the command of the expedition, but being made second, was instructed to follow after his chief with supplies. Federmann avoided making a junction with George, and wandered at the head of about two hundred men, who were faithful to him, seeking glory on his own account, till after three years of labor he emerged in April, 1539, from the mountain passes upon the plains of Bogotá. Two years before this (in 1537) Gonzalo

[1] Cf. Karl Klüpfel, in the *Bibliothek des literarischen Vereins in Stuttgart*, no. xlvii. (1859); Karl Klunzinger, *Antheil der Deutschen an der Entdeckung von Südamerika*, Stuttgart, 1857 ; and K. von Klöoen's "Die Welser in Augsburg als besitzer von Venezuela," in the *Berliner Zeitschrift für allgemeine Erdkunde*, v. 441.

[2] Cf. Schomburgk's *Raleigh's Discovery of Guiana*, p. 17. Raleigh's enumeration of the various searches for Eldorado in this book are annotated by Schomburgk.

[3] An account of an earlier expedition by Federmann in this region, *Indianische Historia*, recounting experiences in 1529-1531, was printed

Ximenes Quesada, following up the Magdalena River, had arrived on the same plateau, and completed the conquest of New Granada. The year following (1538), Sebastian de Belalcazar, marching north from Quito, had reached the same point.[1]

Thus the three explorers from three directions came together. They joined forces and descended the Magdalena to Santa Martha, where Pedro Fernandez de Lugo, the associate of Quesada, died, while Quesada himself proceeded to Spain to obtain the government of the newly discovered region. Meanwhile Hernan Perez, a brother of Quesada, being left

El Licenciado Gonzalo Ximenes de Quesada descubrio el nuevo Reijna de Granada

QUESADA.[2]

in 1557 at Hagenaw. Ternaux, in the first volume of his *Voyages*, etc. (Paris, 1837), gave a translation of it, with an introduction. His route, as marked by Klunzinger in the book already cited, is not agreed to by Dr. Moritz Weinhold, in *Uber Nicolaus Federmann's Reise in Venezuela,* 1529–1531, printed in the *Dritter Jahresbericht des Vereins für Erdkunde zu Dresden,* 1866, *Anhang,* p. 93; also in 1868.

[1] Cf. Markham's *Travels of Cieza de Leon,* p. 110; and his *Narrative of Andagoya,* p. xxv.

[2] Fac-simile of engraving in Herrera, iii. 213.

in command in Bogotá, committed the usual cruel excesses upon the Chibchas, but finally left them, to follow another adventurer who had arrived in the track of Federmann, with the same stories of the golden city. So the recreant Governor joined the new-comer Montalvo de Lugo, and together they marched eastward on their golden quest. He returned to Bogotá in a year's time, wiser but not happier.

Meanwhile a new expedition was forming on the Venezuela side. Among the followers of George of Spires had been one Philip von Huten,[1] who after George's death, and when Rodrigo Bastidas had succeeded him, was made the commander of an expedition which left Coro in 1541 by vessels, and, prepared for an inland march, landed at Barburata. The next spring he got on the track of Quesada and resolved to follow it; but the expedition only journeyed in a circle, and after suffering all sorts of hardships found itself at the point of setting out. Huten, undaunted, again started with a smaller force. He encountered and made friends of the Uaupe Indians, and under their guidance proceeded against the towns of the Omaguas, where they encountered resistance; and Huten being wounded, the invaders retreated, and brought to an end another search for Eldorado. The expedition had added a new synonym, Omaguas, for the attractive lure.

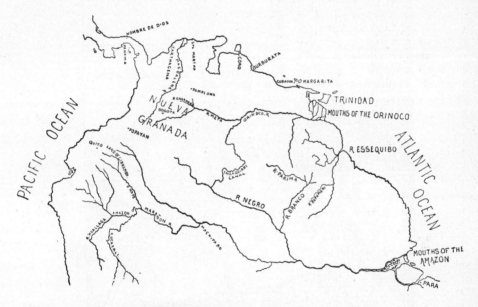

SKETCH MAP, AMAZON AND ELDORADO.

Huten, on his return to Coro, found that Carbajal had seized the government. This brutal soldier now executed Huten, and held his iniquitous sway until the licentiate Juan Perez de Tolosa arrived with the imperial authority in 1546, when Carbajal was in turn put to death. Thus ended the German efforts at South American discovery on this side of the continent.

Meanwhile Gonzalo Ximenes Quesada's visit to Spain had failed in making him the Governor of New Granada, as he had hoped. Luis Alonzo de Lugo, the son of Quesada's associate, was the successful applicant for the position. The new Governor arrived in 1542, but a *residencia* interrupted his career, and Pedro de Ursua, a nephew of Armendariz, the judge who had taken the *residencia*, was sent to Bogotá to take charge. Thence his patron sent him on the old quest for the rivers flowing over golden sands. He failed to find Eldorado; but he founded the city of Pampluna in the wilds, and ruled its stately

[1] He is sometimes called Uten, Utre, Urra, etc.

lots for two years. Then Armendariz had his downfall in turn, and Pedro de Ursua in 1549 found favor enough with those who then administered the government to get command of another expedition to Eldorado, during which he founded another city, which he had to abandon in 1552 because the natives attacked it so persistently. Next, Pedro was put in command of Santa Martha, and began to fight the Indians thereabout; but seeking a larger field, he started for Peru. His fame was sufficient to induce the authorities at Panamá to engage him to quell the Cimarrones, who infested the Isthmus. In two years Ursua accomplished this task, and then went on to Peru, where at Lima, in 1559, the new viceroy Cañete appointed him to lead a well-equipped expedition to Eldorado and the Omaguas. If the fabled city should not be reached, the quest for it would draw away from Cañete's province the prowling ruffians whom the cessation of the civil wars had left among the settlements. But it was thought the quest was more likely to be successful than any previous one had been, since Viraratu, a coast chieftain of Brazil, had with two Portuguese recently ascended the Amazon, and had confirmed to Cañete the old stories of a hidden lake and its golden city.

Pedro de Ursua started in boats down the Huallaga to the Marañon, and so on to the neighborhood of Machiparo. At this point, on New Year's day, 1561, conspirators murdered Ursua, threw off allegiance to Spain, and made Fernando de Guzman their sovereign. One Lope de Aguirre was the leader of the insurrection, and it was not long before Guzman paid the penalty of his life in turn, and Aguirre became supreme. The conspirators went on to the mouth of the Negro, but from this point authorities differ as to their course. Humboldt and Southey supposed they still kept to the Amazon until they reached the sea. Acuña, Simon, Acosta, and among the moderns Markham, suppose they ascended the Negro, crossed by the Cassiquiari canal to the Orinoco, and so passed on to the ocean; or if not by this route, by some of the rivers of Guiana. Mr. Markham[1] balances the testimony. Once on the ocean, at whatever point, Aguirre steered his vessels for the north and west till they came to the island of Margarita, then colonized by the Spanish. Having seized this settlement, Aguirre led his followers across the intervening waters to Venezuela, with the aim of invading and conquering New Granada; but in due time a Spanish force led by Gutierrez de la Peña confronted the traitor and his host, and overthrew them. Many of Aguirre's men had deserted him; when killing his own daughter, that she might not survive to be stigmatized as a traitor's child, he was set upon and despatched by his conquerors.

The earliest account of the expedition of Ursua and Aguirre is a manuscript in the Royal library at Madrid written by one of the company, Francisco Vasquez, who remained with Aguirre under protest till he reached Margarita. Vasquez's story was a main dependence of Pedro Simon, in the sixth of the *Primera parte de las Noticias historiales de las Conquistas de Tierra Firme en las Indias Occidentales*, published at Cuenca in 1627. Simon, who was born in Spain in 1574, had come to Bogotá in 1604, in time to glean much from men still living. After many years of gathering notes, he began to write his book in 1623. Only one part, which included the affairs of Venezuela and the expedition of Ursua and Aguirre, was printed. Two other parts are in existence; and Colonel J. Acosta, in his *Compendio histórico del descubrimiento y colonizacion de la Nueva Granada en el siglo décimo sexto*, published at Paris in 1848, made use of them, and says they are the most valuable recital of the sixteenth century in existence which relates to these regions.[2] The account of Simon, so far as it relates to the expedition of Ursua, has been translated by William Bollaert, and properly annotated by Mr. Markham; it constitutes the volume published by the Hakluyt Society in 1861, called *The Expedition of Pedro de Ursua and Lope de Aguirre in search of Eldorado and Omagua in 1560–1561*. It has a map which marks the alternative courses of Aguirre.[3]

---

[1] Introduction of his *Search for Eldorado*.

[2] Manuscript copies of these parts are in the Lenox Library.

[3] Cf. Markham's introduction to this volume; H. H. Bancroft's *Central America*, ii. 61. *The Expedition of Orsua and the Crime of Aguirre*, by

CASTELLANOS.[1]

The main dependence of Simon, besides the manuscript of Vasquez, was a metrical chronicle by Juan de Castellanos, *Elegias de Varones ilustres de Indias*, the first part of

Robert Southey, was published at London in 1821. This was written for Southey's *History of Brazil*, but was omitted as beyond its scope, and first published in the *Edinburgh Annual Register*, vol. iii. part 2, and then separately.

[1] A fac-simile of the portrait in his *Elegias*, p. 10.

which, containing, besides the accounts of Ursua and Aguirre, the exploits of Columbus, Ponce de Leon, Garay, and others, was printed at Madrid in 1589.[1] De Bry makes use of this versified narrative in the eighth part of his *Grand Voyages*. Castellanos' first part is reprinted in the *Biblioteca de Autores Españoles*, 1847–1850, where are also to be found the second and third parts, printed there for the first time. The text is there edited by Buenaventura Carlos Aribau. Ercilla has recorded his opinion of the faithfulness of Castellanos, but Colonel Acosta thinks him inexact. These second and third parts recount the adventures of the Germans in their search for Eldorado, and record the conquests of Cartagena by Lugo, of Popayan by Belalcazar, and of Antischia. A fourth part, which gave the conquest of New Granada, though used by Piedrahita, is no longer known.

Castellanos could well have derived his information, as he doubtless did, from men who had made part of the exploits which he celebrates ; and as regards the mad pranks of Aguirre, such is also the case with another contemporary account, preserved in the National Library at Madrid, which was written by Toribio de Ortiguera, who was at Nombre de Dios in 1561, and sent forces against Aguirre when that conspirator was on his Venezuela raid. The story written from the survivors' recitals does not materially differ from that of Vasquez. He gives also a short account of the expedition of Gonzalo Pizarro and Orellana, later to be mentioned.

Lucas Fernandez Piedrahita was a native of Bogotá, and, like Garcilasso de la Vega, had the blood of the Incas in his veins. He became a priest, and was successively Bishop of Santa Martha and of Panamá, and after having lived a life of asceticism, and been at one time a captive of the buccaneers, he died at Panamá in 1688, at the age of seventy. He depended chiefly in his *Historia General de las Conquistas del nuevo Reyno de Granada*,[2] on the *Compendio* of Ximenes de Quesada, no longer known, the *Elegias* of Castellanos, and the *Noticia* of Simon. He borrows liberally from Simon, and says but little of Aguirre till he lands in Venezuela. Aguirre's career in the *Historia de la Conquista y poblacion de Venezuela* of Oviedo y Baños is in like manner condensed from Simon, and is confined also to his final invasion of the main. The book is rare, and Markham says that in 1861 even the British Museum had no copy.[3] The general historians, De la Vega, Herrera, and Acosta, give but scant accounts of the Ursua expedition. Markham[4] points out the purely imaginative additions given to Aguirre's story in Gomberville's translation of Acuña, misleading thereby not a few later writers. Much the same incorrectness characterizes the recitals in the *Viage* of the Ulloas, in Velasco's *Historia de Quito* (1789).

The faithlessness of Orellana and his fifty followers in deserting Gonzalo Pizarro in 1540, while this leader was exploring the forests of the Cinnamon country, is told in another place. Orellana, as has been said, was sent forward in an improvised bark to secure food for Pizarro's famished followers, but was tempted to pursue the phantom of golden discovery. This impulse led him to follow the course of the river to the sea. It gave him the distinction of being the discoverer of the weary course of the great Amazon. In his intercourse with some of the river Indians he heard or professed to hear of a tribe of women warriors whom it was easy, in recognition of the classic story, to name the Amazons. At one of the native villages on the river the deserters built themselves a stancher craft than they had escaped in ; and so they sailed on in a pair of adventurous barks, fighting their way past hostile villages, and repelling attacks of canoes, or bartering with such of the Indians as were more peaceful. In one of the fights, when Orellana landed his men for the

---

[1] Ticknor, *Spanish Literature*, ii. 471. There are copies in the Boston Public, Harvard College, and Lenox libraries.

[2] Printed at Amberes in 1688 ; Cf. Carter-Brown, vol. ii. no. 1,364. There are copies in Harvard College and Lenox libraries. Cf. H. H.

Bancroft, *Central America*, ii. 62. The book is worth £5 to £10. Only the *Parte primera* was printed ; it comes down to 1563.

[3] There are copies in the Lenox and Harvard College libraries.

[4] *Search for Eldorado*, p. xliii.

conflict, it is affirmed that women led the native horde. From a prisoner they got signs which they interpreted to mean that they were now in the region of the female warriors, and not far from all the fabled wealth of which they were in search. But the marks of the tide on the banks lured them on with the hope of nearing the sea. They soon got unmistakable signs of the great water, and then began to prepare their frail crafts for encountering its perils. They made sails of their cloaks. On the 26th of August they passed into the Atlantic. They had left the spot where the river Napo flows into the Amazon on the last day of December, 1541; and now, after a voyage of nearly eight months, they spread their sails and followed the coast northward. The vessels parted company one night, but they reached the island of Cubagua within two days of each other. Here they found a Spanish colony, and Orellana was not long in finding a passage to Spain. The story he had to tell was a thrilling one for ears eager for adventure, and a joyous one for such as listened for the tales of wealth. Orellana might be trusted to entrap both sorts of listeners.

The King was the best of listeners. He gave Orellana a commission to conquer these fabulous countries, and in May, 1544, Orellana sailed with four ships and four hundred men. Misfortune followed him speedily, and only two of his vessels reached the river. Up they went for a hundred leagues or so; but it was quite different making headway against the current from floating down it, as he had done before. His men died; his vessels were stranded or broken up; he himself became ill, and at last died. This ended the attempt; and such of his followers as could, made their way back to Spain; and New Andalusia, as the country was to be named, remained without a master.

Of the expedition of Gonzalo Pizarro there is no account by any one engaged in it; but we have the traditions of the story told by Garcilasso de la Vega in the second part, book third, of the *Royal Commentaries*, and this account is put into English and annotated by Mr. Markham in the *Expeditions into the Valley of the Amazons*, published by the Hakluyt Society in 1859, — and to this book its editor contributes a summary of the later explorations of the valley. Orellana's desertion and his experiences are told by Herrera in his *Historia General;* and this, which Markham calls the best account possessed by us, is also translated by him in the same publication. Wallace, in his *Amazon and Rio Negro*, has of late years suggested that the woman-like apparel of the men, still to be found among the tribes of the upper Amazon, gave rise to the belief in the story of the female warriors.[1]

The form which the story of Eldorado oftener took, and which it preserved for many years, gave representation of a large inland sea, called finally Parima, and of a golden city upon it called Manoa, the reminiscences of Martinez's tale. Somehow, as Mr. Markham thinks, these details were evolved in part out of a custom prevalent on the plains of Bogotá, where a native chief is said to have gilded himself yearly, and performed some rites in a large lake. All this array of wealth was clustered, in the imagination of the conquerors of northern Peru, about the fabled empire of the Omaguas; and farther south the beckoning names were Paytiti and Enim. Whatever the names or details, the inevitable greed for gold in the mind of the Spanish invaders was quite sufficient to evolve the phantom from every impenetrable region of the New World. In 1566 Martin de Proveda followed in the track of Ursua; but sweeping north, his men dropped by the way, and a remnant only reached Bogotá. He brought back the same rumors of rich but receding provinces.

In 1568 the Spanish Government mapped out all this unknown region between two would-be governors. Pedro Malaver de Silva was to have the western part, and Diego

<hr>

[1] Schomburgk, in his *Raleigh's Discovery of Guiana* (p. lvi), enumerates the various references to the Amazon story among the early writers on South America. Cf. Van Heuvel, p. 123, Note. Eldorado, chaps. vii. and viii. Acuña's account in 1641 is translated in Markham's *Expeditions into the Valley of the Amazons*, sect. 71; and also

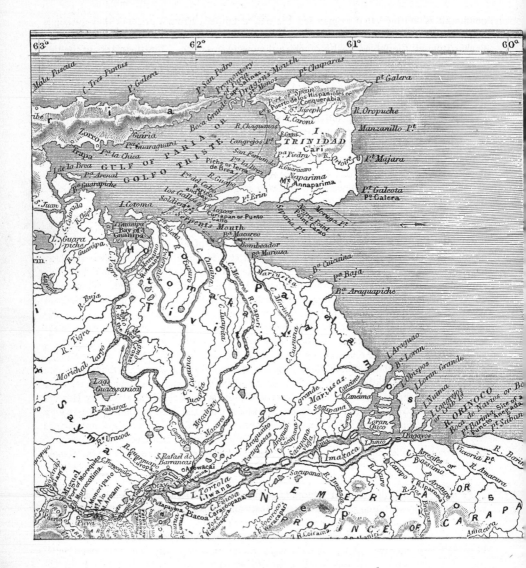

THE MOUTHS OF THE ORINOCO.[1]

Fernando de Cerpa to have the eastern as far as the mouths of the Orinoco. Both of the expeditions which these ambitious heroes led came to nothing beyond their due share of trials and aimless wandering; and one of the leaders, Silva, made a second attempt in 1574, equally abortive, as the one survivor's story proved it to be.

Markham says that the last expedition to achieve any important geographical discovery was that of Antonio de Berreo in 1582. He had received by right the adventurous impulse, through his marriage with the daughter or heiress of Gonzalo Ximenes de Quesada. He followed down the Cassanare and the Meta, and pursued the Orinoco to its mouth. The English took up the quest when Raleigh sent Jacob Whiddon in 1594 to

1 This is a portion of the map given by   ery of Guiana, published by the Hakluyt Society
Schomburgk in his edition of Raleigh's Discov-   in 1848.

explore the Orinoco. Berreo, who was now the Spanish governor of Trinidad, threw what obstacles in the way he could ; and when Raleigh arrived with his fleet in 1595, the English leader captured the troublesome Spaniard, and was confirmed in his belief, by what Berreo told him, that he could reach the goal. This lure was the lying account of Juan Martinez, already mentioned. The fortunes of Raleigh have been told elsewhere,[1] and the expeditions which he conducted or planned, says Markham, may be said to close the long roll of searches after the fabulous Eldorado.

Nearly the whole of the northern parts of South America had now been thridded by numerous adventuring parties, but without success in this fascinating search. There still remained an unknown region in Central Guiana, where were plains periodically inundated by the overflow of the Rupununi, Essequibo, and Branco (Parima) rivers. Here must Eldorado be ; and here the maps, shortly after this, placed the mysterious lake and its auriferous towers of Manoa down to a comparatively recent time. According to Humboldt [2] and Schomburgk,[3] it was after the return of Raleigh's and Keymis's expedition that Hondius was the first in his *Nieuwe Caerte van het goudreyke landt Guiana* (1599),[4] to introduce the Laguna Parima with its city Manoa in a map. He placed it between 1° 45′ and 2° north latitude, and made it larger than the Caspian Sea.

We find the lake also in the *Nieuwe Wereldt* of De Laet in 1630, and in the editions of that year in other languages. Another Dutch geographer, Jannson, also represented it. Sanson, the French geographer, puts it one degree north of the equator in his *Terre Ferme* in 1656, and is particular enough to place Manoa at the northwest corner of a squarish inland sea ; but he omits it in his chart of the Amazons in 1680. We find the lake again in Heylin's *Cosmographie* of 1663, and later editions; in Blaeu's *Atlas* in 1685. Delisle omits the lake in 1703, but gives a legend in French, as Homann does in his map in Latin, " In hac regione aliqui ponunt lacum Parima urbemque Manoa del Dorado." In another of Delisle's maps a small lake appears with the legend : " Guiane proprement dite ou Dorado, dans laquelle quelques-uns mettent le lac Parime." We have it again in the map in Herrera, edition of 1728; and in 1729. Moll, the English geographer, likewise shows it. In the middle of the century (1760) the maps of Danville preserve the lake, though he had omitted it in an earlier edition; and the English edition, improved by Bolton in 1755, still continues it, as does an Italian edition (Venice) in 1779. The original Spanish of Gumilla's *El Orinoco* (2d edition, Madrid, 1745) has a map which gives the lake, and it is repeated in the French edition at Avignon in 1758, and in a later Spanish one at Barcelona in 1781. Kitchen's map, which was prepared for Robertson's *History of America*, again shows it ; and it is in the centre of a great water system in the large map of La Cruz, made by order of the King of Spain in 1775, which was re-engraved in London the same year. It is also represented in the maps in the *Historia de la nueva Andalucia*, of Antonio Caulin,[5] Madrid, 1779, and in the *Saggio di Storia Americana*, Rome, 1780. Conrad Mannert's map, published at Nuremberg in 1803, gives it ; as do the various editions of François Depons' *Voyage dans l'Amerique méridionale*, Paris, 1806. The lake here is given under thirty degrees north latitude, and Manoa is put at the northeast corner of it. The same plate was used for the English version "by an American gentleman," published in New York in 1806 ; while the translation published in London in 1807,

---

[1] Vol. III. p. 117, etc. One of the latest accounts is contained in P. G. L. Borde's *Histoire de l'ile de la Trinidad sous le gouvernement espagnol*, 1498, etc. (Paris, 1876–1883, vol. i.). Abraham Kendall, who had been on the coast with Robert Dudley, and is the maker of one of the portolanos in Dudley's *Arcano del mare*, was with Raleigh and of use to him. Kohl (Collection, no. 374) gives us from the British Museum a map which he supposes to be Raleigh's.

[2] *Personal Narrative*, chap. 17.

[3] *Raleigh's Discovery of Guiana*, published by Hakluyt Society (1848), p. li.

[4] Schomburgk says that Levinus Hulsius availed himself of this map in constructing his *Americæ pars Australis*, which accompanies the *Vera Historia* of Schmiedel, published at Nuremberg in 1599. Cf. Uricoechea, *Mapoteca Colombiana*, p. 90, no. 5.

[5] He was in the boundary expedition of Solano. Humboldt calls this map the combination of two traced by Caulin in 1756.

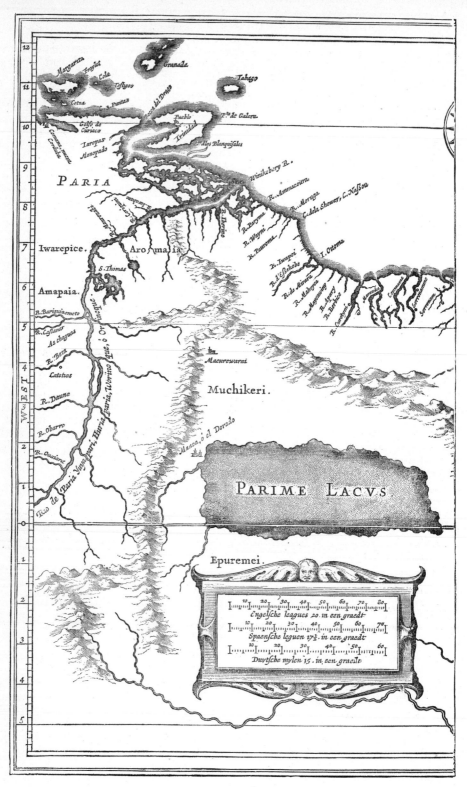

DE LAET, 1630.

apparently the same with a few verbal changes, has a like configuration on a map of reduced scale. One of the latest preservations of the myth is the large map published in London by Faden in 1807, purporting to be based on the studies of D'Arcy de la Rochette, where the inland sea is explained by a legend: " Golden Lake, or Lake Parime, called likewise Parana Pitinga, — that is, White Sea, — on the banks of which the discoverers of the sixteenth century did place the imaginary city of Manoa del Dorado." I have seen it in German maps as late as 1814, and the English geographer, Arrowsmith, kept it in his maps in his day.[1]

It was left for Humboldt to set the seal of disbelief firmly upon the story.[2] Schomburgk says that the inundations of extensive savannas during the tropical winter gave rise, no doubt, to the fable of the White Sea, assisted by an ignorance of the Indian language. Nevertheless, as late as 1844, Jacob A. van Heuvel, in his *Eldorado, being a Narrative of the Circumstances which gave rise to Reports in the Sixteenth Century of the Existence of a Rich and Splendid City in South America*, published in New York, clung to the idea; and he represents the lake somewhat doubtingly as in 4° north, and between 60° and 63° west, in the map accompanying his book.

Later in the seventeenth century the marvellous story took on another guise. It was remembered that after the conquest of Peru a great emigration of Inca Indians had taken place easterly beyond the mountains, and in the distant forests it was reputed they had established a new empire ; and the names of Paytiti and Enim, already mentioned, were attached to these new theatres of Inca magnificence. Stories of this fabulous kingdom continued to be hatched well on into the eighteenth century, and not a few expeditions of more or less imposing strength were sent to find this kingdom. It never has been found; but, as Mr. Markham thinks, there is some reason to believe that the Inca Indians who fled with Tapac Amaru into the forests may for a considerable period have kept up their civilization somewhere in those vast plains east of the Andes. The same writer says that the belief was not without supporters when he was in Peru in 1853; and he adds that it is a pleasant reflection that this story may possibly be true.[3]

The most considerable attempt of the seventeenth century to make better known the course of the Amazon was the expedition under Texeira, sent in 1639 to see if a practicable way could be found to transport the treasure from Peru by the Amazon to the Atlantic coast. Acuña's book on this expedition, *Nuevo descubrimiento del gran Rio de las Amazons*,[4] published at Madrid in 1641, is translated in Markham's *Valley of the Amazons*, published by the Hakluyt Society. It was not till 1707, when Samuel Fritz, a Bohemian and a missionary, published his map of the Amazons at Quito, that we find something better than the vaguest delineation of the course of the great river.[5]

It is not the purpose of the present essay to continue the story of the explorations of the Amazon into more recent times ; but a word may be spared for the strange and sorrowful adventures along its stream, which came in the train of the expedition that was sent

[1] This enumeration has by no means mentioned all the instances of similar acceptance of the delusion.

[2] Cf. his *Cosmos*, Eng. tr., p. 159 ; *Views of Nature*, p. 188. He asks : " Can the little reed-covered lake of Amuca have given rise to this myth? . . . It was besides an ancient custom of dogmatizing geographers to make all considerable rivers originate in lakes." Cf. also Humboldt's *Personal Narrative* and Southey's *History of Brazil*.

[3] Markham's *Valley of the Amazons*, p. xlv.

[4] This book is rare. It was priced by Rich in 1832 (no. 234) at £8 8s. The unsatisfactory French translation by De Gomberville was printed at Paris in 1682. Dufossé recently priced this edition at 150 francs. The original Spanish is said to have been suppressed by Philip IV. but such stories are attached too easily to books become rare. There was a copy in the Cooke sale (1884, no. 10). The *Carter-Brown Catalogue* (vol. ii. no. 484) shows a copy.

[5] It can be found in Stocklein's *Reise Beschreibungen*, a collection of Jesuit letters from all parts of the World. Markham's *Valley of the Amazons*, p. xxxiii.

out by the French Government in 1735 to measure an arc of the meridian in Peru, for comparing the result with a similar measurement in Lapland. The object was to prove or to disprove the theory of Sir Isaac Newton that the earth was flattened at the poles. The commissioners — Bouguer, La Condamine, and Godin (the last accompanied by his wife) — arrived at Quito in June, 1736. The arc was measured; but the task did not permit them to think of returning before 1743, when La Condamine resolved to return by descending the Amazon and then making his way to the French colony of Cayenne. He and his companion, a Spanish gentleman seeking some adventure, had their full content of it, but safely accomplished the journey.

Another of the commissioners, Godin, having tarried a few years longer in Peru, had finally proceeded to Cayenne, where he made arrangements for embarking for France. Through the favor of the Portuguese Government he had been provided with a galiot of sixteen to twenty oars on a side, to ascend the river and meet his wife, who on receiving a message from him was to leave Peru with an escort and come down the river and meet him. Illness finally prevented the husband from proceeding; but he despatched the vessel, having on board one Tristan, who was charged with a letter to send ahead. By some faithlessness in Tristan, the letter miscarried; but Madame Godin sent a trusty messenger in anticipation, who found the galiot at Loreto awaiting her arrival, and returned with the tidings. The lady now started with her father and two brothers; and they allowed a certain Frenchman who called himself a physician to accompany them, while her negro servant, who had just returned over the route, attended them, as well as three Indian women and thirty Indian men to carry burdens. They encountered the small-pox among the river Indians, when their native porters deserted them. They found two other natives, who assisted them in building a boat; but after two days upon it these Indians also deserted them. They found another native, but he was shortly drowned. Then their boat began to leak and was abandoned. On pretext of sending assistance back, the French physician, taking with him the negro, pushed on to a settlement; but he forgot his promise, and the faithful black was so impeded in attempting alone the task of rescue, that he arrived at the camp only to find unrecognizable corpses. All but the lady had succumbed. She pushed on alone through the wilderness, encountering perils that appall as we read; but in the end, falling in with two Indians, she passed on from one mission station to another, and reached the galiot.

Thus a hundred years later than Orellana, the great river still flowed with a story of fearful hazards and treachery.

CHAPTER IX.

MAGELLAN'S DISCOVERY.

BY REV. EDWARD E. HALE, D.D.

FERNANDO DA MAGALHAENS, or Magalhâes, whom the French and English call Magellan, was a Portuguese gentleman of good family. He was educated, as well as his time knew how to educate men, for the business which he followed through his life, — that of a navigator and a discoverer. He was a child when Columbus first came home successful from the West Indies; and as a boy and young man he grew up, in the Court of King John the Second of Portugal, among people all alive to the exciting novelties of new adventure. As early as 1505 he went to the East Indies, where he served the Portuguese Government several years. He was in the expedition which first discovered the Spice Islands of Banda, Amboyna, Ternate, and Tidor. Well acquainted with the geography of the East as far as the Portuguese adventurers had gone, he returned to Portugal.

King Emmanuel was then upon the throne. Spain owes it to an unjust slight which Magellan received at the Portuguese Court, that, under her banner, this greatest of seamen sailed round the world and solved the problem of ages in reaching the east by way of the west. Magellan was in the service of the King in Morocco in a war which the Portuguese had on hand there. He received a slight wound in his knee, which made him lame for the rest of his life. Returning to Portugal, on some occasion when he was pressing a claim for an allowance customary to men of his rank, he was refused, and charged with pretending to an injury which was really cured. Enraged at this insult, he abandoned his country. He did this in the lordly style which seems in keeping with a Portuguese grandee of his time. He published a formal act of renunciation of Portugal. He went to Spain and took letters of naturalization there. In the most formal way he announced that he was a subject of the King of Spain, and should give service and life to that monarch, if he would use them.

Magellan had a companion in his exile; this was Ruy Faleiro, a gentleman of Lisbon, who had also fallen into disgrace at Court. Faleiro,[1] like

---

[1] On Faleiro's contributions to the art of navigation, see Humboldt's *Cosmos*, Eng. tr., ii. 672.

Magellan, was a thorough geographer; and the two had persuaded themselves that the shortest route to the Spice Islands of the East was to be found in crossing the Western Ocean. We know now, that in this conviction they were wrong. Any ordinary map of the eastern hemisphere includes the Spice Islands or Moluccas, as well as Portugal, because the distance in longitude east from Lisbon is less than that of the longitude measured west. It has been proved, also, that the continent of America extends farther south than that of Africa. This, Magellan and Faleiro did not know; but they were willing to take the risk of it. Spain has always held the Philippines, — the prize which she won as the reward of Magellan's

AUTOGRAPH OF MAGELLAN.

great discovery, — under the treaty of 1494, which gave to her half the world beyond the meridian of three hundred and seventy leagues west from Ferro. She has held it because Magellan sailed west, and so struck the Philippines; but, in fact, those islands lie within the half of the world which the same treaty gave to Portugal.

By mistake or by design, the Philippines, when they were discovered, were moved on the maps twenty-five degrees east of their true position on the globe. The Spaniards made the maps. The islands were thus brought within their half of the world; and this immense error was not corrected till the voyages of Dampier.[1]

Charles V. was no fool. He recognized at once the value of such men as Magellan and Faleiro. He heard and accepted their plan for a western voyage to the spice regions. On the 22d of March, 1518, he bound himself to fit out an expedition at his own cost on their plans, under Magellan's orders, on condition that the principal part of the profits should belong to the Throne. Through years of intrigue, public and private, in which the Spanish jealousy of Sevillian merchants and others tried to break up the expedition, Charles was, for once, faithful to a promise. We must not attempt here to follow the sad history of such intrigues. On the 10th of August, 1519, the expedition sailed under Magellan. Poor Faleiro, alas! had gone crazy in the mean time. What proved even a greater misfortune was that Juan of Carthagena was put on board the "San Antonio" as a sort of Japanese spy on Magellan. He was the marplot of the expedition, as the history will show. He was called a *veedor*, or inspector.

---

[1] [It will be remembered that the original Bull of 1493 fixed the meridian 100 leagues (say 400 miles) west of the Azores or Cape De Verde Islands, supposing them to lie north and south of each other; whereas the limit in force after June 7, 1494, was 370 leagues (say 1,080 miles) west of the Azores, since Portugal, complaining of the first limit, had negotiated with Spain for a new limit, the Pope assenting; and this final limit was confirmed by a convention at Tordesillas at the date above given. Cf. Popellinière, *Les trois mondes*, Paris, 1582; Baronius, *Annales* (ed. by Brovius, Rome), vol. xix.; Solorzano, *Politica Indiana*. — ED.]

MAGELLAN.[1]

There is something pathetic in contrasting the magnificent fleet with which Magellan sailed, under the patronage of an emperor, with the poor little expedition of Columbus. With the new wealth of the Indies at command, and with the resources now of a generation of successful discovery, the Emperor directed the dockyards of Seville to meet all Magellan's wishes in the most thorough way. No man in the world, perhaps, knew better than Magellan what he needed. The expedition, therefore, sailed with as perfect a material equipment as the time knew how to furnish. It consisted of five ships, — the "Trinidad" and "San Antonio," each of

[1] [Fac-simile of an engraving in Navarrete's *Coleccion*, vol. iv. It is also reproduced in Stanley's *First Voyage round the World by Magellan* (Hakluyt Society, 1874); in Cladera's *Investigaciones históricas;* in the *Relacion del ultimo viage al estrecho de Magellanes de la fragata de S. M. Santa Maria de la Cabeza en los anos de 1785 y 1786* (Madrid, 1788); in the *Allgemeine geographische Ephemeriden* (November, 1804), p. 269; in August Bürck's *Magellan oder die erste Reise um die erde,* Leipsic, 1844; in Rüge's *Ge-* schichte des Zeitalters der Entdeckungen, p. 402; and in the *Carter-Brown Catalogue,* i. 81.

There are two portraits in De Bry, — one a full length in the corner of a map of America which accompanies the narrative of Benzoni in part vi., and of Herrera in part xii. ; and the other on a map of the two hemispheres in part xi.; also repeated in Schouten's *Journal* (1618). There are similar pictures in Hulsius, parts vi. and xvi. Cf. the *Catalogue* (no. 135) of the Gallery of the New York Historical Society. — ED.]

HERNANDO DE MAGALLANES.
Cavallero Portugues. descubridar del Estrecho de su nombre.

MAGELLAN.[1]

120 Spanish *toneles*, the " Concepcion," of 90, the " Victoria," of 85, — long famous as the one vessel which made the whole voyage, — and the " Santiago," of 75. For the convenience of the translators this Spanish word *toneles* is generally rendered by the French word *tonneaux* and the English word *tons*. But in point of fact the *tonele* of Seville was one fifth larger than the *tonelada* of the north of Spain, which nearly corresponds to our ton; and the vessels of Magellan and Columbus were, in fact, so much larger than the size which is generally assigned to them in the popular histories.[2]

[1] Fac-simile of the engraving in Herrera, i. 293.   [2] [See note, Vol. II., p. 7. — ED.]

MAGELLAN.[1]

[1] Fac-simile of the engraving in Ogilby's *America* (p. 79), — the same used in Montanus's *Nieuwe Wereldt*.

On the 20th of September the fleet had cleared the River Guadalquivir, and was fairly at sea. Six days afterward it touched at Teneriffe for supplies; and here was the first quarrel between Magellan and his watchman, Juan de Carthagena. Up to this point entire secrecy had been maintained by Magellan as to the route to be pursued. Juan de Carthagena claimed the right to be informed of all things regarding it. Magellan refused, probably with considerable scorn. When off Sierra Leone, a few days after, a similar quarrel broke out; Magellan arrested Carthagena with his own hand, and put him in the stocks. Of course this was an insult the most keen, and was meant to be. The other captains begged Magellan to release the prisoner, and he did so; but still he kept him under the arrest of one of their number.

From Sierra Leone they ran across to Brazil and anchored again for supplies in the magnificent Bay of Rio de Janeiro. By their narrative, indeed, on the return of the first vessel, was this great estuary made widely known to the world. It is now known that Magellan was not the first discoverer. Pero Lopez had explored the bay five years before; and as early as 1511 a trader named John of Braga, probably a Portuguese, was established on one of its fertile islands. Indeed, it is said that the hardy seamen of Dieppe had been there as early as the beginning of the century. Its first name was the Bay of Cabo-Frio.

The meridian of Alexander's Bull had been meant to leave all the American discoveries in the possession of the King of Spain. But, unfortunately for him, Brazil runs so far out to the east that a meridian three hundred and seventy leagues west of the Azores gives Portugal a considerable part of it; and in point of fact the western boundary of Brazil has been accommodated quite nearly to the imaginary line of the Pope. To Magellan and his company it made no difference whether they were on Portuguese or Spanish soil. They found the Brazilians friendly. "Though they are not Christians, they are not idolaters, for they adore nothing. Natural instinct is their only law."

This is the phrase of Pigafetta, the young Italian gentleman to whose *naïve* book we owe our best and fullest account of the great voyage. It is clear enough that all the crews enjoyed their stay in the Bay of Santa Lucia, by which name they called our Bay of Rio de Janeiro. It was in the heart of the Brazilian summer, for they arrived on the 13th of December. They had been nearly three months at sea, and were well disposed to enjoy tropical luxuries; and here they stayed thirteen days. Pigafetta describes the Brazilian hammocks;[1] and from his description Europe has taken that word. The same may perhaps be said of the mysterious word "canoe," which appears in his narrative under the spelling "canots."[2]

---

[1] But the word *hamac* is Haytian, not Brazilian. The hammock itself had been noticed by Columbus. Peter Martyr describes it, and Oviedo figures it in narrating the second voyage. [Cf. Schomburgk's *Raleigh's Discovery of Guiana*, pp. 40, 65. — ED.]

[2] [See p. 17 of Vol. II., for a contemporary drawing of a canoe. — ED.]

It was Pigafetta's first taste of the luxuries of the South American fields and forests, and he delighted in their cheapness and variety. "For a king of clubs I bought six chickens," he writes; "and yet the Brazilian thought he had made the best bargain," — as, indeed, in the condition of the fine arts at Santa Lucia, he had. A knife or a hook, however, bought no more; yet the natives had no tools of metal. Their large canoes, which would carry thirty or forty people, were painfully dug out by knives of stone from the great trees of which they were made. The Spaniards ate the pineapple for the first time. Pigafetta does not seem to have known the sugar-cane before; and he describes the sweet potato as a novelty.

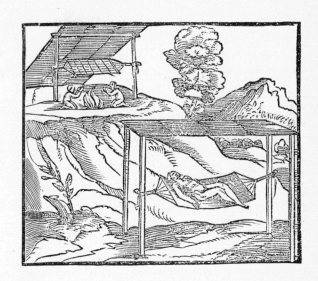

INDIAN BEDS.[1]

"It has almost the form of our turnip, and its taste resembles that of chestnuts." Here, also, he gives the name "patata," which has clung to this root, and has been transferred to the white potato also. For a ribbon, or a hawk's bell, the natives sold a "basketful." Their successors would doubtless do the same now.

The Spaniards found the Brazilians perfectly willing to trade. They went wholly naked, — men and women. Their houses were long cabins.[2] The people told stories, which the navigators believed, of the very great age of their old men, extending it even to one hundred and forty years. They owned that they were cannibals on occasion; but they seem to have eaten human flesh only as a symbol of triumph over conquered enemies. They painted their bodies, and wore their hair short. Pigafetta says it was woolly; but this must have been a mistake. Although he says they go naked, he describes a sort of vest made of paroquet's feathers. Almost

---

[1] [This is Benzoni's representation of the hammocks which are used by the natives of the northern shores of South America (edition of 1572, p. 56). See also the second volume, p. 11. — ED.]

[2] Which they called *boi*, according to Pigafetta; but this name has not been traced since his time. The Brazilian name of house was *oca*. Of twelve "Brazilian" words given in Pigafetta, five found their way into European languages. But, oddly enough, three of these were not Brazilian, but were "ship-language," and borrowed from the West Indies. These are *cacich* for "king," *hamac* for "bed," *maiz* for "millet;" perhaps *canot* is to be added. But *Setebos*, the name of their god or devil, is Pigafetta's own. Shakspeare was struck by it, and gives it to Caliban's divinity.

PART OF SOUTH AMERICA IN THE PTOLEMY OF 1522.[1]

all the men had the lower lip pierced with three holes, and wore in them little cylinders of stone two inches long. They ate cassava bread, made in round white cakes from the root of the manioc.[2] The voyagers also observed the pecari[3] and those curious ducks "whose beak is like a spoon," described by later travellers.[4]

After a pleasant stay of thirteen days in this bay, Magellan took the squadron to the embouchure of the River La Plata, which had been discovered four years before by Juan Diaz de Solis, who lost his life there. The Spaniards believed the tribe of the Quérandis, before whose terrible *bolas* he had fallen, to be cannibals; and they were

other maps of South America. Cf. Münster's map of 1540. Vespucius, in his letter to Lorenzo de' Medici, was the first to describe the cannibalism of the Brazilians. Cf. Thevet, *Singularitez de la France antarctique*, chap. xl., on their cannibalism. — ED.]

[2] Jatropha manihot.

[1] [A part of the "Tabula Terra Nova" in the *Ptolemy* of 1522, showing the acts of cannibals. Similar representations appeared on various

[3] Sus dorso cistifero (Linnæus).

[4] Anas rostro plano ad verticem dilatato (Linnæus).

probably right in this supposition. Continuing the voyage southward, Magellan's fleet observed the two islands now marked as the "Penguins" and "Lions." The historian of the voyage notes the penguins and "sea-wolves" which were then observed there. Passing these islands, they opened a harbor, since known as Port Desire, where they spent the Southern winter. It is near the latitude of 50° south. Magellan supposed it to be in 49° 18'. Hardly had they arrived in this harbor, in itself sufficiently inhospitable, when the mutiny broke out which had been brewing, probably, since Magellan's first insult to John of Carthagena. The announcement made by Magellan that they were to winter here gave the signal for the revolt. On Palm Sunday, which fell on the 1st of April that year, he invited the captains and pilots to meet on his vessel to attend Mass and to dine with him. Two of the captains, Mesquita and De Coca, accepted the invitation and came with their staffs. Mendoza and Quesada did not come. Juan de Carthagena, it will be remembered, was under arrest, and he, of course, was not invited. The same night Quesada, with De Carthagena and thirty men, crossed from the "Concepçion" to the "San Antonio," and made an effort to take Mesquita prisoner. At first they succeeded; but the ship's master, Eliorraga, defended him and his so bravely that, with succor from Magellan, he retained the command. The purpose of the conspirators seems to have been simply to return to Spain without wintering in so bleak a home. The three rebels sent to Magellan to say that they would recognize him as their commander, but they were sure that the King did not propose such an undertaking as this to which he was committing them. Of course, under the guise of respect, this was to exact submission from him. Magellan bade them come on board the flagship. They refused. Magellan kept the boat which they then sent him, and despatched six men, under Espinosa, to the "Victoria" to summon Mendoza. Mendoza answered with a sneer. Espinosa at once stabbed him in the neck, and a sailor struck him down with a cutlass. Magellan then sent another boat, with fifteen men, who took possession of the "Victoria." In every case the crews seem to have taken his side against their own captains. The next day, the 3d of April, he obtained full possession of the "Santiago" and "Concepçion."

On the 4th of that month he quartered the body of Mendoza and published his sentence as a traitor. On the 7th he beheaded Quesada, whose own servant, Molino, volunteered as executioner. When Drake arrived here, fifty-eight years after, he supposed he found the bones of Mendoza or Quesada under a gibbet which was still standing. Juan de Carthagena and the priest Pedro Sanchez de la Reina were convicted as partners in the mutiny, and sentenced to remain when the ships sailed. This sentence was afterwards executed. Magellan doubtless felt that these examples were sufficient, and he pardoned forty of the crew; but, as the reader will see, the spirit which prompted the mutiny was not yet extinguished.

They had lived here two months without seeing any of the natives, when one day, according to the narrative of Pigafetta, a giant appeared to them when they least expected to see any one. " He was singing and dancing on the sand, and throwing dust upon his head, almost naked. The captain sent one of our sailors on shore, with orders to make the same gestures as tokens of peace. This the man did; he was understood, and the giant permitted himself to be led to a little island where the captain had landed. I was there also, with many others. The giant expressed much astonishment at seeing us. He pointed to heaven, and undoubtedly meant to say that he thought we descended from heaven.

" This man," continues Pigafetta, "was so tall that our heads hardly came up to his belt. He was well formed; his face was broad and colored with red, excepting that his eyes were surrounded with yellow, and he had two heart-shaped spots upon his cheeks. He had but little hair, and this was whitened with a sort of powder. His dress, or rather cloak, was made of furs well sewed, — taken from an animal well known in this region, as we afterwards found. He also wore shoes of the same skin."

It seems desirable to copy this description in detail, because here begins in literature the vexed question as to the existence of giants in Patagonia. Whether there ever were any there is now doubted, though the name " Patagonian " is the synonyme of giant in every European language. While the narrative of Pigafetta is thus distinct in saying that one giant only appeared at first, another authority, with equal definiteness, says that six men appeared; and it afterwards appears that two of these, at least, were larger than the Spaniards.

The comparison of the details of this last narrative in Herrera with that of Pigafetta illustrates curiously the perplexity of all historical inquiry; for we are here distinctly told that there were six who appeared on the shore and seemed willing to come on board. A boat was sent for them, and they embarked on the flagship without fear. Once on deck, the Spaniards offered them a kettle full of biscuit, — which was enough, as they supposed, for twenty men; but, with the appetite of hungry Indians, the six devoured it all immediately. They wore mantles of furs, and carried bows and arrows. The bows were about half a fathom long; the arrows were barbed with sharp stones. All were shod with large shoes, like the giant.

On another day two Indians brought on board a tapir, and it proved that their dresses were made from the fur of this animal. Magellan gave them in exchange two red dresses, with which they were well satisfied. It is not till the next day that Herrera places the visit of the giant. That author says that the Indian expressed a wish to become a Christian, and that the Spaniards gave him the name of John. Seeing the crew throwing some mice overboard, he asked that they might be given to him to eat. For six days he took all the mice the ship could furnish, and was never afterward seen.

More than twenty days later, four Indians of the first party returned to the ships, and Magellan gave orders that two of them should be seized to carry home. The men were so large that the Spaniards could not make them prisoners without treachery. Loading the poor giants with more gifts than they could well carry, they finally asked each to accept an iron chain, fitted with manacles. The two Indians were eager enough to accept the fatal present, and were easily persuaded to have the chains fastened to their legs, that they might the more easily carry them away. They found, alas! as so many other men have found, that what they took for ornament was a cruel snare; but, thus crippled, they were overpowered. Their screams of rage were heard by their companions on shore. It was after this treachery that the natives first attacked the Spaniards. Seeing fires at night, Magellan landed a party for exploration. Seven Spaniards found the tracks of Indians and followed them ineffectually. As they returned, however, nine Indians followed, attacked them, and killed one Castilian. But for their shields, all the Spaniards would have been killed. The Spaniards closed upon them with their knives, and put them to flight, visited their camp, and feasted from the store of meat they found there. The next day Magellan sent a larger party on shore and buried the dead Castilian.

The reader is now in possession of all the statements from which we are to decide the much-disputed question whether, in the time of Magellan, Patagonia was a land of giants. He is to remember that Pigafetta, who was the friend and fellow-voyager of the giant Paul, one of the two captives, does not in other instances go out of his way to invent the marvellous, though he often does repeat marvellous stories which have been related by others. It is to be observed that none of the voyagers pretend to have seen any large number of Patagonians. The largest number seen at one time was nine; and even if these were different from the six who came to the ship, fifteen is the largest number of the native visitors to the squadron. Of these, according to one account, in which three at least of the authorities agree, two are of extraordinary height, so that the heads of the Spaniards reached only to their girdles. It is also said that the feet or shoes of all were large, " but not disproportionate to their stature." For three hundred years, on this testimony, it was perhaps generally believed that the Patagonians were very large men. The statement was positively made that they were nine feet high. But as other voyagers, especially in this century, more and more often brought home accounts in which no such giants appeared, there was an increasing distrust of the original Spanish narrative.

Especially when navigators had to do with the wretched Kemenettes and Karaikes of the Straits, who are a tribe of really insignificant stature, was indignation liberally bestowed on the old traveller's story; and when, in 1837, the original narrative of the Genoese pilot was brought to light by Navarrete, — a simple and unexaggerated story; when it proved that he made no allusion whatever to any persons of remarkable height, — the whole giant story was declared to be an invention of Pigafetta, and the gigantic size of the Patagonians was denounced as a mere traveller's fable. Such criticism probably goes too far.

The simple facts may be taken, and the hasty inference may be disregarded. Every travelling showman will testify to the fact that there occasionally appear men, even under the restrictions of civilization, who are so tall that the Spaniards, not of a large race, would only come to their girdles.[1] If Pigafetta is to be believed, two such men came to Magellan's squadron. Tall men came to Cook's squadron at Honolulu, a hundred years ago, who were quite above the average of his men.

GIANT'S SKELETON AT PORTO DESIRE.[2]

Magellan supposed that these were typical men, that they were specimens of their race. Because he supposed so he captured them and tried to carry them to Spain. Magellan was mistaken. They were not specimens of their race; they were extraordinary exceptions to it. But the ready tribe of geographers, eager to accept marvels from the New World, at once formed the conclusion that because these two were so large, all Patagonians would prove to be so.

Pigafetta drew no such inference, nor is there any evidence that the Spaniards ever did. On the other hand, six Spaniards, with their knives, closed fearlessly on nine of these men, and routed them in a hand-to-hand fight. We may fairly conclude that the delusion which modern criticism has dispelled was not intentionally called into being by the navigators, but was rather the deduction drawn from too narrow premises by credulous Europe.[3]

---

[1] O'Brien, the Irish giant, was eight feet four inches high. His skeleton is in the College of Surgeons in London.

[2] [Fac-simile of a part of the cut of Porto Desire (no. 22) in Lemaire's *Speculum orientalis occidentalisque*, etc., 1599. —ED.]

[3] [Cf. note on the alleged height of the Patagonians in Thevet's *La France antarctique*, Gaffarel's ed., p. 287. Schouten testifies to finding bones in a grave ten feet and more of stature; and Pernetty's *Voyage aux Isles Malonines* (Paris, 1770) gives the testimony of an engraving to their large stature (Field, *Indian Bibliography*, no. 1,200). There is a cut of two

The next voyagers who saw these people were Drake's party. Fletcher, writing in the *World Encompassed*, after fifty-eight years, says distinctly in his narrative of Drake's arrival at this same Port Julian: "We had no sooner landed than *two young giants* repaired to them." Again, speaking of the same interview, "he was visited by two of the inhabitants, whom Magellan named Patagous, or rather Pentagours, from their huge stature." And afterward he resumes the matter in these words: "Magellane was not altogether deceived in naming them giants, for they generally differ from the common sort of men both in stature, bigness, and strength of body, as also in the hideousness of their voice. But yet they are nothing so monstrous or giant-like as they are reported, there being some Englishmen as tall as the highest of any we could see. But peradventure the Spaniards did not think that ever any Englishman would come thither to reprove them, and thereupon might presume the more boldly to lie, — the name Pentagones, five cubits, viz. seven foot and half, describing the full height (if not somewhat more) of the highest of them."

QUONIAMBEC.[1]

This last sneer is in Fletcher's worst vein. The etymology of "Pentagones" is all his own. Magellan's people say distinctly that they named the Patagonians from their large feet, — taking the phrase "large feet" from the large shoes which they wore to protect their

enormous Patagonians standing beside a European in Don Casimiro de Ortega's *Resumen histórico del primer viage hecho al rededor del mundo, emprendido por Hernando de Magallanes* (Madrid, 1769). Statements of their unusual height have been insisted upon even in our day by travellers. One of the most trustworthy of recent explorers (1869–1870) of Patagonia, Lieutenant G. C. Musters, says that the men average six feet, some reaching six feet four inches; while the average of the women is five feet four. — ED.]

[1] [Fac-simile of a copper-plate engraving in the English version of Thevet's *Portraitures and Lives* appended to North's *Plutarch* (Cambridge, England) p. 86. Thevet in his text says of this "giant-like man," "I have seen him and sufficiently observed him upon the River of Janaira. He had a great body, proportionably gross, exceeding strong. His portraiture I brought from that country, with two green stones in his cheeks and one on his chin." — ED.]

feet from cold. The language is distinct: "Their shoes go four inches above the great toe, and the space is filled with straw to keep them from the cold." These shoes, of this same form, are figured by modern artists, who have drawn for us the Tehuelches of to-day. It is quite possible that the false etymology which made "Patagonian" mean "Five-cubit man" was the real foundation for the general notion of the gigantic size of the race.

From these winter quarters Magellan despatched the "Sant Iago" to examine the coast. The vessel was unfortunately lost on the rocks, but all the crew were saved. Two sailors returned to the rest of the squadron with news of the disaster, and the commander sent back supplies. They were near a hundred miles away from him, but he kept them supplied with provisions; and they were able to rescue a part of the stores and equipage of their vessel. At the end of two months, in which they encamped upon the shore, they rejoined him. It is observed that with them the winter was so cold that for water for their daily use they were obliged to melt ice.

After taking possession of Patagonia in the name of the King of Spain, by planting a standard on a hill which they called Monte Cristo, Magellan sailed on the 24th of August from this inhospitable bay. He now carried out the cruel sentence of the Court on Juan de Carthagena and the priest Pedro Sanches. He landed them with a supply of biscuit and wine, and left them to their fate.

Two days after, following the coast, he entered the River of Santa Cruz and narrowly escaped shipwreck there. He was able to supply himself with wood, water, and fish. On the 11th of October he observed an eclipse of the sun.[1]

Still keeping on, during the 21st of October, the day which the Church consecrated to the "Eleven thousand Virgins," they discovered a strait, to which Magellan gave that name. It was the entry to the famous channel, four hundred and forty miles long, according to his estimate, which has for so many years borne his name. The depth of water near the shore, which has since been observed, attracted the attention of the Spaniards. The mountains which looked down upon it were high, and covered with snow.

The crew and the captains, even after the hard experience of the mutineers, did not hesitate to express their unwillingness to enter the blind and narrow channel before them. Magellan summoned the commanders and made to them a formal declaration, of which the substance has been preserved. He told them that their sovereign and his had sent them for this very purpose, to discover this strait and to pass through it. If they were faithless as to its issue, he declared that he had seen in the archives of the King of Portugal a map, drawn by Martin Behaim, in which the strait

---

[1] Herrera gives the observation in some detail; but M. Charton says it was not visible there.

was indicated, and that it opened into the western ocean. The squadron should not turn back, he said; and he gave his order for the continuation

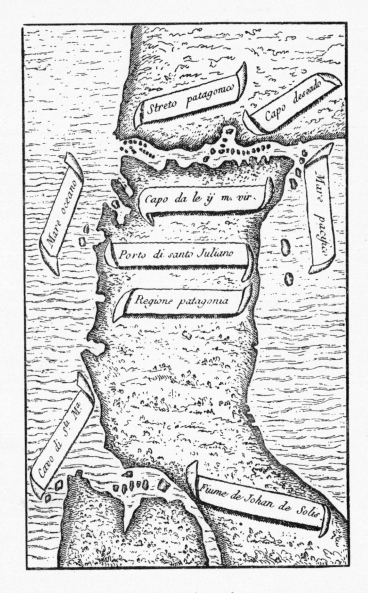

PIGAFETTA'S MAP.[1]

of the voyage in this determination. If the vessels separated, the commander of each was to keep on until he had reached the latitude of

1 [This fac-simile is made from the cut, p. 40 of the French edition of Amoretti's *Premier voyage autour du monde par Pigafetta*, Paris, l'an ix (1801). The reader will observe that the north is at the bottom of the map. There is a reversed sketch of it elsewhere. — ED.]

75° S. If then the strait had not been found, any commander might turn eastward; yet he was not to seek Spain, but to sail to the Moluccas, which were the objective of the voyage; and the proper sailing directions were given for reaching those islands by the route through the Indian Ocean.

The geographers have been at a loss to reconcile this statement, — that Martin Behaim had already drawn the strait upon a map or globe, — with Magellan's claim to be its discoverer. But, as the reader knows, there was no lack of straits or of continents on the various maps before Magellan's time which could be cited for any theory of any cosmographer. We know the history of navigation well enough to understand that, whatever drawings Magellan might have seen or cited, nothing can shake his reputation as the far-sighted discoverer of the channel to which, without any hesitation, the world has given his name.[1]

His firmness had so much effect that the captains went back to their ships, pretending to accede to his wishes. With the " Trinidad " and " Victoria," Magellan waited at the entrance of the channel while he despatched the " San Antonio " and " Concepçion " to complete the survey of it westward. Hardly had the squadron divided, when a terrible tempest broke upon both parts of it, lasting thirty-six hours. Magellan's ships lost their anchors, and were at the mercy of the wind in the open bay. The other vessels seem to have run before the gale. At the moment when their people thought themselves lost, they opened the first " reach " — if it may so be called — of the strait; they pushed through it till they came to the bay now known as " Bouçault Bay." Crossing this, with increasing confidence, they came into the second channel, which opens into a second bay larger than the first. After this success they returned to report their progress to their commander.

He and his officers, meanwhile, had begun to fear that their companions had been lost in the tempest. A column of smoke on shore was supposed to be a signal of the spot where they had taken refuge. But in the midst of such uncertainty their vessels reappeared, and soon fired shots from their guns in token of joy. They were as joyfully welcomed; and, as soon as they could tell their news, the re-united squadron gladly proceeded through the two channels which they had opened. When they arrived in the bay which had been the farthest discovery of the pioneer vessels, they found two channels opening from it. At the southeast is that marked " Supposé " on Bougainville's map; and to this channel Magellan directed Mesquita in the " San Antonio," and Juan Serrano in the " Concepçion."

Unfortunately the sailing-master of the " San Antonio " was Stephen Gomez, who hated Magellan with a long-cherished hatred. When Magellan first arrived in Spain, Gomez was, or thought he was, on the eve of starting on an expedition of discovery under the patronage of the Crown.

---

[1] [See the section on " The Historical Chorography of South America." — ED.]

Magellan's grand plan had broken up this lesser expedition; and instead of commanding it, Gomez had found himself placed in a subordinate post under his rival's command. He now took his chance to revenge himself as soon as he was directed to survey the new channel. Before night fell he had escaped from the surveillance of the "Concepçion." At night he caballed with the Spaniards of his own crew; they rose upon their captain Mesquita, a Portuguese, the loyal cousin of Magellan, and put him in irons. Without delay they then escaped from the squadron; and returning, through the channels they had traced, to the Atlantic, they sailed for home. Touching at the forlorn harbor where they had wintered, they picked up the two mutineers who had been left there. Indeed, it is fair to suppose that their whole plot dated back for its origin to the unsuccessful enterprise of the winter.[1]

Magellan, on his part, waited for the "San Antonio," which had been directed to return in three days. Though the channel which she was to explore passed between mountains covered with snow, we are told that the strait where Magellan awaited them lay between regions which were "the most beautiful in the world." On the southern side they had, once and again, observed fires in the night, and they gave to that land the name of "Tierra del Fuego," "the Land of Fire," which it has ever since preserved. They did not see any of the natives on either coast. The sailors caught so many fish which resembled the sardines of their home, that the name of "River of Sardines" was given to a stream which makes its outlet there. Finding that the "San Antonio" had left him, and probably suspecting her treachery, Magellan went forward through the southwestern channel with the "Victoria" and the "Trinidad."

It is at this point that we are to place a formal correspondence which has been preserved by a Portuguese historian[2] as passing between Magellan and one of his captains on the question of advancing. These letters are dated the 22d of November, 1520. Martin Mendoza, in his reply to Magellan's letter, agrees that until the 1st of January they should persevere while the days are long, but urges that the vessels should lie by in the darkness. He is as resolute in expressing the conviction that they should be out of the strait before the month of January is over, — that is, that they should turn about, if necessary, on January 1, if they had not then reached the Pacific, so as to be well in the Atlantic again by the first of February; that then they should give up the original object of the voyage and sail to Cadiz. The document seems genuine; but, as the reader will see, there was no occasion for using its counsels. Before the 1st of January they were free of the strait forever.

While his squadron loitered in hope of the "San Antonio's" return, Magellan sent forward a boat to explore the channel. On the third day

---

[1] [For Gomez' subsequent career see Dr. Shea's chapter on "Ancient Florida," in Vol. II., and chapter i. of Vol. IV. — ED.]

[2] Juan de Barros.

she returned to him with the joyful news that they had opened the western mouth of the strait.

The Pacific was found! The chroniclers say that the crews wept for joy; and they may well have done so. They gave to the Cape — which made the western end of Tierra del Fuego, on this channel — the name of the "Desired Cape," "Cabo Deseado," which it still retains.

The squadron did not at once follow. Magellan put back for the other vessels, and met the "Concepçion" alone. He sent back the "Victoria" this time to search for his faithless consort. If she were not found, his orders were that a standard should be planted on high ground, at the foot of which should be buried a letter, with an account of the destination of the squadron. Two similar signals were left, — one on the shore of the first bay, and one on the Isle of Lions, in the channel. But the "Victoria," as the reader knows, did not find the "San Antonio;" she was far away. And with three vessels of his squadron only, Magellan passed out from the strait which had detained him so long, into the ocean. They fairly entered upon it on the 28th of November.

Pigafetta, in his joy at leaving this strait, which had been the scene of so much anxiety, describes its natural advantages in glowing colors. "In fine, I do not believe there is a better strait than this in the world," he says. They gave to it the name of "Strait of the Patagonians;" but the world has long since known it by the name of its discoverer. "There may be found at any half-league a good harbor," — such is the Italian historian's statement, — "with excellent water, cedar-wood, sardine-fish, and an abundance of shell-fish. There are also herbs on shore, some of which are bitter, but others are good to eat, — especially a sort of celery,[1] which grows near the springs, of which we made excellent food." Cook found celery of the same kind two centuries and a half later, as well as abundance of *Cochlearia*. So great are the advantages of such supplies for the health of crews in danger of scurvy, that he thought the passage into the Pacific by the Straits of Magellan preferable to that by Cape Horn.[2] In later days his advice has always been followed by vessels having the aid of steam.

Thus ended the only glimpse which Spaniards had of Patagonia for many years. Magellan's act of possession held, however; for the country has no attractions to make it a stake for wars or other controversy. Magellan looked his last upon it as his squadron gladly steered northward; and after leaving his Cape Victory, — for he gave that name to the southwestern point of America, — neither he nor his landed again on this continent.

The poor giants who had been so cruelly enslaved never reached Spain. One was on the "San Antonio" with Serrano, who deserted his commander in the strait. This one died before they had crossed the Atlantic. The other was on board the "Trinidad," the flagship, with Magellan and Piga-

---

[1] Apium dulce.   [2] See Cook's *First Voyage*, i. 70, 74.

fetta, the historian of the expedition. He became fond of Pigafetta; and when he saw him produce his writing tablet and paper, he knew what was expected of him, and of his own accord began to give the names of different objects in the Patagonian language.[1] One day when he saw Pigafetta kiss the cross, he told him by signs that *Setebos* would enter him and make him a coward. But when he was himself dying — of scurvy, most likely, which was decimating the crew — he asked for the cross himself, kissed it, and begged to be baptized. His captors baptized him, gave him the name of Paul, and he died.

It would have been natural for Magellan, now that he had attained the South Sea, to sail by a direct route to the Moluccas, of which he was in search. Till a very late period the geographers have supposed that he did; and his track will be found on most of the large globes, to a period comparatively recent, laid down on a course a little west of northwest, — as, indeed, Pigafetta says they ran.

It was not observed by these globe-makers, and in fact to many of them it was not known, that, if Magellan had taken such a course, he would have run directly into the teeth of those northwest winds which blow with great regularity in that part of the Pacific, and he would have met a steady current in the same direction. In such computations, also, it was forgotten that Magellan supposed the Pacific to be much narrower than it is, and that when he left the straits he did not anticipate so long a voyage as he had. But the fortunate discovery of the log-book of one of the "pilots" now gives us the declination of the sun and the computed latitude for every day of the Pacific voyage. It appears that Magellan held well to the north, not far from the coast of South America, till he had passed, on the west, the islands of Juan Fernandez and Masafuera without seeing them, and only then struck to the northwest, and afterwards to the west.[2] He thus came out at the equator at a point which, by their mistaken computation of longitude, was 152° W. of the meridian of Ferro, 159° 46' west of our first meridian of Greenwich.

The Pacific is now known to us as an ocean studded with islands, the inhabitants of which are well provided with food from their own land, and water.[3] It was, however, the remarkable fortune of Magellan in this voyage to sail more than ten thousand miles and see but two of these islands, both of which were barren and uninhabited. He found no bottom close to the shore. At the second of the two islands he stopped to fish for sharks,

[1] Pigafetta has preserved the vocabulary of ninety words which in this way he made. The words, he says, are to be pronounced in the throat. A few of the words are these: Ears, *sanc*; eyes, *ather*; nose, *or*; breast, *othey*; eyelids, *sechechiel*; nostrils, *oresche*; mouth, *piam*; a chief, *hez*.

[2] This might have been inferred from Pigafetta's map of the strait, in which the western shore of Patagonia and Chili are well laid in;

but that inference seems to have escaped the globe-makers.

[3] Most observers forget, however, when they look upon a map of this ocean, that the name of an island or group upon the map may cover a hundred, not to say a thousand, times as much space on the paper as the island or group takes up on the surface of the world. Dr. Charles Darwin calls attention to such forgetfulness, in the *Voyage of the Beagle*.

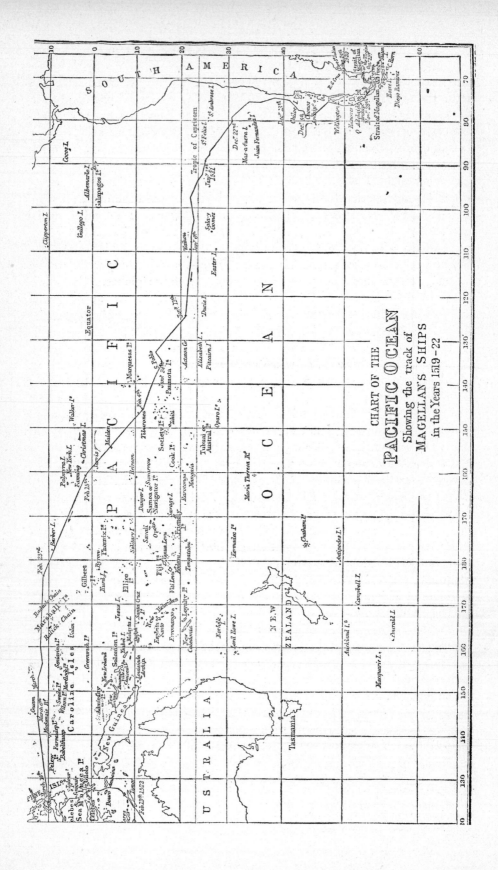

CHART OF THE
PACIFIC OCEAN
Showing the track of
MAGELLAN'S SHIPS
in the Years 1519–22

and gave it the name "Shark's Island," or "Tiburones." The crew were
so impressed by their dismal welcome that they called the two "Desven-
turadas," the "Unfortunate Islands." These two islands, the first-born to
Europe of the multitudes of the Pacific Ocean, cannot now be identified.[1]

On the 6th of March the voyagers at last saw two more small islands.
Soon a number of small sails appeared, the islanders coming out to meet

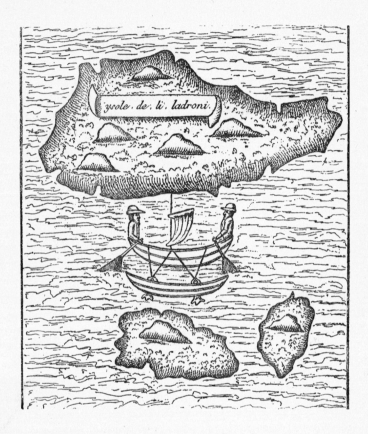

ysole. de. li. ladroni.

THE LADRONES.[2]

the ships. Their little boats had large triangular-shaped sails of matting,
and they seemed to fly over the water. The Spanish seamen saw for the
first time the curious catamarans of the natives of these waters.

Magellan was tempted to land at a third and larger island. This was
either the one since known as Guahan, or that known as Rota; Magellan
called it Ivagana. So many of the natives swarmed upon his ship, and they
were so rapacious in stealing whatever they could lay their hands on, that
he found himself almost at their mercy. They begged him to land, but

[1] The identification attempted on the map
(taken from the Hakluyt Society's volume on
Magellan) is one of many conjectures.

[2] [This fac-simile is made from the Paris edition of Amoretti's *Pigafetta*, p. 62, and shows
the catamaran of the natives. — ED.]

stole the boat attached to the stern of his ship.   At last Magellan did land, in a rage.   He burned some of their huts, several of their boats, got back his own, and killed seven men.

The squadron, after this encounter, continued its westward course, followed by a hundred canoes.   The savages now showed fish, as if they wished to trade; but the women wept and tore their hair, probably " because we had killed their husbands."

To this group the Spaniards gave the name of "Ladrones, the robbers," which it has ever since retained.   After three hundred leagues more of westward sailing, the tired navigators, half starved and dying of scurvy, made the discovery of Zamal, now called Samar, the first of the group since known as the Philippines, — a name they took from Philip the Second. Magellan called them the Archipelago of St. Lazarus, because he first found how large a group it was on St. Lazarus' day, the fifth Sunday in Lent.

In these islands the navigators were, at first, most cordially received. By means of a Malayan interpreter they were able to communicate with the natives.   Before six weeks were over, with rapidity which may well have seemed miraculous, they had converted the king and many of the princes and people to what they deemed Christianity.   But, alas! the six weeks ended in the defeat of the Spanish men-at-arms in a battle with a rival prince, in the death of Magellan and the murder of Serrano, who had been chosen as one of those who should take his place.   The surviving Spaniards withdrew as well as they could from their exasperated allies.

They were obliged to destroy one of their ships, which was leaking, and thus were left with only two.   One of these, the "Trinidad," they despatched eastward to the American coast; but she failed in this voyage, and returned to the Philippines.   In the other vessel, the "Victoria," Sebastian del Cano and his crew, after spending the rest of that year in the East Indies, sailed for Europe.   They left the Island of Timor on the 11th of February. Though they had nothing but rice and water for their supplies, they dared not touch at the Portuguese establishment at Mozambique.   After they doubled the Cape of Good Hope, on the 6th of May, they lost twenty-one men in two months.   Their provisions had failed entirely when, on the 9th of July, they touched at Santa Argo, in the Cape de Verde Islands.

Even now they did not dare tell the Portuguese at that island who they were.   They pretended they came from the coast of America.   When they found that the day was Thursday, they were greatly astonished, for by their own journals it was Wednesday.   Twice they sent their boat ashore for a load of rice, and it returned.   The third time they saw that it was seized. One of the sailors had revealed their secret, and the jealous Portuguese would no longer befriend them.

The poor "Victoria," with such supplies as she had received, was obliged to run direct for Spain.   On the 6th of September she entered the bay of San Lucar again.   By their own computation they had sailed 14,460 leagues. Of sixty men who sailed in her from the Moluccas there were but eighteen survivors; of these almost all were sick. Of the other forty-two, some had deserted at Timor, some had been condemned to death for their crimes, and the others had died. This was all that was returned of two hundred and thirty-seven persons who had sailed three years before on this magnificent expedition.

Del Cano was received at Court with the greatest courtesy. The Emperor gave him a pension of five hundred ducats, and for armorial bearings a globe with the device —

"PRIMUS CIRCUMDEDISTI ME."

The "Victoria" was richly stored with cloves and other spices. Of these the sale was carefully managed, and the proceeds were enormous. The foresight of Magellan was completely justified, and the profits of the expedition alone immediately tempted the Emperor to fit out another. The "Victoria" afterward made two voyages to the West Indies, but never returned to Spain from the second, and her fate is not known. An ancient representation of her (from Hulsius) is the distinguishing sign on the cover of the volumes issued in our day by the Hakluyt Society.

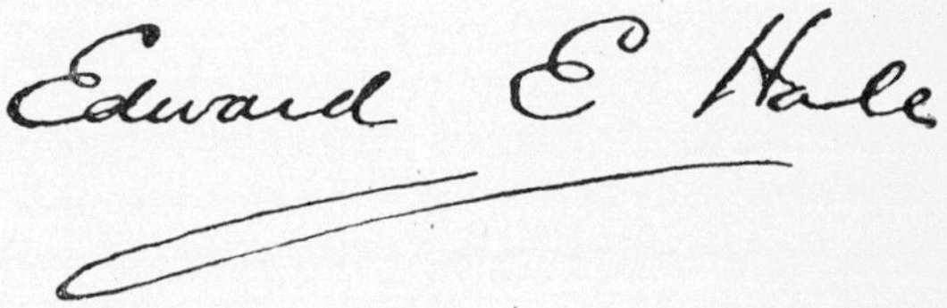

Edward E. Hale

CRITICAL ESSAY ON THE SOURCES OF INFORMATION.

BY EDWARD E. HALE AND THE EDITOR.

PIGAFETTA, who was born in Vicenza not long after 1490, was accordingly from twenty-five to thirty years old when he accompanied Magellan.[1] He kept a diary of the voyage, a copy of which he gave to the Emperor; and later, in Italy, he wrote out a more extended account, copies of which he gave to distinguished persons. Of this ampler narrative four separate texts, in as many manuscripts, are preserved to us.

No. 1 is in French, *Navigation et descouvrement de la Indie superieure faicte par moi Antoine Pigafete, Vincentin;* on paper, in the National Library at Paris. It gives the full vocabulary of the Giants' language, which is also reprinted in Amoretti. Students engaged in the study of the geography of the East Indies should not be satisfied with the few copies given by Amoretti of the maps and representations of the islands there. In this copy, which is divided throughout into short chapters, there are many more of these

---

[1] He died in 1534. A brother-in-law of Magellan, Duarte Barbosa, who was killed at the same time with his chief, prepared a manuscript in 1516, which was printed by Ramusio in Italian as *Sommario di tutti li regni dell' Indie orientali.* This paper, describing from such sources as were available the eastern regions, had not a little influence on Magellan. The original Portuguese was printed by the Lisbon Academy in their *Noticias Ultramarinhas,* in 1813.

maps than have been engraved. It is impossible to look at them without believing that they give some idea of the size and even the shape of the islands visited. Charton calls this paper manuscript the oldest of those in France. No one can decide such a question. The illustrations in the vellum manuscript certainly seem to be nearer the originals than those in this coarser paper one.

No. 2 is a richly illuminated vellum document, with a text somewhat softened in the coarse parts. This may have been the copy known to have been given to Louise of Savoy by Pigafetta. This manuscript is also in the Paris library. The writing is elegant, and the maps are very prettily done in body color. They are much more elegant than the maps in the paper manuscript, which are in rough water-color by some one of no great artistic skill. The representations given by Amoretti of a few of the designs are sufficiently good for all practical purposes. But the picture of the boat with outriggers, illustrating the customs of the Ladrone Islands, is much more artistic in the vellum manuscript than it is in Amoretti's engraving.

No. 3, the most complete, was owned by M. Beaupré, at Nancy, in 1841, when Tho-massy described it; was sold in the Potier sale in 1851 (no. 506), and passed into the Solar Collection, and in 1861 (Solar sale, no. 3,238) it was bought by a London dealer, and reached finally the collection of Sir Thomas Phillipps, who bought it at the Libri sale (no. 1,139) in 1862. It is a question with critics whether Pigafetta composed his work in French or in Italian; for there is also a manuscript (no. 4) in the later language, poorly conceived, however, and mixed with Spanish, preserved in the Ambrosian Library at Milan. This was the manuscript published by the Abbé C. Amoretti; it is written in the character known as *cancelleresco*, on paper folios, of which the handwriting is of the time of Pigafetta; and it was once owned by the Cardinal Frederic Borroméo. Raymond Tho-massy[1] gives several reasons for believing that the French text is the original, but we have not been satisfied that it was so.[2]

In the earliest edition of Pigafetta which we have, — one without date, and in French, edited by Antoine Fabre, — the text is represented as being a translation from the Italian. It is possible that, being an abridgment, it might have followed some abstract which had been made in that language, possibly an account which in 1524 Pigafetta asked permission to print,[3] of the Doge and Council of Venice. This original French edition is called *Le Voyage et Navigation faict par les Espaignolz es isles de Mollucques;* and is usually thought to have been printed in 1525. It is in Gothic type, except the last four leaves, which are in Roman, as are all the notes.[4] Harrisse cites[5] an Italian edition of Pigafetta with the letter of Maximilian, as published at Venice in 1534;[6] but there is little reason to believe such an edition to exist.

The earliest undoubted Italian edition was printed, however, in 1536, and it was pro-fessedly a translation from Fabre's French text, and there is reason to believe that Ramusio may have been instrumental in its publication.[7] It has the name neither of author nor of printer, but is supposed to have been issued at Venice. It is called *Il Viaggio fatto da gli Spagnivoli a torno a'l mondo.*[8]

---

[1] *Bulletin de la Société de Géographie*, September, 1843.

[2] Pigafetta himself mentions a manuscript, *Uno libro scripto de tutti le cose passate de giorno in giorno nel viaggio*, written by his own hand, and presented by him to Charles the Fifth. Harrisse thinks it was written in French, and describes the manuscripts, *Bibl. Amer. Vet. Add.*, pp. xxx–xxxiii.

[3] This petition is given in Stanley's *Magellan*, and in Harrisse's *Bibl. Amer. Vet. Add.*, p. xxviii.

[4] *Bibl. Amer. Vet.*, no. 134; Carter-Brown, no. 86; Brunet, iv. 650; Des Brosses, *Navigations aux*

terres Australes, i. 121; Panzer, viii. 217; Anto-nio, *Bibliotheca Hispana Nova*, ii. 376.

[5] On the strength of *Livres Curieux*, p. 29.

[6] *Bibl. Amer. Vet.*, no. 192.

[7] Ramusio included it in his *Viaggi* in 1554, with annotations.

[8] *Bibl. Amer. Vet.*, 215; *Bibliotheca Heber-nana*, ix. 3,129; *Bibliotheca Grenvilliana*, no. 548; Stevens, *Nuggets*, no. 2,753; Libri, 1861, no. 288; Carter-Brown, i. 118; Court, no. 372. There is also a copy in the Lenox Library. Wiley, of New York, priced a copy in 1883, at $145.

Amoretti published the Ambrosian manuscript (no. 4, above) in 1800, at Milan, under the title of *Primo viaggio intorno al globo terracqueo ossia ragguaglio della navigazione alle Indie orientali d[i] Magaglianes*, 1519–1522. *Pubblicato per la prima volta da un codice manuscritto della Biblioteca Ambrosiana di Milano, e corredato di note da C. Amoretti con un transunto del Trattato di navigazione dello stesso autore. Milano,* 1800.[1]

About a month after the return of Del Cano in the "Victoria," Maximilian Transylvanus (a son-in-law of Cristóbal de Haro, who had been a chief advocate of the voyage at the Spanish Court) wrote to the Cardinal Archbishop of Salzburg a brief account of the voyage, in a letter dated at Valladolid. Oct. 24, 1522;[2] and when it was printed at Cologne in January, 1523, as *De Moluccis insulis,* and in the following November and again in February, 1524, at Rome, as *De Hispanorum in orientem navigatione,* its text constituted the earliest narrative of the voyage which was given in print.[3] It was afterward printed in connection with the earliest Italian edition of Pigafetta ; and the English reader will find it in the volume on Magellan published by the Hakluyt Society.

Ramusio also tells us that Peter Martyr wrote an account of Magellan's voyage, gathered from the lips of the survivors, which he sent to Rome to be printed, but that in the sack of that city by the Constable de Bourbon it disappeared. We have but one point of this Martyr narrative preserved to us, and that is the loss of one day which the "Victory" had experienced in her westering voyage, — when arriving in Seville on the 6th of September, 1522, as her crew supposed, they found the Sevillians calling it the 7th.[4]

There are two modern gatherings of the most important documentary illustrations of this famous voyage, — the one made by Navarrete, and the other published by the Hakluyt Society. The former constitutes the fourth volume of Navarrete's well-known *Coleccion ;* and among the variety of its papers printed or cited largely from the public archives, illustrating the fitting out of the fleet, its voyage, and the reception of Del Cano on his return, a few of the more important may be mentioned. Such is a manuscript from the library of San Isadro el Real de Madrid, purporting to be by Magellan himself; but Navarrete does not admit this. He prints for the first time an original manuscript account in the Seville archives, usually cited as the Seville manuscript, which bears the title of *Extracto de la habilitacion,* etc. It gives an enumeration of the company which composed the force on the fleet. The Navarrete volume also contains the log-book of Francisco Albo, or Alvaro, printed, it is claimed by Stanley (who also includes it in the Hakluyt Society volume), from a copy in the British Museum, which was made from the original at Simancas. It

[1] A French version of this text was issued at Paris in 1801 ; and the Italian text was again printed in 1805. Pigafetta's story is given in English in Pinkerton's *Voyages,* i. 188; in German in Sprengel's *Beyträgen,* and in Kries's *Beschreibung von Magellan-Reise.* Gotha, 1801. Cf. a bibliography of the manuscript and printed editions of Pigafetta in the *Studi biografici e bibliografici,* published by the Società Geografica Italiana (2d ed., 1882), i. 262.

[2] The date in Navarrete is October 5.

[3] All three of these editions are in the Lenox Library, and the first two are in the Carter-Brown. Cf. Harrisse, *Bibl. Amer. Vet.,* nos. 122, 123, 124. Leclerc priced the Cologne edition at 500 francs, and the Rome (1523) at 350. *Bibl. Amer. Vet.* nos. 376, 377. Dufossé (nos. 11,003, 12,348) puts the Cologne edition at 500 francs, and again (no. 14,892) at 380. The *Court Catalogue* (Paris, 1884) shows the Cologne edition (no. 220) and the Rome (1524) edition (no. 221).

Brunet is in error in calling the Roman edition the earliest. A Cologne copy in the Murphy sale (1884) brought $75 ; *Catalogue,* no. 2.519. One in F. S. Ellis's *Catalogue* (1884), no. 188, is priced at £42. Cf. Sabin, xi. 47,038–47,042; Carter-Brown, no. 75; Graesse, iv. 451; Ternaux, no. 129. It was also inserted in Latin in the *Novus Orbis* of 1537 (p. 585), and of 1555 (p. 524), and in Johannes Bœmus's *Omnium gentium mores,* etc., Antwerp, 1542 ; in Italian in Ramusio (i. 347); in Spanish, in Navarrete (iv. 249, dated October 5, and not 24). The narrative in Hulsius (no. xxvi.) is taken from Ortelius and Chauveton. Cf. Panzer, vol. vi., no. 375; Stevens, *Nuggets,* no. 1,868; *Bibliotheca Grenvilliana,* p. 454; Ternaux, nos. 29, 30; Graesse, iv. 451, 452; *Bibliotheca Heberiana,* i. 4,451; ii. 3,687; vi. 2,331; vii. 4,123; Leclerc, no. 69; *Bibl. Amer. Vet. Add.,* no. 136.

[4] *Bibl. Amer. Vet.,* p. 229, where other missing accounts are mentioned.

follows the fortunes of the fleet after they sighted Cape St. Augustine. Muñoz had found in the Archives of Torre de Tombo a letter of Antonio Brito to the King of Portugal, and Navarrete gives this also.[1] A letter of Jean Sebastian del Cano to Charles V., dated Sept. 5, 1527, describes the voyage, and is also to be found here.[2]

The Hakluyt Society volume borrows largely from the lesser sources as given in Navarrete, and among other papers it contains the brief narrative which is found in Ramusio as that of an "anonymous Portuguese." It also gives an English version of what is known as the account of the Genoese pilot, one Joan Bautista probably. This story exists in three Portuguese manuscripts : one belongs to the library of the monks of S. Bento da Sande; another is in the National Library at Paris; and from these two a text was formed which was printed in 1826 in the *Noticias Ultramarinhas* (vol. iv.) of the Lisbon Academy of History, as "Roteiro da viagem de Fernam de Magalhâes" (1519). A third manuscript is in the library of the Academy of History at Madrid. As edited by Luigi Hugues, it is printed in the fifteenth volume of the *Atti della Società Ligure di Storia Patria*.

The narrative in the preceding text has shown that the precise statements of latitude made by the Genoese pilot have wholly destroyed the value of all speculations as to the route of Magellan from the Straits to the Ladrones which were published before this "Roteiro" became known. The track laid down on the older globes is invariably wrong, and Magellan's course was in reality that along which the currents would easily have propelled him, being that of the Antarctic stream of the Pacific, which Humboldt has explained.[3] Stanley also points out that the narrative given in Gaspar Correa's *Lendas da India* is the only authority we have for the warning given to Magellan at Teneriffe by Barbosa; and for the incident of a Portuguese ship speaking the "Victoria" as the latter was passing the Cape of Good Hope.

One Pedro Mexia had seen the fleet of Magellan sail, and had likewise witnessed the return of Del Cano. A collection of miscellanies, which he printed as early as 1526, under the title of *Silva*, and which passed through many editions, affords another contemporary reference.[4] It is hardly worth while to enumerate the whole list of more general historical treatises of the sixteenth and even seventeenth centuries,[5] which bring this famous voyage within their scope. It seems clear, however, that Oviedo had some sources which are not recognizable now, and some have contended that he had access to Magellan's own papers. Herrera in the ninth book of his eleventh Decade in the same way apparently had information the sources of which are now lost to us. The story of Magellan necessarily made part of such books as Osorius's *De Rebus Emmanuelis gestis*, published at Cologne in 1581, again in 1597, and in Dutch at Rotterdam in 1661–1663. Burton in his *Hans Stade* (p. lxxxvi) calls the *Relacion y derrotero del Viaje y descubrimiento del estrecho de la Madre de Dios, antes llamado de Magallanes por Pedro Sarmiento de Gamboa*, published in 1580, an unworthy attempt to rob Magellan of his fame.

---

[1] Cf. *Bibl. Amer. Vet.*, p. 229.

[2] Cf. J. A. Schmeller's *Uber einige älten handschriftliche See-karten*, Munich, 1844, which is an extract from the *Abhandlungen d. Baier. Akad. d. Wissensch.*, iv. 1. It is announced (1884) that Harrisse is preparing an annotated edition of the letter.

[3] Cf. Reclus, *Ocean*, bk. i., chap. ix. and Chart.

[4] Cf. *Bibl. Am. Vet.*, nos. 80, 81, 132, 133, 161; Carter-Brown, i. 212, 283, 336; ii. 221; Sabin, xii. p. 90; *Ticknor, Catalogue*, p. 226.

[5] Among them may be mentioned, for instance, such books as Argensola's *Conquista de las islas Malucas*, Madrid, 1609, which a hundred years later was made familiar to French and English readers by editions at Amsterdam in 1707, and by being included in Stevens's *Collection of Voyages* in 1708, while the German version appeared at Frankfort in 1711 (cf. Carter-Brown, ii. 77; iii. 92, 104, 119, 147); Gotard Arthus's *India Orientalis*, Cologne, 1608; Farya y Sousa's *Asia Portuguesa*, Lisbon, 1666–1675. The final conquest of the Philippines was not accomplished till 1564, when by order of Philip II., Miguel Lopez de Legaspi led a fleet from Navidad in New Spain. For this and the subsequent history of the island see Antonio de Morga's *Philippine Islands* (Mexico, 1609) as translated and annotated for the Hakluyt Society by H. E. J. Stanley, 1868. Cf. Pedro Chirino's *Relacion de las islas Filipinas*, Rome, 1604 (Rich, *Catalogue of Books* (1832), no. 99; Sabin, *Dictionary*, iv. 12,836).

The modern studies of Magellan and his career have been in good hands. Navarrete when he made his most important contribution of material, accompanied it with a very careful *Noticia biográfica* of Magellan, in which he makes exact references to his sources.[1]

A critical life of Magellan was prefixed by Lord Stanley to his Hakluyt Society volume in 1874. R. H. Major in his *Prince Henry the Navigator* included an admirable critical account, which was repeated in its results in his later volume, *Discoveries of Prince Henry*.

A paper on the search of Magellan and of Gomez for a western passage was read by Buckingham Smith before the New York Historical Society, a brief report of which is in the *Historical Magazine*, x. (1866) 229; and one may compare with it the essay by Langeron in the *Revue Géographique* in 1877.

A number of more distinctive monographs have also been printed, beginning with the *Magellan, oder die Erste Reise um die Erde nach dem vorhanderen Quellen dargestellt* of August Bürck, which was published in Leipsic in 1844.[2] Dr. Kohl, who had given the subject much study, particularly in relation to the history of the straits which Magellan passed, published the results of his researches in the *Zeitschrift der Gesellschaft für Erdkunde in Berlin* in 1877, — a treatise which was immediately republished separately as *Geschichte der Entdeckungsreisen und Schiffahrten zur Magellan's Strasse*. In 1881 Dr. Franz Wieser, a professor in the University at Innspruck, examined especially the question of any anterior exploration in this direction, in his *Magalhâes-strasse und Austral Continent auf den globen des Johannes Schöner*, which was published in that year at Innspruck.[3] About the same time (1881) the Royal Academy at Lisbon printed a *Vida e Viagens de Fernão de Magalhães, com um appendice original,* which, as the work of Diego de Barros Arana, had already appeared in Spanish.

The bibliography of Magellan and his voyage is prepared with some care by Charton in his *Voyageurs,* p. 353 ; and scantily in St. Martin's *Histoire de la Géographie,* p. 370.

[1] Cf. also a notice by Navarrete in his *Opúsculos,* i. 143, with (p. 203) an appendix of "Pruebas, ilustraciones y documentos."

[2] Sabin, iii. 9,208.

[3] Wieser has also drawn attention in the *Mittheilungen des Instituts für österreichische Geschichtsforschung,* v. (heft iii.) to "ein Bericht des Gasparo Contarini über die Heimkehr der Victoria von der Magalhâes'schen Expedition," with ample annotation.

EDITORIAL NOTE. — A section on the "Historical Chorography of South America," tracing the cartographical history of that continent, together with a note on the "Bibliography of Brazil," is reserved for Vol. VIII.

INDEX.

INDEX. 633

INDEX. 633

by Navarrete, v; accompanied by Vespucius, 149, 153.
Olano, Lope de, 194.
Old World, map of (1490), 41.
Olibahali, 258.
Olid, Cristóbal de, 214, 351; at the second siege of Mexico, 376; in Honduras, 200, 383; his defection, 384, 411.
Oliva, Anello, *Hist. du Pérou*, 576.
Oliva, F. P. de, his account of Columbus, 66.
Oliva, Johannes, his map, 461.
Olives planted in Peru, 547.
Oliveros, 241.
Omaguas, 581; fabled empire of, 585.
Oña, Pedro de, *Arauco Domado*, 572.
Oñate, Juan de, 461, 504.
Once a Week, 66.
Ondegardo, Polo de, 545, 552; career, 571; *Relaciones*, 523, 571; his manuscripts, 571.
Ongania, his *Raccolta di mappamundi*, 107.
Onondaga, Spanish at, 283.
Oostanaula River, 247.
Opmeer, P. van, *Opus chronographicum*, 72.
Ordaz, Diego, 351; his expedition, 579.
Ordenanzas reales, 347.
Ordinationes legumque collectiones, 401.
Ordoñez de Montalvo, *Las sergas de Esplandian*, 443.
Oregon (river), 469.
Orellana, Francisco de, 188; with Gonzalo Pizarro, 528; courses the Amazon, 447, 528, 584; Herrera's account, translated by Markham, 563; goes to Spain, 585; returns and dies, 585. *See* Amazon.
Orgoñez, R., 525; defeats Alvarado, 526; defeats Manco, 526; killed, 527.
Orinoco River, 133; discovered by Columbus, 20; explored, 579; map of the mouths, 586, 588; explored by Whiddon, 586.
Orista, 282.
Orizaba, 358.
Oropesa, 525, 552, 562.
Orozco y Berra, 418; *Cartografia Mexicana*, 93, 166, 375; *Vallée de Mexico*, 375.
Orozco, Juan de, 504.
Orsenius, Ambrose, 471.
Orsenius, Ferd., 471.
Ortega, C. de, *Resumen*, 603.
Ortega, C. F., 418.
Ortelius, account of, 471; genealogy of, 471; life by Van Hulst, 471; portraits referred to, 471, 472; notice by Macedo, 471; his list of authorities, 93, 471; editions of his *Theatrum*, 471, 472; which is the original text? 471; *additamentum*, 471; French and German translations, 471; his mappemonde described, 472; map of the New World, 472; epitomes of, 472; map of new Spain, 472; of Florida, 472; of Peru, 472; last edition, by himself, 472; *Il Theatro del mondo* (1598), 439; map (1582), 186.
Ortis, Alonso, *Los tratados*, 57.
Ortiz, Diego, 553.
Ortiz de Matienzo, Juan, 238.
Ortiz of Narvaez' expedition, 245; with De Soto when he died, 252.
Osimo, d', *Colomb et Marchena*, 3.
Osorius, *De rebus Emmanuelis gestis*, 616.
Osorno, 524; founded, 549.
Ostro (south), 94.
Osuna, Duque d', 89.
Otina, 279.
Otmar, Johannes, 157.
Ortubia, Juan Peres de, 233.
Otumba, 358, 369; victory at, 370, 374.
Ovalle, *Historica relatione*, 576; *Historica relacion*, 576; English version, 576.

Ovando, Nic. de, 21, 201; deporting natives from the Lucayan Islands, 328; at Hispaniola, 23.
Overland Monthly, 288.
Oviedo y Baños, *Venezuela*, 584.
Oviedo y Herrera, *Vida de Santa Rosa*, 560.
Oviedo y Valdés, G. F. de, 197; in Peru, 563; his account of Peru, 563; his career, 209, 343; *Sumario*, 343, 345; official chronicler, 343; *Historia de las Indias*, 343, 345; critical estimation of his history, 563; published with Peter Martyr, 563; printed complete, 346; correspondent of Ramusio, 343; knew Cortés, 343; hated by Las Casas, 314, 345; bibliography of, 345; *De la natural hystoria*, 343, 345; facsimile of title, 344; his arms, 345; *Coronica*, 345; his autog., 346; *Histoire naturelle*, 346; *Libro* xx, 346; dies, 346; unprinted parts of his *Historia*, 346; life by Amador de los Rios, 346; *Histoire de Nicaragua*, 346; letter from (1543), 410 · and Magellan's papers, 616.

PABLOS, JUAN, 400.
Paca, 559.
Pacaha, 251.
Pachacamac, 519; temple of, 517.
Pachama, 558.
Pacheco, J. F., *Coleccion*, vii, 498.
Pacific coast, discoveries on, 431; chronology of explorations on, 431.
Pacific Ocean, 177; heard of by Columbus, 211; discovered, 195, 608 (*see* Balbóa); various names, 439; (Mar Pacifico) 452; (Mare del Sur) 223, 227, 228, 450, 451; (Mare del Sul) 229; (Mare del Zur) 459; named in Pigafetta's map, 605; maps of (1513), 440; (1518) 217; chart of Magellan's tract, 610; trade-winds, 454.
Pacific Railroad Reports, 502.
Padilla. *See* Davilla.
Padilla, Juan de, 484, 497, 503.
Padilla, Mota, *Nueva Galicia*, 468.
Paesi novamente retrovati, 205.
Paez, Juan, 445.
Pafallaya, 250.
Pagus Hispanorum, 265.
Paillamacu, 561, 563.
Palafox y Mendoça, *Virtudes del Indio*, 343.
Palencia, Fernandez de, career, 569; *Historia del Peru*, 569; called "El Palentino," 569.
Palentino, el. *See* Palencia.
Pallastrelli, B., *La moglie di Colombo*, 85.
Palmas, Rio de, 242, 281.
Palos, 5, 6.
Palos, Juan, likeness of, 287.
Pampluna, 581.
Panamá, 228, 229, 435, 509; documents in, ix; founded, 198, 199, 212, 505 (1566), 451. *See* Peralta.
Paniagua, 569.
Pánuco, 229, 353, 382, 386; Rio, 203 (1520), 218, 225; named, 237.
Panzer, *Annalen*, 159.
Paposo, 524.
Para, 581.
Parana, 459.
Parana Patinga, 589.
Pardo, Captain, 278.
Pardo, Juan, 504.
Pares, Juan de, 507.
Parestrello at Porto Santo, 38; his family, 90. *See* Perestrello.
Pareto, Bartolomeus, sea-chart, 38.
Paria, 114, 169, 177, 218, 223, 588; (Chili) 525; discovered, 187; gulf of, 586 (map), 61; (1511) 110; name of, 231.
Paria, University of, 90.
Parias, 121, 432; (in Schöner's globe) 118.
Paricura, 188. *See* Amazon.

Parima (lake), 585; first in maps, 587; in later maps, 587, 588; disappeared, 589.
Parima (river), 581.
Paris, Société de Géographie de, their *Recueil de voyages*, 30.
Parita (gulf), 198.
Parkman, F., *Pioneers of France*, 293, 298.
Parmentier of Dieppe, 105.
Parmigiano, picture of Columbus, 76.
Parra, Iacinto de, 560; *Rosa Laureada*, 560.
Parrots, land of (Brazil), 598.
Pas, Crispin de, 72, *Effigies regum*, etc., 72.
Pasamonte, 194, 210, 211.
Pasqual, *Descubr. de la sit. de la America*, 58.
Pasqualigo, 107.
Passado, Cape, 507.
Pastene, J. B., 530; his likeness, 531.
Pasto, 509.
Pastro y Cueva, B. de, 561.
Patagonia, giants in, 600: dress of, 600. *See* Giants (*regio gigantum*), 432.
Patalis, 433.
Patinamit, 383.
Patiño, 267.
Paucartambo River, 519.
Pauli, Reinhold, 337.
Paulitschke, *Afrika-literatur*, 40.
Paullu, Ynca, 524, 553.
Pauthier, G, edits Marco Polo, 30.
Payta, 519, 546.
Paytiti, 585, 589.
Paz, M. de, 511.
Pearl coast, 20, 106, 169.
Pearl-fishery, 187.
Pearl Islands, 197, 198, 199, 505, 509.
Pecari, 598.
Pecciolen, M. N., his map, 461.
Pedrarias, Davilla, 209; *Lettere di Pietro Arias*, 567; authorities on, 211; his character, 196. *See* Avila.
Peignot, *Répertoire*, 163.
Pelantaru, 562.
Peña, Gutierrez de la, 582.
Peña, Nuñez de la, *La Gran Canaria*, 36.
Peñalosa, Diego de, his discovery of Quivira, 503, 504.
Penco, 548; bay, 531.
Penguins (islands), 599.
Pensacola, 246, 250, 257, 295; discovered, 236.
Peralta, C. de, 510.
Peralta, Joan Suarez de, *Las Yndias*, 421.
Peralta, Manuel M. de, *Costa Rica, Nicaragua y Panama*, ix, 213.
Perestrello, 2. *See* Parestrello.
Perez de el Christo, Cristóval, *Islas de Canaria*, 36.
Perez, Juan, 469.
Perkins, F. B., translates Lemoyne, 296.
Pernambuco, 228.
Pernetty, *Voyage*, 602.
Perthes, Justus, *Mittheilungen*, 471.
Peru, 433, 435, 436, 446, 450, 459 (1541), 177; "Conquest and Settlement of," by Markham, 505; first rumors of the country, 505; origin of name, 505; Ribero first uses it in maps, 505; likenesses of the viceroys, 532; under Gasca, 539; revolt under Giron, 543; Andrea Hurtado de Mendoza, viceroy, 545; Zuñiga, viceroy, 547; sun-worship in, 551; Castro, governor, 551; Toledo, viceroy, 552; relations of natives with the Council of the Indies, 556; Inquisition introduced, 557; Henríquez, viceroy, 557; F. de Torres, viceroy, 560; Mendoza (fourth marquis of Cañete), 560; described in the Dutch Apianus, 184; negroes introduced, 560; Luis de Velasco, viceroy, 561; sources of information, 563; in Gomara, 412; Xeres on, 345; gold sent to Europe, 566, 578;

VOL. II. — 80.